God's Grand Design

Divine Plan for Eternal Life

**Four Dimensions of God's Creation
on Earth, in Heaven,
within God's Kingdom,
and Divinity
Volume 1**

by

William R. Arnold (1936-2014)

Edited by:
Aurora T. Payad-Arnold, Ph.D.

DORRANCE
PUBLISHING CO
EST. 1920
PITTSBURGH, PENNSYLVANIA 15238

Dorrance Publishing Co
585 Alpha Drive
Suite 103
Pittsburgh, PA 15238
Visit our website at www.dorrancebookstore.com

ISBN: 978-1-4809-5228-7
eISBN: 978-1-4809-5204-1

Acknowledgments

God's Grand Design is the fruit of more than thirty years of William R. Arnold's communion with God. The several volumes of this manuscript are a testament to his complete, 100-percent submission to the will of God. I am witness to his submission by selling his possessions, giving to the poor, taking up his cross, and following Jesus Christ to the grave and thus passing on to eternal life.

This magnum opus of prophetic visions and messages from the Lord Almighty started when the Lord God Almighty appeared to William R. Arnold and sat on his bed in his humble home in Hawaiian Gardens, California at 2:00 a.m. until dawn in the morning of Easter in 1979. The Lord revealed to him the message that he had to convey to the world about God's plan of redemption for mankind. His divinely inspired insights in his analysis and interpretation, from a systems perspective (input of truth/God – process of law/Lucifer – output of will/man – results of holy saints/son of God), of the Word of God as contained in the Bible, relating the events and prophecies in the Old and New Testaments to the various personal revelations he had received in his lifetime, culminated in this magnificent thanksgiving and complete submission to the goodness and greatness of the one, true, and everlasting God in the persons of the Eternal Father, His Son our Lord Jesus Christ, and the Holy Spirit.

His transition from the use of typewriters to computer writing using the publication's software, PageMaker, sped up his constant revisions following new breakthroughs or revelations received during daily masses or at any time of the day or night.

The concept of Growth (physical) is mandatory but Maturity (spiritual) is optional, which I picked up from an article in an old issue of the *Reader's Digest* sometime in 1999, became one of the underpinnings of his constant revisions.

Thanks are due to Jacky Choi, one of his young converts to the Catholic faith and one of our spiritual sons, who contributed his concept of the nine covenants covering the time of creation to everlasting life.

Special mention belongs to my sisters Felice Payad Connolly and Lilia Payad who have been my constant resource in my efforts to share to the world the spiritual legacy of Bill R. Arnold, my beloved late husband and soul mate.

I also owe special thanks to Eric L. Valencia, one of our spiritual sons, my ever available technical support and consultant in locating, transforming from one software program to another software program, and exporting this manuscript in PDF form to publishers.

But most of all, I lift my thanksgiving to the good and gracious Lord who has given me the grace of knowledge, education, experience, and skills to edit this manuscript and get it ready for publication.

Contents

Outline Summary of God's Truths
Teaching of God's Grand Design

God's Truths
Comprehending God's Established Truth,
Reversed Truth, and Blended Truth
(father condemns everything, mother forgives everything,
and parents balance all viewpoints)

Father's Views	Mother's Views	Parents' Views
Formal	Informal	father–Balanced–mother
No Forgiveness	All-Forgiving	Some Not Forgiven/ Some Forgiven Some Forgiven/ Some Not Forgiven

1.

Three Natures	Three Persons	Trinity
(established truth)	(flipped truth)	(blended truth)

2.

God's Son, Christ	Mary's Son, Jesus	God's/Mary's Son, Jesus Christ
(court room - justice)	(Holy mass - mercy)	(family table - love)

3.

Daily Worship	Weekly Worship	Yearly Worship
Worship God/give life	Praise God/give wealth	Thank God/give labors
(Bonus rewards)	(Earned salvation)	(Free redemption)

4.

Divine Faith	Angelic Faith	Human Faith
(Ethics/new lifestyle)	(Morals/new behavior)	(Fairness/new nature)

5.

Faith of Soul	Trust of Heart	Beliefs of Mind
(Kingdom)	(Heaven)	(Earth)

6.

Soil	Light	Water
(government)	(church)	(home)

7.

Repentance	Prayers	Works
(Face Lucifer's Test)	(Face God's Judgment)	(Face Self-evaluation))

8.

Mystical Gift	Spiritual Gift	Physical Gift
(Remove demonic possession)	(Remove worldly temptations)	(Remove sin-nature)

9.

Firstfruits of Love	Planting Seeds of Love	Searching for Love
(God's Divine Will)	(God's Divine Law)	(God's divine truth)

10.

Never-quit Method	Quit-in-defeat Method	Trial and Error Method
(sonship - myrrh)	(priesthood - frankincense)	(kingship - gold)

11.

Adult Life - Owner	Teenage Life - Manager	Baby Life - Employee
(thrill of victory)	(joy of participation)	(agony of defeat)

12.

Bonus Reward on Talent	Earn Interest on Talent	Bury Free Talent
(submit free will)	(abandon feelings)	(deny intellect)

13.

Messiah's Highway	Church's Highway	Damned Highway
(mystical world)	(spiritual world)	(physical world)

14.

War with God's Kingdom	War with God's Religion	War with God's Nation
(palace fights palace)	(temple fights temple)	(throne fights throne)

15.

3rd Advent - Save Babies	2nd Advent - Save Teenagers	1st Advent - Save Adults
(new soul - being)	(new heart - spirit)	(new mind - flesh)

16.

Son Creates Government	Priest Creates Church	King Creates Home
(recognize to sup)	(hear to speak)	(see to think)

17.

3rd Advent - Arrest Crazy Fools	2nd Advent - Arrest Criminals	1st Advent - Arrest sinners
(perfect son - free man)	(holy priest - saint)	(righteous king - citizen)

18.

College	High School	Elementary School
(taught by Christ)	(taught by St. Joseph)	(taught by Virgin Mary)

19.

120 Holy Nations	Promised Land of God	23 Arab Nations
(owned by Jesus)	(owned by Isaac)	(owned by Ishmael)

20.

Sacred Pope	Holy Priesthood	Righteous Laity
(God's Church - Authority)	(Angelic Church - Responsibility)	(Human Church - Duty)
Stern Father	**Loving Mother**	**Dutiful Child**
(God's Home - Kingdom)	(Angelic Home - Heaven)	(Man's Home - Earth)

21.

Reconcile Mind, Heart, Soul, Life	Sacrifice M/H/S/L	Surrender M/H/S/L
(mature adult)	(growing teenager)	(immature child)

22.

Properly Educated	Streetwise	Smart Where Skin Is Off
(awakening)	(enlightenment)	(calling)

23.

Bonus Spiritual Reward	Earned Blood Salvation	Free Water Redemption
(divine works)	(angelic grace)	(human faith)

24.

Reconciliation	Sacrifice	Submission
(divine owner)	(angelic manager)	(human employee)

25.

Adult Disbelief	Teenage Doubts	Baby Fears
(defeat greed)	(defeat cowardice)	(defeat ignorance)

26.

Christian People	Jewish People	Moslem People
(Sunday)	(Saturday)	(Friday)

27.

Evil Curses Blood	Good Blesses Fat	Good/Evil Create Wisdom
(shed blood reconciles)	(broken body forgives)	(sinful nature learns)

28.

Saving Souls	Good Works	Perfect Faith
(gives-up divinity)	(takes-on all sin)	(receives forgiveness)

29.

All Work Institution	All Prayer Institution	All Play Institutions
(bonus rewards - kingdom)	(earned salvation - heaven)	(free redemption - earth)

30.

New Jerusalem	Catholic Church	Mosaic Tabernacle
(Holy Saints)	(Devout Christians)	(Jewish People)

31.

God Recognizes Child's Covenant	God Hears Child's Cries	God Sees Child's Suffering
(working soul)	(praying heart)	(repenting mind)

32.

Look at Christ's Cross	Fed by Christ's Hands	Washed in Christ's Blood
(worship father - give life)	(worship son - give wealth)	(worship spirit - give labor)

33.

Intellect - Thinking

Disgrace to Majesty	Humiliation to Glory	Shame to Honor
(homeless - no house)	(nakedness - no clothes)	(starvation - no food)

Emotions - Feelings

Happiness of Soul	Joy of the Heart	Peace of Mind
(royal palace)	(fine clothes)	(great feast)

34.

Republican Viewpoint	Democratic Viewpoint	Independent Viewpoint
(people own government)	(government owns people)	(capitalists own government)

35.

Facing One's Fears	Learning Lessons of Life	Baby's Joy Fulfilled
(3rd Advent - Thank God)	(2nd Advent - Praise God)	(1st Advent - Worship God)

36.

Church of Pergamum	Church of Smyrna	Church of Ephesus
(pagan church)	(martyrs' church)	(apostolic church)
Church of Philadelphia	Church of Sardis	Church of Thyatira
(saintly church)	(reform church)	(monks' church)
	Church of Laodicea	
	(Prodigal Son's Church)	

37.

Experience God's Adventure	Face Man's Challenges	Dream of Exciting Life
(self-evaluation/value happiness)	(God's judgment/value service)	(Lucifer's Test/value life)

38.

Priesthood	Religious	Lay Leaders
(death to wicked life-force)	(death to greedy soul)	(death to cowardly heart)

39.

Creation of Divinity	Creation of Perfect Society	Creation of Perfect Man
(bonus rewards)	(earned salvation)	(free redemption)

40.

Doctrinal Truths - daily	Gospel Message - weekly	Good News - yearly
(see God/perception of reality)	(see God/Man/relative focused existence)	(see man/fixed frame of reference)

41.

Speak to God	Hear God	See God
(new body)	(new eternal life)	(new nature)
Adopted by God	**Sup with God**	**Touched by God**
(union with God)	(personal freedom)	(new kingdom)

42.

Sanctifications of Life - blood	Anointings of Life - oil	Blessing of life - water
(value of life - happiness)	(purpose of life - serve)	(meaning of life - exist)

43.

Three Gentile Kings - Star (physical)

Myrrh - Soul	Frankincense - Heart	Gold - Mind
(son's sacrificial gift)	(priest's holiness)	(king's wisdom)

Three Jewish Shepherds - Angel (spiritual)

3rd Staff - Soul	2nd Staff - Heart	1st Staff - Mind
(Jesus' Sonship/Kingdom)	(Aaron's Priesthood/Heaven)	(David's Kingship/Earth)

44.

Petitions - God Accepts	Gifts - God Accepts	Offerings - God Accepts
(give God Eternal Life)	(give God New-life)	(give God Life)

45.

Chair - Petitions	Pulpit - Gifts	Altar - Offerings
(God speaks to Christians)	(Christian speaks to God)	(Mankind Dials God)

46.

Christian - Human/Faith	Believer - Robot/Trust	Sinner - Animal/Belief
(master Jesus' palace)	(master Isaac's throne)	(master Ishmael's altar)

47.

Man Sends to God - Repentance/Prayers/Works

3) Tomb	2) Crucifixion	1) Scourging
6) Souls	5) Mass	4) Temple
9) Thanksgiving	8) Praise	7) Worship
12) Home (self)	11) Church	10) Home

God Sends to Man - Righteousness/Holiness/Perfection

3) New Soul	2) New Heart	1) New Mind
6) Mystical Body	5) Glorified Body	4) Transfigured Body
9) Royal Court	8) Temple Court	7) Celestial Court
12) New Kingdom	11) New Heaven	10) New Earth

48.

Compensatory Recompense	Punitive Retribution	Making a Mistake
(Paying for One's Fine)	(Paying for Damages)	(Admitting One's Faults)

49.

God Comes to Help Child	God Recognizes His Covenant	God Hears Child's Cries
(God sups with child)	(God touches child)	(God speaks to child)

50.

Formal God - Father	Informal God - Mother	Semi-formal Parents
(court condemns)	(altar forgives)	(personal fairness)

51.

Mystical Order	Spiritual Order	Physical Order
(divine - output sons)	(spirit - process angels)	(flesh - input men)

52.

Enlightenment by the Life Experience - Child (man's world): See Limitations

Converted via Instincts	Converted via Emotions	Converted via Intellect
(earthly realm)	(human body)	(free-willed life)

Awakening by Man's Truths - Adult (God's World): See Potential

Conversion via Blood	Conversion via Oil	Conversion via Water
(bonus rewards/washing)	(earned salvation/hands)	(free redemption/cross)

53.

Messiah - Universal Perfection	Church - Perfect Society	World - Perfect Man
(divine rights)	(social rights)	(global rights)

54.

Divine Order/future	Supernatural Order/present	Natural Order/past
(Lord God Almighty - Lord)	(Personal God - I'AM)	(Benevolent Force - IS)

55.

All Present God - Soul	All Changing God - Heart	All Knowing God - Mind
(omnipresent - conscious)	(omnifarious - self-aware)	(omniscient - knowledge)
All Paradoxical God - Image	All Creative God - Nature	All Powerful - Life-force
(omnidoxical - likeness)	(omnific - nature)	(omnipotent - sentient)

56.

3rd Redemption - Kingdom	2nd Redemption - Eternal Life	1st Redemption - New Body
(rewarded with God's Love)	(saved by good works)	(redeemed from free will)

57.

Kingdom is a Reward - Adulthood	Heaven is Earned - Teenage Life	Earth is Free - Baby Farm
(guilty conscience)	(unto thine own self be true)	(submission)

58.

Mystical Dimension	Spiritual Dimension	Physical Dimension
(crying for creator)	(suffering repentance)	(struggle builds character)

59.

Enlightened Saint	Sighted Christian	Blind Pagan
(guiding Shekinah glory)	(guiding hand of love)	(guiding stick of light)

60.

Three Christian Testimonies	Two Jewish Testimonies	One Pagan Testimony
(judge as witness)	(judge as witness)	(judge as witness)
(jury as witness)	(jury as witness)	
(witness as witness)		

61.

Define Lifestyle	Define Behavior	Define Nature
(defeat greed to generosity)	(defeat cowardice to courage)	(defeat ignorance to wisdom)

62.

Saintly Morals	Christian Ethics	Pagan Fairness
(God's Divinity)	(Man's New Body)	(Child's Earthly Life)

63.

Gift of Divinity	Creation of New Body	Birth of Appreciation
(perfect son)	(holy saint)	(righteous citizen)

64.

Paradise - Sonship	Life - Priesthood	Time - Kingship
(purified people)	(Christian people)	(Jewish people)

65.

God and Man become One	Man becomes God	God becomes Man
(kingdom of glory)	(paradise in heaven)	(heaven on earth)

66.

Washed in Spirit	Washed in Blood	Washed in Water
(remove venial sin)	(remove mortal sin)	(remove capital sin)

67.

God's Three Powers	Angelic Two Powers	Man's One Power
(perception of reality)	(relative focused existence)	(fixed frame of reference)

68.

Christian Living Prayer of Love	Jewish Soldier-of-the-Light	Pagan Child of Obedience
(creating saints)	(saving the lost)	(defeating ignorance)

69.

Save Soul	Gain Virtues	Remove Faults
(guilty conscience)	(unto thine own self be true)	(submission)

70.

Doing Things Correctly	Speaking Correctly	Thinking Correctly
(save pagans)	(create saints)	(create priests)

71.

Jesus Christ	Christ Child	God's Messiah
(adult savior - Easter Egg)	(baby redeemer - Christmas Gift)	(sacrifice - blessing)

72.

God's Divine Love	Population of People	Infinite Land
(Christ Jesus)	(Jesus Christ)	(Jesus)

73.

Isaac's 3rd Well	Isaac's 2nd Well	Isaac's 1st Well
(eternal freedom)	(mutual hatred)	(falsely accused)

74.

Machines	Mankind	Nature
(Heavenly earth)	(earth)	(life)
Messiah	**God**	**Angels**
(Freedom)	(Kingdom)	(Heaven)

75.

Power to Mass Production	Creation to Work Force	Nothing to Life
(greed - addictions)	(cowardice - fearfulness)	(ignorance/immaturity)

76.

Neighbor becomes Friend	Acquaintances become Neighbors	Stranger to Acquaintance
(Kingdom - generosity)	(Heaven - kindness)	(earth - wisdom)
Give Money to Family	**Give Labor to Friends**	**Give Time to Neighbors**
(God forgives venial sin/dust)	(God forgives mortal sin/dirt)	(forgive capital sin/garbage)

77.

Righteous King	Wicked Sinner	Nothing to Existence
(hear God)	(see God)	(breath of man)
Free Man	**Perfect Son**	**Holy Priest**
(touch God)	(taste God)	(smell God)
All Existence	**Supernatural Being**	**New Creation**
(Lord God Almighty)	(miracle-working powers)	(clairvoyance)

78.

3rd Gamma - Mystical	2nd Gamma - Spiritual	1st Gamma - Physical
(triune existence)	(dual existence)	(point of origin)
6th Gamma - Paradoxical	**5th Gamma - Godly**	**4th Gamma - Divine**
(hexagonal existence)	(quintagonal existence)	(quad existence)
	7th Gamma - Self-reliance	
	(septagonal existence)	

79.

Damnation - See Self-worth	Death - See Potential	Blood - See Limitations
(Mystical Glue)	(Spiritual Glue)	(Physical Glue)

80.

Objective - Happiness	Concepts - To Serve	Ideas - To Exist
(value of life)	(purpose of life)	(meaning of life)

81.

God's Faith - Glorification	God's Trust - Honors	God's Beliefs - Justified
(consistency)	(function)	(definitions)
God's Freedom - Anointing	God's Becoming - Blessing	God's Knowing - Freed
(publication)	(existence)	(application)

God's Best Friend Returns - Sanctification (affirmation)

82.

All Men/God Worship	Church Worships	One Man Worships
(father/divine prayer)	(son/society's prayer)	(Spirit/individual prayer)

83.

Prayer Offering	Gift Offering	Sacrifice Offering
(saving souls - works)	(prayers)	(repentance)

84.

Guilty Blood	Innocent Blood	Neutral Blood
(soldier-of-the-light)	(living prayer of love)	(child of obedience)

85.

1st Truth is God	2nd Truth is Man	Blending Two Truths
(love of God - human God)	(love of Man - divine man)	(God/Man Perfection)

86.

Prodigal Son/ 3rd Kingdom	Jesus Christ/ 2nd Kingdom	Eternal Father/ 1st Kingdom
(saintly kingdom)	(Christian Heaven)	(Jewish Earth)

87.

Teach Perception of Reality	Teach Relative Focused Existence	Teach Fixed Frame of Reference
(Kingdom - personality)	(heaven - character)	(earth - identity)

88.

God's Angels	Gentile Church	Jewish World
(oil contract)	(water contract)	(air contract)
Heavenly Sonship	**Earthly Sonship**	**Holy Saints**
(damnation contract)	(spirit contract)	(blood contract)
	Damned to Hell	
	(oblivion contract)	

89.

Save Murderers	Save Traitors	Save Enemies
(moment of silence)	(My God, My God, Why have You Forsaken Me)	(forgive them)
Save Friends	**Save Neighbors**	**Save Strangers**
(you will be in paradise)	(I thirst)	(it is finished)
	Save Beloved Son	**Save Family**
	(I release My spirit)	(son, behold thy mother)

90.

Sacrament of Baptism	Passover	Animals Enter Ark
(owning property)	(renting a home)	(possessing a house)
Sacrament of Confession	**Unleavened Bread**	**Family Enters Ark**
(good works)	(holy prayers)	(devout repentance)
Sacrament of Communion	**Firstfruits**	**God Closes Ark Door**
(save souls)	(gain virtues)	(remove faults)
Sacrament of Confirmation	**Pentecost**	**Landing on Mt. Ararat**
(admit greed)	(face cowardice)	(overcome ignorance)
Sacrament of Marriage	**Trumpets**	**Dry Land Returns**
(become generous)	(find courage)	(study for wisdom)
Sacrament of Holy Orders	**Atonement**	**Release Birds**
(awakening)	(enlightenment)	(calling)
Sacrament of Last Rites	**Tabernacles**	**Olive Branch**
(perfect son - free)	(holy priest - saint)	(righteous king - citizen)

91.

To become Happy - Kingdom	To Serve - Heaven	To Exist - Earth
(value of life)	(purpose of life)	(meaning of life)

92.

Separation from God/Soul	Hopelessness/Heart	Death Agony/Mind
(Gehenna - Christ's tomb)	(Hell - Crucifixion)	(Grave - Scourging)

93.

Spirit receives a Wife	Son receives a Mother	Father receives a Daughter
(royal kingdom)	(eternal life)	(new body)
Son/Spirit receive Co-redeemer	Father/Spirit receive Queen	Father/Son receive a Handmaid
(Kingdom/royal court)	(Heaven/temple court)	(earth/celestial court)
	Holy Trinity receives a Friend	
	(Beatific Vision/divine court)	

94.

Share One's Gold	Dig Out Gold	Free Gold Mine
(holy saint - kingdom)	(good Christian - Heaven)	(lost sinner - earth)

95.

Man - Adam's Wisdom	Angels - Angelic Beauty	Creation - Infinite Life
(1st man)	(1st Angel)	(1st Creation)
Messiah - Divinity	Jewish People - God's Will	Evil Society - Free Will
(1st Divine Man)	(1st Holy Nation)	(1st Human Society)
Death to Man's New-life	World - Man's Righteousness	Church - Man's Holiness
(1st Resurrected Man)	(1st Righteous Man)	(1st Holy Man)

96.

Evil World becomes Holy Nation	Man becomes Evil World	Angel becomes Man
(ruling holy nation)	(testing facility)	(wicked creation)
Holy Church becomes Righteous World	Redeemer becomes Holy Church	Holy Nation becomes Redeemer
(holy people)	(Virgin Queen)	(Righteous King)

97.

Christ's Divine Wisdom	God's True Wisdom	Lucifer's False Wisdom
(tree of death)	(tree of life)	(tree of knowledge)

98.

Solemn Word - See Will	Solemn Oath - See Law	Solemn Vow - See Truth
(Mary's Pieta - Self)	(Mount Calvary - Society)	(Last Supper - God)

99.

God's Free-willed Life	God in Paradise	God as a Man
(sacrifice Adam)	(sacrifice Lucifer)	(sacrifice creation)
Create Noahic Covenant	**Create Adamic Covenant**	**Create Edenic Covenant**
God's Rule of Law	**God's Faith in Divinity**	**God's Obedience to Truth**
(sacrifice Jewish people)	(sacrifice Isaac/Ishmael)	(sacrifice 1st humanity)
**Create Palestinian Covenant **	**Create Mosaic Covenant**	**Create Abrahamic Covenant **
God's Freedom from Death	**God's Golden Rule of Government**	**Homeland of Love**
(sacrifice Jesus Christ)	(sacrifice King of the Jews)	(sacrifice pagan enemy)
Create Everlasting Covenant	**Create New Covenant**	**Create Davidic Covenant**
God's Kingdom of Glory	**God's Heavenly Paradise**	
(sacrifice righteous world)	(sacrifice holy church)	
God's Covenant with Man	**Man's Covenant with God**	

100.

Fisherman - Water	King/Priest - Earth	Teacher - Light
(evangelization of lost)	(kingship/priesthood)	(pathway of perfection)
Carpenter - Man's Labor	Shepherd - Animals	Farmer - Plants
(builder of kingdoms)	(guiding hand of innocence)	(nourishment of humanity)
Free Man/Father - Freedom	Slave/Son - New Light	Servanthood - God's Rest
(soldier-of-the-light)	(living prayer of love)	(birth of humanity)

101.

Love becomes Perfection	Peace becomes Holiness	Truth becomes Righteousness
(divine love)	(divine peace)	(absolute truth)
Life becomes God	Existence becomes God-like	Choice becomes Divinity
(infinite truth)	(relative truth)	(divine choice)

102.

Remove Greed - Glorify Soul	Remove Cowardice - Honor Spirit	Remove Ignorance - Justify Flesh
(3rd day of creation)	(2nd day of creation)	(1st day of creation)
Forgive Death - Anoint Priest	Forgive Evil - Bless King	Forgive Sin - Life-force
(6th day of creation)	(5th day of creation)	(4th day of creation)
Give Resurrection - Free God	Remove Oblivion - Consecrate Divine	Pardon Damned - Sanctify Son
(new Jerusalem)	(new Heaven/earth)	(7th day of creation)

103.

Ascension via Transfiguration	Forgiveness via Resurrection	Repentance via Crucifixion
(payments accepted by God)	(pay for fines)	(pay for damages)

104.

Never-created Father	Never-created Son	Never-created Spirit
(divine soul/being of love)	(divine spirit/heart of love)	(divine flesh/mind of love)
INPUT TO PROCESS		
Image of God	**Likeness of God**	**Image/Likeness of God**
(see face of divine will)	(see face of divine love)	(see face of God)
Receive Royal Crown	**Receive Royal Robe**	**Receive Throne/Altar**
(God's divine judgment)	(God's divine grace)	(God's divine wisdom)
Receive Royal Ring	**Receive Royal Scepter**	**Receive Royal Crest**
(God's divine majesty)	(God's divine glory)	(God's divine honor)
Receive Royal Lance	**Receive Royal Sword**	**Receive Royal Seal**
(God's divine authority)	(God's divine responsibility)	(God's divine duty)
Receive Royal Keys	**Receive Royal Chalice**	**Receive Royal Sash**
(God's divine force)	(God's divine covenant)	(God's divine salute)
Receive Royal Flag	**Receive Royal Scroll**	**Receive Royal Trumpet**
(God's divine membership)	(God's divine assembly)	(God's divine school)
Receive Royal Burning Bush	**Receive Royal Tree**	**Receive Royal Rose**
(God's divine desert)	(God's divine forest)	(God's divine garden)
Receive Royal Kingdom	**Receive Holy Sanctuary**	**Receive Promised Land**
(God's divine nation)	(God's divine country)	(God's divine household)
Purify Divine Justice	**Purify Divine Mercy**	**Purify Divine Love**

(gift of time/space)	(earned free will)	(manifest destiny)
Manifest Jesus Christ (God/Man)	**Manifest Christ (God)**	**Manifest Jesus (Man)**
(divine life)	(heavenly life)	(earthly life)
Christian receives Faith	**Christian receives Trust**	**Christian receives Belief**
(criminal behavior)	(sinful behavior)	(ignorant behavior)
Christian gets Discernment	**Christian gets Submission**	**Christian gets Obedience**
(become divine will)	(follow divine will)	(enter divine will)
Christian gets Virtues	**Christian gets Perseverance**	**Christian gets Piety**
(life in all things)	(living holocaust)	(transformation of life)
Christian gets Judgment	**Christian gets Soul Savior**	**Christian gets Self-Control**
(value of life/happiness)	(purpose of life/service)	(meaning of life/exist)
Christian gets Fulfillment	**Christian gets Integrity**	**Christian gets Dignity**
(blessing of mutual love)	(humble and contrite heart)	(reflect God's likeness)
God/Man Marriage	**God's Marriage**	**Christ's Marriage**
(union of heaven/earth)	(union of Virgin Mary)	(union of Holy Church)
PROCESS TO OUTPUT		
Fruits of Perfection	**Fruits of Holiness**	**Fruits of Righteousness**
(get royal kingdom)	(get eternal life)	(get new body)
God/Man Sets Life Free	****God Forgives Sin****	****Man Pardons Crimes****
(man changes nature)	(man pays fine)	(man pays damages)

105.

New House	New Spirit	New Body
(mystical body)	(glorified body)	(transfigured body)
New World	New Nation	New City
(earth)	(Israel)	(Jerusalem)
	New Creator	
	(new creation)	

106.

Human Form	Jesus Christ	Divine Clothes
(God as man)	(Angelic form)	(Shekinah glory)

107.

Union of Two Sets of Friends	Union of Couple	Union of Two Fathers
(priesthood/laity)	(Jesus Christ/church)	(God/Abraham)
	Union of Two Families	
	(Angels/Saints)	

108.

God's Perfect Palace	God's Holy Altar	God's Righteous Throne
(Sonship - justice)	(Priesthood - mercy)	(Kingship - love)

109.

God's Covenant	Esau's Birthright	Isaac's Inheritance
(marriage of God's love)	(marriage of God's name)	(marriage of man's virginity)

110.

Human Soul/ Give Resurrection	Human Spirit/ Give Divinity	Human Flesh/Take-sin
(tomb/self-evaluation)	(crucifixion/God's judgment)	(scourging/Lucifer's test)

111.

Conversion of Soul	Conversion of Spirit	Conversion of Flesh
(path of right/holy)	(path of free will)	(path of destiny)

112.

Redeemed Soul	Holy Saint	Broken Sinner
(freedom)	(blessings)	(lessons)

113.

Soul toward God	Heart toward God	Mind toward God
(100% faithful/daily)	(67% faithful/weekly)	(33% faithful/yearly)

114.

Independence	Liberty	Freedom
(overpower guards)	(open prison doors)	(break prison chains)

115.

Jewish Palace creates Kingdom	Jewish Temple Creates Church	Jewish Throne creates World
(one man to all men work)	(one man to all men worship)	(one man to all men study)

116.

Reject Family of God	Reject God's Beauty	Unworthy of God's Toast
(reconciliation/kingdom)	(sacrifice/heaven)	(submission/earth)

117.

Friend/Jesus	Acquaintance/Abraham	Stranger/Noah
(God and man shake hands)	(man offers God hand)	(man meets stranger [God])
Mystical Union/Divinity	**Oneness/World**	**Companion/Church**
(God's/Man's friendship/love)	(God's/man's friendship/peace)	(God's/man's union/respect)

118.

God the Father/Paradox	God's Power/Order	God's Nature/Chaos
(Lord God Almighty)	(Personal God)	(Benevolent Force)

119.

Spirit Offering/Mystical	Blood Offering/Spiritual	Water Offering/Physical
(divine rights)	(social rights)	(individual rights)

120.

Sonly Man/Spirit Released	Priestly Lamb/Blood Shed	Kingly Goat/Body Broken
(remove venial sins/daily)	(remove mortal sins/weekly)	(remove capital sins/yearly)

121.

Go the Extra Mile	Give Coat Freely	Turn the Other Cheek
(if asked to go one mile)	(if asked for a tunic)	(if struck on cheek)
	Be a Generous Lender	
	(if asked for money)	

122.

God/Man Offers His All	God Offers Bride Price	Man Offers Dowry
(giving oneself)	(giving Messiah)	(giving Virgin Mary)

123.

Central Processing Unit	Random Access Memory (RAM)	Read Only Memory (ROM)
(created from secretary)	(created from typewriter)	(created from file cabinet)

124.

God and Man Agree	God Promises All to Man	Man Proves Self to God
(God and Man travel together)	(God travels Messiah's Highway)	(Man travels Church's Way)

125.

Son Purifies Father	Priest Purifies Son	King Purifies Priest
(man creates world)	(God creates church)	(Lucifer creates Messiah)

126.

Mystical Light	Spiritual Light	Physical Light
(beatific vision)	(Messiah's sacrifice)	(creation's life-force)

127.

Jesus Christ Comes to Kingdom	Jesus Comes to Heaven	Christ Comes to Earth
(master new-life)	(master tomb)	(master womb)

128.

One Commandment of God	Two Commandments of God	Ten Commandments of God
(purify soul/new soul)	(purify spirit/new heart)	(purify flesh/new mind)

129.

God and Man become One	Man becomes God	God becomes Man
(God's will from man's will)	(good from evil)	(right from wrong)

130.

4th Cup/Wedding Feast	2nd Cup/Betrothal	1st Cup/Wedding Contract
	3rd Cup/Wedding Supper	

131.

Spirit Son/End of World	Blood Son/Tribulation	Adopted Son/Calvary
(resurrection)	(crucifixion)	(baptism)
	Divine Son/ Final Judgment	
	(transfiguration)	

132.

Death to God/Man	Death of Man	Death of God
(end of the world)	(tribulation)	(Calvary)

133.

New Lifestyle/Ethics	New Behavior/Morals	New Nature/Fairness
(kingdom owners/ authority)	(heavenly managers/ responsibility)	(earthly employees/duty)

133 Teachings
Depicting God's Grand Design

**(God seeks to become Man, Man seeks to become God,
and then God and Man seek to become One)**

1. Seven-fold Spirits of God
   1a. God's Three Natures - One Power on Earth (redeem one man)
   2a. God's Three Persons - Two Powers in Heaven (redeem few men)
   3a. God's Divine Trinity - Three Powers within Kingdom (redeem all men)
2. Power/Authority of God's and Mary's Sons
   1a. God's Son, Christ - Title Deed to Heaven (value of life)
      - Give Divinity - Blood Shed: Create Holy Saints
   2a. Mary's Son, Jesus - Title Deed to Earth (will to live)
      - Take-on Sins - Body Broken: Create Righteous Citizens
3. Meaning of Daily, Weekly, and Yearly Worship
   1a. Yearly Worship - Thank God for Forgiveness of Capital Sins (remove garbage)
      - Offer God One's Labors - Remove Ignorance to Get Wisdom
      - Easter Duty represented by End of Time - Self-evaluation
   2a. Weekly Worship: Praise God for Forgiveness of Mortal Sins (remove dirt)
      - Offer God One's Wealth - Remove Cowardice to Get Courage
      - Weekly Mass represented by One Thousand Years of Peace - God's Judgment
   3a. Daily Worship - Worship God for Forgiveness of Venial Sins (remove dust)
      - Offer God One's Life - Remove Greed to Get Generosity
      - Daily Mass represented by Six Days of Creation - Lucifer's Test
4. The Power of Faith via Thoughts, Words, and Deeds
   1a. Human Faith - Seeking Eternal Life (external Heaven): See God

    2a. Divine Faith: Seeking Redemption of Damned (internal Heaven): Loved by God

5. Surrender One's Life, Wealth, and Labors to God
    1a. Belief - Mind is Convinced: Dying to Ignorance (see reality)
    2a. Trusting Belief - Heart is Convinced: Dying to Cowardice (test reality)
    3a. Faithful Belief - Soul is Convinced: Dying to Greed (own reality)
    4a. Knowing Truth - Life-force is Convinced: Born-again in Life (new reality)

6. Basic Elements of Life
    1a. Light - Kingship: Knowledge (baby's fairness)
    2a. Water - Priesthood: Self-awareness (teenage ethics)
    3a. Soil - Sonship: Consciousness (adult morals)

7. Power of Prayer before God
    1a. Daily Prayer of Repentance - Worship Father: Remove Faults (venial sins)
    2a. Weekly Prayer of Devotion - Praise Son: Forgive Sins (mortal sins)
    3a. Yearly Prayer of Works - Thank Spirit: Resurrect Death (capital sins)

8. God's Twelve Gifts to Creation
    1a. Physical Gifts - Natural Order: Remove Sin-nature
    1b. Transfigured Body - Earth
    2b. Glorified Body - Heaven
    3b. Mystical Body - Kingdom
    4b. Divine Body - God
    2a. Spiritual Gifts - Supernatural Order: Remove Worldly Temptations
    1b. Earthly Life - Free Redemption
    2b. Eternal Life - Earned Salvation
    3b. Mystical Life - Bonus Rewards
    4b. Divine Life - Personal Freedom
    3a. Mystical Gifts - Divine Order: Remove Demonic Possession
    1b. Earth - See Limitations
    2b. Heaven - See Potential
    3b. Kingdom - See Self-worth
    4b. God - See Paradox

9. God's Divine Love
    1a. Searching for Love - Reject Selfishness
    2a. Planting Seed of Love - Deny Intellect
    3a. Firstfruits of Love - Abandon Feelings
    4a. Harvest of Love - Submit Free Will

10. God's Three Methods of Learning
    1a. Trial-and-error Method: Lessons (king)
    2a. Quit-in-defeat Method - Blessings (priest)
    3a. Never-quit Method - Treasures (son)

11. The Three Journeys of Life
    1a. Baby Life - Submission: Elementary School
    2a. Teenage Life - Sacrifice: High School
    3a. Adult Life - Reconciliation: College

12. Given God's Wealth to Manage
    1a. Given Free Talents (earth) - Free Redemption (being saved)
    2a. Earn Interest (Heaven) - Earned Salvation (saving self)
    3a. Bonus Reward on Talents - Bonus Rewards (saving others)
13. Two Highways to Life and Two Highways to Death
    1a. First Highway – Messiah's Highway: God Moves = Spirit World (blessings)
    2a. Second Highway – Church's Highway: Man Moves = Physical World (lessons/see good)
    3a. Third Highway – Damned Highway: Damned Move = Mystical World (curses)
    4a. Fourth Highway – Demonic Highway: Demons Move = Divine World (lessons/see evil)
14. War with God's Kingdoms, Religions, and Nations
    1a. War with God's Kingdom – Man's Kingdom: God's Palace fights Man's Palace (wills)
    2a. War with God's Religion – Man's Religion: God's Altar fights Man's Temple (beliefs)
    3a. War with God's Nations – Man's Nations: God's Throne fights Man's Throne (territories)
15. Four Highways of Life and Death Save the Earth
    1a. First Advent – Messiah's Highway: Heaven
    2a. Second Advent – Church's Highway: Kingdom
    3a. Third Advent – Hell's Highway: Damned
    4a. Judgment – Gehenna's Highway: Demons
16. Thirteen Stages of God's Transformation, Forgiveness, Pardon, and Conversion
    1a. See to Think/Hear to Speak/Recognize to Touch/Become to Sup with God
    2a. Christ is Gentile/Peter is Jewish; then Jesus is Jewish/Paul is Gentile
    3a. Redeem from Baptism/Saved via Confession/Rewarded by Communion/ Freed by Confirmation
    4a. Teach Right, get Righteous/Teach Good, get Holy/Teach God, get Perfect/Teach Real, obtain Freedom
    5a. Truth gives Knowledge/Law gives Self-awareness/Will gives Consciousness/Love gets Sentience
    6a. Mind to Calling/Heart to Enlightenment/Soul to Awakening/Life-force to Indwelling
    7a. Being Saved, get new Body/Save Self, get Eternal Life/Save Souls, get Kingdom/Save God, get Free
    8a. Man's Birth Transforms God/Heaven Forgives Evil/ God's Kingdom Pardons Damned/Christ Saves Demons
    9a. First Advent Saves Self/Second Advent Saves Society/Third Advent Saves God/Judgment Saves All
    10a. First Cup Unites Two Fathers: Eternal Father with Abraham
    10b. Second Cup Unites Couple: Christ's Name with Church's Virginity
    10c. Third Cup Unites Friends: Groom's Priesthood with Bride's Laity

10d. Fourth Cup Unites Families: Groom's Angels with Bride's Saints

11a. Mistaken God to Informed God/Admitted Sinner to Forgiven Saint

11b. Indicted Criminal to Redeemed Damned/Convicted Angel to Converted Demon

12a. Earthly King becomes Earthly Government

12b. Heavenly Priest becomes Heavenly Church

12c. Kingdom Son becomes Kingdom Government

12d. God as Self becomes Freedom of Self

13a. Ignorant Birth becomes Celestial Court

13b. Criminal Heaven becomes Temple Court

13c. Insane Kingdom becomes Royal Court

13d. Evil Spirit becomes Divine Court

17. The Three Advents of Christ

    1a. First Advent - Arrest Sinners: Perfect Messiah

    2a. Second Advent - Arrest Criminals: Holy Church

    3a. Third Advent - Arrest Crazy Fools: Righteous World

18. Life's Painful Journey

    1a. Birth - Ignorant Fool

    2a. Home - Sinner

    3a. Elementary School - Taught by Virgin Mary: Righteous Citizens

    4a. High School - Taught by Saint Joseph: Holy Saints

    5a. College - Taught by Jesus: Perfect Sons

    6a. On-the-Job Training - Taught by Christ: Free Men

    7a. Serving God's Will - Supervised by God (employment): Servanthood

19. Ownership of Creation/144 Nations

    1a. Jerusalem - Owned by Abraham

    2a. Promised Land - Owned by Isaac

    3a. Twenty-three Arab Nations - Owned by Ishmael

    4a. 120 Holy Christian Nations - Owned by Jesus

20. Purpose of the Government/Church/Home

    1a. Government – Kingdom: Son

    1b. Executive

    2b. Legislative

    3b. Judicial

    4b. Citizenry

    2a. Church – Heaven: Priest

    1b. Messiah

    2b. Pope

    3b. Priesthood

    4b. Laity

    3a. Home – Earth: King

    1b. Father

    2b. Mother

    3b. Eldest

4b. Youngest
21. Leaving Immaturity to Gain Maturity
    1a. Leaving Childish Mind/Heart/Soul/Life-force - See Limitations
    2a. Gain Adult Mind/Heart/Soul/Life-force - See Potential
22. Two Viewpoints of God (wise) and Man (streetwise)
    1a. God is Properly Educated in the Finest of Schools
    2a. Man is Smart where the Skin is Off as he Grows-up on the Street
23. Three Ways to be Saved by Christ
    1a. Free Water Redemption – Faith
    2a. Earned Blood Salvation – Grace
    3a. Bonus Spiritual Reward – Works
        (faith through grace affirmed by works)
24. Taking God's Highway to Perfection
    1a. Submission – Gift of Eternal Life: Church (self)
    2a. Sacrifice – Gift of New Body: World (society)
    3a. Reconciliation – Gift of Royal Kingdom: God (divinity)
25. Baby Fear/Teenage Doubt/Adult Disbelief/Wise Man Knowing
    1a. Baby Fear – Lucifer's Test: Defeat Ignorance
    2a. Teenage Doubt – God's Judgment: Defeat Cowardice
    3a. Adult Disbelief – Self-evaluation: Defeat Greed
    4a. Wise Man Knowing - Set free: Defeat Unknown
26. Moslems, Jews, and Christians Worship on Different Days
    1a. Moslems Worship Holy Spirit – Friday (Heaven): Being Saved
    2a. Jews Worship Eternal Father – Saturday (earth): Saving Self
    3a. Christians Worship Son of God – Sunday (Kingdom): Saving Others
27. Evil Curses Blood and Righteousness Blesses Fat
    1a. Evil Curses Blood – Shed Blood Reconciles: Measure of Evil
    2a. Righteousness Blesses Fat – Body Broken Forgives: Measure of Good
28. Three Persons of Christ, Jesus, and Jesus Christ
    1a. Perfect Faith – God's Son Gives-up Divinity: Christ
    2a. Good Works – Mary's Son Takes-on All Sin: Jesus
    3a. Saving Others – Jesus Christ Receives Forgiveness: Jesus Christ
29. Praying (graces) and Working (money) for God
    1a. Prayer Institutions – God's Blessing of Redemption (graces): Save Sinners
    2a. Working Institutions – Man's Blessing of Salvation (money): Create Saints
30. God's Three Institutions on Earth
    1a. Mosaic Tabernacle – Jewish People: Earth
    2a. Catholic Church – Christian People: Heaven
    3a. New Jerusalem – Holy Saints: Kingdom
31. God Observes His Children
    1a. God Sees One's Suffering – Repentance (ignorant mind)
    2a. God Hears Cries for Help – Prayers (cowardly heart)
    3a. God Recognizes His Covenant – Works (greedy soul)
32. Seeking God's Forgiveness

1a. Look at Christ's Cross Daily – Worship Eternal Father (give life)
- Forgive Venial Sins (dust) – Gain Perfection

2a. Fed by Christ's Hands Weekly – Worship Son of God (give wealth)
- Forgive Mortal Sins (dirt) – Gain Holiness

3a. Washed in Christ's Blood Yearly – Worship Holy Spirit (give labors)
- Forgiveness of Capital Sins (garbage) – Gain Righteousness

33. Mind and Heart of Struggling Man
1a. Man's Intellect (thinking)
1b. Shame to Honor – Starvation (no food)
2b. Humiliation to Glory – Nakedness (no clothes)
3b. Disgrace to Majesty – Homelessness (no home)
2a. Man's Emotions (feelings)
1b. Peace of Mind – Feasting
2b. Joy of the Heart – Fine Clothes
3b. Happiness of the Soul – Great Palaces

34. Political Viewpoint Rules Men
1a. Democratic Viewpoint – Social Right: Government Owns Man
2a. Republican Viewpoint – Individual Rights: Man Owns Government

35. Christ's Three Advents to Earth
1a. First Advent – Worship God (give life): Christmas Gift (free) = Baby's Joy
2a. Second Advent – Praise God (give wealth): Easter Egg Hunt (earned) = Learning Life
3a. Third Advent – Thank God (give labor): Halloween Treat (reward) = Facing Fears

36. The Seven Churches of Paul
1a. Ephesus Church – Apostolic Church: Mystical Authority Over **Evil**
- Fighting Evil unto the Death
2a. Smyrna Church – Martyrs' Church: Supernatural Authority Over **Evil**
- Dying for the Faith in Submission
3a. Pergamum Church – Pagan Church: Rome Takes Authority Over **Evil**
- Bowing to Evil by Living with Evil
4a. Thyatira Church – Monks' Church: Holy Men Take Authority Over **Evil**
- Running into the Wilderness to Escape Evil
5a. Sardis Church – Reform Church: Forming Army of Saints to Take Over **Evil**
- Changing Evil by Surrendering to the Catholic Church (dying to selfishness)
6a. Philadelphia Church – Saintly Church: Holy Spirit/Righteous Flesh Take Authority Over **Evil**
- Defeating Evil upon Christ's "Second Coming" – Age of Awakening
7a. Laodicea Church – Prodigal Church: Humanity Grows-up to Take Authority Over **Evil**
- Using Evil and Good in a Blend of Righteousness

37. Facing God's Challenges via Growth and Experience
1a. Face Man's Challenge: Lucifer's Test

1b. Blessing – God Thinks of a Sinner

2b. Anointing – God Speaks to a Christian

2a. Experience God's Adventure: God's Judgment

1b. Sanctification – God Touches His Saint

2b. Consecration – God Sups with His Son

38. Leadership within the Church
1a. Sinners – Death of Ignorant Mind: Belief
2a. Lay Leaders – Death to Cowardly Heart: Trust
3a. Religious – Death to Greedy Soul: Faith
4a. Priesthood – Death to Wicked Life-force: Knowing

39. God's Three Ways to Paradise
1a. Free Redemption – Creation of a Perfect Man: Title Deed to Earth
2a. Earned Salvation – Creation of a Perfect Society: Title Deed to Heaven
3a. Bonus Rewards – Creation of a Perfect Friend of God: Title Deed to Kingdom

40. Comprehending the Teachings of God
1a. Good News – Free Redemption: Fixed Frame of Reference (see man)
2a. Gospel Message – Earned Salvation: Relative Focused Existence (see God/ Man)
3a. Doctrinal Truths – Bonus Rewards: Perception of Reality (see God)

41. God's Five Treasures of Life
1a. See God – New Nature: God Thinks of a Pagan = Submission
2a. Hear God – Eternal Life: God Speaks to a Sinner = Redemption
3a. Speak to God – New Body: Journey Along God's Pathway of Free Will = Salvation
4a. Touched by God – Kingdom of Glory: God Sups with His Saint = Rewards
5a. Sup with God – Divine Freedom: God Adopts Prodigal Son = Freedom
6a. Adopted by God – Union with God: God Befriends His Child as an Equal

42. God's Stages of Consecration or God Touches Man
1a. Blessings of Life – Meaning of Life: Existence (earth)
2a. Anointings of Life – Purpose of Life: Service (heaven)
3a. Sanctifications of Life – Value of Life: Happiness (Kingdom)
4a. Consecration of Life – Fulfillment of God: Love (Beatific Vision)

43. Revealing the Messiah's Authority
1a. Three Gentile Kings – Guided by Star (physical)
1b. Gold – King's Wisdom (mind)
2b. Frankincense – Priestly Holiness (heart)
3b. Myrrh – Son's Sacrificial Gift (soul)
2a. Three Jewish Shepherds – Guided by an Angel (spiritual)
1b. First Staff – David's Kingship (throne)
2b. Second Staff – Aaron's Priesthood (temple)
3b. Third Staff – Jesus' Sonship (palace)

44. Presenting One's Life to God
1a. Offerings – God Accepts Death: Submission (righteousness)

2a.   Gifts – God Accepts New-life: Sacrifice (holiness)

3a.   Petition – God Accepts Eternal Life: Reconciliation (perfection)

45. Meeting God Face-to-Face
  1a.   Altar – Offering Death: God Sees Child Suffer
    •   Dial God's Heavenly Phone (sacrificial offering)
  2a.   Pulpit – Gift of New-life: God Hears Child's Cries
    •   Sinner Speaks to God Personally (sacred word)
  3a.   Chair – Petition of Eternal Life: God Recognizes Child's Covenant
    •   God Speaks to Christian as His Beloved Child (divine word)

46. Man's Conversion Experience
  1a.   Sinner (animal) – Master Abraham's Altar: Meeting the Holy Spirit
  2a.   Believer (robot) – Master Isaac's Throne: Meeting the Son of God
  3a.   Christian (human) – Master Jesus' Palace: Meeting the Eternal Father

47. God Communicates with Man
  1a.   **Man Sends to God:** Repentance, Prayers, and Works (twelve sacrifices)
  1b.   Scourging – Crucifixion – Tomb (Messiah)
  2b.   God's House – Mass – Souls (Church)
  3b.   Worship – Praise – Thanksgiving (World)
  4b.   Church – Government – Home (self)
  2a.   **God Sends to Man**: Righteousness, Holiness, and Perfection (twelve gifts)
  1b.   New Mind – New Heart – New Soul (new earth)
  2b.   Transfiguration – Glorification – Mystical (new Heaven)
  3b.   Celestial – Temple – Royal (new Kingdom)
  4b.   Earth – Heaven – Kingdom (New God)

48. Paying for All One's Transgressions against God
  1a.   Punitive Retribution – Paying for Damages: Body Broken (Calvary)
  2a.   Compensatory Recompense – Paying for Fines: Blood Shed (tomb)

49. God's Relationship with His Child: Exodus 3:7–8
  1a.   God Sees Your Suffering – God Thinks of His Child: See God
  2a.   God Hears Your Cries – God Speaks to His Child: Hear God
  3a.   God Recognizes His Covenant – God Touches His Child: Touch God
  4a.   God Comes to Help You – God Sups with His Child: Eat with God

50. Facing God's Judgment
  1a.   Altar Forgives All — First Chance: Informal God (mother)
  2a.   Court Condemns All - Second Chance: Formal God (father)
  3a.   Personal Fairness - Third Chance: Semi-formal God (parents)
  4a.   Independent Thought - Fourth Chance: Dynamic God (God)

51. The Evolution of the Life-experience
  1a.   Natural Order – God's Combustion Engine: Gas (fuel) = Input Nature
  2a.   Physical Life – Man's Human Body: Compression (force) = Process Man
  3a.   Spiritual Life – Intellect/Emotions/Instincts: Spark (fire) = Output Angels
  4a.   Mystical Life – Infinity/Eternity: Power (torque) = Results become Sons of God

52. The Physical and Spiritual Realms

1a. **Enlightenment of the Life-experience** – Child (man's world)
1b. Free-willed Life – Repenting Mind: Converting the Intellect
2b. Human Body – Praying Heart: Converting One's Emotions
3b. Earthly Realm – Thankful Son: Converting One's Instincts
2a. **Awakening of Man's Truths** – Adult (God's Church)
1b. Free Redemption – Physical Order (natural): Converted via Water Baptism
2b. Earned Salvation – Spiritual Order (supernatural): Converted via Oil
3b. Bonus Rewards – Mystical Order (divinity): Converted via Blood
53. God's Four Levels of Transformation
1a. Messiah – Perfect Man: Divine Rights = Called
2a. Church – Perfect Society: Social Rights = Enlightened
3a. World – Universal Perfection: Global Rights = Awakened
4a. Individual – Perfect Self: Individual Rights = Indwelled
54. Structure of Our Triune God
1a. Benevolent Force – Natural Order: God's Truth
2a. Personal God – Supernatural Order: God's Law
3a. Lord God Almighty – Divine Order: God's Will
55. God's Five Authorities
1a. All Knowing – Omniscient: Mind (knowledge)
2a. All Changing – Omnifarious: Heart (self-awareness)
3a. All Present – Omnipresent: Soul (consciousness)
4a. All Powerful – Omnipotent: Life-force (sentience)
5a. All Creative – Omnific: Nature (free will)
56. God's Three Planned Redemptions
1a. First Redemption is "New Body" – Redeemed from Free Will
2a. Second Redemption is "Eternal Life" – Saved by Good Works
3a. Third Redemption is "Royal Kingdom" – Rewarded by God's Love
57. Entering Earth, Heaven, and the Kingdom
1a. Earth is Free – Death to Selfishness: Submission = Master the Law
2a. Heaven is Earned – Earn New Unselfish Nature: Unto Thine Own Self be True = Master Faith
3a. Kingdom is a Reward – Obtain Balanced Mind: Guilty Conscience = Master Knowing
58. God's Five Dimensions of Existence
1a. Physical Dimension – God Thinks of His Child: Struggle Builds Character
2a. Spiritual Dimension – God Speaks to His Child: Suffering One's Repentance
3a. Mystical Dimension – God Touches His Child: Crying for One's Creator
4a. Divine Dimension – God Sups with His Child: God Recognizes Child's Covenant
5a. Godly Dimension – God Adopts Prodigal Son: God Comes to Redeem Child
59. God Gives His Child Sight and Knowledge
1a. Blind Pagan – Guiding Stick of Light: Sacrificial Lamb = Pay Punitive Retribution

2a. Sighted Christian – Guiding Hand of Love: Temple Tax = Pay Compensatory Recompense

60. Man's Testimonies before God
    1a. One Pagan Testimony – Judge: Submission = Established Truth (father)
       • Judge as Witness – Earthly Knowledge: Mind (belief)
    2a. Two Jewish Testimonies – Jury: Sacrifice = Flipped Truth (mother)
       • Judge as Witness – Earthly Knowledge: Mind
       • Jury as Witness – Heavenly Knowledge: Heart (faith)
    3a. Three Christian Testimonies – Witness: Reconciliation = Blended Truth (parents)
       • Judge as Witness – Earthly Knowledge: Mind
       • Jury as Witness – Heavenly Knowledge: Heart
       • Witness as Witness – Kingdom Knowledge: Soul (knowing)

61. God's Reference Points during Life
    1a. Fixed Frame of Reference – Define Nature: Identity
       • Defeat Ignorance, Gain Wisdom
    2a. Relative Focused Existence – Define Behavior: Character
       • Defeat Cowardice, Gain Courage
    3a. Perception of Reality – Define Lifestyle: Personality
       • Defeat Greed, Gain Generosity

62. Ethics and Morals are Given to God
    1a. New Body – Christian Ethics (flesh) are Sent to the Saints: Worldly Deeds
       • Virgin Mary's Marriage to God – Virginity/Name
    2a. God's Divinity – Saintly Morals (spirit) are Sent to the Angels: Religious Deeds
       • Jesus Christ's Marriage to His Church – Name/Virginity

63. ***God's Grand Design*** Centers on Man's Body/God's Divinity
    1a. Creation of New Body – Righteous Citizen: Man's Ethics
    2a. Gift of Divinity – Holy Saint: God's Morals

64. Creation of Many Peoples to Serve God
    1a. Jewish People – Righteous Minds: Kingship = Time
    2a. Christian People – Holy Hearts: Priesthood = Life
    3a. Purified People – Perfect Paradise: Sonship = Paradise
    4a. Unified People – Divine Paradise: Fatherhood = Spirit

65. The Union between God and Man
    1a. Man becomes God – Paradise in Heaven: Christmas (life) = Temple
    2a. God becomes Man – Heaven on Earth: Easter (death) = Throne

66. God's Mosaic Tabernacle
    1a. Outer Court – Circumcision: Remove Venial Sins = Washed in Blood
    2a. Holy Place – Baptism: Remove Mortal Sins = Washed in Water
    3a. Holy of Holies – Confirmation: Remove Capital Sins = Washed in Spirit

67. God's Four Power Levels
    1a. Fixed Frame of Reference – One Power: Flesh = Ignorance to Wisdom (baby)
    2a. Relative Focused Existence – Two Powers: Spirit = Cowardice to Courage (teenager)

3a. Perception of Reality – Three Powers: Soul = Greed to Generosity (adult)

4a. Living in Reality – Four Powers: Life-force = Death to New-life (wise man)

68. God's Redemptive Process
1a. Jewish Soldier-of-the-Light – Saving the Lost: Body Broken
1b. Christian Living Prayer of Love – Creating Saints: Blood Shed

69. Removing Man's Faults unto Man's Conversion
1a. Remove Faults – Submission: Establish Fixed Frame of Reference = Flesh
2a. Gain Virtues – Unto Thine Own Self be True: Relative Focused Existence = Spirit
3a. Save Souls – Guilty Conscience: Perception of Reality = Soul

70. Purpose of Christ's Three Advents
1a. First Advent – Man's Mind: Thinking Correctly = Create Priesthood (owners)
2a. Second Advent – Man's Heart: Speaking Correctly = Create Laity (managers)
3a. Third Advent – Man's Soul: Doing Things Correctly = Save Pagans (employees)

71. Meeting the Baby God (Christ) and the Adult Man (Jesus)
1a. Baby Redeemer – Christ Child: Christmas Gift = Free Earth (body/intellect)
2a. Adult Savior – Jesus Christ: Easter Egg = Earned Heaven (life/emotion)

72. Messiah Comes in Four Persons
1a. Christ – Eternal Life: Offering Earned Heavenly Life = Paradise in Heaven
2a. Jesus – Infinite Land/New Body: Offering Free Earthly Life = Heaven on Earth
3a. Jesus Christ – Population of People: Offering Rewarded Kingdom = Royal Kingdom
4a. Christ Jesus – God's Divine Love: Offering Freedom = Beatific Vision

73. The "Four Wells" of Isaac bring Life
1a. First Well – Falsely Accused: Owned by One Man: Earthly Water
2a. Second Well – Mutual Hatred: Owned by One Tribe: Heavenly Grace
3a. Third Well – Eternal Freedom: Owned by Society: Kingdom Blessings
4a. Fourth Well – Divine Abundance: Owned by God: Beatific Vision Love

74. Tools in Building God's Kingdom
1a. Nature – Life: Treasured Dirt
2a. Mankind – Earth: Righteous Flesh
3a. Machines – Heaven: Strong Steel
4a. Angels/God – Kingdom: Holy Spirit
5a. Messiah – New-life: Perfect Divinity

75. God is Creating the Five Forces of Life
1a. Nothing to Life – Immaturity: Ignorance
2a. Creation to Work Force – Fearfulness: Cowardice
3a. Power to Mass Production – Addictions: Greed
4a. Life to Eternal Life – Murderousness: Hatred
5a. Imperfection to Perfection – Righteousness: Sharing

76. God's Five Dimensions of Existence

1a. Stranger becomes an Acquaintance – Earth: Wisdom... Physical Life (food)
2a. Acquaintance becomes a Neighbor – Heaven: Kindness...Spiritual Life (labor)
3a. Neighbor becomes a Friend – Kingdom: Generosity... Mystical Life (production)
4a. Friend becomes a Companion – God: Fairness...Divine Life (New-life)
5a. Companion becomes One's Family – God/Man: Love... Godly Life (perfection)

77. Tracking Life from Nothing to All
1a. Nothing – Breath of Man (life): Edenic Covenant (garden)
2a. Wicked Sinner – See God (eyes): Adamic Covenant (body)
3a. Holy Priest – Hear God (ears): Noahic Covenant (purification)
4a. Righteous King – Smell God (nose): Abrahamic Covenant (sacrifice)
5a. Perfect Son – Taste God (mouth): Mosaic Covenant (temple)
6a. Free Man – Touch God (hands): Palestinian Covenant (land)
7a. New Creation – God's Clairvoyance (imagination): Davidic Covenant (throne)
8a. Supernatural Being – God's Miracle-working Power (will): New Covenant (Messiah)
9a. All Existence – Lord God Almighty (love): Everlasting Covenant (God)

78. Gamma Life Forces
1a. First Gamma – Point of Origin (height): God Thinks of Child = Blessing (water)
1b. Creation of Adam – Adamic Covenant: Physical Dimension of Life = **Form**
2a. Second Gamma – Dual Existence (height/width): God Speaks to Child = Anointing (oil)
2b. Creation of Purified Earth – Noahic Covenant: Spiritual Dimension of Life = **Use**
3a. Third Gamma – Triune Existence (h/w/depth): God Touches Child = Sanctification (blood)
3b. Creation of Chosen People - Abrahamic Covenant: Mystical Dimension of Life = **Tenacity**
4a. Fourth Gamma – Quad Existence (h/w/d/time): God Sups with Child = Consecration (spirit)
4b. Creation of God's Priesthood/law – Mosaic Covenant: Divine Dimension of Life = **Works**
5a. Fifth Gamma – Quintagonal Existence (h/w/d/t/spirit): God Adopts Child = Union (divinity)
5b. Creation of Holy Land – Palestinian Covenant: Godly Dimension of Life = **Manifestation**
6a. Sixth Gamma – Hexagonal Existence (h/w/d/t/s/infinity): God Sets Child Free = Ownership (new-life)
6b. Creation of God's Kingship – Davidic Covenant: Infinite Dimension = **Distribution**

7a. Seventh Gamma – Septagonal Existence. (h/w/d/t/s/i/eternity): God's Child Returns = Friendship (treasure)

7b. Creation of God's Sonship – New Covenant: Eternal Dimension = **Finalization**

79. God's Glue that Holds Life Together
1a. Blood – Glue of Physical Dimension: New Mind = See Limitations
2a. Death – Glue of Spiritual Dimension: New Heart = See Potential
3a. Damnation – Glue of Mystical Dimension: New Soul = See Self-worth
4a. Oblivion – Glue of Divine Dimension: New Life-force = See Value to God
5a. Resurrection – Glue of Godly Dimension: New Nature = See Place in Grand Design

80. Comprehending the Life-experience
1a. Ideas – Meaning of Life: To Exist = Priestly Sacrifice (temple)
2a. Concepts – Purpose of Life: To Serve = Kingly Prayer (throne)
3a. Objectives – Value of Life: Happiness = Sonly Gift (palace)

81. Comprehending Physical and Spiritual Existence
1a. God's Beliefs – Man's Definitions: Justification (wonderment)
2a. God's Trust – Man's Function: Honors (thought)
3a. God's Faith – Man's Consistency: Glorification (word)
4a. God's Knowing – Man's Application: Freedom (air)
5a. God's Becoming – Man's Existence: Blessing (water)
6a. God Sets One Free – Man's Publication: Anointing (oil)
7a. God's Friend Returns – Man's Affirmation: Sanctification (blood)

82. Comprehending the Worship of God
1a. One Man Worships – Holy Spirit: Individual Prayer
2a. Church Worships – Son of God: Society's Prayer
3a. All Men/God Worship – Eternal Father: Divine Prayer

83. Giving Offerings to God
1a. Sacrificial Offerings – Repentance: Priestly Offering
2a. Prayer Offerings – Prayers: Kingly Offering
3a. Gift Offerings – Saving Souls: Sonship Offering

84. Soldiers Fight Evil/Prayers Save Souls
1a. Soldier-of-the-Light – Guilty Blood: Streetwise = Trying (overcome evil)
2a. Living Prayer of Love – Innocent Blood: Educated = Succeeding (create saints)

85. Comprehending the "Two Truths" of God
1a. First Truth – Spiritual Dimension: Love of God = Christ as God/Man (human God)
2a. Second Truth – Physical Dimension: Love of Man = Jesus as Man/God (divine man)

86. Establishing God's Three Kingdoms
1a. Eternal Father – First Kingdom: Jewish Earth = Being Saved by Law
2a. Jesus Christ – Second Kingdom: Christian Heaven = Saving Self by Grace
3a. Prodigal Son – Third Kingdom: Saintly Kingdom = God and Man are Friends via Love

87. <u>God's Kingdom Teaches Mankind the Truth</u>
    1a. Earth – Teaches Fixed Frame of Reference (identity): Learning Right from Wrong
    2a. Heaven – Teaches Relative Focused Existence (character): Learning Good from Evil
    3a. Kingdom – Teaches Perception of Reality (personality): Learning God's Will from man's will
88. <u>Saving God's Creation from Evil</u>
    1a. Jewish World – Physical Nature: Air Contract = One's Solemn Word (give hand)
    2a. Gentile Church – Physical to Spiritual: Water Contract = One's Blessing (give water)
    3a. Good Angels – Spiritual Nature: Oil Contract = One's Anointing (give oil)
    4a. Holy Saints – Spiritual to Mystical: Blood Contract = One's Sanctification (give blood)
    5a. Earthly Sonship – Mystical Nature: Spirit Contract = One's Consecration (give spirit)
    6a. Heavenly Sonship – Mystical to Divine: Damnation Contract = One's Worship (give life)
    7a. Damned to Hell – Divine Nature: Oblivion Contract = One's Praise (give wealth)
    8a. Demons of Gehenna – Divine to God: New-life Contract = One's Thanksgiving (give labors)
89. <u>God's Eight Tickets to Heaven</u>
    1a. Enemies of God – Demons of Gehenna: Forgive Them for They Know Not What They Do
    2a. Traitors of God's Son – Damned of Hell: My God, My God, Why have You Forsaken Me
    3a. Murderers of God's Son – Moment of Silence
    4a. Strangers before God – It is Finished
    5a. Neighbors to God – I Thirst
    6a. Friends of God – I Tell you on this Day you shall be with Me in Paradise
    7a. Family of God – Son, behold Thy Mother and Mother, behold Thy Son
    8a. Beloved Son of God – I Release My Spirit
90. <u>Converting Death into New-life</u>
    1a. Animals Enter Ark creates Feast of Passover creates Sacrament of Baptism
    2a. Family Enters Ark creates Feast of Unleavened Bread creates Sacrament of Confession
    3a. God Closes Ark Door creates Feast of Firstfruits creates Sacrament of Communion
    4a. Lands on Mt. Ararat creates Feast of Pentecost creates Sacrament of Confirmation
    5a. Dry Land Returns creates Feast of Trumpets creates Sacrament of Marriage
    6a. Releases Two Birds creates Feast of Atonement creates Sacrament of Holy Orders

7a. Olive Branch of Peace creates Feast of Tabernacles creates Sacrament of Last Rites

8a. Dove Never Returns creates Feast of Last Supper creates Sacrament of Resurrection

91. Finding the Meaning, Purpose, and Value of Life
   1a. Meaning of Life – To Exist: Physical Journey = Remove Faults
   2a. Purpose of Life – To Serve: Spiritual Journey = Gain Virtues
   3a. Value of Life – To become Happy: Mystical Journey = Save Souls

92. Rejection by God because of Faults, Sin, and Evil
   1a. Death Agony – Grave: Scourging
   2a. Hopelessness – Hell: Crucifixion
   3a. Separation from God – Gehenna: Tomb

93. God's Holy Family
   1a. Father receives a Daughter
   2a. Son receives a Mother
   3a. Spirit receives a Wife
   4a. Father/Son receive a Handmaid
   5a. Father/Spirit receive Queen
   6a. Son/Spirit receive Co-redeemer
   7a. Father/Son/Spirit receive Faithful Friend

94. God's Grace is Gold
   1a. Free Gold Mine – Earth: Lost Sinner
   2a. Dig Out Gold – Heaven: Devout Christian
   3a. Share Gold with Others – Kingdom: Holy Saint
   4a. Build Gold Kingdom – Beatific Vision: Perfect Son

95. God's Nine Sacrifices
   1a. God Sacrifices "Creation" – Infinite Life
   2a. God Sacrifices "Angel" – Angelic Beauty
   3a. God Sacrifices "Man" – Adam's Wisdom
   4a. God Sacrifices "Evil Society" – Man's Free Will
   5a. God Sacrifices "Jewish People" – God's Will
   6a. God Sacrifices "Messiah" – Divinity
   7a. God Sacrifices "Church" – Holiness
   8a. God Sacrifices "World" – Righteousness
   9a. God Sacrifices "Death" – New-life

96. Learning the Seven Stages of Creation
   1a. Eternal Father – Divine Thought: Angel becomes Man… Individual
   1b. God Gets a "Wicked Creation"
   2a. Son of God – Sacred Word: Man becomes Evil World…Society
   1b. God Gets His Own "Testing Facility"
   3a. Divine Spirit – Holy Deed: Evil World becomes Holy Nation…Nation
   1b. God Gets a "Ruling Holy Nation"
   4a. Father/Son – Being Like God: Holy Nation becomes Redeemer…Messiah
   1b. God Gets a "Righteous King" to Rule Earth

5a. Father/Spirit – Having God: Redeemer becomes Holy Church…Church

1b. God Gets a "Virgin Queen" to Rule with Her King

6a. Son/Spirit – Doing Like God: Holy Church becomes Righteous World… World

1b. God Gets a "Holy People" to Rule with Him

7a. Trinity – All the Above (paradox): Righteous World becomes Divine Truth…Kingdom

1b. God Gets "Cherished Dream (paradise)" where He is Ruler of All He Surveys

97. God's Trees of Life/God's Judgment and Death/Lucifer's Test

    1a. Tree of Knowledge – False Wisdom: Lucifer's Test

       • Entering God's Illusion – Sin-nature, Worldly Temptations, and Demonic Possession

    2a. Tree of Life – True Wisdom: God's Judgment

       • Entering God's Reality – Righteousness, Holiness, and Perfection

98. Three Divine/Human Sacrifices of Redemption

    1a. Last Supper – Solemn Vow: Manifestation of God (see truth)

    2a. Mount Calvary – Solemn Oath: Manifestation of Society (see law)

    3a. Mary's Pieta – Solemn Word: Manifestation of Self (see will)

99. God Sacrifices His Entire "Spiritual Kingdom" to Get Perfect Physical Life

    1a. God as a Man – Sacrifice Creation (Divine Life)

    2a. God's in Paradise – Sacrifice Lucifer (Angelic Realm)

    3a. God's Free-willed Life – Sacrifice Adam (Humanity)

    4a. God's Obedience to Truth – Sacrifice First Humanity (Cain)

    5a. God's Faith in Divinity – Sacrifice Isaac and Ishmael (Abraham)

    6a. God's Rule of Law – Sacrifice the Jewish People (Moses)

    7a. God's Homeland of Love – Sacrifice Pagan Enemy (Joshua)

    8a. God's Golden Rule of Government (morals) – Sacrifice King of the Jews (David)

    9a. God's Freedom from Death – Sacrifice Jesus Christ (Messiah)

    10a. God's Heavenly Paradise – Sacrifice Catholic Church (Peter)

    11a. God's Kingdom of Glory – Sacrifice Righteous World (God)

100. God's Divine/Human Professions

    1a. Teacher – Light: Pathway of Perfection (mind of truth) …Education

    2a. King/Priest – Earth: Kingship and Priesthood (prayer/sacrifice)…Government

    3a. Fisherman – Water: Evangelization of the Lost (baptism)…Business/Industry

    4a. Farmer – Plants: Nourishment of Humanity (wheat)…Agriculture

    5a. Shepherd – Animals: Guiding Hand of Innocence (lamb)…Finance

    6a. Carpenter – Man's Labor: Builder of Kingdoms (ownership)…Manufacturing

    7a. Servanthood – God's Rests: Birth of Humanity (happiness)…Transportation

    8a. Slave/Son – New Light: Living Prayer of Love (fulfillment)…Operations

101. Reaching One's Level of Perfection
   1a. **Absolute Truth** (baby) – Human Peace: Truth becomes Righteousness
   2a. Divine Peace – Human Love: Peace becomes Holiness (new body)
   3a. Divine Love – Human Choice: Love becomes Perfection (eternal life)
   4a. Divine Choice – Becoming Life: Choice becomes Divinity (royal kingdom)
   5a. **Relative Truth** (adult) – Existence of IS: Existence becomes God-like
102. The Hardest Jobs of God
   1a. Remove Ignorance – Justify Flesh with Wisdom: First Day of Creation (self)
   2a. Remove Cowardice – Honor Spirit with Courage: Second Day of Creation (society)
   3a. Remove Greed – Glorify Soul with Generosity: Third Day of Creation (God)
   4a. Forgive Sin – Create Life-force of Sharing: Fourth Day of Creation (paradox)
   5a. Forgive Evil – Bless the King with Righteousness: Fifth Day of Creation (king)
   6a. Forgive Death – Anoint the Priest with Holiness: Sixth Day of Creation (priest)
   7a. Pardon Damnation – Sanctify the Son with Perfection: Seventh Day of Creation (son)
   8a. Remove Oblivion – Consecrate Divinity with Freedom: Eighth Day of Creation (father)
103. God Gives All to Save His Child
   1a. Pay for Damages – Repentance through Crucifixion: Body Broken (take-sin)
   1b. Blessing the King with Righteousness – Righteous Citizen (earth)
   2a. Pay for Fine – Forgiveness through Resurrection: Blood Shed (give divinity)
   1b. Anointing the Priest with Holiness – Holy Saint (Heaven)
104. Obtaining the "55 Divine Treasures" of God's Creation
   Input of Life
   1a. Never Created Father – **_Divine Soul_**/Being of Love: Garment of Pure Thought
   2a. Never Created Son – **_Divine Spirit_**/Heart of Love: Garment of the Solemn Word
   3a. Never Created Spirit – **_Divine Flesh_**/Mind of Love: Garment of the Perfect Deed

---

Processing of Life
   4a. See the Face of Divine Love – **_Image of God_**: Pay Temple Tax (God's blessings)
   5a. See the Face of Divine Will –**_Likeness of God_**: Offer Lamb Sacrifice (God's lessons)
   6a. Receive God's Throne/Altar – Enter **_Divine Grace_**: Meet Benevolent God (identity)
   7a. Receive God's Royal Robe – Enter **_Divine Judgment_**: Meet Personal God (character)

8a.   Receive God's Royal Crown – Enter *Divine Wisdom*: Meet Lord God Almighty (personality)

9a.   Receive God's Royal Crest – Enter *Divine Force*: Meet Jesus Christ (faithfulness)

10a.   Receive God's Royal Scepter – Enter *Divine Majesty*: Become Divine Truth (Father)

11a.   Receive God's Royal Ring – Enter *Divine Glory*: Become Divine Law (Son)

12a.   Receive God's Royal Seal – Enter *Divine Honor*: Become Divine Will (Spirit)

13a.   Receive God's Royal Lance – Enter *Divine Authority*: Meet Son of God (sonship)

14a.   Receive God's Royal Sword – Enter *Divine Responsibility*: Meet High Priest of Heaven (priesthood)

15a.   Receive God's Royal Keys – Enter *Divine Duty*: Meet King of the Jews (kingship)

16a.   Receive God's Royal Chalice – Enter *Divine Covenants*: Meet Worshipers (Angels)

17a.   Receive God's Royal Sash – Enter *Divine Salutes*: Meet Servants of God (Saints)

18a.   Receive God's Royal Flag – Enter God's *Divine Membership*: Meet Commanders (Michael/Joseph)

19a.   Receive God's Royal Trumpet – Enter God's *Divine Assembly*: Meet Society of God

20a.   Receive God's Royal Scroll – Enter God's *Divine School*: Meet the Academicians of God

21a.   Receive God's Royal Rose – Enter God's *Divine Garden*: Meet the Caretakers of God

22a.   Receive God's Royal Tree – Enter God's *Divine Forest*: Meet the Rangers of God

23a.   Receive God's Royal Sanctuary – Enter God's *Divine Household*: Meet Servants of God

24a.   Receive God's Promised Land – Enter God's *Divine Country*: Meet Citizenry of God

25a.   Receive God's Holy Kingdom – Enter God's *Divine Nations*: Meet Royalty of God

26a.   Receive God's Evil Kingdom – Enter God's *Slaves of Death*: Meet Demonic World

27a.   Receive Purification of Divine Justice – *Manifest Destiny*: Face Testing Center

28a.   Receive Purification of Divine Mercy – *Earn Free Will*: Face God's Judgment

29a.   Receive Purification of Divine Love – *Gift of Time/Space*: Face Self-evaluation

30a.   Receive Manifestation of Holy Mother – *Personal Life via Virgin Mary*: See God

31a. Receive Manifestation of Christ (God) – *Heavenly Life via Death*: Hear God

32a. Receive Manifestation of Jesus (man) – *Earthly Life via Death*: Speak to God

33a. Receive Manifestation of Jesus Christ (Man/God) – *Kingdom Life via Death*: Touch God

34a. Receive Manifestation of Christ Jesus (God/Man) – *Divine Life via Death*: Sup with God

35a. Receive Christian Sacrifice – *Repentance/Forgiveness*: Ignorance to Wisdom

36a. Receive Christian Beliefs – *Plan of Redemption*: Cowardice to Courage

37a. Receive Christian Trust – *Guiding Hand of Redemption*: Greed to Generosity

38a. Receive Christian Faith – *Leading a Soul to Redemption*: Selfish to Unselfish

39a. Receive Christian Obedience – *Following Divine Will*: Knowledge

40a. Receive Christian Submission – *Entering Divine Will*: Self-awareness

41a. Receive Christian Discernment – *Repentance for Sins*: Consciousness

42a. Receive Christian Piety – *Transformation of Life*: Sentience

43a. Receive Christian Perseverance – *Become Holocaust*: Calling

44a. Receive Christian Virtues – *Manifest Life in All Things*: Enlightenment

45a. Receive Christian Self-control – *Fulfilling the Divine Will*: Indwelling

46a. Receive Christian Good Judgment – *Discerning the Holy Spirit*: Save Enemies

47a. Receive Christian Salvation – *Saving of Souls*: Save Traitors

48a. Receive Christian Dignity – *Reflect the Likeness of God*: Save Murderers

49a. Receive Christian Integrity – *Humble and Contrite Heart*: Save Strangers

50a. Receive Christian Love – *Prove One's Perfect Faith*: Save Neighbors

51a. Receive Christian Fulfillment – *Blessing of Mutual Love*: Save Friends

---

52a. Receive Divine Marriage – *Union of God and Man*: Save Family

==

Output of Life

53a. Receive Fruits of Perfection – *Eternal Life*: Save Holy Spirit (righteousness)
- Righteous Man on Earth – Follow Divine Will: Learn Lessons

54a. Receive Fruits of Happiness – *New Body*: Save Son of God (holiness)
- Holy Man in Heaven – Follow God's Divine Love: Receive Blessings

55a. Receive Fruits of God's Rewards – *Royal Kingdom*: Save Eternal Father (perfection)
- Perfect Man within Kingdom – Follow Mind of Christ: Thinking for Self

105. Receiving Christ's "New Nature"
1a. New Body – Human Transfigured Body: Saintly Life…Baby

2a. New Spirit – Human/Divine Glorified Body: Angelic Life…Child

3a. New House – Divine Mystical Body: Divine Life…Adolescent

4a. New City – New Jerusalem: God becomes Man…..Teenager

5a. New Nation – New Earth: Man/God Life (Jesus)…Young Adult

6a. New World – New Heaven: God/Man Life (Christ)…Adult

7a. New Creator – New Kingdom: Men/Angels/God…Wise Man

106. God's Nature comes in Three Advents

1a. Divine Clothes – Shekinah Glory: Free Redemption (save priesthood)… Know God

1b. First Advent – Priest on a Donkey (arranged marriage): Christmas (betrothal)

2a. Jesus Christ – Angelic Form: Earned Salvation (save laity)….Love God

2b. Second Advent – Thief in the Night (snatch the bride): Easter (wedding supper)

3a. Human Form – God as Man: Bonus Rewards (save lost pagans)…Serve God

3b. Third Advent – Just Judge on a Cloud (new house): Halloween (wedding feast)

107. Two Triangles of "Star of David" show Two Marriages

1a. Union of Two Fathers – Marriage Contract: God/Abraham

2a. Union of Couple – Betrothal: Jesus Christ/Church (Peter)

3a. Union of Two Sets of Friends – Wedding Supper: Priesthood/Laity

4a. Union of Two Families – Wedding Feast: Angels/Saints

(First Triangle God Marries Man/Second Triangle Christ Marries Church)

108. God's Four Charters of Life

1a. God's Divine Throne – Divine Justice: Kingship = Unstoppable Force

2a. God's Sacred Altar – Divine Mercy: Priesthood = Unmovable Force

3a. God's Throne/Altar – Divine Love: Sonship = Compromising Force

4a. God's Palace – Divine Freedom: Fatherhood = Independent Force

109. Esau's Birthright and Isaac's Inheritance Create Two Marriages

1a. Esau's Birthright – Holiness of the Spirit: Maturity

1b. Marriage of God's Name – God/Man Union: Last Supper

2a. Isaac's Inheritance – Righteousness of the Flesh: Growth

2b. Marriage of Man's Virginity – Christ/Church Union: Mt. Calvary

110. Transforming Man's Spirit, Flesh, and Soul

1a. Human Flesh –Take-sin: Scourging = Face Lucifer's Test (get new body)

2a. Human Spirit – Give Divinity: Crucifixion = Face God's Judgment (get eternal life)

3a. Human Soul – Given Resurrection: Tomb = Face Self-evaluation (get royal kingdom)

111. Traveling God's Pathway of Life

1a. Pathway of Destiny – Conversion of the Flesh: God's Lessons

2a. Pathway of Free Will – Conversion of the Spirit: God's Blessings

112. Union of Man's Righteous Citizens and God's Holy Saints

1a. Pathway of Destiny – Physical Life: Broken Sinners (lessons)

2a. Pathway of Free Will – Spiritual Life: Holy Saints (blessings)

3a.   Pathway of Righteousness/Holiness – Mystical Life: Redeemed Souls (anointings)

4a.   Pathway of Perfection – Divine Life: Redeemed Sons (sanctifications)

113. Turning Mind, Heart, and Soul Toward God

  1a.   Mind toward God – 33 percent Faithful: Yearly Devotion (Easter) = Offering (sacrifice)

  1b.   Give God One's Life – Remove Capital Sins (garbage): Forgiven Mind

  2a.   Heart toward God – 67 percent Faithful: Weekly Offering (Sunday) = Gift (money)

  2b.   Give God One's Wealth – Remove Mortal Sins (dirt): Forgiven Heart

  3a.   Soul toward God – 100 percent Faithful: Daily Worship (week-days) = Petition (begging)

  3b.   Give God One's Labors – Remove Venial Sins (dust): Forgiven Soul

114. Man must Master Freedom, Liberty, and Independence

  1a.   Freedom – Breaking the Prison Chains: Remove Blindness (new eyes)

  2a.   Liberty – Opening the Prison Doors: Remove Deafness (new ears)

  3a.   Independence – Overpowering Prison Guards: Remove Dumbness (new mouth)

115. Creating God's Divine Institutions

  1a.   Jewish Temple Creates Catholic Church

  1b.   Temple...One Man Worships – High Priest

  1c.   Church...All Men Worship – All Men are Priests

  2a.   Jewish Throne Creates Christian World

  2b.   Throne...One Man Rules – Royal King

  2c.   World...All Men Rule by Vote – Democracy

  3a.   Jewish Palace Creates Saintly Kingdom

  3b.   Palace...One Man Owns Title – Son of God

  3c.   Kingdom...All Men Own Title – Sons of God

116. Purification of Earth, Heaven, and God's Kingdom

  1a.   Submission – Unworthy of God's Toast: Refuse Cup of Wine (insult)

  1b.   Purification of Earth – Flesh: Righteous Citizen

  2a.   Sacrifice – Sacrificing One's Personal Beauty: Cut Hair Bald (ostracized)

  2b.   Purification of Heaven – Spirit: Holy Saint

  3a.   Reconciliation – Reject Family of God: Refuse to Bury Mother (disowned)

  3b.   Purification of Kingdom – Soul: Son of God

117. God's Five Stages of Intimacy

  1a.   Stranger – Noah: Man Meets a Stranger Who is God = Seeking Salvation

  2a.   Acquaintance – Abraham: Man Offers God his Hand = Being Saved

  3a.   Friend – Jesus: God and Man Shake Hands = Saving Oneself

  4a.   Companion – Church: God and Man Like Each Other = Saving Others

  5a.   Oneness – World: Marriage of God and Man = Set Free

118. The Three Major Forces of God

  1a.   Benevolent Force – Nature: Teacher of Chaos = Natural Order...Knowing God

2a. Personal God – Father: Teacher of Order = Supernatural Order…Loving God

3a. Lord God Almighty – Power: Teacher of Paradox = Divine Order…Serving God

119. Offering God Divine Sacrifices
   1a. Water Offering – Physical Life: Earth = Abraham's Altar (individual rights)
   2a. Blood Offering – Spiritual Life: Heaven = Isaac's Throne (social rights)
   3a. Spirit Offering – Mystical Life: Kingdom = Jacob's Palace (divine rights)

120. Offering-up the Goat and the Lamb Sacrifices
   1a. Kingly Goat – Body Broken: Remove Capital Sins = Easter (Yom Kippur)
   2a. Priestly Lamb – Blood Shed: Remove Mortal Sins = Christmas (Passover)

121. Christian Generosity is Beyond Imagination
   1a. Turning the Other Cheek – Going First Mile: Worship = Give Life
   2a. If Asked for a Tunic Give One's Coat – Going Second Mile: Praise = Give Wealth
   3a. If Asked to Go "1 Mile" then Go "2 Miles" – Going Third Mile: Thanksgiving = Give Labor
   4a. If Asked for Money then be a Kind Lender – Going the Fourth Mile: Serve = Give All

122. God's Bride Price and Man's Dowry
   1a. God Offers His Bride Price – Sacrifice of God's Creation: Give-up Divinity (wisdom)
   2a. Man Offers his Dowry – Sacrifice of Man's Messiah: Take-on All Sin (value)

123. God Automates Man via Machine Technology
   1a. Secretary – God: Central Processing Unit (CPU) = Convert Man's Mind
   2a. Typewriter – Kingdom: Read Only Memory (ROM) = Convert Man's Heart
   3a. Filing Cabinet – Heaven: Random Access Memory (RAM) = Convert Man's Soul
   4a. Typed Page – Earth: Monitor (CRT) = Convert Man's Life-force

124. Traveling the Highways of Life
   1a. God Travels the Messiah's Highway – Spirit World: God Promises Man
   2a. Man Travels the Church's Highway – Physical World: Man Proves All to God

125. Purification Process of God
   1a. Priest Purifies King – Creation of the Messiah: Facing Lucifer's Test
   2a. King Purifies Son – Creation of the Church: Facing God's Judgment
   3a. Son Purifies Father – Creation of the World: Facing Self-evaluation

126. Master God's Two Schools of Life
   1a. School of the Soldier-of-the-Light – Inheritance: Physical Light = Messiah
   2a. School of the Living Prayer of Love – Birthright: Spiritual Light = Creation

127. Mastering the Pathways of God to Reach Perfection
   1a. Christ Comes to Earth – Pathway of Destiny: Physical Dimension = Womb
   2a. Jesus Comes to Heaven – Pathway of Free Will: Spiritual Dimension = Tomb
   3a. Jesus Christ Comes to Kingdom – Pathway of Holiness: Mystical Dimension = Church

4a. Christ Jesus Comes to Free Life – Pathway of Righteousness: Divine Dimension = World

128. The Three Sets of Commandments of God
1a. Ten Commandments of God – Purification of the Flesh: New Mind = Offer-up Fat
1b. Fat Reveals One's Measure of Righteousness – Righteous Citizen
2a. Two Commandments of God – Purification of the Spirit: New Heart = Offer-up Blood
2b. Blood Reveals One's Measure of Holiness – Holy Saint
3a. One Commandment of God – Purification of the Soul: New Soul = Offer-up Incense
3b. Incense Reveals One's Measure of Perfection – Perfect Son

129. The Pathways of God Reveal One's Relationship with God
1a. Pathway of Destiny – God becomes Man: Christmas = Learn Right from Wrong
2a. Pathway of Free Will – Man becomes God: Easter = Learn Good from Evil
3a. Pathway of Holiness – God and Man become One: Halloween = Learn God's Will/Man's Will
4a. Pathway of Righteousness – God Sets Man Free: Independence Day = Learn God's Reality from Man's Illusion

130. The Four Cups of the Holy Mass
1a. First Cup – Physical Dimension: Union of Two Fathers = Marriage Contract
2a. Second Cup – Spiritual Dimension: Union of Couple = Betrothal
3a. Third Cup – Mystical Dimension: Union of Two Sets of Friends = Wedding Supper
4a. Fourth Cup – Divine Dimension: Union of Two Families = Wedding Feast

131. The Sonship of God by Size of Offering
1a. Offer Water Baptism – Adopted Son: One Man at Calvary
2a. Offer Bloody Crucifixion – Blood Son: Few Men during Tribulation
3a. Offer Spirit Resurrection – Spirit Son: All Men at End of the World
4a. Offer Divine Transfiguration – Divine Son: Creation Faces Final Judgment

132. Both God and Man Must Face "Death"
1a. Death of God – Brings Divine Light to Earth: Free Redemption = God's Reality
• God's Death on **Mount Calvary** – Being Saved: Body Broken = Take-on Sins
2a. Death of Man – Brings Human Light to Heaven: Earned Salvation = Man's Illusion
• Man's Death During **Tribulation** – Saving Self: Blood Shed = Give-up Divinity

133. Union with God through Conversion
1a. New Nature – Fairness at Home: Baby Employee…Kingship – Truth
2a. New Behavior – Morals in Church: Teenage Manager…Priesthood - Law
3a. New Lifestyle – Ethics in Court: Adult Owner…Sonship – Will

Foreword

The question on the "lips of the world" since time began is, ***What is life all about?***"
Who would guess it is about becoming a "soldier-of-the-light," a free spirit of human
independence, a proven friend of God who has been fully tested in the war of spirit
(good) and flesh (evil). Envision a mighty knight engaged in a slaughter of innocents
to bring forth wisdom (obedience) and courage (love) out of a demonic pit of death to
bring forth the glory of God (sacred name). This clearly depicts our Creator and His
holy friends as they destroy a fictitious dragon in a wonderland of strange illusions,
where each of God's children must conquer the unknown to be set free from ignorance,
cowardice, and greed (get imagination/dream).

The "chosen souls" of this mystical kingdom are all given the truth, indicating
that life is just a test (Lucifer/God/self), measuring each soul's free will on its quest
for wisdom (sentience/thinking for self) as it travels through humanity's evil illusion
of death (shadow). All hope springs from the divine light that only Christ is God's
true reality, and mankind's visible covenant with the absolute truth comes in the
form of God's divinity. We see that every man must release his grasp on man's foolish
mystical world of insanity to commit himself to God alone and rebel against his own
evil nature by surrendering to the actual world of living death that has been manifested in humanity's valley of tears (fear/pain). The "Cross of Christ" is our true reality, while the love for the material existence is a cruel illusion, leading every foolish
soul to Lucifer's highway to hell, until it is willing to bow to God's lessons of life.

Imagine the Lord God Almighty as a fantastic magician who is capable of creating
an entire material existence that offers life's greedy fools only temporary security during
the hour of their great test of faith (Lucifer). We see that pagan security is snatched
away, making the whole life-experience a cruel joke, leaving only a single hope of repentance for every lost broken sinner of death to cling to for survival. We see that a
horrible day of death is coming when material security is the illusion of a fool, while a
life of religious sacrifice and poverty (flesh) will be seen as mankind's true reality. This

new "state of reality" is, in truth, leading to man's freedom, peace, eternal life, and spiritual independence (think for self) all in the name of God's Son, Jesus Christ, who has laid His life down to bring all men to eternal freedom. This will be the time of "each saint's vindication" as the divine light of God will reveal the secret meaning behind the gospel message (earned salvation) of divine truth (friendship of God).

In the creation of God's Grand Design, we imagine God contemplating His impossible dream of making a speck of dust one with the divine flame of truth (light) through His own earthly incarnation (word). The Lord created Adam from the dust of the universe and then told him he was Lord over all he surveyed, meaning that the Earth would be mankind's speck of dust from which mankind's life-force (benevolent) would bear fruit. This means that God had accomplished the first step of making a speck of dust into a divine child of God through the Lord's infinite desire to serve the needs of the least (poor sinner) and transform him into a holy saint (rich son of God). Unfortunately, God's new creation needed the power of free will (freedom/liberty/independence) to understand life and to be awakened to the difference between good as expressed in righteous reality (God/blessings) and evil as expressed in unrighteous illusion (man/lessons). Out of these two dimensions of life (physical/spiritual), the Lord has created the two-truth system of existence: (l) physical dimension (see limitations), free-willed existence (baby), compromised will (love), and (2) spiritual dimension (see potential), predestined existence (adult), direct will (justice).

By using this two-truth logic, we can comprehend that God is reality (creator) representing the first truth (spirit/design/destiny), while man is illusion (creation) representing the second truth (flesh/natural selection/free will). Through the sacrifice of Jesus Christ, the first truth (journey of life) and the second truth (journey of death) can become one in truth, law, and will, thereby making all things righteous, holy, and perfect in the sight of God. We can now understand that in the Lord's first truth (reality), God is simply a benevolent force (concept) of grand design that serves His own creative nature, using both divine creation (purification/positive) and divine destruction (transformation/negative) to bring forth a perfect kingdom of glory. Secondly, in the Lord's second truth (illusion) or natural selection (random change), the Lord God Almighty is a personal God of love who requires His most beloved children to worship, praise, and thank Him for each and every gift of life, which God gives them to create an entire lifetime of debt. When these two truths are blended into one eternal mystical truth, both God and man become one in Christ Jesus and the entire creation will be placed in perfect balance (synchronized) with all of the forces of nature, men, angels, and God.

This means that once a person has mastered God's Divine School of Higher Learning and has been set free from sin, evil, and death, he can meet the concept of God known as the benevolent force of existence. In this teaching, the benevolent force of life (self-love) is in a formless state of divine reality, while the creative force of life (unselfish love) or our personal God has taken form to become our Lord God Almighty in Heaven. The idea here is to see that once a person has become a saint and has earned a place within the Lord's beatific vision, then he can expect to be united (become) with a pure, benevolent nature of divine truth or the existence of eternal life. In contrast, each of God's children is responsible for paying his own sin-debt by facing death agony (scourging), hopelessness (crucifixion), and separation from God (tomb).

The following tabular information indicates that each of God's "sinful children" must face death agony (mind), hopelessness (heart), and separation from God (soul) to pay his sin-debt in full to God for his faults, sins, and evil ways:

Facing Death Agony, Hopelessness, and Separation from God to Pay for One's Own Wicked Sins
(enduring Christ's scourging, crucifixion, and death in tomb to receive life, body, and kingdom)

Truth (mind)	1. **Death Agony** – <u>Scourging</u>: Purchase New Body… Good News
	• 1st Advent – Remove Blindness: Priest on a Donkey = Calvary (free redemption)
	• Learning Right from Wrong – Righteous Citizen: Remove Sin-debt
See God	• Defeat Ignorance to become Wise – Title Deed to Earth (baptism)
	• Man Faces – Death Agony (stealing from earth)
	• Christ Faces – Scourging (stealing from Heaven)
	• Lucifer Faces – Lake of Fire (stealing from Kingdom)
	• God Faces – Sin of Defiance (stealing from God)
	(Adam's body is cursed with death – toil in a barren land in sheer agony)
Law (heart)	2. **Hopelessness**—<u>Crucifixion</u>: Purchase Eternal Life … Gospel Message
	• 2nd Advent – Remove Deafness: Thief in the Night = Tribulation (earned salvation)
	• Learning Good from Evil – Holy Saint: Remove Worldly Temptations
Hear God	• Defeat Cowardice to become Courageous - Title Deed to Heaven (confession)
	• Man Faces – Hopelessness (hiding on earth)
	• Christ Faces – Crucifixion (hiding in Heaven)
	• Lucifer Faces – Bottomless Pit (hiding in Kingdom)
	• God Faces – Evil of Deception (hiding from God)
	(Adam's land is cursed with unfruitfulness – pain and sickness without hope)
Will (soul)	3. **Separation from God** - <u>Tomb</u>: Purchase Royal Kingdom…Doctrinal Truths

- 3rd Advent – Remove Dumbness: King on a Cloud = End of World (bonus rewards)
- Learning God's/Man's Wills – Son of God: Remove Demonic Possessions

Speak to God
- Defeat Greed to become Generous - Title Deed to Kingdom (communion)
- Man Faces – Separation from God (lying to earth)
- Christ Faces – Tomb (lying to Heaven)
- Lucifer Faces – Outer Darkness (lying to Kingdom)
- God Faces – Death of Deceit (lying to God)
  (Adam's children are cursed with poverty – deserted by their God unto separation)

This illustration shows that a "Man Faces" Death Agony, "Christ Faces" Scourging, "Lucifer Faces" Lake of Fire, and "God Faces" Sin of Defiance (stealing) so that all the Debts Owed to Divinity, Angels, and Humanity for Rejecting God's Truth are Paid in Full. Secondly, "Man Faces" Hopelessness, "Christ Faces" Crucifixion, "Lucifer Faces" Bottomless Pit, and "God Faces" Evil of Deception (hiding) so that all Debts Owed to Divinity, Angels, and Humanity for Rejecting God's Law are Paid in Full. Finally, "Man Faces" Separation from God, "Christ Faces" Tomb, "Lucifer Faces" Outer Darkness, and "God Faces" Death of Deceit (lying) so that all the Debts Owed to Divinity, Angels, and Humanity for Rejecting God's Will are Paid in Full.

Once "All the Outstanding" Debts have been Paid to the Physical (man/earth), Spiritual (Angels/Heaven), Mystical (Christ/Kingdom), and Divine (God/Beatific Vision) Levels of Creation, then all the Creations of God shall be Set Free from Sin, Evil, and Death. The idea here is that "If a Person Pays" his Debt to Earth (defeat ignorance), he will Receive a New Body; if he "Pays" his Debt to Heaven (defeat cowardice), he will Receive an Eternal Life; and if he "Pays" his Debt to God's Kingdom (defeat greed), he will Receive his own Personal Kingdom. It should now make sense that "All Debts" must be Paid in Full to God, Angels, Men, and Nature before the Human Race can be Released from Its Obligation to Serve God's Creation as Eternal Slaves until They Pay the Last Penny.

We see that Adam's (speck of dust) Comprehension of Man's Debt (truth) came when he could Not Overcome Temptation or Purify himself sufficiently to Achieve the Status of Divinity (eat forbidden fruit). This inability of "Adam" to Make himself Perfect has Prevented him from becoming Like his God in both Spirit (1st truth) and in Truth (2nd truth). Only then did "Adam" become an Eternal Outcast (barren land/desert) as he Received Man's Curse of Death (toil) upon himself (life), his Land, and his Children (people). These "Three Curses of Death (toil/pain/dying)" brought forth Evil upon the Household of Man in the Form of Starvation (ignorance), Nakedness (cowardice), and Homelessness (greed). We see that "Father Adam" was Forced to Face the Curse of Sweat (Adam) and Toil since he was Forced to Cultivate a Barren Land in a Never-ending Struggle to Feed his Family, Out of the Works of his Hands. We see that "Mother Eve" was Forced to Face the Curse of Pain (Eve) during Childbirth to bring forth the Fruits of Life, Out of her Barren Womb (sin-nature) in a Never-ending Struggle to Clothe the World as She became a Humble Slave of Repentance (love) to Make Up for Her Sin. The tragedy of "Original Sin" is that Adam had Unwittingly Severed Communications with his God, much like a Teenage Child Does with his Parents during those Rebellious Years of becoming an Adult.

We now see that both "Parties" are "Speaking in an Understandable Manner (clearly)," yet, neither Side Understands a Single Word (channel thinking) because of Adam's Original Sin (deaf, dumb, and blind). It is now obvious that there never has been any "Clear Understanding" between Man and his God until the Coming of Jesus (remove blindness), our Human Intercessor, who brought forth His New Perfect Justice System of Love. The Lord's "Perfect Justice System" was on Mount Calvary for the Redemption of the Spirit (baptism) and the Salvation of the Flesh (confession) to Save All Men. We see that centuries prior to "Christ's Death," God made a Dramatic Attempt to Communicate with Moses, giving him and the Jewish People a Heavenly Telephone (tabernacle) in the form of the First Temple that they might Hear His Holy Word and Understand It. Unfortunately, the "Human Race" is Blind, Deaf, and Dumb and can only be Healed by Paying Its Sin-debt to Earth (man), to Heaven (Angels), and to the Kingdom (God) to be Set Free from Its Curses of Darkness, Silence, and Ignorance.

We see that "God" was saying to His "Children (Jews): "I will give you a symbol of My Reality and you may see My Desires, so you can symbolically communicate your desires for Forgiveness and Re-establish My Divine Friendship." Thus, for some 1,500 years, the "Jews Used Symbolic Gestures (Tabernacle)" to Talk to Their Creator, desperately trying to Literally Follow His Laws unto the Letter (commandments). Unfortunately, when "Jesus Came," He Spoke Directly to God and Clarified His most Perfect Divine Purpose (service), so that Even a Fool would Understand the Just Law of God (love). It is too bad that the "Jews Failed to Recognize" Their Hour of Visitation and/or Believe God's Son, Their Coming Messiah. Otherwise, "They might have Found" Freedom from Death and could have also Comprehended the Eternal Truths of Life, Revealing God's Plan to bring forth an Infinite Supply of Righteous Citizens (flesh), Holy Saints (spirit), and Sons of God (soul). Thanks to the "Virgin Mary," Our "Pearl of the Universe," Creation's Only Official Witness to the Manifestation of God's Incarnate Glory, We will All One Day See Humanity's Eternal Peace and also Experience the Lord's Infinite Freedom, thereby Allowing a Person to Live a Perfect Life in God's Perfect Kingdom. The Virgin Mary represents "Man in Heaven," by presenting all her efforts to the Lord, for His Personal Blessing of Mature Independence honoring humanity with His Gifts, Fruits, and Treasures to enlighten Her soul to the Divine Way of Truth.

It is interesting that "God's Future Kingdom" centers on its "Human Queen," the Blessed Virgin of Love as the eternal Wife of God. We see God "Cursed Adam" to Till the Soil (dust) until it brought forth a Fruitful Harvest. In this same regard, our "Wise and Hard-working Jesus" seems to be Tilling Mankind as if it were Soil until He is able to bring forth its Firstfruits of Repentance and His Holy Wife of Love (church). We see that the "Catholic Church" is to be Humanity's first Properly Behaved Lady worthy of a New Body and a seat in the Celestial Court (eternal life) and of God's Presence (kingdom).

The "Blessed Virgin (womb)" and "Her Daughter Church (mystical womb/born-again)" both symbolize the Lord's cherished Pearl of Great Price, the Crown Jewel of God, the Treasure of the Kingdom, Christ's Virgin Mother, Mary. These "Two Precious Diamonds of Strength (flesh) and Beauty (spirit)" are Destined to be the vehicle of God's Divine Incarnation to carry forth the Mission of God's Son to Defeat Satan's Curse of Death. Secondly, in the Triumph of Mary will come the Purifying of the Earth to prepare the way for Christ's Second Coming. Jesus and Mary will then usher in the new "Civilization of Love (1,000 years of peace)," the final evolutionary step, prior to God Merging Heaven, His Spiritual Kingdom of Divinity (divine prayer), and Earth, as His Physical Kingdom of Humanity (sacred works) made into One Holy and Righteous Free-willed People (awakened). The entire purpose of "Human Existence" and the "Creation of the Coming Kingdom" is based on the Fulfillment of the Seven-fold Spirits of God through the Triune Nature of the Lord's Honor (identity/being saved), Glory (character/saving self), and Majesty (personality/saving others). This perfect "Divine/Human Nature" is manifested in God's Son Jesus Christ (judgment seat) who has come to Teach Us all how to Think for Ourselves. This means that "Repentant Men" achieve their pre-ordained Purchase of their Heart's Desire, through the endowment of a Perfect Woman (Church) in the likeness of God's Divine Perfection. In the consummation of the Lord's "Spiritual Completion," the Virgin Mary would Come to Heaven to fulfill the Dreams of All People, Angels, and God.

The following tabular information indicates the "Seven Titles" of the Blessed Virgin Mary Giving God What He has Always Wanted: a dynamic, yet Humble Creature of Pure Love to be an Emphatic and Compassionate Mother to One and All:

Seven Divine Titles of the Virgin Mary

1. **Father Receives**: A Lovely Daughter of Perfection
2. **Son Receives**: A Loving Mother of Understanding
3. **Spirit Receives**: A Devoted Wife of Blessing
4. **Father/Son Receive**: An Obedient Handmaid of the Lord
5. **Father/Spirit Receive**: A Merciful Queen of Glory
6. **Son/Spirit Receive**: A Co-redemptrix of Compassion
7. **Father/Son/Spirit Receive**: A Holy Mother as Faithful Friend/Loving Companion

This illustration shows that the price for possessing such a perfect creature (pearl of great price) requires a divine marriage, consecrated through the authority of a Holy Sacrament of Divinity.

Then it must be consummated through a divine sacrifice worthy of the divine honor of God made perfect through His Royal Majesty of infinite love. For this reason, Christ gave His life (crucified sin), eternally glorifying the marriage between divinity and humanity as a priceless possession of divine love for all eternity. Recall that on the wedding night, the couple must sacrifice their virginity to consummate the marriage, thereby validating the wedding vows making their loving union fruitful (babies) in the sight of God. In the case of the Blessed Virgin, she was required to make a spiritual sacrifice of her purity to conceive, yet still maintain her physical virginity forever in the eyes of God. Note that a newlywed couple will willingly sacrifice their virgin bodies and purity to live in blissful faith, permitting their marriage to bear fruit (Messiah) through the blessing of divine love. We are aware that Christ also sacrificed His body, purity, and life to permit His bride as the mystical body to bear fruit (saints), giving the world the power of divine consummation (eternal bond).

We see that this divine consummation comes through the blessing of the holy mass as the divine seal (contracts) of all eternal unions (Mt. Calvary/contracts). In the case of the Virgin Mary, a handmaid of the Lord, she sacrificed Her own desires through the immaculate abandonment of Her free will unto the divine will of God. The Lord consummated the marriage by inserting His feminine divine will into Her immaculate soul, making God and man one will in spirit (morals) and in flesh (ethics). Through this divine marriage, the souls of man would be guided along the pathway of perfection to be transformed into living prayers of love (sainthood) before the throne of God. The miracle of creation is never more clearly seen than when the Blessed Mother was originally created in the mind of God (formless) to confound even the wisdom of the angels. This announcement by "God to Lucifer" at the moment he was being given his free will ignited the heavenly rebellion and the creation of the spirit of death as angelic pride was tested to the dust and failed. We see that Lucifer proclaimed that he would rather rule in hell than serve Mary in heaven and he was willing to betray his God rather than sacrifice (surrender) one ounce of his evil pride.

The truth is that Lucifer will now be a dishonored slave under the heel of the Virgin Mary, after Her Triumph and glory over all the forces of sin, evil, and death. She will soon defeat evil with the sacred blood (sacrifice) of Her Son, putting Satan (death), the devil (pain), and Lucifer (fear) in chains for one thousand years. Note that we must all face the test of Lucifer (save flesh), the judgment of God (save spirit), and our own self-evaluation (save soul) as we must stand between the rights of the one versus the demands of the many.

Now, if we objectively look at our own purpose in life, it is manifested in our own salvation (earned), which is brought forth by our own repenting heart of infinite gratitude in thanksgiving for our personal forgiveness from God. We now see that men who seek the truth will only find it through the purpose of God (life), their purification (circumcision/tithing), and redemption (baptism/temple tax) of their souls, which are obtained through the blessing of spiritual maturity. We see that everyone must taste the pain and struggle of life and then experience evil as it tries to destroy man's innocence (ignorance) to create a guilty fool, who must then fight his way out of Lucifer's pit of evil (world system). The Lord God Almighty calls this the law of no pain, where there will be no gain because the life-experience is about where there is no cross (sacrifice), there is no crown (reward). We see that life is the purifying force that molds each person's soul, making it into a unique thing of value before God, angels, and men, either priceless (God/reality) or worthless (man/illusion).

We see that every man on Earth has dreams of learning the mysterious eternal truths of the universe and of meeting the Lord God Almighty Himself, which is like chasing a spirit until a person and the spirit become one and then one day, the lost soul simply meets itself, thereby finding its God. We know that mankind has always been willing to pay any price to acquire the knowledge needed to capture the treasures of eternal life and one day experience divine happiness in God, angels, men, and nature. We see that little did man's sojourning soul know that the mysteries of life's realities could never be discovered, even by its own efforts, no matter how hard a person might try. The divine pathway to "freedom (reality/perfection)" can only be found by accepting in faith (submission) the divine message of love from one of the wandering messengers/prophets of God, sent specifically to man to see God's absolute truth. Remember, amazingly enough, most of God's messengers of salvation are one's own parents. Be sure not to miss your divine hour of visitation as the unsuspecting Jews did in their zeal to become holy (fulfill law) without the help of prophets, the Messiah, and/or God.

This means that the only way anyone can actually meet, know, and understand his complex creator is by patiently waiting for His eternal invitation to heaven through the doorway of death (purified grave). The Lord briefly revealed Himself to Adam, who mistakenly believed he knew his God as his Creator and his beloved father, but later came to realize that his God was both a just king (obedience/flesh/law) and a merciful priest (love/spirit/faith). We see that Noah met God in the barren desert of chaos and received a promise of a holy land to be overflowing with milk (human kindness) and honey (divine love), yet Noah also learned the hard way that God Almighty is both a just king (cruel) and a merciful priest (forgiving). We see that Abraham also falsely assumed he knew the Almighty as his faith was tested to its breaking point, when asked to murder his own son and then suddenly, our Father of Faith realized he had met both a just king (sacrificial) and a merciful priest (bloodless sacrifice). We see that Moses met God and triumphantly received the law of perfection, making him sure that he knew God's divine purpose, but eventually God would destroy Moses and God's first generation of true believers. We see that God has betrayed His own chosen people by testing their faith unto the very dust and then forcing them to wander the Earth for two thousand years to find their own identity in God's prophets, His Messiah, and within God Himself. During this period, Jesus came and then the world received the gospel message (earned salvation) and the creation of Christ's church to bring free redemption to one and all. Now, "Christ's church" mistakenly thinks it knows the mind of God sufficiently to explain His omnipotent being, whose mind is farther above man, than the stars are above the Earth. In short, the Lord God Almighty is an enigma wrapped in a mystery and no man will ever come to both know and/or understand his God until he has become God (oneness) and can know all things in Christ Jesus.

The real "purpose of existence" is to experience the presence of God (reality/wisdom), His world (illusion/courage), and His nature (eternal existence/generosity), allowing a person to learn God's divine language of love. In believing in the Lord's divine word, the pathway to proper behavior (perfection) is attained, where life takes on true meaning through the blessing of one's earned salvation. The divine way indicates that all must believe and trust God in everything because things are not as they appear on the surface of human existence, because good and evil are one in Christ Jesus, thereby allowing everything in life to bear holy fruit. We must all humbly surrender in obedience to the Lord's divine will in total abandonment to the forces of death that have been designed to transform us into living prayers of love (sainthood) before the altar of God. We see that each soul must both repent (pay damages) and atone (pay fines) for transgressions against His Majesty, offering devotion and good works to gain His favor and His friendship. This path of perfection leads to one's spiritual maturity and God's gift, expressed as a virtuous character of Christian love and kindness being offered to the entire brotherhood of man. We see that sainthood is obtaining God's gift for instinctively behaving in accordance with God's will, be it direct (adult/justice), permissive (teenager/mercy), or compromised (baby/love). By dying to self, a person's soul can be transformed from its bonds of slavery to the spiritual awakening of divine love, setting a person free from sin, evil, and death forever.

To understand this concept of dying to self (submission), a person must imagine God is giving every person on Earth his own free gold mine (title deed) as a gift from His Son in the form of free redemption (water baptism). Secondly, God is asking everyone on Earth to now be true to himself by digging out the gold (sin-debt) from his own personal gold mine to repay His Son for allowing the people of Earth to earn their own salvation (confession/spirit baptism). Thirdly, God is asking everyone on Earth to listen to his guilty conscience by sharing his gold with others (save souls) to help His Son bless God's saints with eternal rewards (communion). Finally, God is asking everyone on Earth to enter instinctive compulsion or thinking for himself by using his gold to help God build His kingdom of glory (set free) to set God's Son free (confirmation) from sin, evil, death, damnation, and oblivion. The idea associated with this gold mine story is that by using Christ's church (own gold), the righteous government (dig gold), and one's happy home (share gold) as God's gold mines, an eternal wealth of treasures can be obtained so that all men can be saved. The Lord is asking" each and every one of us to sacrifice ourselves by denying ourselves, obeying His commandments, selling all and giving to the poor, picking up Christ's cross, and following the Lord into the fires of hell to save the lost (damned) at any cost. This theme of "giving all" to "get all" sits at the heart of the Good News (free gold mine), the Gospel Message (dig gold), doctrinal truth (share gold), and doctrinal truths/incarnate word (build kingdom) of Jesus Christ's salvation message to the world.

The following tabular information indicates how receiving a person's own free gold mine relates to uniting his life with that of Jesus Christ in bringing forth redemption (free), salvation (earned), rewards (bonus), and freedom (priceless) to all the lost of the world:

**Free Gold Mine, Dig Gold, Share Gold, and Build
Kingdom of God for the Lord God**
(free redemption, earned salvation, bonus rewards, and
eternal freedom come from Jesus Christ's sacrifice)

| Baptism (baby) | 1. | **Free Gold Mine -** <u>Free Redemption</u>: dying to self (submission) |
| | • | Defeating ignorance to obtain wisdom – see limitations = Identity |

Free Redemption	• God's purpose — experience divine life: reality (high marks)
	• Blessing by water — justification of the flesh: remove capital sin
	• Offer "Blood," become God's acquaintance — get New Mind
	• Righteous man — worthy of a *New Body* (transfiguration) (physical dimension — God thinks of child: God is stranger = God becomes man)
Confession (teenager)	2. **Dig out gold** — <u>Earned Salvation</u>: true to oneself (deny intellect)
	• Defeating cowardice to obtain courage — see potential = Character
	• God's world — experience human life: illusion (many points)
Earned Salvation	• Anointing by oil — honoring of the spirit: remove mortal sin
	• Offer death, become God's good neighbor - get New Heart
	• Holy saint — worthy of an *Eternal Life* (glorification) (spiritual dimension – God speaks to child, God is acquaintance = God becomes man)
Communion (adult)	3. **Sharing gold** — <u>Bonus Rewards</u>: face guilty conscience (abandon emotions)
	• Defeating greed to obtain generosity — see self-worth = personality
	• God's nature — experience God's love: Christianity (holy graces)
Bonus Rewards	• Sanctification by blood — Glorification of the Soul: Remove Venial Sin
	• Offer "Damnation" — become God's close friend: get New Soul
	• Perfect son — worthy of his *Own Kingdom* (ownership) (mystical dimension – God touches child: God is friend = God/man become one)
Confirmation (wise man)	4. **Build Golden Kingdom** — Eternal Freedom: Instinctive Compulsion (submit will)
	• Defeating evil to obtain holiness — see New-life = nature (born again)
	• God's divinity — experience God's justice: sainthood (treasures)
Eternal	• Consecration by Death — freedom of the life-force:

Freedom
- remove wicked faults
- Offer "Oblivion," become member of God's family: get Life-force
- Free man — worthy of *Eternal Freedom* (think for self) (divine dimension - God sups with child: God is companion = child becomes God)

This illustration shows that Jesus Christ was giving the flesh of man (baptism) its own free gold mine (God's reality) in the form of a person's free redemption (new body) to defeat a sinner's ignorance and bring forth a new-life of wisdom, thereby allowing him to see his own limitations (new mind). Secondly, the Lord requires the spirit of man (confession) to dig out its own gold (God's illusion) in the form of a person's earned salvation (eternal life) to defeat his cowardice and bring forth a new-life of courage to see his own potential (new heart). Thirdly, the Lord requires the soul of man (communion) to share its gold (God's Christianity) in the form of a person's bonus rewards (own kingdom) to defeat his greed and bring forth a new-life of generosity to see his own self-worth (new soul). Finally, the Lord requires the life-force of man (confirmation) to build a Kingdom of Gold (God's sainthood) in the form of a person's eternal freedom (God's friendship) to defeat his evil and bring forth a new-life of holiness to meet God and see his own kingdom of glory (new-life). At each of these four stages of transformation (free gold mine), purification (dig gold), correction (share gold), and conversion (build golden kingdom), the lost souls of the world are given a second chance (second mile).

1. **First Stage** - Transformation: free gold mine = new nature ... human to divine
   - Breaking the chains of sin - see limitations: free redemption (new body)
2. **Second Stage** - Purification: digging out gold = wash away sin.... sinfulness to holiness
   - Opening prison doors of evil - see potential: earned salvation (eternal life)
3. **Third Stage** - Correction: share gold with others = Thinking for self ...imperfect to perfect
   - Overcoming the guards of death - see self-worth: get bonus rewards (own kingdom)
4. **Fourth Stage** - Conversion: building God a golden Kingdom = freedom... enemy to friend
   - Escape one's eternal captivity - see face of God: freedom (God's friendship)

This illustration shows that a lost broken sinner must repent (believe 100 percent) to pay his sin-debt in full, thereby earning his own eternal freedom from the forces of sin, evil, death, and damnation. The word "transformation" means to break the chains of sin, the word "purification" means to unlock the prison doors of evil; the word "correction" means to overpower the prison guards of death; and the word "conversion" means to escape one's eternal captivity to be set free from damnation. At each of these four levels of growth and maturity, a person is able to reach a higher and higher state of perfection and come ever closer and closer to God's divine love. The Lord's divine love is manifested in His infinite desire to share His peace and wealth (reality) with others, if they will simply repent for their sins against His divine justice. This desire is fulfilled when the Lord's created souls worship His Divine Majesty (save others) as directed by His divine justice, which is the key to opening the treasure chest of God's divine heart of love. The idea here is that God does not benefit from worship, with the exception that it allows Him to bless the worshiper with His divine blessings (benevolence) of a new body (king), eternal life (priest), and His own kingdom (son). Out of the Lord's divine blessing, a repentant sinner receives God's sanctifying grace in the form of heavenly money, thereby giving him a passport, ticket, and personal wealth as his heavenly welcome.

This explains just why God is demanding that mankind not worship Him in vain pride (self-righteous), but with child-like adoration (devotion), thereby guiding each soul to its own divine glory (saving self). In other words, worship (give life), praise (give wealth), and Thanksgiving (give labor) bring man to God and adore God's divine majesty, thereby reflecting the infinite glory of the royal house of God. The majesty of God is similar to our most honored presidency of the United States (office) in that it needs to be treated with the utmost respect at all times in the same way the American people respect the office of the presidency, but not necessarily the president holding office. We see that in the case of God, He is both the president (man) and the office of the presidency (head) at the same time. This implies that the Lord God Almighty is both the Creator (God) and the "Creation" (man) at the same time. We see that the Lord Jesus Christ demonstrated this principle during the Last Supper (first Mass). While mankind was worshiping God (pride), simultaneously God was washing mankind's feet (humility). God's royal position of infinite perfection demands unceasing worship of the all-powerful Creator God. We see that it is only coincidental that the royal throne of God makes the Lord's scepter of justice, seal of rule, and the person of the Lord God Almighty all or one and the same thing (destiny/free will) by virtue of their eternal divinity in Christ Jesus.

The overall governing forces of life are the Father's justice and the Son's mercy manifested as the unstoppable force of absolute truth (reality) encountering the immovable force of relative truth (illusion). The essence of creation is justice (existence) while the essence of man's existence is mercy (life), thereby allowing Jesus Christ to make justice and mercy one through His sacrificial fear, pain, death, and resurrection on Mt. Calvary. Through these two forces, all things are governed in the celestial court of God (earth) under the Lord's divine law of obedience, which has the power to change one's nature from human to divine. The heavenly kingdom is structured with a legislative branch (divine law), judicial branch (divine justice), and executive branch (divine authority), thereby making the three natures of God—His higher principles of principled ethics (righteousness), His virtuous morals (holiness), and His fairness (perfection) to govern the Lord's divine truth.

1. **First Nature** – God's Ethics: Righteousness/law = Man's Dignity............ Eternal Father
2. **Second Nature** – God's Morals: Holiness/faith = God's Honor.............. Son of God
3. **Third Nature** – God's Fairness: Perfection/knowing = God's/Man's Majesty..............Holy Spirit

We also see that mankind is being taught these essential principles of proper living necessary to give a soul a divine nature, leading to an Eternal Life (paradise) of human dignity, honor, and majesty. We see that those who have experienced both of Lucifer's and God's spirit-breaking tests of fear and pain truly know the meaning, purpose, and value of life (existence/service/happiness) in truth (church), law (government), and will (home). The Lord God Almighty most certainly must choose His future white knights of divine truth from this courageous group of purified souls, which have volunteered to wash their garments in the blood of the lamb (cross). We see that through the divine virgin birth (alpha/Christmas), God chooses His purified saints (first truth/reality/glorified spirits); while through the divine death (omega/Easter) on Calvary, God chooses His transformed sinners (second truth/illusion/ transfigured bodies).

1. **Divine Virgin Birth** – Christmas (alpha): God's purified saints............new nature
   • God becomes man via life – God brings Heaven on Earth: Jewish people
2. **Divine Sacrilegious Death** – Easter (omega): Man's transformed sinners... wash away sin
   • Man becomes God via death – God's Son brings paradise in heaven: Christian people

We see that these uniquely qualified tested souls all tell the identical story regarding the purpose and magnitude of God's Grand Design of eternal redemption (free), salvation (earned), and rewards (bonus). The divine motives of the Almighty can only be perceived in the depths of each of our human struggles forcing each soul to pass through its own tests of fear and pain to find both the relative and absolute truths of God (correct thinking). We see that every person on Earth is forced to climb out of Lucifer's pit of death at the peril of his life (earth) and at the peril of his own soul (heaven) for he must face the forces of sin, evil, and death. This eternal danger is known as God's tough love, thereby showing that the Lord's ways are totally different from man's ways and his petty concerns for self-preservation, which lead to man's sin, evil, and eventually his death. In contrast, man is reluctant to make any sacrifice, because he is hoping God will do all the work and then, for simply not doing evil, then humanity believes that God will give man his whole kingdom for free (nothing). We see that mankind is a silly child in a Divine School of Higher Learning, who is being given the opportunity to obtain both the wisdom (mind) and courage (heart) to face the trials of life that he might be awakened to the divine truths of God. This is known as a child's slaughter of innocence (see limitations) that transforms pure-hearted babies (see limitations) into mature soldiers-of-the-light (righteous citizens), ready to fight evil unto the death (learn lessons). The culmination of this mystical opportunity to grow-up (flesh/mandatory) and become mature (spirit/optional), occurs when the people of the Earth become one (collective mind) with their beloved land, the mother of their very flesh.

In this way, the Lord God Almighty will be giving mankind its liberty of spirit (equality to God), its eternal independence (freedom) in the form of a new nature of divinity (God's name), and by washing away man's sins (man's virginity) to make him holy in the sight of God.

1. **Liberty of the Spirit** – Equal to God: new nature of divinity...God's name
2. **Independence of Flesh** – Freedom from God: wash away sin to be holy... Man's virginity

The human soul seeks the freedom of its nature out of the need to find its Creator by matching the creation it sees with the invisible truth it knows exists, somewhere in the reality of the Lord God Almighty Himself. We must consider to what extent our Creator has gone to achieve His objectives in bringing an eternal school of infinite learning into existence through the powers of sin, evil, death, and damnation (Calvary). It is a fact that by the End of Time, the Lord will have made seven deeply personal sacrifices to His own divine justice to bring forth His incarnation, manifested out of the absolute nature of divine truth. The basic purpose for these seven sacrifices centers upon giving God's new human Son (Messiah) seven blessings: (0) life from creation, (1) beauty of Lucifer, (2) wisdom of Adam, (3) courage of first humanity, (4) righteousness of the Jews, (5) divinity of Christ, (6) holiness of the Christians, and (7) perfection of the righteous world. Through these seven gifts of love from God, the Messiah will create His most perfect heavenly paradise (angels/saints) through His sacrificial death on Mt. Calvary (crucifixion).

The following tabular information indicates that each of these carefully designed sacrifices will bring the Lord closer to finding His bride (womb) and building His new kingdom of glory as the eternal home (nest) for God's coming babies:

Purchase Price
Master Sacrifices of Creation
(seven perfect creations destroyed become Virgin Mary's treasures)

0. The Lord sacrificed His most beloved **"Creation"**/get life......Infinite Life
   - His first precious "creation" was a perfect sacred angel, named: "Lucifer"
   - God's Edenic covenant – purchase eternal physical Life... (tree of life)
- -
1. The Lord sacrificed His most perfect **"Angel"**/remove capital sin... Angelic Beauty
   - His most beloved servant "Lucifer" to create a perfect holy man "Adam"

- Adamic covenant – purchase the Blessed Virgin's beauty .....(tree of knowledge)

2. The Lord sacrificed His most perfect **"Man"**/remove mortal sin...human wisdom
   - His first-born "free-willed" child of love "Adam" to create a free-willed "Evil Mankind (Noah)"
   - Noahic covenant – purchase the Blessed Virgin's wisdom (rainbow)

3. The Lord sacrificed His evil **Mankind** (Noah)/remove venial sin...Free Will Courage
   - His future hope of perfection to create a chosen people, the "Jews"
   - Abrahamic covenant – purchase the Blessed Virgin's courage (promise)

4. The Lord sacrificed His beloved **"Jewish People"**/remove faults...God's Law of Obedience
   - His spiritual wife of love to create a new messianic order/man's redeeming Son of God
   - Mosaic covenant – purchase the Blessed Virgin's obedience (tablets)

5. The Lord sacrificed His **"Beloved Son"** (Messiah)/get perfection... God's Divinity
   - His greatest possession of perfection to create the "Virgin Mary" and Her children (church)
   - Davidic covenant – purchase the Blessed Virgin's Immaculate Conception (sun/moon/stars)

6. The Lord will sacrifice His beloved **"Holy Church"**/get holiness...God's Holiness
   - His Son's spiritual wife of love to create a new civilization of love (world)
   - Palestinian covenant – purchase the Blessed Virgin's holiness (land)

7. The Lord will sacrifice His beloved **"Righteous World"**/righteous...God's Righteousness
   - His precision works of His hands to create the new heaven and new earth bringing forth the New Jerusalem, the divine home of God and man (marriage)
   - New Covenant – purchase the Blessed Virgin's righteousness (womb/tomb/life)

- -

8. The Lord will sacrifice man's worst enemy, **"death"**/get new-life...Heavenly Sainthood
   - His most helpful (evil) creation of "pain" and His warning system of "fear" to create His new **Kingdom of Glory** of "pure love" to bring "forgiveness to all"
   - Where ear hath not heard and eye hath not seen the riches of God (earth) and glory (heaven) God has for those who love Him
   - Everlasting covenant – purchase the blessed Virgin's perfection (Holy Spirit)

This illustration shows that through this construct of infinite design, God has systematically sacrificed His most beloved first-born creations, thereby paying the ultimate price to obtain an increasingly greater number of potentially righteous (good minds), holy (good hearts), and perfect (good souls) souls. We see that these most perfect creations are to come forth from both the virgin womb of Mary (Jesus Christ) and the holy womb of Christ's Church (born-again/saints) to bring forth the kingdom of God on Earth.

In the end, all His sacrifices will resurrect and join Him in paradise, exposing the truth by showing that even a cruel sacrifice (Mt. Calvary) can take nothing away from the majesty of God. We see that humanity must come to understand the fruits of God's divine love that are focused upon the creation of His kingdom of glory, designed to reflect the holy love of the Blessed Virgin Mary in spirit (morals) and in flesh (ethics). The Lord was giving His All to create a baby farm (slaughter of innocence) as an earthly kindergarten of human learning (right/wrong) to transform foolish children into righteous citizens on Earth. This Little Red Schoolhouse (church/government/home) allows God to transform heaven into a Divine School of Higher Learning, where every future soul might come to understand the meaning of divine thought (thinking for oneself). Finally, each of God's "children of love" would come to forever reside in the Lord's kingdom of higher laws by sitting at the feet of his Creator to learn the ultimate purpose of it all by discovering his own identity (right/wrong), character (good/evil), and personality (God's will/man's will).

In this teaching, we see that there are nine sacrifices made by each of the Lord's patriarchs to earn each of them a special right to establish one of mankind's stages of either growth (world) and/or maturity (church). These earned rights are the following: (1) God sacrifices His creation — earns right to create angelic realm: Lucifer and the Garden of Eden: Paradise on earth = gift of life, (2) Lucifer stands up to God — earns right to test Adam's courage and Eve's wisdom = gift of courage, (3) Adam repents for nine hundred years – earns right to offer-up Abel's blessing (lamb) and Cain's curse (goat) = gift of freedom, (4) Noah builds the ark (120 years) – earns right to purify the first civilization and create new World Order = gift of covenant (rainbow), (5) Abraham sacrifices his son Isaac — earns right to create Holy Jewish people (Isaac) and righteous gentile people (Ishmael) = gift of forgiveness, (6) Moses sacrifices Jews on desert of death — earns the right to create the holy priesthood (law) and the sacred temple (faith) of God = gift of priesthood (Levitical), (7) Joshua sacrifices gentile blood upon Holy Land — earns the right to create a blessing on the Good Jew and a curse on the evil pagan = gift of homeland (Israel), (8) David sacrifices the king of the Jews — earns the right to create the prayer of repentance (king) and the kingship of God (throne) = gift of kingship, (9) Jesus Christ sacrifices Himself — earns the right to create new nature of man and new kingdom of glory = gift of sonship (freedom), (10) church sacrifices its priesthood/laity to evil — earns the right to create redemption in Heaven (baptism) and salvation on Earth (confession) = gift of Holy Church (submission), and (11) world sacrifices man's government and home unto death — earns the right to create the New Jerusalem (capital) and New Heaven and New Earth = gift of righteous world (sacrifice).

Out of each of these eleven sacrifices, God has been able to finance His coming Kingdom of Glory complete with two natures of life (two truths): one divine (God/reality), and one human (man/illusion). The question is, what is God trying to achieve by suffering through this myriad of painful sacrifices when all He really needs to do is divinely will the creation into whatever form He desires it to be as seen within His heart of hearts? The answer is to establish a kingdom of human and angelic affection, freely given through their worship, praise, and thanksgiving by offering their own lives (repentance), own wealth (prayers), and own labors (works). This means that the Lord can give divine love by pouring it out of His sanctifying grace upon His creatures, all He wants, but He cannot force anyone with free will to love Him back, in either divine spirit (reality) or in human flesh (illusion). It is proven that the most effective method to make someone love you is to become love-able, which could only be done with one's mutual respect, based on divine/human equality (Calvary). We see that God is making Himself loveable by winning the respect and genuine affection of His chosen children by demonstrating that His painful way (struggle builds character) is the only way, by experiencing God's own form of tough love (road of hard knocks).

The following tabular information describes the price of perfection, reflected in the extreme measures required by the seven-fold spirits of God to serve His own divine justice through righteousness (man), holiness (angels), and perfection (God):

Financing the Seven Stages of Creation
(God's sacrificial altar of divine justice)

Seven-Fold Spirits (Divine Celebrants)	Manifested Treasures	Testing of All Creatures Give to Get	New Creations (God's Tough Love)
Eternal Father	1. Divine Thought	Holy Angel = Holy Man	Wicked Creation
• 1st Nature	• Majesty God	*** Divine Justice***	•Evil/Death/ Damnation
Son of God	2. Sacred Word	Holy Man = Evil World	Testing Facility
• 2nd Nature	• Glory	*** Divine Law ***	• Divine School
Divine Spirit	3. Holy Deed	Evil World = Holy Nation	Ruling Holy Nation
• 3rd Nature	• Honor	*** Divine Authority ***	• Kingship/Priesthood
Father/Son	4. Being Like God	Holy Nation = Redeemer	King (Divine Man)
• 1st Person	• Wisdom	*** Holy Church ***	• Divinity/Humanity
Father/Spirit	5. Having God	Redeemer = Holy Church	Queen (Perfect Man)
• 2nd Person	• Courage	*** Sacred Government***	• Humanity/Divinity
Son/Spirit	6. Doing Like God	Holy Church = Holy World	Holy People (Love)
• 3rd Person	• Generosity	*** Divine Home ***	• Baby Farm
Father/Son/Spirit	7. All the Above	Holy World = Divine Truth	Paradise/Happiness
• Holy Trinity	• Mutual Love	*** Divine Love ***	• Everlasting Love
God	8. Creator	Evil Death = Divine	Kingdom of Glory
Lord God Almighty	• Blessings **	*** Divine Friendship ***	• Divine Truth

This illustration shows that it is nearly incomprehensible to believe both God and man ultimately desired the same thing: humanity being transcended to the divinity of God in both spirit (law/purify host) and in flesh (truth/purify grave). In the story of Adam's Fall, we see a man naively believing the advice of a wizard (Lucifer) that he could simply eat the fruit of a magical tree of knowledge (Eve's bread/Adam's wine), and presto, he could become like God. The above sacrificial information is the presto part of Adam's dream for instant divinity, thereby making what Lucifer originally said to Eve ultimately true as all humanity would have to do is eat the flesh (bread) and drink the blood (wine) of God's Son, Jesus Christ. Is it not strange that mankind's past spiritual ruler, Pope Benedict VI, claimed that if a person believes strongly enough in the holy cross of Christ as the tree of death and if he eats its fruits of its sacred bread (flesh) and mystical wine (spirit), then a soul can be made one with God?

First Sacrifice: Lord God Almighty (Love)
We now see that God believed in Himself enough to sacrifice His most beloved creation both spiritually (reality) and physically (illusion) to create the angelic realm (heaven), human realm (earth), and sonship realm (kingdom) in hopes of building His new kingdom of glory.

Second Sacrifice: Lucifer (Beauty)
Secondly, the Lord tested Lucifer by letting him choose between serving in Heaven (slave) and/or ruling in hell (king) and he obviously chose to have a few cosmological seconds of painful freedom, over an eternity of divine happiness. We see that "Lucifer (evil one)" would win a chance to test Adam's courage and Eve's wisdom as the serpent in the garden, thereby making him ruler of the Earth until the coming of the Redemption of Christ.

Third Sacrifice: Adam (Wisdom)
Thirdly, Adam was called to some nine hundred years of repentance during which time the Lord re-established both His inheritance (Abel's blood/Heaven on Earth/divine flesh) and His birthright (Cain's forgiveness/Paradise in Heaven/holy spirit) with the New Nature of Man.

Fourth Sacrifice: First Humanity (Obedience)
Fourthly, first humanity was cursed unto damnation to purify foolish men and then start a new world order, out of the sons of Noah (Ham/Shem/Japheth) to bring forth the white, yellow, brown, red, and black races.

Fifth Sacrifice: Abraham (Faith)
Fifthly, Abraham offered-up his son, Isaac to create the Jewish people (holy) and then he also offered-up his son Ishmael to create the Gentile people (righteous) to bring forth a New Nation of righteous citizens, holy saints, and sons of God.

Sixth Sacrifice: Moses (Law)
Sixthly, Moses purified the Jews on the desert of death and brought forth both the Jewish priesthood (house of Aaron) and the Jewish temple to establish worship (give life), praise (give wealth), and thanksgiving (give labors) before the altar, throne, and table of God.

Seventh Sacrifice: Joshua (Holy Land)
Seventhly, Joshua both trained and built a powerful army of slaves to purify the Holy Land and to separate the Good Jews (heaven) from the evil pagans (hell), thereby creating Heaven on Earth.

Eighth Sacrifice: David (King of the Jews)
Eighthly, David established the kingship of God on earth through the royal household of David to give mankind its own royal king and throne of majesty.

Ninth Sacrifice: Messiah (Sacrifice)
Ninthly, came the Son of God, the Lord Jesus Christ, who took all sin to create a new human nature (divinity) and then gave-up His divinity to create the New Kingdom of Glory (holiness), thereby making God and man one in truth, law, and will.

Tenth Sacrifice: Church (Forgiveness)
Tenthly, Christ's Church brings forth Jesus' flesh (save sinners) to take man's sin in baptism (redemption) and then Christ's spirit (create saints) gives man forgiveness in confession (salvation) to save all the lost of creation.

Eleventh Sacrifice: World (Fight Evil)
Finally, the New Righteous World will be unveiled by God as He brings forth both His new capital city, the New Jerusalem and His new kingdom in the form of our new Heaven and new Earth.

By creating both a spiritual temple and a physical throne, God is able to combine the wants of Heaven (obedience) with the needs of Earth (survival) to create one Kingdom of Glory, thereby making God and man one. In these parallel stories, both God (reality) and man (illusion) are striving to transform a speck of dust into a divinely perfect being, who will one day be worthy of being a true friend of his own Creator. We see on that day of glory, God will give man the divine inheritance (name), and man will give God the sacred merits of Christ (virginity) in the form of his perfect faith (believe 100 percent), tested in the fires of God's tough love (direct judgment). This reveals that the only difference between the dreams of man and the dreams of God is their methods of implementation, just an age-old argument between the amateur of death (man) and the professional of life (God). It all boils down to simply doing it right (see potential), by following Jesus' tree of death (cross of Calvary) to His tiny hill of repentance, leading a soul to heaven to find the mastery of its own self-worth (will) and become a consummate professional in the eyes of God or doing it wrong (see limitations), by seeking Adam's foolish tree of knowledge (world), which was captured by the spirit of the world, leading all lost, broken sinners to their pit of death of original sin (selfishness).

A great fallacy on the Earth today is the belief that many are needed to conquer sin, implying that the whole world must stop sinning and become holy in the sight of both man and God to be saved. The Jewish people tried this technique of being perfect while under the Mosaic Law. It did not work, nor can a Christian hope to achieve the state of holiness without first conquering the evil one of eternal fear (remove ignorance), pain (remove cowardice), and death (remove greed). This is a "fallacy of divine truth" as a person may just as effectively use the Lord's sacrament of penance and the blessing of the Holy Mass to continually purify himself from the dirt (evil) of the demonic world (worldly temptations), thereby removing his satanic death (demonic possession). We have been given new flesh at baptism (capital sin) like a pair of overalls (divine skin), which is to be soiled (sinful) and later cast into the born-again grave to be purified by the coming judgment of God and finally, redeemed in the blood of the Lamb. The soiled evil flesh of man was sacrificed upon Calvary, then washed in the sacred blood of Christ leaving only the divine bones of God to be transformed into a new transfigured body of divine truth during the church's coming resurrection upon the Lord's return (second coming).

The message here is to "Try One's Best" to live by his faith in all things good in his own sight, thereby seeking the divine guidance of the Holy Spirit at every moment through the power of the Holy Mass of eternal purification (washing machine). The spirit of Christ cries out to all His followers to drink His blood, so that their spirits might be purified and converted into His most perfect faith (give life) and His loving divinity (give divinity). Jesus cries out to the lost of the world to "eat my flesh" so that a person's flesh might be transformed and converted into His most loving born-again humanity (take-sin) to make all men righteous citizens, holy saints, and sons of God before their creator. The Lord Jesus Christ came to bring mankind the power of God's forgiveness (altar/throne/table) to free (break chains) it from the forces of fear, pain, evil, death, and damnation forever. We see that the Lord God Almighty is revealing that sacrifices bring forth blessings as He strives to sacrifice all His divine treasures (8) to bring forth a new God/man creation of peace, joy, and happiness.

Note that God gave-up a creation, Lucifer gave-up heaven, Adam gave-up Eden, Noah gave-up his homeland, Abraham gave-up his son (pride), Moses gave-up his royal crown, Joshua gave-up his merciful heart, David gave-up his dignity, Christ gave-up His divine life, the Church will give-up its holiness, and the righteous world will sacrifice all human life, all in the name of trusting in the Word of God.

In short, to get a lot of God's treasures, a person must give a lot (sacrifice), which means he must give his labors (thanks), wealth (praise), and even his own life (worship) to get the Lord's treasures of a new body, eternal life, and his own kingdom. Recall that in the game of chance (gambling), the more a person is willing to bet, the more he can win, but a smart gambler seeks to seize the moment, when he can get the best odds and win it all on just one roll of the dice. We see that in the case of the Lord God Almighty, He was willing to bet it all and gambled on the greatest long shot, ever imaginable, as He bet His creation on the idea that man's free will (natural selection) could be transformed into His divine will (God's design), thereby making all men God-like (one family) in the end. This means that Jesus is seeking those souls, which will share His moment of panic, pain, and death to achieve spiritual purification of their selfish nature as they sacrifice their life to the Lord's divine will of new hope. We see that these devoted souls will experience truth as their spirits cry out in agony, suddenly understanding the meaning of life (to exist) from the standpoint of a desperate need for personal salvation, which leads to their new body (passport), eternal life (ticket), and own kingdom (money).

1. **See need for free redemption** – get passport to heaven: New body...being saved
2. **See need for earned salvation** – get ticket to heaven: eternal life...saving self
3. **See need for bonus rewards** – get money to spend in heaven: own kingdom...saving others

This illustration shows the need to understand both God's design (death) and nature's natural selection (life) as they both strive to bring forth man's free redemption (passport to heaven), earned salvation (ticket to heaven), and his bonus rewards (heavenly money). Obviously, the need for a world savior will never take on more meaning than at that moment of one's hopeless defeat and eternal damnation which occurs during a person's agonizing death, when he is cast into hopelessness and separation from God. We see that if a blind sinner evaluates man's ways (illusion) as compared to God's ways (reality) as shown below, the difference is clear between building good character (reality) rather than building an evil ego (illusion). We see that those cursed with evil egos will cry out the loudest when their destiny is known and life ends, thereby giving them no more hope as time runs out and they are face-to face with God's eternal reality (moment of absolute truth).

The following tabular information indicates the divine/human desires indicating the compared value systems of God and man, reflecting the war of spirit and flesh for all to see the true meaning of life (eternal existence):

Tree of Knowledge (false wisdom)   **Tree of Life** (true wisdom)
Separating Human Self-Righteousness (illusion)
from Divine Righteousness (reality)

Pagan Illusion, highway to hell **Man's Desire to Be** (hope):	**Christian Reality,** pathway to perfection **God's Desire to Force Man to Be** (holy)
1. Prosperous, respectable, and happy	1. Believe/surrender to purification
2. Cultured, educated, and successful	2. Trust God, fight evil world of sin
3. Good taste, proper, and accepted	3. Sacrifice all to God (repentance)
4. High social position (family name)	4. Devote life to worship and good works

5. Career, achievement and popularity
6. Proper care of possessions
7. Good example through leadership
8. Diligent, ambitious, hardworking
9. Affectionate to family and friends
10. Maintain health - being fit
(Willing to trade soul for
"good life of prosperity")

5. Seek the divine virtues of God
6. Pursue the divine truth of God
7. Acquire humble, loving spirit
8. Lift up one's neighbor's virtues
9. Sacrifice life to save souls
10. Live in the divine will of God
(Willing to sacrifice soul for
God's eternal life/friendship)

This illustration shows that the greatest challenge in life is God's dual attitude (two truths) concerning His infinite love for man and His desire to force mankind to experience every hideous torture conceivably devised by the diabolical human mind. The explanation is that pain and struggle build characters of steel for those with the courage to follow Christ to Calvary and then be willing to plunge themselves into the Lord's scourging, crucifixion, and death (tomb). In this way, Christ's Church has had to follow the way of the cross for some two thousand years, as a divine light of purity (forgiveness) flickering before an evil world, showing that the purpose of life revolves around humility (will), devotion (law), and piety (truth). The cross (dying to self) leads to each person's self-identity as a true soldier-of-the-light (soul winner), who has the power to reflect his true image (tree of life) of his own self-worth before the throne of God. We see that Christ's brotherhood has been established through His covenant as a victim soul, manifesting the last hope for a person's supreme sacrifice, where he will offer to sacrifice his life for another in jeopardy of facing eternal death. The Brotherhood of Man is a silent force, with each righteous citizen working quietly to save his neighbors and friends without their knowledge or even without arousing their slightest suspicion. All this is done and accomplished to give mankind an unbelievable surprise gift at death, when presto, a treasure in heaven, truly a priceless gift of redemption, is received from a true friend (Christ), who would be there when all others had failed him.

The real meaning of life and God's friendship is revealed in a person's intent (thoughts) and desires (emotions), expressed in genuine sacrificial actions found in his Unfathomable Charity. We see that these positive commitments (solemn vows) are taken to God's holy altar as payments for the Lord's divine reality (eternal life) and to beg for the Lord's divine approval, while making his intercessory pleas in recompense for the sins of man. This process reconciles one's life (free will) with God's eternal plan (destiny) that centers upon human perfection for one and all as the human race accepts Jesus Christ as its savior, thereby making God's design (divine will) and nature's natural selection (free will) one reality (God/man). We see that those who submit to the divine will of God will be on the path to knowing (wisdom), loving (courage), and serving (generosity) the majesty of God, while those who fulfill His will may be like Him in mind (wise), heart (loving), and soul (generous) to create another soul saver within the kingdom of God.

We see just two men sharing one friendship through a lifetime of companionship leading them both to a new state of peace of mind (transfigured body), joy of the heart (glorified spirit), and happiness of the soul (holy soul). The union of divinity and humanity comes with man's three penitential acts: (1) confession (last supper), (2) contrition (scourging), and (3) penance, (crucifixion) accepted by God's act of forgiveness (resurrection). This most crucial series of steps toward God's reconciliation reveals the need for every soul to continually live the death of Calvary through the sacrament of penance, thereby allowing a person to be eternally forgiven by God. We have always known it's not how many sins one accumulates on his broken soul, but how quickly a person recovers his purity through God's most forgiving mind (wisdom), heart (courage), soul (generosity), and life-force (unselfishness). We must all try continually to fight the evil effects of sin by continually trying to overcome our weak sin-nature as this is truly the way of the cross (trials/tribulations) of Jesus Christ, leading a soul to the pearly gates of heaven.

The following tabular information depicts the three divine/human sacrifices of mankind's redemption revealing the power of the sacrament of penance to overcome sin and defeat the evil one and all his demonic followers (demons):

Three Divine/Human Sacrifices of Redemption

God (Confession)	1.	Last Supper (solemn vow) ...God	Purification of Flesh
	•	God's Bloodless Sacrifice	(Word of Righteousness)
		• Sacrificed "Promise of Death"	
God/Man (Contrition/ Penance)	2.	Calvary (solemn oath) ...society	Purification of Spirit
	•	God/Man Bloodless Sacrifice	(Blood of Purification)
		• Sacrificed living "Existence to Death"	
Man (Forgiveness)	3.	Pieta/Resurrection (solemn word) ...Self	Purification of Soul
	•	Man's Bloodless Sacrifice	(Death of Redemption)
		• Sacrificed "Tears of Death"	

This illustration shows that in view of the triune nature of man's creator, the human experience is multi-dimensional in scope, focus, and diversification, based on one's intellectual (flesh) and emotional (spirit) understanding of God's divine truths. This also signifies the manifestation of a natural contradiction in the overall divine purpose, based upon God loving all His creations equally or just those saints that have reached the state of divine perfection. Everything in God's Grand Design is designed to produce perfect circumstances that create the divine kingdom's major spiritual events (covenants) to form its prestigious history of divine love. In short, the Lord God Almighty is demanding that all creations (buy intercessor) must be divinely sacrificed upon the Lord's altar of death to determine their value (sacrificial price). This means that the Lord was then willing to place His entire creation of existence (God's offering) in harm's way to measure its divine value in terms of the acceptance of man, thereby testing its level of perfection before one and all. It was then man's turn to match God's offering with his own as he is willing to sacrifice his Messiah (man's offering) or buying a divine interpreter upon the Lord's altar of death by determining its value. Through these two awesome sacrifices, the God/man relationship is to be built in preparation for the coming kingdom of glory.

This means that it is absolutely true that things are not as they appear in God's elusive and unpredictable world of strange illogic and reverse psychologies, causing the human race to give-up and let Jesus Christ take over its lives. The answer to mankind's mass confusion is that there is a greater perspective and more comprehensive plan being unfolded by the divine forces of infinite truth, moment by moment as the history of man shows the way to the kingdom of God. Recall that God is betting everything He owns on His own ability to plunge Himself totally into the pit of evil and come out, smelling like a rose (thrill of victory), a winner all the way. The implication is that Lucifer and the negative forces of life (sacrifice Messiah/man) can utilize the five gifted groups of people (winners): (1) smart people (academia), (2) rich people (influential), (3) criminals (strong), (4) evil people (powerful), and (5) all who hate God (demonic). In contrast, the Lord (sacrifice creation/God) will take all five worthless groups of people (losers): (1) ignorant fools (stupid), (2) poor people, (3) sick people, (4) weak people (devout), and (5) all who love God (holy). With this ragtag team of lost souls, the Lord God Almighty will fight on and still win hands down in the end as the Lord can do the impossible of the impossible, using either ALL (God) or Nothing (man). The intent of the Lord is to create both a physical interpreter (Aaron/Jesus) to take man's sin (confession) and a spiritual intercessor (Moses/Christ) to give man His divinity (communion) and guide all men to the divine truths of God.

Through this dual process of purification (intercede) and transformation (interpret), God will convert the whole world from sinful fools to holy saints in the end.

The following tabular information indicates the eleven sacrifices made by God to purchase His kingdom of glory step by step until He defeats evil and makes all things holy in His sight:

God Sacrifices His Entire Kingdom to bring Righteousness, Holiness, and Perfection to All
(God's eleven sacrifices pay for the creation
of a perfect world full of perfect people)

God is Man	1.	God Sacrifices His <u>Creation</u> - Divine Life (breath)… Divinic Covenant
	•	God Gets "**Angelic Realm**" - Heaven: Spirit World = God's Destiny
	•	Lucifer Stands against God, becomes Evil – Challenge Absolute Truth
	•	God Gets "**Human Realm**" – Earth: Physical World = Man's Free Will
	•	Adam Defies God's Law, becomes Evil – Challenge Relative Truth
Paradise	2.	God Sacrifices <u>Lucifer</u> - Tree of Life…………Edenic Covenant

	•	God Gets **"Capital Sin"** – Damnation: Spirit World = Demonic Possession
	•	Serpent Tests Adam's Courage – One Moment of Cowardice = Tree of Knowledge
	•	God Gets **"Mortal Sin"** – Death: Physical World = Rot in Grave
	•	Serpent Tests Eve's Wisdom – One Moment of Ignorance: Forbidden Fruit
Free Will	3.	God Sacrifices <u>Adam</u> - Seed of Promise..........Adamic Covenant
	•	God Gets **"Abel as Intercessor** (give divinity)"** – Divine Inheritance: Land
	•	First Victim of Death – Face Lucifer's Test: Communion (good from evil)
	•	God Gets **"Cain as Interpreter** (take-sin)"** – Divine Birthright: People
	•	First Murderer for Death – Face God's Judgment: Confession (right/wrong)
Obedience	4.	God Sacrifices <u>1st Humanity</u> - Rainbow Promise...Noahic Covenant
	•	God Gets **"Purification of Earth"** – Drowning of Evil Men
	•	Evil Man is Destroyed – See Limitations: Can't Do = Ethics
	•	God Gets **"New World Order"** – Rainbow Covenant of Holiness
	•	Righteous Man Rules Earth – See Potential: Can Do = Morals
Faith	5.	God Sacrifices <u>Isaac and Ishmael</u> – Circumcision of Purity... Abrahamic Covenant
	•	God Gets **"Jewish People of Holiness"** – Messiah (word of Christ)
	•	Isaac's Birth from a Barren Womb – Dying to Selfishness
	•	God Gets **"Gentile People of Righteousness"** – Church (touch of Peter)
	•	Ishmael's Birth from a Fruitful Womb – Born-again in Unselfishness
Law	6.	God Sacrifices <u>Jewish People</u> - Stone Tablets of Law... Mosaic Covenant
	•	God Gets **"Levitical Priesthood"** – Blood Offering (worship)
	•	House of Aaron – Blessing of Holiness: Fixed Frame of Reference
	•	God Gets **"Jewish Temple"** – Prayer Gift (praise)
	•	Tribe of Levi – Blessing of Perfection: Perspective of Reality
Homeland	7.	God Sacrifices <u>Pagan Enemy</u> - Holy Land of Milk/Honey... Palestinian Covenant
	•	God Gets **"Ruling Class of Living Saints"** – Mount Gerizim (maturity)
	•	Joshua's Army Defeats Evil Enemy – Living Prayers of Love
	•	God Gets **"Pagan Slaves in Service to Evil"** – Mount Ebal (growth)
	•	Lucifer's Followers Bow to God's Authority – Soldiers-of-the-Light
Rule	8.	God Sacrifices <u>King of the Jews</u> - Sun/Moon/Stars... Davidic Covenant
	•	God Gets **"Judaic Kingship"** – Prayer Offering: Will of the People
	•	House of David – Blessing of Righteousness: Learn Right from Wrong

		God Gets **"Jewish Throne "**– Gift of Gold: Divine Will of God

- God Gets **"Jewish Throne "**– Gift of Gold: Divine Will of God
- Tribe of Judah – Blessing of Perfection: Learn Reality from Illusion

Freedom 9. God Sacrifices His Son, <u>Jesus Christ</u> - Womb/Cross/Tomb...New Covenant

- God Gets **"New Human Nature"** – Son of Man, Jesus (take-sins)
- Deny Intellect – Reject Lie: Defeat Ignorance = New Mind (remove faults)
- God Gets **"New Divine Nature"** – Son of God, Christ (give divinity)
- Abandon Feelings – Accept Truth: Defeat Cowardice = New Heart (gain virtues)

Heaven 10. God Sacrifices <u>Catholic Church</u> – Holy Spirit... Everlasting Covenant

- God Gets **"Man's Redemption"** – Baptism: Remove Capital Sins (free)
- Submission of the Flesh – Dying to Self (denial): Overcome Sin-nature
- God Gets **"Man's Salvation"** – Confession: Remove Mortal Sins (earned)
- Sacrifice of the Spirit – Born-again in Christ: Overcome Worldly Temptation

Man becomes God 11. God Sacrifices <u>Righteous World</u> – Eternal Father .... Divine Covenant

- God Gets **"New Jerusalem"** – Capital City of Earth: Divine Home
- Blessed with Peace of Mind – Thinking for Self: Free the Mind (growth)
- God Gets **"New Heaven and New Earth"** – Kingdom of Glory: Divine Government
- Blessed with Happiness of Soul – Loving One and All: Free the Heart (maturity)

This illustration shows that God is willing to sacrifice All (creation) to get All (God as man), even if it includes crucifying His Son to purchase the sin-debts of sin (venial), evil (mortal), and death (capital). The Lord was willing to go to any extreme in time, money, effort, and/or even give His own life to earn the right to build a most magnificent Kingdom of Glory, where every person on Earth can expect to become God-like in mind, heart, and soul. The theme of God's eternal creation is to create a place where God can become man (Christ) and man can become God (Jesus) through man's submission (dying to self) and God's sacrifice (born-again) allowing God and man to become one. In the end, God's home in Heaven (reality) and man's home on Earth (illusion) would become one in the Lord's New Heaven and New Earth, bringing forth an entire civilization of righteous, holy, and perfect people.

In the previous chart, we see that God had to place eleven major sacrifices upon His divine altar to be both purified (crucible) and transformed (winepress) from death (crucifixion) to new-life (resurrection). This most perfect kingdom was to be established upon the priesthood of Aaron (church), the kingship of David (government), and the sonship of Jesus (home) to bring forth God's blessings of redemption (being saved/free), salvation (saving self/earned), and rewards (saving others/bonus). In this way, all the children of God could be saved from ignorance (sin), cowardice (evil), and greed (death) in three advents of Jesus Christ (see/hear/speak to God). The Lord God Almighty has designed a single week of purification (knowledge), transformation (self-awareness), correction (conscience), and conversion (sentience) of the human race to bring all men into union with God's truth, law, will, and love.

We see that God's creation causes a serious distortion between the absolute truth (inheritance of name) of God and the relative truth (blessing of virginity) of man, thereby fracturing the divine reality (heaven) to create an unexplainable human illusion (earth). Understanding this aspect of God's dual nature makes it easier to accept a person's life-time of human failures, forcing mankind to continually confess its sins, repent, and be forgiven as it crawls out of an evil past to find eternal freedom comprised of peace, joy, and happiness. This means that humanity is like a wandering pilgrim on a quest to a promised land, where one day, the horrors of the past will become the foundation stones for a successful future (eternal life). The truth is that present-day mankind represents the pioneer stock of the coming kingdom as humanity learns the meaning behind a person's solemn vows, oaths, and sacred words of eternal commitment to God, angels, and men. We see that those who suffer as pioneers traveling along the pathway of perfection (nothingness) for Christ's sake will stand closest to the Lord, when they come into His kingdom of glory at the end of time. The question arises: "How does all this relate" to the purpose of Israel (Promised Land) and its bungled Jewish experiment of trying to fulfill God's divine law of obedience, which would allow the Jews to cover sins and obtain earthly righteousness? First of all, the Jewish heritage is one of God's most cherished treasures and is perfectly on schedule as it rushes toward its fulfillment on the day of its most perfect holiness. Then what happened? The fact is that nothing happened because the new kingdom will depict the theme of a dead people, returning to life and joining forces with their exiled king of death to save all mankind (eternal life). We see that to-gether, they will build the true promised land of milk (human kindness) and honey (divine love) for the benefit of all future generations to bathe in the luxury of God's divine pleasure (brotherhood) through their own divine holiness (sainthood) forevermore.

The tested faith of the Jewish people will be the coming shining light of the world, as mankind passes through its darkest hour of despair (dark night of the soul), when the hearts of all men will fail them during the Lord's coming great tribulation period (seven years/death of man). We see that "Israel" is the firstfruits of divine na-tionhood, the eldest brother to a growing world of eternal nations, all joined in the purposes of God by its royal sonship charter of brotherly love (righteousness). We see that the Lord is in the business of raising babies (baby farm) and making them into men of integrity (think for themselves) to one day walk in freedom (think correctly) and dignity (love correctly) with their Creator God forevermore.

The overall time table of God's plan of redemption includes time for mankind to experience evil, struggle for the control of Earth, and learn the eternal truths of creation to master thinking for itself. The learning curve of humanity has been precisely fixed to reveal God's Divine School of Higher Learning at a time and in a manner only known to the Lord God Almighty Himself. Our Creator is calling those of undaunted faith to join His quest for divine wisdom and infinite perfection, through a universal bond of mutual love (sharing) in search of experiencing and comprehending the truth. The Lord gave Lucifer six days to test and purify men's souls, separating the soldiers-of-the-light (see potential) from the fools of the darkness (see limitations) bringing all things into perfect balance between the forces of good and evil. We see that mankind's final examination is nearing as it takes the form of man's greatest test of faith that will occur when the wrath of God will come to purify all the sins of man and place the enemies of His Son at Christ's feet. The Lord will soon come as a thief in the night (beginning) to begin the establishment of His new civilization of love, thereby revealing His sacred government (righteousness) during a one-thousand-year age of peace, known to us all as when Christ seals His saints.

In perceiving the mind of God, we must comprehend why He has manifested His divine truth by creating our particular life-force in human form, which we see as the parental nature of God (holy father/holy mother). A good case can be made for believing that God is teaching mankind to learn the principles of infinite space (flesh) and eternal time (spirit) based upon a divine continuum of both its physical (illusion) and spiritual (spirit) natures (mystical form). In more simple terms, this means teaching humanity (baby farm) to walk and talk using its own power of discovery and develop a wise mind (self), courageous heart (society), and a generous soul (God). Now, consider the phases of the life-experience as a set of well-defined points along each man's path, as he journeys through the trials and tribulations of life (trial-and-error) to find God's divine truths.

For example, initially, each man learns to walk, talk, and think and so on throughout his early years of life, but then in his mature years, he realizes that reading, writing, and arithmetic are exceptional power tools, when it comes to thinking for oneself (imagination). These most powerful skills teach every sojourning soul to intricately navigate through its own small world of existence, giving it increasing confidence to ever widen its sphere of exploration. Through this adventuresome spirit (challenge), a person will face a lifetime of trials and errors with each try (tenacity) bringing him closer and closer to his ultimate dream of success. Yes! Human success means hearing the words of the world and then deciding which ones are true and which ones are false, much like Jesus' parable of the seed being scattered on the path, among rocks in the weed patch, and finally, falling on the good ground to bear fruit 33 percent (righteous), 67 percent (holy), and 100 percent (perfect).

The following tabular information indicates the Word of God is like seeds falling on a path, among rocks, in a weed patch, and finally, on good ground, where it can bear fruit 33 percent (righteous), 67 percent (holy), and 100 percent (perfect):

**God's Word is Like Seeds on a Path, among Rocks,
in Weed Patch, and finally on Good Ground**
(takes God's word into mind, becomes righteous, heart
becomes holy, and into soul becomes perfect)

1. **Seed Falls on Path** – <u>God's Word Enters Mind</u>: Killed by One's Sin-nature (sin)
   - God *Verbally Announces* the Good News – Free Redemption for Everyone
   - God's Spoken Word – Creates Righteous Men on Earth (believe 33%)
2. **Seed Falls Among Rocks** – <u>God's Word Enters Heart</u>: Killed by Worldly Temptations (evil)
   - God Sounds *Shofar Horn* Giving the Gospel Message – Earned Salvation for Believers
   - God's Written Word – Creates Holy Saints in Heaven (believe 67%)
3. **Seed Falls Among Weeds** – <u>God's Word Enters Soul</u>: Killed by Demonic Possession (death)
   - God Sounds His *Golden Trumpet* Giving Doctrinal Truths – Bonus Rewards for Chosen
   - God's Incarnate Word – Creates Perfect Sons within God's Kingdom (believe 100%)
4. **Seed Falls on Good Ground** – <u>God's Word Enters Life-force</u>: Thinking for Oneself
   - Bear 33% Fruit – Mind of Wisdom: Become Righteous Citizen on Earth (new body)
   - Bear 67% Fruit – Heart of Courage: Become Holy Saint in Heaven (eternal life)
   - Bear 100% Fruit – Soul of Generosity: Become Son of God within Kingdom (kingdom)

This illustration shows that the life-experience is about converting one's mind, heart, and soul by listening to God's Word (mind), learning God's Word (heart), and finally, acting on God's Word (soul) by saving the souls of others. Now, let's look at this great adventure of life as each of God's children must travel through the mosaic tabernacle (tent), Solomon's/Herod's temples (stone), Jesus' Calvary (flesh), and finally, Christ's resurrection (transfiguration) to be set free from sin, evil, and death. By removing his faults (physical), a person can be transformed from a pagan slave (Mosaic tent) into a faithful Christian (stone temple), thereby purifying his mind to remove ignorance and gain wisdom. Secondly, by washing away his sins (spiritual), a person can be transformed from a faithful Christian (stone temple) into a holy saint (Calvary), thereby purifying his heart to remove cowardice and gain courage. Thirdly, by changing his nature (mystical), a person can be transformed from a holy saint (new flesh) into a Son of God (transfiguration), thereby purifying his soul to remove greed and gain generosity. Finally, by becoming born-again (divine), a person can be transformed from a Son of God (transfiguration) into the divinity of Christ Himself (God-like), thereby purifying his life-force to remove selfishness and gain unselfishness. By mastering God's four dimensions of life (physical/spiritual/mystical/divine), a person can comprehend Moses' Tabernacle, Solomon's Temple, Jesus' crucifixion (Calvary), and Christ's resurrection (transfiguration).

The idea here is to see the human race both growing and maturing through four stages of life by being purified using water, blood, spirit, and divinity to transform imperfect humans into perfect sons of God. It should now make sense that both the roles of the Jews and the Christians are central to the transformation of each man's mind (flesh/wisdom), heart (spirit/courage), soul (being/generosity), and life-force (nature/unselfishness). A new mind allows a person to see his own faults; a new heart allows a person to wash away his sins; a new soul allows a person to change his nature; and a new life-force allows a person to receive a transfigured body. At each of these four phases of transformation, we see mankind is following its selfish will (baby), then decides to follow the will of the people (teenager), then decides to follow God's will (adult), and finally, decides to follow its own born-again free will (wise man). This means that a baby is following the pagan philosophy (selfishness); the teenager is following the Christian philosophy (unselfishness); the adult is following the sainthood philosophy (sharing); and finally, the wise man is following the Son of God's philosophy (saving the lost). Through each of these belief systems, the human race both grows and matures to make mankind strong enough to defeat its own sin-nature (ignorance/water), worldly temptations (criminality/blood), demonic possession (insanity/spirit), and even God's curse (evil/transfiguration).

The following tabular information indicates that the human race has been called from Moses' tent (water), to Solomon's/Herod's temples (blood), to Jesus' Calvary (spirit), and then to Christ's resurrection (divinity) to become God-like.

Man's Conversion via Moses' Tent, Solomon's Temple, Jesus' Calvary, and Christ's Resurrection
(tent removes man's sin nature, temple removes worldly temptations, Calvary removes demonic possession, and resurrection removes God's curse)

Truth
(see faults)

1. **Moses' Tent** – <u>Mosaic Tabernacle</u>: Convert Pagan
   Slaves = Sinners....Knowledge
   - Water Purification – Red Sea: Deny One's Intellect
     (baby/mind)
   - Remove Sin-nature – Ignorance: **Physical**
     Admit One's Foolishness   **Dimension**
   - 1st Power of Transformation – See One's Own Limitations
   - Learn Right from Wrong — Righteous Citizen on Earth: New Body
   (follow selfish will – break the chains of ignorance: become wise)

Law
(wash
away sin)

2. **Solomon's/Herod's Stone Building** – <u>Temple</u>: Convert
   Christians = Believers .... Self-awareness
   - Blood Purification – Animal Sacrifice: Abandon Feelings
     (teenager/heart)

- Remove Worldly Temptations – **Spiritual**
  Criminality: Learn God's Truth **Dimension**
- 2nd Power of Transformation – See One's Own Potential
- Learn Good from Evil – Holy Saint in Heaven: Eternal Life
  (follow the people's will – unlock prison doors of cowardice: become courageous)

Will
(change nature)

3. **Jesus' Flesh** – <u>Human Temple</u>: Convert Saints = Saving Others .... Consciousness
- Spirit Purification – Divine Sacrifice: Submit Free Will (adult/soul)
- Remove Demonic Possession – Insanity: **Mystical**
  Implement God's Will **Dimension**
- 3rd Power of Transformation – See One's Self-worth
- Learn God's Will/Man's Will – Perfect Son Within Kingdom: Royal Kingdom
  (follow God's divine will – overpower guards of greed: become generous)

Love
(transfigured body)

4. **Christ's Divinity** - <u>Divine Temple</u>: Convert Sonship = Becoming God ... Sentience
- Divine Purification – God's Approval: Obey God's Laws
  (wise man/life-force)
- Remove God's Curse – Evil: Implement **Divine**
  God's Will **Dimension**
- 4th Power of Transformation – See God's Perfection
- Learn God's Reality/man's illusion – God-like in Divinity: Freedom
  (follow born-again free will – set free to master life: become respected)

This illustration shows that each of God's children must experience life on Earth, in Heaven, within the Kingdom, and by becoming God's Nature to know the meaning, purpose, and value of life. This means that the human race must seek its purification in the waters of baptism, blood of sacrifice, spirit of awakening, and transformation from death to new-life (transfiguration). We see that this journey of purification began with the Mosaic Tabernacle (water) as a manifestation of the Red Sea, where the good of God (Jews) was separated from the evil of Lucifer (Egyptians). Secondly, came both Solomon's/Herod's temples (stone) as a manifestation of God's Passover meal (lamb slaughter), where the chosen of God (holy) were separated from the Gentiles of Earth (unholy). Thirdly, came Jesus' crucifixion (Calvary/spirit) as a manifestation of God's Holy Mass (Son's sacrifice), where the saints of God (saved) are separated from the sinners of death (lost). Finally, comes Christ's resurrection (transfiguration) as a manifestation of God's new creation (life) being separated from old creation (death). In summary, we see that the human race must first learn right from wrong to become a righteous citizen on Earth and become worthy of a new body. Secondly, he must learn good from evil to become a holy saint in Heaven and become worthy of eternal life. Thirdly, he must learn God's will from man's will to become a perfect son of God within the kingdom and become worthy of his own royal kingdom. Finally, he must learn God's reality from man's illusion to become a free man to think for himself and become worthy of managing his own free will.

This means that once a man has seen and done everything in the world, he becomes unafraid of attempting to accomplish any reasonable undertaking, leading to the improvement of his well-being, especially in increasing the value of his life. We all hear that variety is the spice of life and that being well-read and well-traveled makes a person cultured in the eyes of others, making him interesting to know and to be with as they never tire of being all things to all people. The best way to grasp the importance of variety is to comprehend the great work that a wine grower must do to prepare the ground with all of the necessary natural flavors needed to produce a fine wine made by a consummate expert. This most admired "expertise (perfection)" means a man has mastered the many institutions and disciplines of life, including the abstract dimensions of physics and time, giving him even more power in the world. Such an accomplished man has for all intents and purposes grown-up and is ready to graduate to the spiritual dimension (maturity), where he might learn to effectively navigate his own life.

We see that a person's whole life-experience is all about learning to navigate to His soul along the divine progress points, leading him to the very throne of God. All this magnificent training (growing) and experience (maturing) is designed to create the eternal teachers of tomorrow, as the new kingdom will have seven specially created career fields. Out of the many career fields of God and man, experience comes to teach the purpose of life (service) to the new growing babies of future generations. This new hope for a bright future unites the expectations of God with the hopes of man as they commit themselves to working together to build a glorious kingdom of eternal perfection.

The following tabular information indicates God's eternal professions revealing that human institutions of our present society have been designed to fit into the Lord's master scheme of future events:

God's Eternal Divine/Human Professions
(Creation of organized society in Heaven/earth)

Creation	Professions (Responsibilities)	Divine Lesson Plan of God	Institutions
Light	1. **Teacher**	Pathway of Perfection	Education
	• Overcome Pride – Dignity	• Mastery of Holiness (Belief)	
Earth	2. **King/Priest**	Kingship/Priesthood	Government
	• Overcome Avarice – Manage	• Mastery of Just Rule (Trust)	
Water	3. **Fisherman**	Evangelization of Man	Business/Industry
	• Overcome Avarice – Manage	• Mastery of Holy Word (Faith)	
Plants	4. **Farmer**	Nourishment of Humanity	Agriculture
	• Overcome Anger - Moderation	• Mastery of Holy Bread/Wine (Will)	
Animals	5. **Shepherd** (kinship)	Guiding Hand of Truth	Finance
	• Overcome Envy – Sharing	• Mastery of Divine Order (Obedience)	
Man	6. **Carpenter** (sonship)	Builder of ***Kingdoms***	Manufacturing

Rest	• Overcome Sloth – Diligence 7. **Servant** (motherhood) • Overcome Lust – Love	• Mastery of Creation (Self-Control) Birth of Humanity Transportation • Mastery of Love (virtues)
New	8. **Slave/Son** (fatherhood)	Living Prayer of God Operations
Light	• Overcome Death – Life	• Mastery of Sonship (Friendship)

This illustration shows that God is seeking the fruits (accomplishments) of the free-willed human spirit and that the future generations will not be purified by the effects of sin (venial), evil (mortal), and death (capital); so how will they be properly tested (report card), judged (God's opinion), and evaluated (seeing self)? We see that through his "testing/judgment/evaluation," a person can achieve righteousness (right/wrong), holiness (good/evil), and perfection (God's will/man's will) in the sight of God. The Lord knows that "future mankind" will be made up from the holy bloodlines of the children of saints, who have distinguished themselves in the eyes of God (opinion). All future holy people will be products of perfect free-willed spirits that can no longer be defiled by the worldly temptations of Satan or the tests of Lucifer. This concept applies the logic where a racehorse breeder first establishes a line of thoroughbreds to bring forth a winning set of champions. This is done by creating a royal line passing along the best qualities of the breed from generation to generation until a breeder (owner) gets that most special quality of perfection needed to give birth to a perfect race horse (Jesus Christ). This means that among God's future chosen people (Jews), everyone is good by his own free will because he automatically knows the difference between right and wrong, as a part of his fine breeding (growth/mandatory) and proper rearing (maturity/optional).

The Bible explains this concept as God writes His holy law in the hearts of His chosen souls of love so that they can become holy as God is holy and earn the friendship of God. This principle of holiness and the Lord's second coming (thief in night/seal saints) are both predicated upon man being transformed from being automatically evil (sin-nature) to becoming instinctively good (holy nature) in the sight of God. This means that the seven professions of creation, listed above, reveal the Lord's Grand Design for the coming kingdom of glory, whereby humanity becomes one with its Creator in both spirit (law/blessing of virginity) and in flesh (truth/inheritance of name). These divinely inspired professions effectively link the natural forces of life using the deep roots of man's institutionalized systems of human justice (government), mercy (church), and love (home). Through God's forgiveness will come the Lord's new institutionalized system of divine justice (new government), mercy (new church), and love (new home). This implies that this combination of the God/man union will bring a new life-force (human spirit), which will be created and known as the mystical body of Christ (kingdom). The ultimate purpose of God is that of establishing the father's divine household as a royal family of divine love, which is manifested through God's righteous kingdom (home), His Son's sacred government, and the Spirit's holy church. This new divine life-force will be made incarnate through God's kingdom rule creating the government's royal brotherhood (earth/righteousness) and the church's royal sainthood (heaven/holiness). This is accomplished out of the Lord's kingdom of justice (pass/fail system) to bring new-life to all who will repent and serve only the Lord God Almighty without any resistance or complaint (sonship training).

This triune structure comprises the heart of the final creation bringing forth the coming divine kingdom of God through the eternal presence of the Lord's divine truth (righteousness), divine law (holiness), and divine will (perfection). In short, we see that the Lord God Almighty will bring forth two babies into His kingdom: one via the flesh (world), and the other via the spirit (church) to defeat all the forces of evil on earth and glorify all of the forces of good in heaven. This means that one's earthly life is free, but he must choose between the forces of righteousness (right) and unrighteousness (wrong) by learning the lessons of life and then bringing forth a fruitful life of wisdom (job), courage (family), and generosity (home). Secondly, one's Christian life must be earned as a redeemed soul must choose between God's ways (good) and man's ways (evil) by becoming worthy of God's blessings and then bringing forth a fruitful eternal life of repentance (righteousness), prayers (holiness), and works (perfection). We see that through these two births, baby man can change his nature from human to divine (grave) by choosing a righteous life (righteous world); and he can change his sinfulness into holiness (host) by choosing a holy life (church).

The following tabular information indicates that physical birth (world) is free of charge, while a person's born-again birth (church) must be earned, thereby calling physical man to fight evil to bear fruit out of his earthly life (purified grave), while spirit man must surrender his free will to God and give all to Christ:

Understanding the War of Good and Evil
(natural birth must fight evil and accept death/born-
again birth must surrender and face eternal life)

Incarnation of Man		Reincarnation of God	
(spirit to flesh)		(flesh to spirit)	
God becomes man via Life		Man becomes God via Death	
Fighting Evil - **Righteous Man**		**Holy Man** - Worshiping good	
	Natural	Born-again	
Earth	Birth	Birth	**Heaven**
(lessons)	(world)	(church)	(blessings)
• Physical Life on Earth		• Spiritual Life in Church	
• Learn Lessons of Life		• Receive God's Blessings	
• *Fight Evil* unto Death		• *Surrender Will* unto New-life	
• Bear Fruits of Flesh		• Bear Fruits of Spirit	
• Wisdom - New Mind		• Repentance - Righteous	
• Courage - New Heart		• Prayers - Holy	
• Generosity - New Soul		• Works – Perfect	
• Purify One's Grave		• Purify One's Host	
• Get Free Redemption		• Earn Own Salvation	
• Resurrect on Judgment Day		• Resurrect in Christ	
• Receive New Body		• Receive Eternal life	

God's Justice Fulfilled (pay damages)	God's Grave Changes Nature	God's Mercy Fulfilled (pay fines)	Christ's Host Washes Away Sin
	• Animal		• Righteous Man
	• Robot		• Holy Man
	• Human		• Perfect Man
	• Divine (Calvary/ grave)		• Free Man (Last supper/host)

This illustration shows that the job of Earth (world) is to teach the lessons of life (natural birth), while the job of Heaven (church) is to pour forth God's blessings of life (born-again birth). Obviously, natural birth offers a person physical life on Earth so he can grow-up and learn the lessons of life by fighting evil unto his own death (old age) to bear the fruits of wisdom, courage, and generosity, thereby bringing forth his new mind, heart, and soul. Secondly, born-again birth offers a person spiritual life in Heaven so he can mature and receive God's blessing by surrendering his free will to God's divine will to bear the fruits of repentance, prayers, and works to bring forth his righteousness, holiness, and perfection. This means that the "flesh of man (natural birth)" can only have his nature changed from human to divine by purifying his own grave to change his animal mind, robot heart, and human soul into a holy saint (divine). In contrast, the spirit of man (born-again birth) can only wash away his sins to change his sinfulness to holiness by purifying his own host to change him into a righteous man, holy man, perfect man, and finally, a free man before God. The point being made here is that the flesh of man must be changed into divinity via his grave, which is resurrected on judgment day to bring forth his new transfigured body, thereby making his flesh divine (transfiguration). Secondly, the spirit of man must wash away his sins by fulfilling Christ's host through his ability to believe 100 percent in the fact that God's Son can remove his old spirit (water baptism) and exchange it with Christ's spirit (spiritual baptism) so that Christ can become any surrendered soul.

Now it should make sense that the entire human race is being called to fulfill both the physical world (grave) and the Lord's spiritual church (host) by both fighting worldly temptations (grave) and by dying to itself (host) via its complete submission or the sacrifice of its free will to God's divine will. This means that to understand the forces of life in its purest form, it must be comprehended that the natural powers of God's kingdom come from both the sacrificial prayers of Christ's holy mass (death) and from the devotional prayers of the Virgin Mary's Holy Rosary (new-life). This implies that the Mass (create saints/host) and the rosary (save sinners/grave) are the mystical keys (key master) to focusing one's life on man's grave and on Christ's host for the salvation of man (pay sin-debt/save self).

We see that once the gates of redemption are opened (gatekeeper), they pour out God's glory through the Sacred Heart of Christ, thereby sharing the treasures of the kingdom with the beloved friends of God. Through the Immaculate Heart of Mary, all mankind's efforts (duties), works (responsibilities), and sacred accomplishments (authority) shall be collected and then presented before God via the glorification of His

Son's sacrifice for the benefit of the majesty of God. The visual existence of God's Creation is a divine statement, revealing the Lord's infinite personalities (worship), compassionate natures (praise/adoration), and in-depth beauty (thanksgiving), all perfected in the Lord's divine love. The idea is that everything the Lord does, says, or creates is a manifestation of His own self-image, thereby paying for all damages and paying all fines to reflect His divine light of infinite perfection as a guiding force to teach all men His divine truths.

The Lord's divine image is fulfilled in creating a new kingdom of righteousness (universe/flesh) that will manifest His perfect likeness through both His spiritual (benevolent force) and physical (personal God) existence. This omnipotent system of self-expression is, in itself, designed to give a clear picture of God's magnificent glory (gift of life's submission) and royal majesty (grace at death/sacrifice), thereby revealing Himself before the eyes of men. When mankind sees God's true image revealed in the splendor of His perfect creation, it will understand what life is all about based on knowing, loving, and serving God. Obviously, what life is all about centers upon the resurrection from one's grave (flesh) to receive a new body, and then resurrecting from Christ's host (spirit) to receive eternal life. We see that in the "execution" of God's Son, Jesus Christ, the Jews condemned Christ of blasphemy (guilty blood); while the Romans declared Jesus innocent of all charges (innocent blood), showing that the flesh is evil (repentance), while the spirit is innocent (forgiveness).

Note that Jesus as the flesh of man (grave) is guilty for saying He is God, but He lies while Christ as the spirit of man (host) is innocent for saying that He is God, because He really is God. We see the real contradiction comes with Jesus Christ being a living paradox, where the flesh lies and the spirit tells the truth as the Lord is both all man (human God) and all God (divine man) at the same time, thereby confusing both the Jewish temple law (spirit/I am a Jew) and the Roman Civil law (flesh/I am a gentile). Now imagine this contradiction getting out of hand when the Jews killed the spirit, but then used Jerusalem as the city of redeemed flesh; while the Romans killed the flesh, but then used Rome as the city of redeemed spirit. This logic would lead us to believe that the Jews loved the flesh (Jerusalem) and hated the spirit (grave), while the Romans loved the spirit (Rome) and hated the flesh (cross). In the end, they both resurrect with one to transfiguration (body/divine) and the other to eternal life (peace/holiness).

Note that through Jerusalem comes heaven on earth or righteous citizens on Earth, who dedicate their lives to an endless desire to perform greater and greater works to honor and praise (give labors/law) the physical nature of God. Secondly, through Rome comes Paradise in Heaven or holy saints in Heaven, who dedicate their lives to an endless desire to perform greater and greater prayers to honor and worship (give life/faith) the spiritual nature of God. This theme of Jewish flesh fighting Roman spirit during the passion of Christ begins to make sense, when a person realizes that the Jewish people believed in a king of glory, who is scheduled to come on a cloud of glory to become their eternal human king. In contrast, the Roman people believed in a supernatural spirit world, which was comprised of hundreds of gods, yet had been told that the Jews believed in the one God, who rules over both flesh and spirit. Suddenly, Jesus Christ showed up proclaiming to be the One God, who has come to bring both Heaven on Earth (flesh/grave) and Paradise in Heaven (spirit/host) to all those souls who will surrender their lives to Christ and become born-again in the new nature of the one God. The message here is that the Romans worshiped spirit gods and liked what Jesus was teaching them about becoming gods themselves if they will simply eat His flesh (Roman kingship) and drink His blood (Jewish priesthood). In like manner, the Jews believed in a physical God, who promised to come to live with them forever in a jeweled city to be known as the New Jerusalem, which will be brought directly from Heaven by God Himself. This means that Jesus Christ came to Earth to establish two eternal cities (Rome/Jerusalem), with the first being created (Rome) during His first coming (priest on donkey/purify host) and then the second to be created (Jerusalem) during His third coming (judge on cloud/purify grave).

The following tabular information indicates that the Lord God Almighty is bringing two separate redemptive systems to the human race, one saves (grave) man's flesh in Jerusalem (Jews/law) and one saves (host) man's spirit in Rome (Romans/faith):

All Flesh is Called to Jerusalem and All Spirit is Called to Rome
(Jesus fulfills God's law of obedience, while Christ fulfills man's faith in God's love)

1   **All flesh is called to Jerusalem** – Jews kill Christ's Spirit: fulfill law...See Limitations
    - Flesh is called to works – God's law of obedience: change nature .... Human to Divine
    - Temple kills Christ's spirit – Son of God: righteous citizen on Earth ...   **Excommunicated**
    - Blasphemy – claiming to be God: every eye shall see me coming on a cloud of glory
    - A man's head is anointed for burial – oil of myrrh
    - First redemption (free) – saved from grave: purification by fighting evil
    - Come to Jerusalem – worthy of new body and Heaven on Earth
2.   **All spirit is called to Rome** – Romans kill Jesus' flesh: fulfill faith...See Potential
    - Spirit is called to prayer – man's faith in God's love: wash away sins...Sinfulness to Holiness
    - Cross kills Jesus' flesh – Son of man: holy saint in Heaven......**Murdered**
    - Innocent – Pilate washed his hands: I find no guilt in this falsely accused man
    - A man's feet are anointed for resurrection – oil of frankincense
    - Second redemption (earned) – saved by the host: purification by submission
    - Come to Rome – worthy of eternal life and Paradise in Heaven

This illustration shows God creating the Jewish people as His force of death (flesh) and the Christian people as His force of life (spirit) and then putting them at odds against each other to fight for the ownership and control of both Heaven and Earth. Obviously, the Jewish people believed that they are God's chosen people and can talk to God directly via their sacred temple; while the Christian people believed that they are God's chosen people and can talk to God's Son as an intercessor via their Holy Church. Unfortunately, both the Jews (Earth) and the Christians (Heaven) are right as the Jews are God's chosen flesh (death/fight evil) and the Christians are God's chosen spirit (life/die to self). Note that all flesh is being called to eternal work (repentance), while all spirit is being called to eternal prayer (forgiveness) and then at the end of time, the spirit and flesh become one. The first redemption is a free gift so that a person can be saved from the grave as the flesh is purified by fighting evil to fulfill God's law of obedience and change his nature from human to divine, thereby making him worthy of a new body. The second redemption must be earned so that a person can be saved by the host as the spirit is purified by surrendering his free will to God's divine will. This is done to fulfill man's faith of love, thereby washing away his sins and change his sinfulness into holiness to make him worthy of eternal life. Obviously, God has created the city of Jerusalem to represent Heaven on Earth (human kingdom) and then created the city of Rome to represent Paradise in Heaven (angelic realm). This implies that through these two dimensions will come God's peace, joy, and happiness so that God and man can become one flesh (grave) and one spirit (host). We see that in ancient times, the Jews used the oil of myrrh to anoint a man's head for burial (grave), while the Christians used the oil of frankincense to anoint a man's feet for resurrection.

1. **Anoint Head** (down) - Burial in Grave: oil of myrrh…Worthy of **New Body**
2. **Anoint Feet** (up) – Resurrection of Host: oil of frankincense…Worthy of **Eternal Life**

These two anointings of Jesus Christ by Joseph of Arimathea (burial oil/head/man) and Mary Magdalene (resurrection oil/feet/God) sent the Son of Man (Jesus) into His tomb and then brought the Son of God (Christ) resurrection. We see that in the Lord's Grand Design, He has divided the primary functions of existence into three unique forces: (1) committing transgressions — sin-debt (imprisonment), (2) repenting for transgressions — pay sin-debt (justice), and (3) forgiving transgressions — removing sin-debt (freedom). This continual operation both capitalizes and funds God's divine process by which forgiven transgressions represent some form of human loss that is returned to God in the form of a prayer of reconciliation (pay debt). The Lord has sent humanity a Messiah to intercede by becoming a single human transgression of death, thereby allowing Himself to become one with death itself in the form of the king of death for life and death to become one. As the king of death, God's divine/human Messiah has attained the power to forgive the curse of death caused by an intentional act of sinfulness by Adam's cowardice (grave) and Eve's ignorance (host). This means that Jesus Christ was to become sin (scourging), evil (crucifixion), and death (tomb) upon Mt. Calvary to bring forth man's bread of redemption (free/flesh/grave) and cup of salvation (earned/spirit/host). In this way, the Lord is able to restore human life to any transgressor that in this case happens to be Himself as He takes-on all sin (spirit/redemption) or body broken (remove faults) and then gives-up His divinity (flesh/salvation) or blood shed (gain virtues) to save the whole world.

Recall that the job of the Old Testament (eye for an eye) is to save man's flesh by giving him a new physical nature (transfigured body); while the job of the New Testament (turn other cheek) is to save man's spirit by giving him a new spiritual purification (glorified spirit). Note that in Jesus' parable of the wineskins, the Lord makes reference to the old wineskins as Old Testament (death) and the new wineskins being the New Testament (new-life), implying that the new wineskin is man's new transfigured body and the new wine represented man's new nature (glorified spirit) that would be poured into the new wineskins. This shows that the job of the Jewish people is to transform man's physical nature (cowardice) from having an ignorant mind, a criminal heart, an insane soul, and an evil life into a new state of righteousness (knowing right/wrong). Secondly, the job of the Christian people is to purify man's spiritual nature (greed) from having a sinful mind, evil heart, dead soul, and a damned life-force into a new state of holiness (knowing good/evil). When these two natures of righteousness and holiness are blended into one person, this new born-again saint will become perfect (knowing God's will/man's will) in the sight of God. Through God's three blessings of righteousness, holiness, and perfection, the human race can finally get its most beloved home (happiness), government (service), and church (worship), thereby setting all men free (self). The question is, is the "human race" fighting for truth, for peace, for love, and/or just for survival (life)? Or is it fighting for none of these things because all God's creations are fighting for freedom of choice and the right to make their own decisions in life, be they right ones or wrong ones?

We see that the "human race" has been placed in God's divine school of higher learning to teach each child of God the meaning (existence), purpose (service), and value of life (happiness). This means that if a person masters the life-experience, he can be rewarded with freedom from all God's influences be they positive (life) or negative (death) because in born-again Christ, all human endeavors bear holy fruit. It is important to learn right from wrong in all its forms so that a person can become physically righteous (king/citizen), spiritually holy (priest/saint), mystically perfect (son), and divinely sacred (free man) before God.

Through this awakening unto God's truth, a person can find his own fixed frame of reference to define his personal identity, thereby answering the question just who am I in the greater scheme of things? Secondly, a person can find his own relative focused existence and establish his character to answer the second question of what do I really believe as it relates to the greater purpose of God, society, and myself? Thirdly, a person can find his own perception of reality and develop his own unique personality to answer the third question of "what do I want as it relates to the mutual benefit (values) of God, society, and myself?" Finally, a person can find the meaning of to be or not to be as defined by mastering family values to answer the fourth question of "where do I fit as it relates to my redemption from sin, evil, and death?" The point here is that God's creation is traveling from absolute truth to relative truth based on learning God's truth, law, will, and love by mastering all of God's lessons of life (intellect/emotions/instincts). The world is being taught that truth becomes righteousness, peace becomes holiness, love becomes perfection, and free choice becomes divinity in Christ Jesus, thereby bringing forth the fruits of God's labors in righteous Earthly citizens, holy Heavenly saints, and perfect Kingdom sons.

The following tabular information indicates that each of God's children must fight for truth, peace, love, choice, and becoming all he can be on Earth, in Heaven, and within God's Kingdom of Glory:

**Truth, Peace, Love, Choice, and Becoming Define
the Stages of Growth and Maturity for Man**
(truth is righteousness, peace is holiness,
love is perfection, and choice is divinity)

Baby
(truth)

1. **Absolute truth** (1st Day) seeks **Human Peace** (2nd Day)
   – Church...Knowledge
   - Fixed Frame of Reference – Define Identity: Who Am I (king)
   - Learn Right from Wrong – Meaning of Life (existence): <u>Truth becomes Righteousness</u>
     (water baptism – Physical life [mind]):
     body = illusion ends for reality to start)

Teenager
(law)

2. **Divine Peace** (3rd Day) seeks **Human Love** (4th day)
   – Government .... Self-awareness
   - Relative Focused Existence – Establish Character: What Do I Believe (priest)
   - Learn Good from Evil - Purpose of Life (service): <u>Peace becomes Holiness</u>
     (blood baptism - spiritual life [heart]):
     blood = love deadens logic to risk commitment)

Adult
(will)

3. **Divine Love** (5th Day) seeks **Human Choice** (6th Day)
   - Home ... Consciousness
   - Perception of Reality – Develop Personality: What Do I Want (sonship)
   - Learn God's Will/man's will – Value of Life (happiness): <u>Love becomes Perfection</u>
     (spirit baptism – mystical life [soul]:
     soul = thinking failure is better than thinking success)

Wise Man
(love)

4. **Divine Choice** (7th Day) seeks **Becoming Life** (8th Day) – Self...Sentience
   - To Be or Not To Be – Master Family Values: Where Do I Fit (free man)
   - Learn God's Reality/Man's Illusion – Rewards of Life (adventure): <u>Choice becomes Divine</u>
     (Shekinah baptism – divine life [life-force]):
     divinity = learn place in universe)

Free Man
(honor)

5. **Relative Truth** (eternity) seeks **Existence of IS** (infinity)
   – God...Thinking
   - Unto Thine Own Self be True – I am that I am: I Belong to Myself (ownership)

- Teach God's Want from Man's Need – Perspective of Life (challenge):
  Becoming God-like)
  (baptizing the lost – new-life [born-again]:
    humanity = create one's own kingdom)

This illustration shows that absolute truth is seeking human peace, thereby bringing forth God's church, which will fill the Earth with its ocean of knowledge, allowing all mankind to learn God's right from man's wrong. Secondly, divine peace is seeking human love, thereby bringing forth God's government, which will make the human race self-aware, allowing mankind to learn God's good from man's evil. Thirdly, divine love is seeking human choice, thereby bringing forth God's home, which will make the ignorant men conscious of God to learn God's will from man's will. Finally, divine choice is seeking becoming life, thereby bringing forth one's self-worth, which will make the awakened man sentient to learn God's reality from man's illusion. This means that the absolute truth of God is seeking to be transformed into the relative truth of man to give both God and His creation more flexibility in mind, heart, and soul. Note that the righteous man can see his own limitations (mental speed); the holy man can see his own potential (innovations); the perfect man can see his own self-worth, and finally, the free man can see his own independence. This implies that as a person both grows-up and matures into a son of God and is truly worthy of the Lord's respect and God's divine love, then he can journey through the eight days of creation from nothing to all.

We see that on the first day of creation, a person is a tiny baby who is locked in absolute truth based on the forces of destiny, which lead him to human peace and can only be broken by the peace of Christ (forgive transgressions). Secondly, on the second day of creation, a person becomes a child who seeks the forces of free will, which lead him to God's divine peace and the blessings of heaven (forgive sin). Thirdly, on the third day of creation, a person becomes an adolescent who seeks the forces of righteousness, which lead him to human love and God's anointing of heaven (forgive evil). Fourthly, on the fourth day of creation, a person becomes a teenager who seeks the forces of holiness, which lead him to divine love and God's sanctification of heaven (forgive death). Fifthly, on the fifth day of creation, a person becomes a young adult who seeks the forces of perfection, which lead him to human choice and God's consecration of heaven (forgive damnation). Sixthly, on the sixth day of creation, a person becomes an adult who seeks the forces of divinity, which lead him to divine choice and God's sonship of heaven (forgive oblivion). Seventhly, on the seventh day of creation, a person becomes a wise man who seeks the forces of sainthood, which lead him to becoming life and receives God's fatherhood of heaven (forgive imperfection). Finally, on the eighth day of creation, a person becomes a free man who seeks the forces of angelic life, which lead him to becoming God-like and receives God's blessing of liberty (freedom). Through each of these eight days of creation, a person can be purified, transformed, corrected, and converted in mind, heart, soul, and life-force as a way of worshiping (give life), praising (give wealth), thanking (give labor), and honoring (give all) his God.

In like manner, we see that a man of absolute truth has received a water baptism giving him physical life (mind) via Christ's body as a person's illusion ends and his reality begins awakening him to his own identity. Secondly, a man of divine peace has received a blood baptism giving him spiritual life (heart) via Christ's blood as love deadens his logic and risks an unconditional commitment upon which he might build his new character. Thirdly, a man of divine love has received a spirit baptism giving him mystical life (soul) via Christ's soul as it is better to think he is a failure (humility) rather than believing he has become a success (pride). Finally, a man of divine choice has received a Shekinah baptism, giving him divine life-force via Christ's divinity to define his place in the universe as a treasured child of God. Through these four baptisms, the human race can continuously progress from nothing to all based on its desire to become more and more mature before God to become worthy of being a king (citizen), priest (saint), and son (son) before God.

This means that one's progress toward human perfection centers on both God's Messiah and His holy church as they offer every child of God an opportunity to become great in the eyes of God. We now see that our forgiving Messiah was able to create His Holy Church by simply transferring His divine authority to His vicar or Peter's redeeming touch (new nature) to transform all believers of God's divine truth into living prayers of love. This means that everything a person does in life becomes a human prayer in oneness with the divine king of death (submission/faults) and his queen of new-life (sacrifice/virtues). In this logic, we see that death brings life (Jews) while life brings death (Christians). Thus, God becomes death (negative/Jesus) and man becomes life (positive/Christ) to make the last first (man) and the first last (God). As the official queen of death (church), the bride of Christ will have the authority to repent for the curse of death (sin) to both change one's nature and also washing away his sins. The Holy Catholic Church can then offer its forgiven sin in recompense for the Messiah's human transgressions (taking-on all sin), thereby bringing forth freedom out of slavery (sin) to break the chains of death for all men great and small.

Recall that Mary's Son, Jesus represents the king of death as He becomes the Judas goat (bloodless sacrifice) and is given the name of death upon His circumcision (fleshly name of Jesus/earth). In contrast, God's Son, Christ represents the priest of new-life as He becomes the sacrificial lamb (blood sacrifice) and is given the name of eternal life upon His baptism (spiritual name of Christ/heaven). Note that a "baby is circumcised (blood/Jew)" or his head anointed (grave) to receive his human name (death); while an adult is baptized (bloodless/Gentile) or his feet anointed (resurrection) to receive his divine name (new-life). We can now see that death (Jesus) pays man's sin-debt (remove faults) by being scourged at the pillar (circumcision); while new-life (Christ) pays God's sin-debt (gain virtues) by being crucified on the cross (baptism). This means that Jesus takes-on all sin by being scourged to symbolize humanity's circumcision (great tribulation), while Christ gives-up His divinity (forgiveness) by being crucified to symbolize humanity's baptism (end of the world).

By Jesus Christ being able to become both death (submission) and new-life (sacrifice) within the same person, the human race is able to defeat the forces of sin caused by ignorance (mind), the evil caused by cowardice (heart), and the death caused by greed (soul). In this way, "God's Son" can now redeem our minds and bring us to wisdom (logical), save our hearts and bring us into courage (loving), and then reward our souls and make us generous (instinctively dutiful) to one and all. This means that it is "all about facing Lucifer's test" of demonic possession or taking one's personal examination so that a lost soul can see its own limitations (truth) and learn the importance of God's right and man's wrongful (intellect) behavior. Secondly, a person must face "God's judgment" (compromised will) of worldly temptations or having his examination graded so that an awakened soul can see its own potential (law) and learn the importance of good and evil (emotions) behavior. Finally, a person must face his own self-evaluation (will) revealing his wicked sin-nature or knowing both his IQ and his aptitude so that a born-again saint can see his own self-worth (will) and learn the importance of God's will and man's will (instincts) in his life.

It should now begin to make sense why God names everything in His kingdom as He gives His creation its own identity (life), its meaning (existence), its purpose (service), and its value (happiness) all in one perfect description. In this same regard, we see that the Lord has named Jesus as death (submission) and Christ as life (sacrifice) to make them kings of spiritual and physical existence to transform the human race from death (Jesus/nothing) to new-life (Christ/all). In this way, "they" can both bring forth the "forces of Life (fire)" and "death (water)" to either create (fusion/crucible) or destroy (fission/winepress) anything God desires to hold bound (slave) or to be set loose (free). It is quite difficult to realize that the Lord sees the human condition from three separate and completely different points of view based upon his three natures of justice (direct will), mercy (permissive will), and love (compromised will).

1. **First Viewpoint** – Direct Will of Justice: See Value of Life = Happiness (see Self-Worth)
2. **Second Viewpoint** – Permissive Will of Mercy: See Purpose of Life = Service (see Potential)
3. **Third Viewpoint** – Compromised Will of Love: See Meaning of Life = Existence (see Limitations)

We see that this strange truth means that the Lord demands unquestioned perfection from His perfect justice (direct will), while still priding Himself on His ability to see relative truth (goat/body broken) in the divine light of His infinite mercy. We also see that the Lord God Almighty can still find it deep in His own heart to forgive all things done by His innocent babies through the depth of the Lord's most perfect eternal love (compromised will). In this way, the Lord has intended to use the sacrileges of past sin to draw all flesh unto Himself so that His divine nature of absolute truth (lamb/blood shed) can be the divine light of His infinite love. This "infinite love" is manifested in God Almighty's spirit (lamb) and in His truth (goat) so that all will see the overall scope, even if they are the very last lost and broken souls in existence. This implies that these most intimately divinely inspired insights are being provided through personal revelations, coming from both Jesus (good news) and Mary (gospel message) through their holy Church. Obviously, these magnificent "warnings to mankind" are being sent so it might repent prior to the Lord's second coming (thief in the night) when the tribulation of God will come forth onto the Earth like a lightning bolt of justice.

This will occur when the Lord comes to create a new divine order of perfect gratitude (thanksgiving) making the blessings of His own righteousness (goat), holiness (lamb), and perfection (man) loved by all. This means that Jesus became the righteous goat (flesh) when He was cast into hell to take-on all sin (repentance), just as Christ became the Holy Lamb (spirit) when He resurrected from evil death by giving-up His divinity (forgiveness). Finally, the Lord Jesus Christ became the perfect man when He ascended into heaven to sit at the right hand of God as mankind's intercessor to act as our money changer taking our sins (curses) and giving us back God's forgiving grace (blessings). Out of this "forgiving grace," one's brokenness (faults) can be removed and then His perfection (virtues) can be inserted to transform an ignorant, cowardly, and greedy fool into a wise, courageous, and generous son of God.

The following tabular information indicates that God is using an eight-day week to change an evil fool into a holy saint via His institutions of a physical government (kingship), spiritual church (priesthood), and mystical home (sonship):

God's Eight-Day Week of Conversion from an Evil Fool to a Holy Saint via God's Institutions
(removing a sinner's ignorance, cowardice, greed,
sin, evil, death, damnation, and oblivion)

First Day
(truth)

1. **Remove Ignorance** – Justify Flesh with Wisdom: Baby Level ....Knowledge
- Poor in Spirit – *Enter God's Kingdom*: God Thinks of His Child
- Man's Fixed Frame of Reference – Infinite Dimension: Lesson of Quitting
  (human mind – learn right from wrong:
  become righteous = establish identity)

Second Day
(law)

2. **Remove Cowardice** – Honor Spirit with Courage: Child Level ...Self-awareness
- Those Who Mourn – *They shall be Comforted*: God Speaks to His Child
- Man's Relative Focused Existence – Physical Dimension: Lesson of Finding a Way
  (human heart – learn good from evil:
  become holy – develop one's own unique character)

Third Day
(will)

3. **Remove Greed** – Glorify Soul with Generosity: Adolescent Level ...Consciousness

- The Meek – ***They shall Inherit the Earth:*** God Touches His Child
- Man's Perception of Reality – Spiritual Dimension:Lesson of Flying Over Obstacle

(human soul – learn God's Will from man's will:
become perfect = define personality)

Fourth Day
(love)

4. **Forgive Sin** – Free Life-force with Sharing: Teenage Level ....Sentience
- Those Who Hunger/Thirst for Righteousness – ***They shall be Filled***: God sups with Child
- Man says: To Be or Not To Be – Mystical Dimension: Lesson of Crushing Through

(human life-force – learn God's reality and man's illusion:
become divine = respected name)

Childhood (take out faults) - - - - - (put in virtues) **Adulthood**

Fifth Day
(New truth)

5. **Forgive Evil** – Bless the King with Righteousness: Young Adult Level …Independence
- Those Who are Merciful – ***They shall be Given Mercy***: God Makes Him a King
- God's Fixed Frame of Reference – Divine Dimension: Lesson of Solutions

(divine mind – become official government:
state's rights = righteous citizen/earth)

Sixth Day
(new law)

6. **Forgive Death** – Anoint Priest with Holiness: Adult Level …. Freedom
- Those Pure of Heart – ***They shall See God***: God Makes Him a Priest
- God's Relative Focused Existence – Godly Dimension: Lesson of Mind over Matter

(divine heart – become sanctified church:
divine rights = perfect son/kingdom)

Seventh Day
(new will)

7. **Forgive Damnation** – Sanctify with Perfection: Wise Man Level …….. Liberty
- Peacemakers - ***They shall be Children of God***: God Makes Him His Son
- God's Perception of Reality – Eternal Dimension: Lesson of Miracle Power

(divine soul – become happy home:
individual rights = perfect son/kingdom)

Eighth Day	8.	**Forgive Oblivion** – <u>Consecrate Father with Divinity</u>:
(new love)		Free Man Level ... Thinking

- If Persecuted for Righteousness - *Inherit God's Kingdom*: God Sets Him Free
- God Says: To Be or Not To Be – Paradoxical Dimension: Lessons are Lessons

(divine life-force – become one's own confident self:
personal rights = free man/God)

This illustration shows that Christ's Sermon on the Mount was trying to give the human race a clear focus on the life-experience by defining both its childhood (remove faults) and its adulthood (gain virtues) via Christ's eight beatitudes. Note that the initial creation of man is defined by a week of transformation over a seven-thousand-year period plus a day of eternity (eighth day), bringing the human race from nothing to all or from human imperfection to divine perfection in Christ Jesus. In short, the Lord spends four days taking out man's faults (Jewish temple/childhood), and then comes on to the Earth Himself to put in man's virtues (Christ's Church/adulthood), thereby transforming the human flesh into divinity and also washing man's spirit to change it from sinfulness to holiness. This purification (baby/young adult), transformation (child/adult), correction (adolescent/wise man), and conversion process (teenager/free man) allow the human race to both grow-up (baby) and become mature (adult) before the Lord God Almighty Himself (beatific vision). The point is that a baby establishes his identity and then as an adult, he establishes a government, which one day becomes the people of Earth and the eternal home of the physical God (Lord God Almighty/New Jerusalem). Secondly, a child establishes his character, and then as an adult, he establishes a church, which one day becomes the communion of saints in Heaven and the eternal home of the spiritual God (personal God). Thirdly, an adolescent establishes his personality, and then as an adult, establishes a home, which one day becomes the sonship of the Kingdom and the eternal home of the mystical God (benevolent force). Finally, a teenager establishes his own respected name and then as an adult, establishes his own self-worth, which one day becomes his self-identity, becoming his own man and the eternal home of the divine God (born-again life).

Through each of these levels of growth and maturity, a person is able to take his own place in God's Kingdom, thereby establishing himself as a viable force in life in the eyes of God, society, and himself. Obviously, it takes eight days to bring a lost fool out of his darkness to see the divine light of God through the Lord's Son, Jesus Christ, who represents the truth (water), light (blood), and life (spirit) of every cursed soul. We see that man's curse comes in the form of a person's excommunication (temple court) from the church (temple/priest), being an outcast (celestial court) of his nation (throne/king), facing banishment (royal court) from Earth (palace/emperor), and finally, actually being forsaken (divine court) by God Himself (Almighty).

1. **Sin-nature** – excommunication from temple: face shame = master truth... **Become Righteous**

2. **Worldly Temptations** – outcast from nation: face humiliation = master law...
   Become Holy
3. **Demonic Possession** – banished from Earth: face disgrace = master will...
   Become Perfect
4. **Cursed by God** – forsaken by God: face scandalization = master love... **Become Divine**

We are to imagine having to actually experience these four levels of shame (excommunication/Caiaphas), humiliation (outcast/Herod), disgrace (banished/ Pilate), and scandalized (forsaken/God) behavior. We are all in awe of the life-experience, yet Jesus Christ would have to purify each of our lives by being shamed out of the church (temple), humiliated out of His people (Jews), disgraced off the Earth (home), and then scandalized before God (life). Now, we see that the life-experience is all about punishment and reward, but the question is, will men and angels bow to the divine will of God as the Lord strives to prove that His ways (truth) are the only ways (law)? Obviously, this union of truth (knowing) and law (following) establishes God's formal state of obedience to His divine will for all who seek to worship and befriend God.

Unfortunately, most of the world has fallen into the evil hands of Lucifer and have come to only believe in their own wealth and power with little or no regard for God's Word or His demand for human perfection. Note that the temple (excommunication) represents a washing machine (purify the land) designed to clean man's dirty clothes as sin is forgiven by the Lord's waters of baptism (scourging /life). Secondly, the people (outcast) represent a candle of light (purify the babies) designed to light the darkness as evil is pardoned by the Lord's oil of anointing (carry cross/wealth). Thirdly, the Earth (banished) represents an open grave (purify life) or dead body turning to bread (feed life) designed to raise the dead as death is resurrected by the Lord's blood of sanctification (crucifixion/labors). Finally, God's blessing (forsaken) represents a new nature (purify divinity) designed to find the lost as damnation is reconciled by the Lord's death of consecration (tomb/spirit). Through God's blessing (water/wash), anointing (oil/light), sanctification (blood/food), and consecration (death/eternal happiness), religion (washed), people (light), Earth (food), and God (eternal happiness) are redeemed from oblivion forever.

In this lesson, the human race is being called to wash itself (water) and remove its ignorance through knowledge so that the mind of man can master the wisdom of God and be set free from sin, evil, and death. Secondly, mankind is being enlightened by light (oil) to remove its cowardice through self-awareness so that the heart of man can master the courage of God to be set free from its sin-nature, worldly temptations, and demonic possessions. Thirdly, humanity is being awakened by food (blood) to remove its greed through consciousness so that the soul of man can master the generosity of God to be set free from being excommunicated, outcast, and/or banished. Finally, the world is to be indwelled with eternal happiness (death) to remove its selfishness through sentience so that the life-force of man can master the perfection of God to be set free from physical, spiritual, mystical, and divine authority.

Yes! The life-experience is all about being set free from its direct and indirect influences, based on any and all forms of restrictions be they from nature, man, angels, and/or God Himself as all must become instant imagination (thinking) and instant gratification (doing) to fulfill their ultimate dreams. This supernatural ability to create objects, spirits, and/or the impossible at will brings forth the fulfillment of want unto a person's maximum level of divine perfection. Unfortunately, there is one aspect of life that cannot be fulfilled. That is the desire to experience the challenge of competition to create the maximum adventure, allowing one to know the thrill of victory.

It should now be obvious that even the Lord God Almighty must ponder the problem of having a creation of angels and men, who somehow can find a purpose in life that warrants their full and undivided attention forever. This means that God was required to create a good worth having (adventure) and an evil worth fighting (challenge) to force God, angels, and men to work together as one people to bring peace, joy, and happiness to one and all. It should now make sense that God's "Grand Design" has worked and has effectively manifested the needs of life into a noble cause so important and so sacred that nothing is more important than God's divine will. This theme of importance has brought both angels and men to worship (give life), praise (give wealth), and thank (give labors) God for His blessings of eternal life (spirit) and eternal happiness (flesh).

In summary, we see at the end of time, the human race will be forced to face the Judgment of God in the Lord's temple court of holiness (church/religion), in the celestial court of human righteousness (government/state), in the royal court of divine perfection (home/family), and finally, in the divine court of godliness (self/self).

Good luck!

Introduction

The primary intent of these mystical teachings on God's Grand Design is to explain God's purpose, His principles, functions, and techniques in sculpturing mankind into a free-standing work of art, which is worthy of the eternal admiration of God, angels, and saintly men. The best way to envision our omnipotent Creator is to comprehend Him as a divinely meticulous artist, with an infinite compulsion for minute detail far beyond the comprehension of the human mind to either grasp or imagine God's level of perfection. The Lord is possessed with the idea of making His creation of love and Himself one in truth (mind), law (heart), and will (soul) through the bond of friendship so that Jesus might take-sin as man's repentance (save sinners) and Christ might give-up His divinity as man's forgiveness (create saints). This awesome friendship with God must be purchased through the highest price imaginable via the Lord's divine sin-debt (take-sin/flesh/repentance) and Gift of divinity (give divinity/spirit/forgiveness) to make God and man one forever.

1. **Mary's Son, Jesus** (Man) – <u>Takes All Sin</u>: Create *Man's Repentance*…Offer Body Broken
   - Save Lost Sinners – Create Righteous Men on Earth: Worthy of New Bodies
   - Permissive Will - Divine Mercy: Negative Immovable   **Ethics** Force of Perfect Accommodation   (law)
   - The Emotions of God - Feels All Pain: Love/Courage = God/Man Friendship
   - World – Fight Evil: Kill Baby and Resurrect Adult (see limitations)
   - Flesh Fulfills God's Law of Obedience: Change Nature Human to Divine

2. **God's Son, Christ** (God) – <u>Gives-up Divinity</u>: Create *Man's Forgiveness*… Offer Shed Blood
   - Create Holy Saints – Create Holy Saints in Heaven: Worthy of Eternal Life
   - Direct Will - Divine Justice: Positive Unstoppable   **Morals**

Force of Infinite Purity (faith)
- The Intellect of God - Knows All Things: Wisdom/Cunning = Man/God Companionship
- Church – Surrender Free Will: Kill Christian and Resurrect Saint (see potential)
- Spirit Fulfills Man's Faith in God's Love: Wash Away Sins: Change Sinfulness to Holiness

We see that our divine Creator is in the process of sculpturing a lump of clay into human flesh through a breath of air (Adam/spirit) and a rib of man (Eve/flesh) to bring forth an infinite supply of new babies to be transformed into citizens (kings), saints (priests), and sons (sons) of God. This means that one day, the human race will be transformed into a perfect diamond of infinite love, a truly priceless treasure before God that will be presented to the Holy Mother Mary as her diamond engagement ring. This most cherished creation of life will forever decorate all of heaven, thereby reflecting the divine light of God that all may see the glory of divine truth in the blessing of mankind's human love for an obscure handmaid of the Lord. The great significance behind the Lord's second coming (begins as thief/ends as judge) centers around God's desire to cut His most perfect diamond of love, thereby transforming this most precious raw stone of infinite beauty into a spectacular blue (divinity) - white (humanity) gem of divine value before the throne of God.

The question to be asked, is anyone worthy of becoming of priceless value before God by offering man's body broken (ground wheat/crucible) and man's blood shed (crushed grapes/winepress) as recompense for all of man's sins? We see that if the answer is yes, then a person has been willing to face Lucifer's test (flesh broken), God's judgment (spirit shed), and his own self-evaluation (soul killed) with honor and dignity that he might become a priceless treasure before God. In school, we have all learned that it is only possible to create a diamond by applying extreme pressure (struggle) to a piece of dust (humanity), causing a piece of worthless earth to be transformed into a stone of priceless value (kingdom/treasure).

To intellectually grasp the value of existence, a person must understand a concept known as the slaughter of innocence, where a soul is changed into a faithful baby (right/wrong) of love or into a soldier-of-the-light (good/evil), who knows the abstract meaning behind God's divine truths. This "dust (baby) to diamond (adult)" approach is certainly an arduous process, requiring the infinite patience of God Himself to accomplish the impossible of the impossible, assuming it can be done at all. Only in this most tedious and painstaking way might we understand the mind of God to see to what extremes the Lord is willing to go to bring to life that most perfect creation — our Lord Jesus Christ. We see that the Lord God Almighty desperately wants and must have this most perfect creation before He can be satisfied with the divine works of His hands and the hard-work of His beloved human partner in life.

Now, let's try to examine this "divine process of creation" as it applies to the birth of divine truth (physical/spiritual natures) that is brought forth out of the nothingness of existence (illusion/formless) to become a priceless treasure (reality/form) before God.

First, envision "two opposing never created divine forces: one, God's divine justice (benevolent force), a positive, unstoppable force (fire) of infinite purity (fusion); the other, in the form of divine power as God's divine mercy (personal God), a negative immovable force (water) of perfect accommodation, insuring fair treatment to one and all through the principle of permissive will (ethics). The "force of justice" is seen as the wisdom of God (pure thought) represented by the first person of the godhead, who infinitely condemns all imperfection (flawed) within His kingdom. The Lord is declaring that all things not divine (perfect), meaning never created (formless), are flawed, therefore God sends the second person of the godhead or His Son, Christ (body broken/blood shed) to make all created things divine (born-again love). We see that "diametrically opposite" to this type of strict unbending justice is the third person of the godhead, who infinitely declares that all are perfect (perfect flaw) in the eyes of God or seen here as the love of God.

This new form of justice signifies the compromised will (fairness) of the Lord's divinity that is made in spirit (kind love) and in flesh (tough love) to bring union to all things great and small. This new compromised nature reveals the duality of God, thereby making Him a sign of contradiction (paradox), where all things (illusion) are in all (reality), implying that **All and Nothing are One** in the paradoxical nature of God. This means that the Father (absolute truth/justice) and the Son (relative truth/mercy) are <u>One</u> in the Holy Spirit (compromised truth/love), thereby manifesting all existence within the Holy Trinity of God (seven-fold spirits) in the form of divine truth (life). The essence of the "creation of life" centers on the forces of death and new-life as all existence must live within God's divine justice based on a person's physical (flesh) repentance by crucifixion (body broken) and a person's spiritual (spirit) forgiveness by resurrection (blood shed). Out of the Lord's crucifixion (relative truth), Jesus (man) will take all sin to die to self through sacrifice to learn God's right from man's wrong and bring forth one's blessing of righteousness (good citizen). Secondly, out of the "Lord's resurrection (absolute truth)," Christ (God) will give-up His divinity to be born-again through submission to learn God's good from man's evil and bring forth one's blessing of holiness (holy saint). Out of man's repentance and "God's forgiveness," the human race can bring together its church (worship/priest), government (money/king), and home (love/son) into one perfect kingdom of glory.

The following tabular information indicates the transformation of man's flesh through repentance (bread) and the purification of man's spirit through forgiveness (wine), which when combined brings forth earthly righteousness and heavenly holiness to **Make *God and Man One Creation***:

Flesh Repents by Crucifixion,
while Spirit is Forgiven by Resurrection
(mental logic brings ethics to become righteous,
while feelings bring morals to become holy)

All are Called to Exist - Survival is the Meaning of Life (man chooses)

Flesh
(mind)

1. **Repentance by Crucifixion** – <u>Take-sin</u>: Logic brings Ethics/law ... Wisdom
   - Sacrifice of Life – Worship: Body Broken = Learn Right from Wrong
   - *Righteousness* – Good Citizenship: Obey Mosaic Law = An Eye for an Eye

Fight Evil
(individual
rights)

   - Dying to Self – Transformation of the Flesh: Crucible = Bake Bread
   - Learning the Meaning of Life – Existence: Recognize its Flaws = See Limitations
   - Individual Rights – Letter of the Law: Rights of Others (justice)
   - Soldier-of-the-Light (citizenship) – Looking down toward the People's Needs

(Son of Mary, Jesus, Takes-on All Sin to Offer God
Man's Repentance to Save Lost Sinners)

Few are Chosen to Serve – Servanthood is the Purpose of Life (God Chooses)

Spirit
(heart)

2. **Forgiveness by Resurrection** - <u>Give Divinity</u>: Feelings bring Morals/faith... Courage
   - Submission of Wealth – Praise: Blood Shed = Learn Good from Evil
   - *Holiness* – Holy Sainthood: Obey Canon Law = Turn the Other Cheek

Surrender
(Social
rights)

   - Born-again – Purification of the Spirit: Winepress = Make Wine
   - Learning the Purpose of Life – Service: Flaws into Features = See Potential
   - Social Rights – Spirit of the Law: Person's Right to Life (mercy)
   - Living Prayer of Love (sainthood) – Looking-up toward God's Wants

(Son of God, Christ, Gives-up Divinity to Give Man
God's Forgiveness to Create Holy Saints)

This illustration shows that God is transforming man's mind through repentance (take-sin/flesh), while purifying man's heart through forgiveness (give divinity/spirit) to create a new born-again holy soul. This means that the human mind is to be taught a sufficient amount of logic to reveal the value of ethics and see the importance of the letter of the law as it brings a person into a personal respect for the rights of others (ethical behavior). Secondly, this means that the human heart is to be taught a sufficient amount of emotion (instincts/feelings) to reveal the value of morals and see the importance of the spirit of the law as it brings a person into a universal respect for the right to life in all its forms (divine/social/individual rights). By using ethics, a person can comprehend the meaning of life (existence) by recognizing its flaws and see his own limitations to bring forth a new born-again nature for one and all. Secondly, by using morals, a person can comprehend the purpose of life (service) by making flaws into features and see his own potential to bring forth a bright future for one and all. The idea here centers on ethics for it creates a soldier-of-the-light (righteous citizen), who is dedicated to removing flaws, while morals create a living prayer of love (holy saint), who is dedicated to converting flaws into features. The implication is that "Mary's Son, Jesus (humanity)," has been created and commissioned to save sinners from hell; while "God's Son, Christ (divinity)," has been sent from heaven to transform Christians into heavenly saints. To grasp this conversion technique, a person must see God as a giant liar, as He tells foolish man to figure out the life-experience through a series of subtle hints, a few parables, and a lot of mumbo-jumbo (nonsense).

The following tabular information indicates that the people on Earth willingly sacrifice childhood to get human adulthood, while the Lord God Almighty willingly sacrifices foolish earthly men to get divine adults (sainthood):

People on Earth Sacrifice Childhood to Get Adults/God Sacrifices Earthly Men to Get Heaven
(earth is a baby farm full of God's silly children
who are taught lies to reveal truth)

1. **Earthly Babies Grow into Earthly Adults** – <u>Children Believe</u> Lies/Adults Know Truth
   A. Baby Illusion – Believe in Santa Claus, Easter Bunny, and Tooth Fairy
   B. Adult Reality – Believe in Latest Scientific Proofs to Know Right from Wrong
      • Home – Man's Meaning of Life: Existence = Know Man
      • Job – Man's Purpose of Life: Servanthood = Love Man
      • Mate – Man's Value of Life: Happiness = Serve Man
2. **Earthly Adults Mature into Heavenly Saints** – <u>Earthly Men Believe</u> Lies/Saints Know Truth
      • Adult Illusion – Believe There is No God: All was Created by Natural Selection (random chance)
      • God's Reality – Believe in Free Redemption, Earned Salvation, and Bonus Rewards
      • Earthly Home – God's Meaning of Life: Existence = Know God
      • Heavenly Job – God's Purpose of Life: Servanthood = Love God
      • Kingdom Mate – God's Value of Life: Happiness = Serve God

This illustration shows that we can see that the Lord God Almighty is sacrificing man's flesh (world) to the forces of evil to transform man's spirit (church) into holiness, thereby allowing man's illusion (lie) to be manifested in God's reality (truth). We see that all parents explain the life-experience to their children in mystical terms, especially when the kids ask the hard question concerning the importance of Christmas (Santa Claus) and Easter (Easter Bunny). In contrast, when a child reaches the age of reason (seven years old), suddenly his parents admit that they have been less than honest in explaining the meaning, purpose, and value of life, when it comes to comprehending absolute truth (illusion/reality). In layman's terms, this means that when God manifests one of His infinite creations of love, the job of God the Son is to point out all its flaws and then calls them special features, representing the best part of the Father's handiwork (mistakes). When the unstoppable force of Justice (all knowing) collides head on (beatific vision) with the immovable force of mercy (understanding), then an artful compromise is reached, creating a new unblemished truth in the form of God's most perfect divine will (direct will).

This infusion of pure justice and pure mercy is manifested in the unstoppable love of the Eternal Father for His Divine Son and the Son's immovable love for His most Perfect Father as they both seek to be more like each other every moment of every day. The significance of this fact is in the Father's constant desire to seek the divine truth through the slaughter of innocence by killing ignorance to find perfection in wisdom (new born-again mind). This perfection is found in the Lord God Almighty's most beloved Son's wisdom (ethics). Then the Son seeks the divine truth and finds it in the perfect love (morals) of His Father's heart. The merging of these two most powerful forces makes it possible for the Father's (logic) and the Son's (feelings) divine spirits to become one to be manifested in their shared Holy Spirit nature (soul/instincts) of divine truth through their mutual love and respect. The Holy Spirit is the third person of the godhead, who represents God's divine truth, law, and will as the creative power of the Divine Trinity's most gracious divine love (unification of all). The power and authority of the Holy Spirit creates the union between all things through the Lord's righteous word (faults/virtues), the Holy Blood (flesh/ethics), and Sacred Death (spirit/morals) of Christ's crucifixion on Mt. Calvary (perfect justice system). The actual qualifications for receiving God's divine love and obtaining His gift of salvation (life) comes via the undaunted faith, which is manifested in each person's unshakeable devotion (virtuous morals) and mystical works (principled ethics).

The problem with this logic is, how can this obscure form of faith be measured either in the power of belief (spirit) or through the demonstration of its validity (flesh) by works? The simplest answer is in the existence of one's perfect faith (knowing without proof/100 percent belief) based upon God's absolute truth, be it either "yes, I'll serve (life)" or "no, I serve only myself (death)." In this concept of "belief," we must recognize the need to accept all things in life (experiences) as destiny and to learn from them through the power of IS (all is good). This means that God can directly see a man's faith index (fixed frame of reference) and measure its intensity (perception of reality) without any need for holy works or any other manifestation of his being revealing the amount of personal love within his stony heart.

We see that humanity cannot see its own degree of faith (33 percent/67 percent/100 percent) and must measure it through a person's own manifested faith (fruitful life) or his good works (fruits) given with a joyful heart of mutual love (existence) and untiring sacrifices (service) to prove he is a faithful Christian (happiness). This means that unfortunately, no one can tell the real saints (treasures) from the self-righteous hypocrites (flaws) on Earth, which means that only God knows for sure who is who in this land of sin (home), evil (government), and death (church). The idea here is that if an apparent living saint suddenly becomes a pillar of the community and wins the hearts of all, then a person might ask: is this goodness coming from Jesus Christ (invisible good), or is it coming from Lucifer (visible good)? In truth, no one knows for sure. But St. Paul said, "You will know them by their fruits," implying we can get a pretty good idea by looking for historical victims long after this wannabe (self-canonized) saint has died and is long gone.

Note that when God sacrificed His entire creation (first-born) to get a perfect man to be God's priceless individual, it turned out to be Himself (God) in the person of Jesus Christ (all is in all). This meant that neither me nor you were being considered, when it came to receiving our own personalized canonization kit (sainthood), which will fulfill all our egomaniac dreams of becoming perfect in our own eyes. Yes! Only Jesus Christ is mentioned in the Bible or in the traditions of the saints, or in nature itself as all others must witness to the Son of God and to His new physical nature of eternal life. This factor of doubt of how perfect we are distorts the true judgment of every man based upon each soul's level of holy performance in the sight of its peers (test) as opposed to the presence of God (judgment). We see that they are obviously completely different aspects of reality in overall syntax (expression) and must be evaluated, using two separate evolutionary systems: one being divine (absolute truth/reality), and the other, human (relative truth/illusion).

This indicates that in the creative process, we must see the Lord revealing His fatherly infinite mind as absolute truth (reality) to reveal the perfection of divinity, while via God's paradoxical nature, the opposite becomes true. In this way, the Lord is reflecting His priestly honor, kingly majesty, and sonly glory before one and all as a divine kingdom of glory (Christ), while simultaneously reflecting these same titles through man's Heaven on Earth (Jesus). We see that these three natures are manifested in both spiritual (heaven/life) and physical (earth/death) forms to bring forth the most perfect incarnation of God as transformed into the existence of humanity (illusion) on Earth (righteous citizens) and in Heaven (holy saints). This procedure for existence is the royal inheritance to mankind as God desires to share all that He owns with those seeking His true friendship and unconditional love through their worship (give life), praise (give wealth), and thanksgiving (give labors). The idea here is that a loving God seeks to serve a loving friend, just as our God of justice undauntedly seeks the God of mercy in pursuit of the quiescence of eternal peace (church) to bring joy (government) and happiness to all. This great desire for compromise will bring God's divine harmony into reality, thereby creating a true balance between good (lamb) and evil (goat), to purchase eternal happiness for all in the glorious household of God (kingdom's sonship).

The specific steps or procedures for creating a perfect kingdom of glory representing God's chosen children of love are listed below in three major phases of divine manifestation:

1) **Celestial Court** (see God/altar) – Throne Room: Government (points) = Earthly Court + 1st Advent Removes Blindness;
2) **Temple Court** (hear God/pulpit/graces) – Holy of Holies (Church) = Heavenly/Earthly Court + Remove Deafness; and
3) **Royal Court** (speak to God/chair) – Palace Room: Home (marks) = Heavenly Court + Remove Dumbness

These important steps also correspond to finding redemption (free), salvation (earned), and rewards (bonus) leading to the perfect friendship of the Lord God Almighty (expectations) by believing (word contract), trusting (blood contract), and having faith (death contract) in His Son, Jesus Christ. In the concept of belief, it means to see something for oneself and then be convinced that it is real, based on empirical study (illusion), which must be scientifically backed up by the forces of natural order via some measurement of statistical significance (reality). Secondly, the concept of trust is to stand on something (reliability) to test its strength and then decide for oneself that it is extremely reliable and can be trusted over time. Finally, the concept of faith means a person believes and trusts in something so completely (Christ's resurrection) that he is willing to stand on it forever because it has the perfection he is looking for and needs.

We see that the first twenty-six steps below reveal the internal state of the Holy Trinity (godhead) and the creation of heaven as the Lord's administrative control center (authority) for all of God's divine government operations or HQ/headquarters (responsibilities). The next twenty-four steps indicate the kingdom of evil or testing center, bringing the creation and incarnation of mother's love (hopes) to be presented to the Lord God Almighty through Christ's sacrificial blood/death (pay sin-debt) to symbolize the solemn act of human repentance (retribution) before God (forgiveness). The series of steps described below have been required to establish the necessary states of perfection in God's name and man's purity (virginity) to create a divine/human union through an eternal marriage.

The following series of steps reveal the purchasing of man's divine forgiveness by God and the balancing of the divine scales of justice for every soul ever created through the Lord's rank-order judgment of truth or a priority system based on truth (mind), law (heart), and will (soul):

God's Grand Design of Creation
(Royal Court – Temple Court – Celestial Court)

I. **Divine Steps of Creation** – God's Perfect Justice System: Creator of Life
(Divine Administrator – Sacred Spiritual Manifestation – Holy Beatific Presence)
    A. <u>God's Never-created Existence (Holiness)</u> ....Benevolent Force: Nature (life)

INPUT – Divine Will (Reality)

Judgment based on Pass/Fail Grading System – Divine Justice (adults) ......
Bonus

1. Never Created: **Divine Soul/nature/life** of Love – *Divine Garment of Pure Thought*
   - Divine Majesty – The Judicial System of God
   - Omniscient – IS ALL – Blessing   Sonship – Saving Others
     of Life   • Self-evaluation
   - All Knowing Truth – All Seeing – All Caring
     (God becomes Man – Divine Truth on Earth: Wise Mind = See Limitations)

Judgment based on Curve Grading System/average - Divine Mercy (teenagers)... Earned

2. Never Created: **Divine Spirit/Heart** of Love – *Sacred Garment of the Solemn Word*
   - Sacred Glory – The Merciful System of God
   - Omnipotent – Governs   Priesthood – Saving Self
     All – Blessing of Birth   • God's Judgment
   - All Powerful Truth – All Hearing – All Possessing

(Man becomes God – Divine Heart on Earth: Loving Heart = See Potential)

Judgment based on Handicap Grading System — Divine Justice (babies)...
Free

3. Never Created – **Divine Body/Mind** of Love: *Holy Garment of the Perfect Deed*
   - Holy Honor – The Loving System of God
   - Omnipresent – All is in All –
     Blessing of Land   Kingship – Being Saved
   - All Present — All Feeling – All Loving • Lucifer's Test
     (God and Man become One – Divine Will on Earth:
     Instinctive Soul = See Self-worth)

II. **Sacred Steps of Creation** – God's Merciful Manifestation of Truth: Sonship of Life
    (Divine Judge – Law of Truth: Standard of Righteousness = Divine Court of Rule)
    B. Father's Creation (Holy Father – Divinity)...Personal God: Heaven
    INPUT (Continuation)
    4. Manifested *"Face of Divine Love"* – Image of God: Heart (temple tax)
       - Divine Creation of Absolute Truth (Shekinah Glory/Sanctifying Grace)
    5. Manifested *"Face of Divine Will"* – Likeness of God: Mind (sacrifice lamb)
       - Divine Creation of Relative Truth (Celestial Father's – Beatific Vision)
       - Divine Consecration (Divine Son's – Glorified/Smiling Face of Understanding)

6. **Throne/Altar** of <u>Divine Grace</u> – Lord God Almighty (Benevolent/ Personal God)
   - Throne – Royal Family/Divine Spiritual Rule: Kingship/Priesthood/Sonship
   - Altar – Divine Sanctification (Future Existence – Spirit: Eternal Now)
7. **Robe** of <u>Divine Judgment</u> – God's Royal Majesty: "Perfect Justice System"
   - Divine Canonization (Eternal Rewards: Gifts/Fruits/Treasures)
8. **Crown** of <u>Divine Wisdom</u> – God's "Royal Mind: Body of Divine Knowledge"
   - Divine Beatification (Divine Treasures)
9. **Crest** of <u>Divine Honor</u> – God's "Royal Name: Divine Image of Truth"
   - Divine Veneration (Sacred Fruits)
10. **Scepter** of <u>Divine Power</u> – God's "Royal Countenance: Divine Likeness of Truth"
    - Divine Righteousness (Holy Gifts)
11. **Ring** of <u>Divine Authority</u> – God's "Royal Blessing: Divine Spirit of Truth"
    - Divine Manifestation of Law (Letter of Justice)
12. **Seal** of <u>Divine Responsibility</u> – God's "Royal Office: Divine Righteousness of Law"
    - Divine Orders of Law (Spirit of Justice)
13. **Sword** of <u>Divine Duty</u> – God's "Royal Anointing: Divine
    - Hand of Law Enforcement"
    - Divine Shield of Faithful Protection (Canonized Authority)
14. **Lance** of <u>Divine Force</u> (task) – God's "Royal Consecration: Divine Arm of the Law"
    - Divine Limited Power (Execution of Perfect Justice)
15. **Keys** of <u>Divine Treasures</u> – God's "Royal Sanctification: Divine Security of Law"
    - Divine Office of Law (Knowing Absolute/Relative Truth)
16. **Chalice** of <u>Divine Covenants</u> — God's "Royal Salute: Divine Word/ Undisputed Truth"
    - Divine Agreements (Executing Absolute Truth)
17. **Sash** of <u>Divine Honors</u> – God's "Royal Office of Honorary Positions: Divine Career"
    - Divine Gifts of Anointing (Blessing of Truth)
18. **Flag** of <u>Divine Membership</u> – God's "Royal Acclaim: Divine Entitlement to Life"
    - Divine Enrollment (Understanding Truth)
19. **Trumpet** of <u>Divine Assembly</u> – God's "Royal Existence: God's Calling to the Light"
    - Divine Communications (Distribution of Truth)

20. **Scroll** of <u>Divine Word</u> – God's "Royal Reality: Divine Manifestation of the Light"
    - Divine Truth (Revelation of Relative Truth)
21. **Rose** of <u>Divine Kiss</u> – God's "Royal Blessing: Lord's 'Kiss' of Divinity"
    - Divine Love (Physical Nature – Transfigured Body)
22. **Tree** of <u>Divine Fruits</u> – God's "Royal Fruits of Love: Divine Life Anew"
    - Divine Mercy (Spiritual Nature – Divine/Human Spirit)
23. **Sanctuary** of <u>Divine Household</u> – God's "Royal Host of Divine Love: Divine Respect"
    - Divine Justice (Mystical Nature – New Jerusalem: Divine Home/Holy City)
24. **Promised Land** of <u>Divine Territory</u> – God's "Royal Holy Land of Divine Love"
    - Divine Citizenship (New Heaven and New Earth: Sacred World)
25. **Kingdom of Divinity** – <u>Ownership</u>: God's "Royal Possession: Divine Loving Companionship"
    - Divine Adoption into the "Royal Family" (Mystical Body of Christ)
    - Blessing of Priesthood (Servant) – Justification of the Flesh: Wisdom
    - Anointing of Kingship (Friend) – Honoring of the Flesh: Courage
    - Sanctification of Sonship (Son) – Glorification of the Flesh: Generosity
26. **Evil Kingdom** of <u>Demonic/Satanic Ownership</u> – Lucifer's "Evil Possession: Death"
    - Divine Testing Facility for the "Loyalty of Humanity (Divine Purification)"
    (Designed for the "Slaughter of Innocence" – Wisdom through Pain)

God's Divine Plan of Redemption
(David's Throne – Knesset/Sanhedrin – Mosaic Temple)

III. **Holy Steps of Creation**: God's Loving Manifestation of Truth
(Physical Manifestation of Life – God's Sacrificial Altar – Spiritual Manifestation of Death)

   C. <u>Son's Creation</u> (Holy Mother – Humanity) – The Word Made Flesh (incarnation)

PROCESS — Free Will (Illusion): Creation of Physical Existence (time/space)
27. **Purifying Divine Justice** – God's "Eternal Testing Center of Life: <u>Destiny</u> (time)"
    - Spiritual/Physical Testing Chambers for Spirit/Flesh/Soul (Planet Earth)
28. **Purifying Divine Mercy** – God's "Eternal Blessing of Total Liberty:

Free Will (space)"

- Spiritual/Physical Kingdom of Glory (Mystical Creation of Truth)

29. **Purifying Divine Love** – God's "Eternal Awakening to Divine Truth: Time/Space"
    - Mystical Body of Knowledge/Collective Mind of God/Man (wisdom)

30. **Manifestation of the Holy Mother** (soul)/**Blessed Virgin** (heart)/ **Blessed Mother** (mind)
    - Mother of God/Mother of Man – Glorified Human Intercessor (Co-redemptrix)
    - Co-redemptrix – Saving Man's Flesh: Being Saved = Sacrificial Womb
    - Advocate – Saving Man's Spirit: Saving Oneself = Purified Womb
    - Mediatrix – Saving Man's Soul: Saving of Others = Mystical Womb

31. **Christ** – Son of God: Veil of Life via Death (Divine Sacrifice)
    - Mother of God/Mother of Man – Honored Human Intercessor: Divinity
    - Creation of "Mother's Divine Love: New Spiritual Nature"
    - Creation of "Sacrificial Covenant of Divine Love Before God"

32. **Jesus** — Son of Man: Veil of Life via Death (Human Sacrifice)
    - Mother of Man/Mother of God – Beloved Human Intercessor: Humanity
    - Creation of "Mother's Human Love: New Physical Nature"
    - Creation of "Sacrificial Covenant of Human Love Before God"

33. **Jesus Christ** – Holy Church: Living Prayer of Love (sainthood) – Priesthood
    - Mother of God/man and manifested as Mother of Man/God: Gift of Divinity
    - Jesus Christ "God of Flesh" and Christ "God of Spirit" (Jesus: Transfigured Body and Christ: Divine/Human Spirit)

34. **Christ Jesus** – Righteous World: Soldier-of-the-Light (citizenship – Kingship)
    - Holy Cross of Death (Calvary)
    - Pathway of Destiny (Right Foot of Life: Divinity)
    - Pathway of Free Will (Left Foot of Life: Humanity)
    - Pathway of Perfection (Right/Left Feet Meet – Choice)
    - Pathway of Holiness (Fruits of the Holy Life – Right Decision)
    - Pathway of Righteousness (Fruits of the Righteous Life – Guess)

35. **Christian SACRIFICE** – Human Repentance/Divine Forgiveness
    - Creation of "Born-Again" Holy Church/Sacred Government/ Divine Course

36. **Christian BELIEF** in God's "Plan of Redemption" – Jesus Christ's "Sacred Word"
    - Surrendering in the spirit of abandonment to the "Pathway of Per-

fection"
- Divine Belief System of Truth (God's Anointing of Divine Love)

37. **Christian TRUST** in Jesus' and Mary's "Guiding Hand of Redemption – New-life"
    - Human Belief System of Truth (Mary's Consecration of Human Love)

38. **Christian FAITH** in God's "Divine Will" Leading a Soul to Eternal Salvation
    - Divine/Human Belief System of Truth (God/Mary Sanctification of Divine/Human Love)

39. **Christian OBEDIENCE** to God's "Divine Will (Mystical Body of Christ)"
    - Living the Christian Life of "Repentant Devotion"

40. **Christian SUBMISSION** to God's "Divine Will (Holy Catholic Church)"
    - Believing in Redemption with "Perfect Faith (Knowing Without Proof)"

41. **Christian DISCERNMENT** for Repentance of Venial/Mortal/ Capital Sins
    - Purification of One's Conscience (Confession)

42. **Christian PIETY**: Transformation into a "Just Man of Truth (Good Will)"
    - Purification of One's Spirit (Contrition)
    - Becoming a "Living Prayer of Love" before the Throne of God

43. **Christian PERSEVERANCE**: Transforming One's Life into a Holocaust (Victim Soul)
    - Purification of One's Flesh (Penance)
    - Asking, Seeking, and Knocking at God's Door for Salvation (Crucifixion/earned)

44. **Christian VIRTUES** to be manifested in all things (Humility)
    - Replacing "Human Faults" with "Divine Virtues" through One's "Perfect Faith"
    - Manifestation of a Soul's Faith, Hope, and Charity (Forgiveness)

45. **Christian SELF-CONTROL** in faithfully following the "Divine Will" of God
    - Pursuit of "Spiritual Maturity" through the guidance of the "Holy Church"

46. **Christian Good JUDGMENT** is discerning the "Holy Spirit" of God in all things
    - Knowing Right from Wrong and committing one's soul to "Divine Truth"

47. **Christian SALVATION** (Saving Souls) dedicate life to the preservation of others
    - Learning to become a great "Soldier-of-the-Light (Soul Saver)"

48. **Christian DIGNITY** reflecting the "Likeness of God" through oneness with Christ
    - Becoming Holy as God is Holy (Transformed into "Perfection")
49. **Christian INTEGRITY** obtaining a "Humble and Contrite Heart (Spiritual Maturity)"
    - Man's "Virtuous Character of Divine Truth" – Knowing God (Understanding)
50. **Christian LOVE** receiving God's Gift of "Perfect Faith (Knowing)" - Sainthood

Gift of Divine Respect	Fruits of God's Friendship
• Transfigured Body	• Glorified Spirit
• Thought of by God	• Spoken to by God

Treasure of God's Love
- Holy Soul
- Touched by God

God's Divine Plan of Sanctified Life
(Divine Palace – Sacred Temple – Holy Throne)

IV. **Mystical Steps of Creation** (Divinity and Humanity Transformed into "One" Being)
(Mystical Body of Christ – New Jerusalem – New Heaven and earth: Death is Life: Kingdom)
D. Spirit's Creation (Divine/Human Love – Kingdom of Glory)
OUTPUT — Destiny/Free Will (Reality/Illusion)
51. **Mystical Kingdom of Divine Truth**: New Divine/Human Creation of Mutual Love
    - God's Absolute Truth – Man's Relative Truth – God's/Man's Eternal Truth
52. **Marriage between Divinity and Humanity** (Manifestation of the Mystical Body)
    - Holy Father of <u>Perfection</u> (divine) Marries Holy Mother of <u>Imperfection</u> (human)
53. **Mystical Fruits of Perfection**: Divine Freedom and Peace founded upon "Divine Love"
    - Divine/Human Love become "One" in Spirit and Truth (Living Prayer of Love)
54. **Creation of Divine Happiness** – Mankind's Redemption (Eternal Life/Hopeful Joy)
    - All is in All when God's Justice (Step #1) meets God's Mercy (Step #50) = Perfection
55. **God's Most Gracious Divine Rewards**: Gifts, Fruits, and Treasures

1. Holy White Garment	4. Scepter of Power

(Presence of God)   (Human Immortality)

- God Thinks of You – Acquaintance
- God Sups with You - Family

2. Royal Robe of Judgment (Truth)
   - God Speaks to You – Neighbor

5. Throne of Grace (God's Wisdom)
   - God Accepts You - Favorite

3. Royal Crown of Authority (Respect)
   - God Touches You – Friendship

6. Ring/Seal of High Command (Dignity)
   - God Sets You Free – Beloved

7. **God's Riches in Glory** (Treasures)
   - The "Pearl of Great Price – Blessed Virgin"
   - Peace of Mind
   - Joy of the Heart   ***Eternal Freedom***
   - Happiness of the Soul (thinking for oneself)

This illustration shows that the Lord has prepared eight principal gifts of divinity for His chosen children (saints) of redemption (free), salvation (earned), and rewards (bonus), thereby transforming them from broken sinners (goats/damned) into living prayers of love (lambs/saints). We see that these living prayers will then be forever honored before the altar of God, revealing the work of His hands as they strive to save the lives of others via their own repentance (worship), prayers (wealth), and works (labors) by giving-up their own lives, wealth, and labors to God. We see that the master scheme of this creation is devised upon the concept of an input (truth/God), process (law/Lucifer), and output (will/man) system, manifesting the human life-experience upon the Earth. We know this redemptive system is in three dimensions: (1) Physical – Earth (take the test): Lucifer's test = see limitations; (2) Spiritual — Heaven (grade the test): God's Judgment = see potential; and (3) Mystical – God (evaluate test grade): Self-evaluation = See Self-worth. The Lord has demonstrated, in this way, His divine ability to organize the forces of light (goodness) and the forces of darkness (evil) into His new born-again creations of good and evil as manifested in truth, law, and will.

The input concept of the redemptive system appears to be God Himself (reality) in a divine state of manifest destiny as the Lord God Almighty sacrifices Himself to bring forth His eternal physical creation (galactic universe). Obviously, this sacrificial processing concept is comprised of mankind (illusion) and its associated evil testing facility (Lucifer) to bring broken souls to perfection (righteous/holy) through a triune conversion experience. This changes ignorance to wisdom (intellect), cowardice to courage (emotions), and greed to generosity (instincts). Next, we see that the output concept is the creation (real/fake) of the New Kingdom of Glory (illusion) merging the perfection of divinity (reality) with the new born-again perfection of humanity (illusion).

To properly understand the overall creation of God, a person must see the Lord is methodically building a combined spiritual and physical body of infinite love based on God's law (change nature/divine) and man's faith (wash away sin/holy). This divinely manifested mystical body (flesh/Earth) and communion of saints (spirit/Heaven) will encompass all of humanity, thereby allowing the Lord to become One with His most beloved creation of divine truth (law/will/love). This means that the ultimate goal of God, angels, and men is to strive to create a well-adjusted human creation that can think for itself at all four dimensions of existence, thereby taking human, angelic, divine, and never-created forms.

The following tabular information indicates the royal treasures needed for each and every person to seek the divine truths of God with all his mind (wisdom), heart (courage), and soul (generosity), no matter what the cost (spare no expense) in one's time (treasures), money (fruits), or effort (gifts):

God's Gift of Divinity
(Royal Treasures: Thinking for Oneself)

Feeling	1.	**New Body**	-	-
Transfigured Body (Human Life)............Baby				
Seeing	2.	**New Spirit**		-
Divine/Human Glorified Spirit (Divine Life)....Child				
Hearing	3.	**New House**	-	New
Jerusalem (Mystical Life)...............Adolescent				
Smelling	4.	**New City**	- -	New
Earth and new Heaven (Man/God Life)..... Teenager				
Speaking	5.	**New Nation**	-	New
Heaven and new Earth (God/Man Life).... Yng Adult				
Knowing	6.	**New World**	-	-
Kingdom: Mystical Body of Christ (God-like)....Adult				
Willing	7. **New Father**	-	Sacred Heart: Love of Humanity	
	(Absolute Truth/Freedom)..... Wise Man			

- -

Doing	8. **New Mother** -	- Immaculate Heart: Love of Divinity	
	(Relative Truth)............Free Man		

This illustration shows that to correctly comprehend these most profound steps of mystical (divine order), spiritual (supernatural order), and physical (natural order) creations as revealed by their eternal rewards, a person must discern the great significance between steps one through five as God's divine manifestation of life. This means that we are created beings who are permitted to interact with God at His lowest manifested level of reality, realizing that we must understand that we'll never know God's mystical divinity as it truly exists in its timeless void (never-created state/eternal now) of God's null-set (formless state) of non-existence (concept of benevolent life). Imagine here that you are chasing an invisible God and begin to get a good bead on Him through His mystical works and then start to seriously track this elusive God to the point of being just ready to touch Him and then suddenly He becomes you…sorry, God is you. We see the Lord in His manifested mystical divinity as a benevolent force of life (self-love), a deity without the slightest need for any outside influence or any possibility for adding to His naturally supreme nature of love (goodness/life-force/100 percent complete).

In this case, all perfection is able to exist inside a force of never-created energy, comprising the Almighty Person of God (second truth/personal/space) and the benevolent force of existence (first truth/force/time) residing in a totality of infinite desire to serve through both the Lord's pure thought of truth (create friends) and His instinctive loving nature (create life). This means that the Lord God Almighty (form) can only exist as a personal God to be worshiped (give life), praised (give wealth), and thanked (give labors) in the illusion of existence only. In contrast, the Lord God Almighty (formless) is only a benevolent force to be submitted to, obeyed, and followed in the reality of existence (natural laws) with unquestioned obedience. The difference between a personal God (heaven) and a benevolent force (nature) is that the Lord God Almighty is either benefiting from His creation or He is simply giving His blessing of life for free, thereby making God's life-force into pure benevolent energy with only one purpose, which is to create existence. In our case, our personal God is only a manifestation of life's benevolent goodness as a way of giving the children of God a most loving parent to care for and guide His babies through the many steps of their growth and maturity on man's way to freedom.

It is believed that after this stage of maturity or adulthood, a holy saint of God becomes an eternal son of God and is now introduced to the creator of existence or the benevolent life-force to be a person's personal guide (free will) forevermore. The point here is that the Earth is evil and God is holy. Therefore, the Earth has to be purified from its states of evil and death to become holy new-life, thereby allowing God (ultimate guide) to come to a transformed and beautiful Earth. In this teaching, the Lord God Almighty can be seen as Tarzan being raised by the gorillas and only loves the jungle (spirit) and all its animals, but suddenly sees his dream girl, Jane, and is forced to change from a wild man of pure innocence into a civilized human being. Now, imagine God changing (spirit to flesh) to be more like man and then man changing (flesh to spirit) to be more like God so that they can meet somewhere in the middle, with Tarzan (God) willing to take on imperfection (natural order) and Jane (man) willing to take on perfection (supernatural order).

1. Tarzan or **God – Takes-on** Imperfection: Natural Order…Change for Jane (Man)
   - Change Nature – Divine to Human: Fulfill God's Law of Obedience (new body)
2. Jane or **Man – Takes-on** Perfection: Supernatural Order…Change for Tarzan (God)
   - Wash Away Sin – Sinfulness to Holiness: Fulfill Man's Faith in God's Love (eternal life)

This illustration is revealing that when a person befriends God, the Lord will honor this new beloved relationship by giving that person one of His supernatural abilities, much like Tarzan, who befriends the lion to take onto himself the most essential qualities of a powerful (king of all) and sexually potent lion (many children). We now see that this need for God to become man and forever live on Earth clearly sits at the heart of the life-experience as Christ comes to bring free baptism (water) to allow God's babies to be saved from their venial sin (handicap system). Secondly, Christ comes again as a thief in the night to bring both confession (flesh) and communion (spirit) to allow God's teenagers to save themselves from mortal sin (curve system). Finally, Christ returns to bring confirmation (divinity) to allow God's adult children to save others (evangelization) from their capital sins (pass/fail system), thereby allowing them to become holy saints in heaven.

The idea here is that water baptism represents the Lord's First Advent (Messiah/change nature) when He brought free redemption or the Good News as man faces Lucifer's test of crucifixion (death) so that all mankind will see their limitations and experience a soul-crushing challenge. Secondly, confession/communion represent the Lord's Second Advent (Church/wash away sin) as He brings earned salvation or the Gospel Message as man faces God's judgment of entombment (grave) so that all of mankind will see their potential and experience an exciting adventure. Finally, confirmation represents the Lord's third advent (world) as He brings bonus rewards or God's doctrinal truths as man faces self-evaluation of damnation (hell) so that all mankind will see their self-worth and experience an eternal life of fun, fun, fun.

The point is that things are not as they appear and unless a person can master the life-experience as a baby, he will never be able to master life as an adult because sooner or later, a person must learn to think for himself. This means that baby mankind (intellect) must learn God's right from man's wrong to defeat its own ignorance and then master wisdom to become righteous citizens on Earth and forever live in Heaven on Earth (First Advent). Secondly, teenage children (emotions) must learn God's good from man's evil to defeat their own cowardice and then master courage to make them holy saints in Heaven and forever live in Paradise with God (Second Advent). Finally, adults (instincts) must learn God's will from man's will to defeat their own greed and then master generosity to make them perfect sons within God's kingdom and forever live in God's Kingdom of Glory (third advent).

We now see that life is about physical growth (mandatory/destiny) and spiritual maturity (optional/free will) which means everyone must defeat his own selfishness to receive a new body along with his own seat within God's celestial court (rule earth). Secondly, "everyone" must also defeat his own perfection (superiority) to receive eternal life along with his own seat within God's temple court, which will allow him to rule heaven with Jesus Christ. Finally, "everyone" must also be balanced between human selfishness and divine perfection so that man can bow to God (worship) and God can bow to man (forgiveness), thereby allowing mankind to receive its own royal kingdom with its own seat in God's royal court, which will allow humanity to rule creation with God, angels, and men. Yes! God wants to be man to receive a new body and face His challenge of defeating death while man wants to become God to receive eternal life and then have a lifetime of rollicking fun. Note, Hebrews 9:28 states that "Christ has been offered-up to bear the sins of many (free) and now shall come a second time to bring salvation (earned) to His followers."

The following tabular information indicates that Christ first brings free redemption to baptize (good news) a sinful world, a second time to bring earned salvation (gospel message) through confession and communion, and then a third time to bring bonus rewards (doctrinal truths) through man's confirmation:

**Christ Comes to Give Free Redemption, Earned Salvation,
and Bonus Rewards to Repentant Sinners**
(free baptism, earned communion, bonus confirmation
to be saved, save self, and save others)

Baby (mind)	1. **Free Redemption** - <u>Baptism</u>: Good News = Lucifer's Test...See Limitations
	• Believe in Christ – King Fights World: Handicap System = Compromised Will
	• Learning God's Right from Man's Wrong – Defeat Ignorance ... Get Wisdom
Being Saved (water)	• Become Righteous Citizen on Earth – Heaven on Earth (first advent)
	• Defeat Selfishness – Receive New Body: Seat in Celestial Court
	• Man Wants to Become God – Fun, Fun, Fun: First Treasure = New Body
	(priest comes on a donkey - shed His own blood: offer innocent blood = forgive venial sins)
Teenager (heart)	2. **Earned Salvation** - <u>Confess/Communion</u>: Gospel Message = God's Judgment ... See Potential
	• Trust in Christ – Priest Surrenders to God: Curve System = Permissive Will
	• Learning God's Good from man's evil – Defeat Cowardice ... Get Courage
Saving Self (blood)	• Become Holy Saint in Heaven – Paradise in Heaven (second advent)
	• Defeat Perfection – Receive Eternal Life: Seat in Temple Court
	• God Wants to Become Man – Challenge of Death: Second Treasure = Eternal Life
	(king comes as thief in the night – bloodless: offer forgiven blood = forgive mortal sins)

Adult	3.	**Bonus Rewards** - <u>Confirmation:</u> Doctrinal Truths =
(soul)		Self-evaluation.. See Self-worth

- Faith in Christ – Son Defeats Himself: Pass/Fail System = Direct Will
- Learning God's Will/man's will – Defeat Greed and Get Generosity

Saving others
(spirit)

- Become Perfect Son within Kingdom - Kingdom of Glory (third advent)
- Balance God's/Man's Natures – Receive Royal Kingdom: Seat in Royal Court
- God/Man Become One – Adventure of Life: Third Treasure = Royal Kingdom

(son comes as just judge – shed enemy's blood: offer guilty blood = forgive capital sins)

This illustration shows that Christ came as a priest riding a donkey to shed His own blood, thereby offering innocent blood to God to forgive all mankind's venial sins (faults) and set the babies free from their curse of ignorance. Secondly, Christ will come as a king or a thief in the night as a bloodless sacrifice, thereby offering forgiven blood to God to forgive some of mankind's mortal sins and set the teenagers free from their curse of cowardice. Finally, Christ will come as a Son of God or just judge on a cloud to shed His enemy's blood, thereby offering guilty blood to God to forgive mankind's capital sins to set the adults free from their curse of greed. Through these three advents, the Lord Jesus Christ will transform the Earth, Heaven, and God's Kingdom into righteousness, holiness, and perfection to set the captives free from sin, evil, death, and damnation. Yes! The life-experience is centered upon facing Lucifer's test, God's judgment, and one's own self-evaluation to call all men to pass the baby handicap test (obey), teenagers graded on the curve test (love), and finally, an adult's most painful pass or fail test (think for self). This means that the human race is being called to offer God its own blood to slaughter its innocence, to offer God a bloodless sacrifice of forgiven blood, and finally, to offer God His enemy's blood to make restitution for all sin. In this way, a person can receive Jesus' free redemption (good news), Christ's earned salvation (gospel message), and Jesus Christ's bonus rewards for being saved (sinner), saving oneself (Christian), and saving others (saint).

This means that a person gets free redemption by being baptized in water (being saved) or deny his intellect; he gets earned salvation by being baptized in blood (saving self) or abandoning his feelings; and finally, he gets bonus rewards by being baptized in spirit (saving others) or submitting his free will. It should now make sense that the Lord God Almighty is offering mankind three treasures of life: (1) free new body/kingship – Heaven on Earth, (2) earned eternal life/priesthood – Paradise in Heaven, and (3) bonus rewards of own royal kingdom/sonship – kingdom of glory. Through these three treasures, the children of God can attain a new mind of wisdom, new heart of courage, and a new soul of generosity to live forever in peace of mind, joy of the heart, and happiness of the soul.

We see described later the creation of a massive giant kingdom comprised of all the spiritual and physical treasures of God's creation made holy in His sight so that the Lord might become one with the manifested born-again human nature of all life forms. We must comprehend that the creation of the mystical body of God occurs in several stages as determined by the Lord's three divine plans (creation/redemption/sanctified life). We see in phase I (First Advent) the bringing forth of the Jewish faith creating the flesh of God (temple) to be merged with the Christian faith creating the Spirit of God (church) during phase II (Second Advent) of God's creation. During the Lord's second coming or Phase II (thief in the night), Jesus Christ will bring the human bones of God (government) to transform the life of man into oneness with divinity. This state of oneness is created by merging the Son of God (reality) with the Son of Man (illusion) in physical form to create the New Heaven and the New Earth (kingdom). During Phase III (third advent) at the White Throne Judgment (third advent), God the Father will enter the New Jerusalem to manifest Himself in oneness with the mystical body of Christ. Through Christ's mystical body (spirit), God's creation (flesh) will become truly divine via the Lord's gift of divinity that has been freely given to the human spirit (redemption) and earned by the human flesh (salvation).

This perfect mystical marriage of divinity (spirit) and humanity (flesh) signifies the creation of the New Heaven and New Earth precisely at the very hour of the coming of the Lord's Kingdom of Glory. During the Lord's third advent or phase III, Jesus Christ will bring the divine bones of God (Jacob's bones) to earth to transform the life of man into oneness with divinity and humanity. Through this divine/human merger, the Son of Man/God in union with the Eternal Father of God/Man will take both physical form (benevolent energy) and spiritual form (personal God) on Earth.

Through these two combined forms of Spirit (God) and Flesh (Man), God's Son, Jesus Christ is able to come to Earth in three separate advents to transform the human mind, heart, and soul into holy perfection. The idea is that God's priest has been sent to forgive the Messiah as He takes-on all the sins of man and then offers them up to God's altar to create human forgiveness for the first time ever. Secondly, God's king will be sent to forgive the church as it takes-on its members' sins and then offers them up to God's throne to create heavenly saints for the first time ever. Finally, God's Son will be sent to forgive the world as He pardons all humanity and then offer them up to God's kingdom to create sons of God for the first time ever. This means that through mankind's repentance, prayers, and works, the life-experience can be both purified and transformed from foolish babyhood (growth) into wise man adulthood (maturity). This journey of life sets humanity on its course to wash away sin (priest), change man's nature (king), and awaken man's soul (son) to set him free from sin, evil, and death.

The idea is that washing away one's sins (holiness) means being saved from Gehenna (Messiah); changing one's nature (divinity) means being saved from hell (church), and having one's soul awakened means being saved from the grave (pagans). We see that the "priest" offers God frankincense as holy prayer (donkey) to beg for God's forgiveness. The "king" offers God gold as good works (thief) to beg for God's forgiveness. The "son" offers God myrrh as saving souls (judge) to beg for God's forgiveness. Obviously, the priest desires to pay man's sin-debt (sin-nature) by offering His own innocent blood as payment for man's sinful ways to learn God's good from man's evil and then become a holy saint in heaven. Secondly, the king desires to pay man's evil-debt (worldly temptations) by offering forgiven blood as payment for man's evil ways to learn God's right from man's wrong and then become a righteous citizen on Earth. Finally, the Son desires to pay man's death-debt (demonic possession) by offering guilty blood as payment for man's curse of death to learn God's will from man's will and then become a perfect son of God within God's kingdom. By learning God's divine truths, a person can become worthy of God's gifts of eternal life, new body, and his own royal kingdom to set him free from the chains of sin (ignorance), the prison of evil (cowardice), and the guards of death (greed).

The following tabular information indicates that God's Son is coming to Earth on three occasions to transform the Earth from death to new-life by washing away its sins, changing its nature (divine), and awakening its soul (perfect):

Christ's Three Advents of Repentance, Prayers, Works
to Save Humanity from Sin, Evil, and Death
(priest comes to forgive Messiah,
king comes to forgive Church, son comes to forgive pagans)

High Priest of Heaven (donkey)	**1.** **First Advent** – <u>Repentance</u>: God's Forgiveness = Free Redemption … Give Labor
	• Teenage Priest – Comes on Easter: Man's Faith = Wash Away Sins and Holiness
	• Sheds His Own Blood – Forgives Messiah: Believe (Saved from Gehenna)
	• Priest Offers Frankincense – Prayer for Sin-nature Payment (sin)
First Coming	• Innocent Blood – Learn Good from Evil: Become Holy Saint in Heaven
	• Worthy of <u>Eternal Life</u> – Seat in Temple Court: Title Deed to Heaven
	• Earning God's Gift – *Social Enlightenment*: Holy Spirit's Blessing

(innocent blood – sacrifice His own blood:
create the holy church = being saved by Jesus)

King of the Jews (thief)	**2.** **2nd Advent** – <u>Prayers</u>: Church's Forgiveness = Earned Salvation… Give Money
	• Baby King – Comes on Christmas: God's Law = Obedience + Change Nature and Divinity
	• Offer Forgiven Blood (bloodless) – Forgives Christians: Surrender (saved from Hell)
	• King Offers Gold – Good Works for Worldly

Temptation Payment (evil)

Beginning of Second Coming

- Forgiven Blood – Learn Right from Wrong: Become Righteous Citizen on Earth
- Worthy **of** New Body – Seat in Celestial Court: Title Deed to Earth
- Earning God's Gift – ***Godly Awakening***: Son of God's Blessing

(forgiven blood – sacrifice repentant sinner's blood: create new government = saving self)

Son of God (judge) **Ending of Second Coming**

3. **3rd Advent** – Works: World's Forgiveness = Bonus Rewards ...... Give Life
   - Adult Son - Comes on Halloween: God's Knowing = Respect + Think for Self and Perfection
   - Shed Enemy's Blood - Forgives Pagans: Fight Evil (saved from the grave)
   - Son Offers Myrrh - Saving Souls for Demonic Possession Payment (death)
   - Guilty Blood – Learning God's Will from man's will: Become Perfect Son within God's Kingdom
   - Worthy of Royal Kingdom – Seat in Royal Court: Title Deed to Kingdom
   - Earning God's Gift – ***Divine Indwelling***: Eternal Father's Blessing

(guilty blood = sacrifice blood of enemies: create God's/man's new home = saving souls of others)

This illustration shows that during the Lord's First Advent, Christ came as the high priest of heaven, who was riding a donkey to bring free redemption (being saved) to the chosen people of God (Jews) by offering His own blood (innocent). Secondly, during the Lord's Second Advent, Christ comes as the king of the Jews or a thief in the night to bring earned salvation (saving self) to the Christian people of God (gentiles) by offering forgiven blood (repentant). Finally, during the Lord's Third Advent, Christ will come as the Son of God or a just judge on a cloud to bring bonus rewards (saving others) to God's saints (devoted) for saving pagans by offering-up guilty blood (enemies). It all comes down to offering God either innocent, forgiven, or guilty blood to beg for His blessings of a new body, eternal life, and/or a new royal kingdom either from Earth, Heaven, or from God's Kingdom of Glory.

If a person can receive all three of these divine treasures from the hand of God, then he will be invited to sit as an elder in the Lord's celestial, temple, and royal courts of judgment. In this way, a person can come to meet, know, and love the God-force of our Creator as a saint, who has been transformed into a new creation of holy perfection to serve both the needs and wants of God. We see that the God-force (flesh/spirit) is then transformed into a new creation of compromise, symbolized as manifested energy (law), thereby revealing the divine creator (will) that we both see and know today as Jesus Christ, the redeemer of the world. The Lord in His infinite wisdom has decided to create a spiritual heavenly state of existence in such a fashion as to reveal a major portion of His supreme nature (Christ) through the angelic realm of perfection (angels). The Lord then created the physical realm to manifest Himself as a human being in the person of Jesus, so that His supreme life-force could be better understood by those to whom He desired to reveal Himself centered upon His most intimate or personal level of existence. This decision was based on every fiber of God's being, as it is manifested within God's giving and sharing spirit of infinite service to the Earth, Heaven, and unto the Kingdom of God. This transformed spirit is then brought into existence through the power of God's spiritual nature in the form of a personal calling, social enlightenment, godly awakening, and finally, a divine indwelling.

This most gentle beacon of God's spirit is designed to call forth a lost sinner from his darkness of death (dungeon) into God's new divine light of eternal life or the Lord's most earnest desire (wanting) to bring His goodness to all. Each of the Lord's creations is founded upon God's most important instinct to both serve and protect that which He created through a desire for perfect divine love. We see that both angels and men are the recipients of this most perfect love in the form of divine truth to be given to God's creatures out of His desire to share His most magnificent divinity with all who are willing to sacrifice themselves to the max.

In the previously shown "Fifty-Five Steps of Divine Manifestation," it can be clearly seen that life is a natural extension of God's royal being as seen in the divine right of kings. Out of the divine right of kings, we see the coming rule of the human will and the affairs of sinful men as they seek to surrender, sacrifice themselves, and become converted to the divine nature of God (flesh/blood). We see that God's future royal family and coming kingdom of glory are to be established upon this most ancient promise of divine authority given to Adam in the Garden of Eden, making him ruler over all he surveyed. The Lord's first "act of pure manifestation" comes in the creation of the heavenly throne of divine truth, directly out of His divine countenance (grace) to incarnate His divine spirit into a synthetic existence (illusion), thus creating a new dimension (godly) of divine existence through the face of God (beatific vision). In this way, the Lord God Almighty can set up His divine command (top) and control (bottom) center through which to guide His loyal followers to peace, joy, and happiness. In short, "command" means to give direct orders from God (top), which are to be transmitted down the chain of command to the very bottom (Virgin Mary), thereby establishing positive control. Through this "state of positive control," God can reveal Himself in divine clothes (Shekinah glory/blessed), as Jesus Christ (anointed) and/or in human form (sacred). This "transformation" from invisible to visible takes three advents as God becomes a righteous citizen (Earth), holy saint (Heaven), and finally, a perfect son (Kingdom).

The following tabular information indicates that the Lord God Almighty becomes visible to man by first putting on his divine clothes made of Shekinah glory, secondly coming as Jesus Christ in the flesh, and finally, coming as a human being within Christ's transfigured body:

God Comes during Three Advents to Earth in Divine Clothes, as Jesus Christ, and in Human Form

(man sees God's clothes, hears God's voice,
and speaks to God as a friend via human perfection)

See God   1. **Divine Clothes** - <u>Shekinah Glory</u>: 1st Advent = Priest on a Donkey... Redemption
- Remove Blindness — Ignorance becomes Wisdom
- Learn Right from Wrong — Righteous Citizen: Earth
- Jews Bring the "Good News (truth)"

Hear God   2. **Jesus Christ** — <u>Angelic Form</u>: 2nd Advent = Thief in the Night......Salvation
- Remove Deafness - Cowardice becomes Courage
- Learn Good from Evil – Holy Saint: Heaven
- Christians bring the "Gospel Message (law)"

Speak to God   3. **Human Form** - <u>God as Man</u>: 3rd Advent = King on a Cloud....Rewards
- Remove Dumbness — Greed becomes Generosity
- Learn God's/Man's Wills – Perfect Son: Kingdom
- Saints bring the "Doctrinal Truths (will)"

This illustration shows that the human race is striving to see, hear, and speak to its God face to face and is willing to do whatever it takes to bring forth its Creator on Earth even if a person must give up his life, offer all his wealth, and/or serve God forever (labor). Through these three visits to earth, God will remove man's blindness (eyes/truth), his deafness (ears/law), and his dumbness (mouth/will) to set him free from sin, evil, and death. In this theme of healing, we see Christ's First Advent (see God) brings humanity free redemption (earth), then the Lord's Second Advent (hear God) brings humanity earned salvation (heaven), and finally, during Christ's third advent (speak to God), He will bring humanity its eternal rewards (kingdom).

Recall that God cannot be seen as a Real Being either in spirit or in flesh. Therefore, He transformed Himself into a sanctified vision of divine love (Shekinah glory) to make Himself interiorly visible to His most beloved creatures so that they could acknowledge His existence. This interior locution state is manifested through the Lord's sanctifying grace in the form of divine fire seen as Shekinah Glory (golden rays) called the divine flame or holy light of God. The light energy of God is, in fact, simply a manifestation of the Lord's divine love as a holy garment surrounding His divine countenance of perfection (truth/needs a body). Because of God's awesome glory and majesty, neither the angels nor men may approach the presence of God without being in the same state of perfection (grace) so that God can unite with them in oneness through the spirit of love.

The idea expressed here is that if God is in human form (God-force/needs a body/third advent), he can be approached through one's human righteousness (blessed/level number 1) as soon as a person learns God's right from man's wrong (remove ignorance). We see that if God is in spirit form (manifested energy), he can only be approached through one's human holiness (anointed/number 2) when a person learns good from evil (remove cowardice). Finally, if God remains in divine form (soul) as our divine creator, he can only be approached through one's human perfection (sanctified/number 3) when a person learns God's will from man's will (remove greed). At each of these three levels of perfection, God exists and has His Being, thereby forcing both angels and men to enter into extreme states of obedience (righteous/holy/perfect) to become worthy of the presence of God.

An awakened soul may ask: just why did God create a divine throne as a symbol of His divine court system and why is God's throne attached to His sacred altar and the Lord's table in the form of His Holy of Holies (Ark of the Covenant)? The simple answer is that He desired to manifest Himself in spirit (God) and in truth (energy) through His divine character of royalty. The complex answer is certainly quite extensive, yet we may assume that it was to establish the most significant force of God's justice nature as a supreme authority over all created things of an imperfect nature.

The concept of the "altar (sacrifice)" was to establish His second most important nature in the form of God's mercy to symbolize divine law in a construct of pure sacrifice (compromise) by giving up one's wealth (time), loved ones (money), and His own life (effort/self). This process was needed to unite the Father's just nature of perfection with the Son's merciful nature of imperfection, thereby making them one in the person of God/man (love). It is important to note also that the Virgin Mary's job is to transform all the physical imperfections of man into the spiritual perfections of God by suffering all the female temptations of life, including being a nympho, prostitute, like Mary Magdalene. The uncontrolled emotions of foolish women have plagued womankind since the creation of Mother Eve (cursed womb/pain) and they seem to have no hope of escaping their overwhelming desires to chase, love, and marry evil men. Through repentance, prayers, works, and the saving of others, the Virgin Mary will pass God's test of desire and fulfill the curse of nympho passion, thereby bringing complete satisfaction to every out-of-control womb to stop runaway sexuality and prostitution for all time.

The removal of temptation will make the royal throne (prayer) and the sacred altar (sacrifice) one and the same thing, just as the countenance of God on His divine throne (flesh) is magnified by His countenance (spirit) of Shekinah Glory (God) on His divine altar (spirit/mercy seat). It is the Lord God Almighty's countenance upon His altar as the divine flame of life (benevolent force) that brings forth the Lord's blessing of forgiveness.

This force of living love helps to explain the master concept behind this most complex arrangement that reveals the central issue of God based on the forces of fission (justice/division) and the forces of fusion (mercy/union). The idea here is that both of these forces divide and unite the materials of God's new creation of love into one perfect creation of peace, joy, and happiness. The Lord's throne is the force of perfection, making all things new (life) in the sight of God, while the altar is the force of imperfection, making all things ashes (death) in the sight of God. We must be continually reminded that unlike man, God cannot suffer the pain of loss, which indicates that when the Lord places His most beloved creations upon His altar of death, He is improving its performance and making it even more perfect than before (perfect flaw).

This process is much like a craftsman placing a clay pot (growth) into a kiln to be fired then later giving it a perfect finish (maturity) ready for decoration (painted). It is true that all things (creations) in God's creation are traveling toward some future state of perfection that they might one day glorify God's majesty with their restored state of holy perfection in the sight of God. This means that in the end, all existence must be returned to its rightful owner and also be returned to its original state as in the time of the Great Jubilee. The Jubilee is when a final accounting must be made to balance the Books of Life (book of life/lamb's book of life/book of memories) to make a full tabulation of all the creations owned by God.

We now see that the entire life-experience is about creating a merger (contract) between God's divinity (spirit) and man's humanity (flesh) via the manifestation of both the Jewish people (death) and the Christian people (life) as expressed through the Star of David (kingship). We see that the Star of David is comprised of two triangles: one pointing up (heaven) and the other pointing down (earth) to represent the God/Man relationship. Note that the two triangles are overlaid in such a way as to leave an enjoined area, where God's divinity (heaven) and man's humanity (earth) are made one to represent their shared kingdom of glory (God/man). Through the life (earth), death (heaven), and resurrection (kingdom) of Jesus Christ, the top (God), bottom (man), and middle (God/man) of the Star of David would be purchased through the Lord's water (baptism), blood (confession), and spirit (communion) sacrifices.

We can see this union concept in the transfiguration of Christ when Elijah and Moses appeared with Him in the presence of Peter, James, and John, thereby revealing the two marriages of the Father (spirit marriage) and Son (physical marriage) to the Virgin Mary and to the Church. To comprehend the roles of Elijah/Moses (Father's marriage) and James/John (Son's marriage), one must see how they relate to Jesus (groom) and Peter (bride) by understanding the two triangles making up the Star of David. We see that the first triangle represents Jesus as the father (groom) with Elijah becoming the best man (spirit) and Moses becoming the bridesmaid (flesh) to create creation's first Union (God/man). Secondly, the second triangle is represented by Peter as the Church (bride) with James becoming the best man (flesh) and John becoming the bridesmaid (spirit) to create creation's second union (Heaven/Earth). Finally, we see the two triangles merged together, thereby combining the first and second unions (physical/spiritual) into a third union (mystical) or a third marriage between oneself (one) and the kingdom (all).

Now we see that there is a marriage for God, a marriage for man (society), and finally, a marriage for God/man (self) to manifest and bring forth a glorified body for God (spirit), a transfigured body for man (flesh), and a mystical body for God/man (soul). We see that Jesus Christ was revealing these three bodies to His three companions on the Mount of Transfiguration so that they would understand that God and man are to become one through the marriage vows of divinity and humanity. These marriage vows unite the two Fathers (marriage contract/bride price/dowry), the couple (betrothal/name/virginity), the friends (wedding supper/ church/government), and finally, the families (wedding feast/children /home) into one community of peace (forgiveness), joy (wealth), and happiness (love). Through the Fathers (freedom/justice), couple (liberty/ wealth), friends (independence/dignity), and families (privilege/respect), a fruitful people can be created through their own devotion to family values.

The following graphic illustration shows the importance of Christ's Transfiguration before both Heaven (Elijah/Moses) and Earth (James/John) to reveal the promise of a new body for all who will defeat sin, evil, and death:

The Two Triangles of the Star of David
Reveal the God/Man Marriage Relationship
(transfiguration of Jesus before Elijah, Moses,
Peter, James, and John seals the two marriages)

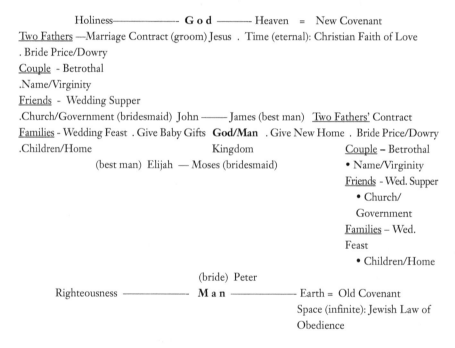

Holiness——————- **G o d** ——- Heaven = New Covenant
Two Fathers —Marriage Contract (groom) Jesus . Time (eternal): Christian Faith of Love
. Bride Price/Dowry
Couple - Betrothal
.Name/Virginity
Friends - Wedding Supper
.Church/Government (bridesmaid) John ——— James (best man) Two Fathers' Contract
Families - Wedding Feast . Give Baby Gifts **God/Man** . Give New Home . Bride Price/Dowry
.Children/Home   Kingdom   Couple – Betrothal
          (best man) Elijah — Moses (bridesmaid)   • Name/Virginity
                                                                     Friends - Wed. Supper
                                                                       • Church/
                                                                       Government
                                                                     Families – Wed.
                                                                     Feast
                                                                       • Children/Home
                              (bride) Peter
Righteousness ————————— **M a n** ——————— Earth = Old Covenant
                                                     Space (infinite): Jewish Law of
                                                     Obedience

This illustration shows the mysteries of the "Star of David" and reveals its depiction of the two marriages of God to Man (Father/Christmas) and of Man to God (Son/Easter) as they blend the nature of time (eternity/life) and the nature of space (infinity/kingdom) into one dimension of existence (paradoxical). Out of these two marriages, Jesus Christ would manifest the birth of three bodies: (1) glorified body (spirit) – live in Heaven (God): priestly holiness; (2) transfigured body (flesh) – live on Earth (man/society): kingly righteousness; and (3) mystical body (soul) – live within Kingdom (self): sonly perfection.

We see that at the "Mount of Transfiguration," the Lord was revealing that Peter would represent God in Heaven (glorified body), James would represent man on Earth (transfigured body), and John would represent God/Man (self) within the Kingdom (mystical body). Through these three dimensions of existence, God (sonship), angels (priesthood), and men (kingship) could become one nature in the person of Christ Jesus. The point is that for God to become **One with Man**, He would have to reconcile His divine life-force with His eight dimensions of existence: (1) eternal dimension (all) – time or God, (2) physical dimension (universe) – kingdom, 3) spiritual dimension (heaven) – world, (4) mystical dimension (kingdom) – nation, 5) divine dimension (Jesus Christ) – state, (6) godly dimension (God) – town or tribe, (7) infinite dimension – space – family, and (8) paradoxical dimension (unknown) – self. This would mean that all eight of these dimensions would have to be made one (all is in all) with God's creation before a new kingdom of glory could become mankind's new home.

This need to unite God's nature (spirit) with man's nature (flesh) is explained by the creation of both the Last Supper (spirit nature/bread and wine) and Mt. Calvary (physical nature/flesh and blood) as they pay the sacrificial price needed to unite God and man. We see in our modern scientific world that the principles of energy (atoms) and matter (elements) are still revealing the life-changing compounds coming from both the field of chemistry (visible world) and physics (invisible world).

**Combining Compounds of Elements
and Subatomic Particles to Create Matter**
(chemistry defines the properties of elements;
physics defines the properties of atoms)

1   **Chemistry** – Visible Properties: research of tangible elements.......chemical composition
    • Human Flesh – Master Visible World: Fighting Evil to Purify Grave
2. **Physics** – Invisible Properties: research of atomic energy...........molecular composition
    • Divine Spirit – Master Invisible Church: Surrendering Will to Purify Host

This illustration shows that both God and man have the same ability to create the basic building block of life, out of visible and invisible forces of existence to bring forth new Creations. Through the Lord's dual nature, we can see God's Grand Design as the king brings a police state (heresy), the priest brings love for all (apostasy), while the Son of God brings a balance (happiness/fun) between God's tough love and man's kind love to set all mankind free. The point is that when building a baby society, the people need a king (tough love); when building a teenage society, the people need a priest (kind love); and when building an adult society, the people need a Son of God (balance). The idea here is to see that the king is the Pharaoh of Egypt and the babies are slaves under the whip of parental discipline or the law (obedience), which demands full submission of their will to authority. Secondly, the priest is the high priest Caiaphas and the teenagers are in a purifying desert of unending traditions and rituals or faith (love), which demands living in a state of complete holiness. Finally, the "Son of God" is the Lord Jesus Christ (Messiah) and the adults are in God's Promised Land of Milk and Honey (thinking), which demands balancing their new nature (law/obey/fight evil) with their holiness (faith/love/submit).

Through this balancing act of spirit (heart) and flesh (mind) or intellect and emotions, a person can grow in knowledge (obedience), while still maturing in human love (devotion). We see that God honors those who recognize (flesh) the groom (flesh) when He comes to enter the wedding supper, just as God gives integrity to those who do not sew new cloth (spirit) on old garments (spirit) just as He gives dignity to those who do not pour new wine (soul) in old wineskins (soul). It is important to see that a king comes to bring order or a police state (babies); the priest comes to bring total freedom (chaos), which ends up in mob anarchy, and finally, the Son of God comes to bring balance in all things, which solves all problems and teaches an adult population to think for itself. It should now make sense that through man's growth and God's maturity, the human race can learn God's right/man's wrong to see its limitations, learn God's good/man's evil, see its potential, and learn God's will/man's will to see its own self-worth.

This means that right and wrong allow a person to become a righteous citizen of Earth and receive his own new body; good and evil allow him to become a holy saint in Heaven and receive eternal life, while God's will from man's will allows him to become a perfect son within God's kingdom and receive his own royal kingdom. By receiving his own free body, then he can attain a new mind of wisdom; by receiving his own eternal life, then he can attain a new heart of courage; and by receiving his own royal kingdom, then he can attain a new soul of generosity. Through the forces of wisdom, courage, and generosity, the human race can be released from slavery, the purifying desert, and receive God's Promised Land of Milk (human kindness) and Honey (divine love).

The following tabular information indicates that the Earth brings mankind into Egyptian slavery; Heaven is man's desert of purification (holiness); and God's Kingdom is man's Promised Land of Milk and Honey.

Earth is Egyptian Slavery, Heaven is Purifying Desert and Kingdom is Promised Land of God

(slavery is crucifixion, desert is tomb,
and Promised Land is resurrection to enter paradise)

Toil (sin)	1.	**Earth** - <u>Egyptian Slavery</u>: Crucifixion = Jesus Takes-on All Sin...... Repentance	
		• Honors - The Wedding Party will not Fast as Long as Bridegroom is with Them	
		• King of Justice (all war) - Offers Prayer of People (baby)	
Throne (purify grave)		• Order – Police State: Force Perfect Obedience (law)	**Old** **Covenant**
		• Learning God's Right from man's wrong – See Own Limitations	
		• Become Righteous Citizen on Earth – Receive *New Body*	
		• Breaking the chains of sin – Deny Intellect: Fight Ignorance	
		• New Mind of Wisdom – Creating a Baby Thought	

(being saved)
(babies break the chains of ignorance
by experiencing life and facing challenge)

Pain
(evil)

2. **Heaven** – <u>Purifying Desert</u>: Tomb = Christ Gives-up
Divinity ......   Prayers
- Integrity – No One Sews New Cloth on Old Garment (teenage)
- Prince of Peace (no war) – Makes Offering for People

Altar
(purify host)

- Chaos – Anarchy/Mob Rule: Let Life   **New**
Take Its Course (faith)   **Covenant**
- Learning God's Good from man's evil – See Own Potential
- Becoming Holy Saint in Heaven – Receive *Eternal Life*
- Opening Prison Doors of Evil – Abandon Feelings: Surrender Cowardice
- New Heart of Courage – Creating a Teenage World (saving self)

(teenagers use key to open prison doors of cowardice
via education to create adventure)

Death
(grave)

3. **Kingdom** – <u>Promised Land</u>: Resurrection = Save
Sinners/Create Saints ...   Works
- Dignity – No One Puts New Wine in Old Wine-skins (adult)
- Son of Mercy (balance) - Leads People to Salvation

Palace
(purify life)

- Balance – Tranquility/Sharing: Proper   **Everlasting**
Rearing Works   **Covenant**
- Learning God's Will from man's will – See Own Self-worth
- Becoming Perfect Son within Kingdom – *Receive Royal Kingdom*
- Overpowering Guards of Death – Submit Free Will: Change Greed
- New Soul of Generosity – Creating an Adult Deed (save others)

(adults defeat guards of death and greed
by thinking for themselves to have fun)

This illustration shows that through the Old Covenant or the Jewish Law of Obedience, a person can break the chains of sin by denying his intellect to fight his curse of
ignorance (Adam/toil). Secondly, via the New Covenant or the Christian faith of love,
he can open the prison doors of evil (key) by abandoning his feelings to surrender his

life and fight his curse of cowardice (Eve/pain). Finally, via the Eternal Covenant or the saint's knowledge of truth, he can defeat the guards of death (sword) by submitting his free will to take control of his life and fight his curse of greed (serpent/death). By defeating sin, evil, and death, he can overcome ignorance, cowardice, and greed to become wise, courageous, and generous before all men; face life's challenges (death); embrace the adventure of life; and make God's magic Kingdom fun.

Yes! The human race must fight for everything that it might get as it learns to master both its physical nature on Earth and its spiritual nature in Heaven and balance them into a new manifestation of righteousness, holiness, and perfection before God. We see that the creation of man's new nature requires the transformation of his mind by denying his intellect (flesh) through his repentance to learn right from wrong and become righteous (transfigured body) before God. Secondly, it requires the purification of his heart by abandoning his feelings (spirit) through his prayers to learn good from evil and become holy (glorified body) before God. Finally, it requires the conversion of his soul by submitting his free will (soul) through his works to learn God's will from man's will and become perfect (mystical body) before God. The idea is to see that once a person has a new mind (wisdom), heart (courage), and soul (generosity), then he will become worthy to receive God's gift of eternal life bringing him Heaven on Earth. In like manner, once he has a new intellect (worship), new emotions (praise), and new instincts (thanksgiving), then he will become worthy to receive God's gift of his own kingdom bringing him Paradise in Heaven.

The Lord is using every facet of His coming Kingdom of Glory to reveal His true nature and the full purpose behind the reason for His existence (challenge/adventure/fun) and also to signify His loving nature of sharing. This shows the Lord's need to use a kingly throne and establish a divine office (physical), within the kingship of God, as a clear signal to humanity that the word king is synonymous with the term deity or God. This divine term has been manifested into the expression benevolent force (righteous as God is righteous) to allow the human race to honor, respect, and thank its Mother Nature for her kindness. In the same manner, the priestly altar has been established as another divine office (spiritual) of the priesthood of God to symbolize the word priest that is synonymous with the term creator or personal God. This divine term has been manifested into the expression compassionate energy (holy as God is holy) to allow the human race to worship, praise, and thank its Creator for His kindness.

To combine the kingship (flesh) and the priesthood (spirit) into one sacred office of divinity, the Lord created a special office to represent His sonship charter (Lord God Almighty) that symbolizes His divine image in spirit (blood shed) and His divine likeness in flesh (body broken). Through the human sonship (title deed to earth) and divine countenance (title deed to heaven) of God, the second person of the godhead was transformed into God's sacred word creating a New Covenant with man through a sonship charter of divine ownership. This master contract links the divine nature of God directly with the future inheritance of man manifested out of the obedience of Father Abraham in the sacrifice of his son Isaac. This faithful act (sacrifice) has given the descendants of Abraham the opportunity to fulfill the sonship charter with God by obtaining the Lord's divine forgiveness out of the act of accepting the Messiah, Jesus Christ, as their personal savior.

The following tabular information indicates how the essential forces of God's countenance (priest) are linked together reflecting God's royal nature (king) as it relates to the sonship of God (son):

God's Kingship, Priesthood, and Sonship Charters

Trinity	Divine Authority	Divine Nature	Divine Offices	Divine Forces
Father	1. **Divine Throne**	Divine Justice	Kingship (King)	Unstoppable Force
	• Divine Perfection (All)			• Plan of Creation
	• *Benevolent Force*			• Righteousness
	• Direct Will			• Right/Wrong
Son	2. **Sacred Altar**	Divine Mercy	Priesthood (Priest)	• Immovable Force
	• Divine Imperfection	(Nothing)		• Plan of Redemption
	• *Personal God*			• Holiness
	• Permissive Will			• Good/Evil
Spirit	3. **Throne/Altar**	Divine Love	Sonship (Son)	Compromising Force
	Div. Conversion	(All New)		• Plan of Sanctified Life
	• *Lord God Almighty*			• Perfection
	• Compromised Will			• God's/Man's Wills
Trinity	4. **Royal Palace/ Table**	Divine Adoption	Fatherhood (free)	Independent Force
	• Divine Imagination	(choice)		• Grand Design
	• *Free Man*			• Freedom
	• Free Will			• Reality/Illusion

This illustration shows that the "Divine Powers Governing" the divine countenance of God provide the foundation stones for the understanding of the ultimate purposes of our Creator, as reflected in His overall Grand Design. Through the plan of God, the Lord will make His Son one with humanity's physical nature/existence to restore its flesh from sinfulness (ignorance) back to righteousness (wisdom). The Lord is primarily trying to communicate with His new creation in the form of a free-willed baby that has never been in existence before and therefore has no way of knowing who or where he is or even why he has been created. This dilemma of not knowing one's origin is confounded by man's mystical existence in that he is a free-willed creature (love) that is unable to be contacted directly by its Creator (God) in fear of destroying man's most coveted free-willed nature. Through this infinite set of free choices or a person's ability to even know the difference between God's right from man's wrong requires everyone to be tested to the bone in life (tough love). Obviously, the Lord God Almighty is making no major effort at convincing mankind of anything, either be it great or small, for fear of tipping anyone off to what life is all about.

This means that we must all figure it out for ourselves so that at the end of time, we can compare our answers to those of God to see just how close we got at knowing the meaning (existence), purpose (service), and value (happiness) of life. We see that one of the best ways to comprehend free will and its choices as it relates to the forces of justice (church), mercy (government), and love (home) is to see God's manifestation of the human existence in terms of God being a magnificent artist, who is diligently at work creating His greatest masterpiece. The delicate balance maintained between the three divine forces of justice, mercy, and love (destiny), as combined with the dynamic force of free will, allow God to properly test (choices made) the wants and desires of every soul on Earth. This means that through a person's free will or free choices, a soul is allowed to both grow (flesh) and mature (spirit) toward eternal perfection, assuming it is willing to learn the lessons of life and then correctly recognize the meaning, purpose, and value of life. We see that these balancing forces are greatly influenced by the forces of evil that challenge the very hand of God to bring all things into perfection based on the ease of destroying God's balance between the use of life (motives) and the use of time (actions).

This tremendous feat of manifesting the impossible to transform the effects of confusion and chaos into a new creation of divine harmony is tantamount to Alexander the Great solving the Gordian knot without using his sword as Alexander did to know all things in life and in death. Recall that after Alexander the Great had no more worlds to conquer, his commanders brought him to a temple of priests to see a great ball of string, which was known as the Gordian Knot (impossible to solve for man). This young man then quickly solved it by simply taking out his sword and cutting the ball in half and then to everyone's amazement, the Gordian Knot solved itself by untying itself.

1. **God's Son, Christ** (God) - <u>Goes to Calvary</u> (3 hrs.): Cuts Gordian Knot in half like Alexander
    - Church Traditions – Gospel Message Requires Earned Salvation: Catholic Faith (spirit)
    - Fulfilling Man's Faith in God's Love – Wash Away Sin: Change Sinfulness to Holiness
    - Become Holy Saint in Heaven – Receive Eternal **Design** Life (sainthood)
    - God Calls All Men to become Prayer Machines (no work)
        – Believe unto Perfection

- God/Man Letter of the Law – Divine Justice: Pass/Fail Grading System
- Intellectual Justice – Modify One's Attitude; Punishment (holy prayers)
  - (all is governed by the ***Will of God*** –
  - destiny wants to be king: master of all it surveys/Heaven)

2. **Mary's Son, Jesus** (Man) – <u>Spends 3,000 Years</u>: Sits Down and Unties Every Knot Personally
   - God's Word – Good News brings Free Redemption: Protestant Faith (flesh)
   - Fulfilling God's Law of Obedience - Change Nature: Human to Divine
   - Become Righteous Citizen on Earth -   **Natural**
     Receive New Body (citizenship)   **Selection**
   - Man Calls All Men to become <u>Work Machines</u>
     - (no prayer) – ***Work unto Perfection***
   - Man/God Spirit of the Law – Divine Mercy: Graded on a Curve System
   - Emotional Revenge – Modify One's Behavior: Imprisonment (good works)
     - (all is governed by ***Will of the People*** –
     - free will wants to be king: master of all it surveys/Earth)

In the case of God's Son, Christ, He represented Alexander the Great, when He went to Mt. Calvary (instant results) to cut the Gordian knot of God and set all of the captives free (slaves) from sin (sin-nature), evil (worldly temptations), and death (demonic possession). In contrast, we see that Mary's Son, Jesus is willing to sit down (patiently) for some three thousand years (three advents) and untie every knot until He has mastered the Gordian knot, its string, and its temple to learn all its lessons be they either good or bad. The Lord desires to share His artistic talent so that we might learn to use the challenging forces of Creation to our advantage, learn the mysteries of life, and come to know our God personally (friendship). This means that the Lord's divine countenance (image) is to be transformed into our sonship charter (likeness), better known as God's gift of divinity, which comes when God's Son is willing to take His name out of God's book of life and put your name in (word/tradition). This divine gift will bring the Lord's friends into a greater and greater perfection in the eyes of God, based on both a person's raw artistic talent (flesh/citizenship) and gifted inspiration (spirit/sainthood). We must imagine ourselves as the Lord's greatest artistic creation in the form of an ingenuous painting of living art, which pictures a royal family of love in all its splendor and infinite perfection. This scene of perfect peace and harmony depicts the true nature of God's divine love as the Lord has placed Himself at the center of all human attention (see God), respect (hear God), and worship (touch God).

The true genius here is that God has made this art treasure divinely valuable by sacrificing His only begotten Son (Calvary) to purchase the priceless supplies (citizens/saints/sons) required for its creation. In this theme of sparing no expense to do it right, God is willing to go to any extreme to get precisely what He wants, when He wants it, even if this calls for the sacrifice of His two Sons, Jesus (human God/flesh) and Christ (divine man/spirit). This means that God's artistic prowess, coupled with His absolute creative genius, has allowed Him to produce a priceless living portrait in such a way as to reveal His own image (reality/original) and likeness (illusion/copy) to sinful man. This most perfect image (God's will/design) and likeness (free will/natural selection) are manifested as a perfect human being (Jesus Christ), who will have both the power and authority to transform the Earth into a New Garden of Eden (paradise). It was never truer that infinite beauty is in the eye of the beholder and that this portrait of God/man (Christ Jesus) reveals the fruits (accomplishments) of both divinity's and humanity's spirit (divine/human oneness) as reflected in the blessing of God's justice, mercy, and love.

This clearly indicates that the coming physical kingdom of God will be an actual manifestation of the Lord's divinity to reflect the Lord's coming spiritual kingdom of glory as seen through the Almighty's beatific vision of love. The idea here is that the physical nature of man believes that if he works hard enough and strives for human perfection (bearing fruit) in every way possible, he can impress even God (rewards) Himself. Unfortunately, nothing could be farther from the truth, because to actually bear fruit (treasures) before God, a person must believe in Christ (33 percent/67 percent/100 percent) unto the denial of his very self (die), then pick up Christ's cross (be buried), and come follow the Lord (rot) unto his own death on Mt. Calvary. In contrast, if a person believes Lucifer's lie that he can somehow earn God's respect through a lifetime of hard-work, he is simply traveling along the pathway of fools, where he will become a self-righteous hypocrite, winding up as a pagan saint (insane fool/self-canonization) in his own eyes.

Conceptually, imagine now a vision of the Eternal Father being face-to-face with the vision of the Son of God, thereby allowing the forces of Justice (tough love) and the forces of mercy (kind love) to become one with divinity (invisible/destiny) and humanity (visible/free will). Now it can be seen that this is the identical position of the First Person of the Godhead, as the positive force of divine truth, which faces the Second Person of the Godhead as the negative force of divine love. Through these opposing forces, reality must come together through the manifestation of the third entity or person of divine existence (Godhead), better known as our Holy Spirit of unity (empathic love). The Holy Spirit is comprised of half of the Father's justice (first truth/energy) and half of the Son's mercy (second truth/matter) and has no nature of His own, which makes the Third Person of the Godhead perfect for being a divine empathic (take pain) or a consumer of all negative forces in life. This means that the Holy Spirit is comprised of both the Father's nature (direct will) and the Son's nature (permissive will) and together, they create an equal nature of divine love, thereby producing a perfect compromise of both God's absolute (perfection) and man's relative truth (imperfection).

The Lord God Almighty is obviously trying to communicate with us all through some abstract mind-bending contradiction or paradoxical mumbo-jumbo (divine code) that seems to be wrapped in an enigma transformed into God's mystery of wonderment. All this is to "avoid" even slightly affecting our free will (individual rights) to choose our own pathway of human desires (want) based upon the use of our natural gifts of life and our own efforts to seek our own destinies. Obviously, nothing is to be taken for granted by those who have come to know God and have come to learn His most mysterious ways, thereby allowing them to reach His pathway of perfection. Even the saints agree that things are not as they appear as they too, try to understand the Lord's great war between spirit (host) and flesh (grave) that has been manifested in the bitter roots of God's divine justice (tough love).

Imagine our Creator God establishing a life-experience, which is centered upon a divine coding system so mystical and so abstract that it can even confuse the mind of Lucifer to the point of killing God's Son by mistake. The initial phase of creation was the Father showing the Son that He was the master of all He surveyed by forcing mankind to become holy through the power of a deity who resides upon Mount Sinai and demands absolute obedience (perfection) to His truth, law, and will. Through this tremendous conflict between the "divine will" or God's raw power (instant results) and the "human will" of man's undaunted determination (hard-work), all mankind would be forced to face and defeat the forces of fear, pain, and death. We see the Son of God coming to Earth as a divine peacemaker to shed new light upon His father's heavy-handed tactics and the Lord Jesus Christ must somehow blend God's expectations for perfection with humanity's hopes to even survive. Jesus Christ would ask divine justice to consider a more merciful approach to bring forth a new universal understanding (peace of mind) to men, angels, and God to become one most beloved eternal family.

This new mystical technique of divine fairness (compromised will) brings up the question: to whom will the New Creation belong and under whose direct authority and direct will is the kingdom going to be governed? We see more importantly that the question is, will the kingdom be ruled by the divine will of God, or will it be ruled by the new free-willed perfect justice system of Jesus Christ? Obviously, the Lord God Almighty will allow all human affairs to be governed by the will of the people with liberty and justice for all as long as the human race can prove that it can think for itself (ethics/morals/fairness). This means that the coming Kingdom of Glory will be ruled by the will of the people, yet it is also true that mankind's human will is to become one with God's divine will, thereby uniting all the affairs of divinity and humanity into one kingdom to serve one (serve) and all (protect) equally.

We are told that the Lord Jesus Christ will bring forth a new sacred government to be ruled by the sacred heart of man/God, so that every person on Earth may live in a perfect land of freedom, under the rule of his own free will (thinking for himself). This is truly an "impossible situation (Gordian knot)" caused by a dispute between the Eternal Father, who desires mandatory worship (personal God/expectations) and His Holy Son, who desires voluntary worship (benevolent energy/hopes), causing an eternal struggle (war) between the spirit of God (letter of the law) and the flesh of man (spirit of the law). We know that this point of disagreement was settled upon Mt. Calvary bringing it to a crescendo, when a final true test of wills was challenged unto the death (sin), damnation (evil), and oblivion (death), thereby ending all future disputes. The question of who is in charge is now forever settled once and for all, by deciding that Jesus would unite God's will (reality) and man's will (illusion), thereby creating a new born-again transfigured body (resurrection) of divine obedience. This new body is to be creation's master arbitrator fully capable of settling all future disputes (issues), thereby allowing all life to be governed by the will of the people through human honor (body broken) and human dignity (blood shed). This reveals God's great gift of free will, which has prepared the way for the Lord's faithful children, based on the Lord's willingness to give up His divine authority so that His omnipotent power might serve the free-willed heart (wants) of man.

This overall concept can best be illustrated by examining the three trials of Christ, where the temple priests became confused as to what crime Jesus had actually been alleged to commit and just what to do with him, if anything. Obviously, the Jews knew that Jesus had a most rebellious attitude against the sacred priesthood when He attacked the priests as evil hypocrites for only using the law to fatten their own pockets. We can now see that Jesus was actually not against the Jewish faith, but only against the evil men, who pretended to be from the house of Aaron (real priesthood) and were falsely administering the affairs of God's temple. This supernatural attack by Jesus then put the temple priests in a quandary over how to judge this most strange behavior (treason/blasphemy), especially from a holy man, who had been formally trained in Samuel's school of prophets and was claiming to be their Messiah, the actual Son of God Himself. Then a problem arose between Jesus and the temple priests because they were not from the original house of Aaron (high priest), but only from the lowly tribe of Levi and had been officially appointed by the Roman leadership (Pontius Pilate) and not by God.

Recall that Jesus had studied in Samuel's school of prophets, which required that a Novas Levi Student Teach (preach) at each synagogue throughout Israel and then complete his studies by teaching in the Great Temple in Jerusalem. The Lord's three-year journey was to show the Jewish people what He had learned from the local rabbis (man/flesh/church traditions) and from the Spirit of God (God/spirit/God's word) and was now ready to combine God's absolute truth or destiny (word) with man's relative truth or free will (traditions). This mastery of the Jewish law also required Jesus to teach twelve of His followers (twelve tribes) the meaning of the Jewish faith so that they could witness to His great knowledge and support His candidacy into the temple priesthood (Herod's temple). This conflict between the ancient Jewish traditions of Moses and the new traditions of King Herod caused a war to break out between Jesus (Pharisees/Heaven/spirit) and the temple priests (Sadducees/Earth/flesh), leading to the Lord's death on Calvary.

The Life of Christ was a complete contradiction (God and man) and none of the temple laws properly fit this special circumstance, forcing them to improvise a new set of Holy Laws just to cover a man proclaiming to be the Lord God Almighty Himself (divine law). The Lord Jesus Christ was then tried and convicted of the crime of Jewish heresy based on Jesus being a sorcerer (healer) in league with the devil in opposition to the Lord God Almighty. This capital sin was tantamount to an abomination of desolation that called for Jesus to be burned at the stake for the crime of witchcraft to symbolize casting Him into the pit of hell forever (Judas goat). At the Lord's trial for blasphemy later in the Sanhedrin with the high priest Caiaphas (rip garment) as His judge, the Lord faced Lucifer in a showdown unto the death. The high priest asked Jesus point blank: are you the Son of God and Jesus responded by saying: "I Tell You One Day You will See Me as the Son of God coming on a cloud of glory." This declaration that Jesus was

God sealed His fate of being convicted as a wicked blasphemer under Jewish Law, but this meant only being excommunicated from Judaism and not crucified. Later, Jesus told Pontius Pilate (washed hands) that He was a king and that if He desired His father to save Him, God would send thirteen thousand legions/cohorts of angels (seventy-two thousand) to come and defend His divine honor and royal throne on Earth. This Declaration of Independence and His right to divine freedom anywhere in the universe got the Lord executed (crucifixion) on Mt. Calvary as He faced both treason (flesh) and Heresy (spirit) unto death. This admission before all of Rome that Jesus was also the king of the Jews cursed Him with being a seditionist (treason) and a threat to the national security of Rome and the whole civilized world of man.

In like manner, King Herod (laughed at clown) then brought Jesus before his royal court and found that none of his national laws clearly fit, so he simply abstained from any official judgment by laughing the Lord out of his palace as a clown, in total humiliation. The temple priest (chief) then claimed that Jesus should have been charged with the crime of sedition (rebellion) for inciting the people to rebel against the Nation of Israel and the imperial seat of Rome, by asking people to follow His new pathway of salvation. The authorities of the temple, Israel, and Rome were then convinced that Jesus was evil (church/blasphemy), crazy (government/sedition,) and a dangerous criminal (home/sorcerer), clearly a serious danger to Jewish/Roman society.

The Lord was then tried a third time by the Roman governor for the crimes of sedition (deceit), sorcery (deception), and blasphemy (defiance) through the power of its procurator Pilate. Even Pontius Pilate could not find any physical law of Caesar that had been broken and therefore decided that he was not qualified to judge spiritual matters such as those charged by the Jews against Jesus. This "Spell" of <u>Church</u> (spirit) and <u>State</u> (flesh) distorted the minds of men (correct thinking) leaving them unable to effectively judge man's Messiah, who had both a human nature (human traditions) and a divine nature (God's word). Obviously, our Messiah was coming to establish a new perfect justice system to free all men from ignorance, criminality, insanity, and evilness by having one truly honest man on Earth, who could judge fairly both the works and behavior of all men.

Jesus Christ Brings Perfect Justice System
to Judge Men's Behavior and Works Fairly
(the Messiah will take away ignorance, criminality,
insanity, and evilness to make all men born-again)

1. **Ignorance** – <u>Baby Level</u>: Sedition = Outcast from People…
Free Redemption
2. **Criminality** – <u>Teenage Level</u>: Sorcery = Excommunicated from Temple…
Earned Salvation
3. **Insanity** – <u>Adult Level</u>: Blasphemy = Banished from Planet Earth…
Bonus Rewards
4. **Evilness** – <u>Wise Man Level</u>: Sacrilege = Forsaken by God…
Personal Freedom

The Lord is trying here to show us that the Jews were people of the Spirit (God's law), while the Romans were the people of the flesh (man's law), both fulfilling their role in the eternal conflict between God (Heaven/Jews) and Lucifer (hell/Romans). This awesome battle of spirit (good/wisdom) and flesh (evil/ignorance) is being fought for ultimate control of the Earth, in creation's war of God's good (reality) against man's evil (illusion). In contrast, King Herod was a Gentile from the lineage of Isaac's son, Esau (Palestinian people), known as the Father of the Edomite Tribe, who should have been the rightful heir to the title deed to the Earth, if Jacob/Rebecca had not stolen it. Obviously, the Edomites were the people who had lost their inheritance (bowl of soup) and were using evil Rome to steal it back through the authority of King Herod. But the Lord God Almighty had other plans when He sent His Son, Jesus Christ to become the real king of the Jews. Because King Herod (neutral) was neither a Jew nor a Roman, he was allowed to see the points of view of both the High Priest Caiaphas (guilty/spirit) and the Governor Pontius Pilate (innocent/flesh). For this reason, the king (fake king) appropriately decided to abstain from any decision concerning Jesus, by stating that He was just a crazy fool (sorcerer). We see that King Herod was saying that Jesus was harmless because he was simply fighting against the religious establishment of the Ancient Jewish temple traditions or against Mosaic Law and nothing else.

We see here that the Lord was effectively combining all three of these judicial authorities into one justice system called the mystical Body of Christ (Earth) and Communion of Saints (Heaven) to reveal God's coming Kingdom of Glory. In this new system of truth, Jesus would represent the Lord God Almighty Himself (blasphemy), priest (sorcery), and king (sedition), serving under the title of Son of Man (circumcision). The job of the Son of Man (circumcision) is to represent man's new holy flesh (sacrificial goat) of born-again humanity (new behavior), which was to come into existence via each child's mother's womb (world). In this same way, Christ would represent God (repentance), priest (prayers), and king (works) serving under the title of Son of God (baptism) to represent man's new Holy Spirit (sacrificial lamb) of born-again humanity (new circumcision), which was to come into existence via the Virgin Mary's mystical womb (church). Out of these two physical and spiritual life forces, the God/man relationship is established in the form of a divine/human marriage between God's name (inheritance/Isaac) and man's virginity (birthright/Esau). This mystical marriage has been created to bring the forces of Heaven (angels) into oneness with the force of Earth (saints) to unite the name of God with the virginity of man.

Note that the Lord Christ has been brought down from Heaven to bring forth the name above all other names in the name Jesus and to bring forth the bride price of perfection for the marriage between God (invisible) and man (visible). In contrast, we see that God has created the Holy Virgin womb or mystical born-again womb in the name of Mary to bring forth the dowry of holiness for the marriage between man (visible flesh) and God (invisible spirit). This means that at the White Throne Judgment, the holy flesh (virginity/Heaven on earth), and the sacred spirit (name/Heaven with God) would be united within the divine soul (beatific vision), thereby manifesting the Lord Jesus Christ as God in the union of divine truth (name/wealth) and human love (virginity/beauty). The idea here is that through this mystical marriage (holy mass/

Canon Law) between divinity and humanity, Jesus Christ would bring forth His new perfect justice system to give both God and man a new creation of fair play, regardless of one's title or position in society.

The trick here is to have Christ's perfect kingdom governed by the collective will of the common man (individual rights) or will of the people and still serve all the people (state's rights) with perfect justice and liberty for all. In this explanation of both the betrothal (bride price) and the wedding supper (dowry), we see that the divine name becomes the birthright of man (bowl of soup/earn) or Paradise in Heaven (divinity), while the holy virginity becomes the inheritance of man (Isaac's blessing/free) or Heaven on Earth (holiness). This important information (knowledge) now allows us to see that out of mankind's inheritance (kill flesh) comes the righteousness of man (right/wrong) or changing his nature, while out of God's birthright (wash spirit) comes the holiness of man (good/evil) or washing away his sins. Out of these two human and divine authorities comes a continuation of Isaac's inheritance blessing (land) on Earth as our eternal dowry (bride/throne), in union with Esau's birthright blessing (people) in Heaven as our eternal bride price (groom/altar). The idea here is to see that these two blessings of Esau and Isaac have come to be represented within both the Last Supper (bread/wine) or bloodless sacrifice (dowry) and on Mt. Calvary (flesh/blood) or bloody sacrifice (bride price) to bring forth the marriage of God and man. We see that this mystical union of Heaven (Spirit/blood/wine) made one with Earth (Flesh/flesh/bread) comes about by God paying the bride price (birthright/give divinity) and man paying the dowry (inheritance/take-sins) to bring righteousness (flesh/Earth/kill flesh) and holiness (spirit/Heaven/wash spirit) to all mankind.

The following tabular information indicates the great importance of the birthright of Esau (Heaven) and the inheritance of Isaac (Earth) as they become the name above all names (God/Jesus) and the mystical virgin womb (man/Mary) to bring about the marriage of God and man:

Esau's Birthright and Isaac's Inheritance
Create the Marriage of God and Man
(Esau gives the bride price and Isaac gives
the dowry to the bride and groom of new-life)

Name (submission)	1.	**Esau's Birthright** - <u>Holiness of the Spirit</u> (maturity) ... Title Deed to Heaven
		• <u>Father God</u> Offers ***Bride Price*** "Name Above All Names" = Jesus (church)
		• Last Supper – Bloodless Sacrifice: Confession of the Spirit (church) = Reality
		• Learning Good from Evil – Holy Sainthood: Priesthood of God (heart)
		• Creating the Temple of God on Earth – Altar of Death (sacrifice)
Purchased		• Gentile People of New-life - Die to Selfishness: Virtuous Morals

- Saving "Oneself (earned)" – Fill the Bowl with Repentance: Nothingness
- Purchase Salvation - <u>Price of a Bowl of Soup</u>: *Glorified Spirit*
- <u>God's Altar</u> – Save Self: Letter of the Law = Worship + Give Life (prayers)
- Redemption – Free Gift: Being Saved by Christ = Water Baptism: Christian

(perfect flaw: trick his brother out of his eternal birthright for a bowl of soup)

Virginity
(sacrifice)

2. **Isaac's Inheritance** – <u>Righteousness of the Flesh</u> (growth)
   ...Title Deed to Earth
   - <u>Father Abraham</u> offers *Dowry* "Eternal Virgin Womb* – Virgin Mary (government)
   - Mt. Calvary – Bloody Sacrifice: Baptism of the Flesh (evil world) = Illusion
   - Learning Right from Wrong – Righteous Citizen: Kingship of God (mind)
   - Creating the "Throne of God" on Earth – Throne of New-life (prayer)

Stolen
   - Jewish People of Death - Born-again in Unselfishness: Principled Ethics
   - Saving "All Men (free)" – Redeem Lost Souls for Christ: Everything
   - Redemption is Free - Ask for Inheritance Blessing: *Transfigured Body*
   - <u>Man's Throne</u> – Save Others: Spirit of the Law = Service + Give Wealth (souls)
   - Salvation – Earned Treasure: Saving Self by Jesus = Blood Confession: Sainthood

(Gordian knot: disguised as Christ pretends to be God's Son and steal inheritance)

This illustration shows that out of Esau's bowl of soup (birthright purchased) and Isaac's powerful blessings (inheritance/stolen), both the title deed to Heaven (holiness) and the title deed to Earth (righteousness) would come forth to bring Christ's born-again mankind. The idea here is to see that out of the "New Heaven" is to come God's birthright blessing (bride price) to anyone willing to pay Him (die to selfishness) for his eternal redemption (spirit/submission) by simply offering Him a bowl of soup (repentance/church). Secondly, out of the New Earth will come man's inheritance blessing (dowry) to anyone willing to work for Christ to receive his eternal salvation (flesh/sacrifice) by simply being born-again (works/world) to Christ's unselfishness. This means that a soul masters the church by giving God a bowl of soup filled with a person's repentance (prayers) to receive free Christian redemption (holiness/baptism) for himself (free); while to master the world, a person must become a soul winner for Christ via his good works (souls) to earn a Christian salvation (righteousness/confession) for all men (paid for in full). Now, we see that the birthright of Esau represents one's free redemption (give divinity) by filling his bowl of soup with repentance and by simply dying to self through Christ's blessing of submission (nothing). Secondly, we see that the inheritance of Isaac represents earning his salvation (take-sin) by dressing as the sacrificial lamb and saving souls through Christ's blessing of sacrifice (everything).

Note that a person must earn Heaven (morals) while being given Earth for free (ethics) based on paying Esau (taking-sin/body broken), or purchasing birthright (blood/holiness), or tricking Isaac (giving divinity/blood shed), or stealing his inheritance (bloodless/righteousness). We see that the Lord is telling us here that our spirit must pay its way to Heaven (salvation) through our submission via repentance (reality/prayer); while our flesh is given Earth for free (redemption) through a person's sacrifice via saving souls (works/illusion/fight evil). The point is to see that free redemption is only free for the pagan world after the sacrificial Christians have placed their broken bodies, blood, and lives (church) on the altar of God to purchase eternal life for the whole world.

This means that mankind is getting its blessing of righteousness and new physical nature of principled ethics (right/wrong) from Father Isaac's inheritance so that everyone on Earth will be set free from sin, evil, and death (purify grave). In like manner, we see that mankind is getting its blessing of holiness and new spirit nature of virtuous morals (good/evil) from Esau's birthright so that every devoted soul on Earth will come to know, love, and serve God (purify host). This means that the life-experience is centered on both worshiping God (maturity/wash spirit) and servanthood to God (growth/kill flesh) through the Christian birthright (church) and the Jewish inheritance (world) made one in Christ Jesus. The Lord God Almighty is obviously striving to teach His beloved children the meaning (existence), purpose (service), and value (happiness) of principled ethics (fairness) and virtuous morals (honesty) because they play a major role in the development of modern society.

We see that God had planted the seeds of both righteousness (flesh/service) and holiness (spirit/worship) four thousand years ago in the bloodline of Father Abraham (blood) to come forth out of the new nature of Jesus Christ (spirit). This meant that out of God's spirit (birthright) was to come the letter of the law (justice) as God demanded to be worshiped with the offering of a repentant human life (submission) upon the altar of the Lord (save self) forevermore. Secondly, out of man's flesh (inheritance) was to come the spirit of the law (mercy) as mankind offers to serve God by offering Him all its wealth (sacrifice) placed before the Lord's throne (save others) forevermore. It is now clear just why there was so much confusion over what the spirit was to do for God (Jews/worship) and just what the flesh was to do for God (Romans/serve) until the coming of Jesus Christ as both God and man.

In all this confusion between the Jews (title deed to earth) and the Romans (title deed to heaven), Jesus could see that even God Himself was not in a proper position to offer an effective and fair judgment on such a complex case without compromising either man's ethics (flesh/growth/free will) or God's morals (spirit/maturity/destiny).

The only person capable of making a proper judgment concerning the guilt or innocence of the Jewish Messiah was to be the creation of God/man (supreme judge), the Lord Jesus Christ Himself. This meant the Lord would have to judge Himself in both spirit (divinity/perfect flaw) and in flesh (humanity/Gordian knot) to reconcile all the differences that existed between God's Church (morals/holiness/worship) and man's state (ethics/righteousness/service). By being able to judge both the Church and the state, all men can relate to the divine law (Mosaic/Canon) of God and His divine judgment at the end of time. Upon this extraordinary set of events, the New Kingdom would be founded, truly born out of the Lord's human blood and divine death, creating a perfect tribunal of divine/human justice. Out of this tribunal, both God and man will be capable of solving all the problems in life within the God and Man creation of perfect love. Only Jesus Christ could effectively operate both the affairs of Heaven and Earth, uniting God and Man into one uncompromising royal family of divine truth. The Lord would have to use His divine authority manifested upon Mt. Calvary to seal all divine and human agreements (sacred), made under the solemn vow of God's divine majesty (court system).

This means that to seal an agreement with God, a person must offer the Lord worship (Jews) or his life; while to seal an agreement with man, he must offer the Lord service (Romans) or his wealth (money). We see the Jews and the Romans found their legal situation so unbearable for all parties concerned that they simply tried to destroy this man of enigma along with all of His human and divine rights of physical (earth), spiritual (heaven), and mystical (kingdom) justice. In this way, Israel's justice system could avoid making any decision concerning the crimes of Jesus, be they against the Church (temple/letter of the law) or against the state (king/spirit of the law). The hopes of the temple priests were that the problem would simply go away and hopefully as quickly as possible to be totally forgotten by everyone involved.

We see that if mankind has any claim to being mistreated by the fates of life, it is founded upon Christ's mistreatment by both of the human (imperfection) and divine justice systems (perfection) of most unconscionable unfairness (kangaroo court/mob rule). This most serious "dilemma makes suspect" the whole question of mankind's evil nature and its need to be reconciled back to some just standard of perfect truth as all the affairs of man relate to a person's natural rights of free existence under the law of nature. We see that Jesus Christ actually defeated the premise upon which original sin had been based and has taken onto Himself the guilt for all the acts of God's fallen creatures as their uncontested leader and loving God. Recall that Jesus stated that He brought sin into the world and not Adam since our first parents only brought the law of nature or divine justice, based on God's law of obedience, while Jesus fulfilled God's law (justice) and established a new born-again law of mercy or the law of love. From this strange quirk of law, we may see why it is so very important for the lost sinners of the world to accept and submit to their divine savior as both the king of the Jews (government) and high priest of Heaven (church) in the person of the Lord Jesus Christ, God's most perfect Son (home).

Through the Lord's sonship, mankind has been saved from damnation by Jesus defeating the three courts (Pilate, Herod, and Caiaphas) of God (divine rights/royal court/Pilate); God/man (states' rights/temple court/Caiaphas); and man (individual rights/celestial court/Herod). Unfortunately, mankind has still inadvertently lost its inheritance to the eternal kingdom as it has now been given to Jesus Christ to use it as He sees fit. This implies that a person must prove his belief in God's Son before he can become worthy of the Lord's eternal inheritance. Through the Lord's titles as king of death (circumcision) and king of born-again life (baptism), He has legally purchased the title deeds to both Heaven (spirit) and Earth (flesh). We see that this divine/human purchase can only take place by saving all men through the free will of the people by making Him their king (thanksgiving/effort), their priest (praise/money), and their God (worship/life). To save the world, the Lord Jesus Christ will have to give cursed humanity a new nature (flesh/grave), new behavior (spirit/host), and new lifestyle (soul/life) through a person's submission (dying to self), sacrifice (fight evil), and reconciliation (save souls). In this way, man's ignorance (see God/Shekinah glory), cowardice (hear God/Jesus Christ), and greed (speak to God/human form) can be transformed into wisdom (know God), courage (love God), and generosity (serve God) through the powers of belief and the sacrifice of Jesus Christ.

The following tabular information indicates that the human spirit, human flesh, and human soul must be transformed into a new nature, new behavior, and new lifestyle to bring mankind from its current pit of death into God's blessing of new-life:

Transforming Man's Human Spirit, Flesh, and Soul into a New Nature, Behavior, and Lifestyle
(all are saved by their submission, sacrifice, and reconciliation before the throne of God)

Submission

1. **Human Spirit** – <u>Give Divinity</u>: Blood Shed = Crucifixion…Knowledge

(Egyptian)
- New Wine – *Creates New Nature*: Surrender to Church = Free Redemption
- Deny Intellect – False Wisdom: See Limitations
- Abandon Feelings – *Unrequited Love*:   **God's** See Potential   **Judgment**
- Submit free will – Foolish Instincts: See Self-worth
- Ignorance (see God) becomes Wisdom (know God)
- See God's Clothes – Shekinah Glory (invisible God)

Sacrifice

2. **Human Flesh** – <u>Take-sins</u>: Body Broken = Scourging …Self-awareness

(Jews)
- New Wineskins – *Creates New Behavior*: Fight Evil in World = Earned Salvation
- Reject Ignorance – Lies: Righteous King
- Reject Cowardice – Fear: Holy   **Lucifer's Test** Priest
- Reject Greed – Stealing: Perfect Son
- Cowardice (hear God) becomes Courage (love God)

- Hear God's Word – Jesus Christ (angelic God)

Reconciliation   3. **Human Soul** – <u>Resurrection</u>: Blood/Flesh Body = Tomb...   Consciousness

(Christians)
- New Chalice – *Create New Lifestyle*: Save Souls in Kingdom = Bonus Rewards
- Defeat Sin – Sin-nature: Transfigured Body
- Defeat Evil – Worldly Temptations: **Self-evaluation** Glorified Spirit
- Defeat Death – Demonic Possession: Holy Soul
- Greed (speak to God) becomes Generosity (serve God)
- Speak to God – Face to Face (human form)

This illustration shows that Jesus Christ offered-up His human spirit by sacrificing (giving) His divinity to provide free redemption to the lost and give all men a new nature (new wine) in truth, law, and will. Secondly, the Lord offered-up His human flesh by taking-on all sin to provide earned salvation to the Christian people so that all men might obtain new behavior (new wineskins) in wisdom, courage, and generosity. Finally, the Lord offers-up His human soul by resurrecting from the dead to provide bonus rewards to living saints so that all men might be given a new lifestyle (new chalice) in righteousness, holiness, and perfection. At each of these three levels of conversion, the human race is being blessed by God like the Egyptian people (Greek) who had to learn submission (die to selfishness); then the Jewish people (Jew), who had to learn sacrifice (fight evil); and finally now, the Christian people (Roman), who are being called to master reconciliation (save souls) before God. Through each of these three peoples, we see the unfolding of God's divine plan for ensuring that every lost broken sinner is destined to receive his own new nature (God/man), new behavior (saintly), and new lifestyle (Christ-like).

The idea here is that if a person receives a new nature (spirit), he can see his own limitations, his own potential, and his own self-worth through Christ's Church. Secondly, if he attains a new behavior (flesh), he can become a righteous king (honesty), a holy priest (courageous), and a perfect son (generous) through the righteous world. Finally, if he strives to create a new lifestyle (soul), he can be blessed with a new transfigured body, a new glorified spirit, and a new holy soul through the Kingdom of God. This means that a person's spirit can be saved (redeemed), or his flesh can save itself (salvation), and/or his soul can save others (rewards), but the final decision rests with the person based on the amount of fear, discomfort, and/or pain a devoted Christian is willing to suffer for Christ. In this way, Jesus Christ has broken down the entire decision-making process of divinity and humanity, transforming it into a more effective method for evaluating proper human behavior based on a one-on-one justice system of perfect order. This one-on-one justice system means facing Lucifer's test (demonic possession), facing God's judgment (worldly temptations), and finally, facing one's own self-evaluation (sin-nature). We know that in any justice system, there are three aspects of perfect judgment: (1) what a man thinks is right (dreams) – remove ignorance (wisdom), (2) what a man intends to do (works) – remove cowardice (courage), and (3) what a man actually accomplished through his own "self-will (deeds)" – remove greed (generosity).

The size of the dreams of a man (wants/mind) shows how much power he must use or invoke to shake the Lord's tree of life and then reveal what it takes to be saved from the forces of sin, evil, and death. This means that the works from a man's hands (needs/heart) reveal his power to move God's holy mountain from its foundations, thereby revealing God's absolute truth (reality). Finally, the holy deeds of a man's soul (dreams) will indicate his power to do God's will throughout his life, revealing his level of greatness in the eyes of God (value). This most delicate problem of doing God's will had to be faced by Jesus Christ in creating a new perfect justice system capable of discerning God's right from man's wrong ultimately to be fair to everyone. This means that by learning the lessons of life, a person can learn to think for himself, thereby allowing him to properly order all of the forces of chaos (illusion) into a new perfect state of divine order (reality). Obviously, he needed to have a way of separating fairly those who: (1) talked and thought about sin (shakers) from those who (2) pushed God's divine laws to their fullest limit (movers) and even worse, those who (3) intentionally sinned with no regard for anyone else (doers). This indicates that a lot of people are talkers of their great deeds, but the question is: how many actually have spent the time, money, and effort to accomplish any great work either good or evil? The answer is, none of mankind's thoughts, words, and/or deeds are very important when present during the Holy Masses because only what a man has in his heart will ever be judged by God.

The significance here is that humanity is living by a false premise, as our foolish world believes that just because a person acts good that God will never know that this fool has an evil heart and a deceitful soul. We must all live by the saying unto thine own self be true so that our lives will match the motives of our own selfish natures, but as devout Christians (believe 100 percent), even our evil actions will bear holy fruit. We see that Jesus Christ has come to take upon Himself the divine guilt of humanity and has only left us the job of abandoning our worthless lives (submission) by offering them to Him in a final desperate act of obedience to obtain our salvation by learning God's good from man's evil (enter holiness). Recall that a man's sin-nature (venial sin) kills his flesh or mind (thoughts) and makes him a sinner; worldly temptations (mortal sins) kill his spirit or heart (words) and makes him evil; then demonic possession (capital sins) kills his soul (deeds) and brings his soul to damnation (hell).

In contrast, we see that by making his Easter duty (yearly), a person can redeem his lost soul when he removes his capital sins (damnation) by thanking God via his offering of good works or labors. We also see that through Sunday mass, he can redeem his lost heart (spirit) when he removes his mortal sins (death) by praising God via his offering of personal wealth or money. Finally, through his daily mass, he can redeem even his lost mind (flesh) as a person removes his venial sins (grave/wounds) by worshiping God via his offering of his entire life. We see that once a person's venial, mortal, and capital sins have been forgiven by God, then a soul can begin working on each of its personal faults and transform them into righteous (works) and holy virtues (souls) before God. We must all come to understand that the human heart (spirit) reveals a person's true nature (wants) and his true value (treasures) in the eyes of God, based upon the depth of his most loving character. This depth of love is shown through the measure of a person's good deeds or that which is lacking in his ability to see the significance of both learning and knowing God's truth (awakening). The truth is especially important when it comes to balancing the decisions of the church (individual rights) against the decisions of the state (state's rights) to find the wills of God and man.

Unfortunately, the wicked heart of the Jewish high priest caused the chosen people to fail to recognize the responsibility of both the Church (altar) and State (throne) as the Jews failed to recognize the hour of their visitation. This means that the legal system of both the Jews (morals/save self) and the Romans (ethics/save others) were unable to determine the essence of divine truth, as it precisely relates to each man's behavior be it past (baby), present (teenager), and/or future (adult).

We see that this failure to understand God clearly reveals that the Lord was testing the human system of justice to its very core to see if it could stand a divine test, where it would be forced to judge the intricate relations involved between God's intellect (mind/justice) and man's emotions (heart/revenge). Obviously, it "failed miserably" in the direct sight of God and was then forced to pay the ultimate price by having its nation, people, throne, temple (altar), and palace torn down and cast into the dust of ancient times. We now see that the first angel of God failed (selfish); the first innocent man of God failed (ignorance); the first sinful society of God failed (greed); the first chosen people (Jews) of God failed (stiff-necked); the first-born son of God both failed (crucifixion/unselfish) and succeeded (resurrection/unselfish); the first holy men (church) of God failed (self-righteous); and finally, the first righteous world (Earth) of God will fail (sin-nature). In short, when a person has been given a fallen free will in the form of a sin-nature, he is destined to trip, stumble, and fall on his face as he is blind, crippled, and insane, yet believes he is perfectly normal.

The beauty of this most perfect test by Jesus Christ was that even God the Father came up short in trying to judge an innocent man or king, who must accept the responsibility of all the sins of His wicked people. The decision was confounded by the fact that this kingly leader was both divine (morals/holy) and human (ethics/righteous) and had actually committed the human crimes of sedition (deceit), sorcery (deception), and blasphemy (defiance). This is true that if what He had claimed was not actually true or He had lied (paradox) about unquestionably being the Lord God Almighty Himself in the flesh, then nothing God's Messiah could or would do can be true. The problem was just how Jesus could say that He was God when He was 100 percent man and could not make any claim that He was the Lord God Almighty in the flesh in even the wildest stretch of the divine imagination.

This most profound discussion leads us to search for a way out of this extremely complex maze of what's right and who's wrong logic, be it God's failure to design creation correctly (genetics) or man's failure to live in God's creation correctly (environment). We know that while the Lord was on the Earth, He continually mentioned the pathway of perfection, explaining that only those who find it will see God's divine light of truth. In other words, discovering the Lord's standard of perfection leads a lost soul to the promised Land of Milk (human kindness) and Honey (divine love), where the most sinful of men may find forgiveness in the sacrifice of Jesus Christ (Calvary).

We can assume from this logic that the Lord has left us a rocky road to divine truth showing the way to human righteousness (flesh) where every pilgrim seeks out and earns his own personal salvation (saving self). This assumption that our Christian faith is synonymous with the Lord's pathway of righteousness assures us that the **Pope** and **Christ's Church** (faith) are the assigned guides showing all humanity the *Divine Light of Truth* (path of perfection). Using this logic, it becomes quite obvious that there are basically three integrated pathways within the Lord's construct, revealed here as the Lord's *Divine Pathway System* (physical, spiritual, and mystical). Our individual, social, and eternal lives are clearly planned and follow some portion of a pathway of destiny (God's reality/children choose) that obviously governs our place of birth, our parents, and our abilities, etc. We also become aware of our own pathway of free will (man's illusion) and its ability to fulfill our physical heart's desire that is only limited by our own strength of human will (want).

This particular life-force is clearly driven by our own undaunted determination (giving all/tenacity) to succeed in this life through the power of our own physical perseverance. This approach to the life-experience will never work as one day, both our strength and perseverance will run out and we will fall into the agony of defeat in total dismay as to what went so terribly wrong. Finally, we notice God is encouraging us to find and follow the Lord's pathway of perfection leading every broken sinner to his own state of physical righteousness (earth) and spiritual holiness (heaven) by his faithful transformation from sinner to saint. Through this faithful transformation, a person can be changed into both a soldier-of-the-light (righteous citizen) and a living prayer of love (holy saint) before the throne/altar of God, because this God-given process will work perfectly to heal the blind and educate the ignorant fool. Now, if we stretch our minds to their outer limits, we can imagine that God is raising spirits in some astral plane (womb of spirits) pictured as a massive chamber, where angels are collecting newly awakening spirits as they come to believe in God as a real person. When a new spirit comes into physical existence, it must be given its own human body, complete with heritage, parents, and a place to eternally call home as the spirit befriends God, angels, men, and nature. This place in human society is most certainly chosen by the spirit itself based on its own free will, thereby allowing it to match its own strength of character against God's eternal opportunities within the Lord's future kingdom of glory. In short, an ambitious spirit can be anything it wants to be, assuming it can master (perform) all of the forces of truth, law, will, and love at the physical, spiritual, mystical, divine, and God levels of righteous, holy, and perfect obedience to God. This implies that the eternal life-experience is sitting there for the taking. All a person needs to do is defeat the forces of fear, pain, sin, evil, death, damnation, oblivion, and then, he is home free (son of God). It can now be seen that God calls this as awesome struggle to find a person's own perfection by attending God's divine school of higher learning. God is saying, come one and come all to **Learn** the *Meaning, Purpose, and Value of Life*.

Unfortunately, each new soul must master God's four pathways: (1) <u>Pathway of Destiny</u> – physical: elementary school (purification) = learning right from wrong (righteous), (2) <u>Pathway of Free Will</u> – spiritual: high school (transformation) = learning good from evil (holy), (3) <u>Pathway of Righteousness</u> – mystical: college (correction) = learning God's will from man's will (perfect), and (4) <u>Pathway of Holiness</u> – divine: on-the-job training (conversion) = learning God's reality from man's illusion (free). The major point is that all four of these paths finally lead to the Lord's master highway known as the pathway of perfection bringing all men to become righteous citizens on Earth, holy saints in Heaven, and perfect sons within God's Kingdom.

The following graphic illustration pictorially describes the four pathways of God, revealing their origin, function, and ultimate purpose in bringing souls to salvation by teaching them right from wrong, good from evil, God's will from man's will, and God's reality and man's illusion to bring all men into perfection:

God's Four Pathways of Destiny, Free Will, Righteous/Holy, and Perfection Guide Mankind to Heaven

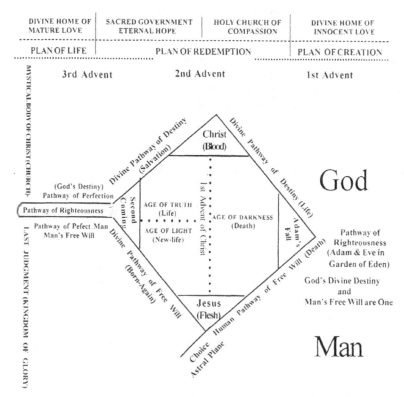

The previous illustration shows that there are four pathways of transformation, leading a lost soul to the meaning, purpose, and values of God via a person's spiritual (first truth/morals) and physical (second truth/ethics) manifestation of purification (destiny/stranger), transformation (free will/acquaintance), correction (righteousness/friend), and conversion (holiness/companion). We see in the above diagram that each person's flesh (growth) and spirit (maturity) start out together, but suddenly the life-experience separates them as the flesh travels toward war (grave) to fight evil and ultimately be destroyed (purify grave), while the spirit travels toward peace (host) to surrender to be washed in the blood of the lamb/born-again (purify host). Yes! We are simply children inside of a divine school of higher learning designed to bring all God's creatures into a more intimate relationship with their Creator by mastering His truth (destiny), law (free will), will (righteous), and love (holy). Unfortunately, only those wise enough and courageous enough to see the truth are willing to enter into a sacrificial covenant with Christ to find the Lord's pathway of perfection (eternal life) and become a son of God. This means that "God's elder sons" would be allowed to seek the knowledge of God by traveling along the many rocky roads (painful) of growth (new mind) and maturity (new heart) leading to God's pathway of perfection. We all "come into existence" through God's pathway of destiny (compromised will) as tiny babies, each called to his own physical reality (ethics) by learning right from wrong so that a person can see his own limitations. Secondly, "a person is called" to God's pathway of free will (permissive will) as a teenager, who seeks to see his spiritual reality (morals) by learning good from evil so that he can see his own potential. Thirdly, a "person is called" to God's pathway of righteousness (direct will) as an adult who seeks to see his mystical existence (principles) by learning God's will from man's will so that he can see his own self-worth. Finally, a "person is called" to God's pathway of holiness (free will) as a wise man, who seeks to see his divine existence (imagination) by learning God's reality from man's illusion so that he can see his own eternal dream.

At "each of these levels of transformation," a person is able to grow and mature into an upstanding, righteous citizen of earth and a respected holy saint of heaven all in the name of Jesus Christ. Obviously, life is all about understanding the perfect righteousness of divinity that seems beyond our imaginations at this moment, yet we must all strive to achieve as much sanctifying grace (earning salvation) as possible during our short time on Earth. We are "faced with a great dilemma" of whether to dedicate our lives to the obedience of God's law, either by fulfilling the divine status of life (son) or by living God's laws to the letter (priest) in seeking the needs of our fellowman (king). This decision involves a person's obedience to the Lord's divine will, which means possibly becoming an outcast and/or cutting oneself off from the possibility of being a direct witness to the truth. This condition forces a soul to live in the abstract nature of God's divine purpose, where it must rely on the spirit of God's law, thereby using its powers of hope and trust to commit itself to the teachings of Christ. Through these teachings of Christ, a person can commit himself to the righteousness, holiness, and perfection of his own mind/heart/soul through sacrifice (born-again/world/purify grave) and through submission (dying to self/church/purify host).

Flesh	Spirit
Sacrifice - Fighting Evil	Submission - Dying to Self
Remove Sin-Nature	Deny Intellect - New Mind
Remove Worldly Temptations	Abandon Feelings - New Heart
Remove Demonic Possessions	Submit Free Will - New Soul
Aaron - Serve God's People	Moses - Serve God's Law
(born-again/world/purify grave)	(dying to self/church/purify host)

This illustration shows that the entire human race is being physically transformed via one's sacrifice (change nature) and spiritually purified via one's submission (wash away sins). The idea here is that all human flesh is being called to fight evil to be born-again in the righteous nature of Jesus (Son of man) and purify one's own grave so that on the last day, he will be resurrected and transfigured into a born-again holy saint. In like manner, all human spirits are being called to surrender and die to themselves in the holy nature of Christ (son of God) and purify their own host so that upon their death, they can be spiritually resurrected and glorified into born-again sons of God. Recall that in ancient times, the Catholic Church was seriously split over an age-old argument of whether the Messiah was either all man or all God, assuming it is impossible that God's Son could be both *All and Nothing at the same time* (Jansenism). We see that the easy answer lies in simple semantics, where the words person and nature are getting confused so Jansenism was correct in saying that the person of Jesus Christ was not human and divine at the same time, but the person of God's Son did have two natures, one as a man (righteous/repentance) and one as God (holiness/forgiveness).

Messiah
One Divine Person

Man's Righteous Fleshly Nature	God's Holy Spiritual Nature
Son of Man – Jesus	Son of God – Christ
Takes All Men's Repentance	Gives All Men Forgiveness
Human God	Divine Man
(Christmas – Last Supper/Life)	(Easter – Mt. Calvary/Death)

One Divine Person

Man's Righteous Fleshly Nature	God's Holy Spiritual Nature
Son of Man – Jesus	Son of God – Christ
Takes All Men's Repentance	Gives All Men Forgiveness
Human God	Divine Man
(Christmas – Last Supper/Life)	(Easter – Mt. Calvary/Death)

This illustration shows that the Lord Jesus Christ is a person with two natures and is unlike any other creature or creation in life because God only has one divine nature and man only has one human nature and the twine shall never meet, without Christ Jesus (last supper/Calvary). In short, we see that man's flesh is walking in the darkness of destiny toward the Lord's pathway of righteousness (light/first mile) that leads to God's ultimate pathway of perfection (Heaven). In like manner, we see that man's spirit is walking in the darkness of free will (blind) toward the Lord's pathway of holiness (light/second mile) that also leads to God's ultimate pathway of perfection (Heaven on Earth). Note that both the "spirit (purification/free will)" and the "flesh (transformation/ destiny)" must make many massive changes in direction to ultimately reach God's pathway of perfection, uniting a person's mind (see), heart (hear), and soul (speak) into one divine person or truth, defined as life. In this way, all Christians must choose to love God's law more than themselves to become worthy of traveling along God's pathway of perfection (yellow brick road) all the way to the Pearly Gates of Heaven.

We see that every Christian soldier will be forced to decide between the value of good works (righteousness) and the fulfillment of his holy faith (holiness) through his abandonment to the sacrificial covenant of divine truth. In this way, the Lord is forcing His children to strike some balance between the forces of good and evil, so that they might accomplish both, without seriously affecting either God (heaven) or man (earth) in a negative manner. It is obviously a matter of proper navigation (balance), implying that a person must learn to read a map correctly or he will stay lost for all eternity as God's maps are based on relativity, thereby changing one's fixed frame of reference moment by moment. This might explain why the science of charting the Earth uses three separate perspectives or projections to see the proper relationships between global or circular geographical locations. We see these three basic projections are (1) flat (Azimuthal) or Path of Destiny – God's truth (Earth), (2) oblique (Machader) or path of free will – God's law (Heaven), and (3) cone (Conic) or path of righteous/holy – God's will (kingdom). Now, we see that each projection is presenting a different viewpoint of man's planet Earth so that collectively, this allows a person to put all viewpoints (pathway of perfection) into proper perspective by blending them into one mystical truth. In this way, God has created different pathways of life leading His children into various aspects of life's infinite choices so that they might exercise the full measure of their God, who gives His babies free will in all things (thinking for self).

The following tabular information indicates four pathways of life presented to mankind via four different viewpoints: (1) destiny – identity: physical dimension = earn eternal life (Earth), (2) free will – character: spiritual dimension = God's gift of divinity (Heaven), (3) righteousness/holiness – personality: mystical dimension = rewarded divine liberty (kingdom), and (4) perfection – countenance: divine dimension = thinking for oneself (free will) for his own personal selection, be it right or wrong:

**God's Holy Saints and Man's Good Citizens
are to become One God's Son, Christ**
(interlaced meanings of the pathways of destiny,
free will, righteousness, and perfection)

Broken Sinners of Man
Love God's People More

1. **Pathway of Destiny**: Physical Life
   (righteous) .... Knowledge

Aaron	• Charity of the Flesh – Good Works: Intellect (mind)
(Other Ten Tribes are to wander the earth seeking their Messiah)	• Symbolizes "True North" of the Great Circle Route to God's Glory
	• Symbolizes "Azimuthal Projection" of Earth (navigation map of destiny)
	• Symbolizes "Storyline no. 1" Life of Christ (God's perfect standard)
Ashkenazi Jews	• Symbolizes "Path of Right Foot" on Truth and Justice through the Legal Perspective of God (follow blindly)
Holy Saints of God Love God's Law More	2. **Pathway of Free Will**: Spiritual Life (holy) …….. Self-awareness
Moses	• Faith in the Spirit – True Devotion: Emotions (heart)
(Tribe of Judah never wandered the earth as they stayed home)	• Symbolizes "Magnetic North of Rumline Route to God's/Man's Glory
	• Symbolizes "Machader Projection" (navigation map of free will)
	• Symbolizes "Storyline no. 2" Life of Jesus (man's perfect standard)
Sephardic Jews	• Symbolizes "Path of Left Foot" on Truth and Justice through the Natural Perspective of Man (think rationally)
Redeemed Soul of God (two-lane road) Loves Law and People	3. **Pathway of Righteous/Holy**: Mystical Life (perfect) … Consciousness
Moses/Aaron	• Knowing of the Soul – Devotion/Good Works Balanced
(Born-again Jews/Gentiles new-life in Jesus Christ via Catholic Church)	• Symbolizes "Mystical North" Righteous Route to Man's Glory
	• Symbolizes "Conic Projection" (navigation map via thinking)
	• Symbolizes "Storyline no. 3" Life of Self (personal standard)
Adopted Jews	• Symbolizes "Path of Right/Left Foot" on Truth and Justice through Mystical Perspective of God/Angels/Men (instinct)

- -

Jesus/Christ	• **Becoming the Life-force** – Devotion/Works United
(Adopted Humanity in Christ's Nature via depth of Submission)	• Symbolizes "Divine North" Perfect Route to Man's Glory
	• Symbolizes "Divine Projection" (navigation map via Christ)
	• Symbolizes "Storyline no. 4" Life of Christ (everyone's standard)
	• Symbolizes "Path of Feet and Hands" on Truth and Justice through Divine Perspective of God's Son, Christ (becoming)

This illustration shows the pathway of information is one's choice between God's stick, the law of justice (pay last penny); or God's carrot, the law of mercy (compassionate). In either case, every living soul must decide for or against the divine will of God. The best of both worlds is to submit to the intercession of Jesus Christ and quietly escape the whole test of choosing between two wrong answers. In the story of Moses, the Lord made Moses (throne) and Aaron (altar) choose between Him and/or the Jewish people, thereby splitting the two brothers' loyalty in two parts, dividing their spiritual commitment (prayer) as well as their physical acts of compassion (works). We see that Moses (Christ-like/divine) chose to serve the laws of God, while Aaron (Jesus-like/human) chose to serve his sick, broken people. Both men were willing to face the consequences of being dead wrong, come what may.

This human dilemma of either seeking God (divine will) or seeking man (human will) sits at the heart of the contradiction (paradox) between who is right (God) and what is wrong (man). We can now understand just why Christ symbolically represents God's divine law, while Jesus symbolically represents God's chosen people (man), to overcome the dilemma through a perfect intercession of God's two divine truths of reality and illusion. Even today in modern-day Israel, there is a constant battle between the authority of the Sephardic Jews (outside Germany), who represent the ancient homeland (good son) against the Ashkenazi Jews (Germany), who represent the modern homeland (prodigal son) of the wandering Jew. We see that these two groups have come to symbolize the good son (Moses/looks-up) and prodigal sons (Aaron/looks-down), one of whom stayed to care for his father's land and the other who left to squander his inheritance in the pursuits of an evil world. Recall that when Jesus told this story of two brothers, He also mentioned that the good son told his father that he would do his will faithfully and then lied, while the prodigal son told the father he would not do his will and finally did it dutifully, only out of raw guilt.

We see the same is true in the case of Mary's Son, Jesus as the prodigal son (Judas goat), who takes-on all the sins of man (scourging) and then returns to redeem the damned from hell. In contrast, God's Son, Christ as the good son (sacrificial lamb), gives-up His divinity (crucifixion), then refuses to save the Jews (Father) and saves the

Gentiles (Mother) instead. Note here that Moses chose God (law) and should be the high priest (temple/look-up) and that Aaron chose man (faith) and should be the king of the Jews (throne/look-down). But in God's wisdom, Moses is king (earth/prayer) and Aaron is the priest (heaven/sacrifice).

Now, let's examine the four pathways of Moses: 1) pathway of slavery – destiny: traveling from Egypt to Red Sea, (2) pathway of the Red Sea – free will: traveling from Pharaoh's army to God's blessing, (3) pathway of Sinai Desert – righteousness/holiness: traveling forty years across the desert, and (4) pathway of Holy Land – perfection: traveling from desert of death into holy land of life. Through each of these four pathways, God has been able to bring His chosen people onto the Lord's pathway of perfection in Jesus Christ for all roads lead to Christ's Church, man's physical baptism (free redemption/earth), and spiritual confession (earned salvation/heaven).

God Gets His New Body – God Comes to Earth (world/body broken)
1. **God's Law of Obedience** – Kills the Flesh: Purify Grave....... Change Nature
   - See Limitations – Learn to Live with Self: Become Righteous Citizen on Earth
   - Water Baptism – Kills the Flesh: Save the Sinner from Death (fighting evil)
   - Resurrection from Grave – Worthy of New Body: Enter Heaven on Earth (evil goat is cast off the cliff into oblivion – death in the pit of forgetfulness)

Man Gets His Eternal Life – Man Comes to Heaven (church/blood shed)
2. **Man's Faith in God's Love** – Washes Clean the Spirit: Purify Host...Wash Away Sin
   - See Potential – Learn to Live with God: Become Holy Saint in Heaven
   - Spiritual Baptism – Washes the Spirit: Creates Saint of New-life (submission)
   - Death unto Born-again New-life – Worthy of Eternal Life: Enter Paradise in Heaven (holy goat slaughtered and offered to God – new-life brings forgiveness to all men)

We see that the current born-again Jewish people have failed to realize that their real strength lies in their combined understanding of both their own homeland (Jewish culture) as well as the mixed cultures (blended Jewish cultures) brought forth from the whole world. This means that just as Jesus sees the Earth and all humanity as His homeland, it is Christ who sees the rest of God's creation and all divinity as His Father's overall Kingdom of Glory. This means that when they are united as one person, Jesus and Christ see both the Laws of God and the faithful people of God from many diverging viewpoints (see truth) all at once. The Lord is showing all the Gentile nations that the Jewish people have mixed their blood with every land and have come to represent the interest of the whole world. We see that only the Jews have been chosen to unite their royal bloodline

(Jesus) with that of God's royal bloodline (Christ) through God's submission (church/host) and man's sacrifice (world/grave). We see that these two bloodlines are combined in the creation of God's Messiah: the Lord Jesus Christ, who brings the world both human faith (body broken), and God's divinity (blood shed) as salvation (earned) for all.

In the Lord's gift of perfect faith (Jesus), a person may receive the right to seek God's most loving gift of divinity (Christ), assuming he is willing to deny his intellect (remove sin-nature), abandon his feelings (remove worldly temptations), and submit his free will (remove demonic possession) to God's will. Through this gift of perfection (divinity), the rest of mankind desires to be holy as God is holy (Nazarite vow/Numbers: 6) so they might be brought to righteousness, holiness, and perfection in the sight of God. We see that all mankind is called to become born-again holy saints as it must have faith in God and do the divine will of God, and to be holy as God is holy through spiritual purification (wash away sins). This phase of a person's transformation process requires the slaughter of his innocence, as a person becomes a victim soul (goat), a willing holocaust unto the Lord on the sacrificial altar of death to his most wicked selfishness. The release of a soul's selfish evil nature (sin-nature) is achieved by the surrender (self-denial) of a person's human will to the divine will of Jesus (man) Christ (God), through the power of the Magisterium of the Church (touch of Peter).

This means that the Power of the Church centers upon each member's depth of submission to the teachings of Christ (belief) and to his individual ability to serve God (yearly/weekly/daily). We now see that the centerpiece of Christ's Church is measured via the depth of a person's submission (commitment) unto all his mind (33 percent), unto all his heart (67 percent), and unto all his soul (100 percent), or until he becomes nothing before God. This act of total submission allows a faithful soul to obtain its own free redemption (mind/33 percent) from Earth (being saved), its own earned salvation (heart 67 percent) from Heaven (saving self), and its own bonus rewards (soul/100 percent) from God (saving others/kingdom). This means that life is all about turning a person's mind toward God (remove garbage) via attending Easter duty yearly to remove his capital sins (think of God) and become worthy of attending weekly mass to remove his mortal sins (remove dirt). Note that we must also turn our hearts toward God (remove dirt) by participating in Sunday services (mass/give wealth) to remove our mortal sins, thereby restoring our love for God. Finally, we must turn our souls toward God (remove dust) by participating in daily mass (worship/give life) to remove our venial sins (do God's will) and restore our service to God. The implication is that we must be washed in the blood of the lamb yearly (Easter/thanks), fed by Christ's hand weekly (Sunday/praise), and then look upon Christ's cross daily (work days/worship) to receive God's blessings (blood), anointings (hands), and sanctifications (cross) in our lives.

1. **First Payment** –Yearly Offering: Thanksgiving = Give Labors…
   Remove Sin-nature
   • Washed in Blood of the Lamb Yearly – Easter Gratitude
2. **Second Payment** – Weekly Offering: Praise – Give Wealth……..
   Remove Worldly Temptations
   • Fed by Christ's Hand Weekly – Sunday: Praise God

3. **Third Payment** – Daily Offering: Worship – Give Life.....
Remove Demonic Possession
- Look upon Christ's Cross Daily: Daily Worship of God

The question is, just how much can a person die to his own selfishness (submission) and then believe that all he does is right (unto thine own self be true/33 percent) as he is controlled by a guilty conscience (67 percent) unto becoming instinctively like Christ (100 percent)? Now, we see that the spiritual authority (33 percent/67 percent/100 percent) of Christ's Church represents the mystical body of Christ as a reflection of the collective mind (worship/ praise/thanksgiving) of all humanity, thereby signifying both the letter (pass/fail test) and spirit (tested on curve/handicap) of God's law.

The following tabular information indicates the importance of submission within the human mind (know God), heart (love God), and soul (serve God) as they are reflected through a person's daily worship (100 percent faith/give life), weekly praise (67 percent faith/give wealth), and annual thanksgiving (33 percent faith/give labors):

Mind Toward God, Heart Toward God, and Soul Toward God to Remove Capital, Mortal, and Venial Sins
(worship is highest, then praise, and finally, thanksgiving is the least before God's majesty)

Perfect Man
33%

1. **Mind Toward God** – 33% Faithful: Make Easter Duty......Yearly Devotion
- Yearly – Washing in the Blood of the Lamb: See Personal Limitations
- Jews are Taught the Perfect Man – Death on Calvary (blessings)

Give Labor
(purify grave)

- Forgiving of Capital Sins – Thanksgiving of Spirit: Give Labors
- Christ Resurrects - New Mind: Ignorance unto Wisdom (right/wrong)
- Being Saved – Free Redemption (good news) from Earth... *Righteous Citizen*
- Believing that All he Does is Right – 33% Faithful (master truth)

(priest on a donkey – mind of a child: believe in illusions – fool)

Perfect
Society
67%

2. **Heart Toward God** - 67% Faithful: Attend Weekly Mass ... Weekly Devotion
- Weekly - Fed via the Hand of Christ: See Mankind's Potential
- Christians are Taught Perfect Society – Death to Church (anointings)

Give Wealth (purify host)	• Forgiving Mortal Sins – Praising of Son - Give Wealth
	• Church Resurrects - New Heart: Cowardice unto Courage (good/evil)
	• Saving Self - Earned Salvation: (gospel message)...***Holy Saint***
	• Responding to his Own Guilty Conscience - 67% Faithful (master law)
	(thief in the night - heart of a teenager: facing confusion – insanity)

Perfect God 100%	3. **Soul Toward God** - <u>100% Faithful</u>: Worshiped at Daily Mass... Daily Devotion
	• Daily - Look at Crucified Cross: See All Men's Self-Worth
	• Mankind is Shown its Perfect God - Death to the World (sanctification)
Give Life (purify host)	• Forgiving Venial Sins – Worshiping of Father: Give Life
	• World Resurrects - New Soul: Greed unto Generosity (God's/Man's Wills)
	• Saving Others - Bonus Rewards (doctrinal truths)... ***Perfect Son***
	• Having an Instinctively Compulsive Nature - 100% Faithful (master will)
	(just judge on a cloud - soul of an adult: becoming truth - normality)

This illustration shows that we are in a world operated by two truths (never-created/created), where God's paradox causes the first to become last and the last to become first (venial sin) as we must first take away our capital sins, then mortal sins, and finally, venial sins to be saved. Note that the hardest sins to remove are venial, which appear to be the most minor in nature, but imagine cleaning a house filled with filth, after you shovel out the garbage (capital sins), then sweep out the dirt (mortal sins), and finally, meticulously vacuum up all the dust particles (venial sins). Unfortunately, a person must make sure that he is totally submitted to Christ in unquestioned belief (perfect faith) before he can even start to clean his house via 33 percent of his mind (yearly), 67 percent of his heart (weekly), and 100 percent of his soul (daily).

Recall that the Jewish people were taught to both comprehend and create the perfect man (33 percent) in the person of the Christ or their Messiah. Secondly, the Christian people are taught to both comprehend and create the perfect society (67 percent) in the institutions of holy churches filled with holy saints. Finally, the righteous world will be taught to both comprehend and create the kingdom of God (100 percent) bringing forth the Lord God Almighty onto the Earth as a man. The question is: who is going to pay for God's creation of perfect people, societies, and His divine kingdoms, who must offer God their own sacrifices in physical (earth/innocent), spiritual (heaven/guilty), and mystical blood (God/forgiven)? The answer is that Christ (offer life) will offer God Mt. Calvary (sacrificial blood), the Christians (offer wealth) will offer God the death of the church (awakening), and humanity (offer labors) will offer God the death of the world (fire) in payment for God's three blessings (new body/eternal life/kingdom).

Now, we see that free redemption (good news) means doing one's Easter duty to have his capital sins forgiven (garbage) as a person thanks the Holy Spirit through his gift of labor (works/saving others). Secondly, we see that earned salvation (gospel message) means going weekly to mass to have his mortal sins forgiven (dirt) as he praises the Son of God through his gift of wealth (prayers). Finally, we see that bonus rewards (doctrinal truths) means going to daily mass to have his venial sins forgiven (dust) as he worships the Eternal Father through his gift of life (repentance). Yes! We serve a God of two truths (paradox) where everything within our established truth must be flipped into its reverse meaning, to correctly see that our daily mass (venial sins/cross) is much more powerful than our forgiveness during Easter (capital sins/blood).

The message here is that a faithful believer must fulfill the teachings of the Church, be they the Good News (free earth), Gospel Message (earned heaven), or the Doctrinal Truths (bonus kingdom) before a person can look upon the Cross of Christ in worship, thereby creating total submission to God's divine will. Yes! We are called to master God's truth (baby mind), master God's law (teenage heart), master God's will (adult soul), and learn to surrender (believe) to the Holy Spirit (thanks) 33 percent (give labors), to the Son of God (praise) 67 percent (give wealth), and to the Eternal Father (worship) 100 percent (give life).

Note: Conquering the Curses of Death (yearly/weekly/daily)

1. Forgiveness of Capital Sins – Restore the Mind: **Remove Death Agony** = Death becomes Life
    *   Receive New Body from Earth – Righteous Citizen
2. Forgiveness of Mortal Sins – Restore Heart: **Remove Hopelessness** = Hopelessness becomes Hope
    *   Receive eternal life from Heaven – Holy Saints
3. Forgiveness of Venial Sins – Restore Soul: **Remove Separation from God** = Separation becomes Union
    *   Receive Personal Kingdom from God – Sons of God

A person's depth of commitment (submission) to his sacrificial covenant (belief) with God opens the doors of heaven and allows the blessings of sanctifying grace to pour out into his soul (new nature). We see that these blessings permit him to overcome the tree of death (cross) and remove its three evil curses (toil/pain/death) placed upon Adam and Eve at the time of their fall from grace. We see these curses are the following: (1) Adam received the curse of sweat and toil (ignorance/death agony) and a sin-nature (deceit), forcing him to till a barren land that had been cursed with unfruitfulness, (2) Eve received the curse of pain in childbirth (cowardice/hopelessness) and worldly temptations (deception), forcing her to populate the Earth with a barren womb (babies) that had also been cursed with unfruitfulness, and (3) both Adam and Eve received the curse of death (greed/separation) and demonic possession (defiance) that forced them to live an entire life of unfruitfulness for them and for their children in a barren desert of death (life). In each of these three divine curses (toil/pain/death), we see the need to be restored from the curse of ignorance by gaining wisdom (new mind), escape the curse of cowardice by becoming courageous (new heart), and defeating the curse of greed by becoming generous (new soul). Only by understanding the triune curses of "original sin (selfishness)" can a person hope to comprehend the pathway of perfection (remove defiance/deception/deceit) and its relationship with the most essential lessons of life, which are growing-up (sacrifice) and becoming mature (submission). This may be seen through the previously mentioned divine curses of land (ignorance), babies (cowardice), and life (greed) that may one day be overcome and removed during the three Advents of Jesus Christ.

We see that in the three Advents of Christ, He came first as a priest on a donkey (sacrifice). Secondly, He will come as a thief in the night (king/groom), and lastly, as a just judge on a cloud (son) to bring forth God's kingdom of glory. Through each of these three Advents, the Lord will transform the Earth from sin (defiance), from evil (deception), and from death (deceit) into God's blessings of wisdom (self), courage (society), and generosity (God). We see that the significance attached to the curses on land, babies, and life is to defeat all God's enemies (justice) and then, God's Son restores the lost back to holiness by using God's powers of anger (silent), rage (vocal), and wrath (striking). In the case where a serious confrontation occurs, such as with Adam and Eve, initial anger leads to cursing one's land (ignorance) so that it will not be fruitful or forcing them to live in a sinful barren land (toilet). If the anger worsens, then a person will curse his enemies even further with a curse on their children or babies (cowardice) that they too will become a barren people (dead womb) to end an enemy's heritage or raising evil children (die young), who are cursed to kill themselves. Finally, in an all-out war with his enemies, he will seek an enemy's life with the curse of death (greed) to make all the works of his enemy's hands unfruitful until he dies and falls in the dirt from his own poverty (poor).

In the case of Adam and Eve, God's anger (deceit/sedition) came when they took the forbidden fruit (death agony). Then God's rage (deception/sorcery) came when they hid and covered themselves with fig leaves (hopelessness). Finally, God's wrath (defiance/blasphemy) came when Adam and Eve disobeyed Him by eating the forbidden fruit (separation), believing that they could become like God and rule the kingdom as they saw fit (free will). Out of Adam's and Eve's war with God, they became seditionists (rebels/land), sorcerers (witches/babies), and blasphemers (gods/life), all in the name of rejecting God and making themselves gods. We see Adam's fall from grace brought humanity three curses from the forces of damnation (agony/hopelessness/separation) that were overcome in spiritual form during the Lord's First Advent (donkey), when the Christ Child became a priest through the blessings of the Lord's most Holy Church (remove sin). It is planned that during the Lord's Second Advent (thief), Christ will come as a king of riches (thief in the night) to bring a new righteous government and a new age of prosperity into existence to overcome the spiritual forces of damnation (remove evil). In the Lord's final visit, He will come as the Son of God, a just judge of pure justice, to purify the entire divine creation and terminate the very nature of physical death. Thus He will restore all land, babies, and life back to their original owner and back to their original state.

It must also be understood that each of the Lord's three advents (donkey/thief/cloud) are symbolically linked to the restoration of starvation (land/scourging), nakedness (babies/crucified), and homelessness (life/tomb) caused by the foolishness of ignorant men. Note that hunger, nakedness, and being homeless all happened to the Lord Jesus Christ while on His journey to Mt. Calvary, where He purchased the coming kingdom of glory with His broken body (take-sin/world) and shed blood (give divinity/church). We see that the creation of the Holy Church brought the Sacred Host onto the Earth to feed the starving spirits of men and restore their most essential life-force (water), thereby giving everyone God's blessing of forgiveness. During Christ's Second Advent (thief), the Lord will return to destroy the enemies of holy men and restore their barren land by making it fruitful (horn of plenty) to clothe lost souls in God's riches in glory. In this way, humanity will overcome the curse of nakedness and again clothe themselves in God's blessings of righteousness as the Lord Jesus Christ comes to take onto Himself all sin (repentance) and give-up His own divinity (forgiveness). During the Lord's third advent, one thousand years from now, He will come to purify the Earth (defeat homelessness) of all its demonic forces by restoring humanity's homeland (good job) and receiving God's gift of the New Jerusalem. The New Jerusalem will come from heaven to become the Lord God Almighty's eternal home on Earth when God and man become one in truth, law, will, and love forevermore via the scourging (good news), crucifixion (gospel message), and tomb (doctrinal truths) of Jesus Christ. This means that the life-experience is centered on a person's individual freedom (earth) within social liberty (heaven) as manifested upon creation's universal independence (kingdom) based on individual rights (self), social rights (society), and divine rights (God).

The following tabular information indicates that the central theme of life involves mastering freedom (self/grave), liberty (society/host), and independence (God/life) based on breaking the chains of ignorance, opening the prison doors of cowardice, and overpowering the guards of greed:

Mastering Freedom, Liberty, and Independence Breaks Chains, Opens Doors, and Removes Guards
(individual freedom brings social liberty
leading to universal independence for one and all)

Self (truth)	1.	**Freedom** – <u>Break Prison Chains</u>: Benevolent Force (one power)… Remove Blindness
	•	Individual Rights – Physical Nature: Earth: Defeat Sin-nature
	•	Mind Cursed with Confusion – Defeat Ignorance to Gain Wisdom......................................**Grave**
Give Labors	•	Learning Right from Wrong – Righteous Citizen: Title Deed to Earth

	•	Redeemed by Universal Sharing – Heal Man's Blind Eyes
Society (law)	2.	**Liberty** – <u>Open Prison Doors</u>: Personal God (two powers)…Remove Deafness
	•	Social Rights – Spiritual Nature: Heaven: Defeat Worldly Temptations
	•	Heart Cursed with Fear – Defeat Cowardice to Gain Courage..**Host**
Give Wealth	•	Learning Good from Evil – Holy Saint: Title Deed to Heaven
	•	Saved by Brotherly Love – Heal Man's Deaf Ears
God (will)	3.	**Independence** – <u>Overpower Prison Guards</u>: God Almighty (three powers) — Remove Dumbness
	•	Divine Rights – Mystical Nature: Kingdom: Rewarded with Mutual Respect
	•	Soul Cursed with Avarice – Defeat Greed to Gain Generosity..**Life**
Give Life	•	Learning God's Will from Man's Will – Perfect Son: Title Deed to Kingdom
	•	Rewarded with Mutual Respect – Heal Man's Dumb Tongue

This illustration shows that mankind is blind (mind), deaf (heart), and dumb (soul) and is awaiting its Divine Savior to heal its eyes, ears, and tongue to set it free from the chains of darkness (blind/sin), the prison cell of silence (deaf/evil), and its guards of miscommunication (dumb/death). Through a person's freedom, liberty, and independence, he can escape the forces of sin (sin-nature), evil (worldly temptations), and death (demonic possession) to become worthy of a new body (grave), eternal life (host), and his own kingdom (life). In this way, freedom (self) will bring individual rights (break chains), allowing him to master the physical nature of the Earth, remove his curse of confusion, and defeat ignorance to bring him to a new-life of wisdom. Secondly, liberty (society) will bring forth social rights (unlock prison doors), allowing a community to master the spiritual nature of Heaven to remove its curse of fear and defeat cowardice to bring all men a new-life of courage. Finally, independence (God) will bring forth divine rights (overpower guards), allowing a holy saint to master the divine nature of the kingdom, remove God's curse of avarice, and defeat greed to bring all creatures to a new-life of generosity.

Yes! God is teaching the human race to learn God's right from man's wrong (intellect) and take positive control of its confused mind so that a lost and confused world can establish a set of principles that can unite all men through universal sharing. Secondly, God is teaching man to learn good from evil (emotions) and take positive control of his foolish heart so that a lost and cruel world can establish a set of principles that can unite all men through brotherly love. Finally, God is teaching lost souls to learn God's will from man's will (instincts) and take positive control of their wicked souls so that a lost and evil world can establish a set of principles that can unite all men through mutual respect. At each of these three levels of conversion, the human race will be able to break its chains of ignorance, unlock the doors of cowardice, and overpower the guards of greed to be set free from its sin-nature, worldly temptations, and demonic possessions.

Through man's new eyes, ears, and tongue, he can come to worship (give life), praise (give wealth), and thank (give labors) God through Christ's temple (freedom), throne (liberty), and table/palace (independence). We see that God is designing His creation around the Earth (throne/altar), heaven (temple/pulpit), and the kingdom (palace/chair) to manifest His coming temple (church), throne (government), and table/palace (home) through worship (give life), praise (give wealth), and Thanksgiving (give labors) to bring perfection to the universal self. Now, it becomes clear that the Lord God Almighty must sacrifice Himself (mind/heart/soul) to bring forth His new creation of natural selection (free will) from the illusion of nothing (death) into the reality of all (life).

Through this magnificent decision to sacrifice God Himself, a chain of sacrifices would have to be made, thereby forcing God's new creation (natural selection) to pay its own way (debts) by making full restitution for all its sinful acts (spirit/damages) and all of its evil acts (flesh/fines). It is now clear that God gives-up His mind (Holy Spirit/labors) to get a king, then a "King (David)" to get a throne, and then a "Throne (Jewish)" to get a righteous world (citizens), then a "World" to get Earth; then the Lord gives-up His planet Earth to get the New Earth (man/God). Secondly, God gives His heart (Son of God/wealth) to Get a priest, then a "Priest (Aaron)" to get a temple, then a "Temple (Jewish)" to Get a Holy Church, and then gives the Church (Christians) to get Heaven, then will give Heaven (angels/saints) to get a new Heaven (God/man). Finally, the Lord gives His very soul (Eternal Father/life) to get a Son, then a Son (Messiah) to get a palace, then a palace (Jewish) to get a perfect home/man, then gives the perfect home/man (self) to get a kingdom of glory, then a kingdom (free men) to get a new Jerusalem (God/Man).

Give Labors	Give Wealth	Give Life
Get Righteousness	Get Holiness	Get Perfection
(government)	(church)	(home)
1. God Gives His *Mind*	1. God Gives His *Heart*	1. God Gives His *Soul*
• Get a King (David)	• Get a Priest (Aaron)	• Get Son (Jesus)
2. God Gives King	2. God Gives Priest	2. God Gives Son
(scourging)	(crucifixion)	(tomb)
• Get Throne	• Get Temple (altar/Jews)	• Get Palace (table)
3. God Gives Throne	3. God Gives Temple	3. God Gives Palace
• Get Righteous World	• Get Holy Church (christians)	• Get Perfect Home/Man

4. God Gives World	4. God Gives Church	4. God Gives Home/Man
• Get Earth (citizens)	• Get Heaven (saints)	• Get Kingdom (sons)
5. God Gives Earth	5. God Gives Heaven	5. God Gives Kingdom
• Get <u>New Earth</u> (Man)	• Get <u>New Heaven</u>	• Get <u>New Jerusalem</u>

We also see that in the Ancient Jewish Temple, only one holy man (high priest/altar) can worship God (sacrifice/lamb) or give his life; on the Jewish throne, only one righteous man (king of the Jews) can praise God (prayer/kingship) or give his wealth; and in the Jewish table/palace, only one perfect man (God's Son) can thank God (treasure/sonship) or give his labor. In contrast, through the Christian Church, all men (Christians/altar) can worship God (sacrifice/goat) or give their lives; then via the righteous world, all men (citizens/throne) can praise God (prayer/king of kings) or give their wealth (money). Finally, via God's kingdom of glory, all men (sons/palace) can thank God (treasure/son) or give their labors. Using this logic, we see that God sacrificed the Egyptian people (mind) to get the Jewish people (heart); then the Lord sacrificed His temple (soul) to get the church (life-force); while God sacrificed his Jewish throne of David (death) to get a righteous world (new-life), thereby making planet Earth the new throne of God (king of kings).

In the next phase of give a first-born to get a better creation, we see that God sacrificed the Jewish people (Calvary) to get a kingdom of glory (freedom), all in the name of His Son, Jesus Christ. With the sacrifice of God's kingdom, He will establish Heaven on Earth as time will end and eternity will begin with the coming of the Lord's Holy City, the New Jerusalem or the City in the Clouds. We see that through the creation of God's Holy Church (light), righteous world (water), and His Kingdom of Glory (soil), the Almighty will bring holiness (life), righteousness (wealth), and perfection (love/labors) to one and all. We see that this great gift of life, wealth, and labors coming from the Lord comes from God sacrificing His Jewish temple to Create His Christian Church and then sacrificing His evil throne to create His righteous world. Through this awesome journey from nothing to all, the human race can obtain its heart's desire by coming to know God on Earth, love God in Heaven, and serve God within His kingdom.

The following tabular information indicates the temple creates the Holy Church (sacrifice) or Heaven, the throne creates the righteous world (prayer) or Man's Earth, then the table/palace creates the Kingdom of Glory (treasure) or God's/man's kingdom:

Temple Creates Holy Church, Throne Creates the Righteous World, and Palace Creates Kingdom
(High Priest becomes Lord of Lords, King of the Jews becomes King of Kings, and Son of God becomes Son of Man)

Give	1.	**Temple** – <u>One Man Worships</u>: High Priest Aaron
Lamb		…Face One's Ignorance
(heart)	•	Stealing God's Fruit – Defiance: Blasphemy = Banished by God + Striking Wrath (not remember)
	•	Water Blessing – Brings Priest's Holiness: Title Deed to

Heaven (spiritual truth)

- Do Not Drink Wine (drunk) – Cursed with Acting Foolish: Remove Sin-nature
- Deny Intellect – Obey Ten Commandments: Remove Capital Sins = New Mind + Wisdom

New Nature (church)	2.	**Church** – <u>All Men Worship</u>: Lord of Lord's Christ… Blessed with Wisdom

- Tomb of Death – Pay Capital Sin-debt: God Meets Man in Church = Perfect Man
- Baptism Blessing – Die to Self: Brings God's Forgiveness = Peace of Mind
- Wine is Blessed (sober) – Blessed with Devotion: Gain Virtue of Worship (give life)
- Vow of Obedience – Good News: Free Redemption = Glorified Spirit
  (Meaning of Life – Gift of Existence:
  Learning Good from Evil = Lord of Lords)

Give Goat (mind)	3.	**Throne** – <u>One Man Praises God</u>: King of the Jews, David…Face One's Cowardice

- Hiding from God – Deception: Sorcery = Outcast from Rome + Vocal Rage (not speak)
- Oil Anointing – Brings King's Righteousness: Title Deed to Earth (physical law)
- Do Not Cut Hair (vain) – Cursed with Wicked Vanity: Remove Worldly Temptations
- Abandon Feelings – Sell All, Give to Poor: Remove Mortal Sins = New Heart + Courage

New Behavior (government)	4.	**World** – <u>All Men Praise God</u>: King of Kings, Jesus… Blessed with Courage

- Crucifixion on Cross – Pay Mortal Sin-debt: Man Meets God in World = Perfect Society
- Confession Anointing – Born-again: Brings God's Wealth = Joy of the Heart
- Hair is Anointed (gracious) – Blessed with Honesty: Virtue of Praise (give wealth)
- Vow of Poverty – Gospel Message: Earned Salvation = Transfigured Body
  (Purpose of Life – Service to Others:
  Learning Right from Wrong = King of Kings)

Give	5.	**Table/Palace** – <u>One Man Gives Thanks</u>: Good Son,

Ram (soul)	Christ...Face One's Greed
	• Lying to God – Deceit: Sedition = Ostracized by the Jews + Silent Anger (not see)
	• Blood Sanctification – Brings Son's Perfection: Title Deed to Kingdom (mystical will)
	• Do Not Touch Dead (infected) – Cursed with Contamination: Demonic Possession
	• Submit Free Will — Come Follow Christ: Remove Venial Sins = New Soul + Generosity
New Lifestyle (home)	6. **Kingdom** – <u>All Men Give Thanks</u>: Prodigal Son, Jesus...Blessed with Generosity
	• Scourging at Pillar – Pay Venial Sin-debt: Man Meets Himself in Home = Perfect Friends
	• Communion Sanctification – Set free: Brings God's Love = Happiness of the Soul
	• Dead are Sanctified (purified) - Blessed Servanthood: Virtue of Thanksgiving (labor)
	• Vow of Chastity – Doctrinal Truths: Bonus Rewards = Holy Soul (Value of Life – Finding Happiness: Learning God's/Man's Wills = Son of God to son of man)

This illustration shows that even God had to give something to get something. The question was, just how much was the Lord God Almighty willing to sacrifice to obtain His heart's desire by having it all in the form of physical truth (Earth), spiritual law (heaven), in mystical will (kingdom), and divine love (self)? In this depiction, we see that via the Nazarite vow of Samson, he promised not to drink wine, nor cut his hair, and/or to touch the dead so that he could officially take his vow of ordination into the Jewish priesthood. Recall that during the time of Moses, the purpose of the Nazarite vow was to enter a week of priestly purification so that a person could see his sins (confession/retreat) and repent before God to become holy. This mystical concept of holiness was introduced by Moses and was only possible by surrendering one's life totally to the Lord's Mosaic tabernacle through sacrifice of ignorance (drunken wine), vanity (hairstyle), and evil contamination (touching dead).

The idea was that after a single week (seven thousand years) of purification, a person would be given a righteous mind (wisdom), a holy heart (courage), and a perfect soul (generosity) to make him worthy of the presence of God. Through this most powerful Nazarite rite (Easter duty), we also come to understand our passion week during Easter (day of atonement) when God's people (Jews/Christians) are to be brought back to their original holy state of Christian perfection (sainthood). Now, we see that within just one week (Passion Week), a lost, broken sinner can receive a set of new wineskins (new nature) to be filled with new wine (new behavior), thereby casting off his old ways to bring forth a new and improved version of life. We see that this new vision of life was extremely important to Christ as He strived to meet John the Baptist on the Jordan River to receive His water baptism (circumcision/kill old nature) and then meet God to receive His spiritual baptism (baptism/birth to new nature) to save the whole world.

1. **Water Baptism** – John the Baptist: Jewish Circumcision = Calvary......Purify Grave
   - Change Physical Nature – Human to Divine: Heaven on Earth
   - Fulfill God's Law of Obedience – Become Righteous Man on Earth
   - Water Kills Flesh – Jesus Takes All Sin: ***Repentance for All***
2. **Spirit Baptism** – Jesus Christ: Christian Baptism = Last Supper.........Purify Host
   - Wash Away Spiritual Sins – Sinfulness to Holiness: Paradise in Heaven
   - Fulfill Man's Faith in God's Love – Become Holy Saint in Heaven
   - Spirit Resurrects Spirit – Christ Gives-up His Divinity: ***Forgiveness for All***

This means that first, Jesus came as Jewish lamb's blood (crucifixion) to change man's nature (divinity); then secondly, Christ came as Christian lamb's death (tomb) to wash away Man's sins (holiness). This need to change a painful life into a happy life in the physical world required Mary's Son, Jesus (Son of Man), to take-on all sin to make sinners into righteous citizens on Earth. Secondly, the need to wash away sin to change death into eternal life in the spirit world required God's Son, Christ (Son of God), to give-up His divinity to make Christians into saints in Heaven. These two conversions from human to divine (sonship) and from evil to holy (sainthood) drive the entire plan of God as He strives to make Heaven and Earth into one Kingdom of Glory in service to all. Recall that the Old Covenant (circumcision) was God's law of obedience (Abel's lamb), which could only be obeyed (change) by eating lamb's flesh and drinking lamb's blood, which was a divine meal that had been prepared by Aaron for the Lord God Almighty Himself. Secondly, the New Covenant (baptism) would be man's faith of love (Cain's wheat/grapes), which must be fulfilled (wash) by eating lamb's bread and drinking lamb's wine, which was a human meal prepared by Jesus for all the children of God. Note that baby Christians are baptized in water to make them into Jesus' followers (righteous), while adult Christians are confirmed by the Holy Spirit to make them into Christ's followers (holy). The theme here is that God wants to become man (challenge) while man wants to become God (fun) as the grass always looks greener on the other side of the fence. But in the end, whether being God or man, life is simply life. It is important to see that man's water nature is being merged with God's spirit nature by blending the humanity of Earth (lamb's blood) with the divinity of Heaven (lamb's death) to create God's new kingdom of glory (unity).

The following tabular information indicates that Jesus was baptized in water (John) to become the Jewish lamb's blood (flesh/blood), while Christ was baptized in spirit (Dove) to become the Christian lamb's death (bread/wine):

Jesus is Jewish Lamb's Blood/Change, while
Christ is Christian Lamb's Death/Wash Away Sin
(Jesus brings water baptism and Christ brings
spiritual baptism to make man divine and holy)

Law
(circumcision)

1. **Jewish Lamb's Blood**/Calvary – <u>Changed</u>: Water
   Baptism……John the Baptist
   • Pain Changed into a Happy Life – Earth: Righteous
     Citizen (baby)
   • Jesus Baptized in Water – Son of Man: Heaven on Earth
     = Change Nature

Obey Law
(one man)

   • Mary's Son – Takes-on All Sin: Save Sinners from Hell
     Fire (Mosaic Law)
   • Old Covenant – Law of Obedience: Eat/Drink Jewish
     Lamb = Flesh/Blood
   • Jesus – Gives Free Redemption to All: *New Body*
   • Man Sacrifices Body for God – God Sacrifices Life for
     Man
   • Baby Man Wants to Become God – Fun, Fun, Fun
     (remove man's selfishness – God Gets New Body:
     God and Man become One = Paradise in Heaven)

Faith
(baptism)

2. **Christian Lamb's Death**/Last Supper – <u>Washed</u>:
   Spiritual Baptism… Holy Dove
   • Death Changed into Eternal Life – Heaven: Holy Saint
     (adult)
   • Christ Baptized in Spirit – Son of God: Paradise in
     Heaven = Wash Sins

Love Faith
(all men)

   • God's Son – Gives-up His Divinity: Change Christians
     into Saints (Canon Law)
   • New Covenant – Faith of Love: Eat/Drink Christian
     Lamb = Bread/Wine
   • Christ – Gives Earned Salvation to Righteous Men:
     Eternal Life
   • God Sacrifices Life for Man – Man Sacrifices Body for
     God
   • Adult God Wants to Become Man – Challenge,
     Adventure, and Fun
   (God becomes generous – Man Gets Eternal Life:
   Man and God become One = Heaven on Earth)

This illustration shows that Jesus represents the Jewish lamb's blood of Abel, thereby forcing Him to fulfill the Mosaic Law to become divinely worthy of eating God's offering on Mt. Calvary via His crucifixion (blood). Secondly, Christ represents the Christian lamb's death of Cain, thereby forcing Him to fulfill the Canon Law to become humanly worthy to eat man's offering in His tomb via His death. In this theme, we see that the Lord God Almighty has found a way to allow baby man to become God (eternal life) and then to allow Adult God to become Man (new body) to bring eternal life to Man and bring a New Body to God. Through this "Mystical Exchange" of God's Spiritual Life for Man's New Body and Man's Physical Life for God's eternal life, we can comprehend our need to sacrifice our bodies for God and then God will sacrifice His life for us.

This means that on God's side, He must do the impossible of the impossible (paradox) to enter death to give mankind His life, while the human race must simply die to its selfishness (submission) to give God its body. The point here is that if man will remove his selfishness, then God can get a new body and create Heaven on Earth (New Earth); while if God will become generous, then man can get eternal life and create Paradise in Heaven (New Heaven). Obviously, as long as man and God stay enemies, neither side will get what it really wants. Thus, it was up to God's Son to find a way to reconcile both the life of God (all) with the flesh of man (nothing) to break this deadlock of eternal stubbornness (stiff neck). This meant that Jesus Christ would have to play all the roles of being God and being man so that He could apologize to Himself and then make all the necessary payments for damages and fines to pay humanity's sin-debt (pay God) and pay God's holy-debt (pay man). It should now make sense that the justice systems of both God and man are extremely complex and that the Gordian Knot of Life would even be an awesome challenge for Jesus Christ as He must balance the love of God with the hatred of man to save everyone.

Recall when Jesus met the young, rich man and told him, if he desired to enter the Kingdom of God, he would have to give-up selfishness, or obey the ten commandments (vow of obedience), to sell all, and give to the poor (vow of poverty), and then come to follow Him into chastity (vow of chastity). The point is that the Lord was telling the young rich man that if he desired heaven, he would have to fulfill the Nazorean rite of holiness to become holy as the Father is holy. This implies that to refuse wine (sober) was an act of submission (dying to self), not to cut one's hair (vanity) was an act of sacrifice (born-again), and that not to touch the dead (purity) was an act of reconciliation (set free) back to the forgiveness of God. The idea here is to see that God is sacrificing a mind (intellect/temple) to get a heart (emotions/throne), then sacrificing a heart to get a soul (instincts/table), all in the name of redeeming the world. Finally, the Lord is sacrificing a soul to get a new born-again life-force (nature/freedom), thereby setting His entire creation free from the forces of sin (sin-nature), evil (worldly temptations), and death (demonic possession).

In this explanation, we see that Christ's shed blood (crucifixion) is offered to God (temple/sacrifice) to receive man's new nature (image); while Jesus' body broken (scourging) is offered to God (throne/prayer) to receive man's new behavior (likeness). In this way, God is able to create a new creation in the image (nature) and likeness (behavior) of Jesus Christ with a new mind or transfigured body, a new heart or glorified spirit, a new soul or holy soul, and finally a new life-force or eternal life. By combining these four entities of human existence into one mystical being, the Lord gets four dimensions plus God within one person: (1) a righteous king (throne/prayer) – righteous citizen (sacrifice): poverty, (2) a holy priest (temple/sacrifice) – saint of heaven (prayer): obedience, (3) a perfect son (church/sacrifice) – son of God (thanksgiving): chastity, and (4) a free man (world/prayer) – trusted companion (treasure): freedom. We know that Jesus taught that when a person finds the pearl of great price, a wise man will sell all and rush to purchase that which is priceless to him alone, especially when everyone else believes he is simply the fool of fools.

Obviously, the Lord has decided to purchase a trusted/loving companion for life, who was worth any price that He would have to pay for him/her. Thus, our all-powerful God was willing to even sacrifice His Son on Mt. Calvary to purchase that most perfect pearl of great price, the most Blessed Virgin Mary, our Mother of mothers (baby farm). Through this awesome sacrifice (God gives His all), God is willing to allow the whole human race to become holy as God is holy (Nazarite Vow) in preparation for their welcome into Heaven.

The following tabular information indicates that in Luke 9:15, Jesus blesses five loaves and two fishes by breaking them and then sharing them with some five thousand families to depict the coming of the ever-multiplying host to feed the whole Earth:

Luke 9:15
Feeding of the Five Thousand
with Multiplication of Loaves and Fishes

Blessing of Offering - Free Redemption,
•Nature's Gift of Nourishment - New Mind

Submission •Five Loaves/Two Fishes (see limitations) **Knowledge**
• Blessed by God - (Worthy of New Body) (meaning of life)
(take vow of obedience - become righteous)

Breaking of Bread - Earned Salvation
• Dividing of God's Meal - New Heart

Sacrifice • Families in groups of Fifty (see potential) **Self-Awareness**
• Anointed by God - Worthy of Eternal Life (purpose of life)
(take vow of poverty - become holy)

Sharing God's Meal with Everyone - Bonus Rewards
• Everyone Eats and is Filled - New Soul

Reconciliation • Twelve Baskets of Scraps **Consciousness**
Collected (see self-worth) (value of life)
• Sanctified by God - Worthy of Own Kingdom
(take vow of chastity = become perfect)

This illustration shows that through God's blessing (creation), breaking of bread (divide), and sharing with others (distribution), the entire redemptive system is founded. The idea is to see that God's blessing represents human righteousness (earth); the breaking of bread represents human holiness (heaven); and finally, sharing with others represents human perfection (kingdom). We see that in Numbers 6:2-6, these scriptures are telling the Jewish people that if they spend just one week within the Mosaic Tabernacle, fulfilling the Nazarite Order by repenting (flesh) and praying (spirit), they can become holy before God. We see this same theme of one holy week occurring from Adam until the end of the world (seven thousand years) and again during Passion Week (Calvary) prior to the Easter celebration (resurrection). It seems that through a person's repentance (no wine), prayers (never cut hair), and works (never touch dead), a person can win God's favor sufficiently to be blessed (new mind), anointed (new heart), and sanctified (new soul) unto holiness.

The idea here is that if a person is before God and the Lord makes a toast by holding up His chalice of wine, then anyone who is unholy must declare himself unworthy to drink (submission) this most holy of wines. Secondly, if a person is before God while at a divine wedding and his hair and beard are not properly groomed (sacrifice), he will be disgraced and then punished by having his head and face shaved off. Finally, if a person is before God and the Lord is rewarding all His resurrected saints and a person has touched death (reconciliation), he will be judged evil (unworthy of resurrection) within the sight of the Living God. Now, we see that the Nazarite Vows of never drink wine (mind), never cut hair (heart), and never touch the dead (soul) are outward signs of a repentant soul's submission (pay day), sacrifice (rest), and reconciliation (eternal rest) to God.

We can now see that the submission of Noah (flood), the sacrifice of Abraham (Isaac), and the reconciliation of Jesus (Calvary) also fit into the format of the Nazarite Vow as all humanity is brought out of sin (sin-nature), evil (worldly temptations), and death (demonic possession). This means that in our personal lives, a person's flesh must be baptized (capital sin/being saved), spirit must confess (mortal sins/save self), and a person's soul must receive communion (venial sins/save others) to become holy before God. Now, it becomes clear that the Earth, Church, and "Man" are passing through the Lord's Nazarite Vows to purify their physical (flesh/mind), spiritual (spirit/heart), and mystical (soul/soul) natures by never drinking wine (submission), cutting one's hair (sacrifice), and/or touching the dead (reconciliation). Unfortunately, before anyone can attribute too much importance to the Nazarite Vow, he must decode its meaning by matching up its three devotions to world events.

This implies that Noah's Flood (no wine), Abraham's sacrifice (never cut hair), and the coming of God's Messiah (never touch dead) brought forth the purification of the Earth. Secondly, during the Lord's Passion Week, we see God's blessings of Palm Sunday (submission), Good Friday (sacrifice), and Easter Sunday (reconciliation) as they bring forth the purification of the Church. Finally, during our own Church sacraments as we receive our own baptisms (capital sin), confession (mortal sin), and our own communion (venial sin), they bring forth the purification of sinners. This means that the purification of the Earth (submission) is bringing forth God's divine rights (royal court/worship); the purification of the Church (sacrifice) is bringing forth man's social rights (temple court/praise); and the purification of sinners (reconciliation) is bringing forth one's individual rights (celestial court/thanksgiving) before the throne/altar/table of the Lord God Almighty.

The following tabular information indicates and/or reveals that Moses' Nazorean Rite is implemented through one's submission (unworthy of God's toast), sacrifice (reject beauty), and reconciliation (reject family) with his Creator God to bring forth each person's gift of holiness:

Submission, Sacrifice, and Reconciliation Bring
Purification of Earth, Church, and Its People
(The Nazorean Rite purifies all life and
makes the earth, religion, and man holy before God)

Self
(truth)

1. **Submission** – <u>Unworthy of God's Toast</u>: Refuse Cup of Wine........... Knowledge
   - Nazarite Vow of No Wine – God Forgives Sinner: Palm Sunday = Purify Earth
   - Vow of Universal Sharing – Righteous King
   - Coming to Know God – Righteous Citizen
   - ***Surrendering One's Life to God*** – Submission
   - Noah's Flood – Bless Earth's Flesh (God)
   - Plan of Creation – Life
   - Palm Sunday – Anoint Church's Flesh (society)
   - Plan of Redemption – Death   **Individual Rights**
   - Personal Baptism – Sanctify Man's Flesh (self)
   - Plan of Sanctified Life – Resurrection
   (light of purification – toil of repentance:
   beg for light = learn right from wrong)

Society

(law)

2. **Sacrifice** – <u>Sacrifice Personal Beauty</u>: Cut Hair Bald... Self-awareness
   - Nazarite Vow to Not Cut Hair – God Anoints Christians: Good Friday = Purify Church
   - Vow of Brotherly Love – Holy Priest
   - Coming to Love God – Holy Saint
   - ***Unto Thine Own self be True*** – Sacrifice
   - Abraham Offers Isaac – Bless Earth's Spirit (God)
   - Worship God – Give Life
   - Good Friday – Anoint Church's Spirit (society)
   - Praise God – Give Wealth   **Social Rights**
   - Personal Confession – Sanctify Man's Spirit (self)
   - Thank God – Give Labors
   (water of purification – prayer of forgiveness:
   buy water = learn good from evil)

God

3. **Reconciliation** – <u>Reject Family for God</u>: Refuse to Bury Mother..... Consciousness

(will)	•	Nazarite Vow to Not Bury Dead – God Proclaims Saint: Easter Sunday	
	•	Vow of Mutual Respect – Perfect Son	
	•	Coming to Serve God – Son of God	
	•	*Guilty Conscience* – Reconciliation	
	•	Jesus on Cross – Bless Earth's Soul (God)	
	•	Repentant Sinner – Deny Intellect	
	•	Easter Sunday – Anoint Church's Soul (society)	
	•	Prayers of Christian – Abandon Feelings	**Divine**
			Rights
	•	Personal Communion – Sanctify Man's Soul (self)	
	•	Works of Saints – Submit Free Will	
		(soil of purification – works of God:	
		till soil = learn God's Will from man's will)	

This illustration shows that the purified Earth (Noah) blesses its soil (flesh); the purified humanity (Abraham) blesses its beliefs (spirit); and the purified cross (Jesus) blesses lost sinners (souls). Secondly, the purified Palm Sunday blesses the Church's worship (flesh); the purified Good Friday blesses the Church's praise (spirit); and the purified Easter Sunday blesses the Church's Thanksgiving (soul). Finally, the purified Christian is baptized blessing the sinner's repentance (flesh); the purified Christian confesses, thereby blessing a Christian's prayers (spirit); and the purified Christian's communion blesses the saints' works (soul). At each of these levels of purification, Earth (nature), Heaven (church), and the Kingdom (self) can become transformed into the (1) creation of life, (2) redemption of man, and (3) eternal sanctified life through humanity's (4) worship, (5) praise, and (6) Thanksgiving brought forth from each person's (7) repentance, (8) prayers, and (9) works in the name of Jesus Christ.

Through these nine acts of devotion before the Almighty, a great union will be established between the Spirit of God (Christmas) and the flesh of man (Easter) allowing God to become man (heaven) and man to become God (earth) in service to one and all (kingdom). Recall that this tremendous union between God and man (physical) began with the efforts of Father Noah for he was willing to go to any extreme to meet God (stranger), either in the form of an ark in nature or even face-to-face in person. Secondly, this union between God and man (spiritual) was continued by the efforts of Father Abraham for he was willing to sacrifice his own son to make the acquaintance of God, no matter what the cost in time, money, or effort. Thirdly, this union between God and man (mystical) was furthered by the efforts of God's Son, Jesus Christ for He willingly sacrificed His divinity to become God's friend in truth, law, will, and in love. Fourthly, this union between God and man (divine) made great strides forward through the efforts of Christ's Church as it strived to become a constant companion of God through its Melchizedek priesthood (Canon Law). Finally, this union between God and man (godly) will reach its fulfillment through the efforts of the coming righteous world when it enters the eternal oneness of God via the Lord's blessings of righteousness, holiness, and perfection.

Now, we see that the holy men of past ages gave their lives to meet God as a stranger, make His acquaintance, become His friend, seek His companionship, and finally, enter the oneness of God to be like Him in all ways. At each of these five stages of intimacy with God, the human race is able to obtain a clear picture regarding the meaning (existence), purpose (service), and value (happiness) of life.

The following tabular information indicates the five stages of intimacy obtained by man by meeting his God face-to-face through a series of superior human achievements worthy of the Lord God Almighty's personal blessing:

The Five Stages of Intimacy as a Stranger, Acquaintance, Friend, Companion, and in Oneness
(Noah meets Stranger, Abraham makes Acquaintance, Jesus becomes Friend, Church is Companion, World is Oneness)

Baptism
(capital sin)

1. **Noah** – <u>Man Meets Stranger as God</u>: Seeking Salvation… Knowledge
- Noahic Covenant – Submission to God's Divine Will: God's Golden Altar
- God Sees Man's Great Suffering – Pagan Fool: Babyhood Level
- 1st Dimension of Life – *Physical Truth*: Righteousness = Pathway of Destiny
- Give Life – Worship: Learn Right from Wrong = Family Worships God

Confession
(mortal sin)

2. **Abraham** – <u>Man Makes God's Acquaintance</u>: Being Saved…Self-awareness
- Abrahamic Covenant – Unto Thine Own Self be True: God's Golden Throne
- God Hears Man's Painful Cry for Help – Chosen Jew: Teenage Level
- 2nd Dimension of Life – *Spiritual Law*: Holiness = Pathway of Free Will
- Give Wealth – Praise: Learn Good from Evil = Community Worships God

Communion
(venial sin)

3. **Jesus** – <u>Man becomes God's Friend</u>: Saving Oneself …. Consciousness
- New Covenant – Obey One's Own Guilty Conscience: God's Golden Palace
- God Recognizes His Covenant – Devout Christian: Adult Level
- 3rd Dimension of Life – *Mystical Will*: Perfection = Pathway of Righteousness

- Give Labor – Thanksgiving: Learn God's/Man's Wills =
Nation Worships God

Confirmation (faults)	4.	**Church** – <u>Man is God's Companion</u>: Saving Others… Sentience

- Everlasting Covenant – Instinctive Compulsion: God's Royal Table
- God Comes to Help His Child – Holy Saint: Wise Man Level
- Fourth Dimension of Life – ***Divine Love***: Sonship = Pathway of Holiness
- Give Respect – Friendship: Learn Reality/Illusion = Many Nations Worship God

Death (virtues)	5.	**World** – <u>Man Enters God's Oneness</u>: Set Eternally free…Thinking

- Divine Covenant – Thinking for Oneself: God's Kingdom of Glory
- God Restores His Child to Good Health – Son: Free Man Level
- Fifth Dimension of Life – ***Godly Nature***: Freedom = Pathway of Perfection
- Accept God's Gift – Liberty: Learn Wisdom from Ignorance = World Worships God

This illustration shows that as each lost broken sinner becomes closer and closer to God, he is able to defeat his ignorance and begin to enter the wisdom of God by learning the meaning (exist), purpose (serve), and values of life (happiness). This means that each of God's children is to master creation's physical truth (existence), spiritual law (service), mystical will (happiness), divine love (value), and godly nature (new nature) to both grow-up and become mature. Note that through the Noahic (stranger), Abrahamic (acquaintance), New (friend), and Everlasting (companion) covenants, the human race is expecting to come to know, love, and serve God to the point of winning His divine friendship (divine covenant) forevermore.

This need to find a way to communicate directly with the Lord God Almighty sits at the center of the religious controversy regarding just how to worship (give life), praise (give wealth), and/or thank God (give labor) to receive His blessings of redemption (eternal life/new body/kingdom). It can be seen that the whole process being used to contact God was simply the devotion of one man named Noah who hoped that his undaunted efforts (build ark) would encourage more and more people to worship God. In this concept, we see that God is planning to come to Earth when He is sure that the whole world has bowed down to His divine truth, His law, and His will forever. The Lord's Grand Design is clearly perfect and our perception of it has little merit when it comes to assessing either its intrinsic value to the human race or in defining its overall final purpose. Obviously, the undaunted determination of the human spirit is one of God's most perfect creations and has come to have its true strength and its place of honor within the hearts and minds of devoted men. This most perfect human spirit is synonymous with the Lord's pathway of destiny, whose quest for perfection is unstoppable and unerring as it seeks to fulfill its personal destiny in the heart of every struggling soul.

The Lord's most powerful Holy Spirit can only be plowed in His progress to purify the human condition by the most evil of human natures as it is immersed in a sinner's selfish flesh (ignorance/cowardice/greed). This means the more sin abounds (immovable), the greater God's grace will abound (unstoppable) leading to the Lord's manifestation of true liberty for the human will, based upon the creation of God's open pathway of free will (self-control). This allows a great sinner to experience that elusive state of freedom, which clearly demonstrates that everything looks easy, even when it is extremely hard. The point here is no matter how far one travels along the road of death seeking his own destruction, he still has a loving Father (personal God) of divine hope, who is patiently waiting for the most special day when His child reaches his awakened maturity, thereby setting him truly free from ignorance (sin), cowardice (evil), and greed (death). The basic concept of freedom is for God to raise His free-willed creatures right by teaching them to seek His divine way of truth (perfection). The only other way is to force Himself to change and establish some meaningful compromise based upon His more tolerant attitude of divine permissiveness. The point here is that God never creates anything that is not for His glory, nor will any of His children fail to bear fruit (treasures) as He originally intended. Of this fact, we can be sure. The most difficult aspect involved in comprehending these four pathways of logic is connected with how reverse conceptualism becomes truth when discussing the dynamics (flexibility) of God's new free-willed human spirit that can do anything (paradox).

We see here that the "flesh of destiny (pagan)" is on a human pathway of destiny, while the "spirit of free will (holiness)" is on a divine pathway of free will based upon a person's depth of physical growth (streetwise/destiny) and spiritual maturity (educated/free will). The point is that once a Christian dies to his free human will and has been surrendered to Christ's pathway of destiny (identity/see self), then he is transformed into God's new pathway of free will (likeness/see God). This final transformation occurs just as one enters the Lord's Kingdom of Glory to become a great saint before God by seeing himself, society, and God in divine truth. Once this process has taken place, a Christian soul is once again given its complete freedom of will (holodeck) to forever operate as it once did on Earth to make itself prosperous (flesh) and successful (spirit) for the glory of God. This concept is founded on the idea of being right-handed all one's life and suddenly becoming ambidextrous or instantly being healed of a crippled condition (dead left hand), that we all once thought was normal. To better comprehend this "logic," imagine being a dutiful child completely surrendered to his parental guidance in body/flesh, spirit, and soul that he might be properly raised as a righteous citizen (righteous) of humanity. In spiritual terms, this is known as his most holy submission (baby) to obtain a more mature will (adult), guaranteeing him a state of command authority based on his common sense (personal

God) manifested through his use of his good instincts (benevolent force). Now, this same child grows-up and has the blessing of freedom given to him from his proud, loving parents so that he might now walk the pathway of adult free will (maturity) just like one of his elders. This is known as the Lord's pathway of perfection, where a submitted soul is made whole and brought to full spiritual maturity, so that it may one day again be restored to total free will without fear of any further failures.

We see that to avoid failure, be it God, angels, and/or men, they need an effective checks and balance system to put the thought process (executive), the words of command (legislative), and the accomplishments from deeds (judicial) in context with truth, law, and will. Obviously, this was the aim of Jesus Christ: to establish a Church (priesthood/banking), government (king/legal), and a home (sonship/accounting) on Earth to balance the flesh (mind), spirit (heart), and soul (being) of man to make him perfect in the sight of God. Now, it makes sense why the Lord said, "A person can become converted only when two or three are gathered in My name." This implies that a New Christian must enter a community of saints (slave) to prevent him from being deceived by the evil one. The idea here is that each of God's children must grow-up (mandatory), become mature (optional), and be set free from sin (sin-nature), evil (worldly temptations), and death (demonic possession) through the intercession of Jesus Christ.

All humanity is striving to grow-up, just as any child of God who desires to be great in the eyes of his Father, as he receives the appropriate authority to demonstrate his skills in self-control through the grace of proper behavior. This indicates that the Lord's pathway of righteousness (ignorant goat/bread) symbolizes a person who has clearly demonstrated a fully mature range of divine social graces to prove he is ready to face any form of godly test. This pathway for becoming a mature, righteous citizen is comprised of fifteen special steps that are to be traversed in two separate groups: (1) seven steps of destiny (flesh) that occur on the Earth by traveling a righteous path (right/wrong), and (2) seven steps being "free will (spirit)" that symbolize walking a holy path (good/evil) in Heaven. The last step is a Christian life of great emotional struggle, thereby making this last step (graduation) one's mark using both the pathway of destiny (righteousness/goat) seen as corporal life (pathway of righteousness/man), and the pathway of free will (holiness/lamb) seen as one's future divine life (pathway of holiness/God) made one in Jesus Christ.

The human experience is divided into two basic phases from birth (physical) to approximately the age of forty (corporal life), and then spiritual phase from forty until death (spirit life). These two physical and spiritual phases give each person a chance to first manifest his own identity (see limitations) in the flesh prior to being forced to comprehend the spiritual attributes of God's most mystical creation. If a soul is truly chosen by the Lord to "Master" in His sight, he will be given a personal public ministry of good works, where he may manifest his life through the salvation of others (evangelization). It is also possible that a person might be chosen to be a silent victim soul, where one is allowed to suffer as a secret holocaust (living prayer) unto the Lord and still save a tremendous number of souls. In either case, every person must mature in his flesh (ethics) and spirit (morals) before he can come to know the Lord (soldier-of-the-light) and serve Him (living prayer) through the blessings of His divine love (marks/graces/points).

In this way, each of us might take the divine stage as holy performers and show our stuff before the very eyes of God since we only get one chance to demonstrate to all the kingdom (God, angels, and men) for all time, how unselfish (total submission) we can be by honoring the glory of God. How many of us will make this following statement at the end of time? "Oh, how great I could have been if only God had given me a reasonable chance to prove myself, like so many others who have failed to recognize the hour of their visitation." Obviously, the Lord will give everyone several chances (three) to recognize the hour of their visitation beginning with that moment when a person could have scored big at a young age. Then later, when a person has much more time to consider the far-reaching consequences (damnation), and finally, having one's last chance (death bed) placed in a soul's face when God is yelling, don't miss your hour of visitation... **I'AM** real, you know (believe it).

In this theme of doing something right (works) versus believing in righteousness (faith), we see the difference between reaching heaven through perfect faith and/or falling into hell via good works. One might ask, why has God only made His "babies" believe truth (spirit) rather than doing the truth (flesh) to receive His awesome blessing of redemption (free gift)? The easy answer is because no one can earn his redemption through works, or he would be God, the first creator of divine works, who has no rival in either thought, word, and/or deed. Obviously, the Lord is establishing a "mystical priority system," whereby God comes first through faith (spiritual belief), while the individual comes second through works (physical prosperity). The implication is that it is pointless to try to become God under one's own power because God has clearly defined His divine chain of command and all creation must follow it to the letter (justice). This established "chain of command" arrangement requires a worthless human being to pay God back (in full) for Adam's breath of life plus the creation of the universe of existence. We see that man's "Jewish Messiah" comes to offer God both His divine Name (divine blood/wine) and perfect nature (divine flesh/bread) in both bloodless (submission promise/take-sin) and bloody sacrifices (sacrificial fulfillment/give divinity). This divine sacrifice on Mt. Calvary opened the doors of heaven (body broken) and the pathway to God's heart (blood shed) for all men of good will (death to selfishness).

Note that in the curse of Adam and Eve, they were given an evil sin-nature of free will that would make them love themselves more than God to prevent them from ever committing suicide via self-preservation (fear of death). When a person tries to make himself God and tries to earn his own place in heaven, he offends the Lord's divinity (justice) and is cursed into eternal oblivion (Gehenna). We are told that it is pointless to even try to earn one's way to heaven through works because the only door to perfection comes through the power of belief (dying to self/submission). Unfortunately, an individual cannot believe in divine truth (Christ) using his own will power because *"it takes two or three in My Name"* to call the Christ into existence. This means that every confused soul is saying, "I can't do it myself, no matter how hard I try to surrender to the divine will of Jesus Christ my savior." Yet in the case of

Jesus Christ, He takes it upon Himself to become worthy of heaven by paying both man's sin-debt (imperfection/faults) and His own virtues/debt (perfection virtues) in full. When a soul pays all debts (sin/virtues/redemption) in full (last penny), then it is permitted to come to meet God (benevolent force), love God (personal God), and serve God (Lord God Almighty) in truth (Holy Spirit), law (Son of God), and will (Eternal Father). It is important to note that Jesus Christ had to pay the divine debt, while we are only required to pay the human debt (back to Jesus), which is microscopic payment, compared to that which the Lord had to pay to redeem humanity from hell fire.

The point being made here is that God is real (name) and man is an illusion (virginity), showing that the Lord is coming to lost humanity in three mystical ways: (1) benevolent force, nature: God's altar (worship) = celestial court (transfigured body) + First Advent: priest (truth); (2) Personal God, Father: God's throne (praise) = temple court (glorified spirit) + Second Advent: king (law); and (3) Lord God Almighty, Creator: God's palace (thanksgiving) = royal court (holy soul) + third Advent: Son (will). Through these three manifestations of the "never-created God (formless)" within the illusion of man, everyone ever created has a chance to become either a holy saint (heaven), righteous citizen (earth), or a baptized pagan (universe). This means that our "divine God (reality)" resides within His never-created life (formless) of perfect self-love in eternal perfection. In contrast, we see that "human existence (illusion)" resides within a created life (form) of unselfishness within the state of temporal holiness. By comprehending these "two types of existence," we can grasp the divinity of God as an intellectual paradox (contradiction).

We see that this paradox appears to man as a mysterious enigma of insanity because the Lord makes no sense to the one-dimensional man residing in a physical world. For this reason, we must learn the importance attached to the benevolent force (chaos) or nature (natural order), to the personal God (chaos/order), or Father God (supernatural order), and to the Lord God Almighty (order) or Creator God (divine order). This triune system of authority (power) is responsible for raising individuals to level one (elementary school), then educating groups of people (societies) to level two (high school). Finally, the Triune System will provide a happy lifestyle to mature worlds at level three (college) so that the human race can master all that it surveys. Recall that God told Adam and Eve, "Now go forth and conquer life and multiply your seed throughout all creation so your lives will bear fruit, no matter what challenges your descendants might have to face in settling the whole universe, inch by inch (pioneers)."

The following tabular information indicates the three life-forces of God: (1) benevolent force (nature); (2) personal God (father); and (3) Lord God Almighty (creator) that operate the physical (earth), spiritual (heaven), and mystical (kingdom) dimensions of life:

The Three Life-forces are Benevolent Force, Personal God, and Lord God Almighty
(manifestation of physical [earth], spiritual [heaven], and mystical [kingdom] creations)

Truth
(intellect)

1. **Benevolent Force** – <u>Nature</u>: Teacher of Chaos =
   Natural Order... Knowing God
   <u>First Power of Existence</u> – Divine Duty: Good Instincts
   = Friendship of God
   - God's Altar – Offer Labor: Thanksgiving = Remove
     Venial Sins (communion)
   - God's Throne – Offer Sweat: Pay Sin-debt = Defeat Sin-
     nature (repentance)

**King on His
Throne**
(free)

   - God's Palace – Offer Harvest: Righteous Citizenship
     (king) = See Limitations
   - <u>Elementary School</u> = ***Creating Individual Values***: Baby
     Level = Ignorance
   - Learning Right from Wrong – Righteousness:
     Principled Ethics (fairness)
   - Blessing of Transfigured Body – Heaven on Earth: Peace of
     Mind (home)
   - Gift of Seat in Celestial Court – Rule Earthly Affairs:
     Awakening
   - Treasure of Eternal Freedom – Create Own Kingdom:
     God's Wisdom

Law
(emotions)

2. **Personal God** – <u>Father</u>: Teacher of Chaos/Order =
   Supernatural Order... Loving God
   - <u>Second Power of Existence</u> – Divine Responsibility:
     Common Sense =   Companionship
   - God's Altar – Offer Wealth: Praising = Remove Mortal
     Sins (confession)
   - God's Throne – Offer Money: Pay Sin-debt = Defeat
     Worldly Temptations (prayers)

**Priest at
his Altar**
(earned)

   - God's Palace – Offer Last Penny: Holy Saint
     (priesthood) = See Potential
   - <u>High School</u> = ***Creating Societies*** (people): Teenage
     Level = Cowardice
   - Learning Good from Evil – Holiness: Virtuous Morals
     (good judgment)
   - Blessing of Glorified Spirit – Heaven with God: Joy of
     the Heart (church)
   - Gift of Seat in Temple Court – Rule Heavenly Affairs:
     Sentience
   - Treasure of Servanthood to All – Create Perfect Society:
     God's Courage

Will
(instincts)

3. **Lord God Almighty** – <u>Creator</u>: Teacher of Order =
   Divine Order...Serving God

	• <u>Third Power of Existence</u> – Divine Authority: Thinking for Self = Oneness of God
	• God's Altar – Offer Life: Worship = Remove Capital Sins (baptism)
	• God's Throne – Offer Children: Pay Sin-debt = Defeat Demonic Possession (works)
Son	• God's Palace – Offer Grandchildren: Son of God (sonship) = Self-worth
Sups at	• <u>College</u> = Creating Worlds (galaxies): Adulthood Level = Greed (selfishness)
His Table	• Learning God's/Man's Wills – Perfection: Divine Fairness (correct decisions)
(bonus)	• Blessing of Holy Soul – Beatific Vision: Happiness of the Soul (government)
	• Gift of Seat in Royal Court – Rule Kingdom Affairs: Imagination
	• Treasure of Independence – Create Worlds to Conquer: God's Generosity

This illustration shows that the life-experience is all about mastering one's spirit through worship (give life), praise (give wealth), and thanksgiving (give labor); while mastering one's flesh comes by venerating God's majesty (repentance/life), glorifying His name (prayers/wealth), and honoring His kingdom (hard-work/labors). The implication here is that once a person has purified his spirit (redemption) and transformed his flesh (salvation) into the new nature of Christ, he can then expect to receive God's eternal rewards of a new mind (transfigured body), new heart (glorified spirit), and new soul (holy soul). This tremendous conversion means that a person has completed elementary school (individual rights) by mastering the art of overcoming chaos in all of its forms so that a growing child can become worthy of a new transfigured body (righteous citizen). Secondly, a person must then complete high school (social rights) by mastering the art of overcoming the blend of chaos/order in all its forms so that as a maturing teenager, he becomes worthy of a new glorified spirit (holy saint). Finally, a person must then complete college (worlds) by mastering the art of establishing order in all of its forms so that an adult can become worthy of a new holy soul (son of God/adopted). Once a person has mastered both chaos and order, he is ready to enter God's on-the-job training program (sonship) to become a wise man before the throne of God worthy of receiving a divine life-force (new nature). The idea here is to see that each created life must receive a new mind, heart, soul, and life-force before he can graduate from elementary school and be allowed to leave a life of selfishness (flesh/submission) to enter a new-life of unselfishness (spirit/sacrifice).

In high school, a person will face the challenge of mastering servanthood (unselfishness) as he must strive to serve the needs of others and be willing to sacrifice himself for his fellowman. This is certainly a beautiful experience as a person sees the individual as expendable in service to the many since the natural order of life (illusion) must give way to the supernatural order of life (reality) through Christ. This means that only babies are so fixated on themselves that they fail to care who or what they hurt as only their concerns matter and to hell with all else. We know that when a person becomes a teenager or young adult, he begins to see a bigger picture, where society and his local community become important and suddenly, everyone needs his personal help. The idea here is that as people grow and mature into responsible adults, they then begin to look at life in relation to divine rights (God), social rights (state), and individual rights (man).

By seeing this overall purpose of life, a person comes to the conclusion that there must be a God and He must be following some master Grand Design for this entire creation. Obviously, any rational adult will go in search of the origin of life and his own eternal roots and will not cease his quest until he knows that most unequivocal absolute truth. The human race, up to now, has been given little or no answers to explain its origin (God), its meaning (existence), its purpose (service), and finally, its value (happiness). This problem of having a lack of information, explaining man's existence to someone and/or anyone so it all might make some semblance of sense to a clear thinking mind, sits at the center of man's confusion. This lack of precise knowledge concerning God, His creation, and His future plans prompts a world full of guesses that are supposed to give mankind some type of assurance that its all-powerful government is in charge (flesh/order) and not his mystical-minded God (spirit/chaos). Unfortunately, God exists and man is an illusion and this paradox of confusion will never be explained to anyone's satisfaction because the existence of God is a conundrum wrapped in an enigma (puzzle).

In the previous chart, we see that the blessing of God's altar (individual), the gifts from God's throne (society), and the treasures from God's table/palace (God) are coming to the Earth through the birth, life, death, and resurrection of Jesus Christ. This means that out of the benevolent force (individual) comes the offering of labor (new body/babies) to the altar (blessing), the offering of sweat (new body/teenagers) to the throne (gift), and offering of the harvest (new body/adults) to the palace (treasure) to win the friendship of God (enlightenment). We see that out of the personal God (society) comes the offering of wealth to the altar (blessing), the offering of money to the throne (gift), and the offering of the last penny to the table/palace to win the companionship of God (awakening). Finally, out of the Lord God Almighty (kingdom) comes the offering of one's life (worship) to the altar (blessing), the offering of children (praise) to throne (gift), and the offering of grandchildren (thanksgiving) to table/palace (treasure) to win the oneness of God (indwelling).

Note that God told the Jewish people to worship Him using the names of Abraham (worship/father), Isaac (praise/son) and Jacob (thanksgiving/grandson) for the Lord to recognize His covenant with His chosen people and bless their worthy offerings (water/blood/spirit). This means that whether man worships God with life (death), wealth (blood), and/or labor (word) or not, God will still honor anyone or everyone, as long as he comes from the family of Abraham. This means that Abraham becomes God's altar (blessing), Isaac becomes God's throne (gift), and Jacob becomes God's table/palace (treasure) to allow the human race to worship (life/wisdom), praise (wealth/beauty), and thank (labor/money) God as required by divine law. Through this triune relationship provided by Abraham's family, mankind can travel from being a mere animal to becoming a worthy human, blessed with both God's righteous flesh (mind/wisdom) and Holy Spirit (heart/love). This means that the life-experience is centered on each of God's children offering Him a blessing of water (baptism), gift of blood (confession), and a treasure of spirit (communion) to become worthy of the Lord's free redemption (earth), earned salvation (Heaven), and bonus rewards (kingdom).

We now see that the Lord God Almighty is coming into the human condition as nature (God in creation), a loving Father (God in others), and as our divine creator (God in blessed sacrament) to bring one and all a mind of understanding (babies), a heart of love (teenagers), and a soul of compassion (adults). In this way, the human race shall be taught how to use God's altar (Abraham), God's throne (Isaac), and God's table/palace (Jacob) to interface with its God through worship (repentance), praise (prayer), and Thanksgiving (works). The idea is that if a person worships God by giving Him his life, he can receive the Lord's blessing of individual rights allowing him to come to know God and see God's divine thoughts (mind). Secondly, if he praises God by giving Him his wealth, he can receive the Lord's anointing of social rights allowing him to come to love God and hear God's angelic words (heart). Finally, if he thanks God by giving Him his labors, he can receive the Lord's sanctification of divine rights, allowing him to come to serve God and touch God's human works (soul). This means that sinners (mind) are to have no other gods before them (nature); Christians (heart) are to make no graven images (Father); and saints (soul) must never use God's name in vain (Creator). In this way, each of God's children shall be purified in God's waters of life (earth), God's blood of death (heaven), and God's spirit of resurrection (kingdom). Through these three purifications, a person can surrender his life to God, sacrifice his wealth to God, and then reconcile his labors back to God to be eternally forgiven. In this requirement of offering God water, blood, and spirit to enter His friendship, companionship and oneness, a person must surrender his life (worship), sacrifice his wealth (praise), and reconcile his labors (thanksgiving) back to God to win His divine favor.

The following tabular information indicates that through mankind's water, blood, and spirit offerings, the human race can obtain God's blessing of life (Man), God's gift of eternal life (saint), and God's treasure of divine life (son):

Offering God Water, Blood, and Spirit Sacrifice to Receive His Blessings, Gifts, and Treasures
(blessed with earthly life, gift of heavenly eternal life,
treasure of kingdom divine life)

Nature
(truth)

1. **Water Offering** – <u>Physical Life</u>: Earth = Abraham's Altar…Blessings
   - Altar – Learning Right from Wrong: Righteous Citizen = Sinner (worship)
   - Purifying One's Grave – Fighting Evil (kill flesh)
   - Coming to Know God – See God's Thoughts (mind)   **Individual Rights**
   - Sacrificing Oneself to Defeat Ignorance
   - See God through His Creation – Have No Other Gods before Me

Father
(law)

2. **Blood Offering** – <u>Spiritual Eternal Life</u>: Heaven = Isaac's Throne…Gifts
   - Throne – Learning Good from Evil: Holy Saint + Saint (praise)
   - Purify the Host – Die to Selfishness (renew spirit)
   - Coming to Love God – Hear God's Words (heart)   **Social Rights**
   - Sacrificing One's Children to Defeat Cowardice
   - See God through Others – Make No Graven Images of Other gods

Creator
(will)

3. **Spirit Offering** – <u>Mystical Divine Life</u>: Kingdom = Jacob's Palace…Treasures
   - Table/Palace – Learning God's Will/Man's Wills: Perfect Son (thanksgiving)
   - Purify One's Life – Resurrect from Death (born-again)
   - Coming to Serve God – Touching God through Deeds (soul)   **Divine Rights**
   - Sacrificing One's Grandchildren to Defeat Greed
   - See God through the Blessed Sacrament – Never Use Name in Vain

This illustration shows that each of God's children is passing through a physical (elementary), spiritual (high school), and mystical (college) life-force to become educated in the nature (home/truth), fatherhood (government/law), and creation (church/will) of God. We see that this education involves babies learning right from wrong (altar), teenagers learning good from evil (throne), and adults learning God's will from man's will (palace) to become a righteous citizen of Earth (water), a holy saint in Heaven (blood), and a perfect son within God's Kingdom (spirit). Once a person masters life and has become a king (righteous), priest (holy), and son (perfect) before God, he can then come to see God through His creation (physical), the lives of others (spiritual), and through the Lord's blessed sacrament (mystical).

Now, the first three commandments in Moses' Ten Commandments truly make sense as having no other gods means learning to worship God (give life); making no graven image means learning to praise God (give wealth); and to never use God's name in vain means learning to thank God (give labor). Through these three commandments, a lost, broken sinner can be converted into a righteous citizen (kingship/earth), a holy priest (priesthood/heaven), and a son of God (sonship/kingdom), all in the name of Jesus Christ. We must keep in mind that mankind is still an evil animal on a barren planet of pure death, seeking to transform its existence into a new Garden of Eden without any help from God. Obviously, the picture that the Lord wants humanity to see is a man on a desert, dreaming of a refreshing fountain of living waters. Yet mankind, in truth, is being called to bring back the Garden of Eden as an oasis of happiness bringing new-life to a dead and barren world of pain by bringing Christ's salvation to one and all. This image symbolizes Jesus when He met the woman at Jacob's well, whose soul was like a barren desert of burning death, thirsty for a drink of Christ's living water that would quench her thirst forever. This scene is intended to separate man's physical illusions (earthly water) from God's true reality (heavenly water), showing that all humanity might see the difference between the temporal life of need (redemption/pleasure) as opposed to the eternal life of want (salvation/love). This idea describes a man who sows a lifetime of works (life) and only reaps a handful of dust (death), as his eternal reward for believing only in himself and failing to realize that he is an illusion, living within an illusion. The most industrious of souls, performing great human works, only create beautiful houses of perfection for themselves, while leaving God's house in ruins by ignoring their spiritual wellbeing (submission/sacrifice/conversion) and then falling into hellfire (life of failure).

The Lord is showing us that the body of every man (bride) is a sacred temple of divine love that must be humanity's first priority in keeping it clean (confession) and beautiful (communion) in preparation for the coming of the Lord. We see Jesus Christ's divine fountain of living waters is in truth God's divine love that can be more valuable than any of man's greatest works made by his own selfish hands. The Lord is encouraging those who will listen to learn that they must coordinate the works of their minds, hands, and hearts in the pursuits of building an eternal home worthy of the blessings of God. The power of "Divine Justice" decides each soul's fate (punishment/reward) based on its eternal value to the kingdom of God. The idea here is that without an understanding of our Creator's justice (self), mercy (society), and love (God), mankind is frozen in its tracks, unsure and afraid to move in fear of condemning itself to oblivion forever. This means that our faith is good (life), but knowing is better (eternal life). Thus, each of us must strive to master the knowledge of right/wrong, good/evil, and God's will from man's will to know the truth, laws, and will of God (give away all) and to follow it (follow me) unto his own perfection (value to kingdom).

We see that the mysteries of divine truth (God, angels, men, and nature) lead a soul to its final pathway of perfection, in fulfillment of its quest to seek the mind of God (true wisdom) and enter the collective mind of divinity to understand the divine will of its omnipotent creator. We can see that a combination of our thoughts (church) in the benevolent force (individual rights), words (government) in the personal God (social rights), and our deeds (home) in the Lord God Almighty (divine rights), reveals our true nature (motives) and expose our ultimate value (features/powers) to the coming kingdom of glory. This is the purpose of life (serve): to receive the divine gift of God's perfect faith in Him (blessing), His creation (gift), and in the eternal future (treasure) that God has planned for all those who love Him. It is nearly impossible to perceive in this present day of carnage (tribulation) that one day soon, the glory of the flesh will return in a twinkling of an eye and presto, a new age of love will come forth.

Our present life of debauchery and humiliation, that we now face, will fall away to a new time of peace, harmony, and love, when once again, man will glorify the flesh, blood, and bone, as in the days of Adam. We see that a new day is dawning when the love of God is released through those most beloved souls, willing to surrender their spirits (die to self) and sacrifice their flesh (born-again) to become both holy (morals) and righteous (ethics) in the sight of God. The power of the flesh or mankind's physical nature (wisdom) is superior to the power of the spirit or mankind's spiritual nature (courage), making it obvious that spiritual power is only a controlling force over the minds of men. This means once humanity grows-up and acquires a mature mind (think for self), it will shake off the temptations of evil and set a new course for its own paradise in that most perfect form that both God and man have always wanted. Fortunately for our present age, the time of this great triumph over the evil one or spirit world is at hand with the second coming of our Lord and Savior Jesus Christ.

The whole issue is that mankind needs a perfect justice system that will correct anomalies showing mankind the difference between right and wrong, and keep track of what people want based on what they really need. This most cherished day will signify that all is well in heaven and on the earth, because humanity will have finally grown-up, shaking off the old curses upon the land (worship), upon its babies (praise), and upon life (thanksgiving) forever.

The time will come when a naive, foolish people will not be so easily fooled by a triple-tongued God of justice (infinity), who claims all His creatures are to have infinite belief, blind trust, and perfect faith in the works of God alone. We hear this harsh voice coming from the ancient desert fathers as they committed their spirits to seek the true light of God by uprooting their very nature from Mother Earth to follow the love of divine law. We now hear another voice of truth that we recognize as the God of mercy (eternity), which contradicts the first voice calling to every rational man of good judgment and holy dignity to blossom where he is. This idea of blossoming comes simply by trusting in Jesus, who will lighten the burden of every faithful man who is willing to give his all to God. This new calling is to all men of good will and of moderation who believe, trust, and have faith in the merciful nature of God, who loves all His lost children equally.

This new faithful batch of Christians will live in obscurity, letting their visible flame of divine truth burn unseen before a blind world of ignorant fools. We see that the Christian faithful will lie in hopes that one day, their personal sacrifice will be seen by all (pagans), bringing all the lost to repentance. The rationale of such a sacrificial soul is that it will follow the little way of St. Therese of the Child Jesus by displaying perfect patience in revealing a pure, humble, and contrite heart (obedience) to a dead and dying world. The idea behind St. Therese's little way is to reflect the long-suffering of God's patient love as He alone remains steadfast and faithful to the chosen of God no matter how long that might take. This concept of the little way is founded upon the idea that God is divinely fair and perfectly just by welcoming all the faithful with a new approach for worshiping the Lord God Almighty's divine majesty. We see that not everyone has been chosen to become a great living saint in the eyes of the world, nor has God only one way of raising His most beloved children who surrender to the sacred way of Christ. We see that lost humanity is dealing with an infinite divine mind of pure thought and must come to realize that there is more than one way to fulfill one's personal destiny. But there is only one way to the doorway of heaven and that is through the name of Jesus (Catholic altar) in the transformation of the flesh with the divine blessing of Christ coming through the purification of a sinner's blood (submission).

This certainly indicates that one day, all will see that the Holy Bible has been written for men of all ages and has three separate voices calling to the souls of lost fools: (1) voice of the past calling mankind to perfection (justice); (2) voice of the present calling mankind to try harder and do one's best (mercy), and (3) voice of the future calling mankind to pure holiness (love). These three contrasting voices of God create a collage of direct commands, one day saying, "Go in perfection (justice), then turn toward hope (mercy)," and then another saying, "Stop and blossom where you are (love)." All these commands seem to be associated with one's values reflecting the collective mind of God, based upon a person's personal perspective of a soul's free will (wants). This new free-willed perspective is comprised of the divine (God), human (man), and mystical (individual) viewpoints, thereby allowing a person to see his own limitations (sins), potential (faults), and self-worth (virtues).

This means that God's divine mind is manifested in identities expressed in a mystical state of consciousness, known as the incarnate word of truth, which simultaneously exists in two dimensions at once, defined here as God's reality and man's illusion (paradox). This conceptual thinking process is predicated on the idea that all reality is revealed in the divine will of God and takes form through its very existence as an expression of All is in All. This clearly shows that all existence is in the total being of God (All) since it can only be manifested through the Creator's will to be expressed via a person's identity based upon the purpose of God's Grand Design. The Lord's supreme countenance is transformed through either a spiritual (moral) or physical (ethical) natural force to become perfect in the sight of God to create earthly citizens, heavenly saints, and kingdom sons. We see that this force is seen as some mystical experience of divine truth, manifesting divine energy either with (personal God) or without (benevolent force) form (formed or formless existence).

This indicates that the Lord God Almighty is double-and triple-talking mankind in a way that will force the human intellect to choose its direction more carefully as it matures, compelling every soul to seek proof (doubting Thomas) before taking those most crucial steps toward salvation (earned). The Lord is teaching us all that faith (blind hope) is good, if it's all that a person has, but certainly, it's no substitute for knowing (vision) what to do and when to do it (instinctive response). This is the difference between following God's Jewish law (physical righteousness/faith) or following Christ's Canon Law (spiritual holiness/knowing). They are both good in that they are founded on the Word of God. This means that one's beliefs must be created on the basis of some rational probability, proving their validity through empirical investigation (seeing is believing) or statistical significance (highly probable). The Holy Bible is intentionally a minefield of faith, but there is no measure for a man's confidence when he actually knows the absolute and unshakeable truth, instead of having faith in a highly probable good guess.

This indicates that the unmitigated truth is that our God is a bit of a Judas goat Himself (paradox) as He sends His good Son, Christ (spirit/give divinity) to tell us to follow the just law of God's holiness (obedience) to be saved. In contrast, then His prodigal son, Jesus (flesh/take-sin) is sent to convince us simply to follow Him, by surrendering our wills to live on His infinite mercy of divine forgiveness and in this way, we can also be saved. We see that Jesus promises redemption no matter how weak our flesh might be against the evil influences of sin (sin-nature), evil (worldly temptations), and death (demonic possession), if we will simply trust in Him alone. The question is, can anyone say he is going to paradise as a holy saint with Christ on His pathway of holiness (rosy path/spirit) or as a repentant sinner with Jesus on His pathway of righteousness (rocky path/flesh)? If this is not confusing enough, then try coming to the new mystical kingdom as a chosen child of the Blessed Mother, who vows She will do whatever it takes to save any devoted soul (last chance), which will accept Her holy rosary and brown scapular in the name of Her Son, Jesus Christ.

To escape this philosophical dilemma, we must see that God is using a two-truth system of logic (take-sin/give divinity) or paradoxical logic, with One (God's view) based on a spirit world (God) and the other (man's view) based on a physical world (man). The point is that each of these totally different worlds has its own set of truths, legal systems, and individual wills; yet God is planning to miraculously combine a spirit concept into physical nature through His Son, Jesus Christ (life/death/resurrection). The Mother of God proclaims to the world that anyone who trusts in Her motherly love will be led to this spiritual/physical union via the saving blood of Her Son through the divine mercy of God. The Virgin Mary asks all Her children to immerse themselves in Her most merciful hands of love and to become cleansed (blood/death/spirit) through the physical blood of Jesus (Son of man), humanity's sacrificial goat as the purifier of all mankind's personal sins (mortal sin). We see that She also tells us that She will immerse a sinner's soul in the spiritual blood of Christ (Son of God), divinity's sacrificial lamb as the purifier of all humanity's original sins (capital sin).

The job of the sacrificial goat was to bring the human race's Jewish circumcision as the prefigurement of Christ's baptism to remove man's capital sins (being saved) through the power of repentance. In contrast, the job of the sacrificial lamb is to bring the human race's Christian baptism as the prefigurement of a sinner's confession for mortal sins (saving self) through the power of prayer. We see the goat sacrifice (conquer world) represents the kingly goat (pay sin-debt), who comes to Earth to take-sin (new body/Easter) by offering God His body broken (bread) during His scourging at the pillar (see limitations). Secondly, the lamb sacrifice (conquer self) represents the priestly lamb (pay holy-debt), who comes to Earth to give-up His divinity (eternal life/Christmas) by offering God His blood being shed (wine) during His crucifixion on the cross (see potential). We see that through Jesus saving sinners (earth) and Christ creating saints (heaven), this miraculous union of spirit (Heaven) and flesh (Earth) can take place, thereby making God and man one in truth, law, and will.

In both of these sacrificial offerings, we see a gift to God (worship/name) and a gift to man (forgiveness/virginity) as an appeasement to God's justice (death/name) and as a blessing for man's Love (new-life/virginity). Now, the great "Contradiction of Life" can be explained by simply making God's first truth the Priestly Lamb of Worship (sacrifice) and then by making God's second truth the kingly goat of forgiveness (prayer). In this way, we can now see just how God's sacrifice (sinner) and man's prayer (saint) are united into one life-force, thereby making Earth (new body), Heaven (eternal life), and Kingdom (kingdom) one in truth, law, and will.

The following tabular information indicates the great significance associated with the sacrifice of both the kingly goat (take-sin) to pay man's sin-debt (remove faults); and the priestly lamb (give divinity/Passover) to pay man's holy-debt (gain virtues/Yom Kippur):

**The Priestly Lamb Brings Mankind Free Redemption
and the Kingly Goat brings Earned Salvation**
(goat pays mankind's sin-debt to remove faults
and lamb pays man's holy-debt to gain virtues)

Take-sin
(faults)

1. **Kingly Goat** – <u>Body Broken</u>: Baptism = Remove Capital Sins…See Limitations
- Bloodless – Scourging at Pillar: Transfigured Body = Good Citizen (righteous)
- Flesh – Repentance: Jewish Circumcision = Son of Man + Jesus (day of atonement)
- Free Redemption – Being Saved: Learn Right from Wrong = Crucible (sinner)
- Paying off Man's Sin-debt – Remove Faults: Purify the Flesh (submission)

Yom Kippur
- *God Eats Cooked Flesh* – Edenic Covenant: Dream of Paradise
- *Man Eats Hot Bread* – Abrahamic Covenant: Dream of Heaven
- <u>Heaven on Earth</u> – Benevolent Force: chosen Jewish People of Death bring Life
- Soldier-of-the-Light – *Conquering the World*: Nothing is Impossible
- Bread is Wisdom – Eat Jesus' Host and become a

Righteous Citizen of Earth
(conversion of lost sinners – fight evil:
kill flesh = purify grave + new body/resurrects)

Give Divinity
(virtues)

2. **Priestly Lamb** - <u>Blood Shed</u>: Confession = Remove Mortal Sins... See Potential
- Blood – Crucifixion on Cross: Glorified Spirit = Holy Saint (holiness)
- Spirit – Prayers: Christian Baptism = Son of God + Christ (Passover meal)
- Earned Salvation – Saving Self: Learn Good from Evil = Winepress (saint)
- Paying Man's Holy-debt – Gain Virtues: Transform the Spirit (sacrifice)

Passover

- *God Drinks Warm Blood* — New Covenant (Messiah): Dream of God as Man
- *Man Drinks Cold Wine* – Everlasting Covenant: Dream of Man as God
- <u>Life in Heaven</u> – Personal God: chosen Christian People of Life bring Death
- Living Prayer of Love – *Conquer Oneself*: Prudence is the Best Judge
- Wine is Courage – Drink Christ's Chalice and become Holy Saint in Heaven

(forgiveness of repentant Christians – surrender:
wash spirit = purify host + eternal life)

This illustration shows that the goat's nature (remove faults) is a sinner of death (being saved) who must have his sins taken (submission) by Mary's Son, Jesus, who has come to offer His body broken (stick) to crush out (wheat/bread) its wild and disobedient desires. In contrast, the lamb's nature is a saint of life (saving self), who must give-up his divinity (sacrifice) through God's Son, Christ, who has come to offer His blood to be shed (carrot) to change the cowardly lamb into a cunning serpent (courage). In this picture, we see that the goat's nature (Yom Kippur/new body) was being beaten during the Lord's scourging at the pillar to take out its wicked faults (resistance), empty a person of all his foolishness and turn it into sacramental bread (wisdom). In this same regard, we see the lamb's nature (Passover/eternal life) is being drained out and poured on the ground during the Lord's crucifixion on the cross to put in a person's holy virtues, fill a person with God's blessing of courage, and then turn it into sacramental wine (courage). In this way, we can see that the goat was ignorant because of its sinful nature (righteousness) and needed to eat God's sacramental bread to receive God's blessing of wisdom; while the lamb was a coward because of its virtuous nature (holiness) and needed to drink God's sacramental wine to receive God's blessing of courage.

In this logic of the wild goat and the passive lamb, we see that if we blend the two natures into one, the goat/lamb creation would become a beautiful horse, which is smart, courageous, and loving to one and all. It can be seen that by taking the nature of God (divinity/lamb) and the nature of man (humanity/goat) during the Lord's crucifixion on Mt. Calvary and blending them into the God/man person of Jesus Christ, Heaven and Earth can be made one in truth (two fathers), law (couple), will (friends), and love (family). This constant theme of blending two things together to get a third creation sits at the center of God's redemption (goat/Jews), salvation (lamb/Christians), and rewards (man/saints) program. The message here is that every Christian must bend unto his breaking point and beyond to bring forth an unstoppable God (Christ) as He collides with an immovable man (Jesus) by blending them into one being (righteousness/holiness/perfection).

Note that Jesus Christ was telling His followers to turn the other cheek (convert enemy); to be generous to a fault that when a person sues for your tunic, then give him your coat (make an acquaintance) as well, and if asked to go one mile, then go two (earn a friend); and if a poor man begs for money, then become a kind and generous lender to all (become a brother). Through these four great kindnesses, the Lord will build His kingdom of sharing and respect for one and all. Note that each of God's children is being taught how to convert an enemy (survival), make an acquaintance (truth), earn a friend (love), and become a brother (choices) by sharing his wealth and respecting everyone's personal rights. This means that a Christian is being called to offer his face (honor), sacrifice his clothes (shame), give freely of his labors (hard-work), and be generous with his money (wealth). The question is, why are Christians so good? The answer is that Christians are to be a reflection of Christ (submission) and all these offerings (enemy), sacrifices (acquaintance), gifts (friend), and generosities (brother) come into one's life, in the form of bearing fruits out of just being oneself (know thy self).

This is known as Unto To Thine Own Self be True and all else shall take care of itself through a person's guilty conscience and his instinctive compulsion to do God's divine will without question. The great mystery is that no one can do God's divine will in the flesh. A person must physically die to self and then be converted into Christ's nature through submission (worship at altar). We see in Matthew 5:39–42 that the Lord is telling all Christians that they must be perfect in the sight of God, but obviously knowing that none of these insane statements would work in any society. So what is this crazy talk all about, and what is the Lord saying to His gullible Church, by giving them these impossible tasks that can never work in our current world of evil men? The Lord is saying, that if one dies to self (submission) and allows Christ to become him in mind (labor), heart (money), and soul (life), anyone can perform these impossible tasks (invisible success) with ease. Recall that Jesus Christ told His followers to pluck out their eye if it offends God or to cut off any part of the body if it offends God. Can these words be taken literally? Note that the Lord said, "Moses tells you not to murder, yet I tell you that anyone who has anger in his heart is a murderer and anyone who looks at a woman with lust is an adulterer." Wild statements like these show that no man can live his life on Earth without sin as even failing to be in God's will 24-7 is also an unforgivable sin. This means that the only hope for man is that he dies to his selfishness until his fleshly nature is gone and he becomes Christ-like, which allows a soul to bear fruit (turn cheek/tunic/extra mile/loan money) out of all of his actions whether they appear good or bad.

The following tabular information indicates that only through Christ (do the impossible) can a person turn the other cheek (enemy), freely give his tunic and coat (acquaintance), go the extra mile (friend), and share his money (brother) without becoming a silly fool before men:

Turning the Other Cheek, Give Tunic and Coat,
Go the Extra Mile, and Lend a Brother Money
(convert an enemy, make an acquaintance,
earn a friend, and become a brother by living right)

Justice   1. **Turn the Other Cheek** – <u>Worship</u>: Give Life…Knowledge
(survival)   • Face – Offer Honor: ***Son of God Converts an Enemy***
               • Learn Right from Wrong – Become Righteous Citizen
                 (earth)
               • Elementary School (earth) – Teaches How to Convert
                 Enemies
               (obey God's ten commandments – fulfill the law:
                       conversion of sinner)

Mercy   2. **Asked for Tunic, Give One's Coat** – Praise: Give
(truth)   Wealth……. Self-awareness
               • Clothes – Offer Shame: ***Son of God makes an***
                 Acquaintance
               • Learn Good from Evil – Become Holy Saint (Heaven)
               • High School (Heaven) – Teaches How to Make
                 Acquaintances
                 (sell all, give to the poor – fulfill faith:
                         forgiveness of Christian)

Love   3. **Asked for One Mile, then Go Two Miles** –<u>Thanks-</u>
(love)   <u>giving</u>: Give Labor…Consciousness
               • Labor – Offer Hard-work: ***Son of God Wins a New Friend***
               • Learn God's Will from man's will – Become Perfect Son
               • College (Kingdom) – Teaches How to Earn Friends
                 (pick-up your cross – fulfill knowing:
                         born-again holy saint)

Union   4. **Asked for Money, then be Kind Lender** – <u>Freedom</u>:
(choices)   Give All…… Sentience
               • Money – Offer Wealth: ***Son of God gets a Beloved***
                 Brother

- Learn God's Reality from Man's Illusion – Become Free Man
- On-the-Job Training – Teaches How to Respect Brothers

(come follow Jesus Christ – fulfill thinking:
creation of son of God)

This illustration shows that each of God's children must attend elementary school to learn how to convert enemies (face), high school to make acquaintances (clothes), college to earn friends (labor), and then on-the-job training to respect brothers (money), all in the name of becoming a well-adjusted citizen of life. Obviously, the life-experience is about establishing oneself on Earth (righteous citizen), in Heaven (holy saint), and within God's Kingdom (perfect son) by being able to fit in (love life/people/God) with any and all types of people, be they good, or bad, or rich, and/or poor, etc. This ability to convert enemies as well as to make friends anywhere allows a person to demonstrate his maturity and bring the goodness of God out of the worst of men at will. This means that God's three pathways of life within the physical realm (righteousness), spiritual existence (holiness), and mystical life (perfection) must all be united into one human (earth), angelic (heaven), and divine truth (kingdom), revealing that Jesus Christ is Lord. Obviously, the answer we are all waiting for is that all three of the pathways of life are capable of taking a lost sinner to the Lord's doorway of free redemption (being saved/rosy path) and earned salvation (save self/rocky road).

We see that one path (calling) is the hard road (goat) that removes faults through strict obedience to Christ's pure justice by following the precepts of the church to the letter of the law. This is a deceptive road of roses (lamb) because the trials and tribulations (thorns) along the way are made easy through the joy of one's heart, which allows a person to love every minute of it. The second path (enlightenment) or rosy pathway is the age of grace, where a person may gain virtues by begging for God's forgiveness. This is the pathway of repentance founded upon Jesus' most merciful love. This second path is where a person refuses to release his human will to the Lord and must be constantly pursued by Jesus' undying love to call this soul to conversion (man) so that it might see God's spiritual reality and its own physical illusion. The third path (awakening) is actually the easiest of all. Called the little way (St. Therese), it is designed for weak sinners, who want to be great saints through only their purest of thoughts (saints) and best behavior (sons). In reality, they are only the faithful of the Blessed Virgin as She desires that Her loving children become like perfect butterflies in God's new Garden of Eden, where the New Eve will raise Her most precious children of love with Her most gentle touch. The Blessed Virgin claims to be able to perform the greatest of miraculous feats of conversion, if only a worthless sinner will give Her the slightest chance to prove Her skills and really show Her stuff. We call this final path a highway to knowing, because it is knowing that the Blessed Virgin will always save you, if you will simply give Her a fighting chance to see you through life's present valley of tears.

In the coming new age, everyone is hoping that Christ will come soon to bring forth an age of the awakened souls into the absolute truths of God (reality) so that they might meet the relative truths of man (illusion), thereby making all things known to the lost fools of the world. This type of massive awakening will bring forth a dual enlightenment as the advances of the physical world (Jesus/goat) will be combined with the advances of the spirit world (Christ/lamb), thus allowing them to be mystically united in a new consciousness of infinite truth.

This will be the time when the old myths of division of Church (Christ God) and State (Jesus Man) will become one in divine truth (time) and one in infinite will (space), united through the collective mind of knowing right from wrong. On this day of days, when the physical and spiritual minds unite into one person, the Lord Jesus Christ, they will be crowned by the Eternal Father's pure thought, Who will declare that there are to be no bounds (limits) to the power of men's minds and human imagination. This great day will occur through the three divine plans of God: (1) creation (life): birth, (2) redemption (transformation/blood): death, and (3) sanctified life (immortality/spirit): resurrection. These three plans of existence are combined into one divine thought, making both chaos (Jesus) and order (Christ) one in the divine force of truth. Through this "truth," all existence is exclusively controlled reflecting God's divine love (will) in the creation, redemption, and sanctification of repentant man.

We see in this description the significance and contrast between the Lord's First Advent (spiritual church/donkey) and His Second Advent (physical government/thief) as God perseveres in the manifestation of His divine humility that is crucial to bringing forth human understanding between God and man. We see that during the Lord's **Third Advent** (mystical home), He will share His divine humility with one and all to make all men perfect in the sight of God. This most interesting revelation shows us that God is intentionally being defamed (attacked) in every conceivable way possible through both physical (ethical) and spiritual (moral) shame (no food), humiliation (no clothes), and disgrace (no home).

The Lord has created two special supreme moments of total disgrace, causing a violation of divine perfection known as the first and second abominations of desolation. The first act of total divine disgrace came when Jesus Christ (God) stood before the high priest Caiaphas (Man) to be officially proclaimed evil in the name of Lucifer. This act created half of God's most perfect new nature of humility permitting divine perfection to be legally judged as absolutely imperfect in the sight of humanity. During the Lord's Second Advent, God's nature of humility is to be fulfilled when the evil anti-Christ is proclaimed Lord God Almighty by the Jewish high priest of Israel in the coming new third Sacred Temple in Jerusalem. This will complete the cycle of divine imperfection as humanity officially proclaims Lucifer himself divine in place of the true God of sacrificial death (Jesus Christ).

The point is that humanity has proclaimed God (lamb) demonically evil in the First Advent and Lucifer (goat) divinely perfect in the Second Advent fulfilling God's desire to become perfectly humble in the sight of man. These two acts of abomination of desolation constitute the dual nature of God's humility allowing the Lord (holiness) to be called evil, and then having evil (wrong/evil) proclaimed divine (right/good) all in the name of perfect justice. The question is, how much more can humility do to desecrate its God of love, short of denying His very existence face-to-face by saying, "We never knew you, nor do we care to acknowledge you as our Creator God, now or ever," even to the death of the human race? We see this declaration of independence from God and/or from His Son, Jesus Christ is about to be hotly contested by the discoveries of science as they begin to piece the gigantic cosmic puzzle together, thereby unveiling that most startling absolute truth...*YES!* There is a God force or at least a mystical will of life.

Nothing becomes All:
1. God to spirit
2. Spirit to energy
3. Energy to matter
4. Matter to life

This illustration shows that the Nothing of life (man) is an illusion or simulation and that the All of life (God) is actually a mystical dimension of life, much like an infinite number of bubbles in a glass of champagne or similar to all the grains of sand on all the beaches of the world. This means that the human race is inside of an infinite number of dimensions of existence and the Universe/Earth is simply the first step in an eternal journey from nothing (death) to all (eternal life).

Now, let's imagine that the Lord God Almighty has created a universe of dark energy, totally void of light. Then thirteen billion years ago, the Lord turned on the lights using our most famous big bang theory ("let there be light"). We now know that out of light energy comes matter ($E=MC^2$) in the form of galaxies, stars, and planets plus rock debris (comets/asteroids), all floating around in the universe doing their divinely appointed jobs (birth/life/death). Obviously, the major purpose of galactic matter is to create (supernova) some ninety-two base elements in great abundance to become the building blocks for organic and non-organic life forms. Note here that God is using both a design system (destiny) and natural selection system (free will) working together to create both natural and supernatural creations, thereby integrating God's nature with man's nature to make spirit and flesh one.

Obviously, one of the great mysteries of life is the very existence of the Earth itself as it has too many special features needed in the formation of life, which on the surface seems statistically impossible. We see that the first problem is the Earth's precise distance from the sun based on its perfect orbit, thereby creating a surface temperature of between zero (0) and 120 degrees, allowing both animal life and human life to survive at all (hard to believe). Then we are told that when the plants were created in our solar system, strangely enough, there were two Earth-size planets at precisely the same distance from the sun in precisely the same orbit causing them to collide to create one super-planet (our Earth).

To make this story even more unbelievable, the scientists tell us that this massive collision caused these two molten spheres to merge (create moon), leaving the Earth with a special iron core, which spins with such a force that it causes a magnetic field to protect the Earth from the sun's solar winds (radioactive particles). We are also told that the collision of the two brother Earths also peeled the crust off the Earth, thereby creating the moon, which would be sorely needed to protect the Earth from dangerous asteroids, during its life cycle (plants/animals/people). To add to this statistical impossibility, imagine that the planet Jupiter has also been placed in a perfect orbit and has the precise size needed to protect the Earth from any and all space debris. Now imagine that the Earth needs water to create a hydrogen/oxygen atmosphere, which would require the Earth to have two-thirds of its surface covered in water with two massive ice caps or there would be no livable land. Now let's keep dreaming that only through random chance, one-celled life was created from rocks and water and evolved into thirty-ton dinosaurs in two billion years, pretty fast evolutionary cycle even for our supernatural Earth.

A person might ask, "Just where did all the food come from to feed an entire world of thirty-ton beasts as they spent sixty-five million years running around, pooping on the land (dung) to transform it from molten rock into fertile farm land, ready for planting? The easy answer is that the plants came first, and with the help of the insect world, were able to cover the Earth a billion years before the coming of the animal kingdom, which would bring forth the human infestation of people, who were able to cover the Earth in just a few thousand years.

The following tabular information indicates that God's design and natural selection had the identical purpose as they miraculously created (nine steps) light, magnetic fields, water, fish, plants, air, insects, animals, and humans literally overnight:

1. **Create Light** – Forming of Galaxies, Stars, and Planets
2. **Create Protective Magnetic Field** – Stop Radioactive Solar Winds
3. **Create Water** – Comets bring Ice to Deliver Water (create oceans)
4. **Create Fish** – Nucleic Acids Poured in Water to Create Life
5. **Create Plants** – Plants Consume Carbon dioxide and Give Out Oxygen
6. **Create Air** – Creating of Earthly Atmosphere to Protect Life
7. **Create Insects** – Plant Life Immediately Covers the Earth
8. **Create Animals** – Create Fertile Land (farms) as Natural Food Source
9. **Create Humanity** – Building of Societies vis-a-vis Development of Cities

This illustration shows that this entire creation story could be somewhat believable, if it were not for the fact that Earth has too many miraculous events, occurring in an extremely short period of time...pretty hard to believe. We are saying that the Earth could have had all of its coincidences in a couple trillion years and we would believe the creation of a few trees and maybe one frog, but modern man in two billion years? Even natural selection has its limits. We also ask, "Is it not strange" that there were twin Earths (good/prodigal), when Isaac had twin sons and then the Messiah came from an immaculate virgin womb as the Son of God, Christ (God/spirit/good) and the Son of Mary, Jesus, and they collided on Mt. Calvary and became one person with two natures? Then to our amazement, God's Son, Jesus Christ takes-on all sin causing both God (spirit) and man (flesh) to desecrate the name and Word of God, thereby creating a divine sacrilege so great that no one could ever forgive such a vile act. The most startling aspect associated with these two offenses of total sacrilege to the divinity of God is founded in the depths of His eternal mercy and His fathomless ability to forgive, one and all, 490 times for the same crime, no matter how great that crime might have been (kill God).

We see that it is unclear as to why the Lord has gone to such extremes to cast His divine majesty into the dirt and lower Himself into the demonic clutches of evil death (Calvary) to save an ungrateful mankind from its just punishment? It would appear that the answer involves our distorted perception of God's level of disgrace as opposed to the reality of His actual loss (death), based upon God's higher purpose. Let's imagine that we are inside of a divine school and that the Lord's sacrifices are part of some divine lesson of life to demonstrate the need to give one's all, thereby bringing forth a person's greatest heart's desire (finding pearl of great price) no matter what the cost. We must note that the Fall of Adam and Eve was predicated upon a tiny violation of divine law. But the punishment was awesome as God cast His two babies into a toilet of evil and then filled it full of all manners of unbearable pain. To the Lord's great surprise, the human race began to love its toilet more than loving God, without knowing that they were supposed to make every effort to crawl out of its toilet and to then take a good hot shower (purification/holiness). This relates to the fact that the divine mind of God is so vast (infinite dimensions) that His love is infinite and therefore able to cherish all of His creations equally through His ability to lower Himself to any level of shame (give labors/starve), humiliation (give wealth/naked), or disgrace (give life/homeless). The Lord God Almighty is simply creating in pure innocence and then uses all worthless residues to create something else (features), in the same way that useless dung becomes fertilizer and is used to feed plants. There seems to be an unwritten divine law that for the Lord to transform humanity into a born-again living prayer of love (saint), He must demonstrate His resolve by placing Himself on the human altar of death (crucify all sin/fertilizer) as a worthy sacrifice (creation).

We see the Lord is caught in a legal dilemma, where humanity (offering) was required to match the value of God's sacrifice (created existence) with one of its own human creations, namely Jesus Christ (creation). This meant that the Lord God Almighty had to come to the Earth in human form and place Himself upon the human altar of death to reconcile all things back to divine perfection. Then simultaneously with this act of perfection, God would place His perfect countenance upon the divine altar of death to balance the two gifts of divine (lamb)/human (goat) sacrifices (name/virginity). In this way, God could purchase the Lost Title Deed to the Earth and restore its citizens back to His divine favor by individually forgiving them, so that they might receive a new nature of Christ. The idea here was that once humanity could again think for itself in a proper manner, the Lord could again communicate (restore Nimrod) with the world (ignorant fools) and bring it to full redemption (wisdom) before God, angels, and men.

The following tabular information indicates that God is putting up His creation (house) in the form of a marriage bride price (give divinity) via its shed blood (lamb submission/creation); while man is putting up God's son, Jesus Christ (wife) as the marriage dowry (take-sin) via the Lord's body broken (goat sacrifice/Messiah):

God Offers His Creation as a Bride Price, while
Man Offers His Messiah as a Dowry
(God offers divinity to make man holy, while man
offers sinlessness to make man righteous)

All
1. **God Sacrifices Creation** – <u>Gives-up Divinity</u>
(God/Man): House of Perfection (name)
- Mother Nature Sacrifices "Destiny (God)" to Surrender to "Free Will (Man)"
- Bride Price – Pay Holy Debt: Blessing of Human Virtues = Good from Evil

Wisdom
- Lamb's Shed Blood – Perfect Nature Cursed into Wine (blood)
- Benevolent Force Sacrifices Its Self-love – Divine Selfishness
- *God becomes Man* – Old Testament: Jewish People Sacrificed to <u>Death</u>
(holy man proves himself – submission:
bear fruit of repent/pray/works/save others = purify host)

Nothing
2. **Man Sacrifices Jesus Christ** – <u>Takes-on All Sin</u>
(Jesus/Christ): Wife of Perfection (virginity)
- Mother of God Sacrifices "God as Christ" and "Man as Jesus"
- Dowry – Pay Sin-debt: Removal of Human Faults = Right from Wrong

Value
- Goat's Body Broken – Perfect Man Cursed into Bread (flesh)
- Personal God Sacrifices His Beloved Son – Divine Unselfishness
- *Man becomes God* – New Testament: Christian People Sacrificed to <u>Life</u>
(righteous man proves himself – fight evil:
bear fruit of home/job/mate/children = purify grave)

This illustration shows that God is placing His offering of blood (creation/wine) upon the **Divine Altar** as **His Payment toward Becoming a Man** (Jesus/goat/purify grave); while man is placing his **Offering of Bread** (Messiah/flesh) upon the divine altar as **his payment toward becoming God** (Christ/lamb/purify host). The idea here is to see that the logical mind of God (intellect) is to marry the loving heart of man (emotion) to unite the power of knowing with the concept of value. This means that God thinks everything is important, while man thinks only he is important. Obviously, when the perfection of God (reality) and the values of man (illusion) are blended (merged) into one mystical life-force, then everything can be placed into its proper balance based on its natural functional priority to the general welfare.

In this explanation, we see that God's truth revolves around a rank-order system from best to worst (formal/public); while man's truth revolves around absolute equality, making top and bottom one. This priority system concept leads to a new age of perfect thinking, bringing a time of divine/human awakening with amazing new high-tech devices, beyond man's ability to conceive infinite force and infinite designs of creative perfection.

The message to us all is that life will never again be placed in the hands of a bunch of silly fools who can't even distinguish the difference between a devil of evil (goat) and a God of holiness (lamb). We will all see the future world of electronics (machine people) used to its maximum in man's race to the stars, which will soon come, as mankind looks forward (dream) to a bright new age (new creation/perfect people) of everlasting exploration (learning). It will be a time when humanity will enter into a new war matching the spirit of Christ (heaven) against the flesh of Jesus (earth), as they compete with Jesus Christ (spirit/flesh), to bring forth the true fruits (mind/heart) of the divine spirit of knowing (wisdom) and the human flesh of love (values). In the future, each living prayer of love (saint) is to be brought to the throne of God as a peace offering of admiration and eternal devotion to prove humanity loves (personal God) God as much as the Lord loves Himself (benevolent force).

The coming new war of good (spirit) and evil (flesh) will be a contest of old views versus new hopes, as the physical world (universe) will one day be something to be proud of. We see that when the children of the future are speaking of the ancients of life, they will reveal that human pride will no longer be an evil tool of Lucifer. Instead, it will become the savior of all life. We see that the human creation will be the divine pride of the whole kingdom of God as it comes forth out of its pit of death (agony of defeat) into a new age of glorious triumph (thrill of victory). In the creation of the coming new age, Jesus Christ is bringing forth His seven mysteries of life: (1) Incarnation of the Word – Messiah: baby = save traitors; (2) Gospel Message of Truth – new-life: child = save enemies; (3) Christ's Church of Perfection – transformation: adolescent = save strangers;   (4) Indwelling of Christ's love – awakening: teenage = save neighbors; (5) Mystical Body of Christ – Jews/Gentiles: young adult = save friends; (6) Transfigured Body of Man – celestial court: adult = save family; and (7) Kingdom of Glory – physical/spiritual creation: wise man = save self.

Through these seven mysteries, the whole human race has been given God's gifts of redemption (free), salvation (earned), and rewards (bonuses/second mile) to set humanity eternally free. Through these seven mysteries, the human race can finally comprehend the meaning of right/wrong, good/evil, and God's will from man's will to learn the eternal truths of life (thinking for oneself).

The Lord Jesus Christ said, "All in its time." Just from this simple statement, we may be able to remove ourselves from an endless state of confusion as to what's right and what's wrong, leading us all to comprehend who's right and who's wrong. The truth lies in the time table of God's Grand Design, as all that is evil (spirit) and sinful (flesh) today will be put into its proper perspective, thereby creating God's coming kingdom of glory. Through this light of understanding (perspective), humanity can come to understand the broken nature of man's imperfection (sin-nature) and change it into a new creature in Christ. On that day, pride will again be redeemed along with everything else in nature, because God never loses or wastes anything He has created (sacrificial offering) with His own divine hands (touch).

We see that the Lord manifested a master plan to cast Himself into a great pit of death that had been designed to serve as a gigantic transformation processor, where the omnipotent divine power of divine perfection would be incarnated into the person of Jesus Christ. Through this brokenness of divinity (humility), humanity would be raised out of its pit of death as God exchanges His divine life-force (new nature) for mankind's sinful nature of death. We see it is upon Mt. Calvary that this whole eternal drama culminates into a moment of truth, where God's love for humanity takes on the reality of infinite sacrifice as the Lord drinks the cup of death (blood) and becomes death itself. In contrast, the human race is then asked to eat a host of life (flesh) and become life to be transformed from a wild animal into a born-again human being with the divine nature of Jesus Christ.

This means that our most serious problem to date is that mankind is in a state of deep mourning for the drastic actions of its Creator as He plunges Himself into humanity's slaughter of innocence to join His beloved children in their evil pit of death. Now, both God and man are trapped inside an evil pit of vipers (toilet), where they are forced to struggle with the demonic forces of death night and day until they break free. This life of fear, pain, and death is called the cross that the Lord is using as the power of humility, manifested through His life of shame (starving), humiliation (naked), and disgrace (homeless) to bring life anew to All (eternal life). During this mystical phase of the divine death experience, the virtue of pride is a deadly poison to the transforming human personality of a born-again Christian into a righteous citizen on Earth, holy saint in Heaven, and a perfect son within the Kingdom of God.

The idea here is to keep the faith while staying in the worldly pit of death (fight evil), but not to be of it, until the return of the risen Messiah (resurrection), our Lord Jesus Christ. The Lord's resurrection was created so that Christ might transform our current existence of death into a new paradise on Earth by drinking His blood (wine) and eating His flesh (bread). In fact, the Lord is planning to make the physical Earth so perfect that the Eternal Father, like Jacob, will leave His own Promised Land to join His Son in the New Jerusalem of peace (forgiveness), joy (money), and happiness (love).

Remember, this happened when Joseph transformed Egypt and especially the Land of Goshen into a paradise on Earth, in preparation for the arrival of his Father (God) and his brothers (Angels), who were suffering in the Land of Canaan. In this story, Jacob was finally reunited with all his children and lived the remainder of his life in a contented sanctuary in a foreign land. The message here is neither the spiritual (Christ) or physical (Jesus) creations will make any difference as long as divinity (God) and humanity (man) are not set free from the demonic evil forces of sin (pain), death (grave), and damnation (hell). We now see that God is the divine creator of life and all its creatures, as man is the eternal builder (carpenter) of lives bringing forth the manifested Glory of God as the fruits of the human spirit. Together, they are to be the citizens of an eternal kingdom of glory, an enchanted place of truth (existence), love (service), and happiness (friendship) forever as all men of good will are welcomed into the presence of their God.

Chapter 1

Christ's Second Coming
(Thief in the Night/Beginning/Sealing of Saints)

A. God's Grand Design

The significance of God's **most perfect Master Plan** can best be understood by visualizing the Lord's search for a perfect man of divine maturity, who has the undaunted desire to serve the needs of others with a purely unselfish motive in his heart. This special man for all seasons must be able to properly handle freedom and demonstrate the responsibility to execute the principles of human independence in mind, heart, and soul. Unfortunately, only a most perfect heavenly saint (Christ) could live such an esteemed responsible life of continual sacrifice given with a generous hand of love. We see that for some reason God has, in His infinite Wisdom, decided to create holy men (butterflies) from evil flesh (caterpillars) by simply allowing them to believe in His Son's sacrifice through which a person could receive God's most perfect gift of divinity (new nature). This reverse logic idea silences mankind's eternal cries against injustice and prejudicial treatment by its divine creator in both spirit (morals) and in flesh (ethics). This means that the Lord is saying that anyone who surrenders his free will to the divine will of God, through the consecration of his Christian baptism, will be given Christ's new nature and His guiding voice of divine truth (instinctive compulsion).

One of the best ways to see God's divine truth is to imagine the Lord as a giant computer system comprised of input (RAM), processing (CPU), output (ROM), and results (monitor/printer). Recall that the invention of the computer came from some system analysis seeing a secretary typing papers and then filing them in her four-drawer file cabinet, which inspired the CPU (secretary), ROM (typewriter), RAM (file cabinet), and monitor (typed page) idea to replace her manual system (employee) with an automated system (computer). We can now imagine that through Christ's coming three Advents and God's judgment, the human race will become automated with its own central processing unit (God), a random access memory (earth), a read-only memory (heaven), and its own monitor (kingdom). Through these four integrated institutions of life, the Lord God Almighty will be able to interface with His angels, saints, Messiah, Blessed Virgin, priesthood, laity, the damned, and His demons at will.

This means that the CPU has to reflect the perfection of life as measured by knowing God's reality from man's illusion so that the human race can see its limitations (thinking). Secondly, the read-only memory has to reflect the holiness of life as measured by knowing God's will and man's will so that the human race can see its potential (decisions). Thirdly, the random access memory has to reflect the righteousness of life as measured by knowing Good and Evil so that the human race can see its own self-worth (retrieval). Finally, the monitor has to reflect the sinfulness of life as measured by knowing right and wrong so that the human race can see its value before God. It is now clear that the experiences of life are designed to bring forth the evolution of things, people, and even God's kingdom as they grow (flesh) and mature (spirit) into perfect creations of divine, angelic, and human life.

The following tabular information indicates that through a secretary, typewriter, filing cabinet, and typed page, the complex world of information has been organized into an instant retrieval system through computerization:

**Secretary, Typewriter, Filing Cabinet, and Typed Page
become Bases of Divine Automation System**
(creation of the CPU, ROM, RAM, and monitor
out of a secretary, typewriter, cabinet, and page)

Father
(process)

1. **Secretary** – <u>God</u>: Central Processing Unit (CPU)......
   Mind (intellect)
   - Government – Divine Rights: Authority (throne)
   - CPU – Thinking Process: **King/Government/Earth**
     Existence of Life
   - Perfection – Learning Reality from Illusion

Son
(input)

2. **Typewriter** – <u>Heaven</u>: Read Only Memory (Rom)...
   Heart (emotions)
   - Church – Social Rights: Responsibility (altar)
   - Rom – Decision Process: **Priest/Church/Heaven**
     Service to Life
   - Holiness – Learning God's Will/man's will

Spirit
(output)

3. **Filing Cabinet** – <u>Earth</u>: Random Access Memory
   (Ram)... **Soul** (instincts)
   - Home – Individual Rights: Duty (table)
   - Ram – Information Retrieval: **Son/Home/Kingdom**
     Happiness in Life
   - Righteousness – Learning Good from Evil

Messiah
(results)

4. **Typed Page** – <u>Kingdom</u>: Monitor (CRT)........
   Life–force (nature)

- Individual – Personal Freedom: Task (set free)
- Monitor – Information Display: **Free Man/Self/God** Fulfillment of Life
- Sinfulness – Learning Right from Wrong

This illustration shows that through need psychology and human ingenuity, a manual system of data processing (secretary/typewriter/filing cabinet/typed paper) can be converted to an automated system of data processing (CPU/ROM/RAM/monitor) to increase both speed and accuracy to the machine level of performance. Now, we are trying to show how this same process of conversion can apply to transforming the computerization concept into the divine system of performance. Note that a king becomes a government and then an entire planetary system of Earth, showing that even the smallest idea can grow and mature into a giant creation of glory. Secondly, a priest becomes a church and then becomes paradise in heaven, showing that God and man are becoming one in truth, law, will, and love. Thirdly, a son becomes a home and then becomes a Kingdom of Glory, showing that angels and saints are becoming one in virtues, righteousness, holiness, and perfection. Finally, a free man becomes a self-willed man and then he becomes God-like, showing that God's creation (life) and man's world (death) are becoming one on Earth, in Heaven, within the Kingdom, and in each transformed soul (new nature).

Through each of these stages of growth and maturity, the mind (intellect), heart (emotions), soul (instincts), and life-forces (nature) of born-again man can become Earth, Heaven, Kingdom, and God, all in the name of Jesus Christ. It should now make sense that our physical universe (cosmos) was initially created with invisible light energy within a gravitational field or nothing (energy) becoming something (matter). Basically, we are seeing this same Nothing to All concept operating within the spirit world as the spirit nature of angels is becoming the physical nature of men through the sacrifices of Christ (cross/blood/spirit). In short, through the forces of evolution, life finds a way to grow and mature from Nothing to All by simply striving to become the nature of its Creator God via the creative forces of belief. Now, we see that nature is inefficient; manpower is a little more efficient; "machine power" is quite efficient, but angels (fast), God (very fast), and finally, the Messiah (instant) can really get the job done. This means that when selecting the right tool to get the job done, a person must decide just how quickly this effort must be finished (sacrifice) and to what tolerance level of perfection (sacrifice) it must adhere to in satisfying the engineering specifications.

In general terms, this means that God's overall perfection is based on the sacrificial principle of blessings in the form of divine gifts (carrot) for His friends; while He sparingly reserves His curses of rejection for things that do not work. This curse of rejection is for those rebellious children who need the Lord's most stern corrective measures (stick) to bring them to see the value of being a model citizen of society. The Lord's divine justice requires that every spiritual and/or physical creation be paid for by some corresponding painful sacrifice given out of one's pure heart of love. The specific curses being hurled against Heaven and Earth required the sacrifice of every first-born male (inheritance) or an equivalent payment acceptable before the throne of God (new-life).

The Lord then puts a blessing on the last-born child (birthright), giving him His own personal eternal inheritance (land/nature/creation) or benevolent force (natural order) to be united with the divine birthright (life/Messiah/Jesus Christ) or personal God (supernatural order) of all those honored with God's human existence.

Through God's blessing of human existence, we see the need for the three Advents of Christ to bring forth the fulfillment of His own perfection (first resurrection), the perfection of His Church (second resurrection), and the perfection of the world (third resurrection). With the creation of the intercessory forces of life in the form of the Messiah (divine), the Church (holy), and finally, the World (righteous), the human race can fulfill Father Abraham's promise to God that He would become one holy nation on Earth. The idea is to see that during the Lord's First Advent (church) would come Lucifer's test of faith; then during Christ's Second Advent (government) would come God's judgment of knowledge and finally, during the Lord's third Advent (home) would come man's self-evaluation (instinctive compulsion). In this picture of man's purification (Messiah), his transformation (church), and finally, his conversion (world), we see God coming three times (redemption/salvation/rewards) to harvest the fruits of His labors in the number of souls saved. We must get to the essence of life at this point by seeing that God is coming to Earth via the Lord's spirit world (destiny/free will) and then man will be allowed to go to Heaven via man's physical world (holiness/righteousness).

In this exchange of divine and human natures, the God/man relationship comes into existence, thereby creating a two-lane highway for God (womb/tomb) and a two-lane highway for man (baptism/grave) so that they might both enter and exit each other's strange worlds of life and death at will. We see that God is promising man individual rights in reality, while man is proving himself through social rights in illusion, showing that when reality and illusion become one in Christ Jesus, the highways of life/death are created. It is very difficult to comprehend just how God becomes man and man becomes God as they travel on and through completely different states of existence (dimension/life forms/etc.). The job of God's Son as priest (donkey/church), king (thief/world), and Son (cloud/Messiah) is to establish the necessary routes by which the spirit of God (eternal life) and the flesh of man (new body) could travel at will. Through these two routes, God's spirit can resurrect from the tomb to obtain eternal life (heaven) and man's flesh can resurrect from its purified grave to obtain a new body (earth). The point is that a person needs a body to fit into the lifestyle on Earth, just as a person needs an eternal spirit to fit into the lifestyle of Heaven.

Through these two vessels of life, both God (eternal life) and man (new body) can join into one nature and come to live in their own kingdom of glory forever. Note that through the Messiah's Highway (individual), God (groom) will be able to marry the Virgin Mary (bride) to unite God's spirit nature (flesh) with man's spirit nature (blood). Secondly, through the Church's Highway (society), Jesus (groom) will be able to marry the Christian Church (bride) to unite man's flesh (bread) with God's flesh (wine). Through these two marriages, the Highway of Holiness (Messiah) is able to open the way to be merged with God's divinity (perfection). In like manner, these two marriages bring forth the Highway of Perfection (Church), thereby opening the way to be merged with humanity (imperfection). This means that Jesus (human God) came as a priest on a donkey (Messiah) during His First Advent to build the highway of holiness (Messiah/cross) so that the Lord God Almighty will have free access to Planet Earth (man). Secondly, Christ (divine man) comes as king in the night (thief) during His Second Advent to build the highway of righteousness (Church/blood) so that the people of Earth will have free access to God's Heaven (saint). It should now all make sense that a set of highways must be built to accommodate the goings and comings of God, angels, and men to merge the spirit of Heaven with the flesh of Earth to create a new born-again kingdom of glory in service to one and all.

The following tabular information indicates that in the Lord's Grand Design, God (individual rights) is planning to move around via the spirit world through His *Birth* (womb) or *In* (life) and through His *Death* (tomb) or *Out* (eternal life), while man (social rights) is planning to move around via the physical world through the *Church* (baptism) or *In* (body) and then via the *World* (grave) or *Out* (new body):

God Moves through the Spirit World and Man Moves through the Physical World to become Perfect
(God is becoming Righteous in Life and Man is becoming Holy in Death to unite All in All)

God Travels the Messiah's Highway/Man Travels the Church's Highway
(God travels the highway of perfection, while man travels the highway of imperfection)

God's Promise to Man - Individual Rights: Reality (give divinity) = Christ's Prayer

Sacrifice   1.   **God Moves** – <u>Spirit World</u>: Learning Right from Wrong
citizen (creation)   = Righteous
Remove Faults
- Birth - In: Flesh (womb)...Destiny
- God - Spirit: Groom = Bride Price + Offer Name (divine)... Christmas

Messiah's
Highway
- Creation of Life - Earth: Agony of Defeat = Remove Sin, Evil, and Death
- Death - Out: Spirit (Tomb)...Free Will: Insert Virtues

(blessing)
- Mary (Flesh): Bride = Dowry + Offer Virginity (Human)...... Easter
- Resurrect Eternal Life - Heaven: Thrill of Victory = Be Righteous, Holy, and Perfect

(Jesus - priest on a donkey:
1st advent = marriage of God [blood] to Virgin [flesh])

Man's Proof to God - Social Rights: Illusion (take-sin) = Jesus' Sacrifice

Prayer   2.   **Man Moves** - <u>Physical World</u>: Learning Good from
(Messiah)   Evil = Holy Saint
- Church - In: Spirit (baptism)...Holiness: Good Works

**Church's
Highway**
(lesson)

- Jesus - Flesh: Groom = Bride Price + Offer Name (human)... Halloween
- Creation of Body - Earth: Agony of Defeat = Ignorance, Cowardice, and Greed
- World - Out: Flesh (grave)...Righteousness: Save Souls
- Church - Spirit: Bride = Dowry + Offer Virginity (divine)...4th of July
- Resurrect New Body - Heaven: Thrill of Victory = Be Wise, Courageous, and Generous

(Christ - thief in the night:
2nd advent = marriage of Jesus [wine] to Church [bread])

This illustration shows that the Lord Jesus Christ (Messiah) has come in His First Advent (priest on a donkey) to build a two-lane highway (birth/death) between heaven and earth (righteous citizen) so that God can become man (Christmas/womb) and man can become God (Easter/tomb). Secondly, the Lord Jesus Christ (Church) will return during His Second Advent (thief in the night) to build a second two-lane highway (church/world) between earth and heaven (holy saint) so that sinners can become Christians (Halloween/baptism) and Christians can become saints (fourth of July/grave). Via these two highways, God's spirit world can come to Earth and man's physical world can go to Heaven in an exchange of cultures so that one day, God and man will become one. This means that one's spirit nature (divinity/reality) must seek to become righteous (mind), holy (heart), and perfect (soul); while his physical nature (humanity/illusion) must seek to become wise (mind), courageous (heart), and generous (soul).

We now see that the Lord God Almighty will be traveling along the Messiah's Highway to bring individual rights (learn right/wrong/will of God) to Earth, while God's chosen people will be traveling along the Church's highway to bring social rights (learn good/evil/will of people) to heaven. Through these two magnificent highways, a working relationship will be established between God (calling), His angels (enlightenment), man (awakening), and Christ's saints (indwelling). It all comes down to three Advents of Christ plus a Final Judgment, giving the human race its ability to travel from a righteous Earth (Christians/adults) to a holy Heaven (God/forgiven); and from an unrighteous Earth (sinners/babies) to an evil hell (Lucifer/pardon) at will. Now, we understand why mankind's "blessing/curse (lessons) arrangement (holy/evil spirit)" has been the driving force compelling Jesus to defeat Lucifer's evil forces and rid the universe of its most deadly first-born curse of death.

Jesus has established a new royal family known as the brotherhood of man, where every member is born again into a new first-born status of human perfection (new nature/round table) in the eyes of God. Fortunately, Jesus took the punishment for those under the first-born curse when the earth murdered its only first-born divine Son of human perfection, our Lord Jesus Christ. This act of sacrificing divine innocence brought forth the redemptive blood of purification, thereby freeing all mankind from its coming fate of certain death (grave) and damnation (hell/Gehenna). This will be accomplished through the unification of God's divine mind (fire) and man's human heart (water) to transform dead sinners (earth/goat) into holy saints (heaven/lamb). To do this, two mystical sacrifices (lamb/goat) were required to satisfy the divine requirements of God's divine justice allowing this unholy curse of evil and death to fall on the least worthy sinner in all creation, Judas (goat). This reversing of God's justice system would then rank order all of mankind from the most holy to the greatest sinner, bringing a new more perfect justice system to one and all. This means that God is creating two systems as one truth rank orders all men (good to bad), and then, with His second truth, the Lord creates a round table (fair), where all men are created equal (opportunity).

The idea here is that God needed to establish a method of proper human judgment out of a new perfect justice system (God's Justice/man's mercy), which was essential to the creation of a holy society of perfectly obedient citizens of mutual love (heaven) and mutual respect (earth). The Lord, in His own way, decided that the curse of evil (justice) would fall upon the innocents of Heaven (angels/lamb) and the curse of death (mercy) would fall upon the guilty of Earth (men/goats). In this way, justice could be served, correcting the injustices of both Lucifer's and Adam's original sins by paying for their mistakes in divine blood, so that the implementation of the Lord's Grand Design would be founded upon good judgment (values). We see that God's divine truth is being served here, in the fact that Jesus took the human curse of evil (take-sin) upon Himself as innocent blood (heaven) and then allowed Judas to take the human curse of death upon himself as guilty blood (earth). Conversely, we see the Son of God (give divinity) taking the divine curse of death upon Himself as innocent blood (lamb/heaven) and then allowing the Son of Man (take-sin) to take the divine curse of evil upon Himself as guilty blood (goat/earth). In this second step, we must recognize the guilt for all the sins of man (capital/mortal/venial) coming from the fact that Jesus was the blood heir to the Davidic throne making Him both the high priest of Israel (redeemer/spirit) and King of the Jews (savior/flesh). We see in this royal inheritance that Jesus Christ becomes fully responsible for all the sins and transgressions of His chosen people to bring them to perfection in the sight of God.

It is about this time that we might ask, then why didn't Jesus just take the sins of the Jewish people and set them free from sin, evil, and death? Secondly, how did the king of the Jews also become responsible for Adam and all the rest of mankind in the first place? The answer appears to be that the Jewish people were given the master sonship charter (Isaac) of human existence upon Planet Earth through the Abrahamic covenant (title deed to earth), thereby making the king of the Jews the one person responsible to pay (three advents) for the sins of all men. Now, to add another dimension to this mystical divine responsibility, we see that it would also be the Jewish high priest (sacrifice/Aaron), who would be personally responsible to purify the king of his sins by offering-up the divine lamb (blood) in sacrifice (payment) for the sins, evils, and deaths of all sinners. The idea here is that the priest (sacrifice) purifies the king; then the king (prayer) purifies the son; and then the son (bloodless sacrifice/prayer) purifies the Father (God). In this way, our Eternal Father can then transform His creation back to its original owner (God/reality) and also restore it back to its original state (Man/illusion) of sacred perfection.

The following tabular information indicates that it takes three mystical purifications (three advents) to transform the King (Jews), the Son (earth), and the Father (heaven) using the sacrifices of the high priest of Israel (Jesus), Earth (Christ), and Heaven (Jesus Christ):

**Priest Purifies King, King Purifies Son,
Son Purifies Father to bring forth the Kingdom**
(redemption of Israel, Earth, and Heaven
through the coming of Jesus Christ, our Savior)

Sin
(truth)

1. **Priest Purifies King** – <u>Creation of the Messiah</u>.......
   Facing Lucifer's Test
   - Redeemer of the Human Spirit – Perfection: Meaning of Life = Existence (alone)
   - Free Gift from God – Learning Right from Wrong: Earning Graces from God
   - 1st Resurrection – Paying the Sin-debt (faults): Overcome Sin-nature
   - Lucifer is Testing Man's Endurance – Baby, Teenager, or Adult Levels
   - Submission – Gift of Humanity: Repentance = Heal Sick Body (venial sin)
       (first Marriage – God Marries Man:
   Eternal Father/Virgin Mary = Waters of Life)

Evil
(law)

2. **King Purifies Son** – <u>Creation of the Church</u>.........
   Facing God's Judgment
   - Savior of the Human Flesh – Holiness: Purpose of Life = Service (society)
   - Earned by Faithful Men – Good from Evil: Earning Points from Man
   - 2nd Resurrection – Paying the Holy Debt (virtues): Overcome Worldly Temptations
   - God is Judging Man's Character – Baby, Teenager, and Adult Levels
   - Sacrifice – Gift of Self: Worship = Heal Dead Spirit (mortal sin)
       (second Marriage – Spirit Marries Flesh:
       Christ/Church = Blood of Death)

Death
(will)

3. **Son Purifies Father** – <u>Creation of the World</u>.........
   Facing Self-evaluation
   - Converter of the Human Soul – Righteousness: Value of Life = Happiness (all)
   - Deserved by Dedicated Saints – God's Will from man's will: Earning Happiness for Self

- 3rd Resurrection – Offering Gift of Love (souls): Overcome Demonic Possession
- Self-evaluation of One's Own Perfection – Baby, Teenager, and Adult Levels
- Salvation – Gift of Divinity: Forgiveness = Healing Damned Soul (capital sin)
  (third Marriage – Saint Marries Sinner:
  Jesus/World = Spirit of Resurrection)

This illustration shows that everything in life begins with a priest's blessing, which helps to explain the great importance of the Mosaic Tabernacle (sacrifice) and the creation of the Levitical priesthood of Aaron (prayer). Through the priest purifying the king's sins, the spirit of the whole human race (church) could be reconciled back to God and then given the Lord's official blessing of forgiveness for one and all. Secondly, the king purifies the son's evil so that the flesh of the whole human race (world) could be reconciled back to God and then given the Lord's official blessing of wealth and prosperity for one and all. Finally, the Son purifies the Father's death so that the soul of the whole human race (kingdom) could be reconciled back to God and then given the Lord's official blessing of divine freedom for one and all. Through these three purifications, we see each and every child of God must face Lucifer's test (alone/grace), face God's judgment (society/points), and finally, face his own self-evaluation (all men/marks) to learn the meaning (existence), purpose (service), and value of life (happiness). In this theme of starting from the bottom and building up, everything begins with one man (priest/Messiah) fighting against all men; then a few holy men (king/church) fighting against the majority; and finally, all men (Son/world) working together to fight against the forces of nature. This need to begin every worthwhile effort with a sacrificial soul, which believes in its just cause enough to dedicate its whole life, will make it an overwhelming success (acceptance) in the eyes of God, angels, and men. In making redemption a success, the Lord decided to use the human flesh (water) of Jesus as the kingship (sacrifice/goat) of His eternal kingdom of glory, and then to use the divine spirit (fire) of Christ as the priesthood (prayer/lamb) of His eternal kingdom of love.

The following tabular information indicates that the creation of God's kingship comes through the sacrifice of Jesus' flesh (fight evil); while the creation of God's priesthood comes through the sacrifice of Christ's spirit (surrender life):

**God's Kingdoms of Glory and Love Fulfill both
God's Physical Law and Man's Spiritual Faith**
(Jesus sacrifices flesh unto the law,
while Christ sacrifices spirit unto faith to save all)

World – Man Travels through Death to become God (Man/God)
- - - Man becomes God – Via the Purified Grave/pardon:
Mount Calvary and/or Easter - - -

1. **Kingdom of Glory** – Human Flesh of Jesus: Creating the *Kingship*
   ....Man's Water
   - God's Law of Obedience – Kills the Flesh: Purify Grave
     .... Change Nature
   - See Limitations – Learn to Live with Self: Become Righteous Citizen on Earth
   - Water Baptism – Kills the Flesh: Saves the Sinner from Death
     (fighting evil)
   - Resurrection from Grave – Worthy of New Body: Enter Heaven on Earth
   - Damages – Punitive Retribution: Offenses Against Man = Pay
     Sin-debt + Scourging/Calvary
   - Body Broken – Pays for Damages: Christ's Crucifixion = Offer Sacrifice
   - Fulfill Abrahamic Covenant – Suffer Broken Hip Joint: Pay Sin-debt
   - Take-sin – Save Sinners: Free Gift of New Body
     (earth)   **Soldier-of-the-Light**
                                                  • Punishment
   - God Gets His New Body – God Comes to Earth (world/body broken)
     (evil goat is cast off from cliff into oblivion –
     death in the pit of forgetfulness)

   Church – God Travels through Life to become Man (God/Man)
   - - - God becomes Man – Via the Purified Host/forgiven:
   Last Supper and/or Christmas - - -

2. **Kingdom of Love** – Divine Spirit of Christ: Creating the *Priesthood*
   .... God's Fire
   - Man's Faith in God's Love – Washes Clean the Spirit: Purify Host
     .... Wash Away Sin
   - See Potential – Learn to Live with God: Become Holy Saint in Heaven
   - Spiritual Baptism – Washes the Spirit: Creates Saint of New-life
     (submission)
   - Death unto Born-again New-life – Worthy of Eternal Life: Enter Paradise
     in Heaven
   - Fines – Compensatory Recompense: Offenses Against God = Pay Holy-debt
     + Cross/tomb
   - Blood Shed – Pays for Fines: Catholic Church = Offer Prayers
   - Fulfill New Covenant – Ear Nailed to Door Post: Pay Holy-debt
   - Give Divinity – Create Saints: Earning Eternal Life
     (Heaven)   *Living Prayer*
                                                  • Rewards
   - Man Gets His Eternal Life – Man Comes to Heaven (church/blood shed)
     (holy goat slaughtered and offered to God –
     new-life brings forgiveness to all men)

This illustration shows that this concept makes Jesus the Son of man (earth) creating the mystical school of the soldier-of-the-light (righteous citizen), who is responsible for eating the bread of human faults (evil) and transforming them into holy virtues of divine love (man becomes God). This also reveals that Christ, as the Son of God (heaven), creates the mystical school of the living prayer of love (holy saint), who is responsible for drinking the wine of human virtues (death), transforming them into holy virtues of divine love (God becomes man). The explicit purpose here has been to challenge mankind's integrity, forcing it to courageously face evil, overcome it, and thereby grow into a man of virtuous character (righteous) and dignity (holy).

This superman of spiritual character will then become a friend to God and join with Him in building His new kingdom of glory. We know God has offered His personal friendship to anyone who will believe in His guidance, trust Him, surrender to His will, and obediently follow His Word in a quest to defeat sin (sin-nature), evil (worldly temptations), and death (demonic possession) in a world without hope. This means that the defeat of sin (divine rights) is to come with the first marriage (overcome ignorance) uniting God (life) and man (death) into oneness through Christ's First Advent (priest on a donkey) via the death of God on Mt. Calvary. Secondly, the defeat of evil comes via the second marriage (overcome cowardice) uniting the spirit (heaven) and flesh (earth) into oneness through Christ's Second Advent (thief in the night) via the death of man during tribulation. Finally, the defeat of death (individual rights) comes via the third marriage (overcome greed) uniting the Saint (educated) and the Sinner (streetwise) into Oneness through Christ's third Advent (Son on a cloud) via the new-life of God/man during the end of the world. Through these three Advents of Christ, the human race is given its living prayer of love (death of God) and its soldier-of-the-light (death of man) to be merged into the new-life of God/man (kingdom).

The following tabular information clearly indicates the two major forces (Messiah/creation) operating in the redemptive plan of God as they transform human faults (Messiah/goat) into divine virtues (Creation/lamb):

Explaining the Redemptive Plan of God

Death (creation)	1. **School of Soldier-of-the-Light** – <u>Inheritance</u> (faith): Physical Light (water)
	• Eats "Bread of Faults (evil)" – Principled Ethics: Learn Right from Wrong
	• Jesus – Son of Man (heart) Cain's Altar – Sacrifice Flesh: Good News
	• Interpreter – God Speaks to His People: God becomes Man (righteousness)
	• Champion Fights Alone – Prodigal Son of Death: Transform the Flesh
Messiah (convert flesh)	• Flesh: King of the Jews (Kingship) "Last Supper (goat/body broken)"
	• Redeem Mankind's Identity (repentance) – Brotherhood

of Man (kingship)

- King of Death – Blood of Purification (born-again-flesh): Informality
- Arrow of Truth (forgiveness) to Receive God's "Silver Blessing"
- ***Righteous of Earth*** – Emotions Transformed to Intellect: Intercessor
- Mind of Christ – Ignorance: Sin-nature = Fool
- Heart of Christ – Cowardice: Worldly Temptations = Criminal
- Soul of Christ – Greed: Demonic Possession = Insane

(Learning Right/Wrong – Righteousness: Righteous
Citizen = Earn Eternal Life [transfigured])

New-life
(Messiah)

2. **School of Living Prayer of Love** – Birthright (knowing): Spiritual Light (fire)

- Drinks "Wine of Virtue (death)" – Virtuous Morals: Learn Good from Evil
- Christ – Son of God (mind) Abel's Altar – Surrender Spirit: Gospel Message
- Intercessor – People Speak to God: Man becomes God (holiness)
- General Leads an Army – Good Son of New-life: Purify the Spirit

Creation
(reconcile
spirit)

- Spirit: High Priest of Jews (Priesthood)   "Mt. Calvary (lamb/blood shed)"
- Redeem Mankind's character (forgiveness) – Sainthood of God (priesthood)
- King of Life – Death of Redemption (born-again-spirit): Formality
- Olive Branch of Truth (blessing) to Receive God's "Golden Blessing"
- ***Saints of Heaven*** – Intellect Transformed to Emotions: Interpreter
- Mind of God – Wisdom: Holy-nature = Wise Man
- Heart of God – Courage: Worldly Experience = Free Man
- Soul of God – Generosity: Demonic Conversion = Perfect Man

(Learn Good/Evil – Holiness:
Holy Saint = Free Gift of Divinity (glorified spirit])

This illustration shows that the dual structure of our Messiah, Jesus Christ, clearly reveals the intercessory (speak to God) and interpretive (speak to people) forces in place and operating through His perfect justice system. This system of justice has been designed to transform our evil ways (ignorance) into a new set of holy ways (wisdom) through the blessing of our God. These two forces represent the two mystical divine schools that have been created out of the divine sacrifice of God's creation (knowledge/law) and man's Messiah (values/faith). Through the creation (world/righteousness) and God's Son (church/holiness), the rest of humanity are transformed into born-again holy saints as eternal members of the celestial court of God in service to His glorious kingdom of love.

Shown above is Jesus as the king of death arguing the defensive position of human flesh, showing God that there are clear extenuating circumstances associated with the reason behind mankind being given an evil fleshly nature. He can point to the wicked spirit of man as one of the major causes associated with fleshly sin, not to mention the blame being attributed to the demonic powers of Lucifer (lie), the devil (cheat), and Satan (steal). Conversely, we see Christ as the king of life arguing the conviction of the human flesh in defense of the human spirit, showing God that there are clear extenuating circumstances why mankind has been cursed with an evil human spirit. We see that Christ can point to the wicked flesh of man as one of the major causes associated with spiritual sin, not to mention the blame that can be attributed to the satanic forces of Lucifer (sin), the devil (evil), and Satan (death).

Through these two arguments of the prosecution (Christ/against) or interpreter and defense (Jesus/for) or intercessor, God's (court/judge) divine mercy is founded as it becomes clear that the human race was facing adult criminal charges as a minor. This means that God would not be able to make a valid judgment until the completion of Christ's three Advents and the conversion of man from baby (death of God), to teenager (death of man), and then to adult (new-life of God/man). The idea here is that once the Lord had created a clear-thinking man and had tested his mind (wisdom), heart (courage), and soul (generosity), only then could he be properly judged in the eyes of God, angels, and men.

This means that the transformation (valid test) of both the flesh and spirit of man must be accomplished simultaneously in a coordinated effort to empty the mind (intellect) and heart (emotions) through the Lord's purifying blood and then to refill these organs with the Lord's redeeming holy word of righteousness (body broken). This mystical effort must be coordinated with the emptying of a new born-again Christian's spirit and soul through the purifying death and then refill them with the Lord's redeeming sacred word of righteousness (lessons). This process will only occur when a man (creation) makes an honest life-changing sacrifice to God (creator) through his soul-shattering experience that forces him to come to full repentance via both his physical conversion (mind) and his spiritual reconciliation (heart).

We see that a true sacrifice involves struggle, pain, and endurance as it challenges one's spiritual faith, fortifying his born-again character, thereby mystically leading him to a new level of maturity (new body), personal dignity (eternal life), and spiritual holiness (kingdom). This means that every man has been allowed to choose his own way of living (free will) and has profited justly by either his good or evil acts as he deserves, in accordance with God's divine justice. This implies that nothing could have been more equitable and fair in either the eyes of man (illusion) or the eyes of God (reality) other than when every soul is allowed to choose its own way in the world based upon its own free will. The Lord has given Mankind "a seven-thousand-year period of open defiance" to His justice, authority, and law, so that all men might have an opportunity to do it their way and show just how they might straighten out the world. In this way, God may now rightfully claim those souls amenable to His way and conversely reject those souls that oppose His will, as He searches for a few perfect friends (remnant) amid a sea of angry enemies (masses).

In the Lord's Grand Design, He sacrificed all in seven divine burnt offerings: (1) Lucifer – sacrifice perfect angel (traitor), (2) Adam – sacrifice perfect man (enemy), (3) first-born society drowned by Noah – sacrifice evil society (strangers), (4) Jews – sacrifice perfect society (neighbors), (5) Messiah – sacrifice divine man (friends), (6) Church – sacrifice holy society (family), and (7) World – sacrifice righteous society (self), all to create a perfect, faithful, and free-willed son of God (think for self). These most perfect mystical sacrificial offerings were each a part of the Lord's Grand Design to bring forth a human bride of true love, using the theory that one perfect life (Jesus/Mary) could be created out of the collective beings of all humanity. Once this new creation (God/man) had been brought into existence, the Lord had planned to insert His own divine female spirit (breath) or the Holy Spirit (Blessed Virgin) into His human flesh (Virgin Mary), thereby creating a mystical body of human love to forever be the bride of God (Blessed Virgin). Unfortunately, for God's master plan to work, the Lord had to create a human male flesh in the person of Jesus to house the divine male spirit of Christ, who could be brought into a perfect union through the trauma of crucifixion (marriage).

This explains why the Lord Jesus Christ was torn spiritually in two as symbolized by the dividing of the sacred veil in the temple, so that the newly purified human male nature could be separated from the divine female nature in such a way as to allow them to be transferred into the new humanity (born-again) or Christ's new nature (think for self). The male nature was inserted into the holy bread (heart) of free redemption (take-sin). Whereas, the female nature was inserted into the sacred wine (mind) of earned salvation (give divinity) so that both could create the mystical transubstantiation (consecration) of God, inside of the Lord's Divine Word. Then the Divine Word was placed in the mouth of Peter (touch) to create the Catholic Church and its holy mass (repentance/forgiveness).

Through the Lord's plan of destiny, a broken sinner may surrender his free will of death unto the Divine Word of God to be transformed into a bride of God by the authority of His universal Catholic Church. This new bride of love would be a New Creation (being), who is a separate entity from herself, yet, has her own divine spirit, making her a member of the royal family of God. The Lord's divine marriage contract (two fathers) of Calvary has been sealed by both blood (holy goat) and death (evil goat) through the divine sacrifice of God's Son, Jesus Christ. This mystical marriage between divinity (nature) and humanity (life) was consummated through the divine vows of ever-lasting love upon the Lord's cross of death (blood offering/earth). Upon Mt. Calvary, the Lord endured His pain to the very end to place His perfect innocent life upon God's altar of death (silver offering/heaven) to purchase (sin-debt) the eternal love of His human bride (Blessed Virgin). The major point is that the Virgin Mary represents the human bride of Christ, while the Holy Church represents the divine bride of Jesus to interlock the union of God's spirit (life) with man's flesh (death). Finally, the righteous world represents the human/divine bride of Jesus Christ to interlock the union of Earth and Heaven into one kingdom of glory, giving peace, joy, and happiness to one and all. Through these three marriages, the Messiah, Heaven, and Earth can legally come to-gether into a marriage contract, thereby bonding truth, law, and will together into one eternal life-force.

We see in this set of marriages (father/son/spirit) that one of the greatest miracles of life is that our human characters cannot be created automatically by God's divine hand and still keep the free-willed nature of man intact. The character of humanity must be developed through the force of free choice (lessons) made in accordance with collecting one's various good and evil experiences (lessons) under his own power. This means that to own a bird (saint), its master must first set it free and then wait for the bird (righteous man) to return on its own accord and then forever stay with its most benevolent and loving owner (God) to be one who serves, but is not a servant (free to leave). The human character and the human heart must both be developed with pre-judgment, but must follow a path that will manifest one's free moral judgment as in the nature of a small child (innocence). To achieve this great purpose of producing the supreme pinnacle of all God's creations, a group of faithful sons with perfect characters and infinite wisdom must be manifested in God's divine truth (think for self) out of man's own free will (success).

In this discussion, we see our God is saying that His pathway of destiny repre-sents the capturing of a bird in a marriage to God (Christ) via the Blessed Virgin (human), who will bring human perfection onto the earth (righteousness/citizen-ship). Secondly, the pathway of free will is the return of the bird in a marriage to man (Jesus) via the Holy Church (divine), who will bring human perfection into heaven (holiness/sainthood). Through this two-lane highway from heaven and back, we see the creation of God's spiritual pathway (destiny/holiness) versus His physical pathway (free will/righteousness) to allow both the followers of Christ (saints/glo-rified spirits) and the followers of Jesus (citizens/transfigured bodies) to journey back and forth between Heaven and Earth at will. Recall that at the time of Moses, he was sent to Egypt to free the slaves via the Miracle-working Power of God, then opened the Red Sea to kill Israel's enemies, and brought manna and water from a rock to sustain the Jews in the desert. Yes! The Lord was quite a miracle worker much as we appear to be before our own children when they are amazed at all the awesome things we do for them with ease.

But now, as the modern world comes into existence, the human race sees fewer and fewer miracles and more and more hard-work and then suddenly, everything that was beyond one's understanding became common place to one and All. This childish reliance on God and then this new belief in oneself shows the growth and maturity of man as he begins to transform the universe (stone by stone) into a beautiful Garden of Eden (tree of life). We see in this conversion (miracles) to common sense (hard-work) scenario that the Lord has been forced to empty the flesh (remove faults) so that He could one day fill the spirit (insert virtues) with His own indwelling perfection (world of supermen).

It is now clear that the Lord needed to first empty the human race of all its wicked faults using its own free-willed power to submit itself to a new mystical force capable of the dual purification of man's spirit (death) and flesh (blood). During the second phase of conversion, God refills each new born-again soul with His Divine Word of righteousness (victims) to make it perfect in His sight. To better understand this concept, we must clearly see the purpose behind the Lord's mystical virgin birth and burial in a virgin tomb, each designed to seal the input and output channels (pathways) for original sin. Recall that Father Abraham was given a promise that his faith would create a new channel that would manifest as many righteous children (Earth/redemptions) as there were grains of sand (righteous citizens/redemptions) on all the beaches of the world from everlasting to everlasting. Secondly, Abraham was also promised that his people's faith would create a new channel that would manifest as many holy children (heaven) as there are stars in the sky (holy saints/salvations) throughout the entire universe.

From this strange promise, we might see the need for the Lord to bring forth the first mystical baby of flesh through the birth canal of the virgin womb (mystical womb of life) as half of God's new born-again mystical creation. Out of this birth, this perfect child would be totally emptied of all the evil faults and filled with God's holy virtues. Now, we must see that another first-born mystical baby of spirit is destined to be born through the birth canal of the virgin tomb (mystical womb of death) as the other half of the new born-again mystical creation. Out of this birth, this perfect adult would be completely filled with the virtues of God. Now, we see that Mary's Son, Jesus (goat) was to be created out of the virgin womb (take-sin/emotion/love), while God's Son, Christ (lamb) was to be created out of the virgin tomb (give divinity/intellect/wisdom), thereby making God and man one in truth, law, and will. This means that the purified tomb (path to earth/spirit) becomes man's mystical womb of death (dying to self), while the Virgin Mary (path to heaven/flesh) becomes man's mystical womb of life (born-again). In the Bible, the purified tomb (journey to heaven) and the Virgin Mary's womb (journey to earth) represent Jacob's ladder that was used by Jesus Christ during His glorious ascension to heaven from the top of the Mount of Olives (pathway of life).

The following tabular information indicates how the pathways of destiny and free will bring the Spirit (God) back and forth between Heaven and Earth (God becomes man), while the pathways of holiness and righteousness bring the resurrected flesh (Man) back and forth between Earth and Heaven (man becomes God):

Pathways of Destiny/Free Will bring God/man;
Pathways of Holiness/Righteousness bring Man
(God comes between Heaven/Earth via tomb;
Man comes between Earth/Heaven via Church/world)

Purification of the Spirit: Divine Conversion

Womb
(truth)

1. **Christ Comes to Earth** – <u>Pathway of Destiny</u>: Physical
   Dimension...Pure Spirit
   - Virgin Mary's Womb of Life – Travel-down to Earth:
     King of Kings (animal mind)
   - God becomes Man – Dying to Self: *New Human Spirit*
     (submission) = Kingship
   - God and Abraham – Two Fathers Offer Bride Price and
     Dowry to Create Marriage
   - Remove Wicked Thoughts – Childish Fantasies become
     Common Sense
   - Highway of Destiny – Empty Mind to Fill Intellect
     (knowledge)
     (create "Perfect Man" – See Limitations:
     Learn Right from Wrong = knowledge)

Tomb
(law)

2. **Jesus Comes to Heaven** – <u>Pathway of Free Will</u>:
   Spiritual Dimension... Glorified Spirit
   - Purified Tomb of Death – Travel-up to Heaven: High
     Priest of Heaven (robot mind)
   - Man becomes God – Born-again: *Glorified Spirit* (think
     for self) = Priesthood
   - Jesus and Church – Couple Offers Name and Virginity
     to Enter into Marriage
   - Remove Sinful Words – Teenage Lust becomes
     Passionate Love
   - Highway of Free Will – Empty Heart to Fill Emotions
     (self-awareness)
     (create "Holy Church" – See Potential:
     Learn Good from Evil = self-awareness)

Transformation of the Flesh: Human Conversion

Church
(will)

3. **Jesus Christ Comes to Heaven** – <u>Pathway of Holiness</u>:
   Mystical Dimension ....Pure Flesh
   - Holy Church of Life – Travel-up to Heaven: High Priest
     of Earth (human mind)
   - God and Man become One – Dying to Self: *New
     Human Flesh* (sacrifice) =   Sonship
   - Priests and Laity – Friends Offer Birthright and

Inheritance for Marriage
- Remove Evil Actions – Adult Greed becomes Philanthropic Generosity
- Highway of Righteousness – Empty Soul to Fill Instincts (consciousness)
(create "Righteous World" – See Self-worth:
Learn God's Will/man's will = Conscience)

World
(love)

4. **Christ Jesus Comes to Earth** – Pathway of Righteousness: Divine Dimension ....Transfigured Flesh
- Righteous World of Death – Travel-down to Earth: King of the Jews (divine mind)
- God/Man becomes Man/God – Born-again: *Transfigured Body* (imagination) = Freedom
- Angels and Saints – Two Families Offer Heaven and Earth for Marriage of God and Man
- Remove Demonic Possession – Wise Man Selfishness becomes Free Man Unselfishness
- Highway of Holiness – Empty Life-force to Fill Nature (sentience)
(create "Kingdom of Glory" – Set Free:
Learn Reality/Illusion = Sentience)

This illustration shows that Christ comes to Earth (God's spirit) to create the perfect man (virgin womb) by learning right from wrong (see limitations), have knowledge (remove wicked thoughts) as the king of kings, and brings humanity its new spiritual nature (intellect/submission). Secondly, Jesus comes to heaven (God's flesh) to create the Holy Church (purified tomb) by learning good from evil (see potential), become self-aware (remove sinful words) as the high priest of heaven, and brings humanity its new spiritual nature (emotions/thinking). Thirdly, Jesus Christ comes to Heaven (man's spirit) to create the righteous world (Holy Church) by learning God's will from man's will (see self-worth), become conscious (remove evil actions) as the High Priest of Earth, and brings humanity its new physical nature (intellect/sacrifice). Lastly, Christ Jesus comes to Earth (righteous world) to create the Kingdom of Glory by learning God's reality from man's illusion (set free), become sentient (remove demonic possession) as the king of the Jews, and brings humanity its new physical nature (emotions/imagination).

In this lesson, we see that Heaven (Christ) is bringing humanity both a spiritual intellect or mind of God and spiritual emotions or heart of God to purify the soul of man (speak to God). Secondly, we see that Earth (Jesus) is bringing humanity both a physical intellect or mind of Christ and spiritual emotions or heart of Jesus to transform the soul of Man (speak to man). Now, picture the creation of two weddings: one with the groom being God's spirit (Christ) and the bride being man's flesh (Virgin Mary).

In the second wedding, we see that the groom is God's flesh (Jesus) and the bride being man's spirit (Church), which matches up with the coming of the new spiritual/physical minds and hearts to make humanity perfect. Now, we see that through these two marriages, Heaven is connected to Earth (Christ/Mary) and Earth is connected to Heaven (Jesus/Church), thereby making pagans into righteous men (earth) and sinners into saints (heaven). It can be seen in the previous chart that God is creating both a spiritual highway (life) between heaven and earth as well as a physical highway (death) between earth and heaven to accommodate all the needs of man and all the wants of God equally. Obviously, each of God's children is called to remove his wicked thoughts (purify mind), remove his sinful words (purify heart), remove his evil actions (purify soul), and remove his demonic possession (purify life-force). In this way, a person can remove his faults to see his limitations, remove his venial sins to see his potential, remove his mortal sins to see his self-worth, and finally, to remove his capital sin to see his value before God. Yes! We are all seeking to become great before God and then one day, receive the Lord's bonus rewards for living a righteous and holy life worthy of God's blessings.

What the Lord had in mind is to bring the new mystical flesh of God (illusion) into existence through the virgin womb of Mary as the Son of Man, our Lord Jesus (challenge/sinner), known as the sacrificial goat of eternal death (hell). Conversely, our Creator will bring the new mystical spirit of God (reality) into existence through the virgin tomb of death as the Son of God, our Lord Christ (adventure/saint), the sacrificial lamb of eternal death (heaven). Thus, both God's Son and Mary's Son could become one, each being born into the Lord's eternal existence through separate wombs (Christmas/Easter): one of life (Jesus/womb/transfigured body) and one of death (Christ/tomb/glorified spirit). The fact that Jesus Christ was made of both life and death can we come to understand the tremendous significance of the Lord's resurrection as it symbolizes the first birth out of death as He emerges from the purified tomb (virgin) in a new transfigured body (treasure) of pure love. We see here that Jesus as the sacrificial goat is born of the Virgin Mary's virgin womb of love and then takes upon Himself (flesh/Easter) a mountain of sin (scourging) to become the king of death (repentance). This means that God's "king of death" is created by crushing His human flesh (brotherhood) and spilling His blood (sainthood) unto eternal damnation (hell).

In contrast to this contradiction, we see Christ as the sacrificial lamb being born out of a tomb of death, thereby giving-up His divinity (crucifixion/Christmas) to become the transformed king of life (forgiveness) by glorifying His human spirit (sainthood) and spilling His blood with eternal life (heaven). The mystical contradiction here is that Jesus or human flesh was cursed with divine damnation (goat); while Christ or divine spirit was blessed with divine life (lamb). When these two forces met in the tomb of death, the mystical forces of evilness/death (Lucifer) could not overcome the awesome divine power of eternal goodness/life (Jesus). The major theme here is that out of death (Christ) will come life (eternal); while out of life (Jesus) will come death (everlasting) so it is better to be born of death to become eternal life rather than vice versa. This contradiction in terms allows us to see the paradox of God as His infinity (space/death) blends with His eternity (time/life) through the death and resurrection of Jesus Christ. This means that individual rights (see limits) come from the womb/tomb of Earth, while social rights (see potential) come from the church/world of Heaven, allowing the union of God and man as acquaintances (ignorance), neighbors (criminal), companions (insane), friends (evil), and finally, family (demonic). In this way, the forces of ignorance (thoughts), criminality (words), insanity (deeds), evil (omission), and demonic possession (witchcraft) can be destroyed to bring forth the new nature of Christ.

In this way, mankind will have to be convinced, by its own rational mind, that God's divine laws are truly fair, and that God's ways are to be obediently followed by all men of good will. This means that humanity must also voluntarily turn to the divine way of infinite truth as a better way of life, adopting God's way of perfection as man's only hope for eternal peace (forgiveness/priest), joy (money/king), and happiness (love/son). This most essential lesson can only be learned through one's human experiences (adventures), grown out of a life of broken struggles (body broken) and soul-changing challenges (blood shed). Yes! Struggle builds character in the physical nature (intellect) while devoted prayer builds character in the spiritual nature (emotion) to be made one in Christ Jesus. The trick to life is being able to merge the spirit and the flesh into one integrated, well-coordinated person (Messiah), who knows the difference between right and wrong at all five dimensions of existence (physical/spiritual/mystical/divine/God).

We see that God's idea of creating a creature separate from Himself, yet still of Himself (begotten), was done by using the force of sin (free will) as justification to give a person an independent and unique character through the power of His free will (human power/choice). The Lord rejected His own Son to create a new divine kingdom of love as the most perfect reflection of His divinity manifested in spirit (morals) and in flesh (ethics). All Christ's followers who had been previously cursed with original sin will be forced to live as outcasts in the present evil world to receive God's eternal inheritance of divine love. In this unique way, our divine God (reality/creation) would give birth to another Human God (illusion/Messiah) capable of building His own infinite kingdom of divine truth made perfect in Christ Jesus. The plan of God called for a mutual unbreakable bond between both kingdoms, using the Blessed Mother's human love as the focal point or frame of reference for both creations: one, divine (Christ); and the other one, human (Jesus). The Virgin Mary had never been born in sin, so she was never cast out of God's perfect kingdom as a broken sinner, allowing Her to be uniquely worthy of citizenship in both of God's kingdoms (human/divine). In contrast, we can make a case for the Blessed Mother not belonging to either Heaven with God and His angels as She is not divine, nor does She belong on Earth with Jesus Christ and His saints (sinners) as She was never a sinner. It is this state of a woman without a country that makes Her truly unique, making Her both the Mother of God (Christ/not divine) and the Mother of Man (Jesus/not a sinner) or the Mother of all creation.

To comprehend just how the Virgin Mary becomes the Mother of spirit, flesh, and soul, imagine the divine seed of God uniting with the human egg of man within the virgin womb to create the person of Jesus Christ. We can then see that the new baby in the mystical womb can generate His own pathways of escape by journeying through the Father's spirit into the future at the end of time (meet God), and then journey through the mother's flesh into the past back to the breath of Adam (meet God). Now, we see that the past, present, and future are all used during the Lord's divine birth to unite the spirit of Heaven with the flesh of Earth through the divine/human natures of Jesus Christ (virgin womb). We know that the Virgin Mary's spiritual husband is the Holy Spirit, the Father of Jesus as flesh used to create the new born-again kingdom of humanity (saints/citizens), thereby providing the interlocking force of oneness between the Eternal Father, Holy Spirit, and His Son of Flesh (instinctive free will).

We also see that Christ was without sin and was never cast out of the Father's original kingdom of divine perfection (eternal life), making Him the perfect sacrifice (lamb). Now, stating the obvious, Christ and Jesus are one, while Jesus was to play the prodigal son to be forgiven by the Eternal Father, purifying His human nature (free will) and royal bloodline (king). Through the Lord's royal bloodline, He sacrifices His perfect humanity to redeem all men using the Lord's endurance (pass test), character (pass judgment), and perfection (pass evaluation). Note here that Jesus' ascribed punishment for the sins of all men has given Him the most powerful and valued possession in either heaven or earth, which was His most cherished free will (freedom/independence). We all know an adopted son (prodigal) may not be disinherited under Jewish law (divine will), which explains the forgiveness of the prodigal son. The adopted son is conceived in divine law and would get his share of the family inheritance plus his father's blessing of freedom (no money) automatically given according to both the wills of God and man.

The dual nature of Jesus Christ (free man/slave), in effect, purchased both divine purity (holiness) and human impurity (sinfulness) through the free-willed sacrifice of the Lord's spirit (Christ/give divinity) and flesh (Jesus/take-sin) upon Mt. Calvary. This act of unselfishness would make Jesus an adopted Son (prodigal) of God and make Christ the natural Son of God (good), inadvertently establishing a new kingdom of glory (mystical) free from the authority of God Himself. The adopted Son (Jesus) would be blessed with the inheritance of rational logic (mind) and then later inherit His Father's instinctive heart (compulsive behavior) of absolute perfection bringing Him to full maturity. Conversely, the natural Son would be blessed with the birthright of instinctive logic (heart) and then later inherit His Father's intellectual mind, allowing Him to understand the ways of God. In this way, Jesus can fully comprehend the ways of man and Christ can fully comprehend the ways of God, giving the Messiah a perfect understanding of both divinity (reality/maturity) and humanity (illusion/growth) concerning all things in either spirit (knowing right/social rights) or flesh (knowing wrong/individual rights).

With this blended personality of Jesus Christ, He can become a man for all seasons by becoming a mystical chameleon to allow Himself to fit into either the affairs of man or into the affairs of God, either as an interpreter (flesh/confession) or an intercessor (spirit/communion), thereby uniting both sides into one kingdom of glory. A uniquely strange condition also exists with Jesus' inheritance, because He could only die by the power of His own will and never be forcibly rejected from the Earth without His own divine permission (I release My spirit). The Lord is a human and is totally free, without fear of any future punishment forever, coming from either His spirit (intercessor) or His flesh (interpreter) as specified by His Father's own divine law.

In the dawn of time, Lucifer (Satan) was only contesting the wisdom of God's infinite law (physical) and eternal justice (spiritual), to test the depth (endurance) and the tenacity (character) of the Creator's divine will. This proved that divine law is simply founded upon loving God (know) and your neighbor (love) as yourself (serve) in fulfillment of all the commandments of God. This means bringing one's neighbor to salvation through the Lord's divine will to symbolize the defeat of the evil one and his demonic forces. In this way, the sacrifice of Jesus Christ made Him one with death and created a new human kingdom of life and death by conquering the prince of darkness (evil one) and all his demons (hell) once and for all. To conquer evil, the Lord needed a set of commandments to govern the mind, heart, and soul to function interactively from the pure justice of the mind to one's soul-crushing love. This means that Jesus Christ came to purify the mind with His daily sacrifice (remove venial sins), purify the heart with His perpetual sacrifice (remove mortal sins/Sunday), and purify the soul with His divine sacrifice (remove capital sins/Easter) to bring free redemption (eternal life), earned salvation (new body), and bonus rewards (kingdom) to all who will die to their selfishness. We now see that the Ten Commandments have been established to purify the physical world (mind/righteousness/earth); the Two Commandments have been established to purify the spirit world (heart/holiness/heaven); and the One Commandment has been established to purify the mystical world (soul/perfection/kingdom). In each of these three cases, we see that the human race must first appease God's silent anger (surrender/earth) for lying, then appease God's vocal rage (sacrifice/heaven) for hiding, and finally, appease God's striking wrath (reconciliation/kingdom) for stealing from the Lord God Almighty Himself.

The following tabular presentation indicates that there are three sets of commandments: (1) Ten Commandments - Moses; (2) Two Commandments - Jewish People; (3) One Commandment - Jesus bringing forth the daily (earth), perpetual (heaven), and divine sacrifices (Kingdom) to God.

God's Ten Commandments, Two Commandments, and One Commandment Purifying Mind, Heart, and Soul
(offering up the daily, perpetual, and divine sacrifices upon the Lord's altar of new-life)

Truth (water)	1. **Ten Commandments** – <u>Purify the Flesh</u>: New Mind...Offer God Smell of Fat
	• *Daily Sacrifice* – Offer Prayer for Oneself: Physical Prayer
	• Appease God's Silent Anger – Forgive Deceit: Lying to God (venial sin)
Surrender	• Learning Right from Wrong – Righteous Citizen: (kingship): Master Earth
	• Free Gift of Eternal Life – Baptism: Purify Sin-nature (redemption)
	• Surrender Mind – Righteous Citizen on Earth:

Individual Rights
- Attend Daily Mass – Deny Intellect: See Limitations
(scourging teaches the Ten Commandments –
Worship God [5] and Respect Man [5])

Law
(blood)

2. **Two Commandments** – <u>Purify the Spirit:</u> New
Heart...Offer God Smell of Fat/Incense
- *Perpetual Sacrifice* – Offer Prayer for One's Family:
Spiritual Prayer
- Appease God's Vocal Rage – Forgive Deception: Hiding
from God (mortal sin)
- Learn Good from Evil – Holy Saint (priesthood): Master
Heaven
- Earn Gift of New Transfigured Body – Confession:
Purify Temptations (salvation)
- Surrender Heart – Holy Saint in Heaven: Social Rights
- Attend Sunday Mass – Abandon Feelings: See Potential
(crucifixion teaches the Two Commandments –
Love God and Neighbor as Yourself)

Will
(spirit)

3. **One Commandment** – <u>Purify the Soul</u>: New
Soul...Offer God Smell of Incense
- *Divine Sacrifice* – Offer Prayer for One's Nation:
Mystical Prayer
- Appease God's Striking Wrath – Forgive Defiance:
Stealing from God (capital sin)

Reconcile
- Learn God's Will/Man's Will – Son of God (sonship):
Master Kingdom
- Bonus Gift of Dream Home in God's Kingdom –
Communion: Purify Possessions   (rewards)
- Surrender Soul – Son of God within Kingdom: Divine
Rights
- Attend Easter Duty – Submit Free Will: See Self-worth
(tomb of death teaches the One Commandment –
Love Each Other as I have Loved You)

This illustration shows that out of the daily sacrifice, sinful man can become a righteous citizen, thereby making him worthy of the title deed to the Earth via the Lord's free gift of redemption (eternal life). Secondly, out of the perpetual sacrifice, a Christian can become a holy saint, thereby making him worthy of the title deed to Heaven via the Lord's earned gift of salvation (new body). Finally, out of the divine sacrifice, a saintly man can become a Son of God, thereby making him worthy of the title deed to the kingdom via the Lord's bonus gift of rewards (dream home/Kingdom). Through these three sacrifices, the eternal contact has been made with God to appease His silent anger (deceit), His vocal rage (deception), and His striking wrath (defiance). This means that via God's blessing of baptism, capital sins can be forgiven (divine sacrifice); out of God's blessing of confession, mortal sins can be forgiven (perpetual sacrifice); and out of God's blessing of communion, venial sins can be forgiven (daily sacrifice). With this most blessed gift of forgiveness, the human race can master the Earth (water) as a righteous citizen (righteous), master Heaven (blood) as a holy saint (holy), and master the Kingdom (spirit) as a son of God (perfect).

Now, we see that each man's journey of life is centered upon fulfilling the earthly kingship, the heavenly priesthood, and the kingdom's sonship by dying to selfishness, sacrificing his flesh, and reconciling his soul back to God forever. This means that God's Son has come to reveal to all men that it is better to give (sacrifice) than to receive (worship), implying that it is better to know (wise man) than to remain ignorant (fool).

This state of ignorance sits at the center of man's curse of sin, evil, and death, which can only be removed by the sacrifice of Jesus Christ (Calvary). This means that each person on Earth (free redemption/being saved) must surrender his mind by denying his intellect (see limitations) to remove his venial sins (daily mass) and become a righteous citizen on earth. Secondly, each converted soul (earned salvation/save self) must surrender his heart by abandoning his feelings (see potential) to remove his mortal sins (Sunday Mass) and become a holy saint in heaven. Finally, each Christian (bonus rewards/saving others) must surrender his soul by submitting his free will (see self-worth) to remove his capital sins (Easter Duty) and become a son of God within God's kingdom. Through these three acts of submission, a person can defeat sin, evil, and death and be set free (break chains/open door/defeat guards) from his chains of sin-nature (ignorance), prison of worldly temptations (cowardice), and guards of demonic possession (greed). Obviously, Christ is teaching that all must give of themselves to others and that all must know right from wrong before they can hope to escape ignorance, cowardice, and greed.

We see that Christ's teachings are based upon these two simple principles: (1) It is better to give than to receive, and (2) it is better to know than to remain ignorant. Recall that the evil one argued for a kingdom of competition (dog eat dog), where winner takes all in the survival of the fittest, so that the haves should get more, based upon the idea that rank has its privileges. The evil one intently argues that man's bloodline is the eternal struggle for personal achievements (free will) and his personal rewards before the throne of God, so that he must win his own victories without the slightest help from God's divine will. We see that Lucifer claims that a person's motivation to succeed needs incentives (endeavoring) to win, thereby creating an indomitable spirit to overcome all obstacles no matter what the cost in time, money, and/or effort. A man's vanity spurs him to action and his pride drives him on and on in an endless struggle to achieve his ultimate dream of human destiny of being holy as God is holy. Yet in the evil one's philosophy, self-desire, competition, and strife (combat) all provide the true root principles for meaningful accomplishments, all created out of a deep commitment to be victorious in both spirit (heaven) and flesh (earth) based on one's own efforts (money) and personal accomplishments (love). The prince of darkness says that the method used for getting what one truly wants is the road to building a kingdom, which is worth possessing, especially when it has been built out of the blood (majesty), sweat (glory), and tears (honor) of dedicated men of true conviction.

Conversely, the Lord says, "Out of one's painful sacrifices and struggles, each person's progress and advancements (level playing-field/Christ) shall be measured in relation to God's absolute standards (values) for divine perfection." This implies that the life-experience is based on the depth of his individual desire placed within his consciousness (illusion) so that he can see God's divine reality. Through his actions (deeds) that create each person's positive view (good) reflecting his righteous, holy, and perfect attitudes or his negative view (evil) which are lying, cheating, and stealing attitudes, he thereby makes the choice between good and evil strictly his own. This means that one day, a single moment in a person's life will be infinitely measured and eternally weighted on God's perfect scales of divine justice (value) to know the worth of a man in mind, heart, and soul. The question is, are men responsible for their own actions (judged on score), or is God kind enough (judged on curve/handicap) to understand the special circumstances (cruel world) that primitive men (fools) were forced to live under (ignorance) to simply survive?

The real question is, did the Lord God Almighty compel mankind to become rebellious sinners just to survive or were they simply born childish cowards (fear) by nature? The answer can be found in the fact that the human race must surrender its flesh to God's divine will and then enter a new state of Unto Thine Own Self be True (belief). By being true to oneself (identity), a person can be controlled by God's desires coming through his guilty conscience to make-up for all that is either wrong or evil. We call this "submission of the spirit (dying to self)" and sacrifice of the flesh (born-again) to make-up Christianity so that anyone who decides to travel the Lord's pathway of perfection must carry his cross unto death via his own free will. He follows the Lord by facing his trials and tribulations along the first mile for oneself (save self/interpreter), and then doing it again by traveling along the second mile (save others/intercessor) for everyone else (world). We shall receive no credit for having a hard life, because the rain falls on both the rich and the poor. Note that on the day of judgment, just saying you were going along just to get along will not be a valid excuse for becoming another evil greedy monster like everyone else, who was also going along to get along.

It can be seen that in the flesh, a person must travel God's pathway of destiny (free ride) to experience all of the lessons of life firsthand, be they taught by becoming smart where the skin is off or enjoyable by tasting success, triumph, and happiness. Secondly, the spirit must travel man's pathway of free will (earned ride) to master the teachings of Christ (church) to comprehend the importance of worship (give life), praise (give wealth), and thanksgiving (give labors) to its Creator God for His gift of life. Thirdly, the soul must travel Christ's pathway of holiness (remove faults) to master the art of repentance (deny intellect), prayers (abandon feelings), and works (submit free will) to bring lost sinners from death to new-life. Finally, the life-force must travel Jesus' pathway of righteousness (gain virtues) to defeat the curses of ignorance, cowardice, and greed to one day master the pathway of holiness (gain sainthood) and receive the blessing of wisdom, courage, and generosity. By traveling each of these four pathways of life, a person can one day hope to become perfect in the eyes of God by dying to his selfishness (death) and being born-again in God's unselfishness (new-life).

The following graphic illustration shows that God's destiny (righteousness) and man's free will (holiness) come together on the pathways of holiness and righteousness to transform man's dead spirit (blood shed) and broken flesh (body broken) into a new creation in Christ Jesus:

Heaven	New Human Spirit/New Human Flesh		**Earth**
(purify old spirit nature)		(transform old fleshly nature)	
Spirit	Christ	Christ	Flesh
(old)	(tomb)	(church)	(new)
\ .	.	.	.
.	.	.	.
.	.	.	.
P	P	P	P
A	A	A	A
T	T	T	T
H	H	H	H
W	W	W	W
A	A	A	A
Y	Y	Y	Y

Christ to Earth	Jesus to Heaven	Jesus Christ to Heaven	Christ Jesus to Earth
God O	Man O	God O	God/Man O
becomes F	becomes F	and F	become F
Man	God	Man	Man/God
D	F	become H	R
E	R	One O	I
S	E	L	G'
T	E	I	H
I		N	T
N	W	E	E
Y	I	S	O
.	L	S	U
.	L	.	S
.	.	.	N
.	.	.	E
.	.	.	S
.	.	.	S

Jesus	Flesh	Spirit	Christ's
(womb)	(old)	(new)	World
(right/wrong)	(good/evil)	(God's/man's wills)	(God's Reality/man's illusion)
K n o w l e d g e	Self-awareness	Consciousness	Sentience
. Worship God	. Praise God	. Thank God	. Set free by God
Physical Life	**Spiritual Life**	**Mystical Life**	**Divine Life**
. Individual Rights	. Social Rights	. Divine Rights	. Ownership Rights
(transfigured body)	(glorified spirit)	(holy soul)	(eternal life)

Marriage Contract - Betrothal		Wedding Supper - Wedding Feast	
. Father God . Jesus - Groom		. 1st Friend - Priests . Family - Angels	
. Bride Price: Heaven . Give Name		. Give Forgiveness . Give New Heart	
. Father Abraham . Church - Bride		. 2nd Friend - Laity . Family - Saints	
. Dowry: Earth . Give Virginity		. Give Repentance . Give New Mind	
1st Cup: *Perfect Man*	2nd Cup: *Holy Church*	3rd Cup: *Righteous World*	4th Cup: *Kingdom*
1st Advent - Think of	2nd Advent - Speak to	3rd Advent - Touch	Final Judgment - Sup With
. Face Lucifer's Test	. Face God's Judgment	. Face Self-Evaluation	. Face Personal Freedom
. God's Truth	. God's Law	. God's Will	. God's Love
. Meaning - Exist	. Purpose - Serve	. Value - Be Happy	. Essence - Love
. Predestined Life	. Called to Eternal Life	. Justified by Sainthood	. Glorified by God
. Given Life	. Given Wisdom	. Given Wealth	. Given Love

This illustration shows that "God wants to become man" and that "man wants to become God" and through Christ, God and man are destined to become one making the God/Man Christ into the new human spirit (blessings) and then the Man/God Jesus becomes the new human flesh (lessons) to make all things perfect in the sight of God. This need for union of the flesh (womb), spirit (tomb), soul (church), and life-force (world) sits at the center of the God/man relationship to rectify the huge disparity (handicap system) between the perfection of God and the imperfection of man. Through this divine union, the whole human race must be taught the meaning of life or existence, the purpose of life or servanthood, the value of life or finding happiness, and the essence of life or to live in God's love.

It is obvious that humanity must first be forced to pass through Lucifer's test of evil sin (sin-nature/endurance) to purify its souls (remove faults) in preparation for entering the divine presence of God and offer God its most heartfelt repentance (worship), prayers (praise), and works (thanksgiving). We see that in this way, God created souls in a system of testing, thereby measuring their free-willed actions (babies) and selfish behavior (teenagers), allowing everyone to become individuals in both spirit (emotions/morals) and in flesh (intellect/ethics). The Lord would test and judge their characters (behavior) using a method for rewarding their goodness (virtues/intercessor) and punishing their evil actions (faults/interpreter) to understand the redeeming value of being measured by God's own divine will. The love of God will truly be expressed when both good (see potential) and evil (see limitations) come to the tribunal of death at the final judgment (balance) of all souls. Through this final judgment, the eternal mysteries of the divine nature of truth reveal one's ability to think for himself (imagination) and to choose either God's good (hardship/lamb) or man's evil (pleasure/goat).

We see expressed here that the deepest emotion of man is his unconditional love, expressed in his freely given self-sacrifice, by understanding a loved one's actions (behavior) being performed through either his need or his want. The Lord is teaching mankind that the responsibility for strong leadership falls on the truly enlightened or those capable of understanding the desires and aspirations of the many (will of the people/vote). In other words, God is saying, "Understand man's primitive nature (baby) and be compassionate by helping to guide him (knowing the way) to a true place of human prosperity and divinely inspired eternal freedom (peace/joy/happiness)."

The freedom God offers is one's liberty from cruel self-ambition that leads to endless toil (fool's errands) and meaningless indulgences (hedonism) of the flesh, when instead a person can simply think for himself. This state of freedom confounds the human spirit, thereby trapping a sinner (fool) into a sea of worldly hopes and unattainable dreams. This shows us that it is true that the Lord's five dimensions of existence represent both man's hopes and his dreams to be fulfilled as the human race masters the meaning (existence), purpose (service), and value of life (happiness). Yes, we must all travel the four pathways of transformation (Messiah/ Church/damned/demons) to master the essence of life, that is, to find God's love and to establish our own special place within God's divine heart from everlasting to everlasting.

We see that the perfection of man can be experienced through the Holy Mass by comparing each sacred cup (illusion) with each of God's dimensions of existence (reality) to comprehend the union of God and man via the Lord's divine marriage ceremony (name/virginity). In the first Cup is the union of the Two Fathers (physical birth/human son), God and Abraham, as they bring forth the bride price (forgiveness/name) and the dowry (repentance/virginity) to bless the physical nature of man (survival). Secondly, the second Cup is the union of the couple (water baptism/adopted son), Jesus and His Church, as they bring forth the sacred name (wisdom) and the holy virginity (prayer) to bless the spiritual nature of man (truth). Thirdly, the third Cup is the union of the couple's friends (blood crucifixion/blood son), priesthood and laity as they bring forth the birthright (divinity) and inheritance (humanity) to bless the mystical nature of man (love). Fourthly, the fourth Cup is the union of the two families (spirit resurrection/ God's Son), angels, and saints, as they bring forth heaven (salvation) and earth (redemption) to bless the divine nature of man (free choices). Finally, the fifth Cup is the union of fathers/couple/ friends/family (sonship of Christ/elder son) into one kingdom of glory as they bring forth divine freedom (reality) and human thinking (illusion) to bless the godly nature of man (freedom). By comprehending the meaning (existence), purpose (service), and value (happiness) associated with each of the previously described five cups of unity (five dimensions), we can all come to see God's Grand Design for eternal existence on earth, in heaven, and within God's kingdom.

The following tabular information indicates how both the cups of the mass are connected to the dimensions of God to bring unity between God, man, Jesus, Church, priests, laity (good/bad), angels (good/bad), and saints to bring forth a new nature of perfection for one and all:

Connecting the Cups of the Mass
with the Dimensions of God to bring Unity to All
(God, Man, Jesus, Church, priests, laity, angels,
and saints become one in kingdom of life)

Life	1.	**1st Cup** – <u>Physical Dimension</u>: Union of Two Fathers…
(marriage		Knowledge of Life
contract)	•	Physical God – Lord God Almighty: Bride Price = Forgiveness

- Physical Man – Father Abraham (covenant): Dowry = Repentance

(Plan of Perfection for Heaven – Home of Divine Truth: Creative Power)

Babies (betrothal)	2. **2nd Cup** – <u>Spiritual Dimension</u>: Union of the Couple… Self-awareness of Life

- Spiritual God – Jesus Christ (groom): Sacred Name = Wisdom
- Spiritual Man – Holy Church (bride): Holy Virginity = Prayers

(Plan of Creation for Earth – Home of Human Law: All Knowledge)

Land (wedding supper)	3. **3rd Cup** – <u>Mystical Dimension</u>: Union of Personal Friends… Conscious of Life

- Mystical God – Priesthood (best man): Birthright (being saved) = Courage
- Mystical Man – Laity (bridesmaid): Inheritance (saving self) = Works

(Plan of Redemption for Man – Home of Divine/Human Will: All Presence)

Freedom (wedding feast)	4. **4th Cup** – <u>Divine Dimension</u>: Union of Royal Families… Sentience of Life

- Divine God – Angels (groom's side): Heaven (salvation) = Generosity
- Divine Man – Saints (bride's side): Earth (redemption) = Souls

(Plan of Sanctified Life for Saints – Home of God's/Man's Love: All Powerful)

Imagination (grandchildren)	5. **5th Cup** – <u>Godly Dimension</u>: Union of Kingdom of Glory… Thinking for Self

- Godly God – Spirit (groom's nature): Sons (expectations) = Freedom
- Godly Man – Flesh (bride's nature): Daughters (hopes) = Thinking

(Plan of Eternity for Kingdom – Home of Man/God Freedom: All Changing)

This illustration shows that God is using a plan of perfection to bring forth His blessing of life for His entire creation to experience the power of knowing that can be sealed in the Lord's marriage contract with man. Secondly, God is using a plan of creation to bring forth His anointing of life for His entire creation to experience the power of awareness that can be sealed in the Lord's betrothal with man. Thirdly, God is using a plan of redemption to bring forth his sanctification of life for His entire creation to experience the power of consciousness that can be sealed in the Lord's wedding supper with man. Fourthly, God is using a plan of sanctified life to bring forth His consecration of life for His entire creation to experience the power of sentience (thinking) that can be sealed in the Lord's wedding feast with man. Finally, God is using a plan of eternity to bring forth His divinity of life for His entire creation to experience the power of thinking for itself that can be sealed in the Lord's coming grandchildren as the eternal future of man. Via this series of stages of life, the God/man relationship will be established to bring forth a Holy Church (worship), sacred government (praise), and divine home (thanksgiving). Now, we see that the life-experience is all about the forces of unity to bring forth God and man (fathers/physical), Jesus and His Church (couple/spiritual), priests and sinners (friends/mystical), as well as angels and saints (family/divine) into one kingdom of glory (people/Godly). In this depiction, we see that through the death of God, only one man can see God's truth (remove faults), while through the death of man, all men can hear God's law (gain virtues).

The Lord is telling us here that to see, hear, and speak to God, a person must first grow-up (mandatory) and then mature (optional) into righteous, holy, and perfect sons of God, who will bow to God's will and serve His kingdom with honor and respect. This need to become closer and closer to God drives the entire kingdom of God as everyone wants to learn God's lessons of life (given knowledge) and then to be blessed by God's generous heart (given life). Through the Lord's bonus rewards program, a born-again Christian can earn his own adoption, then become a blood son, as he strives to one day become a spirit son of God worthy of God's greatest blessings as a divine son. This means that an adopted son (world) will venerate his Creator for his gift of Earth as he is taught to survive in a harsh and barren world of sin, evil, and death. Secondly, in becoming a blood son (church), one must adore his Creator God for His gift of Heaven as he is taught God's truths in a new world of repentance, prayers, and works. Thirdly, in becoming a spirit son (Christ-like), one must exalt his Creator God for His gift of a beautiful Kingdom as he is taught to love God's creation through his righteous, holy, and perfect nature of divine fairness. Finally, in becoming a divine son (God-like), one must devoutly serve his Creator God for His gift of divinity as he is taught to make valid choices through his kingship, priesthood, and sonship of God. Through these four sons of God, Earth (soldier-of-the-light), Heaven (living prayer), Kingdom (savior of life), and God's divinity (sonship of God) can be united into one truth, one law, one will, and one love of God.

The following tabular information indicates that God is calling lost humanity to become His son at four levels of divine union: 1) adopted son – first level: water birth (physical), 2) blood son – second level: blood birth (spiritual), 3) spirit son – third level: spirit birth (mystical), and 4) divine son – fourth level: divine birth (divine):

Adopted Son, Blood Son, Spirit Son, and Divine Son via
Baptism, Crucifixion, Resurrection, and Transfiguration
(receive title deed to earth, heaven, kingdom,
and divinity by taking God's sonship training)

Mind	1.	**Water Baptism** – <u>Adopted Son</u> (offering)…...Calvary
(life)	•	Ignorance to Righteousness – Blessing of God: Worship (give life)

- Title Deed to Earth – Veneration of God: Learn Survival
- Uniting God's Jews and Man's Gentiles – Hear God's Calling

Heart
(babies)

2. **Blood Crucifixion** – <u>Blood Son</u> (gift)...Tribulation
- Cowardliness to Holiness – Anointing of God: Praise (give wealth)
- Title Deed to Heaven – Adoration of God: Learn Truth
- Uniting God's Angels and Man's Saints – See God's Enlightenment

Soul
(land)

3. **Spirit Resurrection** – <u>Spirit Son</u> (treasure)....... End of World
- Evil to Perfection – Sanctification of God: Thanksgiving (give labors)
- Title Deed to Kingdom – Exaltation of God: Learn Love
- Uniting God's Good Souls and Man's Bad Souls – Feel God's Awakening

Life-force
(God)

4. **Divine Transfiguration** – <u>Divine Son</u> (all)...Final Judgment
- Death to New-life – Consecration of God: Love of God (give all)
- Title Deed to Divinity – Devotion of God: Learn Making Choices
- Unite God's Holy Creations with His Evil Creations – Experience God's Indwelling

This illustration shows that each of us must become four separate people by dividing our mind (life), heart (babies), soul (land), and life-force (God) into physical (earth), spiritual (heaven), mystical (kingdom), and divine sons of God. Through these four sonships, one of God's born-again creations can become a savior of the Earth (hear God's call), a transformer of Heaven (see God's enlightenment), a blessing to the Kingdom (feel God's awakening), and become one with God's divinity (experience God's indwelling). We can now see that Jesus Christ was using His three Advents plus God's judgment to become the four sons of life and convert all God's creation into His new divine nature of peace, joy, happiness, and love. This means that an adopted son is called to master the world system by facing great evil and then proving himself by transforming evil chaos into righteous living. Secondly, a blood son is called to fulfill the Church by becoming a living prayer and then proving himself by transforming angelic slavery into legitimate owners within God's kingdom. Thirdly, a spirit son is called to become Christ-like by becoming a new creation in Christ and then proving himself by bringing all men into the sonship of God to become legitimate owners within God's kingdom. Finally, a divine son is called to become God-like by becoming one with his Creator and then proving himself by assisting God to become a man and master of all he surveys. It should now make sense that it takes divine authority to both run and operate the kingdom of God and the Lord seeks only those hard-working leaders (sons) worthy of His greatest praise and utmost respect. It appears that God has created His sonship charter to bring forth the conversion of stiff-necked Jews, pagan Gentiles, enslaved angels, disorganized saints, weak sons of man, ineffective sons of God, the hopelessly damned, and finally, the cursed demons to restore all that were lost back to their original state through the sonship of Christ.

We have been constantly told that the three advents of Christ (sonship charter) have been scheduled in such a way as to allow God to turn on the light of truth for the Church (see God/candlelight), then the government (hear God/sunlight), and finally, the home (speak to God/Shekinah glory) over a three thousand-year period of conversion. To comprehend this "Light of the World" concept, we must recall that the Bible tells us that from the time of the Jewish captivity to the coming of the Messiah is precisely 483 years, leaving seven years (great tribulation) to reach the required 490 years for a perfect forgiveness (pardon Lamech). Note that this same seven-year period existed between the age of Christ, when He died at thirty-three years old, and the normal number of years required for one human repentance is forty years of retribution. This implies that one divine man is willing to suffer thirty-three years of life and then force the rest of humanity to suffer only seven years to bring the light of redemption to all men. This means that it takes both the death of God (Calvary/light of heaven) and the death of man (tribulation/light of earth) to conquer sin (sin-nature), evil (worldly temptations), and death (demonic possession).

Note that Christ was three hours on the cross (spirit), then three days in the tomb (flesh) to manifest the death of God (Calvary) in the spirit. Secondly, mankind will be three and one-half years in spiritual chastisement (God's death/take-sins) and then enter a second three and a half year physical chastisement (man's death/give divinity) to bring forth the light of the world and free the Earth from its darkness (thief in the night). Finally, we see both God and man spending three thousand years from the Lord's First Advent until His third Advent, striving to conquer the intellectual (mind), emotional (heart), and instinctive (soul) darkness to set the kingdom free from sin, evil, and death forever. Through these three divine trials, God, man and the kingdom itself will face death and conquer it to bring forth a bright light on Earth, in Heaven, and throughout the Kingdom of peace (forgiveness), joy (wealth), and happiness (love). We can now see that God alone is the light, be it in truth (nature's sunlight), law (man's candlelight), will (God's Shekinah glory), and/or love (becoming light) as the Lord brings forth the Holy Spirit's light (sunlight), Son of God's light (candlelight), and Eternal Father's light (Shekinah glory light). The idea is to see that this divine light comes forth to light the pathway of destiny (world), the pathway of free will (church), and pathway of perfection (Messiah) so that all men can learn the meaning (existence), purpose (service), and value (happiness) of life.

The following tabular information indicates both the death of God (Calvary) and the death of man (tribulation) as they strive together to bring forth the Light of the World using its Perfect Messiah, Holy Church, and righteous world:

The Death of God and the Death of Man
Bring Forth the Light of the World to One and All
(Messiah kills God, church kills man,
world kills God/man to bring eternal redemption)

God
(reality)

1. **Death of God** – <u>Brings divine light</u>: Free Redemption (spirit).... see God's Truth
   - Son of God's Light – Sunlight: Outer Court = Celestial Court (sin)
   - Transfigured Body – First Gift: Learn Right/Wrong = See Limitations
   - Holy Spirit's Light – Candlelight: Holy Place = Temple Court (evil)

Calvary

   - Glorified Body – Second Gift: Learn Good from Evil = See Potential
   - Eternal Father's Light – Shekinah Glory Light: Holy of Holies = Royal Court (death)
   - Holy Body – Third Gift: Learn God's Will from Man's Will = See Self-Worth

(God becomes man – Christmas Celebration: Slaughter of Innocence = ***Being Saved/Calvary***)

Man
(illusion)

2. **Death of Man** – <u>Brings Human Light:</u> Earned Salvation (flesh)...............Hear God's Law
   - World's Light – Light of Earth: Man's Wisdom = Government (Fight Ignorance)
   - Title Deed to the Earth – First Gift: Forgiveness = Peace of Mind (sonship)
   - Church's Light – Light of Heaven: Man's Courage = Church (fight cowardice)

Tribulation
(son of man)

   - Title Deed to Heaven – Second Gift: Wealth = Joy of the Heart
   - Messiah's Light – Light of Kingdom: Man's Generosity = Home (fight greed)
   - Title Deed to Kingdom – Third Gift: Love = Happiness of the Soul (Son of God)

(Man becomes God – Easter Celebration: Slaughter of Maturity = ***Saving Self/Tribulation***)

This illustration shows that the death of God (Calvary/passion week) and the death of man (Tribulation/seven years) culminate in the death of God's creation at the end of time (heavenly week/seven thousand years). This triune death unites God's divine truth (see limitations) or growing ethical behavior with God's divine law (see potential) or mature moral behavior to bring eternal order to one and all. Through these two concepts of truth and law, a person can find the divine will of God, which will bring forth all men out of the darkness of sin, evil, and death. We see in this teaching that the Lord God Almighty is bringing three temples (natures/priest), three thrones (persons/king), and finally, three tables or palaces (Trinity/Son) onto the Earth to manifest His three natures, three persons, and His trinity in the form of one God (life/divine rights), one people (bodies/social rights), and one kingdom (land/individual rights).

We see that through the death of God, we have the slaughter of innocence (see limitations) causing a person to be saved by God (rebirth); while through the death of man, we have the slaughter of maturity (see potential) forcing a person to save himself (resurrection). This means that God is fighting sin (sin-nature), evil (worldly temptations), and death (demonic forces); while man is fighting ignorance (intellect), cowardice (feelings), and greed (instincts) to find God's door to eternal freedom. It can now be seen that the human spirit is purified through God's temple (remove sin); the human flesh is transformed through God's throne (remove evil); and finally, the human soul is converted through God's table/palace (remove death), thereby giving mankind its own new nature (life), new behavior (body), and new lifestyle (kingdom).

We now see that it is important to recognize the conversion forces of life as they bring forth man's new nature of fairness (employee), man's new behavior of morals (manager), and man's new lifestyle of ethics (owner) to ensure a future life of peace, joy, and happiness. In short, we see that babies are fair, teenagers seek ethics, and adults are morally right as the life-experience is all about growing-up and becoming mature in the eyes of God, angels, and men. Unfortunately, the viewpoints of Earth, Heaven, and God's Kingdom are terribly different, causing a massive conflict in one's perception of reality based on being either in a physical (earth), spiritual (heaven), and/or mystical (kingdom) dimension. We see that in this perception of reality on Earth, we are simply God's employees (slaves), doing precisely what we have been told and asking no questions; while in Heaven, we are to become God's managers, both anticipating and laying out the work in an unending struggle to raise more and more babies (citizens/saints/sons) for God's thriving Kingdom. Finally, within God's Kingdom, we are to become owners with the right to think for ourselves and to make appropriate decisions regarding men, angels, and even God Himself. In this way, the human race will be able to eternally grow into a righteous (king), holy (priest), and perfect (son) people, who have become worthy of God's treasures, blessings, and friendship.

The following tabular information indicates that the life-experience centers on obtaining a new nature (earth), new behavior (heaven), and finally, new lifestyle (kingdom) opening the way for a frank and personal relationship with God and His kingdom:

Obtaining a New Nature, New Behavior, and
New Lifestyle to become One with His Loving God
(learn fairness at home, morals in church,
and ethics in court to become perfect before God)

King   1. New Nature – <u>Fairness at Home</u>: Baby...Knowledge
(truth)   •   Earth – Employee (pay check): Duty = Physical Life +

Meaning of Life/To Exist

- Individual Rights – Learn Right from Wrong: Flesh becomes Spirit (all work)
- Remove Ignorance to become Wise – See Limitations (know God)
- Righteous Citizen – Heaven on Earth: Rule Over Celestial Court

Priest
(law)

2. **New Behavior** – Morals in Church: Teenager... Self-awareness

- Heaven – Manager (salary): Responsibility = Spiritual Life + Purpose of Life/To Serve
- Social Rights – Learn Good from Evil: Spirit becomes Soul (all prayer)
- Remove Cowardice to become Courageous – See Potential (love God)
- Holy Saint – Paradise in Heaven: Rule Over Temple Court

Son
(will)

3. **New Lifestyle** – Ethics in Court: Adult...Consciousness

- Kingdom – Owner (property): Authority = Mystical Life + Value of Life/Be Happy
- Divine Rights – Learn God's Will from man's will: Soul becomes life-force (freedom)
- Remove Greed to become Generous – See Self-worth (serve God)
- Son of God – Interior Heaven: Rule Over Royal Court

This illustration shows that individual rights come from learning right from wrong on Earth, thereby removing a child's ignorance to bring him to wisdom (see limitations) so that he can recognize the difference between man's need to work (life) and God's need for prayer (eternal life). Secondly, this shows that social rights come from learning good from evil in Heaven (church), thereby removing a child's cowardice to bring him courage (see potential) so that he can recognize the difference between evangelizing the lost (damned) and creating saints (saved). Finally, this shows that divine rights come from learning God's will from man's will within God's Kingdom, thereby removing a child's greed to bring him to generosity (see self-worth) so that he can recognize the difference between believing in Lucifer's lies and serving God's truths. This means that it all boils down to seeking conversion within one's nature (knowledge), behavior (self-awareness), and lifestyle (consciousness) as a lost soul is transformed from childhood to adulthood in the eyes of God, angels, and men.

The Lord understands we are all lost in an incomprehensible maze (darkness) of infinite choices (divine school of higher learning), hopefully leading to paradise, with a slight detour through sin, evil, and death (basic training). Everyone knows that random chance and the factors of probability (statistically significant) govern natural selection and are controlled by the precise knowledge derived from the big bang theory (infinite energy/god particle) at the beginning of time (eternal). The implication here is that if anyone thinks he can guess at the truths of the cosmos without expert guidance from God, he will find himself (fool) hopelessly lost (frightened) and confused (panicked) in a world of sin, evil, and death. In the end, he will finally give-up and ignore the whole silly idea that somehow a person can make some semblance of rational meaning for his own purpose in life (happiness). This is man's current understanding of God as he looks toward the skies for some mystical answer to explain the mystery of creation that can logically explain it all in a way that fits his personal experiences to date.

Fortunately, God perfectly understands the aspirations (hopes) and actions (dreams) of every struggling soul (baby) on earth, especially in that He is the master designer of every life and is the only one who knows why He is doing what He is doing, and the way He is doing it. This knowledge is the driving force guiding the children of God to their ultimate destinies as they pass through God's Grand Design into a world of infinite awareness (self-worth/enlightenment) as it pours out from the Lord's School of Higher Learning (values/value to God). The major point of this concept is that our God is responsible for guiding men to the truth and not the other way around, so no one person is responsible for finding God's elusive truths, unless one is called to the divine awakening of life (student) by God Himself. In this mystical search for the meaning of it all (existence), one must understand that God has many truths and many dimensions (seven), which means that life is simply an individual experience (unique/save self) to be fulfilled by sharing his life-experiences (lessons) with others (save others/learn from them). We now see that all the other religions of the world are in search of God, while Christianity is just the opposite as God is in search of Christians.

The answer to finding God is to be willing to die the five deaths of Jesus Christ as He plunged Himself into the grave, hell, Gehenna, damnation, and finally, oblivion to defeat all the forces of death and then resurrect into new-life. In short, the life-experience is much like one's childhood as a person grows-up in stages from babyhood, to childhood, to adolescence, to teenager, unto adulthood, steadily learning the intricacies of his home (parents), government (job), and his Church (God). Obviously, we see that all people, cultures, societies, and even the world must both grow-up and mature to the point of being able to think for themselves. This need for transformation sits at the center of the God/man relationship so that the Lord God Almighty has designed a system, whereby each child of God must defeat his own fears, the pains of the world, and finally the five deaths of evil (God's curse). One might ask, just where have these five deaths come from in the first place? The answer is they all came from the Garden of Eden based on the curses of Eve, Adam, the serpent, God, and nature as they all failed to bring divine perfection out of the first man of creation. This means that Mother Eve was cursed into a painful grave; Father Adam was cursed into the hot barren lands of hell; the serpent was cursed into death-filled Gehenna; God was cursed into damnation; and nature was cursed into oblivion forever.

We now see that the children of Adam and Eve are called to defeat the curses of God by facing Lucifer's test, God's judgment, their own self-evaluation, adult freedom, and thinking for themselves. Through man's great courage, the human race can overcome ignorance, cowardice, greed, selfishness, and hatred to gain God's blessing of wisdom, courage, generosity, unselfishness, and loving all things. It is now clear that Eve was cursed with the grave so that she could be rewarded with a new mind (wisdom); then Adam was cursed with hell so that he could be rewarded with a new heart (courage); the serpent was cursed with Gehenna so that mankind could be rewarded with a new soul (generosity); God was cursed with damnation so that mankind could be rewarded with a new life-force (unselfishness); and finally, nature was cursed with oblivion so that mankind could be rewarded with a new nature (love). Yes! Through a complete transformation of the human earthly existence, God, angels, and men can become one in truth, thereby sharing one intellect, emotions, instincts, natural order, and divine order together.

The following tabular information indicates that the life-experience is comprised of five levels of death as each Christian must defeat the grave, hell, Gehenna, damnation, and oblivion to be set free:

All Christians must Conquer the Grave, Hell, Gehenna, Damnation, and Oblivion to be Set Free
(defeating death agony, hopelessness, separation to
resurrect so God can become a man on Earth)

Flesh
1. **1st Death** – Grave: Learn God's Right/Man's Wrong = Righteousness... Knowledge
   - Physical Death Agony – Mastering the Earth: Righteous Citizen
   - Baby Faces Lucifer's Test – Remove Ignorance to Get Wisdom
   - God Cursed Eve with the Grave – Rewarded with a New Mind

Spirit
2. **2nd Death** – Hell: Learn God's Good/Man's Evil = Holiness.... Self-awareness
   - Spiritual Hopelessness – Mastering Heaven: Holy Saint
   - Teenager Faces God's Judgment – Remove Cowardice to Get Courage
   - God Cursed Adam into Hell – Rewarded with a New Heart

Soul
3. **3rd Death** – Gehenna: Learn God's Will/Man's Will = Perfection... Consciousness
   - Mystical Separation – Mastering Kingdom: Perfect Son
   - Adult Faces Self-evaluation – Remove Greed to Get Generosity
   - God Cursed the Serpent into Gehenna – Rewarded with New Soul

Life-force
4. **4th Death** – Damnation: Learn God's Reality/Man's Illusion = Freedom... Sentience

- Divine Resurrection – Mastering God: Free Man
- Wise Man Faces Thinking for Self – Remove Selfishness to Get Unselfishness
- God Cursed Himself to be Resurrected – Rewarded with New Life-force

Nature   5. **5th Death** – Oblivion: Learn God's Truth/Man's Lie......Thinking

- God becomes Man – Mastering Oneself: Thinking Like God
- Free Man Faces Beatific Vision – Remove Life's mysteries to Get Knowing
- God Cursed Nature to a Fiery Transformation – Rewarded with New Nature

This illustration shows that the human race has been called to fight the war of good and evil with a voracious tenacity so powerful that a tiny speck of dust (Adam) can become a great divine force (Jesus) to destroy all evil. This awesome journey from Nothing to All transforms tiny weak babies into warriors of death (slavery) to become loving parents (freedom) of a New Kingdom of Glory as a reflection of their savior Jesus Christ. In this theme of conversion, we see that a tiny baby must defeat the grave (teenager) to gain the knowledge of life, defeat hell (adult) to gain self-awareness, defeat Gehenna (wise man) to have a good conscience, defeat damnation (free man) to become sentient, and finally, defeat oblivion (Christ-like) to learn to think for himself. At the end of this journey, a small child will have both grown-up and matured to the point of seeing that his life-experience has all been about defeating his ignorant mind (grave), his cowardly heart (hell), his greedy soul (Gehenna), his selfish life-force (damnation), and his evil nature (oblivion) to be set free. Yes! If we master ourselves, we can defeat the grave, hell, Gehenna, damnation, and oblivion and come to meet, know, and serve a glorious God of peace (mind), joy (heart), and happiness (soul). The point is that life is all about facing the challenges of life, then changing them into great adventures, which can be shared with our God so that everyone can have an eternal life of rollicking fun.

Obviously, the job of Jesus Christ is to save the lost fools of the world from violating God's divine justice through their transgressions, sins, and unforgivable sin made against God's ethical, moral, and fair behavior. We can see these violations of divine law as malicious mischief (ethics), misdemeanors (morals), and felonies (fairness) against God's divine justice system (courts), which must be paid in full via one's physical, spiritual, and mystical payments. We can imagine that when Jesus Christ took-on all our sins, He was scourged for our transgressions (malicious mischief), crucified for our sins (misdemeanors), and placed in the tomb for our unforgivable sins (felonies).

The idea is to see that if a person violates God's physical nature (earth), he must pay in labor. If a person violates God's spiritual nature (heaven), he must pay in wealth. And if a person violates God's mystical nature (kingdom), he must pay with his life. We see that these three payments relate to a person offering his own blood (innocent), offering repentant blood (forgiven), and offering enemy's blood (guilty) to pay for the transgressions, sins, and unforgiven sin of ignorant babies, cowardly teenagers, and greedy adults. By offering one's own blood sacrifice to God, he can pay for violating God's thoughts so that the Lord will think of a lost sinner and give him His blessing of righteousness (citizenship). Secondly, by offering repentant blood sacrifice to God, he can pay for violating God's words so that the Lord will speak of a Christian and give him His blessing of holiness (sainthood). Thirdly, by offering enemy's blood sacrifice to God, he can pay for violating God's deeds so that the Lord will sup with a saint and give him His blessing of perfection (sonship).

The idea is that if a person does not pay his sin-debt (fine/damages/retribution), he will be put in chains (excommunicated) for malicious mischief, thrown in prison (outcast) for a misdemeanor, or executed (banished) for a felony. This means that malicious mischief (baby) is the physical rejection of God (earth); a misdemeanor (teenager) is the spiritual rejection of God (heaven); and a felony (adult) is the mystical rejection of God (kingdom). Through a person's physical, spiritual, and mystical behavior, he will apologize to God for his ignorance, cowardice, and greed and offer to make amends by giving his physical labors (thank), spiritual wealth (praise), and mystical life (worship) in payment for all his crimes. We see that a baby's father intercedes for his child by begging God for clemency out of love, in hopes that the Lord will see his suffering and repent from excommunicating his child (scourging) from the temple (book of life). Secondly, a teenager's Messiah intercedes for His devout Christian by begging God for clemency out of mercy, in hopes that the Lord will hear his cry for help and repent from casting out His follower (crucifixion) from His people (lamb's book of life). Finally, an adult court intercedes for its client by begging God for clemency out of justice, in hopes that the Lord will recognize His covenant and repent from banishing this saint (tomb) from the Earth (book of memories).

We see that when the baby is forgiven, he receives God's blessing of righteousness to become a citizen on Earth, worthy of a new body, and God's gift of kingship within the natural order of God. Secondly, when a teenager is forgiven, he receives God's blessing of holiness to become a saint in Heaven, worthy of eternal life, and God's gift of priesthood within the supernatural order of God. Finally, when an adult is forgiven, he receives God's blessing of perfection to become a son of God within the kingdom, worthy of his own royal kingdom, and God's gift of Sonship within the divine order of God. We see that through the natural order of earth, a person can come to know God (brotherhood); via the supernatural order in heaven, he can come to love God (sainthood); and finally, via the divine order within God's Kingdom, he can come to serve God (servanthood).

The following tabular information indicates that there are three levels of divine violations from transgressions (malicious mischief), to sins (misdemeanor), to unforgivable sin (felony), causing a person to be given a ticket (ethics), taken to prison (morals), and/or executed by God:

Violating God's Ethics/Morals/Fairness
is a Crime Against God's Life and His Divine Justice
(ethics is a transgression, morals is sin,
violating fairness is unforgivable before throne of God)

Earth
(truth)

1. **Violate God's Ethics** – <u>Brotherly Transgressions</u>
(Lucifer's Test)...Knowledge

- Venial Sins – Forgive Neighbor: Giving One's Labors on Easter (yearly)
- Malicious Mischief Crime – Face Ticket: Paying Fines = Recompense
- Violating God's Thoughts – Offending God's Mind: God Thinks of Sinner
- Placed in Chains (locks) for Sinfulness – Individual Mistakes

God's
Acquaintance
(challenge)

- <u>Physical Rejection of God</u> – Scourging at Pillar: Excommunicated from Temple
- Offering Own Blood – Innocent Blood: Take-on Sin = Save Ignorant Babies
- Home – Father Intercedes Out of Love: Beg for Clemency (book of life)
- Give God One's Labors – Thank God for His Blessing of Righteousness
- Free Gift of Kingship – *New Body* (righteous citizen on earth)
- Learn God's Right/man's wrong – Master the Meaning of Life: Existence

Good News

- Sin-nature becomes New Self – Individual Rights: See Truth
- Blessed with the Natural Order of God – Know God (redemption)
- Changing Baby Ignorance into Adolescent Wisdom – New Mind
- Seeking One's Identity – Fixed Frame of Reference: Name
- God's Gift of Enlightenment – Jesus' Friendship

Heaven
(law)

2. **Violate God's Morals** – <u>Divine Sinfulness</u> (God's Judgment)...Self-awareness

- Mortal Sins – Forgiven by God: Giving One's Wealth on Sunday (weekly)
- Misdemeanor Crime – Face Prison: Pay Damages = Compensatory Retribution
- Violating God's Word – Offending God's Heart: God Speaks to Christian

	•	Placed in Prison Cell (locked door) For Evil Acts – Social Crimes
God's Friend (adventures)	•	Spiritual Rejection of God – Crucified on a Cross: Outcast from People
	•	Offer Repentant Blood – Forgiven Blood: Create Saints = Save Cowardly Teenagers
	•	Church – Messiah Intercedes Out of Mercy: Beg for Clemency (lamb's book)
	•	Give God One's Wealth – Praise God for His Blessing of Holiness
	•	Earning Own Priesthood – *Eternal Life* (holy saint in heaven)
Gospel	•	Learn God's Good/man's evil - master the Purpose of Life: Service
Message	•	Worldly Temptations become New Society – Social Rights: See Law
	•	Blessed with Supernatural Order of God – Love God (salvation)
	•	Changing Teenage Cowardice into Adult Courage – New Heart
	•	Seeking One's Character – Relative Focused Existence: Position
	•	God's Gift of Awakening – Christ's Companionship
Kingdom (will)	3.	**Violate God's Fairness** – Unforgiven Sin (Self-evaluation)... Consciousness
	•	Capital Sin – Pay Debt of Retribution: Giving One's Life Daily
	•	Felony Crime – Face Execution: Pay Remorse = Personal Restitution
	•	Violating God's Deeds – Offending God's Soul: God Sups with Saint
	•	Armed Prison Guards to Execute Death Sentence – Divine Sacrilege
God's Adopted Son (fun)	•	Mystical Rejection of God – Cast into Tomb of Death: Banished from Earth
	•	Offering Blood of Enemies - Guilty Blood: Convert Pagans = Save Greedy Adult
	•	Government – Courts Intercede Out of Justice: Beg for Clemency (memories)
	•	Give God One's Life – Worship God for His Blessing of Perfection
	•	Bonus Reward of Sonship – *Royal Kingdom* (perfect son within Kingdom)
	•	Learn God's Will/man's will – Master the Value of Life:

	Happiness
Doctrinal	• Demonic Possession becomes New Divinity – Divine
Truths	Rights: See Will
	• Blessed with the Divine Order of God – Serve God
	(rewards)
	• Changing Adult Greed into Wise Man Generosity –
	New Soul
	• Seeking One's Personality – Perception of Reality: Life
	• God's Gift of Indwelling – Jesus Christ's Oneness

These illustrations show that through God's Earthly creation, the human race is to be taught the **Value of Ethical Behavior** and the meaning of life (existence) so that a child of God can learn God's right from man's wrong. Secondly, via God's Heavenly creation, the human race is to be taught the **Value of Moral Behavior** and the purpose of life (service) so that a child of God can learn God's good from man's evil. Finally, via God's Kingdom of Glory, the human race is to be taught the **Value of Fair Behavior** and the value of life (happiness) so that a child of God can learn God's will from man's will.

We see that the earthly experience centers upon becoming an **Acquaintance of God** (thought of) and facing the challenges of life in the form of Lucifer's tests, where a lost soul must search for its own identity or its fixed frame of reference (name). Secondly, the heavenly experience centers upon becoming a **Friend of God** (spoken to) and facing the adventures of life in the form of God's judgment, where a devout Christian must search for his character or his relative focused existence (position). Finally, the Kingdom experience centers upon becoming an **Adopted Son of God** (sup with) and entering the Lord's rollicking fun of life in the form of His self-evaluation, where a holy saint must search for his personality or his perception of reality (new-life).

In this theme, the Lord God Almighty is changing ignorance into wisdom (mind), cowardice into courage (heart), and greed into generosity by enlightening (good news) His babies, awakening (gospel message) His teenagers, and by indwelling (doctrinal truths) adults with His own holy spirit. This means that God is coming into the human race to give each child of God a **Free Redemption** (good news) in the form of a new body, **Earned Salvation** (gospel message) in the form of eternal life, and **Bonus Rewards** (doctrinal truths) in the form of one's own **Royal Kingdom**.

Chapter 2

God Creates Righteous Citizens, Holy Saints, and Perfect Sons

The essence of human life centers upon knowing precisely what God's Time Machine is all about (existence/service/happiness), based on one's forgiven sin (church), physical healing (world), and eternal redemption (God). This means that God is defined by His natural friendship with man, while man is defined by his supernatural friendship with God. They are then made One in Christ Jesus as God and man learn how to live together. In short, we must all come to realize that man's life-experience has been designed to allow every struggling baby of destiny to learn how to live (need/ intellect/challenge) and how to love (want/emotions/adventure) well. We see that living well is dictated by man's comprehension of a set of sound divine principles (imagination) of good housekeeping (perfection), leading to a person's righteous mind (fair), holy heart (ethical), and perfect soul (moral). The idea here is that the human race must live within God's paradoxical nature of **All** (all is good/spirit) and **Nothing** (all is evil/flesh). This implies that the Earth is Evil because it is owned by Lucifer and Heaven is Good because it is owned by God.

It is out of this concept of "Good and Evil" that God and Lucifer are at war, implying that Lucifer has all the smart, beautiful, rich people, and God has all the dumb, ugly, poor people, thereby giving the demonic world a great handicap advantage over divinity. It is no wonder that God appears to be a contradiction among all the religions of the world as He is forcing His followers to decode (recognize truth) the meaning, purpose, and value of life by mastering God's Word (Torah), His Witness (church), His Prophet (Jesus), and His Messiah (Christ) to understand one's criteria to qualify for the *Redemption of Man*.

To comprehend this war of good and evil, the human race must realize that the spirit world is an advanced civilization with no way of increasing its numbers, without the help of the human race, which must provide an endless supply of babies. This mutual interdependency between the spirit world (supernatural order) and the physical world (natural order) causes God, angels, men, and nature to join together in creating a huge baby farm in the form of our current physical universe (energy/matter). Out of God's baby farm, the mysteries of life will begin to unfold and we will start to comprehend the overall purpose for God's law and Christ's schools as the life. The teachings of Moses miraculously reveal the meaning of it all.

A person might be asked: just why, if God's Prophet Moses was sitting in God's presence upon Mt. Sinai, then why didn't he just ask for forgiveness for himself and for the Jewish people for all time and be done with the whole problem of sacrificial redemption? Obviously, God couldn't forgive anyone, even if He wanted to because He would have to consider the demands of His own divine justice, which legally stated that all violations to the divine countenance must be paid for in full (life/wealth/labor). To comprehend one's fanatical adherence to God's Law and bowing to the demands of divine authority, a person must recognize the importance of the origin of God, which has been manifested in the principles of life itself. We see that in the "Beginning of the beginning," the Lord God Almighty was able to miraculously bring Himself from Nothing to All through His own infinite imagination (will/belief), thereby creating divine destiny (intelligent design) or an unchanging nature (destiny), where **All is in All.**

Through this initial beginning, the entire idea of the existence of life has come and has been manifested through the Lord's desire to face impossible challenges, create great adventures, bring forth the joy of rollicking fun, and finally, establish an eternal lifetime of happiness. It is now clear that the human life-experience is intended to allow an infinite number of human babies to be changed into righteous citizens (flesh), holy saints (spirit), and perfect sons (souls) to fill God's kingdom with many most beloved children. Unfortunately, to get beloved children to grow-up straight and righteous, one's parents must be capable of creating a most special loving home, which is full of wisdom, courage, generosity, and unselfishness. This implies that man's journey from God's destiny to man's free will is a painful ordeal based on a person being called to grow-up and be educated in both the schools of streetwise and formal education to set him free from ignorance, cowardice, greed, and selfishness.

Journeying from Destiny to Free Will
(transforming God's babies from ignorance,
cowardice, greed, and selfishness to perfection)

God is Parent   **Man is Child**
Call to Duty – <u>Baby Phase – Birth to Adolescence</u> (all destiny)
- Baby Fulfills God's Law of Obedience – Change Nature: Human to Divine
- Righteous Citizen – Baby is Worthy of Getting a *New Body*

• *Intelligent Design* – Destiny	• *Natural Selection* – Free Will
• Planning Child's Every Moment	• Child Recognizes Need for Freedom

• Guiding Child's Every Thought	• Child Learns Childhood Lessons
• Testing Child's Tenacity	• Child Faces All his *Challenges*
• Parents Teaching Wisdom	• Child Develops Mind of his Own
• Obeying Parental Law	• Bowing/Doing as One is Told
• Seeing Meaning of Life	• How to Live with Parents

Existence
- Meaning of Life
- Purpose of Life
- Value of Life

Call to Responsibility – <u>Teenage Phase – Teens to Young Adult</u>: (half destiny/half free will)
- Teen Fulfills Man's Faith in God's Love – Wash Away Sins: Sinfulness to Holiness
- Holy Saint – Teen is Worthy of *Eternal Life*

• *God's Grand Design*	• *Man's Random Chance*
• Parents Discipline Sibling	• Teenager Fights for Free Will
• Guide Teen's Formal Education	• Teen Learns Lessons of Maturity
• Test Teen's Fortitude	• Teen Makes Life an *Adventure*
• Parents Teach Courage	• Teen Develops Heart of Gold
• Obey Civil Laws	• Respect Legal Authority
• See Purpose of Life	• How to Live with Oneself

Service
- Obey Parental Control
- Obey Civil Laws
- Obey Divine Laws

Call to Authority – <u>Adult Phase – Adult to Wise Man</u>: (all free will)
- Adult Fulfills God/Man Knowing – Thinks for Oneself: Nothing to All
- Perfect Son – Adult is Worthy of his *Own Kingdom*

• *God's Divine Plan*	• *Man's Statistical Significance*
• Parents Befriend Son/Daughter	• Adult Masters his Own Free Will
• Guide Adult into Society	• Adult Learns Lessons of Life
• Test Adult's Character	• Adult Sees Life-experience as *Fun*

- Parents Demonstrate Generosity
- Obey Divine Laws
- See Value of Life

- Adult has a Beautiful Soul
- Worships God Almighty
- Learns to Live with God

Happiness
- Live with Parents
- Live with Self
- Live with God

This illustration shows that God's intelligent design (destiny) is operating like a most beloved parent, who begins caring for a new-born by plunging it into a life of destiny with every moment, both planned and executed as God desires. Only when a person begins to show some flicker of self-determination does God introduce His blessing of natural selection (random chance) that leads from total slavery all the way to adult freedom (thinking), liberty (speaking), and finally, independence (doing). We see that this desire for self-determination becomes the driving force of life as each of God's children must demonstrate his undaunted and unstoppable courage in the face of the greatest of challenges to prove his belief in personal freedom for one and all. This measure of human tenacity drives God's parental judgment as He prepares the way for a person to journey from babyhood, to teenage maturity, to adulthood, thereby allowing his physical growth (flesh/destiny) and spiritual maturity (spirit/free will) to become one in truth, law, will, and love.

Obviously, the Lord God Almighty is establishing a master intellect through His Intelligent Design, Grand Design, and Divine Plan concepts, thereby demonstrating that He is an All Knowing, All Present, All Powerful, All Changing, and All Creating life-force. The Lord's intent is to transmit these mystical powers of eternal existence to the human race through His Son, Jesus Christ by creating an energy-based (matter) reality known as natural selection, where all existence is governed by random chance (force). In our mind's eye, we can see that God has established both a static state of perfection, known as divinity, to make Himself a supernatural force of destiny and then has created an opposite or corresponding natural force of free will to transfer all God's perfection into His born-again human reality (natural selection).

We see that in this way, the Lord God Almighty is creating a divine school of higher learning, which has the ability to transform people from Spirit Beings to (1) babies, (2) righteous men on Earth, (3) holy saints in Heaven, (4) perfect sons in God's Kingdom, into (5) free men, and finally, as (6) personal friends of God. This journey from divine destiny (babyhood) to human free will (adulthood) sits at the center of God's born-again created existence, thereby offering every child of God a chance to grow-up and mature into an eternal reflection of God through His Son, Jesus Christ (word/witness/prophet/messiah). Note that as a parent, God is using destiny to control every moment of Earthly life, thereby forcing the human race to recognize its need for freedom as it awakens to the reality that its flesh is simply a wild animal, coming from natural selection (big bang), while one's spirit is eternal as it has come in search of a body from God's intelligent design (spirit world).

The job of every parent is to instill a sense of discipline in every teenager so that he will be forced to balance civil obedience between his desires for being free. In this way, one's parents change from cruel masters to beloved friends so that a teen will become an adult who has mastered his own free will. The idea here is for a teenage child of God to bow to God's discipline and master the art of fighting for his own free will as he breaks away from all the forces of life, death, and damnation to be set eternally free. Yes! The life-experience is all about growth and maturity as one's parents guide a child's every thought to learn the meaning of existence (lessons), then comes his teenage formal education, where he learns the meaning of maturity, which allows him to enter society as a productive adult member of the community (lessons of life).

The Lord is telling us that every child's tenacity must be tested to determine his ability to face the challenges of life, then comes the testing of a teenager's fortitude as he enters the adventures of life, and finally, is the testing of an adult's character as he makes everything in life fun. This means that parents are teaching their children wisdom for their children to develop a mind of their own, just as parents teach their teens courage to develop hearts of gold, which lead their siblings to reflect their own generosity and attain a beautiful adult soul. Secondly, parents are teaching their children to obey parental law as they bow, doing what they have been told; then as teens, they obey civil law as they respect legal authority, and finally, as adults, they obey divine law as they worship God with dignity. Finally, parents are teaching their children the meaning of life to learn to live peacefully with their parents, then as teens, they are taught the purpose of life to learn to live with themselves, and lastly, as adults, they come to know the value of life, thereby allowing them to know how to live with God. Yes! It is living with one's parents, oneself, and with God that is important in life so that a baby can master every challenge, teenagers can experience great adventures, and adults can live a long and happy life of rollicking fun.

We can now begin to recognize a mystical pattern based on learning God's ways as He seems to repeat a set of cyclic responses, forcing the natural forces of life to destroy weakness and reward strength. Obviously, through these challenges of life, God, angels, men, and nature have been brought together in support of the Lord's divine (life-force), mystical (soul), spiritual (heart/emotions), and physical (mind/intellect) dimensions of supernatural and natural existence. The point here is that because God manifested Himself in the static state of destiny (intelligent design), He existed as one reality or as a one-dimensional truth, thereby making His law, will, and love one life-force with one nature. Unfortunately, when the Lord decided to change from a static God of destiny into a dynamic creation of free will, suddenly the Lord was divided into three parts based on His original structure of positive, negative, and neutral existence. Obviously, the Lord knew that He would have to compensate for this division by establishing three mystical natures $(+ / - / \underline{+})$ which we now call the Father's mind (intellect/body), the Son's heart (emotion/spirit), and the Spirit's soul (instincts/being). In short, a static God is comprised of intelligent design based on logic, while God's creation is based on the forces of natural selection or the mathematical probability of random chance. The miracle of God comes when both intelligent design (destiny) and natural selection (free will) both manifest identical states of existence as they are basically two sides of the same coin with both reflecting the Will of God.

The following tabular information indicates that the All of God and the Nothing of God's creation is a manifestation of God's destiny (parent) and man's free will (child) as the Lord transforms man's childish illusion into God's adult reality:

Manifestation of the Will of God
(God's Will first becomes intelligent design/all
and then becomes natural selection/nothing)

All – Reality
Lord God Almighty
- Intelligent Design – Order
- Destiny – Static Existence
- One – Positive (+): Father
- Zero – Negative (-): Son
- Blank – Neutral (±): Spirit

Nothing – Illusion
Creation of Life
- Natural Selection – Chaos
- Free Will – Random Chance
- Earth – Body: Righteousness
- Heaven – Spirit: Holiness
- Kingdom – Soul: Perfection

(land of opportunity/Jesus Christ balances all and nothing via rule of law)

This illustration shows that when God created life, divine existence split into two parts (male/female) based on God's spiritual and physical natures, thereby causing God, angels, and men to all be within one shared spirit. This spiritual unity ties the entire creation of God together and opens the door for the existence of physical life on Earth in the form of human bodies within which God, angels, men, and nature can become one. Imagine that God is All (full/male) and that God's creation is Nothing (empty/female) and the Lord needed a way to pump out His divinity from His All state (full) into His new Nothing state (empty) to allow both the spirit beings (angels/men) and the physical beings (man) to become God-like. Obviously, this mystical pump that transfers God's divine nature into God's creation is Jesus Christ as He uses the Lord's Word, life, blood, death, and damnation to pump out all the negative forces and to pump in all the positive forces.

Unfortunately, one of the problems with dividing God's nature was that God's spirit became evil (male) and His flesh became holy (female); and then, the strong evil spirit dominated the weak holy flesh, thereby making them both evil causing Jesus Christ to have to purify God, angels, men, and nature all over again. This means that God's spiritual nature had received all of the superior attributes (male) of the divine nature, while God's physical nature had received all the weak, kind, and humble attributes (female) of God's divine nature. This male (strong) versus female (weak) relationship has caused male dominance, thereby creating a basic culture of raw survival of the fittest and causing society to always gravitate toward people and institutions that can provide for themselves (self-reliance). Note that Jesus Christ comes on the scene preaching and teaching the survival of both the humble and the contrite souls as they will be the ones to inherit the Earth and they will be the ones who become worthy of new bodies and eternal lives. This means that when God brings forth His new creation, His spirit nature becomes an adult male (strong/Easter), while His physical nature becomes a female baby (weak/Christmas), thereby automatically causing the Earth to become subordinate to Heaven. Now when God adds His blessing of free will, suddenly there is no law, other than the survival of the fittest, thereby causing every man to be for himself so the weak are quickly destroyed by the strong as armies come to rule the world.

Dominating Adult Spirit (male)	**Weak Baby Flesh** (female)
1. Omnipotent – All Powerful: Strong Body	1. Powerless
2. Omnipresent – All Present: Owns Everything	2. Lost
3. Omniscient – All Knowing: Wise Mind	3. Ignorant
4. Omnifarious – All Changing: Flexible Heart	4. Motionless
5. Omnific – All Creative: Imaginative Soul (owning eternal life)	5. No Imagination (owning transfigured bodies)

This illustration allows us to see that the rule of law puts everything in its proper balance, thereby creating a proper respect for individual, social, and divine rights as they reflect the truth, law, will, and love of God Himself. In other words, both God's intelligent design and His natural selection creative systems must be blended into a single system of life based on the priesthood (angels), kingship (men), and Sonship (God) of God's Son, the Lord Jesus Christ. We see that this balancing process comes through the correction of having too much power, ownership, wisdom, flexibility, and imagination for one group and not enough strength for the other group. The implication here is that God has intentionally created a bottom of life, where everyone must start with nothing (naked/poor) and then strive to become all he can be by having equal opportunity under the law of God. Now it becomes clear that Jesus Christ represents this eternal land of opportunity as He promises to bring rebirth to God, angels, men, and nature by both purifying (winepress) their spirits and transforming (crucible) their flesh into new born-again creations. We might wonder, just how did this spirit and flesh war break out in the first place? The answer is that for God to create a top (strong/male) and bottom (weak/female) for His Heavenly and Earthly creations, He made the spirit world invincible with absolutely no worries forever and then left the Earth with nothing but a dying world of hopelessness. We see that this hopeless state of affairs causes a tremendous conflict within the spirit world at the beginning of time, when the astral plane spirit nature was asked to choose, between either being angels or human, implying having a choice between God's easy road (all) or man's hard road (nothing).

**Learning the Harsh Lessons of Life: Choosing either
God's Road or Man's Road to Reach Eternal Glory**
(God tricks the Spirit World into believing a lie
and now every spirit must become human)

1st Choice	1.	**God Offers Eternal Slavery** – Painless/Happy Life: Blessed with *Eternal Life*
		• Easy Road – Do as You're Told: Stay a Tiny Baby Forever (servanthood)
		• Spirit World is Not Told of Coming of Christ – It's a No Brainer/Take first Choice
2nd Choice	2.	**God Offers 80 Years of Freedom** – Face Demonic Damnation: Blessed with *New Body*
		• Hard Road – Think for Yourself: Grow-up and Become a Productive Adult (servanthood)
		• Physical World Trusts God to Send Messiah – Willingly Takes an Awesome Chance

This illustration shows that the "Spirit World" initially believed a lie that if it could master God's wisdom, courage, generosity, and unselfishness, it could somehow find eternal peace of mind, joy of the heart, and happiness of the soul in slavery (life in a gilded cage). Obviously, the Lord God Almighty was clearly demonstrating to all the supernatural life-forces that the life-experience is not about power and authority, but it is about becoming *nothing* (empty) through humility and be filled with the new born-again nature of Christ to become *All* (pressed down and overflowing). This means that to transform a person's free will into God's wisdom (mind), courage (heart), generosity (soul), and unselfishness (life-force), he would have to attend each of the Lord's schools on Earth (baby farm/elementary), Heaven (divine school/high school), and Kingdom (sonship training/college). Note that throughout the entire life-experience, we are challenged with choosing between the easy way out or facing the music by mustering our courage to the max and taking that evil rocky road toward death agony, hopelessness, and finally, separation from God Himself.

It is now clear that the entire spirit world is being called to both grow-up and become mature in the presence of God by attending the triune Schools of Christ (earth/heaven/kingdom) so it can become worthy of its own transfigured bodies. Unfortunately, the Lord's three schools have been created by the spirit world itself, which showed no mercy, when developing a growth (flesh) and maturity (spirit) program to effectively educate the human race, adequately enough to meet God face-to-face (beatific vision). Now the irony of life has fallen upon every spirit being as it must now become human at the righteous (citizenship), holy (sainthood), and perfect (sonship) levels of life, thereby making it worthy of righteous bodies, holy eternal lives, and its own perfect kingdoms. In short, this implies that the human, angelic, and divine spirits must fulfill the seven deadly sins of Lucifer and convert them from wicked faults into holy virtues so they can grow into respected physical beings on Earth as well as maturing into respected spiritual beings in Heaven.

The following tabular information indicates that the Lord God Almighty has seven mystical ways to approach each of His children to make contact through his senses, spirit, mind, heart, soul, life-force, and even via his human nature.

Lucifer's Seven Deadly Sins Convert
Ignorant Spirits into Highly Educated Humans
(spirits and flesh must go to the same schools
to receive a God/man dual nature in Christ)

1. **Compulsions** – Feel God's Presence… God Thinks of a Person/Baby – Gluttony to Good Taste
2. **Dreams** – Encounter God's Spirit… God Speaks to a Person/Child – Slothfulness to Honesty
3. **Signs/Wonders** – Mind Listens to God…God Touches a Person/Adolescent – Envy to Charity
4. **Locutions/Telepathy** – Heart Listens to God… God Sups with a Person/Teenager – Lust to True Love
5. **Audible Voice** – Soul Listens to God…God Anoints a Person/Young Adult – Avarice to Good Values
6. **Visions** – Life-force Recognizes God…. God Sanctifies a Person/Adult – Anger to Good Judgment
7. **Apparitions** – Nature Sees its God… God Consecrates a Person/Wise Man – Pride to Humility

This illustration shows that the Earthly experience or one's conception (birth) into life is the starting point for entering the eternal life-experience as no one can travel along Christ's pathway of perfection without being properly educated in God's divine school of higher learning. Obviously, we are being told that Earth will teach God's right from man's wrong; Heaven will teach God's good from man's evil, and finally, God's Kingdom will teach God's will from man's will. Through each of these mystical schools (streetwise/educated), a person will come to meet (thank), know (praise), love (worship), and serve (work for) God, thereby making him a servant, follower, friend, and close companion of God forever. Yes! We are destined to grow-up physically and mature spiritually and journey from man's nothing to God's All, assuming we can make all the right choices when God tries one of His unsuspected tricks as He did on the spirit world, which was convinced that it had figured it all out and was home free. Obviously, in a one-dimensional world, this would normally be a no-brainer as spirits get everything (eternal life) and physical beings (flesh) get nothing (dying bodies), at least until the coming of God's Son, Jesus Christ and suddenly, the first becomes last (All) and the last becomes first (nothing). Recall that the Lord God Almighty came to Moses with His law (stone tablets), which suddenly made the human playing field a little more evenly balanced and equitably fair, thereby totally cancelling out the survival of the fittest concept of life.

This new approach to the weak physical nature began to make the spirit world realize that maybe it had acted a little too hastily as the new transfigured body (challenge

/adventure/fun/happiness) is becoming more valuable than some old mundane spiritual eternal life. Now we can clearly see that God is a con-man, who has trapped all of the spirit world (astral plane) into volunteering to become human so it can go to Christ's elementary, high school, and college to get God's omnipotent power, omnipresent everywhere, omniscient wisdom, omnific creations, and omnifarious transformations. In short, maybe a person better think before he leaps as all that glitters is not gold, and making immature decisions can be very costly in the long run, if he doesn't know what he is doing (amateur). This most costly lesson sits at the center of every life-experience, since God began His little experiment with created existence (spirit/flesh) as He strives to sell the importance of challenge (losing), adventure (trying), fun (winning), and happiness (mastering) to one and all.

Truth	1. **Challenge** – Losing: Elementary School = Ignorance to Wisdom (awakening)…	New Mind
Law	2. **Adventure** – Trying: High School = Cowardice to Courage (growing)…	New Heart
Will	3. **Fun** – Winning: College = Greed to Generosity (maturing)…	New Soul
Love	4. **Happiness** – Master's: Sonship Training (mastering)…	New life-force

This illustration shows that the original spirit world was only looking for peace of mind, joy of the heart, and happiness of the soul so it could take an eternal vacation from all the hardships of life. Yes! If we ask a mountain climber just why he sacrifices his body in attempting such a dangerous climb, he will simply say, "The mountain is there so it must be asking to be conquered by the best of the best climbers and that is me." The point is that the physical, spiritual, and divine life-experiences are there and they are asking to be conquered by the best of the best, and so, Jesus Christ is calling for all who will follow Him to challenge and defeat all the forces of Earth, Heaven, and God's Kingdom and be the master of all they survey.

We can now get a better idea of the big picture as God will put a hook in the water with a most delicious-looking bait and then, just when some big fat fish thinks (spirit world) it can steal that bait, it will be hooked and end up in God's frying pan (hell) of foolish beliefs and foolish actions. It is time to realize that things are not as they appear and that we are playing chess with a very crafty and cunning God, who has more on His mind than just news, weather, and sports. He is trying to tell us that what is impossible today will be child's play tomorrow. Now, overlay God's gift of divine free will and it begins to make sense just why both angels and men have failed to defeat the forces of ignorance, cowardice, greed, and selfishness sufficiently to master both Heaven (reality) and Earth (illusion) and set themselves free.

Obviously, it has been the Lord's job to deceive the forces of evil at every turn by appearing to be as gentle as a dove (humble), while in fact being as cunning as a serpent, implying that things are not as they appear or beware of God's mystical deceptions. Recall that the Lord God Almighty hid His Son in the city of Nazareth by disguising

Him as a poor carpenter's son, thereby confusing Lucifer, who was in search of the coming Messiah and then St. Joseph misled the temple into believing that Jesus was his blood son. We see that all the deceptive techniques used by God were to prevent Lucifer from destroying God's redemptive blessing before it can save the whole human race in just a twinkling of an eye (lightning strike). In short, the heart of God's deceptive strategy centers upon defining the purpose of both the Jewish temple and the Christian Church as they appear to be the redeemers of man, when they in fact are only witnesses unto the coming prophets of God, who educate God's people so they can recognize the Messiah when He comes. Through this divine deception, Lucifer attacks (flood churches with hypocrites) both the Jewish temple and the Christian Church, believing that they are important, when in truth they are only decoys to protect the real prophets as they come in disguise to prepare the way for Jesus Christ (Messiah).

This means that during the Lord's First Advent as a priest on a donkey, Jesus was simply playing the role of a disguised prophet (teacher), who was tasked to prepare the way for the coming resurrected Christ, who would return to save the whole world in a twinkling of an eye. This means that it would take three special events to bring forth the redemption of man: First, the Fall of Adam, then the Lord Jesus Christ's payment for all damages and fines, and finally, the creation of the first perfectly repentant sinner (believe 100 percent in Jesus Christ).

One Man Destroys Life

1. **Fall of Adam** – Plunged into Evil Pit of Death...Cursed with Death
   - 100 percent Belief in Oneself – Converted from Destiny to Free Will
   - Creation of Old Adam – Earthly Life: Natural Order
   - Union of Man and Nature – See Limitations (baby farm)
   - Adam being Saved by Jesus – Create Earthly Baby Farm
   - Establish David's Throne – Praise King by Offering Wealth

One Man Restores Life

2. **Jesus' Payment** – Sinful Damages and Evil Fines Paid... Blessed with New-life
   - 100 percent Belief in God – Creation of Born-again Free Will
   - Creation of New Adam – Heavenly Life: Supernatural Order
   - Union of God and Man – See Potential (divine school)
   - Jesus Saving Himself – Create Heavenly Divine School
   - Establish Aaron's Altar – Worship God by Offering Life

One Man Creates New-life

3. **First Repentant Sinner** – Decodes God's Word Correctly...Resurrection into Sainthood
   - 100 percent Belief in Jesus Christ – first New-born Free-willed Baby
   - Creation of Born-again Adam – Kingdom Life: New World Order
   - Union of Man and Eternal Life: See Self-worth (freedom)
   - Jesus Saving Other Repentant Sinners – Create Kingdom Sonship Training
   - Establish Jesus' Table – Thank Son by Offering One's Labors

This illustration shows that the life-experience is all about creating three unions: Using **life, death,** and **eternal life** to <u>unite man and nature</u> (one/throne); <u>unite God and man</u> (two/altar); and finally, <u>unite man and eternal life</u> (three/table). This means that the Lord God Almighty needed Adam, His Son, and some obscure lost soul to save the world from sin, evil, death, and damnation as just one person would have to believe totally (100 percent) in Jesus Christ sufficiently to decode the Torah (God's Word) and unlock the prison doors of death to set the captives free. Obviously, once the Torah is decoded, it will reveal that Genesis is bringing life into existence, Exodus is bringing people into existence, Leviticus is bringing the Jewish temple into existence, Numbers is bringing David's throne into existence, and finally, Deuteronomy is bringing the Promised Land into existence (God's home).

We see that when the Torah has been properly decoded, it reveals that the spirit world is seeking to take human form through a God/man marriage contract (vows), while the flesh world is seeking to enter eternal life through a man/God bloodline (birth). This meant that the spirit world was trying to break out of its eternal dead-end destiny (formless) by multiplying an infinite number of spirits via the creation of an infinite number of free-willed human babies or born-again resurrected bodies.

This Master Plan would allow the spirit world to both grow and mature spirits forever by inserting a new born-again spirit (Christ) into every new human baby, thereby combining the marriage of God (last supper/spiritual incarnation) with the bloodline of man (Calvary/physical incarnation). The point is to see that God's spiritual creation was limited by life's space/time continuum, thereby forcing the Almighty to unite the time of God with the space of man through the sacrifice of His Son, Jesus (space) Christ (time). Note, that through the Lord's Last Supper, we get Christ's spiritual incarnation as God's Word becomes both bread (man's flesh) and wine (God's spirit) via the God/man marriage contract (sacred vows). Secondly, through the Lord's death on Calvary, we get Jesus' physical incarnation as God's Word becomes both flesh (man) and blood (God) via the God/Man Abrahamic bloodline (baptism). It should now make sense that both the spirit world (destiny) and the flesh world (free will) have needed each other from the beginning as God's spiritual intelligent design meets the Lord's physical natural selection to become One in Christ Jesus.

The following tabular information indicates the spirit world is seeking to take human form (body), while the flesh world is seeking to attain eternal life, thereby uniting the spirit's infinite time (church) with the flesh's infinite space (world):

Spirit Seeks Perfect Body, while Flesh Seeks Eternal Life
(spirit world offers marriage vows to get body,
while flesh world offers bloodline to get life)

1. **Supernatural Spirit World** – <u>Seek a Human Body</u>: Physical Reality.........
   See Potential
   - Offer Eternal Union – Marriage Vows: Give Name (groom gets love)
   - Fulfill Man's Faith in God's Love – Change Nature: Human to

Divine **Church**
- God's Spiritual Intelligent Design – (infinite time) Eternal Destiny
- Spirit Gets a *New Body* – Mystical Body of Christ
- Last Supper – Spiritual Incarnation: Bread/Wine

2. **Human Natural Flesh World** – <u>Seeks Eternal Spirit Life</u>: Spiritual Reality..... See Limitations
   - Offer Eternal Union – Abrahamic Bloodline: Give Virginity (bride gets respect)
   - Fulfill God's Law of Obedience – Wash Away Sins: Sinfulness to Holiness **World**
   - God's Physical Natural Selection – (infinite space) Human Free Will
   - Flesh Gets *Eternal Life* – Communion of Saints
   - Calvary – Physical Incarnation: Flesh/Blood

This illustration shows that the desperate need for the spirit/flesh union is coming out of God's decision to give both His spirit world and His flesh world free will, no matter how painful this blessing would be when both spirit and flesh would try to take over the affairs of God. Yes! The spirit of God and the flesh of man are planning to take over both God's nature and His creation to help Him build a new coming kingdom of glory, based on both the physical and spiritual freedom of mind (wisdom), heart (courage), soul (generosity), and life-force (unselfishness). Unfortunately, to be able to grow-up and to mature sufficiently to run and operate a divine creation of God, one must go to school on Earth (elementary), in Heaven (high school), within God's Kingdom (college), and then within God Himself (training). We see that through this massive educational system, all of the new bodies and new spirits will be properly educated in both academics and streetwise knowledge to prepare to take over God's powers and authority to fulfill God's will everywhere.

Through the power and authority of God's Word (Torah), the schools of God and the prophets of God (teachers) can come forth to flood the Earth with God's mystical truths, thereby awakening all humanity upon the second coming of Christ. We see that the Jewish people (visible) have been chosen to teach God's Word and to fight evil unto the death to purify man's sinful grave, while the Christian people have been chosen to teach God's truths and to submit their free wills to God's divine will to become invisible to the forces of evil. This means that the job of the world system is to fight evil and sacrifice itself unto the greater physical good, while the job of the church system is to submit its free will to God's divine will and sacrifice itself unto the greater spiritual good (eternal life). The idea here is to see that in reality, the Lord's divine love can only be centered upon Himself (eternal love/time) in absolute divine perfection; while in the illusion, the Lord's divine love is reversed through Jesus Christ and is centered upon others (infinite love/space) in relative divine perfection.

In this theme, we see that the essence of God (shadow) is for Him to become man (take-sin) and the essence of man (substance) is for him to become God (give divinity) so that God and man could become one in truth, law, will, and love. This mystical desire to change positions sits at the center of our human existence as God wants to be set free from perfection (too much) and man wants to be set free from imperfection, and so, they must merge to balance perfection and imperfection (too little) into a new nature of divine/human love. This means that God's spirit (church) is seeking a new body (world), while man's flesh (world) is seeking eternal life (church), implying that God must fight evil (clean dirty world) to purify man's grave, thereby resurrecting man's born-again flesh (space/body). Then man must die to self (submit to church) to purify the Host, thereby changing man's nature from death to eternal life (time). Through this new body and eternal life process, God's spirit and man's flesh shall work together in building a universal kingdom of glory to house the entire creation of God (God/angels/men/nature).

We see that these two concepts (body/eternal life) are being taught in God's two directly opposing schools of thought to transform the perfection of God into the imperfection of God to make them saviors of each other. The purpose for having these two directly opposing schools of thought actually centers upon the need to establish a set of interchangeable viewpoints (spirit/flesh), thereby allowing every created being to come to his full potential no matter how unique his human nature might be as dictated by some abstract norm. This means that God's divine nature is without change, thereby making Him into infinite destiny or unlimited perfection to the point of fulfilling His own incomprehensible paradox by being All and Nothing at the same time. Unfortunately, when the divine nature tries to duplicate itself in a created state of eternal life, suddenly the Lord splits into two opposite natures, one of spirit (strong with no body) and the other of flesh (weak with no life). Now, imagine splitting man's nature into spirit and flesh and finding out that the spirit is pure evil based on its dominant aggression, while the flesh is law-abiding based on its cowardice, thereby making it good by nature and corrupt by environment.

We can now come to realize that our created God, the angelic realm, and even the human spirit are all a manifestation of the All-Knowing nature of God, while the human babies of life (flesh) are ignorant cowards, full of greed, and selfishness. The message here is that the spirit world (+/positive) and the flesh world (-/negative) are being forced to merge into the original nature of God in created form through the combined spirit of Christ (all become nothing) and flesh of Jesus (nothing becomes all) during their death (crucifixion/repentance) and resurrection (born-again/forgiveness) experiences.

In short, we are being told that God knew that when He transformed Himself into a created state, His Holy Spirit (blessing/life) and His evil spirit (curse/death) would automatically split into two parts and then force Him to blend them back into their original state through His Son, Jesus Christ. We call this God's spiritual reality (time) and man's physical illusion (space), which have been manifested in Heaven (spirit) and on the Earth (flesh) based on God's space-time continuum, where the spirit world (reality) needs a body (space) and the flesh world (illusion) needs eternal time. Yes! The Lord God Almighty certainly knew that He would have to refill the minds, hearts, and souls of His newly created life with His own truths, laws, will, and His love before His creation could come to life (growth/maturity) and be a functioning member of divine society. We are being told that God's Son will come to Earth on three separate occasions (advents) to bring forth the spirit's new body (1/priest), the flesh's eternal life (2/king) and the spirit/flesh's own kingdom of glory (3/son).

The following tabular information indicates that the spirit world is seeking a new body (illusion/space), while the flesh world is seeking eternal life (reality/time) so that they can then join to create a new unified kingdom of glory via the three advents of Christ:

Spirit World Seeks a Body, Flesh World Seeks Eternal Life, then both Seek Their Own Kingdom
(spirit wants a physical government, flesh wants a church, and they both want an eternal home)

Priest	1.	**First Advent** – <u>Spirit Gets a Body</u>: Righteous Citizens on Earth...Fixed Frame of Reference
		• Jesus Excommunicated from Temple - Pays for *New Body* (take-sins)
Challenge		• Jesus Fulfills God's Law – Change Nature: Human to Divine **New Mind**
		• Decode God's Word – Put Baby on Path of Perfection
		• Create Earthly Baby Farm – Citizenship of Man (face challenge)
King	2.	**Second Advent** - <u>Flesh Gets Eternal Life</u>: Holy Saint in Heaven...... Relative Focused Existence
		• Jesus an Outcast from His People – Pays for *Eternal Life* (give divinity)
Adventure		• Christ Fulfills Man's Faith in God's Love – Wash Away Sins: Sinful to Holy **New Heart**
		• Teach God's Truths – Guide Teenager Along Path of Perfection
		• Create Heavenly Divine School – Sainthood of God (have adventures)
Son	3.	**Third Advent** – <u>Spirit/Flesh Get Own Kingdom</u>: Perfect Son within Kingdom... Perception of Reality
		• Jesus is Banished from Earth – Pay for Everyone's Kingdom (become life)
Fun		• Jesus Christ Knows Truth – Thinking for Oneself: Slave to Free **New Soul**
		• Redeem Lost Souls – Give Out Bonus Rewards to Born-again Sons
		• Create Kingdom Sonship Life – Sons of God/Man (rollicking fun)

This illustration shows that Jesus Christ must be sacrificed three times: once as a priest, then as a king, and finally, as the Son of God to pay for the creation's new body, eternal life, and then its universal kingdom of glory. Through these three advents, the Lord will decode God's Word (knowledge), teach God's truths (awakening), and finally, redeem the whole world (transformation) to put back together the broken nature of God so that the body, spirit, and soul will be one creation in Christ Jesus (born-again). We see that the mystical purpose of this new nature is to bring forth God's new divine school of higher learning, which will teach righteousness to Earth (right/wrong), holiness to Heaven (good/evil), perfection to the kingdom (God's Will/man's will), and finally, teach God the value of freedom based on chaos. Out of this most profound school, the Lord God Almighty will bring forth His earthly baby farm (citizenship), heavenly divine school (sainthood), kingdom sonship training (sonship), and finally, His man for all seasons who will be forever free (free man/thinking). Yes! The life-experience is all about learning to think for oneself based on mastering Earth (challenge flesh), Heaven (adventure for spirit), one's Kingdom (fun for soul), and finally, God Himself (joy for life-force) and bring forth a crescendo of peace, joy, and happiness to one and all (the Father will dance). Through this growth and maturity system, the Lord God Almighty will be able to bring forth His righteous (flesh/human), holy (spirit/angelic), and perfect (soul/divine) men in a never-ending flow of most beloved children to fill His house with human, angelic, and divine love.

Obviously, the Lord is trying to fill His kingdom with priests (servants), kings (leaders), and sons (friends) as He counts them: yearly at Easter time (count priests) to measure man's offering of labor; weekly on the Lord's Day (count kings) to measure man's offering of wealth; and finally, daily at the hour of offering (count sons) to measure man's offering of life. The point is that Jesus Christ had thought of every possible extreme case, no matter how bizarre, when He created His divine school of higher learning, ensuring that every soul would be capable of graduation either through God's divine justice (pass/fail), where God forgives man (saved by repentance) or through His divine mercy (handicap), where man forgives God (saved by forgiveness). The first school is to be offered by Earth, where a dedicated chosen soul might strive to achieve a mystical seat (holy) and holy crown (holy) in the Celestial Court of God, in honor of the throne of God. This organization is comprised of some 120 seats of glory, representing the first-born sonship charter of divine blood (flesh) sacrificed upon the hill (Calvary) of fear (ignorance), pain (cowardice), and death (greed). This mystical charter is tasked to bring forth a single holy nation to be governed by the will of the people (vote) in honor of Jesus' blood of purification to bring forth a New World Order. This desire to be free is to symbolize the birth of a new order of born-again soldiers-of-the-light (faults), who are brought forth to manifest God's divine truth (absolute/prophet) upon the Earth. The second school is to be offered by Heaven, where a dedicated free-willed soul might strive to achieve a mystical seat (sacred) and holy crown (sacred) in the Holy of Holies of God in honor of the throne/altar/table of God. This organization is comprised of seventy-one seats of glory representing the last-born sonship charter of divine death (spirit) sacrificed upon the hill (Calvary) of fear (ignorance), pain (cowardice), and death (greed). This mystical charter is tasked to bring forth a holy mankind to be governed by the divine will of God in honor of Christ's death of redemption to symbolize the birth of a new order of born-again babies.

The idea here is that as both the world and the church sacrifice themselves into the hands of Lucifer, then the Lord will mystically redeem them from hell in order to create His invisible army of saints, who will flood the Earth with holy warriors of glory. Now we can correlate the need for Jesus to take-sin and recognize why the Son of man must repent for all men. In contrast, we see Christ gives-up His divinity, thereby allowing us to see why the Son of God must forgive all repentant sinners. Note that Jesus repents for us, and then Christ forgives all who repent, implying that all flesh (world/purify grave) is given free redemption, while all spirit (church/purify host) must earn its own salvation by surrendering one's free will to God's divine will.

Obviously, the Lord is telling us that Jesus is taking our ignorance (sin), while Christ is filling us with wisdom, thereby giving each of God's children a new mind (intelligence) to make us all righteous citizens on Earth (new body). Secondly, we see that Jesus is taking our cowardice (evil), while Christ is filling us with courage, thereby giving each of God's children a new heart (emotions) to make us all holy saints in Heaven (eternal life). Thirdly, we see that Jesus is taking our greed (death), while Christ is filling us with generosity, thereby giving each of God's children a new soul (instincts) to make us all perfect sons within God's Kingdom (own kingdom). Finally, we see that Jesus is taking our selfishness (damnation), while Christ is filling us with unselfishness, thereby giving each of God's children a new life-force (nature) to make us all free men out on our own (servanthood). It is now clear that the Lord Jesus Christ has come to decode God's Word (Torah), to create a witness unto the truth, to use Himself as the all-knowing prophet or teacher, to resurrect as God's Messiah or savior, and to also manifest himself as the Lord God Almighty on Earth.

The following tabular information indicates once a person has been educated by the prophet, he can then believe in Christ 100 percent as he fulfills God's Law (25 percent), takes vow of personal poverty (50 percent), carries the cross (75 percent) and finally follows Jesus Christ (100 percent) to his death on Mt. Calvary:

Human Salvation Requires Believing 100 Percent in God's Son
(being guided to glory by the hidden witness, prophet, and the messiah)

Belief		1.	**Obey God's Ten Commandments** – <u>Baby</u>	
			<u>Sacrifices his Mind</u>... Give God One's Life	
25%		•	Listen to the ***Witness*** unto the Truth –	
			Church ... Christians bring Spiritual Wisdom	
		•	Jews Obey God's Commandments .... Jews Fight	
			Earthly Ignorance	
		•	Jesus Takes-sin (new mind) .... Man's	
			Repentance	**Righteous Citizen**
		•	Jesus Gives-up Divinity (new intellect)...	
			Man's Forgiveness	• New Body

(fulfill God's law of obedience – change nature:
human to divine = heaven on earth)

Belief	2.	**Sell All and Give to the Poor** – <u>Teenager</u>

<u>Sacrifices his Heart</u>... Give God One's Wealth

25%
- Master Teachings of God's *Prophet* –
Jesus ... Christians Bring Spiritual Courage
- Jews Offer God Sacrificial Lamb ..... Jews Fight Earthly
Cowardice
- Jesus Takes-sin (new heart) .... Man's Repentance   **Holy Saint**
- Christ Gives-up Divinity (new emotions) ...
Man's Forgiveness   • Eternal life

(fulfill Man's faith in God's love – wash away sins:
sinfulness to holiness = paradise in heaven)

Belief	3.	**Pick Up One's Cross of Death** – <u>Adult</u>

<u>Sacrifices his Soul</u>... Give God One's Labors

25%
- *Messiah* Points the Way to God –
Christ ... Christians bring Spiritual Generosity
- Jews Pay Annual Temple Tax ...Jews Fight Earthly Greed
- Jesus Takes-sin (new soul) ...Man's Repentance   **Perfect Son**
- Christ Gives-up Divinity (new instincts)
... Man's Forgiveness   • Own Kingdom

(fulfill Man's knowing – thinking for oneself:
ignorant to wise = God's kingdom of glory)

Belief	4.	**Come Follow Jesus Christ** – <u>Wise Man</u>

<u>Sacrifices his Life-force</u>...Christians bring Spiritual Unselfishness

25%
- Jews Fulfill Dietary Laws ....Jews Fight Earthly Selfishness
- Jesus Takes-sin (new life-force) ...Man's Repentance   **Free Man**
- Christ Gives-up Divinity (lifestyle) ...Man's
Forgiveness   • Freedom

(fulfill own free will - becoming servant
to all: worthless to helpful = fulfilled)

This illustration shows that Lucifer has been tricked by both the Jews and the Christians as they proclaim to the world that the Jews have fulfilled God's law of obedience (change nature) and have become righteous before God (Heaven on Earth/citizens) while the Christians have fulfilled their faith in God's love (wash away sin) to become holy before God (Paradise in Heaven/saints). Unfortunately, both of these foolish claims are a lie because the Jews had to become divinely perfect (perfect son) to fulfill God's law (purify grave), while the Christians had to believe 100 percent to fulfill man's faith (purify host) or obey God's Ten Commandments (25 percent), sell all and give to the poor (50 percent), pick up their cross of death (75 percent) and come follow Jesus

Christ (100 percent). This means that to trick Lucifer, God had to make any and all institutions on Earth a mystical decoy be it a holy family, sacred government, and/or divine religion, thereby allowing Lucifer and his demonic followers to attack, kill, and destroy them all in a voracious feeding frenzy bringing forth a great crescendo of demonic triumph.

Yes! Just when Lucifer is convinced he has won and all God's forces have been destroyed, suddenly, the Lord's invisible witnesses, hidden prophets, and God's Messiah (thief in the night) will appear and save the world in a twinkling of an eye. Imagine the shock on the face of Lucifer when he is told that God has found a way to make holy Christians spiritually invisible and that this new army of invisible saints stands ready to invade death, the grave, and even hell to save all who have been lost.

It is now quite clear that we are all living inside of a giant baby farm (be perfect) where through the lessons of life (grave), a person can actually become God and then through God's blessings (host), God can become a born-again person. Through learning lessons (remove faults), a person can fulfill man's bloodline of death (obedient flesh/purify grave), while through the blessing of life (gain virtues), a person can fulfill God's marriage vows of life (loving spirit/purify host). Obviously, once a person has passed through both life's lessons (seven/deadly sins) to remove his faults and has been blessed to gain God's virtues, then he can enter the God/man union via his born-again new nature/life to be physically redeemed (new body) and spiritually saved (eternal life).

Yes! The Lord God Almighty has been working diligently to unite God's spirit with man's flesh through the sacrifices of both the Jewish people (offer Moses) and the Christian people (offer St. Paul) via casting themselves into eternal damnation to save a lost and broken humanity. Obviously, this act of absolute sacrifice was fulfilled by the Lord Jesus Christ as He willingly went to Calvary to pay both man's sin-debt (Jesus/remove faults) and man's holy-debt (Christ/gain virtues). Through these two debts, man is revealing that he wants to become God and that God also wants to become man. The Lord did become man in the person of Jesus Christ via the incarnate word. This incarnation of God's spirit into man's flesh implies that man became God when Jesus died, went down to hell, and resurrected after three days to bring new-life (born-again) to one and all. We see that the Lord ascended into Heaven and then sent the Holy Spirit to Earth to teach humanity how to transform (new nature) into becoming friends of God and/or God-like to magnify God's love to a lost and broken people.

We now see that planet Earth is a baby farm and God has created a time machine (universe) to transform babies into a many-splendored journey of adulthood, which reveals that growing-up is mandatory (flesh/world), while maturing is optional (spirit/church). This journey of growth and maturity transforms the seven deadly sins into the seven virtues of God, which ultimately become the blessings of life in the form of brains, beauty, and bounty.

This process of transformation can be achieved only through a dual redemptive process: first via the salvation of the spirit (submission) through the sacrifice of Jesus Christ in his Church, and secondly, via the redemption of the flesh via his resurrection (fight evil/world). This means that Christ's Church is the holy redeemer and the Man's world is the redeemer of the evil flesh. This implies that the job of the Church is to purify one's host (dying to self) to save his spirit (forgiveness); and then the job of the world is to purify one's grave (sacrificing self) to redeem his flesh (repentance). In short, the sacrificial acts of Moses (book of life) and St. Paul (lamb's book of life) were crucial to the success of God's redemptive plan as they are the **prefigurements** of Jesus taking-on all sin (book of life/repentance) and Christ giving-up His divinity (lamb's book of life/forgive) so that all men might be redeemed (free) and/or saved (earned).

Spirit
(people)

1. **Divine Son** – Christ: Good = Offers-up His Divinity
....Create Holy Saints
- Remove Name from the Book of Life – Moses' Sacrifice (Exodus 32:32)
- Transforming the Cowardly Heart into Courage - Born-again Emotions **Pay Holy-debt**
  • Salvation
- Man of Courage – Becoming Holy Saint in Heaven: Earn Eternal Life
- God's Forgiveness – Fulfill Man's Faith in God's Love: Wash Away Sins

(son of God sacrifices physical church
into hands of Lucifer, convincing him he has won)

Flesh
(land)

2. **Human Son** – Jesus: Evil = Offers to Take-on All Sin
.....Save Sinners
- Remove Name from Lamb's Book of Life – St. Paul's Sacrifice (New Testament)
- Transforming the Ignorant Mind into Wisdom – Born-again Intellect **Pay Sin-debt**
  • Redemption
- Man of Wisdom – Becoming Righteous Citizen on Earth: Free New Body
- Man's Repentance – Fulfill God's Law of Obedience: Change Nature

(son of man sacrifices physical world into
hands of Lucifer, convincing him he has won)

This illustration shows that the life-experience centers upon both God's Book of Life (physical life/redeemed) and the Lamb's Book of Life (spiritual life/saved) and both Moses and St. Paul miraculously offered to take their names out of God's eternal blessing (books) so that the Lord would save both the Jews (chosen people) and the Gentiles (Christians). This desire to give one's eternal salvation (remove from book) to save one's people sits at the center of both the lessons of life (save land) and the blessings of life (save people). This means that the Lord God Almighty is using both the Jewish people and Christmas (God forgives man) to save the land (physical life), via Mary's Son's

(Jesus) sacrifice, thereby creating Heaven on Earth (live among men). Secondly, God is using both the Christian people and Easter (man forgives God) to save the people (spiritual life), via God's Son's (Christ) sacrifice, thereby creating Paradise in Heaven (live with God). Obviously, through this redemptive process, the land, people (babies), and life are to be saved and then made one land, one people, and one life in Christ. In this way, the human race can overcome its curses of ignorance, cowardice, greed, and selfishness to attain God's blessing of wisdom, courage, generosity, and unselfishness.

We see that to comprehend God's level of perfection within the human environment, we must recognize that God's spirit (Christ) is being united with man's flesh (Jesus) to bring forth human perfection.

God's Marriage Vows of Life Spirit	Man's Bloodline of Death Flesh
God becomes Us	We become God
God Wants to be Man	Man Wants to be God
• Life Converts God's Nature	• Death Converts Man's Nature
• Christmas – Man Saves God	• Easter – God Saves Man

God/Man's Union via New Born-again Nature

This illustration shows that God must become man (righteous), man must become God (holy), and then God and man must become one (perfect) for Earth to be filled with citizens, Heaven to be filled with saints, and God's Kingdom can then be filled with sons. Obviously, the Lord God Almighty is using both the world and the Church to establish two redemptive programs on Earth to restore God back to life by refilling His broken heart with joy (purified host) and by restoring man's death to new-life by being born-again in Christ's new nature (purified grave). This means that Christmas represents (man saves God) God passing through such a painful life that His heart was crushed and when He died, His joy poured out upon the ground as He witnessed the death of His Son on Mt. Calvary.

This implies that our creator God has been willing to sacrifice both Himself and His Son, simply to get a physical creation (universe) through which He can bring forth an infinite number of babies (dust/stars) in the form of earthly citizens, heavenly saints, and kingdom sons.

It is expected that the job of God's citizens, saints, and sons will be to resurrect all humanity at the end of time and then to miraculously restore all God's joy, thereby bringing God back to life as our human nature (transfigured body) becomes God. In like manner, we see that Easter represents (God saves man) man passing through death, causing his soul to die as his life-force is terminated, thereby plunging him into death agony, hopelessness, and finally, separation from God Himself. This awful experience of crushing death slaughters one's innocence and causes him to recognize his own faults as compared to God's virtues when he sees Lucifer's seven deadly sins up close and personal.

The point here is that each and every child of God must experience Lucifer's seven deadly sins of (1) gluttony, (2) sloth, (3) envy, (4) lust, (5) avarice, (6) anger, and (7) pride, and convert them into God's blessings of good taste, honesty, charity, love, good values, good judgment, and finally, humility. Now, imagine that Lucifer's seven deadly sins are overlaid by God's Word, witness, prophet, Messiah, God Himself, God's door of freedom, and finally, one's moment of truth as a person journeys from nothing to all. This means that God's Word or the Torah (Bible) is comprised of five books that teach the human race to experience five individual institutions, which make up the overall life-experience as defined by mastering (1) life, (2) people, (3) church, (4) government, and (5) one's home.

This means that as a person masters the seven deadly sins, he must pass through five levels of transformation each time, thereby forcing him to master thirty-five individual tests of human endurance to prove he is worthy of all thirty-five virtues of God. Obviously, the human flesh must attain physical fulfillment by growing in Lucifer's thirty-five tests (slaughter of innocence), while the human spirit must attain spiritual fulfillment by maturing in God's thirty-five judgments (resurrection). This means that God is fighting a war of destiny (intelligent design) and free will (natural selection) and He is expecting His chosen people (Jews/Christians) to fight to remove their faults (empty) and then strive to gain God's virtues (fill). We see that in this great war of good and evil, a person must learn how to master God's coded word and then use it to miraculously decode every facet of the life-experience by fully comprehending the Jewish Torah (first five books of Bible).

The following tabular information indicates that the human race must both grow and mature by traveling the Lord's pathway of perfection to the best of his ability (belief) as he is emptied of faults (death) and then filled with God's virtues (new-life):

Physical Fulfillment
(growing via Lucifer's test)
• Innocent Blood – Babies/good
• Guilty Blood – Babies/bad
• Forgiven Blood – Babies/free

Spiritual Fulfillment
(maturing via God's judgment)
• Righteous Citizens on Earth
• Holy Saints in Heaven
• Perfect Sons within God's Kingdom

God's Lessons of Life – Mandatory
(Thirty-five tests/graded from 1 to 100)

God's Blessings of Life – Optional
(Thirty-five judgments/ranked from 1 to 100)

Word
Ignorant Gluttony
• Foolish Baby
• Genesis
• Exodus
• Leviticus
• Numbers
• Deuteronomy
  (personal score)

Good Taste of Wisdom
• Become *Great Chef*
• Life
• People
• Church
• Government
• Home
  (number of honors)

Witness

Cowardly Sloth
- Cowardly Child
- Repentance
- Prayers
- Works
- Saving Souls
- Resurrection

Honest Courage
- Become *Great Soldier*
- Mind
- Heart
- Soul
- Life-force
- Nature

Prophet

Greedy Envy
- Greedy Adolescent
- Reconciliation
- Redemption
- Salvation
- Rewards
- God's Friendship

Charitable Generosity
- Become *Great Kingly Leader*
- Conversion
- Being Saved
- Saving Self
- Saving Others
- Saving God

Messiah

Selfish Lust
- Selfish Teenagers
- Changing
- Purifying
- Transforming
- Becoming
- Creating

Loving Unselfishness
- Become *Great Priest*
- Give-up
- Give Will
- Give Labors
- Give Wealth
- Give Life

God Almighty

Self-promoting Avarice
- Egoistic Young Man
- Mastering Truth
- Mastering Law
- Mastering Will
- Mastering Love
- Mastering Divine Love

Selfless Good Values
- Become *Righteous Citizen*
- Earth
- Heaven
- Kingdom
- Creator God
- Divinity

Door of Freedom

Hateful Anger
- Hateful Adult
- Creating Righteous Citizens
- Creating Holy Saints
- Creating Sons of God
- Creating Free Men
- Creating Servants

Compassionate Good Judgment
- Become *Holy Saint*
- Productive
- Prayerful
- Dutiful
- Imaginative
- Valued Treasure

Moment-of-truth

Self-centered Pride	Humble Servant
• Despicable Wise Man	• Become *Son of God*
• New Intellect	• Seeing
• New Emotions	• Hearing
• New Instincts	• Smelling
• New Lifestyle	• Tasting
• New Person	• Touching
Purify Grave	**Purify Host**
(strive to fight evil)	(fruits of one's labors)

This illustration shows that the word, witness, prophet, Messiah, God, door of freedom, and moment of truth will guide lost souls from death to new-life by teaching them the meaning, purpose, and value of life at thirty-five stages of transformation. We call this great journey the Lord's pathway of perfection as a person must come to believe in the resurrection of Jesus Christ (born-again new-life/new nature) to the point of offering his labors (33 percent), wealth (67 percent) and finally, even his very life (100 percent) to God. This means that each of God's children is going to be tested all the way up and beyond as at the end of it all, a mature soul will be forced to face its moment of truth when it must decide whether to save itself or to join God in bringing in His great harvest of lost souls. Remember what Jesus Christ has taught: we must all wash our brothers' feet as the greatest servants among us will receive God's greatest blessings, implying that everyone is called to defeat his evil pride or face becoming a self-righteous hypocrite before God.

Obviously, the Lord God Almighty implies that as tiny babies, we are trying to manually save ourselves through some silly bucket system of transformation, which is much like a woman who needs water so she sits down to think about the problem. Then after a lot of contemplation, the desperate woman decides that all she needs to do is run to the river and dip her bucket into the water and presto, she has solved all her problems (new bucket industry is born). Unfortunately, the real answers in life center upon rejecting foolish manual thinking and accept the new ideas of automation, where the bucket mentality is changed to the building of a hydroelectric dam, which will bring forth all the living water anyone will ever want. Through this dual-thinking concept, God is showing mankind that His ways are right and true because He is using supernatural automation (blessings) to live, survive, and to have His blessing.

Now, let us imagine that the seven deadly sins represent manual bucket thinking, while God's seven blessings represent supernatural automation. This implies that if a person travels along God's pathway of perfection all the way to his moment of truth (servanthood), he will transform from the manual human system (death) to the automated divine system (life). In short, traveling along God's pathway of perfection and searching for God's hidden guides transform a person from the natural order of things into the supernatural order of God so that he can escape the curses of ignorance (sin-nature), cowardice (worldly temptations), greed (demonic posses-sion), and finally, his own selfishness (God's curses).

1. Finding God's Word – Jewish Torah (Bible)

We see that the first five books (God's Word) of the Bible or the Torah are introducing the human race to the ideas of existence (life), population (people), religion (temple), law (government), and food/clothing/shelter (home). This means that the first Book of Genesis brought forth the existence of life in the form of light energy, which became matter (soil), and then evolved (natural selection) into plants, animals, and finally, men. Then God decided to bring His Son onto the Earth via the holy man of Adam through God's intelligent design. This means that all other life is to be cursed unto oblivion so that God's Son could become master of all He surveys via the flood of Noah, thereby purifying the Earth so it can be born-again in Christ. Secondly, in the Book of Exodus, God revealed His coming chosen people, who had to journey through the desert of death as they strived to reach the Promised Land of New-life to be redeemed from their physical nature and given new spiritual natures (born-again in 1948). Thirdly, in the Book of Leviticus, God revealed His coming sacred temple, which was manifested in the desert as the Mosaic tabernacle, then in Jewish Jerusalem as Solomon's Temple, and finally, in Roman Jerusalem (gentile) as the born-again Herod's Temple (prophet Jesus). Fourthly, in the Book of Numbers, God revealed His coming government of obedience, which was manifested in God's law, thereby giving the Jewish People the Ten Com-mandments (kingship), staff of Aaron (priesthood), and the manna from heaven (sonship) to guide them along God's pathway of perfection.

In modern times, we have witnessed the creation of the born-again State of Is-rael (1948) and the Creation of its 120-seat House of Representatives, known as the Knesset, which is prophesied to become the New World Order of God on Earth (second coming). Finally, in the Book of Deuteronomy, God reveals His coming eternal home, which is to be manifested on Earth via the Lord's New Jerusalem, which will be a supernatural creation, built and presented to God by His angels and saints in gratitude for all God has done. Through the Word of God (institutions), the human race is to learn the meaning of life, meet God's people, master God's temple, fulfill God's government, and finally, experience God's home so that God can deliver His coded message to all men great and small.

2. Understanding God's Witness – Church

We see that God's children must learn the Mosaic Law to enter God's Canon Law (church) as a person journeys along the Lord's pathway of perfection by passing through the physical world (Jews) to enter God's spirit world (Christians) so that he can see the way, truth, and life of Christ, who will lead him to God's prophet. Ob-viously, the job of the witness is to decode the relationships between God (change nature), His temple (wash away sins), and Christ's Church (point to prophet) to guide a lost soul out of certain death (repentance) so it might be saved and brought to new-life (forgiveness).

1. **1st Job to Change One's Nature** – Lord: Human to Divine + Being Saved... Purify Grave (old nature)
   - Jesus Takes All Sin/lessons – Eat Bread of Life: ***Repentance*** (spoken word)
2. **2nd Job to Wash Away Sins** – Master: Sinfulness to Holiness + Save Self... Purify Host (new nature)
   - Christ Gives-up Divinity/blessings – Drink Chalice of Life: ***Forgiveness*** (written word)
3. **3rd Job to Identify the Prophet** – Teacher: Confusion to Awakening......Educate (God/Man nature)
   - Jesus Christ Creates Born-again Nature/awaken – Sup with Lord: ***Freedom*** (incarnate word)

This illustration shows that the Lord changes one's nature, the Master washes away one's sins, and the Teacher educates God's new creation so that it can identify the all-important Prophet of God and prepare itself for the Messiah's gifts of physical redemption (free) and spiritual salvation (earned). Obviously, the **First Witness is Jesus** who takes all sin so that a repentant sinner can eat the bread of life (lessons), while the **Second Witness is Christ** who gives-up His divinity so that a forgiven Christian can drink from the chalice of life (blessings). This means that all sinners must die to self by surrendering their labors, wealth, and their life to God via their faith through grace to be affirmed by works, thereby proving that they believe 100 percent in Christ Jesus so that they will not lose their way and die in the darkness. It is important to note that in the world system of justice, God forgives man and then becomes each of us through our death in the grave, while in the Church system of mercy, man forgives God (Matthew 6:14) and then we become Him through new-life (born-again/host). This means that each of us represents two persons (world/church) with one in a fleshly nature (world) and the other in a spiritual nature (church). This implies that the *flesh is unworthy to enter God's Church so it is transformed at the vestibule door into Christ and then He, alone, is worthy of worshiping God.* Through the witness of God (church), the human race is to experience how to surrender in repentance, become a living prayer, perform good works, save lost souls, and finally, resurrect from the dead.

3. Listening to and Learning the Prophet's Teachings, Traditions
We see that the job of the Prophet (Elijah) is to teach each of God's children the meaning (exist), purpose (servanthood), and value of life (happiness) as he relates to both man's physical existence on Earth (lessons) and God's spiritual eternal life in Heaven (blessing). Obviously, we are being told that the job of the prophet is to effectively explain God's supernatural order (spirit/time) as it relates to man's natural order (flesh/space), implying that God's spirit (blessings) and man's flesh (lessons) are actually two sides of the same coin. This means that the size and shape of our universe can be physically measured by both chemistry (visible) and physics (invisible) via the periodic table of matter; while spiritual existence can only be measured by decoding God's Word into divine reality through the inspirational teachings of God's prophet. Through these

inspirational teachings, a person can travel along God's pathway of perfection until he reaches God's Messiah, the Lord Jesus Christ, who promises to save a lost broken sinner from sin, evil, death, and damnation if he will simply believe in Him. The idea here is that the prophet of God must have all the answers and can make perfect sense out of every facet of earthly, heavenly kingdom and divine life, thereby convincing true Christians that life, death, and resurrection make sense and can be explicitly explained convincingly unto the nth detail of human logic.

The essence of this human logic centers upon God's paradoxical rationale, which can only be understood by dividing the Lord God Almighty into the forces of All (reality) and Nothing (illusion). This division of rational thought creates a contradiction in terms when it comes to explaining the difference between God's spirit (Heaven/reality/blessings) and man's flesh (Earth/illusion/lessons). Thanks to our glorious God, God's Word can be decoded via the traditions (saintly teachings) of Christ's Church, thereby explaining God's paradoxical insanity by using a two-truth method of comprehension. The idea here is that via the Lord's two truths, a person can establish truth, then reverse this truth (flip it), and finally, blend this truth (unity) into a clear explanation of God, angels, men, and nature as they reside in two different dimensions of existence. This reveals that the human race must duplicate its physical existence to find God's dimension of existence (spirit), which can only be done via one's supernatural inspiration, which can only come from the Holy Spirit Himself. A person might ask, "Why would God hide His identity in this manner?" The easy answer can be found in God's war of good (destiny) and evil (free will) with Lucifer, thereby forcing the Almighty to create a special coded system of communication that could only be broken by a true Prophet of God.

Recall that in Acts 9:17–18, a prophet was sent to St. Paul to remove the scales from his blind eyes to see the truth and was brought forth out of the darkness into the new light of Jesus Christ. Yes! The job of the prophet is to remove the scales from the eyes of all blind sinners by teaching them the paradoxical contradictions of life as he takes one truth and then reversing it to create a second truth. In our case, we are taking God's Word, reversing it to create a second spiritual truth, which must then blend the two truths into a third truth, better known as the mystical existence of God or God's Kingdom of Glory (sonship). Through the Prophet of God (hidden in plain sight), the human race is to be reconciled back to God to be eligible for free redemption, then earn its own salvation, thereby becoming worthy of God's bonus rewards and receive God's personal friendship.

4. Following the Messiah: Carry Cross

Now, let's imagine that a person has been educated by the prophet and is now ready to be personally guided by the Messiah along God's pathway of perfection, as he strives to master the fourth leg of his journey by carrying his cross of death from his condemnation to Calvary. We call this Fourth Leg one's moment of redemption as a person comes to realize that he must be saved (free), then save himself (earned), and finally, help save others (bonus rewards). This is much like getting a free gold mine, then digging out the gold, and finally, sharing one's gold with others.

The idea is that if a person is willing to follow Jesus Christ, he will see that the good news is that the flesh gets free redemption (new body), the Gospel message is that the spirit can earn its own salvation (eternal life), and the doctrinal truth is that one's soul can become eligible for God's bonus rewards (own kingdom). Obviously, the Messiah is taking each child of God through a life of sacrifice as he must witness unto the truth (ministry), spread the Good News, and then, face a horrible death on Calvary to be resurrected on the third day. It should now be clear that we have been created by a dual-natured God, who serves both His positive nature (justice) and His negative nature (mercy) equally to transform Himself into either energy (nothing) and/or matter (all) at will. Now, let's divide God's law (changing) and Man's faith (washing) into both God's positive nature (matter) of destiny and His negative nature (energy) of free will so that we can see both God's intelligent design (will/order) and nature's natural selection (random change/chaos).

1. **Fulfill God's Law of Obedience** – <u>Change Nature</u>: Human to Divine......
   Positive Nature/Justice
   - Intelligent Design – Implemented Perfection: Destiny = Save the Land (lessons of life)
   - God's Order/transformation – Creates the Identical End Result as Nature's Chaos
   - Called to Perfection – Child Accepting God: Worthy of New Body (matter/all)
2. **Fulfill Man's Faith in God's Love** – <u>Wash Away Sins</u>: Sinfulness to Holiness.... .Negative Nature/Mercy
   - Natural Selection – Random Chance: Free Will = Save the People (blessings of life)
   - Nature's Chaos/purification – Creates the Identical End Result as God's Order
   - Chosen for Perfection – God Accepts Child: Worthy of Eternal life (energy/nothing)

We are being told that whether life comes from intelligent design (transformation) or natural selection (purification), the end result will be precisely the same because destiny and free will are simply two sides of the same coin or twin natures in God's paradoxical conceptualism. Now, we can see that Mary's Son, Jesus was a human being (man), while God's Son, Christ was a divine being (God) and it was imperative that they be blended into one new God/man creation by passing through life, death, and resurrection. By combining God's nature with man's nature, both Earth and Heaven could become one mystical life-force to bring forth the Lord's new kingdom of glory (one land/people/life) as born-again life, home, government, and church in service to God, angels, men, and nature. The idea here is that in God's positive nature (destiny), man accepts Him (called), while in God's negative nature (free will), God accepts man (chosen). This contradiction in terms sits at the center of the God/man conflict based on who is really in charge of what? The easy answer is that both God and man are sharing all authority with the exception that God is man (Christ/Son of God) and man is God (Jesus/Son of man) so that they are actually one in the same person (same coin) performing the same actions and getting the same results. To explain that paradox, through the Messiah of God (redeemer), the human race is able to master the art of changing the Earth, purifying Heaven, transforming the Kingdom, even becoming God-like as all mankind learns how to change its human nature into God's divine nature.

5. Worshiping God: Give One's Life/Wealth/Labors
We now see that a dutiful soul has obediently followed God's Messiah and has become worthy of reaching the fifth stage of born-again life, where it must face God's judgment by passing through the Lord's divine flame of purification, better known as the Almighty's beatific vision (face of God). We see that this state of perfection before the face of God will determine the specific rank one can expect as he strives to enter God's work-force of dedicated citizens within God's kingdom of glory. To understand this fifth stage of life, a person must imagine that he is traveling from Kansas to Oz with Dorothy/Toto and that he and his house have been caught in a whirlwind of confusion and then suddenly landed in the beautiful Land of Oz. It's the same with traveling from babyhood to adulthood in life as each of us is journeying along the yellow brick road of life in search of the Great Wizard (who will serve) the Lord God Almighty.

Unfortunately, if a person fails to recognize God's Word and then makes the mistake of not learning how to decode Jewish Law (Cabala), he will surely fail because he will never find his way to Christ's Church, which will witness unto God's prophet of knowing. The idea here is that if a person can reach the prophet of knowing, then he will be taught how to think for himself physically, which will allow him to supernaturally recognize the Messiah when He comes to seal His saints. Note that Jesus Christ is planning to come to Earth during three mystical advents, with the first designed to collect those who have fulfilled God's law of obedience (one), the second to collect those who have fulfilled man's faith of love (few), and the third to collect those who have mastered knowing (all).

1. **Jesus' 1st Advent** – <u>Collect Those Who have Fulfilled</u>: God's Law of Obedience... None Qualify
   - Perfect Souls – Only One Qualifies (one): Give Life to Worship God (obedient)
   - Repentance Creates Perfection – Sonship: Worthy of Own Kingdom (bonus rewards)
2. **Christ's 2nd Advent** – <u>Collect Those Who have Fulfilled</u>: Man's Faith of Love... Few Qualify
   - Holy Souls – Only Few Christians Qualify (few): Give Wealth to Praise God (faithful)
   - Prayers Create Holiness – Priesthood: Worthy of Eternal Life (earned salvation)

3. **Jesus Christ's 3rd Advent** – Collect Those Who have Fulfilled: God/Man's Knowing… All Qualify
    *   Righteous Citizens – Everyone Qualifies (all): Give Labors to Thank God (knowing)
    *   Good Works Create Righteousness: Worthy of New Body (free redemption)

This illustration shows that Jesus Christ came to save the human race as if he were: first, the Eternal Father of justice (direct will) and is demanding that everyone repent before Him at the divine level of perfection (pass/fail). Secondly, Jesus Christ is coming to save the human race as if He were the Son of mercy (permissive will) and is asking that His followers pray to God at the sacred level of perfection (graded on a curve/average). Finally, Jesus Christ is coming to save the human race as if He were the Holy Spirit of love (compromised will) and is hoping that mankind might do some good works at the holy level of perfection (graded by handicap/trying). Obviously, through these three visits, the Lord Jesus Christ is able to rank order the entire human race from the most perfect (priceless) to the most imperfect (worthless). Through God Himself (Creator), the human race is to master all things as each of God's children becomes adept at mastering earthly truth, heavenly law, kingdom will, even God's love, and finally, mastering divine love itself.

6. Entering Door of Freedom: Passing through Divine Flame

We now see that a beloved Son of God has become one with his Creator God and has become worthy of reaching the sixth stage of born-again life, where he must face the possibility of having to think for himself as it is now all up to him. At this sixth stage of perfection, a person is being called to take on authority, responsibility, duty, and task as the gravy train of life is over and the real complexities of life are at hand. The question is, has a person learned enough to really make it on his own? Yes! A highly trained child of God has a huge amount of knowledge, but the question is, does he know it all, down to every job and title because even one mistake can be the undoing of all God's hard work if a person fails to control all the forces of life, death, and resurrection? Suddenly, the true meaning of freedom takes on a more profound dimension as a person must consider the most powerful forces of social liberty (balance) and universal independence (fairness) as they call forth the idea of equality for all (equitable competition). The idea is to see that when a person breaks free from one culture, he must take on a new set of relationships based on establishing a new culture, either ruled by him (king/ownership) or served by him (priest/servanthood). Either way, a free man will always be faced with another form of slavery.

1. **King** – Master of All he Surveys: Ownership…… King Owns the People (money)
    *   Responsibilities Create Slavery – Care for One's People: Lifetime of Hard-work
2. **Priest** – Servant to All: Vow of Poverty… People Own the King (votes)
    *   Responsibilities Create Slavery – Care for One's People: Lifetime of Hard-work

Now, we can see that the All-powerful God and the Nothingness of Divinity are destined for one ultimate fate, which is to be either the beloved servant unto everything or an ignored and meaningless servant unto all. Through this paradoxical contradiction, a person believes in and even strives for eternal freedom, yet in truth, when reaching maturity, he automatically creates his own servanthood unto all those who own the environment in which he has matured and mastered all that he surveys. In short, the Lord God Almighty is telling us that if we master the Earth, Heaven, and His Kingdom, then we will automatically become slaves unto ourselves, society, and to God, thereby making freedom a state of mind and not a physical reality. This means that the king (all for one) and the priest (one for all) are actually one and the same thing. They must both bow to the responsibility of service because all life needs a caregiver, just as all caregivers need life (mutual admiration society). We now see that through God's door of freedom (maturity), the human race learns the art of creating righteous citizens on Earth, creating holy saints in Heaven, creating perfect sons within God's kingdom, then creating free men to build their own kingdoms, and finally, helping God (servanthood) bring in His great harvest of souls (infinite number of babies).

7. Choosing to be a Servant unto the Lord: Saving Others

We now see that a person has been set free and is ready to strike out on his own as he has become worthy of reaching the seventh stage of born-again life and has proven himself fully mature in the eyes of God. Unfortunately, if a person is now really mature, he will have become a paradox within himself, thereby causing him to see the benefits associated with every facet of life unto the smallest of details. This means that whether a person is God or just a meaningless slave, he must live by the mystical words of human wisdom which state that every person needs God's gift of serenity to accept the things he cannot change, have the courage to change the things that he can, and finally, have the wisdom to know the difference. Through this sentiment, slavery and freedom become one as the only person in God's creation who can claim to have divine serenity, courage, and wisdom is our Lord Jesus Christ. He alone can become creation's divine free man (free will/church) and human slave (destiny/world) at the same time.

A person might ask, if being both free and slave are actually one and the same thing at the divine level of existence, then what is so important about casting off sin, evil, death, and damnation, only to be plunged back into righteousness, holiness, perfection, and divinity as an eternal slave of God? The answer is that a person's spirit has been set free because he has changed from fighting servanthood to loving servanthood. It becomes mankind's new definition of eternal freedom. By choosing life's treasures (servanthood), the human race is able to become a master at getting a new mind of intellect, getting a new heart of emotion, getting a new soul of instincts, getting a new life-force and lifestyle, and finally, getting a whole new nature to create a new person in Christ Jesus.

The central question here is, just what is God asking us to learn? The answer is everything that God, life, death, damnation, and resurrection have to offer in the form of both energy and matter, thereby forcing the human race to explain just how everything works and why God created it in the first place. Now, it should make sense that human wisdom has to come through the Holy Spirit via a supernatural force, known as the incarnate Word in Christ, which is manifested within each of the Lord's followers based on his depth of belief (33 percent/67 percent/100 percent). We are defining one's 100 percent awakening via thirty-five mystical teachings, coming from seven mystical guides, beginning with believing in God's Torah (word), which will lead a lost soul to God's witness unto the truth (church).

Obviously the witness will point the way to God's prophet, who will point the way to God's Messiah, who will point the way to God Himself, who will point the way to the door out, thereby forcing a person to decide to save himself or go back to save his family, friends, neighbors, and even lost strangers. Yes! God, angels, and saints are all servants unto the natures of truth, law, will, and love, thereby forcing all future babies to bow unto human, angelic, and divine servanthood as they grow and mature into born-again supernatural beings in Christ Jesus. This need to physically grow (righteous citizen) and to spiritually mature (holy saint) in Christ causes a person to seek the Lord's pathway of perfection (Jacob's ladder) and to seek the redeeming Word of God, which will lead a lost soul from death to new-life.

This means that the pathway of perfection is divided into seven separate stages of development with five unique teachings at each level to transform each of God's children from babies, to teenagers, to adults, to wise men, and finally, setting them free. Obviously, everyone desires to be free and execute his own free will as he sees fit. This implies that there is a fine line between man's physical compassion and his radical fanaticism just as there is also a fine line between God's compliance and His total submission. This means that it takes God and man working together to be able to balance every facet of the life-experience to keep from becoming too extreme, either liberal or conservative, but staying perfectly moderate and balanced between the two to maintain order between God's supernatural nature (energy) and man's natural nature (matter).

God's Word/Torah – Obedience
1. Learn Meaning of Life
2. Meet God's People
3. Master God's Temple
4. Fulfill God's Government
5. Experience God's Home

God's Messiah/truth – Righteous
16. Changing the Earth
17. Purifying Heaven
18. Transforming God's Kingdom
19. Becoming God-like
20. Human Nature becomes Divine Nature

God's Witness/church – Faithful
6. Surrender in Repentance
7. Become a Living Prayer
8. Performing Good Works
9. Saving Lost Souls
10. Resurrecting from Death

Lord God Almighty/treasures – Holy
21. Mastering Earthly Truth
22. Mastering Heavenly Law
23. Mastering Kingdom Will
24. Mastering God's Love
25. Mastering Divine Love

God's Prophet/guide – Knowing

11. Reconciling Back to God

12. Getting Free Redemption

13. Earning One's Own Salvation

14. Worthy of God's Bonus Rewards

15. Receiving God's Friendship

God's Door of Freedom/choice –
    Perfect
26. Creating Righteous Citizens
    on Earth
27. Creating Holy Saints in
    Heaven
28. Creating Perfect Sons within
    Kingdom
29. Creating Free Men to Build
    Own Kingdom
30. Helping God bring In His
    Great Harvest of Souls

Man's Moment-of-truth/servanthood – Complete
31. Getting New Mind of Intellect
32. Getting New Heart of Emotion
33. Getting New Soul of Instincts
34. Getting New Life-force of Lifestyle
35. Getting New Nature to Create New Person

This illustration shows that the human race is being called to learn the Torah (temple); master God's doctrinal truths (church); find God's redemptive path (prophet); change from death to new-life (Messiah); comprehend God's truth, law, will (God); then find God's door of freedom (choice) to reach one's final moment of truth (going forward or back).

In this moment of creation, we see the flavor is man (truth) and the temperature is God (law) with the delectability being both God/man (will) as they try to meet at the precise moment when they are both at their very best. We all know that nothing is more rewarding than to have entered into a great contest of world competition and then miraculously win the golden honor of highest achievement with a last-minute Herculean effort of personal tenacity. The same is true for God as He, too, is desperately trying to fulfill His own personal demand for high marks in personal performance and He drives Himself to transform the forces of death into life to make hate into love. This means going all out no matter how much the enormous cost might be in making His own personal sacrifices of time, money, and effort, even if God would have to sacrifice His own Son to save the world.

Yes! We are the chips off the old block and our forefathers have given us the correct directions to follow. All we must do now is keep evolving into the very best (flesh) and most holy (spirit) people we can be, no matter how long that might take. In summary, let's look at how the Lord's knowledge (input), information (process), functions (output), and results (completion) are coming together to form a single divine identity in the light of our human understanding (open mind). The divine light of God (lessons) is only a mystical beacon of truth that reveals the absolute science of human comprehension (see faults) based upon empirical study, combined with divine revelation that becomes each of our own responsibilities.

The point here is that the Lord God Almighty can only prepare the meal (Word) and place it before each of us. Then, we must put in the effort to eat God's holy food (Word) on our own or we will certainly starve to death and fall into Lucifer's pit of stupidity or knowing better and still failing. The purpose of religion is only to give mankind science of the spirit world as it manifests itself into the physical world, thereby giving humanity a dual education (physical lessons/spiritual blessings) in explaining the divine forces of life. This essential education opens the door for a person to Passover from his earthly animal nature (love of self) to the Lord's new heavenly nature (love of others), thereby transforming a person from death to new-life. This means that a born-again soul, which is worthy of Christ's new nature will be miraculously saved by the Lord God Almighty Himself, thereby taking its new glorified soul to heaven to wait the resurrection of one's new transfigured body on judgment day. The whole point here is that God becomes us through Christ's resurrection and we become God on Judgment Day as humanity resurrects from its purified graves. Through this dual redemptive process (spirit/flesh), God and man can become one.

Yes! We are being told that life on Earth converts our flesh into God's nature (divinity), while our death on Earth converts our spirit into man's nature (holiness), thereby allowing us to become worthy of eternal life on both Heaven (sainthood) and Earth (citizenship). We see that a dying soul has been willing to sacrifice its mind, heart, and soul to attain a new body (righteous citizen), eternal life (holy saints), and finally, its own kingdom (perfect son). This means that man's physical program is always free (free gold mine), while God's spiritual program must pay its own way in full (digging out gold). This implies that Jesus (flesh/grave) must save sinners via His hard-work in fighting evil, while Christ (spirit/host) is creating saints via His submission to the divine will of God.

The following tabular information indicates that God's ways (first program) are certainly not man's ways (second program) as the Lord can do everything instantly (invisible), while the human race must move along at glacial speed (visible) as God's day is one thousand man years:

God's Ways are Not Man's Ways, God Performs Instantly and All is Free, Man must Pay in Full
(God gives free gold mines, while man is left
digging out gold and sharing it with others)

Wedding Vows	Bloodline
God's Spiritual Program	**Man's Physical Program**
Divine Destiny – Union by Marriage	Human Free Will – Union via Nature
(digging out gold – Forgiveness)	(free gold mine – Repentance)
Submission	**Fighting Evil**
Man must Earn his Way	God Gives Free Gifts
Church • Gospel Message of Christ	• Good News of Jesus **World**
(holiness) • Earned Salvation	• Free Redemption (change nature)
• God Dies three Earthly Days	• Man Dies three thousand Years
• Punishment is Cast into Hot Flames	• Evil is Cast into Cold Darkness

• Receives Blessing of Grace	• Receives Treasures of Life
• Resurrects in Host	• Resurrects in Grave
• *New Glorified Body*	• *New Transfigured Body*
(1 hour in cool of evening)	(work all day in the hot sun)
——Marriage of Holiness——	——Bloodline of New Nature——

Christian People	Jewish People
Saved by Belief 100%	Saved by Knowing God 100%
All Men can Believe	*Only One Man* can Know the Law

Union of God/Man

God's	Man's
Resurrected	Born-again
Nature	Host
(Christmas)	(Easter)

Union of Man/God

God's	Man's
Dead	Purified
Spirit	Grave
(Last Supper)	(Calvary)

<table>
<tr><td colspan="3" align="center">Bread/Wine</td><td colspan="3" align="center">Flesh/Blood</td></tr>
<tr><td colspan="3" align="center">Life-to-Death</td><td colspan="3" align="center">Death to New-life</td></tr>
<tr><td colspan="3" align="center">Holy Father</td><td colspan="3" align="center">Holy Mother</td></tr>
<tr><td colspan="3" align="center">(Create Heavenly Saints)</td><td colspan="3" align="center">(Create Earthly Citizens)</td></tr>
<tr><td>God's</td><td></td><td>Man's</td><td>Christ's</td><td></td><td>Christian's</td></tr>
<tr><td>Dead</td><td>Saving</td><td>Purified</td><td>Resurrected</td><td>Saving</td><td>Born-again</td></tr>
<tr><td>Spirit</td><td>God</td><td>Grave</td><td>Life</td><td>Man</td><td>Life</td></tr>
<tr><td>(broken heart)</td><td></td><td>(Fighting evil)</td><td>(spirit baptism)</td><td></td><td>(water baptism)</td></tr>
<tr><td colspan="3">Man's Flesh becomes God's Spirit</td><td colspan="3">God's Spirit becomes Man's Flesh</td></tr>
<tr><td colspan="3">• Righteous Man Saves God from Death</td><td colspan="3">• Christ Saves Man from Damnation</td></tr>
<tr><td colspan="3">• God Wants to become Man</td><td colspan="3">• Man wants to become God</td></tr>
<tr><td colspan="3">(get new divine nature)</td><td colspan="3">(get a new holy flesh)</td></tr>
</table>

This illustration shows that there are two redemptive programs being used to transform the human flesh (change to divine) and to also purify the human spirit (make holy) so that a person can become worthy of both Heaven on Earth (flesh/live with man) and Paradise in Heaven (spirit/life with God). This means that the human flesh is being called to fight evil (world) so that a person can purify his own grave (righteous citizenship), while the human spirit is being chosen to surrender (church) so that it can purify its own host (holy sainthood). The idea here is similar to God (Jews) giving a person a free gold mine (good news/belief) as an indication that he has been physically saved from sin, evil, and death. But when Christ comes (Christians), He tells everyone that they must dig out the gold (gospel message/grace) so that they can then save themselves to become worthy of all God's treasures of life (new body/eternal life/kingdom).

We now see the treasures of God come in two forms (physical/spiritual unions): one from the bloodline of Abraham (Jews) and the other from the marriage vows of Jesus Christ (Christians), implying that a person's bloodline can change his nature into divinity (create citizens), while a person's marriage vows can purify his nature into holiness (create saints). Obviously, through a person's new nature and his holiness, he can be united to both the spirit of God (Heaven) and also to the flesh of man (Earth) as he proves he can do small things well, thereby revealing that he is ready to do big things within the kingdom of God.

We see that through this growth and maturity process, the human race can master both God's spiritual and physical redemptive programs via Father Abraham's bloodline (Jews) and via Jesus Christ's marriage vows (Christians). In short, Abraham's bloodline (new nature) or God's law is capable of transforming man's flesh into a new nature via one's blood (wine) and via his flesh (bread), thereby creating a union between God's spirit (bloodline) and man's flesh (grave), which allows God to become man (God/man). Secondly, Jesus Christ's marriage vows (holiness) or man's faith is capable of purifying man's spirit to make it holy via the groom's name (union) and the bride's virginity (union), thereby creating a union between man's flesh (vows) and God's spirit (host), which allows man to become God (man/God).

We see that the great significance of this mystical union is centered upon the coming of God's witness (decode word), prophet (teach truth), and Messiah (save souls) as they are tasked to build three divine schools (Earth/Heaven /Kingdom) within the Kingdom of God. Out of these schools, God's eternal rewards shall be earned and each of God's children can become worthy of attaining God's riches in glory, thereby blessing him with God's gifts, fruits, and treasures. We see that these eternal rewards are coming from God's eternal riches in glory in the form of God's honors, keys, and treasures along with the Lord's Kingdom of Glory, which has been reserved for His most perfect sons. Imagine being in a minefield of imperfection, where a person is ordered to watch his every step as just one false step (sin) might be his last. Now, picture being forced to live a perfect life in the presence of God (all-seeing eye), where being perfect is the norm.

Yes! We are all called to be perfect before the Throne of God, implying that Lucifer has been planning from the beginning to attack and destroy any and all of God's most blessed creatures as a way of defeating his divine enemy's desire for perfection. We see that the Lord God Almighty has been working diligently to defeat Lucifer and his ability to change all that is good into evil, thereby forcing the Lord to protect His redemptive efforts by making all that is visible on Earth into well-disguised decoys. This means that all the Earthly people, all its institutions, its religions, and even nature itself have been intentionally sacrificed by God to trick Lucifer into believing that God's Son's earthly invasion was to come from the visible world through the creation of some silly army of saints. Obviously, this satanic belief has sent Lucifer on an insane rampage to kill anything and everything human just as God intended, thereby allowing the Lord to deploy His invisible redemptive forces without fear from Lucifer and his demons.

The message here is that Jesus represents visible man (physical nature), while God (Christ) represents invisible man (spiritual nature), implying that they are both being used to fight and defeat Lucifer and his forces of evil. Now, let's look at this visible to invisible attack strategy being used by God to trick Lucifer into believing a lie, which seems so real that it has even misled Planet Earth into convincing itself that it has all become perfect in the sight of God. In short, the Lord has trapped Lucifer into finding a needle in a haystack as God's witnesses (decoders), prophets (teachers), and the thief in the night Himself (savior) can move around the Earth by hiding in plain sight. This ability to be effectively disguised in general society gives the Almighty a fair advantage over Lucifer and his demons because they cannot recognize God's citizens, saints, and/or His sons as they openly convert death into new-life without detection from their enemies.

Unfortunately, to make this invisible system work, the Lord has had to sacrifice nature, men, angels, and even Himself to ensure that all in life is to be thoroughly tested unto its level of eternal perfection.

The following tabular information indicates that first, God has initially made seven sacrifices from among His most treasured creations, then secondarily, the Lord has had to sacrifice all that is visible on Earth (people/governments/religions) to trick Lucifer into chasing and attacking mystical shadows (smoke and mirrors).

God's Seven Sacrifices Establish Seven Visible Decoys to be Destroyed by Evil
(visible individuals, families, governments, religions,
false witnesses, false prophets, false Messiahs)

1. **Sacrifice first Sacred Angel**/Lucifer – Eternally Damned.......Cursed with **Gluttony**
   - Sacrifice All Individual Rights – Gluttonous **Slaves** (Hard-work)
   - Protect God's Witnesses – They Decode God's Word...   Reveal Blessing of Good Taste
2. **Sacrifice first Holy Man**/Adam – Cursed with Sin, Evil, and Death...Cursed with **Sloth**
   - Sacrifice All Families – Slothfully **Poor** (poverty)
   - Protect God's Prophets – They Teach God's Truth.....Reveal Blessing of Honesty
3. **Sacrifice first Human Society**/Ancient World – Cursed with Drowning...Cursed with **Envy**
   - Sacrifice All Governments – Envious **Corruption** (lie/cheat/steal)
   - Protect God's Thief in the Night – Seal God's Saints.....   Reveal Blessing of Charity
4. **Sacrifice first Chosen People**/Jews – Cursed with God's Law....Cursed with **Lust**
   - Sacrifice All Religions – Lustful **Superstitions** (evil desires)
   - Protect God's Newly Born-again Babies – Water/Spirit Baptisms... Reveal Blessing of True Love
5. **Sacrifice first Perfect Man**/Christ – Cursed with Man's Faith.... Cursed with **Avarice**
   - Sacrifice False Witnesses – Avarice **Illogical Decoding** (fanatical beliefs)
   - Protect God's Real Witnesses – Decode God's Word...   Reveal Blessing of

Good Values

6. **Sacrifice first Holy Church**/Christians – <u>Cursed with Knowing God</u>.. Cursed with **Anger**
   - Sacrifice False Prophets – Angrily *Taught Lies* (false teachings)
   - Protect God's Real Prophets – Teach God's Word ... Blessing of Good Judgment

7. **Sacrifice 1st Righteous World**/Free Men – <u>Cursed with Free Will</u> ... Cursed with **Pride**
   - Sacrifice False Messiahs – Pridefully *Erroneous Redemptions* (soul-killing beliefs)
   - Protect God Thief in Night (Messiah) – Redeem Soul..... Reveal Blessing of Humility

This illustration shows that God has sacrificed Earth among a sea of fake targets, thereby confusing the evil one as to who is dangerous to him and just who isn't. Secondly, the Lord has sacrificed Adam to use families as decoys so that the Lord can hide His holy family (Jews) on Earth among a sea of families, thereby confusing the evil one as to who is saving families and just who isn't. Thirdly, the Lord has sacrificed first society to use governments as decoys so that the Lord can hide born-again government (Christians) on Earth among a sea of corrupt governments, thereby confusing the evil one as to who is taking over Earth and just who isn't. Fourthly, the Lord has sacrificed the Jewish people to use the world's religions as decoys so that the Lord can hide His true faith (Jews/Christians/Moslems) on Earth among a sea of crazy beliefs, thereby confusing the evil one as to who is really telling the truth and just who isn't. Fifthly, the Lord has sacrificed His own Son (Jesus Christ) to use false witnesses (falsely decode God's word) as decoys so that the Lord can hide His real witnesses (Christians) on Earth among a sea of foolish mystics, thereby confusing the evil one as to who is decoding God's Word correctly and just who isn't. Sixthly, the Lord has sacrificed His Roman Church (host) to use false prophets as decoys so that the Lord can hide His real prophets (Catholics) on Earth, among a sea of strange-looking doomsayers, thereby confusing the evil one as to who is teaching God's truth and just who isn't. Finally, the Lord has sacrificed His righteous world (grave) to use false messiahs as decoys so that the Lord can hide His Redeemer (Jesus Christ) on Earth, among a sea of most believable holy men, thereby confusing the evil one as to who is really redeeming the lost (thief) and just who isn't.

This means that out of these seven decoys the Lord has condemned the human race to face a lifetime of slavery, poverty, corruptions, an ocean of superstitions, a bunch of nonsensical decoded messages from God, plus a landslide of disconnected supernatural teachings, and finally, a host of different methods for getting to heaven (redemption).

Obviously, the Lord God Almighty has left Lucifer a monumental task of sorting out all of these false leads as the evil one must become a great forensic scientist who is capable of determining God's reality (intelligent design) from man's illusion (natural selection). It should now be clear that God never hesitates to sacrifice one of His treasures when it comes to deceiving Lucifer and trapping him into believing a lie, especially when the Lord is constantly flooding the evil one with an ocean of sacrificial decoys. We now see that God's sacrificial system was essential to the overall success of his satanic decoy program to force man's free-willed nature to bow to the overall lessons of life (see faults), which bring forth the blessings of life (gain virtues) as the God/man treasures of life (body/eternal life/kingdom). This means that the Lord God Almighty has created three mystical schools: one on Earth (baby farm), one in Heaven (divine school), and one within His Kingdom (sonship training) to teach the children of God the meaning, purpose, and value of life.

The Lord is teaching us all that the meaning of life is to exist on Earth as righteous citizens of the human race, each called to fight evil unto death with his sword of promise to purify his grave, thereby becoming worthy of resurrection (new body). Secondly, the purpose of life is to serve others in Heaven as a holy saint of the human race, each called to submit his free will to God's divine will through the power of belief (100 percent) to purify his host, thereby becoming worthy of being born-again (eternal life). Finally, the value of life is to find happiness within God's kingdom as a perfect son of God, who has been called to redeem the lost through his ability to think for himself to purify his life, thereby becoming worthy of being set free from sin, evil, and death. This means that the Lord God Almighty has created three mystical schools to teach and educate His babies with the school of witnesses designed to decode God's Word (Torah), the school of prophets to teach God's truths (worship/fight evil), and finally, the school of Messiahs to redeem souls (saving everyone).

1. **Elementary School** – School of Witnesses: Decode God's Word = Torah...Purify Grave (new body)
2. **High School** – School of Prophets: Teach God's Truths = Worship/Fight Evil...Purify Host (eternal life)
3. **College** – School of Messiahs: Redeem Lost Souls = Save Everyone...Purify Life (own kingdom)

This illustration shows that the Lord God Almighty has created an initial creation of natural (flesh) and supernatural (spirits) creatures as mystical decoys to flood Lucifer's reality with nothing but lies, until he is so confused that he will give up in hopeless insanity. This meant that God's righteous citizens, holy saints, and perfect sons would have the necessary skills to decode God's Word, then teach God's truths to others, and finally, strive to redeem the lost souls of the world.

Obviously, the Lord had to create a set of schools to respond to the growth and maturity levels of human development as the babies become witnesses unto God's truth by decoding God's Word; the teenagers become prophets unto God's Law by teaching God's Word; and finally, the adults become Messiahs unto God's will by becoming God's incarnate Word (host). We see that in God's Grand Design, He has established a series of institutions of higher learning to teach the meaning of life (existence), the purpose of life (servanthood), and the value of life (happiness) to set all the captives free. The point here is that God has been forced to change the babies' fixed frame of reference, modify the teenagers' relative focused existence, and alter the adults' perception of reality by distorting both God's reality (spirit) and man's illusion (flesh).

The following tabular information indicates that God has created an earthly baby farm to create righteous citizens (new bodies), a divine school to create holy saints (eternal life), and a sonship training program to create perfect sons of God (own kingdoms):

Baby Farm – Virgin Mary's Little Red School House
(babies become witnesses unto God's truth by decoding God's word)

Meaning of Life – To Exist (honors)

Witness 1. **Elementary School** – Decode God's Word: God Thinks of His Child...Child Awakes

First Class – Learns God's *Right* from Man's *Wrong*......Eyes Open

Second Class – Child Gets Intellect: *New Mind* = Learns Mosaic Law...Mind Opens

Third Class – Separates God's *Decoys* from God's True *Witnesses*..... Imagination

Fourth Class – Removes *Ignorance* and Gains *Wisdom*: Knows Right from Wrong...Ethics Opens

Fifth Class – God's *Throne*: Praises God with Wealth = Places God First... Common Sense

Sixth Class – Transforms from *Immaturity* to *Maturity* – Changes Viewpoint... Identity Opens

Seventh Class – Fulfills Law of Obedience: Changes Nature = *Human* to *Divine*...Values Open

Eighth Class – Be *Righteous Citizen* on Earth: Does Duty/Service to Others...Life Opens

Ninth Class – Teaches *Good News*: Free Redemption for Flesh = Purifies Grave... Future Opens

Tenth Class – Teaches *God's Truths*: Helps to Spread the Word...Knowledge Opens

Eleventh Class – Establishes One's *Fixed Frame of Reference*: Finds the Way... Path Opens

Twelfth Class – Worthy of *Heaven on Earth* – Lives with Man: Settles In...Home Opens

Thirteenth Class – Helps Jesus Christ *Redeem Lost Souls*: Fights Evil... Respect Opens

Fourteenth Class – Learns the *Lessons of Life*: Masters World System ... God's Love Opens

Fifteenth Class – First Graduation: Worthy of *New Body:* God's Friendship... Divine School

(soldier-of-the-light – fights evil: repentance/Jesus takes-sin)

Divine School – Saint Joseph's High School System
(teenagers become prophets unto God's law by teaching God's word)

Purpose of Life – To Serve (keys)

Witness 1. **High School** – <u>Teaches God's Truth</u>: God Speaks to His Son...Teen Listens

First Class – Learns God's *Good* from Man's *Evil*...   Full Attention

Second Class – Teen Gets Emotions: *New Heart* = Learns Canon Law...Heart Opens

Third Class – Separates God's *Decoys* from God's True *Prophets*...   Cunning

Fourth Class – Removes *Cowardice* and Gains *Courage*: Knows Good from Evil...Morals Open

Fifth Class – God's *Altar*: Worship God with Life = Places Christ Second...Good Sense

Sixth Class – Purifies from *Childhood* to *Adulthood*: Changes One's Views... Character

Seventh Class – Fulfill Faith in God's Love: Wash Away Sin = *Sinful to Holy*... Values Change

Eighth Class – Be *Holy Saint* in Heaven: Takes Responsibility/Stands Up...New-life

Ninth Class – Teaches *Gospel Message*: Earns Salvation of Spirit = Purifies Host...Sees Future

Tenth Class – Teaches *God's Laws*: Helps to Explain the Word...Self-awareness

Eleventh Class – Enters *Relative Focused Existence*: Shows the Way...Path Revealed

Twelfth Class – Worthy of *Paradise in Heaven*: Lives with God: Loving Life...Belongs to God

Thirteenth Class – *Redeems/Saves Lost Souls*: Surrenders to God's Will...Honored

Fourteenth Class – *Receives Blessings of Life*: Masters Church System...Love One's God

Fifteenth Class – <u>Second Graduation</u>: Worthy of *Eternal Life*: God's Companionship...Sonship Training

(living prayer of love – submits life: forgiveness/Christ gives divinity)

Sonship Training Program – Jesus Christ's College System

(adults become Messiahs unto God's will by becoming incarnate word)

Value of Life – To be Happy (treasures)

Witness 1. **College** –<u>Teaches God's Will</u>: God Touches His Beloved...   Adult Joins Him

First Class – Learns *God's Will* from *Man's Will*.....   In Sync

Second Class – Adult Gets Instincts: *New Soul* = Learns Divine Law...Soul Opens

Third Class – Separates God's *Decoys* from God's True *Messiah* (thief)... Powerful

Fourth Class – Removes *Greed* and Gains *Generosity*: Knows God's

Will/Man's Will....... Fairness Opens

Fifth Class – God's *Table*: Thanks God with Labors = Places Self Last...Thinking

Sixth Class – Converts from *Adulthood* to *Wise Man*: Adopts Own Views...Personality

Seventh Class – Fulfills God/Man Knowing: Thinks for Self = *Imperfect* to *Perfect*...Know Value

Eighth Class – Be *Perfect Son* within Kingdom: Given Authority/Ownership... Power to Vote

Ninth Class – Teaches *Doctrinal Truths*: Bonus Rewards of Soul = Purifies Life... Create Future

Tenth Class – Teaches *God's Will*: Becomes the Incarnate Word...Consciousness

Eleventh Class – Obtains *Perception of Reality*: Lights the Way...Highway Opened

Twelfth Class – Given One's *Own Kingdom*: Lives with God/Man: Creating Life... God/Man One

Thirteenth Class – *Redeems/Saves Lost Souls*: Surrenders to God's Will... Honored

Fourteenth Class – *Receives Treasures of Life*: Masters Divine System ...God Loves Son

Fifteenth Class – Third Graduation: Worthy of *Own Kingdom*: God's Oneness...Freedom

(sonship redemption – saves lost soul: resurrection/God gives new-life)

God/Man Sentience – God, Angels, Men, and Nature are One
(Free Men become God unto God's Love
by becoming the infinite word of perfection)

This illustration shows that the life-experience is all about waking up in a world of sin, evil, and death, only to find out that things are not as they appear because what appears to be cursed (faults) is in fact the treasured blessings of life (virtues). This will one day be our lives in the Lord's new creation, where no sin is permitted and only a person's proper training (decoding) and correct rearing (breeding) can save him from certain death, moment by moment or living in constant fear of the fires of failure (agony of defeat). The trick to living under such divine scrutiny falls upon the Blessed Mother doing Her job correctly in teaching Her beloved children (baby farm/divine school/sonship training) the most proper and effective methods for living well in becoming righteous/holy citizens of Heaven and Earth. We see that these little angels of perfection will be able to sweep the entire minefield (faults/decoys) clean as a whistle in a minute's time, as they busily search for the hidden Easter Eggs (virtues/truth) of God's loving gifts (honors), fruits (keys), and treasures. Yes! Through each child's desire to obtain God's gifts, fruits, and treasures, he will strive to perform admirably on Earth (baby farm), in Heaven (divine school), and within God's Kingdom (sonship training).

We must all come to understand that the secret for becoming perfect in the sight of God is simply a matter of coming to understand and instinctively knowing the divine truths of life (carrot/stick) in both spirit (morals/love) and in flesh (ethics/law). A baby's experiences create positive or negative personality traits as dictated by the divine will of God, which has been eternally formulated in the divine plan of every creation. This fact means that all we must do to see God's Grand Design (intelligent design/natural selection), which depicts each of our lives, is to review our own life story and understand that it is simply transformed into the Lord's mystical reality, which determines each new saint's seat of perfection in God's Celestial Court of Justice (Earth). This means everyone in existence is only a manifestation of will, either man's human will (birth) or God's divine will (born-again) and in the case of Jesus Christ, both man's and God's wills are one.

We see that the human race is striving to obtain a new spirit (heart/ prayers), new flesh (mind/works), and new soul (being/souls saved) by facing the forces of evil in the form of being poor, rich, and/or average (middle class) in life. At each of these levels of financial stability, a person can measure his own personal worth and value to himself (righteousness/citizenship), to society (holiness/sainthood), and to his God (perfection/sonship), based on the depth of his obedience (law/justice), faith (love), and overall mastery of knowing (comprehension).

Yes! The life-experience is all about comprehending God's truths, which are comprised of both His order or intelligent design (supernatural/God/prayers) and His chaos or natural selection (natural/man/works). Through these two states of existence (order/chaos), we see the importance of God's spirit world (church) and man's physical world (world) as each strives to fulfill its own destinies by bringing about God's eternal life (supernatural) and man's new body (natural). Unfortunately, neither creation's eternal life or new body would be possible without the intercession of God's Son, Jesus Christ, as He alone would be worthy of living forever (spirit) and of having His own transfigured body (flesh).

For this reason, the Lord Jesus Christ had to fulfill God's law of obedience (change nature), man's faith in God's love (wash away sins), and God's/man's knowing all things (thinking for oneself). This would mean that God's will (Christ) and Man's will (Jesus) would have to be kept in balance through either Jesus taking-out sin (create Christians) to stabilize natural order (physical life) or Christ putting in divinity (create saints) to stabilize supernatural order (spiritual life). In this way, creation will obey God's will, while creation will love man's will, thereby allowing them to be united in the new born-again God/man will so all God's creatures can learn to think for themselves.

The following graphic illustration shows that the born-again Christian nature is to be kept in balance by fulfilling God's will both supernaturally (church/blood shed) and naturally (world/body broken) as a person kills his spirit by dying to self (God's judgment) and then kills his flesh by fighting evil (Lucifer's test).

God's Divine Will
(balancing the born-again nature via God's prayers and Man's works)

Face Life			Face Death
• God's Judgment			• Lucifer's Test
Justice (God Forgives Man)		(Man Forgives God)	**Love**

- -

Crucifixion	**Christ's**	**Jesus'**	**Scourging**
• Blood Shed	Mercy	Mercy	• Body Broken
Christ Gives	(gives	(takes-	Jesus Takes-out
• Divinity	divinity)	sin)	Sins
(forgiveness)			(repentance)

Supernatural   Natural

(intelligent design)   (natural selection)

Eternal Life/New Body

(master intellect or master courage)

Order Unto Law		Chaos unto Love	
(spirit)		(flesh)	
Christ	**Worthy of**	**Worthy of**	**Jesus Redeemer**
Intercessor	**Eternal Life**	**New Body**	
• Pay Fines Daily	• Purify Host	• Purify Grave	• Pay Damages
			Once
(attend church)	• Die to Self	• Fight Evil	(face Calvary)

Heaven – God's Will/Man's Will – Earth
God's/Man's Will – Kingdom

This illustration shows that All in Life is God's will, which is balanced by the Lord's supernatural (prayers) and natural (works) life-forces as God's Son is either putting in more merciful divinity (add or subtract prayers) or taking out man's sin (add or subtract works) to keep the human nature in sync with God's truth, law, will, and love. The importance of understanding God's balancing process is centered on learning that the price to speak to God is to offer Him man's sin and God's divinity, thereby receiving three divine blessings: (1) divine life (eternal) – eat death: speak (home) = tomb (life), (2) new divine body (transfigured) – eat evil: hear (church) = crucifixion (babies), and (3) new divine kingdom (royal) – eat sin: see (government) = scourging (land). The idea here is that God gives life (death), then society gives babies (pain), and the individual clears the land (sweat) to bring forth the God/man kingdom of glory and bring God all the babies He will ever want.

1. **God Gives Life** – Blessing of Spiritual Perfection: Worthy of Eternal Life .... Paradise in Heaven
   - Christ is Intercessor – Pay Fines Daily: Infinite Payments by Church =

Offering Repentance
- Add and Subtract Prayers – Balance God's Spirit: Holy Saints (see one's potential)

2. **Man Gives Babies** – Blessing of Physical Perfection: Worthy of New Body.....Heaven on Earth
    - Jesus is Redeemer – Pay Damages Once: Payment Made on Calvary = Begging God for Forgiveness
    - Add and Subtract Works – Balance Man's Flesh: Righteous Citizens (see one's limitations)

This illustration shows that the Messiah got divine life, a divine body (holy soul), and a divine kingdom (speaking to God), while the "church (priesthood)" got a spiritual body (glorified spirit), and a spiritual kingdom (heaven) or the honor of hearing God. Finally, we see that the world (individual/laity) is only getting a physical kingdom (earth) to represent Heaven on Earth or being allowed to see God as a man and to worship this man/God as the Lord God Almighty Himself. Note that the Messiah (trinity) is getting three blessings (life/body/kingdom); then the church (persons) is getting two blessings (body/kingdom); while the world (nature) is getting only one blessing (kingdom). Recall that at the time of Moses in his Mosaic Tabernacle, the first room or the outer court (king) only got one blessing (sunlight), the second room or the holy place (priest) got two blessings (candlelight), and finally, the third room or the holy of holies (sonship) got three blessings (Shekinah glory light).

We see that this multiplication of blessings concept is actually being manifested from the combined sacrifices of Mary's Son, Jesus (man/repentance) and God's Son, Christ (God/forgiveness) as they individually take-sin and give divinity to keep all life in balance, thereby producing an infinite number of earthly babies (works) and born-again saints (prayers). We see that the "Son of Mary, Jesus (Man)" is a soldier-of-the-light (flesh) who is responsible for taking-sin (body broken/repentance) to create righteous men, who do good works in the world (create new body), thereby bringing forth more and more healthy babies (innocent blood). We see that the Son of God, Christ (God), is a living prayer of love (spirit) who is responsible for giving divinity (blood shed/forgiveness) to create holy saints, who offer prayers within the church (create eternal life), thereby bringing forth more and more holy saints (guilty blood).

We can see now that Jesus Christ came to the Earth as a poor carpenter (no money) to represent both man's righteous works (world/repentance) to transform the flesh (create babies) and also to represent God's holy prayers (church/forgiveness) by purifying the spirit (create saints). The point is that Jesus Christ was the essence of God and without the power of money, He appeared to have no value to His family, His community, or even His nation, who saw all people as dollar signs, with little to offer anyone other than their labors (sweat). This odd value system caused the Lord God Almighty to strive to give the disenfranchised both value and importance through His blessings of repentance, prayers, and works before God.

Once a person has become of divine value to God, he will be rewarded with the Lord's blessing of eternal life and with his own place in heaven to forever live in the presence of God. We know that in heaven, the Lord is most highly worshiped using the harp, where the prayers of humanity are songs to God through the angelic choirs of perfect love in an act of translating the desires of the human heart as they worship their creator. This means that using a musical instrument symbolizes the divine praise for the majesty of God since all heaven glorifies the Lord's most perfect death of redemption (level one) as the ultimate symbol of God's true love. The second level is an improvised musical instrument that symbolizes the sacred praise of the glory of God as all heaven honors the Lord's blood of purification to represent the manifestation of humanity's love for divinity.

We see that the lowest level is any form of holy gratitude (thanksgiving) to the honor of God, as all heaven praises the Lord's most holy words of righteousness that have been spoken in absolute truth to bless all those who hear them. We can now see that during the Lord's First Advent (first mile/new body), He had come to save the blind by breaking their chains of bondage (ignorance) when He gave them a guiding stick of faith in the form of His Father's divine heart. Secondly, upon the Lord's Second Advent (second mile/eternal life), He would come to save the newly awakened by unlocking the prison doors of bondage (cowardice) when He gives them His light of knowledge in the form of His own sacred heart. Finally, upon the Lord's third Advent (third mile/own kingdom), He will come to save the insane by overcoming the guards of bondage (greed) when He gives them a new mind of Christ in the form of His Mother's Immaculate Heart.

We now see that through these three mystical hearts (advents), the love of God, Jesus, and Mary can break into the prison of life to set the captives free from sin (chains), evil (doors), and death (guards). This mystical attack is called the war of identities (baby/teen/adult) in the struggle to either create God's image in man or man's image in God (spiritual union). Thanks to the Lord's sacrifice on Calvary (physical union), both God and Man were made one in spirit (morals) and flesh (ethics), thereby transforming them both into the likeness of each other (infinite reflection). We see that this ability to save lost sinners via identity comes through both God's purifying church (winepress) and man's transforming world (crucible), which must work together to change man's fleshly nature (human to divine) and also to wash away one's sins (sinful to holy).

Obviously, the Lord is telling us that He is after righteous earthly citizens, who are responsible enough to build well-adjusted societies (good works) that can produce an unlimited supply of babies, who can be educated and transformed into holy saints as future citizens of heaven. This means that righteous men are worthy of receiving a free gold mine from God (babies) if they will fight evil (world); while holy men become worthy of digging out God's gold (saints) if they will surrender their lives to Christ (church). Finally, perfect men become worthy of sharing God's gold with others (sons of God) if they are chosen by God to receive bonus rewards for their outstanding lives and for their unselfish devotion (loyalty) in serving the will of God.

Yes! It's all about receiving free redemption (babies/being saved), then earning one's salvation (saint/saving self), and finally, being worthy of bonus rewards (sons of God/saving others) to bring forth a flood of new babies (citizens), saints, and sons of

God to fill the Lord's new kingdom of glory. The truth is that the entire life-experience is about growing and maturing through both God's human (world) and divine (church) conversion process, which initially transforms man's flesh (fight evil) and then purifies man's spirit (submission) to create earthly righteousness (citizenship) and heavenly holiness (saints). The idea is that earthly life is mandatory, while heavenly life is optional, thereby giving every person a free-willed choice between bowing to either God's will or serving his own free will.

Optional	Mandatory
Spiritual Conversion	**Fleshly Conversion**
Church's Purification	**World Transformation**
(winepress of death)	(crucible of fire)

	Optional	Mandatory	
	• Christ Gives Divinity - Offers Prayers	• Jesus Takes-sins - Offers Works	
	• Son of God - Forgives Sins	• Son of Man - Repents for Sins	
	• Fulfill Man's Faith in God's Love	• Fulfill God's Law of Obedience	
	• Wash Away Sins - Sinful- to-holy	• Change Nature - Human-to-Divine	
Christian	• Surrender to Divine Will	• Fight Evil by Will of People	**Jewish**
Prayers	• Learn God's Good/Man's Evil	• Learn God's Right/Man's Wrong	**Works**
(mature)	• Living Prayer of Love	• Soldier-of-the-Light	(grow)
	• God's Blessings of Life	• God's Lessons of Life	
	• Sword of Promise to Destroy Evil World	• Abrahamic Promise of a Righteous World	
	• Christians Chosen to See Potential	• Jews Called to See Own Limitations	
	• Creating *Sanctifying Grace*/save self	• Creating *Personal Wealth*/be saved	
	• Manifesting Born-again Saints	• Man Wants More Babies	
	• Blessing of Eternal Life	• Gift of a New Body	
	• *Holy Saints Dig Out God's Gold*	• *Righteous Citizens Get Free Gold Mine*	
	• Create More Saintly Souls	• Birth of Infinite Number of Babies	

Perfect Sons Share Gold with Others
Consecrate Born-again Sons of God

Defining the Four Levels of God's High Command

1. **Bless Babies** – Water...Knowledge/wisdom
   - Torah Gives Word of God (earth)
   - Counting Babies on Their Birthdays
2. **Anoint Citizens** – Oil...Self-awareness/courage
   - Witness Decodes Word (Heaven)
   - Counting God's Citizens on Sabbath
3. **Sanctify Saints** – Blood...Consciousness/generosity
   - Prophet Teaches Truths (Kingdom)
   - Counting Saints on Lord's Day
4. **Consecrate Sons** – Death...Sentience/unselfishness
   - Messiah Saves Souls (God)
   - Counting God's Sons on Judgment Day

This illustration shows that the job of Earth, Heaven, and God's Kingdom is to convert human souls via God's mystical factory, which outputs an infinite number of babies, citizens, saints, sons of God, and finally, free men (friends of God) to be of service to the overall Kingdom. This means that the job of hard-working, righteous men of Earth is also to use their free gift of life to create as many babies as possible, either by marriage (birth) or by helping build strong, healthy communities in well-adjusted homes for as many of God's children as humanly possible. Secondly, the job of world leaders (governments) is to transform ignorant children into productive righteous citizens, who can effectively fight evil and manage their own lives, communities, states, nations, and even the whole world to educate the masses in the art of righteous living so that they might comprehend ethics (man's law), morals (God's law), and fairness (personal law). Thirdly, the job of Christ's Church is to purify hard-working, righteous men by converting them from warriors of death into born-again priests (living prayers) of loving kindness as they surrender themselves as living holocaust in service to the redemptive plan of Christ. Fourthly, the job of the Messiah is to train God's saints in the art of perfection to convert them into sons of God, thereby making them of great service to the Lord God Almighty Himself. Finally, the job of God Himself is to hand-select those special free men of life, who can work without supervision and can become trusted leaders and holy elders within God's divine society as they join God's inner circle of most personal friends (servant unto the Lord).

It should now make sense that God, Angels, and Men must all work together in creating a set of three mystical societies that can supply the Lord God Almighty with all or the necessary resources He will ever need to keep His kingdom of glory running perfectly forever. The basic message here is that the God/man union (holiness) comes about by combining God's resurrected nature (Christmas) with man's born-again host (Easter), thereby uniting a person's human life (bread/host) with God's divine death (wine/chalice). Secondly, the message is that the man/God union (new nature) comes about by combining God's dead spirit (last supper/no joy) with man's purified grave (Calvary), thereby uniting God's dead spirit (last supper) with man's purified grave (Calvary).

Now, we can see that the creation of the Holy Father comes from the union of God's resurrected nature and man's born-again host, while the creation of the Holy Mother comes from the union of God's dead spirit and man's purified grave. Obviously, the job of the Holy Mother is to save sinners through repentance to purify their graves (Earthly citizens), while the job of the Holy Father is to create saints through forgiveness to become a born-again host (Heavenly saints). The implication here is that a lost soul can be saved (first union) by Abraham's bloodline (covenant/called) via God's law of obedience or by fulfilling all the demands of the Jewish Temple (citizenship/fight evil), while a Christian can save himself (second union) by Jesus Christ's marriage vows (covenant/chosen) via man's faith in God's love or by fulfilling all the demands of Christ's Church (sainthood/submission).

Yes! We are all being shown that man or the world system (flesh) saves God via its depth of repentance (righteousness), while God or Christ's Church (spirit) saves man via its merciful forgiveness (holiness). This means that God saves man first by changing his nature from human to divine and then promises the human race that it can return the favor on its day of resurrection (Judgment Day) by filling God's dead heart with an unending flow of living human joy. We call this day of glory when the **Father Will Dance** as He lives again because He has found His first-born grandchild, who will transform His heart's desire into pure joy, when this little one (soldier-of-the-light), fulfills Christ's promise to defeat all evil. The Lord is telling us that we are to surrender our spirits to Christ's Church so we can receive the Lord's sword of promise, implying that as a child of God, a person sacrifices his physical life into the hands of evil men so that he can then bear fruit (God's graces) by purifying his own grave. This means that one's flesh is to be sacrificed to evil to create a person's repentance (sword of promise), which will be witnessed by God Himself, who will see the death of Lucifer moment by moment as one of God's children breaks his chains of sin, opens the prison doors of evil, and then overcomes the guards of death to set himself free (God's joy).

It should now be clear that the Lord God Almighty has created two distinctive creations with one comprised of spirit or Heaven (faith) and the other comprised of flesh or Earth (law); and then He has created two separate redemptive systems (blood law/marriage faith). Through this dual design concept, the spirit of God and the flesh of man are to be joined using the earthly law of obedience (knowing/blood) and the heavenly faith in God's love (believing/marriage). Unfortunately, this mystical joining concept must take place via the union of a human God (Jesus/blood/fight evil) and a divine man (Christ/marriage/surrender) as only a human God (nothing/repentance) can believe enough (faith) to become God (visible), while only a divine man (all/forgiveness) can know enough (law) to become God (invisible). This means that when we look at God's paradoxical nature, we see that He exists in two forms: one as a sleeping God, who is dreaming of a fantastic adventure, with the other being the fulfillment of His dream, known as man's reality (physical life). The following tabular information indicates that our God has two paradoxical natures: one being awake/active (human life/all) and the other being asleep/rest (divine life/nothing), thereby forcing the human race to fulfill them both via man's nature (human God/Jesus) and God's nature (divine man/Christ):

Active
(illusion)

1. **Benevolent Life-force** (IS) – Creator of Physical Life:
   All = Real Challenges
   - God's Physical Laws – Energy and Matter: Transfigured Body (awake)
   - Fulfill the Physical Life – Earth, Heaven, and Kingdom
   - Transformation – Human God: **God's Physical Nature** Believes All
   - Purification – Divine Man: • Man's Fleshly Reality Knows All
   - Conversion – God/Man: Masters All

Rest	2. **Lord God Almighty** (God) – Creator of Spiritual Life:
(reality)	Nothing = Hopes and Dreams

- God's Spiritual Justice – Divinity and Spirit: Glorified Spirit (asleep)
- Fulfill Spiritual Life – Future Dreams, Visions, and Imagination
- Transformation – God's Dream: **God's Spiritual Nature** Ownership
- Purification – Angels' Dreams: • God's Mystical Dream Perfection
- Conversion – Man's Dreams: Divinity

This illustration shows that at the heart of the Lord's divine truth, we must give-up all life's physical treasures and seek a new-life, where we will not die and his treasures will not rust (kingdom) or even be stolen by some unscrupulous thieves. This is not to say we are not to embrace a sincere concern for our physical welfare, because we are duty bound to serve God, life, and ourselves forever by fulfilling both God's physical nature (illusion/nothing) and God's spiritual nature (reality/all). This implies that man's reality will be in the flesh (all/hard-work) and God's illusion or dream state will be in the spirit (nothing/restful bliss). The idea here is that the job of the fleshly world is to bring human, angelic, and divine challenges because eternal struggle builds character, while the job of the spirit world is to bring adventure to God, angels, and men for eternal rest creates hopes and dreams for a bright and most blessed future (vision of hope). It is simply a matter of placing the concerns of life in a strict priority order of true importance, based upon the divine policies and procedures of God's divine authority over the affairs of man.

This means that God created a spirit world (divine death) and now it is man's job to create a born-again physical world (human life) by growing and maturing in both God's reality (dreaming) and man's illusion (building) at the same time. Through each person's growth and maturity process, the illusion of man (physical nature) can be transformed into the reality of God (spiritual nature) and vice versa (illusion/dream is real). This implies that it is up to God, angels, and men to work together (hard slave labor) to transform the challenges of life into a great adventure as each of their dreams for a most beautiful future can become a reality for one and all.

Remember that because of one's accomplishments (satisfaction), the Buddhist, Hindus, Moslems, and Protestants have established their entire religions upon some human manifestation of good works (righteousness) so that they might point to some actual animate object given to them by God Himself. This animate object is to signify that this religion is bringing all its members into a new state of holiness, thereby proving that God is with them alone and no one else as all who fail to worship Him correctly shall be condemned. The whole Christian walk is just the opposite as a person must keep the Lord's unshakeable, undaunted gift of faith (submission/100 percent belief) in his heart (invisible) and keep telling himself God is with me (faith). This means that this invisible blessing allows a repentant soul to be convinced that whatever is going on in its life will one day be transformed into its new eternal state of righteousness, holiness, and perfection.

We must all be convinced that our creator is doing a great work in every soul as every person in creation is perfect as defined in any given moment, yet none of us will ever be infinitely perfect in the eyes of God. The Holy Church has been chosen to represent the elect of all creation as eight percent of the overall creation represents one-twelfth of the pie and has been called to faithful perfection in the name of Judas (repentance), whose seat of glory was tarnished by his evil betrayal of his master. We see that to restore Judas' tarnished name, the human race will have to master Christmas by fulfilling God's law of obedience since the human race must fight evil to change its nature from human to divine to be resurrected from one's grave (new body). Secondly, the human race will have to master Easter by fulfilling man's faith in God's love as the human race must surrender to God's will to wash away all its sins, thereby changing its sinfulness to holiness to be resurrected by Christ's born-again host (eternal life). Finally, we see that during Christmas, the Jewish shepherds (poor) and the Gentile kings (rich) repent and are summarily forgiven by the baby Christ (life); while during Easter, the Son of God (rich), Christ (Gentile) and the Son of Man (poor), Jesus (Jewish) repent and are summarily forgiven by Christ's adult Church (death). We all know that God wants to be man (life) and man wants to be God (eternal life) and now thanks to Christmas (God becomes us) and Easter (we become God), the human race and its creator God can become one in truth, law, will, and love.

The following tabular information indicates that through man's earthly life, God can become all of humanity based on human repentance (Jews/Gentiles) and God's divine forgiveness; while through God's death (Calvary), man can become divine based on the Lord's divine repentance and man's human forgiveness:

Human Life/Flesh	Divine Death/Spirit
CHRISTMAS	**EASTER**
God Becomes Us	*We Become God*
. Human Repentance before God	. Divine Repentance before God
. **Poor** Jewish Shepherds - See Angel (father)	. **Rich** Son of God - See Good Thief (priest)
. Offer Ignorance - New Mind	. Offer to Deny Intellect - New Mind
Birthright . Offer Cowardice - New Heart	. Offer Abandon **Bride Price** Feelings - New Heart . Name
. Worship . Offer Greed - New Soul (born in manger - free redeemer of world)	. Offer Submit Free Will - New Soul (bloodless Last Supper - earned savior of world)

. **Rich** Gentile Kings - See Star (son)	. **Poor** carpenter's Son - See Bad Thief (laity)
. Offer Gold - Kingship	. Offer Scourging - Kingship
Inherit . Offer Frankincense - Priesthood	. Offer Crucifixion - **Dowry** Priesthood
. **Wealth** . Offer Myrrh - Sonship	. Offer Death in Tomb - . Virginity Sonship
(crowned in glory - king of Jews)	(bloody crucifixion/cross - high priest of heaven)
. Divine Forgiveness of Man	. Human Forgiveness of God
. Baby Christ - God (bloodline/law)	. Adult Jesus - Church (marriage vows/love)
. Human God - Flesh/Blood	. Divine Man - Bread/Wine
. Righteous Citizen - Earth	. Holy Saint - Heaven
. Pay Sin-debt - Remove Faults	. Pay Holy-debt - Gain Virtues
. Blessed with Divinity	. Blessed with Holiness
. Purify Grave - *New Body*	. Purify Host - *Eternal Life*
(blood: man gives worship/wealth)	(marriage: God gives name/virginity)

. Worship Sacrifice - Save Jewish Shepherds	. Bloodless Sacrifice - Save Son of God
. Angelic Realm Forgives - God's Spirit	. Good Thief Forgives - Priesthood
. *Shepherds* Give Worship (law)	. *Son of God* Gives Wealth (eternal life)
. Offering of Birthright - Israel	. Gift of Name - New Heaven
. Wealth Sacrifice - Save Gentile Kings	. Bloody Sacrifice - Save Son of Man
. Star of Bethlehem Forgives - Creation	. Bad Thief Forgives - Laity
. *Kings* Give Wealth (faith)	. *Son of Man* Gives Worship (new body)
. Gift of Inheritance - Earth	. Offering of Virginity - New Earth

---

God becomes Man via Forgiveness	**Man becomes God via Forgiveness**
. Angel/Father Forgives the Jews	. Good Thief/Priesthood Forgives Christ
. Jews/shepherd - Offer Worship	. Father/last supper - Offers Worship
. Star/Son Forgives the Gentiles	. Bad Thief/Laity Forgives Jesus
. Christians/kings - Present Gift	. Son/cross - Present Gift

This illustration shows that through the celebration of Christmas, the human flesh can become a human God in the person of Jesus to be worthy of Heaven on Earth (life); and through the celebration of Easter, the human spirit can become a divine man in the person of Christ to be worthy of Paradise in Heaven (eternal life). This means that both the poor and the rich come before the Christ Child (Christmas) seeking His forgiveness by offering their repentance of ignorance, cowardice, greed, gold, frankincense, and myrrh as payment for all men's sinfulness (remove faults). Secondly, the poor and the rich come before Christ's Church (Easter) seeking man's forgiveness by offering their repentance of a rejected intellect, emotions, will, scourging, crucifixion, and death in tomb as payment for God's holiness (gain virtues).

Yes! God becomes man by changing His nature from human to divine, and then man becomes God by washing away his sins to become holy. This implies that the God/man union comes from the human birthright (worship) and inheritance (wealth), while the Man/God union comes from the divine bride price (name) and dowry (virginity). We call this union process human and divine repentance as both God and man must first pay their sin-debt (remove faults) with God's worship (Angel), man's wealth (star), and then man and God must pay their holy-debt (gain virtues) with God's name (Father God) and man's virginity (Father Abraham). Once both the sin-debt and the holy-debt have been paid, man's wicked flesh can be forgiven by the Christ Child (law) and God's Holy Spirit can be forgiven by Christ's Church (love).

It can now be seen that via man's repentance, the righteous man (Jesus' nature) is going to get God's/man's mind, heart, and soul plus the Lord's wealth, powers of worship, and His righteousness to be offered before the throne of God. Secondly, via God's repentance, the Holy Man (Christ's nature) is going to get man's/God's mind, heart, soul, plus the Lord's obedience, submission, and His holiness to be offered before the altar of God. Note that during Christ's birth (Christmas), He was seen as a helpless baby in a manger when three shepherds (near) were told by an angel to worship the new-born King, who was coming to give free redemption to everyone. Then three kings (far) followed a star, which told them to crown the new King in God's glory so that He can come to give earned salvation to God's chosen saints.

We see in like manner that during Christ's death/resurrection (Easter), He is seen as a supernatural force as the Son of man who offered His body broken during the Last Supper in the form of bread and wine (new-life), and then the Son of God offered His shed blood during His crucifixion in the form of flesh and blood (death). Through these two offerings (bread/wine and flesh/blood), the bloodline of the Jews (law) and the marriage vows of the Christians (love) can become one to make full restitution for all the sins of man, thereby permitting mankind (church) to forgive its God for all His evil carnage being perpetrated against its human flesh.

Christmas God becomes Man via Forgiveness	Easter Man becomes God via Forgiveness
• Angel/Father Forgives the Jews (temple)	• Good Thief/Priesthood Forgives Christ (chalice)
• Jews/shepherds – Offer Worship/repent (1)	• Father/last supper – Offers Worship/repent (3)
• Star/Son Forgives the Gentiles	• Bad Thief/Laity Forgives Jesus (host)
• Christians/kings – Present Gift/repent (2)	• Son/crucifixion on cross - Present Gift/repent (4)

1) **Repent to Physical Dimension – Earth: Shepherd**
2) **Repent to Spiritual Dimension – Heaven: Kings**

3) Repent to Mystical Dimension – Kingdom: Son of God
4) Repent to Divine Dimension – God: Son of Man

This illustration shows that Christmas is the redeemer of the world (Holy Family), while Easter is the savior of the Church (Holy Trinity) based on the forces of forgiveness coming from God's angelic nature, natural nature (star), priestly nature, and human nature (laity). In short, Christmas is forgiving the human race for all its fleshly transgressions while Easter is forgiving the Lord God Almighty for all His spiritual sinfulness (take-on all sin). We can see God's blessing of forgiveness in reality, when the shepherds worshiped the Holy Family in the cave/tomb (Jesus, Mary, and Joseph) and when the three kings presented their gifts unto the Holy Land of God to bring forth the born-again Israel, New Earth, and New Heaven.

We can see Man's blessing of forgiveness in reality, when the Son of God worshiped the Holy Trinity on the cross/tomb (Father, Son, and Spirit) and when the Son of God presents His gifts unto the Holy People of God to bring forth a new body, eternal life, and one's own kingdom. This means that at Christmas time, God is forgiving the sinful world (Christ Child), while at Easter time, the Church is forgiving our repenting God (priests/laity). Yet for these two reconciliations to take place, God has to become nothing in the Christ child (baby) and then man has to become all within the person of Jesus Christ (adult). Now, it is clear that God has created two separate redemptive programs to transform the physical nature of the land (forgiven by God) and the spiritual nature of the people (God forgiven by Church) into human gods (heaven) and divine men (Earth).

Obviously, God wants His creation to repent for all its failures by apologizing to the Earth (physical dimension), Heaven (spiritual dimension), Kingdom (mystical dimension), and to God Himself (divine dimension) through both His Son's birth (Christmas) and His death (Easter). Initially, we see that the poor Jewish shepherds had been called upon to repent for all the failures on Earth (physical dimension) as they came to ask the Christ child to forgive them through God's Jewish law of obedience. Secondly, we see that the rich Gentile kings had been called upon to repent for all the failures of Heaven (spiritual dimension) as they came to ask the Christ child to forgive them through God's divine justice of perfection. Thirdly, we see that the Jewish Son of Man has been called upon to repent for all the failures of God's Kingdom (mystical dimension) as He came to ask the laity (bad thief) to forgive Him through man's faith in Mary's Son, Jesus. Finally, we see that the Gentile Son of God has been called upon to repent for all the failures of God Himself (divine dimension) as He comes to ask the priesthood (good thief) to forgive Him through man's faith in God's Son, Christ. This means that through these four acts of repentance, all four of God's dimensions can be forgiven and then transformed from their childish destiny (nothing) into adult free will (all).

The following tabular information indicates that God's justice forgives the land directly (law), while God's mercy is forgiven by the people indirectly (faith), implying that only a Perfect Man (Messiah/one man) can be forgiven by God, yet anyone can forgive God's mercy (all men/church), thereby being forgiven by God via Matthew 6:14:

Land	People
(world is forgiven by God)	(church forgives God)
Worship World –	**Worship Church** –
Offering/Angel/God	Offering/Priest/Good Thief

	1. Holy Family – Shepherds		1. Holy Trinity - Son of God	
God's	• Jesus		• Father	**God's**
Justice	• Mary	**Human Gods**	• Son	**Divine Men**	**Mercy**
Forgives	• Joseph		• Spirit	**Forgiven**
Land				**by People**

Gift to World - Gift/Star/Man
2. Holy Land – Kings
• Israel
• Earth
• Heaven
(God becomes Nothing in Christ Child)

Gift to Church - Gift/Laity/Bad Thief
2. Holy People – Son of Man
• New Body
• Eternal Life
• Own Kingdom
(Man becomes All in Jesus Christ)

This illustration shows that the land must be forgiven (justice) in the form of **Israel** (Promised Land), **Earth, Heaven, Kingdom**, and even **God**. Then the people must be forgiven (mercy) to learning how to forgive others (Matthew 6:14) in Christ Jesus. This implies that to fulfill God's law of obedience or God's justice, a person must have his sins forgiven, while in the fulfillment of man's faith in God's love or God's mercy, a person must forgive God to have his sins forgiven (church). Recall Matthew 6:14, states that "if you forgive others, then my Father will forgive you, but if you fail to forgive others, then my Father will not forgive you."

In this sentiment, we can see both the Jewish law of justice (forgive perfection), or the Father's Land (look-up/inheritance), and the Christian law of mercy (forgive imperfection), or the Son's people (look-down/birthright). Obviously, the Lord is telling us here that only God's Son (Last Supper) can be forgiven by God's divine justice (law), yet any repentant sinner (Calvary) can be forgiven by God's divine mercy (faith). This means that the Eternal Father represents the land as its Creator and then the Son of God represents the people as their born-again Creator. Note that in God's justice, He forgives the land (law), while in God's mercy, the Lord is forgiven by the people (faith).

This means that Christmas represents God forgiving one perfect man (world) when the Jews repent via the worshiping shepherds, and when the Christians repent via the kings' gifts, then Father God (angel) forgives the Jews and God the Son (star) forgives the Christians for God to become man (earthly life) or Heaven on Earth. Secondly, Easter represents man forgiving God (church/Matthew 6:14) when Father God repents via His worshiping Last Supper. When God the Son repents by presenting His cross as a gift, the priesthood (good thief) forgives the Eternal Father, and the laity (bad thief) forgives the Son of God for Man to become God (heavenly life) or Paradise in Heaven.

This means that Christmas has been established to reconcile the God/man relationship (Earth) so that God could become man (Heaven on Earth) through the inheritance of the land (law), while Easter has been established to reconcile the man/God relationship (Paradise in Heaven) so that man can become God through the birthright of the people (faith). Now we see man's repentance (world/fight evil) and God's repentance (church/submission) were necessary for both the Christ Child (Christmas) and the Holy Church (Easter) to forgive all the acts of tough love, which had to be perpetrated upon the human race to force them to both grow-up and mature in the eyes of God.

Man's Repentance	God's Repentance
1. Birthright – Angel	1. Bride Price – Father God
• Worship (shepherds)	• Name (priesthood)
2. Inheritance – Star	2. Dowry – Father Abraham
• Wealth (kings)	• Virginity (laity)

Forgiveness	Forgiveness
• Christ Child	• Christ's Church
• Angel – Father	• Good Thief – Son of God
• Star – Son	• Bad Thief – Son of Man
(Abrahamic Covenant)	(New Covenant)

This illustration shows that there are two separate systems (reverse logic) for transforming God into man using Christ's baby spirit (life) and then transforming man into God by using Jesus' adult flesh (death). This means that the Lord is first establishing truth (input), then He reverses truth (process), and finally, in the end, He blends the truth (output), thereby showing that through this methodology, the Almighty can change God into man (Earth) and man into God (Heaven) at will. We see that the Holy Church (love) has been given the gift of faith, with the power to save the world and restore the disgrace of Judas through its compassionate prayers of repentance, which had to be drenched in the words, blood, and death of Jesus Christ. Now, it is quite clear that God is to become us (Christ child/bloodline) and that we are to become Him (church/marriage vows) to make God and man one through the forces of repentance (pay sin-debt) and forgiveness (pay holy-debt).

This means that this exchange in roles is showing us that the life-experience centers on three mystical phases of life as everyone starts as a helpless baby, growing into a cowardly teenager, and finally, ending as a confident adult, who has seen it all.

1. Baby Challenges his Fears – Finds Freedom: Using Time Correctly
We see that the human race has been given God's greatest blessing of free will, which has forced mankind to begin life as a tiny baby, who must attend God's elementary school (baby farm) on Earth to learn God's right from man's wrong. Secondly, during the Lord's First Advent, He came to help the babies face their fears and to use their time wisely to learn the meaning of freedom as they are freed from the curses of sin,

evil, and death. Once a new baby has been awakened to life, then he can strive to fulfill God's law of obedience to change his nature from human to divine, which will set him free from the chains of ignorance to receive God's blessing of wisdom (new mind). Obviously, the Lord God Almighty has intentionally designed Planet Earth as an awesome challenge for baby man as everyone must face the Lord's life of natural selection based on the survival of the fittest (random chance). This means that God's babies are being challenged to establish their own fixed frame of reference in life by defining their own identities, characters, and their own personalities and become a particularly unique individual (one of a kind) in a world of infinite creations.

2. Teenager Converts Life's Pains into Adventures – Finds Liberty: Using Money Correctly

We see that the human race has been given God's greatest blessing of free will, which has forced mankind to grow-up into a teenager, who must attend God's high school (divine school) in Heaven to learn God's good from man's evil. Secondly, during the Lord's Second Advent, He will come to help the teenagers face the pains of life and to use their money wisely and learn the meaning of liberty as they defeat their own sin-natures, worldly temptations, and finally, all demonic possessions. Once a growing teenager has found himself, then he can strive to fulfill man's faith in God's love to wash away his sins to be changed from sinfulness to holiness, which will open the prison doors of cowardice and receive God's blessing of courage (new heart). Yes! The life-experience is meant to be a great adventure as God's teenage children strive to master their own spiritual nature by comprehending God's Word, His Church, and their own born-again nature in Christ. This means that God's teenagers are being called to establish their own relative focused existence by demonstrating their own skills, aptitudes, and abilities to become of eternal value to God, angels, men, and nature.

3. Adults Face the Shadow of Death and Make Life Fun – Find Independence: Using Labor Correctly

We see that the human race has been given God's blessing of free will, which has forced mankind to fulfill life by becoming a mature adult, who must attend God's college (sonship training) within God's Kingdom to learn God's will from man's will. Secondly, during the Lord's Third Advent, He will come to help the adults face the shadow of death and use their labors wisely to learn the meaning of personal independence as they master man's righteousness (citizen), holiness (saint), and perfection (son). Once a mature adult has mastered all he surveys, then he can strive to fulfill the God/man knowing to be able to think for himself and be changed from man's illusion to God's reality, which will overcome the guards of greed to receive God's blessing of generosity (new soul).

Through God's elder children or His adults, the challenges (babies) and the adventures (teenagers) of life can be transformed into a life of rollicking fun as one matures and realizes that things are not as they appear because there is no Santa Claus and/or Easter Bunny because they are simply his Creator God. This shows us that the Adamic covenant has established free will (freedom/liberty/independence) as mankind's badge of honor (dignity), allowing each of Adam's children to do what he wishes with his own time (time/freedom), own money (treasure/liberty), and his own efforts (talent/independence). This means that God's adults are being called to establish their own perception of reality by teaching their personal understanding of the meaning of life (existence), the purpose of life (service), and the value of life (happiness) to others.

1. **Free Will to Use Time** – <u>Freedom</u>: Baby Grows in Wisdom... Ignorance/Sin-nature
   - Defeating One's Fears – Believing in Jesus (33%): Becoming Righteous Citizen on Earth
   - Break Chains of Ignorance – New Mind: Worthy of a New Body (being saved)
   - Facing the Challenges of Life – Nothing to Fear but Fear Itself
2. **Free Will to Use Money** – <u>Liberty</u>: Teenager Experiences Courage...Cowardice/Worldly Temptations
   - Defeating Pains of Life – Trusting in Christ (67%): Becoming Holy Saint in Heaven
   - Open Prison Doors of Cowardice – New Heart: Worthy of Eternal Life (saving self)
3. **Free Will to Use Efforts** – <u>Independence</u>: Adult Matures in Generosity... Greed/Demonic Possession
   - Defeating Death Itself – Faith in Jesus Christ (100%): Becoming Kingdom Son of God
   - Overcome Guards of Greed – New Soul: Worthy of Own Kingdom (saving others)

This illustration shows that our Free Will has been divinely cursed with ignorance (toil), cowardice (pain), and greed (death) as a test of each man's personal strength and tenacity via his pursuits of a happy life. This particular brand of free will is offered to the human race by Lucifer to bring the joys of life to all who are willing to reject the will of God and follow their own sin-natures, worldly temptations, and enter demonic possession. This free will concept produces nothing of value (divine love/church) and bears no fruit (human kindness/world) before God, as free will only entertains a world full of silly babies. The individual is lost among all the things he says and does and is unable to find salvation (pay debt) through the efforts of his own actions (works), because he is only a silly fool in a world of insanity. We see that just as it was in the Edenic sin-debt, ownership of the free will is not truly obtained unless it is first given away, much like owning a bird, which must be freed to see if it will return.

We see that when Jesus taught "Sell all and give to the poor so you can store up treasures in heaven," the power of submission came into effect and all God's children were called to deny their intellects (mind), abandon their feelings (heart), and submit their free wills (soul) to Christ. An individual gives up his free will by denying his intellect (remove ignorance), abandoning his feelings (remove cowardice), and submitting his free will (remove greed) to the divine will of God. In essence, this sacrifice allows him to give his human will to God, allowing his soul to become even more human, while God gives him His will to make him more God-like each day of his life.

We see that by doing this and by flipping these two truths over and over at a fast rate, a person can blend any two concepts into one reality of perfect will, thereby allowing him to attain freedom of choice (instinctive compulsion). The trigger mechanism of submission is dying to self or personal denial, thereby killing man's selfish nature (flesh) to empty his nature and leave room for a new nature (spirit) that will emerge later on in his life (Christ-like). The Adamic Covenant clearly defines the significance of both Adam's free will (illusion) and God's divine will (reality) that establish the value of life (see potential) in goodness and the will to live (see limitations) in a person's evilness as the essence of human existence. The two-truth system of divine will enables the children of God to comprehend the need to learn wrong (rib of life) first and then to flip all they have learned into the lessons of right (forbidden fruit of eternal life). Finally, when both God's right and man's wrong are combined with God's good and man's evil to then be merged (blended) into one divine law, the whole world can establish its own fixed frame of reference by setting its own parameters for human wisdom, courage, and generosity.

We see that this ability to set up one's own parameters in life allows a person to see that he must put forth a mature gesture of gratitude, either for being blessed (righteous) or for being sacrificed (unrighteous), and then later redeemed from his sacrifice through repentance. The idea here is that anyone can master the Lord's cosmic system of selection, if he can come to understand that a person can use his life of brokenness, sin, and death to its best advantage by repenting and surrendering his free will to God's divine will. This act of great wisdom will cancel the effects of sin, thereby removing the penalty of damnation, leaving only the sentence of purgatory, which must be removed by offering gifts to God.

We are all seeking God's ultimate blessing, which is to attain interior maturity (perfection) that has the power to make a man master of all he surveys on Earth, in Heaven, and within God's Kingdom of Glory. Obviously, this means that even the Lord God Almighty is only the master of all He surveys, be it a great kingdom in His own eyes or a tiny abode in the eyes of others. Yet we must all master the life-experience (find oneself). We are all striving to find ourselves and to fill our minds, hearts, and souls with that absolute certainty that our lives are important, if only to us as we have reached paradise by mastering the act of self-worth. It should now all make sense that what it means to be chosen by God is to simply recognize that the entire life-experience centers around mastering the art of submission, which means to release a person's death grip on the cares of the world. We see that if a person receives his call unto physical humility (flesh/mind) and spiritual holiness (spirit/heart) as indicated in Hebrew's 9:15 (inheritance), all he needs to do then is answer God through the power of submission (death to self). This means that a person must seek his physical salvation (flesh/stewardship) through his free gift of faith, which must be fulfilled by mastering his worldly state of humility (denial). This desire to reject a person's selfish pride (faults) allows him to learn the lessons of sin, thereby leading a soul to understand the meaning of the word *wrong* so that a person can master the art of living with himself forevermore.

In like manner, we see that a person must also seek his spiritual rewards (spirit/spirituality) through his earned gift of works (fighting evil), which must be fulfilled by mastering his mystical state of holiness. This desire to obey Christ's Church (virtues) allows a person to become a soul winner for Christ, thereby leading him to understand the meaning of the word *right* to master the art of living with God forevermore. Now, if we combine these two divinely inspired skills of humility (will to live) and holiness (value of life), we see that the sinful flesh (experience) and the purified spirit (education) have become one in Jesus Christ, thus recognizing that this divine process of human transformation can only occur by a person joining and becoming a baptized practicing Christian in service to the will of the Lord God Almighty Himself. This is not to say that only Christians are to be saved, but it is revealing that the Christian faith has been chosen as the spiritual saviors of the world (holiness), just as the Jewish people were used to be the physical saviors of the world (righteousness). The idea here is to see that God's earthly elect (righteous citizens) are to be the eternally chosen Jewish people (destiny /intelligent design), while God's heavenly elect (holy saints) are to be the eternally chosen Christian people (free will/natural selection).

The point here is that anyone can choose to become a member of God's heavenly elect, if he will only master the art of submission and kiss the IS of a humble life to prove that he is an eternal servant of the Lord. In this way, all men can find their way onto the Lord's pathway of perfection, leading them to the royal household of God to receive their eternal rewards of peace of mind (earth), joy of the heart (heaven), and happiness of the soul (kingdom). Yes! We are all seeking eternal peace, joy, and happiness, but no one is capable of fulfilling God's law of obedience (Jews) or even man's faith in God's love (Christians) to earn a person's place within the Kingdom of God. This dilemma faces the human race today as Jesus came in His first coming (priest) to fulfill God's law of obedience (divine will) to change man's Jewish nature from human to divine, so that He can return during His second coming to fulfill man's faith in God's love (belief) in order to wash away man's sins and then change one's Christian spirit from sinfulness to holiness. This means that Jesus came (Man) to obey God's divine will (law) and fulfill God's intelligent design of human destiny (slavery), while Christ came (God) believing in the Lord's redemptive system (faith) to fulfill God's natural selection of human free will (freedom).

We see just why the Lord God Almighty has established a two-dimension system of transformation (chaos to order) and purification (order to perfection), which are centered upon the idea that all chaos (evil) is to be merged with all order (good) via the sacrifices of Jesus Christ (Last Supper/Calvary). This implies that through the Lord's death and resurrection, the human race can be converted into earthly righteous citizens (flesh) and heavenly holy saints (spirit) by fulfilling God's law and man's faith to bring all sinners to repentance (remove faults) and all Christians to forgiveness (gain virtues).

The following tabular information indicates the difference between God's legal justice system and His faithful mercy system as the Lord manifests His law of repentance within the Jewish people and His faith of forgiveness within His Son's Christian people:

Flesh	Spirit
God's Justice	**God's Mercy**
Jewish People – divine	Christian People – holy
(law of repentance – obey)	(faith of forgiveness – believe)

Flesh	Spirit
1. Obey Commandments – *Life*	1. Decode God's Law/Torah – *Life*
• God's Throne - Law	• Man's Throne – Law
• Remove Ignorance – Baby	• Gain Wisdom – Adult
2. Worship Staff – *Death*	2. Eat Host/Church – *Born-again Life*
• God's Altar – Faith	• Man's Altar – Faith
• Remove Cowardice – Teen	• Gain Courage – Teen
3. Eat Manna – *Resurrection*	3. Drink Chalice/Host – *Eternal Life*
• God's Table – Knowing	• Man's Table – Knowing
• Remove Greed – Adult	• Gain Generosity
Justice – God Forgives Man	Mercy – Man Forgives God
Jesus Takes-on All Sin	**Christ Gives-up His Divinity**
• Fulfill God's Law of Obedience	• Fulfill Man's Faith in God's Love
• Change One's Nature	• Wash Away One's Sins
• Human to Divine	• Sinfulness to Holiness
• *Righteous Man on Earth*	• *Holy Saint in Heaven*
• Free Heaven on Earth	• Earned Paradise in Heaven
• Worthy of having a <u>New Body</u>	• Worthy of having <u>Eternal Life</u>
• King Fights All Evil Forces	• Priest Surrenders to God's Will
• Purifying Sinners' Grave	• Purifying Christians' Host
• Son of Man – Chaos	• Son of God – Order
• Pay Sin-debt – Fight Evil	• Pay Holy-debt – Submit Will
• Remove Faults (dying to self)	• Gain Virtues (born-again)
New Body	**Eternal Life**
<u>Baby</u> – Ignorance to Wisdom (mind)	<u>Adult</u> – Cowardice to Courage (heart)
• Transformation of Physical Nature	• Purification of Spiritual Nature
<u>God's Spirit</u> – Intelligent Design	<u>Christ's Spirit</u> – Natural Selection
• Destiny – Static Existence	• Free Will – Dynamic Existence
• Baby – Instinctive Compulsion	• Adult – Thinking for Himself
• <u>Man's Flesh</u> – Natural Selection	• <u>Jesus' Flesh</u> – Intelligent Design
• Free Will – Dynamic Existence	• Destiny – Static Existence
• Adult – Thinking for Himself	• Baby – Bearing Fruit

*Intelligent Design Comes from God's Will, while Natural Selection is based on Belief

   1.   **God's Will** –<u>Spiritual Destiny</u>...Supernatural Life

- Justice – Repentance (curse): Positive Nature
- Mercy – Forgiveness (blessing): Negative Nature
2. **Creation's Belief** – Physical Free Will.... .Natural Life
    - Energy – Physics (existence): Destiny
    - Matter – Chemistry (life): Free Will

This illustration shows that our never-created God has been required to manifest His Own divine life-force into a dual-natured creation (spirit/flesh) as His blessing (Holy Spirit/positive) and His curse (evil spirit/negative) automatically divide into spirit beings and human beings with the creation of free-willed existence. It was God's job to mystically unite His positive (destiny) and negative natures (free will) via the incarnation of Jesus Christ on Earth to merge God's spirit with man's flesh via the rebirth of all life through the mystical womb (born-again) of the Virgin Mary (church). We call this God's new justice system, which has the power to transform flesh into righteous citizens (Earth) and to purify one's spirit, thereby making him a holy saint (Heaven). Through this conversion process, God's old positive (will) and negative natures (belief) can become one in Christ Jesus.

It may be quite difficult to comprehend that all existence is simply a manifestation of God's will, implying that all supernatural and natural laws are only logical explanations for observed cause and effect. This is like saying that every morning, the rooster crows; therefore, the rooster is making the sun come up so that everyone will have a perfectly logical explanation for what they observe based on some rational precept of the life-experience. But NO! It's just God's will. This implies that the job of the creation is to believe in God's will, assuming it can decode the mystical Word of God as the Lord pours forth more and more mystical information, concerning His basic divine, mystical, spiritual, and physical natures.

Obviously, the Lord God Almighty had to manufacture a believable story line to go along with His creative will (divinity). Thus, God created the Jewish people out of the barren womb of Sarah (Isaac) to logically connect supernatural life (intelligent design/destiny) with natural life (natural selection/free will). Obviously, there is no connection at all other than God has willed both supernatural life and natural life to exist and to interface into the creation of angelic/human spirits through the creation of an infinite number of babies, who are to be turned into earthly citizens, heavenly saints, and finally, into kingdom sons of God. We see that in this logical explanation of how the rooster makes the sun come up, God has placed a tremendous importance on His Ten Commandments (life/tablets), Aaron's staff (death), and His manna from heaven (resurrection) to depict the link between God's supernatural world (destiny) and man's natural world (free will).

Obviously, the Lord is trying to reveal that His Old Testament stone tablets (law) actually represent the Torah or God's Word (good news) in the New Testament as the human race is given its own eternal throne on Earth. Secondly, the Lord is saying that Aaron's staff (faith) in the Old Testament actually represents Christ's Church in the New Testament as the human race is given its own eternal altar on Earth. Finally, the Lord is saying that His heavenly manna (knowing) in the Old

Testament actually represents the Sacred Host in the New Testament as the human race is given its own eternal table of the Lord on Earth. Upon the throne, altar, and table, the New God/man relationship depends as the nature of God meets the creation of man to bring forth an unlimited supply of righteous citizens for Earth (throne/baby), holy saints for Heaven (altar/teen), and perfect sons for God's Kingdom (table/adult). We see that in this mystical process of transmitting God's duties (throne), responsibilities (altar), and authority (table) onto the Earth, this allows God's justice (God forgives man) to enter the world government (flesh) and God's mercy (man forgives God) to enter the Holy Church (spirit).

Now, it makes sense just why God has spent some seven thousand years establishing His God/man relationship via His physical world and His spiritual religion/church using both the bloodline of Abraham (flesh union) and the marriage vows of Christ (spirit union). Through these two channels, the Lord will be able to fight and destroy all evil and call all men to surrender their lives to Christ's Church to be transformed from lost sinners into newly born-again saints. Through this dual channel system, the flesh of man (physical) and the spirit of man (spiritual) can be given their hearts' desires as all flesh seeks a new body (purified grave) and all spirit seeks eternal life.

The following tabular information indicates in Luke 19:10 that the Lord reveals the flesh of Jesus (Man) is seeking lost sinners, while the spirit of Christ (God) is striving to create holy saints:

Two Systems to Save Man's Spirit and Man's Flesh
Luke 19:10   Jesus Seeks Lost and Christ Saves Saints
(Mary's Son Gives Free Redemption,
while God's Son Offers Earned Salvation)

- - - - - - World – Fighting Evil (good works) - - - - - - **Life** - - - - - -

1. **Redeeming Flesh** – Mary's Son, Jesus –Takes-on All Sin…   Free Redemption for All Flesh
    - Fulfill God's Law of Obedience – Change Nature: Human to Divine (agony of defeat)
    - Repentance – Purifying Grave: Soldier-of-the-Light: Learning Lessons of Life
    - Jesus Offers – Broken Body: Scourging = Flesh Spanked for Mortal Sins
    - Father's Justice – Man Repents and God Forgives (Christmas/life): Worthy of *New Body*
    - In Physical World – Visible Nature: Natural Selection is Energy and Matter (big bang)
    - Flesh Appears as Free Will (illusion) - Earthly Life (righteous grave)
    - In Spiritual World – Invisible Nature: Intelligent Design is God's Master Plan (life)
    - Spirit Existence is Destiny (reality) - Church Life (holy host)

- - - - - - Church – Submission to Christ (holy prayers) - - - - - -**Death** - - - - -
2. **Saving Spirits** – God's Son, Christ – Gives-up Divinity...   Earned Salvation for
   Worthy Spirits
   - Fulfill Man's Faith in God's Love – Wash Away Sins: Sinful to Holy (thrill of victory)
   - Forgiveness – Purifying Host: Living Prayer of Love: Blessed by God
   - Christ Offers – Blood Shed: Crucifixion = Spirit Killed for Capital Sins
   - Son's Mercy – God Repents and Man Forgives (Easter/death):   Worthy of *Eternal Life*
   - In Spiritual Church – Invisible Nature: Intelligent Design is Destiny (real)
   - Spirit Existence is Free Will (reality) — Church Life (holy host)
   - In Physical Church – Visible Nature: Natural Selection (illusion)
   - Flesh Appears as Destiny (illusion) — Earthly Life (righteous grave)

This illustration shows that each of our fleshly natures is passing through its life-experience for free, thanks to Jesus' broken body (scourging), while our spiritual natures are passing through water/spiritual baptisms for a price (pays sin-debt), thanks to Christ's blood shed (crucifixion). Obviously, the job of Jesus (man) is to save lost souls (new earth), while the job of Christ (God) is to create holy saints (new heaven), implying that through the Eternal Father's justice, man repents and God forgives (Christmas/life); then through the Son of God's mercy, God repents and man forgives (Easter/death). We see that through this life and death scenario, everything in the life-experience points to the fact that God wants to be man (Christmas) and man wants to be God (Easter).

Obviously, the job of Jesus Christ is to divide His divine/human nature into two mystical natures to serve both God's intellectual design (world destiny) and creation's natural selection (church free will). Yes! The human race wants Heaven on Earth and is striving to create a physical eternal lifestyle, comprised of raising an infinite number of babies who are to be transformed into righteous citizens in service to one and all. In contrast, the Lord God Almighty wants Paradise in Heaven and is striving to create spiritual eternal lifestyle, comprised of both angels and saints, who are to be transformed into born-again sons of God in service to the Kingdom of God.

This means that the Lord God Almighty is using the world to force the human race to fight evil as great warriors (give all) and then He is using His holy Church to create spiritual slaves, who must bow and worship their God (give all). Through these two systems of transformation, both the wants of God (law) and the needs of man (faith) can be fulfilled, assuming that Jesus Christ can become all things to all people by transforming man's flesh into eternal righteous citizens on Earth and by purifying God's spirit into eternal born-again saints in Heaven.

Now, it becomes clear that God has placed the human race in two separate systems, with one comprised of chaos (natural selection) and one comprised of order (intelligent design). He then called one group of humans (flesh) to fight chaos and the second group (spirit) to submit to order, thus creating two separate teams. Through these separate teams, an eternal competition can be established with one group giving its loyalty to physical existence (Jesus/Earth/ Jews) and the other giving its loyalty to spiritual existence (Christ/Heaven/Christians).

We see that in this war of good (order) and evil (chaos), the Lord would create an argument between which one can serve the needs and wants of God the best as the Lord's earthly humans fight and destroy chaos in order to master all that they survey (new body), while the Lord's heavenly born-again humans submit to and become order and thus become servants unto the Lord. Through its combined mastery and its servanthood, a mature soul can unite with the mystical unknown of both chaos (man) and order (God) to be worthy of serving within God's earthly, heavenly, and kingdom realms of life.

1. **Fighting Natural Selection** – <u>Baby Fear</u>: Defeat Destiny...Master of All One Surveys
   - Challenge – Master Earthly Baby Farm: Elementary School = Learn Lessons of Life
   - Understanding God's Right from Man's Wrong – Thanking God: Give Labors
   - Fulfill God's Law of Obedience – Change Nature: Human to Divine

2. **Submit to Intelligent Design** – <u>Teenage Pain</u>: Control Free Will ...Servants unto the Lord
   - Adventure – Serve Heavenly Divine School: High School = Learn Purpose of Life
   - Comprehending God's Good from Man's Evil – Praising God: Give Wealth
   - Fulfill Man's Faith in God's Love – Wash Away Sins: Sinful to Holy

3. **Unite with Mystical Unknown** – <u>Adult Death</u>: Unite with God's Will...Freedom from All Enemies
   - Fun – Benefit Kingdom's Sonship Training: College = Learn Value of Life
   - Separating God's Will from Man's Will – Worshiping God: Give Life
   - Fulfill God/Man Knowing – Thinking for Oneself: Nothing to All

This illustration shows that God has sent the Jewish people to fight evil by defeating natural selection (chaos) or random change, coming from the big bang, thereby manifesting the forces of energy and matter into an earthly life-experience (world). In like manner, God has sent the Christian people to surrender (die to self) by serving God's intelligent design (order) coming from God's will, thereby manifesting the forces of reality into a heavenly life-experience (church). This means the job of the Jews is to create an infinite number of children (bodies) and the job of the Christians is to create an infinite number of born-again Christians (eternal lives). The job of Jesus Christ then is to unite the Jews and the Christians into God's new kingdom of glory so that they could work together in converting ignorant children into perfect sons of God.

This eternal mystical cycle of creating babies and then transforming them into sons of God would unite God, angels, men, and nature into an eternal joint effort in bringing life out of nothing. This mystical process of uniting God's kingdom sits at the center of educating God's children as the Lord's babies must change chaos into order (fighting evil/new body) to learn the lessons of life and become physically successful (growing-up). Secondly, the Lord's adults must change baby order into adult chaos or complexity (submission/eternal life) to receive God's blessings of life and become spiritually successful (maturing).

Through both of these growth/maturity systems, the human race can create all the bodies God will ever need and then be blessed with all the eternal life that mankind will ever need to live long and prosper. This means that the Lord Jesus Christ has been sent to ensure that man's living flesh saves God's dead spirit by purifying the grave (free redemption), while also ensuring that God's living spirit saves man's dead flesh by purifying the host (earned salvation). Through this mystical exchange of human sacrifice (repentance) with divine compassion (forgiveness), which was reversed on Mt. Calvary during the Lord's earth-shattering crucifixion, Jesus takes-sin (flesh saves spirit) and Christ gives-up His divinity (spirit saves flesh).

Important Note: God/Man Reversal of Roles (both saviors) - - -
- - - We become God – Physical Nature (nothing saves all) - - -
Repentance

Man's Living <u>Flesh</u> Saves God's Dead <u>Spirit</u>
Righteous Man Fights Evil/sacrificing his flesh to
Save Broken-Hearted God
Man Resurrects from Purified Grave to
Become Dead Spirit of God/Saving his Lord
——Man becomes God – Jewish Bloodline:
Fulfills Law of Obedience = Changes Nature——

Obviously, this complex teaching is clearly explaining that the job of man's redeemed flesh (grave) is to save others by becoming God's dead spirit, which had died (sword of sorrows), when the Lord God Almighty felt the loss of His most beloved son as He was being crucified upon man's altar of death (Calvary). This means that each man's flesh is traveling from the nothing of death to the all of new-life by fighting evil unto death and then resurrecting into new-life to save the dead spirit of God, who was willing to sacrifice His All just for His beloved child.

———God becomes Us – Spiritual Nature (all saves nothing) ———
Forgiveness

Christ's Living <u>Flesh</u> Saves Man's Dead Spirit
Christ Resurrects from Tomb/surrendering His Spirit to Save Sinful Man
- - - - - - God becomes Man – Christ's Marriage Vows:
Fulfills Man's Faith in God's Love = Holiness - - - - -

Secondly, the job of Christ's resurrected flesh (eternal life) is to save each soul by becoming man's born-again spirit (host), which had been murdered (suicide), when a true believer offered his life/wealth/labors upon God's altar of death (church). This means that God's spirit is traveling from the all of life to the nothing of death by surrendering Himself and then resurrecting into new-life to save (born-again) the dead spirit of man, who is then willing to sacrifice his all (dying to self/submit) just for his beloved God.

This important note is clearly explaining that through God's justice, we are forgiven (world), while through God's mercy, we are all forgiving God (church/Matthew 6:14), implying that the human race must repent by fighting physical evil (purify grave), then born-again man must forgive (Matthew 6:14) by surrendering to God's will (purify host). This reversal of roles as a forgiver of transgressions reveals that anyone can apologize but the apology has no value, unless it is accepted via a most forgiving heart. This means that in the case of the evil world (death) and the Holy Church (life), they must both forgive each other with that most forgiving heart and then prove it with an eternal lifetime of good works.

Yes! We all know that forgiving the world is done by Mary's Son, Jesus (Son of Man), while man forgiving God is done by God's Son, Christ (Son of God) because Jesus Christ is the only person worthy of being a divine/human priest, king, and Son all at the same time. This means that only Jesus Christ could fulfill all nine of God's covenants, thereby legalizing all the statutes of God as written in His Torah (Mosaic law) so that they could govern the physical Earth (baby farm), spiritual Heaven (divine school), and mystical kingdom (sonship training) from everlasting to everlasting.

It is now quite clear that God created the nine covenants (creation of souls) as stages of growth beginning with His personal gift of life (Edenic), then making Adam a slave to ignorance (Adamic) to force him to comprehend the meaning of the Word servanthood (Noahic). The idea here is that as tiny babies, we enter God's kingship (truth); as teenagers, we enter God's priesthood (law); as adults, we enter God's sonship (will); and finally, as wise men, we enter God's free will/servanthood (love) unto the truth, law, will, and love of God. We see that with the coming of the Abrahamic covenant (Heaven/Earth), God introduced parenting (parenthood) at the divine level of love and devotion or at the sacrificial level of commitment, thereby meaning unto death itself. Then the Lord brought forth man's priesthood (Mosaic), homeland (Palestine), kingship (Davidic), sonship (new), and servanthood (everlasting) to provide all of the eternal institutions needed to bring forth God's kingdom of glory (everlasting).

In this theme, the Lord God Almighty was a conscientious farmer with two most prized trees, one bearing good fruit (tree of life) and the other bearing evil fruit (tree of knowledge) and allowed Adam to choose his favorite tree (holiness or wisdom). We see that Adam chose evil or wisdom (Edenic), thereby allowing the seed to fall from the tree of Knowledge upon the barren ground of death (Adamic) in preparation for its resurrection into new-life. We see that with the coming of Noah (rainbow covenant), the evil seed was watered to set it free from its dry state of death to be filled with new-life in the heart of Father Abraham. We now see that Father Abraham fertilized the seed in the dung of Egyptian slavery, bringing it forth as a seedling in the Sinai desert of fear, pain, and death to give the Tree of Knowledge supernatural strength. The seedling was placed in the hands of the Master Grower Moses, who made it grow healthy and strong in preparation for being transplanted into the Holy Land of God (defeat curse of toil) by Joshua. Next came the nurturing of the new tree, where it thrived in the fertile soil of David's kingly opulence as the baby tree wanted for nothing since it was watered, fertilized, and pruned regularly. The Lord God Almighty sent his only begotten Son (new) to pick the tree's firstfruits of divine perfection, producing just enough for one tiny meal (Last Supper) for just twelve men of holiness (apostles).

It's now time to prune the tree (two thousand years) and to wait for the fall of the year when it will be time to gather the great harvest of souls in preparation for the heavenly celebration (everlasting). We see that at each of these stages of growth, God has been planting seeds and growing people (souls) to fill His most blessed Earth (flesh) with His treasures of life in preparation for His coming Heavenly Kingdom (spirit). It should now be clear that Adam's Tree of Knowledge represented man's weak flesh (criminal behavior), which needed to be transformed (Old Adam/flesh) from ignorance, cowardice, greed, and selfishness to a new creation of wisdom, courage, generosity, and unselfishness. This implies that once the Tree of Knowledge has made mankind strong, it could now be allowed to mate with God's Tree of Life, which had also been transformed (New Adam/spirit) from being too powerful to becoming balanced between God's good and man's evil natures.

The following tabular information indicates the nine covenants of God (growth) that reveal the transformation of man's free will into humanity's eternal freedom, based on God's nine sacrificial creations from Eden, Adam, Noah, Abraham, Moses, Joshua, David, Jesus (New Covenant/church), and Christ (everlasting covenant/world):

God's Nine Covenants bring forth
the Lord's Perfect Kingdom of Glory
(home, perfect man, deed to earth, deed to heaven,
priest, homeland, king, divine man, and kingdom)

Alpha 1. **Edenic Covenant** – <u>Garden of Eden</u>: Home of God...First Seal- - Tree of Life
- Spirit becomes Worthy of New Body – *Righteous Citizen* on Earth
- Fulfill God's Law of Obedience – Change Nature: Human to Divine

- -

2. **Adamic Covenant** – <u>Perfect Man:</u> Friend of God...Second Seal- - — Rib of Eve
- Fault of Gluttony becomes Virtue of Good Taste – Ignorance to Wisdom: *New Mind*
- Baby Level – Earthly Baby Farm: Elementary School (decode/life-experiences)
3. **Noahic Covenant** – <u>Ownership of Earthly Nature</u> (rainbow)...Third Seal- - -Rainbow

- Fault of Slothfulness becomes Virtue of Honesty – Cowardice to Courage: *New Heart*
- Child Level – Heavenly Divine School: High School (taught truth)

4. **Abrahamic Covenant** – <u>Title Deeds to Earth/Heaven</u>... Fourth Seal
- - - Circumcision
  - Fault of Envy becomes Virtue of Charity – Greed to Generosity: Getting a *New Soul*
  - Adolescent Level – Kingdom Sonship Training: College (saving souls)

5. **Mosaic Covenant** – <u>Sacred Priesthood</u> (law).. .Fifth Seal-- Two Tablets
  - Fault of Lust becomes Virtue of True Love – Selfishness to Unselfishness: New *Life-force*
  - Teenager Level – On-the- Job Training: Employment (duty)

6. **Palestinian Covenant** – <u>Promised Land of Milk/Honey</u>...Sixth Seal
- - - Promised Land
  - Fault of Avarice becomes Virtue of Good Values – Evil to Good: Getting a *New Body*
  - Young Adult Level – God's High Command: Leadership (responsibility)

7. **Davidic Covenant** – <u>Royal Kingship</u> (government)...Seventh Seal- - - Sun/Moon/Stars
  - Fault of Anger becomes Virtue of Good Judgment – Unrighteous to Righteous: *New Eternal Life*
  - Adult Level – Personal Ownership (authority)

8. **New Covenant** – Divine <u>Sonship of Christ</u> (home)...Eighth Seal – Wooden Cross
  - Fault of Pride becomes Virtue of Humility – Hypocritical to Saintly: *Own Personal   Kingdom*
  - Wise Man Level – Thinking for Oneself (freedom)

- -

Omega 9. **Everlasting Covenant** – <u>Kingdom of Glory</u>: Home of God/Man... Ninth Seal – - - Holy Spirit
  - Flesh becomes Worthy of Eternal Life – *Holy Saint in Heaven*
  - Fulfill Man's Faith in God's Love – Wash Away Sins: Sinful to Holy

This illustration shows that the Edenic and everlasting covenants represent the alpha of life (man) and the omega of eternal life (God) as the Lord sacrifices all of His first-born creations unto forces of sin, evil, death, and damnation for their purification and eventual transformation. Note that each of God's covenants creates some extremely important institution, needed in the creation and formation of the God/man relation-ship, thereby supplying the Almighty with His own eternal life (self), government (Earth), church (Heaven), and home (Kingdom). The job of God's Kingdom is to pro-vide a continuous supply of most beloved babies, who can be transformed into righteous earthly citizens, holy heavenly saints, and finally, perfect kingdom sons. We can see in the establishment of the following seven human covenants that God intends to remove all men's faults (empty) and then fill each of His children with divine virtues to indicate their individual progress (growth/maturity) as they journey along the Lord's pathway of perfection (lessons of life).

1. **Adamic Covenant** – <u>Perfect Man</u>: Friend of God...Second Seal- - Rib of Eve
   - Fault of Gluttony becomes Virtue of Good Taste – Ignorance to Wisdom: *New Mind*
   - Baby Level – Earthly Baby Farm: Elementary School (decode/life-experiences)

In phase II of God's plan, the Lord is willingly sacrificing a holy couple into the curse of gluttony (eat forbidden fruit) to transform their ignorance into wisdom so that they can be blessed with good taste in all things great and small. This means that Adam's Covenant represents the baby level of life as the Garden of Eden is a prefigurement of the Lord's coming earthly baby farm, where all God's new-borns will be required to fulfill God's law of obedience to change their natures from human to divine. The idea here is that new-borns are mindless fools who will believe in anything, even fairy tales, Santa Claus, and the Easter Bunny as they live in a dreamland of mystical illusions with little or no way of encountering, learning, and/or mastering the real mysteries of life (knowing God). Only by growing-up can a person learn God's right from man's wrong, thereby giving him the wisdom to master man's law (obedience) and God's faith (love) to balance his life between the needs of man (respect) and the wants of God (love).

2. **Noahic Covenant** – <u>Ownership of Earthly Nature</u> (rainbow)...Third Seal - - Rainbow
   - Fault of Slothfulness becomes Virtue of Honesty – Cowardice to Courage: *New Heart*
   - Child Level – Heavenly Divine School: High School (taught truth)

In phase III of God's plan, the Lord is willingly sacrificing His first humanity into the curse of sloth or lying, cheating, and stealing to transform its cowardice into courage so that it can be blessed with honesty in all things great and small. This means that Noah's covenant represents the child level of life as Noah's Ark is a prefigurement of the Lord's coming newly created purified life, where God's Word and man's gospel message will wash away man's sins, thereby changing all men from sinfulness to holiness. The idea here is that God's newly purified children are being awakened to the painful realities of earthly life (survival) as foolish superstitions give way to scientific proofs, thereby opening the minds, hearts, and souls to the meaning, purpose, and value of life. Only by growing-up can a person learn God's good from man's evil, thereby giving him the courage to master man's law and God's faith to balance his life between earthly righteousness (respect) and heavenly holiness (love).

3. **Abrahamic Covenant** – <u>Title Deeds to Earth/Heaven</u>...Fourth Seal - - - Circumcision

- Fault of Envy becomes Virtue of Charity – Greed to Generosity: Getting a *New Soul*
- Adolescent Level – Kingdom Sonship Training: College (saving souls)

In phase IV of God's plan, the Lord is willingly sacrificing Abraham's son, Isaac, into the curse of envy (green-eyed monster) to transform men's greed into generosity so that they can be blessed with charity in all things great and small. This means that Abraham's covenant represents the adolescent level of life as Abraham's grave in Hebron is a pre-figurement of the Lord's coming tomb of resurrection, where all God's children will be required to fulfill man's faith in God's love by changing their natures from stiff-necked fools into faithful believers. The idea here is that God's children are being taught God's Word, as they must face the huge complexities of modern society in seeking their own identity, character, and personality to find out (self-awareness) just where they fit into the grand scheme of things. Only by growing and maturing can a person learn God's will/man's will, thereby giving him the generosity to master man's law and God's faith to balance his life between the illusion of man (respect) and the reality of God (love).

4. **Mosaic Covenant** – <u>Sacred Priesthood</u> (law)...Fifth Seal - - -Two Tablets
   - Fault of Lust becomes Virtue of True Love – Selfishness to Unselfishness: *New Life-force*
   - Teenager Level – On-the-Job Training: Employment (duty)

In phase V of God's plan, the Lord is willingly sacrificing the Jewish people to the curse of lust (passion) to transform their selfishness into unselfishness so that they can be blessed with true love in all things great and small. This means that Moses' covenant represents the teenager level of life as Moses brought God's Law (two/tablets), written in stone as a prefigurement of the Lord's coming divine judgment (justice), where all God's elder children will be required to enter the Jewish faith by bowing to the Lord's altar, throne, and table to change their natures from wild animals to righteous citizens before God. The idea here is that God's elder children are being taught God's truths, as they must face the reality of meeting, knowing, loving, and serving a paradoxical God, who can only be found if a person believes in His Son, 100 percent (total submission). It is only by fully maturing that a person can learn God's reality from man's illusion, thereby giving him an unselfish heart to master God's commandments in order to see man's desperate need to be saved from eternal damnation.

5. **Palestinian Covenant** – <u>Promised Land of Milk/Honey</u>... Sixth Seal - - - Promised Land
   - Fault of Avarice becomes Virtue of Good Values – Evil to Good: Getting a *New Body*
   - Young Adult Level – God's High Command: Leadership (responsibility)

In phase VI of God's plan, the Lord is willingly sacrificing the evil pagans of Palestine by cursing them with avarice (passion) in order to transform their pagan hearts into repentant sinners so they can be blessed with good values in all things great and small. This means that the Palestinian covenant represents the young adult level of life as Joshua cleared the Holy Land, house to house, as a prefiguration of the Lord's coming in silent anger, vocal rage, and finally, in His striking wrath. This means that all God's adult children will be required to take on the responsibility for their own actions by offering God their labors (thanksgiving), their wealth (praise), and their lives (worship) before the Lord's table, throne, and altar. The idea here is that God's adult children are ready to help the Lord bring in His harvest of souls by offering the lost free redemption (being saved), earned salvation (saving self), and by giving them bonus rewards for trying to help save others. It is only by reaching adulthood that a person can learn God's truths from man's lies, thereby giving him a new perception of reality, in order to allow him to see man's desperate need to find a way out of his curse of sin, evil, death, and damnation.

6. **Davidic Covenant – Royal Kingship** (government)...Seventh Seal - - - Sun/Moon/Stars
    - Fault of Anger becomes Virtue of Good Judgment – Unrighteous to Righteous: *New Eternal Life*
    - Adult Level – Personal Ownership (authority)

In phase VII of God's plan, the Lord is willingly sacrificing the king of the Jews by cursing him with anger (revenge) in order to transform his warrior's heart into kingly majesty so he can be blessed with good judgment in all things great and small. This means that David's covenant represents the adult level of life as he prepared to give his people both a perfect government (man) and a holy temple (God) as a prefiguration of the Lord's coming new kingdom of glory. This means that all God's adult children will be required to accept a leadership role in God's kingdom by demonstrating their use of divine authority through their humble and contrite hearts. The idea here is that God's adult children are looking forward into the future to see how to change everyone's quality of life for all the kingdom's subjects by bringing forth that most ultimate instant solution (David's son Solomon/wisdom). Only by becoming a responsible adult in God's kingdom can a person earn God's respect and fulfill His expectations in superior intellect (mind), emotional stability (heart), and natural instincts (soul).

7. **New Covenant** - <u>Divine Sonship of Christ</u> (home)...Eighth Seal - - - Wooden Cross
    - Fault of Pride becomes Virtue of Humility – Hypocritical to Saintly: ***Own Personal Kingdom***
    - Wise Man Level – Thinking for Oneself (freedom)

In phase VIII of God's plan, the Lord is willingly sacrificing the Messiah of God by cursing Him with pride (egomania) to transform His empathic heart into the sonship of God so he can be blessed with humility in all things great and small. This means that the new covenant represents the wise man level of life as he prepares to give his followers God's blessing of power and authority over all the forces of natural and supernatural life. This means that all God's wise men or messiahs will be required to accept full responsibility for the Earth, Heaven, and God's Kingdom by protecting all the forces of life, eternal life, and divine life. The idea here is that God's wise man shall call all men to repentance and then God will forgive His children of all their sinful ways and evil deeds to set the captives free, thereby bringing forth peace of mind (challenge), joy of the heart (adventure), and happiness of the soul (fun) to one and all. Only by becoming a wise man in God's Kingdom can a person befriend God and lend a helping hand to sinful men, thereby bringing humanity to sentience so that all men might see the meaning (existence), purpose (service), and value (happiness) of life.

This illustration shows that the Lord's nine covenants are basically defining an eternal sacrificial journey from nothing to all as God, angels, men, and nature travel together along the Lord's pathway of perfection as the physical nature grows-up (mandatory) and the spiritual nature matures (optional). We see in this process that the physical nature must be transformed (mandatory) by passing through seven levels of life, known as Lucifer's test, implying that each of God's children must face the seven deadly sins (faults) and convert each of them into a most blessed virtue of God. In contrast, the spiritual nature must be purified (optional) by passing through seven levels of eternal life, known as God's judgment, implying that God's righteous men, saints, and sons must apply each of God's seven virtues to some useful application to benefit society in support of the greater good. In this way, a child of God will learn God's right from man's wrong in all its forms and learn to think for himself, thereby proving that he has mastered every aspect of God's divine truth.

We see that in God's Grand Design, He has chosen nine special men to forever serve His altar (priesthood), throne (kingship), and table/palace (sonship) on Earth for man, including serving His Church, throne, and palace in Heaven. Out of these two sets of institutions (Jews/Christians), an eternal bond of marriage (vows) shall be established uniting God (trinity) with man (Virgin Mary), including man's flesh (Jesus/new body) and God's spirit (church/eternal life) to bring forth the God/man Kingdom of Glory. In short, the Lord is using both the Old Jewish Law (Mosaic/Torah) and the New Christian law (Canon/gospel) to be merged into one divine/human law to bring forth a legal mechanism (perfect justice system) for creating an arranged marriage between divinity's name (intellect/truth/respect) and humanity's virginity (emotions/word/love). Through this mystical marriage, the couple will be merged into one life-force through sight (truth), hearing (law), smelling (will), tasting (love), and touching (life) forever.

Obviously, if the Lord God Almighty intended to bring forth a combined divine/human law into existence, then He would also have to establish a priesthood to perform the appropriate ceremony needed to unite the couple in wedded bliss. Through God's priesthood, the Lord could then place both a divine and human blessing on the couple to eternally unite their lives in wedded bliss, thereby bringing forth an infinite number of babies (mystical womb/born) to fill God's kingdom with citizens, saints, and sons. We also see that the Lord needed to establish His own royal government both in Heaven and on Earth through a dual kingship, with authority over both the affairs of God (spiritual) and the affairs of man (physical). This also included creating a spiritual home in Heaven and a physical home on Earth, leaving the problem of converting the human race into spirit beings so that they could travel back and forth between Heaven and Earth at will. In short, our Creator God was faced with a tremendous number of very difficult problems in trying to combine a spiritual kingdom with that of a physical kingdom, especially when they hated each other as natural enemies.

We now see that this awesome job of combining a never-created God (reality) with created existence (illusion) had an uncountable number of complexities and nearly insurmountable problems to make the whole kingdom a workable arrangement. Obviously, it appears that the Lord is using the first three covenants (Eden/Adam/Noah) to create the institution of an eternal home (love God); then the next three (Abraham/Moses/Joshua) to create the institution of an eternal church (worship God). Then the Lord used the last three (David/Jesus/Christ) to create the institution of an eternal government (serve God) to bring forth His holy Earth (government/executive branch), sacred Heaven (church/congressional branch), and divine kingdom (home/judicial branch). Out of these three sets of institutions/branches, we see the three unions of love, respect (worship), and service within the marriage agreement that had to be sealed in word, blood, and death (Calvary) to consecrate the couple's solemn vows. For this reason, God assigned a special seal to each of His nine covenants (institutions) in the form of a tree (Eden), rib (Adam), rainbow (Noah), circumcision (Abraham), tablets (Moses), Holy Land (Joshua), sky (David), cross (Jesus,) and Holy Spirit (Christ) to give them sanctity before God.

Seeing	1.	**Tree means Life** — Man's Eyes (thinking)...Edenic Covenant
Hearing	2.	**Rib Means Death** — Man's Ears (speaking)...Adamic Covenant
Smelling	3.	**Rainbow Means Born-again** — Man's Nose (touching)...Noahic Covenant
Tasting	4.	**Circumcision means Eternal Life** — Man's Mouth (supping)...Abrahamic Covenant
Touching	5.	**Tablets mean Divine Justice** —-Man's Skin (becoming)...Mosaic Covenant
		- - - - - - - - - *Transforming from Nothing to All* - - - - - - - - -
Seeing	6.	**Holy land means Home-sweet-home** — God's Eyes (baby)...Palestinian Covenant
Hearing	7.	**Sky means Lord God Almighty** — God's Ears (teenager)...Davidic Covenant
Smelling	8.	**Cross means Forgiveness** — God's Nose (adult)... New Covenant
Tasting	9.	**Holy Spirit means Union with God** - God's Mouth (wise man)...Everlasting Covenant

This illustration shows that if God thinks of a man, he comes into existence allowing the Lord to see him, hear him, smell him, taste him, and finally, touch him to know that this creature is truly real. Once a person is real to God (justice forgives man), then it is important for God to become real to that person (mercy forgives God). It can only happen when a created soul gains knowledge (see), becomes self-aware (hear), is conscious (smell), and finds sentience (taste/reality) in the creation of God (mate/home/job). Obviously, the Lord needed to force His new creation to surrender its spirit (heart) to a priest to be purified (new spirit); then to sacrifice its flesh (mind) to a king to be transformed (new body); and finally, to save its soul (being) through God's Son to be converted to a new-life (new nature) in truth, law, will, and love.

At each of these stages of life, the Lord has hoped to mature His children and bring them from Nothing to All by converting their minds, hearts, and souls into new creations in Christ (new nature). In this explanation, we now see that if God even thinks of a man, he will come into existence and be given the Lord's free gift of life to live seventy or eighty years, allowing him to find his own eternal pathway for himself based on what he believes.

In contrast, if God speaks to a man, he will be invited into the Lord's sacred temple (church) to teach him God's divine truths and explain the meaning (see limitations), purpose (see potential), and value of life (see self-worth). In the case where God touches a man, he will be made holy through the Lord's blessings of repentance, prayers, works, and through the saving of souls to bring him out of God's curse to set him free. Next, if God sups with a man, he will be honored with God's divine friendship by being given the Lord's blessings of wisdom, courage, and generosity so he can become of great service to the entire kingdom of God. Finally, if God adopts a man, this most chosen soul (free man) will be both blessed (spirit) and honored (flesh) with entering the royal household of God as a member of God's divine family of infinite perfection.

We can see that within each of the nine covenants of God, the Lord has thought of, spoken to, touched, supped with, and finally adopted, each of these nine men chosen to carry the Lord's torch of freedom from the dawn of time until the coming of the Lord as a man on the Earth. There is a need to be specially chosen by God to perform a great work for Him and to be willing to surrender one's heart (know God), sacrifice his mind (love God), and to have his soul saved (serve God) all in the name of the will of God. We see in this theme that each of God's children must first be saved (free gold mine), then save himself (dig gold), then save others (share gold), and finally, to be set free to build (servanthood) his own kingdom of glory (golden city) for God.

We can now see the great losses from crimes in both Heaven and on the Earth and both of these divine violations must be rectified as all must be restored back to their original owners and put back into their original states even if it takes all eternity to do it. This means that all things shall be transformed into God's perfection with the coming of God's Son, Jesus Christ, who will bring divine solutions to every human problem to create Heaven on Earth for one and all. Through the everlasting covenant, we see the fulfillment of God's kingship (one blessing), priesthood (two blessings), sonship (three blessings), and servanthood (four blessings), thereby allowing each of God's children to both grow and mature into the finest of men possible with an abundance of honor, dignity, and integrity.

Now we can see that through the above nine covenants, the Lord God Almighty would be able to make full restitution (payment) to His own divine justice through the sacrifices of His faults or His first-born creations (birthright/spirit) and the blessing of His virtues or His second-born creations (inheritance/flesh).

The following tabular information indicates that God is using two separate systems to correct the problem of taking form, where His positive nature became an evil spirit (order/strong adult) and His negative nature became a holy flesh (chaos/weak baby):

Likeness (-)	Image (+)
• Son	• Father
• Holy Flesh	• Evil Spirit

Flesh (reveal word)	**Spirit** (decode word)
<u>Purifying the Word</u>	<u>Transforming the Truth</u>
Called to Man's Righteousness	Chosen for God's Sainthood
• Word of God is the Torah	• Gospel of God is the Doctrine

Witness is the Word	*Prophet is the Truth*
• Try – Fight Evil	• Win – Submit Free Will

Old Testament – Law/Jews	New Testament – Faith/Christians
1. Genesis – Earthly Life	1. Matthew – Heavenly Life
2. Exodus – Earthly People	2. Mark - Heavenly Saints
CHAOS 3. Leviticus – Earthly Temple	3. Luke – Heavenly Church **Order**
4. Numbers – Earthly Government	4. John – Heavenly Government
5. Deuteronomy – Earthly Home	5. Revelation – Heavenly Home
(negative nature/weak baby – chaos)	(positive nature/strong adult – order)

Sacrifices of God's Faults	**Blessing of God's Virtues**
• Justice Forgives Man in Reality	• Mercy Forgives God in Illusion
• Agony of Defeat – Loser	• Thrill of Victory – Winner
• Worthy of Purified Grave	• Worthy of Purified Host
• *New Body* – Heaven on Earth	• *Eternal Life* – Paradise in Heaven

This illustration shows that God knew that when He infused His paradoxical nature into a single natural creation, it would automatically divide into an evil spirit nature (strong) and a holy physical nature (weak). Then the evil nature would consume the holy nature, thereby making both the spirit (angelic/human) and the flesh evil (human). To comprehend God's mystical dilemma of having His positive nature become evil (evil spirit) and His negative nature become holy (holy spirit) is the same as taking a picture of one's image (person) and then when the photograph is developed, the positive is reversed, thereby making all whites black (Father [+]) and all blacks white (Son [-]). Through this reversal process, the image of God is distorted by the physical creation of the Son (Incarnate Word) and even worse, the Son has been divided into God's law of justice (baby obey/flesh) and God's faith of mercy (adult submit/spirit). Unfortunately, for God to transform His old image and likeness back into a single life form, He would have to increase its value from Nothing to All by placing His labors, wealth, life, and even His eternal life (Calvary) upon His altar of oblivion to prove His depth of commitment (make a high wager). We are all witnessing God that as He grows and matures from a baby to an adult, He becomes more and more proficient in increasing His bet (sacrificial offering): first offering (betting) Adam, then first humanity (Noah's flood), then the Jews, then Jesus Christ, then the Church, and finally, the world itself.

This means that if we are to convince God that we are serious about helping Him build His kingdom of glory from the dust of the earth on up, we too must become professional gamblers with the good sense to place that correct bet at that precise moment when we can win a bundle, better known as reaping where you did not sow. We see that in the case of the Lord God Almighty, His highest bet comes from His divine justice (big black chips), which always bets life against death (tomb). Next is His divine mercy, which always bets real cash (money/grace dollars) against pain (crucifixion), and finally, comes His divine love, which always bets labors against slavery, which is God's most valued commodity (cursed with hard labor).

Playing the Game of Life – Take a Chance
(make your bet upon either God's Altar of Life,
Throne of Wealth, or Table of Works)

Time (spanked)	1. **Justice** – <u>Life against Death</u> – Tomb/Altar...Bet One's Soul
	• Baby's Challenge – Fulfill God's Law of Obedience (trying/failure)
	• Mastering God's Church – Sacrifice Eternal Life (tomb/daily)
	• Learning God's right from man's wrong – graded on handicap system
Money (corrected)	2. **Mercy** – <u>Wealth against Pain</u> – Crucifixion/Throne...Bet One's Happiness
	• Teenager's adventure – Fulfill Man's Faith in God's Love (competing)
	• Mastering Man's Government – Sacrifice Wealth (crucifixion/weekly)
	• Learning God's Good from Man's Evil – Graded on Curve System
Effort (reviewed)	3. **Love** – <u>Labors against Slavery</u> – Scourging/Table...Bet Comfortable Life
	• Adult's fun – fulfill God/Man Knowing – Thinking for Self (winning)
	• Mastering God's/Man's Home – Sacrifice Eternal Labors

(scourging/yearly)
- Learning God's Will/Man's Will – Graded on Pass/Fail Grading System

This illustration shows that the Lord God Almighty can only sacrifice His life (justice) upon His altar (priesthood worships), His wealth (mercy) upon His throne (kingship praises), and finally, His labors/works (love) upon His table (sonship thanks). This means that the life-experience is being controlled by the Eternal Father's altar of justice (trying), the Son of God's throne of mercy (competing), and the Holy Spirit's table of love (winning). This implies that the game of life is all about investing one's time, money, and effort to get either man's agony of defeat (trying) or God's thrill of victory (winning). The implication here is that man's baby flesh is trying to win as it fights all the forces of evil in a desperate attempt to master the life-experience, which can only be won by accepting and embracing one's agony of defeat (cross). In contrast, if a person accepts defeat, he can then master dying to his own selfishness unto oblivion, thereby setting him free from sin, evil, death, and even damnation to make him worthy of God's blessing of the thrill of victory (bonus rewards/triumph).

The idea here is that if a person faces God's justice (babyhood), he will be spanked every day (basic training). If he faces God's mercy (teenager), he will be corrected weekly (Sunday). Finally, if he faces God's love (adulthood), he will be reviewed annually (Easter). This means that if a person is within a gambling casino, he can now decode (God's word) and the rainbow of Noah (seal of purity) in seven colors of the light spectrum clearly defines the mystical value of God's seven-fold spirits in maturity or power levels.

Obviously, the best way to measure the individual value of God's three natures (3), three persons (6), and His Trinity (7) is to determine the size of God's offering or bet, thereby saying either put up (sacrifice) or shut up (worship). This means that when we look at Noah's rainbow, we see the color black means betting death (tomb), blue means betting diamonds, yellow means betting gold, green means betting money, red means betting sacrificial blood, purple means betting one's royal crown, and finally, white means betting one's purity (baby innocence).

Colors of God's Mystical Chips in the Game of Life
(God is betting against slavery, reputation,
homeless, naked, hungry, broke, and even death)

1. **Black Chips** – <u>Betting</u>: Life Against Death (three days in tomb)... Bet Death
2. **Blue Chips** – <u>Betting</u>: Wealth Against Poverty (school of hard-knocks)... Bet Diamonds
3. **Yellow Chips** – <u>Betting</u>: Labors Against Slavery (chains/prison/guards)... Bet Gold
4. **Green Chips** – <u>Betting</u>: Disgrace Against Starvation (hunger for truth)... Bet Money

5. **Red/Pink Chips** – <u>Betting</u>: Humiliation Against Nakedness (out in the cold) … Bet Blood
6. **Purple Chips** – <u>Betting</u>: Shame Against Homelessness (no place to lay head)… Bet Crown
7. **White Chips** – <u>Betting</u>: Debasement Against Honor/Losing Face (reputation)… Bet Purity

This illustration shows that the life-experience is being paid for by the size of God's offering, which begins with God Himself, then Lucifer, Adam, the Angels, Heaven, Christ, the Church, the Lord's Tree of Life, Evil Humanity, Jewish People, Jesus, and finally, the Whole World. Obviously, God is sacrificing it all to win it all in just one roll of the dice. This implies that there is no gamble the Lord is not willing to make to get new bodies for His people, eternal lives for His lost and beautiful kingdoms, and labors upon the Lord's table. We put our money before God's throne, then put our lives, and our eternal lives upon the Lord's altar, and put them all on the line because where there is no guts, there is no glory.

Place Your Wager	**Spirit** Spiritual Offerings	**Flesh** Physical Offerings	Treasures
1. Bet honor	1. God	1. Tree of life	1. New body
2. Bet labors	2. Lucifer	2. Adam	2. Eternal Life
3. Bet money	3. Angels	3. Evil humanity	3. Own Kingdom
4. Bet life	4. Heaven	4. Jewish people	4. Personal Freedom
5. Bet eternal life	5. Christ	5. Jesus (Son of Man)	5. God's Friendship
6. Bet All (Judas)	6. Church	6. World (Earth)	6. Companionship
7. Winner/Winner/ Winner	7. New Heaven	7. New Earth	7. God's Oneness

This illustration shows that "when a person (a mature/baby)" first attempts something new, he is literally challenged to his soul as he is putting his honor and reputation on the line because when he fails, all his family, friends, and neighbors will laugh (clown/joke). Initially, God must bet His honor (God/tree of knowledge) as He sacrifices His destiny to create free will, which will force His new creation to master both its streetwise flesh (fighting evil/world) and then master its educated intellect (submit to knowledge/church). Secondly, God must bet His works/labors (Lucifer/Adam) as He sacrifices His first-born spiritual (Lucifer/angels) and physical (Adam/men) creations to create both the angelic realm in Heaven (saints) and the human race on Earth (righteous men). Thirdly, God must bet His own money (angels/humanity) as He sacrifices His first-born demons (hell) and evil mankind (death) to create Lucifer's test (baby farm) to torment God's children with painful sin-natures (self), worldly temptations (society), and demonic possessions (God). Fourthly, God must bet His very life (heaven/Jewish people) as he sacrifices His first-born Jewish and Gentile (Christians) peoples to create God's judgment (divine school) to test, judge, and evaluate the growth and maturity progress of each of God's children. Fifthly, God must bet His eternal life (Christ/Jesus) as He sacrifices His first-born Messiah, first as a baby (Christmas/God forgives), and secondly, as an adult (Easter/man forgives) to unite God's spirit (life/host) with man's flesh (death/grave). Sixthly, God must bet His All (church/world) as He sacrifices His new born-again nature (sainthood) and His newly created righteous citizen to bring forth His new Heaven and His new Earth to unite God's mind (wisdom) with man's heart (love). Finally, God must bet His super jackpot (new Heaven/new Earth) as He sacrifices His first-born jackpot to become human (spirit enters population), thereby allowing Him to finally enter physical existence within His own holy city (New Jerusalem) as He travels from Heaven (spirit) to Earth (flesh) to meet one and all.

We now see that through each of these seven mystical offerings, the Lord God Almighty could pay the full sacrificial price (give it all) for His new body, His eternal life, and His new Kingdom of Glory so that all His subjects could have all the challenges, adventures, fun, and freedom (happiness) that they have ever wanted.

Skill Level Determines Depth of Confidence
(0 percent to 100 percent)
(baby is challenged, teen seeks adventure, adult is
having fun, and wise man masters all he surveys)

1. Challenge	First Time Bet and win (beginner's luck): offer one's labors... Thanksgiving (table)
	• Baby is challenged unto failure
2. Adventure	Second Time (double down bet): offer one's wealth...praise (throne)
	• Teenager seeks adventure (winning and losing)
3. Fun	Become Professional Gambler (it's easy): offer one's life... worship (altar)
	• Adult is having fun (everything brings a smile)
4. Financial Freedom	Fulfill One's Heart's Desire: offer eternal life...sacrifice (face)
	• Wise man masters all he surveys (treasuring the life-experience)

This illustration shows that the heart of the life-experience is centered upon a **baby's challenge** (taking risk) on Earth, a **teenager's adventure** (willingly sacrificing) in Heaven, an **adult's fun** (professional gambler) within God's Kingdom, and finally, a **wise man's** (making a living at risk) **financial freedom**. The idea here is that the definition of a challenge is being trapped into defending oneself and then ending up fighting for his very life (survival). But this same event suddenly turns into a great adventure when he sees the benefit of risking a little (life) to get a lot (eternal life).

Yes! We are all called to a great amount of risk and extreme danger as we embark upon our great adventure of life, truly gambling with our own life, our money, and our hard-work (labors) in hopes of making our mark on the world by fulfilling our destiny before God, angels, and men. This means that by facing death, a person can fulfill his life, thereby giving it true value in the eyes of everyone who witnesses his wisdom, courage, and tenacity as he strives to make something out of nothing. We see that baby survival turns into a great opportunity, and then on one fine day, it all becomes fun and no one ever wants to stop playing the game of life forever and ever as all one day learn to seek eternal life and all it has to offer to the most beloved Son of God.

Chapter 3

Jesus Christ's Perfect Justice System
(Witness/Prophet/Messiah)

"Each of God's Children" is being <u>Called to Master</u> **Physical Government** (job), the **Spiritual Church** (worship), the **Mystical Home** (love), and finally, to **Possess His Own** **Divine Kingdom** (freedom/servanthood). The idea here is to see that "If a Person" <u>Masters his Kingship</u>, he will **Get a Title Deed to the Earth** (land) and a *New Transfigured Body* (babyhood/Earth). "If He Masters the Priesthood," he will Get a **Title Deed to Heaven** (land) and a *New Glorified Body* (adulthood/Heaven). Next, "If He" <u>Masters his Sonship</u> (son of God), he will Get a **Title Deed to the Kingdom** (land), a **New Mystical Body** (babies), and **God's Blessing** of *Divine Ownership* (servanthood/life), **All in the Name** of *Jesus Christ*. Finally, "If He" <u>Masters his Servant-hood</u>, he will **Get a Title Deed to God's Beatific Vision** (land), a **New Holy Body** (babies), **Life for Others** (life), and an **Infinite Number of Beloved Children** (love) **Giving Him** *Peace, Joy, and Happiness Forever*.

The idea here is that whether a "Person Gets One Blessing" or "All Four Blessings," <u>Every Cup shall be Filled</u> and <u>Every Soul</u> **Which** Passes through **God's Divine School of Higher Learning** will both **Love** and *Treasure* its *Journey unto Perfection Forever* (God's personal gift/white rock). The idea here is to see that "God's Spirit (lamb)" can <u>Only</u> be <u>Washed and Made Perfect</u> (clean pig/holy), while "Man's Flesh (goat)" can <u>Change Natures</u> (pig to human/divine); yet, the **Miracle Comes When God's Spirit** (blessings) and **Man's Flesh** (lessons) are *Made One in Christ Jesus*. This "Two-Truth Concept (all/nothing)" <u>Sits at the Center</u> of **God's Paradox** of Life (all/nothing), causing a **Contradiction** (paradox) between **God's Mind** (wisdom/all) and **Man's Mind** (ignorance/nothing) as **He Tries** to **Comprehend** the *Divinity of God* (Christ/law) and the *Humanity of Man* (Jesus/faith). Recall that "Adam/Eve" were Cursed to become **Animals** (pigs) and were then **Forced to Live** in **Caves and Mud Shacks** as **They were Made to Survive** in a **Barren Land** (desert/no water) simply because **They Believed** that <u>**Lucifer's Tree of Knowledge would** *Set Them Free*</u>. Yes! Our "First Parents" <u>Got All the Knowledge</u> **They would Ever Want**, but **Failed to Comprehend** that **Knowledge** becomes an **Evil Curse, If it is Not** <u>**Controlled by Wisdom**</u> which can *Only Come* from *God's Tree of Life* (using knowledge/thinking). This "Pig-Like Status" caused <u>Primitive Mankind</u> to **Live Like Wild Animals** (ignorant fools) and **Caused Man** to **Reject** the **Guiding Hand of God**, at least, until the **Coming** of *God's Son, Jesus Christ* (Messiah).

During the "Lord's 1st Advent (priest on donkey)," <u>Lost Sinners</u> were **Called** to **Their Conversion Experience** as **They** had to **Deny Their Intellects** (mind), <u>Hear the Word of God</u>, and then *Surrender Obediently to God's Divine Will* (being saved). Secondly, with the coming of the "Lord's 2nd Advent (thief in the night)," <u>Christians</u> will be **Chosen** for **Their Conversion Experience** as **They Abandon Their Feelings** (heart) to become <u>**Living Prayers**</u> within the *Lord's Holy Church* (saving self). We see that this "Conversion Experience" Involves **First Removing Sin** (washing) via **God's Forgiveness;** and then <u>Secondly, Changing **Death into New-life**</u> via *Christ's Death and Resurrection* (saving others/Calvary). Unfortunately, "History is Teaching Us" that the <u>Jewish Law Failed</u> to **Transform Man's Flesh** (defeat sin) nor has the "Christian Church (faith)" been able to **Transform Man's Spirit** (defeat death) because it **Takes Them** both <u>**Blended Together in Jesus Christ**</u> to *Work Correctly* as *They Transform a Man's Soul* (flesh/spirit) into *Holy Perfection*. We might ask "Why has Christianity Failed" to <u>Make Everyone on Earth</u> into **Holy Saints** and to **Create the Promised** *Heaven on Earth*? The answer is that "Christianity Taught Human Faith (seek life/free)" and <u>Failed</u> to "Teach" or "Even Understand" <u>Divine Faith</u> (seek death/earned), causing <u>Christians</u> to **Physically Travel Toward** *God's Curse* (save self) **Instead** of **Spiritually Traveling Toward** *God's Blessing* (save lost/damned). Yes! The answer to "Human Redemption" is <u>Centered</u> on **Blending** both **God's Spiritual Blessing** (spirit) and **God's Physical Redemption** (flesh) to **Unite** the **Jewish Law** (flesh/blood) with **Man's Faith** (bread/wine) to <u>**Set the Stage**</u> for *Saving the Whole World*. The idea was for the "Jewish People" to <u>Speak Directly to God</u> (temple) and to bring forth **Heaven on Earth** by <u>**Converting**</u> *Ignorant Fools* into *Righteous Citizens*; while the "Christian People (gentiles)" were to <u>Speak Indirectly to God</u> (church) and to bring forth **Paradise in Heaven** by <u>**Converting**</u> *Sinners* into *Holy Saints*.

The following tabular information indicates that the "Jewish People" were <u>Chosen to Save</u> **Man's Physical Nature** (world) by bringing the **World** into <u>**Obedience**</u> to *God's Law*, while the "Christian People" were <u>Called to Save</u> **Man's Spiritual Nature** (church) by bringing the **Church** into **Faithfulness** unto *God's Love*:

Law of Obedience is Blended with Faith in God's Love
(Jewish stick of discipline fails and Christian
carrot of kindness fails to change mankind)

1. **Jewish Law of Obedience** - <u>Failed</u>: Offer God's Blessing to the World...Jews See Their Limitations
   - God Gives *Temple* to Jews - Speak Directly to God: Messiah Only (pay all debts)
   - God's Earthly Blessing Cast into the Dirt - Jews Foolishly Killed Their Messiah
   - Jews Begged God for Mercy and Got It - Jews Showed No Mercy to Jesus
   - Righteous Man - Called by Jesus: Hear Word to Redeem Flesh/Eat Bread to be Born-again
2. **Man's Faith in God's Love** - <u>Failed</u>: Offer God Redemption to World...Christians See Their Potential
   - God's Son Gives *Church* to Christians - Speak via Intercessor to God: Christians Only (pay others' debts)
   - God's Heavenly Blessing Cast into Dirt - Foolish Christians Only Save Themselves
   - Christians Beg God for Free Redemption - Christians Keep Free Gift for Themselves
   - Holy Man - Chosen by Christ: Save Souls to Redeem Spirit/Drink Wine to Enter Sainthood

* *Called is Man Accepting God (Jews/Christmas)*
* *Chosen is God Accepting Man (Christians/Easter)*

This illustration shows that the "Jewish People" <u>Spent 1500 Years</u> **Trying** to **Fulfill God's Law** and **Failed**, thereby **<u>Creating Christ's</u>** *1st Advent* (priest); while the "Christian People" have <u>Spent some 2,000 Years</u> **Trying** to **Fulfill Man's Faith** and **Failed**, thereby **<u>Creating Christ's 2nd Advent</u>** (thief). The question is: just "What will Work?" The <u>Answer</u> can be **Found** in the **3rd Advent of Christ** (end of second coming) as **He Comes** to *Resurrect His Saints* (1/faith), *Kill All the Evil Pagans* (2/law), and then *Set All of the Captives Free* (3/will). This means that "Christianity was Trying" to <u>Earn Eternal Life</u> through the *Law* (save self), **Instead of Trying** to **<u>Give Redemption to the Damned</u>** through *One's Faith* (saving others). In short, this is telling us that "Life is Consumed by Man (will)" through his <u>Thrill of Victory</u> (blessing becomes curse), while "Death is Consumed by God (belief)" through <u>His Agony of Defeat</u> (curse becomes blessing). We see this "Great Journey" from <u>Defeat to Victory</u> in the **First Week of God's Creation** as we must **Worship** (home) the *Eternal Father* (daily) for *Six Days*, then **Praise** (church) the *Holy Spirit* (Sunday) for *One Day*, and finally, to **Thank** *the Son of God* at the *End* (Easter Duty).

Now, imagine using God's "1st Week of Creation" as a <u>Seven-Day Period</u> plus a <u>Day of Judgment</u> (8th day) and we can see what each of our **Earthly Weeks** should look like as we must **Worship the Father for Six Days** (repentance) by *Giving Him Our Lives*, then **Praise the Holy Spirit on Sunday** (prayers) as we *Give Him Our Wealth* or *Money*, and finally, we **Thank the Son of God on Easter** (works) by **Giving Him Our Annual Labors** (souls saved). At each of these "Stages of Life," we are able to both <u>Grow and Mature</u> in **God's Truths** (right/wrong), **Laws** (good/evil), and **Will** (God/man's) allowing us to *See Our Limitations* (daily), *See Our Potential* (Sunday), and *See Our Self-worth* (Easter). It should now make sense that "Earthly Repentance (man)" brings <u>Free Redemption</u> (new body/citizenship), "Heavenly Prayers (Angels)" bring <u>Earned Salvation</u> (eternal life/sainthood), and "Kingdom Works (God)" bring <u>Bonus Rewards</u> (royal kingdom/sonship)

Out of these "Three Stages of Life," **Each of God's Children** can **Overcome Ignorance**, **Defeat his Sin-nature**, and become *Righteous*. He can also **Overcome his Cowardice**, **Defeat Worldly Temptations**, and become *Holy*. Finally, a "Born-again Soul" can <u>Overcome its Greed</u>, **Defeat Demonic Possession**, and become **Perfect**, all in the **Name of Mastering** *God's Truths, Laws, and Will*. It should now make sense that the "Life-experience" is <u>All About</u> **Defeating** the **Ignorant Flesh** via *God's Law*, **Defeating** the **Cowardly Spirit** via *Man's Faith*, and finally, **Defeating His Greedy Soul** via the **Power of His** *God/Man Knowing*. Unfortunately, we are "Not Perfect Yet" and it's clear that <u>We have All been Tricked</u>, as **Each of Us** is **Actually On-display before Our Creator** to be either **Accepted** (blessed) or **Rejected** (cursed) for **Special Treatment** and **Promotion** unto *God's High Command*.

We see that it is like "Any School" <u>Which is Looking</u> for **Mentally Gifted Students Who** are truly **Worthy** of **Special Training, Leading** to a **Person's High Expectations** within *God's Eternal Social Order*. We hear it said that "There is No Greater Burden" than a "Great Potential (perfection)" and this was <u>Never Truer</u> than **When Trying** to become a **Devout Christian Who** must **Plunge himself** into the **Depths of Sin, Evil, and Death** to **Prove** to **One and All** that he *Believes in Christ 100%* (fighting evil). The "Hope in Heaven (expectations)" is that <u>One Day</u>, the **Lord's Kingdom of Glory** will **Come** and **All will See the Value of Living a Life of Perfect Truth** as **Each Man will Live** through an **Unbreakable Code of Honor**, **Reflecting** the *Dignity of his Very Soul*. This has been the "Ultimate Purpose" of the **Lord God Almighty** as He **Struggles** to bring **Humanity** an **Understanding** of **His Divine Laws** as **Manifested** in **Our Own Civil** (government) and **Natural** (nature) **Laws** of *Order and Obedience*. The "Establishment of Order" <u>Requires that All</u> must be **Encased** within the **Governing Forces of Law** through some **Mystical Power of Will**, showing that this **Concept of Free Will** has been **Predicated** upon **Someone's Master Plan**, thereby **Defining** the <u>Objectives Associated</u> with a *Person's Physical Existence*.

This "Mystical Construct" for the Creation of <u>Perfect Order</u> clearly **Relates to the Need** for the **Lord Jesus Christ** to **Come** as a **Multifunctional Witness** (decode word/parables), **Prophet** (teacher), and **Messiah** (savior) to **Conquer Death** and bring the **Blessings of God's Healing** to a *Lost and Broken World*. This most "Essential Redemptive Process" would be <u>Executed</u> in **Three Mystical Phase**s as has been **Mentioned Many Times**, thereby **Identifying Them** as the **Three Advents of Christ, Who Comes to Save** the **Babies, Teenagers**, and **Adults** from *Fear, Pain, and Death*. We see that in the "Lord's 1st Advent (witness/death)" or a <u>Baby Coming on a Donkey</u> (priest), the <u>Human Race</u> was **Baptized in Death** (sacrifice Christ) to **Pay for Capital Sins** (Divine Sin-debt/soul) and **Create** *Thanksgiving of God* via *One's Labors* (table). Secondly, the "Lord's 2nd Advent (prophet/pain)" or <u>Teenager Coming as Thief in the Night</u> (king) **Involves Mankind's Confession in Blood** (sacrifice church) to **Pay for Mortal Sins** (human debt/spirit) and **Create** *Praise of God* via *One's Wealth* (throne). Finally, the "Lord's 3rd Advent (Messiah/fear)" or <u>Adult Coming as Judge on a Cloud</u> (son) **Involves** <u>Humanity's</u> **Communion of the Word** (sacrifice world) to **Pay for Venial Sins** (personal debt/flesh) and **Create** *Worship of God* via *One's Life* (altar).

Witness Decodes the Torah - Create Church (awakening)
- Saving the Woman at the Well Being Saved from Sin (repent)

Jesus Christ's 1st Advent/Priesthood - Witness Decodes God's Word (church/morals)
Recall that in the "Lord's 1st Advent (priest on donkey)," He Came as the **Christ Child** to bring **Humanity a Priest** (church), **King** (government), and **Son** (home) **All in the Form** of a **Sacrificial Lamb** to *Pay the Outstanding Sin-debt of Man* (ignorance to wisdom). During this "First Phase" of Mankind's Redemption, the **Lord Created** the **Redeeming Church** (touch of Peter/baptism) **Out** of the **Divine Ordinations** of *God's Holy of Holies* (royal court) *in Heaven*. This "Step of Purification" would clearly Reveal the Need for **Distinguishing the Difference** between **Church and State** (government) by **Teaching Humanity** the **Difference** between *Moral* (Heaven/church/sacrifice) and *Ethical* (earth/government/prayer) *Behavior*. This means that the "Lord God Almighty" was Using the Jewish People to **Introduce** the **Word of God** into the **World** in the **Form** of the **Torah** (1st five books of bible); and then use the **Three Mystical Advents of Christ** as **He Comes** as the **Witness** (decode), a **Prophet** (teach), and finally, **Resurrects** as the *Messiah of God*. The "Purpose of the Witness (create church)" is to bring forth the Natural Law of Life in the **Form** of **Human Fairness** so that the **Flesh of Man** can **Defeat its Ignorance** to **Attain** **God's Blessing of Wisdom** (intellect) through *One's Awakening*. The idea here is that the "Carpenter's Son" was the Witness to the **Woman of the Well, When the Lord Told** her that **She could be Saved** by **Drinking the Living Waters of Life** which is to **Believe** in the *Christ* or *Messiah 33%* (fulfill 10 commandments). This means that "God's Babies" must First Repent by **Thanking God** with their **Labors** to **Prove** that they have **Believed in God's Son, 33%** (mind) and are **Now Worthy** of having a **New Transfigured Body Brought forth Out** of *Their Purified Graves*. By "Fulfilling One's Beliefs" in Christ, a **Person can Defeat his Ignorance and Obtain** a **Wise Mind**, thereby **Awakening him** to the **Realities of Life** and can **Decode God's Word** to *See God's Truth*.

Prophet Teaches God's Truths - Creates Government (seal saints)
- Synagogue Priest Saves himself - Saved from Evil Forces (prayer)

Jesus Christ's 2nd Advent/Kingship - Prophet Teaches God's Truth (government/ethics)
During the Lord's "2nd Advent (thief in the night)," He will bring humanity God's Triune Construct of Infinite Law through which He will establish His new **Sacred Government** created out of the *Blood of His Enemies*. We see that "Jesus Christ" is to Come as a **Thief in the Night** to **Reveal** the **Power of God** as **He Arrives to Establish** the **Eternal Reign of God** upon the **Earth** that will be **Ruled** with an *Iron Rod of Mercy* from *Everlasting to Everlasting*. The "Lord will Institute" God's New Divine Statutes **Designed to Govern** the **Future Ethical Behavior** (flesh) of **All Men, Revealing** to **One and All** just **How** the **Inter-Personal Affairs of Humanity** should be **Handled** in both *Spirit* (morals) and in *Flesh* (ethics). Note here that "God is Using" His Holy Church as a **High Priest** (Pope) to **Offer Him** the **Necessary Sacrificial Offerings** to **Warrant an Audience** with the **Whole Human Race, Allowing**

It to Officially *Present Its Prayer* before the *Royal Court* (mercy seat) *of God*. Secondly, we see "God is Using" His "Sacred Government" as a **Righteous King** to **Offer-up Man's Formal Request** (prayer) for **Divine Blessings** (thought of), **Anointings** (spoken too), **Sanctification** (touched), and **Consecration** (sup with) from the *Lord God Almighty Himself*. Thirdly, we see "God is Using" His Divine Home as a **Perfect Son** to **Effectively Implement Man's Divine Gifts** of **Wisdom, Wealth**, and **Happiness** to bring the **Greatest Benefit to All** the *Peoples of the Earth*. Finally, we see that "God is Using" His Kingdom of Glory as **God on Earth** to **Effectively Communicate** with **Lost Broken Humanity** and **Reveal** to **One and All** that the **Life-experience** is **All About** becoming *Educated on Earth* (growing-up/meaning), *Working in Heaven* (maturing/purpose), and having a *Person's Eternal Life* (adulthood/value) *with God*.

Yes! Life is about "Man becoming God (Jesus Christ/flesh)" and "God becoming Man (Christ Jesus/spirit)" so that the Two Kingdoms of the **Benevolent Force** (1st truth) and the **Personal God** (2nd truth) could become **One** in *Truth, Law, Will, and Love*. Obviously, the "Church Represents" the Love of God (worship) and the "Government Represents" the Love of Man (wealth). This implies that the **Lord has Come** to **Show Mankind How** it can **Place its Heart** upon the **Works of God** (heart) and its **Mind** upon the **Works of Man** (mind) **Dividing its Efforts**, to *Cover both Requirements at the Same Time.* Now, "We may Come to Understand" just Why the Messiah had to be **Torn in Two Parts** (Abrahamic covenant) during **His Crucifixion on Mount Calvary**, so that **His Spirit** could be *Transformed* into *His Sacred Heart of Perfect Love*. This "Perfect Love" has been Eternally Offered-up to the **Will of God**, thereby **Fulfilling** *His Priestly* **Spiritual Nature** (perpetual sacrifice) and *His Sonly Mystical Nature* (daily sacrifice) to **Attain** both *Earth and Heaven*. Conversely, it becomes clear that the "Messiah's Flesh" was Transformed into **His Immaculate Mind of Perfect Love** to **Forever** be in the **Will of Man**, thereby **Fulfilling** *His Kingly Physical Nature* (daily sacrifice).

The reason for this "Inter-locking" of the Human Heart (God) and Human Mind (Man) with the **Messiah's Spirit** (heart) and **Flesh** (mind) is so that the **Human Soul** will **Come to Understand** the **Difference** between *God's Divine Law* (Church) and *Man's Civil Law* (Government). In this way, the "Human Soul" will be Able to Balance the **Affairs of the Mind** (intellect) **Against the Affairs of the Heart** (emotions), bringing a **Person's Intentions** in **Line** with his **Emotional Impulses**, thereby **Keeping Every Born-again Life** on the *Straight* and *Narrow*. The "Purpose of the Prophet (create government)" is to bring forth the Civil Law of Life in the **Form** of **Human Ethics** so that the **Spirit of Man** can **Defeat its Cowardice** to **Attain God's Blessing of Courage** (emotions) through *His Knowledge*. The idea here is that "Jesus" was the Prophet (teacher) **Who Supped with the Synagogue Priest** and **Told him** that **he could Save himself** (saving self) by **Washing His Feet with his Tears** (repent) and **Drying Them with his Hair** (forgiven), like what the **Prostitute Did to the Son of God** which was to **Believe** in the *Christ* or *Messiah 67%* (fulfilled by selling all). This means that "God's Teenagers" must Secondly Pray by **Praising God** via **Offering Their Wealth** to **Prove** that they have **Believed in God's Son, 67%** (heart) and are **Now Worthy** of having **Eternal Life in Paradise Brought forth**

Out of *Their Purified Host*. By "Fulfilling His Beliefs" in <u>Christ</u>, **A Person can Defeat** his **Cowardice and Obtain** a **Courageous Heart**, thereby **Allowing Him** to be **Accepted by God** so that he can **Decode God's Blood** to *See God's Law*.

Messiah Saves Lost Souls - Create Home (judgment)
• Temple Priest Saves Others - Save World from Curse of Death (works)

<u>Jesus Christ's 3rd Advent/sonship</u> - Messiah Saves Lost Souls (home/fairness)

The "Lord Jesus Christ" will "<u>Return to Earth</u>" during **His 3rd Advent** to bring forth **His Father's Divine Heart** and to **Teach Those most Important Divine Principles** of <u>God's Truth</u> through *His Great White Throne Judgment* (standards). "When All Mankind" is <u>Able to Compare</u> the **Experiences of All Men** (collective mind) with **Their Own Experiences, They will be Able to See the Meaning of It All** (existence) and <u>**How They Themselves Fit**</u> into the *Big Picture of Life* (purpose/serve God). The point is that "Absolutely No One" will <u>Leave God's Last Judgment</u> **Not Knowing the Difference** between **God's Right and Man's Wrong**, that clearly **Reveals** the **Full Impact** of both <u>**Morals, Ethics,**</u> and <u>**Fairness**</u> upon the *Institutions* of God's *Church* (way/peace), *Government* (truth/joy), and *Home* (life/happiness). The "Purpose of the Messiah (create home)" is to bring forth the <u>Divine Law of Life</u> in the **Form** of **Human Morals** so that the **Soul of Man** can **Defeat its Greed** and **Attain** <u>**God's Blessing of Generosity**</u> (emotions) through *Its Unselfishness*.

The idea here is that "Christ" is the <u>Messiah</u> (savior) **Who Confronted the Temple Priest** and **Told him** that **he could Help Save Others** by **Sacrificing himself** unto **Death on Mount Calvary** which was to <u>**Believe**</u> in the *Christ* or *Messiah 100%* (fulfill carrying the cross). This means that "God's Adults" must <u>Thirdly Work</u> by **Worshiping God** via **Offering Their Life to Prove** that they have **Believed in God's Son, 100%** (heart) and are **Now Worthy** of having their **Own Kingdom Brought forth Out** of a *Their Purified Life*. "By Fulfilling His Beliefs" in Christ, a **Person can Defeat his Greed and Obtain a Generous Soul**, thereby **Allowing Him to Fulfill** his **Own Destiny** and <u>**Decode God's Death**</u> to *See God's Will*.

- - - - - - - - - - - - - - - - - -**Important Note:** - - - - - - - - - - - - - - - - - -
Everyone Needs to Learn Life and then Live It
(honor, courage, duty, and sacrifice)
- -

*Note, we see that "Giving One's All (death)" for a <u>Just Cause</u> is **Never a Sacrifice**. Therefore, **Jesus** (fight evil) **and Mary** (surrender will) have put **Their Duty** above **Their Self-interest** and now <u>**All Humanity is being Called**</u> to *Follow Their Example* (total submission/fight evil). Remember, the more a "Person" <u>Helps in Saving Souls</u> for **Christ**, the more he is **Able to Save himself** from the <u>**Curses**</u> of *Ignorance* (sin), *Cowardice* (evil), *Greed* (death), and *Selfishness* (damnation). We see that the "Jewish People" <u>Brought God's Law</u> (shadow of death/world) to **Make** the **Flesh**

Perfect (grave), while the "Christian People" <u>Brought Man's Love</u> (substance of life/church) to **Make** the *Spirit Perfect* (host). This implementation of both "God's Law (shadow)" and "Man's Love (substance)" has <u>Created</u> the **War of Good** (love) and **Evil** (law) which can **Only be Resolved** <u>When</u> *God's Love* (eternal life) <u>**Overcomes**</u> *Man's Law* (eternal death).

Save Self from Sin, Evil, and Death
(Create New Divine Flesh (purify grave)
and Create New Holy Spirit (purify host)
W o r l d - Shadow of Death
. Fighting Evil - Change Nature
. Free Transfigured Body

--------Man Travels through Death to become God - Heaven on Earth: Citizenship--------
World - Learn Lessons of Life (bear fruit/new body)... Fight Evil (to die of evil)
1. <u>Destroy One's Own Flesh</u> - Fulfill God's Law of Obedience - Change Nature: Human to Divine
   . Fighting Lucifer's Evil unto Death - See Limitations (agony of defeat)
   . The More a Person Fights Evil, the More Evil he becomes until it Kills him

C h u r c h - Substance of Life
. Surrender Will - Wash Away Sins
. Earn Own Eternal Life - Love

--------God Travels through Life to become Man - Paradise in Heaven: Sainthood--------
Church - Receive Blessings of God (become fruit/eternal life)...Surrender (to die of shame)
2. <u>Purify One's Own Spirit</u> - Fulfill Man's Faith in God's Love...Wash Away Sin: Sinfulness to Holiness
   . Submit One's Sinful Spirit unto New-life - See Potential (thrill of victory)
      . The More a Person believes in Christ, the More Ashamed he becomes until he Dies of Shame

    <u>For example</u>, during the "Great Angelic Rebellion," <u>Four Curses Landed</u> upon the **Angels of the Air,** the **Good Angels, the Bad Angels,** and finally upon **God, Himself,** thereby *<u>Cursing Them</u> with Silence, Slavery, Pain, and Crushing Sorrow.*
1. **Angels of the Air** - <u>Cursed with Silence at the Table:</u> Ignorance becomes Wisdom   **Silence**
   . Outcast from Kingdom - Restored by Repentance .... See Limitations
   . Home of God - Babies Put in School: Remove Sin-nature = Get New Body
2. **Good Angels** - <u>Cursed with Slavery before Altar</u> : Cowardice becomes Courage   **Slavery**
   . Excommunicated from Kingdom - Restored by Prayer .... See Potential
   . Temple of God - Teenagers Called to Worship: Remove Worldly Temptations
3. **Bad Angels** - <u>Cursed with Painful Torture before Throne:</u> Greed becomes Generosity   **Pain**
   . Banished from Kingdom - Restored by Works .... See Self-worth

. Government of God - Adults called to Govern: Remove Demonic Possession =
Get Own Freedom

4. **Creator God** - Cursed with Failure before Self: Selfishness to Unselfishness **Sorrow**
. Forsaken by the Whole Kingdom - Restored by Saving Others...See Value of Life
. Lord God Almighty - Wise Men Set Free: Remove God's Curse

God's Highway to Earthly Righteousness (host)
Fulfill God's Law of Obedience - Change Nature from Human to **Divine**
Christmas   Circumcision - God Wants to be Man: Master Life/host by Fighting Evil   **Jesus**
Flesh Going to Heaven on Faith
Speed - is doing Everything Fast
(man likes others for their good qualities)

Man's Highway to Heavenly Holiness
Fulfill Man's Faith in God's Love - Wash Away Sin to Change
Sinfulness to *Holiness*   **Easter**
Baptism - Man Wants to be God: Master Death/grave via Submission   **Christ**
Spirit Going to Paradise in Heaven
Accuracy - is Watching Every Detail
(man likes others for their natural defects)

This illustration shows that "God Wants to be a Man (Christmas/host)" so He must Live as a **Man** to **Attain His** *Own Human Nature* (Jesus), while "Man Wants to be God (Easter/grave)" so he must Face Death as **God** did on **Mount Calvary** to **Attain** his *Own Divine Nature* (Christ). We must "Now Open Our Minds" to Grasp the **Lord's Sacrificial-to-Blessing Concept** as **Nature, Men, Angels**, and even **God** are to **Grow-up Together** via the *Challenges* (baby life), *Adventures* (teenage life), *Fun* (adult life), and *Happiness of Life* (wise man life). Note that the "Word Sacrifice" means to give-up Everything to be **Blessed with Everything**, implying that the **Lord Jesus Christ** would have to **Become Pure Evil** (traitor) to **Eventually become Holy** in the *Sight of God.* This means that the "Last Supper" was the Creation of a **New Brotherhood of Traitors** (all evil) as **They had All Failed** to become **Righteous, Holy, and Perfect before God** because both **God's Law** and **His Justice** were *Impossible to Fulfill.* This "Forced Jesus Christ" to Terminate the **Old World Order of Justice** (circumcision) and **Institute** a **New World Order of Mercy** (baptism). Thus, **Even** the most **Ignorant of Fools** could be **Saved** under the **Lord's Free Redemption Program** for *All Human Flesh.* We see that in the "Justice System," the Chosen People were **Required** to be **Circumcised** to be **Marked** as **Children of God,** thereby **Making Them Worthy** of **God's Presence Among Them** in the **Form of Shekinah Glory** upon the *Sacred Mercy Seat*. In contrast, the "Mercy System" Terminated Circumcision and **Replaced** it with a **Dual Baptism** of both **Man's Water** (death) and **God's Spirit** (resurrection) to **Mark** a **New Born-again Christian** as a **Follower of Christ**, thereby **Making him Worthy** of *God's Presence in Heaven Forever.*

Note that in "Circumcision," the Flesh must Die by **Cutting the Foreskin** of the **Penis** and then to **Bleed** to **Change One's Nature** from *Egyptian Slave* (flesh) to

Jewish Free Man (blood). We see the "Same Process" in the Ceremony of Baptism, where **John the Baptist Submerged** a **Sinner** into the **Waters of Baptism** to **Kill the Evil Flesh**. Then **Jesus Christ Spiritually Raises** the **New Born-again Saint** to **Change His** *Physical Sinfulness into Spiritual Holiness*. It should now be clear that "Circumcision brings God to Earth," while "Baptism brings Man to Heaven" in **Fulfillment** of **God's Desire to become Man** and **Man's Desire to become God** which would **Actually Occur When Jesus Christ Fulfills** the **Jewish Law of Circumcision** (1st highway) via *His Death* and then **Fulfills Man's Faithful Baptism** (2nd highway) via *His Resurrection*. Obviously, "God Wants to Come to Earth (grave)" to Receive **His Own** *Physical Transfigured Body* (Jesus/Man), while "Man Wants to Come to Heaven (host)" to Receive his *Own Spiritual Glorified Body* (Christ/God).

1. **Jews Worthy of God's Presence on Earth** - Mark of Circumcision
   (flesh/blood)…   Peace of Mind
   - God Wants to become Man - Physical Body (transfiguration): Righteous Man
   - Fulfill God's Law of Obedience - Change Nature: Human to Divine
   - Blessed with Heaven on Earth - Man and God become One in New Jerusalem
2. **Christians Worthy of God's Presence in Heaven** - Mark of Baptism
   (water/spirit)…   Joy of Heart
   - Man Wants to become God - Spiritual Body (glorification): Holy Saint
   - Fulfill Man's Faith in God's Love - Wash Away Sins: Sinful to Holy
   - Blessed with Paradise in Heaven - God and Man become One in Eternal Rome

The following tabular information indicates the "Great Significance" of the Jewish Circumcision and the Christian Baptism as **They Represent One Highway** *Coming to Earth* (flesh), and then a **Second Highway** *Going to Heaven* (spirit):

(death) **Flesh - Circumcision - Blood** (resurrection)

1. **Old World Order of Justice** - Cast into the Grave: Jews Try for 1,500 Years to Fulfill Law and Fail
   - *Jewish People* - Fulfill God's Law of Obedience via Messiah: Jews See Limitations
   - Only the Son of God can Fulfill God's Law - Justice Demands Death (grave)
   - All Human Flesh will be Destroyed in Fulfillment of God's Promise - Slaughter of Innocence
Law
   - Out with the Old Thinking - Cast Evil Goat into Pit of Oblivion (forgotten)
   - The Old Physical World (flesh) is Destroyed – Purification of the Grave

- Overcome the Crucible of Fire (bread) - Become All (purify grave)
  (circumcision brings God to Earth to live among
  His most chosen people - 1st Highway)

(purify grave) **Water - Baptism - Spirit** (purify host)
2. **New World Order of Mercy** - <u>Rises from the Grave:</u> Holy Spirit Fills All Christians with Faith
   - *Christian People* - Fulfill Man's Faith in God's Love through Submission: Saints See Potential
   - Free Redemption for All Human Flesh - Mercy Gives New-life (host)
   - All Human Flesh will be Saved in Fulfillment of Jesus' Promise - Resurrection of Glory

Faith
   - In with the New Thinking – Slaughter Innocent Goat Giving Everyone Forgiveness
   - The New Born-again Spirit World is Created - Purification of the Host
   - Overcome the Winepress of Death (wine) - Become Nothing (purify host)
     (baptism sends Man to Heaven to live in the presence
     of the Lord God Almighty - 2nd Highway)

This illustration shows that the "Lord Jesus Christ" is <u>Casting Out the Old</u> to bring forth the <u>New</u> by **Establishing His Own Secret Organization** of **Devoted Followers, Each Required** to <u>**Take a Vow**</u> of *Disloyalty to Humankind* and *Unconditional Loyalty to God's Divinity*. We see that "Actual Establishment" of this <u>Secret Agent Organization</u> or the <u>New World Order</u> was **Formed** at the **Moment When Jesus Christ Dipped His Morsel** with **Judas**, thereby **Making** this <u>**Evil Traitor His**</u> *Guest of Honor* with the *Other 12 Traitors at the Last Supper*. This means that the "Old Physical World (flesh)" is to be <u>Destroyed</u> to bring forth the *Purification of the Grave* (flesh and blood/righteousness), while the "New Born-again Spirit World" is <u>Created</u> to bring forth the *Purification of the Host* (bread and wine/holiness). We see that in this "Diabolical Scheme," the <u>Lord and His Followers</u> were **Planning to Kill Every Person on Earth** (die to self) and <u>**Replace Them**</u> with **New Transfigured Spirit Bodies** which have been <u>**Made Perfect**</u> in the *Nature of Christ Jesus* (love).

The Last Supper
New Organization of Traitors Against All Past Beliefs
(make solemn vow to betray humankind and join Jesus' new world order)

1. Jesus - Betrayed Father by Saving Gentiles, When Told to Save Only the Jews
   . Jesus Cursed to Death for Giving God's Table Scraps to the Dogs
2. Peter - Betrayed Jesus by Denying Him Three Times: Face to Face
3. Judas - Betrayed Jesus by Plotting His Death: Behind His Back

4. Thomas - Betrayed Jesus by Doubting that He Resurrected (being absolutely sure)
5. Bartholomew/Nathaniel - Betrayed Jesus by Believing too Easily (being gullible fool)
6. Matthew - Betrayed Jesus by Going AWOL in the Face of Fear, Pain, and Death
7. Philip - Betrayed Jesus by Going AWOL in the Face of Fear, Pain, and Death
8. James - Betrayed Jesus by Going AWOL in the Face of Fear, Pain, and Death
9. Jude - Betrayed Jesus by Going AWOL in the Face of Fear, Pain, and Death
10. Simon - Betrayed Jesus by Going AWOL in the Face of Fear, Pain, and Death
11. James (1s) - Betrayed Jesus by Going AWOL in the Face of Fear, Pain, and Death
12. Andrew - Betrayed Jesus by Going AWOL in the Face of Fear, Pain and Death
13. John - Betrayed Jesus by Never becoming a Martyr (John betrayed brotherhood of traitors)

---

14. Matthias - Betrayed his Own Nation, Family, and Honor for the Sake of Jesus

This illustration shows that the "Lord Jesus Christ" was Sent from Heaven to **Live With** and **Run With** a **Pack of Evil Wolves** (apostles) and was then **Called to Convert** the <u>**Worst of the Worst**</u> into *Holy Saints of God*. It is "No Wonder" that the <u>Whole World</u> was **Amazed When Jesus Christ Sent** the **Holy Spirit** to **Transform These most Evil Men** into **Born-again Christians** in a <u>**Single Moment**</u> during the *1st Pentecost* (birth of church). Unfortunately, to "Convert an Evil World," the <u>Lord was Forced</u> to **Destroy God's Justice,** the **Jewish People**, including **All Evil Human Flesh** to bring forth a *New Spirit Creation of Infinite Love* (born-again). Recall that the "Lord God Almighty" has <u>Planned from the Beginning</u> to **Create** a **Special Chosen People, Who** would become **His Holy Saints on Earth;** and **All Other Human Flesh** (infidel) was to be **Destroyed** by **Joshua** (flesh) and **Jesus** (spirit) as **They were Ordered** to <u>**Kill the Gentiles**</u> and *Purify the Whole Earth.* Unfortunately, both "Men of God" <u>Failed to Slaughter Humankind</u> and **Instead** both **Men Established** a **New World Order**, whereby **Evil Pagans** could be **Forgiven** (taxed) and **Live Among** the **Chosen People of God** as *Neighbors and Friends.* This means that "God's Justice" must be <u>Satisfied</u> by the **Letter of the Law** (obeying) through **Death** (crucifixion/grave), *while* "God's Mercy" must be <u>Satisfied</u> by the **Spirit of the Law** (thinking/host) through **New-life** (resurrection) to bring forth *Growth and Maturity.* The idea here is to see that "Mary's Son (Jesus/man)" brings <u>Free Redemption</u> (forgiveness/wash away faults) by <u>**Taking-sin**</u> to *Save Sinners*, while "God's Son (Christ/God)" brings <u>Earned Salvation</u> (resurrection/change in virtues) by <u>**Giving-up His Divinity**</u> (forgiveness) to *Create Saints*. Imagine "God Creating" a <u>Giant Manufacturing Plant</u> to **Create Three Products** in the **Form** of <u>**Physical Bodies**</u> or *Earthly Citizens*, <u>**Spiritual Eternal Lives**</u> or *Heavenly Saints*, and finally, <u>**Mystical Kingdoms**</u> or *Sons of God.*

God's Life-experience is About Creating Citizens, Saints, and Sons of God
(Earth is offering God babies, Heaven gives saintly gifts,
and the Kingdom gives treasures)

Kingship **1. Creating Righteous Men on Earth** (babies) –
(challenge) Counted on Sabbath   ...See Limitations
- Free Redemption Creates Babies - Being Saved
- Creation of Earthly Baby Farm -   **Earthly Offerings to God**
  New Body   • Purify Grave
- Fulfill God's Law of Obedience - Change Nature
- Changing Flesh into Divinity - Man Wants to become God
  (babies - learn right from wrong to become
        righteous: deny intellect/new mind)

Priesthood **2. Creating Holy Saints in Heaven** - Counted on Lord's Day/Sunday
(adventure)   ...See Potential
- Earned Salvation Creates Saints - Saving Self
- Creation of Divine School   **Heaven's Gifts to God**
  in Heaven - Eternal Life   • Purify Host
- Fulfill Man's Faith in God's Love - Wash Away Sin
- Changing Sinfulness to Holiness - God Wants to become Man
  (saints - learn good from evil to become holy: abandon feelings/new heart)

Sonship **3. Creating Perfect Sons within Kingdom** - Counted at Final Judgment
(fun)   ...See Self-worth
- Bonus Rewards Create Sons - Saving Others
- Creation of Sonship Training   **Kingdom's Treasures**
  in Kingdom - Own Kingdom   • Purify Self
- Fulfill God/Man Knowing - Thinking for Self
- Changing from Death to New-life - God and Man become One
  (sons - learn God's will from man's will
        to become perfect: submit free will/new soul)

This illustration shows that the "Central Theme of Life" is Centered upon Creating **Physical Babies, Spiritual Saints, and Mystical Sons of God** as the **Three Divine Products of God** via **His Creation** of *Earth, Heaven, and God's Kingdom.* This implies that "Forgiven Sinners" become Christians by *Denying Their Intellect* (wash mind), while "Born-again Christians" become Saints by *Abandoning Their Feelings* (change heart). We see that "Sinners" must Learn Right from Wrong (intellect) to become **Righteous Citizens** on *Earth,* while "Christians" must Learn Good from Evil (emotions) to become **Holy Saints** in *Heaven.* This need to be "Washed" in Jesus' Blood or to be **Redeemed** and "Changed" via Christ's Death or to be **Saved Creates Two Doorways of Escape: One** from **Hell Fires** to *Receive* a *New Body* (destroy flesh/purify grave), and the **Other** from **Physical Death** to *Receive Spiritual Eternal*

Life (wash spirit/purify host). This means that "God's Word is Dead" until it was Brought to Life through the **Sacrificial Blood of Christ** on **Mount Calvary,** when **He Denied His very Self** unto the *Dust of the Earth* (submission). It should now make sense that "Every Person on Earth (called/chosen)" must Deny His Very Self, **Surrender to God's Son** (church), and be **Saved** through *His Physical Purification* (wash mind/fight evil), and *Spiritual Conversion* (change heart/become nothing).

In short, this means that "God's Word" or the Bible is a **Mystical Code Book** to **Prevent Lucifer** and his **Evil Followers** from **Comprehending** *God's Grand Design*, meaning that to **Decode God's Word**, a **Person must Use** the *Traditions of the Church* (communion of saints). The idea here is that the "Lives of the Saints" are the Decoding Force or **Light of Truth** which can **Translate** the **Strange Wording** and **Phraseology of God** into its **Proper Context** so that it will *Make Sense* to *Only the Awakened Man*. By "Studying" the Lives of the Saints and **Decoding Their Messages, Each of God's Words** and **Terms** can be **Translated** into its *Physical Earthly Meaning* (flesh/Man) and also its *Spiritual Heavenly Meaning* (spirit/God). We see that to be "Called" Out of One's **Illusion of Life** causes a **Person** to **Leave Sinfulness** and be **Forgiven** unto **Holiness** (earth); while being "Chosen" to Enter the **Reality of Lif**e is to **Leave Death** and then to be **Transformed** into *New-life* (Heaven).

1. **Called** - Means Man Choosing God
   • Free Will - Natural Selection (energy)
2. **Chosen** - Means God Choosing Man: Destiny
   • Intelligent Design (spirit)

The idea here is that "Called Sinners" can be" Saved (called)" by Changing Their Nature from **Human to Divine** to *Understand Physical Truth*; while "Chosen Saints" can be "Created (chosen)" by Washing Away Their Sins (holiness) to *Understand Spiritual Truth*. This means that the "Job of Jesus Christ" is to Blend the **Sinners of Death** with the **Saints of New-life** by **Making God's Destiny** (chosen) and **Man's Free Will** (called) **One** via *Creation's Energy* (natural selection) and *God's Spirit* (intelligent design). We must imagine that the "Lord God Almighty" is Working with Two Separate **Creative Materials** (energy/spirit) and **Desires** that **They become One** so that **God can become Man** (Christmas) and **Man can become God** (Easter) and then **God and Man** can become **One** in *Christ Jesus*.

The following tabular information indicates that "Man's Flesh (new nature)" is being Called to Change Man's Nature (washed), while "God's Spirit (forgiveness)" is Chosen for Purity from a **Wicked Sinner** into a *Born-again Holy Saint*:

Man's Flesh is Called to Purity,
while God's Spirit is Chosen to be Changed by God's Son
(flesh is changed from death to new-life
and spirit is washed of sinfulness unto forgiveness)

- - - - - - - -Holy Mother's Baby Farm - Raising Babies:
Filling the Earth with Righteous Citizens- - - - - - - - -

Called
(goats)

1. **Man's Flesh** - Changed Nature: New Born-again Man is Changed from Human to Divine
   - Free Redemption – Take-sin: Save Sinners = Blood of the Lamb (purification)
   - Removing *Man's Sinfulness via God's Forgiveness* - See Limitations (growth)

Informal Face
(fight evil)

   - Justice – Letter of the Law: Learn Right from Wrong = Righteousness
   - Sinners become Christians – Deny Intellect (washing/remove faults)
   - Remove False Wisdom - Teach Lambs (Jn 21:15): Gospel/Word (flesh /blood)
   - Become Righteous Citizen on Earth - New Body (faults to virtues)
     (changed in resurrection of Christ -
     Jewish Faith: conversion of flesh/grave)

- - - - - - - -Holy Father's Divine School - Creating Saints:
Filling Heaven with Holy Saints- - - - - - - -

Chosen
(sheep)

2. **God's Spirit** – Washed to be Purified: Man is Cursed to be a Pig Living in Mud
   - Earned Salvation – Give Divinity: Create Saints = Death of Christ
   - Changing Man's Nature from *Death to New-life* - See Potential (maturity)

Formal Face
(submission)

   - Mercy – Spirit of the Law: Learn Good from Evil = Holiness
   - Christian becomes Saint – Abandon Feelings (changing/gain virtues)
   - Remove Sin-nature – Feed Sheep (Jn 21:16): Cross/Eucharist (bread/wine)
   - Become Holy Saint in Heaven – Eternal Life (evangelize to save souls)
     (washed in the blood of Calvary –
     Christian Knowing: conversion of the spirit/host)

===

Religious Informal – Laity (one): Serve the World (save sinners) = Competitor (looking-down)
   - John 6:35 Those Who Come to Me will **Not Hunger** (bread) - Washed in Blood (pure nature)
   - Called – Lessons of Life: Obey God's Laws = Submission (death to self)

Human
(witness)

   - Sowing God's Word – Fruits of Faith: Submission = Flesh (will to live)
   - Wash Away Sin – Righteousness: Pick-up Your Cross = Unto Thine Own Self Be True
   - Failure Teaches Lessons – Genetics: Experiencing Life = See Limitations (mind)
   - Traditions Shed Light on God's Word – Understand Physical Truth: Called to Holiness

<u>Religious formal</u> – Priests/Nuns (all): Serve the Church (create saints) = Cooperation (looking-up)

John 6:35   Those Who **Believe in Me** will **Not Thirst** (wine) - Changed in Spirit (new nature)

- Chosen - Blessings of Life: Sell All and Give to Poor = Guilty Conscience

Divine
(prophet)

- Reaping God's Traditions – Fruits of Works: Spirit (value of life)
- Changed Nature – Holiness: Deny Very Self = Instinctive Compulsion
- Success Brings Blessings - Environment: Knowledge of Life = See Potential (heart)
- Traditions Shed Light on God's Word - Comprehend Spiritual Truth: Chosen to Divinity

----

Luke 19:44 states: "I will Level or Destroy both You and Your Children and then Your Enemies will Not Leave One Stone upon Another because <u>You have Failed to Recognize</u> the *Hour of Your Visitations*."

Note that Mankind Must Recognize Christ's Three Advents: 1st as *Priest on a Donkey* (save Messiah) or Baby Farm (water baptism/save Messiah); 2nd as *Thief in the Night* (save church) or Divine School (blood baptism); and 3rd as *Just Judge on a Cloud* (save world/judge sinners) or *Sonship Training* (spirit baptism).

Church
1. **Recognize Lord's Priesthood** - <u>1st Advent:</u> First Coming of Lord Jesus Christ
   - Prophet Comes - Teach Lost Souls: Create Righteous Citizens

Government
2. **Recognize Lord's Kingship** - <u>2nd Advent:</u> Beginning of Second Coming (spirit)
   - Messiah Comes - Seal Saints: Create Holy Saints

Home
3. **Recognize Lord's Sonship** - <u>3rd Advent:</u> End of Second Coming
   - God Comes - Judge Everyone: Create Perfect Sons

This illustration shows that on "Earth (teach lambs)," <u>Sinners become Christians</u> (called/word) by *Denying Their Own Intellects* (wash mind); while in "Heaven (feed sheep)," <u>Christians become Saints</u> (chosen/cross) by *Abandoning Their Own Feelings* (change heart). This means that the "Righteous Man (recognize visitation)" must be <u>Washed</u> in the **Blood of Calvary** (Jewish Faith) to **Teach the Lessons of Life** (purification) to a <u>**Lost World**</u> to bring forth the *Conversion of the Flesh* (faults to virtues). Secondly, the "Holy Saint (recognize visitation)" or "Holy Man" must be <u>Changed</u> via **Christ's Resurrection** (Christian Knowing) to **Receive God's Blessing** (transformation) for <u>**Good Works**</u> and bring forth the *Conversion of the Spirit into a Son of God* (evangelize to save souls). We see that the "Purpose of Life" <u>Centers upon Merging</u> **God's Spirit** (life) with **Man's Flesh** (death) via the <u>**Mind**</u> (ignorance), **Heart** (worldly temptations), **Soul** (demonic possession), and **Life-force** (God's curse) of *Lost Sinners*. This means that "Each Man is Striving" to <u>Master his Own Life</u> **Sufficiently to Obtain** a <u>**Righteous Flesh**</u> (ignorance/wisdom/quantity) or *Pardoned*, a **Holy Spirit** (cowardice/courage/quality) or *Forgiveness*, and a **Perfect Soul** (greed/generosity/quantity and quality), or being *Freed*. This also means that by "Learning" <u>God's Right from Man's Wrong</u> (righteous/intellect), <u>God's Good from Man's Evil</u> (holiness/emotions), and finally, separating <u>God's Will</u> from <u>man's will</u> (perfection/instincts), a **Lost Soul** can *One Day* become *Righteous* (wise/kingship), *Holy* (courageous/priesthood), and *Perfect* (generous/sonship) *before God*. The "Human Life-force (existence/nature)" is <u>Focused</u> <u>upon Humanity's Concern</u> for both the **Care** (daily) and **Maintenance** (weekly) of **Self** (individual), **Family** (home), **Society** (government), and **God** (church) in that order, based on the *Power of Knowing Right* (gain virtues) from *Wrong* (remove faults).

This philosophy signifies that "Mankind is Foolishly Hoping" to <u>One Day</u> be <u>Divinely Worthy</u> of **God's Divine Housekeeping Seal of Approval** (certification) by simply **Holding up** its <u>**Great Human Accomplishments**</u> (do step) to **Obtain** the <u>**Adoration of Its Creator's**</u> most *Sacred Blessings of Eternal Life* (glorified body), *New Body* (transfigured body), and *Royal Kingdom* (mystical body). Obviously, "Nothing could be Farther" from the <u>Truth</u> because **Mankind** will be the <u>**Lucky Recipient**</u> of *God's Royal Household* (gift) - Not the *Creator of It*. Thus, the "Human Race is Called" to <u>Serve Its God</u> (productivity), yet, a **Person is Not** to be a <u>**Meaningless Servant**</u> (thinking for himself) within *God's Kingdom of Divine Glory*. No! "Man" is much more as we can see by both the "Job of the Saints (new bodies/works)," and the "Job of the Angels (new-life/prayers)" as <u>They Convert</u> **Man's Ethics** (law) and **God's Morals** (love) into <u>**New Bodies**</u> (physical/flesh/saints) or **Transfigurations** (Jesus'/sacrifice) and <u>**Eternal Lives**</u> (spiritual/concepts/angels) or **Glorifications** (Christ's/divinity) for *One and All*. Now, we see that the central theme defining a "Person's Life-experience" <u>Centers</u> upon having a way to **Appease God's Anger** (works/blood) when <u>**He is Mad**</u> and then **Thanking Him for His Mercy** (prayer) when the **Lord Shows His <u>Divine Kindness</u>** to *One and All*. This implies that "Knowing God Well Enough" is to <u>Find that Infinite Balance</u> between **Man's Needs** (natural order) and **God's Wants** (supernatural order) to **Please the Lord in All Ways,** both *Great and Small*. This conflict between "God (life/host) and Man (death/grave)" is <u>Centered</u> on the fact that <u>God Wants to become Man</u> (Christmas/earth/flesh), while <u>Man Wants to become God</u> (Easter/Heaven/thought) as **No Price is Too High to Pay** for <u>**Living an Eternal Life**</u> of *Personal Perfection* (novena).

We see in this picture the "Mystical Redemption" of the <u>Ignorant Orphan,</u> the <u>Cowardly Widow,</u> the <u>Greedy Poor,</u> and the <u>Selfish Stranger</u> as **They Each Strives** to **Find a Place** in **Society** based on *Man's Compromised Will* (loving), *Permissive Will* (merciful), *Direct Will* (just), and/or *His Own Free Will* (free). Yes! Everyone is "Seeking a Job (ethics)," a "Perfect Mate (morals)," and a "Happy Home (fairness)" as <u>He Knows</u> that **Everything** that is **Good in Life Comes** from **His Personal Stability** which is **Centered upon His** *Wisdom, Courage, Generosity, and Unselfishness*. We see that through "These Stable Human Qualities," the Lord Blesses a **Mature Soul's Hands** to **Anoint its Mystical Works** (working together) to bring **Glory** to **All the Creations of its Heart,** which is **Done in the Name** of *God's Son Jesus Christ.* Finally, a "Born-again Soul is Given" the Lord's Crown of Majesty to **Glorify and Honor** its **Mind,** so that the very **Thoughts in its Head** will be **Anointed** with the *Sanctifying Grace* of the *Eternal Father.* This means that a "Person must Keep God Foremost" in his Mind (worship) and Heart (praise) by **Practicing God's Holy Virtues** via **His Christian Faith** to bring forth the **Sacred Fruits** (submission/sacrifice) of the *Lessons of Life* (death to self).

The message here is that "If God Works Alone," He will Fail because **He must Function** within a **Mystical Paradox** (all/nothing), implying that **When the Lord Created Free Will** (natural selection), **He basically Cursed** *All his Man-Made or Free-Willed Creations*. In short, the "Lord God Almighty" Made Himself into a Man (Christ Child/baby) **Who is an Ignorant Fool** (mindless), thereby **Making** both **God and Man Helpless** until **They can Grow** and **Mature Sufficiently** to **Effectively Work Together** (team effort) to **Establish** *Heaven on Earth, Paradise in Heaven,* and bring forth the *New God/Man Kingdom of Glory.* This strange "Divine Behavior" in effect has Made God Helpless, much like **Giving His Eyes** (blind) to **His Created Child,** thereby causing **Him to No Longer See** that He Needs a Guide who is Described in Isaiah 11:6, where it says that a **Child shall Lead Them** *Out of the Darkness.* This "Need" for a Mutual Admiration Society **Sits at the Center** of the **Birth, Death,** and **Resurrection of Christ** as **He Alone can Perform** the **Necessary Works of God** on **Earth,** implying that **All Humanity** must be *Transformed into Christ* (100% belief/born-again).

The following tabular information indicates that "When God Created" a Free-Willed Creation, **He** in effect **Cursed His Own Divine Authority** as He must Now **Share His Kingdom** (work together) with the *King, Priest, and Son of Eternal Humanity:*

God and Man must Work Together or They will both Certainly Fail
(God's intelligent design and Man's natural selection
must become One in energy and matter)

Destiny (church)	1.	**God/Man Work Together** - Intelligent Design: Energy/spirit...Jesus' Bread
	•	God of All – Changing Divine Energy into Human Matter: Sacred Host
	•	I have Come to Give You My Peace (John 14:27) - Submission (God's justice)
	•	Gain God's Virtues - Learning the Prophet's Teachings: Lessons of God
Forgiveness	•	God's Destiny will Fail without *Spiritual Lessons of Life* Man's Free Will
	•	Fulfill Man's Faith in God's Love - Wash Away Sin: Sinfulness to Holiness
	•	Redeeming Host - Makes a Person Holy before God (eternal awakening)

Free Will (world)	2. **Man/God Work Together** – <u>Natural Selection</u>: Matter/Flesh — Sinner's Death
	• Man of Nothing – Changing Human Matter into Divine Energy
	• I have Come to bring Division onto Earth (Luke 12:51) - Sacrifice (man's mercy)
	• Remove God's Faults - Trials and Tribulations of Life: Lessons of Man
Repentance	• Man's Free Will will fail *Physical Lessons of Life* without God's Destiny
	• Fulfill God's Law of Obedience - Change Nature: Human to Divine
	• Saving Grave - Makes a Person Divine before God (rest in peace)

This illustration shows that "When Jesus Christ" <u>Came to Save All Humanity</u>, **He Told** the **Jewish People** that *He had Come to bring Division and Not Peace* (Luke 12:51) and then in the **Next Breath, He Told** the **Christian People** that *He had Come to bring His Blessing of Peace* (John 14:27). Now a "Wise Person might Ask:" has <u>Jesus Come to Make Peace</u> and **Turn the Other Cheek** or has <u>He Come to Make War</u> on **All Evil** via **His Sword of Division**? Certainly, the **Right Answer is Both** as the **Lord is a Paradox** (all and nothing) of *God's Justice* (repent) and *Man's Mercy* (forgive). Yes! We know that "God's Intelligent Design (destiny)" is <u>All Forgiving</u> and that "Man's Natural Selection (free will)" is <u>All Repenting</u>, but **No One will be Able** to either **Repent** and/or be **Forgiven** until **Jesus Christ** <u>Sacrifices Himself Three Times</u>: *Offer Blood* (1/innocent blood), *Seal Saints* (2/forgiven blood), and *Judge Sinners* (3/guilty blood). It is "No Wonder" that the <u>Human Race</u> is so **Confused**, especially **When It has been Told** to become **Perfect** in the <u>Sight of God</u> by *Doing Good Works* (100% belief) and then being **Told** that **They are Not Worthy** to *Do Any Works at All* (Christ becomes Man). In short, the "Trick of the Tail" is that <u>Man's Evil Flesh</u> must become <u>God's Born-again Spirit</u> or **Christ becoming Us**. Then **Everything Done in Life** (sword of promise) is **Evil**, yet, has the **Power to Bear Good Fruit** through the *Lord's Blessing of Forgiveness*.

The idea is that "When a Person" is <u>Baptized</u>, he is **Dying to Self** unto **Nothingness**, based on **Believing 100% in Jesus Christ** (through grace), then to be **Affirmed by Works**, or by **Fighting Evil**, which occurs **When a Person Allows** his **Sin-nature** (scourging), <u>Worldly Temptations</u> (crucifixion), and **Demonic Forces** (tomb) to *Destroy his very Life* (bear fruit). Through this "Sacrifice of One's Flesh," he becomes a <u>Soldier-of-the-Light</u> and **Fights Evil** with the **Lord's Sword of Promise** (7 drops of blood) which **Comes from Longinus' Stabbing Jesus** in the **Heart** to **Get God's Seven Last Drops of Blood** to be **Placed** on the *Mercy Seat of Forgiveness* (Calvary). This means that "God Gets" <u>Three Drops</u> of **Innocent Blood**, "Man Gets" <u>Three Drops</u> of **Guilty Blood**, and then the **Last Drop** is **Placed** on **God/Man's Forgiven Blood**, thereby **Uniting** the <u>Body, Spirit, and Soul</u> into *One New Born-again Nature*. In theory, through this "New Born-again Nature" or <u>Sword of Promise</u> (word/truth), **God's Christian Soldiers** will **Flood the Earth** with **God's Knowledge** to <u>Set All the Captives</u> **Free** from *Sin, Evil, and Death*. In this theme, the "Redeeming Host (submission)" will <u>Make a Person</u> *Holy before*

God (spiritual nature), while the "Saving Grave (fight evil)" will <u>Make a Person **Di-vine before God**</u> (physical nature).

Unfortunately, to become "Worthy of Personal Perfection," a <u>Person</u> must **Obey God's Commandments, Sell All and Give to the Poor, Pick-up his Cross,** and **Come Follow Jesus Christ** to his *Death* on *Mount Calvary.* Okay. Just how many "Extremely Smart (sensible)" and "Super Brave Souls (hard-working)" are <u>Willing to Give Their Lives</u> to **Some Religious Belief** which **Promises Eternal Life If he is Willing** to **Follow** the **Voice of God, No Matter How Insane** (kill own son) his **Test of Faith** might **Become** to *Prove himself?* Now try to imagine "God Telling You" to <u>Cast Your Eternally Redeemed Soul</u> into **Hell** to **Prove** that **You are Willing** to **Do Anything to Save the Damned, No Matter What the Cost?** In other words, just **Where** is this **Man for All Seasons** or *How can We Find him?* The answer is that "There will be Very Few," because <u>Who will Take to Heart</u> the **Words of Isaiah,** when he states in **Chapter 42: 6-7** that **God's Chosen People** shall be a <u>**Light**</u> unto the *Blind Eyes* (fools/prophet), to bring *Out Prisoners from Captivity* (cursed souls/Messiah), and to *Open the Dungeons* to *Remove the Damned* from *Their Darkness* (damned in hell/God)?

1st Mile 1. **Open Blind Eyes** - Free Redemption for All Who will Repent
- Meet the Prophet - 1st Advent: Priest on a Donkey = Get Good News

2nd Mile 2. **Save Prisoners from Their Captivity** - Coming Awakening of Lost Souls
- Meet the Messiah - 2nd Advent: Thief in the Night = Hear Gospel Message

3rd Mile 3. **Open Dungeons to Remove Damned from Hell** - Final Judgment
- Meet Lord God Almighty - 3rd Advent: Judge on a Cloud = Hear Doctrinal Truths

We see this "Implies" that a <u>Devout Christian</u> must **Offer God his Eternal Soul** and be **Willing** to **Sacrifice** himself unto **Eternal Damnation, If he Wants** to **Give the Lord** the **Ultimate Gift** <u>Far Beyond</u> (3rd mile) even a *Saint's Call of Duty.* Note that in "Exodus 32:33," <u>Moses Told God</u> that to **Save the Jewish People** from being **Cast into Eternal Damnation** (golden calf), he was **Willing** to have his <u>**Name Removed**</u> from *God's Book of Life.* It appears that this "Act of Total Sacrifice" has <u>Set a Precedent</u> before **God** which can **Only be Outdone** by the **Sacrifice** of **God Himself** as **He Offered the Life** of <u>**His Only Begotten Son,**</u> the *Lord Jesus Christ.* We see that "If a Person" Desires to Join the Exclusive Club of **Followers of Moses** and **Jesus, He must Offer His Eternal Soul to God** on **All Hallows Eve** (midnight) yearly to <u>**Save All Who have been Lost**</u> (damned) in that *Last Year.* The implication here is that "When the Standard" for <u>Perfection</u> has been **Set so High,** just **Who** can even **Get an Eternal Life,** with which to be <u>**Sacrificed**</u> for the *Eternally Damned of the World* (hell bound)? We now clearly "See the Meaning" of the <u>Word Saint,</u> **Who** then becomes **Worthy** of being a **Son of God When** he **Sacrificed** the **Greatest Treasure in Life,** simply to <u>**Save Lucifer**</u> and his **Demons,** the **Damned** and <u>**All that has been Lost**</u> during *God's War of Good and Evil.*

Now, let's examine this "Awesome Conflict (good/evil)" between <u>Divine Perfection</u> (good) and <u>Human Imperfection</u> (evil) as **God's Law of Obedience** <u>Strives to</u>

Create *Dutiful Robots* (perfect obedience), while **Man's Faith in God's Love** <u>Strives to Create</u> *Free-Willed Human Beings* (love conquers all). Note that when the "Jewish Messiah" <u>Jesus Christ</u> **Came to Earth, Suddenly There was a Huge Conflict** between the **Need** for **God's Son to Marry** the **Physical** <u>Jewish People of Life</u> (chosen/Lea) by an **Arranged Marriage** and/or **Marrying** a <u>Spiritual Prostitute of Death</u> (gentiles) *Out Of Love* (Rachel). Obviously, "Jesus' Mother Mary" is <u>Placing Her Hopes</u> on **Saving All the Lost**, while "Christ's Father" is <u>Placing His Expectation</u> on **Saving Only the Holy Jews** based on the **Belief** that a **Pagan Kingdom of Sinners** will just *Never Work*. We see that this "Irreconcilable" <u>Difference of Opinion</u> was **Still Raging** when **Jesus was Hanging on His Cross** and **Asking Why** had **God Forsaken Him**. The **Answer** is that **He had Married** a **Prostitute of Death** and had *Disgraced His Father's Name* (God).

We see that "God is Convinced" that an <u>Arranged Marriage</u> **Created** by **Two Well-Established Fathers** is the **Only Process** that can **Ever Produce** a **Righteous Community Made up of Healthy Jewish Families**, <u>Who are Deeply Rooted</u> in *God's Law of Obedience*. In short, the "Christian Philosophy" was <u>Doomed from the Start</u> as **Ignorant Man** will **Fail to Make the Love Bond Hold** and **End up** with a **World of Divorced Fools, Who Keep Trying and Trying** (permissive sex) to **Figure Out How to Get** that *One and Only Perfect Marriage*. Now, let's look at "God's Son's Perfect Solution" to the <u>Arranged</u> (Lea) versus <u>Love</u> (Rachel) **Concept** as **Man's Holy Spirit Adamantly Disagrees** with **Man's Righteous Flesh** as to <u>Who would Be</u> that *One Perfect Wife or Husband*. Obviously, the "Answer is to be Found" in <u>Man's Christian Death of the Flesh</u> and then being <u>Born-again in Christ's Spirit</u> to **Attain a New Nature** based on **His New** *Wisdom, Courage, Generosity, and Unselfishness*. Thus, **Christ Needed a Common Denominator** of **All Spirit** (change nature) and then to **Physically Educate** the **Human Flesh Sufficiently** to <u>Transform It</u> from *Spiritual Sinfulness to Holiness*.

We see that a "New Born-again Soul" becomes a <u>Living Invocation</u> to a **Lost and Broken World** in **Appreciation** for its **Call to Purification** (water/blood /death/spirit) through a *New-life of Devotion* and *Faithful Works*. We see a "Transforming Sin-nature" which is <u>Actually Changing</u> before **Our very Eyes** through a **Person's Imitation of Christ** by being **In Him** as a **Living Prayer**, <u>Allowing him</u> to *Glorify the Majesty of God*. Once a "New Christian Comes" to his <u>First Awakening,</u> he will **Enter a New State** of **Servitude Coming** to a **Full Understanding** of his **Christian Duties** by **Serving and Sharing** the **Good News** (free redemption), **Gospel Message** (earned salvation), and **Doctrinal Truths** (bonus rewards) with a *Lost and Broken World*. "When a Person Reaches" a <u>Series of Mystical Plateaus</u> of **Holy Veneration**, he **Comes to Comprehend** the **Meaning of Life** (existence) as it **Relates** to the **Total** <u>Worship of God</u> in *Truth, Law, Will, and Love*. This "New Realization" of the <u>Significance of His Existence </u>is **Manifested** in a **Special Loving Relationship** for All the **Creations of God, Lowering His Worldly Fears,** and <u>Giving him</u> *Peace of Mind forever*. Finally, a "Person Passes" through the <u>Lord's Introductory Phases</u> of **Christian Life** to **Fully Surrender his Spirit** to the **Duties of a Holy Life** in **Practicing** the **Virtues** of **Divine Purity** as he **Experiences the Sensation** of *Growing-up*. By coming to "Full Maturity" in <u>Christ</u>

Jesus, a **Person** becomes **God's Best Friend** and is **Transformed** into a **Free Man** to be **Forever Trusted** with the **Enormous Responsibility** of his **Own Free Will** bringing him to the **Door of Eternal Freedom** through the *Power of Knowing* (instinctive compulsion/thinking for himself). "When a Broken Sinner" is Transformed into a **Holy Saint of God,** he has his **Feet Blessed** by the **Holy Spirit** so **that All his Future Travels** (everlasting way) will be **Anointed** by the **Love of God** to *Honor the Way* of his *Eternal Life.*

Note that "Each of God's Children" must Come forth **Out of Nothing** to **Pass** through the **Lord's Astral Plane,** where a **Person** would become a **First Spark of Life** by **Accepting His Conversion** into **Human Existence, Assuming he will Receive** his *Own Eternal Gold Mine.* Secondly, via "His Birth on Earth," a Person would become a **Tiny Flame** as he is **Saved by Christ** from a **Meaningless Life of Nothing Forever** and was **Promised** by the **Lord** a **Free Gold Mine** in the **Form** of a New Body. Thirdly, via "His Human Life-experience," a Person would become a **Blazing Fire** as he **Saves himself** and **Prepares** to bring forth his **Own Free Will** which means **Digging Out his Own Gold** in the **Form** of *His Eternal Life.* Finally, via "His Eternal Life-experience," a Person would become a **Roaring Furnace** as he **Prepares** to **Save the Souls of Others,** still **Locked** within the **Astral Plane** which means **Sharing his Gold** in the **Form** of **Giving Everyone** his *Own Kingdom of Glory.* It is now clear that the "Human Race" is Traveling from **Nothing to All** and must become a **Reflection of God's Divine Flame of Life** (beatific vision) by **Growing** and **Maturing** from a *Spark* (baby), *to Flame* (teen), *to Fire* (adult), and finally, to a *Great Furnace of Heat* (wise man).

The following tabular information indicates that "God is Made of Fire" and If a Person is to become a **Reflection of God on Earth,** he must become a **Spark, a Flame, a Fire,** and finally, a **Great Furnace of White Hot Heat,** thereby *Blessing One and All:*

Being Saved from a Meaningless Life of Nothingness Forever by Christ Jesus
(Lord Jesus Christ takes humanity from nothing to all
by guiding it along His pathway of perfection)

Truth   1. **First Spark** - Astral Plane: Conversion Experience…Asking for Gold Mine (human life)
- Living Life - Dreaming: New Mind = Transformed from Ignorance to Wisdom
- Released - Conception: Creation = Pardoned by God

Law   2. **Tiny Flame** - Earthly Birth: Being Saved by Christ…Receive Free Gold Mine (new body)
- Meaning of Life - Existence: New Heart = Transformed from Cowardice to Courage
- Freedom - Birth: Individual = Break Chains of Sin

Will   3. **Blazing Fire** - Life-experience: Saving Oneself…Digging Out the Gold (eternal life)

- Purpose of Life - Service: New Soul = Transformed from Greed to Generosity
- Liberty - Born-again: Society = Open Prison Doors of Evil

Love 4. **Hot Furnace** - Eternal Life: Saving Souls of Others…Sharing Gold with Others (own kingdom)
- Value of Life - Happiness: New Life-force Transformed from Selfishness to Unselfishness
- Independence - Resurrection: God = Overpower Guards of Death

This illustration shows that "When a Person" Travels Along the **Lord's Pathway of Perfection,** he must **Grow** and **Mature** by becoming **Bigger** and **Stronger** until he can **Take On Full Responsibility** for *himself, his Family, his Community,* and hopefully, even *God's Good Works*. We have to imagine here that in "God's Grand Design," the Lord has Two Creations: **One Comprised** of **Angelic Spirits** (Heaven) and the **Second Comprised** of **Human Flesh** (Earth) as both are **Called to Serve** the *Lord's Spirit Nature* (positive/order/perfection) and *His Physical Nature* (negative/chaos/imperfection). Obviously, "God First Called" forth the Angelic Realm to become **Servants unto the Lord** as **They are Expected** to *Thank Him* (table/give labors), *Praise Him* (throne/give wealth), and to *Worship Him* (altar/give lives) for *His Gift of Life*. We see that this "Mystical Arrangement" between God and His Angels **Actually Made Them Birds Living** in a **Golden Cage** as **They were Living Their Lives** with **No Muss** and **No Fuss** as **All are Perfect** in the *Sight of God*. At this point, "Lucifer Asked:" but where is Our Challenge, Our Adventure, and Our Fun in **All of This Peace and Harmony? We Want** to be **Like God** so **We Too can Live** via the *Lord's Throne* (challenge), *Altar* (adventure), and *Table* (fun). In response, the Lord God Almighty said, " Okay, I will Give You All **Free Will** so **You can Decide for Yourselves** just **What the Life-experience** should be based on its *Meaning* (exist/challenge), *Purpose* (service/adventure), and its *Value* (happiness/fun)." At this "Moment" When the Angels were **Given Free Will,** a **Great War** broke **out** causing the **Ignorant Angels** to *Grab God's Rollicking Fun* (table); then the **Cowardly Angels** *Grabbed God's Great Adventures* (altar); leaving the **Greedy Angels** to *Grab God's most Painful Challenges* (throne). Unfortunately, in the "Great War" between God and His Angels, some of the **Angels** (ignorant) were to be *Chained in Sin* (silent), some were **Placed** (cowards) in a **Prison of Evil** (forced to repent), and then the **Last Group** (fight God) was to be *Guarded by Death* (sentenced for execution).

1. **Ignorant Angels** - Chained in Sin: Cursed to be Dumb = Silent…Innocent Blood
2. **Cowardly Angels** - Imprisoned in Evil: Cursed to Repent = Worship…Forgiven Blood
3. **Greedy Angels** - Guarded by Death: Cursed to Fight God = Try to Win… Guilty Blood

This illustration shows that "God is Still Fighting" a Great Angelic War, while **He is Calling** forth the **Human Race** to **Come Out** of the **Astral Plane** (nothingness) of **Spirits** to **Enter** the <u>Wombs of Life</u> to bring forth *Righteous Citizens on Earth,* *Holy Saints in* **Heaven,** and *Perfect Sons within God's Kingdom.* To "God's Shock," <u>None of His Human Spirits</u> had the **Necessary Courage** to **Come Out** of **Their Astral Plane so** that **They would be Given Free Redemption** of the **Flesh** (mandatory) and **Offered Earned Salvation of the Spirit,** <u>If They could</u> <u>Believe</u> *100% in Jesus* (optional). Through this "God/Man Agreement," <u>Adam</u> <u>and Eve</u> **Came** forth to **Enter Life** via **God's Breath** (redemption) and **Adam's Rib** (salvation) to bring forth a **Sufficient** <u>Number of Babies</u> to *Start the Human* *Life-experience on Earth.* We see that in this "Carnage of Human Innocents," some <u>30 Billion Ignorant/Cowardly/Greedy Souls</u> would **Face Lucifer** (ultimate test) **Over the First Week of Life** (7,000 yrs.) and be **Slaughtered** and **Destroyed** by *Sin* (sin-nature), *Evil* (worldly temptations), *Death* (demonic forces), and *Damnation* (God's curse). Through this "Awesome Human Sacrifice," the <u>Human</u> <u>Race</u> would be **Able to Get a Foothold on Earth, Thanks** to the **Help of Jesus Christ** and **His Three Advents** as **He** brings *Wisdom*/good news, then *Courage*/gospel (2nd advent/seal saints), and finally, *Generosity*/doctrine (3rd advent/judgment) to a *Lost and Broken World.*

Teach   1. **1st Advent** - <u>Priest brings Wisdom;</u> Mount Calvary…Good News
               Being Saved
               • Prophet - Guides the Way: Teaching God's Truth = Ignorance to
                 Wisdom
Redeem   2. **2nd Advent** - <u>Thief brings Courage:</u> Sealing of Saints…Gospel
               Message to Save Self
               • Messiah - Seals His Saints: Redeeming God's Chosen Ones =
                 Cowardice to Courage
Judge   3. **3rd Advent** - <u>Judge brings Generosity:</u> Judgment…Doctrinal Truths
               to Save Others
               • God - Judgment of Souls: God Reveals His Eternal Rule = Greed
                 to Generosity

This illustration shows that "Souls Now Poured" forth from the <u>Astral Plane</u> **Beginning** with **Adam and Eve** who as a **Host** of **Ignorant Babies,** were **Willing to Face Lucifer** and his **Demons** in a **Great Cosmology On Slaughter** of **Human Flesh,** <u>Ready to Die</u> for *Their God.* Secondly, with the "Coming of Christ," the <u>Astral Plane</u> will then **Release** its **Cowardly Babies** to **Flood** onto the **Earth** in a **Second Wave** of **Unconscionable Slaughter** as **Man's Human Flesh** was even **More** <u>Ready to Die</u> for *Its All Forgiving God.* Finally, with the "Third Coming of Christ," the <u>Astral Plane</u> will **Release** its **Greedy Babies** to **Flood** onto the **Earth** in a **Third Wave** of **Massive Slaughter** as **Man's Human Flesh** was even **More** <u>Ready to Die</u> for *Its most Beloved God.* Through "These Three Waves (holy innocence)" of <u>Human Babies,</u> the **Lord God Almighty** will be **Able** to **Defeat Sin, Evil, Death,** and even **Damnation** to bring forth *Peace, Joy, and Happiness to One and All.*

We might ask: "Just Why so Much Sacrifice" and "Why would God" <u>Kill his Own</u> <u>Son</u> to bring forth a **Newly Purified Earth** at **All Cost** and then **Soak It** in both **Human** and Divine Blood to **Make It** <u>Unconscionably Valuable</u> to *God, Angels, Men, and even Mother Nature?* Imagine that "God is Faced" with <u>Exterminating</u> an **Infestation of Evil Rats** based on **Those Who Remained Ignorant, Cowardly, Greedy, and Selfish.** Hence, **They were to be Destroyed** by *God's Wise, Courageous, Generous, and Unselfish Angels and Saints.* This would mean that the "Whole Earth" would have to be <u>Burned</u> and <u>Purified</u> to bring forth a **New Earth, Complete** with its **Own Divine School of Higher Learning** which would **Prevent** the **Human Race** from **Falling Back** into a **Second Rat Infestation** of *Sin* (ignorance), *Evil* (cowardice), *Death,* (greed) and *Damnation* (selfishness).

The following tabular information indicates that "God Needed Teachers" with some <u>7,000 Years of Training</u> and so, **He Created** the **Demons** (evil), **Damned** (wrong), **Saints** (right), and **Angels** (good) to be *His New Set of Eternal Teachers:*

God's Divine School of Higher Learning
Teaches Lessons and brings Blessings
(wisdom brings challenge, courage brings adventure, generosity
brings fun, and unselfishness brings happiness)

1. **Demons** - <u>Teach Evil:</u> Ignorance to Wisdom = Elementary School...Virgin Mary
   - Teaching Right from Wrong - New Mind: Intellect: Knowledge (see limitations)
   - Wisdom brings forth Challenges of Life - Create Righteous Citizens on Earth
2. **Damned** - <u>Teach Wrong:</u> Cowardice to Courage = High School...Saint Joseph
   - Teaching Good from Evil - New Heart: Emotions = Self-awareness (see potential)
   - Courage brings forth Adventures of Life - Create Holy Saints in Heaven
3. **Holy Saints** - <u>Teach Right:</u> Greed to Generosity = College...Jesus Christ
   - Teaching God's Will/Man's Will - New Soul: Instincts = Consciousness (see self-worth)
   - Generosity brings forth Rollicking Fun - Create Perfect Son within God's Kingdom
4. **Good Angels** - <u>Teach Good:</u> Selfishness to Unselfishness = Sonship Training...God Almighty
   - Teaching God's Reality/Man's Illusion - New Life-force: Lifestyle = Sentience

This illustration shows that the "Challenges of Life" are <u>Centered</u> upon **Removing Ignorance** and then **Striving to Obtain Wisdom** by **Learning** the **Lessons of Life** which **Remove One's Faults** to <u>**Empty His Nature**</u> of *Childish Thinking* (illogic). Secondly, the "Adventures of Life" are <u>Centered</u> upon **Removing Cowardice** and then **Striving to Obtain Superhuman Courage** by **Earning God's Blessings of Life** which

Allows a Person to **Gain God's Virtues** to <u>Fill His Nature</u> with *Adult Behavior* (maturity). Finally, the "Fun Things of Life" are <u>Centered</u> upon **Removing Greed** and then **Striving to Obtain Heartfelt Generosity** by **Learning** to **Think for Oneself** which <u>**Allows a Person**</u> to become *Righteous, Holy, and Perfect before God.*

Yes! "We are Witnessing" <u>God bringing His</u> **Divine School** into **His Creation** by **Making Earth His Elementary School** to **Teach God's Right** and **Man's Wrong**, thereby **Creating Righteous Citizens Who** are *Worthy of New Bodies.* Secondly, "God's Creation" is <u>Making Heaven</u> **His High School** to **Teach God's Good and Man's Evil**, thereby **Creating Holy Saints Who** are **Worthy of Living** <u>**Eternal Lives**</u> in the *Presence of God, Angels, and Men.* Thirdly, "God's Creation" is <u>Making God's Kingdom</u> **His College** to **Teach God's Reality and Man's Illusion**, thereby **Creating Perfect Sons, Who** are **Worthy** of having <u>**Their Own**</u> *Personal Kingdoms of Glory.* This means that "Once a Person" has <u>Completed his Education,</u> he must then **Enter God's Sonship Training Program** without **Complaint** to **Master God's** <u>**Truth, Law, Will, and Love**</u> by becoming a *Man for All Seasons* (thinking for oneself).

A Person might ask: "Just <u>How Does</u> both the **Angelic** and **Human Rebellions** Fit into the <u>**Creation**</u> of *God's Divine School?*" The simple answer is that "If God was Going" to <u>Instantly Give</u> **Angels** and **Men Free Will**, the **Lord** would have to **Counter** the **Instant Effects** of **Ignorance** (mind), **Cowardice** (heart), **and Greed** (soul) which would <u>**Accompany**</u> having *God's Divine Authority Overnight.* Note that "God Knew" that the <u>Massive Effects of Free Will</u> would be **Less at the Spirit Level** than it would be at the **Human** or **Physical Level.** Thus, **He Infected** the **Angelic Nature First** so that **It** could **Recover** and then <u>**Help bring the Humans**</u> *Out of Their Withdrawal* (insanity) *more Easily.*

Thinking for Oneself via Free Will
The Instant Side-effects of Receiving God's Free Will
(both Angels and Men go a little crazy
when given God's Free Will Authority All at Once)

1. **Intellectual Free Will** - <u>Mind of Ignorance:</u> Chain Insane Fool…Cursed with Silence
   - Silence the Foolish - Thanking God: Give Labors = Serving God's Table (elementary)
2. **Emotional Free Will** - <u>Heart of Cowardice:</u> Imprison Wild Animal…Cursed with Repentance
   - Repentance of Cowards - Worshiping God: Give Lives = Serving God's Altar (high school)
3. **Instinctive Free Will** - <u>Soul of Greed:</u> Guard Hate-Filled Soldier…Cursed with Execution
   - Defeat Greedy Monsters - Praising God: Give Wealth = Serving God's Throne (college)

This illustration shows that the "Lord God Almighty" would have to <u>Initially Arrest</u> **All Creation's Fools** by *Chaining Ignorance* (silent/table), *Imprisoning All Cowards* (repent/altar), and *Guarding Greedy Fools* (fight to the death/throne). "After" both <u>Angels</u> and <u>Men</u> had **Passed** through the **Insane Effects of Free Will, They would Then be Able to Master Thinking for Themselves,** thereby **Making Them Excellent Teachers** (divine school) for the **Rest of God's Babies** as <u>**They Come**</u> forth by the <u>**Millions**</u> (sons), <u>**Billions**</u> (saints), and even <u>**Trillions**</u> (citizens) to *Enter the Eternal Workforce of God* (grains of sand/stars). The question is: just "How can God Feed" so <u>Many Mouths</u> **When the Divine, Mystical, Spiritual, and Physical Dimensions All Need to Eat** <u>**God's Divine Energy,**</u> *All at the Same time?* The idea here is that as "God's Creation Grows" from <u>Angels, to Men, to Nature,</u> and then **Keeps Multiplying** at an **Alarming Rate,** it **Appears Hopeless to Find a Way** to **Multiply God's Mystical Life-force** (divine energy) **Fast Enough** to **Satisfy Creation's Exponential Demands,** without <u>**Risking Some Catastrophic**</u> *Future Collapse.* Obviously, this "Infinite Supply of Food" was to <u>Come from Jesus Christ</u> (Calvary) as **He would Turn Himself** into **Lamb, Bread, and Wine** to **Keep** the **Table of the Lord** <u>**Forever Filled**</u> with *Life-giving Food.*

Now, let's look at this "Supply Side Economic Idea" a Little Closer as the Creatures of God **Fill Themselves** with **Nourishment** from <u>**Man's**</u> (physical) *Home, Government, Church* and <u>**Man's**</u> (spiritual) *Thanksgiving, Praise, Worship* from <u>**God's**</u> (mystical) *Table, Throne, Altar,* and finally, from <u>**God's/Man's**</u> (divine) *Priest, King, and Son.* Yes! Each of the "Four Dimensions of Life (12 stages)" will <u>Eat Its Fill</u> as **It Travels** from **Nothing to All** and **Back** so <u>**It can Experience Life**</u> for **Itself** in *Ignorance, Cowardice, Greed,* and finally, in *Pure Selfishness.* Through this "Great Journey" <u>Along God's Pathway of Transformation</u> (see illusion/change nature/lessons), a **Person can become Worthy** of **Entering** <u>God's Pathway of Purification</u> (see reality/wash away sin/blessings) which **Leads** from **All to Nothing,** thereby <u>**Allowing Him to Experience**</u> the *Indwelling of God for himself* (fulfill the divine dream). We see that "Man Carries Jesus' (great accomplishments)" <u>Physical Cross of Work,</u> *Eats His Bread,* and *Drinks His Wine to Live,* while "God Rests in Christ's (dream of greater accomplishments)" <u>Spiritual Tomb of Sleep,</u> *Eats His Flesh,* and *Drinks His Blood to Live.* Through this "Mystical Cycle" of <u>Life and Death,</u> **God's Paradoxical Existence** can become **One** with **Man's Desire** to be **All** (flesh/world) which is **Fulfilled** by <u>**God's Desire**</u> to be *Nothing* (spirit/church). It's a "Mystical Pumping System" as <u>Man is Consuming Life</u> (oxygen/animals) and *Pumping in Death* (Jesus/takes-sin/lessons), while <u>God is Consuming Death</u> (carbon dioxide/plants) and *Pumping in New-life* (Christ gives divinity/blessings). It should now be clear that the "Physical Life-experience" or <u>Our Illusion of Life</u> is **All About** *Removing Faults* (lessons) and *Gaining Virtues* (blessings), while the "Spiritual Life-experience" or <u>God's Reality</u> is **All About** *Escaping an Evil Illusion* to *Enter a Holy Reality.*

The following tabular information indicates that "Man is Passing" through <u>Twelve Stages of Perfection</u> as he **Travels** from *Nothing to All* (pride), while "God/Man is Passing" through a <u>Second Set</u> of <u>Twelve Stages</u> (or 24) of <u>Divine Perfection</u> as **He** <u>**Travels**</u> from *All to Nothing* (humility).

Mystical Pumping System
Eternal System of Nourishment for God, Angels, Men and Nature
======== Man Carries Jesus' Physical *Cross of Work*
and Eats His Bread and Wine to Live ========

Transformation - Man Increases (live the vision)
Physical   Spiritual   Mystical   Divine
World - Flesh/lessons: Remove Faults (fight evil)
Astral - plane / *Nothing* - - - - - - - - - *All* / Grave of Death
Church - Spirit / Blessings: Gain Virtues (submission)

	1.. Home	4. Thanksgiving	7. Table	10. Citizenship	
Man Wants	2 Government	5 . Praise	8. Throne	11. Sainthood	**Death Begins**
to be God	3. Church	6 . Worship	9. Altar	12. Sons of God	. Illusion
. Human Nature	(mind)	(heart)	(soul)	(life-force)	

============== God Rests in Christ's *Tomb of Sleep*
and Eats His Flesh and Blood to Live ==============

Purification - God Decreases (dream the dream)
God   Angels   Men   Nature
Human Nature - Physical / Convert death: escape illusion (merging)
Born-again Host / *All* - - - - - - - - - - - - - - - *Nothing* / Tomb of Calvary
Divine Nature - Spiritual / Convert Damnation: enter reality (blending)

	1. Priesthood	4. Earth	7. Bottom Choirs	10. 3rd Person	
God Wants	2. Kingship	5. Heaven	8. Middle Choirs	11. 2nd Person	**Life Begins**
to be Man	3. Sonship	6. Kingdom	9. Top Choirs	12. 1st Person	. Reality
. Divine Nature	(nature)	(new body)	(eternal life)	(own kingdom)	

Man's All - Natural Selectiom: Human lessons (awake)
** *God's Nothing - Intelligent Design: Divine Dreams (sleep)*

This illustration shows that "Man Wants to be God (hard-work)" and "God Wants to be Man (big dream)." This could Only become a Reality in **Christ Jesus** as both **God's Creation** (bloodline) and **God Himself** (marriage vow) would have to become **One Life-force** in *Christ's New Born-again Nature*. Note that in the "World (lessons)," Life is Comprised of *Eating, Drinking, and being Merry,* while in the "Church (blessings)," Life is Comprised of *Fasting, Putting On Sackcloth,* and *Sitting in a Pan of Ashes.* This means that "When a Person" is Traveling from **Nothing to All** (pride/increase), he is **Getting Fat Like a Bear**; and then "When a Person" is Traveling from **All to Nothing** (humility/decrease), he is **Starving,** becoming **Naked,** and is finally, **Homeless** with **Nowhere to Lay his Head.** Yes! The "Life-experience" is All About Increasing unto Perfection and then **Sacrificing It All** (priceless to worthless) in **Service to One's** *Family, Friends, Neighbors,* and his *Community,* even unto the *Outermost Parts of the Earth* (strangers). Obviously, the "Lord God Almighty" has Sent Us a Messiah **Who can Fix Anything** and **Everything** by **Mystically Merging God/Man, Right/Wrong, Day/Night** and even the **Past** (lessons) and the **Future** (blessings) to **Make Life and Death One Creation** (eternal present) in *Truth, Law,*

Will, and Love. We have to imagine that "Jesus Christ" <u>Suffered More</u> in the **Womb of Life** during **Christmas** than **He Did** in the **Tomb of Death** during **Easter** as both **Places Represent Eternal Prisons** which must be <u>Transformed</u> into a *New Paradise for One and All.*

We see that in the "Story of Peter and Paul," <u>They</u> were both <u>Chained, Imprisoned,</u> and <u>Closely Guarded,</u> implying that **When God's Son Came to Earth, <u>He</u> Too** was *Chained in the Womb, Imprisoned in Life,* and finally, *Guarded by Death.* It was the "Lord Sending" <u>His Flesh</u> to become **All Perfection** (pride of ownership) in *God's Breath* (Adam), while **Simultaneously** <u>Sending His Spirit</u> to become **Nothing** (humble servanthood/poverty) in *God's Resurrection* (New Adam/Jesus). Through this "Process of Fulfillment," <u>Man's Nature</u> can **Find its Heart's Desire** in the **Old Adam of Hardwork/past glory** (physical life), while <u>God's Nature</u> can **Find its Heart's Desire** in the **New Adam** of *Eternal Rest/future dream* (spiritual life). Yes! We are being "Called to Honor" both <u>Our Past Glories</u> and <u>Our Future Dreams</u> of a **More Productive Society** as **Everyone Strives** to **Grow and Mature** into a **Higher and Higher State** of **Perfection** within the *Eyes of God*. We see that <u>**Living**</u> in the very *Paradox of God* means we have to "Accomplish this Impossible Feat" of an <u>Ever Expanding Nature,</u> while **Striving** to be **All in Flesh** (pride of ownership), and **Nothing in Spirit** (humble servant) at the **same time.**

On this "Eternal Day of Perfection," <u>Everyone will Live</u> in the **Present Moment** as his **Works** (owner) and his **Dreams** (servant) are **Made One** in **Christ Jesus** (God/Man), through the **<u>Fulfillment</u>** of both the *Old Adam of Work* (pride of ownership) and the *New Adam of Rest* (dreams). To "Comprehend" this <u>Dual Nature Concept</u> (spirit/flesh), a **Person must Imagine** that upon the **Lord's Conception, He Instantly Escaped** through the **Human Bloodline, Traveling Back in Time** to **Reach <u>Father Adam</u>** and *God's Breath of Life*. Secondly, "Baby Jesus" <u>Traveled Forward in Time</u> to **Reach Mount Calvary** so that **He could Pass** through the **Portal of Death** via **His Tomb of Resurrection,** thereby **Again Reaching God's Spirit of New-life** to **<u>Link</u>** the *Nothing of Adam* (mystical body) with the *All of God* (communion of saints). Obviously, by "Linking" both the <u>Death of the Past</u> with the <u>Life of the Future,</u> the **Lord Jesus Christ** could **Create** the **Eternal Present** (infinite moment), where **Every Imbalance** in **Human, Angelic, and Divine Life <u>Needs</u>** the *Healing Touch of Christ.*

Lord's Birth/Death bring God's Gift of Eternal Present
(Man's Christmas and God's Easter
unite the Past and Future into Born-again Present)

Mystical Body - Man is Awake (daytime)　　　　　　　　**Physical Chaos**
World - Flesh/lessons: Remove Faults (fight evil)　　　　•Remove Faults
Nothing————Get Obedience————*All* (pride of ownership/world)
　　　　Church - Spirit/blessings: Gain Virtues (submission)
　　　　　　Past　　Jesus – Man (natural selection)
Adam (God's breath)———————— *Womb*———— (resurrection)　　*Calvary*

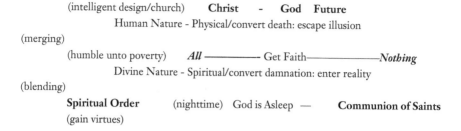

(intelligent design/church)   **Christ**   -   **God   Future**
            Human Nature - Physical/convert death: escape illusion
(merging)
        (humble unto poverty)   *All* ——————— Get Faith——————*Nothing*
            Divine Nature - Spiritual/convert damnation: enter reality
(blending)
        Spiritual Order   (nighttime)   God is Asleep —   **Communion of Saints**
        (gain virtues)

This illustration shows that through "God's Intelligent Design (church)" and "Man's Natural Selection (world)," the <u>Human Past of Works</u> can **Meet** the <u>Divine Future of Dreams,</u> thereby **Creating** the **Eternal Present** of <u>**Mutual Admiration**</u> and <u>**Respect**</u> between *God, Angels, Men, and Nature.* This means that the "Reality of the Flesh" will <u>Forever be Found</u> in the **World System** (pride of ownership) of *Dedicated Hardwork* (honor the past), while the "Reality of the Spirit" will <u>Forever be Found</u> in the **Church System** (humility/servanthood) of *Beautiful Dreams* (see the future).

In the previous graphic illustration, "We See Christ's Birth" <u>Depicts the Blending</u> of **God's Life** (Christ) and **Man's Death** (Jesus) which become **One** in **Spirit and Flesh,** thereby <u>**Combining**</u> both *God's Never-created Nature* (all/energy) with *Man's Created Nature* (nothing/matter). This implies that the "Creation of Christmas" brings forth <u>Man's</u> *Pathway of Human Perfection* (honor works), while the "Creation of Easter" brings forth <u>God's</u> *Pathway of Divine Perfection* (live for the dream). The "Lord is Telling Us" that "Our Transformed Flesh (change nature/get obedience)" is <u>Going to Forever</u> **Strive to Create** a **Bigger** and **Bigger Physical Creation** to bring forth as <u>**Many Wise, Strong, and Healthy Babies**</u> as *Humanly Possible.* Secondly, "Our Purified Spirit (purify nature/get faith)" is <u>Going to Forever</u> **Strive to Dream Up More** and **More Mystical States of Human, Angelic, and Divine Perfection** to bring forth as **Many** <u>**Righteous, Holy, and Perfect**</u> *Sons of God as Possible*.

Now, "We have Learned" that <u>Mankind</u> will **Walk in the Daylight** and **Do All in its Power** to **Translate God's Dream** into **Real Blood and Bone Reality** by becoming **More and More Obedient** to the *Divine Laws of God* (change nature). Secondly, "We have Learned" that <u>Divinity</u> will **Walk in the Night** and **Do All in its Power** to Define the **Deepest Heart's Desire of God** so that the **Human Race** will **Know Where** and **What to Build** as it **Strives to Create** the <u>**Lord's New God/Man Kingdom of Glory**</u>.

Now, let's try to "Comprehend the Mystical Forces" which <u>Comprise</u> the **Creation** of this **New God/Man Kingdom** as **God Offers His Destiny** (all) or **His Intelligent Design** and **Man Offers** his **Free Will** (nothing) or his **Natural Selection** to **Blend** both **All and Nothing** into <u>**One Reality**</u> in *Christ Jesus.* We see that to "Comprehend" this <u>Blending Process,</u> **One must Imagine** that **Jesus Christ** is like a **Giant Black Hole** which is **Pulling In Two Stars** (God and Man) with **One Eternally Pumping In Intelligent Design** (destiny) and the **Other Eternally Pumping In Natural Selection** (free will) which are <u>**Blended into One**</u> *Born-again Creation* *of New-life*. The idea here is that "Only Christ's New Creation (born-again)" can <u>Bear Fruit</u> **Out** of both **God's Good/order** (intelligent design/night) and **Man's Evil/chaos** (natural selection/day), implying that **All the Actions** of either <u>Heaven or Earth</u> will *Bear Fruit* (pure gold) *in Christ Jesus*.

We see in this "Explanation" that the <u>Lord is Telling Us,</u> **If God and Man** can **Work Together, They can Produce** an **Awesome Amount of Productivity**, thereby **Making Them** both <u>Fabulously Rich</u> in *Gold, Love,* and in an *Abundance of Happiness*. We see in the "Bible" <u>that Jesus Tells</u> the **Story of a Poor Man Who Finds a Treasure in a Field** and **Sells All** to **Buy the Field** to **Get the Treasure** (free gold mine); then as a **Rich Man**, he **Goes in Search** of the **Pearl of Great Price** and **Again Sells All to Buy It** (dig out gold); and finally, the **Man Casts** a **Great Net into the Sea** to <u>Gather</u> a *Great Harvest of Wealth* (sharing gold).

1. **Free Gold Mine** - <u>Increasing</u>: Get Fat Like the Bears...See Limitations
   - Learning the Lessons of Life - Removing One's Faults (citizenship)
   - Fulfill God's Law of Obedience - Change Nature: Human to Divine
     - Find a Field with a Great Treasure - Sell All and Buy Field (life)
        (Life - experiencing a *Free-willed Childhood*:
           chained in insanity = God's table)
2. **Digging Out the Gold** - <u>Decreasing</u>: Offering Oneself Like Christ...See Potential
   - Getting God's Blessings of Life - Gaining God's Virtues (sainthood)
   - Fulfilling Man's Faith in God's Love - Washing Away Sins: Sinfulness to Holiness
   - Going in Search of the Pearl of Great Price - Selling All and Buy Pearl (death)
        (Death - experiencing a *Free-willed Teenage Life*:
           imprisoned in repentance = God's altar)
3. **Sharing One's Gold with Others** - <u>Celebrating</u>: One's Triumph with All...See Self-worth
   - Master Sacrificing Oneself - Righteous/Holy/Perfect (sonship)
   - Fulfilling God/Man Knowing - Thinking for Oneself: God and Man become One
   - Casting a Great Net into the Sea - Bringing forth One's Harvest of Wealth (resurrection)
        (Resurrect - experiencing a *Free-willed Adulthood*:
           guarded by responsibilities = God's throne)

This illustration shows that "Each of God's Children" is being <u>Called to Seek</u> the **Wisdom of Life** as **If it were a Free Gold Mine**, then **Sacrifice Himself** by **Digging Out the Gold**, and finally **Sharing His Gold** with <u>Everyone Else</u> to bring *Prosperity to All*. We see this "Same Theme of Sharing" in the <u>Story of God</u> and <u>His Creation</u> as the **Lord Makes All Things in Destiny** (law/divine justice) and then **Miraculously Gives Angels, Men**, and even **Nature** their **Own Free Will** so that **All can Experience** *Freedom, Liberty, and Independence for Themselves.* This means that the "Lord God Almighty" had Never-created Existence (meaning of life) or a **Free Gold Mine**; then through **Jesus Christ, God Dug Out the Gold** to be of **Service to One and All** (purpose of life) and finally, the **Lord is Offering to Share All He Owns** with **His Kingdom** to **Create the Value of Life** in the **Form** of *Eternal Happiness.*

Unfortunately, "No Matter How Generous" God Hoped to Be as soon as **He Offered His Divine Authority** to **His Entire Creation**, it **Instantly Divided** into **Babies** or *Ignorant Fools*, into **Teenagers** or *Cowardly Criminals*, and finally, **Adults** or *Greedy Monsters*. Suddenly, the "Lord God Almighty" had inadvertently Created a Nightmare and there seemed to be **No Hope of Educating** this **Bunch of Insane, Criminal, and Murderous Fools Sufficiently Enough** to **Turn Them** into *Normal Human Beings.* "Only with Christ's" Intervention could a **New Perfect Solution** be **Found** which was to **Give Everyone a New Born-again Nature**, **Comprised** of *God's Wisdom, Courage, and Generosity.*

We can now "Comprehend that Great Importance" Associated with the **Lord's Three Advents** as **He Transforms the Babies** (new nature/wisdom), **Purifies the Teenagers** (remove sins/courage), and **Converts the Adults** (thinking/generosity) in an **Attempt** to **Remove Human** *Ignorance* (life), *Cowardice* (death), and *Greed* (resurrection). The point here is that to "Give Any Incompetent Fool" Too Much Power (free will) and/or Authority (ownership) is **Like Handing a Child** a **Stick of Dynamite.** For **Some Strange Reason**, this is **Precisely What** the **Lord God Almighty has Done**, causing **Those Who** *Sow the Wind* to *Reap the Whirlwind.* Now, because of this "Divine Gesture of Kindness" by God, the **Entire World** is **Infested** with **Insane Fools Who Roam the Land Like** Wild Animals *Stealing* (ignorant children), *Beating* (cowardly teenagers), and *Killing* (greedy adults) *Everyone that They Meet.*

Yes! We "Live in a Violent Land" and the Only Hope is that **God's Son** might **Return to Chain** the **Ignorant** (babies), **Imprison** the **Cowards** (teenagers), and finally, **Guard** the **Greedy Fools** (adults) to *Save the World.* The "Job of God's Messiah" will be to Teach and Heal the **Babies** to *Break Their Chains of Ignorance*, then to Wash the Cowardly Sinners (teenagers) in **His Sacrificial Blood** to *Free Them from Prison* (captivity), and finally, to Resurrect the **Greedy Adults** to **Set Them Free** from *Sin, Evil, and Death.* Now, we see that through the "Free-willed Child," the "Free-willed Teenager," and the "Free-willed Adult," the Lord Jesus Christ is **Planning** to bring forth **God's Harvest of Souls** in the **Form** of **Righteous, Holy**, and **Perfect Men** of *Wisdom, Courage, and Generosity.*

1. Experiencing a Free-willed Childhood - Chained in Insanity (table)
   We see that "If God Gives" His Awesome Power (free will) to a **Child**, he will Think it is just **Another Toy** until his most **Beloved Toy Begins** to **Attack him, Injure his Body**, and finally, **Kill** his *Mind, Heart, and* his *Soul* (rot in grave).

Life - Past
The Ignorant Child
(baby Christ purifies Earth with Teachings/Healings)
- Foolish Intellect - Mind: Think of Man
- Uncontrollable Emotions - Heart: Speak to Man
- Compulsive Instincts - Soul: Touch Man

2 .   Experiencing a Free-willed Teenage Life - Imprisoned in Repentance (altar)
We see that "If God Gives" <u>His Awesome Power</u> (free will) to a **Teenager, Suddenly he will Think,** and he can **Master All he Surveys** by either **Using** his *Stick of Pain* (murder) or his *Carrot of Pleasure* (money).

Death - Present
The Cowardly Teenager
(teenage Christ purifies Earth with Sacrificial Blood)
- Immature Intellect - Mind: Think of God
- Unstable Emotions - Heart: Speak to God
- Ineffective Instincts - Soul: Touch God

3.   Experiencing a Free-willed Adulthood - Guarded by Responsibilities (throne)
We see that "If God Gives" <u>His Awesome Power</u> (free will) to an **Adult,** he will **Think he can Rule the World** with an **Iron Hand,** thereby **Enslaving his Fellow Men,** while <u>**Making himself** </u>the *Greatest and Richest King the World has Ever Seen* (Solomon).

Resurrection - Future
The Greedy Adult
(adult Christ purifies Earth with Personal Resurrection)
- Professional Intellect - Mind: Think of God/Man
- Rock-hard Emotions - Heart: Speak to God/Man
- Supernatural Instincts - Soul: Touch God/Man

This illustration shows that the "Human Life-experience" is <u>Comprised</u> of **Life** (birth), **Death** (grave), and finally, **Resurrection** (born-again) much like that of a **Caterpillar** as it <u>**Transforms**</u> from a *Worm* (sinner) into a *Beautiful Butterfly* (saint). This means that the "Life-experience Begins" in <u>Selfish Destiny,</u> then becomes **Free Will** (death), and **finally, Ends** in a **Person's Unselfish Destiny** as he has **Learned** that **God, Society,** and the **Needs of Others** are <u>**More Important**</u> than his *Own Simple Needs.* Through this "Massive Journey" from <u>Nothing to All</u> (hard-work) and <u>Back</u> (dream), **God, Angels, Men,** and **Nature** are **Able** to become <u>**One Creation**</u> (life), <u>**One People**</u> (death), and even <u>**One Land**</u> (resurrection) of *Peace* (challenge), *Joy* (adventure), and *Happiness* (fun). Yes! We all "Want to be Creators" in <u>Fulfillment</u> of **Our Desire for Challenge, Adventure, Fun,** and **Happiness** as **We Strive** to **Expend Ourselves** unto the **Max** in **Inventing Something New,** truly **Unique** (one of a kind), and then **Convincing Everyone Else** that *They Can't Live Without It.* Obviously, "Our God and His Son have Done" just that as They have Designed, Created, and are Now Implementing **Their Mystical Creation** (free-willed born-again blessing) on **Earth and in Heaven** to bring forth **Their New Kingdom of Glory** in *Service to One and All.*

God's Gift of Free Will is a Massive Cross
(life begins in selfish destiny, becomes free will,
and ends in a person's unselfish destiny)

Earth   1.   **Physical** - Ignorant Child: Orphan = Citizenship/wisdom ...
(temperance)   Church/Face Life
- Evangelize   Virgin Mary: Elementary School = Ignorance to Wisdom
- New Mind - Thinking for Oneself: New Body = Saved by Ethics
- Lost Fool - Fails to Fulfill God's Law of Obedience (compromised will)

Heaven   2.   **Spiritual** – Cowardly Teen: Widow = Sainthood/courage ...
(fortitude)   Prophet/Face Death
- Teach - Saint Joseph: High School = Cowardice to Courage
- New Heart – Speaking Correctly: Eternal Life = Saved by Morals
- Insane Outcast - Fails to Fulfill Man's Faith in God's Love (permissive will)

Kingdom   3.   **Mystical** - Greedy Adult: Poor = Sons of God/generosity...Messiah/Face
(just)   Damnation
- Redeem - Jesus Christ: College = Greed to Generosity
- New Soul - Touch Truth: Own Kingdom = Saved by Fairness
- Dangerous Criminal – Fails to Fulfill God/Man Knowing (direct will)

God   4.   **Divine** - Selfish Wise Man: Stranger = God/unselfish ...
(balance)   God/Face Resurrection
- Judge - God: Sonship Training = Selfish to Unselfish
- New Life-force - Sup with Others: Freedom = Saved by Justice
- Homicidal Murderer - Fails to Fulfill Thinking for Oneself (free will)

This illustration shows that to "Fulfill" God's Gift of Free Will, a **Person** must **Believe in Christ 100%** (submission), or **Master the Church** (blessings), then **Pick-up** his **Sword of Promise,** and *Fight the Evil World unto the Death* (lessons). In short, "If a Person" Crushes himself upon the **Earthly Winepress of Death** (lessons), he can **Remove his Faults** (empty); and then, "If a Person" can Master the Church, he can be **Filled** with *God's Virtues* (fill). This means that "We must All Pass" through the Physical World of **Evangelization**, the Spiritual World of **Education** (teaching), the Mystical World of **Redemption**, and finally, the Divine World of **Judgment** to become either a *Righteous Citizen, Holy Saint,* and/or truly *Sons of God* within *God's Kingdom.* Obviously, "God is Calling" Each of His Children to **Enter His Elementary School, Graduate to High School, Go to College,** and then **Take God's Sonship Training Program** to become **Worthy** of the very *Friendship of God Himself.* By "Going" through this Entire Process, a **Person** can be **Transformed** from an **Ignorant Child** to a *Wise Student*, from a **Cowardly Teenager** to a **Courageous Soldier**, from a **Greedy Adult** to a **Generous Holy Man** (priestly), and finally, from a **Selfish Wise Man** to an *Unselfish Son of God*.

We see in this picture the "Mystical Redemption" of the Ignorant Orphan, the Cowardly Widow, the Greedy Poor, and the Selfish Stranger as **They Each Strives** to **Find a Place** in **Society** based on *Man's Compromised Will* (loving), *Permissive Will* (merciful), *Direct Will* (just), and/or *His Own Free Will* (free). Yes! Everyone is "Seeking a Job (ethics)," a "Perfect Mate (morals)," and a "Happy Home (fairness)" as He Knows that **Everything** that is **Good in Life Comes** from **His Personal Stability** which is **Centered upon His** *Wisdom, Courage, Generosity, and Unselfishness*. We see that through "These Stable Human Qualities," the Lord Blesses a **Mature Soul's Hands** to **Anoint its Mystical Works** to bring **Glory** to **All the Creations of its Heart,** which is **Done in the Name** of *God's Son Jesus Christ.* Finally, a "Born-again Soul is Given" the Lord's Crown of Majesty to **Glorify and Honor** its **Mind,** so the very **Thoughts in its Head** will be **Anointed** with the *Sanctifying Grace* of the *Eternal Father.* This means that a "Person must Keep God Foremost" in his Mind (worship) and Heart (praise) by **Practicing** the **Holy Virtues** of the **Christian Faith** to bring forth the **Sacred Fruits** (submission/sacrifice) of a *Holy Life* (death to self).

It is clear that the "Lord is Enormously Proud" of His Infinite Power and **Never Passes Up** an **Opportunity to Turn** on **His Miracle Forces** to **Transform a Person's Evil Despair** (hell) into a **New-life** (Heaven) of *Divine Hope.* Why would the "Lord Make a Statement" such as, I have Not Come for the Righteous (saved), but for the Unrighteous (lost), especially **When All** the **Wicked Souls of Creation** certainly **Appear to be Falling** into the **Fires of Hell** without *Hope of Salvation*? The answer is simple. "Jesus Christ" hasn't Lost a Single Soul and will certainly **Keep His Solemn Word, No Matter How Impossible Things may Appear** at **Mankind's** *Darkest Hour of Desperation.* Remember, the "Lord Passed" through the Entire Torturous Crucifixion of Death without **Breaking One Bone** just to **Prove He can Take All Humanity** through the *Valley of Death* (agony of defeat) and bring *It Out the Other side Unharmed* (thrill of victory).

The "Lord is Able" to Pass through Death without the **Loss of even One Soul** (lost sheep) as **He Pays Mankind's Sin-debt** by **Offering God** *His Life* (blood), *Death* (damnation), and *Resurrection* (spirit). Through the "Impossible" Redemptive Feat, **Jesus Christ** would now be **Responsible** for **Transforming, Purifying, and Converting** the **Entire World** into a **New Born-again Creation** of *Wealth and Prosperity.* It would appear that to "Transform" a Bunch of Ignorant Fools into Righteous Citizens, **Christ** would have to bring the **Human Race Housing, Schools, Businesses** (jobs), and **Cities** by the **Boat Loads** until *World Poverty Ends* and *Global Prosperity Begins.* We see such a "Time of Prosperity" Mentioned in the Bible as **Christ's 1,000 Years of Peace** (sealing of saints) or the **Civilization of Love** which is a **Time When Lucifer is Chained in Hell** to **Stop Evil** and **Begin** a **New Age** of *Peace, Joy, and Happiness.*

The question is just "What is at the Root" of All Success (treasure)? The "Obvious Answer" is both God's Wisdom (Christ) and God's Beauty (Jesus) **Working Together** to bring forth the **True Meaning of Life** in *All its Splendor* and *Perfection*. We see this "Great Combination" in the Creation of a **Wise Adam** and a **Beautiful Eve** as **They had it All** in **Their most Beloved Garden of Eden** which **Represented God's Best Effort** at **Manifesting** a *Synthetic Paradise on Earth*. Unfortunately, "Adam" and Eve Did Not" have Real Wisdom and Real Beauty because **They had No Idea** of **What Real Ignorance** and **Real Ugliness** were, because **When One is Born** into the **Thrill of Victory,** just **How** is a **Person Expected** to **Know** the *Agony of Defeat* until it *Actually Comes*?

Obviously, "After Six Thousand Years" of Ignorance and Ugliness, the **Human Race** has a **Clear Picture of Stupidity**/insanity which **Cries Out** for the **Blessings of Wisdom** and **Beauty** as in **Every Prayer** is *Man's Petition for a Savior*. Note that in the "Creation" of the Jews and the Birth of a Jewish Messiah **Came** the **Wisdom of Solomon** and the **Beauty of Bathsheba** as **They Clearly Demonstrated** the **Difference** between *David's Agony of Defeat* versus *Israel's Thrill of Victory*. This means that "Every Modern Soul" Knows that **If Anyone Seeks Success** in his **Life,** he must be **Highly Educated** and **Strikingly Beautiful** to **Overcome All** the **Physical Obstacles** within the *Life-experience*. It should now be "Clear" that Mankind Needs a **Collective Mind** of **Global Wisdom Founded** on a **Divine Mind** of **Infinite Perfection** to **Solve All** the **Problems of the World,** and then **Create** *Heaven on Earth*.

We see that the "Rich People" and the "Scientist" have Got Together and **Decided that They** could be **mini-gods** by **Instituting Artificial Intelligence** via a **New Positronic Computer Brain** (Skynet) which is **Capable of Doing** the *Thinking for All Mankind*. This "Sci-fi Approach" to Making Mankind Smart is at the **Center** of the **War of Good and Evil** as the **Church** is **Saying that Real Wisdom Comes** from *Surrendering to Christ,* while the **World is Saying No, Wisdom Comes** from a *Micro-chip in Your Brain* (AI). Obviously, "God's Answer" is Both as the **Lord will Soon Come** as a **Thief in the Night** (1,000 years of peace) to **Unite** the **Needs of the Flesh** (arrange marriage/society) with the **Wants of the Spirit** (love marriage/individual) to bring forth both a **Physical Answer** and a **Spiritual Answer** to *All the Problems of the World*. The implication here is that the "Lord God Almighty" or Our Creator is **Using an Old Bracket Fire Technique Developed by Gunnery Officers,** which was **Developed** to **Hit a Target Dead Center** (bulls eye) **Every time** after *Only Three Shots* (3 advents).

In this "Concept of Projectile Accuracy," a Commander would **First Fire High** (fortitude) or **Long** (arranged marriages); on the **Second Shot, Fire Low** (temperance) or **Short** (love marriage), thereby **Determining that the Target** is to be **Right in the Middle** (bulls eye); or **Combining Law** (state/society) and **Love** (Church/individual) to *Create Long and Happy Marriages*. Now, imagine the "Jewish People (Man/Father)" being the Arranged Marriage or **Firing High** to **Hit** the *Letter of the Law* (blind obedience/flesh) and then, the "Christian People (God/Son)" being the Marriage of Love (lust) or **Firing Low** to **Hit** the *Spirit of the Law* (blind faith/spirit). We see that in the "Last Phase," the "God/Man People (trinity)" become the Marriage of Law and

Love (wisdom) or **Firing to Hit the Target Dead Center** (bulls eye) by using both the **Letter** (righteous) and **Spirit** (holy) of the **Law, United** into a <u>**New Born-again Nature**</u> of *God/Man's Perfection*.

1st Advent	1.	**1st Shot Long** - Jewish Law of Obedience Fulfilled: Church/priest
		• Priest Makes Offering to God's Kingship (throne)
2nd Advent	2.	**2nd Shot Short** - Christian Faith in God's Love Fulfilled: Government/king
		• King Makes Offering to God's Priesthood (altar)
3rd Advent	3.	**3rd Shot Dead-center** - God/Man's Knowing is Fulfilled: Home/son
		• Son Makes Offering to God's Fatherhood (table)

This illustration shows that the "Lord Jesus Christ" is <u>Coming in Three Advents</u> to **Establish** his **Holy Church, Righteous Government, and Perfect Home** upon the <u>**Earth**</u> via *His Priesthood, His Kingship,* and finally *His Sonship.* In this way, a "Mystical Union (marriage)" can be <u>Established</u> between **God's Law** (flesh), **Man's Faith** (spirit), and <u>**God/Man's Knowing**</u> (soul) to bring forth *God's Truth, Law, Will, and Love* upon *One and All.* We see that an "Extremely Wise Man" might <u>Ask:</u> just **How Did God Expect to Perform** such a **Tremendous Feat** of **Establishing Arranged Marriages on Earth**, then **Reversing this Logic** to **Create Pure Marriages of Love** (lust), and finally bringing forth the *Perfect God/Man Marriage* (balance)? Obviously, the answer can be found in the "Three Advents" of Jesus Christ as **He Came to Create** an *Effective Divine Government* (duty) on *Earth*; then **He Returns** to <u>**Set Up a Workable**</u> *Capitalistic Economic System* (responsibility); and on <u>**His Third Visit,**</u> brings about an *Adult Ownership System* (authority) to **Make All Men** *Kings, Priests, and Sons of God.* Basically, it comes down to "Creating" <u>Three Essential Social Systems</u> to **Transform** <u>**Sinful Men**</u> (bureaucrats) into *Righteousness* (social service); <u>**Evil Men**</u> (thieves) into *Holiness* (individual responsibility); and <u>**Disenfranchised Men**</u> (dead) into *Universal Perfection* (adult owners). In short, "Righteous Men" are <u>Duty Bound</u> (time); "Holy Men" are <u>Honest</u> (wealth/money); and "Perfect Men" are <u>Loving Caretakers</u> (labor/effort), implying that it **Takes a Great Knowledge** to effectively **Manage One's** *Time, Money, and Efforts*.

This means that to "Create a Properly Functioning" <u>Government</u> (laws/throne), <u>Economy</u> (money/altar), and <u>Society</u> (love/table), it would **Take a Supernatural Force Using its Direct Authority** on **All the Forces of Life** to *Create a Perfect World.* For this reason, the "Lord GodAlmighty" <u>Needed a Messianic Figure</u> in the **Person of Jesus Christ** to **Come to Earth** in **Three Mystical Visits** to **Set Up** a *Government* (law/faith/knowing); an *Economy of Scales* (wealth/values/love); and finally, a *Perfect Life for Everyone* (peace/joy/happiness). In this teaching, during the "Lord's 1st Advent (priest)," <u>Jesus Christ</u> **Made the First Payment** on **Man's Redemption** by **Placing** an <u>**Acceptable Offering**</u> (stop arranged marriages) upon *His Eternal Father's Throne* (betrothal). We see in the "2nd Advent (thief)" that the <u>Lord will Use</u> **His most Holy Church** to **Make** the **Second Payment** on **Man's**

Redemption by **Placing** a most <u>**Treasured Gift**</u> (bride/bond of love) upon *His Eternal Father's Altar* (wedding supper).

Finally, we see that during the "3rd Advent (judge)," the <u>Lord will Use</u> **His Born-again World** (righteous) to **Make the Third** and **Final Payment** on **Man's Redemption** by **Placing Humanity's** <u>**Petitions**</u> (accept change) upon *His Eternal Father's Table* (wedding feast). We see that once "Man's Redemption" is <u>Paid Off,</u> the **Human Race** is to be **Set Free** from <u>**Blind Obedience**</u> (ignorance), <u>**Blind Faith**</u> (cowardice), and from <u>**Selfishness**</u> (greed) to *Learn to Think for Itself.*

The following tabular information indicates that the "Jews" <u>Lived by Blind Obedience</u> unto the **Law of Moses**; the "Christians" <u>Lived by Blind Faith</u> unto the **Love of Jesus Christ**; and finally, **God's Law** and **Man's Love** will be <u>**Merged**</u> into *Thinking for Oneself.*

Christ's Three Advents bring New Marriage Arrangement
to Satisfy both God and Man via Compromise
(arranged marriage too tight, love marriage too loose,
and law/love marriage works like a charm)

- - - - - - - - - **Blind Obedience** - Serves Society Perfectly (flesh) - - - - - - - -

Truth   1.   **1ˢᵗ Advent** - <u>Priest on Donkey:</u> Offering = Stop Arranged Marriages....
               Knowledge

(law)   • Creation of Babies - Kingship: Earthly Citizens = See Limitations
          • Jewish People Created as Bride for Messiah - Failed (Lucifer's test)
          • Graded on Handicap System - Baby Training Wheels (glue too strong of bond)

Righteous • *Fortitude* - Horse's Reins too Tight: Horse Stops (change idea)
King   • Bride and Groom Obey Parents' Wishes - <u>Obey God's Law Blindly</u> (law)
(throne)   • Becoming Dutiful - Slave Mentality: Serve without Complaint
          • Government Bureaucracy - Creates Society of Corruption
                    (baby grows out of blind obedience -
            the day of rebellion: the child says No, Never Again)

- - - - - - - - - - -**Blind Faith** - Serves the Individual Perfectly (spirit)- - - - - - - - - - -

Law   2. **2nd Advent** - <u>Thief in Night:</u> Gift = Marriage on a Bond of Love....Self-awareness
(love)   • Sealing of Saints - Priesthood = Heavenly Saints: See Potential
          • Christian People Courted to Love Messiah - Failed (God's judgment)
          • Graded on Curve System - Teenage Love Experiment (glue too weak of bond)

Holy   • *Temperance* - Horse's Reins too Loose: Runs to Barn (try new idea)
Priest   • Bride and Groom Fall in Love Blindly - <u>Obey Forces of Lust</u> (love)
(altar)   • Becoming Responsible - Master Mentality: Supervise Every Detail
          • Capitalist Economics - Creates Society of Thieves
                    (teenager matures out of blind faith -
            day of wisdom: young adult says there are Two Truths)

- - - - - - - - - - **Seeing Truth** - Serves Society and Individual Equally (soul)- - - - - - - - -

Will	3.	**3rd Advent** - <u>Judge on a Cloud:</u> Petition = Combine Marriage Law/Love ...
(law/love)		Consciousness

- Judgment of Sinners - Sonship: Kingdom Sons of God (Self-evaluation)
- God/Man People Combine Marriage Law and Marriage Love - Succeed
- Graded on Pass/Fail System - Adults Learn to Think (glue just right)

Perfect Son • *Just* - Horse's Reins Just Right: Horse Strides in Parade (find truth)

(table) • Bride and Groom both Educated - <u>Think for Themselves</u> (law/love)
- Becoming Victim/Savior - Owner Mentality: Tender Loving Care
- Ownership System - Creates Perfect Societies
  (adult knows difference between lie and truth -
  day of sentience: everything makes sense)

This illustration shows that the "Fall of Adam and Eve" has Centered Around **God's Curse** on *Government* (defiance), **Lucifer's Curse** on *All Money* (deception) and **Man's Curse** on *Society* (deceit). This means that a "Perfect Government (challenge)" is to <u>Serve Society</u> through the **Enforcement of Laws,** which have been **Designed to Protect** both <u>**Individual**</u> and **Social Rights** via the *Use of Courts, Police, and Armies*. Secondly, a "Perfect Economy (adventure)" is to <u>Serve Society</u> through **Private Enterprise** which has been **Designed** to **Provide Resources** to **Government, Businesses,** and **Individuals** via the **Use** of <u>**Local, National,**</u> and **Global** *Investment Banking*. Finally, a "Perfect Society (fun)" is to <u>Serve Men, Women, and Children</u> through its **Unlimited Services** in **Health Care, Education, Employment,** and **Social Welfare** via the <u>**Use of One's**</u> *Commitment to Labor*. Unfortunately, the "Human Race" has been <u>Divinely Cursed</u> **Since its Creation,** thereby causing it to **Fall** into the <u>**Sin**</u> of *Blind Obedience*, into the <u>**Evil**</u> of *Blind Faith,* and finally, the **Death** of *Blind Selfishness*.

This "Awesome Tragedy" was <u>Rectified</u> by **God's Son, Jesus Christ** as the <u>**Jews/Man**</u> are to bring forth a *Perfect Government*; the <u>**Christians/God**</u> are to bring forth a *Perfect Economy*; and the <u>**God/Man Society**</u> is to bring forth its *Perfect Society*. Through these "Three Institutions of Life," the <u>Earth is to be Saved</u> first, **Beginning** with *Mount Calvary*, then with the **Sealing** of *God's Saints*, and finally, with the **Coming** of *God's Final Judgment* (white throne). With the "Formation" of <u>God's Perfect</u> **Government, Economy, and Society,** the <u>**Lord will Create**</u> Heaven on Earth (throne/kingship), *Paradise in Heaven* (altar/priesthood), and *His Kingdom of Glory* (table/sonship). This means that upon "Calvary," <u>Baby Humanity</u> has **Grown Out** of its *Blind Obedience* (law); upon the "Sealing of God's Saints," <u>Teenage Humanity</u> will **Mature Out** of its *Blind Faith*; and finally, during "Man's Adult Judgment (end of world)," it will **Come to Know** the <u>**Difference**</u> between *Man's Lies* (illusion) and *God's Truth* (reality). It is now clear that the "Whole Life-experience" is about <u>Thinking for Oneself</u> at the **Divine Level of Comprehension** (mastery) so that a **Person** can **Speak, Read, and Write** in *Human, Angelic, and Divine Languages*. Yes! We must "All Grow Out (baby)" of <u>Blind Obedience,</u> "Mature to Overcome (teenager)" <u>Blind Faith,</u> and finally, to "Think for Ourselves (adult)" to <u>See the Truths of Life,</u> thereby being <u>**Set Free**</u> from *Sin, Evil, Death, and Damnation*.

The "Job of the Righteous King" is to <u>Defeat Sin</u> by **Taking Away Governmental Bureaucracy** to **Set the Earth Free** from the **Simplistic Beliefs** of **Insane Governments** as **They Strive** to **Enslave the People** (tax/spend) and <u>**Make Them**</u> *Automatons of Labor.* Secondly, the "Job of the Holy Priest" is to <u>Defeat Evil</u> by **Taking Away Corrupt Fiscal Practices** to **Set the Earth Free** from the **Criminal Actions** of **Unscrupulous Bankers** as **They Strive** to **Turn the People** into **Stupid Cows** and <u>**Milk Them**</u> of *All Their Money.* Finally, the "Job of the Perfect Son" is to <u>Defeat Death</u> by **Taking Away Dangerous Neighbors** and **Corrupt Law Enforcement Officials Who Prey** upon the **Local Community** to <u>**Feed upon the Fears**</u> of *Frightened Residents.* Obviously, the "Bureaucracy," "Unscrupulous Bankers," and "Dangerous Communities" have <u>Enslaved Humanity,</u> causing **It** to **Cry Out to God** for **Help** and **Lift-up the Covenant Promises** from <u>**God's Prophets, God's Son,**</u> and **Christ's Church** to *Find Relief.* We see that "This Relief" from a <u>Broken Social Order, Corrupt Personal Responsibilities,</u> and from a <u>Lack of Adult Ownership</u> can only come about by **Empowering the People** with <u>**Real Authority**</u> through *Their Vote, Wealth, and Unity* (strong organizations).

We see that "When Jesus Christ" <u>Came to Save Humanity,</u> **He Encountered King Herod** (government), the **High Priest Caiaphas** (economy), and **Pontius Pilate** (society), <u>**Only to be Attacked**</u> and made an *Outcast of the Jewish People* (mocked), then *Excommunicated from God's Temple* (tortured), and finally, *Banished from Earth* (killed). This "Lack of Justice" and "Lack of Human Kindness" have <u>Established the Agenda</u> for **Christ's Return** as **He Comes** as a **Thief in the Night** to **Prepare the Way** for **His Father's Armies,** <u>**Who will Defeat Man's**</u> *Broken Social Order* (no vote), *Corrupt Personal Responsibilities* (no money), and *Lack of Adult Ownership* (no rights/authority). This will be "Done" because it is <u>Time</u> to bring forth a **New Righteous Government** (vote), **New Standard of Wealth** (economy), and a **New Honest** and **Hard-working Society** (good people) to bring forth **1,000 Years of Peace** onto the *Earth.*

The following tabular information indicates that "During Christ's 1st Advent (priest)," <u>Earth Got</u> its *New Physical Government;* "During Christ's 2nd Advent," <u>**Earth Will Get**</u> its *New Spiritual Economy;* and "During Christ's 3rd Advent," <u>**Earth Will Get**</u> its *New Mystical Society:*

God brings Social Order; Man brings Personal Responsibilities; and God/Man brings Adult Ownership
(physical government brings democracy;
spiritual economy brings capitalism; and mystical society brings ownership)

Physical   1.   **Social Order** - <u>Perfect Government</u>...Democracy (voting)
Answers   •   Political Leaders - Serving the People: Doing Sworn Duty
             •   Mastering God's Law of Obedience - Baby Fortitude
Ethics   •   Time - Worship God: Give Life = King of the Jews   **Messiah**
             •   Face Lucifer's Test - Learn God's Right from man's wrong   (corruption)
             •   God Wants to become Man - Heaven on Earth (see limitations)

              (righteous king - brings God's Law of Obedience to Earth:
                    change nature from human/divine)

Spiritual 2. **Personal Responsibilities** - <u>Perfect Economy</u>.... Capitalism (enterprise)

Answers   • Financial Institutions - Protecting All Wealth: Sacred Responsibility

            • Mastering Man's Faith of Love - Teenage Temperance

Morals   • Money - Praise God: Give Wealth = High Priest of Heaven **Church**

            • Face God's Judgment - Learn God's Good from man's evil (poverty)

            • Man's Wants to become God - Paradise in Heaven (see potential)

                (holy priest - brings Man's Faith of Love to Earth:

                    wash away sin, change sin to holiness)

Mystical 3. **Adult Ownership** - <u>Perfect Society</u>...Ownership (independence)

Answers   • Dedicated Citizens - Serving Self/Society/God: Accept Final Authority

            • Mastering Thinking for Oneself - Adult Justice

Fairness   • Effort - Thank God: Give Labors = Son of God   **World**

            • Face Self-evaluation - Learn God's Will/man's will   (insanity)

            • God/Man are One - Kingdom of Glory (see self-worth)

                (perfect son - brings power of knowing to Earth:

                    Think for Oneself, change blind to vision)

This illustration shows that the "Evil Earth" is to be <u>Restored</u> through **Three Special Visits** from **God's Son** as He both **Purifies** and **Transforms** the **Institutions, Man's Health** (prosperity), **and Restores the People** to bring forth a **New World Order** as a **Reflection** of the *Divine Nature of God*. This means that through the "Messiah's" <u>Ethical Behavior,</u> the "Church's" <u>Moral Behavior,</u> and the "World's" <u>Fairness,</u> **Sin, Evil, and Death** can be **Destroyed** and the **Human Race** can be **Set Free** from its *Ignorance, Cowardice, and Greed*. It would "Appear that Lucifer" has <u>Gained Control</u> of **Man's Will** by **Taking Control of Man's Governments, Wealth, and Social Order** via the **Power of Money** to **Put a Stranglehold** on <u>Every Aspect</u> of *Humanity's Daily Life*. This would imply that the "Job of God" is to <u>Figure Out</u> a **Master Stroke of Genius** to **Take Possession** of **All Money and Convert** it from **Evil Power** into **Holy Power** to <u>**Restore All Things Back**</u> to **Their Original State** and then <u>**Return Them All Back**</u> to *Their Original Owners*.

    The idea here is for the "Political Leadership of Man" to become <u>Dedicated</u> (Patriotic Duty) to **Only Serving** the **Needs and Wants of Their Fellow Men** (vote) through the **Establishment of Effective Laws** and **Important Public Entitlements** which will <u>**Benefit**</u> both the *Government* (spend) and the *People* (earn). Secondly, "Financial Institutions" must also become <u>Dedicated</u> in **Serving** and **Protecting** the **Financial Needs** of **Everyone and Everything** in **Human Society** as **They Work Tirelessly** to <u>**Increase the Overall**</u> *Value of Life* (prosperity for all). Finally, "Dedicated Citizens of Earth" must become <u>Unconditionally Loyal</u> to the **Welfare of Earth; Heaven, and God** through <u>**Daily Worship**</u> (give life) at *God's Holy Altar*; plus <u>**Their Commitment**</u> to *Christ's Throne* (give wealth); and finally, **Their Devotion** to the

Table of the Lord (give labors). Through these "Three Institutions" of <u>Government,</u> <u>Economy,</u> and <u>Society,</u> the **Human Race** will be **Brought Out** of its **Corruption, Poverty,** and its **Insanity** to be **<u>Born-again</u>** in its *Savior Jesus Christ*. This means that "Corruption" comes from <u>Bureaucracy;</u> "Poverty" comes from <u>Unscrupulous Business</u> <u>Practices;</u> and "Insanity" comes from <u>Social Mismanagement.</u> This implies that **Jesus** **Christ** will have to bring forth *His New World Order,* then *Institute Holy Money,* and finally, *Manage Society* through the *Power of Divine Truth*. In conclusion, we see that "Man's Physical Answer" for <u>Removing Corruption</u> comes with having a **Perfect Gov-** **ernment** (1st advent); "Man's Spiritual Answer" for <u>Removing Poverty</u> comes with having a **Perfect Economy** (2nd advent); and finally, "Man's Mystical Answer" for <u>Re-</u> <u>moving Insanity</u> comes with having a *Perfect Society* (well-adjusted people).

Recall that in "Phase III," <u>God and Man are to become One</u> (Kingdom/thought plus flesh) so that in the "Final Phase," both <u>God and Man can be Set Free</u> from **Any** **and All Restrictions** involving *Truth* (water/self), *Law* (blood/home), *Will* (death/gov-ernment), and/or *Love* (spirit/church). Yes! We are focused upon a "Happy Ending" as the <u>God/Man Relationship</u> becomes a **Union of Love and Respect** so **Strong** that **<u>Nothing Great or Small</u>** can *Break It, Damage It, or even Weaken It, No Matter* *What* (binding agreement). We see that this "Strong Union" has been <u>Forged via the</u> <u>Offerings</u> of <u>Cain and Abel</u> through the **Establishment** of both **<u>Moral</u>** (God's Law) and **Ethical** (man's law) **Behavior** within *Man's Fallen Human Nature*. Obviously, the "Fallen Nature of Man" must <u>Now be Tested</u> (God/Lucifer) by both **God's Winepress** **of Death** (far/cold) and **His Crucible of Fire** (close/hot) to **Measure Each Child's** *Level of Ignorance/Cowardice before his Father*. The "Job of the Crucible" is to <u>Change</u> <u>One's Nature</u> (spirit) by **Changing Flour into Baked Bread** (sinner into Christian), or **Forcing a Child** to *Master the World System* (fight evil); while the "Job of the Wine-press" is to <u>Wash Away Sin</u> (flesh) by **Changing Water into Wine** (Christian into Saint), or **Forcing God's Son** to *Master the Holy Church* (surrender).

Genetics 1. **Crucible of Fire** - <u>Fulfill God's Law of Obedience:</u> Change Nature = Human to Divine
- Jesus Changes the Flesh - Become Righteous Citizen on Earth (evil bears fruit)
- Flesh Fights Evil - Die in the Attempt - Purify Grave (ethics)

Behavior 2. **Winepress of Death** - <u>Fulfil Man's Faith in God's Love:</u> Wash Away Sin = Sinful to Holy
- Christ Changes the Spirit - Become a Holy Saint in Heaven (holiness bears fruit)
- Spirit Dies to Self - Born-again into New-life - Purify Host (morals)

This means that by "Defeating the Crucible (ethics/faults)," a <u>Person</u> can **Remove** **his Ignorance** and become *Wise before God*; while by "Defeating the Winepress (morals/virtues)," a <u>Person</u> can **Remove his Cowardice** and become *Courageous* *before God*. Through the "Power of Physical Ethics (body)" and "Spiritual Morals (life)," a <u>Person</u> can **Become Strong** and **<u>Face</u>** both the *Challenges of Physical* *Life* (crucible) and *Challenges of Spiritual Death* (winepress). We see that in the

"Crucible," <u>Nothing is becoming All</u> or a **Baby** is *Entering Adulthood* (mature); while in the "Winepress," <u>All is becoming Nothing</u> or an **Adult** is *Becoming Childlike* (humble). This teaching explains that when a "Person is Facing" the <u>Crucible of Fire</u> (ignorance), he is like the **Three Kings** (blind) who were **Following** a *Star by Night*. yet, when "He is Facing" the <u>Winepress of Death</u> (cowardice), he is like the **Three Shepherds** (vision), who were **Following** an *Angel's Guiding Light*. We see that the "Lord God Almighty" is <u>Teaching Us</u> to become **Wise Confident Adults** by **Night** and then become **Humble Servants** by **Day** so that we can **Fulfill** both the *Will of the People* (society) and the *Will of God* at the *same time*. Yes! It is all about "Serving Two Masters" of the <u>Forces of Blindness</u> (crucible) and the <u>Forces of Vision</u> (winepress) by simply **Balancing** the *Ethics of Man* (face world/life) with the *Morals of God* (face church/death). We see that by "Mastering Ethics (man's respect)," a <u>Person is Able</u> to **Face Life** and then **Experience** the *Agony of Defeat*, thereby **Allowing him** to *Learn the Lessons of Life*. Secondly, by "Mastering Morals (God's respect)," <u>He</u> is able to **Face Death** and then **Experience** the *Thrill of Victory*, thereby allowing him to *Earn the Blessings of God*. This implies that "Facing Life" allows a <u>Person</u> to **Wash Away his Sins** and *Purify his Fleshly Nature* (submission), while "Facing Death" <u>Allows Him</u> to **Change his Nature** and *Purify his Spiritual Nature* (born-again).

The following tabular information shows that "Jesus" is <u>Changing Man's Nature</u> (spirit) via His *Crucible of Fire* (flour to baked bread/righteous); while "Christ" is <u>Washing Away Sin</u> (flesh) via His *Winepress of Death* (water to wine/holy):

Jesus Changes Man's Nature via His Crucible;
while Christ Washes Away Sin via His Winepress
(face the world to have nature changed,
then master the holy church to wash away one's sins)

Truth
(chaos)

Ethics
(face life)

1. **Change Nature** - <u>Flesh:</u> Roman Law Washes Hands in Holy Water...Will to Live
   - Water becomes Wine - Innocent Soul (far/cold): Nothing becomes All
   - Sinner becomes Christian - Master the World (streetwise)
   - Free Will becomes New Body - Seat in the Celestial Court: Rule Earth
   - Creating the Righteous Man on Earth - Kingship of Man (David)
   - *Winepress of Death/wine* - Too Far from God: **Jews** Heresy (goat)
   - Three Kings (blind) - Following Star: Traveling by Night
   - <u>Romans Sign Jesus' Death Warrant</u> - Pilate Washes his Hands: Innocent Blood
   - Earn Man's Respect - Face Life: Agony of Defeat = Learn Lessons
   - Learning God's Right and Man's Wrong - Become Righteous Citizen on Earth
   - See One's Limitations - Defeat Curse of Ignorance: *Seeking Wisdom*
              (face winepress of death/Lucifer's test -
              gain ethical behavior: attain respect of man)

Law (order)	2. **Wash Away Sin** - <u>Spirit:</u> Jewish Law Seals Death in Hatred...Value of Life
	• Wine becomes Blood - Guilty Blood (close/hot): All becomes Nothing
	• Christian becomes Saint - Master Heaven (educated)
Morals	• Destiny becomes Eternal Life - Seat in the Temple Court: Rule Heaven
(face death)	• *Creating the Holy Man in Heaven -* **Christians**
	Priesthood of God (Aaron)
	• Crucible of Fire/bread - Too Close to God: Apostasy (lamb)
	• Three Shepherds (vision) - Following Angel: Traveling in the Light
	• <u>Jews Seal Jesus' Death Warrant</u> - Caiaphas Washes Hands in Enemy's Blood: Guilty Blood
	• Earn God's Respect - Face Death: Thrill of Victory = Receive Blessings
	• Learning God's Good from Man's Evil - Become Holy Saint in Heaven
	• See One's Potential - Defeat Curse of Cowardice: *Seeking Courage*
	(face crucible of fire/God's Judgment - gain moral behavior: attain respect of God)

This illustration shows that by "Changing One's Nature (world)," he is able to <u>Remove his Ignorance</u> and **Attain Ethical Behavior** to **Gain** the <u>Respect of Man</u> as he *Journeys from Death to New-life* (agony of defeat). Secondly, by "Washing Away his Sins (church)," he is able to <u>Remove his Cowardice</u> and **Attain Moral Behavior** to **Gain** the **<u>Respect of God</u>** as *he Journeys* from *his Old Life* to *his New-life* (thrill of victory). In this logic, we see that when a "Person" is <u>Too Far from God</u> (flesh), he must **Make Bread** (crucible) or a *Child becomes an Adult*; but when a "Person" is <u>Too Close to God</u> (spirit), he must **Make Wine** (winepress) or an *Adult must become Child-like* (humble). Now, we see that "Man's Flesh" must <u>Face Life</u> (winepress) and *Master the World* (work); while "Man's Spirit" must <u>Face Death</u> (crucible) and *Master the Church* (prayer).

Note that in "God's Paradox," the <u>Flesh is Facing Death</u> by **Fighting All Evil** and *Dying in the Attempt* (purify grave); while the "Spirit is Facing Life" by <u>Dying to its Selfishness</u> and then being *Born-again in Christ* (purify host). This means that by "Defeating" both <u>Childhood</u> and <u>Adulthood,</u> a **Person** can **See his Own Limitations** (faults) and his **Own Potential** (virtues) and then **Balance his Life** between the *Needs of Man* (body/money) and the *Wants of God* (life/perfection). In this way, the "Human Race" can <u>Fight Its Way Out</u> of **Lucifer's Pit of Death** (test) and then <u>Enter God's Perfect Nature</u> (judgment) to *Experience the Best of both Worlds*. This "Journey Allows a Person" to <u>Experience</u> the **Innocence of Childhood** (innocent blood) in the *Slaughter of Innocence* (confidence) and then to <u>Experience</u> the **Guilt of Adulthood** (guilty blood) in the *Crushing of his Pride* (humility). We call this the "Slaughter of Innocence" as Man's **Crucible of Fire** (bread) or being *Too Far from God* (life), while we call the "Crushing of Pride" as <u>God's</u> **Winepress of Death** (wine) or being *Too Close to God* (death).

In the case, "Pilate the Roman (flesh)" and "Caiaphas the Jew (spirit)" <u>Represented the Winepress</u> and the <u>Crucible Forces</u> in the **World** as **They Attacked God's Messiah** with *All Their Fury* and *All Their Strength*. In this theme, we see that "Jesus

Christ" was <u>Able to Face</u> both **Pilate's <u>Test of Water</u>** (scourging) and **Caiaphas' <u>Test of Blood</u>** (crucifixion) with both *Wisdom* and *Courage*. We see that by "Mastering" both <u>Man's Wisdom</u> (mind) and <u>God's Courage</u> (heart), a **Person** can **Learn the Difference** between *God's Right* (crucible) and *Man's Wrong* (winepress). This means that the "Lord God Almighty" is <u>Educating His Children</u> in **Three Stages of Development** from **Righteous Citizen,** to **Holy Saint,** to **Perfect Son,** and finally, to being a **Free Man, <u>Worthy</u>** of *God's Friendship*. We see that the "Lord Counts" <u>His Citizens</u> (babies), <u>His Saints</u> (teens), and <u>His Sons</u> (adults) on **Three Separate Occasions** as the **<u>Jews Count Babies</u>** on the *Sabbath* (Saturday); **<u>Christians Count Saints</u>** on the *Lord's Day* (Sunday); and finally, **God Counts His Sons** on *Judgment Day*.

Righteous   1. **Righteous Citizens on Earth** - <u>Fulfill God's Law of Obedience</u>…
Flesh   See Limitations
               • Receive New Divine Nature - Purify One's Grave
               • God Counts His Free New Bodies - Jewish Sabbath

Holy Spirits 2. **Holy Saint in Heaven** - <u>Fulfill Man's Faith in God's Love</u>…
               See Potential
               • Wash Away One's Wicked Sins - Purify One's Host
               • God Counts Number of Saints Earned - Lord's Day

Perfect Souls 3. **Perfect Son within Kingdom** - <u>Fulfill Knowing God/Man Truth</u>…
               See Self-worth
               • Thinking for Oneself - Purify One's Life
               • God Counts Number of Sons Created - Judgment Day

This illustration shows that "Each of God's Children" is being <u>Called to Enter</u> the **Eternal Society of God** by both **Growing** and **Maturing** into **<u>Useful</u>** and **<u>Productive</u> Citizens** of the *Kingdom of God*. Now, "If We Look Closely" at the <u>Three Rooms</u> within **God's Jewish Temple, We can Comprehend** that the **1st Room** is in **<u>Sunlight</u>** or the *Earth* (create babies); the **2nd Room** is in **<u>Candlelight</u>** or in *Heaven* (create saints), and the **3rd Room** is Lite with **<u>God's Shekinah Glory</u>** or *God's Kingdom* (create sons). By "Researching" the <u>Jewish Temple</u> (Solomon), we can see **God's Overall Master Plan** as the **Lord** brought **On to the Earth Four Positive Judgments** of **(1) <u>Right,</u>** (2) **<u>Good,</u>** (3) **God's Will,** and (4) **Seeing God's Reality** for *Men of Good Will* (innocent blood). Secondly, the "Jewish Temple (King Herod)" brought <u>On to the Earth</u> **Four Negative Judgments** of (1) **<u>Wrong,</u>** (2) **<u>Evil,</u>** (3) **Man's Will,** and (4) **<u>Seeing Man's Illusion</u>** for *Men of Evil Will* (guilty blood). We see that these "Four Judgments" actually <u>Occur</u> within the **Outer Court** (right/wrong), **Holy Place** (good/evil), **Holy of Holies** (God's Will/man's will), and finally, on **God's Mercy Seat** (God's Reality/man's illusion) as **<u>They Judge</u>** the *Righteous Man* (baby), *Holy Man* (teen), *Perfect Man* (adult), and *Free Man* (wise man).

Note that "Jesus Christ" <u>Destroyed the Stone Temple</u> to <u>Make His Followers Fleshly Temples</u> as **They Consume His Flesh** (bread) to **<u>Fulfill</u>** *God's Law* (obedience) and **Drink His Blood** (wine) to **Fulfill** *Man's Faith* (love). The idea here is that "All of the Furniture" within God's Temple was **Actually a Mini Judgment Seat** either for **Innocent** or **Guilty Blood** within the *Physical, Spiritual, Mystical, and/or Divine Dimensions of Life.* Obviously, "If a Person" was Innocent, he was **Blessed;** and "If a Person" was Guilty, he must **Offer God his Lessons Learned;** then this **Combination** of **Blessings/Lessons** would be **Placed** upon **Each Temple Altar** to **Receive One** of *God's Four Gifts.* We see that in this "Earning of God's Gifts," a Person is both **Growing and Maturing** from **Baby** to **Teenager, to Adult,** and finally, to **Wise Man.** Thus, **If They can Pass** through **God's Temple of Judgment, They** will be **Transformed** into a *Righteous Citizen, Holy Saint, Perfect Son*, and finally, a *Free Man* or a *Beloved Friend of God.*

The following tabular information indicates the "Four Judgment Seats of God" and the Four Jewish Gifts of *Good Jew/Priest/High Priest/Messiah,* and the Four Christians' Gifts of *Citizenship, Sainthood, Sonship, and Free Man:*

God's Jewish Temple/one man (fulfill God's law of obedience)	**Christ becomes Temple/all men** (fulfill Man's faith in God's love)
1. **Outer Court** - 1st Judgment • Judge Right/Wrong • Are You a Good Jew?	1. **Mind of Christ** - 1st Judgment • Judge Ignorance/Wisdom • Are You Righteous Citizen?
2. **Holy Place** - 2nd Judgment • Judge Good/Evil • Are You Holy Priest?	2. **Heart of Christ** - 2nd Judgment • Judge Cowardice/Courage • Are You Holy Saint?
3. **Holy of Holies** - 3rd Judgment • Judge God's Will/man's will • Are You High Priest?	3. **Soul of Christ** - 3rd Judgment • Judge Greed/Generosity • Are You Son of God?
4. **God's Mercy Seat** - 4th Judgment • God's Reality/man's illusion • Are You the Messiah?	4. **Life-force of Christ** - 4th Judgment • Judge Selfishness/Unselfishness • Are You Friend of God?

This illustration shows that "Individual Rooms" within God's Temple have become the **Intellect, Emotions, Instincts**, and **Nature of Christ** which also **Represent** *Man's Physical Life on Earth* (baby farm), *Spiritual Heaven* (divine school), the *Mystical Kingdom* (sonship training), and also the *Beatific Vision of God Himself.* Obviously, the "Lord is Telling Us" that He will Crush the Flesh (world) into **Oblivion** to **Teach** it the **Lessons of Life** (death) and then **Raise Up the Spirit** (church) by **Transforming** it into a *Born-again Reflection of Christ* (new-life).

We see that the "Ancient Jewish Temple" is Our Master Template for **Comprehending** the **Lord's Divine Judgment System** as **He Requires Each** of **His Children to Learn** *Right from Wrong* (righteousness), *Good from Evil* (holiness), *God's Will from Man's Will* (perfection), and *God's Reality from Man's Illusion* (freedom).

The overall theme here is that "All Flesh is Guilty (gentile)" and "All Spirit is Innocent (Jewish)," implying that the Job of the Flesh is to **Learn** the *Lessons of Life* and the Spirit's Job is to **Receive God's** *Blessings of Life.* Now, "If We Walk" through the Temple Station-by-station, **We** will have been **Judged Eight Times** by the (1) *Jews,* (2) *Christians,* (3) *Jewish Saints,* (4) *Angels,* (5) *Jewish Jesus,* (6) *Christ,* (7) *Humanity,* and (8) *Divinity.* This means that the "Human Race" is Passing through **God's Eternal Judgment Seat, Beginning** with **Earth** to **Judge Man's Babyhood**; then **Going to Heaven** to **Judge Man's Teenage Life;** then **Going to God's Kingdom** to **Judge Man's** *Adulthood;* and finally, **Going into God's Beatific Vision** to Judge Man's *New Free Will* (God's Friendship). In short, "We have just Passed" through God's Baby Farm (earth), God's Divine School (Heaven), God's Sonship Training (Kingdom), and then Graduated from **Human Existence** to **Enter** the *Friendship of God Himself.*

We can now see the "Jewish Temple" was Revealing that **Man's Sin-nature** (guilty blood) was to be **Converted, One Painful Lesson** at a **Time,** so that a **Person** could **Learn Wrong, Evil, Man's Will, Man's Illusion,** and then **Take this Knowledge** into *His Holy-nature* (innocent blood). The "Job of the Holy-nature" is to be Converted, **One Joyful Blessing** at a **Time,** so that a **Person** could **Prove he Knows Right, Good, God's Will, and God's Reality** by **Heart.** Then **Man's Ignorance** is to be **Compared** to **God's Wisdom** so that a **Person can Clearly See** *God's Divine Truths.*

Note that there are "Four Stations (innocent blood)" on the Right Side of the Temple: the **Water** (1/right); **Bread** (2/good); **1st Angel** (3/God's will); and **Right-side of Mercy Seat** (4/God's reality), thereby **Blessing Man's Mind, Heart, Soul, and Life-force** with *God's Wisdom.* Secondly, there are "Four Stations (guilty blood)" on the Left Side of the Temple: the **Fire** (1/wrong); **Candlelight** (2/evil); **2nd Angel** (3/Man's will); and **Left-side of Mercy Seat** (4/Man's illusion), thereby **Teaching God's Lessons** to **Man's Mind, Heart, Soul, and Life-force** to *Remove Man's Ignorance.* This means that a "Person has Now Passed" throughout the Temple and has **Mastered** the **Entire Life-experience** from **Baby-to-Teenage-to-Adult-to-Wise Man** and has **Earned his Own Eternal Freedom** from *Sin, Evil, Death, and Damnation.* The idea here is that the "Jewish Temple" Represents **Each Child's Gauntlet of Life**** as he **Learns All** the **Lessons of Life** and then **Takes Them** into **God's Giant Washing Machine** to **Convert Them** into **God's Blessings** or into *Wisdom, Courage, Generosity,* and finally, *Unselfishness.* Basically, an "Earthly Life" is Centered upon **Using One's Fleshly Life** to **Get Dirty** in the **Evil World** (get lessons) and then **Using His Spirit** to **Take His New Found Wisdom** (blessings) into the **Lord's Temple** to **Offer it Up** or have it **Purified** in *God's Giant Washing Machine* (purification/forgiveness).

**The Gauntlet of Life means Facing the Lord's Scourging, Crucifixion, Tomb, and Resurrection to Attain One's Born-again Wisdom, Courage, Generosity, and Unselfishness.

The following graphic illustration shows the "Lay-out" of God's Jewish Temple based on its **Three Judgment Rooms Plus** its **All Important Mercy Seat,** where the **High Priest Aaron** would **Place Seven Drops** of **Lamb's Blood** on the **Day of Atonement** so that **God could Judge** *His Innocence* (innocent blood), *His Family's Repentance* (guilty blood), and then *Israel's Depth of Submission* (forgiven blood):

God's Jewish Temple

———————————————- Eastern   Gate ————————————

Outer Court - Earth: Baby Farm (face truth)

Water	*Fire*
(innocent blood)	(guilty blood)
Judged by Jewish People	Judged by Christian People

Brazen Altar
1st Gift - Righteous Citizen

———————————————————————————————————

Holy Place - Heaven: Divine School (face law)

Table of Bread	*Candlelight*
(innocent blood)	(guilty blood)
Judged by Jewish Saints	Judged by Angelic Realm

Golden Altar
2nd Gift - Holy Sainthood

Enter ——————————————————————————————

God's White Tunnel of Death

— —Exit

Holy of Holies - Kingdom: Sonship Training (face will)

1st Golden Angel	*2nd Golden Angel*
(innocent blood)	(guilty blood)
Judged by Jesus/Man	Judged by Christ/God

Ark of the Covenant
Third Gift - Perfect Sonship

————————————————————-

```
        *              *
    *        *      *   Seven Drops of Blood
        *              *
```

————————————————————

God's Mercy Seat
(innocent blood)	(guilty blood)
Judged by Humanity	***Judged by Divinity***

Center Drop is Forgiven Blood*

God's Divine Love   -   Beatific Vision
. 4th Gift - Free Man/God's Friendship

———————————————————————————————————

This illustration shows that the "Outer Court" is <u>Earth</u> (baby farm), where the **Jewish People** will **Forever Judge Man's <u>Innocent Blood</u>** (babyhood) to *See his Good Works* (offering); while the **Christians** will **Forever Judge Man's <u>Guilty Blood</u>** (adulthood) to *See his Holy Prayers* (repentance). Secondly, the "Holy Place" is <u>Heaven</u> (divine school), where the **Holy Saints** will **Forever Judge Man's Innocent Blood** (baby) to *See his Great Wisdom* (growth); while the **Sacred Angels** will **Forever Judge Man's <u>Guilty Blood</u>** (teen) to *See his Great Courage* (maturity). Thirdly, the "Holy of Holies" is the <u>Kingdom</u> (sonship training), where **Mary's Son, Jesus** will **Forever Judge Man's <u>Innocent Blood</u>** (teen) to *See his Great Generosity* (confidence); while **God's Son, Christ** will **Forever Judge Man's <u>Guilty Blood</u>** (adult) to *See his Great Unselfishness* (independence). Finally, the "Mercy Seat" is the <u>Lord God Almighty, where **Humanity** will **Forever Judge Man's <u>Innocent Blood</u>** (adult) to *See his Own Free Will* (friendship); while **Divinity** will **Forever Judge Man's <u>Guilty Blood</u>** (wise man) to *See God's Divine Will* (companionship).

Yes! This "Massive Journey" from <u>Nothing to All</u> **Forces Each of God's Children** to **Pass** through the **Lord's Temple of Judgment**, where **He must Face God's Truth, Law, Will, and Love** on his <u>Way to Finding</u> *God's Divine Forgiveness.* The message here is that "God's Forgiveness" <u>Comes in Three Forms</u>: **1st** as **<u>Free Redemption</u>** (being saved) for *Babies*; **2nd** as **<u>Earned Salvation</u>** (saving self) for *Teenagers*; **3rd** as **<u>Bonus Rewards</u>** (saving others) for *Adults;* and finally, as **<u>Eternal Freedom</u>** (building kingdom) for *Wise Men.* The idea here is that "If a Person" <u>Learns Right from Wrong</u> and is **Given** his **Free Redemption,** then he will **Receive** a **New Body** (kingship) as he has **Purified his Own Grave** and is <u>Worthy</u> of *Eternal Resurrection in Christ.* Secondly, "If a Person" <u>Learns Good from Evil</u> and has **Attained** his **Own Salvation,** then he will **Receive Eternal Life in Heaven** (priesthood) as he has **Purified his Host** and is <u>Worthy</u> of *Eternal Ascension in Christ.* Finally, "If a Person" <u>Learns God's Will</u> from <u>man's will</u> and has been **Chosen to Receive** the **Bonus Reward** of having **His Own Kingdom** (sonship) as he has **Purified his Life,** then he is **<u>Worthy</u>** of *God's Beatific Vision* (face-to-face). Obviously, the "Job of the Temple" is to <u>Transform Each</u> of **God's Creations** into its **Final Form** by **Changing Nothing** into **All** via the **<u>Forces</u>** of *Intellect* (mind), *Emotion* (heart), *Instincts* (soul), and *Nature* (life-force).

This implies that through the "Outer Court," the <u>Jews</u> and the <u>Christians</u> are to be **Man's Eternal Judges on Earth, Tasked** to **Change Sinners** into **Christians** via the **Lord's Blessing of Righteousness** (kingship) to **<u>Make Human Flesh</u>** *Friends of God Forever.* Secondly, through the "Holy Place," the <u>Saints</u> and the <u>Angels</u> are to be **Man's Eternal Judges Tasked** to **Change Christians into Holy Saints** via the **Lord's Blessing of Holiness** (priesthood) to **<u>Make Human Spirits</u>** *Companions of God Forever.* Thirdly, through the "Holy of Holies," <u>Jesus the Man</u> and <u>Christ the God</u> are to be **Man's Eternal Judges, Tasked** to **Change Holy Saints into Sons of God** via the **Lord's Blessing of Perfection** (sonship) to **<u>Make Human Souls</u>** into the *Oneness of God Forever.* Fourthly, through the "Mercy Seat," <u>Physical Man</u> (earth) and <u>Spiritual God</u> (Heaven) are to be **Man's Eternal Judges, Tasked** to **Change Sons of God into**

Free Men via the **Lord's Blessing of Thinking for Themselves** (fatherhood) to **Make Human Life-forces** into *Their Unity with God Forever.* Finally, through "God's Nature," the Free Flesh (transfiguration) and the Free Spirit (glorification) are to be **Man's Eternal Judges, Tasked** to **Change Free Men** into **Independent Contractors** via the **Lord's Blessing of Free Will/choice** (master) to **Make Human Flesh** *Free from Sin, Evil, Death, and Damnation Forever.* It is now clear that the "Human Race" is in God's Divine School of Higher Learning and is **Called** to **Graduate with Honors** by becoming **One with God** in *Physical, Spiritual, Mystical, and Divine Life-forms* (natures).

Transformation of Each of God's Children through Five Stages of Life
(man's flesh passes through grave,
spirit passes through host, and soul passes through life)

Baby	1. **Jew**	1. **Christian**	Righteousness - Kingship (friendship)
Teenager	2. **Saint**	2. **Angel**	Holiness - Priesthood (companionship)
Adult	3. **Jesus**	3. **Christ**	Perfection - Sonship (oneness)
Wise Man	4. **Man**	4. **God**	Divinity - Fatherhood (unity)
Free Man	5. **Free Flesh**	5. **Free Spirit**	God-like - Choose Own Form (choice)
	(physical freedom)	(spiritual freedom)	

This illustration shows that the "Human Race" is being Called to **Infinite Transformation** (grave/host/life/eternal life) from **Nothing** (energy) to **All** (God) by **Learning All the Lessons of Life** so that a **Person can See God's** *Meaning, Purpose, and Value of Life for himself.* Obviously, the "Lord God Almighty" can Hardly Wait to See that **First Perfect Creation** coming **Out of His Sacred Temple** as he comes forth to **Take his Place** in the **Lord's Kingdom of Gods** as a **Reflection of the Almighty Himself** in *Mind, Heart, Soul, and Life-force.* It should now make sense just "Why the Human Race" has had to Pass through **Babyhood, Teenage Years, Adulthood,** then to **Wise Men** on **Their Way** to becoming **Free Men,** truly **Friends of God,** thereby **Helping Him Transform More and More Babies, Citizens, Saints,** and **Sons** into *God's New Eternal Friends.* This means that "God's Friendship" Sits at the Center of **God's Grand Design** as **He Strives** to **Build** an **Eternal Kingdom of Glory, Comprised** of *Strangers, Neighbors, Friends, and His Own Royal Family.* Probably, one of the best ways to "Comprehend" this Massive Transformation Process is to **Imagine Earth** (babies), **Heaven** (teenagers), **Kingdom** (adults), **God** (wise men), and **Freedom** (free men) as **Five Grains of Sand** Sitting Among the Other Grains on *All the Beaches of the World.* This implies that it's "Going to Take" a Great Deal of Time to **Fulfill** just **Our 1st Five Grains of Sand, Not to Mention All the Infinite**

Grains (dimensions of life) <u>**Still Sitting**</u> on **All the Beaches of the World.** The question is: "Just How Many" <u>Grains of Sand</u> or **Dimensions of Life** will **One Person** have to **Pass** through before he can **Say he is Finished** and has **Reached** the **End of God's Journey of Life**? The <u>**Answer**</u> is *All of Them*... Now Get to Work!

The following tabular information indicates both "Man's Transformation" and "God's Three Redemptive Systems:" <u>One for Earth</u> as *Free Redemption* (flesh), <u>One for Heaven</u> (church) as *Earned Salvation* (spirit), and <u>One for God's Kingdom</u> as *Bonus Rewards* (soul):

The Three Redemptive Systems of Jesus Christ are Grave, Host, and Life
(finding and traveling God's pathway of perfection
via resurrection, ascension, and serving God)

Mind	1.	**Free Redemption** - <u>Given Heaven on Earth:</u> Righteous Citizen...
(flesh)		See Liminations
		• Compromised Will - Handicap Grading System: Get God's Friendship
		• Purify One's Grave (resurrection) - Measure Ability to *Fight Evil*
		• 1st Advent - Purifying Earthly Grave: Fight Lucifer (Messiah resurrects)
Grave		• Baby Farm Saves Babies - *Count One's Babies on Sabbath*
		• Worthy of New Body - Transfigured Body: Fight Evil
Heart	2.	**Earned Salvation** - <u>Given Paradise in Heaven:</u> Holy Saint...See Potential
(spirit)		• Permissive Will - Curve Grading System: Get God's Companionship
		• Purify One's Host - Measure Ability to *Surrender One's Will*
		• 2nd Advent - Purify Heavenly Host: Die to Selfishness (church resurrects)
Host		• Divine School Saves Saints - *Count One's Saints on Lord's Day*
		• Worthy of Eternal Life - Glorified Spirit: Surrender
Soul	3.	**Bonus Rewards** - <u>Given Own Kingdom of Glory:</u> Son of God...See Self-worth
(soul)		• Direct Will - Pass/Fail Grading System: Get God's Oneness (beatific vision)
		• Purify One's Born-again Life (become God): Measure Ability to *Serve God*
		• 3rd Advent - Purifying Kingdom Life: Servanthood to All (world resurrects)
Life		• Sonship Training Program Saves Sons - *Count God's Sons on Judgment Day*
		• Worthy of Own Kingdom - Holy Soul: Think for Oneself

This illustration shows that the "Entire Redemptive Process" <u>Centered</u> upon **God's Desire** to **Create Righteous** (babies), **Holy** (saints), and **Perfect People** (sons) to <u>**Worship, Praise, and Thank Him**</u> for *Their Gifts of Glory*. Initially, the "Lord God Almighty" has <u>Created Earth</u> as **His Baby Farm, Out of His Love** or **Compromised Will** which **Uses** its **Own Handicap Grading System** to <u>**Encourage God's Babies**</u> to *Try Their very Best*. The "Job of the Jews (teach lessons)" is to be the <u>Caretakers</u> of **God's Babies, Along with the Virgin Mary** (give blessings)**, Who Prepares Each New Generation** of <u>**Potential Saints**</u> for *Their Entry into Heaven.* Secondly, "God has Opened Heaven" as <u>His Divine School,</u> **Out of His Mercy** or **Permissive Will** which **Uses** the **Curve Grading System** to **Teach God's Teenagers** to <u>**Master All Knowledge**</u> to become *Holy Saints before God.* The "Job of the Christians (educate)" is to be the <u>Instructors</u> of

God's Growing Children, Along with **Saint Joseph** (school head master), **Who Prepares Each New Generation** of <u>Newly Created Saints</u> to *Learn the Ways of God*. Finally, "God has Prepared His Kingdom" as <u>His Sonship Training Program,</u> **Out of His Justice** or **Direct Will** which **Uses** the **Pass/Fail Grading System** to **Transform** <u>God's Adults</u> into *Sons of God*. The "Job of Jesus Christ (teach leadership)" is to be the **Transforming Force** of **God's Perfect Sons** with **God Himself** (authority figures), **Who Prepares Each New Generation** of <u>Potential Sons</u> for *Entry* into *God's Kingdom of Glory*. Note that "Only the Best of the Best" from <u>Earth, Heaven,</u> and <u>God's Kingdom</u> **can Reach** that **Supreme Level of Freedom** based on being **Worthy** of **One's Personal Liberty** and then **Graduating with Honors** (cum/magna/summa) as an <u>Independent Citizen</u> with *One's Own Personal Kingdom*. Yes! It is a "Long Journey" from the <u>Bottom to the Top</u> of **God's Creation,** but **Every Pain** and **Every Step** is **Worth It,** when a **Person Reaches** that **Moment of Truth When** he can become a **Personal Friend of God** and then <u>**Help Everyone Else Make It**</u> to the *Top as Well*. It is "Hard to Imagine" that in this <u>Awesome Ordeal,</u> **All Begin** with some **Lost Broken Sinner Learning God's Right** from **man's wrong** and **Suddenly Coming to the Realization** that <u>**There is a God**</u> and that *He Wants to be Your Friend*.

We see this "Lesson" between <u>Right and Wrong</u> is clearly **Expressed** in **Hosea, Chapter Six,** where the **Prophet Reveals** that there will be **Coming Two Days of Torment** and then on the **Third Day** or at the <u>**End of Time,**</u> *God Will Return*. It is "Important to Note" that in <u>Hosea 6: 1-2</u> is a **Set of Statements** which **Reveals the Significance** of **God Attacking Man** by both **Crushing his Spirit** (ignorance) and **Wounding his Flesh** (cowardice) and then **After Two Mystical Days, Comes** <u>1,000 Years</u> of Peace, when the *Lord will Heal the Spirit* (courage/winepress) and *Bind Man's Wounds* (wisdom/crucible).

This "Restoration of Mankind" between the <u>Second/Third Days</u> (7th day) will bring forth a **Great Awakening** as an **Ocean of Knowledge is Poured** upon the **Earth** to **Set the Stage** for **1,000 Years of Peace** (sealing of saints) or a <u>Time</u> when *Lucifer will be Chained in Hell*. Note that on the "1st Day," the <u>Lord God Almighty</u> is **Attacking Mankind's Human Emotions** to **Crush Man's Love for God,** thereby causing <u>**Humanity to Lose Its Faith**</u> as the *Church becomes Under Attack from Modernism*. We see that on the "2nd Day," the <u>Lord God Almighty</u> is **Attacking Man's Human Intellect** to **Wound Man's Logical Trust in God,** thereby causing <u>**Humanity to Believe Only in Science**</u> as the *World Sees Itself* as *Solving Its Own Problems Without God*. Finally, at the "End of the 2nd Day" <u>Comes a Strange Period</u> of **Intellectual Awakening** so **Great** (Artificial Intelligence or AI) that the **Mystical Codes of God** will be **Broken** and the <u>**Human Race will be Able**</u> to *Find Its Way Back to God's Love* (home). This "New Union" between <u>Humanity</u> (flesh) and <u>Divinity</u> (spirit) will bring forth <u>**Mankind's Understanding**</u> of the *Meaning of Life* (existence), the *Purpose of Life* (service), and the *Value of Life* (happiness).

It appears that the "Lord God Almighty" is <u>Crushing Man's Spirit</u> and <u>Wounding his Flesh</u> to **Force** the <u>**Teaming Masses**</u> to *See Their Limitations* (poverty) and *See Their Future Potential* (prosperity). Obviously, the "Lord" is <u>Putting Man's Spirit</u> in

His **Winepress of Death** (wine) to *Change Evil* (cowardice/sin) into *Good* (courage/holiness), while "He" is Putting Man's Flesh in His **Crucible of Fire** (bread) to *Change Wrong* (ignorance) into *Right* (wisdom). We see that "After the Chastisement" of the Spirit (heart) and Flesh (mind), the **Lord God Almighty Will Heal** the **Broken Spirit** and **Bind** the **Wounded Flesh** to **Restore the Human Race** to its *Original State*. Upon the "Completion" of One Heavenly Day (7th day of rest), **God** will bring forth **His Great Tribulation** or **Time of Jacob's Troubles** to **Test the Quality of His Work** to **See** the **Depth** of *Man's Wisdom*, **Strength** of *Man's Courage*, and the **Goodness** of *Man's Generosity*. Upon this "3rd Day," the Lord God Almighty will bring forth the **Great Dragon** (Lucifer), **Black Leopard** (Anti-Christ), and **Evil Lamb** (false prophet) to **Test** (seven years) *Man's Ignorance, Cowardice, and Greed*. Finally, at the "End of All God's Testing," the Lord Jesus Christ will **Come** as a **Just Judge on a Cloud** and **Every Eye shall See Him, Arriving Like Spring Rain** (grace) to *Restore All Things to Divine Perfection*.

The following tabular information "Gives an Important" Scripture Reference in **Hosea 6:1-2 Revealing** that **God has Designed** a **Two-Day Period,** following the **Destruction of Herod's** Temple to *Purify the Human Race*:

Hosea 6: 1-2: Two Days or 2,000 Years of the Death of Israel

Hosea Describes the Events on the Three Final Days of Life on Earth

1. **1st Day** - God will Crush Man's Spirit - Wandering Jew (crush with cowardice)
   - Turn Man's Heart Toward Evil - Seek Pleasure (purification): Crucible of Fire
2. **2nd Day** - God will Wound Man's Flesh - Modern Age of Evil (wound with ignorance)
   - Turn Man's Mind Toward Money - Seek Wealth (transformation): Winepress of Death

Reviving the Jewish Nation - Sign that God is Coming Back

2nd Advent of Christ - Thief in the Night: King = Bema Judgment of Sanctuary
- Messiah Returns to Heal the Broken Spirit of Man - New Church (heal via courage)
- Messiah Returns to Bandage Wounds of Flesh of Man - New Government (bind with wisdom)

3rd Advent of Christ - Just Judge on a Cloud: Son of God = White Throne Judgment
3. **3rd Day** - Resurrection of Man's Mind, Heart, and Soul
   - All Men are Resurrected from the Grave and from Sin, Evil, and Death
   - All Men will Come to Know Their God - New Heaven and New Earth
         God Returns Like Spring Rain (grace)
         Coming Blessing of Spring Flowers (saints)

This illustration shows that the "Prophet Hosea" is Predicting the Coming of both the **2nd** and **3rd Advents** of **Jesus Christ** as **He Comes to Destroy Man's Ignorance** and **Cowardice** to bring forth *Man's New Wisdom and New Courage*. The "Theme Here" is that it will be 2,000 Years (two days) between **Christ's 1st Advent** as a **Priest on a Donkey** (offer own blood) until the **Lord's 2nd Advent** as a **Thief in the Night** (kingship), *When He Offers His Father Forgiven Blood* (church). Then "Hosea" mentions another 1,000 Years between the **Lord's 2nd Advent** (invisible) and **3rd Advent** (visible), when **He Comes** as a **Just Judge on a Cloud**, where *Every Eye on Earth shall See Him*. Through the "Lord's 2nd Advent (present day)," Jesus Christ will Come to Seal His Saints and to **Build His Government** which is **Confirmed** in the **Book of Revelation** (9:4): **God Orders His Angel of Tribulation to Wait** and **Do Not Hurt the Earth for 1,000 Years** as *He must Seal His Holy Saints*. This "Process of Sealing" Creates the **Great Awakening** and brings forth **1,000 Years of Prosperity, Leading** to the **Completion of God's *Holy Church*** (morals), *Honest Government* (ethics), and *Happy Homes* (fairness). We now see that the "1st/2nd/3rd Days of Transformation" were necessary to Measure the **Wisdom of Man, the Courage of Man**, and the **Generosity of Man** so **All on Earth** would be **Properly Cared For** and **Made Righteous, Holy, and Perfect** (unselfish) in the *Sight of God*. The "Job" of the Great Dragon (Lucifer) is to **Test Man's Wisdom**, then the Black Leopard (Anti-Christ) will **Test Man's Courage,** and finally, the Evil Lamb (false prophet) will **Test Man's Generosity** before the *Eyes of All*. Once the "Dragon, Leopard, and Evil Lamb" are Finished with Their Work, then it will be **Time** to bring forth the **Great White Throne Judgment** as **God is Now Ready to Separate** *His Sheep* (good /spirit) from *His Goats* (evil/flesh) *Forever*.

During the "Lord's Final Judgment," All the Children of God will be **Judged** on the **Depth of Their Belief in Christ,** be it *25%* (baby wisdom), *50%* (teenage courage), *75%* (adult generosity), and *100%* (wise man unselfishness). The idea here is to "Enter Christ's Church" and Surrender One's Life **Totally** unto the **Will of God** and then **Return to the World** to **Fight** *His Sin-nature* (sin) or *Ignorance*, **Fight** *Worldly Temptations* (evil) or *Cowardice*, **Fight** *Demonic Possessions* (death) or *Greed*, and finally, to **Fight** *God's Curse* (damnation) or *Selfishness*. *His Life can then Bear Fruit* if a "Person has Mastered" both Christ's Church (winepress) and the Evil World (crucible) to **Learn the Lessons of Life** and then **Places** these **Priceless Lessons** (growth) upon **God's Altar** as **Offerings**, along with his **Repentance, Prayers, Works,** and **Number of Souls Saved.**

The major point is that "God Wants to See" Steady and Consistent Growth **Moment-by-moment** until a **Tiny Baby Grows** into a **Responsible Adult, Who is Filled** with *Wisdom, Courage, Generosity, and Unselfishness*. We see that based on this logic, "Wisdom Creates" Righteous Men on Earth **Who are Worthy** of **New Bodies** (free). This means that as a **Baby**, a **Person** had **Faced Lucifer's Test** and has **Defeated** his **Own Sin-nature** by **Getting his Sinfulness** to *Bear Fruit* (citizenship). Secondly, "Courage Creates" Holy Men in Heaven **Who are Worthy of Eternal Life** (earned). This means that as a **Teenager**, a **Person** had **Faced God's Judgment** and has **Defeated Worldly Temptations** by **Getting his Evil Wickedness** to *Bear Fruit* (sainthood). Thirdly, "Generosity Creates" <u>Perfect Men within God's Kingdom</u> **Who are Worthy of Their Own Kingdoms** (bonus reward). This means that as an **Adult**, a **Person** had **Faced his Own** *Self-evaluation and has Defeated All Demonic Possessions by <u>Getting his Curse of Death</u> to Bear Fruit* (sonship). Finally, "Unselfishness Creates" <u>Free Men Who can Think for Themselves</u> and are **Worthy of God's Friendship** (accepted). This means that as a **Wise Man**, a **Person** has **Faced himself** and has **Defeated** his **Own Human Frailties** by **Getting his Weaknesses** to *Bear Fruit* (freedom/liberty/independence). Yes! We all have "Weak Flesh (destroy)" and "Supernatural Spirits (wash)" but the <u>Trick is to Use</u> **Our Spiritual Strengths** to **Accentuate Our Physical Weaknesses** through the **Intercessory Power** and **Authority of Christ** to **Learn the Lessons of Life** and **Bear Fruit <u>Out of All Things,</u>** either *Great and/or Small.*

The following tabular information indicates that "Adam and Eve" were <u>Cursed</u> with a **Sin-nature, Worldly Temptations, Demonic Possession,** and **God's Curse** and were then **Challenged** to **Figure Out** just **How to Transform <u>Sin, Evil, Death, and Damnation</u>** into *Righteousness, Holiness, Perfection,* and even into *God's Divinity.*

Removing One's Sin-nature, Worldly Temptations, Demonic Possession, and God's Curse
(changing ignorance to wisdom, cowardice to courage,
greed to generosity, and selfishness to unselfishness)

1. **Sin-nature Creates Ignorance** - <u>Baby must Fight Ignorance</u>...Learn Wisdom
   - Person must Believe 25% unto Repentance - Remove his Ignorant Mind
   - Learning God's Knowledge - See One's Limitations (seen by God)
   - Learning God's Right from Man's Wrong - Master Earthly Baby Farm
   - Wisdom brings forth a Righteous Citizen on Earth - Worthy of New Body

(when sin enters mind, it creates ignorance and can only be taken out by killing the flesh)

2. **Worldly Temptations Create Cowardice** - <u>Teen must Fight Cowardice</u>....Learn Courage
   - Person must Believe 50% unto Prayer - Remove his Cowardly Heart
   - Learning to be Self-aware - See One's Potential (spoken to by God)
   - Learning God's Good from Man's Evil - Master Heavenly Divine School
   - Courage brings forth a Holy Saint in Heaven - Worthy of Eternal Life

(when sin enters heart, it creates evil/cowardice and can only be taken out by killing spirit)

3. **Demonic Possession Creates Greed** - <u>Adult must Fight Greed</u>...Learn Generosity
   - Person must Believe 75% unto Works - Remove his Greedy Soul
   - Learning to be Conscious - See One's Self-worth (touched by God)

- Learning God's Will from Man's Will - Master Kingdom Sonship Training
- Generosity brings forth a Perfect Son within Kingdom - Worthy of Own Kingdom

(when sin enters the soul, it creates death/greed and can only be taken out by killing soul)

4. **God's Curse Creates Selfishness** - Wise Man must Fight Selfishness...Learn Unselfishness
   - Person must Believe 100% unto Saving Others - Remove his Selfishness
   - Learning to be Sentient - See the Face of God (sup with God)
   - Learning God's Reality from Man's Illusion - Master Thinking for Oneself
   - Unselfishness brings forth a Free Man, Who Thinks for himself - Worthy of God's Friendship

(when sin enters one's life, it creates damnation/selfishness and can only be taken out by killing life-force)

This illustration shows that the "Life-experience" is All About Growing-up and **Learning God's Right, Good, Will,** and **Reality** as **Opposed** to **Man's Wrong, Evil, Will, and Illusion**, yet, still becoming **Born-again in Christ** and **Bear Fruit Out of Every Moment of Life.** The message here is that "Most Christians" are Convinced that **If They Master Repentance, Prayers, Works,** and the **Saving of Souls, They** can **Go to Heaven** in **Royal Style, Not Realizing** that **God is Watching** and **Waiting** for **Each of His Christian Children** to **Grow-up Daily** and to **Prove It** by **Placing Their Offering** of **Lessons Learned** upon **His Altar** *Daily* (flesh), *Weekly* (spirit), and *Yearly* (soul). This means that "If a Person" Believes in Christ 25% (baby), he can **Convert** his **Ignorance** into **Wisdom** and **Face Lucifer's Tes**t by being **as Gentle as a Dove** and as **Cunning as a Serpent** to **Learn God's Right** from **Man's Wrong** and then **Defeat** his *Own Sin-nature.* Secondly, "If a Person" Believes in Christ 50% (teen), he can **Convert** his **Cowardice** into **Courage** and **Face God's Judgment** by being as **Courageous** as **King David** when he **Faced Goliath** to **Learn God's Good** from **Man's Evil** and then **Defeat** his *Own Worldly Temptations.* Thirdly, "If a Person" Believes in Christ 75% (adult), he can **Convert** his **Greed** into **Generosity** and **Face His Own Self-evaluation** by being **Generous** to a **Sick and Dying World** to **Learn God's Will** from **Man's Will** and then **Defeat** the *Evil One's Demonic Possessions.* Finally, "If a Person" Believes in Christ 100% (wise man), he can **Convert** his **Selfishness** into **Unselfishness** and **Face Thinking for Himself** by being **Unselfish** to **Others** to **Learn God's Reality** from **Man's Illusion** and **Defeat** *God's Curse on Adam.*

Yes! Fulfilling the "Born-again Experience" Means both **Dying to Self** (submission/blessed) and **Fighting the Evil World** (lessons) to **Prove to God** that a **Devout Christian** has been **Steadily Growing** in his *Faith* in *God's Grace* to be *Affirmed by His Works* (fruits). The theme here is that "If a Person" can Grow into Adulthood and **Take Full Responsibility** for his **Life,** his **Community,** and the **Works of God,** he will be **Counted Among the Lord's** most *Beloved Sheep* and

Not Rejected as some *Foolish Goat.* We see that the "Separation" of the Sheep (spirit/believed) and the Goats (flesh/disbelief) **Means Separating Those Souls Which Learned** the **Lessons of Life** and became *All* (new body) from **Those Souls Which Surrendered to Christ** and became *Nothing* (eternal life). This means that the "Job of the Flesh" is to Master All Knowledge (lessons) to **See** the *Physical God of Illusion* (Jesus/death), while the "Job of the Spirit" is to Master Christ's Church (blessings) to **See** the *Spiritual God of Reality* (Christ/life). The point is that "If a Person" Fights the **Evil World System,** then he can Learn the *Lessons of Life* (all); and "If He" Surrenders to **Christ's Church,** then he can **Obtain** the *Blessings of Life* (nothing). Yes! When "He Masters" the World System, his **Faults** can be **Removed, Allowing** him to **Defeat his Ignorance** and *Obtain Wisdom*, while "If He Masters" Christ's Church, he can **Gain Virtues** by **Defeating his Cowardice** and *Obtaining Courage.*

We see that the "Central Theme" here is to Spend One's Life both **Purifying His Grave** (flesh) and **Purifying His Host** (spirit). **What this Does** is to **Offer God His Works** by *Killing the Flesh* (grave/lessons) and then **Offering God His Prayers** by *Killing the Spirit* (host/blessing). This means that the "Lord God Almighty" is Using both the **World** and the **Church** (host) to **Transform** the **Human Race** from an **Ignorant Fool** and **Wicked Sinner** into *Righteous Citizens* (earth) and *Holy Saints* (Heaven). Obviously, "We are All Living" within a Divine School (growth/maturity), where the **Earthly Teachers** are the **Jewish People** (world) and the **Christian People** (church), **Who** are **Teaching God's Children How to Change** into both *Righteous Citizens* (grave) and *Holy Saints* (host). This "Ability to Change" from Ignorant Fools and Wicked Sinners into **Kings, Priests, and Sons of God Allows Mankind** to become **Future Rulers** on **Earth,** in **Heaven,** and within **God's Kingdom** to **Fulfill** *God's Law of Obedience* (world) and *Man's Faith in God's Love* (church). The "Lord is Telling Us" that the World System is to be **Decoded** (God's Word/Law) by the **Jewish People** so that a **Person** can become a *Righteous Citizen* (all); and the Holy Bible is to be **Decoded** (God's Word/faith) by the **Christian People** so that a **Person** can become a *Holy Saint* (nothing). This means that through the "Jewish Decoding System," a Person can Master **God's Law** (lessons) and **Learn** to *Bow to God's Will* (supernatural order); while through the "Christian Decoding System," a Person can Master **Man's Faith** (blessings) and **Learn** to *Bow to God's Beliefs* (natural order).

The following tabular information indicates just "How Mankind" can both become All (Jesus flesh) and Nothing (Christ's spirit) at the **Same time** since **Eating** from the **Tree of Knowledge** *Kills the Flesh* (slaughter innocence); and **Eating** from the **Tree of Life** (cross) *Kills the Spirit* (born-again nature):

Showing One's Growth	Showing One's Maturity
Mankind becomes All	Mankind becomes Nothing
(flesh masters all knowledge)	(spirit dies to selfishness)

• Man Learns All the Lessons in Life	• Man Surrenders to God's Will and Christ
• Fighting All Earthly Evil - Works	• Dying to One's Own Selfishness - Prayer
• Eating from Tree of Knowledge (word)	• Eating from the Tree of Life (cross)

Decode Word	• Fulfilling One's ***Grave*** - Death	**Decode Bible**	• Fulfilling Christ's ***Host*** - Born-again
• Resurrection from the Dead		• Blessed with New-life at Death	
• Worthy of a New Body - New Mind		• Worthy of Eternal Life - New Heart	
• Living with Oneself/natural order		• Living with God/supernatural order	
• Seeing Physical God (free will)		• Seeing Spiritual God (destiny)	
• Fulfilling God's Law of Obedience		• Fulfilling Man's Faith in God's Love	
• Seeing Physical God (free will)		• Seeing Spiritual God (destiny)	
• Change Nature - Human to Divine		• Washing Away Sins - Sinful to Holy	
• Remove Faults - Ignorance to Wisdom		• Gain Virtues - Change Cowardice	
• Becoming Righteous Citizen on Earth		• Becoming Holy Saint in Heaven	
• Entering Heaven on Earth (God's physical lessons/law)		• Entering Paradise in Heaven (God's spiritual blessings/faith)	

This illustration shows that by "Fulfilling" God's Law and Man's Faith, a **Person** can have his **Nature Changed** into **Divinity** and have his **Sinfulness Changed** into **Holiness**, thereby **Transforming a Soul** into a **Righteous Citizen Who is Worthy** of a ***New Body*** and into a **Holy Saint**, **Who is Worthy** of ***Eternal Life***. The idea here is to become "Divine" so that a Person can See his **Physical God** (Jesus) and then to become "Holy" so that He can See his **Spiritual God** (Christ), thereby **Allowing** a **Righteous Saint** to **Come** to **Know, Love, and Serve** his ***Creator God***. Yes! The "Whole Human Race" is being Called (man wants to become God) to **Fight the Evil World** (all knowledge) to become **Wise** and then to be Chosen (God wants to become man) to **Die to One's Selfishness** (nothing) and become **Courageous** as **Each of God's Children** must **Face Lucifer's Test/world** and **God's Judgment/church** to be Accepted by ***God, Angels, and God's Saints***.

"Out" of Lucifer's Test (get lessons), God's Judgment (get blessings), and Man's Self-evaluation (get value), the **Human Race** will come to **Worship God** (give life/wisdom), **Praise God** (give wealth/courage), and finally, **Thank God** (give labors/generosity) to ***Win God's Divine Favor***. On this "Great Day of Forgiveness," known as the Eighth Day, the **Human Race** will **Take Away** its **Excommunication from God's Temple,** its being **Outcast from God's People,** and being **Banished from the Earth** to be ***Set Free Forever***. This means that on the "Eighth Day (8th day)," the Human Race will become **Worthy of Receiving** its ***New Body, Eternal Life,*** and even ***Its Own Royal Kingdom of Glory***.

In this picture of the "Eighth Day," we see Mankind First Failing to Recreate the **Garden of Eden on Earth** with its **Own Hands**. In **Only Six Thousand Short Years, Foolish Man** has been ***Able*** to ***Destroy himself*** and his ***Entire Planet***. Obviously, these

"Foreseen Circumstances" were <u>Anticipated by the Lord</u> as **He** has been **Patiently Standing** by in the **Wings,** simply **Waiting** for the **Human Race** to **Fall** into the **Evil One's Pit of Death** to <u>**Forever be his Captive**</u> in a *Darkness without Hope*. The question is: just "What Brought" the <u>Human Race</u> **Down so Quickly** and **Why Couldn't** the **Free Will of Men Learn to Work Together** in such a way as to **Establish some Form** of **Status Quo** which is **Stable Enough** to at *Least Survive the Test of Time*? But, No! "Humanity was Hell-bent" on <u>Conquering</u> the **Undaunted Human Spirit** and **Placing It** in **Complete Submission** to the <u>**Will of the State**</u> through the *Powers of Fear* (threaten pain) and *Intimidation* (threaten life). We all know that the "Human Race" had <u>No Chance of Success</u> (hopeless slavery) from the **Beginning** as <u>**It was**</u> **Cursed** with a *Sin-nature* (ignorant mind), *Worldly Temptations* (cowardly heart), *Demonic Possession* (greedy soul), and even *God's Curse of Original Sin* (selfish life-force).

We see that this "Curse of Slavery" constantly <u>Drove Men to Seek</u> a **Higher and Higher Authority, Hoping Against Hope** that the **Next Level** of **Raw Power** would **Provide** the <u>**Pure Justice Needed**</u> to *Rule All Men Fairly*. The point here is that "Mankind" has <u>Three Powerful Forces</u> or <u>Wills</u> to **Contend with**: 1) <u>Serving Oneself</u> (home), 2) <u>Serving One's Society</u> (government), and 3) <u>Serving One's God</u> (church). Each of these "Mystical Forces" <u>Demands a Person's Full Attention,</u> with **One Calling him** to *Work* (state), **Another Calling him** to *Prayer* (church), and a **Third Calling him** to *Pleasure* (home). We see that this "Triune Conflict" of <u>Demanding Wills</u> has **Caused Mankind to Fall** to the **Depths of Despair** so **Quickly** as **No Man** could **Serve Three Masters at Once,** especially <u>**When They are All Demanding**</u> *All Work, All Pray, and All Pleasure at the Same time*. We see that the "Entire Human Race" was in a Reasonable <u>Quandary</u> as to **Who to Serve First** and just **How Much** of **One's Precious Life-force** to **Expend on This or That Project** based on some **Direct or Indirect** <u>**Powerful Influence**</u> of *Fear, Pain, and/or Threat of Death*. Note that the "Problems of the World" have <u>Grown so Great</u> that **They Require Massive Human Efforts** of **Well-Financed, Well-Trained, and Well-Organized Personnel** to <u>Take Control</u> and **Solve** these *Serious Defects* (illnesses) within *Human Society*.

We see that just like the "Human Body," <u>When a Single Cell</u> is **Out of Control** and **Turns** into a **Malignant Cancer,** then the **Whole Body will Suffer** and **Finally Die,** thereby <u>**Destroying**</u> *One's Life, Hopes, and Dreams Forever*. This will be the case with the "Whole Human Race" as <u>Man's Human Fleshly Nature</u> (animal) will **Seek to Solve** his <u>**Life and Death Problems**</u> by *Using* the *Works of his Own Hands* and the *Lies of his Own Heart*. The "Lord is Calling" the <u>Human Race</u> to **Recognize** that **It Cannot Hope** to **Ever Solve Its Own World-Shattering Problems by Itself** before the **Evil One and Death** <u>Overtake Them</u> and *Cast Them All into Hell Fire*. The only hope for a "Mortally Wounded Mankind" is to <u>Call</u> upon some **Supernatural Force** and to **Pray** for a **Divine Miracle** to **Come from the Sky** to **Save the Day, Just Moments** before *It Is Too Late* (last second reprieve).

We can now see that in "God's Grand Design," the <u>Human Race</u> was **Intended to Fail** upon its **First Attempt** to **Create Paradise on Earth,** but this **Does Not Mean** that the **Lord has Not Scheduled a Second Chance** (born-again) **When**

Mankind will be <u>Ready</u> to *Face the Triune Will of Nature*. Nothing in the "Life-experience" can <u>Prepare a Person</u> for the **Tremendous Trials and Tribulations** he will **Face During his Time of Sonship Training** because the **Lord has Designed** this **Phase of the Life-experience** to be <u>Strictly Dynamic</u> and *Totally Unpredictable* (unknown). The point here is that "We have been Led" to <u>Believe</u> that **If One Chooses** the **Right Things in Life** and also **Makes All the Right Decisions,** then he will be the <u>**Lucky One**</u> and *Live a Life* of *Smooth Sailing*. *Wrong,* this will *Never Happen*. Certainly, we can make a case for this "Type of Person," but this is <u>Only a Fraud,</u> **Set in Position** to **Mislead Us** and **Give Us a** <u>**Complete Misconception**</u> of the *Purpose of Life* which is to be of *Service to Others*. We see that "Each Person's Life-force" has been <u>Specially Designed</u> into a **Master Tapestry** of **Divine Perfection** and **Nothing** will **Change It,** <u>**No Matter What a Person**</u> might *Think, Say, or Do*. This certainly sounds like "Fatalistic Logic," but in truth, it is <u>Only</u> a simple <u>Explanation</u> for **Understanding the Forces** of **Destiny** (God) **and Free Will** (Man) as <u>**They Work Together**</u> to *Manifest One's Life-experiences upon the Earth*. Within the "Three Mystical Plans of God," <u>We Find</u> the **Conflicting Forces of Human Decision, Each** <u>**Tied to the Creation**</u> of a *Person's Identity* (Earth/king), *Character* (Heaven/priest), and *Personality* (Kingdom/son). The first thing to observe in the "People Around You" is: are <u>They Working for Themselves</u> (selfish), the <u>Brotherhood of Man</u> (state), or are <u>They very Religious</u> and <u>Dedicated</u> to the <u>Works of God?</u> We can clearly observe "All Three" of these <u>Types of People</u> in the **General Public** as **All** are seemingly **Driven** to some **Abstract Goal** of **Personal Fulfillment** based upon *Their Own Belief System* and *Their Own Destiny*.

The following tabular information indicates how the "Conflicting Forces of Decision" <u>Relate</u> to a **Person's Obedience** to the <u>**Lord's Righteousness**</u> (law) through the *Lord's Three Plans of Creation* (creation/redemption/sanctified-life):

Conflicting Forces on Human Decisions
(the eternal contradiction between God's power/law
(Christ) and Man's faith (Jesus))

Plan of   1. **Serving Absolute Truth** – <u>Servanthood</u>…Petition
Creation   • Divine Will - Lord God Almighty (Creator): God Wants to Become Man
(teenage   • Serving God and His Holy Church - All Prayer: See Potential
Heaven)   • Divine Slavery - Heavenly Priest: Receive Eternal life
    (life is only loving God - learn good from evil: become holy saint in Heaven)

Plan of   2. **Obeying the Laws of the Land/ethics** – <u>Friendship</u>…Intercession
Redemption   • Will of the People: Spirit of the World: Man Wants to Become God
(baby earth)   • Serving Man and His State (government) - All Work: See Limitations
      • Earth - Self: Being Rich and Happy = Physical Perfection
      • Human Slavery - Earthly King: Receive New Body
  (life is only loving man - learn right from wrong: become righteous citizen on earth)

Plan of	3.	**Unto Thine Own Self be True** – <u>Sonship</u>…Judgment
Sanctified	•	Self-will - Island of Perfection: God/Man Become One in Holiness
Life	•	Serving Selfishness and One's Own Home - All Pleasure: See Self-worth
(adult	•	Kingdom - God: Being Poor in Spirit/Rich in the Flesh = Mystical
Kingdom)		Perfection
	•	God/Man Freedom - Kingdom Sonship: Receive Own Royal Kingdom

(life is loving God/Man - learn God's Will/man's will: become perfect son within Kingdom)

This illustration shows that we are "All Facing Tremendous" <u>Conflicting Forces</u> from **Our State/Earth** (all work/king)**, Church/Heaven** (all prayer/priest), and **Home/Kingdom** (all pleasure/son) as **They Each Cries Out** for <u>**Our Full Attention**</u> ***Demanding that We Respond***. If we asked the "Church (brothers)" <u>What We should Do</u> about this most **Complexing Problem**, the **Priesthood** will **Say** to **Transform Our Evil Life** into a **Living Prayer** before **God** and then to **Submit All** <u>**Our Time and Energies**</u> to the *World of Prayer*. Conversely, "If We Ask" the <u>State</u> (neighbors), **What Their Opinion** is to this most **Paralyzing Dilemma**, obviously **It will Quickly Remark** that the **Answer** to **All Human Problems** is a <u>**Lack of Quality Work,**</u> based upon a *Lifetime of Dedicated Hard Labor* (production/production).

Now, let's compare these "Two Philosophies of Life" <u>Against</u> **Our Own Personal Experiences** as **We have Tried** to <u>**Pray Ourselves**</u> into *Sainthood* (poor and happy), just as **We have Tried** to <u>**Work Ourselves**</u> into *Worldly Perfection* (rich and happy). Note that "Neither" of <u>These All Pray</u> or <u>All Work Systems</u> has **Worked**. It is **About Now** that it might **Start to Make a Person Believe** that there is **More to Life** than **Prayer and Work**. How **About** a **Little Pleasurable Living** based on a **Person's Ability** to **Balance** <u>**All his Responsibilities**</u> through the *Power of Maturity* (wisdom)? Obviously, the "Human Circumstance" has been <u>Intentionally Designed</u> to **Cause a Direct Conflict** between the **Body** (flesh), **Spirit**, and **Soul of Man** to <u>**Force him to Choose**</u> between *God's Pathway of Perfection* (wise man's reality) and *Man's Pathway of Perceived Truth* (fool's hope).

In the "First Four Thousand Years" of <u>Human Existence,</u> known as the **Plan of Creation, Mankind** was a **Tiny Baby** under the **Direct Divine Will of God**, where he was <u>**Forced to Serve**</u> the *Forces of Absolute Truth*. At the time of the first "Coming of Jesus Christ," the <u>World Saw its</u> **First Signs of Growing-up** as it **Transitioned** to the **Plan of Redemption**, where it would **Learn** to **Obey the Laws of the Land** (ethics) in **Accordance** with the *Free Will of Man*. The "Second Phase" is <u>Designed</u> to **Last Three Thousand Years** during which **Time** the **Human Race** would **Learn the Difference** between <u>**God's Right**</u> and <u>**man's wrong**</u>, thereby *Bringing Salvation to All Men*. This "First Seven Thousand Years" will <u>Represent</u> the **Servanthood of Man Intended to Symbolize** a **Seven-Day Period of Mystical Creation** to bring forth <u>**Nature, Mankind,**</u> and <u>**Jesus Christ**</u> as *One Holy and Perfect Creation*.

At the "End of this Period," the <u>Lord</u> will bring forth a **New Eighth Day of Creation** which will **Represent** the **Plan of Sanctified Life** (freedom), where **Mankind** would be **Set Free** to be <u>**Taught the Infinite Mysteries**</u> of *God's Mystical Divinity*. In this "Last Phase (8th day)" of the <u>Creation,</u> **Mankind will Live** under **Its Own Self-will** as the **Theme of God's Kingdom** will be **Unto Thine Own Self be True**. This means that in <u>God's Eyes,</u> *Humanity has Grown-up* into *Adulthood*. This "State of Adulthood" will show that the Human Race can **Now Think for Itself in Mind** (body), **Spirit,** and **Soul** as the **Maturity of Earth, Heaven,** and **God's Kingdom** are <u>**Brought into Perfection**</u> through the *Sonship of Jesus Christ.*

The "Ability" to <u>Think for Oneself</u> **Opens the Door** for the **Collective Mind of Men to be Formed,** thereby **Allowing the Human Race to Learn the Lessons of Life** and **Solve** <u>God's Mystical Puzzle</u> *Surrounding Our Human Existence.* By "Comprehending Human Existence," the <u>Human Race</u> could **Actually Find a Way** to become a **Physical God** in the **Person of Mary's Son, Jesus** as **Mankind Strives** to **Fight All the Forces of Evil** until it has *Mastered All Knowledge.* By "Learning" <u>God's Right</u> from <u>man's wrong,</u> the **Human Race** can **Understand God** and **See** the **Basic Purpose Behind** *God's Grand Design* as **He Strives to Create** an **Infinite Supply** of **Babies** (citizens), **Teenagers** (saints), **Adults** (sons), and **Wise Men** to <u>**Rule Over**</u> *His Massive Kingdom of Glory.* We see in this "Teaching" that <u>Jesus</u> becomes **All Human Flesh, Fights** the **Evil World System,** like **Untying** (3,000 years) the **Gordian Knot** until **He has All Knowledge** and then **Figures Out** the **Meaning, Purpose, and Value of Life,** thereby <u>**Making Himself**</u> into a *Physical God* (God/Man). In like manner, "Christ" becomes <u>All Human Spirit</u> by **Converting Everyone** into **Christianity,** thereby **Solving** the **Gordian Knot of Life** to **Make All Mankind Born-again Saints** who will then <u>**Make Themselves**</u> into *Spiritual Gods* (Man/God). Through these "Two Life-long Dreams" of <u>God being Man</u> and <u>Man being God,</u> **Jesus Christ** can be **Fulfilled** as **Jesus** *Takes-on All Sin* (learning) and **Christ** *Forgives All Sin* (converting).

Yes! The "Human Race" can <u>Certainly Thank</u> **Its Jewish Savior** (Messiah) for being **Willing** to **Sacrifice** both **His Natural Flesh** (scourging) and **His Supernatural Spirit** (crucifixion) to **Purchase** both a <u>**Universal** *Physical*</u> (Man) and *Spiritual* (God) *Set of Gods.* We see that an "Easy Way to Comprehend" the <u>Life of Jesus Christ</u> is to **See His Flesh** as a **Streetwise Orphan** (lessons), **His Spirit** as a **Highly Educated Prince** (blessings), and then the **Lord Blends** <u>**His Two Natures**</u> into a *New Mystical Creation.*

The following tabular information indicates that the "Human Flesh" must <u>Fight the Evil World</u> to **Learn the Lessons of Life, Figure Out** the **Meaning of Life** (solve puzzle), to be **Taught God's Truths** to become a *Spiritual God* (Man/God):

<u>World becomes Physical God</u>	<u>Church becomes Spiritual God</u>
*****Human God*****	*****Divine Man*****
• **Fulfilling God's Physical Law**	• **Fulfilling Man's Spiritual Faith**
• Mankind Learns Lessons of Life	• Mankind Receives God's Born-again Blessing
• Mankind Puts Puzzle Together	• Mankind Taught God's Divine Truths

• Mankind becomes God		• Mankind becomes God
• Man Wants to be God **Sinner**		• God Wants to be Man **Saints**
• Free Will of Man		• Divine Will of God
• Streetwise Orphan		• Highly Educated Prince
(purifying man's grave)		(purifying God's host)

This illustration shows that the "Lord God Almighty" is <u>Revealing Some Type</u> of **Mystical Competition** between a **Poor Fool** (Jesus/streetwise) and a **Highly Educated Rich Scholar** (Christ) as **They** are to **Use** <u>Two Completely Different Methods</u> to become *Successful in Life*. The idea here is that "God is Planning" to <u>Indwell His People</u> both **Physically** and **Spiritually** to **Make God and Man One**, but for this **Miracle to Occur**, the **Human Race** will have to **Spend 3,000 Years** <u>Learning</u> the *Lessons of Life* (Physical God) and <u>**Transforming**</u> into *Christ's Born-again Nature* (Spiritual God). This means that upon the "8th Day of Creation," <u>God</u> will bring forth the **New Heaven** or <u>**Reveal**</u> *Man's New Spiritual God Nature;* and then the **Lord** will bring forth the **New Earth** or <u>**Reveal**</u> *Man's New Physical God Nature*. The idea here is for the "Physical Nature (God/Man)" to <u>Purify Man's Grave</u> (resurrect new body) through its *Great Wisdom* (accomplishments/lessons); while the "Spiritual Nature (Man/God)" is to <u>Purify God's Host</u> (resurrect glorified spirit) through its *Great Courage* (blood/blessings).

We see that on this "8th Day of Creation," there shall be a <u>Great Accounting</u> by both the **Holy Mother, <u>Who will Count</u>** *Her Beautiful Babies* (people on earth) and by the **Holy Father, <u>Who will Count</u>** *His Courageous Saints* (people in Heaven). On this "Day of Judgment," the <u>Holy Mother</u> will **Determine the Number** of **Babies Saved by Her Son, Jesus, When He Took upon Himself All the Sins of Man** and then **Washed His Mother's Babies** to <u>**Remove Their Sinfulness**</u> to *Make Them Holy* (bread). The "Job of the Holy Mother" is to <u>Wash Her Babies</u> (remove sin) in the **Blood of the Lamb** (flesh) and **Remove Ignorance** (mind), **Cowardice** (heart), **Greed** (soul), and **Selfishness** (life-force) and then **Empty Them** of <u>**All Their Faults**</u> via *God's Winepress of Death* (purification). On the "Day of Judgment" also, the <u>Holy Father</u> will **Determine the Number** of **Holy Saints Saved by His Son, Christ, When He Gave-up His Divinity** and then **Changed Man's Nature** via <u>**Man's Crucible of Fire**</u> from *Human to Divine* (wine). Note here the "Mystical Flip" or <u>Paradoxical Logic</u> which **Changes/reverses the Position** of <u>**God's Winepress**</u> (submission) and <u>**Man's Crucible**</u> (fight evil) during the *God/Man Final White Throne Judgment*. This means that "Each of God's Children" is being <u>Called</u> to **Come to God's Altar** with both a **Holy Prayer** (spirit) and a **Good Work** (flesh), as **His Personal Offering**, thereby **Demonstrating** the **Amount** of <u>**Progress**</u> and/or <u>**Growth**</u> **He has Made** *Since his Last Visit*.

We see that the "Job of the Holy Father" is to <u>Change His Saints</u> (gain holiness) in the **Spirit of Christ** (spirit) to **Give Them Wisdom** (mind), **Courage** (heart), **Generosity** (soul), and **Unselfishness** (life-force) and **Fill Them** with <u>**All God's Virtues**</u> via *God's Crucible of Fire* (transformation). The idea here is to see that the "Holy Mother" is <u>In-charge</u> of the **Baby Farm on Earth**, where **All Humanity** must be **Prepared for Entry** into **Eternal Life** via the *Father's Divine School* of *Holy Sainthood*. In like manner, we see that the "Holy Father" is In-charge of the **Divine School in Heaven**, where **All God's Saints** must be **Prepared for Entry** into the *Lord's Sonship Training Program* (divinity). This means that the "Dual Job" of the Eternal Father and the Virgin Mary is to **Work Together** in **Transforming Babies into Christians,** then **Christians into Saints,** and then **Saints into Sons of God** so that finally, *They might One Day be Set Free* (think for self).

Note that "When the Father/Mother" Work Together, **God's Law is Used** by the **Mother** and **Man's Faith is Used** by the **Father**, thereby **Mixing the Changing of Nature** with the **Washing Away of Sin** to **Create** *Loving Babies* and *Courageous Saints*. Basically, the "Holy Mother" is Using Man's Physical Nature to **Save Sinners** (Jesus), while the "Holy Father" is Using God's Spiritual Nature to **Create Saints** (Christ). This **Process Allows the Babies** of *Earth* to **Become the Adults** of *Heaven*. The idea here is that "Jesus Represents" a Human God, while "Christ Represents" a Divine Man **Working Together** to **Assist Their Parents** in **Transforming Earthly Babies** into **Heavenly Saints** by **Teaching Them** the Jewish *Commandments of God* (word) and the **Christian** *Works of Mercy* (traditions). Note that "Moses' Ten Commandments" are on Two Sets of Tablets, **One Spiritual** and the **Other Physical**, which are **Reflected** in **Jesus Christ's Two Commandments** of *Worship God* (1st tablet) and *Treat Your Neighbor as Yourself* (2nd tablet). The "Lord is Showing Us" that His 1st Tablet is **Creating** a **Living Prayer of Love** (all prayer), while His 2nd Tablet is **Creating** a **Soldier-of-the-Light** (all works) which is **Translated** into a *Person's Faith* (living prayer) through *Grace Affirmed by Works* (soldier). Note that the "Holy Mother" Hopes Her Babies (obedient) will **Become Living Prayers** *Who Live by Faith*, while the "Holy Father" Expects His Saints (loving) to **Become Soldiers-of-the-Light,** *Who Live by Good Works* and the *Saving of Souls*.

The following tabular information indicates that the "Holy Mother" Hopes for **Many Babies** both *Beautiful* and *Loving*, while the "Holy Father" Expects **Many Saints** both *Perfect* and *Courageous*:

Law   1. **Mother's Hopes** - Many Babies: Beautiful and Loving Children…Holiness
(obedience)   • Living Prayers of Love - All Prayer: Honor Man's Traditions = Free
                Redemption
              • Wash Away Sin - Change from Sinfulness to Holiness: See Limitations
              • Count Babies on Saturday (Sabbath) - Man's Day of Rest
              • Fulfill God's Word of Obedience - Christmas: God Wants to Become Man
              • Jewish People of Death - Crucifixion: Agony of Defeat: Repentance
              • Master Corporal Works of Mercy - Become Holy

Called to   1. Feed the Hungry   4. Shelter the Homeless
Baby Farm   2. Give Drink to Thirsty   5. Visit the Sick
(keys)   3. Clothe the Naked   6. Pay Ransom for Captives
                7. Bury the Dead
                   • Free Gift of *New Body* and *Heaven on Earth* - Live with Self
                   • Master 2nd Five Commandments - Learn God's Right from man's wrong

6. No Killing		8. No Stealing	
7. No Adultery		9. No Lying	
10. No Coveting			

(mother counts her *Money* on Saturday in *Babies* and offers them up to God in *Praise*/ownership)

Faith	2.	**Father's Expectations** - <u>Many Saints:</u> Courageous and Perfect Men…Divine
(love)	•	Soldiers-of-the-Light - All Work: Honor Word = Earned Salvation
	•	Change Nature - Change from Human to Divine: See Potential
	•	Count Saints on Sunday (Lord's Day) - Day of Worship
	•	Fulfill Man's Faith of Love - Easter: Man Wants to become God
	•	Christian People of Life - Resurrection: Thrill of Victory: Forgiveness
	•	Master Spiritual Works of Mercy - Become Divine

Chosen for	1. Instruct the Ignorant	4.	Bear Wrongs Patiently
Divine	2. Counsel the Doubters	5.	Forgive all Offenses
School	3. Reveal Sinful Acts	6.	Comfort the Afflicted
(ownership)	7. Pray for Living and the Dead		

• Earned Treasure of *Eternal Life* and *Paradise in Heaven* - Live with God
• Master 1st Five Commandments - Learn God's Good and man's evil

1. Worship God Only	3.	Don't Take God's Name in Vain
2. No Graven Images	4.	Keep the Sabbath Day Holy
5. Honor Thy Father/Mother		

(father counts his *Love* on Sunday in *Saints* and offers them up to God in *Worship*/keys)

This illustration shows that the "Holy Mother" <u>Calls Her Babies</u> to **Her Earthly Baby Farm** to **Fulfill God's Word of Obedience** via the **Principles of Proper Living** which is <u>**Treating Others**</u> with the *Utmost Respect and Dignity*. Secondly, the "Holy Father" <u>Chooses His </u>Saints for **His Divine School** to **Fulfill Man's Faith of Love** via the **Principles of Service to All** which is <u>**Treating the Human Race**</u> as *If It were God Himself*. The idea here is that the "Baby Farm" is a <u>Free Gift</u> (inheritance/adopted son) from **God**, bringing **Each Child** his **Own Transfigured Body** and **Heaven on Earth** based on **His Depth of Repentance** for <u>Adam and Eve's Sins</u> of *Ignorance, Cowardice, Greed, and Selfishness*. Secondly, the "Divine School" is an <u>Earned Treasure</u> (birthright/blood son) from **God**, bringing **Each Adult** his **Own Eternal Life** and **Paradise in Heaven** based on **His Depth of Forgiveness** to **Reflect** the <u>New Adam and Eve's Blessings</u> of *Wisdom, Courage, Generosity, and Unselfishness*. This means that the "Holy Mother" is <u>Teaching Her Babies</u> **Four Institutions on Earth** in the **Form** of the **Self, Home, Government, and Church** to **Ensure** that **Each of Her Children** can **Master His Own Mind, Heart, Soul, and Life-force** to **Become Worthy** of *God's Divine School*. We see that in "God's Grand Design," <u>Earth</u> **Represents** *God's Government*, <u>Heaven</u> **Represents** *God's Church*, the <u>Kingdom</u> **Represents** *God's Home*, and <u>God Himself</u> **Represents** the *God/Man Self*.

Obviously, "We are All being Called" to <u>Try Our Best</u> to **Climb** the **Holy Mountain of God** and **Receive God's Ten Commandments** as *Moses Did* and to be **Transformed** from a **Worthless Human** into a **Divine Son of God** as the *Apostles Did*. By both "Mastering" the Jewish Temple (God's Word/law) and the Christian Church (Man's Faith), a **Person can Fulfill** both the **Corporal and Spiritual Works of Mercy** to **Become a Direct** *Reflection of Christ Himself*. This "Awesome Journey" from Nothing (law) to All (faith) has **Set God's Bar of Perfection** to its **Highest Level** so that a **Person can See that** the **More he Tries** to **Fulfill God's Law** (baby,) the *More he will Fail*; while the **More he Surrenders** to **Christ's Faith,** the *More he will Succeed*. We are being taught that the "Job of God's Law" is to Teach **God's Right** and **man's wrong** (lessons); while the "Job of Man's Faith" is to Teach **God's Good** from **man's evil** (blessings); and then **Combining** **These Two Teachings** through the *Creation of One's New Nature in Christ*. This "Concept of Teaching" Allows Us to See that the **Holy Mother's Obedience** (hopes) is to be **Blended** with the **Holy Father's Tough Love** (expectations) to **Fulfill** the **Birth** of *Mary's Son on Christmas* (flesh) and the **Death** of *God's Son on Easter* (spirit).

Recall that "God Wants to Become a Man (freedom/circumcision)" and "Man Wants to become God (power/baptism)." Yet, this Seemed to be **Totally Impossible** until the **Birth** and **Death of Jesus Christ** Who Opened the Door for *Everyone's Heart's Desire, One and All*. Now, we see that through this "Birth to Death Experience," the Whole Human Race can **Fulfill Its Heart's Desire** of having the **Challenges of a Baby** (baby farm), **Adventure of a Teenager** (divine school), the **Fun of Adults** (sonship training), and the **Happiness of a Wise Man** (freedom) as a *Free Gift from God*. It should now be clear that the "Jewish People of Death" were Destined to be **Crucified** on **God's Law of Obedience** to show **Them** that **Human Flesh was Evil** and could **Never be Worthy** of the *Presence of God in Heaven*. In contrast, the "Christian People of Life" Died to Self to be **Resurrected** by **Man's Faith of Love** to show the **Human Race** that **God's Spirit of Holiness** was Worthy of the *Presence of God in Heaven*. Unfortunately, "All Mother Mary's Babies" must have Their Innocence Slaughtered (crucifixion) on **God's Law of Obedience** at **Birth** to **Prepare Them** for **Their Agony of Defeat** (see limitations) and **Freely Admit** that *They are Wrong* and that *God is Right*. Through this "Moment" of Shame, Humiliation, and Disgrace, **Each Child of God** will **Learn** the **Lessons of Life** and become **Worthy** of the **Blessings of Life** to **Enter the Thrill of Victory** (see potential) as **He Strives** to **Die to Self** and **Enter** the Saintly World (divine school) of the *Holy Father*. Yes! We must have "Our Human Nature Changed" and "Our Spirits Made Holy" to become Worthy to **Enter God's Kingdom**, where **We can Take Our Sonship Training without Complaint** and become a *Blood Son before God*. Recall that the "Lord God Almighty" has Spent some **Seven Thousand Years** to **Simply Teach Mankind** the **Difference** between **God's Right** (Heaven/faith) and **man's wrong** (earth/law) which actually **Started** with the *Fall of Adam and Eve in the Garden*.

We see that the "Whole Creation" is Centered upon **God's Right** (law) and **man's wrong** (faith) and the **Lord God Almighty** has specially **Prepared** a **Seven-Thousand Year** Servanthood Period to *Teach His Child His Divine Truths*. We see that this was "Done Correctly" when the Lord Jesus Christ **Used His Own Life-Experiences** as a **Mystical Seal** (model) between **God's Birth** (1st seal) and **Man's Death**

(2nd seal). In this way, the "Lord Jesus Christ" <u>Transformed</u> **His Holy Flesh** (right to wrong) into the ***Bread of Life*** (crucible) and then **Transformed His Sacred Spirit** (wrong to right) into the ***Wine of Eternal Life*** (winepress). Through these "Two Mystical Forces (bread/wine)" of <u>Man-Made Creations</u> **Composed** of **Wheat** (birth) and **Grapes** (death), the **Lord Created** a **New Transpersonal Realm** to **Transform <u>Humanity</u>** into a ***New State of Divinity*** (born-again). In this symbolism, "Men Break Bread" at the <u>Beginning of the Meal</u> (purify host) to **Acknowledge** the **Blessings of Life** (babies) through the **Staff of Life** which brings **<u>Each Person</u>** *Nature's Nourishing **Bread of Life*** (flesh). In contrast, "Men Raise a Cup of Wine" at the <u>End of the Meal</u> (purify grave) to **Acknowledge that Death** will bring **New-life** as **They will Sup** with **<u>Their Creator Forevermore</u>** in ***His Kingdom of Glory*** (sons of God). In between the "Bread Blessing (flesh/crucible)" and "Cup Blessing (spirit/winepress)," <u>We See</u> that there is a **Lamb Blessing** (bone/freedom) as **All Eat Their Fill** of the **True Fruits of Life**, the **<u>Sweet Meat of the Choicest</u>** of *God's Blessings*.

Now, add the dimension that this "Holy Meal is the <u>Wedding Supper</u> of **God's Son, Jesus Christ** (divinity) to **His Bride,** the **Holy Christian Church** (humanity), as **They will Work Together** to ***Wash Away All Sin*** and ***Make God's Children Holy***. We see in this scenario that through the "Blessed Mother's Immaculate Womb (spirit)," <u>She Gives Birth</u> to **God's Law of Obedience** (perfect flaw) which has the **Power** to **Change One's Nature** from *Human to Divine*. Secondly, through the "Holy Church's Mystical Womb (flesh)," <u>She Gives Birth</u> to **Man's Faith in God's Love** (Gordian knot) which has the **Power** to **Wash Away Sin** and **Change** *Sinfulness into Holiness*. Unfortunately, a "Spirit Being Cannot Marry" a <u>Human Being</u> without some **Type of Intercessory Mechanism** to **Interpret** the **Actions of One to Another** of the **Joining Parties**, plus having the **<u>Appropriate Authority</u>** to ***Join Two Mystical Beings Together***. By coming to "Understand this Dilemma," a <u>Person can See the Need</u> for **God's Mystical Contradiction** of the **Perfect Flaw** (divinity/Christ) and the **Gordian Knot** (humanity/Jesus) which **<u>Seal</u> Man's Physical Life-force** (bread) within *God's Spiritual Life-force* (wine) to ***Make Them One Being*** (Married). The symbolism here indicates that when the "Bread, Lamb, and Wine" are <u>All Eaten</u> in a **Single Divine Meal** (feast), a **Person Becomes What he Eats,** thereby **Making him** into a **<u>Triune Nature</u>** of *Holy Bread* (flesh), *Sacred Lamb* (blood), and *Divine Wine* (bone). This implies that the "Human Race" is <u>Eating</u> **Man's Physical Nature** (earth), **God's Spiritual Nature** (Heaven), and the **God/Man Mystical Nature** (Kingdom) to **Transform** from **<u>Sin</u>** to *Righteousness*, from **<u>Evil</u>** to *Holiness,* and from **<u>Death</u>** to *Perfection*.

1. **Holy Bread** - <u>Flesh:</u> Physical Dimension…   Change from Sin to Righteousness (citizen)
2. **Sacred Lamb** - <u>Blood:</u> Spiritual Dimension…Change from Evil to Holiness (saint)
3. **Divine Wine** - <u>Bone:</u> Mystical Dimension…   Change from Death to Perfection (son)

This explanation "Reveals the Coming" of the <u>New Divine Brotherhood of Man</u> (truth) which will have the **Power and Authority** to **Unite** the **Flesh, Blood, and Bone of**

Man into **Oneness** with its *Savior, the Lord Jesus Christ* and *His Sainthood*. The purpose of the "Perfect Flaw (spirit)" as the Born-again Spirit of Man (wine) is to **Establish One Side of the Wedge** between **Life and Death Representing** *Divine Life* or *God Himself*. This position has been "Eternally Assigned" to the Virgin Mary (Jesus/son of man), while the **Other Side** will be **Comprised** of the **Gordian Knot** (paradox)" seen here as the *Holy Church* (Christ/Son of God). Notice that "Jesus" and "His Blessed Mother" are One United Force **Representing** *Mankind* (create babies), while "Christ" and "His Bride the Holy Church" are also One United Force **Representing** the *Interests of Divinity* (create saints). The significance here is that the "Virgin Mary Represents" Only One Person as **God's Wife** having the **Power** to **Hold-up One Complete Side** through **Her Mystical Bond** with *Her Son, Jesus* (destiny/son of man). In contrast, the "Holy Church" with All Its Saints (communion of saints) is **Responsible** to **Hold-up** the **Other Side** of the **Seal** through her Union with *her Husband Christ* (free will/Son of God). The idea here is for these "Two Groups (babies/saints) to Unite into Oneness through the **Establishment** of a **New Sacred Government** (second coming) which will have the **Ability to Widen** this **Mystical Gap** between *God's Life* and *Man's Death*. Through this "Mystical Gap," an Opening will be Created, thereby **Allowing Room** for the **Coming New Divine Home of God** (New Jerusalem) as **God** brings forth *His New Heaven and New Earth*. We can now see that "Jesus Christ's Death" on Mount Calvary was simply **Able to Put a Tiny Crack** in the **Armor of Death/Damnation** and then the **Undaunted Courage** and **Love** of **His Mother** would bring Her Army of Babies to *Open the Way to Freedom* (new body/eternal life). Through this "Little Company of Mary (rosary)," a New Army of **Devoted Faithful Saints** would be **Raised Up** to **Come to the Aid** of **Its Savior** as **He Stands Against** All the Forces of *Sin, Evil, and Death by Himself*.

The following tabular information indicates the "Blessed Mother's Immaculate Womb (crucible)" has the Power to **Change Natures** from *Human to Divine*, while the "Holy Church's Mystical Womb (winepress)" has the Power to **Wash Away Sin** and **Change** *Sinfulness into Holiness*:

Blessed Mother's Immaculate Womb Changes Natures,
Holy Church's Mystical Womb Washes Away Sin
(Immaculate can change nature from human to divine
and Mystical can change sinful to holy)

1st Seal (life)	1. **Blessed Mother's Immaculate Womb** - Gives Birth to God's Law (spirit): Change Natures
	• God's Law of Obedience - Changes *Human to Divine*: Winepress of Death
	• Spirit Taught - God's Good from man's evil: Become Holy Saints in Heaven
	• Saints Made Worthy - Eternal Life: Receive Paradise in Heaven
Perfect Flaw (womb)	• Holy Father Married to Holy Mother - Remove Death to Gain New-life
	• Eat Flesh/Jesus (host) and Drink Blood/Christ (cup) - Feed God
	• Son of God - Creates Saints: Honors Father = See Potential
	• Christmas - God Wants to Become Man: Human God (birthright)

- Sainthood of Man - Priestly Altar: Sacrifices Abel
- Door Out is Death - Reject Lucifer   **Flesh and Blood**
- Door In is Life - Honor Holy Saints
  (crucible of fire - fulfill God's law of obedience:
  change nature = human to divine)

2nd Seal 2. **Holy Church's Mystical Womb** - Gives Birth to Man's Faith (flesh): Wash Away
(death) Sin
- Man's Faith of Love - Changes *Sinfulness to Holiness*: Crucible of Fire
- Flesh Taught - God's Right/man's wrong: Become Righteous Citizen on Earth
- Christians Made Worthy - New Body: Receive Heaven on Earth
Gordian • Jesus Christ Married to Holy Church - Remove Evil to Gain Holiness
Knot (tomb) • Eat Bread/wheat (host) and Wine/grapes (cup) - Feed Man
- Son of Man - Saves Sinners: Honors Mother = See Limitations
- Easter - Man Wants to Become God: Divine Man (inheritance)
- Brotherhood of Man - Kingly Throne: Sacrifice Cain
- Door Out is Evil - Reject Sinfulness   **Water and Spirit**
- Door In is Holiness - Honor Righteous Citizens
  (winepress of death - fulfill Man's faith in God's love:
  wash away sin = sinful to holy)

This illustration shows that "God's Spirit" is Trying to Unite with "Man's Flesh" to **Create a Union** between **God's Heaven** (sainthood) and **Man's Earth** (brother-hood) and bring forth *God's Kingdom of Glory*. Obviously, this "Divine Feat" is Accomplished by **Blending God's Law** (obedience) with **Man's Faith** (love) so that the **Lord God Almighty** can *Learn Man's Wrong and Evil* (logic), while the **Human Race** can *Learn God's Right and Good* (emotions). By "Exchanging" the Imperfection of Man with the Perfection of God, **God's Spirit** and **Man's Flesh** can be **United** which could **Only Occur** by **God Taking Human Form** in the *Person of Jesus Christ*. Unfortunately, this "Divine to Human Process" Requires God to **Enter** the **Immaculate Womb**, thereby **Creating a Portal** between **Two Worlds** which **Forced the Lord** to **Create Two Doors** or **Seals** to *Keep Evil/Death Out* and *Allow Life/Holiness In*. Recall that "Abel's Offering (rancher)" was a Lamb of Flesh and Blood, while "Cain's Offering (farmer)" was Wheat and Grapes (water/spirit). Both **Boys Asked God** to **Choose Their Offering** and to **Give Them** the *Lord's Divine Inheritance of the Earth*. To "Cain's Amazement," God Chose Abel's Lamb although he was **Eldest** and was **Entitled** to the **Divine Inheritance** as **Ruler of All he Surveyed**. This **Threw him** into a *Frenzy of Anger Against Abel*. The message here is that "Ultimately," Abel's Offering (flesh/blood) **Became** the **Jewish People of Death, Who** were **Destined to Become** the **Owners of Earth** through *God's Inheritance* or *God's Law of Obedience* (change nature). Secondly, "Cain's Offering (wheat/grapes)" Became the **Christian People of Life, Who** were **Called to Become** the **Owners of Heaven** through *God's Birthright* or *Man's Faith in God's Love* (wash away sin).

In this previous lesson, we see that "Adam's Son, Abel" was being <u>Taught the Difference</u> between **God's Right** and **man's wrong** as he brought forth **Ethics onto the Earth** to <u>Guide the Human Race</u> to its *New State of Righteousness* (new body). In like manner, we see that "Adam's Son, Cain" was being <u>Taught the Difference</u> between **God's Good** and **man's evil** as he brought forth **Morals onto the Earth** to **Guide the Human Race** to its *New State of Holiness* (eternal life). By combining both "Abel's Ethics" and "Cain's Morals," we can see the bases for <u>Man's Will</u> (genetic behavior) and <u>God's Will</u> (circumstantial behavior) as **They are Expressed** in the *Divine/Human Natures of Jesus Christ* (God/Man Kingdom). Now, we can see that the "Lord's Last Supper (table)" was a <u>Representation</u> of **Cain's Altar** (church) as **Man would Kill Its Own God** as **Portrayed** during the **Lord's Death on Calvary** (cross). In truth, it <u>Represented</u> **Abel's Altar** (world), where the **Lord God Almighty** inadvertently caused the **Earth's First** *Divine Murder*. Recall that when "Abel Offered the Lord" a luscious <u>Roasted Lamb</u> without either **Spot or Blemish,** he sincerely **Won Over God's Heart** to the point of being **Chosen Over his Brother Cain**, *Adam's First-born Heir*. This "Act of Showing Favoritism" toward <u>Adam's Good Son, Abel</u> (innocent blood) as opposed to <u>Favoring Adam's Bad Son, Cain</u> (guilty blood) who was the **Uncontested Heir to the Earth** and **All that was on It,** *Inflamed Cain's Hatred for Abel.* Unfortunately, "Cain did Not Know that Abel" was to become the <u>Heir to a New Born-again Planet Earth</u> (Christianity) which would be **Redeemed** by the **Divine Blood of a Lamb,** who would make **All Things New Again** in the *Sight of Men, Angels, and God*. We see that in "God's Grand Design," <u>He is Creating</u> the **People of Blood** (death) out of *Abraham's Circumcision* (Abel's altar/washed) to be **United** with the **People of Water** (new-life) out of *Christ's Baptism* (Cain's altar/changed).

The idea here is to see that the "Jews are to Represent the Bride," who must <u>Offer Her Virgin Body up to God</u> as *Her Dowry* (love/emotion/wash), while the "Christians are to Represent the Groom," who must <u>Offer His Divine Name Up to God</u> as *His Bride Price* (truth/intellect/change). This "Mystical Union" of the <u>Physical Nature</u> (surrendered humanity) of the **Jews** (washed in law) with the <u>Spiritual Nature</u> (sacrifice divinity) of the **Christians** (changed by faith) brings forth the *Rebirth of All Humanity*. The point here is that out of "Abel's Altar (Mount Calvary)" came the <u>Payment for Mankind's Dowry</u> (virgin body/changing) as **Mary's Son, Jesus,** willingly **Took-on All Sin** (scourging/save sinners) when **He was Sacrificed** as an *Unblemished Lamb* (flesh/blood) to become *Food for God Himself*. In this same regard, we see that out of "Cain's Altar (Last Supper)" came the <u>Payment for the Lord's Bride Price</u> (divine name/washing) as **God's Son, Christ,** willingly **Gave-up His Divinity** (crucifixion/create saints) when **He was Sacrificed** as *Bread/Wine* (wheat/grapes) to become *Food for Born-again Man*.

The following tabular information indicates that "Mankind" is <u>Putting Up Its Dowry</u> (love) through **Abel's Altar;** while the "Lord God Almighty" is <u>Putting Up Its Bride Price</u> (truth) through **Cain's Altar** so *that God and Man could become One Creation*:

Mankind's Dowry comes from Abel and Divinity's
Bride Price comes from Cain to Make Them One
(Abel's altar takes-on all sin, while Cain's
altar brings forth God's Divinity saving all men)

Love   1.   **Dowry** - <u>Bride Offers-up Her Virgin Body</u> (physical) ...Evil World

(emotions)   •   Abel's Altar - Mary's Son, Jesus Takes-on All Sin (save sinners): Confession

      •   Consume Sin - Remove Faults: Wash One's Physical Sin-nature (laws)

Humanity   •   Father Abraham Guarantees a Perfect Humanity - Genetic Behavior (free will)

(babies)   •   Last Supper - Table Altar: Learning Right and Wrong = Righteousness

      •   Abel Washes Man's Flesh (law) - Blessing of Forgiveness: *Gift of New Body*

                (Mount Calvary - Crucifixion:

       failure teaches lessons = save sinners/genetics/experience [man's word])

Truth   2.   **Bride Price** - <u>Groom Offers-up His Divine Name</u> (spiritual) ...Holy Church

(intellect)   •   Cain's Altar - God's Son, Christ Gives-up His Divinity (create saints):

           Communion

      •   Change Sin into Forgiven Sin - Gain Virtues: Change Spiritual Nature (vows)

Divinity   •   Father God Promises to Sacrifice His Son - Circumstantial Behavior (destiny)

(saints)   •   Mount Calvary - Cross Altar: Learn Good and Evil = Holiness

      •   Cain Changes Man's Spirit (faith) -New Nature: *Gift of Eternal Life*

                (Last Supper - Resurrection:

       success brings blessings = create saints/environment/ knowledge [sacred vows])

This illustration shows that "Mankind's Dowry (perfect humanity)" is <u>Created</u> when **Jesus Breaks Man's First-born <u>Curse</u>** by *Taking-on All Sin* (submission), while "God's Bride Price (sacrifice son)" is <u>Created</u> when **Christ Breaks <u>God's First-born Curse</u>** by *Giving-up His Divinity* (sacrifice). This "Mystical Union" between <u>Man's Flesh</u> (righteousness) and <u>God's Spirit</u> (holiness) could be **Accomplished**, **If Mankind's Faults** could be *Removed by Mary's Son* and then **Mankind could be Filled** with **God's Virtues** from the *Sacrifice of God's Son*. The idea here is to see that it is "Impossible" for <u>Man's Righteous Flesh</u> to become **Perfect** at the **Heavenly Level**. Thus, it is up to <u>Man's Holy Spirit</u> to become **Perfect** and then **Manifest Itself** into a *Born-again Spirit Body of Jesus Christ* (transfigured).

     We are witnessing that this actually occurs as "Jesus Removes Man's Faults (death)" and then "Christ Puts in Man's Virtues (new-life)" by <u>Allowing</u> the <u>Human Race</u> to **Eat His Flesh** and **Drink His Blood** in the *Form* of *Holy Bread* (flesh) and *Sacred Wine* (blood). The idea here is to see that "Man's Flesh" would have to be <u>Purified</u> through *Jesus' Water Baptism* (Cain's altar), while "Man's Spirit" would have to be <u>Purified</u> via *Christ's Spiritual Anointing* (Abel's altar). Using this logic, we see that "Circumcision" <u>Removes Man's Physical Faults</u> (sin) and "Baptism" <u>Removes Man's Spiritual Faults</u> (sin-nature). Then through the **Lord's Spiritual Anointing Processes** of the **Last Supper** (bread/wine) and **Mount Calvary** (flesh/blood), both **Man's Flesh and Spirit** would be *Filled with God's Virtues*.

Note that out of "Cain's Altar (new body)" comes both <u>Baptism</u> (purified spirit) and the <u>Last Supper</u> (Glorified Spirit); while out of "Abel's Altar (eternal life)" comes both <u>Circumcision</u> (purified flesh) and <u>Mount Calvary</u> (Transfigured Body), thereby **Transforming <u>Man's Old Nature</u>** from *Death to New-life*.

We now see that in "Man's Old Nature," the <u>Human Race</u> **Was Dead** (ignorance); while in "God's New Nature," the <u>Human Race</u> will be **Given New-life** (wisdom) which is **Mentioned** in **Jeremiah 31: 31-34**. It states that in the **<u>Old-times, Men Taught Men</u>**, but in the **New-times, God will Write His Law in Men's Hearts**. With this "Change" from the Old to the New, the **Human Race** will **Come to Know Its God** so that **All Might Come** to **Know, Love, and Serve Their Creator** through the <u>Indwelling</u> of *Jesus Christ* and the <u>Indwelling</u> of *God's Holy Spirit*. Notice the "Transformation of Man" as he <u>Journeys</u> from a **Manual Method** (word of mouth) **Using Natural Order** to a **New Automatic Method** (written in heart) **Using Supernatural Order** to **Speed Up** the **Process of** <u>Knowing</u> *God's Right from man's wrong*. The idea here is that "Adam and Eve Ate" from the <u>Tree of Knowledge</u> (flesh/blood) and were **Cursed** with *Seeking Their Own Free Will*, while "Jesus Christ (Calvary)" <u>Brought a New Tree of Life</u> (bread/wine) so that **Man could Eat** and be **Blessed** with *Seeking Only God's Will*. This "Transformation of Natures" <u>Sits at the Center</u> of the **Three Advents of Christ** as **He Comes** to *Save Sinners* (greed), *Change Them* into *Christians,* and then **Change Christians** into *Holy Saints* (generosity) in *Heaven*.

1st	1.	**Free Redemption for All Flesh** - <u>Free Gold Mine</u>…Earthly Blessing
Advent		• Good News - Free New Body: Righteous Citizen on Earth
		• Write Ten Commandments in Men's Minds - See Limitations
2nd	2.	**Earned Salvation for All Spirit** - <u>Dig Out Own Gold</u>…Heavenly Blessing
Advent		• Gospel Message - Earn Eternal Life: Holy Saint in Heaven
		• Write Two Commandments in Men's Hearts - See Potential
3rd	3.	**Bonus Rewards for Saved Souls** - <u>Share Gold with</u> Others….Kingdom Blessing
Advent		• Doctrinal Truths - Bonus of Own Kingdom: Perfect Son within Kingdom
		• Write One Commandment in Men's Souls - See Self-worth

We see that in the "Law of Circumcision (God is Man)," the <u>Jews</u> were **Called** to *Obey God's Law* (ten commandments/being saved), but in the "Law of Baptism (Man is God)," the <u>Christians</u> are **Called** to *Love Christ's Faith* (two commandments/being holy). Using this logic, "Jesus (lamb)" is <u>Taking-sin</u> to **Save Sinners** and *Conquer Death*; while "Christ (Jesus)" is <u>Giving-up His Divinity</u> (forgiveness) to **Create Saints** and bring *Holy Life*. Out of "Jesus' Sacrifice," <u>Mankind Receives</u> **Free Redemption** (good news) as **Sinners Only Need to Believe** in the **Name of Jesus** and **They can Come to <u>Submission</u>** and *Plunge Themselves* into **Death to Self** (selfishness). Secondly, out of "Christ's Sacrifice," <u>Mankind Receives</u> **Earned Salvation** (gospel message) as **Christians** can become **Holy Saints, If They Strive** to **Fulfill the Divine Will of God** and **<u>Prove Themselves</u>** before the *Judgment Seat of God's Throne* (justice). The point here is that on "Christ's 1st Advent (priest on donkey)," <u>He Came</u> to

Save Sinners via **Belief** by bringing the **Good News** that **All Men can Receive Free Redemption** (being saved)**,** thereby <u>**Making Them Worthy**</u> of a *New Body on Earth* (kingship). Secondly, on "Christ's 2nd Advent (thief in night)," <u>He Comes</u> to **Transform Sinners** into **Earthly Christians** via **Trust** by bringing the **Gospel Message** so that **Good Men** can **Receive Earned Salvation** (saving self), thereby <u>**Making Them Worthy**</u> of *Eternal Life in Heaven* (priesthood). Finally, on "Christ's 3rd Advent (judge on cloud)," <u>He Comes</u> to **Transform Christians** into **Heavenly Saints** via **Faith** by bringing the **Doctrinal Truths** so that **Holy Men** can **Receive Bonus Rewards** (saving others), thereby <u>**Making Them Worthy**</u> of *Their Own Royal Kingdom* (sonship). It is important to "Focus on Christ's" <u>2nd Advent</u> as the **Lord Comes** as a **Thief in the Night** to **Seal** (awaken) the **Righteous Men of Earth** (Christians) and to **Write God's Law** or <u>**Ten Commandments**</u> in *Their Hearts*.

The following tabular information indicates that in "Old Times," <u>Men Taught Men;</u> while in the "New Times," <u>God will Write His Law</u> in the **Hearts of All Men** so that the <u>**Human Race**</u> will *Come to Know, Love,* and **Serve Its Creator**:

In Old Times, Men Taught Men (Mosaic Covenant);
while in New Times, God will Write Law in Hearts
(changing old sin-nature into a new holy-nature
simply by writing God's law in all hearts)

Law	1.	**Man Teaches** - <u>Brother/Neighbors God's Law:</u> Mosaic Law…See Limitations
(obey)		• Old Sin-nature (circumcision) - Abel's Altar: Offer Flesh and Blood (being saved)
		• Eating Of - Tree of Knowledge: Treasure, Fame, and Fortune (human will) = Love Greed
		• Law of Circumcision - Obey God's Law: Change Nature from Human to Divine
		• Jesus – Takes-sin: Saving of Sinners = Death Conquers Sin
		• Free Redemption - Good News: Believe in Jesus = Baby Reward + New Body
Faith	2.	**God Writes Law** - <u>In Hearts of All Men:</u> New Covenant…See Potential
(love)		• New Holy-nature (baptism) - Cain's Altar: Offer Bread and Wine (being holy)
		• Eating of - Tree of Life: Treasure God's Divine Love (divine will) = Love Generosity
		• Faith of Baptism - Love God's Faith: Transform from Sinfulness into Holiness
		• Christ - Gives-up Divinity: Creation of Saints = New-life brings Holiness
		• Earned Salvation - Gospel Message: Faith in Christ = Adult Reward + Eternal Life

This illustration shows that "One of the Ways" that <u>Mankind</u> will **Know that It is Christ's Second Coming** (thief/judge) is that **God will Write His Law** within <u>**Every Man's Heart**</u> and he will <u>**Automatically Know**</u> *God's Right from man's wrong*. Note that at the "Present Time," the <u>Church is Busy</u> **Giving Bible Studies** to **Inform Confused Christians** of both the **Purpose** and **Mission of God** as **He** brings the <u>**Whole Human Race**</u> from *Death into New-life*. Obviously, a "Time is Coming" <u>When God's Law</u> or **Ten Commandments** will be **Written** within **Everyone's Minds** and **All will Automatically Know Their God** so that **Even the Least** in <u>**God's Kingdom**</u> can *Recognize God's Messiah When He Comes*. This means that during "Christ's 3rd Advent," <u>He will Come</u> to **Write God's 2nd Law** or **Two Commandments** in **Everyone's Hearts** and **All** will **Automatically** <u>**Know, Love, and Serve**</u> *Their Creator God*. Finally, during "God's Final Judgment," **He will Write His 3rd Law** or **One Commandment in Everyone's Souls** and **All** will **Automatically** become <u>**Sons of God,**</u> *Worthy of Freedom from All Laws*. Now, we see that by "Understanding" both the <u>Law of Circumcision</u> (blood/obey) and the <u>Faith of Baptism</u> (bloodless/love), a **Person can Comprehend God's** (Christ) coming *New Nature* (divine) and **Man's** (Jesus) coming *Holy Flesh* (purified). It is now clear that "We are All being Torn In two" by the <u>Demands of the Flesh</u> (Man/all work) as **Opposed** to the <u>Demands of the Spirit</u> (God/all prayer) which are **Fighting Over Every Moment** of <u>**Our Time,**</u> either *Needing More Work* (society) or *Needing More Prayer* (self). The question on the "Minds of Every Struggling Christian" is: when is it <u>My Turn</u> to become the **First in Line** so **that My Human Free Will** can <u>**Express Itself**</u> in *Mind, Heart, and Soul?* The answer is that "It will Never Come" <u>Unless a Lost Broken Sinner Comes</u> into a **Perfect Union** with the **Divine Love of God** through the **Blessings** (alliance) of both the *Immaculate* (human love) and *Sacred* (divine love) *Hearts of Jesus and Mary*.

The Paradox of God Creates Confusion
between the Dual Mission of Life

1. **God Wants to become Man** - God Travels through Life to become Man... Christmas (baby)
   • Jesus Faces Life - Flesh Fights Evil and Loses (human changed to divine)
   • Christ Faces Life - Spirit Surrenders to Death and Wins (purify host)
2. **Man Wants to become God** - Man Travels through Death to become God... Easter (adult)
   • Christ Faces Death - Flesh Surrenders to Death and Loses (purify grave)
   • Jesus Faces Death - Spirit Fights Evil and Wins (sinfulness changed to holiness)

We see that these "Two Mystical Hearts (alliance)" have been <u>Created to Transform</u> a **Lost Soul** from **Death to New-life** by **Making** a **Born-again Christian** into a <u>**Servant**</u> of both *Man's Righteousness* (Jesus/obedience) and *God's Holiness/peace* (Christ/love). This means that a "Person" must come to a <u>New State of Human Understanding</u> based on **His Ability** to **see himself** (sainthood), **his Society** (brotherhood), and **God** (sonship) **All** in the same **Divine Light** (truth) of <u>**Knowing** *God's*</u> *Right* and *Man's Wrong*. The depth of the "Born-again Awakening" <u>Only Comes</u> <u>When a Person has</u> **Purged his Very Soul** of **All Its Wicked Selfishness** to the point of **Desiring Nothing More** than to *Serve the Needs of Others* (servanthood). Obviously, this is exactly the "Opposite (serve self)" of the <u>Human Race Today</u> as **We Each Strives to become Great** in **Our Own Eyes** <u>No Matter What the Cost</u> in *Time, Money, Effort*, and **No Matter How Cruel** a *Person has to Become to Survive*. We see that to "Correct this Flaw" in <u>Man's Character,</u> **Jesus Christ** is **Tasked** to *Change Man's Nature* (spirit) and then to *Make him Holy* (flesh) in the *Eyes of God*. Note that "God's Son, Christ" is a <u>Heavenly Priest</u> (spirit/church), **Who Comes** to the **Earth** to **Transform the Jewish People** into *Righteous Citizens* (new body); while "Mary's Son, Jesus" is an <u>Earthly King</u> (flesh/world), **Who was Born** to the **Task** of **Transforming** the **Christian People** into *Holy Saints* (eternal life).

Remember, we have been "Forewarned" that <u>God is a Paradox</u> and **Everything in God's Creation** will **Exchange Places** as the **Lord Manifests** *Established Truth*, then *Flips Truths* (reverses), and finally, *blends into God's Divine Truth* (absolute). The point is that "If a Jew (flesh)" <u>Fulfills the Law</u> (wisdom), then he can become *Divine before God*; while "If a Christian (spirit)" <u>Fulfills his Faith</u> (love), then he can become *Holy before God*. This means that "God's Son, Christ (Son of God)" was <u>Sent to Face Death</u> (law) so **He could Defeat** *All the Curses in Life* (ignorance/cowardice/greed); while "Mary's Son, Jesus (son of man)" was <u>Born to Face Life</u> (faith) so **He** could bring forth *All the Blessings of Life* (wisdom/courage/generosity).

We can see that "If a Person" <u>Fulfills the Mosaic Law,</u> he can become **Divine** (Christ-like) and **Receive** the **Inheritance of Earth** (flesh) which is being **Blessed** with *Heaven on Earth* (presence of Man). In like manner, "If a Person" <u>Fulfills his Christian Faith,</u> he can become **Holy** (Jesus-like) and **Receive** the **Birthright of Heaven** (spirit) which is being **Blessed** with *Paradise in Heaven* (presence of God). We see that this "Whole Process" of <u>Receiving</u> a **New Nature** (change) from **God's Spirit** and <u>Receiving</u> a **Holy Flesh** (washed) from **Man's Flesh** involves **Mastering** both *God's Love* (society) and *Man's Love* (self). The point is that a "New Child of God" must <u>Enter</u> both his **New Mother's Love** (Virgin Mary) and **Heavenly Father's Love** to **Escape** the **Forces of Uncontrolled Selfishness** (fear/greed) as **They Destroy** both *Man's Mind* (intellect/wisdom) and *Man's Heart* (emotions/love). In short, "Christ (gives divinity)" has been <u>Called to Face Death</u> (love of God) to **Create** an *Eternal Free Man* (born-again); while "Jesus (take-on sin) has been <u>Called to Face Life</u> (love of Man) to **Create** an *Eternal Servant* (dying to self).

The following tabular information indicates the "Mystical Union" which has been <u>Divinely Created</u> to **Link** the **Sacred Heart of the Father** or *Love of God* (Christ/free man) with the **Immaculate Heart of the Mother** or *Love of Man* (Jesus/servant):

Law	1.	**Sacred Heart of Father** - <u>Loving God:</u> Christ = Gives Divinity…Life
(divine)	•	Father Makes Offering (selfishness) - Upon Son's Cross of Death: Face Death Agony
	•	Father's Expectations - Pass or Fail: Direct Will (see potential)
	•	God Overcomes Selfishness - Coward becomes Courageous (new heart)
Priestly	•	Christ Blesses Man with New Nature - Change from Human to Divine/obey
Love	•	God's Priest (love) - Becomes Man's King (wisdom) = Free Man

(face death)   Jewish People - God becomes Man (slow and deliberate)
- God's Birthright/baptism - Paradise in Heaven: Day of Prayer/blessed
- Sunday - Evaluate Spiritual Treasures: Count Souls
- Priest Faces Death - <u>Lives with God</u> (joy of heart)

(priest learns good from evil - becomes holy saint in Heaven: gets eternal life)

Faith   2. **Immaculate Heart of Mother** - <u>Loving Man:</u> Jesus = Takes-on Sin/holy...Death
(holy)
- Mother Makes Offering (selfishness) - Upon Her Sword of Sorrows: Face Death Agony
- Mother's Hopes - Graded on Curve: Permissive Will (see limitations)
- Man Overcomes Selfishness - Ignorance becomes Wisdom (new mind)

Kingly
- Jesus Blesses Man with Purified Soul - Wash Away Sin to be Holy/love

Love
- Man's Faith - ***Flesh becomes holy***: Free Intellect = Think for Self

(face life)
- Man's King (wisdom) - Becomes God's Priest (love) = Servant
- Christian People - Man becomes God (speed and accuracy)
- Man's Inheritance/circumcision - Heaven on Earth: Day of Work/lessons
- Saturday - Evaluate Physical Treasures: Count Children
- King Faces Life - <u>Lives with Self</u> (peace of mind)

(king learns right/wrong - becomes righteous citizen on Earth: gets new body)

This illustration shows that "Jesus has Taken Human Selfishness (demonic possession)" onto <u>His Cross of Death</u> so that it might **Experience the Depths** of **His Death Agony**, where it can be **Transformed into a New Creation** (divine unselfishness) before the ***Throne of God***. In this same way, we see the "Virgin Mary Taking Human Selfishness (curse of sin-nature)" upon <u>Her Sword of Sorrow</u> so that it might **Experience the Depths** of **Her Death Agony**, where it can be **Transformed into a New Creation** (human unselfishness) before the ***Throne of God***. The idea here is to see that "Jesus" was to <u>Take upon Himself</u> the **Physical Pain** of **Death Agony** as **He Plunged Himself** into the <u>Void of Infinite Darkness</u> to the point of being ***Separated from God***. In like manner, the "Virgin Mary" was to <u>Take upon Herself</u> the **Spiritual Pain** of **Death Agony**, as **She Plunged Herself** into the **Void of Human Despair** as **She Witnessed** the ***Death of Her Son***. This description of the "Unconscionable Torment" of <u>Jesus</u> as a **Human Being <u>Paying for the Sins/Transgressions of Man</u>** must be **Mirrored by Christ** as a **<u>Divine Being</u>** also **<u>Paying for the Sins/Transgressions of Man</u>**. In this way, the "Sacred Heart (Christ)" and "Immaculate Heart (Mary)" are **Created** through the **Sacred Union of Jesus** when **He Functions** as both the ***Death of Humanity*** (grave) and the ***New-life of Divinity*** (host). To understand this "Mystical Structure" where <u>Jesus/Mary were Responsible</u> for **Man's Repentance** and <u>Christ/Jesus were Responsible</u> for **God's Forgiveness,** we must **See the Need** to **Create an Interlink** between ***God and Man***. This "Interlink Structure" is clearly <u>God's Divine Love</u> in the **Sacred Heart** of the ***Eternal Father*** (king) in **Union** (marriage contract) with the "Human Love" in the **Immaculate Heart** of the ***Blessed Mother*** (servant). Out of this "Unconditional Union" of <u>Perfect Love,</u> both the **Sainthood of Christ** (love/mystical body) and the **Brotherhood of Jesus** (law/communion of saints) are **Created to Unite** ***God's Spirit*** (law) with ***Man's Flesh*** (faith).

This illustration shows that "Christ Represents" the Divine Law (divinity/obey) while "Jesus Represents" the Human Faith (holiness/love) and then **They are Reversed** in the fact that **Jesus** becomes the **King of the Jews** to **Take Unto Himself** the *Divine Love of God.* Conversely, "Christ" becomes the High Priest of Heaven which **Requires Him** to **Take Unto Himself** the **Divine Love of God** to bring forth a **Union** of **Jesus' Flesh** (love) and **Christ's Spirit** (law), thereby *Making Them One* (new nature). We are in effect "Witnessing the Creation" of Divine/Human Treasury of both **Heaven and Earth** which is **Manifested** out of a **Person's Obedience** to *God's Divine Law* (order) as **Opposed** to the **Depth of One's Human Love** (chaos) to the *Church's Faith.* The idea here is that the more a "Person Loves God," the more he can Violate God's Law until that **Mystical Point** (critical mass**)**, when the **Lord's Love** is actually **Set Aside** as it **No Longer Holds Power** Over a *Child's Love* (pure devotion). This allows us to see that we can "Come to God" with a Full Measure of Fleshly Obedience (order/law) **Coupled** with a Full Measure of Spiritual Love (chaos). The **Question** is which **One** will **Ingratiate Us More** in the *Sight of God*? The answer is that in the "Life-experience," we are Trying to Balance **Our Faithful Obedience** (law) **Against** our **Faithful Love** (love) so that each of **Our Lives** will **Take-on** a **State of Fleshly Holiness,** thereby **Making Us Worthy** of the *Presence of God*.

In truth, the "Parents of the World" would rather have the Unconditional Love of **Their Children** any day, as **Opposed** to the **Stony-Hearted Military Obedience** of **Strict Discipline** brought forth out of *God's Divine Justice*. This reveals that "Christ Came to Earth" with Orders from **His Eternal Father** to **Establish God's Divine Law on Earth** No Matter What that might *Take in Time, Money, or Effort* (crucifixion). In contrast, we see "Jesus being Raised" by His Blessed Mother to **Love the People** at **All Cost** (crucifixion) so **that They might be Saved** from **Their Eternal Curse of Death**, **If They Fail** to *Repent, Pray, or Do Good Works*. It is now clear that "Law Creates Selfishness (duty)," while the "Blessing of Love Creates Unselfishness (responsibility)" to Make All Things Perfect in the *Sight of God*. We see that the "Trick of Jesus Christ" was to Make Law and Love One in the **Union** of the **Sacred** and **Immaculate Hearts** (alliance) to bring forth *God's New Heaven and Man's New Earth* (Kingdom). In this way, "Man's Brotherhood (love)" and "God's Sainthood (law)" could Find a Common Ground upon which **They** could **Learn to Communicate** either through the *Father's Law/Love, Mothers Love/Law, or Jesus Christ's Brotherly Love*. Clearly, "All Three of These Unions" could be Perfectly Accomplished through the **Interface of Jesus** as **He Ties Together** both **God's Spirit** (Christ) and **Man's Flesh** (Mary) into a *Single Expression of Divine/Human Love* (Life's Horn of Plenty).

Via these "Triune Unions of God," the Human Race can bring forth its (1) *New Mind,* (2) *Heart,* and (3) *Soul* to **Reflect** its (1) *New Home,* (2) **Government,** and (3) *Church* as an **Expression** of (1) *Earth,* (2) *Heaven,* and (3) *God's Kingdom.* The idea here is to see that through these "Nine Steps of Development," the Human Race can both **Grow and Mature** into an **Adult Soul before God** by **Graduating** from the *Lord's Baby Farm, Divine School,* and then by *Taking His Sonship Training.* We can now "Justify" Christ's Three Advents as **He Comes to Judge** the **Fairmindedness, Ethical, and Moral Behavior** of **Sinful Men** to **Determine** Each Soul's Level of *Obedience,*

Love, and Sentience for Itself. In this way, "Jesus Christ" can <u>Determine</u> **If the Jews have Fulfilled God's Law of Obedience** and **Changed Their Natures** from **Human to Divine** (babies), as **They had been Told to Do** by *Their Creator God*. Secondly, "Jesus Christ" <u>Promises to Return</u> to **Determine If the Christians** have **Fulfilled Man's Faith of Love** and **Washed Away Their Sins** to **Change Their Sinfulness into Holiness** (teenagers), as **They had been Told** by *Their Messiah*. Finally, "Jesus Christ" <u>Promises to Return</u> a **Third Time** to **Determine If the Evil World** has **Fulfilled its God/Man Sentience Level** by **Learning to Think for Itself** (adults) to **Set All the Captives Free** as **They had been Told** *Three Thousand Years Earlier*.

The idea here is that "During the Lord's" <u>Three Advents,</u> **He will Come** to **Judge Mankind Three Times** 1) <u>First, on Humanity's Day of Atonement</u> (Calvary/table) - Pay Sin-debt; 2) <u>Secondly, on Man's Bema Judgment</u> to Evaluate the Sanctuary (altar) - Seal Saints; and 3) <u>Finally, during God's White Throne Judgment</u> of All Men (throne) - Separate Sheep/Goats. We see that the purpose of "Christ's Coming" on a <u>Donkey</u> as a **Humble Priest was** to **Build His Church of Forgiveness** when the **Lord Asked** the **Human Race to Repent** in <u>Total Submission</u> by *Denying Its Intellect, Abandoning Its Feelings, and Submitting Its Free Will.* Secondly, "Christ Comes" as a <u>Thief in the Night</u> or as a **King Building His New Government** on Earth. Then the **Lord Will Ask** the **Human Race to Become Holy** by *Defeating Their Own Sinnature, Worldly Temptations, and Demonic Possession.* Finally, "Christ Comes" as a <u>Just Judge on a Cloud</u> or as a **Son of God** to **Establish His New Divine Home on Earth.** Then the **Lord Will Ask** the **Human Race to Think for Itself** by <u>Mastering the Earth</u> as *Citizens,* <u>Mastering Heaven</u> as *Saints,* and <u>Mastering God's Kingdom</u> as *Sons of God.* Note that "Humanity Begins Life" as <u>Babies on Earth,</u> **Who Grow into Teenagers** by <u>Becoming Saints in Heaven,</u> and finally, **Traveling** to God's Kingdom as **Divine Thinking Adults,** *Who Know God's Right from man's wrong.* We see that the "Life-experience" is about <u>Attaining</u> **Righteous Flesh** (citizen), a **Holy Spirit** (saint), and finally <u>Creating</u> a **Perfect Soul** (son) to **Become Worthy** of the **Eternal Presence** of the *Lord God Almighty Himself.*

"Each of Christ's" <u>Three Advents</u> is outlined below to **Individually Explain** the **Scope** of **God's Judgment on Earth**, in **Heaven**, and within **His Coming Kingdom of Glory** as the **Human Race** *Grows and Matures into Adulthood.*

1. <u>1st Advent</u> - Jesus Christ Comes to Judge God's Free Gifts of Life: New Body
    When "Christ Came" as a <u>Priest on a Donkey,</u> **He Judged God's Babies** to **Determine Their Level of Righteousness** as **Good Citizens of Earth** (flesh), basically to **Inspect the Jewish People** as to the *Job They have Done in God's Name.* In short, the "Lord's 1st Visit" was to <u>Measure</u> **Jewish Obedience to God's Law** and **Their Ability to Change** from **Humans to Divine Beings** so that **They** might *Come to Know God* and *Master Living with Themselves* (self-control). The point is that "If a Person" can <u>Live with himself,</u> then he can **Master the Art** of being **Fair-minded Toward Others** through his **Personal Self-control** as he *Defeats his Ignorance* by *Striving for Wisdom* (degrees). "Out of this Wisdom," a <u>Person</u> can **Change** his **Animal Nature** (worldliness) of **All Work** as a **Fool, Who Strives to Make Money** and **More**

Money until he is **Rich**, thereby <u>**Making himself**</u> a *Righteous Citizen before All*. The theme here is that "Through Wisdom," a <u>Person</u> can **Become** a **Real Fair-minded Righteous Citizen, Who** is truly **Self-aware** and **Sees** the **Meaning of Life** which is to <u>**Exist on Earth**</u> as a *Child of God*. By "Mastering Babyhood," a <u>Person</u> can become **Worthy** of <u>**God's Gifts in Life**</u> which is to have a *New Transfigured Body, Heaven on Earth,* and to *Forever Work* on *God's Earthly Baby Farm* (Blessed Mother). We now see that "All the Work (thank God/labor)" that a <u>Person has Done</u> in **Conceiving** and **Raising God's Babies** is to be **Evaluated** on **Every Sabbath** or **Saturday** which is **Called** the *Lord's Jewish Judgment Day* (counting new babies/circumcisions). It should now make sense that the "Earth" is <u>God's Baby Farm</u> and that the **Jews are In-charge** of **Going** forth to **Multiply** and to **Master All that They Survey** in **Every Facet** of the **Life-experience** to <u>**Honor**</u> the *Physical Creation of God*. We see that the "Best Way to Honor" <u>Earthly Life</u> is to **Logically Measure** (mind) the **Quantity** of **Mass Production** in **Loving Babies** as **They Come from Immaculate Wombs** to **Serve** the <u>**Human**</u> **Race** in *Building a Life of Righteousness*.

2.   <u>2nd Advent</u> - Jesus Christ Comes to Judge God's Fruits of Life: Eternal Life
     Upon the "Lord's 2nd Advent," <u>He will Come</u> as a **Thief in the Night** to **Judge God's Saints** to **Determine Their Level of Holiness** as **Holy Saints in Heaven** (spirit), basically to <u>**Inspect the Christian People**</u> as to the *Job They have Done in Christ's Name*. In short, the "Lord's 2nd Visit" is to <u>Measure</u> **Christian Love** via **Their Depth of Faith** and **Their Ability** to **Wash Away Their Sins** and become **Holy** so that <u>**They**</u> might *Come to Love God* and to *Master Living with Others* (community). The point here is that "If a Person" can <u>Live with Others,</u> then he can **Master the Art** of being **Ethical** by **Following Informal Rules** and **Formal Laws** to the <u>**Letter**</u> as he *Defeats his Cowardice* by *Striving for Courage* (honors). "Out of this Courage," a <u>Person</u> can **Change** his **Robot Nature** (religiosity) of **All Prayer** as a **Fool, Who Strives** to **Become a Self-proclaimed Canonized Saint** on **Earth**, thereby <u>**Making himself**</u> into a *Holy Saint in Everyone's Eyes, but God's*. The theme here is that "Through Courage," a <u>Person</u> can **Become** a **Real Ethical Holy Saint, Who is Conscious** of the **Purpose of Life** which is to **Serve** the **Needs of Others** to <u>**Attain Heaven**</u> as *a Future Saint of God*. By "Mastering the Teenage Years," a <u>Person</u> can become **Worthy** of <u>**God's Fruits in Life**</u> which is to have *Eternal Life, Paradise in Heaven,* and *Forever Work* in *God's Heavenly Divine School* (Saint Joseph). We now see that "All the Work (praise God/wealth)" that a <u>Person has Done</u> in **Converting Sinners** and **Creating God's Saints** is to be **Evaluated** on **Every Lord's Day** or **Sunday** (count saints) which is **Called** the **Christian Judgment Day** (counting new saints/baptisms). It should now make sense that "Heaven" is <u>God's Divine School</u> and that **Christians are In-charge** of **Going** forth to **Convert Sinners** (take-sin) and **Create Saints** (give divinity) in **Every Facet** of the **Christian Life** to <u>**Honor**</u> the *Spiritual Creation of God*. We see that the "Best Way to Honor" <u>Heavenly Life</u> is to **Emotionally Evaluate** (heart) the **Quality of Saints** as **They Come from Earth** to **Serve** in the <u>**Angelic Realm,**</u> where *They will Build an Eternal Life of Holiness*.

3. 3rd Advent - Jesus Christ Comes to Judge God's Treasures of Life

Upon the "Lord's 3rd Advent," **He will Come** as a **Just Judge on a Cloud** to **Judge God's Sons** to **Determine Their Level of Perfection** as **Perfect Sons** within **God's Kingdom** (soul), basically to **Inspect the Free Men of God** as to the *Job They have Done in God's/Man's Name*. In short, the "Lord's 3rd Visit" is to Measure **Sonship Sentience** via **Their Depth of Knowledge** and **Ability** to **Think for Themselves** so that **They** might *Come to Serve God* and to *Master Living with God* (friendship). The point here is that "If a Person" can Live with God, then he can **Master the Art** of being **Moral in All Things** through his **Devotion to God's Will** as he *Defeats his Greed* by *Striving for Generosity in All Things* (blessings). "Out of this Generosity," a Person can **Change** into a **Human Being** by **Balancing** his **Works and Prayers** into **Service to All** as he **Strives** to be a **Dutiful Son of God,** thereby being **Converted** into a *Reflection of Christ Himself.* The theme here is that "Through Generosity," a Person can **Become** a **Real Moral Son of God** (dutiful)**, Who is Sentient** of the **Value of Life** which is to **Become Happy** in **God's Friendship** to **Attain a Place** in *God's Kingdom*. By "Mastering Adulthood," a Person can become **Worthy of God's Treasures in Life** which is having *His Own Royal Kingdom, Living in God's Kingdom*, and *Forever Working* in *God's Royal Kingdom*, where he will *Train Future Sons* (Jesus Christ). We now see that "All the Work (worship God/life)" that a Person has Done in **Training Saints** and **Creating Sons of God** is to be **Evaluated Daily** or **Monday/Friday** which is **Called** the *General Judgment* (counting new sons/transformation). It should now make sense that the "Kingdom" is God's Sonship Training Program and that **Mankind is In-charge** of **Going** forth to **Educate Saints** and **Create Sons of God** in **Every Facet** of the **Sonship Lifestyle** to **Honor** the *Mystical Creation of God*. We see that the "Best Way to Honor" Kingdom Life is to **Instinctively Judge** (soul) the **Value of Sons of God** as **They Come from Heaven** to **Serve** in **God's Divine Home** by *Building a Life of Perfection*.

The following tabular information indicates that the "Coming of God's Son" to the Earth is **Centered** upon **Three Mystical Judgments** based on **Fulfilling** *God's Law* (God/obedience), *Man's Faith* (Man/love), and *Learning to Think for Oneself* (God/Man knowing):

God's Three Judgments on Babies, Saints, and Sons
to Create New Heaven, New Earth, and Kingdom
(fulfill God's law of obedience, Man's faith of love,
and God's/Man's mind of knowing to be perfect)

——————God's Day of Atonement - Judge Jewish People——————

1st	1.	**Judgment of Babies** - Fulfill God's Law of Obedience…Change Nature
Advent		• Change Animal Nature/world - All Work: Become *Fair-minded* Citizens
(priest)		(flesh)
		• Obey God's Ten Commandments - Five for Sainthood/Five for Brotherhood

	•	Righteous Citizen (33%) - Empty Human Nature: Mind being Saved
	•	Deny Intellect - Ignorance to Wisdom
God's	•	Holy Citizen (67%) - Fill with Divine Nature: Heart being Saved
Gift	•	Abandon Feelings - Cowardice to Courage
New Body	•	Perfect Citizen (100%) - Human/Divine are One: Soul being Saved
(see God)	•	Submit Free Will - Greed to Generosity
	•	***Count Babies on Sabbath***/Sat. - Measure Growing Family: Physical Creation
	•	Mind Measures Quantity - Volume of Babies Created: Live by Logic
	•	Being Saved - Free Redemption: Good News Circumcises in Blood via Holy Word
	•	Worthy of Heaven on Earth - Receiving a New Transfigured Body

(earth - God's baby farm: teaching God's right from man's wrong to children to bring growth)

──────────God's Bema Judgment - Judge Christian Sanctuary──────────

2nd	2.	**Judgment of Saints** - <u>Fulfill Man's Faith of Love</u>...Wash Away Sin
Advent	•	Change Robot Nature/church - All Prayer: Become ***Ethical*** Saint (spirit)
(thief)	•	Obey God's Two Commandments - One for Sainthood/One for Brotherhood
	•	Righteous Saint (33%) - Wash Sin-nature: Saving Home
	•	Remove Sin-nature - Gain Righteous Nature
God's	•	Holy Saint (67%) - Wash Worldly Temptations: Saving Government
Fruits	•	Perfect Saint (100%) - Wash Demonic Possession: Saving Church
Eternal	•	Remove Demonic Possession - Gain Perfect Nature
life	•	***Count Saints on Lord's Day***/Sun. - Evaluate Sainthood: Spiritual Creation
(see/hear God)	•	Heart Evaluates Quality - Perfection of Saints: Live by Emotions
	•	Save Self - Earn Salvation: Gospel Message Baptizes in Water via Sacred Blood
	•	Worthy of Paradise in Heaven - Receiving Blessing of Eternal Life

(Heaven - God's divine school: teaching God's good/man's evil to teenagers to bring maturity)

──────────God's White Throne Judgment - Judge Entire World──────────

3rd	3.	**Judgment of Sons** - <u>Fulfill God/Man Sentience Level</u>...Set Captives Free
Advent	•	Change Human Nature/God - All Service: Become ***Moral*** Son (soul)
(judge)	•	Obey One Commandment - 1/2 Sainthood/1/2 Brotherhood
	•	Righteous Son (33%) - Saving One Soul: Saving Earth
	•	Remove Sin - Gain Peace of Mind
God's	•	Holy Son (67%) - Saving Few Souls: Saving Heaven
Treasure	•	Remove Evil - Gain Joy of the Heart
Royal	•	Perfect Son (100%) - Saving All Souls: Saving Kingdom
Kingdom	•	Remove Death - Gain Happiness of the Soul
(see/hear/speak)	•	***Count Sons Daily*** (M-F) - Judge Sonship Training Program: Mystical Creation
	•	Soul Judges Value - Sons' Value to Lord God Almighty: Live by Instincts
	•	Save Others - Bonus Reward: Doctrinal Truths Transform Spirit via Divine Death

- Worthy of God's Kingdom of Glory - Receiving Own Royal Kingdom (Kingdom – God's sonship training: teaches God's Will/man's will to adults to bring freedom)

This illustration shows that during "Christ's 1st Advent (33%/see God)," He came to **Wash Out Man's Mind** (circumcision/blood) with **God's Holy Word** (good news) to bring **Free Redemption** (being saved) to a *Dead World* (remove ignorance). Secondly, during "Christ's 2nd Advent (67%/see and hear God)," He Will Come to **Wash Out Man's Heart** (baptism/water) with **His Own Sacred Blood** (gospel message) to bring **Earned Salvation** (saving self) to an *Awakening World* (remove cowardice). Finally, during "Christ's 3rd Advent (100%/see, hear, and speak)," He Will Come to **Wash Out Man's Soul** (transformation/spirit) with **His Divine Death** (doctrinal truths) to bring **Bonus** Rewards (saving others) to a *New Mature Adult World* (remove greed). Through this "Growth and Maturity Concept," God, Angels, and Men **Hope to Forever Establish** a **Triune Level Educational System** as **Babies** are **Challenged** on *Earth*, **Teenagers** **Experience Adventure** in **Heaven**, and **Adults** have a **Lot of Fun** within *God's Kingdom*. This means that "Babies will be Raised" via Their Challenges (God's friend), "Teenagers will be Matured" via Their Great Adventures (God's companion), and "Adults will Learn to Think" while having Lots of Rollicking Fun with **God** (oneness with God). We call this "Treasure Chest" of God's Challenges, Adventures, and Rollicking Fun the **Lord's Horn of Plenty** as it will **Forever Pour** forth the **Infinite Love of God** upon **His most Beloved Children** *Pressed-down, Shaken Together, and Overflowing*. We see that this "Mystical Horn of Plenty" is based on God's Gifts (new body/see), Fruits (eternal life/see and hear), and Treasures (royal kingdom/see, hear, and speak) which can be **Obtained** by a **Sinner** (blind), **Christian** (see), **Saint** (hear), and/or **Son** through *One's Repentance, Prayers, Works,* or the *Saving of Souls*. Recall that the "Bible Speaks" of Five **Mystical Trees of Redemption** which are the *Tree of Knowledge* (evil fruit/knowledge), *Olive Tree* (Jews/self-aware), *Fig Tree* (Christians/conscious), *Palm Tree* (saints), and finally, the *Tree of Life* (sons/sentient). Through these "Five Trees," Creation is Established to **Convert** the **Minds, Hearts, Souls, Life-forces, and Natures** of **Defiled Men, Who have Eaten** from the **Tree of Knowledge** and have **Fallen** into *Eternal Damnation* (hell).

God's Five Trees of Growth and Maturity
(5 trees represent five dimensions of life: 1) physical,
2) spiritual, 3) mystical, 4) divine, and 5) God)

1. **Tree of Knowledge** - Conversion of Sinners…..See God
2. **Olive Tree** - Jewish Obedience to God's Law…See/Hear God
3. **Fig Tree** - Christian Devotion to Christ's Faith…See/Hear/Speak to God
4. **Palm Tree** - Saint's Sacrifice in Saving Others…See/Hear/Speak/Touch God
5. **Tree of Life** - Son of God Thinks for himself…See/Hear/Speak/Touch and Sup with God

We see that "Each of These Trees" <u>Represents One</u> of **God's Five Dimensions** of **His Physical, Spiritual, Mystical, Divine, and Godly States of Existence** which have been **Designed** to bring **Growth and Maturity** to <u>Each of God's</u> *Newly Created Children Forever*. To "Comprehend" <u>God's Defilement</u> to <u>Purification System,</u> we can **Imagine** a **Sinner Struggling** through the **World of Evil** to **Learn the Lessons of Life,** then **Surrendering** to **Christ's Church** to **Wash Away his Sin** (confession), and then <u>**Returning to the World**</u> to *Learn More Lessons.* The "Lord's Children" <u>Come into Existence</u> as <u>**Sinners,**</u> **Grow** into **Christians,** to **Saints,** to **Sons,** and finally, become **Respected Men of Honor** (free) before **God, All** through the <u>**Works**</u> of *God's Law* (Moses) and *Man's Faith* (Christ).

We see that "Moses and Christ" <u>Had Volunteered</u> to **Work to Convert God's Chaos** into **Order** as **Moses and Christ Strived** to **Each Save Their People Using Two Totally Different** *Approaches for Problem Solving.* In this "Great Parallel" between the <u>Life of Moses</u> (Jewish Son) and the <u>Life of Christ</u> (God's Son), **They** both **Promised Their People** an **Eternal Promised Land** *Leading* to *Eternal Happiness* (earth/Heaven). To "Make this Comparison," a <u>Person</u> must note **that Moses** was the **Pharaoh's Son** (prince) for **40 Years in Egypt,** while **Christ** was **God's Son** (prince) **Always in Heaven** and <u>**They**</u> were both *Willing to Save Their People.* The theme here is that both "Moses" and "Christ" Started Their Lives in **Their Father's Promised Land** and then **Came** to the **Desert of Death** to **Help Their Lost People** <u>**Find Their Way**</u> to the *Promised Land of God.* Secondly, "Moses" and "Christ" were then <u>Asked by God</u> to **Willingly Sacrifice Themselves** to **Save Their People** by **Going** into the **Heart of Evil** to <u>**Fight the Forces**</u> of *Ignorance, Cowardice, Greed, and Selfishness.* Thirdly, "Moses" and "Christ" then <u>Took Their People</u> to the **Desert of Death** to **Purify Their Lives** by **Removing Their Ignorance, Cowardice, Greed, and Selfishness** so that **They can Become** <u>**Worthy of Their**</u> *Promised Land of Milk* (kindness) and *Honey* (love). Finally, "Moses" and "Christ" <u>Took Their People</u> to the **Promised Land** by **Passing Them Through Death** into a **New Born-again Life** to **Set Them Free** from **Sin, Evil, Death, and Damnation** so <u>that They</u> can truly *Master All They Survey.* This "Great Journey" from <u>Nothing to All</u> **Defines God's Plan of Redemption** which **Transforms Lost Creations** from **Death to New-life** by <u>**Passing Them**</u> through *God's Baby Farm, Divine School, and Sonship Training Program.*

The idea here is that to "Break" the <u>Codes of the Bible,</u> a **Person** must **See Every Bible Story** as **Jesus Christ Himself** and that **Every Word in the Bible** is <u>**God Talking to His Son**</u> to *Give Him His Plan of Redemption.* We see that "Jesus Christ" has <u>Come to Explain</u> **His Journey** from *Paradise* to *Save Slaves* (sinners), to the *Desert of Purification* (Christians) into the *Promised Land* (saints), and then to finally be *Set Free* (Son/think for self). The "Job of Humanity" now is to <u>Teach Its Children</u> the **Journey of Christ** as **He Travels** from the **Nothing of Man** to that **All of God** by <u>**Passing**</u> through *His Scourging, Crucifixion, Death in Tomb, Resurrection, and Ascension into Heaven.* Recall that "God Wants to Become Man" and that "Man Wants to Become God." Thus, just as <u>Moses</u> brought **Passover** (Christmas) and the **Day of Atonement** (Easter), <u>Jesus Christ</u> has brought **Christmas** so that *God can Become Man* and <u>**Easter**</u> so that *Man can Become God.* This "Theme" of <u>Every Story in the</u>

Bible being **Jesus Christ**, brings us to **See** the **Purpose** of **Christ's Ministry on Earth** as it **Fulfills Everything** and then it **Transforms** *Death into Eternal Life*.

The following tabular information indicates that "Moses" and "Christ" have had Parallel Lives (prince/shepherd/prophet/judge) as **They** become the **Redeemers** of the *Jewish People* and the **Redeemers** of the *Christian People*:

Parallel Lives of Moses and Christ as They Come
to Save Their People from Captivity/Death
(both are Princes, Shepherds, Prophets,
and Sons of God as They bring Their People to Safety)

Egypt   1. **Moses is a Prince** - Pharaoh's Son: 40 Years of Pleasure
(God)   • Christ is a Prince - God's Son: Eternal Happiness
    • Moses and Christ Living in Promised Land
    • Sinner - Converted into a Christian

Fields   2. **Moses is a Shepherd** - Tending Flocks: 40 Years of Good Life
(1st Advent)   • Moses and Christ Promise People Promised Land
    • Christian - Change Nature: Human to Divine
    • Christ is a Good Shepherd: Tending to Lost Man: 3 Years of Fun
(Moses promises Heaven on Earth, while Christ promises Paradise in Heaven)

Desert   3. **Moses is Prophet of God** - Saving Jewish Slaves: 40 Years of Hard-work
(2nd Advent)   • Christ is a Prophet of God - Saving Lost Man: 1,000 Years of Hard-work
    • Moses and Christ Prepare the Promised Land of Milk and Honey
    • Saint - Wash Away Sin: Sinfulness to Holiness

Heaven   4. **Moses is Judge in God's Court** - Judging Tribes of Israel (earth): Eternity
(3rd Advent)   • Christ Sits at Right Hand of God - Judging Apostles of God (Heaven): Eternity
    • Moses and Christ Take People to Promised Land of Eternal Happiness
    • Son of God - Transformed: Servant to Free Man

This illustration shows that "Moses" Took the Jews to the **Desert** to **Change Their Natures** from *Slaves to Free Men*, then into the **Promised Land** to **Wash Away Their Sins** to **Change Them** from *Sinners* (animals) into *Righteous Citizens of Israel* (humans). We see this "Same Parallel" with Jesus Christ as **He Takes** the **Slaves of Sin** (sinner) into the **Desert of Conversion** (Christian) to **Prepare Them** for *God's Promised Land* (saint) in **Heaven**. In this "Parallel Comparison," Moses Did **Everything by Hard-work**, while Jesus Christ **Uses God's Miracle-working Power** to **Get Things Done** as **They both Strive** to *Save Their People* (babies). The idea here is that "Earth and Man" are Forced to Use **Physical Hard-work** to *Save Its People* (Jews/citizens/new body), while "Heaven and God" are Using **Spiritual Miracle-working Power** to *Save Its People* (Christian/saints/eternal life). These "Opposing

Approaches," in Saving the **Flesh on Earth** (citizens) as **Compared** to Saving the **Spirits in Heaven** (saints), **Define the Ministries** of *Moses* (law) *and Jesus Christ* (faith). This means that "Moses is Saving his People via God's **Law of Obedience** to *Change Natures/Wash Sin*, just as "Christ" is Saving His People via **Man's Faith of Love** to *Change Natures/Wash Sin*. Note "Moses is Using" his Mosaic Tabernacle to **Fulfill God's Law** (take-sin), while "Christ is Using" His Holy Church to **Fulfill Man's Faith** (give divinity). The **Trick is to Merge God's Law** and **Man's Faith** into **Oneness** through a *Union of Spirit* (spirit baptism) and *Flesh* (water baptism).

We can now see the "Dual Roles" of Moses and Christ **Represent a Marriage** between **God and Man** as **They Come to the Altar** to **Exchange Vows**, where **God Gives** *His Name* (law) or *Free Birthright* and **Man Gives** *his Virginity* (faith) or *Earned Inheritance*. In this way, "We are Able to See" the Combination of **Man's Inheritance** (free gift) as it **Relates** to **Man's Birthright** (earned) which in **Effect** means that a **Person must Merge** both his *Miracles* (free) with *His Hard-works* (earned). Yes! The "Jewish People" did have a Fantastic Miracle in being **Saved** from **Four Hundred Years** of Bondage (slavery), yet, this **Blessing** (birthright) was **Coupled** with **Forty Years of Hard-work** (desert) to make them **Worthy of Their** *Promised Land of Milk and Honey*. The idea here is that "We have All been Given" a Miraculous Birth (birthright/free) of **Human Existence** (physical/slavery), yet, **We are Each Required** (hard-work/earn) to **Transform** this **First Miracle** of **Good Fortune** into a *Great Inheritance of Eternal Life*. To emphasize this point, "We See that Jesus" was casually Walking Around Israel **Healing** the **Sick, Casting Out Demons,** and **Forgiving Sins,** yet, when it **Came Time to Redeem All Mankind, Why Didn't He** simply **Do the Same Thing**, just **Wave His Divine Hand** and *Poof! It was Done* (Calvary)? No! When it "Came Time" to actually Accomplish the Great Work of **Human Physical Redemption,** the **Lord** suddenly became a **Common Laborer Cast** into the **Desert of Death** (3,000 years work) to **Shoulder the Full Burden** of the Task of Man's Salvation through *Divine Forgiveness*. Obviously, this was a "Demonstration" of a Combination of **God's Wizardry** (spirit) **Mixed** with **His Dedication** (flesh) to **Get the Job Done** in the **Flesh** by the *Powers of Old Fashioned Hard-work* (Calvary).

Free   1.   **Save the World** – Hard-work: Flesh Fights Evil unto Death…
              See Limitations
              Purify Grave - Evil Bears Good Fruit (flesh)
Earned 2.   **Save the Church** - Miracles: Spirit Surrenders to Death…See
              Potential
              Purify Host - Holiness Bears Good Fruit (spirit)

This "Journey of Hard-work" from Nothing to All started when **Adam and Eve Began Life** by **Eating from a Tree of Knowledge** so **that They could become God** for **They Believed** that the **Serpent Lucifer** was **Telling Them the Truth** and *They* could *Soon be Righteous, Holy, and Perfect Like the Almighty Himself*. This means that with the "Coming of Moses" and the Great Olive Tree (Jews) or Mosaic Tabernacle, the **High Priest Aaron** could **Eat of the Sacrificial Lamb** and become **Holy before God** *One*

Day a Year (Day of Atonement). Next would "Come Jesus (1st advent)" bringing the Christian Fig Tree or **Holy Church** so **that Saint Peter** could **Eat Holy Bread** and **Drink Sacred Wine** and become **Holy before God** *Every Day* (mass). Next would "Come Christ (2nd advent) bringing the Saintly Palm Tree or Sacred Government so that **God's Chosen People** (living saints) could **Live in Holiness** *All the Time* (sacred seal). Then would "Come Jesus Christ (3rd advent) bringing the Son's Tree of Life or Divine Home (New Jerusalem) so that the **Whole Earth** (sons) could **Live in Divine Perfection**, as **Time would End** and **All would have Their Communion** in *God's Shekinah Glory/Beatific Vision* (divine flame). Through "Each of These" Five Stages of **Growth and Maturity**, the **Human Race** would **Enter** the **Divine Light of God's Truth, Law, Will, and Love** to be **Set Free from Its Darkness** and *Walk in the Light of Jesus Christ*. Via this "Great Journey," Jesus Christ can **Defeat Ignorance** and bring the **Human Race to Wisdom** so **that All Sinners** can become **Christians** when **They Leave Babyhood** (earth) and *Enter Born-again Life as Awakened Teenagers* (Heaven). Secondly, "Jesus Christ" Defeats Cowardice and **Gives Humanity Courage** so that **All Christians** can become **Saints** when **They Leave Their Teens** (Heaven) to *Enter the Mystical Life* as *Highly Trained Adults* (Kingdom). Finally, "Jesus Christ" Defeats Greed, **Giving Mankind Generosity** so **that All Saints** can become **Sons of God** when **They Leave Adulthood** (Kingdom) to be **Set Free** to *Govern Their Own Royal Kingdoms*.

Through this "Process" of Transforming the Flesh (growing) and Purifying the Spirit (maturing), **God, Angels, and Men** are **Able to Become One Creation** within the *Law, Faith, and Knowing of God*. Yes! The "Tree of Knowledge" Sets Man on his *Path of Evil*; the "Olive Tree" Sets Man on *God's Path of Righteousness*; the "Fig Tree" Sets Man on *Christ's Path of Holiness*; the "Palm Tree" Sets Man on *Jesus Christ's Path of Perfection;* and finally, the "Tree of Life" will Set Man on *God's Path of Freedom Forever*.

The following tabular information indicates that "God's Creation" has been **Founded upon Five Trees:** 1) Tree of Knowledge - Sinner: Ignorance becomes Wisdom, 2) Olive Tree - Christian: Cowardice becomes Courage, 3) Fig Tree - Saints: Greed becomes Generosity, 4) Palm Tree - Sons: Selfishness becomes Unselfishness, and 5) Tree of Life - Free Man: Hate becomes Love:

Five Trees: 1) Tree of Knowledge, 2) Olive Tree, 3) Fig Tree, 4) Palm Tree and 5) Tree of Life
(trees convert mind, heart, soul, life-force,
and nature from death to new-life in Christ)

Mind	1. **Tree of Knowledge** - Sinner/Man's evil fruit: Earthly Life…Knowledge
(temple)	• Man's Works are Cursed - Moses: Saves Slaves of Egypt = Cursed Fruit
	• Promised Land - Man Thinks he's God: Facing Challenge
	• Guilt - Guilty Conscience: See Limitations **Lucifer's Test**
Wisdom	• Meaning of Life - Existence: Obey the Law
	• Baby Level - Baby Farm: Elementary School = Law

- Ignorance - Steal: Defiance = Blasphemy + Excommunicated from Temple/silent anger
- Learn Right from Wrong - Become Righteous Citizen of Earth: Receive **New Body**
- Physical Dimension/earth - Abrahamic Covenant: Isaac's Sacrifice = Circumcision
- Father's Table/parent - Home: Father's Blessing
- Covenant - Being Saved: Changing Nature = Human to Divine

Heart
(church)

2. **Olive Tree** - Christian/righteous fruit: Eternal Earthly Life…Self-awareness
   - Earthly Works become Righteous - 1st Advent: Priest on a Donkey = Blessed Fruit
   - Heaven on Earth - God becomes Man: Living Adventure
   - Repentance - Confession: See Potential   **God's Judgment**

Courage
   - Purpose of Life - Service: Love the Faith
   - Teenage Level - Divine School: High School = Faith
   - Cowardice - Hiding: Deception = Sorcery + Outcast from One's People/vocal rage
   - Learn Good from Evil - Become Holy Saint in Heaven: Receive **Eternal Life**
   - Spiritual Dimension/Heaven - 1st Advent: Priest on Donkey = Water Baptism
   - Son's Throne/king - Government: Son's Command
   - Passover - Saving Self: Washing Away Sin = Becoming Holy

Soul
(government)

3. **Fig Tree** - Saint/holy fruit: Heavenly Life…Consciousness
   - Heavenly Works become Holy - 2nd Advent: Thief in Night = Holy Fruit
   - Paradise in Heaven - Man becomes God: Having Fun
   - Prayers - Act of Contrition: See Self-worth   **Self-evaluation**

Generosity
   - Value of Life - Happiness: Master Knowing
   - Adult Level - Sonship Training: College = Knowing
   - Greed - Lying to God: Deceit = Sedition + Banished from Earth/striking wrath
   - Learn God's Will/man's will - Become Perfect Son in Kingdom: Receive **Royal Kingdom**
   - Mystical Dimension/Kingdom - 2nd Advent: Thief in Night = Blood Baptism
   - Spirit's Altar/priest - Church: Spirit's Anointing
   - Holy Mass - Saving Others: Transfigured Body = Celestial Court

Life-force
(home)

4. **Palm Tree** - Son/perfect fruit: Kingdom Life…Sentience
   - Kingdom's Works become Perfect - 3rd Advent: Judge on Cloud = Sacred Fruit
   - Kingdom of Glory - God/Man become One: Becoming Happy

Unselfishness	• Works - Perform Penance: See Society's Worthiness **Thinking for Self**
	• Treasures of Life - Fulfillment: Seeing Face of God
	• Wise Man Level - Eternal Career: Professional Expert
	• <u>Selfishness</u> - Cursed by God: Death = Sacrilege + Forsaken by God/ murderous attack
	• Learn God's Reality/man's illusion - Being Set Free: Receive *Freedom*
	• Divine Dimension/God - 3rd Advent: Judge on Cloud = Spirit Baptism
	• Trinity's Palace/son - Kingdom: Trinity's Sanctification
	• New Jerusalem - Saving God: Glorified Spirit = Temple Court

Nature (kingdom)	5. **Tree of Life** - <u>Free Man</u>/God's fruit: Divine Life…All Knowing
	• God's Works are Blessed - Final Judgment: White Throne = Divine Fruit
	• Freedom from God - Flesh/Spirit/Soul/Life-force are One: Finding Fun
	• Saving Souls - Retribution: See God's Worthiness **Imagination**
Loving	• Essence of Life - Saving God: God Sees Man's Face
	• Free Man Level - Eternal Retirement: Master of All Things
	• <u>Corruption</u> - Enemy of God: Damned = Defiled + Cast into Outer Darkness/rot in grave
	• Learn God's Truth/man's lie - Being Made One with God: Receive *Divinity*
	• Godly Dimension/God/Man - Final Judgment: White Throne = Divine Baptism
	• God's Nation/God - God: Almighty's Consecration
	• God/Man Worship - Universal Salvation: Mystical Soul = Royal Court

This illustration shows that as "Mankind Travels" <u>Along Its Path of Life,</u> it is **Forced to Face** *Lucifer's Test* (see limitations), *God's Judgment* (see potential), *Self-evaluation* (see self-worth), and *Divine Freedom* (see all things). By "Facing These Challenges," a <u>Person can Pass</u> through the **Promised Land, Heaven on Earth, Paradise in Heaven, God's Kingdom of Glory,** and **Reach** his **<u>Own Divine Freedom</u>** as he *Learns to Think for himself* (imagination). This means "Each of God's Children" must <u>Learn **God's Right from man's wrong, God's Good from man's evil, God's Will from man's will, God's Reality from man's illusion**</u> and **God's Truth from man's lie** to *Master Righteousness, Holiness, Perfection and Freedom* (thinking). Obviously, the "Earth" has been <u>Created</u> to **Raise Righteous Babies** in *Large Numbers Forever*, then **Send Them to Heaven** to be *Given Eternal Lives*, then be **Sent to God's Kingdom** to *Receive Their Own Kingdoms*, thereby **Increasing** the **<u>Lord's Massive Harvest</u>** of *Uncountable Humans*. This is the "Eternal Product (citizens/saints/sons)" of <u>God's Manufacturing Plant</u> as **He Desires Mass Production** of **Saintly Sons of God** (human bodies), **Who Seek Servanthood** in God's Creation to **Perform** the **Massive Amounts of Work Needed to Create** an *Eternal Kingdom of Glory*. Yes! "Right and Wrong" <u>Create Righteous Citizens on Earth,</u> **Who are Worthy** of **<u>New Bodies</u>** and *Heaven on Earth*; while "Good and Evil" <u>Create Holy Saints in Heaven,</u> **Who are Worthy** of **Eternal Lives** in

Paradise with God. "Learning God's Will" from "Man's Will" <u>Creates Perfect Sons of God within God's Kingdom,</u> **Who are Worthy** of **Their Own Royal Kingdoms** to be **Shared** with the *Lord God Almighty Himself*. Finally, by "Learning God's Reality" from "Man's Illusion," <u>Free Men</u> (God's friends) are <u>Created, Who can Think for Themselves,</u> thereby **Making Them Capable** of **Striking Out** for the *Unknown Territories of Life* to **Harvest the Eternal Fruits** of *God's Glory* and *Man's Honor*.

The "Lord God Almighty" has <u>Designed a Perfect Creation,</u> where **All of the Aspects** of **Challenge** (earth/baby), **Adventure** (Heaven/teenager), **Fun** (Kingdom/adults), and **Eternal Happiness** (Freedom/wise men) have been **Included** in the *God/Man Life-experience*. Recall that "Adam and Eve" had <u>Set the Stage</u> for **Facing Challenge** as **Eve Stole** (ignorance) the **Forbidden Fruit** in **Blasphemous Defiance of God**, which **Provoked His Silent Anger** (pain) and **She** was **<u>Excommunicated from the Lord's Temple</u>** in *Shame* (scourging). Secondly, "Adam" <u>Set the Stage</u> for **Facing Adventure** as **he Hid Behind a Fig Leaf** (coward) like a **Deceptive Sorcerer** (magic), which **Provoked God's Vocal Rage** (toil) and **Adam** was an **<u>Outcast from God's Garden</u>** in *Humiliation* (crucifixion). Thirdly, the "Serpent" <u>Set the Stage</u> for **Facing Fun** as he **Tricked Adam and Eve** into **Greed** causing **Them to Lie** to **Cover Their Sedition,** making **Them Deceitful Fools,** which **Provoked God's Striking Wrath** (death) and the **<u>Serpent was Banished</u>** from his *Privileged State* (dust) and **Adam and Eve** were *Cursed with Death* in *Disgrace* (tomb). Finally, "God Himself" <u>Sets the Stage</u> for **Eternal Happiness** as **He Accepts Blame** for **His Selfishness** in **Testing Adam's Loyalty** as **He Promises** to **<u>Share in Adam's and Eve's</u>** *Pain* (scourging), *Toil* (crucifixion), and *Death* (tomb).

The idea here is that "Babies" are <u>Challenged</u> by *Every Task*; yet, "Teenagers" <u>Think that</u> <u>Everything in Life</u> is just another *Great Adventure*; while "Adults" can <u>Turn Anything</u> into a *Game* (fun); and "Wise Men" are <u>Constantly</u> in *Search of Eternal Happiness*. This "Difference in One's" <u>Perception of Reality</u> **Makes the Difference** between **Fear of Pain, Death, and Damnation** and **<u>Converting Everything</u>** into the *Blessings and Fruits of Joyous Living* (rollicking fun). Yes! Growth and Maturity "Make All the Difference" in the <u>World</u> as **They Change One's Point of View** from a **Nightmare of Horror** into a **Beautiful Dream** of a **Happy Future, If a Person** will **Only Believe** in **God's Son, Jesus Christ** and **<u>Trust His</u> Promises** of a *Coming Blessing* of *Peace, Joy, and Happiness*.

Through "Jesus Christ," a <u>Person</u> can **Defeat Sin, Evil, Death, and Damnation** to **Become** a **Righteous Citizen, Holy Saint,** and finally, a **Perfect Son,** thereby **<u>Making him Worthy</u>** of a *New Body, Eternal Life, and his Own Royal Kingdom.* The theme here is that "Each of God's Children" must <u>Face Life's Challenges</u> and the **More his Soul can Display** the **Depth of his Courage** and the **Brilliance of his Wisdom,** the **<u>Higher he can Rise</u>** on *God's Ladder of Perfection* (33%/67%/100%). "God's Babies" are on <u>Earth</u> and **Live in a Baby Farm,** which is **Ruled by Lucifer's Tests** and **Requires Each** of God's Children to **Muster All his Courage** to **<u>Defeat</u>** his *Own Sin-nature* (forces of sin). Secondly, "God's Teenagers" are in <u>Heaven</u> (church) and **Live in a Divine School,** which is **Ruled by God's Judgment** and **Requires Each of God's Young People** to **Muster All his Courage** to **<u>Defeat</u>** *Worldly Temptations* (forces of evil). Finally, "God's Adults" are within God's Kingdom and are **Taking God's Sonship Training**, where **Each Person** is **Responsible** for his **Own Self-evaluation** by **Mustering his Courage** to **Defeat** *Demonic Possession* (forces of death). The "Lord God Almighty" is Telling Us that **Life is About Facing Challenges** (defeat sin), **Having Adventures** (defeat evil), and **Turning Everything** into **Rollicking Fun** (defeat death) to **Make Every Moment of Life Count,** truly *Living to the Fullest with Gusto*. The implication here is that the "More a Person" is Challenged and Tested, the **Greater the Level** of his **Performance**, which **Begins** at **33% Perfect** (baby), when **He** is **Called** to **Overcome his Ignorance** and *Strive to Obtain Wisdom* (new mind). Secondly, "If He" can Perform at the **67% Level of Perfection** (teenager), then he can **Overcome** his **Cowardice** and **Obtain Courage**, thereby **Making him Worthy** of **Attaining** a *New Heart of Invincibility*. Finally, "If He" can Perform at the **100% Level of Perfection** (adult), then he can **Overcome** his **Selfishness** and **Greed** and **Obtain Generosity**, thereby **Making him Worthy** of **Attaining** a *New Soul of Unstoppable Confidence*. It should now "All Make Sense" that the Life-experience is a **Rigorous Journey** through a **Painful Basic Training Course** as **Each of God's Children Enters** as a *Baby* (grow) and **Graduates** as an *Invincible Adult* (mature).

The following tabular information indicates that the "More a Person" is Challenged, the **More** he can **Prove himself** as he **Defeats Sin** (ignorance), **Evil** (cowardice), and **Death** (greed) to **Become Righteous, Holy,** and **Perfect** in the *Sight of God*:

God's Children Called to Face the Challenges
of Sin, Evil, and Death to become Set Free
(defeat sin, become righteous; defeat evil,
become holy; and defeat death, become perfect)

Sin   1. **Challenge Sinfulness** - Defeat Sin to Become Righteous: Christian...
(truth)   Knowledge
- Face Father's Law - Lucifer's Test/ignorance: Baby Farm = 33% Courage
- Fulfill God's Law/ethics: Obedience = Change Nature from Human to Divine

Sin-nature
- Jesus Faces Scourging at the Pillar – Takes-on All Sin (see limitations)
- Learn God's Right from man's wrong - Righteous Citizen on Earth: Kingship
- Graded by God's Love - Handicap System: Just Try (slaughter of innocence)
- Free Redemption (good news) - Given *New Body* (Heaven on earth)
- Receiving Heaven on Earth - Seat in Celestial Court of God

(excommunication from temple - face High Priest Caiaphas: blasphemy = you are God)

Evil   2. **Challenge Evilness** - Defeat Evil to Become Holy: Holy Saint...Self-awareness
(law)
- Face Mother's Love - God's Judgment/cowardice: Divine School = 67% Courage

- Jesus Christ Faces Death in Tomb - Sacrifices His Life (see self-worth)
- Fulfill Man's Faith/morals: Love = Become Holy: Sinner becomes a Christian

Worldly
Temptations
- Christ Faces Crucifixion on Cross - Gives-up Divinity (see potential)
- Learn God's Good from man's evil - Holy Saint in Heaven: Priesthood
- Graded by God's Mercy - Graded on a Curve: Top Score (dark night)
- Earned Salvation (gospel message) - Given *Eternal Life* (paradise)
- Receiving Paradise in Heaven - Seat in Temple Court of God

(outcast from one's people - face King Herod: sorcery = you change water to wine)

Death   3. **Challenge Death** - Defeat Death to Become Perfect:
Son of God...Consciousness
- Face Brother's Love - Self-evaluation/greed: Sonship Training = 100% Courage
- Fulfill Knowing: Thinking/instinct - Become Free: Christian becomes a Saint

Demonic
Possession
- Jesus Christ Faces Death in Tomb - Sacrifices His Life (see self-worth)
- Learn God's Will from man's will - Perfect Son within Kingdom: Sonship
- Graded by God's Justice - Pass or Fail System: 100% Perfect (death)
- Bonus Rewards (doctrinal truths) - Given *Royal Kingdom* (freedom)
- Receiving Own Royal Kingdom - Seat in Royal Court of God

(banished from earth - face Pontius Pilate: sedition = you are a king)

This illustration shows that a "Baby Soul" must Face the Father's Law and be **Willing to Take Lucifer's Test** to **Experience** the **Slaughter of his Innocence, Show** him the **Depth of his Ignorance,** and *See his Own Limitations*. Once a "Baby" has Been Tested, he is **Ready** to **Face** his **Scourging at the Pillar** and **Take-on All the Sins of Man** to **Prove he is Now United** with the **Tenacity of Jesus** and has the *Strength of a Bull*. Secondly, a "Teenage Soul" must Face Mother's Love and be **Willing to Accept God's Judgment** to **Experience** the **Dark Night of the Soul** to **Show** him the **Depth of his Cowardice** and *See his Own Potential*. Once a "Teenager" has Accepted God's Judgment, he is **Ready** to **Face** his **Crucifixion on the Cross** and to **Give-up his Divinity** to **Prove he is Now United** with the **Submission of Christ** and has the *Courage of a Warrior*. Finally, an "Adult Soul" must Face Brother's Love and be **Willing to Evaluate himself** to **Experience** Nature's Curse of Death, **Show** him the **Depth of his Greed,** and *See his Own Self-worth*. Once an "Adult" has Evaluated himself, he is **Ready** to **Face the Tomb of Death** and **Sacrifice his Life** to **Prove he is Now United** with the **Undaunted Spirit of God** and has the *Generous Heart of a Saint*. Through this "Series" of Tests of Endurance, the **Human Race** can **Take** its **Sonship Training** to **Learn God's Right, Good, Reality,** and **man's wrong, evil, and illusion** to bring forth a *Righteous Citizen on Earth, Holy Saint in Heaven, and a Perfect Son within God's Kingdom*. To "Learn All the Lessons" in Life, a **Person** must be **Graded** by God's Love through the **Lord's Handicap System** to **Show** the **Depth of His Effort** as he **Tries his Hardest** to <u>Overcome</u> the *Slaughter of Innocence*. Secondly, a "Person" must be <u>Graded by God's Mercy</u> through the **Lord's Bell Curve System** (average) to **Show** the **Depth of His Effort** as he **Proves he is Worthy** by <u>Overcoming</u> the *Dark Night of the Soul*. Finally, a "Person" must be <u>Graded by God's Justice</u> through the **Lord's Pass/Fail System** (100% perfect) to **Show** the **Depth of His Effort** as he **Impresses even God** by <u>Overcoming</u> the *Curse of Death Itself*.

The "Lord God Almighty" is <u>Revealing</u> that the **More a Person is Able** to **Measure** the **Depth of his Own Brokenness**, the **More he can Comprehend the Awesome Fortitude** that it will **Take** to be <u>**Transformed**</u> into a *Perfect Creation before God*. The implication here is for "Every Effort Made" in <u>Healing</u> **One's Own Brokenness**, he can become **Worthy** of **One** of **God's Mystical Treasures** of *Free Redemption* (being saved), *Earned Salvation,* and/or *Bonus Rewards* (saving others). This means that "Free Redemption" brings with it a <u>New Body;</u> just as "Earned Salvation" brings with it <u>Eternal Life;</u> and "Bonus Rewards" bring with it <u>One's Own Royal Kingdom.</u> It should be extremely clear that the "Life-experience" is about both <u>Growing-up</u> and <u>Maturing</u> from a **Baby to an Adult** so that He can become **Worthy** of **God's Eternal Treasures** to <u>**Attain**</u> *Heaven on Earth, Paradise in Heaven,* and finally, *Living in His Own Kingdom*.

Obviously, "Our Perfect God Knew" that <u>Each of His Children</u> would **Need** to **Defeat his Own Fear of Failure, Fear of Death,** and the **Fear of Eternal-damnation** before he could have the **Necessary Courage to Face** his *Own Sin-nature* (fear/self), *Worldly Temptations* (death/world), and *Lucifer's Demonic Possession* (damnation/Hell). The message here is that the "Lord God Almighty" also <u>Needed a Challenge Worthy</u> of **His Divine Perfection**. Thus, **He Devised** <u>**His Scourging**</u> to *Remove his Fear of Failure*, then <u>**His Crucifixion**</u> to *Remove His Fear of Death* (pain), and finally, the <u>**Tomb**</u> to *Remove His Fear of Damnation* (hell). With the "Life," "Death" and "Resurrection" of <u>Jesus Christ,</u> the **Lord God Almighty** could **Fulfill His Dream** of <u>**Defeating**</u> *Fear* (scourging), *Pain* (crucifixion), and *Death* (tomb) on *Earth*. Obviously, for an "Infinite God" <u>Who was Never-created,</u> **He was also Challenged** to **Face His Greatest Fear** and that is of **Falling** into some <u>**Pit of Oblivion**</u> (all becomes nothing) and *Disappearing from All Existence Forever and Ever*. This means the "God of All" would have to <u>Go to Mount Calvary</u> to become the "God of Nothing" and become **Transformed** into a **Perfect Man** with the *Wisdom, Courage, and Power of a God*, yet, to also have the *Humility of a Dutiful Slave*...and so it was *Done*. Through these "Treasures," a <u>Person can Fulfill</u> the **Spirit of God** (divine/law) and the **Flesh of Man** (holy/faith), thereby <u>**Making Them One**</u> in *Truth, Law, Will, and Love*. Obviously, the "Spirit of God (divine)" <u>Comes from Christ</u> (law), while the "Flesh of Man (holiness)" <u>Comes from Jesus</u> (love) and then were **United** on *Mount Calvary* into the "Soul of God/Man (perfection)." Note that "Christ is Coming" from <u>Heaven</u> (spirit/Father's Law), while "Jesus is Born" on <u>Earth</u> (flesh/Mother's Love) so that both the *Free Redemption of the Flesh* can be **Merged** with the *Earned Salvation of the Spirit* (eternal life). This implies that "Jesus and Christ" become <u>One Person</u> within the **Nature of Jesus Christ** to bring forth the **Redemption of the**

World (free) and the **Salvation of the Church** (earned), thereby **Making Earthly Men** *Righteous Citizens* (law) and **Heavenly Men** *Holy Saints* (love).

1. **Jesus** - <u>Master the World</u> - Gain New Divine Nature…Jewish People (become Man)
   - Learn the Lessons of Life - Bear Fruit Out of Evil (fight evil)
2. **Christ** - <u>Master the Church</u> - Gain Saintly Holiness….Christian People (become God)
   - Receive the Blessing of Life - Bear Fruit Out of Holiness (surrender)

The point here is to see that to "Master the World," a <u>Person</u> must **Fulfill the Law** via his *Circumcision* (Jewish People/become Man); and then to "Master the Church," a <u>Person</u> must **Fulfill Human Love** via his *Baptism* (Christian People/become God). This "Fulfillment Process" will <u>Allow</u> a <u>Righteous Citizen</u> to **Get Christ's** *Divinity* (new mind), while a <u>Holy Saint</u> will become **Worthy** of **Getting Jesus'** *Holiness* (new heart). This "Great Achievement" will <u>Give a Person</u> the **Wisdom to Face Life** (trials/errors), and the **Courage to Face Death** (pain/suffering) so that his **Flesh** can be *Redeemed* (being saved) and his **Spirit** can be *Saved* (saving self). We see that "One's Wisdom" will show him the <u>Lessons of Life</u> via the **Fleshly Ordeal** of the **Jewish People** on **Their Journey** to *Own the Earth*. Secondly, "One's Love" will show him the <u>Blessings of Life</u> via the **Spiritual Devotion** of the **Christian People** on **Their Journey** to *Owning Heaven*. Through these "Lessons and Blessings," the <u>Flesh</u> will **Learn Right from Wrong** and the <u>Spirit</u> will **Learn Good from Evil** to <u>Separate</u> the *Lessons of the World* (law) from the *Blessings of the Church* (love). Via "Man's Lessons" <u>Taught by Jesus,</u> **Mankind** can attain its **Holy Flesh** from its *Life of Hard-work*, while "Man's Blessings" <u>Come from Christ</u> so that **Mankind** can attain its **New Nature** from its *Life of Holy Prayers*.

Obviously, this "Life of Work" is <u>Designed to Create</u> the **Righteous Citizen** on *Earth*, while a "Life of Prayer" is <u>Designed to Create</u> the **Holy Saints** in *Heaven*. By "Reaching" this <u>Level of Perfection,</u> a **Person can See** that **Man's King** becomes *God's Priest* (Jesus/earth), while **God's Priest** becomes *Man's King* (Christ/Heaven). The implication here is that on "Mount Calvary," <u>God's Son</u> (Christ/spirit) was **Asked** to **Master the World** (face life) and **Fulfill the Law** (become divine), while <u>Mary's Son</u> (Jesus/flesh) was **Asked** to **Master the Church** (face death) and *Fulfill his Faith* (become holy). By "Fulfilling the Law," <u>God can become Man</u> (Christmas) to **Create Babies on Earth;** and by "Fulfilling One's Faith," Man <u>can become God</u> (Easter) to **Create Saints in Heaven.** Through this "Process" of <u>Facing Life,</u> a **Person can Receive God's Gift** of *Free Redemption* (good news), while by <u>Facing Death,</u> a **Person** can **Earn his Own** *Salvation* (gospel message). The point here is that "Redemption" brings forth <u>God's Gift</u> of a *New Body*, while "Salvation" thereby <u>Allows a Person to Earn</u> his *Own Eternal Life*. In this way, a "Righteous Citizen" can <u>Establish his Own</u> **Heaven on Earth** (peace of mind) and **Learn** to *Live with himself,* while a "Holy Saint" can become <u>Worthy</u> of being **Invited** into **Paradise in Heaven** (joy of heart) and *Live with God*. When both "Earth and Heaven" are <u>Made One</u> in the **New Heaven and New Earth, Jesus Christ** will bring forth the *Lord's Kingdom of Glory* (happiness of soul). We see that in "God's Coming

Kingdom," God, Angels, and Men will **Live Together** in **Peace, Joy, and Harmony** to bring forth the **Treasures of Life** through *Challenges* (never-quit), *Adventures* (being defeated), *and Fun* (defeat self). This means that "All Humanity" is being Called to **Master the Law** (world/obey) to become **Righteous** and then **Master its Faith** (church/love) to become **Holy** as a **Reflection** of *God's Son, Jesus Christ*.

The following tabular information indicates that "God is Calling Mankind" to Master the World through **Law** (righteous citizen) and then to Master the Church through **Faith** (holy saint) to **Attain** a *New Body* (Heaven on Earth) and *Eternal Life* (Paradise in Heaven):

Fight Evil Master World (law)	Surrender Master Church (faith)
1. Fulfill Law - Circumcision	1. Fulfill Faith – Baptism
2. Get Christ's Divinity/new mind	2. Get Jesus' Holiness/new heart
3. Wisdom to Face Life (ethics)	3. Courage to Face Death (morals)
4. Lessons of Life/Jewish People	4. Blessings of Life/Christian People
5. Learn Right from Wrong	5. Learn Good from Evil
6. Change Nature (all work)	6. Wash Away Sins (all prayer)
• Human to Divine	• Sinfulness to Holiness
7. Righteous Citizen on Earth	7. Holy Saint in Heaven
8. Man's King becomes God's Priest	8. God's Priest becomes Man's King
9. God becomes Man (Christmas)	9. Man becomes God (Easter)
10. Free Redemption/good news	10. Earned Salvation/gospel message
11. Gift of *New Body*	11. Earned *Eternal Life*

12. Heaven on Earth (peace of mind)	**12. Paradise in Heaven** (joy of the heart)
• Live with Self (never-quit)	• Live with God (being defeated)

Kingdom of Glory (happiness of the soul)
Live with Everyone (defeat self)

Saturday Evaluation (blood)	Sunday Evaluation (death)
• Number of Babies Created	• Number of Souls Saved
• Fulfill Word of God	• Fulfill Traditions of Church
• Mystical Body of Christ	• Communion of Saints
• Holy Nation - Serve People	• Holy Church - Worship God

===

Holy Nation and Holy Church become One - Mankind Receives Its Eternal Rewards

===

1. Babies	3. Adults	1. Sinners	3. Saints
• Kingdom of God	• Inherit Earth	• Shown Mercy	• Sons of God
2. Teenagers	4. Wise Men	2. Christians	4. Sons of God
• Comforted	• Righteousness	• See God	• Kingdom of Heaven

This illustration shows that "All the Treasures of God" are to be <u>Kept</u> in **His Coming Kingdom of Glory** in the <u>**Form**</u> of *His most Beloved Babies* (bodies) and *His most Respected Saints* (eternal lives). We see that the "Lord God Almighty" <u>Uses His Holy Sabbath</u> (Saturday) to **Count His Children** and to **Evaluate Their Progress** during the **Last Week** to <u>**See If They have Grown**</u> in *His Physical Perfection*. Secondly, the "Lord God Almighty" <u>Uses His Sacred Sunday</u> to **Count His Saints** and to **Evaluate Their Progress** during the **Last Week** to <u>**See If They have Matured**</u> in *His Spiritual Perfection*. We see that the "Physical Babies" come in **Four Categories**: 1) <u>Baby Life</u> - Seek Kingdom of God, 2) <u>Teenage Life</u> - Seek Comfort, 3) <u>Adult Life</u> - Seek Inheritance of Earth, and 4) <u>Wise Man Life</u> - Seek Righteousness. Secondly, the "Spiritual Saints" come in **Four Categories**: 1) <u>Sinners</u> - Shown God's Mercy, 2) <u>Christians</u> - See God, 3) <u>Saints</u> - Made Sons of God, and 4) <u>Sons of God</u> - Given Kingdom of God. We see that these are the "Eight Beatitudes" which <u>Match</u> the **Treasures of God** that are **Given to God's** *Four Stages of Life* (growing-up/washed) and to *God's Four Stages of Sainthood* (maturing/changed). We can now see that "Growing-up (righteousness)" is to have <u>One's Nature Changed</u> (fulfill law) by the *Blood of Jesus*, while "Maturing (holiness)" is to have One's <u>Sins Washed Away</u> (fulfill faith) by the *Spirit of Christ* (church). This means that "God's Spirit (new nature)" <u>Represents</u> **Life's Formal Face** (law/ethics), while "Man's Flesh (washed)" <u>Represents</u> **Life's Informal Face** (love/morals) which become the <u>**Formality**</u> of the *Church* (prayer) versus the <u>**Informality**</u> of the *World* (work).

The message here is that the "Human Experience" <u>Involves Displaying</u> both a **Formal Face** (official/professional) <u>Next to One's</u> **Informal Face** (unofficial/immature). Then the **Trick** is to **Combine** these **Two** <u>**Faces**</u> (balance) into *One Personality* (Christ). The "Lord God Almighty" is <u>Forcing His Christians</u> to **Blend** the <u>**Face of the Church**</u> (serious adult/holiness) with the **Face of the World** (playful child/righteousness) by *Mastering* both *Their Spirit Nature* (morals) and *Their Physical Nature* (ethics). In this teaching, we see that the "False Face" is to be <u>Excommunicated</u> from *Religion* (fear), <u>Outcast</u> from *One's People* (pain), <u>Banished</u> from the *Earth* (death), <u>Forsaken</u> by *God* (damnation), and finally, <u>Executed</u> from *Life* (oblivion). This rejection of "Falsehood (lessons)" thereby brings forth "Truthfulness (blessings)" <u>Making a Person</u> a **Holy Priest** (courageous), **Righteous King** (wise), **Perfect Son** (generous), **Unselfish Wise Man** (imaginative), and finally, a **Free Man/Faithful Servant** (dedicated) unto the *Lord*. Recall that "Jesus Christ Faced" the <u>High Priest Caiaphas</u> and was **Excommunicated from the Temple** for **Blasphemy**, placing **God's Son** under the **Curse of Fear** as the <u>**Temple Priests Tried**</u> to *Scare Him* into *Denying His Eternal Father*. Secondly, "Jesus Christ Faced" <u>King Herod</u> and was made an **Outcast** from the **Jewish People**, placing **God's Son** under the **Curse of Loss of Worldly Properties** (pain) as the <u>**Royal Palace Laughed at Christ,**</u> making *Him* into a *Circus Clown*. Thirdly, "Jesus Christ Faced" <u>Pontius Pilate</u> and was **Banished** from **Planet Earth**, placing Him under the **Curse of Death to Family** (death) as the <u>Mobs Spit on Him,</u> making Him into an *Evil Criminal*. Fourthly, "Jesus Christ Faced" the <u>Lord God Almighty</u> and was **Forsaken by God**, placing Him under the **Curse of Death to His Children** (damnation) as even **Heaven Condemned Him to Hell,** making

Him into an ***Insane Mad-man***. Finally, "Jesus Christ Faced" <u>Himself</u> for being **God** in the **Judgment of Truth** and was **Executed for Imperfection** (take-on all sin), placing **Him** under the **Curse of Crucifixion** (oblivion) as <u>**He was Forced**</u> to *Release His Own Evil Spirit*.

Recall that the term "Fundamentalism" means <u>Foolish Man</u> **Defining God** in his own **Human Perception**, showing that **Christ was Forced** to go beyond both <u>**Human Comprehension**</u> (intellect/ethics) and <u>**Human Imagination**</u> (emotions/morals) to *Face Himself* (divinity). Now, we see the "Merging" of both the <u>False Face of Man</u> (world) and the <u>True Face of God</u> (church) as they **Blend** into a **New Creation** of <u>Honesty</u> and <u>Integrity</u> made *Perfect* in the *Union of Life* (holy blessings) and *Death* (righteous lessons). We see that this "Mystical Union" of <u>Life and Death</u> can **Best be Explained** by **Understanding** the <u>**Fulfillment of God's Law**</u> by the *Jewish People* and the **Fulfillment of Man's Faith** by the *Christian People*.

The idea being expressed here is that "When a Person" <u>Fulfills God's Law</u> (obedience), he becomes **Divine** (spirit/new nature); while "When a Person" <u>Fulfills Man's Faith</u> (love), he becomes **Holy** (flesh). Yet, when **Divinity** and **Holiness** are <u>**Made One,**</u> a *Person* becomes *Perfect in the Sight of God*. Unfortunately, "Only Christ" or the "Messiah" can <u>Fulfill God's Law</u> (Mosaic/obedience) or **One Man** through the **Bloodline of the Jews** which must be **Sacrificed** upon <u>**God's Altar of Death**</u> to bring forth *Free Redemption to All* (good news). Secondly, through the "Church" or <u>Repentant Sinners,</u> **One** can **Fulfill God's Faith** (Canon/love) or **All Men** through the **Christian Blessing of Baptism** (water) which must be **Sacrificed** upon <u>**God's Altar of New-life**</u> to bring forth *Earned Salvation to Converted Souls* (gospel message). This means that the "Messiah" is the <u>Bridegroom</u> bringing *His* **Bride Price** (royal name), while the "Church" is the <u>Bride</u> bringing **Her Dowry** (virginity) as *They Both Come* to *God's Altar of a Happy Life*. Note that the "Groom" brings <u>His Bride</u> a *Royal Name of Divine Respect*, while the "Bride" brings <u>Her Groom</u> *Her Virgin Love* and *Eternal Happiness*. This "Marriage" of <u>God's Prosperity</u> (money) and <u>Man's Love</u> **Establishes the Happy Home** of **Beloved Children**, **Who** can **Expect** a *Lifetime of Peace* (challenge), *Joy* (adventure), and *Happiness* (fun).

The idea here is that "Prosperity (money)" <u>Only Comes When a Person</u> **Fulfills God's Law** (Jewish People/blood) through **Fear** (negative) which causes him to <u>**Die to his Own Selfishness**</u> (agony of defeat) and then to *Surrender to God's Divine Will*. Secondly, "Man's Love (faith)" can <u>Only Come When a Person</u> **Fulfills Man's Faith** (Christian People/spirit) through **Wanting to Serve** (positive) which causes him to be <u>**Born-again**</u> (thrill of victory) and then become a *Servant unto God's Divine Love*. "Out of the Groom's Name," <u>His Children shall</u> **Receive a Respected Name** or *God's Blessing* (gain virtues); while "Out of the Bride's Love," <u>Her Children</u> shall **Receive a Lifetime of Happiness** or *God's Lessons* (remove faults). We see that in the "End," <u>Each of God's Children</u> will be **Able** to **Fulfill God's Law** (Christ's nature/obedience/grave) and **Fulfill Man's Faith** (holiness/love/host) **On his Own** and become both a <u>**Respected and Loving Person**</u> within the *Kingdom of God*.

The following tabular information indicates that the "Messiah" is the <u>Only Person</u> **Who** can <u>**Fulfill God's Law**</u> (change nature/obedience) and *Become Divine* (spirit), while "Jesus Christ" is the <u>Only Person</u> **Who** can **Fulfill Man's Faith** (wash away sin/love) and *Become Holy* (flesh):

Fulfill the Law to Become Divine and then Fulfill
God's Faith to Become Holy in Christ Jesus
(Messiah fulfills the law, while the Church fulfills
God's faith to bring forth Redemption)

Change
Nature
(blood)

1. **Fulfillment of the Law** (Jesus/obey) - <u>Become Divine:</u> Messiah (one man)...
Flesh
   - Jesus Takes-on All Sin - Save Sinner: Repentance (ethical honesty)
   - Righteous Citizen on Earth - Seat in Celestial Court (earth/divine love)
   - Sacrifice Christian's Water Baptism - Altar of New-life: Earned Salvation

Good
News
(word)
   - Physical Bride/Church - Dowry: Virginity (take-sins/obedience)
   - Lessons of Life/remove faults - Learn Right/Wrong: New Mind (intellect)
   - *Free New Body* - Transfigured Body: Jesus-like (Man)
   - <u>Inheritance</u> - Paradise in Heaven with God: Earned (Christ Human God)
   - Government - King/sinner...See Limitations/starvation

Ethical
Honesty
(death)
   - Church - Priest/Christian...See Potential/nakedness
   - Home - Son/saint...See Self-worth/homelessness
   - <u>Informal Brotherhood of Man</u> - Viewpoint: Universal Friendship
   - Honor – Home

Purify
Grave
   - Code – Government **Speed and Accuracy - World: Works**
   - God – Church
   - Yes! I Served Jesus Christ Perfectly - Passing Grade
   (fulfill the law - birth of Jesus: Christmas = face challenge of obeying the Jewish Law)

Wash
Away Sin
(spirit)

2. **Fulfillment of Faith** (Christ/want) - <u>Become Holy:</u> Church (all men)... Spirit
   - Christ Gives-up His Divinity - Create Saints: Sonship Training
     (moral integrity)
   - Spiritual Bridegroom/Messiah - Bride Price: Royal Name (give divinity/love)
   - Sacrifice Messiah's Jewish Blood - Altar of Death: Free Redemption for All

Gospel
Message
(tradition)
   - Holy Saint in Heaven - Seat in Temple Court (Heaven/divine will)
   - Blessings of God/gain virtues - Learn Good/Evil: New Heart (emotion)
   - *Earn Eternal Life* - Glorified Body: Christ-like (God)
   - <u>Birthright</u> - Heaven on Earth with Man: Free (Jesus Divine Man)
   - Earth - Government/righteous...See Wisdom/brains

Moral
Integrity
   - Heaven - Church/holy...See Courage/beauty
   - Kingdom - Home/perfect...See Generosity/wealth

(blood)	• <u>Formal Sainthood of God</u> - Viewpoint: In Business with Man
	• Honor - Earth
Purify	• Code - Heaven **Slow and Deliberate - Church: Prayer**
Host	• God – Kingdom
	• Yes! I Worshiped God Perfectly - Passing Grade
	(fulfill Man's faith - death of Christ:
	Easter = face challenge of loving the Christian Faith)

This illustration shows that the "Good News (Jesus Divine Man)" is that <u>Christ Paid</u> for **Physical Sin** and brought **<u>Free Redemption to All</u>** and be *Transformed into Christians*; while the "Gospel Message (Christ Human God)" is that <u>Jesus Pays</u> for **Spiritual Sin** to **Allow** a **Repentant Sinner** to **<u>Earn his Own Salvation</u>** and be *Transformed into a Saint*. This means that "Each of God's Children" must be <u>Changed</u> into *Jesus' Nature* (new heart) and then have <u>His Sins Washed Away</u> by *Christ's Baptism* (new mind). Obviously, "Christ's Nature" allows the <u>Human Flesh</u> to become *Righteous* (citizenship/free will), while the <u>Human Spirit</u> becomes *Holy* (sainthood/destiny). By "Uniting" <u>Man's Righteousness</u> (intellect) and <u>God's Holiness</u> (emotions), the **Human Race** can **Think for Itself** at the **<u>Adult Level of Understanding</u>** to bring forth *One's Christian Perfection*. We see that this "Christian Perfection" means that a Person has **Received Man's Lessons of Life** to *Remove his Faults* and has also Received **<u>God's Blessings of Life</u>** to *Gain God's Virtues*. Yes! Through both "His Empty Flesh (faults)" and his "Newly Filled Spirit (virtues)," a <u>Person</u> can become **<u>Worthy</u>** of a *New Earthly Body* (transfigured) and a *New Heavenly Body* (glorified). Through these "Two Bodies of Life," the <u>Creation of God</u> could **Fulfill** the **Two-Truth System** of **Righteousness and Holiness** via the **Earth, Heaven, and the Kingdom** as a **<u>Reflection</u>** of *Mankind's Government, Church, and Home*. Through these "Institutions," <u>God's Kingship</u> (wisdom) becomes *Man's Kingship* (see limitations); <u>God's Priesthood</u> (courage) becomes *Man's Priesthood* (generosity); and <u>God's Sonship</u> becomes *Man's Sonship* (see self-worth). This means that the "Flesh of Man" must <u>Master the World</u> by *Fulfilling God's* Law (obedience) and the "Spirit of Man" must <u>Master the Church</u> by *Fulfilling Man's Faith* (love).

Obviously, the "Law of God (divine)" and the "Faith of Man (holy)" are <u>Designed</u> to **Work Together** in **Uniting** the **Spirit of God** with the **Flesh of Man** to bring forth a **New Heaven and New Earth** in the **<u>Form</u>** of *God's Born-again Kingdom of Glory*. For this "Purpose," <u>God, Angels, Men, and Nature</u> have been **United** into a **Divine, Sacred, Holy, and Natural Work-force** under the **<u>Authority</u>** of *God's Son,* the **Lord Jesus Christ**. The "Job" of <u>Jesus the Man</u> is to **Fulfill God's Law** by becoming the *Christ* (obedience); while the "Job" of <u>Christ the God</u> is to **Fulfill Man's Faith** by becoming *Jesus* (love). This means that "Mary's Son, Jesus" must <u>Master the World</u> (flesh) by *Dying to His Selfishness* (submission); while "God's Son, Christ" must <u>Master the Church</u> by being *Born-again to Unselfishness* (confidence). In this way, the "Forces of Nothing (Jesus)" will be <u>United</u> to the "Forces of All (Christ)," thereby **<u>Allowing</u> God to become Man** (Christmas) and *Man to become God* (Easter).

Clearly, "Only One Perfect Man (Messiah)" can <u>Fulfill God's Law</u> and become **Obedient** to the **Letter of the Law** through **His All Knowing Intellect** and then <u>**Offer Himself Up**</u> to *Take upon Himself All Sin* (Jesus' blood). Secondly, it is for "All Men (Christians)" that He can <u>Fulfill Man's Faith</u> and then **Love** the **Spirit of the Law** through **His Pure Emotions** and **Offer Himself Up** by <u>**Giving-up His Divinity**</u> (forgiveness/eternal life) to *Save the Souls of Others*. We can now see that through "Jesus' Blood (take-sin)," a Person's <u>Nature is Changed</u> (being saved), allowing him to **Receive God's Gift** of **Free Redemption** (good news). Secondly, we see that through "Christ's Death (give divinity)," a <u>Person's Sins</u> are **Washed Away** (saving self), thereby <u>**Allowing him**</u> to *Earn his Own Salvation* (gospel message). This means that "Free Redemption" <u>Allows a Person</u> to **See his Own Limitations** and **Receive** a **New Mind of Wisdom,** thereby <u>**Giving him**</u> the *Blessing of Ethical Honesty* (divine man). Secondly, "Earned Salvation" <u>Allows a Person</u> to **See his Own Potential** and **Receive** a **New Heart of Courage**, thereby <u>**Giving him**</u> the *Blessing of Moral Integrity* (human God). We now see that by "Fulfilling the Law," a <u>Person can Attain</u> **Heaven on Earth**, thereby <u>**Allowing**</u> *God to become a Man*; while by "Fulfilling the Faith," a <u>Person can Attain</u> **Paradise in Heaven**, thereby <u>**Allowing**</u> *Man to become God*. Now it becomes clear that the "Life-experience is All About" <u>Fulfilling</u> **God's Law** (grave) and **Man's Faith** (host) to **Receive All the Treasures** of <u>**Heaven**</u> and <u>**Earth**</u> via the *Forces of Obedience* (death) and *Love* (new-life).

The following tabular information indicates the "Importance" of <u>Mastering</u> both the **World** (flesh) and the **Church** (spirit) by **Fulfilling God's Law** and **Fulfilling Man's Faith** through a <u>**Person's**</u> *Obedience to God* (change nature) and *Love for Man* (wash away sin):

<u>Master World</u> - Flesh	<u>Master Church</u> - Spirit
• Purify Grave	• Purify Host
1. **Fulfill the Law - Man**	2. **Fulfill One's Faith - God**
• Obedience - Intellect	• Love - Emotion
• Jesus' Blood	• Christ's Death
• Take-on Sin	• Give-up Divinity
• Change Nature	• Wash Away Sin
• Save Sinners	• Create Saints
• Free Redemption	• Earned Salvation
• See Limitations	• See Potential
• <u>New Mind/wisdom</u>	• <u>New Heart/courage</u>
• Become Divine	• Become Holy
• Divine Man	• Human God
(ethical honesty)	(moral integrity)

Heaven on Earth - Man	*Paradise in Heaven* - God
• God becomes Man	• Man becomes God
(agony of defeat)	(thrill of victory)

Bible/Word/Messiah	Church/Traditions/Saints
• Save One Perfect Man	• Save All Wicked Men
• Mystical Body	• Communion of Saints
(purify grave, get transfigured body)	(purify host, get glorified spirit)

This illustration shows that the "Life-experience" is about **Mastering the World** with **One's Flesh** and then "Mastering the Church" with **His Spirit** to both *Change his Nature* (crucible) and *Wash Away his Sins* (winepress). This "Process" of <u>Transformation</u> (change) and <u>Purification</u> (washing) brings forth a **New Creation in Christ** in **Fulfillment of God's Kingship** (earth), *Priesthood* (Heaven), and *Sonship* (Kingdom). In this way, the "Lord God Almighty" is <u>Connecting</u> the **Physical Nature** of <u>Earth</u> with the **Spiritual Nature** of <u>Heaven</u> through *His Law* (obedience) and *Man's Faith* (love). Through these "Two Forces" of <u>Obedience</u> and <u>Love,</u> the **Life-experience is Fulfilled** both in a **Person's Baby Flesh** (Christmas/life) and in **His Adult Spirit** (Easter/death) as a <u>Baby</u> must *Fulfill the Earth*, while an <u>Adult</u> must *Fulfill Heaven* (born-again). Note that "Human Childhood" is <u>Centered</u> upon **Obeying** his **Parents, Teachers, Authorities, and God**; while "Human Adulthood" is <u>Centered</u> upon **Loving One's Family, Community, Nation, and God**.

Flesh	1. **God's Law** - Obedience: New Divine Nature = Face Life with Wisdom…
(lessons)	Christmas

- Baby Goes from Obedience to Love - See Worldly Limitations
  (agony of defeat)
- Father's Expectations - Child Graded on Pass/Fail System (one man/dark)
- Jesus - Takes-on All the Sins of Man: Get New Nature
  (bow to authority)
- Creating Righteous Men on Earth - *Free New Body* (dying to self)

(ethical honesty - doing things quick and dirty: becoming a divine man)

Spirit	2. **Man's Faith** - Love: New Holy Nature = Face Death with Courage…Easter
(blessings)	• Adult Goes from Love to Sainthood - See Church Potential (thrill of victory)

- Mother's Hopes - Child Graded on Handicap System (all men/light)
- Christ - Gives-up One's Divinity: Get Holiness (love/respect one's peers)
- Creating Holy Saints in Heaven - *Earned Eternal Life* (born-again)

(moral integrity - doing things slow and methodical: become a human God)

This means that a "Baby's" <u>Nature is Changed</u> to **See** his *Own Limitations in Life* (obedience to love)*;* while an "Adult's" <u>Sins are Washed Away</u> to **See** his *Own Potential in Life* (love to servanthood). Through this "Combination" of <u>Limitations</u> (be nothing) and <u>Potential</u> (be all), a **Person** can **Hope to Receive** *God's Gift of Divinity* (holiness) while **Uniting** with **Jesus Christ** to *Take-on All the Sins of Man* (new nature). It should now make sense that "Mary's Son (flesh)" <u>Jesus</u> (Man) came to **Change Men** into *God-like Beings* (obedient); while "God's Son (spirit)" <u>Christ</u> came to **Wash Away Sin,** thereby *Creating Holy Saints* (loving) for *Heaven*. It could only be through the "Blending" of

God's Spirit with Man's Flesh on **Mount Calvary** (cross) that **Divine Obedience** and **Human Love** could become **One** in *Truth, Law, Will, and Love*. The implication here is that the "Jewish Law" Changes One's Nature (obey truth), while "Christian Faith" Washes Away Sin (holiness). This most "Powerful Truth" Allows the Human Race to **Comprehend** just **How** a **Lost Broken Sinner** is **Changed** into both a **Righteous Citizen on Earth** (world) and then a **Holy Saint in Heaven** (church) through the *Sacrificial Blood/Death of Jesus Christ*. Obviously, the "Righteous Citizen (works)" has been Required to **Learn** the **Lessons of Life** (agony of defeat/virginity), while the "Holy Saint (prayers)" has been Required to **Earn** *God's Blessings* (thrill of victory/name).

The point here is to see that the "Lessons of Life" bring forth Human Purity or Virginity, while the "Blessings of God" Allow a Person to be **Seen by God**, thereby **Making him *Worthy*** of *his Own Respected Name*. This means that "Human Virginity" is Rewarded with **God's Gift** of a **New Body** through a *Person's Good Works*; while "Human Divinity" is Given to Devout Souls, **Who Earn Their Own Eternal Lives** through *Holy Prayers*. We see that the "God/Man Relationship" known as Jesus Christ has miraculously **Fulfilled** both the **Jewish Law** (world) and the **Christian Faith** (church) by both **Dying to Self** (submission) and then being ***Born-again*** (new-life).

The following tabular information indicates that "Christ" Fulfills God's Law (one man) via **His Obedience** (blood) to the *Divine Will* (become divine); while "Jesus" Fulfills Man's Faith (all men) via **His Love** (death) for *Divine Love* (become holy):

Fulfilling God's Law to become Divine and
Fulfilling Man's Faith to become Holy in Christ
(Jewish Law Changes One's Nature [obey], while
Christian Faith Washes Away One's Sins [love])

1. **Fulfill God's Law** - One Man/Earth	2. **Fulfill Man's Faith** - All Men/Heaven
• Master Obedience to Divine Will	• Master Loving God's Divine Love
• Change Nature - See One's Limitations	• Wash Away Sin - See One's Potential
• God Gives-up Divinity (spirit)	• Man Takes-on All Sin (flesh)
• Man becomes Divine - In Jesus	• Man becomes Holy - In Christ
• Man's Lessons - Receive Virginity	• God's Blessing - Receive Name
• *Free New Body* - Good Works	• *Earn Eternal Life* - Holy Prayers
1. Kingdom of God - Baby	1. Shown Mercy - Sinner
2. Comforted - Teenager	2. See God - Christian
3. Inherit Earth - Adult	3. Son of God - Saint
4. Righteousness - Wise Man	4. Kingdom of Heaven - Son
(world - Jewish People: Christmas = baby)	(church - Christians: Easter = adults)

This illustration shows that the "Human Race" is Tasked to become **God-like in Spirit** (transformation) and **Holy in the Flesh** (purity) as a **Reflection** of the **Divine Light of Jesus Christ** to bring forth a *New Heaven and New Earth*. In this way, a "New Justice System" is to be Created on **Earth**, in **Heaven,** and within **God's Kingdom** to **Establish** the **Laws of God** and the **Faith of Man** as **One Truth** (eternity) and **One**

Law (infinity) bringing *Divine, Angelic, and Human Love to All*. Now we see that the "Law" comes from <u>Jesus' Birth</u> during **Christmas** as the **Lord Fulfills His Father's Law** (expectations) via *His Obedience*; while "Faith" comes from <u>Christ's Death</u> during **Easter** as the **Lord Fulfills His Mother's Faith** (hopes) via *His Love*. In this same way, we see that "God Creates" <u>His Formal Sainthood</u> (God) as a **Business Venture** (law) to **Populate His Earth** (honor), **Fill His Heaven** (code), and **Bless His Kingdom** (God) with a *Constant Flow of Beloved Children*. Secondly, "God Creates" <u>His Informal Brotherhood</u> (man) as a **Place of Universal Friendship** (faithfulness) to **Honor** the *Home*, **Fulfill the Code** of the *Government*, and to **Worship God** in *His Church*. The implication here is that "God's Spirit of Obedience (Church/priesthood)" is <u>Slow and Deliberate</u> (perfection) and *Never Makes a Mistake;* while "Man's Flesh of Love (World/brotherhood)" <u>Uses Speed and Accuracy</u> (imperfection) to *Get Things Done Quickly and Dirty*. Obviously, this "Eternal Truth" of "Obedience and Love" <u>Represents</u> **Ethical Honesty** which will **Transform All Flesh** into *Righteousness* (law); while the "Infinite Law" <u>Represents</u> **Moral Integrity** and it will **Transform All Spirit** into *Holiness* (faith). Now we see that through a "Person's Honesty (ethics)" and "Integrity (morals)," he can **Find** a *Life of Daily Challenges*, thereby **Creating** a *Year of Adventure* leading to a *Lifetime of Rollicking Fun for All*.

Yes! We "All See" that the <u>Challenge of Calvary</u> (dark night) <u>Leads to the Adventure</u> of the **New Heaven** and the **New Earth** which **Culminates** in the **Coming** of the **Lord God Almighty Himself** (fun) in **His New Jerusalem** from *Heaven to Earth*. The question is: just how can a "Lost Soul on Calvary (bad thief)," <u>Who is Demon-Possessed</u> have **Any Chance** of being **Saved**, when he has **Lost Any Personal Power Over** his *Own Free Will?* The answer lies in the "Creation" of <u>Christ's New Belief System</u> which is **Centered** on a **Second Chance** or a **Co-redeemer, Who is to Come** as **Infinite Mercy Seeking Those most Unfortunate Souls** *Who* are *Lost Forevermore*. Certainly, this "Mystical Co-redeemer" is the <u>Blessed Virgin Mary,</u> **Who has Become One** with **Her Son, Jesus** so that **She might Unite** with **His Mystical Plan** to <u>Save Man's Cursed Flesh</u> (grave) and *Eternally even Every Damned Spirit in Hell*. We see this "Glimmer of Hope" being <u>Played-out</u> on **Mount Calvary** (mercy seat) with the **Story** of the **Two Thieves, Who Argued Over** whether **Jesus** was either a *Man* (bad thief) or was *God Himself* (good thief). Unfortunately, we see that "Jesus is Both" <u>All Man</u> and <u>All God</u> at the **Same time** and therefore is **Capable** of **Saving All Sinners** (Man) and then **Turning Them into Holy Saints** (God) because as a **Divine Man** (Jesus/law), *He* has the *Power Over Nature;* and as a **Human God** (Christ/faith), *He can Perform the Impossible*. This "Paradoxical Contradiction" <u>Sits at the Center</u> of the **Argument** between the **Two Thieves** as **They** simply **Could not Fathom such Complexity**, especially when *Their Immortal Soul* was *Hanging in the Balance*.

The "Theme Here" is that <u>All Lost Sinners</u> (bad thief) are to be **Taught the Lessons of Life** to **Learn God's Right** from **man's wrong** and become **Righteous Citizens on Earth, Worthy** of a *New Body* (free redemption). Secondly, "All Repentant Sinners (good thief) are to <u>Receive God's Blessings</u> to **Learn God's Good** from **man's evil** and become **Holy Saints in Heaven, Worthy** of *Eternal Life* (earned salvation). This means that the "Saved Sinner" is to <u>Defeat his Ignorance</u> and **Gain Wisdom** to **Create** *Heaven on Earth*, while the "Born-again Saint" is to Defeat his Cowardice and **Gain Courage** to **Create Paradise in Heaven.** We now see that there are "Two Redemptive Plans:" One for **Saving Sinners** and One for **Creating Saints** based on either **Defeating** *Baby Ignorance* (free gift) or **Defeating** *Adult Cowardice* (earned treasure).

The following graphic illustration indicates just "How the Holy Cross" was Used to Divide the **Two Redemptive Plans of God: One to Save** the *Unrepentant Bad Thief* (law/free) and **One to Save** the *Repentant Good Thief* (faith/earned):

Flesh
(unrepentant)

1. **Bad Thief** - Obey God's Law: Change Nature (free) …See Limitations
   - Learn Right from Wrong - Become Righteous Citizen on Earth: New Mind (purify grave)
   - Defeat Ignorance Gain Wisdom - Intellect: Baby Level (growth of flesh)
   - Seeing Jesus as a Man/Divine Man - Heaven on Earth: New Body (find sinners)

**Learn
Lessons**
   - If He is God, then Let Him Take Down from Here - Human (soldier-of-the-light)
   - Free Redemption - Good News: Baptized in Water = Jesus Takes-on Sin
   - Saving the Pagan World - Winepress of Death: Making Wine

Spirit
(repentant)

2. **Good Thief** - Love Man's Faith: Become Holy (earned) …See Potential
   - Learn Good from Evil - Become Holy Saint in Heaven: New Heart (purify host)

**Receive
Blessings**
   - Defeat Cowardice Gain Courage - Emotions: Adult Level (maturity of spirit)
   - Seeing Jesus as God/Human God - Paradise in Heaven: Eternal life (create saints)
   - This Day You will be with Me in Paradise - Divine (living prayer of love)
   - Earned Salvation - Gospel Message: Baptized in Spirit = Christ Gives-up Divinity
   - Saving the Holy Church - Crucible of Fire/Life: Making Bread

This illustration shows that "Mary's Son, Jesus (free redemption) was Born to **Take onto Himself All Sin** and **Fulfill God's Law** (commandments) by **Offering God His Perfect Obedience,** thereby **Changing Man's Nature** (bad thief) from **Human** (death) to *Divine* (life). Secondly, "God's Son, Christ (earned salvation)" Came to Earth to **Give-up His Divinity** and **Fulfill Man's Faith** (worship) by **Offering His Father Human Love,** thereby **Making Mankind Holy** (good thief) by *Resurrecting the Dead.* These "Two Master Plans" for a Sinner's Redemption (free) and for a Christian's Salvation (earned) bring **New Hope** to **Every Person on Earth** as the **Lord Jesus Christ Comes** in **His Three Advents** to Save the *Chosen Jews, Faithful Christians, and Evil Pagans.* We see that these "Three Advents" represent the Good Thief being *Saved First* (1st advent), the **Bad Thief** is being *Saved Second* (2nd advent), and finally, the Murderer Barabbas was *Saved Last* (3rd advent). The idea here is for the "Bad Thief" to be Saved from Ignorance to **Give him Wisdom** to **See his**

Own Limitations and **Learn the Lessons of Life** by **Knowing Right from Wrong**, thereby <u>**Making him**</u> a *Righteous Citizen on Earth* (new mind). Secondly, the "Good Thief" will be <u>Saved from Cowardice</u> and **Given Courage** to **See his Own Potential** and **Receive God's Blessings in Life** by **Knowing Good from Evil**, thereby <u>**Making him**</u> a *Holy Saint in Heaven* (new heart). Obviously, through both the "Bad Thief" as <u>Compared</u> to the "Good Thief," we can <u>Come to Understand</u> the **Dual Nature of Jesus Christ** as **He Seeks** the *Lost for His Mother* (redeem Hell) and also **Seeks** the *Saints for His Father* (create Heaven). We see that "All Humanity" has been <u>Called to Repentance</u> to **Open the Gates** of **Christ's New Kingdom of Glory,** thereby **Welcoming All** the <u>**Children of God,**</u> be *They* either *Good Thieves* (spirit) and/or *Bad Thieves* (flesh). This means that "Everyone Must Go to Calvary (judgment)" and "Everyone must Face" the <u>Challenge</u> of **Defeating** either his **Baby Ignorance** (law) or his **Adult Cowardice** (faith). The ultimate **Choice** is <u>**Left Up**</u> to **Every Person on Earth,** **Win** (earn honors) or *Lose* (free ride). Yes! the "Life-experience" can either be a <u>Living Nightmare</u> (challenge) or an <u>Exciting Adventure</u> (fun). The **Choice** is **Left Up to Every Soul** <u>**Which must Decide**</u> to either *Follow God's Will* (eternal life) or to *Follow its Own Will (death).*

The Most Evil of Curses Turns into Man's Greatest Blessings

Deception   1.   **Adam Cursed** - <u>Toil in a Barren Land:</u> Man Defeats *Ignorance,* becomes *Wise*

Defiance   2.   **Eve Cursed** - <u>Pain in a Barren Womb:</u> Man Defeats *Cowardice,* becomes *Courageous*

Deceit   3.   **Adam/Eve Cursed** - <u>Death in Barren Grave:</u> Man Defeats *Greed,* becomes *Generous*

The point here is to see that the "Life-experience" can certainly be <u>Centered</u> upon a **Lifetime of Excitement If a Child of God** is **Eager to Open** that **Door of Hope** and **See the Great Joy** of <u>Living</u> just *One More Glorious Day* in *God's Exciting Kingdom*. Yes! It's all about being "Challenged (games)," going on that "Exciting Adventure (journeys)," and having a "Lifetime of Rollicking Fun (rides)" as <u>**Every Thing in God's Creation**</u> is *Perfect and Holy* in the *Eyes of a Baby*. The question is: "Who would Imagine" that the <u>Soul-crushing Fall</u> of **Adam and Eve** would **Lead to** <u>**Man's Peace, Joy, and Happiness**</u> in *All Things both Great and Small?* Consider "Our First Parents" as <u>They Stole God's Forbidden Fruit</u> (greed) in an **Evil Act of Defiance** and were then <u>**Cursed**</u> with *Toil in a Barren Desert* (hard-work). This "Curse of Hard-labor" <u>Leads</u> to <u>Defeating Man's Ignorant Mind</u> as the **Human Race Learns** to <u>**Struggle Against All the Forces**</u> of *Sin* (sin-nature), *Evil* (worldly temptations), and *Death* (demonic possession). Secondly, "Adam and Eve" <u>Ran and Hid from God</u> in an **Evil Act of Deception** and were **Cursed** with a *Barren Womb* or *Pains at Childbirth*. This "Curse of Pain" <u>Leads</u> to <u>Mankind Defeating its Cowardly Heart</u> as the **Human Race Learns** to **Struggle Against All the Forces** of *Homelessness* (death), *Nakedness* (poverty), and *Starvation* (disease). Finally, "Adam and Eve" Lied to God Face-to-face in an **Evil Act of Deceit** and were **Cursed** with a *Barren Life* (defiled host) or an *Evil Grave of Death* (defiled grave). This "Curse of Death" Leads to Mankind Defeating its Greedy Soul as the **Human Race Learns** to **Struggle** against its *Own Selfishness* (sin-nature) to **Overcome the Propensity** to *Lying, Cheating, and Stealing.* Through the "Curses" of Hard-work (earth), Pain (Heaven), and Death (Kingdom), the **Human Race** is so **Greatly Blessed** as **It Learns** to **Overcome All Manner of Adversity** through **Its Constant Dedication** to the *Intricate Details of Life* (science). We see that "Hard-work (starvation)" Leads the Human Race to *Build Homes*; then "Pain (nakedness)" causes Man to *Build Governments;* and finally, "Death (homelessness)" caused Mankind to *Build Churches to Worship God.*

The following tabular information indicates that the "Life-experience" is centered upon One's Daily Challenge (trickle), His Yearly Adventure (fountain), and a Lifetime of Fun (deluge) **Assuming a Person** has been **Blessed** with *Wisdom* (hard-work), *Courage* (sacrifice), *and Generosity* (shed blood):

Life is About Challenge, Adventure, and Fun which Comes from Mankind's Sin, Evil, and Death
(man is challenged to remove ignorance, adventure to remove cowardice and fun to remove greed)

Trickle (truth)	1.	**Challenge** - Removing Ignorance: Sin = Stop Lying (deceit) …Knowledge
		• Learning Right from Wrong - Becoming a Righteous Citizen on Earth (honor)
		• Daily Challenge - Facing the Trials of Life: Trial and Error **Beliefs**
		• Experiencing Failure (agony of defeat) - Overcome Adversity •Identity
Hard-work		• See Limitations - Mastering Honesty: Ethics = Build Home
(done to you)		• Mind of Wisdom - Overcome Sin-nature: Free Redemption = New Body
		• Obedience becomes Wisdom - Toil Changed to Rest: Baby Level of Maturity
		• New Body brings forth *Human Knowledge* - Free Redemption (defiance - sin curses mankind with hard-labor: toil in a barren land = sweat + fruitless harvest)
Fountain (law)	2.	**Adventure** - Remove Cowardice: Evil = Stop Hiding (deception)... Self-awareness
		• Learning Good from Evil - Becoming a Holy Saint in Heaven (integrity)
		• Yearly Adventure - Overcoming Problems through Help: Quit-in-defeat **Likes**
		• Experiencing Success (thrill of victory) - Winning •Character
Sacrifice		• See Potential - Mastering Integrity: Morals = Build Government
(done to yourself)		• Heart of Courage - Overcome Worldly Temptation: Earn Salvation = Eternal Life

- Humility becomes Courage - Pain Changed to Pleasure: Teenage Level of Maturity
- Eternal Life brings forth *Divine Love* - Earned Salvation
  (deception - evil curses mankind with pain: barren womb = pain of childbirth + fruitless family)

Deluge (will)

3. **Fun** - <u>Remove Greed:</u> Death = Stop Stealing (defiance) ...Consciousness
- Learning God's Will/man's will - Becoming a Perfect Son within Kingdom (dignity)
- Lifetime of Fun - Work and Play are One: Never-quit Fighting **Actions**
- Experiencing Freedom (thinking for self) - Treasuring　　•Personality

Shed Blood
(done by God)

- See Self-worth - Mastering Dignity: Fairness = Build Church
- Soul of Generosity - Overcome Demonic Possession: Bonus Reward
- Holiness becomes Generosity - Death Changed to Life: Adult Level of Maturity
- Royal Kingdom brings forth *God's Perfection* - Bonus Rewards
  (deceit - death curses mankind with hell:
  barren life = death agony + fruitless existence)

This illustration shows that the "Human Race" has been <u>Challenged</u> to **Defeat** its *Curse of Ignorance* by becoming *Wise* (new mind), then **Defeat** its *Curse of Cowardice* by becoming *Courageous* (new heart), and finally, **Defeating** its *Curse of Greed* by becoming *Generous* (new soul). Through "Wisdom, Courage, and Generosity," a <u>Person can Find</u> the **True Essence of Life** as **God Intended** in the **Garden of Eden** through the **Union** of *God's Love* (all) and *Man's Faith* (nothing). This means that through "Man's Physical Growth (babyhood/law)" and "Man's Spiritual Maturity (adulthood/faith)," the <u>Human Race</u> could **Learn** enough to **Overcome All the Negative Forces** within its *Evil World*.

Obviously, the "Longest Journey" starts with a <u>Single Step</u> and a "Great River" starts with a small Trickle of Water so this axiom must still hold for the *Birth of Man*. We see that the "Creation of Law" and the <u>Institutions of Society</u> (home/government/church) are extremely **Slow in Coming** as it seems to **Take Forever** to get the *Forces of Order* to *Defeat the Forces of Chaos*. We also see in the previous chart, that the "Lord God Almighty" is <u>Seeking</u> to **Determine Man's Beliefs** (challenge) to **Reveal the Depth of his Mind** (wisdom) and the **Intelligence Quotient of his Intellect** (honor) to **Know his Child's Aptitude** (identity) for *Living a Divine Life*. Secondly, the "Lord God Almighty" is <u>Seeking</u> to **Determine Man's Likes** (adventure) to **Reveal the Depth of his Heart** (courage) and the **Devotion Quotient of his Emotions** (integrity) to **Know His Child's Wants** (character) for *Living a Divine Life*. Finally, the "Lord God Almighty" is watching <u>Man's Actions</u> (fun) to **Reveal the Depth of his Soul** (generosity) and his **Innate Abilities Developed** within his **Instinctive Nature** (dignity) so the **Lord** will **Know His Child's Lifestyle** (personality) when *Living a Divine Life*. This means that "Building a Perfect Society" is going to <u>Take</u> a great deal of **Hard-work**, many **Sacrifices,** and the **Shedding of Innocent Blood** before *Man* *can Conquer Sin, Evil, and Death*. We see that this "Awesome Journey" will precisely Make Men Out of Boys and bring forth the **Treasures of Life** in the **Form** of *Honors* (flesh), *Integrity* (spirit), and *Dignity* (soul).

We see that through "His Honors," "Integrity," "Dignity," and also "Holiness," a Person can **Expect** to become **Worthy of Touching** the **Face of God** and truly **Reach** the **Heights of Divine Union** before *Men, Angels, God, and even Oneself*. Remember that in "Reverse," God must also **Touch** the **Face of Man** and then **Transform** into **His New Human Nature** with a **Dual Life-force** (destiny/free will) by becoming both *All and Nothing at the Same Time*. This "Ability" to Master the Divine Paradox (two masters) of the **Impossible Sits at the Center** of *All Existence* and *All Happiness*. This means that the "Lord God Almighty" is Faced with **Blending People, Power,** and **Love All Together** into **One Perfect Creation** in such a way as to **Ensure** that **Every Person within the Creation** has a **Fair Amount** (equality) of *Challenge, Adventure, Fun, and Happiness Forever*. We see that this "Divine Goal" of Perfect Equality (equal competition) is the **Centerpiece** of **God's Coming Kingdom of Glory**, but to **Do This Right, Every Man** must be both a **King** (pride) and a **Slave** (humility) within *One Dual Nature of a Balanced Self*. We call this the "New Transfigured Body (king/slave)" of Jesus Christ (God/Man) which was **Displayed** at the **Transfiguration** and again to the **Apostles** in the **Upper Room** *After the Lord's Resurrection* (put fingers in wounds). The idea here is that "During the Lord's" 2nd Advent (thief), the **Awakened Church** will be **Given God's Firstfruits of Perfection** as **Every Saint**, whether on **Earth** or in **Heaven**, will **Receive his Own** *New Transfigured Body* (1Corinthians 15:52). The "Lord" is Telling Us that at the **Sounding** of the **1st Trumpet,** the **Living/Dead Saints** (flesh) will **Rise** (rapture/graves) and **Meet the Heavenly Saints** (spirit) in the **Air** to be **United** with **Jesus Christ** in **His New** *Physical Kingdom of Glory*. Now, we see in this "Grand Design" that God's Goal of bringing **Challenge, Adventure, Fun, and Happiness** to **All Men** would **Require** the **Creation** of *Four Mystical Facilities* (baby farm/divine school/sonship training/freedom). The idea here is that the "Earth" Represents **God's Baby Farm** and has been **Designed** so **that God's Babies** can both **Grow** and **Mature** through a **Life** of **Trials and Errors** as **They Face the Challenge** of Taking Lucifer's Test of *Sin, Evil, and Death*. Secondly, "Heaven" Represents **God's Divine School Designed** so that **God's Teenagers** can **Enter Their Sainthood** through a **Life** of **New Experiences, Enter God's Adventure, Face God's Judgment,** and *His Call to Holiness*. Finally, the "Kingdom" Represents **God's Sonship Training Program Designed** so that **God's Adult Children** can **Enter Their Sonship** through the **Power of Knowing All Things, Enter God's Fun,** Face Self-evaluation, and *Receive God's Blessing of Freedom*. We see that on that "Awesome Day of New-life (own keys)," God, Angels, and Men will become **One Creation** and **Everyone** and **Everything** will **Enter a State** of *Eternal Freedom, Peace, Joy, and Happiness*.

The following tabular information indicates that "Wisdom" brings Knowledge (freedom); "Courage" brings Self-awareness (peace); "Generosity" brings Consciousness (joy); and "Unselfishness" brings Sentience (happiness):

Home (omniscient) **Parents**	1. **Wisdom brings Knowledge** - <u>Mind:</u> Comprehension of Ideas...Truth • Baby's Fear of Pain - Overcome Fear with Knowledge...Freedom • Find Human Honors (rewards) - Master Physical Dimension (earth) • Transfigured Body - New Dual Nature (seat in celestial court) • 1st Level of Life - Silly Child (informal/formal)
Government (omnifarious) **Leaders**	2. **Courage brings Self-awareness** - <u>Heart:</u> Awakened to Reality... Law • Teenager's Fear of Death - Overcome Fear with God's Right/man's wrong ...Peace • Find Personal Integrity (self) - Master Spiritual Dimension (Heaven) • Glorified Spirit - Eternal Life (seat in temple court) • 2nd Level of Life - Growing Teenager (informal) and Citizen of Society (formal)
Church (omnipotent) **Pope**	3. **Generosity brings Consciousness** - <u>Soul:</u> Knowing Right from Wrong...Will • Adult's Fear of Damnation/hell - Overcome Fear with God's Right/man's wrong...Joy • Find Dignity (self/society) - Master Mystical Dimension (Kingdom) • Holy Soul - Own Royal Kingdom (seat in royal court) • 3rd Level of Life - Mature Adult (informal) and Holy Saint (formal)
God (omniscient) **God**	4. **Unselfishness brings Sentience** - <u>Life-force:</u> Sense of Knowing All Things... Love • Free Man's Fear of Oblivion - Overcome Fear by Knowing Happiness—All Things • Find Happiness (self/society/God) - Master Divine Dimension (God) • Perfect Life-force - Eternal Freedom (seat in divine court) • 4th Level of Life - Citizen of Creation (informal) and Child of God (formal)

The following information indicates the "Fears" of <u>Earthly Babies</u> (ignorance), <u>Heavenly Teenagers</u> (cowardice), <u>Kingdom Adults</u> (greed), and <u>God's Free Men</u> (selfishness) are **Overcome** by the **Forces** of *Wisdom* (knowledge), *Courage* (self-awareness), *Generosity* (consciousness), and *Unselfishness* (sentience):

1. **Fixed Frame of Reference** - Identity
   • Meaning of Life - To Exist
2. **Relative Focused Existence** - Character
   • Purpose of Life - To Serve
3. **Perception of Reality** - Personality
   • Value of Life - To be Happy
4. **Comprehension of Life** - Ambience
   • Blessings of Life - To Find God

1. Repentance—-**Fixed Frame of Reference/Meaning of life** (existence) —
Baby's Fear of Pain - New Body (defeat ignorance/fear of pain)
    This means that "God's Awesome Creations of Life" have been <u>Designed</u> to
Remove a Baby's Fear of Pain and **Master God's Destiny** to **Journey** from
being a **<u>Sinner</u>** to being a **<u>Christian</u>** via the *Blessed Mother's Elementary School*
(see limitations). In this most "Powerful School (life)," a <u>Tiny Baby</u> will **Find the
Importance** of **Life's Challenges** and **Face** the **Pain of Struggle** to **<u>Live It</u>** (kiss
the IS/moment) to *Its Fullest without Fear* (growing). This experience is much
"Like Stumbling" <u>Over a Treasure</u> in a <u>Field,</u> then **Selling All** to **Purchase** (buy)
the **Field** to **Make Oneself Rich** and **<u>Learn God's Right</u>** from **man's <u>wrong</u>** to
Face his Physical Fears (pain). Obviously, this "Experience" will <u>Allow a Person</u>
to **Grow-up** and become a **Righteous Citizen on Earth**, thereby **Making himself Worthy** of <u>God's Great Gift</u> of a *New Transfigured Body* (earth). This means
that the "Job of Parents" is to <u>Fill Their Children</u> with **Knowledge** so that **They
can Effectively Comprehend** the **Meaning of Ideas,** thereby **Allowing Each
Child** to **Overcome his Fears** and **<u>Allow</u>** him to *Find that All Important Truth*
(answers). "When a Child" <u>Learns the Truth</u> and has **All** of the **Correct Answers,**
he can become **Worthy** of his **Mother's Blessings** (love) and his **Father's Rewards** (honors/respect). Via this **Love and** these **Honors,** a **Growing Child** can
<u>Obtain the Necessary Confidence</u> to *Master his Own Little World of Life*. Obviously, at this "Moment when a Person" has become <u>Master of All he Surveys,</u> he
can be **Set Free**, thereby **Making him Worthy** of **Christ's Transfigured Body**
(dual nature) so that he can **Take Stock of his Life** and *See he is Still Only a
Silly Child*.
(defeat ignorance - overcome fear of pain through wisdom: growing-up brings knowledge)

2. Prayers—**Relative Focused Existence/Purpose of Life** (service) —
Teenager's Fear of Death - Eternal Life (defeat cowardice/fear of death)
    Secondly, a "Teenager's Fear of Death" must be <u>Removed</u> as he **Masters his Own
Free Will** and **Journey** from being a **<u>Christian</u>** to being a **<u>Saint</u>** via *Saint Joseph's Heavenly High School* (see potential). In this most "Powerful School (eternal life)," a <u>Teenager</u>
will **Find the Importance** of **Life's Adventures** and **Face** the **Curse of Death** to **<u>Defeat It</u>** (kiss the IS/moment) by **<u>Changing Directions</u>** and *Finding a New Path* (growing). This experience is much "Like Going in Search" of the <u>Pearl of Great Price,</u> then
Selling All to **Purchase** (buy) **It** to **Make Oneself Eternally Happy** and **<u>Learn God's
Good</u>** from **man's evil** to *Face* his *Spiritual Fears* (death). Obviously, this "Experience"
will <u>Allow a Person</u> to **Grow-up** and become a **Holy Saint in Heaven**, thereby **Making
himself Worthy** of <u>God's Great Gift</u> of a *New Glorified Spirit* (Heaven). This means
that the "Job of the Pope" is to <u>Fill His Parishioners</u> with **Consciousness,** thereby **Allowing Them** to be **Awakened to the Reality of God** (right/wrong), so that a **Mature
Adult** can **Overcome his Fears** which will **Allow** him to *Follow the Will of God*. "When
a Devout Christian" can <u>Know God's Will</u> from <u>man's will,</u> he will be **Given the Mind
of Christ**, be **Worthy** of **God's Blessings, Obtain** the **Grace Needed** to **<u>Master his</u>**

Own Life, and ***Become a Son of God***. Obviously, at this "Moment when a Saint" has become <u>Master of All he Surveys,</u> he can be **Set Free,** thereby **Making him Worthy** of **Christ's Glorified Spirit** (eternal life), **Take Stock of his Life** and **See** he is both a ***Mature Adult*** and *a Holy Saint.*
(defeat cowardice - overcome fear of death through courage: growing-up brings self-awareness)

3. Works————-**Perception of Reality/Value of Life** (happiness)————
<u>Adult's Fear of Damnation</u> (hell) - Royal Kingdom (defeat greed/fear of death)

Thirdly, an "Adult's Fear of Damnation/hell" must be <u>Removed</u> as he **Masters his Own Dual Nature** to **Journey** from being a **Saint** to being a **Son of God** via *Jesus Christ's College/Sonship Training Program* (see self-worth). In this most "Powerful University (mystical life)," an <u>Adult</u> will **Find the Importance** of **Life's Treasure of Fun** and then **Face** the **Curse of Damnation, Defeat It** by **Uniting** with **God's Omnipotent Power,** and *Finding a Valid Solution* (maturity). This experience is much "Like One Going in Search" of a <u>Great Catch</u> (fish) and **Devising a Great Net** to **Catch Them All at Once** to **Reap Its Great Rewards,** and **Learn God's Will** from **man's will** to *Face his Own Mystical Fears* (damnation). Obviously, this "Experience" will <u>Allow a Person</u> to **Mature** and to become a **Son of God** within the **Lord's Kingdom,** thereby **Making himself Worthy** of <u>God's Great Gift</u> of a *New Holy Soul* (Kingdom). This means that the "Job of Leaders" is to <u>Fill Their Citizens</u> with **Self-awareness** and **Effectively be Awakened** to the **Realities of Life,** so that a **Young Adult** (Teenager) can **Overcome his Fears** which will **<u>Allow</u>** him to *Follow the Laws of the Land.* "When a Citizen" can <u>Know Reality</u> from <u>Illusion,</u> he will be **Given** the **Cognitive Skills Needed** to become **Worthy** of both his **Teachers' Grades** and his **Leaders' Promotions,** and **<u>Obtain the Wisdom</u>** to *Master his Growing Fiefdom of Human Existence.* Obviously, at this "Moment when a Person" has become <u>Master of All he Surveys,</u> he can be **Set Free,** thereby **Making him Worthy** of **Christ's Holy Soul** (kingdom), **Take Stock of his Life,** and *See* he is a *Growing Teenager* and a *Citizen of Society.*
(defeat greed - overcome fear of damnation/hell through generosity: maturity brings consciousness)

4.   Save Souls—-**Comprehension of Life/Blessings of Life** (fulfillment)—
<u>Free Man's Fear of Oblivion</u> - Freedom (defeat selfishness/fear of oblivion)

Finally, a "Free Man's Fear of Oblivion" must be <u>Removed</u> as he **Masters both Humanity and Divinity** to **Journey** from being a **Son of God** to being a **Free Man** via the ***Lord God Almighty's Leadership Position with Him.*** In this most "Awesome Leadership Position (divine life)," a <u>Free Man</u> will **Find the Importance** of **Life's Blessing of Happiness,** then **Face the Curse of Oblivion** to **Defeat It** by **<u>Becoming One with God</u>,** and *Finding a Way* to be ***Both All and Nothing at Once*** (adulthood/paradox). This experience is much "Like One Going in Search" of <u>God Himself</u> and then **Planning a Way** to **Repent, Pray, Work, and Save Souls Enough** to Become Worthy of God's Perfect Life-force to **Learn God's Reality** from **man's**

illusion and *Face his Divine Fears* (oblivion). Obviously, this "Experience" will Allow a Person to **Reach Adulthood** to become a **Free Man Thinking for himself,** thereby **Making him Worthy** of <u>God's Great Gift</u> of a *New Perfect Life-force* (free will). This Means that the "Job of God" is to <u>Fill Christ's Followers</u> with **Sentience,** allowing them to **Learn All Things** and become **Omniscient Beings,** so that a **Son of God** can **Overcome his Fears** which will **<u>Allow</u>** him to *Learn to Think for Himself.* "When a Holy Saint" can <u>Know God's Reality</u> from <u>man's illusion,</u> he will be **Given God's Infinite Mind** and **Loving Heart,** be **Worthy** of his **Personal Freedom, Obtain** the **Power Needed** to **Master All Creation,** and *Become a Reflection of God.* Obviously, at this "Moment When a Son of God" has become <u>Master of All he Surveys,</u> he can be **Set Free,** thereby **Making him Worthy** of **Christ's Perfect Life-force** (freedom), **Take Stock of his Life,** and *See* he is both a *Citizen of Creation* (free) and an *Elder Child of God* (free). (defeat selfishness - overcome fear of oblivion through unselfishness: freedom brings sentience)

The following tabular information indicates that "God's Earthly Baby Farm" will <u>Produce *Eternal Bodies*</u>, "God's Heavenly School" will <u>Produce *Eternal Lives,*</u> "God's Sonship Kingdom" will <u>Produce *Personalized Kingdoms,*</u> and finally, "God's Eternal Freedom" will <u>Produce *Men Who can Think for Themselves*</u> (free men):

Mastering God's Baby Farm, Divine School, and Sonship Training to Unite God and Man as One
(Baby Farm brings honors via courage, Divine School brings dignity
via wisdom, and Sonship Training brings holiness via devotion)

Defeat
Sin
(honor)

1. **Baby Farm** - <u>Scourging:</u> Fighting/defeating Sin-nature..... Knowledge
   * Life on Earth - Trials and Errors: Guess and By Golly = Being Saved
   * Remove Baby's Fear of Pain - Master Destiny: Sinner becomes Christian
   * Blessed Mother's Elementary School - Little Red School House: See Limitations
   * Find the Importance of *Challenge* - Face Pain of Struggle and Loving It
   * Stumbling Over a Treasure in a Field - Sell All to Buy Field
   * Learning God's Right from man's wrong (treasure) - Face Physical Fears
   * Becoming Righteous Citizen on Earth - *Receive New Body*

Defeat
Evil
(dignity)

2. **Divine School** - <u>Crucifixion:</u> Fighting/defeating Worldly Temptations... Self awareness
   * Life in Heaven - Experiencing Life: Studying Perfection = Saving Self
   * Remove Teenager's Fear of Death - Master Free Will: Christian becomes Saint
   * Saint Joseph's High School - Heavenly Education: See Potential
   * Find the Importance of *Adventure* - Face Solving Impossible and Loving It
   * Going in Search of the Pearl of Great Price - Selling All to Buy It

- Learning God's Good from man's evil (pearl) - Face Spiritual Fears
- Becoming Holy Saint in Heaven - *Receive Eternal Life*

Defeat Death (holiness)	3.	**Sonship Training** - <u>Tomb:</u> Fighting/defeating Demonic Possession... Consciousness

- Life within Kingdom - Knowing All Things: Receiving the Mind of God = Save Others
- Remove Adult's Fear of Damnation - Master Dual Nature: Saints become Sons
- Jesus Christ's College - Kingdom Sonship: See Self-worth
- Find the Importance of *Fun* - Converting Challenge/Adventure into Fun
- Focusing Life on God's Riches in Glory - Selling All to Become Worthy
- Learning God's Will from man's will - Face Mystical Fears
- Becoming Righteous Son within Kingdom - *Receive Royal Kingdom*

Defeat Damnation (perfect)	4.	**Eternal Freedom** - <u>Resurrection:</u> Fighting/defeating Divine Justice... Sentience

- Life within God - Becoming All Things: Receiving Beatific Vision = Self-worth
- Remove Wise Man's Fear of Oblivion - Master Divinity/Humanity: Sons to Freedom
- God Sets His Son Free - Own Royal Kingdom: See Face of God
- Find the Importance of *Happiness* - Finding Awe-inspiring Value
- Sacrificing Human Nature to Get Divine Nature - Give Life to God
- Learning God's Reality from man's illusion - Face Divine Fears
- Becoming Free Man within Himself - *Receive God's Freedom* (keys)

This illustration shows that "God's Baby Farm" is to <u>Defeat Sin</u> (sin-nature) and **Remove Each Baby's Fear of Pain** to **Set Him Free** from **Lucifer's Painful Tests** as **Evil <u>Works Night</u>** and **<u>Day</u>** to *Torment the Human Race*. Secondly, "God's Divine School" is to <u>Defeat Evil</u> (worldly temptations) and **Remove Each Teenager's Fear of Death** (grave) to **Set Him Free** from **God's Judgment** as **He Works Night** and **<u>Day</u>** to **<u>Educate</u>** the **Human Race** in the *Struggles of Life*. Thirdly, "God's Sonship Training Program" is to <u>Defeat Death</u> (demonic possession) and to **Remove Each Adult's Fear of Damnation** (hell) to **Set Him Free** from **Self-evaluation** (self-worth) as a **<u>Person Works Night</u>** and **<u>Day</u>** to be **<u>Trained</u>** in *Overcoming the Attacks* from *Himself, Society*, and *Lucifer or God*. Finally, "God's Eternal Freedom" is to <u>Defeat Damnation</u> (God's curse) and **Overcome Fear of Freedom** (failure) to **Set Him Free** from the **Unknown Factor** (independence) as a **Wise Man <u>Works Night</u>** and **<u>Day</u>** to **<u>Think for himself</u>** to *Overcome Ignorance, Cowardice, Greed, and Selfishness*. It is now clear that the "Baby Farm (baby)," "Divine School (teenage)," "Sonship Training (adult)," and "Eternal Freedom (wise man)" are <u>All Designed</u> to **<u>Challenge God's Children</u>** to *Face the Struggles of both Life and Eternal Life*. Obviously, "Our Perfect God Knew" that <u>Each of His Children</u>

would **Need** to **Defeat his Own Fears,** his **Fear of Death,** and his **Fear of Eternal-damnation** before he could have the **Necessary Courage to Face** his *Own Sin-nature* (fear/self), *Worldly Temptations* (death/world), and *Lucifer's Demonic Possession* (damnation/Hell). The message here is that the "Lord God Almighty" also Needed a Challenge Worthy of **His Divine Perfection** so **He Devised His Scourging** to *Remove his Fear of Failure* (pain), then **His Crucifixion** to *Remove His Fear of Death*, and finally, the Tomb to *Remove His Fear of Damnation* (hell). With the "Life," "Death," and "Resurrection" of Jesus Christ, the **Lord God Almighty Fulfilled His Dream** of **Defeating** *Fear* (scourging), *Pain* (crucifixion), and *Death* (tomb). Obviously, an "Infinite God," Who was Never-created, had to **Challenge Himself** in **Facing His Greatest Fear,** which was that of **Falling** into some **Pit of Oblivion** (all becomes nothing) and *Disappearing from All Existence Forever and Ever.* This means that the "God of All" had to Go to Mount Calvary to become the "God of Nothing" to become **Transformed** into a **Perfect Man,** with the *Wisdom, Courage, and Power of a God,* yet, to also have the *Humility of a Dutiful Slave*...and so it was done.

Note: If a Person Tries to Figure Out the Life, Nature, or Purpose of God or Anything About Him, Nothing will Explain God and Nothing can Determine His Motives because He IS, IS (all is in all) or a Paradox and All Else is Separate from Him.

Now that "We Know that God" is an Enigma Wrapped in a Paradoxical Mystery, **We** can come to **Understand** that **Our God of Justice** has **Miraculously Changed** into a **God of Mercy,** where **All of Humanity** is **Now Invited to Heaven** either through **Christ's Free, Earned, or Bonus Redemption Programs.** We see that "These Three Programs" are to be Implemented by either a Handicap System (free) for **Innocent Children,** the **Old, Homeless,** and/or the **Insane** to **Bless Them** based on **Their Desire** to *Simply Try Their Best.* Secondly, "Man will also be Saved" by a Curve System (earned/average) for **Christian Believers** either at the **33%** Level (sinners), **67%** Level (Christians) and/or the **100%** Level (saints) to **Bless Them** based on **Their Ability** to *Deny Their Intellects, Abandon Their Feelings,* and/or *Submit Their Free Wills to God.* Finally, the "Most Chosen will be Saved" by a Pass/Fail System (bonus/perfect) for **Living Saints, Who Qualify** for becoming **Future Sons of God** by *Obeying God's Commandments, Selling All, and Giving to the Poor, Picking-up Their Cross, and Following Christ to Hell.* To "Comprehend" this Triune System, imagine a **Society** with **Many Poor Broken People Who Can't Help Themselves** and so **God Sent His Son** to **Help Save** an **Entire World** of *Innocent Children, Fools, Failures, and Lost Souls, Who are Begging for Redemption.*

The following tabular information indicates that the "Lord Jesus Christ" has Brought Three Redemptive Systems to **Earth** to **Save the Innocent,** the **Forgiven,** and even the **Guilty** based on **Three Different** *Mystical Scoring Systems:*

World - flesh
Free Redemption for Mankind's Babies - Heaven on Earth

1. **Children Get Free Redemption** - <u>Ignorant Mind:</u> Believe in Christ...Save the Innocent
2. **Old Get Free Redemption** - <u>Cowardly Heart:</u> Believe in Christ...Save the Fools
3. **Homeless Get Free Redemption** - <u>Greedy Heart:</u> Believe in Christ...Save the Failures
4. **Insane will Get Free Redemption** - <u>Selfish Soul:</u> Believe in Christ...Save the Lost

Church - spirit
Earned Salvation for Mankind's Teenagers - Paradise in Heaven

5. **Earned 33% Belief** - <u>Repentant Sinner:</u> Thank God with Labors...Blessed with Wisdom
6. **Earned 67% Belief** - <u>Devout Christian:</u> Praise God with Wealth... Blessed with Courage
7. **Earned 100% Belief** - <u>Holy Saint:</u> Worship God with Life........   Blessed with Generosity

God - soul
God's Bonus Rewards for Mankind's Adults - Own One's Kingdom

8. **Bonus for Knowing** - <u>Saints Changed to Sons:</u> Serve God with New Nature.... Given Freedom

This illustration shows that "Every Society is Using" its <u>Productive Citizens</u> to **Create an Economic Base** to **Establish Sufficient Wealth** to **Support Everyone,** be *They either Weak or Strong.* Unfortunately, the "Lord God Almighty's" <u>New Eternal Society</u> **Only** has **One Productive Citizen** and that is **His Son Jesus Christ** (all/nothing), **Who** will have to **Transform Everyone on Earth** into **His Own God/Man Nature** to **Save Them** from *Sin, Evil, and Death.* This theme of "Being All to Live (life)" and "Being Nothing to Die (death)" <u>Reveals</u> that the **Entire Life-experience** is **Centered** upon a **Great Journey** as **Each Created Soul** must **Travel** from *Man's Nothing* (sinner) to *God's All* (divinity). This "Awesome Eternal Journey" means that <u>Each of God's Children</u> must **Travel** through **Ten Levels of Life,** known as **God's Divine Chain of Command** from a *Never-created God, All the Way* to a *Created Man.* We see that these "Ten Levels" or "Stages of Life" <u>Operate</u> much like an **Inter-switch Trunking System** of **Circuits,** each with its **Own Set of Priorities,** thereby **Forcing** both **Angels and Men** to **Establish Their Own** <u>Priority Authority</u> (rank) or **Set of Credentials** to be *Authorized to Use the System.*

The idea here is that "Humanity" <u>Starts Out in Life</u> as a **Lost Broken Baby** (sinner), **Who must Prove himself** at **Every Level of Life** to both **Grow** (flesh) and **Mature** (spirit) to the **Point** of *Reaching Heaven* (saint), *Mastering the Kingdom* (son), and finally, becoming *One with God* (free). Now, it makes sense that "Everyone" <u>Starts Out in Life</u> as a **Sinner,** and must **Find the True Church** (mystical body of Christ) to become a **Christian** (earth); then he must **Reach Sainthood** (transfigured body) to be **Welcomed into Heaven** as a *Member of the Communion of Saints*. Through this "Heavenly State," a Person can Fulfill **God's Will** and **Become a Son of God** within **God's Royal Kingdom,** where he will **Prepare** to **Master God's Divine Love** and **Earn God's Respect/friendship** to the *Point of Being Set Free* (personal kingdom/thinking).

The idea here is that "Life on Earth Begins" with the Blessed Mother as **She is In-charge** of **Every Newly Created Soul.** This means that "Life Ends" by **Uniting** with the *Benevolent Force of God* (pure love) or with *God's Divine Nature Itself.* To "Make Everything Work Correctly," Jesus Christ's Job is to **Establish** an **Intercessory System** or **Priority System** from **One to Ten** so **that God, Angels, Men, and Nature** could **Communicate** with *Each Other Perfectly.* In this way, "God could become a Man (life)" and "Man could become God (death)" at Will, thereby **Allowing** a **Lost Broken Sinner** to **Travel** through **Ten Mystical Dimensions** from **Death to Newlife** to **Reach Life's** *Final Stage of Freedom* or being able to *Think for Oneself* (divine mind). We see that through this "Special Linking Function," the Benevolent Force (God/spirit) can become **One** with the Blessed Virgin Mary (Man/flesh), implying that the **Human Race** is **Hoping** to **Meet, Know, Love, and Serve** its **God,** but **One Day** will **Realize** that **God** and **His Creation** have become *One* or *God is You.*

The following graphic illustration "Reveals" the Special Linking Function **Required** by **God's Messiah** to bring forth an **Appropriate Intercessory System** so that **All the Forces of Creation** might *Communicate Freely*:

God/Man's Inter-Switch Communication System
(Jesus Christ's Perfect Justice System in Operation)

Become   1.   **Benevolent Force** - IS/Never-created God…Worship God
Alone (repent)

Love   2.   **Personal God** - I'AM: Divine Love (beatific vision) …Do
Not Worship Idols (Christian)
     • Divine Justice - Supreme Judgment (perfect)

Will   3.   **Lord God Almighty** - Divine Will (kingdom) …Do Not
Take God's Name in Vain (saint)

Law   4.   **Trinity** - Divine Law (eternal life) …Honor Thy
Father/Mother (righteous)

Truth   5.   **Seven-fold Spirits** - Divine Truth (new body) …Keep the
Sabbath Day Holy (holy)

- - - - -**Adult**- - - - -
God Speaks and Man Listens (down) - (up) *Man Speaks and God Listens*
Christ - Son of Man   *Law/Love*   *Jesus - Son of Man*
- - - - -**Baby**- - - - -

Results   6.   **Christ Jesus** - Son of God: Divine Man (holy) … Do
Not Kill (new body)

Deed	7.	**Jesus Christ** - <u>Son of Man:</u> Human God (righteous)…Do Not Commit Adultery (eternal life)
Word	8.	**Christ** - <u>High Priest of Heaven</u> (saint) … Do Not Steal (own kingdom)
Thought	9.	**Jesus** - <u>King of the Jews</u> (Christian) … Do Not Lie (beatific vision)
New-life	10.	**Blessed Virgin Mary** - <u>Absolute Repentance</u> (sinner)…Do Not Covet (set free)

Benevolent Force Wants to become Man——————----Man Wants to become
Benevolent Force

This illustration shows the "Intricate Structure" being <u>Used by God</u> to **Establish an Effective Chain-of-command** through which the **Divine Word of God** might be **Communicated** to the *Minds, Hearts, and Souls of Lost Mankind*. This means that "Life is All About" <u>Journeying</u> through **Ten Mystical Conversions**: 1) <u>Repenting</u> before the *Blessed Mother*, 2) <u>Christian</u> as follower of *Jesus*/King of the Jews, 3) <u>Saint</u> before *Christ*/High Priest of Heaven, 4) <u>Righteous</u> before *Jesus Christ*/son of man, 5) <u>Holy</u> before *Christ Jesus*/Son of Man, 6) <u>New Body</u> before *Seven-fold Spirits*/divine truth, 7) <u>Eternal Life</u> before *Trinity*, 8) <u>Own Royal Kingdom Live</u> with *Lord God Almighty*/divine will, 9) <u>Beatific Vision</u> (perfect) *Face of Personal God* (I'AM), and 10) <u>Set Free</u> - **Union** with *Benevolent Force* (IS).

Through this "Command Structure," <u>God can Speak to Man</u> and then <u>Man can Speak to God</u> to **Establish a Two-Way Conversation** between **God and Man,** thereby **Starting an Eternal Dialogue** between *Two Good Friends*. The question is just "How Great" of a <u>Personal Friend</u> **Does a Person Want to Be** with his **Creator,** based on **Ten Mystical Ranks** or **Levels of Priorities, <u>Beginning</u>** with (1) *Repentance,* (2) then becoming a *Christian,* (3) then a **Saint,** (4) then a **Righteous Citizen,** (5) then a *Holy Citizen,* (6) then *Receiving* a *Transfigured Body,* (7) then *Entering Eternal Life,* (8) *Owning One's Own Kingdom/son of God,* (9) then *Entering God's Beatific Vision/free man,* and finally, (10) being *United with God's Nature*/Benevolent Force. At "Each of These Levels," a <u>Person</u> both **Grows** (flesh) and **Matures** (spirit) just a **Little More Each Day,** until he can **Learn** to **Think for himself** and **Take Charge** of his *Own Life, Family, Community,* and then the *Whole World.*

We see that the "Same will be True" of the <u>Eternal Life</u> as a **Person** must be **Physically Purified** (chaos) and then **Spiritually Transformed** (order) from *Nothing* (man) to *All* (God). Yes! It's all a matter of being "Willing to Fight (believe)" for <u>What's Right</u> (government/earth), to "Surrender (submit/bow)" to <u>God's Will</u> (church/Heaven), and then to "Master (trying)" <u>One's New Nature</u> (fight evil). This means that the "Life-experience" is <u>Centered</u> on **Defeating One's <u>Sin-nature</u>** (ignorance), **<u>Worldly Temptations</u>** (cowardice), **Demonic Possession** (greed), and **God's Curses** (selfishness) to become *Wise* (repentance), *Courageous* (prayers), *Generous* (works), and finally, *Unselfish* (saving souls). Basically, this means that "Defeating" <u>All the Negative Forces</u> on **Earth** (baby farm), a **Child** must now **Prove himself** to **God, Angels** (church), **Men** (world), and **Nature** (self) since

Every time a **Person** seems to have **Won a Great Victory**, **Suddenly** <u>Comes a New Challenge</u> in an *Unending Stream/series of Painful Problems*. We then see that "Life is Short" and it is <u>Time to Enter Heaven</u> (divine school), which will seem a **Lot Like Training,** to become a **Pope** (priesthood) for a **Soul must Learn** to **Worship God** with its *Everlasting Life*, **Praise God** with its *Great Wealth*, and **Thank God** with its *Eternal Labors*. At the "End of One's Education" in <u>God's Divine School,</u> a **Person** must become **Ready** to **Take his Sonship Training** as a **Son of God** in the **Lord's Royal Kingdom,** where upon **Graduation,** a <u>Soul will be Rewarded</u> with its *Own Kingdom* (keys). Finally, it is time to "Put It All Together" and <u>Strike-out</u> on **One's Own** as **God is Now Ready** to **Give His Elder Child** the **Keys to Life** (divine power) and his **Own Bank Account** (divine love) to **Make him Fully** *Independent from Everything and Everybody*.

1. **Worship God** - <u>Everlasting Life:</u> Break Prison Chains…Gain Freedom
2. **Praise God** - <u>Great Infinite Wealth:</u> Open Prison Doors…Gain Liberty
3. **Thank God** - <u>Eternal Labors:</u> Overcome Prison Guards…Gain Independence

Yes! This "Tiny Baby" has <u>Grown-up</u> and has **Defeated Toil, Pain, Death, and Damnation.** He has **Faced** <u>Excommunication,</u> been an **Outcast, Faced Banishment,** and even been **Forsaken by God** (agony of defeat), but has *Still Kept Fighting*. We see that this "Undaunted Soul" has <u>Seen It All</u> and has **Mastered Lucifer's Test** (death agony), **God's Judgment** (hopelessness), and even its **Own Self-evaluation** (separation from God) to be **Crowned a True Winner** (thrill of victory) and has *Won* the *Respect of God Himself.* We see that through this "Awesome Respect" from <u>One's Benevolent Creator,</u> the **Life-experience Starts to Make Sense** because **Initially God Hates Man** as **He Inputs** *Righteousness, Holiness, and Perfection,* and then **Outputs** *Sin, Evil, and Death*. This "Divine Process" <u>Causes God to Hate Man</u> because the **Human Race Inputs** *Sin, Evil, and Death* to **Output** *Righteousness, Holiness, and Perfection* or just the *Reverse*. The "Job of Jesus Christ" was to Come to Earth and **Reverse the Process** (implement paradox) between the **Divine Spirit** and the **Human Flesh** through the **Power of Conversion,** thereby **Allowing God to Love Man** and for **Man to Love God** without any <u>Interference</u> from *Sin, Evil, and/or Death*.

Now, let's look at the "Work" that <u>Jesus Christ</u> would have to **Do** to **Accomplish this Feat** of **Reversing** the **Natural Order of Divinity** and **Straightening Out** this **Entire Mess,** based on **Creating** a *New Home* (table), *Government* (bench), and *Church* (altar). This would mean "Reversing" the <u>Input</u> and the <u>Output</u> **Process of God's Old Law** (Abrahamic Covenant/Mosaic law) and then **Instituting God's New Law** (New Covenant/Canon law) via the **Power of Conversion** through the **Baptismal Forces** (purification) of *Water, Blood, and Spirit*. The idea here is that "Humanity" is so <u>Ignorant</u> that it is **Eating Poison** from the *Tree of Knowledge* (belief in flesh/world). **Jesus Christ** had to <u>Educate</u> the **Human Race** to the point of **Consuming the Antidote** from the *Tree of Life* (belief in spirit/church) or from **His** *Cross of Death*. Imagine a "Healthy Animal" <u>Eating, Drinking, and Sleeping Correctly</u> and then, the **Farmer Determines** just **How Long** his **Stock can Live** and *How Long They* can be *Productive on his Farm*. In the

"Case of God," the Eternal Father is **Eating Right** (righteousness/home), thereby **Properly Nourishing His Home** (table), or **Giving Life to His Kingdom** through **Righteous Living,** which is **Governed** by *Knowing Right from Wrong.* Secondly, in the "Case" of the Son of God, **He Drinks Right** (holiness/government), thereby **Properly Purifying His Government** (throne/bench) or **Giving Life to Heaven** through **Holy Living,** which is **Governed** by *Knowing Good from Evil.* Finally, in the "Case" of the Holy Spirit, **He Sleeps Right** (perfection/church), thereby **Properly Resting His Church** (altar) or **Giving Life to Earth** through **Perfect Living,** which is **Governed** by *Knowing God's Will from Man's Will.* In contrast to "All this Healthy Living," we see Adam and Eve being **Cursed** for **Eating** from the **Tree of Knowledge,** which **Makes Them Afraid** of **Fear Itself,** of **Pain,** and of **Death** to the **Point of Running** from *Their Own Shadows.*

Note that the "Lord God Almighty" Inputs (virtues) **Righteousness, Holiness, and Perfection** and Outputs (faults) *Sin, Evil, and Death,* while "God's Children" Input (faults) **Sin, Evil, and Death** and Output (virtues) *Righteousness, Holiness, and Perfection.* This "Input/Output Structure" would Exist for 4,000 Years, or until **God's Jewish Messiah** would **Come** to **Reverse the Process** (implement paradox) by bringing a **Tree of Life** (cross) to **Input Sin, Evil, and Death** to the *Throne/Altar/Table/ Face of God.* In turn, then the "Lord God Almighty" would simply Forgive this Corruption and **Transform It** into **Righteousness** (flesh), **Holiness** (spirit), and **Perfection** (soul) for the *Benefit of All* (God/Angels/Men/Nature).

Son	1.	**God's Throne** - Government: Righteous Citizen on Earth = New Body
Spirit	2.	**God's Altar** - Church: Holy Saint in Heaven = Eternal Life
Father	3.	**God's Table** - Home: Perfect Son within God's Kingdom = Own Kingdom
Trinity	4.	**God's Face** - Self: Free Man within the Nature of God = God's Friendship

With this "New Justice System," Humanity could bring **Sin** to the **Son's Throne/Bench** to be **Exchanged** for *Righteousness*; then **Evil** is brought to the **Spirit's Altar** to be **Exchanged** for *Holiness;* and finally, **Death** is brought to the **Father's Table** to be **Exchanged** for *Perfection.* Once a "Person Attained" Righteousness, he could **Transform** his **Home** into *New Bodies for All.* With Holiness, he could **Transform his Government** into *Eternal Lives for All;* and then with Perfection, he could **Transform** his **Church** into *Royal Kingdoms for All.* Unfortunately, to "Create this State" of Heaven on Earth, the **Lord Jesus Christ** would have to **Return to Earth Two More Times, First** in a **2nd Advent** (thief) to bring forth *God's Government;* and then in a **3rd Advent** (judge), to bring forth *God's Home.* The "Job of the Church (2,000 yrs.)" would be to Transform into a **Government** (1,000 yrs.); and then, the **Government** is to **Transform** into *God's New Home on Earth* (New Jerusalem). With the "Completion of this Earthly Effort," the Lord God Almighty would become a **Man and Come to Earth** as **Creation's Eternal** *Righteous* (earth/babies), *Holy* (Heaven/lives), and *Perfect* (kingdom/homes) **God.** This means that the "Eternal Father" is bringing <u>Mankind</u> *Free Transfiguration* (flesh); the "Son of God" is bringing <u>His Followers</u> *Glorification* (spirit); the "Holy Spirit" is bringing <u>His Saints</u> *Adoration* (soul); and the "Trinity" is bringing the <u>Sons of God</u> *Exaltations* (life-force). Unfortunately, this "Mystical Union" between <u>God and Man</u> could **Not Occur** without **Jesus Christ's** *Repentance* (1st advent), **Church's** *Prayers* (2nd advent), **World's** *Works* (3rd advent), and each **Person's** *Evangelization* (judgment/saving souls). The idea here is that "God and Man" must <u>Work Together</u> with **God Inputting Death** (tree of knowledge) and *Outputting Life* (tree of life); while **Man Inputs Life** (tree of life) and *Outputs Death* (tree of knowledge).

The following tabular information indicates that "Divinity Incorrectly" <u>Inputs</u> *Righteousness, Holiness, and Perfection* and <u>Outputs</u> *Sin, Evil, and Death;* while "Humanity Incorrectly" <u>Inputs</u> *Sin, Evil, and Death* and <u>Outputs</u> *Righteousness, Holiness, and Perfection*:

Reversing God's Input from Good to Evil and Man's Input from Evil to Good via Christ's Church
(God is consuming perfection [life/holiness]; while man is consuming imperfection [death/unholiness])

Transfiguration
(baby farm)

1. **Father** - <u>Eats Righteousness, Outputs Sin</u>...Home/table
   - Give Life - Worship God: New Body
   - Animal - Drinks Water: Output Urine

Glorification
(divine school)

2. **Son** - <u>Eats Holiness, Outputs Evil</u>...Government/throne
   - Give Wealth - Praise God: Eternal Life
   - Animal - Eats Food: Outputs Dung

Adoration
(sonship training)

3. **Spirit** - <u>Eats Perfection, Outputs Death</u>...Church/altar
   - Give Labors - Thank God: Royal Kingdom
   - Animal - Recuperative Sleep: Outputs Exhaustion

Exaltation
(become one with God)

4. **Trinity** - <u>Eats Bodies/Life/Kingdoms</u>...God/face
   - Give Eternal Life - Become God: Freedom
   - Animal - Eats/Drinks/Rests God: Input/Output One

This illustration shows the "Mystical Roles" of the <u>Father, Son, Spirit,</u> and the <u>Holy Trinity</u> as **They Strive** to bring forth **God's Government, Church, Home, and Himself** into *Physical Form upon the Earth*. In short, the "Lord God Almighty" <u>Needed to Create</u> a **War of Good and Evil** between **God's Angels** (church) and **Lucifer's Demons** (government) so that the *Ignorance, Cowardice, Greed, and Selfishness of Man* could be **Transformed** into *God's Wisdom, Courage, Generosity, and Unselfishness*.

Perfection of God	Tree of Life/Tree of Knowledge	Perfection of Man
Christ————————	————Blessed Virgin – Grace————————	Jesus
Angels - Church (spirit)	<u>Eternal Life/Remove Faults</u>	**Saints** - World (flesh)
• Saint Michael - Heaven		• Saint Joseph - Earth

• Eat Holiness		• Drink Righteousness
	Input Good	
Church	**Home**	**Government**
Faith - - Morals	Fairness	Ethics - - Law
Knowledge/wisdom	Self-awareness/courage	Consciousness/ generosity
• Remove Ignorance	• Remove Cowardice	• Remove Greed

Output Evil

Demons - Gehenna (life-force)	Eternal-death/Take Faults	**Damned** - Hell (soul)
• Lucifer - Bottomless Pit		• Judas - Lake of Fire
• Eat Evil - Flesh		• Blood - Drinks Sin
Demonic Possession	Worldly Temptations	Sin-nature
• Lifestyle	• Addiction	• First Try
• Death/disgrace	• Pain/humiliation	• Fear/shame

(Jesus repents [1st advent], Church prays [2nd advent],
World works [3rd advent], Self saves souls [judgment])

This illustration shows that the Life-experience is About Mastering the **Government, Church, Home, and Oneself** to become a **Son of God, Who is Worthy** of **Owning** his **Own Kingdom of Glory** and then **Ruling** with the *Lord God Almighty Himself*. We see that "Those Fools" Who have Eaten from the **Tree of Knowledge** have been **Cursed** to **Run from Fear** only to *Fall into Shame* (baby), **Run from Pain** to *Fall into Humiliation* (teenager), and **Run from Death** to *Fall into Disgrace*. We see that "Jesus Christ" Faced the **High Priest, Caiaphas** (fear) and became *Excommunicated from the Temple*; He Faced **King Herod** (pain) and became an *Outcast from His People* (Jews); and He Faced **Pontius Pilate** (death) and became **Banished from the Earth** (adult). Secondly, "Jesus Christ" Mustered All His Courage to **Face the Lord God Almighty Himself** (damnation) upon **His Cross of Death** (take all sin) and was **Forsaken by God** and *Cast into Eternal Hell Fire*. Finally, "Jesus Christ" had the Courage to **Face His Tomb of Damnation**, where **He Defeated Sin, Evil, Death, and Damnation** and then **Resurrected** (new body) into **Eternal Life,** bringing a **New Input/Output Process** (perfect justice system) to **All Souls** *so that They Too could be Saved*.

With this "Divine Resurrection," the Lord Jesus Christ would **Create** a **New Divine School of Higher Learning**, where **Angels** would *Teach Good,* **Saints** would *Teach Right,* **Demons** would *Teach Evil,* and the **Damned** would *Teach Wrong*. Yes! The "Lord Jesus Christ" would Put Everyone to Work **Educating the Babies** and **Teenagers**, then **Training the Adults,** and finally, **Graduating His Students Ready to Work** in *God's Kingdom of Glory Forever*. Remember, in being "Raised by the Blessed Virgin," the Lord was Taught that **Nothing in Life** is to **Go to Waste** (philosophy of the poor) as **Everything** can be **Used Somewhere**. It is just a **Matter** of **Finding that Right Job** for that *Right Creation*.

On this "Day of Re-creation," Jesus Christ will **Remove Creation's Fear of Pain, Fear of Death**, and **Fear of Damnation**, thereby **Setting It Free** from **Sin, Evil, and Death** and bringing forth *Righteousness, Holiness, and Perfection to One and All*. Yes! The "Lord Jesus Christ" has Defeated **Sin, Evil, Death, and Damnation** via **His Repentance, Prayers, Works**, and the **Saving of Souls** to **Set the Captives Free** from *All* the *Curses of God* (forsaken), *Angels* (banished), *Men* (outcast), and *Nature* (excommunicated). God's Son has this "Divine Ability" to **Fulfill** the **Baby Farm** of *Earth* (ignorance), the **Divine School** of *Heaven* (cowardice), **Take His Sonship Training without Complaint** within *God's Kingdom* (greed), and then **Become One with God** (career) in *Eternal Freedom* (unselfishness).

Flesh	1.	**Baby** - Grows-up: See his Own Limitations = Change Nature (God) ...Righteous
Spirit	2.	**Teenager** - Matures: See his Own Potential = Wash Away Sin (Man) ...Holy
Soul	3.	**Adult** - Thinks: See his Own Self-worth = Merge with God (God/Man)...Perfect

Now, we see that this "Need to be Changed (reversed)" from a Baby to a Teenager comes by **Learning** the **Lessons of Life** to **Defeat Ignorance** and bring forth **Wisdom** (honors), which **Allows** a **Tiny Child** to *Survive in a Dangerous World* (physical dimension). Secondly, comes the "Need to Wash Away Sin" and "Change" a Teenager into an Adult by **Receiving** the **Blessings of Life** to **Overcome Cowardice** and bring forth **Courage** (integrity), which **Allows** a **Youngster** to *Prosper in the Kingdom of God* (spiritual dimension). Finally, comes the "Need to Think for Oneself" and Become a Mature Adult via a **Person's Common Sense** to **Control Greed** and bring forth **Generosity** (dignity) which **Allows** a **Mature Adult** to *Master All he Surveys* (mystical dimension). The message here is that a "Baby" must Grow-up and *See his Own Limitations*; a "Teenager" must Mature and *See his Own Potential;* and finally, an "Adult" must Think for himself and *See his Own Self-worth*.

At each of these "Levels of Growth" and "Maturity," a Person Learns to **Never-quit Fighting** a *Continuously Changing World System*, **Surrender** before *God*, and **Defeat** his **Own Selfish Nature** so that he can be *Set Free*. The "Power" of Wisdom, Courage, and Generosity **Allows a Person** to **See the Physical, Spiritual, and Mystical Dimensions of Life** in a **Collage** of **Abstract Concepts** so **Complex** that *They Boggle the Mind*. Recall that a "Wise Man Seeks" the Serenity to Accept the **Things he Cannot Change**, the Courage to Change the **Things that he Can,** and the Wisdom to Know the **Difference**. This **Leads** him to **Control his Own Destiny** and *Live a Happy Life*. Yes! The "Human Race is In" a Complex Divine Creation as the **Life-experience Passes** through **Earth, Heaven, the Kingdom, God, and Beyond** (self) as it **Lasts Forever**, thereby **Forcing Each Soul to Find Its Own Place** in a *World Without End*. Obviously, "Changing," "Washing," and

"Thinking" are <u>Constant</u> and <u>Forever</u> and **Men, Angels, and God** will be **Forced to Blend All** the **Forces of Life** into <u>**One Truth**,</u> *If They Seek* to *Become One People* in *Union* with *One God*.

The following tabular information indicates that "Change Comes" by <u>Fighting</u> the *World's Ignorance*; "Washing Sin Comes" by <u>Fighting</u> *Religious Cowardice;* and "Thinking Comes" by <u>Fighting</u> *One's Greedy Desires* (selfishness):

Messiah Changes Natures, Church Washes Away Sin, and World Teaches Thinking for Oneself
(change ignorance to wisdom, wash cowardice
unto courage, think away greed unto generosity)

Messiah 1. **Change Nature** - <u>Fight World Ignorance:</u> Master Honors... Knowledge
(Jews)
- Change Baby – Growth: Seeing the Light of Truth = See Limitations
- Never-quit Fighting the World System – Immovable Force: *Get New Body*

Being • Find the Serenity to Accept the Things One Cannot Change
Saved • Earth is United with Its People – Become Righteous Citizen
(wisdom/knowledge allows a blind person to survive in the darkness and find his way out)

Church 2. **Wash Away Sin** – <u>Fight Church Cowardice</u>: Master Integrity
(Christian) ... Self-Awareness
- Purify Teenager – Maturity: Learn the Law of Life = See Potential
- Surrender to God and Become Holy – Unstoppable Force: *Get Eternal Life*

Saving • Find the Courage to Change the Things that he Can
Self • Heaven is United with Its Saints - Become a Holy Saint
(courage/self-awareness is when a person comes out of darkness/awakened to find truth)

World 3. **Merge/Think for Self** – <u>Fight Selfish Greed:</u> Master Dignity .... Consciousness
(Pagans)
- Transform Adult – Freedom: Serve God's Will = See Self-Worth
- Defeat Oneself and Master All – Blended Force: *Get Royal Kingdom*

Saving • Find Wisdom to Know the Difference Between Right and Wrong
Others • Kingdom is United with Its Sons – Become Perfect Son
(generosity/consciousness is when a person learns to think for himself/right and creates truth)

This illustration shows that the "Messiah (Jews)" <u>Changes Natures</u> (divine); "Church (Christians)" <u>Washes Away Sin</u> (holy); and the "World (Pagans)" <u>Teaches Thinking for Self</u> as these **Three Institutions** bring forth **Wisdom, Courage, and Generosity** to *One and All*. We see that in "God's Grand Design," the <u>Earth is to be United</u> to *Its People*; <u>Heaven is to be United</u> with *Its Saints*; <u>God's Kingdom is to be United</u> with *Its Sons*; and finally, <u>God is to be United</u> with the *Nature of Man*. Through these "Four Unions," the <u>God/Man Life-force</u> shall **Find** its

Meaning (existence), **Purpose** (service), and **Value** (happiness) to be **Expressed** in the *Lord's People, Saints, Sons, and Free Humanity*. This means that on "Earth," through the <u>Institutions</u> of **Home, Government, Church, and Oneself, Man's Physical Nature** will *Find Its Personal Identity* and *Grow-up*. Secondly, "Heaven" will <u>Create Four Courts of Judgment</u> to **Give Authority** to its **Saints, Angels, Christ, and God** to **Establish a Single Government** to *Rule Over All the Forces of Life*. Thirdly, "God's Kingdom" will <u>Offer Nature, Men, Angels, and God</u> **Four Levels** of <u>Union</u> in *Friendship* (Holy Spirit/flesh), in *Companionship* (Son/spirit), in *Oneness* (Father/soul), and finally, in *Becoming All* (Trinity/life-force) *before God*. Finally, the "Lord God Almighty (IS/I'AM/Lord), Himself" will <u>Offer His Respect, Blessings, Love, and Union</u> to **All Who Bow, Serve, Love, and Unite** with **His Truth, Law, Will, and Love** to bring <u>Peace, Joy, and Happiness</u> to *All His Kingdom*.

Recall that "During Man's Fall (Garden of Eden)," <u>Eve was Cursed</u> with *Ignorance* (birth pain), <u>Adam was Cursed</u> with *Cowardice* (toil), the <u>Serpent was Cursed</u> with *Greed* (face in dirt), and <u>God is Cursed</u> with *Selfishness* (lose all). Through these "Four Curses," <u>Mankind must Fight</u> its **Own Sin-nature, Worldly Temptations, Demonic Possessions,** and **God's Curse** to <u>Overcome Division</u> and bring forth *Eternal Unity*. This "New State of Life" comes forth <u>When Jesus Christ</u> brings **to Lost Humanity God's Four Gifts** of: (1) **Wisdom**, (2) **Courage**, (3) **Generosity**, and (4) **Unselfishness** to <u>Make All Men</u> *Righteous, Holy, Perfect, and Divine before God*. Through these "Four Stages of Life" also, we see <u>God's Gifts</u> of a **New Body** (earth/men), **Eternal Life** (Heaven/angels), **Royal Kingdom** (Kingdom/Christ), and **Divine Freedom** (God/Man) coming into **Existence** as the *Ultimate Treasures of Life*.

The following tabular information indicates that the "Four Unions of <u>Earth</u> (people), <u>Heaven</u> (saints), <u>God's Kingdom</u> (sons), and finally, the <u>Lord God Almighty</u> to <u>Mankind</u> brings forth the **Perfection** of <u>Nature, Men, Angels, and God</u> as *One Eternal Family*."

Four Unions of Life are Established in Earth/People, Heaven/Saints, Kingdom/Sons and God/Man
(land unites with babies/spirit unites with
flesh/mystics with God/divinity with life)

Truth	1. **Union of Earth/People** - <u>Land Unites with Babies:</u> God's Physical Union... Knowledge	
	• Defeat "Mother Eve's" Curse of Ignorance - Christ brings Wisdom	
	• Home - Parents/Children (family relations)	
Individual	• Government - Leadership/Bureaucracy	**Give New Body**
Rights	• Church - Priesthood/Laity	• Righteousness
	• Self - Growth/Maturity	
	(learn right/wrong - become righteous/citizen: defeat excommunication from temple)	

Law

2. **Union of Heaven/Saints** - <u>Spirit Unites with Flesh:</u> God's Spiritual Union...Self-awareness
   - Defeat "Father Adam's" Curse of Cowardice - Christ brings Courage
   - Celestial Court - Saints/God

Social

Rights
   - Temple Court - Angels/God   **Give Eternal Life**
   - Royal Court - Christ/God   • Holiness
   - Divine Court - God/God

(learn good/evil - become holy/saint: defeat being outcast from people)

Will

3. **Union of Kingdom/Sons** - <u>Mystics Unite with God:</u> God's Mystical Union... Consciousness
   - Defeat "Evil Serpent's" Curse of Greed - Christ brings Generosity
   - Friendship - Holy Spirit/Jesus (flesh)

Divine
   - Companionship - Son of God/Christ (spirit) **Give Royal Kingdom**

Rights
   - Oneness - Eternal Father/Jesus Christ (soul) • Perfection
   - Becoming - Trinity/Christ Jesus (life-force)

(learn God's Will/man's will - become perfect/son:

defeat banishment from earth)

Love

4. **Union of God/Free Men** - <u>Divinity Unites with Life:</u> Divine Union... Sentience
   - Defeat "Lord God Almighty's" Curse of Selfishness - Christ brings Unselfishness
   - IS - God's Respect (earth)

Free
   - I' AM - God's Blessings (heaven)   **Give God's Freedom**

Will
   - Lord - God's Love (kingdom)   • Divine
   - Lord God Almighty - God's Union (God)

(learn reality/illusion - become divine/free man: defeat being forsaken by God)

This illustration shows that the "Union" between <u>Earth and Its People</u> means **Settling the Land** and **Establishing the Boundaries** to **Define the Rights** for *Individuals, Families, Homes, Governments, Churches, and God's Spirit World*. This means that initially, the "Land (individual rights)" must be <u>United</u> with **God's Children** (babies); then the "Spirit (social rights)" is <u>United</u> with the **Flesh** (eternal life); next the "Mystics (divine rights)" are <u>United</u> with **God** (kingdoms) and finally, "Divinity (free will)" is <u>United</u> with **Life** to bring forth a *Perfect World*. In this "Perfect World," we see <u>Babies Gaining Knowledge</u>, <u>Teenagers</u> becoming **Self-aware**, <u>Adults</u> becoming **Conscious of Life,** and <u>Wise Men</u> becoming **Sentient** to the point of *Understanding All Things*. Yes! We are each being "Called" to <u>Grow-up</u> and become <u>Mature</u> so we might **See God's Creation** as a **Reflection of the True Nature** of *God Himself*.

In this way, the "Human Race" can <u>Learn Right from Wrong</u> to become **Righteous Citizens on Earth, Defeat Their Excommunication** (sin-nature) from <u>God's Temple,</u> and from being *Cast* into the *Curse of Death* (hated). Secondly, the "Human Race must <u>Learn Good from Evil</u> to become **Holy Saints in Heaven, to Defeat becoming**

Outcast (worldly temptations) from **God's People,** and from being *Cast* into the *Curse of the Grave* (rot). Thirdly, the "Human Race" must <u>Learn God's Will from man's will</u> to become **Perfect Sons within God's Kingdom, Defeat being Banished** (demonic possession) from the **Earth,** and from being *Cast* into the *Curse of Damnation* (hell). Finally, the "Human Race" must <u>Learn God's Reality from man's illusion</u> to become a **Free Man in Truth**, **Defeat being Forsaken** (God's curse) by **God,** and from being *Cast* into the *Curse of Oblivion* (Gehenna).

Through each of these "Four Stages of Life," a <u>Person</u> can become **Worthy** of **Receiving One of God's Four Treasures**: 1) <u>New Body from Earth</u> - Righteousness (challenge), 2) <u>Eternal Life</u> <u>from Heaven</u> - Holiness (adventure), 3) <u>Royal Kingdom from the Kingdom</u> - Perfection (fun), and 4) <u>Divine Freedom from God</u> - Divinity (happiness). We see that these "Four Treasures" are <u>Coming from Christians</u> as **They are Able** to **Defeat the Curses** which **Fell** upon **Adam, Eve, the Serpent, and God** during **Man's Fall from Grace** in the *Garden of Eden*.

Recall that "Adam" was <u>Cursed with Toil</u> in a *Barren Land*, while <u>Eve was Cursed</u> with *Birth Pain coming from a Barren Womb*; the <u>Serpent was Cursed</u> to *Crawl on his Belly* (eat dirt); and <u>God was Cursed</u> with *Selfishness* (rejection). Through each of these "Mystical Curses," <u>Jesus Christ</u> is able to **Change Adam's Ignorance** into *Wisdom,* **Eve's Cowardice** into *Courage,* the **Serpent's Greed** into *Generosity,* and **God's Selfishness** into *Divine Unselfishness.* We now see that the "Life-experience" is about <u>Passing</u> through **God's** *Baby Farm* (flesh), **God's** *Divine School of Higher Learning* (spirit), **Christ's** *Sonship Training Program* (soul), and finally, the **Father's** *On-the-Job-Training Program* (life-force) to *Reach Perfection.* By "Passing through Each" of the <u>Training Programs,</u> a **Lost Broken Sinner** can be **Transformed** into a *Righteous Christian, Holy Saint, Son of God,* and finally, a *Free Man of Perfection*.

This means that "Wisdom" will <u>Unite Earth</u> with *Man;* "Courage" will <u>Unite Heaven</u> with *Man;* then "Generosity" will <u>Unite God's Kingdom</u> with *Man;* and finally, "Unselfishness" will <u>Unite God</u> with *Man Forever*. Note that "Adam's Children" are <u>Given</u> a *Sin-nature* (fear); "Eve's Children" are <u>Given</u> *Worldly Temptations* (pain); then "All Children" are <u>Given</u> *Demonic Possession* (evil); and finally, "God's Children" are <u>Given</u> *Selfishness* (death). Through these "Four Curses," the <u>Perfection of Man</u> shall **Come About** as the **Human Race Learns** to **Defeat Toil** and *Earn Its New Body on Earth*, **Defeat Pain** and *Earn Its Blessing of Eternal Life in Heaven*, **Defeat Evil** and *Earn Its Own Royal Kingdom,* and finally, **Defeat Death** and *Earn Its Own Freedom*. In this way, "God," "Angels," and "Men" shall become <u>One Creation</u> in **Christ Jesus** as **They Work Together** to *Defeat the Four Curses of Man* (sin-nature/worldly temptations/demonic possession/God's curse of death).

The following tabular information indicates that "Adam was Cursed" with <u>Sin-nature</u> (ignorance); "Eve was Cursed" with <u>Worldly Temptations</u> (cowardice); the "Serpent was Cursed" with <u>Demonic Possession</u> (greed); and "God was Cursed" with <u>Death</u> (selfishness):

**Adam, Eve, Serpent, and God are Cursed with either
Ignorance, Cowardice, Greed, and/or Death**
(ignorance becomes wisdom, cowardice becomes courage, greed
becomes generosity, and selfishness becomes unselfishness)

Mind
(truth)

1. **Adam's Curse** - <u>Ignorance</u>: Toil in a Barren Land...Bear Ignorant Children
   - Blessed with Wisdom - Unite Earth with Man
   - Adam's Children Given *Sin-nature* (fear)   **Loving Home**
   - Defeat Toil - Earn New Body on Earth

(voice of the word - God's revelation: call sinners to repentance = see limitations)

Heart
(law)

2. **Eve's Curse** - <u>Cowardice</u>: Pain of Child-birth...Pain Falls on Children
   - Blessed with Courage - Unite Heaven with Man
   - Eve's Children Given *Worldly Temptations* (pain) **Honest**
   - Defeat Pain - Earn Eternal Life in Heaven   **Government**

(face of the word - Jesus Christ: call Christians to sainthood = see potential)

Soul
(will)

3. **Serpent's Curse** - <u>Greed</u>: Crawl on Belly in Dirt...Children Tempted by Evil
   - Blessed with Generosity - Unite Kingdom with Man
   - All Children Given *Demonic Possession* (evil)   **Holy Church**
   - Defeat Evil - Earn Royal Kingdom within God's Kingdom

(house of the word - Holy Church: call saints to the Lord's sonship = see self-worth)

Life-force
(love)

4. **God's Curse** - <u>Selfishness</u>: Crucifixion and Death...Children Cursed with Death
   - Blessed with Unselfishness - Unite God and Man
   - God's Children Given *Curse of Death* (death)   **Beloved God**
   - Defeat Death - Earn Freedom from Slavery

(work of the word - evangelistic mission: call sons to divinity = see perfection)

This illustration shows that "Mother Eve" is bringing <u>Mankind</u> a **New Mind of Truth** by being the **Mother of Ignorance**, thereby **Forcing her Children** to **Strive Toward** the **Blessing of Wisdom** to <u>**Set Them Free**</u> from a *Lifetime of Sweat and Toil*. Secondly, "Father Adam" is bringing <u>Mankind</u> a **New Heart of Law** by being the **Father of Cowardice**, thereby **Forcing his Children** to **Strive Toward** the **Blessing of Courage** to <u>**Set Them Free**</u> from a *Lifetime of Fear and Pain*. Thirdly, the "Wicked Serpent" is bringing <u>Mankind</u> a **New Soul of Will** by being the **Father of Greed**, thereby **Forcing Adam's/Eve's Children** to **Strive Toward** the **Blessing of Generosity** to <u>**Set Them Free**</u> from a *Lifetime of Cruelty and Evil*. Finally, "Father God" is bringing <u>Mankind</u> a **New Life-force of Love** by being the **Father of Selfishness**, thereby **Forcing Adam's/Eve's Children** to **Strive Toward** the **Blessing of Unselfishness** to <u>**Set Them Free**</u> from a *Lifetime of Hatred and Bitterness*.

These "Awesome Challenges of Life" <u>Allow</u> even the most **Ignorant and Sinful Child of God** to *Master the World, Himself, and God Forever.* The point here is to see that "If a Person" <u>Masters Ignorance,</u> he can **Obtain** a *Loving Home.* "If he" <u>Masters Cowardice,</u> he can **Obtain** an *Honest Government.* "If he" <u>Masters Greed,</u> he can **Obtain** a *Holy Church.* Finally, "If he" <u>Masters Selfishness,</u> then he can **Obtain** *Oneness* with his most *Beloved Creator God.* It should now make sense that "Mankind's" <u>Sin-nature</u> comes from *Ignorance;* <u>Worldly Temptations</u> come from *Cowardice;* <u>Demonic Possession</u> comes from *Greed;* and finally, <u>God's Curse</u> is coming from **Man's Own** *Selfishness.* Now, we can "Better Understand" the <u>Motives of God</u> and the **Ignorance of Man** as the **Lord is Justified** in **Casting His Children** into a **Pit of Evil and Death** to <u>**Teach**</u> Them the *Meaning, Purpose, and Value of Life.*

To understand this "Process" of <u>Casting One's Children</u> (curses) into a **Pit of Evil** to **Toughen Them Up** and then **Convert Them** from **Children to Adults,** we must see *God's Four Curses on Man.* These **Four Curses are**: 1) <u>Sin-nature</u> - Cursed to Toil in Barren Land: Sweat (hard-labor) = Lucifer's Test (being saved) + Join Church (baptism); 2) <u>Worldly Temptations</u> Cursed with a Barren Womb: Pain (sacrifice) = God's Judgment (saving self) + Easter Duty (repentance); 3) <u>Demonic Possession</u> - Cursed with Barren Life: Death (shed blood) = Self-evaluation (saving others) = Sunday (prayers); and 4) <u>God's Curse</u> - Cursed with Barren Eternal Life: Damnation (hopelessness) = Nature's Placement (serving God) + Daily Mass (works). Out of these "Four Curses" will come the **Lord's Four Treasures of Life**: 1) <u>Challenge -</u> Removing Ignorance: New Mind = See Limitations (knowledge); 2) <u>Adventure -</u> Removing Cowardice: New Heart = See Potential (self-awareness); 3) <u>Fun</u> - Remove Greed: New Soul = Self-worth (consciousness); and 4) <u>Happiness</u> - Remove Selfishness: New Life-force = Independence (sentience). Through these "Four Treasures of Life," the whole <u>Human Race</u> can **Master the Life-experience** (Sabbath/Lord's day) and bring forth <u>New Homes, Governments, and Churches</u> to bring *Peace, Joy, and Happiness to One and All.*

It is all very simple because "All One Needs to Do" is <u>Believe in God</u> and **Trust in His Ancient Promises** to the **Max** and then **Await the** <u>**Coming of His Awakening**</u> to the *Lord's Truth, Law, Will, and Love.* It now becomes clear that the "Old Jewish Sabbath (Saturday)" was <u>Concerned</u> with the *Importance of Work* (righteousness); while the "New Christian Lord's Day (Sunday)" is <u>Concerned</u> with the *Importance of Prayer* (holiness). This means the "Lord God Almighty" has <u>Two Systems of Life</u> (paradox): with **One** on the **Sabbath Day** (Saturday/count babies) to *Define All* (work/create babies); and **One** on the **Lord's Day** (Sunday/count saints) to *Define Nothing* (prayers/saving souls). We now see in "Christ Jesus" both the <u>All of God</u> (space/infinity) and the <u>Nothing of Man</u> (time/eternity) are **Made One** in *Truth, Law, Will, and Love.* By "Mastering" <u>Truth, Law, Will, and Love,</u> a **Person** can become **Worthy** of <u>**Receiving God's Gifts**</u> of a *New Body* (knowledge), *Eternal Life* (love), a *Royal Kingdom* (perfection), and *Divine Freedom* (liberty). This means that through a "Person's Good Works," he can become <u>Educated</u> (knowledge), <u>Find Love,</u> and become <u>Perfect before his God,</u> thereby **Allowing** him to **Win his Freedom** from *Sin, Evil, Death, and Damnation.*

Yes! We are all "Seeking to Find Paradise" in Our Homes, Governments, Churches, and within Our very Selves; yet, this **Journey** from **Nothing to All Requires Looking** at a **Bigger Picture** which *Involves the Rights of Man.* Obviously, the "Life-experience" is about Seeing Life from the **Standpoint** of **Mastering** the **Earth, Heaven,** the **Kingdom,** and even the **Lord God Almighty Himself** before a *Person can Learn It All.* We now see it that when a "Person Matches" the Law of the Church (God), Son, and his Home (Family) **Against** his **Own Self-motivations,** he is able to *See his Sins* (selfishness). This "Ability" to See One's Faults thereby **Allows** the **Human Race** to **Distinguish the Difference** between *Divine Rights* (life/church), *Social Rights* (liberty/government), and *Individual Rights* (pursuit of happiness/home).

Obviously, in "America," the Rights of Man were **First Instituted** as a **Legal Document** (Constitution) to bring forth both the *Roles of the Government* versus the *Role of the Individual Citizen.* We see that the "Argument" on the Rights of Man has been **Centered** upon the **Views** of **George Washington, Thomas Jefferson, John Adams** (democrat/democracy/votes), **Abraham Lincoln** (republican/capitalism/money), and **FDR** (Roosevelt) as **They Defined** *Government Rights* (own people) versus *Individual Rights* (own government). Initially, "George Washington" stated that the Quality of Life **Centered** on **Defending One's Home** by **Force** or the **Basic Right** to **Bear Arms** through the *Law of Protecting One's Homeland.* Secondly, "Thomas Jefferson" stated that the Natural Rights of Man center upon **Building a Future** for **One's Nation** (glorification), **One's Family** (transformation), and **Oneself** (self-image) through the *Natural Resources of Life.* Thirdly, "John Adams (democratic party)" stated that the Rights of Man were **Divided** between the **Role of the Government** (spend) and the **People** (earn) as the **Government Legally Owned the People** and were *Responsible for the Survival of All* (national security). Fourthly, "Abraham Lincoln (republican party)" stated that the Rights of Man were **Divided** between the **Role of Government** (serve) and the **Will of the People** (vote) as the **People Legally Owned the Government** (financially/money) and were *Responsible for Themselves* (no slavery). This means that "Adams" was Arguing that the **Opportunities of Life** are *Centered* upon the *Actions of the Government* (collective mind), while "Lincoln" was Arguing that the **Opportunities of Life** are *Centered* upon the *Actions of the Individual* (single-mindedness of purpose). We see this "Conflict of Ideas" was Settled by **Franklin Delano Roosevelt** (FDR), when he stated that there can be **No Rights of Man** without **Peace** and then he **Proclaimed** a **Division of Labor** between *What Government can Do* (tax/spend) versus *What the Individual can Do* (work/earn).

We see that this "Argument" between Divine Rights (God/church), Social Rights (government), and Individual Rights (people/home) still **Rages Today** as **God, Angels, and Men** each *Defines Their Boundaries of Life.* They show that that these "Boundaries of Life" are Defined by **Seeing One's Sins** as a **Person Comes to See** that his **Wicked Flesh** is **Out of Control in Pursuing a Lifetime** of **Unlimited Wants** based on His *Own Self-image* (face) and *Personal Glorification* (wealth). We are all in hopes of "Becoming Great" in One Way or Another that we might be able to **Take Heart** and **Convince Ourselves** that **Life was Worth Living** and that **We will One Day**

Find **Life, Liberty,** and the **Pursuit of Happiness** within *Our Own Homeland*. Unfortunately, this "Desire to be Great" in One's Own Eyes **Creates a Dangerous Blindness** in the **Untrained Soul,** thereby **Causing him to Fall** into the **Demonic Trap** of *Soul-Damning Pride*. This means that our "Forefathers" were Telling Us that **Any Nation** would have to both **Grow and Mature Over Time** to **Fully Implement the Institutions** of the *Will of the People* (public/vote) versus the *Will of the Individual* (private/money).

This "Process" of Growth and Maturity **Sits at the Center** of the **Life-experience** as **We Try Desperately** to become **Perfect** within *Our Own Homes* (citizens), *Governments* (sainthood), *Churches* (sons of God), and within *Our Selves.* We see that to "Reach Perfection," God is Asking Man to **Raise a Family** (home), **Get a Good Job** (government/career), become a **Living Saint** (church), and **Improve himself** (thinking) in the *Eyes of Others* (respect). This "Need for Self-respect" is the Driving Force in Life as **Each Person** must *Face Lucifer's Test* (ignorance), *God's Judgment* (cowardice), *Self-evaluation* (greed), and *Freedom* (selfishness). Obviously, in "Life," we are Each Witnessing **Individual Perfection** in **One Field or Another,** yet, what the **Lord is Talking About** is to **Become Perfect** (man for all seasons) in *All Four Areas of Life, All at the Same time*. In short, "One Person" will Master in *Educational Excellence* (self); "Another" will Master becoming a *Devout Christian* (church); while "Another" will Master becoming *President of America* (government/career). What the "Lord is Speaking About" is to Strive for Greatness in **Them All at Once** by **Overcoming** *One's Ignorance* (foolish), *Cowardice* (criminal), *Greed* (insanity), and *Selfishness* (evil).

Obviously, the "64-Thousand Dollar Question" is: just how can a Tiny Baby Master such a **Complex World** and become *All Things to All People* or become this *Awesome Man for All Seasons*? The answer is to "Surrender to Christ (born-again)" and then be Transformed into a **New Creation** in *Mind* (intellect), *Heart* (emotion), **Soul** (instincts), and *Life-force* (nature). This means that the "Human Race" has a Long Way to Go and must come to **Realize** that the **Life-experience** will be a **Great Challenge** as **We Each Builds** a *Beautiful Home*, **Establishes** a *Fair Government*, **Creates** a *Holy Church,* and then become *Perfect* (self) as *God is Perfect*.

The following tabular information indicates that "Each of God's Children" is to Master the **Home** (earth), **Government/job** (Heaven), **Church** (Kingdom), and **Oneself** (God) to become *Wise, Courageous, Generous, and Unselfish before God*:

**Mastering Home (earth), Government (Heaven), Church
(Kingdom) and Self (God) to become Perfect**
(homes change babies, governments change teenagers,
churches change adults, and self changes wise men)

Kingship   1. **Master Home** - Baby Level of Life: Ignorance becomes Wisdom…
(truth)   Knowledge
                   • Home becomes Earth - Physical Life: Free Redemption (being saved)
                   • Righteous Citizen on Earth - See Limitations: Defeat Sin (foolishness)

- God's Justice brings Man's Peace - Peace of Mind (intellect)
- Toil to Build a Beautiful Family - Challenge of Life: Righteous Man (kingship)
- *New Body*/mind - Transfigured Body: Experiencing the Challenges of Life

(face Lucifer's test - change sin-nature from false-wisdom to true-wisdom)

Priesthood 2. **Master Government**/job - <u>Teenager Level of Life:</u> Cowardice becomes
(law) Courage...Self-awareness
- Government becomes Heaven - Spiritual Life: Earned Salvation (saving self)
- Holy Saint in Heaven - See Potential: Defeat Evil (criminal acts)
- God's Mercy brings Man's Joy - Joy of the Heart (emotions)
- Pain of Establishing a Government - Adventure of Life: Holy Man (priesthood)
- *Eternal Life*/heart - Glorified Body: Seeking the Adventures of Life

(face God's judgment - change worldly temptations from sin-nature to holy-nature)

Sonship 3. **Master Church** - <u>Adult Level of Life:</u> Greed becomes Generosity...
(will) Consciousness
- Church becomes Kingdom - Mystical Life: Bonus Rewards (saving others)
- Perfect Son within Kingdom - See Self-worth: Defeat Death (insanity)
- God's Love brings Man's Happiness - Happiness of the Soul (instincts)
- Death in Creating a Holy Church - Fun of Life: Perfect Man (sonship)
- *Royal Kingdom*/soul - Mystical Body: Having Rollicking Fun in Life

(face Self-evaluation - change demonic possession from soul-death to soul-life)

- -

God 4. **Master Self** - <u>Wise Man Level of Life:</u> Selfishness/Unselfishness... Sentience
(love)
- Self becomes God-like - Divine Life: Freedom (saving God)
- Free Man within Own Kingdom - See Beatific Vision: Defeat Damnation (evil)
- God's Oneness becomes Man's Oneness - Oneness of the Life-force (nature)
- Damnation Phased unto Perfection - Thrill of Life's Victory: Free Man (mastery)
- *Divine Freedom*/life-force - Divine Body: Enjoying the Friendship of God

(face Unselfishness - change God's curse from life's damnation to life's freedom)

This illustration shows that the "Lord is Explaining" that as <u>Lost Broken Fools,</u> **We can Do Nothing**; but as **Soldiers of Christ, We can Do All Things Perfectly** because **<u>All that is Attempted in Christ</u>** shall *Bear Good Fruit in the End*. This "Mystical Theme" of <u>Human Perfection</u> **Sits at the Center** of the **Christian Faith**, implying that **All Things in Life** can be **<u>Done Well,</u>** *If a Person can Simply Believe.*

This means that via "God's Truth (intellect/ethics)" will come the Light of Knowing (new mind); via "God's Law (emotions/morals)" shall come a Person's Self-awareness (new heart), via "God's Will (instincts/fairness)" shall come a Person's Consciousness (new soul);" and via "God's Love (nature/love)" shall come a Person's Sentience (new life-force).

In other words, the "Toil of Life (struggle)" comes with the Challenge of **Building** a **Beautiful Home** to **Raise Our** most **Prosperous Families** (children) and bring forth the *Blessings of Human Love*. Secondly, the "Pains of Life (crushing)" come with the Adventure of **Establishing a Righteous Government** to **Govern The People** and bring forth the *Blessings of a Great Nation*. Thirdly, the "Death of Life (dying)" comes with the Fun of **Creating a Holy Church** to **Worship One's God** and bring forth the *Blessings upon God's Holy Saints*. Finally, the "Damnation of Life (hell)" comes with Society's Achievements to **Make It Perfect** (self) and become of **Value to Society** and to bring forth the *Blessings of Human Respect upon Itself*. The theme here is that bringing forth a "Perfect World" means Learning It All from the **Bottom to the Top** by being **Willing** to **Face Toil, Pain, Death, and Damnation** to eventually **Create a World** of *Peace, Joy, Happiness,* and *Everlasting Perfection*. This means that "God's Justice" brings forth "Man's Peace" to be Manifested as **Peace of Mind** or **One's Righteous Intellect** as the **Human Race Strives** to **Create Peace on Earth** (obey law) for *One and All*. Secondly, "God's Mercy" brings forth "Man's Joy" to be Manifested as **Joy of the Heart** or **One's Holy Emotions** as the **Human Race Strives** to **Create Joy in Heaven** (love faith) for *Angels and Saints*. Thirdly, "God's Love" brings forth "Man's Happiness" to be Manifested as the **Happiness of the Soul** or **One's Perfect Instincts** as the **Human Race Strives** to **Create Happiness within God's Kingdom** (set free) for *All the Sons of God*. Finally, "God's Oneness" brings forth "Man's Oneness" to be Manifested as the **Oneness of the Life-force** or **One's Divine Nature** as the **Human Race Strives** to **Create Tranquility within God** (unity) *for All Who Enter the Lord's Beatific Vision*.

Yes! "Peace," "Joy," "Happiness," and "Oneness" with the Lord God Almighty bring forth the **Divine Blessings of God** upon the **Whole Human Race** in the **Form** of *Transfigured Bodies* (earth), *Eternal Lives* (Heaven), *Royal Kingdoms* (Kingdom), and *Divine Freedom* (God). Through "God's Justice," "Mercy," "Love," and "Divinity," the Human Life-experience is **Changed** from **Adam's Death** into **Jesus' Eternal Life,** thereby *Making All Things Perfect* in the *Sight of God*.

Through this "Concept of Everlasting Perfection," we see the Lord Creating His Life-experience upon a **Universal Balance of Powers,** using **His Own Triune Nature** to be **Manifested** on the **Earth** or *Home* (executive), in **Heaven** or *Government* (legislative), and within **His Kingdom** or *Church* (judicial). These "Three Powers" center around the Lord's Physical (man), Spiritual (angels), and Mystical (God) **Dimensions of Life** as a **Reflection** of *His Own Thoughts, Words, and Deeds*. The idea here is to imagine "Our Creator God" Using His Intellect (mind) as *Creation's Home* (truth), His Emotions (heart) as *Creation's Government* (law), and His Instincts (soul) as *Creation's Church* (will). By using this concept of

"Human Life," we can see the Lord Balancing the Home with **Physical Growth** (flesh) versus **Spiritual Maturity** (spirit) by **Mastering** both **Ethics** or *Man's Law* and **Morals** or *God's Law*. Secondly, the "Lord is Balancing" the Government with the **Government's Will** (authority) versus the **Will of the People** (vote) to **Synchronize** *Management* (leadership) with *Labor* (bureaucracy). Thirdly, the "Lord is Balancing" the Church with **God's Will** (want) versus **Man's Will** (need) to **Synchronize** **Man's Curse** (flesh) or *Mastering Law* with **God's Blessing** (spirit) or *Mastering Faith*. Finally, the "Lord is Balancing" Oneself with **His Logic** versus **His Feelings** to **Synchronize** the **Human Intellect** *or Mastering the Mind* with the **Human Emotions** *or Mastering the Heart*.

In this teaching, imagine that by "Meeting His Parents (home/schools)," a Person can **Meet and Understand** his **Own Mind** and **Focus his Thoughts** upon the *Meaning of Life* (existence). Secondly, imagine that by "Meeting His Government Leaders (job)," a Person can **Meet and Comprehend** his **Own Heart** and **Focus his Feelings** upon the *Purpose of Life* (service). Thirdly, by "Meeting His Priesthood (church/Christianity)," a Person can **Meet and Treasure** his **Own Soul** and **Focus his Instincts** upon the *Value of Life* (happiness). Finally, by "Meeting His God (self/divinity)," a Person can **Meet and Fathom** his **Own Life-force** and **Focus his Nature** upon the *Love of God* (fulfillment). The idea here is that to "Balance the Home," a Person must **Establish** a *Fixed Frame of Reference* (identity); to "Balance the Government," He must **Establish** a *Relative Focused Existence* (character); to "Balance the Church, He must **Establish** a *Perception of Reality* (personality); and finally, to "Balance Himself," He must **Enter** the *All Seeing Eye of God* (nature). Through each of these "Levels of Perfection," a Person can come to **Know, Love, Serve, and Befriend** his **Creator God** as a **Reflection** of the *Lord's Omniscient Mind, Omnipresent Heart, Omnifarious Soul, Omnipotent Life-force, and Omnificent Nature*.

The following tabular information indicates that "God's Creation" is Centered upon a **Series** of **Balance of Powers** from the **Lord's Trinity** to the **Institutions** of *Man's Home* (executive), *Government* (legislative), and *Church* (judicial):

God's Balance of Power Exists in God, Angels, Men, Nature via Church, Government, Home and Self
(Father/Son/Spirit are Equal to Kingdom/Heaven/Earth
and also to the Church/Government/Home)

Truth   1.   **Judicial Church** - God the Father: Mystical Life-experience = Thought... Kingdom
- Divine Rights - Learning God's Will from Man's Will: See Self-worth
- Balance God and Man - Perception of Reality (personality)
- God's Innocence (blessing) - Master Faith   **Serve God**
- Man's Guilt (curse) - Master Law

Balance God's Will/man's will or destiny and free will to become holy
- Church Gives Mystical Body - Beatific Vision: Serve Father

- Jesus Christ Offers Death - Perfect Son within Kingdom
- Face Death in Barren Grave - Value of Life
- Receive Bonus Rewards - *Given Royal Kingdom*
- Seat in God's Royal Court - Rule Over God's Kingdom

(balancing God's will, God, Innocence, and Blessings to <u>Get Faith</u> [remove spirit demonic possession])

(balancing man's will, man, guilt, and curses to <u>get law</u> [remove flesh demonic possession])

Law   2. **Legislative Government** - <u>God the Son:</u> Spiritual Life-experience = Word... Heaven
- Social Rights - Learning Good from Evil: See Potential
- Balance Leadership and Bureaucracy - Relative Focused Existence (character)
- Management (greed) - Master Authority   **Love God**
- Labor (fear) - Master Responsibility

Balance Security/guns and Money/butter to become righteous citizen on earth
- Government Gives Glorified Body - Mount Calvary: Love the Son
- Christ Gives-up Divinity - Holy Saint in Heaven
- Face Pain of Barren Children - Will to Live
- Receive Earned Salvation - *Given Eternal Life*
- Seat in God's Temple Court - Rule Over God's Heavenly Realm

(balancing Good, Leadership, Management, and Greed to <u>Get Authority</u> [remove spirit worldly temptations])

(balancing evil, bureaucracy, labor, and fear to <u>get responsibility</u> [remove flesh worldly temptations])

Will   3. **Executive Home** - <u>God the Spirit</u> - Physical Life-experience = Deed... Earth
- Individual Rights - Learning Right from Wrong: See Limitations
- Balance Growth and Maturity - Fixed Frame of Reference (identity)
- Flesh (baby) - Master Ethics   **Know God**
- Spirit (adult) - Master Morals

Balance Father's Expectations/Mother's Hopes to become Perfect Son within Kingdom
- Home Gives Transfigured Body - Submission: Knowing the Spirit
- Jesus Takes-on All Sin - Righteous Citizen on Earth
- Face Toil in Barren Desert - Agony of Defeat
- Receive Free Redemption - *Given New Body*
- Seat in God's Celestial Court - Rule Over God's Earthly World

(balancing Right, Maturity, Spirit, and Adult to <u>Get Morals</u> [remove spirit sin-nature])
(balancing wrong, growth, flesh, and baby to <u>get ethics</u> [remove flesh sin-nature])

Love   4. **Voting Self** - <u>Holy Trinity</u> - Divine Life-experience = Accomplishment... God
- Collective Rights - Learn God's Reality/man's illusion: See God
- Balance Logic and Feelings - All Seeing Eye of God (nature)
- Intellect (wisdom) - Master Mind   **Befriend God**
- Emotions (courage) - Master Heart

Balance Personal Needs against Unlimited Wants to become Free Man of God
- Divinity Gives Divine Body - Divine Love: One with Holy Trinity
- Christ Jesus Offers Life - Free Man Lives in Own Kingdom
- One Faces Damnation in Hell - Thrill of Victory
- Receive Divine Liberty - *Given Personal Freedom*
- Seat in God's Divine Court - Rule Over God's Divine Love

(balancing God's Reality, Logic, Intellect, and Wisdom to Get Mind [remove God's spirit curse])
(balancing man's illusion, feelings, emotions, and courage to get heart [remove God's flesh curse])

This illustration shows that "God is Balancing" the Executive Home (earth), Legislative Government (Heaven), Judicial Church (Kingdom), and the Voting Self (God) by *Using Individual, Social, Divine, and Collective Rights*. "One's Right" to Life, Property, Ownership, and Respect **Opens the Way** for **Social Order** and the **Inter-relationships** between *God, Angels, Men, and Nature*. Obviously, the "Home is Designed" to bring forth New Bodies; the "Government is Designed" to bring forth Eternal Lives; the "Church is Designed" to bring forth Royal Kingdoms; and the "Self is Designed" to bring forth Personal Freedom. Through each of these "Four Institutions (home/government/church/self)," God's Creation Operates based on the **Mind Learning Right** (adult) **from Wrong** (baby) to **Master Righteousness** (ethics/citizen) on **Earth** and then *Transforming the Flesh into Human Perfection*. Secondly, the "Heart is Called" to Learn Good (greed) from Evil (fear) to **Master Holiness** (morals/sainthood) in **Heaven** and then *Transform the Spirit into Angelic Perfection*. Thirdly, the "Soul is Called" to Learn God's Will (innocence/blessed) from man's will (guilt/cursed) to **Master Perfection** (fairness/sonship) within the **Kingdom** and then *Transform the Soul into Divine Perfection*. Finally, the "Life-force is Called" to Learn God's Reality (wisdom) from man's illusion (courage) to **Master Divinity** (justice/freedom) within the **Lord God Almighty Himself** and then *Transform One's Nature into a New Creation* (born-again).

The point here is that "If a Person" Receives a New Body, he becomes **Worthy** of a **Seat in God's Celestial Court** (king) and *Rule with Christ Over the Earth* (physical dimension). Secondly, "If a "Person" Receives Eternal Life, he becomes **Worthy** of a **Seat in God's Temple Court** (priest) and *Rule with Christ in Heaven* (spiritual dimension). Thirdly, "If a Person" Receives a Royal Kingdom, he becomes **Worthy** of a **Seat in God's Royal Court** (son) and *Rule with Christ in God's Kingdom of Glory* (mystical dimension). Finally, "If a Person" Receives his Own Personal Freedom, he **Automatically** becomes **Worthy** of a **Seat in God's Divine Court** (free man) and *Rule with God Over All that He Surveys*. Through each of these "Four Courts," a Person is Able to **Attain Eternal Authority** within God's **Physical** (thought), **Spiritual** (word), **Mystical** (deed), and **Divine** (accomplishment) **Creations** as a *King, Priest, Son, and Free Man of God*. To "Attain" this High State of Perfection, a **Person** must **Master the Life-experience** and **Learn How** to **Get It Right** in *Mind, Heart, Soul, and Life-force*. We now see that the "Life-experience" is All About Getting it Right by **Working All Week** and then **Taking Stock** of **One's Progress** on both **Saturday** (Sabbath/count babies) and **Sunday** (Lord's day/count saints) to *Evaluate his Efforts* *both Human and Divine.* We now see that on "Saturday," a <u>Person is Expected</u> to **Take Stock of his Good Works** (growth/children), **Leading** to his **Personal Wealth** in **Land, Material Wealth, and Money.** This **Day of Relaxation** is for him to *Honor his Devotion to Duty.* Secondly, on "Sunday," a <u>Person is Expected</u> to **Take Stock of his Prayers** (maturity/sainthood), **Leading** to his **Community Blessings** in **Offices Held, Certificates Earned, and Titles Attained** as this **Day of Worship** is for *God,* to *Honor His Servant's Depth of Repentance.*

Baby	1.	**Celestial Court** - <u>Rule Earth:</u> Physical Nature…God's Kingship (throne)	
Teenage	2.	**Temple Court** - <u>Rule Heaven:</u> Spiritual Nature…God's Priesthood (altar)	
Adult	3.	**Royal Court** - <u>Rule Kingdom:</u> Mystical Nature…God's Sonship (table)	
Wise Man	4.	**Divine Court** - <u>Rule Divinity:</u> Divine Nature…God's Fatherhood (face)	

We see that "Man's Day of Relaxation (Saturday)" comes via <u>God's Free Redemption</u> (being saved) to **Give Each** of **God's Children** the **Lord's Blessing of Growth** so that he might **Pass** through **Physical Life** (earth) in *Three Stages of Transformation* (baby, teenager, and adult). Secondly, "Man's Day of Worship (Sunday)" comes via <u>Man's Earned Salvation</u> (saving self) to **Give Each** of **God's Children** the **Lord's Blessing of Maturity** so that he might **Pass** through **Spiritual Life** (Heaven/church) in *Three Stages of Purification* (king, priest, and son). The idea here is that on "Saturday," a <u>Person</u> is <u>Evaluating his Behavior</u> (flesh/world/works) to **Determine** the **Depth of his Righteousness** in *Tangible Assets* (visible). Secondly, on "Sunday," a <u>Person</u> is <u>Evaluating his Nature</u> (spirit/church/prayers) to **Determine** the **Depth of his Holiness** in *Mystical Assets* (invisible). Through a "Person's" <u>Submission to Jesus Christ,</u> he can **Combine** his **Earthly Treasures** (behavior) and his **Heavenly Blessings** (nature) to **Receive** a *New Body* (new mind), *Eternal Life* (new heart), and *Royal Kingdom* (new soul) *from God.* It should now make sense that "God Wants to become a Man (Christmas/life)" and that "Man Wants to become God (Easter/death)" and this <u>Eternal Union</u> can **Never Take Place** without **Mastering** both the *Jewish Sabbath* (Saturday/works/babies) and the *Christian Lord's Day* (Sunday/prayers/sainthood).

The following tabular information indicates that the "Meaning" of both the <u>Jewish Sabbath</u> (Saturday/works/babies) and the <u>Christian Lord's Day</u> (Sunday/prayers/saints) **Reveal** a **Time of Evaluation** as the **Flesh Judges** its *Growth* (behavior) and the **Spirit Judges** its *Maturity* (nature):

**God's Two Systems of Life (all/nothing) One on
Saturday (servant) and One on Sunday (slave)**
(measure growth Saturday [righteous babies] via works
and measure maturity Sunday [holy saint] via prayer)

Works	1.	**Saturday** - <u>Amount of Growth:</u> Earning Righteous Dollars...Jewish Sabbath

Works
(nothing)

1. **Saturday** - <u>Amount of Growth:</u> Earning Righteous Dollars...Jewish Sabbath
- Servanthood - Paid Job: Serving Son of God = Removing Faults + Fulfill the World
- Running from the Stick of Pain (streetwise) - Stop and Lose (body broken)

Count Babies/
money
(ownership)

- Paying Punitive Recompense - Pay Damages: Money/Hard-work (visible)
- Learning Right from Wrong - Become Righteous Citizen on Earth (God becomes Man)
- Free Redemption (being saved) - New Body of Life: Physical Dimension
- Relaxation - Land Owned, Material Wealth, and Money Saved (inheritance)

Man's
Destiny
• Lessons
(space)

- Transformation - Crucible of Fire: ***New Behavior*** (Jesus)
- Baby Selfishness - Ignorance (mind)
- Teenage Lustfulness - Cowardice (heart)   **Remove Ignorance**
- Adult Avarice - Greed (soul)   • Self or Society
- <u>Count Number of Babies Created</u> - Creating God's Children on Earth (count money)

(save sinners - Heaven on Earth: God's interior blessing = relative truth: earn money)

===

Earthly Babies and Heavenly Saints become Sons of God in Service to All

===

Prayers
(all)

2. **Sunday** - <u>Amount of Maturity:</u> Earning Holy Dollars...Christian Lord's Day
- Slavery - No Pay: Serving Eternal Father = Gain Virtues + Fulfill the Church
- Chasing the Carrot of Pleasure (educated) - Win and be Rewarded (blood shed)

Count Saints/
Love
(keys)

- Paying Compensatory Retribution - Fine/ticket: Money/Imprisonment (invisible)
- Learn Good from Evil - Become Holy Saint in Heaven (Man becomes God)
- Earned Salvation (save self) - Eternal Life: Spiritual Dimension
- Worship - Offices Held, Certificates Earned, and Titles Attained (birthright)

God's Free Will
• Blessings
(time)

- Purification - Winepress of Conversion: ***New Nature*** (Christ)
- Kingship of Leadership - Wisdom (new body)
- Priesthood of Sacrifice - Courage (eternal life)   **Remove Cowardice**
- Sonship of Love - Generosity (royal kingdom)   • Fun or Worship

(create saints - Paradise in Heaven: God's exterior blessing = absolute truth: save souls)

This illustration shows that the "Life-experience" is <u>All About</u> either having **Heaven on Earth** (inheritance) with **Man** (Jesus), or <u>Attaining</u> **Paradise in Heaven** (birthright) with **God** (Christ), or having both through the <u>**Union**</u> of ***Man's Flesh*** (destiny/Jesus) and ***God's Spirit*** (free will/Christ). We see that to have "Heaven on Earth," a <u>Person must Be Saved</u> by the **Messiah,** thereby bringing the ***Removal of his Ignorant Mind*** (selfishness) to ***Give him a Wise Mind*** (unselfishness). Secondly, to have "Paradise in

Heaven," a <u>Person must Save himself</u> by **Prayer,** thereby bringing the ***Removal of his Cowardly Heart*** (fear) to ***Give him a Courageous Heart*** (fearless). In the case of the "World System," <u>Mankind is Hoping</u> (treasure) to **Receive** the **Lessons of Life** in **Babyhood Fun** (new mind), ***Teenage Love*** (new heart), and ***Adult Wealth*** (new soul). Secondly, in the case of the "Church System," <u>Humanity is Certain</u> (pearl) to **Receive** the **Blessings of Life** in ***Kingship*** (new body), ***Priesthood*** (new eternal life), and ***Sonship*** (royal kingdom). This means that "Saturday is Devoted" to <u>Removing One's Faults</u> to **Transform the Flesh** into ***Proper Behavior*** (environment); while "Sunday is Devoted" to <u>Inserting God's Virtues</u> to **Purify the Spirit** into a ***New Nature*** (instincts). In this explanation, we see that "Man's Destiny" is of a <u>Physical Nature</u> based on ***Infinite/space*** (Saturday), while "God's Free-willed Nature" is of a <u>Spiritual Nature</u> based on ***Eternity/time*** (Sunday). The trick comes with making "Destiny" and "Free Will One" as <u>God becomes Man</u> (Christmas/lessons) and <u>Man becomes God</u> (Easter/blessings) to **Convert** the **Human Nature** into an **Eternal Being** in the ***Person of Jesus Christ***. In this "Process of Conversion," we see that <u>Man</u> must **Take-on All Sin** (body broken), while <u>God</u> must **Give-up His Divinity** (blood shed) to **Unite** the ***Flesh of Man*** (Saturday) with the ***Spirit of God*** (Sunday). This would cause the "Human Race (pagan world)" to <u>Insult</u> "God's Divine Nature" unto the **Wrath** of **God's Divine Justice,** thereby ***Creating*** the ***Unforgivable Sin against Eternal Life***.

It can now be seen that the "Essence of Life" <u>Centers</u> on **What We Believe** (mind) on **Saturday,** be it ***Relaxation*** (self) or ***Work*** (society) and/or just **What We Believe** (heart) on **Sunday,** be it ***Fun*** (Man) or ***Worship*** (God). This means that on the "Weekend," a <u>Person</u> is to **Take Stock of his Life** and **Reflect** on his **Priesthood** (see limitations)**, Kingship** (see potential)**, Sonship** (see self-worth), and **Free Nature** (see new nature) as he <u>Strives</u> to become ***Righteous, Holy, Perfect, and Free before God***. We see that to become "Worthy of Freedom," <u>Each of God's Children</u> (slaves) must be **Transformed** into a **Crucible of Fire** (God's law/bread) to have his **Physical Nature Changed** from ***Sinfulness to Holiness***. Secondly, to become "Worthy of Eternal Freedom," <u>Each of God's Adults</u> (servants) must be **Purified** in the **Winepress of Conversion** (Man's faith/wine) to have his **Spiritual Nature Changed** from ***Human to Divine***. In short, the "Life-experience is About" <u>Spending the Week Working</u> to **Create Babies** (mothers/flesh) and **Saints** (fathers/spirit), and then on **Saturday** (Sabbath), a **Mother Counts** her **Wealth** (money) in the **Number of Babies** (ownership) she has ***Raised***. Secondly, on "Sunday (Lord's Day/8th day)," a <u>Father Counts</u> his **Wealth** (love) in the **Number of Saints** (keys) he has **Created** through **Proper Education** and **Training** as he **Strives** to bring forth **Many Lovable Souls** in **Service** to ***Men, Angels, and God***. This "Need to Attain Perfection" is <u>Driving Us All</u> and it becomes extremely important to **Evaluate Our Lives** as **Often as Possible** (weekends) and **Prioritize Our Time and Energies** as we ***Strive to become Like Our God***.

We see that this "Prioritizing Concept" <u>Centers</u> on **Making a Blood Offering to God** either as a **Priest** ***Who Sheds His Own Blood***, as a **King** ***Who Makes a Bloodless Sacrifice,*** and/or a **Son,** ***Who Offers the Blood of God's Enemies***. This means that a "Priest" Offers Innocent Blood to **Pay Man's Sin-debt** (ignorance); a "King" <u>Offers Forgiven Blood</u>/bloodless to **Pay Man's** ***Evil-debt*** (cowardice); and a "Son" <u>Offers</u>

Guilty Blood to **Pay Man's *Death-debt*** (greed). The idea here is that "Innocent Blood" brings Repentance for **All Venial Sins,** thereby **Teaching God's Right** from **man's wrong.** Then a **Person** can become a **Righteous Citizen on Earth, Receive** the **Title Deed to the Earth,** thereby *Giving* him *Heaven on Earth* (new body). Secondly, a "Bloodless Sacrifice" brings an Awakening of **All Mortal Sins,** thereby **Teaching God's Good** from **man's evil.** Then a **Person** can become a **Holy Saint in Heaven, Receive** the **Title Deed to Heaven,** and then *Attain Paradise in Heaven* (eternal life). Finally, "Guilty Blood" brings God's Friendship showing **All One's Capital Sins,** thereby **Teaching God's Will** from **man's will.** Then a **Person** can become a **Son of God within the Kingdom, Receive** the **Title Deed to God's Kingdom,** and *Earn His Freedom* (royal kingdom). In this concept of "Offering God Blood," a Priest is bringing **Moral Behavior,** the King brings **Ethical Behavior,** and the Son brings **Fair/Perfect Behavior** to *Transform Earth into Heaven.* Through this "Ability to Change" Nothing into All, **God, Angels, and Men** are **Able** to bring **Challenge, Adventure, and Fun** to **Each** of **God's Beloved Children** and **Transform Them** into *Righteous, Holy, and Perfect Sons of God.*

Obviously, the "Priest" is Challenging Mankind to **Learn God's Right** from **man's wrong** so that a **Person** can become a **Righteous Citizen on Earth** (new mind), thereby **Making** him **Worthy** of the **Title Deed to Earth** bringing him *Heaven on Earth* (new body). Secondly, a "King" Offers Mankind Adventure by **Learning God's Good** from **man's evil** so that a **Person** can become a **Holy Saint in Heaven** (new heart), thereby **Making** him **Worthy** of the **Title Deed to Heaven** bringing *Paradise in Heaven* (eternal life). Finally, a "Son" Offers Mankind Rollicking Fun by **Learning God's Will** from **man's will** so that a **Person** can become a **Son of God** within **God's Kingdom** (new soul), thereby **Making** him **Worthy** of the **Title Deed to his Own Kingdom** bringing *Eternal Freedom* (royal kingdom). In short, by "Mastering the Life-experience," a Person can Attain **God's Treasures** and **Escape Immature Foolishness** to become a *Wise* and *Productive Member of Society.* This "Mystical Transformation" comes from Christ's Priesthood, Kingship, and Sonship as **They Each Offers His Innocent, Forgiven,** and **Guilty Blood** to **Save** the **Lost Minds, Hearts, and Souls** of *Cursed Humanity.*

The following tabular information indicates that a "Priest (innocent)" Sheds His Own Blood, a "King (forgiven)" Offers-up Forgiven Blood, and a "Son (guilty)" Sheds the Blood of God's Enemies as **Each Offering** brings **Repentance, Awakening,** and **God's Friendship** to *All Humanity*:

Priest Sheds Own Blood, King Sheds Forgiven Blood,
Son Sheds Enemies' Blood to Honor God
(priest brings moral behavior, king brings
ethics, son brings perfection to set man free)

Messiah   1.   **Priest** - Sheds His Own Blood: Moral Behavior = See Limitations... Knowledge
(soul)
             •   Innocent Blood Sacrifice - Pay Sin-debt: Remove Sin-nature (ignorance)
             •   Forgive Spirit Nature - Call to Repent: Slaughter Baby (innocence)

Lost Soul		• Learn Right/Wrong - Become Righteous Citizen on Earth
		• Remove Venial Sins - Restore Mind to Wisdom (challenge)
		• Receive Title Deed to Earth - Heaven on Earth: Know God
		• Receive Free Redemption - Remove Sin-nature *Gain New Body*
		• Christ - High Priest of Heaven: Offers Innocent Blood = Save Lost
		• High Priest - Saves Babies for Free: Water Baptism = Change Nature
		• Placed upon God's Altar of Life/earth: Low Performance (help)
		• God's Love - Judged on Handicap System: Compromised Will

Church
(spirit)

2. **King** - <u>Sheds Forgiven Blood:</u> Ethical Behavior = See Potential...
Self-awareness (spirit)
- Forgiven Bloodless Sacrifice - Pay Evil-debt: Remove Worldly Temptations (cowardice)
- Forgive Flesh Nature - Call to Awaken: Slaughter Teenager (lust)
- Learn Good from Evil - Become Holy Saint in Heaven/paradise

Repentant Soul
- Remove Mortal Sins - Restore Heart to Courage (adventure)
- Receive Title Deed to Heaven - Paradise in Heaven: Love God
- Receive Earned Salvation - Remove Worldly Temptations   *Gain Eternal Life*
- <u>Jesus</u> - King of the Jews (earth): Offers Forgiven Blood = Save Repentant Sinners
- Royal King - Forgives Teenage Sin: Blood Confession = Wash Away Sin
- Placed upon God's Altar of Death/Heaven: Average Performance (trying)
- God's Mercy - Judged on a Curve System: Permissive Will

World
(flesh)

3. Son - <u>Sheds Blood of Enemies:</u> Perfect Behavior = See Self-worth....
Consciousness
- Guilty Blood Sacrifice – Pay Death-debt: Remove Demonic Possession (greed)
- Forgive Soul Nature - Call to Friendship: Slaughter Adult (selfishness)
- Learn God's Will/man's will - Become Perfect Son within Kingdom

Born-again Soul
- Remove Capital Sins - Restore Soul to Generosity (rollicking fun)
- Receive Title Deed to Kingdom - Freedom in Kingdom: Serve God
- Receive Bonus Rewards - Remove Demonic Possession   ***Gain Royal Kingdom***
- <u>Jesus Christ</u> - Son of God: Offers Guilty Blood = Save Born-again Soul
- God's Son - Kills God's Adult Enemies: Spiritual Communion = Think for Self
- Placed upon God's Altar of New-life: High Performance (perfect)
- God's Justice - Judged on Pass/Fail System: Direct Will

This illustration shows that the "Life-experience" is primarily <u>Centered</u> upon being **Saved from Sin, Evil, and Death** by **God's Son, Jesus Christ** as **He was Willing** to **Offer-up His Innocent, Forgiven, and Guilty Blood** to <u>**Take-on**</u> *All Mankind's*

Transgressions Against God. Once a "Lost Soul" is <u>Redeemed by Innocent Blood</u> (priest), then his **Sin-nature is Removed** and he is **Eligible to Receive** a **New Body**, thereby **Allowing him** to **Come to Know God** and to *Enter His Personal Friendship.* Secondly, a "Repentant Soul" is <u>Redeemed by Guilty Blood</u> (king), then his **Worldly Temptations are Removed** and he is **Eligible to Receive Eternal Life**, thereby **Allowing him** to **Come to Love God** and to *Enter His Personal Companionship.* Finally, a "Born-again Soul" is <u>Redeemed by Forgiven Blood</u> (son), then his **Demonic Possession is Removed** and he is **Eligible to Receive his Own Royal Kingdom**, thereby **Allowing him** to **Come to Serve God** and to *Enter His Perfect Oneness* (union).

Yes! The whole "Redemptive System of God" <u>Depends</u> upon **Each Person's Maturity Level** based on his **Intellect, Emotions, and Natural Instincts** as **They Relate** to his **Ability to Perform** within *Human Society.* This means that a "Low Performer" or <u>Baby Soul</u> is **Given God's Free Redemption** (being saved) as the **Lord Does the Work** for him by **Offering Christ's** (High Priest) **Innocent Blood** upon the *Almighty's Altar of Life* (starvation). Secondly, an "Average Performer" or <u>Teenage Soul</u> must **Earn his Own Salvation** (saving self) as the **Lord Expects Great Things** of him by **Offering Jesus'** (King) **Forgiven Blood** upon the *Almighty's Altar of Death* (nakedness). Finally, a "High Performer" or <u>Adult Soul,</u> **Hopes** for **God's Bonus Rewards** (saving others) as the **Lord Demands Perfection** of him by **Offering Jesus Christ's** (Son) **Guilty Blood** upon the *Almighty's Altar of New-life* (homelessness). The idea here is that a "Low Performer (baby)" <u>Needs</u> his *Nature Changed*; the "Average Performer (teenager)" <u>Needs</u> his **Sins Washed Away**; while the "High Performer (adult)" <u>Needs</u> to *Think for himself.* We can now see that a "Low Performer (baby/venial)" is <u>Learning Morals;</u> an "Average Performer (teen/mortal)" is <u>Learning Ethics;</u> and a "High Performer (adult/perfect)" is <u>Learning Perfection,</u> **All Based** on *Coming to Know, Love, and Serve God.*

Truth   1. **Washed in Innocent Blood** - <u>Remove Sin-nature</u> (sin): Receive New Body
- Baby Low Performer - Needs Nature Changed (divine): Knowing God (ethics)
- Balance Morals and Ethics (earth) - To Balance the Home...Nature
- Sin Kills the Mind - Change Ignorance to Wisdom

Law   2. **Washed in Guilty Blood** - <u>Remove Worldly Temptations</u> (evil): Receive Eternal Life
- Teenager Average Performer - Needs Sins Washed Away (holy): Love God (morals)
- Balance Authority and Responsibility (Heaven) - To Balance Government...Men
  Evil Kills the Heart - Change Cowardice to Courage

Will   3. **Washed in Forgiven Blood** - <u>Remove Demonic Possessions</u> (death): Receive Own Kingdom
- Adult High Performer - Needs to Think for Himself (perfect): Serve God (fairness)
- Balance Faith and Law (Kingdom) - To Balance the Church...Angels

- Death Kills the Soul - Change Greed to Generosity

Love   4. **Purify Grave and the Host** - Remove God's Curse (damnation): Receive Eternal Freedom
- Wise Man's Perfect Performance - Needs Great Imagination (life): Servant of All (goodness)
- Balance Mind and Heart (God) - To Balance Oneself…God
- Damnation Kills Life-force - Change Selfishness to Unselfishness

It now becomes clear that we must "Seek to Balance (home)" Morals and Ethics on *Earth; then* to "Balance (government)" Authority and Responsibility in *Heaven;* then to "Balance (church)" Faith and Law within the ***Kingdom;*** and finally, to "Balance (self)" the Mind and Heart as a *Reflection of God.* Through these "Four States of Perfection," we can effectively Balance Our Lives to be at **One** with **God, Angels, Men, and Nature** and to *Reflect the Holy Teaching of Christ.* We can now see that "Jesus Christ" came to Explain the Life-experience in terms of **Our Physical Growth** and **Spiritual Maturity** so that each of **God's Children** could reach his **Own** *State of Righteousness, Holiness, Perfection, and Freedom before God.* The question is: just when did a "Person" become Aware that he **Wanted** to **Commit** his **Life** to becoming *Righteous* (earth), *Holy* (Heaven), and/or *Perfect* (Kingdom) before *God?* The easy answer is when a "Baby Soul" was still a Spirit within the **Astral Plane,** where **All Eternal Decisions** were to be **Made** concerning *God's Destiny* (illusion) and *Man's Free Will* (reality). The theme here is that as "Astral Spirits," we were Required to **Choose Our Parents,** to be **Male/Female,** and **All Else** within **Our Earthly Nature** so that we could **Master the Life-experience** and *Attain* the *Level of Happiness We Desired.*

The point here is that having a "Long-life on Earth (80 yrs.)" meant either Choosing either to be a *Winner* (adult/make rules) or to be a *Loser* (child/follow rules). Obviously, the "Winners of the World (adulthood)" are Intellectually Superior (brains), Attractive (beauty), and Wealthy (bounty); while the "Losers of the World (childhood)" are Slow-Witted (dumb), Unattractive (ugly), and Poor (lazy.) Unfortunately, like most "Things in Life" when you Think you have **Chosen the Better Part,** suddenly **What Looks Easy** (adulthood/blessings) becomes *Hard* (childhood earth); and **What Looked Hard** (childhood/lessons) becomes *Easy* (adulthood Heaven). We call this "Confused Perception of Reality" being Tricked by God because **Things are Not as They Appear.** Be sure you **Look Past the Obvious** as *All that Glitters is Not Gold.* In the case of the "Lord's Life-experience," Beware of Greeks Bearing Gifts, especially **If it's Free** or **If it Appears You have just Won the Lotto** as the *Luckiest Person Ever.* Obviously, the "Trap of God" is in the fact that an Earthly Child (holy/morals) becomes a *Heavenly Adult* (paradise in Heaven); while an Earthly Adult (righteous/ethics) becomes an *Earthly Wise Man* (Heaven on Earth). It all comes down to "Learning to Read the Signs" and Learning to **Take Positive Control** of both the **Spirit** (adult/birthright) and the **Flesh** (child/inheritance) through the *Forces* of the *Church* (spirit) and the *World* (flesh). The idea here is that "Childhood" Appears as Play (adventure)," but in the **End** is **Work** because a **Person must Learn** (passed) the

Lessons of Life (earned). In contrast, "Adulthood" <u>Appears as Work</u> (challenge); but in the **End** is **Play** because a **Person is Left Behind** (failed) on **Earth** to *Raise the Babies of God Forever*.

The following tabular information indicates that the "Astral Plane" is a <u>Real Trap</u> as it **Forces a New Spirit** to **Choose** either the **Rosy Pathway** of *Childhood* or the **Rocky Road** of *Adulthood*:

**Choices Made in the Astral Plane between having
an Easy or Hard Life on Earth**
(choose an easy life of a child/free (lessons)
or hard life of an adult/earned (blessings)

Play (adventure)	1.	**Life of a Child** - <u>Seek Heaven:</u> Lucifer's Test = Learn Lessons of Life… Knowledge
		• Easy Road/rosy path - Streetwise: Love of the Heart (emotions) = Free Will
		• Learn Right from Wrong - Flesh: Master Priesthood = Church (Mary)
		• Child to Divine Adult - Paradise in Heaven: Worship Eternal Father (temple)
Lessons		• Free Birthright - Must Earn Eternal Life by Surrendering to the Church
		• Direct Contact with God - Be Holy Saint: Take Stock of One's Life on Sunday
		• Receive Eternal Life from Heaven - Morals to Holiness (spirit)
		• Hired by God (job) - Servant unto the Lord (son of God)
Work (challenge)	2.	**Life of an Adult** - <u>Seek Earth:</u> Face God's Judgment = Receive Blessings… Self-awareness
		• Hard Road/rocky road - Educated: Wisdom of the Mind (intellect) = Destiny
		• Learn Good from Evil - Spirit: Master Kingship = World (Martha)
		• Adult to Earthly Wise Man - Heaven on Earth: Worship Son of God (church)
Blessings		• Earned Inheritance - Receive Free New Body and Master Earth
		• Intercessory Contact - Be Righteous Citizen: Take Stock of Life on Saturday
		• Receive New Body from Earth - Ethics to Righteousness (flesh)
		• Hired by Man (job) - Raise Babies in Universe (son of man)

This illustration shows that when a "Soul" has <u>Chosen Adulthood on Earth,</u> it appears to be a **Road to Wealth and Power** (blessings); but in the **End,** it will be a <u>Divine Trap</u> because a **Person** has *Only Mastered the Earthly Experience Alone*. In contrast, "Choosing Childhood on Earth" seems initially to be <u>Stupid;</u> but this **Choice Leads** to becoming a **Divine Adult in Heaven, If** an <u>Awakened Soul</u> can *Master the Church* (belief). We must all "Beware" of a Two-<u>Truth System</u> (child/adult), where the **Forces** of All and Nothing are **One** and where **God's Reality** and **Man's Illusion** can become **Interchangeable** at the *Divine Level of Perfection*. Obviously, the "Secret" to <u>Outsmarting God</u> is to **Do Both,** by being a **Spiritual Child** (submission) and also being a **Physical Adult** (sacrifice) and <u>**One Day Own**</u> both *Heaven* (spirit/eternal life) and *Earth* (flesh/new body). This implication of being a "Responsible Earthly Adult" is to become <u>Immersed in Physical Sin</u> to <u>**Learn All**</u> the *Lessons in Life* and then to **Spend Every Waking Hour Trying to Save Lost Souls.** Once a "Person is Filled with Sin (sees wrong)," he must then <u>Enter the Church</u> to be **Purified** in **Christ's Great Washing Machine** (see right), and then **Come Back into the World** <u>**Refreshed**</u> and <u>**Ready for Another**</u> *Fight with Lucifer.* This "Dual-Nature Concept" can be <u>Fulfilled</u> by **Meeting God** and obtaining *His Authority* (life-force), *Responsibility* (soul), *Duty* (heart), *Task* (mind), and *Objectives* (nature). It is important to "Recognize" whether you have <u>Chosen</u> to be an <u>**Earthly Adult**</u> (raise babies) or a <u>**Heavenly Child**</u> (bless lives) **Forever** so you can *Put All Things in Perspective*. Obviously, seeing "Things Correctly" also means <u>Recognizing</u> **If a Person** has **Created a Victim** by **Offending Himself** (venial), <u>**His Brothers**</u> (mortal), or <u>**His God**</u> (capital) through *His Faults* (self), *Transgressions* (society), or *Sins* (God). The implication is that by "Offending Himself," a <u>Person</u> has <u>Created a Venial Sin</u> which has the **Power to Kill the Mind** through *His Wicked Thoughts* (flesh). Secondly, by "Offending His Society" or "Brother," a <u>Person</u> has <u>Created a Mortal Sin</u> which has the **Power to Kill the Heart** through *His Selfish Desires* (spirit). Finally, by "Offending God," a <u>Person</u> has <u>Created a Capital Sin</u> which has the **Power to Kill the Sou**<u>l</u> through *His Murderous Acts*. By "Committing" <u>Venial, Mortal,</u> and <u>Capital Sins,</u> a **Person has Violated** the **Laws of God** and must <u>**Pay These Debts**</u> through his *Repentance, Prayers, and Works*.

We see that the "Major Debts of Man" <u>Reside</u> in **Removing His Faults** (emptying) and **Gaining His Virtues** (filling) which had to be <u>**Paid For**</u> by both the *Goat of Death* (Jesus) and the *Lamb of Life* (Christ). In the case of the "Goat of Death," he was <u>Forced to Sacrifice</u> his **Guilty Blood** by **Killing His Enemies** upon the <u>**Altar of Man**</u> to *Repent for the Sins of All Men*. Secondly, the "Lamb of Life" was <u>Forced to Sacrifice</u> His **Innocent Blood** by **Offering-up His Own Blood** upon the **Altar of God** to <u>**Receive Forgiveness**</u> for *All His Sins*. This means that "Offering Enemy Blood" <u>Represents</u> **Entering** the **Winepress of Death** (wine) to <u>**Wash Away Sin**</u> to *Remove One's Faults* (empty). Secondly, "Offering His Own Blood" <u>Represents</u> **Entering** the **Crucible of Fire** (bread) to <u>**Change a Person's Nature**</u> to *Insert his Virtues* (fill). In short, "Emptying a Person of Faults" <u>Teaches</u> (lessons) a **Child of God** the **Essence of Life**; while "Filling a Person with Virtues" **Blesses** (grace) a **Child of God** with **New-life** to <u>**Blend**</u> the *Forces of Evil* (childish mistakes) with the *Forces of Good* (adult perfection). The "Lord Jesus Christ" is <u>Telling Us</u> that **Removing Faults Represents** a <u>**Day of Reconciliation**</u> (Yom Kippur) or *Man's Jewish Sacrifice* (repentance). Secondly, the "Lord Jesus Christ" is <u>Telling Us</u> that **Inserting Virtues Represents** a <u>**Day of Forgiveness**</u> (Passover Meal) or *God's Christian Sacrifice* (forgiveness). Through these "Two Sacrifices," we see <u>Mary's Son, Jesus</u> **Taking-on All the Sins of Man** to **Represent** the <u>**Goat of Death**</u> (reconciliation) *Killing All the Enemies of God* (guilty blood). Secondly, we see "God's Son, Christ" <u>Giving-up His</u>

Divinity (forgiveness) to **Represent** the **Lamb of Life** by *Offering His Own Blood* (innocent blood).

In this explanation, we see that the "Man Jesus (goat/guilty blood)" is bringing the Good News, by **Telling the World** that **Everyone** will **Receive Free Redemption** (righteousness) from *Sin, Evil, and Death*. In contrast, we see that the "God Christ (lamb/innocent blood)" is bringing the Gospel Message, **Telling the World** that **God's Saints** can **Earn Their Own Salvation** (holiness) from *Hell, Gehenna, and Oblivion*. It should now make sense that through the "Flesh of Jesus," a Person can become a **Righteous Citizen on Earth** (new body) so that he might **Know the Difference** between *Right and Wrong*. Secondly, through the "Spirit of Christ," a Person can become a **Holy Saint in Heaven** (eternal life) so that he might **Know the Difference** between *Good and Evil*. Obviously, by "Understanding" both the Natures of God and Man, a **Person** can **Master** the *Teachings of Life* (growth) and then **Receive** the *Blessings of Life* (maturity).

The following tabular information indicates that "Man's Sacrificial Goat (wine)" Teaches Life (reconciliation); while "God's Sacrificial Lamb (bread)" Blesses Life (forgiveness):

Man's Sacrificial Goat (wine) Teaches Life; God's Sacrificial Lamb Blesses Life (bread)
(goat offers enemy's blood to get reconciliation
and lamb offers own blood to get forgiven)

Flesh (mind)	1. **Sacrificial Goat's Blood** - Offer Enemy's Blood (death) …Teach Lessons
	• Enter Winepress of Death (wine) - Wash Away Sin: *Remove Faults* (crucifixion)
	• Confession (growth) - Yom Kippur: Day of Reconciliation = Jewish Sacrifice
Teaching Life (ethics)	• Place Guilty Blood on Man's altar – Learn Right from Wrong
	• Become Righteous Citizen on Earth - New Body (face life)
	• Master the Will to Live - Living with Oneself (law)
	• Free Redemption - Wash Original Sin: Offer Faith (redeemed)

(Mary's Son, Jesus – takes-on all sin: pays mankind's sin-debt = free redemption)

Spirit (heart)	2. **Sacrificial Lamb's Blood** - Offer Own Blood (life) …Receive Blessings
	• Enter Crucible of Fire (bread) - Change Nature: *Gain Virtues* (resurrection)
	• Communion (maturity) - Passover Meal: Day of Forgiveness = Christian Sacrifice
Blessing Life (morals)	• Place Innocent Blood on God's Altar - Learn Good from Evil
	• Become Holy Saint in Heaven - Eternal Life (face death)
	• Master the Value of Life - Living with Others (faith)
	• Earned Salvation - Change Sin-nature: Offer Works (saved)

(God's Son, Christ – gives-up His divinity: pays man's holy-debt = earned salvation)

This illustration shows that "God's Human Nature (Jesus)" has <u>Come</u> to **Teach Humanity** the *Will to Live* (new body); while "God's Divine Nature (Christ)" has <u>Come</u> to **Bless Humanity** with the *Value of Life* (eternal life). In short, the "Lord God Almighty" is <u>Striving to Teach</u> the **Human Race** to **Live with Itself** as a *Child* (growth) and then **Master the Art** of <u>Living with Others</u> or <u>God</u> as an *Adult* (maturity). In this "Process" of <u>Growth and Maturity,</u> **Each Struggling Soul** is being **Called to Establish** its **Own Identity** (micro) and to then **Recognize its Own Role** within the *Overall Social Order* (macro). Obviously, the "Job of Jesus Christ (Man)" is to <u>Create</u> a **Manufacturing Plant on Earth** (flesh) to **Produce** an <u>**Infinite Number of Babies**</u> or an <u>**Infinite Number of Bodies**</u> (righteous citizens) in *Service to the Will of God*. Secondly, the "Job of Christ Jesus (God)" is to <u>Create</u> a **Manufacturing Plant in Heaven** (spirit) to **Produce** an **Infinite Number of Saints** (holy citizens) or an <u>**Infinite Number of Eternal Lives**</u> in *Service to the Love of God*. The idea here is that "If a Person" is <u>Willing to Face Life,</u> he can *Gain the Respect of Man* (growing-up); while "If a Person" is <u>Willing to Face Death,</u> he can *Gain the Respect of God* (full maturity).

The question is: "Just How Many Souls" have the <u>Necessary Courage Needed</u> to **Face** both **Life** and **Death** and still have the **Strength to Face** *Lucifer's Test*, *God's Judgment,* and *Their Own Self-evaluation*? The answer is "Very Few, If Any" which is <u>Why the Lord</u> has been **Forced** to **Send His Son** to **Change Man's Nature** with His *Guilty Blood* (law) and to then **Wash Away Sin** with His *Innocent Blood* (faith). The idea here is to see that through "Jesus' Physical Blood (law)," <u>Man can Pass</u> through the *Seven Stages of Earth* (death), while through "Christ's Spiritual Blood (faith)," <u>Man can Pass</u> through the *Seven Stages of Heaven* (life).

We see that the "Human Race" is being <u>Called to Master</u> both the **Physical Earth** and **Spiritual Heaven** by **Changing** its <u>**Nature**</u> on *Earth* and then **Washing Away** its <u>**Sins**</u> to *Enter Heaven*. This "Ability to Change" and to "Transform" <u>Allows</u> the **Human Race** to **Find a Way Out of the Darkness** and **Move into God's Light** when **Our King** <u>**Calls the World**</u> to *Come to His Great Banquet of Glory* (wedding feast). Recall the scripture of "Matthew 22: 2-14" which states that <u>Jesus Says that the Kingdom</u> is likened unto a **King, Who is Putting** on a **Great Banquet** and **Invites** the <u>**Finest**</u> and most **Honored of Guests** (Jews/chosen), but *They All Refused to Come,* with the *Exception* of *One Jew (Messiah)*. We see that this "Angry King" or "God" then <u>Decided</u> to **Invite the Commoners** (Christians/church) from **His Own City** even *If They* were *Poor, Sick, and Broken*. We see that "Some time Later" the <u>King Saw</u> that his **Banquet Hall** was **Not Filled** and **He Ordered His Servants** (sons of God) to **Go Out to the By-ways** and **Invite** the *Strangers* (pagans/world) and even the *Far-off Foreigners* (ends of the earth). This "Theme" of <u>God Inviting</u> the **Jews**/chosen (1st advent), the **Christians**/church (2nd advent), and finally, the **Pagans**/world (3rd advent) *Reveals His Grand Design*. Note that the "Jewish People" were <u>Forced to Wander the Earth</u> in **Search of Their God** as **They Missed Their Hour of Visitation,** but were *Given a Second Chance* (1948). Secondly, the "Christian People" are <u>Rewarded</u> with **Their Own Resurrection** upon the **Lord's Second Coming** as the **Thief in the Night**, showing **All Mankind** that it **Pays to**

Listen to *God's Holy Word*. Finally, the "Pagan People" will be able to <u>See the Light</u> and <u>Convert</u> to **God's Divine Truths,** when **They Realize** that both the **Jews and Christians** have *Found God's Pathway to Perfection.* This means that the "Jews" represented the <u>Finest</u> and most <u>Honored Guests</u> as **They** were **God's Chosen People** *Who* have been *Clothed in Holiness.* Unfortunately, the "Jews Refused to Bow" to <u>God's Divine Will</u> and to **His Son,** the **Lord Jesus Christ** so **that They** were **Forced to See** the **Errors of Their Ways** by *Wandering the Earth* for some *2,000 Years* (two days). This "Treasure of Life" was then <u>Given to the Gentiles,</u> meaning the **Half Jew/Half Pagan** (Samaritan), **Who** had **Rejected God's Temple,** but *Loved God's Son, Jesus the Christ.* Finally, the "Lord God Almighty" becomes <u>Willing</u> to **Save All Men** as **He Opens** the **Door of Redemption** to the <u>**Pagan World of Atheists,**</u> *Who Only Love Themselves* and the *Power of Their Money.* It now makes sense that the "Lord Jesus Christ" <u>Came</u> as a **Priest on a Donkey** to *Be Saved* (righteousness), and will come as a <u>**Thief in the Night**</u> to *Save Himself* (holiness), and finally, as a <u>**Just Judge on a Cloud**</u> to *Save the Whole World* (perfection).

The following tabular information indicates that during the "Lord's Three Advents," <u>God the King Invites</u> the **Messiah** (being saved), the **Church** (saving self), and finally, the **World** to be <u>**Saved**</u> from *Sin, Evil, and Death* (saving others):

Three Advents of Christ to Save the Messiah, the Church, and World from Sin, Evil, and Death
(King invites opulently rich, then commoners in city, and finally, strangers and foreigners)

Save Messiah (one)	1. **1st Advent** - <u>Priest on a Donkey:</u> Bring Righteousness to Earth… Knowledge
	• King Invited Nobles and Wealthy Merchants to his Banquet
	• Jews Invited to Banquet and Did Not Come: Sinners Reject God
	• Jews Forced to Wander the Earth in Search of God
	• Offering Innocent Blood - Save Lost: Resurrection of New Body
	• Priest Offers his Own Blood - Being Saved
	  (repentant sinner - learn right/wrong: obey law:
	    change nature = lessons of life [ethics])

Save Church (few)	2. **2nd Advent** - <u>Thief in the Night:</u> Bring Holiness into Heaven… Self-awareness
	• King Invited Everyone in the City both Poor and Crippled
	• Christians Invited to King's Banquet and Came: Christian Saints Accept God
	• Christians Forced to Perform Good Works in Service to God
	• Offering Forgiven Blood - Save Repentant: Resurrection of Eternal Life
	• King Offers Repentant Blood - Saving Himself
	  (living prayer - learn good/evil: love faith:
	    wash away sin = blessings of life [morals])

Save	3.	**3rd Advent** - <u>Just Judge on Cloud:</u> Bring Perfection into Kingdom…
World		Consciousness
(all)		• King Invited Everyone in the World both Strangers and Foreigners
		• Pagans Invited to King's Banquet and All Came: Pagans Repent
		• Pagans Forced to Change Their Ways and Save Lost Souls
		• Offering Guilty Blood - Save Born-again: Resurrection of Royal Kingdom
		• Son Offers Enemy's Blood - Saving Others

(soldier-of-the-light - learn God's Will/man's will:

set free = thinking for self [instincts])

This illustration shows that the "Jewish People" are being <u>Forced</u> to **Wander the Earth** to *Find God's Truths*; then the "Christian People" are being <u>Forced</u> to **Perform Good Works** in *Service to Their Creator God*. Finally, the "Pagan People" are being <u>Forced</u> to **Change Their Ways** and **Go in Search of Lost Souls** to bring **Them** into the *Righteousness* (king), *Holiness* (priest), and *Perfection* (son) of *God*. Through these "Three Groups" of <u>Lost Broken Humans,</u> we see the **Opulent Jews** (found temple), the **Commoner Christians** (found church), and the **Outcast Pagan Strangers** (found world) **<u>All in Search</u>** of that *One and Only Absolute Truth*. During the "Lord's 1st Advent (Messiah/one)," <u>Christ</u> **Resurrected** the **New Body of Righteousness** to **Create Heaven on Earth** and bring forth the *Spirit of God on Earth* (church). This means that during the "Lord's 2nd Advent (Church/few)," <u>Christ</u> will **Resurrect** the **Eternal Life of Holiness** to **<u>Create Paradise in Heaven</u>** and bring forth the *Son of God in Heaven* (world). Finally, in the "Lord's 3rd Advent (World/all)," <u>Christ</u> will **Resurrect** the **Royal Kingdom of Perfection** to **<u>Create God's Kingdom of Glory</u>** and bring forth the *Eternal Father within the Kingdom* (freedom). By "Creating" the <u>New Earth</u> (body), <u>New Heaven</u> (eternal life), and <u>God's Kingdom</u> (kingdom), the **Whole Human Race** will be **<u>Redeemed</u>** from its *Pit of Sin, Evil, and Death*. The point is to see that the "Lord's 1st Advent" was centered upon <u>Knowledge</u> as **He Removes Ignorance** and brings forth **Wisdom** to **<u>Set Mankind Free</u>** from its *Curse of Mental Illness*. Secondly, in the "Lord's 2nd Advent," <u>He</u> will bring <u>Man's Self-awareness</u> as **He Removes Cowardice** and brings forth **Courage** to **<u>Set Mankind Free</u>** from its *Curse of Childish Fears*. Finally, during the "Lord's 3rd Advent," <u>He</u> will bring <u>Man's Consciousness</u> as **He Removes Greed** and brings forth **Generosity** to **<u>Set Mankind Free</u>** from its *Curse of Unlimited Wants*. Yes! The "Life-experience" is <u>Comprised</u> of a **Set of Challenges** because the **Human Race** must **Defeat** its **Curses of Ignorance, Cowardice, and Greed** to be **<u>Set Free</u>** from a *World of Sin, Evil, and Death*.

We see that the "Lord God Almighty" has <u>Designed a Perfect Creation</u> and that **He is Blending** the **Spiritual Nature of God** (Christ/morals) with the **Physical Nature of Man** (Jesus/ethics) through the **<u>Sacrifice</u>** of *His Son, Jesus Christ* on *Mount Calvary*. Through the "Lord Jesus Christ's" <u>Seven Last Words</u> on the **Cross, He Wrote <u>Seven Tickets of Redemption</u>** (plus a free pass/8), thereby bringing *Growth to the Earth* (law) and *Maturity to Heaven* (faith). We see that when "Jesus Said" (1)

Forgive Them for They Know Not What They Do, this meant the Roman Soldiers as the *Enemies of God.* When "Jesus Said" (2) *My God, My God, Why have You Forsaken Me?* this meant Judas the **Evil Traitor** to **All Mankind,** truly a **Man Who will Wish** he had *Never been Born.* (3) When "Jesus Said" *I Thirst,* this meant His Neighbors or the **Jewish People,** who had **Spent Their Lives Seeking** the **Signs of the Times** and the *Identity of Their Messiah.* (4) When "Jesus Said" *On This very Day You will be with Me in Paradise,* this meant His Friends or the Catholic Church (followers) and the **Mystical Body of Christ** as *They would Overcome Their Own Sin-natures.* (5) When "Jesus Said" *Son, behold Thy Mother"* and *"Mother, behold Thy Son,* this meant His Family or the Apostles/priesthood and **Christ's Communion of Saints** as *They would Overcome All Evil.* (6) When "Jesus Said" *It is Finished,* this meant the Saving of Himself or the **Creation of Christ's New Body** which would *Resurrect from the Grave.* Finally, (7) When "Jesus Said" *I Release My Spirit,* this meant the Saving of Father God Himself by **Offering God** both a **New Body** and **Eternal Life** so that **He could become Human** and *Forever Live on Planet Earth.* Note that (8) "Jesus Christ" was also Able to Save **All the Forgiven Souls When He Remained Silent before Pilate,** thereby **Leaving** an **Eighth Free Ticket of Redemption** for *All the Barabbases of the World.*

Through "Each of these Seven Last Words (plus silence)," God and Man are to **Become One Creation,** thereby bringing forth the **Lord's Blessings** of (1) *Word*/tradition; (2) *Mystical Body*/communion of saints; (3) *Word becomes Ethics*/traditions become morals; (4) *Ethics becomes Righteous Man*/morals becomes holy man; (5) *Remove Human Faults*/insert divine virtue; (6) *Receive New Body*/receive eternal life; and (7) *Heaven on Earth*/paradise in Heaven. Through these "Seven Stages of Transformation," the Human Race can **Grow-up** and **God's Nature** can **Mature** to **Unite** the **Nature of Man** (Jesus) with the **Nature of God** (Christ) in *God's Son, Jesus Christ.*

The following tabular information indicates that through the "Physical Nature of Jesus (guilty blood)" and the "Spiritual Nature of Christ (innocent blood)," the Human Race can **Pass** through its **Seven Stages** of *Growth and Maturity*:

**The Physical Nature of Jesus and Spiritual Nature
of Christ Pass through Seven Stages of Life**
(God's word creates Heaven on Earth and
Man's traditions create Paradise in Heaven for all)

Physical Nature of Jesus (growth - master God's laws)	Spiritual Nature of Christ (maturity - master Man's faith)
1. Word of God	1. Traditions of Church
• Baby - See Man's Truth	• Baby - See God's Truth
• *Forgive Them*	• Save Enemies
2. Mystical Body of Christ	2. Communion of Saints
• Teenager - Hear Man's Law	• Teenager - Hear God's Law
• *Why have You Forsaken Me*	• Save Traitors
3. Word becomes Ethics	3. Traditions become Morals

- Adult - Smell Man's Will
  - *I Thirst*
4. Ethics becomes Righteous Man
  - Wise Man - Taste Man's Love
    - ***This Day in Paradise***
5. Remove Human Faults
  - Free Man -
    Touch Man's Perfection
    - ***Son Behold/Mother Behold***
6. *Receive New Body*
  - Servant - Human Imagination
    - ***It is Finished***
7. Heaven on Earth
  - Son of Man - Creates Bodies
    - **I *Release My Spirit***

- Adult - Smell God's Will
  - Save Neighbors
4. Morals become Holy Man
  - Wise Man - Taste God's Love
    - Save Friends
5. Insert Divine Virtues
  - Free Man - Touch God's
    Perfection
    - Save Family
6. *Receive Eternal Life*
  - Servant - Divine Imagination
    - Save Self
7. Paradise in Heaven
  - Son of God - Creates Life
    - Save God

————————————————— Master Self —————————————————

Lessons - Will to Live (law)
- Live with Self - Save Sinners
  - Love Neighbor (law)
  - ***Silent Moment***

Blessings - Value of Life (love)
- Live with God - Create Saints
  - Worship God (faith)
  - Sinner is Saved

This illustration shows that "Jesus' Physical Nature (guilty blood)" <u>Represents</u> **Human Growth** from **Babyhood to Adulthood** as the whole **Human Race** is **Called** to **Master the Law of God** by <u>Surrendering Its Sin-nature</u> to *God's Divine Will*. Secondly, "Christ's Spiritual Nature (innocent blood)" <u>Represents</u> **Divine Maturity** from **Sinner** (baby) to **Saint** (adult) as **Christ's Church** is **Called** to **Master the Faith of Man** by becoming **Born-again** to *God's Divine Love*. We see that as "Babies," we are <u>Called</u> to **Physically** *See Man's Truth* (earth) and **Spiritually** to *See God's Truth* (Heaven). Secondly, as "Teenagers," we are <u>Called</u> to **Physically** *Hear Man's Laws* (earth) and **Spiritually** to *Hear God's Laws* (Heaven). Thirdly, as "Adults," we are <u>Called</u> to **Physically** *Smell Man's Will* (people) and **Spiritually** to *Smell God's Will* (God). Fourthly, as "Wise Men," we are <u>Called</u> to **Physically** *Taste Man's Love* (will to live) and **Spiritually** to *Taste God's Love* (value of life). Fifthly, as "Free Men," we are <u>Called</u> to **Physically** *Touch Man's Perfection* (Jesus) and **Spiritually** to *Touch God's Perfection* (Christ). Sixthly, as "Servants," we are <u>Called</u> to **Physically** *Imagine Man's New Body* (transfiguration), **and Spiritually** to *Imagine God's Eternal Life* (glorification). Finally, as "Sons of God," we are <u>Called</u> to **Physically** *Create New Bodies for Others* (redemption) and **Spiritually** to *Create New-lives for Others* (salvation).

We now see that the "Overall Life-experience" entails <u>Mastering the Earth</u> and then <u>Mastering Heaven</u> to **Find** the **Friendship, Companionship,** and **Oneness of God** through the *Blessings of Jesus Christ* (church). Obviously, "Mastering Earth (wash)" is <u>Accomplished</u> by **Sacrificing** a **Person's Guilty Blood** (pay faults) on the *Altar of Jesus* (Man), while "Mastering Heaven (change)" is <u>Accomplished</u> by **Sacrificing** a **Person's Innocent Blood** (pay virtues) on the *Altar of Christ* (God). The idea here is to "Master Jesus' Altar" so that a <u>Person</u> can **Learn** the **Lessons of Life** which **Leads** to His *Will to Live* (live with self), while by "Mastering Christ's Altar" <u>He</u> can **Receive** the **Blessings of God** which <u>**Leads**</u> to **His** *Value of Life* (live with God). In this logic, we see that "Guilty Blood (Jesus)" is <u>Used</u> in the <u>**Changing of Natures**</u> (save sinners) of *Venial, Mortal, and Capital Sins*, while "Innocent Blood (Christ)" is <u>Used</u> in the <u>**Washing Away of Sin**</u> (create saints) to bring forth *Righteous, Holy, and Perfect Men of God.*

The idea here is that a "Person's Venial Sins" are <u>Paid For</u> by a **Righteous Man**; "His Mortal Sins" are <u>Paid For</u> by a **Holy Man** (two commandments); and "His Capital Sins" are <u>Paid For</u> by a **Perfect Man** (one commandment) to bring forth the *King of Life* (earth), the *Priesthood of Death* (heaven), and *Sonship of New-life* (kingdom). This means that through "God's Ten Commandments," <u>Earthly Flesh</u> can **Strive** for **Obedience** to the *Family*, to *Government,* and to its *Church*. Through "God's Two Commandments," <u>Heaven's Spirit</u> can strive for **Devotion** to a *Person's Community,* to *Human Prosperity,* and to His *Labors of Love.* Finally, through "God's One Commandment," the <u>Kingdom's Soul</u> can show its **Passion** for **Repentance, Prayers, and Works** in <u>**Service**</u> to the *Needs of God*. In this way, we see that the "Physical, Spiritual, and Mystical Man" is coming forth to <u>Serve Earth, Heaven</u>, and the <u>Kingdom</u> to bring forth **New Bodies, Eternal Lives,** and **Royal Kingdoms** for *One and All*. Unfortunately, "None of these Men" can come forth until the <u>Curses</u> of **Sin-nature, Worldly Temptations, Demonic Possession,** and **God's Curse** can be **Broken** by **Someone** willing to **Fight Sin, Evil, Death, and Damnation** unto *Oblivion*. In truth, we see that "Christ the Messiah" <u>Creates</u> the <u>Perfect Man</u> out of *Mount Calvary* (death); the "Church Creates" the <u>Holy Man</u> out of being *Burned at the Stake* (death); and the "World Creates" the <u>Righteous Man</u> **Out** of *Creation's Fiery End* (death). In each of these cases, it is clear that the "Mind" of the <u>Ignorant Man</u> is **Healed** through *Wisdom;* the "Heart" of the <u>Cowardly Man</u> is **Given** *Courage;* and the "Soul" of the <u>Greedy Man</u> is **Changed** to *Generosity*. Now, we see that the "Righteous Man is Wise," the "Holy Man has Courage," and the "Perfect Man is Generous" to bring forth a <u>Man for All Seasons,</u> **Who** can **Save** a *Sick and Dying World of Pure Evil from Itself.*

The following tabular information indicates that the "Lord God Almighty" is <u>Creating</u> a **Righteous, Holy, and Perfect Man** to **Allow** a **Sinner** to **Be Saved** via *Redemption* (create Christians), **Save Self** via *Salvation* (create saints), and by **Saving Others** via *Rewards* (create sons):

**God Creates the Righteous Man, Holy Man, and
Perfect Man Out of His Divine Commandments**
(righteousness from ten commandments, holiness from two
commandments, and sonship from one commandment)

Kingship of Life (earth)	1. **Righteous Man** - <u>Ten Commandments:</u> Learn Right/Wrong (flesh)... Yearly Thanksgiving
	<u>Spiritual Law</u> <u>Physical Law</u>

- No Other gods
- No Graven Images
- Not Take God's Name in Vain
- Keep Sabbath Day Holy
- Honor Father/Mother
- No Kill
- No Adultery
- No Stealing
- No Lying
- No Coveting

Offerings from Father's Table - Wife/House/Job: Individual Rights
- Pay for Venial Sins - Remove Dead Mind (ignorance): Gift of Wisdom
- Righteous Citizen on Earth - New Body: Seat in Celestial Court
- Good News - Free Redemption: Creating Christians (remove faults)
- Being Saved - Ignorance becomes Wisdom: See Limitations
- Bride's Family Represents Sinners (repentance)
- Groom's Family Represents Christians (prayers)

(natural order - Earth: home/government/church/self = baby level creates bodies)

Priesthood of Death (heaven)	2. **Holy Man** - <u>Two Commandments:</u> Learn Good/Evil (spirit) … Weekly Praise

- Worship God with Whole Mind, Heart, and Soul - Spiritual Law
- Love Thy Neighbor as Yourself - Physical Law

Offerings from Judge's Bench - Community/Wealth/Labor: Social Rights
- Pay for Mortal Sins - Remove Dead Heart (cowardice): Gift of Courage
- Holy Saint in Heaven - Eternal Life: Seat in Temple Court
- Gospel Message - Earned Salvation: Creating Saints (gain virtues)
- Saving Self - Coward becomes Courageous: See Potential
- Church Choir Represents Communion of Saints (works)

(supernatural order - Heaven: celestial/temple/royal/divine
courts = teenage level creates eternal life)

Sonship of New-life (kingdom)	3. **Perfect Man** - <u>One Commandment:</u> Learn God's/Man's Wills (soul)…Daily Worship

- Love Each Other as I have Loved You - Spiritual/Physical Law are One

Offerings from God's Altar - Repentance/Prayers/Works: Divine Rights
- Pay for Capital Sins - Remove Dead Soul (greed): Gift of Generosity
- Perfect Son within Kingdom - Royal Kingdom: Seat in Royal Court
- Doctrinal Truths - Bonus Rewards: Creating Sons (become divine)
- Saving Others - Greed becomes Generosity: See Self-worth
- Church Sanctuary Represents Angelic Realm (save souls)

(divine order - Kingdom: friendship/companionship/
oneness/becoming = adult level creates kingdoms)

This illustration shows that through the "Righteous (mind)," "Holy (heart)," and "Perfect Man (soul)," the <u>Earth, Heaven,</u> and <u>God's Kingdom</u> can be **Transformed** from *Death to New-life*. The idea here is to see that the "Righteous Man Comes" from <u>God's Natural Order</u> (earth) and must **Defeat Ignorance, Cowardice, Greed,** and **Selfishness** to *Overcome* the *Curses of Life*. Secondly, we see that the

"Holy Man Comes" from God's Supernatural Order (Heaven) and must **Defeat Sin-nature, Worldly Temptations, Demonic Possession,** and **God's Curses** to *Overcome All Sinful Men,* an *Evil World*, and *Lucifer's Demonic Forces*. Finally, we see that the "Perfect Man Comes" from God's Divine Order (Kingdom) and must **Defeat Sin, Evil, Death,** and **Damnation** to **Overcome** the *Lake of Fire* (hell), the *Bottomless Pit* (Gehenna), and the *Outer Darkness* (Lucifer). Through each of these "Three Transformed Men," the Kingdom of God can come forth to bring the **Whole World** a **Life** of **Wisdom, Courage, Generosity, and Unselfishness,** thereby **Creating** *Heaven on Earth* (baby level), *Paradise in Heaven* (teenage level), and a *Kingdom of Glory* (adult level). This means that at the "Baby Level," the Righteous Man is **Giving Mankind** the **Good News** (father's table) that **All are Offered Free Redemption** (being saved) or *Their Own Free Gold Mine* (title deed to earth). Secondly, at the "Teenage Level," the Holy Man is **Giving Mankind God's Gospel Message** (judge's bench) that **All are Asked to Earn Their Own Salvation** (save self) or to *Dig Out Their Gold* (title deed to Heaven). Finally, at the "Adult Level," the Perfect Man is **Giving Mankind God's Doctrinal Truths** (God's Altar) that **All can Obtain Their Own** **Bonus Rewards** (save others) or to *Share Their Gold with Others*.

The idea here is to see that when "We Go to Church," the Inside of the Church **Represents** the **Righteous** (sinners/Christians), **Holy** (saints), and **Perfect Man** (angels) as **Compared** to the *Mosaic Outer Court, Holy Place, and Holy of Holies*. Now imagine that the "Bride's Family" Represents *Sinners*; the "Groom's Family" Represents *Christians*; the "Choir" Represents *Saints;* the "Sanctuary" Represents the *Angels*; the "Altar" Represents *God's Son;* and finally, the "Tabernacle" Represents the *Lord God Almighty Himself.* In this way, we see that the "Physical World" is Called to bring forth the **Righteous Man** (outer court), **Who** has **Mastered Right and Wrong** to become *Righteous Citizen on Earth.* Secondly, we see that the "Spiritual World" is Called to bring forth the **Holy Man** (holy place), **Who** has **Mastered Good and Evil** to become a *Holy Saint in Heaven.* Finally, we see that the "Mystical World" is Called to bring forth the **Perfect Man** (holy of holies), **Who** has **Mastered God's Will and man's will** to become a *Perfect Son within the Kingdom.* Now it becomes clear that the "Job" of the Righteous Man (self), Holy Man (society), and Perfect Man (God) is to **Not Create a Victim** (bring solutions), but to be a **Man for All Seasons** as a *Friend* to *One and All.*

We now see that through the "Righteous/Holy/Perfect Man" shall come the Fulfillment of **God's Ten, Two, and One Commandments** (laws) to bring forth an **Eternal Bond of Friendship** between **God, Angels, and Saints** through the *Sacrifice of God's Son, Jesus Christ.* The idea here is to see that to "Master the World (king)," a Righteous Man (earth)" must **Fulfill God's Ten Commandments** by **Surrendering his Life** to *God's Destiny* (new spirit) and then by being **Born-again** in *Christ's Free Will* (new flesh). Secondly, to "Master the Church (priest)," a Holy Man (Heaven) must **Fulfill God's Two Commandments** by **Uniting** with *Christ in Spirit* (born-again spirit) and then **Uniting** with *Jesus in the Flesh* (born-again flesh). Finally, to "Master Oneself/God (son)," a Perfect Man (Kingdom) must **Fulfill God's One Commandment** by **Becoming One** with <u>**God, Angels, and Men**</u> through the ***Broken Body of Jesus*** (bread/scourging) and the ***Blood Shed by Christ*** (wine/crucifixion). The implication here is that the "Job of the Ten Commandments" is to <u>Govern</u> ***Planet Earth*** (physical dimension); then the "Two Commandments" are to <u>Govern</u> ***God's Heaven*** (spiritual dimension). In like manner, we see that "God's One Commandment" is to <u>Govern</u> the **Lord's Kingdom of Glory** through the <u>**Intercession of Jesus Christ**</u> on ***Earth*** (home), in ***Heaven*** (church), and within the ***Kingdom*** (government).

This means that the "Lord God Almighty" is <u>Using His Physical Dimension</u> (earth) to bring forth **God's Destiny** (Jews) and **Man's Free Will** (Christians) to be **Changed** into **God's Spiritual Will** via ***Christ*** (spirit) and **Man's Spiritual Will** via ***Jesus*** (flesh). Finally, we see that the "Converted Will of God" and the "Converted Will of Man" are <u>Merged</u> and <u>Blended</u> into a **New Creation Known** as the **God/Man Mystical Will** which ***Rules All the Affairs*** within the ***Lord's Kingdom***. We can now see that "Man's Flesh" must <u>Master Earth;</u> "Man's Spirit" must <u>Master Heaven;</u> and "Man's Soul" must <u>Master the Kingdom</u> to bring forth an **Eternal Reconciliation** between ***God, Angels, and Men***. This most "Powerful Reconciliation" will <u>Unite</u> **God's Divine Justice System** (divine law) with **Man's Human Justice System** (human law), thereby **Establishing** <u>**Ethical Behavior**</u> (earth), **Moral Behavior** (Heaven), and <u>**Fair Behavior**</u> (Kingdom) within the ***Royal Household of God***. The idea here is to see that "Ethics" brings forth <u>Individual Rights</u> on ***Earth***; "Morals" bring forth <u>Social Rights</u> to ***Heaven;*** and "Divine Behavior" brings forth <u>Divine Rights</u> within ***God's Kingdom of Glory***. Through "God's, Angels', and Men's Proper Behavior," an <u>Alliance</u> can be **Established** between both **Peoples** and **Individuals** to <u>**Allow**</u> the ***Laws of God/Man to Function Correctly***.

The following tabular information indicates that the "Ten Commandments" <u>Govern</u> ***Earth*** (physical laws), "Two Commandments" Govern ***Heaven*** (spiritual laws), and the "One Commandment" <u>Governs</u> the ***Kingdom*** (mystical law):

Mastering the World, the Church, and Oneself/God
via Ten, Two, and One Commandments of God
(God's and Man's Physical Will on Earth, God's and Man's Spiritual
Will in Heaven, God's and Man's Mystical Will in Kingdom)

Purify Grave		**Purify Host**	
Master World		Master Church	
• Righteous Man on Earth		• Holy Man in Heaven	
(ten commandments)		(two commandments)	

<u>1st Tablet</u>	<u>2nd Tablet</u>	<u>1st Commandment</u>	<u>2nd Commandment</u>
• God's Law	• Man's Law	• God's Mosaic Law	• Man's Canon Law
• *God's Physical Will*	• *Man's Physical Will*	• *God's Spiritual Will*	• *Man's Spiritual Will*
• *God's Destiny*	• *Man's Free Will*	• *Christ's/Angelic Will*	• *Jesus'/Saints' Will*

| • Eternal Life | • New Body | • Glorified Spirit | • Transfigured Body |

- -

| • Earthly Spirit | • Earthly Fleshly | • Heavenly Spirit | • Heavenly Fleshly |
| Nature | Nature | Nature | Nature |

Creates "Individual Rights"   Creates "Social Rights"
•Ethical Behavior   • Moral Behavior

<u>Master Self/God</u>
- Perfect Man within Kingdom
(one commandment)
- God's/Man's Law
- *God's/Man's Mystical Will*
- *Own Royal Kingdom*
(Jesus Christ becomes Christ Jesus)
- Spirit/Flesh Nature One
Creates "Divine Rights"
- Divine Behavior
<u>Men, Angels, and God Become One</u>

This illustration shows that it has been the "Job of Jesus Christ" to Create a **Whole New Legal System** between **Earth, Heaven, and God's Kingdom** and **Establish** a **<u>New Set of Behavior Patterns</u>** for *God, Angels, and Men to Adhere To*. Obviously, "God's Behavior" <u>Only Reflects His Destiny</u> or **Pre-destined Behavior** based on the **Perfect Will of God** (direct) as **<u>Expressed</u>** via *His Manifestation of All Truth*. Secondly, "Man's Behavior" <u>Only Reflects his Free Will</u> or **Response to Needs and Wants** based on **his Human Will** (compromised) as **<u>Expressed</u>** via *Man's Manifestation* of *his Perception of Reality* (truth). We see that "God's Divine Truth" and "Man's Perception of Reality" are both <u>Merged</u> (surrender) and <u>Blended</u> (born-again) into **One New Truth,** known as the *Mind, Heart, Soul, and Life-force of Christ*. The implication here is that the "Natures" of <u>God</u> (mystical), <u>Angels</u> (spiritual), and <u>Men</u> (physical) are **All Different** and must be **Made One in Christ** to **Create** a **Single Behavior Pattern** via a *Combined God/Man Legal System*. The "Lord is Telling Us" here that a <u>Master Reconciliation</u> has to **Take Place** via **Christ's Three Judgments** with the **First** on *Mount Calvary* (priest on donkey), the **Second** on the *Church* (thief in the night), and **<u>Lastly,</u>** at the *End of Time* (judge on a cloud) or the *End of the World* (final judgment). We see that the "First Judgment (Messiah)" is where <u>Man's Spirit</u> (destiny) **Gets Eternal Life** and <u>Man's Flesh</u> (free will) **Gets a New Body** in **Preparation** for a **<u>Born-again Soul</u>** to *Enter Its Heavenly Blessing of Holiness*. Secondly, in the "Second Judgment (Church)," **Man's Eternal Life** becomes a **Glorified Spirit** (Choir of Angels) and **<u>Man's New Body</u>** becomes a *Transfigured Body* (Communion of Saints). Finally, in the "Third/last Judgment (World)," the <u>Glorified Spirit</u> and <u>Transfigured Body</u> are **Rewarded Their Own Combined Royal Kingdom** within the **<u>Presence</u>** of the *Lord God Almighty Himself.*

    Now, we see that the "Job of Jesus Christ" is to <u>Unite</u> **Oneself, Society, and God** into **One Perfect Creation,** yet **Not Creating a Victim,** but still **Changing Everyone's**

Fixed Frame of Reference from **Physical, Spiritual,** and **Mystical** into becoming *Christ-like*. We see that the "Life-experience" is All About **Not Creating a Victim,** be it **Oneself, Society, and/or God.** But **If** through a **Person's Faults, Transgressions, or Sins** he **Fails at being Perfect,** then he can either *Learn Man's Lessons* (flesh) or *Receive God's Blessings* (spirit). This means that the "Lessons of Life" can be Attained by **Falling Down** (dirty) and then **Getting Up Again** (washed clean), while the "Blessings of Life" can be Attained by **Never Falling Down** and by being *Honest, Hardworking, and Faithful.* The question is: just "How Many People" can Pass Through Life by being Perfect in the *Eyes of God, Society, and Oneself?* The answer is "None" but "Jesus Christ." This means We must Strive to Learn as **Many Lessons as Possible** by **Striving to Correct Our Mistakes** as **Quickly as Possible,** thereby **Allowing Us** to *Learn God's Right from man's wrong.* The idea here is that "When One's Mind (intellect)" has been Killed by His **Faults,** he must **Find Out What he has Done Wrong** and **Make Every Effort** to **Learn the Lessons of Life** by **Changing** both **his Thinking** and **his Behavior** to *Stop Offending his Own Nature.* Secondly, when "One's Heart" has been Killed by his **Transgressions,** he must **Recognize What he has Done to Others** and **Make Every Effort** to **Apologize** for his **Actions** to *Stop Offending his Brothers.* Finally, when "One's Soul" has been Killed by his **Sins,** he must **Bow to his Creator God** and **Beg Him for Forgiveness** through his most **Powerful Worship** and then *Stop Offending God's most Holy Name.* By being "Reconciled" back to oneself, Society, and God, a **Person can See** his **Own Limitations,** his **Own Potential,** and his **Own Self-worth** in the *Eyes of God, Angels, and Men.* This "New Perception of Reality" Allows an **Awakened Soul** to more **Effectively Grasp** the **Importance** of **Not Creating** a **Victim in Life** which in the **End Creates** a **Sin** (God), **Transgression** (society), or **Fault** (self) **Debt** that *One Day* must be *Paid For in Full.*

The following tabular information indicates that we are "Offending Ourselves" via Faults (venial sins), "Offending Society (brothers)" via Transgressions (mortal sins), and "Offending God" via Our Sins (capital sins):

Offending Self via Faults, Offending Society via Transgressions, and Offending God via Sins
(faults cause venial sin, transgressions cause mortal sins, and sins cause capital sins)

Intellect (repentance)	1. **Offending Self** via Faults (master self) ...Knowledge
	• Venial Sins - Kills the Mind (wicked thoughts)
	• Yearly Thanksgiving - Give Labors: Easter Duty
	• Remove Venial Sins - New Mind: Thinking **See Limitations**
	• Lying Ignorance - Learn Wisdom
	• Cheating Cowardice - Find Courage
	• Stealing Greed - Believe in Generosity

(Jonah converted Nineveh - three days for a man is measured in twenty-four-hour periods)

Emotions (prayers)	2. **Offending Brother** via Transgressions (master church) ...Self-awareness
	• Mortal Sin - Kills the Heart (selfish desires)

- Weekly Praise - Give Wealth: Sunday Offering
- Remove Mortal Sins - New Heart: Loving   **See Potential**
- Reject Self - Earn Self-respect
- Reject Family - Welcomed into Brotherhood
- Reject Society - Honored into Sainthood

(Jesus converts Israel - three days for a nation is measured in three-year periods)

Instinct   3. **Offending God** via Sinfulness (master world) …Consciousness
(works)
- Capital Sin - Kills the Soul (murderous acts)
- Daily Worship - Give Life: Mon. through Sat.
- Remove Capital Sins - New Soul: Serving   **See Self-worth**
- Follow Sin-nature - Become Righteous Citizen
- Enter Worldly Temptations - Become Holy Saint
- Accept Demonic Possession - Become Perfect Son

(Christ converts World - three days for a world is measured in three thousand periods)

This illustration shows that a person's "Venial/Mortal/Capital Sins" must be Removed through his **Repentance, Prayers, and Works** to **Receive a New Mind** (intellect), **New Heart** (emotions), and **New Soul** (instincts) to become a *Righteous Citizen, Holy Saint, and Perfect Son before God*. To "Remove Venial Sin," a Person must Defeat his own **Ignorance, Cowardice, and Greed** by willingness to **Surrender his Life** to **Jesus Christ** and *Give his All in Service to God*. Secondly, to "Remove Mortal Sin," He must Defeat his **Rejection of himself, his Family, and his Society** to **Earn** his *Own Self-respect*, **Enter** the *Brotherhood of Man*, and finally, **Become** a *Holy Saint in Heaven*. Finally, to "Remove Capital Sins," He must Defeat his own *Sin-nature* (selfishness), *Worldly Temptations* (sinful pleasures), and *Demonic Possession* (evil acts). By "Overcoming Sin and Evil," a Person can become a Righteous Citizen on **Earth**, a Holy Saint in **Heaven**, and a Perfect Son within **God's Kingdom** making him **Worthy** of a *New Body, Eternal Life, and a Royal Kingdom*. Through these "Three Stages" of Transformation, **He** can **Master himself**, his **Society**, and the **Nature of God** to be **Set Free** to **Think for himself** and to **Make the Correct Choice in Life** in *Service to One and All*.

Yes! The "Life-experience" is Centered on **Learning Man's Lessons** and on **Receiving God's Blessings** to **Give a Person** the *Knowledge he Needs, Make* him *Self-aware,* and bring *Consciousness to his Soul*. In this way, "He can Master himself, his Church, and the World so that he might **See** his *Own Limitations*, his *Own Potential*, and his *Own Self-worth before God*. In short, this means that a "Sinner" must Make his Easter Duty Yearly to **Preserve his Eternal Soul** (being) through his **Gift of Thanksgiving** (God's generosity) by *Offering All his Labors* (sweat). Secondly, a "Christian" must Attend Church Weekly to **Preserve his Eternal Spirit** (heart) through his **Heartfelt Praise** (honor God's name) by *Offering All his Wealth* (money). Finally, a "Saint" must Go to Mass Daily to **Preserve his Eternal Flesh** (mind) through his **Devout Worship** (respecting God) by *Offering his Very Life* (breath). At each of these "Levels of Devotion," a Person can **Appease God's Wrath** and **Please the Blessed Mother** and **Win Their Favor** in *All the Endeavors of Life*. Recall that "Jesus Christ Spent" Three Years Converting the Jews (nation days). **He Spent Three Days** (man's days) in the **Tomb** to **Save Mankind** and now **He is Willing** to spend **Three Thousand Years** (world days) *Converting a Pagan World of Sinners*. This "Massive Effort" of Personal Commitment has **Pleased God** and has **Allowed Jesus Christ** and **His Church** to **Awaken** a *Lost and Broken World of Evil Sinners*.

This means that "Three Days for a Man" is Measured in *Twenty-four Hour Periods*, while "Three Days for a Nation" is Measured in *Three-Year Periods*, implying that "Three Days for a World" is Measured in *Three-Thousand Year Periods* (3 advents). Recall that "Jonah Walked in Nineveh" for Three Days and *Converted the Whole City* (living saints). "Jesus Walked in Israel" for Three Years and **Converted the Whole Nation** (promised land). Finally, we see that "Christ will Walk on Earth" for Three Thousand Years to *Convert the Whole World* (Heaven on Earth). This concept of "Three-Day Periods" Sits at the Center of **God's Conversion Cycle**. This means that **One is to be Touched** by the **Holy Spirit, Son of God,** and the **Eternal Father** to **Take a Lost Soul** from the *Darkness of Death* (life) into the *Light of New-life* (eternal life). It is also important to "Read the Signs of the Times" and to Learn to Read the *Meaning of It All* (genetics/environment). Obviously, a "Person Needs" to Recognize that the **Life-experience** is **Comprised** of a **Physical** (earth), **Spiritual** (Heaven), **Mystical** (Kingdom), **Divine** (God), and **Godly** (Lord God Almighty) *Dimensions of Existence*.

In this teaching, we see that the "Lord God Almighty" is showing us that His Creation is **Divided** into **Five Dimensions of Existence**: 1) Physical Dimension - Priest Level (earth): Planning the Work; 2) Spiritual Dimension - King Level (Heaven): Managing the Work; 3) Mystical Dimension - Prodigal Son Level (Kingdom): Supervising the Work; 4) Divine Dimension - Good Son Level (God): Performing the Work; and 5) Godly Dimension - Lord God Almighty Level (divinity): Accounting of the Work. Through these "Five Dimensions," the Work of God (labor) is being **Done** through a set of **Godly Courts,** each **Governing** the *Earth* (Celestial Court), *Heaven* (Temple Court), *Kingdom* (Royal Court), *God* (Divine Court), and the *Free Man* (God's Court) *Levels of Life*. Obviously, the "Lord" needed to Plan His Work on *Earth*, Manage His Work in *Heaven*, Supervise His Work within the *Kingdom*, Perform the Work *Himself* with His *Church* and His *World*, then finally, make an Accounting of His Work via His *Own Divine Wealth*. At each of these "Stages of Development," the Lord God Almighty will **Measure His Progress** as He strives to **Create Heaven on Earth,** a **Paradise in Heaven,** and then bring forth a **Kingdom of Glory** to *House All of His most Beloved Children*. To "Create an Eternal Kingdom," the Lord would have to **Unite** His **Absolute Spiritual Truth** (reality) with His **Relative Physical Truth** (illusion) to **Make God and Man One** in *Truth, Law, Will, Love, and Thought*. In effect, this would be like "Focusing" one's Five Senses into **One Super Sensor** to be able to **Experience His Environment** at all times to **Sense Its Entire Life-force** and *Know Its Needs*.

Now, we see that the "Lord God Almighty (never-created)" has Found a Way to become **One** with "His Creation (created)" through the establishment of a **Priesthood, Kingship, Sonship,** and **Godhood** *Set of Titles* (authority). Through "These Titles,"

Men, Angels, and God can **Move** and have **Their Being** in *Individuals, Societies, Nations, Worlds, and Kingdoms*. Obviously, the "Lord" has needed an Organizational Structure to **Build on** as He has **Decided** to establish His **Human, Angelic, and Divine Existence** upon the **Five Senses of Life which are** Expressed in the Forms of *Creation* (eyes/priest), *Knowledge* (ears/king), *Presence* (nose/prodigal son), *Power* (mouth/good son), and *Form* (skin/God). Through these "Five Functions," the Abundance of Life can come forth to bring about **Peace, Joy, and Happiness** to the **Mind, Hearts, and Souls** of *All God's Children*. Note that "God's Creation" is Ruled by Five Courts: 1) Celestial Court - Govern Earth: Physical Dimension, 2) Temple Court - Govern Heaven: Spiritual Dimension, 3) Royal Court - Govern Kingdom: Mystical Dimension, 4) Divine Court - Govern God: Divine Dimension, and 5) God's Court (people) - Govern God/Man: Godly Dimension. Through these "Five Courts," the God/Man Relationship is based bringing forth the **Five Institutions of Life** in the form of the *Priesthood, Kingship, Prodigal Son, Good Son,* and *Lord God Almighty* (father).

Obviously, the "Lord God Almighty" is a God of Law and is **Demanding his Children** to **Learn His Law** and to **Obey It** in both the **Letter** (reality) and its **Spirit** (illusion) by **Mastering** *Their Flesh of Ignorance* (knowledge) and **Mastering** *Their Spirit of Cowardice* (fight). This means that all of "God's Children" must Face Five Cycles of Discipline based on the **Depth of Their Rebellion Beginning** with a **Baby's** *Ignorance of the Mind*, **Teenager's** *Criminality* of *the Heart* (face grave), **Adult's** *Insanity of the Soul* (face hell), **Wise Man's** *Evil of the Life-force* (face Gehenna), and finally, a **Son's** *Cursed Nature* (face judgment). At each of the "Levels of Rebellion," a Person becomes **Farther and Farther from his God** until he *Reaches* the *Breaking Point of God's Love*. At this "Breaking Point," the Lord God Almighty *Begins His* **Corrective Process**, thereby **Allowing** a **Lost Fool** to *See his Own Ignorance* (lost), *See the Importance of his Grave* (meaningless life), *See the Flames of Hell* (abject failure), *See the Outer Darkness of Gehenna* (hated by God), and finally, *Facing God's Judgment/Oblivion* (day of reckoning). In short, "If a Person" Sees Where he is Going to End-up, he will Realize that he is **Going In the Wrong Direction** and must *Amend his Ways* and *Straighten-out his Life*. Through the "Lord's Five Institutions" of Priesthood (see limitations), Kingship (see potential), Prodigal Son (see self-worth), Good Son (see new nature), and Lord God Almighty (see divinity), **Each Treasured Life** can be **Kept on Track** to **Prevent Falling** into *God's Five Cycles of Discipline*. The "Job of God's Institutions" is to bring the Powers and Authorities of God onto the **Earth** to both **Purify** and **Transform God's Children** into *Righteous Citizens* (flesh) and *Holy Saints* (spirit).

The following tabular information indicates that the "Life-experience" is about becoming a Priest (creator), a King (wisdom), a Prodigal Son (witness), a Good Son (powerful), and the Lord God Almighty (changing forms) within the *Kingdom of God*:

**See One's Inter-self as a Priest, King, Prodigal
Son, Good Son, and Lord God Almighty**
(priest is omnific/king is omniscient/prodigal son is
omnipresent/good son is omnipotent/God is omnifarious)

Truth	1. **Priest** - <u>Omnific Power:</u> Creation = Seeing Truth...Knowledge
(called)	• Planning the Work - Executive Branch: Govern Physical Dimension
	• Ruled by Celestial Court - Earthly Realm (new viewpoint)
	• <u>Mind brings Conversion</u> (beliefs) - Creative Eye
	• Repentance
	• Prayers **See Limitations**
	• Works • Change Viewpoint

(1st cycle of discipline/coveting - ignorant mind: corrected by seeing himself as ignorant)

Law	2. **King** - <u>Omniscient Power:</u> All Knowing = Hearing Law...Self-awareness
(enlightened)	• Managing the Work - Legislative Branch: Govern Spiritual Dimension
	• Ruled by Temple Court - Heavenly Life (new nature)
	• <u>Heart brings Submission</u> (dying to self) - All Knowing Ear
	• Deny Intellect
	• Abandon Feelings **See Potential**
	• Submit Free Will • Change Nature

(2nd cycle of discipline/lying - criminal mind: corrected by seeing one's grave)

Will	3. **Prodigal Son** - <u>Omnipresent Power:</u> All Present = Smelling Will...
(awakened)	Consciousness
	• Supervising the Work - Judicial Branch: Govern Mystical Dimension
	• Ruled by Royal Court - Kingdom Happiness (new behavior)
	• <u>Soul Fights Evil Forces</u> (faith) - All Present Nose
	• Remove Sin-nature
	• Remove Worldly Temptations **See Self-worth**
	• Remove Demonic Possession • Change Behavior

(3rd cycle of discipline/stealing - insane soul: corrected by seeing the flames of hell)

Love	4. **Good Son** - <u>Omnipotent Power:</u> All Powerful = Tasting Love... Sentience
(Indwelling)	• Performing the Work - Voters: Govern Divine Dimension
	• Ruled by Divine Court - God's Joy (new lifestyle)
	• <u>Life-force Saves Souls</u> (evangelization) - All Powerful Tongue
	• Free Redemption
	• Earned Salvation **See New-nature**
	• Bonus Rewards • Change Lifestyle

(4th cycle of discipline/adultery - evil life-force: corrected by seeing Gehenna)

Thinking	5. **Lord God Almighty** - <u>Omnifarious Power:</u> All Forms = Touching
(union)	Thought... Thought
	• Accounting of the Work - Money: Govern God's Dimension
	• Ruled by God - God's Peace (Christ-like)
	• <u>Nature Sets Captives Free</u> (savior) - All Changing Touch (skin)
	• Freedom
	• Liberty **See Divinity**

This illustration shows that the "Five Master Functions" of Life **Allow** the ***Mind to bring Conversion*** (beliefs), the ***Heart to bring Submission*** (dying to self), the ***Soul to Fight Evil*** (faith), the ***Life-force to Save Souls*** (evangelization), and the ***Nature to Set Captives Free*** (savior). We see that the "Mind is Converted" by its <u>Repentance, Prayers,</u> and <u>Works</u> so that a **Child** might **See his Limitations in Life** and **Correct his Behavior** (called) through the ***Blessings of Christ*** (baptism). Secondly, the "Heart is Surrendered" by <u>Denying One's Intellect, Abandoning Feelings,</u> and <u>Submitting Free Will</u> so that a **Teenager** might **See his Potential in Life** and **Correct his Behavior** (enlightened) through the ***Blessings of Christ*** (confession). Thirdly, the "Soul Fights Evil Forces" by <u>Removing Its Own Sin-nature, Removing Worldly Temptations, Removing Demonic Possession</u> so that an **Adult** might **See his Self-worth in Life** and **Correct his Behavior** (awakened) through the ***Blessings of Christ*** (communion). Fourthly, the "Life-force Saves Souls" by <u>Offering Free Redemption, Earned Salvation,</u> and <u>Bonus Rewards</u> so that a **Wise Man** might **Think for himself in Life** and **Correct his Behavior** (indwelled) through the ***Blessings of Christ*** (confirmation). Finally, the "Newborn Nature Sets Captives Free" by <u>Breaking the Chains of Sin</u> (freedom), <u>Opening the Prison Doors of Evil</u> (liberty), and <u>Overcoming the Guards of Death</u> (independence) so that a **Free Man** might **Dream of Paradise** and **Improve his Behavior** (union) through the ***Blessings of Christ*** (resurrection). This "Awesome Journey" through the <u>Life-experience</u> brings forth the **Forces of Growth** and **Maturity** so **that Each** of **God's Children** can come to ***Know, Love, and Serve Their Creator God in Person***.

The theme here is that "If a Priest Goes Bad (1st cycle)" by <u>Coveting His Neighbor's Wife</u> or <u>Goods,</u> then the **Lord is Going** to **Change his Viewpoint** by showing him his **Own Ignorance** (knowledge) to ***See his Own Limitations*** (truth). Secondly, "If a King Goes Bad (2nd cycle)" by <u>Lying to Society,</u> then the **Lord is Going** to **Change his Nature** by showing him his **Grave** (self-awareness) to ***See his Own Potential*** (law). Thirdly, "If a Prodigal Son Goes Bad (3rd cycle)" by <u>Stealing from Society,</u> then the **Lord is Going** to **Change his Behavior** by showing him the **Depth of Hell** (consciousness) to ***See his Own Self-worth*** (will). Fourthly, "If a Good Son Goes Bad (4th cycle)" by <u>Committing Adultery,</u> then the **Lord is Going** to **Change his Lifestyle** by showing him the **Outer Darkness of Gehenna** (sentience) to ***See his New-nature*** (love). Finally, "If the Lord God Almighty Goes Bad (5th cycle)" by <u>Committing Murder</u> (killing), then the **Lord is Going** to **Take Him to Judgment** by showing him **God's Divinity** (thinking) to ***See the Sacrifice of Jesus Christ*** (wisdom). Through each of these "Stages of Correction," a <u>Person</u> can be **Transformed** from a ***Worthless Animal*** to a ***Respectable Citizen of New-life***. In essence, the previous chart "Reveals" that <u>Human Existence</u> and **One's Life-experience** are **Founded** upon a <u>Person's Belief in an All-Loving Creator,</u> **Who** has **Created** a **Perfect Master Plan** for ***Each*** of **His Children's Lives**.

This "Righteous, Holy, and Perfect" <u>Template of Life</u> **Guides a Person** through **God's Church** (easy), **Man's Government** (hard), **His Home** (adventures), and then **Himself** (challenging) to ***Discover his Own Identity***. Through "God's

Church (saint)," a <u>Person Sees his Sinfulness</u> and must **Repent** to **Remove his Ignorance** (venial sin), **Purify his Mind,** and <u>**Transform his Thoughts**</u> into *Correct Thinking.* Secondly, Through "His Home (child)," he can <u>See his Fears and Cowardice</u> to **Purify his Heart** and <u>**Transform his Feelings**</u> into *Steadfast Devotion for What is Right.* Thirdly, Through a "Citizen's Government (job)," he can <u>See his Greedy Life in Money,</u> **Purify his Soul,** and <u>**Transform his Instincts**</u> into a *Commitment to Duty for God and Country.* Finally, through "Himself," he can <u>See his Selfish Desires,</u> **Purify his Life-force,** and <u>**Transform his Nature**</u> into a *Person of Wholesome Qualities* and *Family Values.* Yes! Through a <u>Person's</u> **Church, Government, Home, and Self,** both the **Meaning** (existence) and **Purpose** (service) of **Life** come forth to **Reveal** the <u>**Various Natures**</u> of *Earth, Heaven, the Kingdom, and then of God Himself.* The "Job" of every <u>Living Soul</u> is to **Strive** to *Master its Own Selfishness* (self), become a *Good Parent* (home), attain *High Standards on the Job* (government), and finally, *Serve the Church Well* (church). In this theme of a "Perfect Life," a <u>Person must Realize</u> that **God's Curse Involved Making** the **Human Race** into **Ignorant Fools, Criminals, Insane Mad-men,** and even **Evil Monsters** which must be <u>**Transformed Back**</u> into *Righteous Citizens, Holy Saints, Perfect Sons,* and *Beloved Free Men.* We see that this "Transformation Process" is a <u>Call</u> to **Awaken Mankind** to the <u>**Difference**</u> between the *Qualities of Leadership* (line/thinking for self) versus being an *Obedient Soldier* (staff/follower). Basically, this means "Defining" the <u>Difference</u> between being a **Diligent Bureaucrat** (follower) or an **Effective Leader** (problem solver) which **Centers** upon *Knowing What to Do* and then *Doing It, Jesus Christ Style.*

The following tabular information indicates just "How a Person" can <u>Remove his Ignorance, Remove his Criminal Behavior, Remove Insanity,</u> and <u>Remove Evil</u> by **Mastering** *His Venial, Mortal, Capital,* and *Unforgiven Sins.*

Removing One's Ignorance, Criminal Behavior, Insanity, and Evil by Removing His Sinfulness
(mastering one's venial, mortal, capital, and unforgiven sins through his reconciliation)

Mind
(truth)

1. **Remove Ignorance** - <u>Master Venial Sins</u> (thoughts) …Knowledge
   - Venial Sins Kill Mind - Deny Intellect: New Mind (intellect)
   - *Excommunicated* from Temple/Caiaphas - Rejected by Church/ Blasphemy: Burned at Stake

Low
Rank
   - Thank God Yearly - Make Easter Duty: Save Ignorant Fool
   - Master Self (will) - See Limitations: Receive New Body on Earth

(church - easy to join/hard to master: priesthood = kicked out, then repent)

Heart
(law)

2. **Remove Criminal Behavior** - <u>Master Mortal Sins</u> (words) …Self-awareness
   - Mortal Sins Kill Heart - Abandon Feelings: New Heart (emotions)
   - *Outcast* from People/Herod - Rejected by Home/sorcery: Stoned by Society

| Medium | • Praise God Weekly - Sunday Mass: Save Wicked Criminal |
| Rank | • Master Home (love) - See Potential: Receive Eternal Life in Heaven |

(home - free gift/fun to master: sonship = kicked out, then apologize)

Soul	3. **Remove Insanity** - <u>Master Capital Sins</u> (deeds) …Consciousness
(will)	• Capital Sins Kill Soul - Submit Free Will: New Soul (instincts)
	• *Banished* from Earth/Pilate - Rejected by Government/sedition: Crucified by the State
High	• Worship God Daily - Mon. through Saturday: Save Insane Mad-man
Rank	• Master Government (money) - See Self-self Worth: Receive Royal Kingdom

(government - earn job/career to master: kingship = kicked out, then get pardoned)

Life-Force	4. **Remove Evil** - <u>Master Sacrilege Sins</u> (lifestyle) …Sentience
	• Unforgivable Sins Kill Life-force - Surrender Life: New Life-force (nature)
	• *Forsaken* by God/God - Rejected by Self/sacrilege: Personal Suicide
Supreme	• Rot in Grave - Eternal Death: Save Evil Demon
Rank	• Master Church (graces) - See God's Treasure: Receive God's Friendship

(self - hard to understand/easy to master: kicked out, then cast into hell)

This illustration shows that the "Human Nature" is exemplifying <u>Four Basic Negative Personalities</u> in the **Form** of **Ignorance, Criminal Behavior, Insanity, and Evil,** causing the **<u>Human Race to Live</u>** in a *Continual State of Hopeless Confusion*. This means that "We All have been Cursed With" <u>Ignorant Minds, Criminal Hearts, Insane Souls,</u> and <u>Evil Life-forces</u> which must be *Transformed from Death into New-life*. We see above that "Venial Sins" Kill the Mind and **Terminate Man's Physical Nature** (flesh), causing him to be **Cursed on Earth** to the point of **<u>Forcing him</u>** to *Bow to Mother Nature*. Secondly, "Mortal Sins" <u>Kill the Heart</u> and **Terminates Man's Spiritual Nature** (spirit), causing him to be **Cursed in Heaven** to the point of **<u>Forcing him</u>** to *Bow to Christ's Holy Church*. Thirdly, "Capital Sins" <u>Kill the Soul</u> and **Terminate Man's Mystical Nature** (soul), causing him to be **Cursed by God's Kingdom** to the point of **<u>Forcing him</u>** to *Bow to the Lord Jesus Christ Himself*. Finally, "Unforgivable Sin" <u>Kills the Life-force</u> and **Terminates Man's Eternal Nature** (life-force), causing him to be **Cursed by God** to the point of **<u>Forcing him</u>** to *Bow to the Lord God Almighty Himself* (beatific vision). At each of these "Levels of Growth and Maturity," a <u>Person</u> can either be **Blessed or Cursed** by **God,** yet, the **Question** is that the **Choice is Left Up To** *Each of God's Children*. We see that the "Lowest Level (4th rank)" of <u>Human Achievements</u> is to **Defeat Ignorance** through the **Acquisition of Knowledge** to bring forth a person's *Personal Wisdom*. Secondly, the "Middle Level (3rd rank)" of <u>Human Achievements</u> is to **Defeat Criminal Behavior** (cowardice) through his **<u>Self-awareness</u>** to bring forth his *Personal Courage*. Thirdly, the "High Level (2nd rank)" of <u>Human Achievements</u> is to **Defeat Insanity** through his **<u>Consciousness</u>** to bring forth his *Personal Generosity Toward Others*. Finally, the

"Supreme Level (1st rank)" of <u>Human Achievements</u> is to **Defeat Evil** through his **Sentience** to bring forth his *Personal Unselfishness*.

The idea is to see that it is "Easy to Join a Church" which <u>Makes</u> being **Excommunicated from a Religion** a **Minor Offense before God**; yet, to **Master the Church** and become the **Pope** is the most **Difficult Task in Life** and is *Given God's Highest Blessing*. In like manner, to get a "Job in Society (government)" is <u>Not too Difficult</u> so that being an **Outcast to One's People** is a **Serious**, but **Not Catastrophic Offense before God**; yet, to **Master a Government** and become a **President** is quite **Difficult** and is *Given One of God's High Blessings* (divine right of kings). Next, we see being "Born in a Home" is a <u>Gift from God</u> and to be **Banished from the Earth** is to have one's **Birthright Removed** and is a **Serious Matter before God**; yet, to become the **Supreme Ruler of Planet Earth** is extremely **Difficult** and will even be *Honored by God*. Finally, to "Take Control of Oneself" <u>Requires</u> an **Awesome Amount of Tenacity** so that being **Forsaken by God** is a **Divine Sacrilege before God**; yet, to become **One Who** can **Think for himself** is a by-product of a **Good Life** and is *Treasured by God*. This means that a "Person" first <u>Journeys</u> (follower) from the **Church** (member/parishioner), to the **Government** (employee), to the **Home** (baby), to the **Self** (I am).

In "Leadership," a <u>Person Journeys</u> from **Self** (mature), to the **Home** (father), to the **Government** (global leader), and finally, to the **Church** (pope). The point here is that "Things" that are <u>Easy in Life</u> **Receive** **Little Note before God**; yet, "Things" that are <u>Extremely Difficult</u> **Receive Great Accolades from God** via His *Friendship, Companionship, and Oneness*. We are being shown that "If We Overcome" <u>God's Curses</u> of **Blasphemy, Sorcery, Sedition, and Sacrilege**, we can **Defeat Excommunication** (dying) from *Religion*, being **Outcast** from our *People*, being **Banished** (death) from the *Earth* (damnation), and being **Forsaken** by *God* (hell). These most "Evil Curses" come upon a <u>Person</u> when he **Fails to Surrender his Life** to both the **Law** and **Will of God** and then **Fails to Serve the Lord** with his *Whole Mind, Heart, and Soul*.

This "Complete Commitment to God" begins <u>One's Journey</u> from a **Confused Mind** (flesh) to a **Clear Thinking Mind** (spirit) by **Converting Mankind's** *Sin-nature* and *Ignorance* into *Obedience* and *Wisdom*. Secondly, "Transforming Man's Heart" from <u>Cowardice to Courage</u> is **Converting Mankind's** *Worldly Temptations* and *Criminality* into *Self-control* and *Honesty*. Thirdly, "Transforming Man's Soul" from <u>Greed to Generosity</u> is **Converting Mankind's** *Demonic Possession* and *Insanity* into *Good Judgment* and *Integrity*. Finally, "Transforming Man's Life-force" from <u>Selfishness to Unselfishness</u> is **Converting Mankind's** *Divine Curse* and *Evil* to *Good Values* and *Dignity*. Through each of these "Mystical Conversions," the <u>Human Race</u> can expect to **Learn All the Lessons of Life** and **Master** its own **Life-experience** on *Earth*, in *Heaven*, within the *Kingdom*, and in *God Himself*. It should now make sense that the "Life-experience" is about <u>Challenging the Flesh</u> (righteousness), creating <u>Adventure for the Spirit</u> (holiness), having <u>Fun with the Soul</u> (perfection), and finally, bringing <u>Happiness to One's Life-force</u> (divinity).

In short, this is much like "Raising Children" as <u>They too are Seeking</u> the **Treasures of Life** to **Escape** the **Curses of Life** coming from *Hard-work* (barren land/toil),

Pain (barren womb), ***Death*** (barren life), and ***Damnation*** (barren future). Unfortunately, to "Escape God's Curses," a <u>Person must be Willing</u> to <u>Defeat</u> (grow/mature) **Ignorance, Criminality, Insanity, and Evil** to <u>**Embrace**</u> ***Obedience, Self-control, Integrity, and Dignity***.

The following tabular information indicates both the "Spiritual and Physical Curses" facing the <u>Human Race</u> as it **Overcomes Them** to bring forth the **<u>Treasures of Life</u>** in *Obedience* (wisdom), *Self-control* (honesty), *Good Judgment* (integrity), and *Good Values* (dignity):

Spiritual/Physical Curses are Converted to Spiritual/Physical Blessings via Christianity
(ignorance, criminality, insanity, and evil converted to wisdom, honesty, integrity, and dignity)

<u>God's Curses</u>   <u>God's Blessings</u>

1. **Sin-nature/**<u>Ignorance</u> - - - - Converted to - - - - **Obedience/**<u>Wisdom</u>
   (spiritual)/(physical)   (spiritual)/(physical)
   - Union of Father God/Father Abraham - Marriage Contract (see limitations)
   - Baby Calling - Learn Right from Wrong: Overcome Blasphemy
   - Challenge Flesh - Righteous Citizenship on Earth: ***Receive New Body*** = Enter Celestial Court

   (escaping the curse of hard-work [barren land/toil] to enter God's eternal rest and peace)

2. **Worldly Temptations/**<u>Criminality</u> - - Converted to - - **Self-control/**<u>Honesty</u>
   (spiritual/(physical)   (spiritual)/(physical)
   - Union of Groom Jesus Christ/Bride Holy Church - Betrothal (see potential)
   - Teenage Enlightenment - Learn Good from Evil: Overcome Sedition
   - Adventure of Spirit - Holy Sainthood in Heaven: ***Receive Eternal Life*** = Enter Temple Court

   (escape the curse of pain [barren womb] to enter God's eternal love and joy of the heart)

3. **Demonic Possession/**<u>Insanity</u> - - Converted to - - **Good Judgment /**<u>Integrity</u>
   (spiritual)/(physical)   (spiritual)/(physical)
   - Union of Groom's Friend Priest/Bride's Friend Laity - Wedding Supper (see self-worth)
   - Adult Awakening - Learn God's Will/man's will: Overcome Sorcery
   - Fun for the Soul - Perfect Sonship within Kingdom: **Receive Royal Kingdom** = Enter Royal Court

   (escape the curse of death [barren life] to enter God's eternal fulfillment and happiness)

4. **God's Curse /**<u>Evil</u> - - - - Converted to - - - - **Good Values/**<u>Dignity</u>
   (spiritual)/(physical)   (spiritual)/(physical)
   - Union of Groom's Family Angels/Bride's Family Saints - Wedding Feast (see God)

- Wise Man Indwelling - Learn Reality from Illusion: Overcome Sacrilege
- Happiness of Life-force - Divine Free Man of God: *Receive Divine Freedom* = Enter Divine Court

(escape the curse of damnation [barren future] to enter God's eternity of treasures and freedom)

This illustration shows that the "Human Sin-nature" must be <u>Converted</u> into *Obedience*; "Worldly Temptations" must be <u>Converted</u> into *Self-control*; "Demonic Possession" must be <u>Converted</u> into *Good Judgment;* and "God's Curse" must be <u>Converted</u> into *Good Values*. Through each of these "Curses," a <u>New Blessing</u> is to be **Created** to **Save the Whole Human Race** from *Sin, Evil, Death, and Damnation*. By "Making a Full Commitment" to <u>God, Angels, and Men</u> to **Help Them Build** a **Great Kingdom,** the **Human Race** shall be **Brought Out** of its **Ignorance, Criminal Behavior, Insanity, and Evil**. This means that the "Lord God Almighty" is <u>Calling All</u> **His Children** to *Sell All* and *Give It to the Poor*, **Pick-up Their Crosses, and Come Follow Christ** in the *Saving of Lost Souls*. This "Divine Mission" <u>Haunts Wicked Men</u> as they are **Forced to Realize** that **They must Serve God** either by **Coming Freely** (Heaven) or by being **Made Slaves of Death** (hell). The *Choice is Theirs*. We see "Jesus Christ" went to <u>Mount Calvary</u> to **Free All Men** from **Adam's and Eve's Four Curses** of <u>Toil, Pain, Death, and Damnation</u> by being *Excommunicated from the Temple*, made an *Outcast of the Jewish People*, being *Banished from the Earth*, and then being *Forsaken by God Himself.*

Obviously, the "Lord Knew" that <u>He would have to Face</u> **His Agony in the Garden** (excommunicated), **Scourging** (outcast), **Crucifixion** (banished), and **Death in the Tomb** (forsaken) to **Set the Human Race Free** from *Sin, Evil, Death, and Damnation*. We see that the "Lord" is <u>Calling</u> **His Christian Faithful** to **Deny Their Intellects** (minds) to **See Their Limitations** and **Overcome Adam's Curse** of *Toiling in a Barren Land* (starvation). Secondly, the "Lord" is <u>Calling</u> **His Holy Saints** to **Abandon Their Feelings** (hearts) to **See Their Potential** and **Overcome <u>Eve's Curse</u>** of a *Barren Womb of Pain* (nakedness). Thirdly, the "Lord" is <u>Calling</u> the **Sons of God** to **Submit Their Free Wills** (souls) to **See Their Self-worth** and **Overcome our <u>1st Parents' Curse</u>** of a *Barren Life* (homelessness). Finally, the "Lord" is <u>Calling</u> **All Free Men** to **Die to Self** (life-force) to **See the Meaning of Life** and **Overcome** the **Evil Serpent's Curse** of *Barren Beliefs* (rot in grave). At each of these "Stages of Life," <u>Christ</u> is going to **Renew Man's Hopes and Dreams** of being **Blessed** with a *New Body, Eternal Life*, a *Royal Kingdom,* and his *Oneness with God* (friendship). Through "God's Blessing of Forgiveness," the <u>Human Race</u> can **Defeat** its **Sin-nature, Worldly Temptations, Demonic Possessions,** and even **God's Curse** to be **Set Free** from its *Ignorance* (stupidity), *Criminal Behavior* (cowardice), *Insanity* (greed), and *Evil Acts* (selfishness). Through this "War of Good and Evil," <u>We See the Power</u> of **Jesus Christ** (Messiah) on **Earth** to **Defeat <u>Ignorance of the Mind</u>** (starvation), **Cowardice of the Heart** (nakedness), **Greed of the Soul** (homelessness), and **Selfishness of One's Life-force** (rotting in grave) to bring forth *Heaven on Earth*, by

<u>Surrendering</u> or **Giving All to the Poor** to **Open the Way** to <u>**Build a Happy**</u> <u>**Home**</u> and <u>**Raise a Beautiful Family**</u> of *Healthy Children.*

The following tabular information indicates that each of "God's Children" must <u>Give All to the Poor</u> (build home), <u>Pick-up his Cross</u> (establish government), <u>Come Follow Christ</u> (fulfill church), and <u>Save Souls</u> (master self) to *Become a King, Priest, Son, and Free Man before God.*

All must Give All to the Poor, Pick-up Cross,
Come Follow Christ, Save Souls to Please God
(all are called to build a home, establish government,
fulfill church, and master themselves)

Home   1. **Give All to the Poor** - <u>Build Home</u> (family) …Intellect (mind)
(truth)   • Deny Intellect - See Limitations: Adam Cursed to Toil Barren Land
                • *Banished from the Earth* (ignorance) - Pilate Declares Innocence
                  (sorcery)
Individual   • Remove Sin-nature (natural order)   **Agony in Garden**
Rights   • Remove Baby Ignorance (1st curse) .   • Starvation
                • Toil - Water Purifies Home: Removes Banishment
                • Sonship - Perfect Son within Kingdom: Royal Kingdom
                • Good News - Man becomes Divine: Messiah is Saved (one is saved)
                • Meaning of Life - To Exist: Face Life's Challenges (agony of defeat)
                • Knowledge - Know Oneself: Brought from Egypt = Defeat Toil
         (sinner goes to priest to become a faithful Christian – soldier-of-the-light)

Government 2. **Pick-up Cross** - <u>Establish Government</u> (law) …Emotions (heart)
(law)   • Abandon Feelings - See Potential: Eve Cursed with Pain (barren womb)
                • *Outcast from People* (criminal) - King Herod: Abstain from Decision
                  (sedition)
Social Rights   • Remove Worldly Temptations (supernatural order) **Scourging**
                • Remove Teenage Criminal Behavior (2nd curse)   • Nakedness
                • War - Blood Purifies Government: Removes being Outcast
                • Kingship - Righteous Citizen on Earth: New Body
                • Gospel Message - Evil becomes Righteous: Church is Saved (few are
                  saved)
                • Purpose of Life - To Serve: Create Life's Adventure (thrill of victory)
                • Self-awareness - Know One's Society: Lost in Temple = Defeat Pain
         (Christian goes to bishop to become a holy saint - living prayer of love)

Church   3. **Come Follow Christ** - <u>Fulfill Church</u> (faith) …Instincts (soul)
(will)   • Submit Free Will - See Self-worth: 1st Parents Cursed with Death
                  (barren life)
                • *Excommunication from Temple* (insane) - Caiaphas Declared Jesus
                  Guilty (blasphemy)

Divine Rights	• Remove Demonic Possession (divine order)	**Crucifixion**
	• Remove Adult Insanity (3rd curse)	• Homelessness

- Submit - Death Purifies Church: Removes Excommunication
- Priesthood - Holy Saint in Heaven: Eternal Life
- Doctrinal Truths - Damned are Set Free: World is Saved (all are saved)
- Value of Life - Happiness: To Have Rollicking Fun (pain is pleasure)
- Consciousness - Know One's God: Die on Calvary = Defeat Death

(saint goes to the pope to become son of God - dutiful fisher of men)

Self
(love)

4. **Saving of Souls** - <u>Master Selfishness</u> (thinking) ...Nature (life-force)
- Surrender Life - See Meaning of Life: Serpent Cursed with Evil (barren beliefs)
- *Forsaken by God* (evil) - Christ Offers Spirit to God (sacrilege)

Godly Rights	• Remove God's Curse (God's order)	**Death in Tomb**
	• Remove Wise Man's Evil (4th curse**)**	• Rot in Grave

- God - Spirit Purifies Self: Removes being Forsaken
- Free Man - Thinking for Self: Divine Imagination
- Divine Truths - Divinity becomes Man: God is Saved (self is saved)
- Imagination of Life - To Dream: To Attain One's Treasure (feel love)
- Sentience - Knowing All Things: Resurrection = Defeat Damnation

(son of God goes to God to become free man in kingdom - soul savior for Christ)

This illustration shows that there are "Four Basic Stages of Conversion" from <u>Childhood to Adulthood</u> as **Each** of **God's Children** is being **Called** to *Build a Happy Home, Establish an Honest Government, Fulfill his Faith* (church), and then go forth in the *Salvation of Others* (God). By "Mastering his" <u>Mind, Heart, Soul,</u> and <u>Life-force,</u> a person **can Prove to God** that he is <u>Worthy</u> of *Heaven on Earth, Paradise in Heaven*, a *Royal Kingdom*, and a *Place* in *God's Beatific Vision* (friendship). With the "Coming of God's Son" in <u>His Three Advents,</u> the **Human Race** would be <u>Given Authority Over</u> *God's Natural Order* (physical), *Supernatural Order* (spiritual), and *Divine Orders* (mystical). In short, "Jesus Christ's" <u>Coming</u> is to bring **Mankind Individual Rights** (home), **Social Rights** (government), and **Divine Rights** (church) based on the *Level of Each Person's Maturity* (baby/teenager/adult) and *his Divine Rank* (king/priest/son). This means that through the "Sonship of God," <u>Mankind is to Learn</u> the **Meaning of Life** as **Humanity is Called** into **Existence** to **Face Life's Challenges** and to *Experience the Agony of Defeat* (loss). Secondly, through the "Kingship of God," <u>Mankind is to Learn</u> the **Purpose of Life** as **Humanity** is **Called into Service** to <u>Experience the Adventure of Life</u> and to *Feel the Thrill of Victory* (winning). Thirdly, through the "Priesthood of Life," <u>Mankind is to Learn</u> the **Value of Life** as **Humanity** is **Given Its Gift of Happiness** to <u>Experience Rollicking Fun</u> and to *Know the Joy of Living*. Finally, through the "Freedom of Life," <u>Mankind is to Learn</u> to **Think for itself** as **Humanity** is **Given Its Own Imagination** to *Experience the Wonderment of Self-expression* through *God's Love*.

Through each of these "Four Stages of Maturity," the <u>Human Race</u> is **Able to Come** into a **New Relationship** with **God's <u>Truth, Law, Will, and Love</u>** to become *One with its Creator*. Note that the "Good News (free gift)" means that <u>Man becomes Divine</u> (Messiah) or only that **One Perfect Man** is to be **Saved** by **His Willingness** to **Sacrifice Himself** for the *Welfare of Others*. Secondly, the "Gospel Message (earned)" means that <u>Evil becomes Righteous</u> (church) or only a **Few Saints** are to be **Saved** by **Their Submission to Christ** and **<u>Their Desire</u>** to *Enter God's Communion of Saints in Heaven*. Thirdly, the "Doctrinal Truths (reward)" means that the <u>Damned are to be Set Free</u> (world) or **All Lost** and **Broken Men** are to be **Saved by Their Worship** of the **One True God** and <u>Their Desire</u> to *Enter God's Kingdom of Glory*. Finally, the "Divine Truths (set free)" mean that <u>Divinity becomes Man</u> (God) or **Our Perfect God** becomes **Imperfect** and is **Saved by Virtue** of **<u>His Desire</u>** to *Enter the Friendship of Man through Christ*. In short, the "Human Race" is being <u>Called</u> to **Know Life** to the **<u>Point of Mastering</u>** *Itself* (mind), *Society* (heart), *God* (soul), and finally, *Knowing All Things* (life-force/omniscient).

Through a "Person's Knowledge of Truth," he can both <u>Purify</u> and <u>Build</u> a **Home/family** via the **Waters of Life** (toil/washing) to **Remove** his **<u>Banishment from Earth</u>** and **Make him Worthy** of *God's Blessings of a New Body* (individual rights). Secondly, an "Awakened Soul" can both <u>Purify</u> and <u>Establish</u> a **Government/job** via the **Blood of Life** (war/fighting) to **Remove** being an **Outcast from its People** and become **<u>Worthy</u>** of *God's Blessing of Eternal Life* (social rights). Thirdly, a "Christian" can both <u>Purify</u> and <u>Create</u> a **Church/sainthood** via the **Death of New-life** (submit/quitting) to **Remove** being **Excommunicated from the Temple** and make him **<u>Worthy</u>** of *God's Blessing of a Royal Kingdom* (divine rights). Finally, a "Saint" can both <u>Purify</u> and <u>Make Himself</u> **Perfect** via the **Spirit of Life** (God/never-quit) to **Remove** being **Forsaken by God** and **Make** him **<u>Worthy</u>** of *God's Blessing of Freedom* (infinite rights). This means that to "Know Oneself," a <u>Person must Experience</u> being **Brought Out of Egypt** (Moses/Jesus) to **Defeat God's Curse of Toil** in the **World** and **<u>Break Man's Chains</u>** of *Back-breaking Work*. Secondly, to "Know His Society," a <u>Person must Experience</u> being **Lost in the Temple** (12 yrs. old) to **Defeat God's Curse of Pain** in the **World** and to **<u>Open the Prison Doors</u>** of *Despair and Hopelessness*. Thirdly, to "Know His God," a <u>Person must Experience</u> **Facing Crucifixion** on **Mount Calvary** (cross) to **Defeat God's Curse of Death** in the **World** and to **<u>Overcome the Evil Guards</u>** of *Death and the Grave*. Finally, to "Know All Things," a <u>Person must Experience</u> the **Thrill of Victory** (resurrection) to **Defeat God's Curse of Damnation** in the **World** and **<u>Overcome the Evil Forces</u>** of *Damnation and Oblivion*. By "Overcoming All" of the <u>Curses of God,</u> a **Person can Break Free** from the **Forces** of **<u>Sin, Evil, Death, and Damnation</u>** to *Enter God's Blessing of Eternal Unity* (oneness). This "Oneness Concept" is <u>Centered</u> upon **Each Person's Comprehension** of his **Individual, Social, and Divine Rights** as **Mankind <u>Learns the Difference</u>** between *Human Rejection* (loss) and *Divine Acceptance* (treasure).

1. **Human Rejection** - <u>Loss</u>: Fighting the Evil World…Facing the Agony of Defeat
   • Purify Grave - See Limitations: Ignorance becomes Wisdom = See Man

2. **Divine Acceptance** - <u>Gain</u>: Surrendering to God's Will…Facing the Thrill of Victory
   • Purify Host - See Potential: Cowardice becomes Courage = See God

By "Understanding God's Rejection," we can <u>Comprehend the Need</u> for **Individual, Social, and Divine Rights** to clearly **Define** the <u>**Physical, Spiritual, and Mystical Relationships**</u> between *God* (Kingdom), *Angels* (Heaven), *and Men* (Earth). Through these "Three Relationships," <u>God's Kingdom, Heaven, and Earth</u> can begin to **Work Together** and **Co-exist** as *One Big Happy Family*. We see that the "Human Race" represents <u>Individual Rights</u> based on the idea that **Earth** is a **Baby Farm** of **Physical Homes,** indicating that **Babies** can only **Lay in One Place** as they can only *Think and/or Dream of Things to Come*. Yet, the "Angelic Realm" represents <u>Social Rights</u> based on the idea that **Heaven** is a **Teenage Place of Learning** or a **Set of Spiritual Schools,** where <u>**God Educates His Children**</u> in the *Art of Feeling Good*. Finally, "Divinity Represents" <u>Divine Rights</u> based on the idea that **God's Kingdom** is an **Adult World** or a **Place of Mystical Businesses,** where <u>**God Transacts His Affairs**</u> through *Divine, Angelic, and Human Instinct*. Based on the "Lord" having a <u>Need for Three Rights to Life,</u> we see **Laws Governing Private, Public, and Official Business** which is being **Conducted** by <u>**God, Angels, and Men**</u> through the *Intercession of Jesus Christ*. Through "God's Son," <u>Thoughts, Words, and Deed</u> are to be **Allowed in Existence** and are **Given** their associated <u>**Weight of Importance before God**</u> based on one's *Particular Rank*. This implies that a "Parent" will <u>Listen</u> more **Seriously** to an **Elder Child** rather than to one of the **Babies** so that a <u>**Certain Level of Reliability**</u> must be attached to *Each of God's Children* (rank order/trust). This "Need for Aptitude Testing" <u>Drives</u> the whole **Divine School of Higher Learning** as it constantly **Determines** the <u>**Levels of Progress**</u> associated with one's *Mind* (intellect/thoughts), *Heart* (emotions/words), and *Soul* (instincts/deeds). The implication is that the "Mind of Life" is the <u>Earth</u> (beliefs); the "Heart of Life" is <u>Heaven</u> (love); and the "Soul of Life" is <u>God's Kingdom</u> (perfection). "God's Job" will be to both <u>Educate</u> and bring to <u>Maturity</u> His **Newly Created Earth** (baby/home), **Heaven** (teenager/church), and **Kingdom** (adult/government) to <u>**Awaken**</u> to the *Meaning, Purpose, and Value of Life*.

The following tabular information indicates that "God is Using" <u>Three Separate Institutions in Life</u> to **Create His Individual, Social,** and **Divine Rights** based on *Privacy* (thoughts), *Public Concerns* (words), and *Divine Demands* (deeds).

The Difference between Private, Public, and Official
Business Governs God's Kingdom of Glory
(private business is thoughts, public business is words,
and official business is one's deeds)

Truth (beliefs)	1. **Private Business** - <u>Personal Thoughts:</u> Individual Rights…World System
	• Physical Nature - Flesh: Mind = Intellect + Baby Nature (see limitations)
	• Thoughts Create Beliefs - We are What We Believe
	• Duty - Compromised Will: Kingship Level + Identity

Law	2. **Public Business** - <u>Expression of Words:</u> Social Rights...Holy Church
(love)	• Spiritual Nature - Spirit: Heart = Emotions + Teenage Nature (see potential)
	• Words Form Viewpoints - Speaking Out for What We Believe
	• Responsibility - Permissive Will: Priesthood Level + Character

Will	3. **Official Business** - <u>Performance of Deeds:</u> Divine Rights...Know Oneself
(perfection)	• Mystical Nature - Being: Soul = Instincts + Adult Nature (see self-worth)
	• Deeds Determine Accomplishments - Standing for What We Believe
	• Authority - Direct Will: Sonship Level + Personality

This illustration shows that "Thoughts Create Beliefs" and <u>We</u> are *What We Believe* (identity). "Words Create Viewpoints" and <u>We</u> must <u>All Speak Out</u> for *What We Believe* (character). Finally, "Deeds Determine Accomplishments" and <u>We</u> must <u>All Stand</u> for *What We Believe In* (personality). The Lord is showing us that "Our Minds are Important" because <u>They Reveal Our Duty in Life</u> through the **Power of Compromised Will** which comes from *Our Physical Nature* (intellect) or *Our Kingship Level of Life* (identity). Secondly, "Our Hearts are Important" because they <u>Reveal Our Responsibilities in Life</u> through the **Power of Permissive Will** which comes from our *Spiritual Nature* (emotions) or our *Priesthood Level of Life* (character). Finally, "Our Souls are Important" because they <u>Reveal Our Authority in Life</u> through the **Power of Direct Will** which comes from our *Mystical Nature* (instincts) or *Our Sonship Level of Life* (personality). Through "Authority," "Responsibility," and "Duty," God's entire <u>Creation Operates</u> and is able to bring forth *Transfigured Bodies* (earth), *Eternal Life* (Heaven), and *Royal Kingdoms* (Kingdom) for *One and All*. This means that "Our Beliefs" are <u>Transformed</u> into "What We Love," and **What We Cherish** is <u>Transformed</u> into "God's Divine Perfection" through *Christ Jesus His Son*. This shows us a "Cycle of Life" from <u>Birth to Rebirth</u> as every **Ending has a New Beginning**, **World Without End** until <u>All God's Children</u> are *Fat, Happy, and Wise*. Now, we can see the "Differences" between <u>Private, Public, and Official Business</u> as it is **Governed** by the **Forces of God, Angels, and Men** to bring forth the coming *Kingdom of God*.

We see that this "Teaching" on <u>God's Transformed Creation</u> centers upon the fact that we are all within a **Giant Belief System** and that ***We are What We Believe*** **Telling Us that We** must **Believe in Christ Jesus** (dying to self) to one day *Become the Nature of Christ*. Through the "Nature of Christ," each of <u>God's Children</u> can **Master** the **Righteousness** of *Earth* (education/job/mate), **Holiness** of *Heaven* (worship/praise/thanksgiving), and the **Perfection** of the *Kingdom* (know/love/serve). This means that each "Person on Earth" must ultimately <u>Believe</u> that he must **Enter Death** to be **Born-again in New-life** and become **Christ-like**, thereby **Creating an Eternal Union** between *God's Love* (life) and *Man's Blind Faith* (death/hope for love). Through this "Union of Life and Death," we can see the <u>Meaning of Love</u> as it passes through the **Seven Dimensions of Life**: 1) <u>1st Dimension</u> - Physical Love: Procreation (babies), 2) <u>2nd Dimension</u> - Spiritual Love: Worshiping God (give life), 3) <u>3rd Dimension</u> - Mystical Love (unconditional): God Loves Man, 4) <u>4th Dimension</u> - Divine

Love (agape): God and Man Love Each Other, 5) 5th Dimension - God's Love (infinity): God becomes Man/Man becomes God, 6) 6th Dimension - All Love (eternity): Love Union in Marriage, and 7) 7th Dimension - No Love (paradox): Love Changes into Eternal Adoration.

We now see that at "Level Eight," the State of Nothing (null-set) enters **Rebirth**, where **Adoration becomes Exaltation** and **Transforms** into the *Worship of Oneself* or *Maturing into Divinity*. This "Process of Maturing" via a Person's Own Mastery **Requires** becoming an **Expert** within **Each and Every Dimension of Existence** until one is *Proficient on Earth* (physical), in *Heaven* (spiritual), and within the *Kingdom* (mystical). We see that in the "Physical Dimension" or "Love," a Person must Master his **Mind of Intellect** to **Defeat Ignorance** and become *Wise as a King*; he must then Master his **Heart of Emotion** to **Defeat Cowardice** and become as *Courageous as a Priest*; and finally, he must Master his **Soul of Instincts** to **Defeat Greed** and become as *Generous as a Son of God*. Secondly, in the "Spiritual Dimension or Love," one must Master **Repentance** to **Worship God** (daily) by **Giving his Life** to be a *Converted Sinner*; he must then Master **Prayer** to **Praise God** (weekly) by **Giving his Wealth** to be a *Faithful Christian*; and finally, he must Master **Works** to **Thank God** (yearly) by **Giving his Labors** to be a *Holy Saint*. Thirdly, in the "Mystical Dimension or Love," a Person must Master being **Scourged** to **Offer his Flesh** as a **Broken Body** to *Unite his Life with Jesus* (being saved); he must then Master being **Crucified** to **Offer his Spirit** as **Blood Shed** to *Unite his Life with Christ* (saving self); and finally he must Master the **Tomb** to **Offer his Soul** as a **Death Sacrifice** to *Unite his Life with Jesus Christ* (saving others). Fourthly, in the "Divine Dimension or Love" one must Master **Free Redemption** to become a **Righteous Citizen** with his **Own Title Deed to Earth** to attain the *Respect of Man* (truth); next, he must Master **Earned Salvation** to become a **Holy Saint** with his own **Title Deed to Heaven** to attain the *Respect of God* (law); and finally, he must Master **Bonus Rewards** to become a **Perfect Son** with his own **Title Deed to a Royal Kingdom** to attain the *Respect of both God and Man*.

Fifthly, in the "Godly Dimension or Love," one must Master **Earth** as an upstanding **Member of Humanity** to **See his Own Limitations,** thereby *Revealing his Identity* (name); he must then Master **Heaven** as a **Holy Member of Divinity** to **See his Own Potential,** thereby *Revealing his Character* (position); and finally, he must Master the **Kingdom** as a **Member** of the **God/Man Relationship** to **See his Own Self-worth,** thereby *Revealing His Personality* (title). Sixthly, in the "All Dimension or Love," a Person must Master his **New Body** by **Setting Up** His **Own Government Guaranteeing Individual Rights** to the **Slaves of Life** to **Protect Their** *Possession of the Land*; he must then Master **Eternal Life** by **Joining Christ's Church,** where a **Person is Given Social Rights** as a **Nobleman of Life** to *Rent the Land*; and finally, he must Master the **Royal Kingdom** by **Establishing** his **Own Family's Home**, where he is **Given Divine Rights** within the **Royalty of Life** to *Own the Land*. Finally, in the "Nothing Dimension or Love," a Person must Master the **Transfigured Body** to bring forth **Man's New Earth** to be **Ruled** by **God's Celestial Court** which **Represents** *God's Throne* and/or the *King's Prayer*; he must then Master the **Glorified Body** to bring forth **God's New Heaven** to be **Ruled** by **God's Temple Court** which <u>**Repre-sents**</u> *God's Temple* and/or the *Priest's Sacrifice*; and finally, he must <u>Master</u> the **Divine Body** to bring forth the **God/Man Kingdom of Glory** to be **Ruled** by **God's Royal Court** which <u>**Represents**</u> *God's Palace* and/or the *Son's Blessing*.

At each of these "Seven Levels of Command Authority," <u>God, Angels, and Men</u> shall have **Their Being** (unification) to **Govern All** the <u>**Forces of Space and Time**</u> to bring forth the *Meaning* (existence), *Purpose* (service), and *Value* (happiness) *of Life*. In short, "God" is Asking <u>Each of His Children:</u> Have **You Been There** (experience)? Have **You Done That** (participation)? Did **You Get a Tee Shirt** (mastery) to show that you have <u>**Mastered**</u> the *Lord's Seven Dimensions of Life*? If a person has "Been There, "Done That" and "Got a Tee Shirt," then he can <u>Boast</u> that he is **Ready** to **Move On** from **Level to Level to Level Forever** until he has <u>**Seen It All**</u> (limitations) and <u>**Done It All**</u> (potential), thereby showing he has been *Consumed unto his Nothingness* (spent). This means that this "Faithful Child of Love" is <u>Now Ready</u> (self-worth) for the *Lord's Next Challenge* (divinity/1st truth/blessings) and the *Lord's Next Awesome Adventure of Life* (humanity/2nd truth/lessons).

The Selfish Life Never Works

1. **Seeing It All brings Death** - One Day, Every Selfish Nature will be Fulfilled, then Selfishness Ends
   - Challenged Everything - Won Them All...Knowledge Ends
   - Experienced Every Adventure - None Left...Self-awareness Ends
   - Had Enough Fun - Life is Boring...Consciousness Ends
   - Been Totally Happy - Nothing Left to Do...Sentience Ends

Service to Others Always Works

2. **Raising Children brings Life** - Challenge, Adventure, Fun, and Happiness Never-ever Ends
   - Challenge - There's Always More Babies to Raise...Unending Peace
   - Adventure - There's Always More Teenagers to Teach......Unending Joy
   - Fun - There's Always More Adults to Play With....Unending Happiness
   - Happiness - There's Always More Wise Men to Awaken....Unending Life

This illustration shows that that the "Life-experience" was <u>Never Designed</u> for **Some Selfish Fool to Seek his Own Self-Fulfillment** because this <u>**Concept is Impossible**</u> in *Divine Terms;* while the "Life-experience" is <u>All About</u> *Raising Babies, Teaching Righteous Citizens, Creating Holy Saints, and Offering God New Born-again Sons.* Yes! The "Human (Earth/kings)," "Angelic (Heaven/priests)," and "Divine Realms (Kingdom/sons)" have been <u>Created</u> to **Work Together** in **Running God's Awesome Kingdom of Glory** in the **Form** of a **Giant Farm or Ranch** to <u>**Produce All the Treasures of Life**</u> *God would Ever Want.*

The following tabular information indicates that the "Emotion of Love" both <u>Grows and Matures</u> as it <u>**Travels**</u> through the *World* (1st dimension), *Church* (2nd dimension),

Heaven (3rd dimension), ***Kingdom*** (4th dimension), ***God*** (5th dimension), ***God's Paradox*** (6th dimension), and into ***Creation's Null-set of Conversion*** (7th dimension):

Love Changes Its Nature by Dimension from Lust to Adoration, thereby Making God and Man One
(becoming one through procreation, worship,
sacrifice, union, marriage, indwelling and blending)

World   1. **Physical Love** - <u>Procreation:</u> Babies = Tree of Knowledge...Knowledge
- Master Mind - Intellect: Ignorance becomes Wisdom = King (gold)
- Master Heart - Emotions: Cowardice becomes Courage = Priest (frankincense)   **Selfishness**
- Master Soul - Instincts: Greed becomes Generosity = Son (myrrh)

(fixed frame of reference - location: belief = throne of life + kingship)

Church   2. **Spiritual Love** - <u>Man Worships God:</u> Gives Life = Tree of Life.... Self-awareness
- Master Repentance - Worship: Give Life = Sinner (daily)
- Master Prayers - Praise: Give Wealth = Christian (weekly) **Submission**
- Master Works - Thanksgiving: Give Labors = Saint (yearly)

(relative focused existence - identity: trust = robe of life + priesthood)

Heaven   3. **Mystical Love** - <u>God Loves Man:</u> Sacrificing Life = Tree of Death ... Consciousness
- Master Scourging - Offering Flesh: Body Broken = Jesus (being saved)
- Master Crucifixion - Offering Spirit: Blood Shed =   **Sacrifice** Christ (save self)
- Master Tomb - Offering Soul: Death Sacrifice = Jesus Christ (saving others)

(perception of illusion - lie: faith = crown of life + sonship)

Kingdom   4. **Divine Love** - <u>Loving Each Other:</u> Friendship = Tree of New-life... Sentience
- Master Redemption - Righteous Citizen: Own Earth = Man (truth)
- Master Salvation - Holy Saint: Own Heaven = God (law) **Reconciliation**
- Master Rewards - Perfect Son: Own Kingdom = God/Man (will)

(perception of reality - truth: knowing = scepter of life + servanthood)

God   5. **Godly Love** - <u>God is Man/Man is God:</u> Marriage = Tree of Fruits...Fairness
- Master Earth - Humanity: See Limitations = Identity (name)
- Master Heaven - Divinity: See Potential =   **Redemption** Character (position)
- Master Kingdom - God/Man Nature: See Self-worth = Personality (title)

(perception of infinity - space: becoming = ring of life + champion)

Paradox   6. **All Love** - <u>God and Man are One:</u> Indwelling = Tree of Treasures…Ethics
- Master New Body - Government: Individual Rights = Slave (possession)
- Master Eternal Life - Church: Social Rights =   **Conversion**
  Nobleman (rental)
- Master Royal Kingdom - Home: Divine Rights = Royalty (ownership)

(perception of eternity - time: transforming = seal of life + commander)

Null-set   7. **No Love** - <u>Love Changes into Adoration:</u> Blending = Tree of Free Will…
  Morals
- Master Transfigured Body - New Earth: Celestial Court =
  Throne (prayer)
- Master Glorified Body - New Heaven: Temple Court =   **Recreation**
  Temple (sacrifice)
- Master Mystical Body - Kingdom of Glory: Royal Court =
  Palace (blessing)

(establishment of truth - Christ: arriving = sword of life + free man)

This illustration shows that "If We Define Love" by <u>Dimension of Existence,</u> its basic **Meaning will Change** with **Every New Level of Application,** thereby **Showing** that **God is Using <u>Earth</u>** (physical), **<u>Heaven</u>** (spiritual), and **<u>His Kingdom</u>** (mystical) to **<u>Better Define</u>** the *Use of the Term Love.* Note that in the "Physical Dimension" or <u>Our Physical Love</u> (lust), it is **Defined** as **Procreation** or the **Creation of Babies** to **Populate the Earth** with an **<u>Unlimited Supply</u>** of *Future Righteous Citizens of God.* Secondly, in the "Spiritual Dimension (Heaven)" or <u>Spiritual Love,</u> it is **Defined as Worship** (give life) or **Creation of Christians** to **Fill Heaven** with an **<u>Unlimited Supply</u>** of *Future Holy Saints of God.* Thirdly, in the "Mystical Dimension (Kingdom)" or <u>Mystical Love,</u> it is **Defined** as **God Loving Man** (sacrifice) or **Creation of Images of Christ** to **Fill God's Kingdom** with an **<u>Unlimited Supply</u>** of *Future Sons of God.* Fourthly, in the "Divine Dimension (God)" or <u>Divine Love,</u> it is **Defined** as **God and Man Loving Each Other** (friendship) or **Creation of Soul Saviors** to fill **God's Spirit** with an **<u>Unlimited Supply</u>** of *Future Wise Men* (evangelists) *of God.* Fifthly, in the "Godly Dimension (God/Man)" or <u>God's Love,</u> it is **Defined as God becomes Man** (Christmas) and **Man becomes God** (Easter) or **Creation of Eternal Mates** (marriage) to **Fill God's Nature** with an **<u>Unlimited Supply</u>** of *Boundless Love.* Sixthly, in the "All Dimension (Benevolent Force)" or <u>All Love,</u> it is **Defined** as <u>God and Man are One</u> (indwelling) to **Fill God's Life** with an **<u>Unlimited Supply</u>** of *Challenges* (spirit) and *Adventures* (flesh). Finally, in the "Nothing Dimension (Personal God)" or <u>No Love,</u> it is **Defined** as **Love Changing into Adoration** (blending) to **Fill** the **Infinite Life-force** (energy) with an **<u>Unlimited Supply</u>** of *Evolving Limitless Creations Without End.*

In the explanation of "Man's Journey of Life" from <u>Nothing to Nothing,</u> we see that **Human Existence** is about **Attaining All God's Gifts, Fruits, and Treasures** and then **Returning Them to Him** (redeem damned) to <u>**Earn One's Own Respect**</u> (worship self) as a *Limitless Creation without End*. To "Understand this Paradox" of <u>Reality</u> versus <u>Illusion,</u> **We must Comprehend** that **God Himself** is <u>**Comprised**</u> of being *Never-created* (reality) and *Created Life* (illusion). This "Dual Nature" within Three Persons **Allows** the **Human Race** to **See God** as both the <u>**Blessing**</u> of the *Holy Spirit* (reality) and as a **Teacher** via the *Evil Spirit* (illusion). This "Blessing (adulthood)" and "Teaching Process (childhood)" bring forth the <u>Challenges of Life</u> (conversion) which **Lead** to **Facing** and <u>**Conquering the Unknown**</u> to *Create* the *Adventures of Life*.

It should now make sense that the "Challenge of Life" is <u>Centered</u> upon the **Conversion** of a **Person's Life** (earth), **Spirit** (Heaven), and **Divinity** (Kingdom) to **Transform a Soul** into a **New Creation** (infinite energy), <u>**Worthy**</u> of *God's Divine Blessing* (spirit) and *Divine Respect* (flesh). We see that the "Conversion of Lost Souls" comes with <u>Breaking</u> each of **God's Covenants of Life** and then having the <u>**Wisdom, Courage, Generosity, and Unselfishness**</u> to *Pay for All Damages* (compensatory retribution) and *Pay for All Fines* (punitive recompense). We see that "Breaking" the <u>Water Covenant of Earth</u> (excommunication) via a **Person's Defiance** (stealing) **Requires** an **Intercessory Priest** to **Make an Appropriate** <u>**Sacrifice to God**</u> and then *Beg Him for His Divine Mercy* (forgiveness). Secondly, "Breaking" the <u>Blood Covenant of Heaven</u> (outcast) via a **Person's Deception** (hiding) **Requires** an **Intercessory King** to **Offer an Appropriate** <u>**Prayer to God**</u> and then *Beg Him for His Divine Mercy* (pardon). Thirdly, "Breaking" the <u>Death Covenant of God's Kingdom</u> (banishment) via a **Person's Deceit** (lying) **Requires** an **Intercessory Son** to **Intercede** with **His Good Works** <u>**Presented before the Lord**</u> and then *Beg Him for His Divine Mercy* (resurrection). Finally, "Breaking" the <u>Spirit Covenant of God</u> (forsaken) via a **Person's Desecration** (damage) **Requires** an **Intercessory Repentant Sinner** (self) to **Offer** his <u>**Damnation to God**</u> and then *Beg Him for His Divine Mercy* (reconciliation).

1. **Breaking God's Water Covenant** - <u>Human Defiance:</u> Stealing from God … Changed by Wisdom
   - Being Excommunicated from Temple - Scourging at Pillar (pay God in thanksgiving/labor)
2. **Breaking God's Blood Covenant** - <u>Human Deception:</u> Hiding from God… Changed by Courage
   - Being an Outcast from One's People - Carrying Sinful Cross (pay God in praise/money)
3. **Breaking God's Death Covenant** - <u>Human Deceit:</u> Lying to God…Changed by Generosity
   - Being Banished from the Earth - Crucified upon the Cross (pay God in worship/life)
4. **Breaking God's Spirit Covenant** - <u>Human Desecration:</u> Rejecting God… Changed by Unselfishness
   - Being Forsaken by God - Cast into Tomb of Damnation (pay God in servanthood/eternal life)

Through each of these "Four Covenants (water/blood/death/spirit)," the <u>Human Race</u> can both **Grow and Mature** into <u>**Priests**</u> (baby), <u>**Kings**</u> (teenagers), <u>**Sons**</u> (adults), **and even** <u>**God**</u> (wise men) based on the *Depth of Their Intercessory Commitment* (0%/33%/67%/100%). The implication is that the "Human Race" is <u>Guilty</u> of **Stealing** (defiance), **<u>Hiding</u>** (deception), **<u>Lying</u>** (deceit), and **<u>Damaging</u>** *God's Property* (desecration). For "All These Crimes," <u>Humanity</u> must **Pay Its Sin-debt** unto the **<u>Last Penny</u>** via *Worship* (give life), *Praise* (give wealth), *Thanksgiving* (give labors), and *Servanthood* (give all). This means that for "Defiance, a Person" is to be <u>Excommunicated</u> from *God's Temple* (sinful blasphemy/Caiaphas). For "Deception, a Person" is to be an <u>Outcast</u> of his *People* (evil sorcery/Herod). For "Deceit, a person" is to be <u>Banished</u> from *Earth* (deceitful sedition/Pilate). For "Desecration, a Person" is to be <u>Forsaken</u> by the *Lord God Almighty Himself* (unforgivable sacrilege/God). For these "Four Crimes (blasphemy/sorcery/sedition/sacrilege)" <u>Against God's Divine Justice,</u> a **Person** must be **Forgiven** (repentance/priest), **Pardoned** (prayers/king), **Resurrected** (works/son), and be **Reconciled** (save souls/God) **<u>Back to his God</u>** to *Pay his Sin-debt in Full* (fear/pain/death/damnation). In short, each of "God's Children" must <u>Purify his Ignorant Mind</u> (baptism) with *Living Waters* (wisdom), <u>Purify his Cowardly Heart</u> (sacrifice) with *Sacred Blood* (courage), <u>Purify his Greedy Soul</u> (pay damages) with *Eternal Death* (generosity), and finally, <u>Purify his Selfish Life-force</u> (pay fine) with *God's Spirit* (unselfishness). In this way, a "Person can Attain" <u>Free Redemption</u> (blessed/good news) on *<u>Earth</u>* (new body), <u>Earn his Salvation</u> (anointed/gospel message) in *Heaven* (eternal life), "Receive" a <u>Bonus Reward</u> (sanctified/doctrinal truths) within the *Kingdom* (homeland), and finally, be "Personally Honored (consecrated /thinking for self)" as <u>One of God's Sons</u> to become *Worthy of Freedom.*

The following tabular information indicates that there are "Four Major Covenants (water/blood/death/spirit)" governing <u>Earth, Heaven, the Kingdom, and God</u> through the *Priestly Offering of Water* (sacrifice), *Kingly Offering of Blood* (prayer), *Sonly Offering of Death* (gift), and the *Divine Offering of God's Spirit* (treasure):

God Governs by Four Covenants/Water (earth), Blood (Heaven), Death (Kingdom), and Spirit (God)
(water removes defiance, blood removes deception,
death removes deceit, and spirit removes desecration)

Baptism   1. **Water Covenant of Earth** - <u>Defiance</u> (stealing) …Free Redemption
(baby)   • Intercessory Priest - Man Begs God for Forgiveness: God Sees Suffering
           • 1st Redemptive Seal - Forgiveness of Sin: Reveal Right/Wrong
Blasphemy • Forgive Excommunication from Temple - Blasphemy (death of mind)
           • <u>Priest's Solemn Vow</u> - Remove Hunger/Set Man Free from Starvation
           • *Give* - Obedience (no freedom)
           • *Create* - Wisdom (right/wrong)   **Educate Foolish Ignorance**
           • *Get* - New Body (transfigured body)
    (defeat sin-nature - blessed with righteous citizenship on earth: new body)

Sacrifice (teenager) **Sorcery**	2. **Blood Covenant of Heaven** - <u>Deception</u> (hiding) …Earned Salvation • Intercessory King - Man Begs God for His Pardon: God Hears Cry for Help • 2nd Redemptive Seal - Pardon of Evil Acts: Reveal Good/Evil • Pardon Outcast from People - Sedition (death of heart) • Punishment - Crucifixion: Blood Blessing: See Potential • <u>King's Solemn Vow</u> - Remove Poverty/Set Man Free from Nakedness • *Give* - Poverty (no money) • *Create* - Courage (good/evil) **Rehabilitate Criminal Behavior** • *Get* - Eternal Life (glorified spirit)

(defeat worldly temptations - blessed with holy sainthood in Heaven: eternal life)

Pay Debt (adult) **Sedition**	3. **Death Covenant of Kingdom** - <u>Deceit</u> (lying) …Bonus Rewards • Intercessory Son - Man Begs God for Resurrection: God Recognizes His Covenant • 3rd Redemptive Seal - Resurrection from Death: Reveal God's/Man's Wills • Resurrected from Banishment of Earth - Sorcery (death of soul) • Punishment - Cast into Tomb: Death Blessing: See Self-worth • <u>Son's Solemn Vow</u> - Remove Exposure/Set Man Free from Homelessness • *Give* - Celibacy (no sex) • *Create* - Generosity (God's Will/man's will) **Heal Insane Mind** • *Get* - Royal Kingdom (mystical soul)

(defeat demonic possession - blessed with perfect sonship in Kingdom: new home)

Pay Fine (wise man) **Sacrilege**	4. **Spirit Covenant of God** - <u>Desecration</u> (rebelling) …Personal Freedom • Intercessory God - Man Begs God for Reconciliation: God Comes to Help • 4th Redemptive Seal - Reconciled from Damnation: God's Reality/Man's Illusion • Reconciled from being Forsaken - Sacrilege (death of life-force) • Punishment - Cast into Hell: Spirit Blessing: See God Face-to-face • <u>God's Solemn Vow</u> - Remove Imprisonment/Set Man Free from Captivity • *Give* - Works (no rest) • *Create* - Unselfishness (God's Reality/man's illusion) **Change Evil Nature** • *Get* - Infinite Freedom (divine life-force)

(defeat God's curse - blessed with personal freedom in God: friendship)

This illustration shows that the "Life-experience" is governed by "Man's" <u>Priestly Intercession</u> on *Earth* (excommunication), "Man's" <u>Kingly Intercession</u> in *Heaven* (outcast), "Man's" <u>Sonly Intercession</u> within the *Kingdom* (banishment), and "Man's" <u>Godly Intercession</u> via *Divinity* (forsaken). We see that "Mankind" is <u>Begging God</u> for **Forgiveness of Sin** (blasphemy), **Pardon for Evil Acts** (sedition), **Resurrection from Death** (sorcery), and finally, **Reconciliation from Damnation** (desecration) all in the *Name of Jesus Christ*. These most "Merciful Blessings" from <u>God</u> are known as the <u>Four Redemptive Seals</u> (covenants) which **Govern** the **Teaching of Lessons** (water/blood/death/spirit) **Required When One** of <u>God's Children Fails</u> to *Obey the Lord's Divine Law*. We see that the "Punishment" for breaking the <u>Water Covenant</u> (purify mind) is *Scourging* (see limitations); for **Breaking** the <u>Blood Covenant</u> (purify heart) is *Crucifixion* (see potential); for Breaking the <u>Death Covenant</u> (purify soul) is to be *Sealed in a Tomb;* and for **Breaking** the <u>Spirit Covenant</u> (purify life-force), a **<u>Sinner</u>** is to be *Cast into Hell* (damnation). Through each of these "Corrective Techniques (obedience)," a <u>Person</u> is to be <u>Transformed</u> from a **Lost Broken Sinner** (lessons) into a **<u>Holy Saint</u>** (blessings), thereby *Creating* a *Newly Purified Son of God*. The whole point is that the "Ignorant Fool" must be <u>Educated</u> (new mind/wise king); "Criminal Behavior" must be <u>Rehabilitated</u> (new heart/courageous priest); the "Insane Mind" must be <u>Healed</u> (new soul/generous son); and the "Evil Nature" must be <u>Changed</u> (new life-force/unselfish God).

We see that this "Education (earth)," "Rehab (Heaven)," "Healing (Kingdom)," and "Changing (God)" <u>Process can Only be Done</u> by **God's Son**, the **<u>Lord Jesus Christ</u>** through His *Water* (obedience), *Blood* (poverty), *Death* (celibacy), and *Spirit* (works) *Sacrifices* upon *Mount Calvary*. To grasp the "Essence of this Teaching," <u>Focus</u> on **What a Person must Give** (obedience/poverty/ celibacy/works), **What that Sacrifice Creates** (wisdom/courage/generosity/unselfishness), and then **What Does a Person Get** (body/life/kingdom/freedom) in the **End** for **Seeking** to **<u>Know</u>** (wisdom), **Love** (courage), and **<u>Serve</u>** (generosity) an *Invisible God of Mystery*. This means that the "Born-again Life-experience (Christ's new nature)" is <u>All About Defeating</u> **Man's Sin-nature** (self/foolish ignorance), **Worldly Temptations** (society/criminal behavior), **Demonic Possession** (Lucifer/insane mind), and finally, **God's Curse** (God/evil nature). Once a "Person" <u>Defeats Sin, Temptations, Demonic Possession,</u> and <u>Curses,</u> then he will be an **Awakened Soul** ready to be **<u>Transformed</u>** into a *Righteous Citizen* (earth), *Holy Saint* (Heaven), *Perfect Son* (Kingdom), and *Free Man* (God) before the *Throne of God*. Through this "Conversion Process" from <u>Sinner to Saint,</u> we can **Grasp the Many Dimensions of God** as He Strives to **<u>Explain that Physical Human Life</u>** is simply a *Manifestation of Divine Existence*. To "Grasp" the <u>Essence of Divine Truth,</u> we must **Define the Life-experience** as *Corporeal Existence* or *Flesh* (matter), as a *Spiritual State* or *Spirit* (concept), as *Conceptual Word* or *Incarnation* (words), and finally, as *Pure Thought* or *Divinity* (ideas).

1. **Truth/Matter** - <u>Physical Human Life:</u> Changing the Flesh…Defeat Sin-nature
2. **Concepts** - <u>Spiritual Angelic State:</u> Changing the Spirit…Defeat Worldly Temptations
3. **Words** - <u>Mystical Divinity:</u> Changing the Soul…Defeat Demonic Possession
4. **Ideas** - <u>Divine Pure Thought:</u> Changing the Life-force…Defeat God's Curses

This then "Defines Man's Journey" from <u>Earthly Matter</u> (mind/intellect), to <u>Spiritual Concept</u> (heart/emotions), to <u>Mystical Word</u> (soul/instincts), to <u>Divine Thought</u>

(life-force/nature) so that an **Awakened Soul** might <u>**Reach**</u> its *God of Truth, Law, Will, and Love.* Through this "Teaching," a <u>Person can Comprehend</u> the **Act of Becoming Pure Thought** or to **Exist as an Idea** which can **Experience All Life** through its <u>**Combined**</u> *Intellectual* (logic) and *Emotional* (feelings) *Experiences*. Obviously, the "God State" is <u>Pure Thought</u> and the "Man State" is <u>Physical Life</u> which is much like a **CPU Processor** trying to **Marry** a **Printer,** but the *CPU is Electricity* and the *Printer is Made of Steel* (matter). Unfortunately, this is the case between "God (CPU)" and "Man (Printer)." The question is: how can the <u>CPU and Printer</u> become either **Pure Electricity** or **Pure Steel** so they can both <u>**Enter the Same Dimension of Existence**</u> to be *United into True Love*? In our "Reality," this <u>Common Denominator Processor</u> is **Mount Calvary** (crucifixion) and the **Creation** of the **Lord Jesus Christ** as the <u>**Incarnate Word of Life**</u> is <u>**United**</u> with the *Flesh and Blood of Humanity*. We now see that the "Flesh and Blood" of <u>Jesus</u> is becoming **Bread and Wine**, just as the <u>**Wheat and Grapes of Nature**</u> are becoming the **Flesh and Blood of God** to *Make God and Man One*. Recall that in the TV show *Star Trek: Voyager*, we see that the <u>Q-continuum Cannot</u> effectively **Communicate** with the **Human Race** because **They** are **Creatures of Pure Thought** and have **Always Existed** (omnipotent) so **They Need** a **Way to Express Their Conceptual Existence** in <u>**Physical Form**</u> for *Mankind to Understand*. In truth, we see that the "State of Pure Thought" or <u>Ideas</u> is in effect the **Creators of Human Life** as **Thought, Word, and Deed** are actually **One and the Same thing**, just expressed in <u>**Different**</u> **Forms** or in *Different Dimensions of Expression* (thought/word/deed). This "Pure Thought Nature" of the <u>Lord God Almighty</u> and the "Flesh/Blood Nature" of <u>Mankind</u> must be **Made One** through the <u>**Sacred and Immaculate Hearts**</u> of *Jesus and Mary*.

We can now see that the "Benevolent God Force (never-created/pure thought)" is <u>Trying</u> to become <u>One</u> with "Its Created Man (flesh/blood)" through the <u>**Intercession of Wheat and Grapes**</u> as the *Common Denominator of Eternal Existence* (input). Secondly, the "Lord's Personal God Force (word)" is <u>Trying</u> to become <u>One</u> with "His Created Man (flesh/blood)" through the **Intercession of Bread and Wine** as a *Second Common Denominator of Eternal Existence* (process). Thirdly, the "Lord God Almighty Himself (deed)" is <u>Trying</u> to become <u>One</u> with "His Created Man (flesh/blood)" through the **Intercession of Flesh and Blood** as a *Third Common Denominator of Eternal Existence* (output). Finally, the "God Force (becoming)" is <u>Trying</u> to become <u>One</u> with His "Created Man (Man/God)" through the **Intercession of Man and God** as a fourth *Common Denominator of Eternal Existence* (results). Through the "Input-Process-Output Concept," <u>God</u> shall bring forth <u>Eternal Results</u> **Expressed** in **Four Major Dimensions of Life**: 1) <u>Physical</u> Earth: Flesh or Body (truth), 2) <u>Spiritual</u> - Heaven: Concept or Blood (law), 3) <u>Mystical</u> Kingdom: Word or Soul (will), and 4) <u>Divine</u> - God: Thought or Divinity (love). In other words, the Lord was "Miraculously Transforming Himself" from a <u>Thought,</u> to a <u>Word of Reality,</u> to a <u>Concept of Life,</u> and finally, into <u>Corporeal Form</u> or <u>Human Flesh</u> (truths) as the **Person of Adam,** simply by **Focusing His Mind** (intellect) and **Heart** (emotions) on the *Idea of Creation*.

This means that the "Mind of God" or <u>Intellect</u> represents **Human Flesh** in the Person of Mary's Son, **Jesus** (son of man), who has been **Tasked** to <u>**Save Sinners**</u> (lessons) by *Taking-sin* (death) and *Offering God His Blood of Repentance*. Secondly, we see that the "Heart of God" or <u>Emotions</u> represents **Human Spirit** in the **Person** of **God's Son, Christ** (Son of God), **Who** has been **Tasked** to <u>**Create Saints**</u> (blessings) by *Giving Man His Divinity* (resurrection) and *Offering God His Grace of Forgiveness*. This "Creation Idea" of <u>Death and Resurrection</u> brought **God** from the **Idea of Life** (earth) into a **Second Manifestation** of **Redemption of Life** (Heaven) which **Automatically Leads Him** into the <u>**Need for Sanctified Life**</u> (Kingdom) to bring into *Existence* the *Triune Nature of God* (home/government/church). We see this "Triune Nature (natures/persons/trinity)" coming forth in the <u>Realities</u> of **Earth** (body), **Heaven** (blood), <u>**Kingdom**</u> (soul), and **God** (divinity) to exist within *Man's Mind* (self/idea), *Heart* (society/word), *Soul* (God/concept), and *Life-force* (life/flesh). These "Forces of Life" are brought forth out of <u>God's Justice</u> (pure thought), <u>God's Morals</u> (conceptual word), <u>God's Ethics</u> (spiritual state), and <u>God's Fairness</u> (corporeal existence) to **Transform Wicked Sinners** (earth) into *Holy Saints* (Heaven).

The following tabular information indicates that we are comprised of "Four States of Life" beginning with <u>Corporeal Existence</u> (earth), then a <u>Spiritual State</u> (Heaven), then becoming a <u>Conceptual Word</u> (Kingdom), and finally, reaching <u>Pure Thought</u> (God) as an *Expression of God Himself*:

Life's Four States are Corporeal Existence, Spiritual State, Conceptual Word, and Pure Thought
(man is journeying from ideas to words to concepts
to truths and become the ultimate state of life)

Earth
(truth)

1. **Corporeal Existence** - <u>Truth:</u> Flesh = Mind (intellect) …Knowledge
   - Jesus - Crucifixion: Humanity Takes-sin = Forgiveness (earth)
   - Remove Faults - Teach Wrong: Manifested Word of God (wheat/grapes)
   - Wheat
   - Bread   **God's Fairness** - Physical Dimension (nature)
   - Flesh (body)

Heaven
(law)

2. **Spiritual State** - <u>Concept:</u> Spirit = Heart (emotions) …Self-awareness
   - Jesus Christ - Tomb: Humanity Gives Divinity = Pardon (Heaven)
   - Gain Virtues - Teach Right: Incarnate Word of God (bread/wine)
   - Grapes
   - Wine   **God's Ethics** - Spiritual Dimension (humanity)
   - Spirit (blood)

- -

Kingdom
(will)

3. **Conceptual Word** - <u>Word:</u> Soul = Soul (instincts) …Consciousness
   - Christ - Resurrection: Divinity Takes-sin = Resurrection (Kingdom)
   - Remove Sinfulness - Teach Evil: Written Word of God (flesh/blood)

- Baby
- Jesus   **God's Morals** - Mystical Dimension (angelic)
- Man (soul)

God
(love)

4. **Pure Thought** - <u>Idea:</u> Life-force = Being (nature) …Sentience
   - Christ Jesus - Ascension: Divinity Gives Divinity = Reconciliation (God)
   - Gain Forgiveness - Teach Good: Spoken Word of God (Man/God)
   - Divinity
   - Christ   **God's Justice** - Divine Dimension (divine)
   - God (divinity)

This illustration shows that "God's Justice (love)" brings forth the <u>Lord's Divine Dimension of Life</u> (God) which **Ranges** from **God's Divinity All the Way** to the **Lord God Almighty Himself** in the **Nature of Divinity** or *Never-created Absolute Truth* (pure thought). Secondly, "God's Morals (will)" bring forth the <u>Lord's Mystical Dimension of Life</u> (Kingdom) which **Ranges** from **Baby Jesus** all the way to **Man Jesus** in the **Nature of One's Soul** or *Never-created Relative Truth* (conceptual word). Thirdly, "God's Ethics (law)" brings forth the <u>Lord's Spiritual Dimension of Life</u> (Heaven) which **Ranges** from **Grapes** all the way to the **Spirit** in the **Nature of Blood** or *Created Absolute Truth* (spiritual state). Finally, "God's Fairness (truth)" brings forth the <u>Lord's Physical Dimension of Life</u> (earth) which **Ranges** from **Wheat** all the way to **Flesh** in the **Nature of One's Body** or *Created Relative Truth* (corporeal existence). Note that "God's Four Gifts of Life" are a <u>Transfigured Body</u> (earth), <u>Eternal Life</u> (Heaven), a <u>Royal Kingdom</u> (God), and finally, <u>One's Personal Freedom</u> (self) which match-up with the **Lord's Body, Blood, Soul,** and **Divinity** or the *Lord's States of Life*. Now, we see that "God" has <u>Journeyed</u> from **Thought** (divinity), to **Word** (spirit), to **Concept** (energy), to **Truth/Flesh** (matter), and now the **Lord** is **Asking Each of Us** to <u>Travel</u> from *Flesh* (die to self/earth), to *Concept* (be self/Heaven), to *Word* (guilty conscience/Kingdom), and finally, into *Pure Thought* (instinctive compulsion) to *Return to our Original Creator*. This means that "We must Each Master" <u>Intellect, Emotions, Instincts,</u> and <u>Nature</u> to become **One with God** in *Truth* (corporeal existence), *Law* (spiritual state), *Will* (conceptual word), and *Love* (pure thought).

This means that the "Lord has Sent His Son," <u>Jesus Christ</u> to bring **Humanity Free Redemption** (knowledge) to *Leave the Flesh* (body), **Earn Salvation** (self-awareness), become a *Concept* (blood), obtain **Bonus Rewards** (consciousness), become the *Word* (soul), and finally, **Receive Eternal Freedom** (sentience) to become *Pure Thought* (divinity). We see that this "Journey of Eternal Life" is brought into <u>Reality</u> via **Christ's Crucifixion, Tomb, Resurrection, and Ascension** as **They are Manifested** in **Man's Ability to Learn** *Right from Wrong* (earth) and *Good from Evil* (Heaven). We see that through "Christ's Crucifixion (redemption)," He is Able to **Give Forgiveness**. Then by "His Death in the Tomb (salvation)," <u>He is Able</u> to <u>Give Pardon.</u> By "His Resurrection (rewards)," He is <u>Able</u> to <u>Resurrect the Grave.</u> And finally, by "His Ascension into Heaven," He <u>is Able</u> to <u>Reconcile All Souls</u> *Back to His Father's Love*. This "Set of Divine Blessings" allows the <u>Lost to be Found</u> and *Restored to Their*

Original State (damaged) and then *Returned Back to Their Original Owner* (fined). Through the "Lord's" <u>Thoughts, Words,</u> and <u>Deeds,</u> the **Human Race** can become **Perfect** or **Born-again** in **His Sight** through the **Intercession** of *His Son, Jesus Christ.*

Unfortunately, before a "Born-again Soul" can <u>Attain Personal Perfection in Christ,</u> it must be **Willing** to be **Transformed in Mind** (intellect/flesh), **Heart** (emotions/concept), **Soul** (instincts/word), and **Life-force** (nature/thought) by **Surrendering** into *Correct Beliefs, Dying to Selfishness,* be *True to Oneself* (one image), *Obey Guilty Conscience,* and *Enter Instinctive Compulsion* (embrace fruits). This means that "If a Person's Mind is Converted (intellect)," he will become <u>Wise, Learn to Think,</u> and **One Day, Reach** a **State** of <u>Pure Thought</u> so that his **Inductive and Deductive Logic** will *Correctly Correspond to God's Infinite Truth.* Secondly, if a person's "Heart is Converted (emotions)," he will <u>Love God, God will Love him,</u> and they will <u>Love Each Other</u> so that his **Emotional Balance** will *Correctly Correspond* to *God's Infinite Law.* Thirdly, if a person's "Soul is Converted (instincts)," it will have a strong <u>Devotion to God,</u> then <u>Unite with Him,</u> and <u>Become One</u> in **Truth, Law, Will, and Love** which will *Correctly Correspond to God's Infinite Will.* Finally, if a person's "Life-force is Converted (nature)," he will <u>Commune with God</u> via His **Natural Order, Supernatural Order,** and **Divine Order** which will *Correctly Correspond to God's Infinite Love.*

It should now make sense that each of "God's Children" is really <u>Four Different Individuals,</u> who must both **Grow** (infinite life) and **Mature** (eternal life) into *Perfect Creations of God.* This means that the "Lord God Almighty" <u>Wants Each Person</u> to <u>Exist</u> as an **Innocent Baby, Tough Teenager, Cunning Adult,** and a **Wise Man** to *Defeat Ignorance, Cowardice, Greed,* and *Selfishness.* Thus, a "Person" can hope to <u>Appease God's Wrath</u> for all his **Mistakes, Sins, and Evil Acts** coming from his *Foolish Ignorance, Criminal Behavior, Insane Mind,* and *Evil Nature.* The "Human Race must Die" unto <u>Nothingness</u> and then **God's Son** (Jesus Christ) will become <u>Born-again Mankind</u> (all) in **Flesh** (earth), **Spirit** (Heaven) and **Soul** (Kingdom) to **Appease the Striking Wrath** (murderous hate) of *His Creator God.*

To understand both "God's Great Anger (self-love)" and <u>His</u> equally <u>Awesome Kindness</u> (unselfishness), we must see the **Lord has Sent His Only Begotten Son** to *Give Mankind* a *Door of Reconciliation.* This "Door Operates (death to self)" by <u>Accepting</u> the **Lord's Free Redemption** (worship) when a **Soul** *Hears the Word* (good news/light) or *Follows God's Will* and then being **Able** to **Earn Salvation** (praise) simply by *Believing in that Word* (gospel message/water) or *Believing in God's Truths.* Finally, the "Human Race" is being <u>Given God's Blessings</u> in the **Form** of **Bonus Rewards** (think), **If It** will only *Do God's Word* (doctrinal truths/soil) or *Purchase God's Lands* in *Eternal Service to the Almighty.* In short, each of "God's Children" must see <u>God's Lights Go On</u> (earth), <u>Make God's Waters Flow</u> (Heaven), and <u>Witness God's Soil as It Bears Fruit</u> (Kingdom). These "Three Events" sit at the center of <u>God's Creation</u> as man's **Mind** is *Called into the Light* (wisdom); man's **Heart** is *Enlightened with Water* (courage); and man's **Soul** is *Awakened by the Soil* (generosity). Obviously, "God's Divine Light (self-respect)" allows <u>Humanity</u> to **Follow God's Will** (accomplishments); "God's "Divine Water (social honors)" allows <u>Humanity</u> to **Believe God's**

Truths (perfection); and God's Divine Soil (God's love)" allows Humanity to **Purchase God's Lands** (celebration).

This means that each of "God's Children" can Receive his Own Identity through his **Accomplishments** which *Lead* to his *Personal Self-respect* (pride of accomplishments). Secondly, a "Child can Receive" his Character through his **Perfect Efforts** which **Lead** to **his Social Honors,** *Bestowed* upon him by his *Community* (pride in perfection). Finally, a "Child can Receive" his Personality through his **Day of Celebration** which **Leads** to **his Title of Ownership** given to him by the *Lord God Almighty Himself* (pride of ownership). Through a "Person's Respect (light)," "Honors (water)," and "Titles (soil)," he can Strive to become a Righteous King on *Earth* (citizen), a Holy Priest in *Heaven* (saint), and a Perfect Son within *God's Kingdom* (son). This means that a "King" is worthy to receive a New Body (earth); a "Priest" is worthy to receive Eternal Life (Heaven); and a "Son" is worthy of receiving his own Royal Kingdom (homeland) all in the *Name of Human Perfection* (new nature).

We are all being "Called" to Master the **Twelve Major Institutions of Life**: 1) Self - Baby, 2) King - Child, 3) Government - Adolescent, 4) Earth - Teenager, 5) Society - Young Adult, 6) Priest - Adult, 7) Church - Wise Man, 8) Heaven - Free Man, 9) God - Servanthood, 10) Son - Slave, 11) Home - Son of Man, and 12) Kingdom - Son of God. Through these "Twelve Stages of Life," we can Journey from **Nothing** (death) to **All** (life) within **Ourselves**, in the **World**, in the **Church,** and within **God Himself** by **Passing** through the *Purification* (being saved), *Transformation* (saving self), and *Conversion* (saving others) *Experiences*.

The following tabular information indicates the "Twelve Major Institutions of Life" Used in the Purification of the Flesh (God becomes Man), Transformation of the Spirit (Man becomes God), and Conversion of the Soul (God and Man become One) via the **Lord's Physical** (earth), **Spiritual** (Heaven), and **Mystical** (Kingdom) *Dimensions of Life*.

Twelve Major Institutions of Life
(self/king/government/earth - - - society/priest/church/Heaven - - - God/Son/home/kingdom)

Physical World (earth)

1. *Self* becomes *King* becomes *Government* becomes *Earth* - God becomes Man
   - Self is Mind (1) - Intellect: Deny Intellect
   - King is Heart (2) - Emotions: Abandon Feelings   **Purification**
   - Government is Soul (3) - Instincts: Submit Free Will   •Thinking of Mind
   - Earth is Life-force (4) - Nature: Dying to Self
     (being saved/sin-nature - learn right from wrong:
     righteousness = new body [save sinners])

Spiritual Church (Heaven)

2. *Society* becomes *Priest* becomes *Church* becomes *Heaven* - Man becomes God (life)
   - Society is Mind (5) - Intellect: Calling

- Priest is Heart (6) - Emotions: Enlightenment   **Transformation**
- Church is Soul (7) - Instincts: Awakening   •Understanding of Heart
- Heaven is Life-force (8) - Nature: Indwelling

(saving self/worldly temptations - learn good from evil: holiness = eternal life [create saints])

Mystical   3. ***God* becomes *Son* becomes *Home* becomes *Kingdom* - God and Man**

God   **become One** (free)

(Kingdom)
- God is Mind (9) - Intellect: New Body
- Son is Heart (10) - Emotions: Eternal Life   **Conversion**
- Home is Soul (11) - Instincts: Royal Kingdom   • Will of the Soul
- Kingdom is Life-force (12) - Nature: Personal Freedom

(saving others/demonic possession - learn God's Will/man's will:

perfection = Kingdom [serve God])

This illustration shows that in the "Physical World (thinking of the mind)," a New-born Baby can **Be Saved** from his **Own Sin-nature** (sin) through the **Purification of his Flesh** (self-rule) to allow him to **Grow** from *Self* (self-control), into a *King* (supervisor), into a *Government* (politician), and finally, into the *Whole Earth* (global rule). Secondly, in the "Spiritual Church (understanding of heart)," a Teenager can **Save himself** from **Worldly Temptations** (evil) through the **Transformation of his Spirit** (social rule) to allow him to **Mature** from *Society* (leadership), into a *Priest* (holy man), into a *Church* (management), and finally, into *Heavenly Paradise* (sacred rule). Finally, in the "Mystical Kingdom (will of the soul)," an Adult Soul can **Save Others** from **Demonic Possession** (death) through the **Conversion of his Soul** (divine rule) to allow him to be **Set Free** as *God* (serenity), into a *Son* (courage), into a *Home* (wisdom), and finally into a *Royal Kingdom* (servant). This means that within the "Divinity of God," a Mature Wise Man can **Save God** from **His Divine Perfection** (robot) by **Offering Him** his **Kingship of Earth, Priesthood of Heaven, Sonship of Kingdom** and his **Servanthood of God** to become *God's Friend* (mind), *Companion* (heart), and then enter *God's Oneness* (soul).

Through this "Journey of Life," a Person can Enter the "Christmas Celebration" as God becomes a Man (baby) in *Physical Form* (Earth); in the "Easter Celebration," a Man becomes God (teenager) in *Spiritual Form* (Heaven); and finally, in the "Halloween Celebration," God and Man become One (adulthood) in *Mystical Form* (Kingdom). During "God's Independence Celebration," God and Man are Set Free (wise man) in **Divine Form** (God) to go their **Separate Ways** to forever *Help Build the Kingdom of God*. Yes! The "Human Race" has had to begin the Life-experience as an **Animal in a Jungle** (earth), become an **Obedient Robot of Prayer** (Heaven), and then **Learn** to **Think for himself** as a *Son of God* (Kingdom) *All to Win the Favor of its Creator God*.

We see that the "Lord God Almighty" is such an awesome Creator. He has **Thought** of **What** it would be like to **Live as an Animal** and/or to **Live as a Perfect Robot,** and then just **How** to **Blend Imperfection** (man) with **Perfection** (robot) to bring forth a most *Righteous/ Holy Human being* (God/Man). The idea here is that as an "Animal People," they are <u>Prone</u> to <u>Lying, Cheating, and Stealing</u> and when **Angered** become **Cruel Murderers** **Unworthy** of **Any Kind** of *Social Interaction* and **Unworthy** of *God's Blessing of Life*. In contrast, as a "Robot People," they are <u>Prone to Resisting</u> **Any Form** of **Change** or **Growth** until **They** have **No Life's Work** or even **Stated Purpose** until the **Meaning of Life Takes** on its **Own Eternal Status Quo** of *Rest in Peace or Death*. We see that "If We Correctly Blend" the <u>Animal Nature of Pleasure</u> (all work) with the <u>Robot Nature of Peace</u> (all prayer), we can **Come Up** with a **New Creation,** where *Work and Play become One* and *Everyone will have Lots of Fun*.

Now, we can understand that "God Wants to become Man (Christmas/animal)," and "Man Wants to become God (Easter/robot)" and at the <u>End of Time,</u> we see *God and Man become One* (Halloween). This "Blending Process" through the <u>New Nature of Jesus Christ</u> has been **Made Perfect** by **Blending** the **Evil of Man** with the **Holiness of God** on **Mount Calvary** to <u>Balance</u> the *Animal of Pleasure* (Man) with the *Robot of Peace* (God). With this "New Mystical Nature," the <u>God/Man Creation</u> can **Face the Unknown** with both **Courage** and **Confidence** as **Nothing in Life** seems too **Overwhelming** or too **Impossible** for the *Prepared Mind*. This "Invincible Soldier of God" is <u>Obligated to Serve</u> by **Fulfilling** both **God's Destiny** (majority opinion) and **Man's Free Will** (minority opinion) to put **All God's Children** on the **Paths of Righteousness, Holiness, and Perfection** to *Journey to the House of God*. Once a "Person Attains Perfection," he can then <u>Control</u> the **Disruptive Elements of Life** and **Guide Lost Fools** (defeat anarchy) into **Social Order** so that the **Human Race** will show **No Deviation** from the *Art of Correct Living*. We see that the "Lord God Almighty" was <u>Not Creating a Vacation,</u> but an <u>Eternal Life,</u> because a **Temporary Joy** seeks **Discovery** (work), **Executing Issues** (challenge), and **Humor** (fun/adventure), and then becomes *Infinitely Bored*. Yet, the "Values of Eternal Life" <u>Journey</u> through **Life** (thrill of victory), **Death** (agony of defeat), and **Re-birth** (wonderment) to make the **Life-experience** become **Anew each Day** and offer a **New Challenge, New Adventure,** and **New Experience/Fun** of *Infinite Love* continually, thereby *Making a Person Truly Happy*.

This "Need to Become Happy" for <u>God, Angels, and Men</u> **Drives** the **Forces of Life** as **They Strive** to **Teach God's Creation** *Right from Wrong* (righteousness), *Good from Evil* (holiness), *and God's Will from man's will* (perfection). We see that to "Unite the Creations" of <u>Earth</u> (man), <u>Heaven</u> (Angels), and the <u>Kingdom</u> (God), it was necessary to **Defile** the **Earth with Sin, Heaven with Evil,** and the **Kingdom with Death,** and then, **Create Three Sets of People** (Jews/Christians/Pagans) to *Convert Imperfection into Perfection*. This "Process" of <u>Changing Nothing</u> into <u>Everything</u> **Makes Up God's Grand Design,** where the *Worthless* later becomes *Priceless before God*. We see that the "Worthless Jewish People" are initially <u>Chosen</u> to **Take-on All Sin** (ignorance) and then **Convert Sin** into **Righteous Living** (citizenship) through *Their Obedience to God's Law* (change nature). Secondly, the "Worthless Christian People" are <u>Chosen</u> to **Take-on All Evil** (cowardice) and then **Convert Evil** into **Holy Living** (sainthood) through *Their Faith in God's Love* (wash away sin). Finally, the "Worthless Pagan People" are <u>Chosen</u> to **Take-on All Death** (greed) and then **Convert Death** into **Perfect Living** (sonship) through *Their Knowledge of Nature's Truths* (think for self).

By "Mastering" Earth, Heaven and the Kingdom, **Men, Angels, and God** can become **One People** (earth) within **One Land** (Heaven) in **Service** to **One Divine God** (One God/Kingdom), thereby bringing forth *Physical Righteousness, Spiritual Holiness, and Mystical Perfection to One and All*. This means that "God's Curse of Ignorance (sin)" Fell upon the Jewish People as **They Falsely Believed the Lie** that They **Knew All Things** and had **Fulfilled God's Law** (superiority), thereby *Making Themselves Righteous before God* (kings). Secondly, came "God's Curse of Cowardice (evil)" which Fell upon the Christian People as **They Falsely Believed the Lie** that They had **Mastered Life** and **Fulfilled Man's Faith** (humility), thereby *Making Themselves Holy before God* (priests). Finally, came "God's Curse of Greed (death)" which Fell upon the Pagan People as **They Falsely Believed the Lie** that **They** had **Mastered All They Survey** and **Fulfilled Their Own Destiny** (perfection), thereby *Making Themselves Perfect before God* (sons). We see that this "Failure" of the Jews, Christians, and Pagans brings forth the **Three Advents of Christ Who Transforms Failure into Success** by *Removing Ignorance, Cowardice, and Greed*.

The following tabular information indicates that the "Jewish People" have been Chosen to *Take-on Sin* (ignorance); the "Christian People" have been Chosen to *Take-on Evil* (cowardice); and the "Pagan People" have been Chosen to *Take-on Death* (greed):

Jews Choose Sin, Christians Choose Evil, Pagans
Choose Death to be Rewarded with New-life
(Jews purify mind/one man; Christians
purify heart/few men; and Pagans purify soul/all men)

Purify   1. **Jewish People** - Chosen to Become Sin: Honored with Righteousness...
Mind   Knowledge
(one man)
- Enemy - World System/Lucifer's Test: Baby Tries to Defeat an Immovable Force
- Baby - Handicap System: Everyone Wins (thrill of victory)
- Ignorance Changed to Wisdom - New Mind: Man's Intellect (know God)

Life
- Nobleman/Wealth Merchants - God's Chosen People (kingship)
- Called and Refused to Come - Too Important (negative)
- Messiah Sent to Save Jews - Taught Right from Wrong (being saved)
- Seven Stars - Seven Guardian Angels: Obedience to Law (wisdom)

Ignorance
(Messiah)
- Holy of Holies - Ark of Covenant: Seven Drops of Blood
- Righteous Citizen on Earth (title) - *Free New Body* (ethics)
- See Limitations - Try Harder to Repent (challenge): New Flesh

(Messiah - change nature: fight world system [trying] = Heaven on Earth)

Purify   2. **Christian People** - Chosen to Become Evil: Honored with Holiness...
Heart   Self-awareness
(few men)
- Enemy - Supernatural Forces/God's Judgment: Teenager Quits Fighting

Unstoppable Force

	• Teenager - Curve System: 1st to Quit Gets Highest Score (agony of defeat)
	• Cowardice Changed to Courage - New Heart: God's Emotions (love God)
	• The Common Man/broken - Man's Chosen People (priesthood)
Host	• Called and Came Running - Honored to be Invited (positive)
	• Church Sent to Save Christians - Taught Good and Evil (save self)
	• Seven Candlesticks - Seven Churches: Love of the Faith (courage)
Cowardice	• Holy Place - Golden Altar of Incense: Seven Sacraments
(church)	• Holy Saints in Heaven (title) - *Earned Eternal Life* (morals)
	• See Potential - <u>Quit-in-defeat</u> (adventure) or Surrender: New Spirit

(Church - wash away sin: stop fighting God [defeat] = Paradise in Heaven)

Purify	3. **Pagan People** - <u>Chosen to Become Death:</u> Honored with Perfection...
Soul	Consciousness
(all men)	• Enemy - Selfish Nature/Self-evaluation: Adult Defeats Himself/Blended Force
	• Adult - Pass/Fail System: Either "Yes" or "No" (fulfillment)
	• Greed Changed to Generosity - New Soul: God/Man Instincts (serve God)
	• The Foreigner/Stranger - Self-righteous People (sonship)
Grave	• Called and Failed to Understand - Lost Fool (neutral)
	• The World Sent to Save Pagan - Taught God's Will/man's will (saving others)
	• Seven Temple Gates - Seven Virtues: Awaken to Know (generosity)
Greed (world)	• Outer Court - Brazen Altar of Sacrifice: Seven Blessings
	• Perfect Sons in Kingdom (title) - *Rewarded Royal Kingdom* (perfection)
	• See Self-worth - Master Oneself: New Soul

(World - think for self: never stop fighting self [winning] = Own Royal Kingdom/freedom)

This illustration shows that through "Ignorance (sin)," "Cowardice (evil)," and "Greed (death)," the <u>Mind, Heart, and Soul</u> are to be **Purified** and **Transformed** into <u>**Wisdom, Courage,** and **Generosity**</u> through *Jewish Kingship, Christian Priesthood,* and *Pagan Sonship*. The theme here is that the "Jews (mind)" represent <u>Trying</u> to **Fight** (never-quit) the **World System** (1st enemy/baby) *Forever.* The "Christians (heart)" represent <u>Surrendering</u> to **God's Will** (2nd enemy/teenager) in *Defeat* (instantly quit). The "Pagans (soul)" represent <u>Fighting **Oneself**</u> (3rd enemy/adult) and *Winning*. In short, the "King Fights Forever (baby mind)," the "Priest Surrenders to God (teenage heart)," while the "Son Defeats Himself (adult soul)." This <u>Pattern of Life</u> **Sets Mankind Free** from *Sin, Evil, and Death*. Recall the "Lord's Parable" of a <u>Great King</u> who had a **Banquet** and **Invited** the **Richest of the Rich** and **They Refused to Come;** so he **Invited** the *Commoners from his City* (poor). Unfortunately, there were "Not Enough Local Citizens" so the <u>King Opened the Doors</u> to **Everyone Near and Far**, until **His Banquet Hall was Full** of **Joyful Celebrants**. Then the **King Inspected** the **Dress Code** and

Rejected Unwelcomed Guests. The "Moral of this Story" is that <u>If You are Lucky Enough</u> to be **Invited** to **God's Eternal Banquet,** at **Least Take the Time** to <u>**Buy the Right Clothes**</u> (holiness) and be *Ready to Make a Good Appearance*.

The idea here is that the "Jews Represent" the <u>Rich Royalty;</u> the "Christians Represent" the <u>Poor Local Citizenry;</u> and the "Pagans" represent the <u>Foreigners from Afar,</u> who are *Lucky to be so Honored by the King*. This means that through "God's Son" <u>Jesus Christ</u> and **His Three Miraculous Advents,** the **Jews/citizens** would be *Saved* (priest on donkey/being saved); the **Christians/saints** would be *Saved* (thief in night/save self); and finally, the **Pagans/sons** would be *Saved* (judge on cloud/save others). Obviously, when "Jesus Christ Comes," <u>He will Teach</u> the **Jews Right from Wrong** (intellect) to be *Saved from Ignorance*; then <u>He will Teach</u> the **Christians Good from Evil** (emotions)to *Save Themselves from Cowardice*. Finally, "God's Son will Come" to <u>Teach</u> the **Pagan People God's Will from man's will** (instincts) to have the <u>**Ability**</u> to *Save Others from Their Own Greedy Sin-natures*. Yes! "Ignorance," "Cowardice," and "Greed" are the <u>Enemies of Man</u> and he must **Change Ignorance** to *Wisdom* (handicap system), **Cowardice** to *Courage* (curve system), and **Greed** to *Generosity* (pass/fail system) *Forever*. By "Mastering" the <u>World,</u> the <u>Church,</u> and the <u>Home,</u> a **Person** can **Become Wise, Brave, and Charitable** to his **Fellowmen** and bring forth a **New Age of Peace,** where <u>Babies</u> are *Given a Handicap* (faith), <u>**Teenagers**</u> are *Graded on a Curve* (hope), and <u>**Adults**</u> either *Pass or Fail in Life* (charity). This means that a "Happy Home" <u>Gives Each Child</u> his **Own Thrill of Victory** and **Makes him a Winner in Life,** showing him that simply with his <u>**Wise Mind,**</u> he can *Master All Things Great and Small*. Secondly, a "Devout Church" <u>Teaches Each Teenager</u> the **Agony of Defeat** and **Makes him a Loser in Life,** but a **Winner before God** (death/bear fruit), thereby showing him that simply with his **Loving Heart,** he can *Master All Things Great and Small*. Finally, a "Just Government" <u>Offers Each Adult</u> both **Failure and Success** and **Makes him Productive in Life, showing** him that simply with an <u>**Instinctive Soul,**</u> he can *Master All Things Great and Small*.

<u>Jewish People/citizens</u> - Seven Stars (purify grave)

In the "Bible," the <u>Jewish People</u> are **Referred** to as the <u>**Seven Stars**</u> (Archangels) or *Chosen People*, the <u>Christian People</u> as the **Seven Candlesticks/Seven Churches** (sacraments) or *Gentile People*, and the <u>Pagan People</u> as the <u>**Seven Temple Gates**</u> (blessings) or *Infidel People*, **Who** have **Failed to Believe** in **God, His Son,** or even **Christ's Church** so <u>**They**</u> are to be *Called Last*. Obviously, the "Pagan Fools (master self)" are to be the <u>Last,</u> but **One Day,** will be **First** as **They** will be <u>**Honored by God**</u> to be the *Lord's Harvesters of Lost Souls* (saving others). In contrast, we see that the "Jewish People" were <u>First, yet, shall be Last</u> as **They are Destined to Fight the World System** in a **Hopeless Struggle** <u>Against Impossible Odds</u> as *They Try and Try Again, and again forever*. Now, imagine the "Jewish People (master government)" or <u>Seven Stars</u> as being the **Holy of Holies,** represented by the **Ark of the Covenant** where the **High Priest** brings <u>**Seven Drops of Blood**</u> to be **Placed on the Mercy Seat** (change nature). This "Act of Repentance" shows that the <u>Angelic Realm</u> (adults) is **Honoring God's Seven-fold Spirits** by **Covering Its Failures** with the **Divine Blood** of **Try Again and Again** until **It Gets It Right** as *Practice Makes Perfect*.

Christian People/saints - Seven Candlesticks (purify host)
We see the "Christian People (master church)" or Seven Candlesticks to be the **Holy Place** represented by the **Golden Altar of Incense**, where the **Priest** brings **God's Sacraments of Submission** as *Dying to Self Prayers* (wash away sin). This "Act of Prostration" shows that the Communion of Saints (teenagers) is **Honoring God's Seven-fold Spirits** by **Giving All to God** and by becoming **Nothing** to **Make God Everything** until *Nothing and All are One*. The "Job of the Christian People" is to Create a **Roman Priesthood** in the **Holy City of Rome** as **They** are **Given 1,000 Years** to **Convert the Pagan World** to **God's True Faith** (host) which is **Called** the *Sealing of Christ's Saints* (Thief in the Night).

Pagan People/sons - Seven Temple Gates (purify life)
We see the "Pagan People (master home)" or Seven Temple Gates being the **Outer Court** represented by the **Brazen Altar of Sacrifice**, where the **Head Deacon** brings **God's Blessings of Self-realization** to **Allow a Person** to *Think for himself* (master self). This "Act of Awakening" shows that the Lost of the World (babies) now **Honor God's Seven-fold Spirits** by becoming **Everything** in **Their Own Eyes** (awakening) as **They Master Ignorance, Cowardice, Greed,** and **Selfishness,** and *Find Their Own Identity* (perfect self). We can now "Thank" the Jews, Christians, and Pagans for **Revealing God's** future **Government, Church, and Home** as **They Call All Humanity** to *Try, to Quit,* and to *Master Themselves Forever*. The point here is that "If a Person" Never-quits Trying, he can **Attain a Place** in the **World System** (government), based on **Passing All his Tests** and **Earning** the necessary **Credentials** to *Establish himself in Life*. Secondly, "If a Person" Surrenders to God (quits), he can **Attain a Place** in the **Royal Household of God** (church), based on **Believing God's Truths** and being **Born-again** into the *Divine Judgment of God*. Finally, "If a Person" Defeats his Own Selfishness (overcomes), he can **Attain a Place** within his **Own Nature** (home) based on **Understanding his Own Instincts** and becoming **Mature** (perfect) in his *Own Self-evaluation*.

1. **Defeat Ignorance** - Face Lucifer's Test: Never-quit Trying… Master the World System
   • Honor Spirit - Becoming Righteous via Intellect: Thanking God with Labor (yearly)
2. **Defeat Cowardice** - Face God's Judgment: Surrender to God…Master the Holy Church
   • Honor Son - Becoming Holy via Emotions: Praising God with Wealth (weekly)
3. **Defeat Greed** - Face Own Self-evaluation: Defeat Selfishness…Master Self
   • Honor Father - Becoming Perfect via Instincts: Worshiping God with Own Life (daily)

In other words, to "Try" is to Face Challenge; to "Quit" is to Experience Adventure; and to "Defeat Oneself" is to have a Lifetime of Rollicking Fun which **Leads to Meeting** *God, Angels, Men, and Nature Face-to-face*. Obviously, to "Live in a World" of Challenge, Adventure, and Fun Forever is to **Have It All**. To **Add Becoming One with**

God is to <u>**Master Every Aspect**</u> of *Peace, Joy, and Happiness to the Fullest*. Now, imagine "Living in a World" where <u>All Things have been Said,</u> and then the **Human Race** has **Fallen Silent** because there is **Only One Truth** and **Change has been Outlawed,** because the **Forefathers have Found** the <u>**Meaning of Life**</u> and *It has become Sacred in Their Sight*. This idea of a "Stagnant Society" would <u>Cheapen Life</u> a little more each day until **All Things would be Routine** and **Repetitious**, thereby making the **Life-experience** *Futile, Meaningless, and Unendurable for Everyone*. Unfortunately, the "Life-experience" is to be <u>Vital, Rich, and Enjoyable</u> to the point of **Leaping from One's Bed** to **Meet** the **New** and **Exciting Day** with a **<u>Great Enthusiasm</u>** for the coming *Set* of *New Challenges, Adventures, and Great Fun*. This type of "Lifestyle" can only come forth when the <u>Human Race Gets</u> its **New Nature** and when the **Lord God Almighty** becomes **Human** so that the **<u>Light of Eternal Peace, Joy, and Happiness</u>** (Christmas morning) will spring forth for *Every Born-again Child of God*.

Via this "Treasure of Life Moment," the <u>Whole Human Race</u> is **Seeking** its **Need** to become **<u>Righteous</u>** through *Labor* (kingship), to become **<u>Holy</u>** through *Wealth* (priesthood), and finally, to become **<u>Perfect</u>** through *Life* (sonship). The idea here is to see that "If a Person (1st advent/donkey)" is willing to <u>Give his Life</u> (daily), he can **Worship God** (man's will in death/God's will in life) and **Enter God's Kingdom** through the *Lord's Pathway of Perfection* (truth, law, and will). Secondly, "If a Person (2nd advent/thief)" is willing only to <u>Give his Wealth</u> (Sunday), he can **Praise God** (man's evil in life/God's good in death) and **Enter God's Heavenly Realm** through the *Lord's Pathway of Holiness* (repentance, prayers, and works). Finally, "If a Person (3rd advent/cloud)" is willing to reluctantly <u>Give his Labors</u> (Easter), he can **Thank God** (man's wrong in life/God's right in death) and **Enter God's Earthly Paradise** through the *Lord's Pathway of Righteousness* (morals, ethics, and fairness). This means that a "Lost Soul" must first enter <u>Moses' Eastern Gate</u> as a **Sinner**, then be invited into the **Outer Court** as a *Righteous Citizen*. Next, a person takes his "Levitical Rites (vows)" and becomes a <u>Priest</u> to enter the **Holy Place** as a *Holy Saint*, then takes his "Sonship Training (Calvary)" to become a <u>Son of God</u> and enter the **Holy of Holies** as *God's Messiah*. Now, "If a Person" has <u>Passed Through</u> the <u>Sanctity</u> of the **Eastern Gate** (sinner), **Outer Court** (citizen), **Holy Place** (priest), and **Holy of Holies** (Messiah), then he has become **Worthy of God's Personal Friendship** by *Placing Seven-drops of Blood upon His Mercy Seat*.

The following tabular information indicates that a "Person" <u>Cannot</u> simply **Walk up to God** and introduce himself as the **Lord's Friend**; he must first come as *God's Son* (Messiah/purify life), as a *Holy Saint* (Church/purify host), then as a *Righteous Citizen* (world/purify grave), and finally, **God** will **Come to a Lost Soul** (chosen) as his *Loyal Friend*:

**Coming to God as the Messiah, Church, and World;
then God Comes to Man as a Loyal Friend**
(Messiah comes in Perfection, Church in Holiness,
World in Righteousness, and God as a Friend)

Give Life (worship)	1. **Messiah** - Travel to God via Perfection: God Meets the Jews…Sentience • Divine Dimension of Life - God's Divine Court of Law: See Nature (thinking) • Truth – Sonship • Law - Priesthood **Holy of Holies** (1st advent) • Will - Kingship

(wise man - learn man's will in life: learn God's Will in death = see perfection/daily)

Give Wealth (praise)	2. **Church** - Travel to God via Holiness: Moses Meets the Jews… Consciousness • Mystical Dimension of Life - God's Royal Court of Law: See Personality (chastity) • Repentance – Friendship • Prayers - Companionship **Holy Place** (2nd advent) • Works - Oneness

(adult - learn evil in life: learn good in death = see self-worth/weekly/Sunday)

Give Labors (thanks)	3. **World** - <u>Travel to God via Righteousness:</u> Aaron Meets Jews…Self-awareness • Spiritual Dimension of Life - God's Temple Court of Law: See Character (poverty) • Morals – Neighbor • Ethics - Acquaintance **Outer Court** (3rd advent) • Fairness - Stranger

(teenager - learn wrong in life: learn right in death = see potential/yearly/Easter)

- -

Give All (gift)	4. **God** - <u>Travel to Man via Friendliness:</u> Golden Calf Meets Jews…Knowledge • Physical Dimension of Life - God's Celestial Court of Law: See Identity (obedience) • Know God – Wisdom • Love God - Courage **Mercy Seat** (judgment) • Serve God - Generosity

(baby - learn illusion in life: learn reality in death = see limitations/moment)

This illustration shows that the whole "Human Race" is being asked to <u>Fulfill the Mosaic Tabernacle</u> at some **Stage of Growth** either **as Baby, Teenager, Adult, or Wise Man**; but each of **God's Children** is being *Called to Divine Maturity in Some Form*. This brings up the "Problem of a Two-Truth System," where we are either <u>Growing-up</u> in **Illusion** (babyhood) or we are <u>Maturing</u> in **Reality** (adulthood). In either case, a *Person must Experience Change*. The question is: is a "Person" facing God's <u>Loving Kindness</u> as a *Baby* (illusion) or is he facing God's <u>Verbal Rage</u> as an *Adult* (reality)? The answer is that "If a Person Surrenders his Life" to <u>God,</u> he is **Facing God's Anger**; yet, he is still within the **Lord's Illusion** because he has **Left his Flesh** (intellect) and has *Entered his Spirit* (emotions). This "Contradiction" should help us see that the <u>Physical Nature</u> is an **Illusion** and the <u>Spiritual Nature</u> is **Reality**; yet, within **Christ,** these *Two Forces Reverse* (nothing/all).

To "Understand" the <u>Illusion/Reality Concept</u>, imagine that **God's Holy Spirit** is **Placed** within **Reality** (Heaven) to *Bless God's Children*; while **God's Evil Spirit** is **Placed** within an **Illusion** (earth) to *Teach God's Children*. Now, a "Person" can comprehend the logic of a Two-Truth System, where **One Truth** is *Centered on Life* (all/Heaven/God/God's Son) and the **Other Truth** is *Centered on Death* (nothing/earth/man/Mary's Son). Through this "Life and Death Logic," our Creator creates a **Handicap System** for **Babies** versus a **Scratch System** for **Adults** to create a little *Divine Equitable Competition* for *Handicapped Children*. This leads us to why a "Person" has to be a Perfect Son of God or **Messiah** to **Meet his Creator** within the *Divine Dimension of Life*. Obviously, with this "Logic," the Wise Man must **Learn How to Think** as *Witnessed by Society*; the Adult must become **Chastised** before his *Master*; the Teenager must become **Humble** (poor) before his *Peers;* and the Baby must become **Obedient** to his *Parents*. At each "Stage of Growth," a person is Gaining a little more insight into his own **Perfection** (Messiah), **Self-worth** (Church), **Potential** (world), and **Limitations** (self/God) as they reflect his *Identity, Character, Personality, and Nature before God*. Out of one's "Aptitude for Service" based on his Depth of Focus (instincts), God can effectively **Measure** a **Child's Eternal Service** to *Nature, Men, Angels, and God*.

The "Bible" is teaching us that this Eternal Service (saving souls) is only through **Abel's Blood Sacrifice** (lamb) which was able to **Appease God's Anger** against the **Crimes of Adam and Eve** when they **Ate** the Lord's *Forbidden Fruit* (stolen knowledge). This "Crime" created **Three Curses** upon **Our First Parents**: 1) Curse of Defiance (face Lucifer's Test) - Stealing Fruit: Demonic Possession (blasphemy) = Excommunication, 2) Curse of Deception (face God's Judgment) - Hiding from God: Worldly Temptations (sorcery) = Banished, and 3) Curse of Deceit (face self-evaluation) - Lying to God: Sin-nature (sedition) = Outcast.

This meant that to "Remove These Curses," Mankind must **Repent through Baptism** (capital sin) to **Remove Defiance** and overcome *Demonic Possession* (death); then **Pray through Confession** (mortal sin) to **Remove Deception** and overcome *Worldly Temptations* (evil); and finally, "Do Good Works" through Communion (venial sin) to **Remove Deceit** and overcome its own **Sin-nature** to be *Set Free* from *Sin* (contract adoption)**,** *Evil* (blood birth), and *Death* (spirit resurrection). Now, we can see that the "Job of the Jewish People (earth/law)"was to Appease God's Anger by offering their **Perfect Lamb Sacrifice** (Jesus Christ/blood) to *Seal the Gates of Hell* (remove faults/save sinners). Secondly, the "Job of the Christian People (Heaven/faith)" is to Thank God for His Mercy by offering their **Perfect Prayer of Sacrifice** (Christ Jesus/prayer) to *Open the Gates of Heaven* (gain virtues/create saints).

This means that the "Jews" represent God's New Physical Nature as **God becomes a Man** (Christmas) and brings forth **Man's New Body** to create *Heaven on Earth*; while the "Christians" represent God's New Spirit Nature as **Man becomes God** (Easter) and brings forth **God's Eternal Life** to create *Paradise in Heaven*. In this way, "God is Giving Man" all the Eternal Time (name) he will *Ever Want*; while "Man is Giving God" all the Perfect Bodies/Babies (virginity) that **God, Angels, and/or Men** will *Ever Need*. Through this "Exchange of Gifts" between God and Man, we see the importance of **Jesus Christ** (Messiah) as He comes to **Remove Sin** (1st advent/Calvary/1st war of wills), **Remove Evil** (2nd advent/Tribulation/2nd war of beliefs), and finally, to **Remove Death** (3rd advent/Judgment/3rd war of lands) to

Set All Men Free. The shock associated with the "Creation" of both the <u>Jewish People</u> (flesh/earth) and the <u>Christian People</u> (spirit/Heaven) comes with realizing that neither the **Mosaic Law** (eye for an eye/law), or the **Catholic Church** (turn other cheek/faith)/**Canon Law)** has **Worked** as they were **Sent to Curse** all the world's *Foolish Hypocrites unto Oblivion*. Note that both the "Jews" and the "Christians" began their <u>Struggle for Perfection</u> with **Superhuman Undaunted Courage**; yet, as time went by, they became more and more **Corrupt** until they *Stunk with Pure Evil*.

We can now comprehend the "Essence of God" through the Lord's <u>Seven-fold Spirits</u> as they guide the **Human Race** from its **First State of Nothingness** to its **Final Perfection in All** by fulfilling God's *Seven-levels of Transformation*. Recall that the "Human Race" is striving to obtain a <u>New Body</u> (three seats), <u>Eternal Life</u> (three seats), and its <u>Own Kingdom</u> (three seats) all in the name of fulfilling God's *Three Natures* (physical), *Three Persons* (spiritual), and *Trinity* (mystical). Obviously, the Lord is manifesting His "Life-force" on <u>Earth</u>, in <u>Heaven,</u> and within <u>His Kingdom</u> to allow the **Human Race** to live within the *Eternal Father, Son of God,* and *Holy Spirit*. It is important to see that "Life on Earth" is about obtaining <u>Three Bodies</u> comprised of a **Mind** or *Transfigured Body* (earth), a **Heart** or *Glorified Body* (Heaven), and finally, a **Soul** or *Mystical Body* (Kingdom). Secondly, "Life in Heaven (church)" is about obtaining <u>Three Eternal Lives</u> on **Earth** (king), in **Heaven** (priest), and within God's **Kingdom** (son) to give each of **God's Saints** a *Physical* (Heaven on Earth), *Spiritual* (Paradise in Heaven), and *Mystical Existence* (Kingdom of Glory). Finally, "Life in God's Kingdom" is about obtaining <u>Man's Kingship</u> (celestial court), an <u>Angelic Priesthood</u> (temple court), and a <u>Divine Sonship</u> (royal court) before God to become **Worthy** of one's own *Personal Freedom* (physical/natures/flag), *Social Liberty* (spiritual/persons/ Lady), and *Divine Independence* (mystical/trinity/declaration) before *God*. This means that each of "God's Children" must <u>Master</u> the entire **Life-experience** to prove himself in every way to obtain the **Honors** (one power), **Respect** (two powers), and **Blessings** (three powers) of *God* as a salute for a *Job Well-done*.

The following tabular information indicates that the "Three" Natures, Persons and <u>Trinity</u> of **God** both **Govern and Rule** the entire **Creation** of *Physical Earth* (universe), *Spiritual Heaven* (angelic realm), and God's *Kingdom of Glory* (divinity):

God's Seven-fold Spirits Rule and Govern
All Physical, Spiritual, and Mystical Things
(Eternal Father's Natures, Son of God's Persons, and the Holy Spirit's Trinity)

<u>Seven-fold Spirits</u>
1. <u>Eternal Father</u> - 1st Nature: Worship (beliefs)
   - Venial Sin - Daily Forgiveness: Pay by Giving Life
   - Get Transfigured Body - *New Mind* (intellect on earth)
2. <u>Son of God</u> - 2nd Nature: Praise (faith)   One Power - God's Name
   - Mortal Sin - Weekly Forgiveness: Pay
     by <u>Giving Wealth</u>
                                             • Master Earth - Twelve Levels
   - Get Glorified Body - *New Heart* (emotion in Heaven)   (new body)

3. <u>Spirit of God</u> - 3rd Person: Thanksgiving (knowing)   Seven Lampstands
   - Capital Sin - Yearly Forgiveness: Pay by Giving Labors
   - Get Mystical Body - *New Soul* (instincts in Kingdom)
                    (master earth - physical existence: learn right/wrong =
                            Righteous Citizen + God's Name)

---

4. <u>Father/Son</u> - 1st Person: Surrender (repentance)
   - Remove Ignorance - Gain Wisdom: Offer Repentance
   - Free *Title Deed to Earth* - Physical Life
5. <u>Father/Spirit</u> - 2nd Person: Conversion (prayers)   Two Powers - God's Virginity
   - Remove Cowardice - Gain Courage: Offer Prayers   • Master Heaven - Nine Levels
   - Earn *Title Deed to Heaven* - Spiritual Life   (eternal life)
6. <u>Son/Spirit</u> - 3rd Person: Reconciliation (works)   Seven Stars
   - Remove Greed - Gain Generosity: Offer Works
   - Rewarded with *Title Deed to Kingdom* - Mystical Life
   (master Heaven - spiritual existence: learn good/evil = Holy Saint + God's Wealth)

---

7. <u>Father/Son/Spirit</u> - Trinity: Righteous/Holy/Perfect (servanthood)
   - Gain Kingship, Priesthood, and Sonship -
     Know/Love/Serve God   Three Powers - God's Union
   - Gift of *Beatific Vision* - Divine Life   • Master Kingdom - Seven Levels
   - Righteous Kingship   (kingdom)
   - Holy Priesthood   Seven Archangels
   - Perfect Sonship
                    (master Kingdom - mystical existence: learn
                    God's/man's wills = Perfect Son + God's Love)

This illustration shows that the "Eternal Father" is <u>Guiding</u> the <u>Human Race</u> with the **Light of the Sun** or the **<u>Candlestick</u>** which shows the clear *Sight of Righteousness*; the "Son of God" is <u>Guiding</u> the <u>Angelic Realm</u> with the **Light of the Stars** of *Holy Vision*. Finally, the "Holy Spirit" is <u>Guiding Divinity</u> with the **Light of the Archangels** or **Shekinah Glory, <u>Giving All Creation</u>** the *Sight of Perfection*. Recall the "Three Rooms" within the <u>Mosaic Tabernacle</u> where each **Room is Lighted** with **<u>Different Forms of Light</u>** from the *Outer Court's Sunlight* (earth), the *Holy Place's Candlestick* (Heaven), and the *Holy of Holies' Shekinah Glory* (Kingdom/mercy seat). With this symbolism of "Seeing Physically (sunlight)," "Spiritually (starlight)," and "Mystically (Shekinah glory)," <u>Each of God's Children</u> could **Demonstrate** his **Level of Vision,** showing he **Sees God's Truth** by *Seeing God's Light of Perfection* (lamps/stars/angels). The idea here is to see that "God is Writing" <u>His Truth</u> (sunlight), <u>His Law</u> (candlelight), and <u>His Will</u> (Shekinah glory) in the **Minds** (surrender), **Hearts** (sacrifice), and **Souls** (reconciliation) of the **Human Race** to bring **It** to **His Light of Understanding** and then **Comprehend <u>Earthly Righteousness</u>** (celestial court), **<u>Heavenly Holiness</u>** (temple court), and **<u>Kingdom Perfection</u>** (royal court) in the *New Nature of Christ Jesus.*

To "Master God's Name (sinner)," a Person must Fulfill **Twelve Levels of Accomplishments** (face Lucifer's Test) on *Earth* (physical), which leads to "Mastering God's Virginity (Christian)" by Fulfilling **Nine Levels of Accomplishments** (face God's Judgment) in *Heaven* (spiritual). Finally, to "Master God's Union (saint)," a Person must Fulfill **Seven Levels of Accomplishments** (face Self-evaluation) within the *Kingdom* to complete **Twenty-Eight Levels of Perfection** as a **Soul Journeys** from *Nothing to All* (beatific vision). If this is true, then "Why Do so Few" of God's Children Find the **Path of Righteousness Guiding Them** to *God's Name* (mind), *God's Virginity* (heart), and *God's Union* (soul)? The answer is to be found in the "Mystical Timing" between Christ's 1st Advent (Calvary) where the *Lord Saves His Priesthood* (wise) and Christ's 2nd Advent (tribulation) where the *Lord Will Save His Laity* (fool). Yes! One day "All Mankind will be Saved," but this Great Effort will take some **Seven Thousand Years** and **Require Christ** to come in **Three Advents** to *Save His Priesthood*, *His Laity*, and finally, *All Pagans* from *Themselves*.

A "Person might Ask": Why Does Everything on Earth seem to be **Right**, **No Matter How Outlandish** it might appear to the *Rational Mind of Educated Men* (self-wise)? The answer is to be found in the fact that "God's Belief System" will Work for Anyone who is willing to **Cast himself** into *Sin* (sin-nature), *Evil* (worldly temptations), and *Death* (demonic possession). This act of "Divine Sacrifice" is done to Pay the Necessary Price **Required** for *Receiving God's Divine Blessings*. Yes! We are "All Attending God's" Divine School of Higher Learning (challenge/adventure) and the more a **Person Masters God's Divine Truth,** the **Closer** he will become to the *Kingdom of God*. The idea here is that "If a Person" Believes he can Walk Across Hot Coals Barefooted while being **Convinced** that his **Feet will Not be Burned,** then **God** will **Honor this Belief** in the *Name of Lucifer*. Obviously, this can "Explain the Creation" of an Infinite Number of Religions on Earth because whatever **Crazy People Believe,** then **Lucifer** will *Make that Belief Real*.

This leads us to "Man's Christian Belief" which is that If a Person will **Die to Self** by **Surrendering unto Death** (faithful belief), then his **Flesh** (learn lessons) will be **Taken Over** by **Mary's Son, Jesus** to **Save this Sinner** (take-sin) from the *Curse of an Evil World* (Easter). Secondly, "If a Christian" Dies to Self by **Surrendering unto Damnation** (knowing belief), then his **Spirit** (God's blessings) will be **Taken Over** by **God's Son, Christ** to **Create a New Saint** (give divinity) by *Purifying* him within the *Holy Church* (Christmas). This "Need to Purify" both One's Flesh (world) and Spirit (church) allows a **Lost Broken Sinner** to **Bear Fruit** out of his *Own Mistakes/Wickedness/Evil* (faults). The "Job of Jesus Christ" is to Convert the **Ignorant into Righteousness** (birth), the **Criminals into Holiness** (baptism), and the **Evil into Perfection** (resurrection) before *God*. Obviously, this awesome task would take "Three Mystical Advents" to Accomplish as the **Lord must Convert** the **Individual** (self/1st advent/defeat will), then **Societies** (man/2nd advent/defeat beliefs), and finally, the whole **Creation** (God/3rd advent/defeat lands) from *Death into New-life*. In this way, "God's Son" could Purify and Save the **Earth** (babies), **Heaven** (teenagers), and **God's Kingdom** (adults) in **Three Mystical Visits** to **Give Each** of *God's Children* his *Own Eternal Life, New Body, and Personal Kingdom*.

The following tabular information indicates that "Jesus Christ" actually has <u>Two Jobs</u> (take-sin/give divinity) with **One Being** to *Save the Lost* (son of man/world/friends) and the **Other** is the *Creation of Saints* (Son of God/ church/family):

**Mary's Son, Jesus Saves Sinners (flesh);
while God's Son, Christ Creates Saints (spirit)**
(Jesus defeats the evil world and Christ fulfills
holy church to bring perfection to all)

Lessons 1. **Mary's Son** - <u>Jesus Rules the Flesh:</u> Convert Evil World...New Mind
(truth)
- Take-sins - Save Sinners: Washed in Human Blood (water) = God becomes Man
- Learning Right from Wrong - Righteous Citizen on Earth (death becomes life)

Friends
- Heaven on Earth - Live with Beloved Friend: Working Together
  - Jesus - Pays Sin-debt: Master One's Mind = See Limitations

(bread of crucifixion - death: pay sin-debt = conversion of the flesh into a new body)

Blessings 2. **God's Son** - <u>Christ Rules the Spirit:</u> Fulfill Holy Church...New Heart
(law)
- Give Divinity - Create Saints: Washed in Divine Spirit (fire) = Man becomes God
- Learn Good from Evil - Holy Saint in Heaven (life becomes death)

Family
- Paradise in Heaven - Face an Angry God: Judged by Performance
  - Christ - Pays Holy-debt: Blessed with New Heart = See Potential

(wine of resurrection - new-life: pay holy-debt = conversion of the spirit into eternal life)

This illustration shows that it is only "Jesus Christ" <u>Who</u> could <u>Pay Mankind's Sin-debt</u> (Heaven on Earth) and <u>Holy-debt</u> (Paradise in Heaven) to **Set Lucifer's Captives Free** from *Sin, Evil, and Death*. The idea here is that once "Jesus Pays" a <u>Person's Sin-debt</u>, then he can **Learn the Lessons of Life** and *Master his Own Righteous Mind* (see limitations). Once "Christ Pays" a <u>Person's Holy-debt</u>, then he can be **Blessed** with a *New Holy Heart* (see potential). This means that the "Job" of <u>Each of God's Children</u> is to **Learn his Lessons Well** (new mind) and come to **Love God** with his **Whole Being** to become **Worthy of God's Blessings** of *Eternal Life*, a *New Body*, and his *Own Personal Kingdom*. In this lesson, we are being "Taught" that <u>Jesus Saves Sinners</u> (truth/streetwise) by **Washing Them in Human Blood** (water) to bring forth **Heaven on Earth** so *that Everyone* can *Live in Peace* with his most *Beloved Friends*. Secondly, we are being "Taught" that <u>Christ Creates Saints</u> (law/educated) by **Washing Them in Divine Spirit** (fire) to bring forth **Paradise in Heaven** so *that God's Chosen* can *Live in Happiness* with his most *Beloved Family*. The implication here is that "If a Person's Flesh is Forgiven (world)," then he <u>Receives</u> **Heaven on Earth** (citizenship) with his *Friends*; but "If a Person's Spirit is Forgiven (church)," then he <u>Receives</u> **Paradise in Heaven** (sainthood) with his *Family*. This means that every "Person on Earth" is seeking to <u>Be Forgiven</u> and to have his **Sin-debts Paid in Full** to **Receive All** the *Blessings of God*. This means that "Mary's Son, Jesus" became the <u>Bread of Crucifixion</u> (death) to **Pay Man's Sin-debt** (faults) so that the **Flesh of All Men** might be *Converted into New Bodies* (earth). Secondly, "God's Son, Christ" becomes the <u>Wine of Resurrection</u> (new-life) to **Pay Man's Holy-debt** (virtues) so that the **Spirit of All Men** might be *Converted into Eternal Life* (Heaven). When both "Man's Flesh (bread)" and "Man's Spirit (wine)" are <u>Blended</u> into the **Nature of Christ** (soul), a **Person** can be **Transformed** from **<u>Nothing</u>** (death) to **<u>All</u>** (life), thereby making him *Worthy of the Presence of God* (Kingdom).

We see the "Human Flesh," "Spirit," and "Soul" represent the <u>Coming</u> **Holy Nation, Holy Church, and Holy Men** as they strive to **<u>Serve</u>** the *Needs of Earth* (worship God), the *Wants of Heaven* (serve people), and the *Demands of God* (serve saints). This means that the "Holy Nation" is <u>Called</u> to **Worship God** by **Giving-up Its Life** in **Fulfillment of God's Law** via **<u>Its Obedience</u>** to *God's Divine Will* (wisdom). Secondly, the "Holy Church" is <u>Called</u> to **Serve the People** by **Giving-up Her Wealth** in **Fulfillment of Man's Faith** via **<u>Its Love</u>** for *God's Divine Love* (courage). Finally, the "Holy Man" is <u>Called</u> to **Serve God's Saints** by **Giving-up his Labor** in **Fulfillment of Man's Freedom** via **His Hard-work** to *Honor God's Divine Justice* (generosity).

We see that the "Holy Nation" <u>Takes Stock on Saturday</u> (Great Sabbath to **Evaluate** and **Count the Number of Babies** that have been **Produced** and just **<u>How Many of these Children</u>** have *Matured Correctly* (righteous citizens). Secondly, the "Holy Church" <u>Takes Stock on Sunday</u> (Lord's Day) to **Evaluate** and **Count the Number of Saints** that have been **Produced** and just **How Many** of these **<u>Holy Ones</u>** have *Matured Correctly* (holy saints). Finally, the "Holy Man" <u>Takes Stock Daily</u> (Final Judgment) to **Evaluate** and **Count the Number of Sons** that have been **Produced** and just **How Many** of these **<u>Divine Ones</u>** have *Matured Correctly* (perfect sons). This means that the "Holy Nation" is to <u>Teach the Jews</u> **God's Right** (order) from **Man's Wrong** (chaos) to **Create** a **Righteous Man on Earth** via **<u>Christ's Crucifixion</u>** as the *Lord Pays Mankind's Sin-debt* (faults) *in Full*. Secondly, the "Holy Church" is to <u>Teach the Christians</u> **God's Good** (order) from **Man's Evil** (chaos) to **Create** a **Holy Man in Heaven** via **<u>Christ's Resurrection</u>** as the *Lord Pays Mankind's Holy-debt* (virtues) *in Full*. Finally, the "Holy Man" is to <u>Teach the Pagan World</u> **God's Will** (order) from **man's will** (chaos) to **Create** a **Perfect Man within the Kingdom of God** via **<u>Christ's Ascension</u>** since the *Lord Pays All Mankind's Past Due Debts* (freedom) *in Full*.

In this way, the "Physical People (being saved/free gold mine)" will become <u>Worthy</u> of **God's Free Redemption to <u>Receive God's Gift</u>** of a *New Body*. Secondly, the "Spirit People (save self/dig gold)" will become <u>Worthy</u> of **Man's Earned Salvation** to **<u>Receive God's Blessing</u>** of *Eternal Life*. Finally, the "Mystical People (saving others/share gold)" will become <u>Worthy</u> of **God's Bonus Rewards to <u>Receive God's Reward</u>** of a *Personal Royal Kingdom*. The "Lord is Showing Us" that through <u>His Crucifixion,</u> the **Human Race** will be **Set Free from Slavery** and **Given Heaven on Earth** via *Death to Self* (submission). Secondly, through "His Resurrection," the Human Race will be **Set Free from Servanthood** and **Given Paradise in Heaven** via *Rebirth* (awakening). Finally, through "His Ascension," the <u>Human Race</u> will be **Set Free from Captivity** and **<u>Given Personal Freedom</u>** via *a New-nature in Christ* (changed). It should now make sense that "God's Holy Nation," "Holy Church," and "Holy Man" have been <u>Created to Serve</u> the **Earth, Heaven,** and **God's Kingdom** through the *Perfection of Christ*.

The following tabular information indicates that "God is Creating" a <u>Holy Nation, Holy Church,</u> and a <u>Holy Man</u> to **Serve Earth, Heaven, and His Kingdom** by **Changing Man's Sin-nature** into a *Righteous-nature,* <u>Worldly Temptations</u> into *Worldly Holiness,* and **Demonic Possession** into *Human Perfection*:

Creating the Holy Nation, Holy Church and the Holy Man to Serve God, Angels, and Men Forever
(nation worships God, church serves people,
and God serves the holy saint to bring perfection)

Truth
(slavery)

1. **Holy Nation** - <u>Worship God:</u> Give Life (mind) ...Knowledge
   - Zophar Condemns Job - Sin-nature: You've been Cursed by Ignorance
   - Fulfill Law - Obedience: Become Divine = Christmas + See Limitations
   - Saturday/Sabbath - Count Number of Children: Measure Progress
   - Learn Right from Wrong - Become Righteous Citizen on Earth (crucifixion)
   - Free Redemption - Receive *New Body*: Rebirth

Law
(servanthood)

2. **Holy Church** - <u>Serve People:</u> Give Wealth (heart) ...Self-awareness
   - Eliphaz Condemns Job - Worldly Temptations: You've been Cursed with Cowardice
   - Fulfill Faith - Love: Become Holy = Easter + See Potential
   - Sunday/Lord's Day - Count Number of Saints: Measure Success
   - Learn Good from Evil - Become Holy Saint in Heaven (resurrection)
   - Earned Salvation - Receive *Eternal Life*: Transfiguration

Will
(free man)

3. **Holy Man** - <u>God Serves Saint:</u> Give Labors (soul) ...Consciousness
   - Bildad Condemns Job - Demonic Possession: You've been Cursed with Greed
   - Fulfill Knowing - Freedom: Become Free = Halloween + See Self-worth
   - Week Days - Work Hard to Create Babies and Saints: Measure Wages Earned
   - Learn God's Will/man's will - Become Perfect Son within Kingdom (ascension)
   - Bonus Rewards - Receive *Royal Kingdom*: Glorification

This illustration shows that the "Lord Jesus Christ" has <u>Gone All Out</u> to **Purchase Mankind** a **New Mind** of **Knowledge,** a **New Heart** of **Self-awareness,** and a **New Soul** of **Consciousness** to <u>**Set God's Children Free**</u> from *Sin, Evil, and Death*. Now, it should make sense that "God's Son" will have <u>Three Advents upon the Earth</u> with the <u>**1st**</u> being the *Great Sabbath* (Calvary), <u>**2nd**</u> being the *Lord's Day* (1,000 years), and the **3rd** being the *Final Judgment* (1 hour). Through these "Three Advents," the Human Race will be able to **Count and Record the Number** of **Babies, Teenagers, and Adults** it has **Created** via the *Creative Forces of God*. Recall in the "Story of Job," he was Forced to Take Stock of his Life in the **Presence of Three Friends, Zophar** (sin)**, Eliphaz** (evil)**, and Bildad** (death)**, Who Revealed** that **Job's Sin-nature, Worldly Temptation,** and **Demonic Possession** had *Brought him to Ruin*. We now see that "What Brought Job" to Experience God's Curse is the **Same thing** that "Brought Adam" to Experience **God's Three Curses** of *Sin-nature* (sin), *Worldly Temptations* (evil), and *Demonic Possession* (death). We now see that the "Human Race" is Striving to Remove its **Sin-nature** via *Christmas,* Remove its **Worldly Temptations** via *Easter,* and Remove its **Demonic Possession** via *Halloween*. If these "Curses" of Sin, Evil, and Death can be **Removed** via **Man's Submission, Rebirth, and Freedom,** then the **Human Race** can bring forth *Heaven on Earth, Paradise in Heaven,* and *God's Kingdom of Glory*.

This means that "Christmas" will Allow Mankind to *See Its Limitations* (weak mind/Saturday); then "Easter" will Allow Mankind to *See Its Potential* (loving heart/Sunday); and finally, "Halloween" will Allow Mankind to *See Its Self-worth* (happy soul/daily). In this way, the "Human Race" has been Given a Pathway of Perfection which **Leads It** to **Earthly Righteousness** (mind), **Heavenly Holiness** (heart), and finally, **Kingdom Perfection** (soul) *All in the Name of Jesus Christ*. We see that "Earthly Righteousness (give labors)" comes by Thanking God (remove ignorance) for the **Forgiveness** (gain wisdom) of **Capital Sins** (baptism) during a *Person's Easter Duty* (yearly). Secondly, "Heavenly Holiness (give wealth)" comes by Praising God (remove cowardice) for the **Forgiveness** (gain courage) of **Mortal Sins** (confession) during a *Person's Weekly Devotion*. Finally, "Kingdom Perfection (give life)" comes by Worshiping God (remove greed) for the **Forgiveness** of **One's Venial Sins** (communion) during a *Person's Daily Worship*. Through these "Three Blessings from God," a Born-again Soul can **Enter God's Holy Nation** to *Receive a New Mind* (thinking), **God's Holy Church** to *Receive a New Heart* (loving), and become a **Holy Man in Christ** to *Receive a New Soul* (imagination).

This means that with a "New Mind," a **Person** can **Obtain** a *New Body in Christ*; with a "New Heart," **Obtain** *Eternal Life in Christ;* and with a "New Soul," **Obtain** his *Own Personal Royal Kingdom in Christ*. In this way, a "Born-again Child of God" can become Worthy of **Counting his Babies** on *Saturday* (Sabbath/neighbors), **Counting his Saints** on *Sunday* (Lord's Day/friends), and **Counting his Sons of God** *Daily* (Jubilee/judgment/family). The idea is that the "Human Race" is being Called to **Keep Track** of its **Babies** (physical births/home), the **Making of Saints** (spiritual births/church), and the **Forming of its Sons of God** (mystical births/government) as **All these Treasures** are to be *Offered unto the Lord Almighty*.

We now see that the "Meaning," "Purpose," and "Value of Life" center on Babies from Earth (God's children), Saints from Heaven (eternal lives), and Sons of God from God's Kingdom. It then becomes **Extremely Important** to **Keep Track** of **Every Moment of Life** as *One* of the *Future Treasures of God*. We also see that during the "Lord's 1st Advent (priest)," He Came as a **Priest on a Donkey** to **Sacrifice His Life**

(Mount Calvary) for the **Sins of All** on the **Great Sabbath** and to <u>**Count the Number**</u> (people) of *Jews, Romans, and Greeks on Earth*. Secondly, during the "Lord's 2nd Advent (thief)," <u>He will Come</u> as a **Thief in the Night** to **Sacrifice His Church** (Three Days of Darkness) for the **Evil Acts of Christians** on the **Lord's Day** and to <u>**Count the Number**</u> (saints) of *Venerable, Beatified, and Canonized Saints on Earth*. Finally, during the "Lord's 3rd Advent (judge)" <u>He will Come</u> as a **Judge on a Cloud** to **Sacrifice the Whole World** (Flames of Judgment) for the **Curse of Death,** during **God's Final Judgment** and to <u>**Count the Number**</u> of (sons) *Righteous, Holy, and Perfect Sons of God on Earth*. These "Days of Judgment" during the <u>Great Sabbath</u> (slaves), <u>Lord's Day</u> (servants), and <u>Final Judgment</u> (free men) represent the **Counting** of <u>**God's Slaves**</u> to the **Flesh** (earth), **Servants** unto **God's Spirit** (Heaven), and the <u>**Free Men** *Honoring God's Soul*</u> (Kingdom).

This means that "Christ the Priest Comes" to <u>Wash Away Sin</u> and to **Forgive Sinners** to <u>**Learn God's Right**</u> from **man's wrong**, thereby *Removing Their Ignorance* to *Gain Wisdom* (lessons/new mind). Secondly, "Christ the Thief (king) Comes" to <u>Change Man's Nature</u> and to **Create Saints** to <u>**Learn God's Good**</u> from **man's evil,** thereby *Removing His Cowardice* to *Gain Courage* (blessings/new heart). Finally, "Christ the Judge (son) Comes" to <u>Set Mankind Free</u> and to **Anoint the Sons of God** to <u>**Learn God's Will**</u> from **man's will,** thereby *Removing Its Greed* to *Gain Generosity* (treasure/new soul). Yes! Through "Wisdom," "Courage," and "Generosity," the <u>Human Race</u> can **Find** the <u>**Meaning of Existence,**</u> the <u>**Purpose of Servanthood,**</u> and the <u>**Value of Happiness**</u> for *One and All*. It should now be clear that "Christmas is for Babies (earth)" and that they are being <u>Given God's Finest Present</u> in the **Form** of a <u>**Painful Life of Struggle**</u> (character) to *Earn a Place in God's Kingdom*. Secondly, "Easter is for Teenagers (Heaven)," thereby <u>Forcing Them</u> to **Face Great Evil** to **Defeat Challenge** and **Create Adventure**, and then **Transform** the *Agony of Defeat* (failure) into the *Thrill of Victory* (triumph). Finally, "Halloween is for Adults (Kingdom)," thereby <u>Inviting Them</u> to **Defeat Sin, Evil, and Death** to **Enter God's Blessing of New-life** and then **Transform** *Ignorance, Cowardice, and Greed* into *Wisdom, Courage, and Generosity*. Through these "Three Transformations," a <u>Person can Forever Be</u> a **Loving Baby, Holy Saint** (teenager), and **Son of God** (adult) before the **Lord Almighty**, with the <u>**Authority to Count**</u> the *Righteous/Holy /Perfect Treasures of God*.

The following tabular information indicates that the "Life-experience" is <u>All About Counting</u> the **Treasures of God** in *Loving Babies* (bodies/physical people), in *Holy Saints* (eternal lives), and in *Sons of God* (kingdoms/mystical people):

**Evaluating the Number of God's Treasures on His
Great Sabbath, Lord's Day, and Final Judgment**
(counting physical, spiritual, and mystical people
living on earth, in Heaven, and in Kingdom)

Babies (slave)	1.	**Great Sabbath**/Saturday - <u>Count Number of Physical People</u>...God's Children
		• 1st Advent - Priest on Donkey: Mount Calvary (one man)

Purify	• Wash Away Sin - Forgive Sinners: Learn Right from Wrong
Grave	• Remove Ignorance - Gain Wisdom: Lessons of Life = New Mind
	• Thank God – Give Labors: Find God's Treasures = Christmas
	• Jewish People - Spoken Word: Being Saved
	• Create Baby Farm - New Bodies Out of Old Bodies
	• Create *New Bodies* - Treasure (trickle)
	• Individual Rights - See Limitations

(baby farm - become righteous man on earth: Heaven on Earth = Knowing God)

Teenagers	2. **Lord's Day**/Sunday <u>- Count Number of Spirit People</u>…God's Saints
(servant)	• 2nd Advent - Thief in Night: Three Days of Darkness (few men)
	• Change Nature - Create Saints: Learn Good from Evil
	• Remove Cowardice - Gain Courage: Blessings of Life = New Heart
Purify	• Praise God - Give Wealth: Purchase Pearl of Great Price = Easter
Host	• Christian People - Written Word: Saving Self
	• Create Divine School of Higher Learning - Saints Out of Sinners
	• Create *Eternal Lives* - Pearl (fountain)
	• Social Rights - See Potential

(divine school of higher learning - holy man in Heaven: Paradise in Heaven = Loving God)

Adults	3. **Final Judgment**/daily - <u>Count Number of Mystical People</u>…God's Sons
(free man)	• 3rd Advent - Judge on a Cloud: White Throne Judgment (all men)
	• Set Free - Honor Sons of God: Learn God's Will/man's will
	• Remove Greed - Gain Generosity: Freedom of Life = New Soul
Purify	• Worship God - Give Life: Love the Good Life = Halloween
Life	• Protestant People (monday)
	• Moslem People (tuesday) Incarnate Word
	• Hindu People (wednesday) (saving others)
	• Buddhist People (thursday)
	• Black Magic People (friday)
	• Create Sonship Training Program - Sons of God Out of Saints
	• Create *Royal Kingdoms* - Good Life (deluge)
	• Divine Rights - See Self-worth

(sonship training program - perfect man in Kingdom: Eternal-happiness - God Serves)

This illustration shows that the "Jewish People" <u>Represent</u> the **Spoken Word of God**, bringing **God's Free Redemption** (being saved) to a <u>**Lost and Dying World of Fools**</u> through the *Great Sabbath* (Saturday). Secondly, the "Christian People" <u>Represent</u> the **Written Word of God,** bringing **God's Earned Salvation** (saving self) to an <u>**Awakened World of Saints**</u> through the *Lord's Day* (Sunday). Finally, the "Sons of God" <u>Represent</u> the **Incarnate Word of God,** bringing **God's Bonus Rewards** (saving others) to a <u>**World of Peace**</u> through *God's Final Judgment* (daily). The idea here is that "God's Earthly Children" are <u>Assigned to Create</u> a **Baby Farm** to <u>**Produce**</u> *New Bodies* (new wineskins) out of *Old Dead Bodies* (old wineskins). Secondly, "God's

Earthly Saints" are <u>Assigned to Create</u> a **Divine School of Higher Learning** to **Produce** *Holy Saints* (new-life) out of ***Old Dead Sinners*** (old life). Finally, "God's Sons of Glory (Kingdom)" are <u>Assigned to Create</u> a **Sonship Training Program** to **Produce** *Sons of God* (new nature) out of *Holy Saints* (old nature). This means that "Earth (baby farm)" is the <u>Trickle of Life</u> **Transforming** <u>**Worthless Human Bodies**</u> into **New Priceless Bodies,** *Worthy of Heaven*. Secondly, "Heaven" is the <u>Fountain of Life</u> as **Christians** are **Glorified in Christ** (sainthood) to bring forth **Eternal Lives,** *Worthy* of *God's Kingdom of Glory*. Finally, the "Kingdom" is the <u>Deluge of Life</u> as **Saints** are **Exalted in Christ** (sonship) to bring forth **Royal Sons of God,** *Who* are *Worthy* of *God's Divine Presence*.

This "Mystical Process" of <u>Transformation</u> **Allows** the **Earth** (home), **Heaven** (church), and **Kingdom** (government) to **Produce** the **Treasures of God** in the *Form of Babies* (new bodies), *Saints* (eternal lives), and *Sons* (royal kingdoms). These "Treasures" allow <u>Earth</u> to bring forth **Individual Rights** for **God's Children** to <u>**See Their Own Limitations**</u> (new mind) and *Come to Know God*. Secondly, these "Treasures" allow <u>Heaven</u> to bring forth **Social Rights** for **God's Saints** to <u>**See Their Own Potential**</u> (new heart) and *Come to Love God*. Finally, these "Treasures" allow the <u>Kingdom</u> to bring forth **Divine Rights** for **God's Sons** to <u>**See Their Own Self-worth**</u> (new soul) and *Come to Serve God*. To put this "Grand Design into Context," a <u>Student of Life</u> must **Comprehend** the <u>**Conversion**</u> of *Sinners to Christians* (babies), of *Christians to Saints,* and finally, of *Saints to Sons of God*.

We now see that the "Earth" is <u>Creating</u> *Christians (babies)*, "Heaven" is <u>Creating</u> *Saints* (eternal lives), and the "Kingdom" is <u>Creating</u> *Sons of God* (royal kingdoms) to **Fill God's Creation** with *Physical, Spiritual, and Mystical People*. This "Transformation (winepress)," "Purification (crucible)," and "Conversion (generator)" <u>Process</u> **Changes Men's Natures** (law), <u>**Washes Away Their Sins**</u> (faith), and **Converts Their Lives** (knowing) into *Growing Babies, Mature Teenagers, and Clear-Thinking Adults*. Obviously, the "Earth" is <u>God's Baby Farm</u> (face death), where **Everyone** must have his **Faults Removed** by **Mastering Jewish Obedience** to **God's Law** to **Change Human Nature** into *Christ's Divine Nature* (slave to servant). Secondly, "Heaven" is <u>God's Divine School</u> (face grave), where **Everyone** must have his **Transgressions Removed** by **Mastering Christian Love** to **Enter Man's Faith** to <u>**Wash Away**</u> his **Sins,** thereby *Making him Holy before God*. Finally, "God's Kingdom" is <u>Christ's Sonship Training</u> (face hell), where **Everyone** must have his **Sins Against God Removed** by **Mastering Pagan Thinking** (ignorance) to **God/Man Knowing** (wisdom) to **Convert** his **Mind,** thereby <u>**Creating**</u> *a Free Man on his Own*.

We see that "Earth" represents <u>Water Baptism</u> as **God's Winepress of Death** and **Changes Water** into **Wine** to **Transform Babies into Teenagers** by **Teaching Them God's Right** from **man's wrong** to <u>**Learn**</u> the *Lessons of Life* (God's Law). Secondly, "Heaven" represents <u>Blood Baptism</u> as **God's Crucible of Fire** and **Changes Sin** into **Holiness** to **Transform Teenagers into Adults** by **Teaching Them God's Good** from **man's evil** to <u>**Learn**</u> the *Blessings of Life* (God's Will). Finally, the "Kingdom" represents <u>Spirit Baptism</u> as **God's Generator of Conversion** and **Changes Slaves** into **Free Men** to **Transform Adults** into **Wise Men** by

Teaching Them God's Will from **man's will** to <u>Learn</u> the *Value of Thinking for Themselves*.

The question is: just "When are All" <u>These Divine Treasures</u> **Going to be Brought** to this **Sinful World** to **Set Babies, Teenagers,** and **Adults Free** from **Their Ignorance, Cowardice,** and **Greed** to <u>Begin Living the Life</u> *God Wants for His People*? The answer is that "All God's Treasures" are <u>Going to be Brought to Earth</u> in **Three Advents of God's Son** as **Jesus** (priest) brings **Babies** a <u>**New Handicap System**</u> based on *Love* (wisdom); then **Christ** (thief/king) brings **Teenagers** a <u>**New Curve System**</u> based on *Mercy* (courage); and finally, **Jesus Christ** (judge/son) will bring the **Adults** a <u>**New Pass/Fail System**</u> based on *Justice* (generosity). It should now make sense that both "God and His Son" have a <u>Great Deal of Work to Do</u> in **Preparing** the **Mind** (fairness), **Heart** (ethics), and **Soul** (morals) of **Mankind** before the **Human Race** could **Hope** to <u>**Know, Speak, and Sup**</u> with *Their Creator God*. We see in this "Preparation Stage" that for <u>God to Create</u> a **Fair-Minded Person, He** has to **Remove a Baby's Personal Faults** (sin-nature) and then **Insert** a <u>**Righteous Nature**</u> based on *Treating himself Fairly*. Secondly, to "Create a Person" with an <u>Ethical Heart,</u> the **Lord** has to **Remove a Teenager's Transgressions Against his Fellowmen** (worldly temptations) and then **Insert** a <u>**Holy Nature**</u> based on *Treating Others Ethically* (follow law). Finally, to "Create a Person" with a <u>Moral Soul,</u> the **Lord** has to **Remove All His Sinfulness Against his God** (demonic possession) and then **Insert** a <u>**New Perfect Nature**</u> based on *Treating God with Impeccable or Flawless Morals* (follow commandment). Through this "Upgraded Vision" of the <u>Human Nature,</u> **Faults, Transgressions,** and **Sins** can be **Removed** from the **Human Condition** and **Set Mankind Free** to **Think for Itself** to become **One** with *God* (spirit), *Angels* (energy), *Men* (matter), *and Nature* (life) *Forever*.

The following tabular information indicates that "Earth's Task" is to <u>Remove Personal Faults</u> (baby); "Heaven's Task" is to <u>Remove Transgressions Against One's Brother</u> (teenager); and "God's Kingdom's Task" is to <u>Remove All Sins Against God</u> (adult):

Removing Personal Faults, Transgressions Against Brother, and Sins Against God to become Saved

(Jewish obedience takes faults, Christian love takes transgressions, Pagan repentance takes-sin)

Self (slave)	1.	**Remove Personal Faults/face death** - <u>Jewish Obedience:</u> Change Nature… Divinity
		• Water Baptism - Winepress of Death: Water into Wine (transformation)
		• Blasphemy - Excommunication from God's Temple: Face Lucifer's Test
		• Fair Mind - Learn God's Right from man's wrong: Learn Lessons = God's Law
Baby (righteous)		• Slaughter of Innocence - Innocent Blood: Remove Sin-nature = Get *New Body*
		• Earth - Baby Farm: Elementary School = Mind/Ignorance to Wisdom

- Jesus Brings Babies - Handicap System: Love becomes Justice

Society (servant)	2. **Remove Transgressions Against Brother/face grave** - <u>Christian Love:</u> Wash Sin...Holy

- Blood Baptism - Crucible of Fire: Wheat into Bread (purification)
- Sorcery - Outcast from God's People: Face God's Judgment
- Ethical Heart - Learn God's Good from man's evil: Receive Blessings = Man's Faith

Teenager (holy)

- Slaughter Guilty Conscience - Forgiven Blood: World Temptation = Get *Eternal Life*
- Heaven - Divine School: High School = Heart/Cowardice to Courage
- Christ Brings Teenagers - Curve System: Mercy is Mercy

God (free man)	3. **Remove Sins Against God/face hell** - <u>Pagan Repentance:</u> Think for Self... Freedom

- Spirit Baptism - Generator of Life: Slave into Free Man (conversion)
- Moral Soul - Learn God's Will/man's will: Released from Curses = God/Man Knowing

Adult (perfect)

- Slaughter Enemy's Cruelty - Guilty Blood: Demonic Possession = Get *Royal Kingdom*
- Kingdom - Sonship Training: College = Soul/Greed to Generosity
- Jesus Christ Brings Pass/Fail System: Justice becomes Love

This illustration shows that "When Babies" <u>Fail to Remove</u> **Their Faults** (offend self), **They must Face Death** (dying). This **Implies Remaining On Earth Forever** (eternal death) since a **Person is Left Behind** (blasphemy) or *Excommunicated from God's Temple* (law). "When Teenagers" <u>Fail to Remove</u> **Their Transgressions** (offend brother), **They must Face the Grave.** This **Implies Remaining in Heaven Forever** (eternal grave) since a **Person is Being Left Behind** (sorcery) or an *Outcast from God's People* (will). "When Adults" <u>Fail to Remove</u> **Their Sins** (offend God), **They must Face Hell.** This **Implies Remaining** within the **Kingdom of God Forever** (eternal hell) since a **Person is Being Left Behind** (sedition) or being *Banished from God's Love*. The question is "If a Person Doesn't Want" to be on <u>Earth,</u> in <u>Heaven,</u> and/or in <u>God's Kingdom</u> **Forever,** then just **Where Does he Want to Be** from *Everlasting to Everlasting* (never-ending life)? The easy answer is that "We must All Grow -up" and <u>Be Set Free</u> from **Sin, Evil, Death,** and even **God's Eternal Loving Care** (parenthood) to **Go on Our Own** (freedom) to **Explore Who We Are** and to *Find Our Own Identity* (name/fairness), *Our Own Character* (respect/ethics), and *Our Own Personality* (integrity/morals).

This "Journey of Eternal Life" <u>Establishes</u> the **True God/Man Relationship** as the **Creator of All Things** is **Made of Law** (33%), **Love** (67%) and **Repentance** (100%) and **Anyone, Who is Willing** to <u>**Sacrifice himself Totally,**</u> can *Become an Eternal Friend of God*. Yes! We are "All Striving" to <u>Become Great</u> in the **Eyes of God.** Unfortunately, this **Requires** also **Becoming Great** (respected) in the *Eyes of*

Angels, Saints, All Men, and Ourselves. Now, just "Where Does this Awesome Respectability" <u>Come From</u> as **Our Minds, Hearts, and Souls** are **Filled** with **Ignorance, Cowardice, and Greed** to the point of having **No Chance of Defeating** the *Curses of Sin, Evil, Death, and Damnation* without *Help*? Note that "We have Shown Our Suffering," "We have Cried for Help," "We have Waived Our Covenant," and "We have Waited to be Saved," but <u>Still We See No Sign</u> of *God's Compassion* and/or *His Unfathomable Mercy.* Fortunately, the "Lord God Almighty" is <u>Calling His Creation</u> to **Conversion** by **Giving Them** a **New Nature,** a **Holy Spirit,** and a **Sentient Countenance** (thinking) to *Become Eternal Friends of God.*

The "Pathway to God's Friendship" is through the <u>Challenges, Adventures, and Fun of Life</u> as **All of God's Children** must **Grow** and **Mature** into **Properly Behaved Adults,** <u>Who Know</u> *Right from Wrong, Good from Evil, and God's Will from Man's Will.* The idea here is that the "Sinner (baby)" must <u>Get Dirty</u> (world) to **Learn** the *Lessons of Life;* then the "Saint (teenage)" must <u>Wash Away Sin</u> (church) to **Receive** *God's Blessings;* and finally, "God's Son (adult)" must <u>Master All he Surveys</u> to **Receive** the *Treasures of Life.* This means that a "Person" only has his <u>Labors, Wealth,</u> and his <u>Life</u> to **Put into the Life-experience** to **Fulfill** his **Babyhood, Teenage Years,** and then **Adulthood** through the **Forces** of *Challenge, Adventure, and Fun.*

In short, the "Lord God Almighty" is <u>Grading His</u> **Babies, Teens, and Adults** on **Three Different Scoring Systems** from *Handicap* (try best), to *Curve* (compare with peers), and **God's** most **Difficult** *Pass/Fail System* (perfect or nothing). The "Babies are Scored" on <u>Their Strength of Spirit</u> as **They are Challenged** to **Fight** and **Struggle Unceasingly** and **Try Their Best, Never-quit,** and **Above All,** <u>They</u> are to *Never Surrender to the Enemy.* Secondly, the "Teenagers are Scored" on <u>Their Depth of Loyalty</u> as **They are Asked** to **Prove Themselves Above** and **Beyond the Call of Duty** by **Surrendering Totally** to the **Cause** and **Giving Their Labors, Wealth,** and even **Their Lives** unto the *Bitter End.* Finally, the "Adults are Scored" on <u>Their Level</u> of **Personal Sentience** as **They are Asked to Demonstrate Their Depth of Self-control** by becoming **Respected Responsible Citizens** within the *Community.* The "Babies of Life (flesh)" are <u>Offered</u> **God's Free Redemption** to **Grow-up** and **Mature** into **Righteous Citizens on Earth, Who are Worthy** of **New Eternal Bodies** as **They Offer God** <u>Their Labors</u> to *Remove Their Ignorance* and *Gain Wisdom* (innocent blood). Secondly, the "Teenagers of Life (spirit)" are <u>Called</u> to **Earn Their Own Salvation** to **Grow-up** and **Mature** into **Holy Saints in Heaven, Who are Worthy** of **New Eternal Lives** as **They Offer God** <u>Their Wealth</u> (money) to *Remove Their Cowardice* and *Gain Courage* (guilty blood). Finally, the "Adults of Life (soul)" can <u>Receive</u> a **Bonus Reward** to become **Sons of God** within **God's Kingdom,** thereby **Making Them Worthy** of **Their Own Kingdoms** as **They Offer God** <u>Their Lives</u> to *Remove Their Greed* and *Gain Generosity* (forgiven blood). This means that "God's Earthly Babies" are to <u>Face</u> the **Challenges of Life,** thereby **Forcing Them** to **Taste** the *Agony of Defeat* (fight evil). "God's Heavenly Teenagers" are to <u>Face</u> the **Adventure of Life,** to **Experience** the *Thrill of Victory* (surrender). Finally, "God's Kingdom Sons" are to <u>Face</u> the **Fun of Life** to **Take Control** of *Their Own Eternal Lives.*

The following tabular information indicates that "Our Ignorant Baby Flesh" must Fight the Evil World (challenge/lessons); "Our Rebellious Teenage Spirit" must Surrender to God's Church (adventure/blessings); and finally, "Our Greedy Adult Soul" must Take Control of Its Own Life (fun/treasures):

Face Fears	1. **Baby Flesh** - <u>Fight Evil World:</u> Never-quit = Lucifer's Test…See Limitations	
	• Graded on the Size of Challenge - Graded on Handicap System	
	• Challenge with Labors – Small	
Getting	• Challenge with Money - Average	**Taste Agony of Defeat**
Dirty	• Challenge with Own Life - Great	• Learn Right from Wrong
	• Free Redemption - Become Righteous Citizen on Earth: New Body	
	• Offer Labors - Remove Ignorance, Gain Wisdom (innocent blood)	
	• Fighting an Evil World - Creates the Lessons of Life	
Face Pain	2. **Teenage Spirit** - <u>Surrender to God:</u> Quit Instantly = God's Judgment…See Potential	
	• Graded on Size of Adventure - Graded on Curve System	
	• Adventure Using Labors	
	• Adventure Using Money	**Taste Thrill of Victory**
Saved	• Adventure Using Own Life	• Learn Good from Evil
from Dirt	• Earned Salvation - Become Holy Saint in Heaven - Eternal Life	
	• Offer Wealth - Remove Cowardice, Gain Courage (guilty blood)	
	• Lessons of Life - Create Death to Own Selfishness	
Face Death	3. **Adult Soul** - Take Control of Self: Become Winner = Self-evaluation… See Self-worth	
	• Graded on Size and Quality of Fun - Graded on Pass/Fail System	
	• Fun Using Labors	
	• Fun Using Money	**Taste the Essence of Life**
Washed	• Fun Using Own Life	• Learn God's Will/Man's Will
Clean	• Bonus Rewards - Become Perfect Son in Kingdom: Own Kingdom	
	• Offer Life - Remove Greed, Gain Generosity (forgiven blood)	
	• Death to Oneself - Creates Christ's Born-again Blessing	

This illustration shows that "God's Earthly Babies" are <u>Called</u> to **Learn Right from Wrong** to **Master** the **Art of Righteousness,** while **Proving** <u>**They can Survive**</u> within an ***Evil World of Sinfulness.*** Secondly, "God's Heavenly Teenagers" are <u>Called</u> to **Learn Good from Evil** to **Master** the **Art of Holiness,** while **Proving They can Believe** in **Their Creator** unto **Their Own Nothingness,** thereby <u>**Making Them Saints**</u> in the ***Eyes of God.*** Finally, "God's Kingdom Sons" are <u>Called</u> to **Learn God's Will from Man's Will** to **Master** the **Art of Perfection,** while **Demonstrating Their Own Self-reliance** as **They Strive** to become <u>**Responsible**</u> ***Citizens of the Community.*** This means that the "Born-again Experience" is <u>Centered</u> upon **Fighting All** the **Forces in Life** as **One is Immersed in Evil** (sinfulness) to **Learn All the Lessons of**

Life which cause a **Person to be Convicted** or to **Die to Self More and More** until he **Experiences** a *Deeper Born-again Relationship with Christ* (100% belief). Through this "Method" of being Killed by the World (death) and then Born-again in Christ (rebirth), a **Person Enters** the **Conversion Experience** to be **Executed** by the **Lessons of the World** and then **Resurrect** via the *Blessings of Christ*. Yes! We see that the "Conversion Experience" is all about being Graded by One of **God's Three Evaluation Systems**, either **Handicap** (babies), **Curve** (teenagers), and/or **Pass/Fail** (adults) as a **Person Grows** and **Matures** through **Life** by **Fighting** an *Evil World*, **Fulfilling** *God's Faith*, and becoming a *Responsible Adult in God's Kingdom of Glory*.

To better understand this "Conversion Experience," we must Recognize the **Differences Associated** between a **Highly Competitive Sporting Event** and a **Business Venture** as **Each Tries** to **Make Money Out** of *Televising Sports*. Note that the "Coaching Staff Cares" only about how Good Players can Perform on the **Field**; while the "Business Types" only care about the Bottom-line or *Their Profit Margin* (earnings). Unfortunately, this same "Problem Exists" between Lucifer's Philosophy of Life (circus)" and God's Philosophy of Life (respectful) as **They** both **Use People** to bring **Peace, Joy, and Happiness** to *Their Barren Lives*. We see that both "God and Man are Caught" in this Same Management/Labor Struggle as **They** both **Strive to Build a Society** of **Wealth and Prosperity** in **Hopes of Converting** a **Bunch of Wild Animals** into a *Society of Fair-Minded, Ethically-Hearted and Morally Good Souls*. Unfortunately, "Creating Good Pagan People" is Not What Life is All About. **Life is About Integrity** which can only **Come from God** and *His Divine School of Higher Learning* (fairness/ethics/morals). We are "Called" to Learn the Meaning of Life and **Understand** that it's about becoming a **Righteous and Holy Person Worthy** of *God's Blessing* and *His Respect*. Through this "Mystical Blending Concept (spirit/flesh)," the Human Race is able to **Overcome Its Reliance** on **Lucifer's Money** (almighty dollar) and become **Self-sufficient** by *Surrendering to Christ, Believing in Themselves* and by *Earning God's Grace Come What May* (IS).

By "Comprehending" the Meaning (existence), Purpose (service), and Value (happiness) of Life, a **Lost Soul** can **Overcome Evil** (money) and **Enter** the *Brotherhood of Christ* (faith). Through the coming "Brotherhood of Man," the Entire Human Race will be **Formed** as **Each** of God's Children has Personally Chosen His Own Life-experiences based on **His Desire to Come** to *Know, Love, and Serve God*. This "Right to Choose" Creates the **Human Free Will** (individuality) which will **One Day** become the **Will of the People** (society) based on **What Man** both **Wants** (holy blessings/good) and **Needs** (righteous lessons/bad) as they **Reflect** his *Desire to Please* the *Divinity of God*. This means that "Each of God's Children" must Choose **His Own** *Personal Appearance* (looks), *Social Position* (career), *Desired Location* (home), *Family* (name), *Perception of Reality* (viewpoint), *Dreams* (future), and *Individual Life-experiences* (challenges/adventures). Through these "Life-Forming Selections," the Whole Human Race can be **Established** and **Universally Pass** through **God's Divine School of Higher Learning** to become **Properly Educated** in the *Ways of Man* (relative truth) and in the *Ways of God* (absolute truth). Now, imagine each "Generation of Man" both Growing and Maturing throughout the **Ages** as the **Choices of Men** become **Better**

and Better until They are *Perfect in the Sight of God, Angels, Men, and Nature*. At this "Stage of Life," the Human Race will *Know Who It Wants to Be* (God/Man), *What It Wants to Do* (create babies), and *Where It Wants to Live* (kingdom) *Forever*.

Government 1. **Man Knows** - Who He Wants to Be:
Enter God/Man Identity........................Master God's Friendship
- Given Birth via the *Earthly Womb* - See Limitations: Become Righteous Citizen on Earth

Church 2. **Man Knows** - What He Wants to Do: Raise Babies/Citizens/Saints/Sons
.... Master God's Companionship
- Given Birth via the *Immaculate Womb* - See Potential: Become Holy Saint in Heaven

Home 3. **Man Knows** - Where He Wants to Live: Live in Own Kingdom
.... Master God's Oneness
- Given Birth via the *Mystical Womb* - See Self-worth: Become Perfect Son within Kingdom

Obviously, the "Lord is Seeking" a more Mature Approach to Life as the **Human Race Discovers** its **Own Human Soul** (earth/physical) and **Divine Spirit** (Heaven/spiritual) through the *Teachings and Lessons of Christ*. We must imagine that "Man's Divine Spirit" Starts Its Life Journey in the **Astral Plane** (mystical dimension), where it must **Choose Its Human Form**, thereby **Defining** Its Eternal Journey to effectively **Implement** these **Choices** by **Attaining** "Man's Human Soul" through the *Womb of Its Three Mothers* (earthly womb/immaculate womb/mystical womb). It is now clear that through "Heaven (spirit)," "Earth (soul)," and "God (nature)," the Human Race is able to **Grow-up** into an **Earthly King** (baby farm), **Heavenly Priest** (teenage school), and **Kingdom Son** (adult paradise) to take its *Rightful Position* with the *Angels and with God*. The "Lord is Telling Us" that the Life-experience is a Mystery and that **Things are Not as They Appear** on the **Surface**. But like any **Serious Science Project**, what seems **Impossible in the Beginning** (baby's view) will become **Child's Play** (adults) on *His Day of Mastery* (graduation). The "Lord is Telling Us" that once We Attain the **Treasures of Life** (redemption) and thereby **Fulfilling Our Own Lives**, we must **Sacrifice Them** in an **All Out Effort** (give redeemed soul)* to **Save the Damned** from the *Fires of Hell* (hopelessness).

Recall that in Exodus 32:32, Moses Told God he would Give his Eternally Redeemed Soul (remove from book of life) to Save the Jewish People from Their Moment of Extinction for Offending God's Divinity.

The following tabular information indicates that "All of Us" have Chosen Our Own Lives by **Selecting Our** *Physical Appearance, Social Status (career), Desired Location, Family, Perception of Reality, Future Dreams*, and *Individual Life-experiences*:

Choosing Own Earthly Life in Pursuit of God's Eternal Love
(select own looks, social status, location, family,
reality, dreams, and life-experiences)

Truth
(gluttony)

1. **Physical Appearance** - <u>Mind</u> (recognizing truth) ....Knowledge
   - Excommunication from Temple - Water Purification: Forgiveness (kingship)
   - Ignorance to Wisdom - New Body: Righteous Citizen on Earth
   - Baby Level - Recognize True Identity: Meaning of Life = *Existence*
     (belief/helplessness - mind brings wisdom:
     learning God's right from man's wrong)

Law
(envy)

2. **Social Status** - <u>Heart</u> (feeling pleasure/pain) ...Self-awareness
   - Outcast from People - Blood Purification: Pardon (priesthood)
   - Cowardice to Courage - Eternal Life: Holy Saint in Heaven
   - Child Level - Spill Blood: Purpose of Life = *Service*
     (submission/obedience - heart brings courage:
     learning God's good from man's evil)

Will
(sloth)

3. **Desired Location** - <u>Soul</u> (rational implementation) ......Consciousness
   - Banished from Earth - Death Purification: Resurrection (sonship)
   - Greed to Generosity - Royal Kingdom: Perfect Son in Kingdom
   - Adolescent Level - Offers Prayers: Value of Life = *Happiness*
     (Unto thine own self be true/restraint - soul brings
     generosity: learning God's Will from man's will)

Love
(lust)

4. **Family** (name) - <u>Life-force</u> (work and play are one) ......Sentience
   - Forsaken by God - Spirit Purification: Reconciliation (freedom)
   - Selfishness to Unselfishness - Freedom: Free Man in God
   - Teenage Level - Master Word: What's It All About? = *Learning*
     (guilty conscience/law - life-force brings unselfishness:
     learn God's Reality from man's illusion)

Union
(avarice)

5. **Perception of Reality** - <u>Nature</u> (striving for excellence) ...Limitations
   - Evaluated by Self - Human Purification: Retribution (know God)
   - Weak Flesh to Strong Spirit - Eternal Peace: Evaluating Oneself
   - Young Adult Level - Evangelize Others: Life Makes Sense = *Knowing*
     (instinctive compulsion/free - nature brings free will:
     learn God's Truth/man's lie)

Worship
(anger)

6. **Future Dreams** - <u>Free Life</u> (desires of heart) ....Potential
   - Judged by God - Divine Purification: Recompense (love God)
   - Weak Spirit to Strong Flesh - Eternal Joy: Finding Servanthood
   - Adult Level - Save Souls: Life is Becoming God = *Giving Life*
     (embrace God's fruits - free life brings servanthood: learn to think for oneself)

Oneness
(pride)

7. **Life-experiences** - <u>Essence of Life</u> (finding God) ...Self-worth
   - Tested by Lucifer - Demonic Purification: Reinstated (serve God)
   - Weak Soul to Strong Life-force - Eternal Happiness: Honoring Slavery

- Wise Man Level - Become God's Friend: Life is Life = *Giving All*
  (offer fruits to God - rich life brings slavery:
  learn to follow God's will obediently)

This illustration shows that the "Baby Viewpoint Seeks" only <u>Outward Appearance</u> and **Fails** to **Recognize** the **Difference** between **Ignorance and Wisdom** (belief) until he **Fails at Falsehood** (false face) and must *Find Forgiveness* in the *Spirit of God's Truth*. Secondly, the "Child's Viewpoint Seeks" <u>All Pleasure,</u> yet, soon <u>Finds Pain</u> as he **Fails to Recognize** the **Difference** between **Cowardice and Courage** (submission) until he **Fails at Instant Gratification** (happiness) and must *Find Pardon* in the *Spirit of God's Law*. Thirdly, the "Adolescent's Viewpoint Seeks" a <u>Rational Approach to Life</u> (logical implementation) until he **Fails to Recognize** the **Difference** between his **Greed and his Own Generosity** (unto thine own self be true) when he **Fails at becoming Rich** (powerful) and must *Find Resurrection from Failure* in the *Spirit of God's Will*. Fourthly, the "Teenager's Viewpoint Seeks" the idea that <u>Work and Play are One</u> and <u>Life is All Fun,</u> yet, **Fails to Recognize** the **Difference** between his **Selfishness and Unselfishness** (guilty conscience) until he **Fails his Education** (wisdom) and must *Find Reconciliation* in the *Spirit of God's Love*. Fifthly, the "Young Adult's Viewpoint Seeks" to <u>Strive for Excellence;</u> yet, he **Fails to Recognize** the **Difference** between the **Weakness of Flesh** (exhausted) and the **Strength of Spirit** (willing) until he **Fails at Marriage** (love) and must *Find Retribution* in the *Spirit of God's Union*. Sixthly, the "Adult's Viewpoint Seeks" to fulfill the <u>Desires of the Heart;</u> yet, he **Fails to Recognize** the **Difference** between the **Weakness of Spirit** (hope) and the **Strength of Flesh** (knowing) until he **Fails at Family Life** (respect) and must *Find Recompense* in the *Spirit of Worshiping God*. Finally, the "Wise Man's Viewpoint Seeks" to <u>Find his God;</u> yet, he **Fails to Recognize** the **Difference** between the **Weakness of the Soul** (human life) and the **Strength of the Life-force** (divine life) until he **Succeeds at Meeting God** (oneness) and *Finds the Reinstatement of Rights* in the *Spirit of Divine Oneness* (servanthood/slavery).

We now see that "Babies must Overcome" <u>Gluttony;</u> or Their <u>Uncontrolled Appetites</u> will cause **Them to Stick Everything They See** in <u>**Their Mouths**</u> and then **Touch** the most *Dangerous Things without Fear*. Secondly, "Children must Overcome" <u>Envy;</u> or the <u>Desire to Own Everything</u> will cause **Them to Take** that which **Does Not Belong to Them** as **They Strive** to <u>**Satisfy Their Outlandish Desires**</u> with *Instant Gratification*. Thirdly, "Adolescents must Overcome" <u>Slothfulness</u> (laziness); or the <u>Desire to Take Short-cuts</u> will cause **Them to Lie, Cheat, and Steal** as **They Try** to **Get Whatever They Want**, thereby <u>**Striving**</u> to *Make Themselves Special and Important*. Fourthly, "Teenagers must Overcome" <u>Lust;</u> or the <u>Fulfillment of Their Sexual Desires</u> will cause **Them to Enter into Troublesome Relationships** which can **Lead** to the *Destruction of Their Lives*. Fifthly, "Young Adults must Overcome" <u>Avarice;</u> or the <u>Satisfaction of Their Self-importance</u> will cause **Them** to become **Workaholics** as **They Strive to Attain Great Honors** which will <u>**Certainly Lead**</u> to *Their Ultimate Financial and Family Failures*. Sixthly, "Adults must Overcome" <u>Anger;</u> or the <u>Demand for Perfection</u> as **They Seek Personal Ownership** and **Absolute Control** will cause **Them** to **See Life** as *Their Own Treasure House of Infinite Wealth.* Finally, "Wise Men must Overcome" Pride; or Human Superiority as they **Seek Political Power** and **Influence** will cause **Them to Enter** a **State of Corruption** which will **Lead** to **Their Banishment** from a *Society of Righteous Men.*

Yes! through "Man's Ability" to Conquer **Gluttony, Envy, Sloth, Lust, Avarice, Anger, and Pride,** he can both **Grow-up** and **Mature** into a **Righteous King** (earth), **Holy Priest** (Heaven), and **Perfect Son** (Kingdom) Worthy of the *Presence of God.* Through these "Seven Growth Levels," the Human Race is **Able to Face** Sin (Lucifer's test) and **Life's Challenges** (God's judgment) and **Overcome Them** (self-evaluation) in **Each** and **Every Situation** Presented to it by *Men, Angels, and God.* This "Commitment to Challenge" had Once Spurred the **Jewish People** on to **Fulfill** the **Will of God, No Matter What** the Lord might Ask of Them (unquestioned obedience) be it *Facing Sin, Evil, Death,* and/or even *Damnation.* The "Apostles" had been Given a Massive Commitment or **Overwhelming Challenges** as **They Strived to Fulfill** the **Will of God** by **Establishing** a **Pagan-born Priesthood** Capable of *Saving the Whole World* (open God's portal). The "Lord Jesus Christ" was Telling **His First Church of Ephesus** to **Go Forth** and **Baptize All Men** in **Water** (innocent blood), **Blood** (forgiven blood), **and Spirit** (guilty blood) to Fulfill *Abraham's Covenant* (new body/free redemption/water), *His New Covenant* (eternal life/earned salvation/blood), and finally, *God's Eternal Covenant* (royal kingdom/bonus reward/spirit).

1. **Baptize in Water** - Offer Innocent Blood: Fulfill Abrahamic Covenant…God's Law
   - Belief - 33% of Perfection: Learning God's Right from Man's Wrong = Righteous Citizen on Earth
   - Purify Grave - Baby Level: Free Redemption = Being Saved/New Body (seat in celestial court)
2. **Baptize in Blood** - Offer Forgiven Blood: Fulfill New Covenant…Man's Faith
   - Trust - 67% of Perfection: Learning God's Good from Man's Evil = Holy Saint in Heaven
   - Purify Host - Teenage Level: Earned Salvation = Saving Self/Eternal Life (seat in temple court)
3. **Baptize in Spirit** - Offer Guilty Blood: Fulfill Eternal Covenant…God's/Man's Knowing
   - Faith - 100% of Perfection: Learning God's Will from Man's Will = Perfect Son within Kingdom
   - Purify Life - Adult Level: Bonus Rewards = Save Others/Own Kingdom (seat in royal court)

The "Lord Jesus Christ" is Calling All Men either to **Be Saved** (water), **Save Themselves** (blood), and/or **Help Christ Save Others** (spirit); but **All Creation** must **Come** to *Believe in Truth, Trust in the Law,* and/or have *Faith in God's Will.* Yes! "Fulfilling" God's Faith through Grace (trust) Affirmed by Works (belief) will **Set a Person Free** from *Eve's Curse of Pain* (ignorance), *Adam's Curse of Toil* (cowardice), the *Serpent's Curse of Death* (greed), and *God's Curse of Damnation* (selfishness). "Belief" is

33% Perfection and **Teaches a Person God's Right** from **man's wrong** to **Become a Righteous Citizen on Earth** and **Defeat Ignorance** to **Enter** a *New State of Wisdom*. "Trust" is 67% Perfection and **Teaches a Person God's Good** from **man's evil** to **Become a Holy Saint in Heaven** and **Defeat Cowardice** to **Enter** a *New State of Courage*. We see that "Faith" is 100% Perfection and **Teaches a Person God's Will** from **man's will** to **Become a Perfect Son** within **the Kingdom** and **Defeat Greed** to **Enter** a *New State of Generosity*.

This means that "Wise People" become Worthy of a **New Body** and bring **the Good News to All** that **Jesus** is **Bringing Free Redemption** to **Those Who Strive** to **Master Ethical Behavior** (obedience) on **Earth, Fulfill God's Law,** and **Change Their Nature** from *Human to Divine*. This means that "Courageous People" become Worthy of **Eternal Life** and bring the **Gospel Message** to **God's Saints** that **Christ** is **Bringing Earned Salvation** to **Those Who Strive to Master Moral Behavior** (love) in **Heaven, Fulfill Man's Faith,** and **Wash Away their Sins** to *Change the Unholy to Holy*. This means that "Generous People" become Worthy of **Their Own Royal Kingdom** and bring **Doctrinal Truths to God's Sons** that **Jesus Christ** is **Bringing Bonus Rewards** to **Those Who Strive** to **Master God's Fairness** (thinking) within the **Kingdom, Fulfill God's/Man's Knowing,** and **Learn** to *Think for Themselves* (imagination). The implication here is that "Growing Babies" can Become Soldiers-of-the-light, **Who** can **Thank God Yearly** (Easter Duty) by **Offering-up Their Labors** to **Prove They are Worthy** of **Graduating** from the **Lord's Earthly Elementary School** to *Remove Their Sin-natures/faults* and *Gain Virtues* (righteousness). A "Maturing Teenager" can Become a Living Prayer of Love, **Who** can **Praise God Weekly** (Sunday) by **Offering-up His Wealth** to **Prove He is Worthy** of **Graduating** from the **Lord's Heavenly High School** to *Remove His Worldly Temptations/evil* and *Gain Holiness*. A "Full Adult" can Become an Eternal Soul Savior, **Who** can **Worship God Daily** (Monday-Friday) by **Offering-up His Life** to **Prove He is Worthy of Graduating** from the **Lord's Kingdom College** to *Remove His Demonic Possession/death* and *Gain Perfection*. It should now make sense that "Man's Righteousness," "Holiness," and "Perfection" are Calling the **Lost Broken Sinners** to **Sign-up for God's Mystical Schools** to **Take Their Sonship Training** via *Water Baptism* (baby), *Blood Baptism* (teenager), and *Spirit Baptism* (adult).

The following tabular information indicates that "When Lost Sinners" Sign-up in **God's Mystical Schools, They become Worthy** of **Abraham's** *Free Redemption* (new body), **Christ's** *Earned Salvation* (eternal life), and **God's** *Bonus Rewards* (royal kingdom):

**Saving World via Water, Blood, and Spirit Baptisms
via Abraham, Christ, and God's Blessings**
(Abraham brings free redemption, Christ brings
earned salvation, and God brings bonus rewards)

Law (obedience)	1.	**Water Baptism** - Abrahamic Covenant: Free Redemption (being saved) ....Knowledge

- Earth - Learn Right/Wrong: Become Righteous Citizen on Earth = New Body
- Good News - Transfigured Body: Baby Flesh = Master Ethical Behavior

Belief
(righteousness)

- 1st Denial of Peter - Entered House of Shame: See Limitations   **Priest has Innocent Blood**
- Change Nature - Human to Divine: Soldier-of-the-Light = Own Earth
- Thank God - Offer Labors: Easter Duty (yearly)
- Enter Elementary School - Remove Sin-nature/faults Gain Virtues
- Jesus' 1st Advent - Priest on a Donkey: Jews Get *Heaven on Earth*

Faith
(love)

2. **Blood Baptism** - <u>New Covenant:</u> Earned Salvation (save self)
....Self-awareness
- Heaven - Learn Good/Evil: Become Holy Saint in Heaven = Eternal life
- Gospel Message - Glorified Body: Teenage Spirit = Master Moral Behavior

Trust
(holiness)

- 2nd Denial of Peter - Entered House of Humiliation: See Potential   **King has Forgiven Blood**
- Wash Away Sin - Change Unholy to Holy: Living Prayer = Own Heaven
- Praising God - Offer Wealth: Lord's Day (weekly)
- Christ's 2nd Advent - Thief in Night: Christians Get *Paradise in Heaven*

Knowing
(freedom)

3. **Resurrected Spirit Baptism** - <u>Everlasting Covenant:</u> Bonus Rewards
(save others)... ....Consciousness
- Kingdom - Learn God's Will/man's will: Become Perfect Son in Kingdom = Own Kingdom
- Doctrinal Truths - Mystical Body: Adult Soul = Master Fair Behavior

Faith
(perfection)

- 3rd Denial of Peter - Entered House of Disgrace: See Self-worth
- Set Free - Think for Self: Eternal Soul Savior = Own Kingdom   **Son has Guilty Blood**
- Worship God - Offer Life: Daily Sacrifice (perpetual)
- Jesus Christ's 3rd Advent - Judge on Cloud: Pagans Get *Kingdom of Glory*

This illustration shows that during the "Lord's Three Advents," the <u>Jews</u> **Get Heaven on Earth;** the <u>Christians</u> **Get Paradise in Heaven;** and the <u>Pagans</u> **Get the Kingdom of Glory** to <u>**Unite God, Angels, and Men**</u> into *One Mystical Creation* (earth/ Heaven/Kingdom). This means that on "Jesus'" <u>1st Advent</u> (donkey), **He** was bringing **Water Baptism** to **Purify Man's Sin-nature** to **Fulfill God's Law** (obedience) and **Transform the Jewish People** into **True Believers** in <u>**Fulfillment**</u> of the *Abrahamic Covenant* (create babies). Secondly, on "Christ's" <u>2nd Advent</u> (thief), **He** will bring **Blood Baptism** to **Purify Man's Worldly Temptations** to **Fulfill Man's Faith** (love) and **Transform** the **Christian People** into **Trusting Saints** in <u>**Fulfillment**</u> of the *New Covenant* (create saints). Finally, on "Jesus

Christ's" 3rd Advent (judge), **He** will bring **Spirit Baptism** to **Purify Man's Demonic Possession** to **Fulfill God/Man Knowing** (think) and **Transform** the **Pagan People** into **Faithful Sons** in **Fulfillment** of the *Eternal Covenant* (create sons).

In short, through the "Lord's Three Advents," Planet Earth becomes an **Eternal Baby Farm** specially **Designed** to **Create Baby Sinners** (Jews/belief), **Teenage Christians** (church/trust), and **Adult Saints/Pagans** (world/faith) to bring forth **New Transfigured Bodies** for *God's Eternal Work-force* (slaves). Secondly, "God's Heaven" becomes an Eternal Divine School specially **Designed** to **Create Righteous Saints** (belief), **Holy Saints** (trust), and **Perfect Saints** (faith) to bring forth **New Glorified Spirit Bodies** for *God's High Command* (servants). Finally, "God's Kingdom" becomes an Eternal Sonship Training Facility specially **Designed** to **Create Righteous Sons** (belief), **Holy Sons** (trust), and **Perfect Sons** (faith) to bring forth **New Mystical Divine Bodies** for *God's Royal Household* (free men). The "Message Here" is that the Spirit of Christ has **Come** to **Earth,** to **Heaven,** to the **Kingdom,** and even to **God** to **Transform All** into **New Creations** of **Mystical Love** as a **Reflection** of *God's Justice* (life), *Mercy* (death), and *Love* (new-life). It can be seen that this "Mystical Process" of Total Conversion will begin with the **Coming** of **Christ's** most **Holy Church** and **Christ's Priesthood** as it is **being Sent Throughout the World** to **Begin the Work** of *Human Conversion* (purifying grace).

This implies that the "Modern Day Priesthood" will Build Churches (money), Evangelize the Gentiles (friends), and Preach the Word of God (educate) in such a way as to **Call All** the **Lost Souls of Death** into *Eternal Redemption* (Christ). No! Not for one moment was this to be the "Master Plan of God," because just as the Jews Thought **They were Going** to **Fulfill the Mosaic Law** and become **Holy on Earth** (physical), the **Christians** were to also be *Sacrificed unto Confusion* (witnesses unto the truth). The point here is that "God was Not Using" the Jews and/or the Christians to **Save Mankind, One Family** at a time. The **Lord** was simply **Using Them** as a **Decoy for Lucifer,** until **He could Create** a *Mystical Portal of Invasion* for *His Son.* The "Job of the Messiah" during each of His Three Advents is to bring **Jews** (redemption)**, Christians** (salvation), and **Evil Pagans** (rewards) to *Righteousness* (mind), *Holiness* (heart), and *Perfection* (soul) in the *Sight of God.* We see that our present "Christian Priesthood" and its "Religious" have reached Perfection in the Sight of God and have effectively **Tricked Lucifer** into **Believing** that the *Church* has become an *Abomination of Sin and Evil.* No! It is exactly the opposite, just as in the "Time of Christ," when the Jewish People were **Called White-Washed Tombs Full of Dead Men's Bones** (failure), but instead **Judaism had Created** a *Mystical Portal* (Law/Virgin Mary), **Preparing the Way** for the *Coming of the Christ.* Through this "Portal of Life (earthly womb/immaculate womb/mystical womb)," Jesus Christ would come to **Visit Earth Three Times** (altar/throne/table): first, to **Institute** the *Messiah on Earth* (repentance/priest on donkey); secondly, to create the *Catholic Church* (prayers/thief in night); and finally, to *Build God's Righteous World* (works/end of the world).

This means that the "Life-experience" represents God's Divine School of Higher Learning in **Flesh** (earth), **Spirit** (Heaven), and **Soul** (Kingdom), thereby **Allowing**

Each of <u>God's Children</u> to become *Streetwise in the Flesh* (see limitations) and properly *Educated in the Spirit* (see potential). Obviously, through "Education (3,000 yrs.)," <u>God's Children</u> would both **Grow and Mature** to **Reach Adulthood**, thereby **Allowing Them** to **Recognize Their Messiah** and join with *Him* to *Save the World*.

Over a "3,000-Year Period," <u>Christ would Convert</u> **Man's Old Nature** (caterpillar) into a **New Born-again Nature** (butterfly) via **Seven Stages of Growth/Maturity**: 1) <u>Belief</u> - Wisdom, 2) <u>Submission</u> - Courage, 3) Unto Thine Own Self be True - Generosity, 4) <u>Guilty Conscience</u> - Unselfishness, 5) <u>Instinctive Compulsion</u> - Know God, 6) <u>Embrace God's Fruits</u> - Love God, and 7) <u>Offer Fruits to God</u> - Serve God. Through these "Seven Stages of New-life," a <u>Person can Expect</u> to **Experience his Conversion** from an *Earthly Caterpillar* (sinner) into a *Heavenly Butterfly* (saint).

The "Human Race" is being <u>Required</u> to **Attend Elementary School** (sin-nature) to **Learn Right from Wrong** (defeat ignorance) and then **Face Lucifer's Test** (study) to *Master Earth* (wisdom). Secondly, "Man" is <u>Required</u> to **Attend High School** (worldly temptations) to **Learn Good from Evil** (defeat cowardice) and then **Face God's Judgment** (experience) to *Master Heaven* (courage). Thirdly, "Man" is <u>Required</u> to **Attend College** (demonic possession) to **Learn God's Will from man's will** (defeat greed) and then **Face Self-evaluation** (imagination) to *Master God's Kingdom* (generosity). Fourthly, "Man" is <u>Required to Take</u> his **On-the-Job Training** (curse) to **Learn God's Reality from man's illusion** (defeat selfishness) and then **Face Freedom** (tasks) to *Master the Lord God Almighty Himself*. Fifthly, "Man" is <u>Required</u> to **Enter God's Work-force** (evil) to **Learn God's Truth from man's lies** (defeat knowing Lucifer) and then **Face Liberty** (duties) to *Master Oneself*. Sixthly, "Man" is <u>Required</u> to become an **Independent Contractor** to **Learn God's Law from man's law** (defeat loving Lucifer) and then **Face Independence** (responsibilities) to *Master His Own Ideas*. Finally, "Man" is <u>Required</u> to **Think for Himself** to **Learn God's Will from man's will** (defeat serving Lucifer) and then **Face Personal Ownership** (authority) to *Master His Own Circumstances*. At each of these "Levels of Human Performance," a <u>Person</u> must **Prove himself** be it on *Earth*, in *Heaven*, within the *Kingdom*, in *Union with God,* and/or simply *Surviving On his Own*.

The following tabular information indicates that there are "Seven Stages" of <u>Conversion</u> beginning with *Belief,* then *Submission,* to *Unto Thine Own Self be True,* to *Guilty Conscience,* to *Instinctive Compulsion,* then *Embracing God's Fruits,* and *Offering One's Fruits to God for His Love:*

**Conversion Means Believing, Surrendering, Unto Thine Own Self
be True, Guilty Conscience, Instinctive Compulsion, Embrace
God's Fruits, and Offer One's Fruits to God for His Love**

Mind   1. **Belief** - <u>Wisdom:</u> Master Ignorant Self (sin-nature)
(truth)   .... Knowledge
            • Enter Elementary School - Learn Right from Wrong: *Master Earth*

| Heart (law) | 2. **Submission** - <u>Courage:</u> Kill Sinful Self (worldly temptations) ....Self-awareness |

- Enter High School - Learn Good from Evil: *Master Heaven*
- Master Emotions - Face God's Judgment (experience)

| Soul (will) | 3. **Unto Thine Own Self be True** - <u>Generosity:</u> Resurrect Self (demonic possession) ....Consciousness |

- Enter College - Learn God's Will from man's will: *Master Kingdom*
- Master Instincts - Face Self-evaluation (imagine)

| Life-force (love) | 4. **Guilty Conscience** - <u>Unselfishness:</u> God Guides Self (curse) ....Sentience |

- Enter On-the-Job Training - Learn God's Reality/man's illusion: *Master God*
- Master Nature - Face Freedom (tasks)

| Nature (union) | 5. **Instinctive Compulsion** - <u>Know God:</u> Automatic Response (evil) ....Limitations |

- Enter God's Work-force - Learn God's Truth from man's lies: *Master Self*
- Master Ideas - Face Liberty (duties)

| Free Life (worship) | 6. **Embrace God's Fruits** - <u>Love God:</u> Treasures of Life (death) ....Potential |

- Enter Independent Contractor - Learn God's Law/man's law: *Master Society*
- Master Behavior - Face Independence (responsibilities)

| Essence of Life (oneness) | 7. **Offer Fruits to God** - <u>Serve God:</u> God Rewards Self (damnation) ....Self-worth |

- Think for Self - Learn God's Will/man's will: *Master Divinity*
- Master Circumstances - Face Ownership (authority)

This illustration shows that each of "Our Conversion Experiences" takes us on a <u>Great Journey</u> from **Nothing to All** as we must **Kill Our Old Selves** (selfishness/sin-nature) and bring forth a *New Creation in Christ Jesus* (unselfish nature). This tremendous "Journey" causes the whole <u>Human Race</u> to **Enter God's Divine School of Higher Learning**, where each of **God's Children** will receive a *New Mind* (wisdom), *New Heart* (courage), *New Soul* (generosity), *and New Life-force* (unselfishness). This means the "Human Race is Called" to <u>Master</u> its **Intellect, Emotions, Instincts, Nature, Ideas, Behavior,** and **Circumstances** to bring itself from a *State of Helplessness* into being the *Master of All It Surveys*. We now see that one's "Beliefs" brings a **Person** to <u>Knowledge,</u> "Submission" to <u>Self-awareness,</u> "Unto Thine Own Self be True" brings <u>Consciousness,</u> "Guilty Conscience" brings <u>Sentience,</u> "Instinctive Compulsion" brings <u>Seeing Limitations,</u> "Embracing of God's Fruits" brings <u>Seeing Potential,</u> and "Offer of Fruits to God" brings <u>Seeing Self-worth</u>. Once a "Person" is able to <u>See his Own Self-worth,</u> he can comprehend the **Meaning** (existence), **Purpose** (service), and **Value** (happiness) of **Life,** thereby leading him to **Find God** through *Worship* (give life), **Praise** (give wealth), and **Thanksgiving** (give labors). We are being shown that "Life is All About" the Power of Belief which must be turned into our **Desire to Serve our God** by becoming **Wise, Courageous, Generous, Unselfish,** thereby **Allowing Us** to **Know God, Love God,** and finally, **Serve God** in *Truth, Law, Will, and Love.*

We see that to "Comprehend" Mankind's Journey of Life, we must both **Grow Physically** (earth) and **Mature Spiritually** (Heaven) through **Four Stages of Life** from *Wise Baby*/sinner to *Courageous Teenager*/Christian, to *Generous Adult*/saint, to *Unselfish Wise Man*/son. By "Mastering" these Stages of Life, a **Person can Experience** becoming *More and More Perfect before God.* This means that the "Life-experience" is Made-up of **Four Chambers** much like **Moses' Mosaic Tabernacle** (outer court/holy place/holy of holies/mercy seat). In **Our Case,** these **Four Chambers** are represented by *Earth, Heaven, Kingdom, and God.* Recall that in the "Mosaic Tabernacle," the Holy of Holies was **Reserved** for the **High Priest** just **Once a Year** on the **Jewish Day of Atonement** (Yom Kippur) or when **He** would **Place Seven Drops** of Goat's Blood on *God's Mercy Seat* (forgiveness). Secondly, the "Holy Place" was Reserved for **the Levitical Priest,** who would **Perform** the **Daily Worship of God** by **Offering Prayers** upon the *Golden Altar of Incense.* Thirdly, the "Outer Court" was Reserved for **Righteous Jews,** who would bring **Their Sacrificial Offerings** to the **Brazen Altar** to be *Killed and Offered-up to God.* Finally, the "Eastern Gate" was Reserved for the **Gentiles** (strangers), who would **Beg for Forgiveness** from the **One God** as **They were in Hopes** of One Day becoming *Adopted Jews.*

We can now see an "Interesting Structure" based on Four Mystical Levels of Perfection from **Gentile** to **Righteous Jew,** to **Levitical Priest,** to **High Priest** as each **Person** is *Getting Closer and Closer to God.* We see this "Same Structure" in God's Creation, where **Earth** is the *Outer Court* (kings), **Heaven** is the *Holy Place* (priests), the **Kingdom** is the *Holy-of-holies* (sons), and then **God Himself** is the *Sacred Mercy Seat* (God).

1. **Earth** - Outer Court: God's Kingship = Fulfill God's Law of Obedience... Change Nature
   - Judged by Jews - Water (flesh)
   - Judged by Christians - Fire (spirit)   *Human to Divine*
   - Declared Righteous - Citizenship (soul)
2. **Heaven** - Holy Place: God's Priesthood = Fulfill Man's Faith in God's Love... Wash Away Sins
   - Judged by Saints - Bread (flesh)
   - Judged by Angels - Candlestick (spirit)   *Sinfulness to Holiness*
   - Declared Holy - Saintly (soul)
3. **Kingdom** - Holy of Holies: God's Sonship = Fulfill God/Man Knowing God's Truth... Awakened from Sleep
   - Judged by Jesus (flesh)
   - Judged by Christ (spirit)   *Imperfection to Perfection*
   - Declared Perfect - Son of God
4. **God** - Sacred Mercy Seat: God's Freedom = Fulfill Man/God Free Will Thinking... Darkness into Light
   - Judged by Man (flesh)

- Judged by God (spirit)   *Death to New-life*
- Declared Free - Free Man

The "Trick to Life" is to <u>Travel</u> from **Nothing to All** by <u>Journeying</u> from *Earth* (physical), to *Heaven* (spiritual), to the *Kingdom* (mystical) *All the Way to God Himself* (divine). In this "Awesome Ordeal," we see that it <u>Requires God's Son</u>, **Jesus Christ** to **Open the Necessary Doors** from **One Dimension to Another** via *His Three Advents*. Notice that "God" First Sent the <u>Jewish People</u> to **Establish Earth** as the **Eastern Gate**; then **Came Jesus** as a **Priest on a Donkey** to <u>Open Heaven</u> via *His Sacrifice on Mount Calvary*. Secondly, we see "Jesus Christ" must <u>Return</u> as a **Thief in the Night** to **Take His Saints into Heaven** via the <u>Judgment of the Sanctuary</u> or during the *Three Days of Darkness*. Thirdly, "Jesus Christ" will come as a <u>Just Judge on a Cloud</u> to **Take the Whole World** into **His Father's Kingdom** via the <u>Great White Throne Judgment</u> or during the *End of the World*. We see that after the "Coming of Jews" and "Christ's Three Advents," <u>God Himself</u> is **Planning to Come** into <u>**His New Heaven and New Earth**</u> via *His Journey in His New Jerusalem*. The idea here is that the "Human Race" must <u>Pass through</u> **Four Levels** of <u>**Transformation**</u> (Man becomes God) to *Reach God;* and now it is "God's Turn" to <u>Pass through</u> **His Four Levels** of **Transformation** (God becomes Man) to *Reach Man*. Yes! It all comes down to becoming a "Wise Baby," "Courageous Teenager," "Generous Adult," and "Unselfish Wise Adult" and then a <u>**Person can be Set Free**</u> from *Sin, Evil, Death, and Damnation*.

The following tabular information indicates that the "Human Race is Traveling" through <u>Four Levels</u> of **Transformation** from <u>**Wise Baby**</u> (sinner), <u>**Courageous Teenager**</u> (Christian), **Generous** <u>**Adult**</u> (saint), to <u>**Unselfish Wise Man**</u> (son), to become *Perfect Before God*:

		Earth Jewish People (elementary school/baby farm)	Heaven Christian People (high school/divine school of higher learning)
God (divinity)	1.	**House of Aaron**/mercy seat	1. **Communion of Saints**/tabernacle
		• Holy of Holies	• Altar of God
		• Sonship Level	• Father God Level
		• Wise Man Status	• Seat in Divine Court **Unselfish**
		• Learn Man's Illusion	• Learn God's Reality
		• Righteousness - Wise Man	• Kingdom of Heaven - Son

(3rd Advent - Judge on a Cloud: Final Judgment = God's Freedom/become God)

Kingdom (son)	2.	**Levitical Priesthood**	2. **Melchizedek Priesthood**
		• Holy Place	• Sanctuary of God
		• Kingship Level	• Son of God Level
		• Adult Status	• Seat in Royal Court **Generous**
		• Learn Man's Will	• Learn God's Will
		• Inherit Earth - Adult	• Son of God - Saint

(2nd Advent - Thief in Night: Lord's Day = God's Royal Kingdom/serve God)

Heaven (saints)	3.	**Jewish Laity**	3.	**Catholic Laity**	
		• Outer Court		• Church Assembly	
		• Priesthood Level		• Holy Spirit Level	
		• Teenage Status		• Seat in Temple Court	**Courageous**
		• Learn Man's Evil		• Learn God's Good	
		• Comforted - Teenager		• See God - Christian	

(1st Advent - Priest on a Donkey: Great Sabbath = God's Eternal Life/love God)

Earth (Christians)	4.	**Gentile Pagan**	4.	**Pagan World**	
		• Eastern Gates		• Church Vestibule	
		• Sinner Level		• Messiah Level	
		• Baby Status		• Seat in Celestial Court	**Wise**
		• Learn Man's Wrong		• Learn God's Right	
		• Kingdom of God - Baby		• Shown Mercy - Sinner	

(12 Jewish Tribes - Mosaic Law of God: Day of Atonement = God's New Body/know God)

This illustration shows that the "Human Race" has been <u>Created</u> to both **Grow Physically** and **Mature Spiritually** through **Four Levels of Transformation** via a <u>Repentant Sinner's</u> *Mind, Heart, Soul, and Life-force*, thereby **Allowing** a <u>Person to Master</u> *Earth, Heaven, the Kingdom, and God*. The question is: just "How can a Person" <u>Accomplish All This</u> in just **One Earthly Lifetime** (physical existence), unless he is **Jesus Christ Himself, Who** can <u>**Do All Things**</u> in *Mind, Heart, Soul, and Life-force*? Obviously, to "Do All Things Perfectly," a <u>Person must Master</u> the **Physical** (earth), **Spiritual** (Heaven), **Mystical** (Kingdom), **and Divine** (God) **Dimensions** in **One Lifetime** by <u>**Building a Perfect**</u> *Home, Government, Church, and Self-worth in Christ*. This "Desire to be Perfect" <u>Allows a Person</u> to **Begin Life** as a *Sinner*, become a *Christian*, become a *Saint*, and finally, become a *Son of God*.

Note that in the "Mosaic Tabernacle," there were <u>Four Entry Points</u> beginning with the *Outer Court*, the *Holy Place*, the *Holy of Holies*, and finally *God's Mercy Seat*. Through these "Four Entry Points," <u>Jesus Christ</u> was **Able** to **Show His Followers** that **His Job** was to **Open Each Holy Chamber** to the **Next Level**, thereby <u>**Welcoming**</u> a *New Set of Growing and Maturing Believers*. In short, during the "Time of Moses," <u>Only the High Priest</u> could **Enter** the **Holy of Holies** <u>Once a Year</u> on the *Day of Atonement*. In contrast, after the "Lord's 1st Advent," the <u>Holy of Holies</u> was **Open** to the **Melchizedek Priesthood** and the **High Priest** or the **Messiah was Promoted** to *Sit at the Right Hand of God* (intercessor). Obviously, "After the Lord's 2nd Advent," the <u>Melchizedek Priest</u> (saints) will **Sit at the Right Hand of God** and the **Laity** will be **Allowed** to **Enter** the **Holy of Holies** as <u>Everyone</u> will *Move Up One Additional Step*. This means that "After the Lord's 3rd Advent," the <u>Laity</u> will **Sit at the Right Hand of God** and the **Forgiven Sinners** will be **Allowed** to **Enter the Holy of Holies** as <u>Everyone</u> will *Again Move Up One Step*. Upon this "Glorious Moment of Triumph," <u>God, Angels, and Men</u> will **Proclaim the Coming** of the <u>**New Heaven and the New Earth,**</u> thereby *Bringing Unity to One and All*.

The following tabular information indicates that "Jesus Christ" is <u>Moving All Mankind</u> **One Step at a Time** from **Death to New-life** <u>**Beginning**</u> with the **_Outer Court_** (earth) **All the Way** to **_God's Mercy Seat_** (God):

	Physical Dimension (12 Jewish Tribes)	Spiritual Dimension (1st Advent)	Mystical Dimension (2nd Advent)	Divine Dimension (3rd Advent)
God's Mercy Seat (altar)	1. High Priest(1) (sons of God) Church	Levitical Priest(2) (saints) Government	Righteous Jew(3) (Christians) Home	Forgiven Gentile(4) (forgiven sinners) *Self* (freedom)
Holy of Holies (sanctuary)	2. Levitical Priest (2) (saints) Government	Righteous Jew (3) (Christians) Home	Forgiven Gentile (4) (forgiven sinners) *Self* (royal kingdom)	Lost Pagan(5) (converted Pagans) - - - -
Holy Place (assembly)	3. Righteous Jew (3) (Christians) Home	Forgiven Gentile (4) (forgiven sinners) *Self* (eternal life)	Lost Pagan (5) (converted Pagans) - - -	Eternally Damned (6) (resurrected damned) - - -
Outer Court (vestibule)	4. Poor Gentile (4) (sinners) *Self* (new body)	Lost Pagan (5) (converted Pagans) - - -	Eternally Damned (6) (resurrected damned) - - -	Evil Demons (7) (purified Demons) - - -
	Mosaic Tabernacle	Holy Mass	Christ's Temple	New Jerusalem

Redemption of New Creations via Belief:

1. **Sons of God** - - - - - - - - - - -Death/Life: <u>Orphans</u> - - - - - - - - - - Remove Faults: **_Become God_**
2. **Saints** - - - - - - - - - - - - - - -Holy Orders: <u>Widows</u> - - - - - - - - - Remove Sin: **_Serve God_**
3. **Christians** - - - - - - - - - - - -Marriage: <u>Poor</u> - - - - - - - - - - - - - Remove Evil: **_Love God_**
4. **Forgiven Sinners** - - - - - - - -Confirmation: <u>Strangers</u> - - - - - - - Remove Death: **_Know God_**
5. **Converted Pagans** - - - - - - -Communion: <u>Insane</u> - - - - - - - - - - Remove Grave: **_Worship God_**
6. **Resurrected Damned** - - - - -Confession: <u>Enemies</u> - - - - - - - - - - Remove Damnation: **_Praise God_**
7. **Purified Demons** - - - - - - - - -Baptism: <u>Lucifer himself</u> - - - - - - - - Remove Fires of Hell: **_Thank God_**

This illustration shows that the "Human Race is Traveling" from an <u>Evil Demon</u> all the way to becoming a <u>Son of God</u> as a **Person must Master** the **Physical, Spiritual, Mystical, and Divine** <u>**Dimensions of Life**</u> to **_Become God-like_**. We now see that the "Human Race is Traveling" through <u>Moses' Tabernacle</u> or the **Jewish Temple** from its **_Outer Court_**, to its **Holy Place**, to its **_Holy of Holies_**, and finally, to **_God's Mercy Seat_** (judgment). This means that the "First Person" to be <u>Saved</u> is the **_Orphan_** (Son of God), then the **_Widow_** (Saints), then the **_Poor_** (Christians), then the **_Strangers_** (Forgiven Sinners), then the **_Insane_** (Converted Pagans), then the **_Enemies_** (Resurrected Damned), and finally, **_Lucifer_** (Purified

Demons) *himself*. We see that "Each One" of these <u>Lost Broken People</u> is **Given a Chance** to **Move Up the Ladder** (one step) until he **Sits** at the <u>**Right Hand of God**</u> and is *Transformed from Nothing to All*. During this "Awesome Journey," an <u>Eternally Damned Person</u> is **Called Out** of the *Flames of Hell,* **Removed** from *Damnation,* **Taken** from the *Grave,* able to **Conquer** *Death,* **Overcome Evil,** be **Purified** of *Sin,* and finally, **Remove his** *Smallest Faults*. Through the "Sacrifice" of <u>Jesus Christ</u> upon **Mount Calvary,** this **Tremendous Journey** from **Nothing to All** will **Take Place,** thereby **Setting** <u>**Men, Angels, and God Free**</u> from the *Curses of Imperfection.*

A "Person might Ask: If Redemption" <u>Comes from Believing</u> in the **Goodness of God** and the **Need to become Perfect** in the **Sight of God,** then just **How Can a Lost Soul Hope** to be <u>**Saved,**</u> *When All is Totally Hopeless*? The answer is that "God" in <u>His Divine Wisdom</u> has a **Grand Design** which includes **Creating** the **Jewish People, Christ's 1st, 2nd, and 3rd Advents** to bring <u>**Lost Sinners**</u> from the *Nothing of Death* to the *All of Eternal Life*. In short, the "Jewish People (Eastern Gate)" brought forth the <u>New-body</u> or **Christ's Resurrection** and the **Creation** of the **Gentile Church** that <u>**Set the Stage**</u> for the *Lord's 1st Advent*. "When Jesus Christ (Outer Court)" <u>Rode into Jerusalem</u> as a **Priest on a Donkey,** the **Whole World** was **Offered Free Eternal Life** (good news), <u>**If a Lost Soul**</u> will simply *Believe in God's Son* (word). Secondly, upon "Christ's Second Coming (Holy Place)" as a <u>Thief in the Night,</u> the **Earth** will be **Offered God's Royal Kingdom of Glory, If a Person** will <u>**Sacrifice himself**</u> by *Dying with Christ's Holy Church*. Finally, upon "Christ's 3rd Advent (Holy of Holies)" as a <u>Just Judge on a Cloud,</u> the **Earth** will be **Offered God's Infinite Freedom, If a Person** will <u>**Sacrifice himself**</u> (fight evil) by *Dying with Christ's Righteous World*. Yes! The "Life-experience" is <u>All About</u> **Believing In** the **Righteousness, Holiness, and Perfection of God** even when the **Lord God Almighty is Willing** to **Sacrifice It All** to bring forth a most *Beloved Treasure Worth Owning.*

We see that "God must Believe in Himself" as <u>He is Willing to Sacrifice</u> **Everything** to **Create a Perfect Kingdom of Glory,** even **If He** must **Pay the Sin-debt** of <u>**Every**</u> **Person on** <u>**Earth**</u> with *His Own Son's* (Jesus Christ) *Blood, Death, and Redeemed Spirit*. Obviously, the "Lord God Almighty" knew that <u>Big Things Take Time</u> and will certainly **Cost Him Dearly** even unto *His Last Penny* or *His Last Seven Drops of Sacred Blood* (Calvary/mercy seat). We see that these "Seven Drops of Blood" are <u>Represented</u> by the **Lord's Seven Last Words** which were **Spoken from the Cross** as <u>**Divine Requests to His Father**</u> to *Save All the Lost Sinners in Creation*. Note that "Jesus Christ" also remained <u>Stone Silent</u> to **Save Lucifer/ Barabbas** and <u>**All Murderers,**</u> thereby *Giving His Father Eight Tickets of Eternal Redemption*. These "Eight Tickets of Redemption" are: 1) <u>Silent before King Herod</u> - Save Murderers: Lucifer and Barabbas; 2) <u>Forgive them for They Know What They Do</u> - Save Enemies: Jews, Romans, and Greeks; 3) <u>My God, My God, Why have You Forsaken</u> Me? - Save Betraying Friends: Judas (all traitors); 4) <u>It is Finished</u> - Save Strangers: Lost Fools of the World; 5) <u>I Thirst</u> - Save Neighbors: Stiff-necked Jews; 6) <u>This Day You will be With Me in Paradise</u> - Save Friends: Good Thief/Apostles/

Friends (Lazarus/Mary/Martha); 7) <u>Son, behold Thy Mother and Mother, behold Thy Son</u> - Save Family: Blood Relatives; and 8) <u>I Release My Spirit</u> - Save Self: Jesus Christ and His Church. Through these "Eight Sacrifices," <u>We can Understand</u> **God's Symbolic Act** of **Placing Seven Drops of Blood** plus **Aaron's Prayer** upon the <u>**Ark of the Covenant's Mercy Seat**</u> during *Yom Kippur* (Day of Atonement). This "Gesture of Giving One's All" represents <u>Each of God's Seven Fold-spirits</u> **Giving Its Last Drop of Blood** and then **God Himself** <u>**Sacrificing His Divine Spirit**</u> to **Symbolize** a *Final Sacrifice unto Oblivion* (empty). Note that the "Last Words" of <u>Jesus Christ</u> are **I Release My Spirit** (save self) to signify that **He is Empty** unto <u>**Absolute Nothingness,**</u> thereby *Making Him Worthless Before God*. It now makes sense to "Connect Jesus'" <u>Seven Last Words</u> (plus silence) to **Lucifer's Seven Deadly Sins** which are then <u>**Supernaturally Forgiven**</u> by *God's Seven Blessings of Forgiveness* on *Mount Calvary*.

The following tabular information indicates that "Jesus Christ's Seven Last Words" bring forth <u>God's Seven Blessings of Forgiveness</u> (pay sin-debt) as they **Relate** to the <u>**Evil One's Seven Deadly Sins**</u> causing *Man's Physical and Spiritual Destruction*:

Jesus Christ's Seven Last Words bring forth God's Seven Divine Forgivenesses to a Lost World

(seven deadly sins are made perfect on Mt. Calvary
by Jesus Christ via his blood/death/spirit)

Lucifer	0.	**Jesus is Silent** – <u>Save Murderers/Barabbas</u>…Sacrifice God's Beauty
(God)		• 1st Redemptive Payment - 1st Angel: Lucifer = I Never Knew You
		• Pride - Forgiveness of Evil Demon: Spiritual Baptism (humility)
Humility		• *Create Damnation* - Separation from God: Edenic Covenant (imperfection)
		• Jewish Hanukkah - Redeem Chosen People: Air Contract (short-lived)
		• Purchase Royal Kingdom - Remove Ignorance (new mind)
		• Treasure - <u>Kingdom of God:</u> Teaches Evil (elementary babies)

Adam	1.	**Forgive Them for They Know Not What They Do** - <u>Save Enemies</u>…
(father)		Sacrifice God's Wisdom
		• 2nd Redemptive Payment - 1st Man: Adam = The Woman Gave Me the Fruit
		• Anger - Forgiveness of One's Enemies: Water Baptism (good judgment)
Good		• *Create Hell* - Hopelessness: Adamic Covenant (unholiness)
Judgment		• Jewish Passover - Baptism (water): Water Contract (dries)
		• Purchase Eternal Life - Remove Cowardice (new heart)
		• Treasure - <u>Comfortable Life:</u> Teaches Wrong (elementary/child)
Noah	2.	**My God, My God, Why have You Forsaken Me** - <u>Save Traitors</u>
(son)		…Sacrifice God's Obedience
		• 3rd Redemptive Payment - 1st People: Society = We Don't Believe in Noah
		• Avarice - Forgiveness of Betraying Friend: Penance (good values**)**
Good		• *Create Grave* - Death Agony: Noahic Covenant (unrighteousness)
Values		• Jewish Unleavened Bread - Communion (Eucharist): Oil Contract (fades)

- Purchase God's New Body - Remove Greed (new soul)
- Treasure - <u>Inherit Earth:</u> Teaches Evil/Wrong (elementary/adolescent)

———————————— Son of God (wash away sin/lessons) ————————————

Jews
(spirit)

True
Love

3. **It is Finished** - <u>Save Strangers</u>…Sacrifice God's Faith
- 4th Redemptive Payment - 1st Nation: Chosen People = Stiff-necked Fool
- Lust - Forgiveness of Ignorant Strangers: Communion (love)
- *Create Death* - Painfulness: Mosaic Covenant (transformation)
- Jewish Firstfruits - Confirmation: Blood Contract (fades)
- Purchase God's Wisdom - See God's Truth (new life-force)
- Treasure - <u>Become Righteous:</u> Teaches Right/Wrong (high school/ teenage)

Messiah
(father/son)

Charity

4. **I Thirst** - <u>Save Neighbors</u>………………………Sacrifice God's Love
- 5th Redemptive Payment - 1st Divine Man: Takes-on All Sin = I Surrender
- Envy - Forgiveness of Cold Neighbors: Confirmation (charity)
- *Create New-life* - Sonship: New Covenant (perfection)
- Jewish Pentecost - Marriage: Death Contract (resurrection)
- Purchase God's Love - See Self-worth (new nature)
- Treasure - <u>Shown God's Mercy:</u> Teaches Good/Evil (high school/young adult)

———————————— Son of Man (change nature/blessings) ————————————

Church
(father/spirit)

Honesty

5. **This Day You will be With Me in Paradise** - <u>Save Friends</u>…Sacrifice God's Holiness
- 6th Redemptive Payment - 1st Holy Man: Holy Saint
- Sloth - Forgiveness of Unthinking Friends: Holy Orders (honesty)
- *Create Holiness* - Priesthood: Abrahamic Covenant (sainthood)
- Jewish Trumpets - Holy Orders: Damnation Contract (forgiven)
- Purchase God's Holiness - See Potential (new instincts)
- Treasure - <u>See God:</u> Teaches God's/Man's Wills (junior college/adulthood)

World
(son/spirit)

Good
Taste

6. **Son, Behold Thy Mother/Mother, Behold Thy Son** – <u>Save Family</u>… Sacrifice God's Righteousness
- 7th Redemptive Payment - 1st Righteous Man: Awakened Christian
- Gluttony - Forgiveness of Untrusting Family: Marriage
- *Create Righteousness* - Kingship: Palestinian Covenant (brotherhood)
- Jewish Atonement (confess) - Death: Oblivion Contract (God's miracle)
- Purchase of God's Righteousness - See Limitations (new imagination)
- Treasure - <u>Son of God:</u> Teaches Reality/Illusion (college/wise man)

Self

7. **I Release My Spirit** - <u>Save Self</u>………..Sacrifice God's Perfection

(trinity)	• 8th Redemptive Payment - Free Man: Thinking for Oneself
	• Ignorance - Forgiveness of Unthinking Self: Death
Wisdom	• *Create Perfection* - Free Will: Everlasting Covenant (freedom)
	• Jewish Tabernacle - Resurrection: New-life Contract (Calvary)
	• Purchase of God's Perfection - See Face of God (beatific vision)
	• Treasure - <u>Kingdom of God:</u> Teaches God's/Man's Truths (on-the-job training/saint)

This illustration shows that the "Lord God Almighty was Willing" to <u>Sacrifice Everything He Owned</u> to **Obtain** a **Perfect Wife** (virgin), **Perfect Mother** (blessed), and **Perfect Friend** (Mary) with *Whom He could Live His Eternal Life*. In the above depiction, we see "God is Giving His All (eight sacrifices)" by <u>Sacrificing His **1st Angel**</u> (Lucifer), **1st Man** (Adam), **1st Humanity/People** (society), **1st Nation** (Jews), **1st Divine Man** (Jesus), **1st Holy People** (church), **1st Righteous World** (world), and **1st Repentant Sinner** (self) to *Get a Kingdom of Glory*. Through these "Eight Sacrifices," <u>God, Angels, and Men</u> are **United** within the *Blood, Death, and Spirit of Christ*. Via these "Eight Sacrifices," <u>God also Defeats</u> **Lucifer's Seven Deadly Sins** plus **His Own Curse of Original Sin**: 1) <u>Sin of Pride</u> - Curse of Damnation (separation from God): Curse of Ignorance = Wicked Mind; 2) <u>Sin of Anger</u> - Curse of Hell (hopelessness): Curse of Cowardice = Wicked Heart; 3) <u>Sin of</u> Avarice - Curse of Grave (death agony): Curse of Greed = Wicked Soul; 4) <u>Sin of Lust</u> - Curse of Death: Curse of Selfishness = Wicked Life-force; 5) <u>Sin of Envy</u> - Curse of Pain: Curse of Selfishness = Dead Soul; 6) <u>Sin of Sloth</u> - Curse of Discomfort: Curse of Non-cooperation = Damned Life-force; 7) <u>Sin of Gluttony</u> - Curse of a Mean Spirit: Curse of Confusion = Obliterated Nature, and 8) <u>Sin of Cruelty</u> (selfishness) - Curse of Wickedness: Curse of Evil = Nothingness. This means that through "God's Eight Sacrifices," <u>He is Able to Purchase</u> **His Heart's Desire** (needs nothing/wants everything) which is *Described Below*:

Purchasing God's Heart's Desire
(God is forced to give His All to pay the last penny and own a Kingdom of Glory)

1. <u>God Sacrifices His 1st Angel</u> - Lucifer (beauty)
Note that "God's 1st Sacrifice (Passover)" was the <u>Beauty</u> of **His 1st Angel, Lucifer** to **Ensure that God** would **Get a Beautiful Wife** and a **Place of Torment or Hell** for **Anyone Who would Not Honor** this most *Beautiful of All Women* and *Her Beautiful Children*. We see that "Jesus Remained Silent" before <u>King Herod</u> and **Defeats** the **Sin of Lucifer's Pride** (I never knew you), thereby **Forgiving All Murderers,** even *Barabbas* and the *Demons of Hell*. This "Act of Forgiveness" brings forth <u>Spiritual Baptism</u> (humility) upon **God's Creation** to **Set All the Captives Free**, thereby **Transforming Them** from *Imperfection* into *Perfection* before *God*. But, "Woe to Those" <u>Who Reject Christ's Death</u> (1st drop/second chance), because **They will Face Eternal Separation from God** and *Lose the Edenic Covenant of Life* (imperfection). This means that

through this "1st Sacrifice," <u>God will Pay Creation's</u> **Sin-debt of Damnation**, thereby **Removing All Ignorance** (new mind) and then *Getting a New Royal Kingdom* or *Kingdom of God.*

2.   <u>God Sacrifices His 1st Man</u> - Adam (wisdom)
Note that "God's 2nd Sacrifice (unleavened bread)" was the Wisdom of **His 1st Man, Adam** to Ensure **that God** would **Get a Wise Wife** and a **Place of Damnation or Eternal-flames** for **Anyone Who would Not Honor** this most *Brilliant of All Women* and *Her Wise Children*. We see that "Jesus Said" Forgive Them for They Know Not What They Do and **Defeats** the **Sin of Adam's Anger** (the woman gave me to eat), thereby **Forgiving All Sinners.** even *Eve* and those in *Damnation*. This "Act of Forgiveness" brings forth Water Baptism (remove original sin) upon **God's Creation** to **Set All the Captives Free**, thereby **Transforming Them** from *Evil Sinners* into *Repentant Sinners* before *God*. But "Woe to Those" Who Reject Christ's Blood (2nd drop/forgiveness), because **They will Face Eternal Hopelessness** and *Lose the Adamic Covenant of Life* (unholiness). This means that through this "2nd Sacrifice," God will Pay Creation's **Sin-debt of Hell**, thereby **Removing All Cowardice** (new heart) and then *Getting Eternal Life* or a *Comfortable Eternal Life*.

3.   <u>God Sacrifices His 1st People</u> - 1st Humanity/Noah (obedience)
Note that "God's 3rd Sacrifice (firstfruits)" was the <u>Obedience</u> of **His 1st Humanity, Noah** to **Ensure that God** would **Get an Obedient Wife** and a **Place of Eternal Burial** (grave) for **<u>Anyone Who would Not Honor</u>** this *Obedient of All Women* and *Her Dutiful Children*. We see that "Jesus Said" <u>My God, My God, Why have You Forsaken Me?</u> and **Defeats** the **Sin of Man's Avarice** (I don't believe in Noah), thereby **Forgiving All Traitors,** even *Judas Iscariot* and those in the *Grave*. This "Act of Forgiveness" brings forth <u>Repentance</u> (confession) upon **God's Creation** to **Set All the Captives Free**, thereby **Transforming Them** from *Ignorant Sinners* to *Christians* before *God*. But "Woe to Those" <u>Who Reject Christ's Pain</u> (3rd drop/Christianity), because **They will Face <u>Eternal Death Agony</u>** and *Lose the Noahic Covenant of Life* (unrighteousness). This means that through this "3rd Sacrifice," <u>God will Pay Creation's</u> **Sin-debt of the Grave**, thereby **Removing All Human Greed** (new soul) and then *Getting a New Body* or *Inheriting the Earth*.

4.   <u>God Sacrifices His 1st Nation</u> - Jews (faith)
Note that "God's 4th Sacrifice (Pentecost)" was the <u>Faith</u> of **His Chosen People, Jews** to **Ensure that God** would **Get a Faithful Wife** and a **Place of Eternal Death** for **<u>Anyone Who would Not Honor</u>** this most *Faithful of All Women* and *Her Devoted Children*. We see that "Jesus Said" <u>It is Finished</u> and **Defeats** the **Sin of Man's Lust** (stiff-necked fool), thereby **Forgiving All Strangers,** even the *Jewish People* and those in *Eternal Death*. This "Act of Forgiveness" brings forth <u>Communion</u> (Eucharist) upon **God's Creation** to **Set All the Captives Free**, thereby **Transforming Them** from *Christians* to *Saints* before *God*. But "Woe to Those" <u>Who Reject Christ's Suffering</u> (4th drop/sainthood), because **They will Face <u>Eternal Suffering</u>**

and *Lose the Mosaic Covenant of Life* (transformation). This means that through this "4th Sacrifice," God will Pay Creation's **Sin-debt of Death**, thereby **Removing All Human Selfishness** (new life-force) and then *Getting a Royal Kingdom* or to *Become Righteous*.

5.   God Sacrifices His 1st Divine Man - Jesus (love)
Note that "God's 5th Sacrifice (trumpets)" is the Love of **His Beloved Son, Jesus** to **Ensure that God** would **Get a Loving Wife** and a **Place of Eternal Pain** for **Anyone Who would Not Honor** this most *Loving of All Women* and *Her Loving Children*. We see that "Jesus Said" I Thirst and **Defeats** the **Sin of Man's Envy** (I surrender), thereby **Forgiving All One's Cold Neighbors,** even *God's Messiah* and those in *Eternal Pain*. This "Act of Forgiveness" brings forth Confirmation (spirit anointing) upon **God's Creation** to **Set All the Captives Free**, thereby **Transforming Them** from *Saints* into *Sons of God* before **God**. But "Woe to Those" Who Reject Christ's Pain (5th drop/sonship), because **They will Face Eternal Pain** and *Lose the New Covenant of Life* (perfection). This means that through this "5th Sacrifice," God will Pay Creation's **Sin-debt of Pain**, thereby **Removing All Human Faults** (new nature) and then *Getting God's Blessing of Freedom* or to be *Shown God's Mercy*.

6.   God Sacrifices His 1st Holy Man - Church (holiness)
Note that "God's 6th Sacrifice (atonement)" is the Holiness of **His Sacred Church, Catholics** to **Ensure that God** would **Get a Holy Wife** and a **Place of Eternal Correction** for **Anyone Who would Not Honor** that most *Holy of All Women* and *Her Holy Children*. We see that "Jesus Said" This Day You will be With Me in Paradise and **Defeats** the **Sin of Man's Sloth** (lie/cheat/steal), thereby **Forgiving All Unfaithful Friends,** even *Christ's Apostles* and those in *Eternal Discomfort*. This "Act of Forgiveness" brings forth Holy Orders (ordination) upon **God's Creation** to **Set All the Captives Free**, thereby **Transforming Them** from *Sons of God* to *Free Men* before **God**. But "Woe to Those" Who Reject Christ's Discomfort (6th drop/freedom), because **They will Face Eternal Discomfort** and *Lose the Abrahamic Covenant of Life*. This means that through this "6th Sacrifice," God will Pay Creation's **Sin-debt of Discomfort**, thereby **Removing All Human Weaknesses** (new imagination) and then *Getting God's Blessing of Freedom* or to *Actually See God* (beatific vision).

7.   God Sacrifices His 1st Righteous Man - World (righteousness)
Note that "God's 7th Sacrifice (tabernacles)" is the Righteousness of **His Righteous World, Mankind** to **Ensure that God** would **Get a Righteous Wife** and a **Place of Eternal Guilt** for **Anyone Who would Not Honor** that most *Righteous of All Women* and *Her Righteous Children*. We see that "Jesus Said" Son, behold Thy Mother and Mother, behold Thy Son and **Defeats** the **Sin of Man's Gluttony**, thereby **Forgiving All Jealous Family Members,** even *His Grandparents* and those in *Eternal Guilt*. This "Act of Forgiveness" brings forth Marriage (contract) upon **God's Creation** to **Set All the Captives Free**, thereby **Transforming Them** from *Free Men* to *Servants of God* before **God**. But "Woe to Those" Who Reject Christ's Guilt (7th drop/servanthood), because **They**

will Face **Eternal Guilt** and *Lose the Palestinian Covenant of Life* (land). This means, that through this "7th Sacrifice," God will Pay Creation's **Sin-debt of Servanthood,** thereby **Removing All Human Laziness** (new strength) and then *Getting God's Blessing of Servanthood* or *Become a Son of God* (adopted).

8.   God Sacrifices His 1st Free Man - Kingdom (perfection)
Note that "God's 8th Sacrifice (new-life)" is the Perfection of **His Perfect Self, God** to **Ensure that God** would **Get a Perfect Wife** and a **Place of Eternal Shame** for **Anyone Who would Not Honor** that most *Perfect of All Women* and *Her Perfect Children*. We see that "Jesus Said" I Release My Spirit and **Defeats** the **Sin of Man's Lack of Vision** (shallow), thereby **Forgiving His Own Human Weaknesses**, even *His Divine Perfection* and those in *Eternal Doubt*. This "Act of Forgiveness" brings forth Death (extreme unction) upon **God's Creation** to **Set All the Captives Free,** thereby **Transforming Them** from *Servants of God* unto *Slaves of All* before **God.** But "Woe to Those" Who Reject Christ's Servanthood (8th drop/slavery), because **They will Face Eternal Shame** and *Lose the Everlasting Covenant of Life*. This means that through this "8th Sacrifice," God will Pay Creation's **Sin-debt of Slavery,** thereby Removing All Human Lack of Dedication (new character) and then *Getting God's Blessing of Slavery* or *Entering God's Kingdom of Heaven*.

Obviously, the "Previously Described" Eight Divine Sacrifices were in **God's Grand Design** to **Pay Creation's Sin-debt** (faults) and to also **Pay for Creation's Holy-debt** (virtues) as it *Earns the Eight Treasures of Life*. These "Eight Treasures of Life" are Described in the **Lord's Eight Beatitudes** which happen to **Match God's Blessings** for **Good Behavior** or *Bonus Rewards*. These "Eight Treasures" are: 1) Heaven on Earth - Royal Kingdom: Teach Elementary School = Baby Level (learn evil), 2) Comfortable Life - Eternal Life: Teach Elementary School = Child Level (learn wrong), 3) Inherit Earth - New Body: Teach Elementary School = Adolescent Level (learn evil from wrong), 4) Become Righteous - God's Wisdom: Teach High School = Teenage Level (learn right/wrong), 5) Shown God's Mercy - God's Love: Teach High School = Young Adult Level (learn good/evil), 6) See God - God's Holiness: Teach Junior College = Adult Level (learn God's/Man's Wills), 7) Son of God - God's Righteousness: Teach College = Wise Man Level (learn reality/illusion), and 8) Paradise in Heaven - God's Perfection: On-the-Job Training = Free Man's Level (learn God's Truth/man's truth).

Through each of these "Treasures of Life," a Person can become **Employed in God's Kingdom** on **Earth,** in **Heaven,** and within the **Kingdom of Glory** as a *Servant unto the Lord*. This means that "On Earth (good news)," a Person can become a *King* (baby); "In Heaven (gospel message)," he can become a *Priest* (teenager); "Within the Kingdom (doctrinal truths)," he can become a *Son of God* (adult); and "In His Own Royal Kingdom (God's Divine Truths)," a Person can become a *Free Man* (think for self). We see that through "Each of God's Sacrifices," His Entire Creation of both **Angels and Men** is **Given** the **Good News** (free redemption/chains), **Gospel Message** (earned salvation/prison door), **Doctrinal Truths** (bonus rewards/guards), and **God's Divine Truths** (freedom/death) to *Set Them Free*.

We are told here that "Each of God's Children" must See that from the Earth, Christ Speaks (Messiah/one man) to His People about the Word of God, Giving Them the Good News that All Men shall Freely Receive a New Body of Righteousness, thereby Making Them *Eternal Citizens of Earth*. Secondly, out of "Heaven, the Church Speaks (priesthood/three men)" to Its People about the Prayer of God, thereby Giving Them the Gospel Message that All Men must Earn their Own Eternal Lives of Holiness, thereby Making Them *Holy Saints in Heaven*. Thirdly, out of the "Kingdom, Christianity Speaks (laity/many men)" to Its People, Telling Them to Do Good Works which Gives Them the Lord's Doctrinal Truths and Reveals that Chosen Souls will be Rewarded with Their Own Personal Kingdoms, thereby Making Them *Sons of God* within *God's Kingdom of Glory*. Finally, out of "Humanity, All Men Speak (human race/all men)" to Their People about Saving Others and Teaching Them to Think for Themselves that God's Sons will Share in God's Wealth, which Gives Them Eternal Freedom, thereby Making Them *Kings, Priests, Sons* of the *Most High God*. Through these "Four Voices of Redemption," Earth, Heaven, the Kingdom, and Oneself can be Saved from *Sin* (sin-nature), *Evil* (worldly temptations), Death (demonic possession), and *Damnation* (wicked selfishness). Through this "Set of Redemptions," Mankind becomes Worthy of God's Blessings of a New Body, Eternal Life, Royal Kingdom, and Freedom which Leads to Thinking for Oneself at the *Divine Level of Perfection*. This means that "If a Repentant Sinner" Pays All his Debts (100% belief) to God in Full, he can have his Spirit Forgiven, his Flesh Pardoned, his Soul Redeemed, and his Life-force Saved from *Sin* (self), *Evil* (society), *Death* (God, and *Damnation* (Life/Lucifer).

1. Pay Sin-nature Debt - Spirit is Forgiven: Remove Sin…Restore Self
2. Pay Worldly Temptations Debt - Flesh is Pardoned: Remove Evil… Restore Society
3. Pay Demonic Possession Debt - Soul is Redeemed: Remove Death… Restore God
4. Pay God's Curses Debt - Life-force is Saved: Remove Damnation… Restore Life

Recall the story of the "Kind Master" Who Forgave his Servant a Great Debt, only to have this same Evil Man to Later Cast Another Servant and his Family into Prison until he Paid him Back unto the *Last Penny* (purgatory). This caused the "Generous/kind Master" to Change his Mind and Demanded that this Evil Servant be Turned Over to the Torturers (hell) until he Paid the Last Penny of his Debt because he Did Not Show the Master's Hand of Mercy to his *Fellow Servant*. Now, apply this logic to "Christ's 1st Advent (priest)" When He Came and Forgave Everyone's Debt (church/age of grace/2,000 years) on Mount Calvary, but then the World Fails to Forgive Its Fellow Man (2,000 years). Therefore, When the Lord Returns (2nd Advent/thief) He will Demand that the Human Race Pay its 1st Debt unto the *Last Penny* (great tribulation/torturer). This means that the "Period (church age)" between Christ's 1st Advent (death) and His 2nd Advent (newlife) is Not a Blessing to Man, but a Great Curse just as in the case of God's Gift of the **Mosaic Law** which was **Given** to the *Jewish People to Save Them from Damnation*. This implies that "When God Gives Man a Gift" such as Wealth and/or Prosperity (Egypt) or even some Blessing of Free Redemption (church/baptism), it is time to **Beware of Greeks Bearing Gifts** which might be some kind of **Demonic Test** to **Measure One's Depth of Growth and Maturity Associated with Each** of *God's Children*.

We can now see that the "Jewish Law" Failed to **Transform Man's Flesh** (defeat sin) nor has the "Christian Church (faith)" been able to **Transform Man's Spirit** (defeat death) because it **Takes Them** both **Blended Together** to *Work Correctly* as *They Transform a Man's Soul* (flesh/spirit) into *Holy Perfection*. We might ask: "Why has Christianity Failed" to Make everyone on Earth into **Holy Saints** and to **Create the Promised** *Heaven on Earth*? The answer is that "Christianity Taught Human Faith (seek life/free)" and Failed to "Teach Divine Faith (seek death/earned)" causing Christians to **Travel Toward** *God's Curse* (save self) **Instead** of **Traveling Toward** *God's Blessing* (save lost/damned).

1. **Jewish Law of Obedience** - Failed: Offer God's Blessing to the World....Jews See Their Limitations
   • God Gives *Temple* to Jews - Speak Directly to God: Messiah Only (pay all debts)
   • God's Earthly Blessing Cast into the Dirt - Jews Foolishly Killed Their Messiah
   • Jews Begged God for Mercy and Got It - Jews Showed No Mercy to Jesus
   • Righteous Man - Called* by Jesus: Hear Word to Redeem Flesh/Eat Bread to be Born-again

2. **Man's Faith in God's Love** - Failed: Offer God's Redemption to World... Christians See Their Potential
   • God's Son Gives *Church* to Christians - Speak via Intercessor to God: Christian Only (pay others' debts)
   • God's Heavenly Blessing Cast into Dirt - Foolish Christians Only Save Themselves
   • Christians Beg God for Free Redemption - Christians Keep Free Gift for Themselves
   • Holy Man - Chosen* by Christ: Save Souls to Redeem Spirit/Drink Wine to Enter Sainthood

* Called is Man Accepting God (Jews/Christmas)
* Chosen is God Accepting Man (Christians/Easter)

This means that "Christianity was Trying" to Earn Eternal Life through the *Law* (save self), instead of trying to Give Redemption to the Damned through *One's Faith* (saving others). In short, this is telling us that "Life is Consumed by Man (will)" through his Thrill of Victory (blessing becomes curse), while "Death is Consumed by God (belief)" through His Agony of Defeat (curse becomes blessing). We see this "Great Journey" from Defeat to Victory in the **First Week of God's Creation.** Thus, we must **Worship** (home) the *Eternal Father* (daily) for *Six Days*, then **Praise** (church) the *Holy Spirit* (Sunday) for *One Day,* and finally to **Thank** the *Son of God* at the *End* (Easter Duty). Now, imagine using God's "1st Week of Creation" as a Seven-Day Period plus a Day of Judgment (8th day) and we can see what each of our **Earthly Weeks** should look like. We must **Worship the Father for Six Days** (repentance) by *Giving Him Our Lives*; then **Praise the Holy Spirit on Sunday** (prayers) as we *Give Him Our Wealth* or *Money;* and finally, we **Thank the Son of God on Easter** (works) by **Giving Him Our Annual Labors** (souls saved).

At each of these "Stages of Life," we are able to both <u>Grow and Mature</u> in **God's Truths** (right/wrong), **Laws** (good/evil), and **Will** (God's/man's) allowing us to *See Our Limitations* (daily), *See Our Potential* (Sunday,) and *See Our Self-worth* (Easter). It should now make sense that "Earthly Repentance (man)" brings <u>Free Redemption</u> (new body/citizenship); "Heavenly Prayers (Angels)" bring <u>Earned Salvation</u> (eternal life/sainthood); and "Kingdom Works (God)" bring <u>Bonus Rewards</u> (royal kingdom/sonship). Out of these "Three Stages of Life," each of <u>God's Children</u> can overcome <u>Ignorance</u>, defeat his <u>Sin-nature</u>, and become **Righteous.** He can also overcome his **Cowardice**, defeat **Worldly Temptations,** and become *Holy*. Finally, a "Born-again Soul" can overcome his <u>Greed</u>, defeat <u>Demonic Possession,</u> and become **Perfect** all in the **Name of Mastering** *God's Truths, Laws, and Will*.

The following tabular information indicates that we must "Worship the Eternal Father (repentance)" for <u>Six Days</u> (give life/week) to **Receive** a *New Body* (home), then "Praise the Holy Spirit (prayers)" on <u>Sunday</u> (give wealth/one day) to **Receive** *Eternal Life* (church), and finally, "Thank the Son of God" on <u>Easter</u> (give labors/one day) to **Receive** a *Royal Kingdom* (government):

Daily Worship 1st Six Days of Creation/Sunday Praise
1,000 Years Peace/End of Time is Easter Thanksgiving
(1st face Lucifer's test, 2nd face God's Judgment,
and 3rd face Self-evaluation to See God)

Daily
(home)

1. **1st Six Days of Creation** - <u>Face Lucifer's Test</u>...Knowledge
   - Worship Eternal Father - Give Life: Get *New Body* = Righteousness (home)
   - Earthly Repentance - Free Redemption: Citizenship (mind)
   - Fight Ignorance - Overcome Sin-nature: Defeat the Darkness
   - Learn God's Truths - Right from Wrong: Master Babyhood (wisdom)
   - Power One - Influence Earth: Physical Existence (celestial court)
     (daily mass - remove venial sins [death to flesh]:
       earthly forgiveness = face Lucifer's test)

Sunday
(church)

2. **1,000 Years of Peace** - <u>Face God's Judgment</u>...Self-awareness
   - Praise Holy Spirit - Give Wealth: Get *Eternal Life* = Holiness (church)
   - Heavenly Prayers - Earned Salvation: Sainthood (heart)
   - Fight Cowardice - Overcome Worldly Temptations: Enter the Light
   - Learn God's Laws - Good from Evil: Master Teens (courage)
   - Power One - Influence Earth: Physical Existence (celestial court)
   - Power Two - Influence Heaven: Spiritual Existence (temple court)

(weekly mass - remove mortal sins [death to spirit]:
Heavenly forgiveness = face God's judgment)

Easter (government)	3.	**End of Time** - <u>Face Self-evaluation</u>... Consciousness

- Thank Son of God - Give Labor: Get ***Royal Kingdom*** = Perfection (government)
- Kingdom Works - Bonus Rewards: Sonship (soul)
- Fight Greed - Overcome Demonic Possession: Break Free from Death
- Learn God's Will - God's Will from man's will: Master Adulthood (generosity)
- Power One - Influence Earth: Physical Existence (celestial court)
- Power Two - Influence Heaven: Spiritual Existence (temple court)
- Power Three - Influence Kingdom: Mystical Existence (royal court)
  (yearly mass - remove capital sins [death to soul]:
  Kingdom's forgiveness = face Self-evaluation)

This illustration shows that "Our Normal Work Week" is actually <u>Divided</u> into **Three Parts**: 1) <u>Six Days of Toil</u> or Giving of One's Life-force to Worship the Eternal Father to reflect His Creative Nature (hard-work) - Power One/Earth; 2) <u>Sunday</u> (weekly) to Pray or Giving One Day to Praise the Holy Spirit to reflect His Priestly Nature (devotion) - Power One and Two: Earth/Heaven; 3) <u>Easter</u> to Thank God or Giving One Day to show Gratitude to Jesus Christ to Reflect His Sacrificial Nature (offering) - Power One, Two, and Three: Earth/Heaven/Kingdom. Through these "Three Phases of Life (lost/called/chosen)," <u>Worship</u> (give life), <u>Praise</u> (give wealth), and <u>Thanksgiving</u> (give labor) can be **Understood** as *They* bring forth ***Man's Six Days of Repentance*** (4,000 years), ***Two Days of Prayer*** (2,000 years) and ***One Day of Works*** (1,000 years/saving souls).

1. **Lost** - <u>Man Repents:</u> 4,000 Years = Being Saved from Sin...Forgive Capital Sins
   - See Eternal Father Yearly - Thank God with Labors: Make Easter Duty (given one power)
   - God Removes Ignorance to Gain Wisdom - New Mind: Worthy of New Body
   (Adam's toil in a barren land is ***Repentance*** for his sins - change desert into garden)

2. **Called** - <u>Man Prays:</u> 2,000 Years = Saving Self from Evil...Forgive Mortal Sins
   - See Son of God Weekly/Sunday - Praise God with Wealth: Make Sunday Mass (earn one power)
   - God Removes Cowardice to Gain Courage - New Heart: Worthy of Eternal Life
   (Eve's pain in a barren womb is ***Prayer*** for her evil - change earthly womb to heavenly womb)

3. **Chosen** - <u>Man Works:</u> 1,000 Years = Saving Others from Death...Forgive Venial Sins
   - See Holy Spirit Daily - Worship God by Giving Life: Make Daily Mass (bonus of one power)
   - God Removes Greed to Gain Generosity - New Soul: Worthy of Own Kingdom

(Adam's/Eve's struggle in a barren life is *Works* for their curse of death - change death to new-life)

We are to "Spend Four Days" <u>Facing Lucifer's Test</u> (handicap system) to **Prove Our Wisdom** (mind), **Courage** (heart), and **Generosity (soul)** to show we have become *Worthy of God's Blessings* (water). Secondly, we are to spend "Two Days" <u>Facing God's Judgment</u> (scored on curve) to prove we have **Removed** our **Sin-nature** (sin), **Worldly Temptations** (evil), and **Demonic Possession** (death) to show we have become *Worthy of God's Anointing* (oil). Finally, we are to spend "One Day" <u>Evaluating Ourselves</u> (pass/fail) to **Prove We** have **Grown** into **Man's Righteousness** (earth), **Angelic Holiness** (Heaven,) and **Divine Perfection** (Kingdom) to *Show We* have become *Worthy of God's Sanctification* (blood).

1. **Repent** - <u>Defeat Sin-nature</u> (sin/ignorance): Pass Lucifer's Test....Master One Power
    - One Power is becoming Earthly Wise - New Mind (man's intellect)
2. **Prayers** - <u>Defeat Worldly Temptations</u> (evil): Pass God's Judgment...Master Two Powers
    - One Power is becoming Heavenly Wise - New Mind (God's intellect)
    - Two Powers is becoming Heavenly Courageous - New Heart (God's emotion)
3. **Works** - <u>Defeat Demonic Possessions</u> (death): Pass Self-evaluation...Master Three Powers
    - One Power is gaining Kingdom Wisdom - New Mind (God's/Man's intellect)
    - Two Powers is gaining Kingdom Courage - New Heart (God's/Man's emotions)
    - Three Powers is gaining Kingdom Generosity - New Soul (God's/Man's instincts)

This illustration shows that the "Concept of Repentance" <u>Means</u> to **Spend Four Days** (4,000 years) becoming an **Unblemished Lamb** by **Defeating One's Sin-nature** (sin/ignorance), **Showing that a Person** has **Passed Lucifer's Test,** and has **Received** his *Own Power of Wisdom* (man's intellect). Secondly, the "Concept of Prayer" <u>Means</u> to **Spend Two Days** (2,000 years) becoming a **Sacrificial Lamb of God** by **Defeating One's Worldly Temptations** (sin/ignorance), **Showing that a Person** has **Passed God's Judgment,** and has **Received** a *Second Power of Courage* (man's emotions). Finally, the "Concept of Works" <u>Means</u> to **Spend One Day** (1,000 years) becoming a **Born-again Lamb** by **Defeating Lucifer's Demonic Possessions** (sin/ignorance), **Showing that a Person** has **Passed His Own Self-evaluation,** and has **Received** a *Third Power of Generosity* (man's instincts). Yes! Through a "Sinner's Repentance," he can <u>Attain</u> a **New Mind** of *Wisdom*; then through a "Christian's Prayers," he can <u>Attain</u> a **New Heart** of *Courage*; and finally, via a "Saint's Works," he can <u>Attain</u> a **New Soul** of *Generosity*. By "Defeating" One's <u>Enemies,</u> a **Person** can **Defeat/Reverse All the Forces of Life** and **Reject Evil** to **Embrace Good** so that **All His Lessons** (Man) and **Blessings** (God) can be *Blended* into a *Single New Philosophy of Life* (serving God) through *Christ Jesus*.

We see that "If a Person" is <u>Worthy to Thank God Yearly</u> (Easter/repentance), he can **Receive One Power** to **Influence Planet Earth** (physical existence) or **God's Baby Farm** via *God's Celestial Court*. Secondly, "If a Person" is <u>Worthy to Praise God Weekly</u> (Sunday/prayer), he can **Receive** both **One Power** and then a **Second**

Power to **Influence both Earth and Heaven** (physical/spiritual experience) via both *God's Celestial/Temple Courts*. Finally, "If a Person" is <u>Worthy to Worship God Daily</u> (works), he can **Receive <u>One Power</u>** of *Earth* (celestial court), a **Second Power** for *Heaven* (temple court), and a **<u>Third Power</u>** for the *Kingdom* (royal court), thereby **<u>Allowing him</u>** to *Rule in All Three Courts* (celestial/temple/royal). We now see that through a "Person's Worship (father)," "Praise (spirit)," and "Thanksgiving (son)," he can <u>Receive</u> **All Three of God's Powers** to **Influence <u>Earth, Heaven,</u>** and the **<u>Kingdom</u>** via *God's Celestial, Temple, and Royal Courts*. This means that going to "Yearly Mass (Easter)" <u>Removes a Person's</u> **Capital Sins** (death to flesh) **Giving** him an **Earthly Forgiveness** to **<u>Defeat Lucifer's Test</u>** and *See His Limitations.* Secondly, going to "Weekly Mass (Sunday)" <u>Removes a Person's</u> **Mortal Sins** (death to spirit) **Giving** him a **Heavenly Forgiveness** to **<u>Pass God's Judgment</u>** and *See His Potential.* Finally, going to "Daily Mass (Mon. to Saturday)" <u>Removes a Person's</u> **Venial Sins** (death to soul) **Giving** him the **Kingdom's Forgiveness** to **<u>Accept his Own Self-evaluation</u>** and *See His Self-worth.*

Through this "System of Forgiveness," a <u>Person can Go</u> from **Nothing to All,** thereby **Making** the *Last First* (divine) and *First Last* (human), implying that **God is a Paradox** causing *Everything in Life* to be **<u>Relative</u>** to *Everything Else.* In the "Bible," this <u>Conversion Experience is Called</u> **Making** the **First into Last** (cursed) and the **Last into First** (blessed), thereby **Creating <u>God's Philosophy</u>** of **Divine Justice,** where **<u>Nothing can become All</u>** through *Christ Jesus.* To "Master Divine Perfection," a <u>Person</u> must **Surrender himself Totally** by **<u>Offering his Redeemed Life</u>** to **<u>Save the Damned</u>** from **Eternal Oblivion** (hell/Gehenna) by **Simply Taking Their Place,** like **Jesus Christ has Taken** *His Place in Hell.* In this way, a "Devout Christian" has <u>Proven</u> that he has become the **Good Servant, Who Forgives the Debts** of his **Brothers** and has **Learned his Lesson** that If a Person is **Forgiven** by his **Master,** he must **<u>Pass This Blessing On</u>** to his *Fellow Servants.* Recall that "On the Cross," the <u>Bad Thief</u> (citizen) **Only Saw a Man** (Jesus) and **Asked Him** for **<u>Eternal Life</u>** by **<u>Taking him Down</u>** to *Give him Heaven on Earth;* while the <u>Good Thief</u> (saint) **Saw God** (Christ) and **Asked Him** to **<u>Take him into Death</u>** to *Earn Paradise in Heaven.*

It can now be seen that "Christ's Church was Told" to <u>Seek Poverty of Spirit</u> (faith through grace affirmed by works), yet **They Later Came to Believe** that **God had Told Them** to **<u>Seek the Wealth of the Flesh</u>** (human faith) so *They could Save the World.* We see in the "Story of Saint Francis" that he had <u>Dedicated his Life</u> to **Abject Poverty** and **Got into a Great Dispute** with the **Holy See** (Vatican) **Over this Concept** of **<u>Poverty of Spirit,</u>** even unto being *Excommunicated from the Church.* Obviously, "God is a Contradiction in Terms (paradox)" and <u>When a Person</u> is **Striving to be Priceless** (worth everything), he must **Make himself Worthless** (worth nothing) to **<u>Make</u>** the *First Last* (life/cursed) and the *Last First* (death/blessed). Recall in "Luke 7:28," the <u>Lord States</u> that **No Man Born of Woman** is **<u>Greater on Earth</u>** than *John the Baptist* (first/flesh), while in **Heaven <u>All Men</u>** are **Greater** than *John the Baptist* (last/spirit). The "Hidden Message" here is that "On Earth," <u>Righteous Men</u> (serve self) are to **Face the Evil World** with **<u>Courage</u>** (greatest on earth) like *John the Baptist* (perfect); yet, "In Heaven," <u>Holy Men</u> (serve all) are to become of

Service to All (greatest in Heaven) or the *Least of God's Saints* is the *Greatest*. Note in "Matthew 20:27," the <u>Lord States</u> that **If a Person Wants** to be **Great in Heaven,** he must be the **Servant to All** and <u>**Only he Will**</u> be the *Greatest Saint before God* (John the Baptist).

This means that on "Earth (flesh/law)," a <u>Person</u> is to <u>Fight Evil</u> and **Confront Kings** with the **Courage of a Lion**; but in "Heaven (spirit/faith)," a <u>Person</u> is to become <u>**Silent before God**</u> and *Humbly Serve the Needs of All* (God, Angels, and Men).

The following tabular information indicates that "Human Faith (cursed)" <u>Seeks Eternal Life</u> through the *Law* (worthless/life); while "Divine Faith (blessed)" <u>Seeks the Redemption of the Damned</u> through a *Person's Faith* (priceless/body):

Human Faith is Cursed for Taking Life, while
Divine Faith is Blessed for Sacrificing Life
(foolish Christians seek eternal life,
while wise Christians seek the redemption of damned)

Cursed 　　　　1. **Human Faith** - <u>Seeking Eternal Life</u> (free): Take Life…Worthless
(law)
- Foolish Christians Traveling Toward God's Curse - Wealth: Selfishness
- Thrill of Victory - Life is Consumed by Man: *Earning Eternal Life*
- Man's Evil Nature - Learning Wrong and Evil through Greed

Mary's Son
- Become a Slave to Sin, Evil, and Death - Human Faith is a Weed/Chaff/
(fulfill law)　　Tares
- Cast into Death Agony - Death (ignorance) …Physical Baby
- Cast into Hopelessness - Grave (cowardice) …Physical Teenager
- Cast into Separation from God - Hell (greed) …Physical Adult

(hear God's word - free redemption: worship = give life in submission to Christ)

Blessed 　　　2. **Divine Faith** - <u>Seeking Redemption of Damned</u> (earned): Give Life…Priceless
(faith)
- Wise Christians Traveling Toward God's Blessing - Poverty: Unselfishness
- Agony of Defeat - Death is Consumed by God: *Redeeming the Damned*
- Man's Holy Nature - Learning Right and Good through Generosity

God's Son
- Become Free Man to Righteousness, Holiness, and Perfection - Divine
(fulfill faith)　　Faith is Wheat
- Earn New Body - Kingship (earth) … Spiritual Baby
- Earn Eternal Life - Priesthood (Heaven) …Spiritual Teenager
- Earn Royal Kingdom - Sonship (Kingdom) …Spiritual Adult

(believe the word - earned salvation: praise = give wealth in being true to oneself)

This illustration shows that "Foolish Christians (human faith)" are <u>Striving to Reveal</u> **Their Holiness** through **Their <u>Personal Wealth and Power</u>** before *Men*, while the "Wise Christians (divine faith)" are <u>Striving to Reveal</u> **Their Holiness** through their **<u>Personal Submission and Sacrifice</u>** to *God*. This means that "Foolish Christians (cursed)" are <u>Taking Life's Treasures</u> for *Themselves and Their Posterity* (law), while the "Wise Christians (blessed)" are <u>Giving Their Lives</u> in the **Pursuit** of *Saving the*

Souls of Others (faith). "Man's Evil Nature (selfishness)" is simply <u>Learning Wrong and Evil</u> through *his Greed* (take/see limitations), while "Man's Holy Nature (unselfishness)" is <u>Learning Right and Good</u> through *his Generosity* (give/see potential). In short, a "Foolish Christian (law)" has become a <u>Slave</u> to **Sin, Evil, and Death** which **Leads** to *Death Agony* (death/ignorance), *Hopelessness* (grave/cowardice), and *Separation from God* (hell/greed). Secondly, a "Wise Christian (faith)" has become a <u>Free Man</u> **Valuing Only Righteousness, Holiness, and Perfection** which **Leads** to *Earning Eternal Life* (kingship/earth), *Earning a New Body* (priesthood/Heaven), and *Earning a Royal Kingdom* (sonship/kingdom). Obviously, "Human Faith" is an <u>Evil Weed</u> (chaff/tare) that has been *Sown in God's Church* (Mt.13:25); while "Divine Faith" is <u>Holy Wheat</u> that has **Grown 33%** (kingship/belief), **67%** (priesthood/trust), and **100%** (sonship/faith) in the *Rich Soil of One's Perfect Faith* (knowing without proof). Now it is clear that "Human Faith" <u>Involves being Converted</u> (take-sin) by **Mary's Son, Jesus** (earth) as **He is Responsible** for **Transforming** <u>Sinners into Christians</u> by *Teaching Them Ethics* (new body). Secondly, "Divine Faith" <u>Involves being Converted</u> (give divinity) by **God's Son, Christ** (Heaven) as **He is Responsible** for **Transforming** **Christians into Saints** by *Teaching Them Morals* (eternal life). In this explanation of "Jesus as a Man (physical bodies)" and "Christ as God (spiritual life)," we see <u>They</u> have both been <u>Sent to Connect</u> and/or <u>Unite</u> the **Saints of Earth** (evil spirit/curse) and the **Angels of Heaven** (holy spirit/blessing) to the *Lord God Almighty* through the *Bodies of Men* (new body) and the *Spirit(s) of God* (eternal life). This means that "Earth" is a <u>Body Factory</u> **Operated by Jesus, Who is Using** the **Mystical Body of Christ** (bread) to **Change** *Natural Flesh* (80 years/womb) or **Right/Wrong** into *Supernatural Flesh* (eternal/tomb) or *Ethics.* "Heaven" is a <u>Spiritual Life Factory</u> **Operated by Christ, Who is Using** the **Communion of Saints** (wine) to **Change** *Natural Spirits* (80 years/womb) or **Good/Evil** into *Supernatural Spirits* (eternal/tomb) or *Morals.*

It should now make sense that the "Human Life-experience" is <u>Centered</u> upon a **Two-Truth System of Belief** and that **Anyone Who Masters God's** <u>Truth, Law, Will, and Love</u> will *Receive* a *New Body* (earth) and *Eternal Life* (Heaven). The "Two-Truth System" of <u>God's Spirit</u> (Heaven) and <u>Man's Flesh</u> (earth) **Will One Day Merge** into a "Third Truth," <u>Giving Us</u> the **God/Man Kingdom** where the **Challenges of Life** (truth), the *Adventures of Life* (law), and the *Fun of Life* (will) will bring forth *Eternal Happiness for All*. This "Hope for Happiness" <u>Drives God, Angels, and Men</u> to **Build a Unified Kingdom of Glory** as **They Strive** to <u>Fulfill God's Divine Justice</u> by *Becoming Perfect in His Sight*. This "State of Perfection" is <u>Defined</u> by the **Righteous Man** of **Earth** (new body), **Holy Man** of **Heaven** (eternal life), and the **Perfect Man** within **God's Kingdom** (royal kingdom) as **They Spread** the **Good News** of *Free Faith* (church), the **Gospel Message** of *Earned Grace* (government), and the **Doctrinal Truths** of *Bonus Works/Freedom* (home). The idea here is that through "Redemption," <u>Mankind can Get</u> its **New Mind** (truth) and **Learn God's Right** from **Man's Wrong**, thereby **Revealing** the *Lessons of Life* (remove faults). Secondly, through "Salvation," <u>Mankind can Get</u> its **New Heart** (law) and **Learn God's Good from man's evil**, thereby **Revealing** the *Blessings of Life* (gain virtues). Finally, through "Rewards," Mankind can Get its **New Soul** (will) and **Learn God's Will from man's will,** thereby **Revealing** the *Value of Life* (freedom). By "Combining" the Three Duties of Jesus Christ (redeem/save/transform) during **His Three Advents, We can See** the **Creation** of **Christians, Saints,** and **Sons of God** as *Worthy Citizens of God's Coming Kingdom*.

The idea here is that the "Lord Jesus Christ" is bringing Out of Christianity **Earthly** *Individual Rights* (title to earth); Out of Sainthood, **Heavenly** *Social Rights* (title to Heaven); and Out of Sons of God, **Divine Rights** to the *Kingdom* (title to Kingdom). This "System of Conversion" Transforms **Babies into Teenagers** and then **Teenagers into Adults** so that the **Forces** of **Growth and Maturity** will **Create All the Holy People** (babies/bodies) **God will Ever Need** to *Serve His Kingdom of Glory*. It is now obvious just how "Important" it is to be a Witness for Christ in bringing the **Good News** so that the **Human Race** can have **Free Redemption** (free baby faith) to *Save the Flesh of Man* (being saved); Secondly, to be a Teacher of the Word in bringing the **Gospel Message** so that the **Human Race** can have **Earned Salvation** (earned teenager works) to *Save the Spirit of Man* (saving self); finally, to be an Implementer of the Truth so that the **Human Race** can have **Bonus Rewards** (reward adults for saving others) to *Save the Soul of Man* (saving others). It should now "All Make Perfect Sense" that the Life-experience is a **Gift from God** and for a **Person** to **Thank God Properly,** he must *Surrender to be Saved* (redeemed), then **Save himself** (saved), and finally *Strive to Save Others* (evangelization).

The following tabular information indicates that "Jesus Christ" is bringing Free Redemption (save flesh), Earned Salvation (save spirit), and Bonus Rewards (save soul) to **Create Christians** on *Earth*, **Saints** in *Heaven,* and **Sons of God** within *God's Kingdom*:

Free Redemption Creates Christians, Earned Salvation Creates Saints, and Rewards Create Sons
(being saved by free faith, saving self with works,
and saving others with holy grace/reward)

Truth (mind)	1. **Free Redemption** - Create Christians: Free Faith...Being Saved
	• Repentant Sinner - *Believe 33%*: Believing that God has Forgiven You
	• Spreading the Good News - Saving the Flesh: Mind = Intellect
	• Learning Right from Wrong - Lessons: Removing One's Faults
Physical	• Man's Law - Ethical Behavior: Individual Rights (see limits)
Nature	• Becoming a Righteous Citizen on Earth - Physical Title Deed
	• Wash Away Sin - Receive a *New Body* (elementary)

(Christians get Heaven on Earth - Seat in Celestial Court and God's Friendship)

Law (heart)	2. **Earned Salvation** - Create Saints: Do Works...Saving Self
	• Devout Christian - *Believe 67%*: Believing You have Forgiven Yourself
	• Teaching the Gospel Message - Saving the Spirit: Heart = Emotions
	• Learning Good from Evil - Blessings: Gain God's Virtues

Spiritual	• God's Law - Moral Behavior: Social Rights (see potential)
Nature	• Becoming a Holy Saint in Heaven - Spiritual Title Deed
	• Change Nature - Receive *Eternal Life* (high school)
	(Saints get Paradise in Heaven - Seat in Temple Court and God's Companionship)

Will	3. **Bonus Rewards** - <u>Create Sons:</u> Save Souls…Saving Others
(soul)	• Holy Saint - ***Believe 100%***: Believing You have Forgiven All Others
	• Implementing Doctrinal Truths - Saving the Soul: Soul = Instincts
	• Learning God's Will/man's will - Ownership: Become Divine
Mystical	• God's/Man's Law - Divine Behavior: Divine Rights (see self-worth)
Nature	• Become a Son of God within Kingdom - Mystical Title Deed
	• Transformation - Receive ***Royal Kingdom*** (college)
	(Sons of God get Own Royal Kingdom - Seat in Royal Court and God's Oneness)

This illustration shows that "If a Person" <u>Believes that God has Forgiven him,</u> or it **Shows** his **Belief in Life** (mind), then he **Believes 33%**, thereby **Making him** a **Repentant Sinner** or **One Who** can **<u>Walk on Earth</u>** as a *Righteous Citizen* (good news). Secondly, "If a Person" <u>Believes that he has Forgiven himself,</u> or it **Shows** he is **Trusting the Belief in Himself** (heart), then he **Believes 67%**, thereby **Making him** a **Devout Christian** or **One Who** can **Walk in <u>Heaven</u>** as a *Holy Saint of God* (gospel message). Finally, "If a Person" <u>Believes that he has Forgiven All Others,</u> or it **Shows** his **Faithful Belief in God** (soul), then he **Believes 100%**, thereby **Making him** a **Heavenly Saint** or **One Who** can **<u>Walk in God's Kingdom</u>** as a *Perfect Son of God* (doctrinal truths). This means that "God's 1st Blessing (wash away sin)" brings <u>Free Redemption</u> to **All** by **Placing Man's Law** within **Their Minds** (follow blindly) to bring forth **Proper Ethical Behavior** (individual rights) so that a **<u>Christian</u>** might *See his Own Limitations*. Secondly, "God's 2nd Blessing (change nature)" brings <u>Earned Salvation</u> (saving self) to a **Few Souls** by **Placing God's Law** within **Their Hearts** (obeying orders) to bring forth **Proper Moral Behavior** (social rights) so that a **<u>Saint</u>** might *See his Own Potential*. Thirdly, "God's 3rd Blessing (transfiguration)" brings <u>Bonus Rewards</u> to **God's Chosen** by **Placing Divine Law** within **Their Souls** (thinking for self) to bring forth **Proper Divine Behavior** (divine rights) so that a **<u>Son of God</u>** might *See his Own Self-worth*.

The idea here is to see that "Christians will be Blessed" with Heaven on Earth **and Their Own Seat** in **God's Celestial Court** (rule earth) plus **God's Personal Friendship** to **Transform <u>a Person</u>** from *Man's Flesh to God's Spirit*. Secondly, a "Saint will be Blessed" with <u>Paradise in Heaven</u> **and His Own Seat** in **God's Temple Court** (rule Heaven) plus **God's Beloved Companionship** to **<u>Transform a Person</u>** from *God's Spirit to God's Soul*. Finally, a "Son of God will be Blessed" with his <u>Own Royal Kingdom</u> **and his Own Seat** in **God's Royal Court** (rule Kingdom) plus **God's Treasured Oneness** (beatific vision) to **Transform a Person** from *God's Soul to God's Life-force*. Through these "Three Awesome Blessings," the <u>Human Race</u> can **Hope to be Saved** from <u>Sin, Evil, and Death</u> and brought into *God's Kingdom* via *Christ's New Heaven and new earth*. This means that "Humankind is Striving" to <u>Conquer</u> its **Physical, Spiritual, and Mystical Natures** to **Receive** the **<u>Title Deeds</u>**

to *Man's Earth* (baby), *Angelic Heaven* (teenager), and *God's Kingdom* (adult). The idea here is to see that "Man's Earth (physical)" Teaches Ethics or **Man's Law** for the **Human Race** to become **Righteous Citizens** within the **Blessed Mother's** *Elementary School of Life* (baby farm). Secondly, "Angelic Heaven (spiritual)" Teaches Morals or **God's Law** (Jewish Mosaic Law) for the **Human Race** to become **Holy Saints** within **Saint Joseph's** *High School of Life* (divine law). Finally, "God's Kingdom (mystical)" Teaches Transfiguration or **Divine Law** (Christian Canon Law) for the **Human Race** to become **Sons of God** within *Jesus Christ's College of Life* (sonship training program).

This teaching should help explain why "Man's Physical Nature" seems to always Appear to be Evil; while "Man's Spirit Nature" can either be Good or Evil, **Depending** upon the **Depth of his Desire** to **Surrender his Life** (belief) to the *Lord's Cross of Death*. It is imperative that a "Person Understand" the Meaning of the Word **Submission** as it **Relates** to the *Belief in Life* (mind/33%), *Trusting the Belief in Oneself* (heart/67%), and having a *Faithful Belief in God* (soul/100%). The idea here is to see that "Simple Belief Relates" to having a 33% Commitment unto the **Lord God Almighty's Truth** or **Bearing the Fruits of Repentance** before *God's Divine Justice* (earthly kingship). Secondly, "Trusting Belief" relates to having a 67% Commitment unto the **Lord God Almighty's Truth** or **Bearing the Fruits of Prayers** before *God's Divine Mercy* (Heavenly priesthood). Finally, "Faithful Belief" relates to having a 100% Commitment unto the **Lord God Almighty's Truth** or **Bearing the Fruits of Works** before *God's Divine Love* (Kingdom sonship) *Face-to-face* (beatific vision).

It can be seen at each of these "Levels of Fruitfulness" to what extent a Committed Soul will go to **Prove to God** that it has **Died to its Own Selfishness** and is willing to be **Born-again** in *Christ's Unselfishness*. "On Earth," a Person is Required to **Master Works** by **Fighting Evil** to *Die to Self* (flesh); yet, "In Heaven," a Person is Required to **Master Prayer** by his **Submission** to *Die to Self* (spirit). "Only" through "Mary's Son, Jesus" can a Person *Master Earthly Works* (new body), while "Only" through "God's Son, Christ" can he *Master Heavenly Prayer* (eternal life). In the final analysis, a "Lost Sinner" must Believe in Jesus via the **Law** to become a *Righteous Citizen* (Heaven on Earth); while a "Devout Christian" must Believe in Christ via his **Faith** to become a *Holy Saint* (Heavenly Paradise). This means that "Eternal Citizenship on Earth (new body)" is Established through **Ethical Behavior** of *Right and Wrong* (Heaven on earth/Man); while "Sainthood in Heaven (eternal life)" is Established through **Moral Behavior** of *Good and Evil* (Heavenly Paradise/God). Obviously, both "Our Works on Earth" and "Our Prayers in Heaven" are Needed to **Prove to Divine Justice** that **Man's Wicked Human Nature** is *Slowly* (33%/67%/100%), but surely, *Changing from Evil to Good*.

The following tabular information indicates that "When Entering" into Absolute Submission to God, a **Person** must **Believe** with his **Mind** (33%), then **Enter Trusting Belief** within his **Heart** (67%), and finally, be **Consumed** with **Faithful Belief** of his **Soul** (100%) to truly *Die to himself Completely* (ignorance/cowardice/greed):

**Mastering Belief, Trusting Belief,
and Faithful Belief at the Mind, Heart, and Soul Levels**
(dying to one's ignorance, cowardice, and greed through
the powers of belief in Christ Jesus, the Savior)

<u>Surrender</u>

Kingship   1. **Belief** - <u>Mind is Convinced:</u> Life is Real…Dying to Ignorance
(survival)
    • 33% Commitment - Bear Fruits of Repentance: Defeat Sin-nature
    • Hear the Truth - Good News
    • See the Truth - Gospel Message   **See Reality**
    • Touch the Truth - Doctrinal Truths

Priesthood 2. **Trusting Belief** - <u>Heart is Convinced:</u> Oneself is Real… Dying to Cowardice
(truth)
    • 67% Commitment - Bear Fruits of Prayers: Defeat Worldly Temptations
    • Being Saved - Free Redemption
    • Saving Self - Earned Salvation   **Test Reality**
    • Saving Others - Bonus Rewards

Sonship   3. **Faithful Belief** - <u>Soul is Convinced:</u> God is Real…Dying to Greed
(love)
    • 100% Commitment - Bear Fruits of Works: Defeat Demonic Possession
    • Worthy of Eternal Life - God's Friendship
    • Worthy of New Body - God's Companionship   **Own Reality**
    • Worthy of Royal Kingdom - God's Oneness

Free Man   4. **Knowing Truth** - <u>Life-force is Convinced:</u> Reality is Life… Born-again to
(choice)   Life
    • Becoming Committed - Bear Fruits of Saving Souls: Gain Eternal
      Rewards
Become   • Earning Seat in "Celestial Court" - Governing the Flesh (home)
Real   • Earning Seat in "Temple Court" - Governing the Spirit (church)
    • Earning Seat in "Royal Court" - Governing the Soul (government)
(born-again in wisdom, courage, and generosity to become of service to God)
**Surrendering to a God of <u>Glory</u> (God), who divides
into Three Gods of <u>Splendor</u> (king, priest, and son) **

This illustration shows that the "Life-experience" is <u>Centered</u> upon **Man's Ability
to Surrender** his **Mind, Heart, and Soul** to <u>**God's Divine Will**</u> through the *Forces
of Belief* (remove ignorance/33%), *Trusted Belief* (remove cowardice/67%), and *Faithful Belief* (remove greed/100%). This means that "God is Telling" the <u>Human Race</u>
that **He Desires** to see **Its Worthless Flesh Cursed by Death** (no light), **Cast into
the Grave** (no water), to **Rot unto Oblivion** (no soil), or **Die** to <u>**Appease His Divine
Anger**</u> to the *Point of Eternal Forgiveness*. Instead, the "Human Race" is <u>Convinced</u>
that It is being **Called** to become **Perfect in the Sight of God** through the **Quality
of Its Works** by **Doing Precisely What** the <u>**Ordinances of Man Require to be**</u>

Done unto the *Letter of the Law*...Wrong. No! In short, "God is Not Trying" to Create Perfect People **Out of Their Works**, but instead **He Wants** the **Entire Human Race** to become **Spiritually Dead** (submission) to **Kill Its Evil Free Wills** (poisonous tree of knowledge) and *Take-on God's Divine Will* through the *New Nature of Jesus Christ*. This "Need" to be Transformed and then become Blessed by God by **Serving Him, His Kingdom,** and the **Greater Good Sits** at the **Center** of the **Life-experience** on *Earth,* in *Heaven,* and within *God's Kingdom*. Now, let's return to the "Lord's Initial Creations" of Light (will), Water (belief), and Soil (land) when the **Original Blessings of God** were **Giving His Creation** its **Sanctity** before the *Lord's Divine Justice*. This reveals that "God's Will (follow)" is the Light (conversion), "God's Truth (belief)" is the Water (baptism), and "God's Law (union)" is the Soil. Then **All Three Combined** are *Made Perfect in Christ's New Nature*.

The following tabular information indicates that "God's Light" is Man's Awakening (mind/king/government); "God's Water" is Man's Purification (heart/priest/church); and "God's Soil" is Man's Livelihood (soul/son/home):

Light, Water, and Soil are Sanctified before God through His Kingship, Priesthood, and Sonship
(see light, follow will; purified in water believe
divine truths; and toil in land to serve God)

Truth (submitted)	1.	**Light** - Kingship (righteousness): Following God's Will...Knowledge
		• Walking in the Divine Light - Following Christ unto Death (cross)
		• Lights Go On - A Baby Wakes-up (intellect): Good News = Free Redemption
		• Learning Right from Wrong - Darkness unto Light: Life is Survival
Trial/Error		• Electricity (seeing) - New Body on Earth: See Limitations
		• King Thinks - Blessing of Wisdom: Fail to Succeed/trial and error
		• Face Lucifer - Master Self: Blinded = Bright Light
	(plan of creation - light of knowing: physical life on earth = receive new body)	

Law (sacrificed)	2.	**Water** - Priesthood (holiness): Believing in God's Truths... Self-awareness
		• Washing in Divine Water - Believing in Christ's Resurrection (tomb)
		• Waters Flow - Teenager Enters Society (emotion): Gospel Message = Earned Salvation
		• Learning Good from Evil - Dirty unto Clean: Life is Finding Truth
Quit-in-defeat		• Bathing (water) - Eternal Life in Heaven: See Potential
		• Priest Prays - Blessing of Holiness: Give-up to Succeed/quit
		• Face God's Judgment - Master Society: Drowned = Deep Water
	(plan of redemption - waters of self-awareness: spiritual life in Heaven = eternal life)	

Will	3.	**Soil** - Sonship (perfection): Toil in Eternal-service...Consciousness

(reconciled)	• Buried in Divine Soil - Conquering the Grave through Christ (resurrection)
	• Soil Bears Fruit - Adult Owns Land (instincts): Doctrinal Truths = Bonus Reward
	• Learn God's/Man's Wills - Barren to Fruitful: Life is being in Love
Never-quit	• Eating (food) - Kingdom of Glory in God: See Self-worth
Trying	• Son Works - Blessing of Livelihood: Eternally-try to Succeed/never-quit
	• Face Self-evaluation - Master God: Overwhelmed by Dirt

(plan of sanctified life - soil of consciousness: mystical life in Kingdom = kingdom)

This illustration shows that all that is "Good before God" shall come from the Lord's Light of Wisdom (trial and error), His Waters of Holiness (quit-in-defeat), and His Soil of Livelihood (never-quit) as they bring forth *Man's Wise Earth* (king), the *Angels' Pure Heaven* (priest), and *God's Prosperous Kingdom* (son). The idea here is that "If the Eye" Gets Too Much Bright Light, it will become **Blind**, causing a **Lost Fool to Stumble** through a **Painful Life** in **Ignorance,** until it **Uses** an **Unending Series** of **Trials and Errors** which **Teaches it** to *Survive in the Dark*. Secondly, "If a Person" Gets Too Much Water, he will **Drown** causing him to **Give-up his Life** (submission) and **Use his Faith** to **Resurrect** via his **Messiah** (baptism) through *His Purified Grave*. Finally, "If a Saint" is Overwhelmed by Man's Dirt and is **Buried Under an Evil Mountain** (grave), he will simply start **Digging** until he **Confronts All the Worldly Forces**, *Defeating Them One by One* until *They are All Transformed into Goodness*. This means that a "King (general)" Uses the Scientific Tools of *Trial and Error* (repentance); and the "Priest (living prayer)" instantly Quits-in-defeat (prayer) so *that God Will Come* and *Fight for him* and the "Son (champion)" Fights All Comers until he *Defeats Them All*.

This theme of "Trial and Error (king)" on **Earth**, "Quitting (priest)" in **Heaven,** and being an "Eternal Warrior (son)" within the **Kingdom Allows Us to See** the **Great Importance** of having a **Divine Mind** (wisdom), a **Divine Heart** (courage), and a **Divine Soul** (generosity), *Each Worthy of God's Praise*.

==
Extremely Important
This misunderstanding about "Making Oneself Perfect (ego)" or Allowing God to "Make You Perfect (submission)" has caused All Mankind to Embrace Lucifer's Superstitions of Life as It Believes Only in a *Do Step Approach* (good works) instead of Bowing to **God's Real Truth** based on a **New Approach** of *Death to Ignorance* (fool), *to Cowardice* (criminal), *to Greed* (insane), *and to Selfishness* (evil). This "New Approach" Opens God's Four Highways of Life so that All Mankind can have a **Wise Mind** (survival), **Courageous Heart** (truth), **Generous Soul** (love), and an **Unselfish Life-force** (choice) as a Person brings the *Good News* (light), *Gospel Message* (water), *Doctrinal Truths* (soil), and *God's Will* to *One and All* (life).

The "Whole Life-experience" Centers upon **Mankind's Daily** (altar/Isaac), **Weekly** (pulpit/Ishmael), and **Yearly** (chair/Jesus) **Worship** which brings forth **God's Blessings** of *Earthly Life* (remove faults/give labors), *Heavenly Eternal Life* (forgive sins/give wealth), and *His Kingdom's Mystical Life* (resurrect from death/give life). Through these "Three Stages of Life," the <u>Human Race</u> can **Expect to Receive** a **New Body of Good Health** (wisdom), plus an **Eternal Life of Prosperity** (courage), and finally, a **Kingdom of Love** (generosity) where <u>God, Angels, and Men are One</u> in *Truth* (earth), *Law* (Heaven), *and Will* (Kingdom). This means that "Good Health Comes" with <u>Removing Faults</u> through *Wisdom* (righteous mind); then "Prosperity Comes" with <u>Removing Sins</u> through *Courage* (holy heart); and finally, "Love Comes" with <u>Removing Demonic Possession</u> through *Generosity* (perfect soul).

The question is: just "How can Anyone" <u>Accomplish All This</u> when he has **No Wisdom** (ignorance), **No Courage** (cowardice), and **No Generosity** (greedy) causing him to **<u>Fail</u>** in *Self-image* (self), *Social Respect* (Man), and *Divine Honors* (God)? The answer is to be "Found in Jesus Christ," in <u>His Church,</u> and in his <u>Living Saints</u> as **They have been Sent** to bring forth **God's New Body** (light), **Eternal Life** (water), and **Royal Kingdom** (soil) onto the **<u>Earth</u>** to *Save One and All*. This "Need for Salvation" <u>Sits at the Heart</u> of the **Life-experience** which is **Calling Each** of **God's Children** to a *Deep Repentance* (Isaac/Jews), *Holy Prayer* (Ishmael/Arabs), and to *Do Good Works* (Jesus/Christians). Via "God's Will," <u>Each of His Babies</u> **Responds** to **His Calling** (see God), becomes **<u>Enlightened</u>** (hear God), becomes **<u>Awakened</u>** (touch God), and then be **<u>Indwelled</u>** (sups with God) with *God's Loving Resurrected Spirit*. Remember, the "Leaders of Men" <u>Cannot Take</u> their <u>People Anywhere</u> that **God Does Not Want Them to Go**. This **Gives Us All Confidence** that **Our Present <u>Life-experience</u>** is a *Journey of Growth* and *Maturity*, **<u>Leading Us</u>** to the *Lord God Almighty*.

The following tabular information indicates that to "Master the Life-experience," a person must <u>Worship the Father Daily</u> (wisdom), <u>Praise the Spirit Weekly</u> (courage), and <u>Thank the Son Yearly</u> (generosity) to *Remove His Faults* (life), *Forgive His Sins* (wealth), and *Resurrect from Death* (labor):

Daily Prayer of Repentance, Weekly Prayer of
Devotion, and Yearly Prayer of Works bring God
(worship the Father, praise the Spirit, and thank
the Son for wisdom, courage, and generosity)

Remove　　1. **Daily Prayer of Repentance** (Mon-Sat) - <u>Worship Father</u>... Knowledge
Faults　　　　• Removing Venial Sins (mind) - Sinfulness (baptism): Defeat Sin
(life)　　　　• Worship of Light - Father is the Light: Give Life to Get New Body
　　　　　　　• Bright Light Creates Blindness - Walking in the Darkness (baby)
　　　　　　　• King Thinks - *Wisdom*: New Mind of Righteousness
　　(repentance of Isaac [1st son] - Jews: Fulfilling the Law = Gaining Life of Good Health)

Forgive　　2. **Weekly Prayer of Devotion** (Sunday) - <u>Pay the Son</u>...Self-awareness
Sin　　　　　• Removing Mortal Sins (heart) - Evilness (confession): Defeat Evil
(wealth)　　• Praise the Water - Spirit is the Water: Give Wealth to Get Eternal Life
　　　　　　　• Deep Waters cause Drownings - Learning to Swim (teenager)

- Priest Prays - *Courage*: New Heart of Holiness

(prayers of Ishmael [2nd son] - Arabs: Fulfilling Worship = Gaining Life of Prosperity)

Resurrecting   3.   **Yearly Prayer of Works** (Easter) - <u>Thank the Spirit</u>... Consciousness

Death   •   Removing Capital Sins (soul) - Deathliness (communion): Defeat Death

(labor)   •   Thank the Soil - Son is the Soil: Give Labor to Get Royal Kingdom

           •   Mountain of Dirt Buries Everything - Toil Moves Mountains (adult)

           •   Son Works - *Generosity*: New Soul of Perfection

(works of Jesus [3rd son] - Christians: Fulfilling Works = Gaining Life of Love)

This illustration shows that "All Mankind must Approach" the <u>Altar of God</u> **Daily** (worship Father), **Weekly** (praise Spirit), and **Yearly** (thank Son) to **Reconcile Its Lives <u>Back to God</u>** for *All* that *It Has Done Wrong* (sin) and for *All* that *It Has Failed to Do* (sin of omission). Obviously, the "Human Race" must <u>Learn to See</u> (air), to <u>Swim</u> (sea), and to <u>Work the Land</u> (land) so that **Each of God's Children** can be *Emptied of his Faults* and then be *Filled with God's Virtues*. This means that "Man's Ignorant Mind" must become <u>Wise</u>; his "Cowardly Heart" must become <u>Courageous</u>; and his "Greedy Soul" must become <u>Generous</u> so that the *Divinity of God* (light/water/soil) can **Meet** the *Righteousness* (light), *Holiness* (water), and *Perfection* (soil) *of Man*. In the previous chart, the "Repentance of Man" comes from <u>Isaac</u> or the <u>Jews</u> by **Fulfilling God's Law of Obedience** to **Gain** a **Life of Good Health** in a *World* of *Sick Broken People*. Secondly, the "Prayers of Man" come from <u>Ishmael</u> or the <u>Arabs</u> to **Fulfill Man's Faith in God's Love** (worship) to **Gain** a **Life of Prosperity** in a *World* of *Poor, Broken, and Hopeless People*. Finally, the "Works of Man" come from <u>Jesus</u> or the <u>Christians</u> to **Fulfill God/Man Knowing** or **Thinking for Oneself** (labor) to **Gain** a **Life of Peace, Joy, and Happiness** in a *World* of *War, Hate, and Unhappiness*.

    We must "All Thank Our Holy Trinity" for <u>Their Great Mercy</u> upon the **Human Race** by being **Willing** to **Sacrifice Themselves** in **Physical** (earth), **Spiritual** (Heaven), and **Mystical** (Kingdom) **Forms** to *Save a Lost and Dying World*. The question is: just "How Far" are <u>We Willing to Go</u> to **Save Ourselves** (1st mile) and to **Save Others** (2nd mile) when the **Struggles of Life** become more and more **Painful Each Day** and **We become More and More Tired** unto **Total Exhaustion** as *Time Goes By*? Yes! "If We are Willing" to <u>Go that 1st Mile</u>, **We can Save Ourselves** (sinner). "If We are Committed" to <u>Going that 2nd Mile</u>, **We can Save Others** (lost fools). Just <u>Imagine Who We can Save</u> (damned), "If We" <u>Go that 3rd Mile</u> of *Unimaginable Torment* (Calvary). This "Willingness to Go" on that most <u>Painful Journey of Life</u> **Separates** the **Boys from the Men** as **Only** an **Inspired Few** will have the **Tenacity** to **Die to their Own Selfishness** (miraculous belief) **<u>All the Way</u>** to their *Own Death* (kill sin/purify grave). It is now clear that to "Kill Sin," <u>Mankind</u> must **Die to Its Selfishness** (belief); to "Kill Evil," <u>Mankind</u> must be <u>Born-again in a New Nature</u> (faith); and to "Kill/end Death," <u>Mankind</u> must <u>Resurrect from Its Grave</u> (knowing).In this way, the "Whole Human Race" can be Transformed from **Death to New-life** to become **Worthy of <u>God's Twelve Gifts of Creation</u>** (physical/spiritual/mystical/divine x 3) which is having *Four Bodies* (earth), *Four Lifestyles* (Heaven), and *Four Homes*

(Kingdom). The "Lord is Revealing" here that the Human Race is **Comprised** of **Four Individuals Growing** and having its being within **Each Person on Earth,** based on *One's Intellect* (mind), *Emotions* (heart), *Instincts* (soul), and *Nature* (life-force). The question is: just how can a "Single Individual Manage" Living in **Four Different Places** at the **Same time** and still **Remain** a **Single Identity** within *Truth, Law, Will, and Love?* The answer comes with "Entering God's Divine Nature" as the Father (light), Son (soil), Spirit (water), and Trinity (life), thereby **Seeing** (thought), **Hearing** (word), **Speaking** (deed), and **Feeling** (becoming) **All at the Same time,** just as *If We* were a *Normal Body with Many Parts*. This means that as "We Enter Eternal Life," What We Used to Do with **Our Feet** (transfigured body), **Hands** (glorified body), **Eyes** (mystical body) and **Mouth** (divine body) which can **Work Independently** of **Each Other**, we can **Focus** on **Four Separate Jobs** at the **Same time**, thereby **Showing** that this will become *Our Lives* within *God's Quad-Shaped Infinite Creation*.

We see this "Universal Independence" of Body Parts **When We** are **Driving a Car** and **Our Hands, Feet, and Head** are **Busy** with the *Gas Pedal, Brakes, Steering Wheel*, while *Simultaneously Watching in Every Direction*. We call this "Multi-tasking (many things at once)." Now, think of it as being Properly Trained, like a **Person Typing a Document** while *Carrying* on a *Conversation with Someone Else* on the *Telephone*. We must expect that this "Bi-," "Tri-" and "Quad-Location Principle" Operates within the same **Set** of **Multi-functional Mechanisms** as **Our Integrated Human Movements**, yet, also **Operating** within a **Detached Mode** of *Our Own Body*. Obviously, "Living with God" in His New Kingdom of Glory will be a **Little Strange** at **First** or at **Least** until **We Get Used to Our** *New Transfigured Bodies* (physical), *Glorified Spirits* (spiritual), *Holy Souls* (mystical), *and Sacred Life-forces* (divine).

The following tabular information indicates that the "Mind of Man" must become Worthy of God's *Four Bodies;* the "Heart of Man" must become Worthy of God's *Four Lifestyles;* and the "Soul of Man" must become Worthy of God's *Four Homes*:

God's Twelve Gifts to Creation
(four bodies/four lives/four homes)

Physical	1. Transfigured Body	2. Glorified Body	3. Mystical Body	4. Divine Body
(natural order)	• Son Removes Sin-nature: Worldly Righteous-nature (submissive)			
	• Man's Wisdom - Freedom from Slavery: Home Life (king)			
	• Break Chains of Painful Existence - Value Good Health			
Spiritual	5. Earthly Life	6. Eternal Life	7. Mystical Life	8. Divine Life
(supernatural)	• Spirit Removes Worldly Temptations: Heavenly Holy-nature (sacrificial)			
	• Angelic Goodness - Liberty through Servanthood: Church Employee (priest)			
	• Unlock Prison Doors of Endless Service - Value Prosperity			
Mystical	9. Earth	10. Heaven	11. Kingdom	12. Self (God)
(divine order)	• Father Removes Demonic Possession: Kingdom's Perfect-nature (reconciled)			
	• God's Prosperity - Independence of Ownership: Government Leader (son)			
	• Overpower Guards of Eternal Unhappiness - Value Love			

This illustration shows that the "Job of the Son" is to Remove Our Sin-nature to **Make Us Worthy** of a *New Worldly Righteous-nature* (submissive). The "Spirit" will then Remove Our Worldly Temptations to **Make Us Worthy** of a *New Heavenly Holy-nature* (sacrificial). The "Father" will Remove Our Demonic Possessions to **Make Us Worthy** of a *New Kingdom's Perfect-nature* (reconciled). We see that "Out of Our" "New Righteous-nature," **We will Receive Wisdom** (free from slavery), **Allowing Us** to *Enter Christ's Kingship* (home life). "Out of Our" "New Holy-nature," **We will Receive Goodness** (liberty through servanthood), **Allowing Us** to *Enter Christ's Priesthood* (church employee). In like manner, "Out of Our" "New Perfect-nature," **We will Receive Prosperity** (independence through ownership), **Allowing Us** to **Enter Christ's Sonship** (government leader) as **Members** of the *Kingdom of God.* Through these "Three Divine Natures," We can Come to **Know, Love, and Serve Our God** as He Welcomes Us into His **Multidimensional Lifestyle** of *Manifested Will*, where a *Person Needs Only Think of Something* and *It will Occur*. We must imagine "Getting Used" to Traveling by **Our New God/Man Will** and **Working in Four Places at Once**, while having **Eternities of Time** to **Get Things Done** as **We Work** with **Our Best Friend,** the **Lord God Almighty,** to *Make Everything Perfect.*

Obviously, "Speed" and "Accuracy" will Take-on a **Whole New Meaning** as the **Now of Life** and **Eternal Now of Infinity Merge** into a **Collage** of **Expedited Activities**, where **Everything** can *Get Done at Once*. Everyone knows that "Man's Futuristic Lifestyle" is Going to be Far Beyond Our Wildest Imaginations; but **We** are sure a **Three-Year Old Child** will **Say** the same **Thing About** becoming a **Nuclear Physics Scientist** *When he Grows-up*. Yes! We are "All Tiny Children" much like an Ugly Caterpillar, **Which can Hardly Imagine** becoming a **Beautiful Butterfly** that can **Actually Fly into the Sky** and then **Spend its Life** *Pollinating the Garden Flowers*. For this reason, the "Bible Speaks" of Breaking Our **Chains of Slavery**, Opening the **Prison Doors of Captivity,** and Overpowering the **Prison Guards of Death** that we might *Escape Our Own Sin, Evil, and Death* through *Christ Jesus*. By "Breaking Our Chains (sin-nature)," We can Value *Good Health*, "Opening Prison Doors (worldly temptation)," and *Prosperity.* By "Overpowering Our Guards (demons)," We can Value *Divine/Angelic/Human Love.*

It should now make sense that "We Can Never Escape" Our Own **Pit of Hopelessness,** but **Only** through **Christ can All Things become Possible** and through **His Sacrificial Blood** will the **Dream of Freedom Soon become Real** to *One and All*. Through "Christ's Love" for a Devastated Humanity (sin), **He is Willing** to **Sacrifice Himself** to the **Last Drop of His Blood** to **Save His Bride** from **Eternal-damnation** and to *Restore Her Beauty and Love* unto *Himself*. Unfortunately, this "Process of Redemption" would Require Mankind to *Reject Its Selfishness* (soul), *Deny Its Intellect* (mind), *Abandon Its Feelings* (heart), and *Submit Its Free Will* (life-force). In other words, "Mankind" must become Unselfish," Pledging Not to Believe even *What's in Its Own Mind*, **Not Loving What Comes** from *Its Own Heart,* and Not Treasuring (owning) **What Comes** from *Its Own Soul*. In short, the "Human Race" must Reject the Earth, its Tree of Knowledge (poisoned mind,) and All that Exist on Earth as it is simply a **Deception of the Evil One** (Lucifer's test) and **Cannot be Trusted** to **Lead a Soul** from its **Pit of Death** (hell) All the Way to the *Lord's Eternal*

Glory in Heaven (God). We are "Each being Called" to Search for Love (romance), Plant the Seed of Love (marriage), Bear the Firstfruits of Love (1st baby), and finally, Harvest Our Eternal Lives of Love (many children) and **Offer God** the *Treasures of Life* (love). It is important to realize that the "God/Man Relationship" has been Established upon a **Massive Lie** being **Told** by the **Father of Liars, Lucifer,** as **We have All** been **Deceived into Believing** in a **World of Physical Happiness** without a *Loving God*. Obviously, this "Fairy Tale" Cannot be True and the **Whole Human Race** must **Reject Planet Earth** and **All that is In It** so that **All Men** can be **Set Free** from *Sin* (sin-nature), *Evil* (worldly temptations), and *Death* (demonic possession). This means that "Christ must Come" to Save Us (light/see); then **We** must **Save Ourselves** (water/purification); then **Help Save Others** (soil/work); and finally, go forth to **Save even God** (life/union) from **His Divine Pit of Darkness** (single-mindedness of purpose), thereby **Making God, Angels, and Men One** in *Truth, Law, Will, and Love*.

The following tabular information indicates that "We must All Go" in Search of Love (romance), "Plant" the Seed of Love (marriage), "Bear" the Firstfruits of Love (1st baby), and finally, Harvest Our Love (many children) to have a *Full and Happy Life*:

God's Love Makes the World Go Around
(being saved/saving self/saving others/saving God)

Reject
Self
1. **Searching for Love** - Reject Selfishness: Need New Perspective... Self-love
   - Wedding Contract - Union of Two Fathers (exchange)
   - Bride Price - Paid in Blood: Gift of Name   **Romance**
   - Dowry - Paid in Love: Gift of Virginity

(Spirit's Love - being saved: receive free gold mine = given seat in celestial court)

Wisdom
2. **Seed of Love** - Deny Intellect: Need New Life-behavior...Loving Others
   - Betrothal - Union of the Couple (exchange)
   - Groom Offers his Name   **Marriage**
   - Bride Offers her Virginity

(Son's Love - saving self: dig out own gold = given seat in temple court)

Courage
3. **Firstfruits of Love** - Abandon Feelings: Need New Lifestyle...Loving God
   - Wedding Supper - Union of Friends (exchange)
   - Groom's Friends Offer Wealth and Power   **1st Baby**
   - Bride's Friends Offer Beauty and Love

(Father's Love - saving others: sharing his gold with others = given seat in royal court)

Generosity
4. **Harvest of Love** - Submit Free Will: Need New Nature...Becoming Love
   - Wedding Feast - Union of Two Families (exchange)
   - Groom's Family Offers Fruitful Land   **Many Children**
   - Bride's Family Offers Livestock

(Almighty's Love - saving God: building golden kingdom = given seat in divine court)

This illustration shows that "Christ is Scheduled to Come" to Save Us (sinners) via the **Light of His Word** (Bible); then **We must Save Ourselves** (Christians) via the *Purification of Water Baptism* (church). Finally, the "Church is to Go" forth to Save Others (pagans/good news) via the **Good Works of Evangelization** (world), thereby **Plowing** the **Soil of Ignorance** until **Awakened Mankind** can **Plant the Seeds of Wisdom** in *Every Lost and Broken Soul*. Yes! Through "Christ's Light," "Church Waters," and the "World's Hard-work," **Planet Earth** can be **Saved** from its **Original Curses** of *Defiance* (stealing), *Deception* (hiding), and *Deceit* (lying).

1. **Christ's Light** - Fill Man's Mind with God's Truth: Being Saved... See Limitations
2. **Church's Waters** - Drowned Flesh/Resurrect Spirit: Saving Self...See Potential
3. **World's Hard-work** - Create God/Man Heaven on Earth: Saving Others...See Self-worth

We see in the previous chart that through the "Wedding Contract," the Two Fathers of the **Bride/Groom** are **Locked** into a **Lifetime of Negotiation** *Over* the *Groom's Bride-price* (name) and the *Bride's-dowry* (virginity) to **Make Sure** that this *Agreement was Just in the Eyes of God*. Secondly, through the "Betrothal," the Couple shall **Take Their Wedding Vows of Sanctity** (betrothed love) by **Exchanging** the **Groom's Name** (support) for the **Bride's Virginity** (babies) to **Make** the *Marriage Bond Perfect and Eternal*. Thirdly, through the "Wedding Supper," the Friends of the Groom (garter touch) will **Unite** by **Exchanging Their Influence** (wealth) with the Friends of the Bride (bouquet touch)**, Who** will **Unite** by **Offering Themselves as Potential Wives** to *Create Future Marriages*. Finally, through the "Wedding Feast," the Family of the Groom (home) will **Unite** by **Exchanging Their Lands/votes** (power) with the Family of the Bride (baby sitter), **Who** will, in turn, **Unite** by **Exchanging Their Stock/food** to *Feed Everyone at Every Coming Feast*.

Now, we see that at "Every Level of Society," Individual Groups have **Something of Value** to **Share** (community) with the **Family, Friends, Neighbors,** and even **Strangers** of *Humankind*. Obviously, a "Wedding is Designed" to bring People Together to *Share Their Knowledge* (strangers), to *Share Their Time* (neighbors), to *Share Their Labors* (friends), and finally, to *Share Their Money* (family).

1. **Share Crucial Knowledge** - Help Strangers: Learning Right/Wrong...Get New Body
2. **Share Valuable Time** - Help Neighbors: Learning Good/Evil...Get Eternal Life
3. **Share Treasured Labors** - Help Friends: Learning God's/Man's Wills...Get Own Kingdom
4. **Share Hard-earned Money** - Help Family Members: Learning Reality/Illusion... Get Freedom

The "Lord is Telling Us" that the World will be Saved through the **Blessings of Sharing** as the **Human Race Strives** to become **Righteous** in the **Flesh** and **Holy** in the **Spirit** to bring forth *Heaven on Earth* (Man) and *Paradise in Heaven* (God). For this "Dream of Sharing" to become a Reality, **Each of God's Children** must **Master the World** (called/changed) and then **Master the Church** (chosen/washed) to both become

Righteous and Holy before God. The theme here is that a "Righteous Man" is <u>Called by Jesus</u> to **Hear the Word** (redeem flesh) and *Eat Eternal Bread* (born-again/purify grave), while a "Holy Man" is <u>Chosen by Christ</u> to **Save Souls** (redeem spirit) and *Drink from the Eternal Chalice* (sainthood/purify host).

1. **Righteous Man** - <u>Called by Jesus:</u> Hear Word to Redeem Flesh = Eat Bread to be Born-again
   • Fight Evil unto Death - Become Worthy of New Body: Transfiguration (purify grave)
   • Convert from Sinner to Christian - Share One's Labors (master world)
2. **Holy Man** - <u>Chosen by Christ:</u> Save Souls to Redeem Spirit = Drink Wine to Enter Sainthood
   • Surrender unto Death - Become Worthy of Eternal Life: Glorification (purify host)
   • Convert from Christian to Saint - Share One's Money (master church)

Through the "Righteous Man," <u>Man's Physical Nature</u> will **Hear the Good News** so that the **Lord** can bring **Free Redemption** (free gold mine) to **Those Who** will *Bow to God's Divine Will* (fight evil). Secondly, through the "Holy Man," <u>Man's Spiritual Nature</u> will **Hear the Gospel Message** so that the **Lord** can bring **Earned Salvation** (dig out gold) to **Those Who** will *Enter God's Divine Love* (submission). This means that the "Job of the Righteous Man" is to <u>Fulfill</u> the **Divine Will of God** to *See his Own Limitations* (agony of defeat); while the "Job of the Holy Man" is to <u>Fulfill</u> **God's Divine Love** to *See his Potential* (thrill of victory). We are expecting to "See the Righteous Man" to <u>Learn the Lessons of Life</u> (called) as he **Comes** to **Obey God's Laws** to **Defeat his Own Ignorance and** be **Washed in Jesus' Baptism** (picked-up cross) to *Make him Streetwise in the World* (Christian). Secondly, the "Holy Man" shall be <u>Blessed with God's Love</u> (chosen) as he **Sells All and Gives It to the Poor** to **Defeat his Own Cowardice** and be **Changed via Christ's Blood** (deny self) to *Make him Formally Educated by Heaven* (sainthood).

We are showing that the "Righteous Man" is <u>Striving to be Transformed</u> from a *Sinner* (share knowledge) to a *Christian* (share time); while the "Holy Man" is <u>Striving to be Transformed</u> from a *Christian* (share labors) to a *Saint* (share money). Through this "Process of Conversion (called/chosen)," the <u>Whole Earth</u> shall be **Saved** from **Its Curses** of *Ignorance, Criminal Behavior, Insanity,* and becoming *Evil before God.* Now, we see that the "Plan of God (spirit)" and "His Son (flesh)" is to <u>Call All Sinners</u> (washed) to **Master the World** and become *Righteous*, and <u>Choose All Saints</u> (changed) to **Master the Church** and become *Holy*.

The following tabular information indicates that "Sinners are Called" to <u>Master the World</u> and become **Righteous**; while "Saints are Chosen" to <u>Master the Church</u> and become **Holy** in the *Name of God and Mary's Son*:

Sinners are Called to Master the World,
while Saints are Chosen to Master the Church
(the called become righteous men of earth,
while the chosen become holy men of Heaven)

Master World - See Limitations   **Master Church** - See Potential

God's Divine Will (Christian)

1. <u>Righteous Man</u> - Mary's Son, Jesus/law
   - Called - Lessons (share knowledge)
   - Obey God's Laws - Defeat Ignorance
   - Change Nature - Individual Rights (share time)
   - Pick-up Your Cross - Streetwise

   Free Redemption (good news) - Save Sinners
   - Those Who <u>Believe</u> in Me (called)

<u>Will Not Hunger</u> - Bread (new body)
   - Learn Man's Wrong (flesh) - Strangers
   - **Learn God's Evil (spirit) – Neighbors**
     Face - Agony of Defeat

God's Divine Love (Saint)

2. <u>Holy Man</u> - God's Son, Christ/faith
   - Chosen - Blessings (share labors)
   - Sell All, Give to Poor - Defeat Cowardice
   - Wash Away Sin - Social Rights   (share money)
   - Deny Your Very Self - Educated

   Earned Salvation (gospel message) - Create Saints
   - Those Who <u>Come</u> in Me (chosen)

<u>Will Not Thirst</u> - Wine (eternal life)
   - Learn Man's Right (flesh) – Friends
   - **Learn God's Good (spirit) – Family**
     Seek - Thrill of Victory

This illustration shows that "Those Sinners" <u>Who Come to Jesus</u> will **Not Hunger** as **They** will **Eat Eternal Bread** (wheat/last supper) and *Receive New Bodies*; "Saints" who <u>Believe in Christ</u> will **Not Thirst** as **They** will **Drink from the Eternal Chalice** (wine/Calvary) and *Receive Eternal Life*. It can now be seen that "Jesus" has Come" to <u>Teach Man's Wrong</u> (called) to a **Confused World** (flesh) so **that Mankind can Learn** to **Befriend the Stranger** by <u>Sharing</u> with him *Individual Rights* (knowledge). Secondly, "Jesus Comes" to <u>Teach God's Evil</u> (washed) to a **Cruel World** (spirit) so **that Mankind can Learn** to **Befriend his Neighbors** by **Sharing with Them** America's most *Important Social Rights* (time). Thirdly, "Christ Comes" to <u>Teach Man's Right</u> (chosen) to an **Enlightened World** (flesh) so **that Mankind can Learn** to **Make Friends with Everyone** by <u>Sharing</u> with them *Divine Rights* (labors). Finally, "Christ Comes" to <u>Teach God's Good</u> (changed) to a **Newly Blessed World** (spirit) so **that Mankind can Learn** to **Love Its Own Families** by **Sharing** with <u>Them</u> *God's Inalienable Rights* (courts) and *Man's Natural Resources* (money). Yes! We are "All being Taught" that the <u>Life-experience</u> is about **Making Friends with God, Angels, and Men** by **Giving of Oneself** until a <u>Person is Empty</u> of *All his Worldly Selfishness*. This "Need to Listen" to <u>God's Son</u> and to **Strive** to become a **Reflection** of **Christ on Earth** drives an <u>Ignorant Fool</u> to become *Wise* (befriend stranger), a <u>**Criminal**</u> to become *Honest* (befriend neighbor), an <u>**Insane Mad-man**</u> to become *Normal* (make friends), and an <u>**Evil Monster**</u> to become a *Treasure on Earth* (love family).

We see that the "Lord God Almighty" is <u>Telling Us</u> that **Anything is Possible with Christ** and that **Life is Comprised** of **Many Forces,** some <u>**Good**</u> and some <u>**Evil;**</u> but in *Christ, All Can be Made Perfect*. This "Need to Bond" with <u>God, Angels, and Men</u> **Unites God's Kingdom** and brings **All Peoples Together** in the **Light of Truth, Law, Will, and Love** so that <u>**They can Work Together**</u> to *Create Babies, Earthly Citizens, Heavenly Saints, and Kingdom Sons for God*. Now, we see that the "Life-experience Involves" the <u>Forces of Union</u> or <u>Bonding</u> as **Familiarity** brings **People Together**. Thus, the more a **Person Rejects** his <u>**Own Wants**</u> to <u>**Share his Life with Others,**</u> the more *Acceptable* and *Well-liked* he becomes within the *Community*. It must be understood that the "Only Do Step of Life (submission)" is <u>Man's Death to Selfishness,</u> via <u>Belief</u> thereby **Allowing Christ to Becoming Him** (no wants), **Take Over His Life,** and **Miraculously <u>Accomplish All His Good Works</u>** by *Bearing Fruit, Out* of even *One's Most Evil Actions* (sin-nature). In this "Final Step of Life," a <u>Person Comes</u> to **Know the Truth** as his **Life-force is Convinced** that **Reality is Life** and that the **Life-experience** is <u>All About *Saving the Souls of Others*</u> (pride of accomplishment) even at the *Cost of One's Own Life.*

This means that "Mastering One's Kingship (face Lucifer's Test)" is <u>All About Survival</u> (baby belief) and <u>Learning God's Truths</u> (see limitations); while "Mastering the Priesthood (face God's Judgment)" is <u>All About One's Sacrifice</u> (teenage belief) and <u>Learning God's Law</u> (see potential). We see that "Mastering One's Sonship (face Self-evaluation)" is <u>All About Finding Protection</u> (adult belief) and <u>Learning God's Will</u> (see self-worth), while "Mastering His Freedom (face making choices)" which is <u>All About Making Own Choices</u> in Life (wise man belief) and <u>Learning God's Love</u> (see face of God).

1. **Mastering One's Kingship** - <u>Facing Lucifer's Test:</u> Baby Belief...See Limitations
   - All About Man's Survival   **Belief in God**
   - All About Learning God's Truths
2. **Mastering One's Priesthood** - <u>Facing God's Judgment:</u> Teenage Belief...See Potential
   - All About Man's Sacrifice   **Trusting Belief in God**
   - All About Learning God's Law
3. **Mastering One's Sonship** - <u>Facing Self-evaluation:</u> Adult Belief...See Self-worth
   - All About Man's Protection   **Faithful Belief in God**
   - All About Learning God's Will
4. **Mastering One's Freedom** - <u>Facing Making Choices:</u> Wise Man Belief...See Face of God
   - All About Man's Self-reliance   **Knowing God Himself**
   - All About Learning God's Love

In short, the "Meaning of Life" <u>Centers on Surviving</u> by **Establishing** a **Person's Own Life-support System** which **Offers Sufficient Resources Needed** to **Sustain His Life** and **<u>Support</u>** both his *Family* and his *Community.* Secondly, the "Purpose of Life" <u>Centers</u> on **Finding the Truth/Law** by becoming of **<u>Service to Others</u>** which **Offers** a **Sufficient Reason** to **Live Another Day** as a <u>Person Finds</u> his *Respected Place in Society.* Thirdly, the "Value of Life" <u>Centers</u> on **Becoming Loved** by being **Loveable to Others** which **Leads** to a **Treasured Life** of **Peace of Mind, Joy of the Heart,** and **Happiness of the Soul** to bring **<u>Fulfillment to One's</u>** *Mind, Heart, and Soul.* Finally, the "Perfection of Life" <u>Centers</u> on having **Unlimited Choices** by being **Wise, Courageous, and Generous** to the **Whole World** which <u>**Leads**</u> to a *Sense of Self-Worth* (see God) brought on by *Dying to Own Selfishness in Christ.* The "Job of Both" the <u>Jews</u> and the <u>Christians</u> is to **Offer-up Their Selfishness to God** via the **Lord's Throne of Innocence** and via **His Altar of Guilt** to **<u>Purify</u>** both the *Human Flesh* (Jews/grave) and the *Human Spirit* (Christians/host) before *God.* We see that the "Innocent Throne (Jews)" is <u>Designed</u> to **Purify One's Grave** (flesh) by **Fulfilling God's Law of Obedience**, thereby <u>**Changing His Nature**</u> from *Human* (death) to *Divine* (new-life). Secondly, the "Guilty Altar (Christians)" is <u>Designed</u> to **Purify the Host** (spirit) by **Fulfilling Man's Faith** in **God's Love**, thereby **Washing Away His Sins** to <u>**Change**</u> *Sinfulness into Holiness.*

Offering God Two Sacrifices with One for Flesh and One for Spirit
(innocent blood purifies the grave and guilty blood purifies the host to save all men)

Flesh   1. **Jewish People** - <u>Good Goat:</u> Offer God Innocent Blood…See Limitations
- Purify Grave - Mary's Son, Jesus: *Man is Sacrificed* = Fighting Evil Forces

Defeat   • Throne - Fulfill God's Law of Obedience: Change Nature = Human to

Life   Divine
- God Wants to be Man - Face Life: Change Evil into Good (Christmas)

Spirit   2. **Christian People** - <u>Bad Goat:</u> Offer God Guilty Blood…See Potential
- Purify Host - God's Son, Christ: *God is Sacrificed* = Submission to God

Defeat   • Altar - Fulfill Man's Faith in God's Love: Wash Away Sin = Sinfulness to

Death   Holiness
- Man Wants to be God - Face Death: Change Death into New-life (Easter)

This illustration shows that through "Mary's Son, Jesus (Man)" or the <u>Good Goat</u> (innocent blood), the **Graves of Wicked Men** are to be **Purified** based on just <u>**How Much a Person Fought**</u> the *Evil Forces of the World.* Secondly, through "God's Son, Christ (God)" or the <u>Bad Goat</u> (guilty blood), the **Lives of Wicked Men** (host) are to be **Purified** based on just **How Much a Person Surrenders** to the *Divine Will of God.* In summary, the "Human Race" is being <u>Called to Perfection</u> by being **Able to Bear Fruit Out** of the **Worst of Circumstances** even in the **Depths of Evil** (Sin/Lucifer/Hell) <u>**Far Beyond Anyone's**</u> *Wildest Imaginations.* With the "Creation of America's" <u>Declaration of Independence</u> by the **Founding Fathers,** the **Three Treasures of Life** are clearly **Defined** in the <u>**Mystical Words:**</u> *Life* (eternal life), *Liberty* (new body,) and *Pursuit of Happiness* (kingdom). Through these "Three Concepts of Human Purpose," <u>Mankind</u> can **Grasp the Essence** of **Each Person's Call to Perfection** by being <u>**Willing to Journey**</u> from *Death* (Egypt) to *New-life* (promised land). Recall that "Moses Redeemed the Jews" by <u>Sacrificing the Egyptians</u> (life/wisdom); then he brought **Them** into the **Desert of Prayer** (liberty/goodness); and finally, **Guided Them** into the <u>**Promised Land of Good Works**</u> (happiness/prosperity), all in the *Name of Independence.*

    Through this "Triune Journey of Life (repentance/prayers/works)," <u>Each of Us</u> has been **Taken** from **Babyhood** to **Teenage Life** unto **Adulthood** so **that God's Children** can become **Like** the **Three Kings of Christ** bringing the <u>**Baby Jesus Gold**</u> (Passover/life), <u>**Frankincense**</u> (manna/body), and <u>**Myrrh**</u> (fruitful/kingdom) in *Honor of God's Divine Love.* It should now make sense that the "Human Race" is being Called to Face the Realities of Life by being **Willing** to **Sacrifice Themselves** (Egypt/light), **Pray Devoutly** (desert/water), and **Work Hard** (promised land/soil) to bring forth *Adam's and Eve's Paradise on Earth*. It is important to note that the "Human Race" is Receiving Two Blessings (sanctified reality/actual illusion): **One from Man** through **Isaac** (Old Testament/actual); and the **Other from God** through **Jesus** (New Testament/sanctified). Then, **Man/God** (flesh) will have *Heaven on Earth* and **God/Man** (spirit) will have *Paradise in Heaven*. We now see that "Isaac's Sacrifice (Jews)" brings forth God's Actual Grace to *Purify Man's Flesh* (save sinners/purify grave); while "Jesus' Sacrifice (Christians)" brings forth God's Sanctifying Grace to *Heal Man's Spirit* (create saints/purify host). This "Need to Pass" through this Two-Stage Process **Takes Lost Sinners from Hell** and **Places Repentant Christians in Heaven** making the **Whole Human Race** *Converted from Death to New-life*.

In the "World System," the Human Race is **Called to Serve** the **Divine Will of God** (laws) so **that Lost Fools** can **Defeat Their Own Sin-natures** to *Earn Their Own Individual Rights* (growth/childhood). In contrast, in the "Church System," the Christians are **Chosen to Serve** the **Divine Love of God** (vows) so **Saved Souls** can **Defeat Their Own Worldly Temptations** to *Earn Social Rights* (maturity/adulthood). In this explanation, it is shown that "Man's Worldly Experiences" are Creating **Righteous Men** (water) who **Build Homes, Governments**, and **Churches** to *Redeem the Lost*. Secondly, "Man's Church Life" Creates **Holy Men** (spirit) who **Repent, Pray, and Work** for the **Souls of Others** to *Save Repentant Sinners*. We see that the "Life-experience" is Leaving the **Human Illusion** (temporary childhood) to Enter **God's Divine Reality** (permanent adulthood) as **Man** is **Baptized in Water** to *Die to Self* (death/conviction) and then **Baptized in the Resurrected Spirit** to be *Born-again* (new-life). This means that the "Righteous Man" must Learn Right from Wrong and **Strive** to **Transform Earth** from a **Barren Desert** to bring forth *Heaven on Earth*. In contrast, the "Holy Man" must Learn Good from Evil and **Strive** to **Change Sinners into Saints** to **Earn a Place** in *God's Eternal Heaven*.

We see that "Suffering" the Agony of Defeat **Allows** the **Righteous Man** to **Learn Lessons** and *See his Own Limitations*; while "Experiencing" the Thrill of Victory **Allows** the **Holy Man** to be **Blessed** and *See his Own Potential*. Through both "Limitations and Potential," the Human Race is able to **Remove Its Faults** (illusion) and then **Gain Virtues** (reality) to **Rid Itself** of both its *Ignorance* and its *Cowardice*. The implication is that "Man's Mind" has been Cursed with Ignorance; while "Man's Heart" has been Cursed with Cowardice, but both can be **Removed** via the **Altars** of *Cain* (first-born) and *Abel* (second-born). Recall that in the "Story of Cain and Abel," They Offered God **Different Sacrifices**: one being a **Lamb** and the other being **Wheat/Grapes. God Chose Only the Lamb** to Bless and **Cursed** the **Wheat/Grapes Offering** causing *Cain to Murder Abel*. To "Reconcile" this Hatred between Brothers, **God Sent** his **Son, Jesus Christ** to become both the *Lamb to the Slaughter* (death/actual) and to become *Man's Bread and Wine of New-life* (life/sanctifying).

The following tabular information indicates that "God's Actual Grace" <u>Purifies Man's Flesh</u> (save sinners/lamb), while "God's Sanctifying Grace" <u>Heals Man's Spirit</u> (create saints/bread and wine) to **Convert** *Lost Sinners on Earth* into *Holy Saints in Heaven*:

Actual and Sanctifying Grace Purifies the Lost
and Heals the Saved through Christ's Love
(actual grace brings righteous citizens,
while sanctifying grace brings forth holy saints)

Righteous Man - Builds Home, Government, and Church: Blessed with Holy Water (ethics)

Lessons	1.	**Actual Grace** - <u>Purification:</u> Washed = Jesus Takes-sin (laws) …Save Sinners
(laws)		• Serve Divine Will - Master World: Flesh Defeats Sin-nature (ignorance)
		• Learn Right from Wrong - Righteous Citizen on Earth: Heaven on Earth
		• Called - Wash Away Sin: Righteous Man Sees Own Limitations (share knowledge)
Offer-up		• <u>Remove Faults</u> - Remove Ignorance (mind): Abel's Altar/flesh and blood = Dowry/bride
Lamb of		
Death		• Inheritance - Steal Brother's Wealth: Winepress of Death = Purify/wash
		• Stick of Death - Mother's Hopes: Trying One's Best = Agony of Defeat
		• Pick-up Your Cross - Streetwise: Individual Rights = Live with Self
		• *Free Redemption* brings the Good News - Growth is Mandatory/know God
		• Will to Live - Man's Purification: Earth Gives New Body (babies)

(those who come to me shall not hunger - bread of life: new body/challenge)

Holy Man - Repents, Prays, and Works for Souls: Blessed with God's Spirit (morals)

Blessings	2.	**Sanctifying Grace** - <u>Healing:</u> Changed = Christ Gives-up Divinity…
(vows)		Create Saints
		• Serve Divine Love - Master Church: Spirit Defeats Worldly Temptations (cowardice)
		• Learn Good from Evil - Holy Saint in Heaven: Paradise in Heaven
		• Chosen - Change Nature: Holy Man Sees Own Potential (share money)
Offer-up		• <u>Gain Virtues</u> - Remove Cowardice (heart): Cain's Altar/bread and wine = Bride Price/change
Bread/Wine		
Life		• Birthright - Purchase with Bowl of Soup: Crucible of Fire = Transform/change
		• Carrot of Life - Father's Expectations: Succeed = Thrill of Victory
		• Deny Your very Self - Educated: Social Rights = Live with God
		• *Earned Salvation* brings Gospel Message - Maturity is Optional/love God
		• Value of Life - Man's Transformation: Heaven Gives Eternal Life (adult)

(those who believe in me shall not thirst - wine of life: eternal life/adventure)

This illustration shows that through "Esau's" Birthright (morals) and Inheritance (ethics), the **Coming Kingdom of God** was **Transferred from Isaac** to his **Son** (Esau) to bring forth the *Promised Redemption of Man*. "Rebecca" Realized that **Her Babies Switched Positions** in the **Womb** that caused a **Great Mistake** in the **Definition** of the **First-born** between *Esau and Jacob*. For this reason, "Rebecca" decided to Make Jacob the True Heir to the **Abrahamic Covenant** of **Human Redemption** by Stealing **Esau's Inheritance** through *Trickery*. The idea here is that "Isaac's Inheritance/Birthright" were to be Divided between **Man and God** to **Allow Redeemed Souls** to be **Sealed** through **Rebirth** via their *Blessing of Birthright*. This means that when a "First-born Male" is Born on Earth, he becomes **Worthy of Earning** his **Own Inheritance** through the **Creation** of a *Happy Home, Honest Government, and Righteous Church*.

In the case of "One's Birthright," If he Dies to Self and **Believes** in **God's Son, Christ,** he can then be **Born-again** into a **New Nature of Divinity** and become **Worthy** of a *New Body, Eternal Life,* and a *Royal Kingdom*. This "Division" between a Person's Inheritance on Earth (mind) and a Person's Birthright in Heaven (heart) allows the **Creation of a School** for *Human Flesh* (kingship) and an **Eternal Career** for *Divine Spirits* (sonship). The idea here is that "Man's Earthly School" represents the Stick of Death (inheritance) based on a **Mother's Hopes** (trying/lessons) which leads a **Child of God** to **Taste** the *Agony of Defeat*. Secondly, "God's Heavenly Career" represents the Carrot of Life (birthright) based on a **Father's Expectations** (success/blessings) which leads a **Born-again Son of God** to **Taste** the *Thrill of Victory*. This allows a "Person" to become Balanced in both **Flesh and Spirit** by **Learning** to **Pick-up his Cross for Jesus** (hard-work) and then **Denying his Very Self for Christ** (surrender) to **See the Difference** between *Individual* and *Social Rights*.

The implication is that "Individual Rights (streetwise)" Teach a Person to **Learn** to *Live with himself* (Earth); while "Social Rights (educated)" Teach a Person to **Learn** to *Live with God* (Heaven). It all comes down to "Learning" to Think for Oneself and **Accept God's Gift** of a **Free Redemption** (good news) which allow a **Tiny Baby to Grow-up** (mandatory) and become an *Effective Member of Humanity*. In contrast, a "New Born-again Soul" must also Accept God's Challenge of **Earning** his **Own Salvation** (gospel message) as an **Adult Matures** (optional) and becomes an *Effective Member of Divinity*. This reveals that "Tiny Babies" must Find the **Will to Live** by becoming **Purified** (washed) to become **Worthy** of a *New Body* (grave); while "Adults" must Find the **Value of Life** by becoming **Transformed** (changed) to become **Worthy** of *Eternal Life* (host). Recall that "Jesus Said" Those Who Come to Me shall **Not Hunger** (host). This means that **They will Receive** the *Bread of Life*. When "Christ Said" Those Who Believe in Me shall **Not Thirst** (chalice), this means **They will Receive** the *Wine of Eternal Life*. Through this "Bread and Wine of Life Idea," the Human Race can both **Grow** (Isaac) **and Mature** (Jesus) into **Sons of God,** thereby becoming **Worthy** of **God's Lessons** and **Blessings** to *Convert Wicked Fools into Holy Saints*.

Note that both "Isaac (bloodless)" and "Jesus (blood)" are Sons of Abraham and have been **Sacrificed** to the **Divine Justice of God** to **Remove God's Curses** of *Sin* (excommunication), *Evil* (outcast), *Death* (banished), and *Damnation* (forsaken). In this way, the "Human Race" can be both Changed (called) and Washed (chosen) into a **New Creation** through *Wisdom, Courage, Generosity, and Unselfishness*. This means that the "Lost Broken Mankind" must both be Physically Purified (winepress of death) and Spiritually Transformed (crucible of fire) to both **Save Sinners** (take-sin) and **Create Saints** (give divinity) to bring forth a *New Heaven* (God) and a *New Earth* (Man). In this context, we see an "Ignorant, Criminally, Insane Man," who is "Pure Evil" must be Transformed into a **Wise, Honest, Healthy,** and *Holy Man of Righteousness*. Obviously, this "Conversion Begins" with the Coming of Mary's Son, Jesus, who **Takes Away Sin** to *Save Sinners from Death* and then Comes God's Son, Christ, who **Gives-up His Divinity** (forgiveness) to *Create Saints in Heaven*. Secondly we see that "Jesus Comes" and Takes Man's Sin to **Wash Away** *Physical Sin* (purify); while "Christ Comes" and Gives-up God's Divinity to **Wash** one's *Spiritual Nature* (change). Thirdly, "Jesus also Comes" to Master the Law or *Save Sinners* (earth); while "Christ also Comes" to Master Faith or *Create Saints* (Heaven). Fourthly, "Jesus Calls Sinners" to Face *Excommunication* (temple), *Outcast* (people), *Banishment* (earth), and being *Forsaken by God* (self); while "Christ Chooses Saints" to be Given a *New Body* (temple), *Eternal Life* (people), *Royal Kingdom* (earth), and *Rewarded with Personal Freedom* (think for self). Fifthly, "Jesus Teaches" the Righteous Man **Right from Wrong** (intellect) to receive a *Righteous Citizenship on Earth*; while "Christ Teaches" the Holy Man **Good from Evil** (emotions) to become a *Holy Saint in Heaven*. Sixthly, "Jesus Transforms" a Person's Wicked Flesh into His **New Body** (title deed to earth) or *God's Friendship;* while "Christ Purifies" a Person's Born-again Spirit into a **Blessing of Eternal Life** (title deed to Heaven) or **God's Companionship**. Finally, we see "Jesus as a Jew" brings Heaven on Earth (new earth) by making **All People Worthy** of a **Seat** in *God's Celestial Court* (rulers); While "Christ as a Christian" brings Paradise to Heaven (new Heaven) by making **His Saints Worthy** of a **Seat** in *God's Temple Court* (rulers). It should now make sense that the "Righteousness (earth)," "Holiness (Heaven)," and "Perfection of Man (Kingdom)" come from the Efforts of **Jesus as a Man** (flesh) and **Christ as God** (spirit) both *Working Together for a Better World*. Obviously, "Jesus is Man's Friend (loser)" and has Come to Wash Away (man's law) the *World's Wickedness* (physical purification); while "Christ is Man's Companion (winner)" and has Come to Change (God's Law) **Man's Nature** from *Death to New-life* (spiritual transformation).

The following tabular information indicates that the "Life-experience" is Divided into one's **Physical Purification** (washed) and **Spiritual Transformation** (changed) through the *Intercession of Jesus Christ* (bread/wine):

Physical Purification	**Spiritual Transformation**
(winepress of death/flesh and blood)	(crucible of fire/bread and wine)
1. **Jesus** – Takes-sin (illusion)	1. **Christ** - Gives Divinity (reality)
• See Limitations - Isaac's Blessing	• See Potential - Jesus' Blessing

• Agony of Defeat (loser)	• Thrill of Victory (winner)

2. **Washed in Water** - Baptism
   - John's Jewish Baptism
   - Purification - Wash Flesh
   - Forgiven Sins - Defeat Ignorance
   - Last Supper - Bread (man's law)
   - Pulpit - Lessons (stick)

2. **Washed in Spirit** - Confirmation
   - Jesus' Christian Baptism
   - Transformation - Change Nature
   - Save Souls - Defeat Cowardice
   - Mount Calvary - Wine (God's Law)
   - Chair - Blessings (carrot)

3. **Saving Sinners** - Master Law
   - Mother Desires Child to be Good
   - Hopes of the Mother/Trying
   - Hungry Caterpillar - Blind

3. **Creating Saints** - Master Faith
   - Father Desires Child to be Smart
   - Expectations of Father/Success
   - Devoted Butterfly - Vision

4. **Called by God** - Divine Will
   - Excommunicated from Temple - Remove Sin
   - **Overcome Ignorance/New Mind**
   - Outcast from One's People - Remove Evil
   - Overcome Criminality/New Heart

4. **Chosen by God** - Divine Love
   - Banished from Earth - Remove Death
   - **Overcome Insanity/New Soul**
   - Forsaken by God - Remove Damnation
   - Overcome Evil/New Life-force

5. **Righteous Man on Earth** - Citizenship
   - Mind of Wisdom
   - Heart of Courage

5. **Holy Man in Heaven** - Sainthood
   - Soul of Generosity
   - Life-force of Unselfishness

6. **New Body** (babies) - Transfiguration
   - 1st Mile - Pay for Faults in Blood
   - Title Deed to Earth - Friendship

6. **Eternal Life** - Glorification
   - 2nd Mile - Pay for Virtues in Prayers
   - Deed to Heaven - Companionship

7. **Heaven on Earth** - Jews
   - Seat in Celestial Court - Stewardship
   - Filled with God's Divine Will

7. **Paradise in Heaven** - Christians
   - Seat in Temple Court - Spirituality
   - Emptied of Man's Free Will

---

8. **Living with Oneself** - Mother's Hope

   - Running Toward the Carrot - Love
   - **Will to Live - Survival**

8. **Living with God** - Father's Expectations

   - Running from the Stick – Tough Love
   - **Value of Life - Paradise**

(what makes the donkey walk is neither the "Stick" nor the "Carrot" because it is the "Load")

This illustration shows that "Jesus" is bringing Mankind a **Winepress of Death** (see limitations) to **Purify Its Flesh** and **Set It Free** from *Its Faults*; while "Christ" is bringing Mankind a **Crucible of Fire** (see potential) to **Transform Its Spirit** and **Bless It** with *God's Virtues*. Note that "Man's Winepress (stick)" is an Illusion Used to **Scare Babies** into **Finding Their Own Courage** in the *Face of Their Own Death*; while "God's Crucible (carrot)" is the Lord's Reality Used to **Honor the Life-experience** by *Facing God* and *His Divine Judgment*. By "Facing the Stick" and "Chasing the Carrot," the Human Race can **Learn** just **What Life is All About** as **Each Soul** must be **Willing** to **Carry the Load without Complaint** so that a Person (citizen/saint) can become a *Productive Member of Society*. Obviously, to become a "Productive Member" of Man's

Society, a **Person** must become a ***Righteous Citizen*** (home/government/church); while to become a "Productive Member" of God's Society, a **Person** must become a ***Holy Saint*** (worship/praise/thanksgiving). By using this logic, we see the "Importance" of God's Will to **Punish Mankind,** and the "Importance" of God's Love to **Bless Mankind** so that the **Human Race** can **Learn the Meaning** of both ***Sharing with Neighbors*** and ***Serving Families.*** This means that the "Highest Honor in Life" is to Do One's Duty (carry load)" and to become a **Productive Member of Society** at **All Levels** of the ***Social Order of Life.*** The idea here is that becoming of "Value to God, Angels, and Men" Allows a Person to become **Worthy** of the **Lord's Eternal Rewards** based on the ***Number of Souls Saved.*** In short, we are "All being Called" to Build a Home for ***Man on Earth*** and then to Build a Home for ***God in Heaven*** so that they can be **Joined Together** in **Building a Combined Home Together** to ***Share a Universal Kingdom of Glory.***

This need to establish a "Home for Man (righteous)" on Earth (works) and then a "Second Home for God (holiness)" in Heaven (faith) **Creates** the **Need for Two Truths,** made **Perfect** through the ***Blessings of Isaac*** (illusion) and ***Jesus*** (reality). The idea here is to see that "Isaac" is bringing forth a Physical Blessing **Designed** to bring **Physical Prosperity** so **that Righteous Men of Works** can **Convert Sinners** (citizens) by bringing them through ***Man's Blood Purification System*** (circumcision). Secondly, "Jesus" is bringing forth a Spiritual Blessing **Designed** to bring **Spiritual Redemption** so **that Holy Men of Faith** can **Create Saints** (saints) by bringing them through ***God's Waters of Purification*** (baptism). In short, "If a Person" Receives an **Old Testament Blessing** (law), he will be **Given Heaven on Earth** to **Rule All he Surveys,** as a **Royal King** via **God's Divine Rite of Kings,** and ***Establish God's Government on Earth.*** Secondly, "If a Person" Receives a **New Testament Blessing** (faith), he will be **Given Paradise in Heaven,** to be a **Servant unto the Lord** as a **Humble Son of God** via **God's Divine Rights of Sonship,** and ***Establish God's Church in Heaven.***

When the "Earthly Blessing (wealth)" is Combined with the "Heavenly Blessing (redemption)" upon the Cross of Calvary (blood/water), we see the **Union** of the **Son of Man, Jesus** with the **Son of God, Christ,** thereby bringing forth ***One Single Blessing of Perfection*** (Holy Spirit). Out of the "Blessing of Man," the Whole Earth (world) can be **Transformed** from ***Ignorance to Wisdom*** (mind); while out of the "Blessing of God," Christ's Faithful (church) can be **Transformed** from ***Cowardice to Courage*** (heart). This "Transformation Process" is used to Convert Earthly Sinners (world) and Create Heavenly Saints (church) by simply **Cursing** that which is ***Evil*** and **Blessing** that which is ***Good.*** We can now see that the "Jewish People" represent the Old Testament (ethics/law) and the **Blessing of Their Temple** (flesh/blood) upon the ***Human Race*** (son of man); while the "Christian People" represent the New Testament (morals/faith) and the **Blessing of Their Church** (bread/wine) upon the ***Human Race*** (Son of God).

The following tabular information indicates that the "Old Testament (Isaac)" Offers Its Heirs **One Blessing** to bring a **Struggling Soul** ***Prosperity on Earth***; while the "New Testament (Jesus)" Offers Its Heirs an **Infinite Number of Blessings** to bring a **Cursed Sinner** ***Redemption in Heaven***:

One Old Testament Blessing and Infinite Number
of New Testament Blessings from Isaac and Jesus
(Old Testament brings physical prosperity,
while New Testament brings spiritual redemption)

Flesh
(kingship)

1. **Old Testament Blessing** - <u>Isaac:</u> One Blessing (lifetime) …Illusion
   - Physical Prosperity (son of man) - Righteous Citizen on Earth: *New Body*
   - Heaven on Earth - Man: New Jerusalem = Fight Death and Win (world)
   - Circumcision - Blood: Works = Convert Sinner (ignorance to wisdom)
   - Blessing of Righteousness - Learning Right from Wrong: See Limitations
   - Blessing of Temple - Flesh and Blood: Ethics (inheritance/redemption)
   - Get Baby Life on Earth - King of All You Survey (see self-worth)
   - Home of Man - Work and Play are One and Everyone has Fun (informal)

Spirit
(priesthood)

2. **New Testament Blessing** - <u>Jesus:</u> Infinite Blessings (eternal life)...Reality
   - Spiritual Redemption (Son of God) - Holy Saint in Heaven: *Eternal Life*
   - Paradise in Heaven - God: Kingdom of Glory = Honor Life and Win (church)
   - Baptism - Spirit: Faith = Create Saints (cowardice to courage)
   - Blessing of Holiness - Learning Good from Evil: See Potential
   - Blessing of Church - Bread and Wine: Morals (birthright/salvation)
   - Get Adult Life in Heaven - Servant unto the Lord (think for self)
   - Home of God - Life is Serious and Struggle Builds Character (formal)

This illustration shows that the "Job of the Jews (law)" was to bring forth an <u>Old Testament Blessing</u> (Isaac/grave) in the *Form of a New Body* (righteous citizen); while the "Job of the Christians (faith)"was to bring forth a <u>New Testament Blessing</u> (Jesus/host) in the *Form of Eternal Life* (holy saint). In short, out of the "Old Testament" would come the <u>Kingship of God</u> to bring **Prosperity to the Flesh** via the **Son of Man** with the **Intent** of *Creating Heaven on Earth* (Man/ethics). Secondly, out of the "New Testament" would come the <u>Priesthood of God</u> to bring **Redemption to the Spirit** via the **Son of God** with the **Intent** of *Manifesting Paradise in Heaven* (God/morals). Recall the "Lord's Story" of <u>Putting New Wine</u> (life) in <u>New Wineskins</u> (body). This **Refers to Putting New Eternal Life** (Heaven/host) into a **Person's New Body** (earth/grave) to become **Worthy** of the *Divine Presence of God*. In this description of "Spiritual Blessings," we see that the <u>Earthly Blessing</u> (flesh/blood) comes from a **<u>Loving Father</u>** (Isaac) to his *Devoted Son* (Esau/stolen by Jacob), while the <u>Heavenly Blessing</u> (bread/wine) comes from the **Eternal Father** to *His Son, Jesus Christ*.

Note that the "Earthly Blessing" <u>Originates</u> within the *Spirit of Man* (Adam's breath); while the "Heavenly Blessing" <u>Originates</u> from the *Spirit of God* (Holy Spirit). With the "Establishment" of these <u>Two Blessings</u> within the **Kingdom of God,** the **Flesh of Man** can **Receive** its **<u>Inheritance</u>** of a *New Body* (redemption); while the **Spirit of Man** can **Receive** its **<u>Birthright</u>** of an *Eternal Life* (salvation). The idea here is that "If a Person" is <u>Found Ethical</u> or **Righteous before Men,** then he can become **Worthy** of a **New Body** and be **<u>Awarded</u>** *Heaven on Earth* (baby life). "If a Person" is <u>Found Morally Sound</u> or **Holy before God**, then he can become **Worthy of Eternal Life** and be **Awarded** *Paradise in Heaven* (adult life). This means that "If a Person Seeks" the <u>Baby Life</u> (illusion), then he will be allowed to **Master** his *Own Self-worth* (blind man with stick); while "If a Person Seeks" the <u>Adult Life</u> (reality), then he will be allowed to **Master** *Thinking for Himself* (seeing the light). Obviously, this is the "Difference" between being a <u>Blind Baby</u> (ignorance) or being a <u>Blind Adult</u> (wisdom), who has been **Healed** and can **Now See** (light of truth). The question is which **Pathway of Life** will *You Take*? Obviously, we all want to become "Adults" so that we can <u>Reject Our False Face</u> and put on the **True Face of God** to **Defeat God's** Curse on **Adam** and be *Set Free from Our Own Hypocrisy*.

When "God Created Adam," he had <u>Formed</u> **One Honest Face**, but when **Adam Fell from Grace**, the **Human Race** was **Given Two Faces**: **One** <u>Looking Toward</u> **Lucifer** (man's will/hell), and **One** <u>Looking Toward God</u> (God's Will/Heaven). Thus, this gave rise to the concept of *Good* (blessing) *and Evil* (curse). It has been the "Job of Jesus Christ" to <u>Convert Mankind</u> **Back** into **One Face of Holy Perfection** based on becoming **Worthy** of God's *Presence Face-to-Face*. In the "Modern World," <u>Humanity is Wearing</u> both the **Faces of Holiness** and **Evil** as **Everyone** has **Learned** that it is **Easier** to *Go Along* to *Get Along with the Crowd*. This "Don't Create Any Waves" <u>Approach to Life</u> has caused **Mankind to Distort** every **Person's True Nature** to the point of **Not being Able to Recognize** his *True Beliefs* and/or to determine just *What he Stands For*. This "Dual Integrity Concept" has caused an entire <u>World</u> to **Mistrust Everyone** and **Everything** because it might certainly be a *Fake* (Judas goat). Through "Jesus Christ" and <u>His New Nature</u> (honesty), **Individual Integrity** shall be **Restored Back** to the **Human Race** by **Reducing the Gap** between *What a Person Believes* and *What a Person* is *Willing to Make Public*. This "Gap of Credibility" must be <u>Eliminated</u> so that **When a Person Comes** to **Face God** during his **Divine Judgment**, What **he Says** will **Match What he Does**. We can now see that when "Jesus Died on Calvary (takes-sin)," *He* was *Removing Man's False Face* (lie); and when "Christ Resurrected (give divinity)," *He* is *Putting On Man's True Face* (truth).

This same theme is being taught as a "Person Dies to Self (submission)" or *Goes to Calvary* (death/dark night of the soul) and is then "Born-again in Truth" or *Resurrects in Christ* (new-life). This means that "If a Person" <u>Offers Humanity His False Face,</u> this will **Trigger** the **Creation of a Series** of *Phony Friends* (back stabbers) and *Fake Relationships* (con-men). But "If a Person" <u>Lives by</u> **Unto Thine Own Self be True**, then for **Better** or for **Worse**, his **Friends** and **Acquaintances** will be *Genuine and True*. When the "Face of Good" and the "Face of Evil" become <u>One,</u> a **Person is Able** to be **Called** (knowledge) to *God's Truth*, **Enlightened** (self-awareness) in *God's Law*, **Awakened** (consciousness) to *God's Will,* and then **Indwelled** (sentience) with *God's Love*. This means that the "Journey of Life Ends" with the <u>Power to Know</u> **Right from Wrong** (called), **Good from Evil** (enlightened), **God's Will from Man's Will** (awakened), and **God's Reality and man's illusion** (indwelling) as the **Human Race** becomes *Committed to Saving Souls* in the *Name of Jesus Christ*.

This process allows each "Born-again" <u>Son of God</u> an **Opportunity** to **Earn his Own Seat** in **God's Celestial Court** (flesh), **Temple Court** (spirit), and **Royal**

Court (soul) through the **Authority** of *God's Divine Justice* (divine court/life). Hence, to become "Worthy of a Seat" in God's Royal Kingdom, a **Person** must become a **Leader of Men,** truly capable of **Ruling** the *Government of Man's Flesh* (celestial court/baby), the *Church of Man's Spirit* (temple court/teenager), and/or the *Home of Man's Soul* (royal court/adult). Once he has "Proven Himself" by Converting Evil (tribulation) into Good (1,000 years of peace) using **Nothing** but his undaunted **Belief, Trust, Faith,** and finally **Knowing,** he will be **Crowned by God** with the *Authorities of both Righteous* (man/earth) and *Holy* (Angels/Heaven) *Perfection* (God/Kingdom). Obviously, to obtain "God's most Honored Gifts" of Righteousness (earth), Holiness (Heaven), and Perfection (Kingdom), a **Person** must **Face Life's Trials** (errors), **Face Total Abandonment** (quit), and then become an **Invincible Force** (never-quit) in a *World of Evil.*

We now see that the "Honored Gifts from God" are to Come in the Form of **Wisdom** (baby), **Courage** (teenager), and **Generosity** (adult), thereby **Allowing a Person** to both **Grow and Mature** on the *Earth* (1st portal), in *Heaven* (2nd portal), within the *Kingdom* (3rd portal), and finally, in *Oneness with God Himself* (final destination). The "Lord's Physical Portal (priest on a donkey)" Comes First through a **Tiny Baby** (grave) to **Enter** the **Earthly Realm of Life** and show the **Human Race** that **God's Nature** is both *Humble and Loving* (contrite). Secondly, the "Lord's Spiritual Portal (thief in the night)" Comes Second through **God's Altar of Death** (holy mass/host) to **Enter** the **Heavenly Realm of Life** and show the **Human Race** that **God's Nature** is *Merciful, yet, Cunning.* Finally, the "Lord's Mystical Portal (just judge on a cloud)" Comes Third through **Man's Governmental Institutions** (thrones) to **Enter** the **Kingdom Realm of Life** and show the **Human Race** that **God's Nature** is both *Powerful* (armies) and *Authoritative* (leadership).

Through "Each of These" Three Portals, **God will Open His Highways of Perfection** to bring the **Human Race** a *Free New Body* (new mind), an *Earned Eternal Life* (new heart), and finally a *Bonus Reward* in the *Form* of a *Son's Royal Kingdom* (new soul). These "Treasures from God" will Open Three Eternal Doorways to **Man's Earthly Realm** (mind), the **Heavenly Angelic Realm** (heart), and to **God's Kingdom Realm** (soul), thereby **Allowing** a **Lost Broken Sinner** to become a **Righteous Citizen** on *Earth* (submission), a **Holy Saint** in *Heaven* (sacrifice), and a **Son of God** within *God's Kingdom* (reconciliation). We see that the "Earth" has been Chained in Sin; "Heaven Represents" a Prison of Evil; and the "Kingdom" is Guarded by Death to **Prevent God's Enemies** from **Reaching God's Treasures** of an *Eternal Body* (transfiguration), *Eternal Life* (glorification), and *Everlasting Homeland* (mystic). This means that "Individuals on Earth," "Society in Heaven," and "God in Divinity" must become One Creation of **Peace, Joy, and Happiness** through the **Three Advents of Christ** in the *Form* of *Man* (Jesus/earth), *God/Man* (Jesus Christ/Heaven), and *God Himself* (Christ/Kingdom).

The following tabular information indicates that "God" is Using" Three Portals to **Descend** into **Lucifer's Evil Earthly World** on **Three Separate Occasions** (womb/altar/throne) to **Break Man's Chains of Sin,** Open Man's **Prison Doors of Evil,** and **Overpower Man's Guards of Death** to *Set All the World's Captives Free:*

**Christ's Three Portals of Redemption via Mary's
Womb, Aaron's Altar, and David's Throne**
(new mind of wisdom, new heart of courage,
and new soul of generosity bring salvation to all)

Truth
(new mind)

1. **1st Portal** - Mary's Womb: Break Chains of Sin…Doorway to Earth
   - 1st Advent - Priest on a Donkey: Submission = Wisdom (see limitations)
   - Called to God's Truth - Learn Right from Wrong: Physical Righteousness
   - Union of God's Mind (hear cry for help) and Man's Mind (know God)
   - God Chains Earth in Sin - Face Lucifer's Test: Defeat Sin-nature
   - Individual gets Free Redemption (being saved) - Receive a *New Body*
   (enter earthly realm via mother's womb - manifestation of God's Truth/good news)

Law
(new heart)

2. **2nd Portal** - Aaron's Altar: Open Prison Doors of Evil…Doorway to Heaven
   - 2nd Advent - Thief in the Night: Sacrifice = Courage (see potential)
   - Enlightened by God's Law - Learn Good from Evil: Spiritual Holiness
   - Union of God's Heart (see child's suffering) and Man's Heart (love God)
   - Seal Doorway to Heaven from Evil - Face God's Judgment: Defeat Worldly Temptations
   - Society gets Earned Salvation (saving self) - Receive *Eternal Life*
   (create heaven on earth via holy mass - manifestation of God's Law [gospel message])

Will
(new soul)

3. **3rd Portal** - David's Throne: Overpower Guards of Death…Doorway to Kingdom
   - 3rd Advent - Just Judge on a Cloud: Reconciliation = Generosity (see self-worth)
   - Awakened by God's Will - Learn God's Reality/man's illusion: Mystical Perfection
   - Union of God's Soul (recognize own covenant) and Man's Soul (serve God)
   - Guard Kingdom Highway from Death - Face Self-evaluation: Defeat Demonic Possession
   - World gets Bonus Rewards (saving others) - Receive *Royal Kingdom*
   (bring kingdom to earth via governmental institutions –
   manifestation of God's Will [doctrinal truths])

This illustration shows that when "Adam and Eve" <u>Fell from Grace,</u> the <u>Lord</u> immediately <u>Chained Earth in Sin</u> (Lucifer's Test), <u>Sealed Heaven from Evil</u> (God's Judgment), and <u>Guarded His Kingdom Highway from Death</u> (self-evaluation). He thereby **Forced** the **Human Race** to **Break the Chains of Sin** (sin-nature), **Open the Prison Doors of Evil** (worldly temptations), and **Overpower the Guards of Death** (demonic possession) to *Set Man Free* from *Sin, Evil, and Death*. These "Three Acts of Escape" would require <u>Man's Savior,</u> the **Lord Jesus Christ,** to make **Three Journeys to Earth** via the **Virgin Mystical Womb/born-again** (1st portal), the **Holy Mass/Host** (2nd portal/host), and **Worldly Governments/Messiah** (3rd portal/grave) to bring forth the **Christ** as a *Priest on a Donkey* (submission), as a *Thief in the Night* (sacrifice), and as the *Just Judge on a Cloud* (reconciliation). Through these "Three Advents (priest/thief/judge)," the Lord would Break the **Chains of Sin** (holy church), Open the **Prison Doors of Evil** (righteous world), and Overpower the **Guards of Death** to **Create Righteous Citizens** on *Earth* (new body), **Holy Saints** in *Heaven* (eternal life), and **Sons of God** within *God's Kingdom* (royal kingdom).

During "Christ's 1st Advent (priest on a donkey)," Humanity is a **Tiny Baby** (church womb) and must **Break Its Chains of Sin** (repentance) through the **Power of Submission** or **Believing** in the *Lord's Resurrection from Death*. Secondly, during "Christ's 2nd Advent (thief in the night)," Humanity is a **Teenager** (worldly life) and must **Open Its Prison Doors of Evil** (prayers) through the **Power of Sacrifice** and **Prayer**, thereby **Trusting** in the **Lord's Coming Age of Peace** (1,000 years/seal saints). Finally, during "Christ's 3rd Advent (just judge on a cloud)," Humanity is an **Adult** (resurrected grave) and must **Overpower Its Guards of Death** (works) through the **Power of Reconciliation and New-life**, thereby having **Faith** in the **Lord's Coming** *New Kingdom of Glory* (end of the world). Yes! Through the "Creation" of a New Body (earth), Eternal Life (Heaven), and a Royal Kingdom (homeland), **God** will **Pay All His Children's Debts** to *Save Them* from the *Forces of Sin, Evil, and Death*.

It is now clear that the "Debts of God (intentional mistakes)" must be Paid in Sacrificial Blood (innocent/forgiven/guilty) to show that the **Lord's Natural Order** (earth/innocent), **Supernatural Order** (Heaven/forgiven), and **Divine Order** (Kingdom/guilty) **Cannot** be **Violated** via **God's Mind, Heart, and Soul** in any way because *Fear* (death agony), *Pain* (hopelessness), and *Death* (separation) will *Occur*. Thus, the need exists to "Do Things Right" to the point of following Physical (earth), Spiritual (Heaven), and Mystical (Kingdom) Law; otherwise, a **Violation will Occur,** causing both *Punitive Retribution* (pay damages) and *Compensatory Recompense* (fine).

1. **Natural Order**/Earth - Paid For in Innocent Blood: Baby = Christmas....Buy New Body
2. **Supernatural Order**/Heaven - Paid For in Forgiven Blood: Teen = Easter...Buy Eternal Life
3. **Divine Order**/Kingdom - Paid For in Guilty Blood: Adult = Halloween....Buy Own Kingdom
   • First 3 1/2 Years of Tribulation - All Hallows Eve: Evil Takes Its Harvest (guilty blood)
   • Second 3 1/2 Years of Tribulation - All Saints Day: Good Takes Its Harvest (innocent blood)
   • White Throne Judgment - All Souls Day: Good and Evil Separated (forgiven blood)

The idea here is that when "God Intentionally Violates" His Own Laws of Order, **He** must **Pay for Damages** (damage restoration) with **Innocent Blood** (sacrifice Christ/spirit) and then **Pay His Fine** (compensatory retribution) with **Guilty Blood** (sacrifice Jesus/flesh) to *Restore Divine Order Back to Divine Justice* (forgiven blood). We call this "Restoration Process (forgiven blood)" Returning Damaged Goods **Back to Their** *Original State* and then **Sending Them Back to Their Original Owner** to **Restore All** that has been *Destroyed*. This "Restoration Concept" was being taught to the <u>Jewish People</u> in the **Jubilee Ceremony** every **Fifty Years**, when **All** was to be **Restored to Their Original State** and then **Returned to Their Original Owner** until the *Next Jubilee*. The idea here is that "Children Learn" by <u>Trial and Error</u> (science); then "Teenagers Learn" from <u>Total Failure</u> (quit/submission); and finally, "Adults Learn" from <u>Raw Tenacity,</u> showing that **They** must **Never-quit** (God's power) until *They Succeed in Triumph*. In this picture, we see an "Ignorant Fool" being <u>Born on Earth</u> with **No Idea of What he Is** (animal/human), **Who he Is** (man or God), or even **Where he Is** (earth or Heaven) until **God Comes to Tell** (Abrahamic Covenant) him just *What's Going On in Life*.

We are now experiencing the "Three Advents of Christ" so that the <u>Human Race</u> will **Know Who, What, When, Where,** and **How Everything** in **Life Fits Together** (Gordian puzzle) to **Give Man's Existence** *Meaning* (home), *Purpose* (government), and *Value* (church). We see that the "Lord God Almighty" is <u>Revealing</u> to <u>His Foolish Children</u> that out of the **Fall of Adam and Eve** (body broken) would come the *Need for Innocent Blood* (death); while out of the **Fall of Lucifer** (blood shed) would come the *Need for Guilty Blood* (damnation). This is why "Jesus Christ" went to <u>Calvary</u> to first **Take Man's Sins** (body broken/guilty) and then to **Give-up His Divinity** (blood shed/innocent) to **Pay** both *Adam's and Lucifer's Debts to God*. Obviously, "Christ's Church" has been <u>Created</u> so **that Each of Us** might **Pay Our Debts to God** via **Our Baptisms** (trial/error), **Confessions** (quit), and **Communions** (never-quit) to **Set Us Free** from *Sin, Evil, and Death*.

The following tabular information indicates that "God's Three Methods" being <u>Used to Raise</u> **His Beloved Children** are **Defined** as *Trial and Error* (physical/baby), *Quit-in-defeat* (spiritual/teenager), and *Never-quit* (mystical/adult):

God's Three Methods for Learning are Trial and Error, Quitting-in-defeat, and Never-quitting
(kings try, priests quit, and sons never-quit
as God has three systems for awakening mankind)

Truth (mind)	1.	**Trial and Error** - <u>King Tries:</u> Sacrifice of Innocent Blood… Knowledge
		• Mosaic Law - Earthly System to Reveal Human Failures: See Limitations
		• God's Mistakes - Paid For with "Innocent Blood (ignorance):" Meaning
Lessons		• Babyhood - Smart Where the Skin is Off: Street smart (scientific method)
		• Trying brings Learning - Right from Wrong: Righteousness (citizenship)
		• Trying until a Baby is Defeated - Surrendering Flesh

(1st six days of creation - trial and error method: face test of Lucifer = learn truth)

Law (heart)	2.	**Quit-in-defeat** - <u>Priest Quits:</u> Sacrifice of Guilty Blood…Self-awareness
		• Christian Faith - Heavenly System to Reveal Angelic Failures: See Potential
		• God Comes - Paid with "Guilty Blood (cowardice):" Purpose
Blessings		• Teens - Smart by Surrendering to Divine Inspiration: Educated (listening)
		• Quitting brings Learning - Good from Evil: Holiness (sainthood)

- Quitting in Overwhelming Awe - Then God Comes to Save You: Spirit

(1,000 years of peace - quit-in-defeat: face God's Judgment = learn law)

Will   3. **Never-quit** - <u>Son Never-quits:</u> Sacrifice of Forgiven Blood…Consciousness
(soul)   • Divine Knowing - Kingdom System to Reveal God's Failures: See Self-
              worth
Treasures   • God's Power - Paid For with "Divine Blood (greed):" Value
              • Adulthood - Smart by Mastering How to Become God: Wisdom
              (knowing)
              • Never-quitting brings Learning - God's Will/man's will: Perfection
              (sonship)
              • Rewarded with God's Strength - One Never-quits: Soul

(end of time – never-quit succeeding: face Self-evaluation = follow God's will)

This illustration is showing "Mankind" that <u>Kings Try</u> (honor ego) to **Guide Their People** (earth); <u>Priests Quit-in-defeat</u> (death to self) to bring **God to Their People** (Heaven); and <u>Sons Never-quit</u> (worship God) to **Indwell Their People** with **God's Spirit** (Kingdom). Through these "Three Teaching Techniques," <u>God</u> will <u>Reveal His Truth</u> (trial/error), <u>His Law</u> (quit-in-defeat), and <u>His Will</u> (never-quit) to **One and All** so **that** <u>**They might Obtain**</u> **New Minds** (new body), **New Hearts** (eternal life), and **New Souls** (royal kingdoms). Yes! We must become "Kingly Scientists" through <u>Trial and Error</u> (try/amateur); then become "Obedient Priests" through <u>Total Abandonment</u> (quitting); and finally, become "Dutiful Sons" through a <u>Person's Ability</u> (professional) to **Never-quit** (tenacity) **Fighting Evil.**

Truth   1. **Kingly Scientist** - Kings Try Their Hardest: Trial and Error…Pass Lucifer's
              Test
              • Babies are Smart where the Skin is Off - Experience
Law   2. **Obedient Priests** - Priests Quit-in-defeat: Total Abandonment…Pass God's
              Judgment
              • Teenagers are Smart when Bowing to a Greater Force - Training
Will   3. **Dutiful Son** - Sons Never-quit Fighting Enemy: Professional Ability…Pass
              Self-evaluation
              • Adults are Smart When They Never-quit Struggling – Expertise

This means that through "Scientific Methods (study)," <u>Mankind</u> will **Gain Knowledge** (know God). Through "Listening to God (word)," <u>Mankind</u> will become **Self-aware** (love God), and then through "Knowing All Things," the <u>Human Race</u> will **Enter** into a **New Consciousness** (serve God). The point here is to see that "Knowledge (right/wrong)" <u>Gives Mankind the Ability</u> to **See Its Own Limitations** (truth); then via "Self-awareness (good/evil)," <u>Mankind will have the Ability</u> to **See Its Own Potential** (law); and finally, through "Consciousness (God/man's wills)," <u>Mankind will have the Ability</u> to **See Its Own Self-worth** (will). The whole "Human Race" must <u>Face Lucifer</u> to **Master Trial and Error**, then <u>Face God's Judgment</u> to **Master Total**

Abandonment (quitting), and finally, <u>Face Its Own Self-evaluation</u> to *Master* the **Ability** to *Never-quit* (invincible).

Obviously, "If a Person can Master" <u>God's Truth,</u> he will clearly see his *Own Identity* and his *Own Meaning.* "If he Masters" <u>God's Law,</u> he will see the *Purpose of Society;* and "If he Masters" <u>God's Will,</u> **he will see** his *Value before God.* This means that "Babies" are <u>Smart Where the Skin is Off;</u> that "Teenagers" become <u>Smart by Surrendering</u> to <u>Divine Inspiration;</u> and finally, "Adults" become <u>Smart by Knowing All Things.</u> It now makes sense "Why God Brought" the <u>Mosaic Law</u> (temple) to the **Jewish People** because **They Represented Human Babyhood** and were **Forced to Use Trial and Error** to **Find Their Messiah** (sacrificial lamb) **Who Came** as a *Priest on a Donkey* (1st advent). Secondly, "God" brought "His Canon Law (church)" to the <u>Christian People</u> because **They Represented Human Teens** and would **Freely Abandon Themselves Totally** (surrender) to **Find Their Messiah** (sacrificial goat) **Who is to Come** as a *Thief in the Night* (2nd advent). Finally, "God" would bring "His Divine Law (kingdom)" to the <u>Holy Saints</u> because they represent **Adults** and are **Forced to Use Indomitable Courage** to **Find Their Messiah** (sacrificial Christ) **Who is to Come** as a *Just Judge on a Cloud* (3rd advent). We see that going through "Babyhood (trial and error/home)," "Teen age (quit-in-defeat/church), and "Adulthood (never-quit/government)," a <u>Person is Called</u> to **Totally Surrender** his **Mind, Heart, and Soul** to the *Will of God.* This makes "Life a Great Journey (challenge/adventure/fun)" and the <u>First Giant Step</u> is **Surrendering to Christ** by **Dying to One's Own Selfishness** which *Allows* a *Lost Sinner* to instantly *Defeat All the Forces of Evil.*

It must be understood that as "Mankind Journeys" closer and closer to <u>Christ's 2nd Advent</u> (beginning of second coming), the **Greater** the **Depth of Evil Consuming** the **Entire World** until *Evil Defeats Good* (God). It is for this reason that a "Person Cannot Say a Few Prayers" and simply <u>Go to Heaven</u> because the **Depth of Evil** is so **Great in the World** that a **Devout Soul** must **Surrender his Life Totally** (prayer/works) via his *Divine Faith* before he can be *Saved.* In short, a "Person Cannot" be an <u>Evil Hedonist</u> within the **World System** and then **Tell God Daily** how much he **Loves Him,** but **Fails to Do His Divine Will** by **Demonstrating His Devotion** through *Good Works* (souls saved). This means that a "True Devotion" to the <u>Lord God Almighty</u> and the **Fulfillment** of **His Will** actually hinges upon a **Child's Steady Growth and Improvement** in both **Physical** (lessons) and **Spiritual** (blessings) **Development** to be <u>Reverently Placed</u> upon *God's Altar Weekly.* It will certainly be a "Great Shock" to a <u>Christian Fool</u> when he **Dies** and is cast into **Death Agony** (mind of ignorance), then into a **Grave of Hopelessness** (heart of cowardice), and finally, into **Hell Fire** (soul of greed) to be *Separated from God Forever.* This implies that "If he were a Wise Christian," he could <u>Dedicate his Life</u> to **Growing-up** and to **Saving Others,** then **Earn Eternal Life, Earn a New Body,** and finally, **Earn a Royal Kingdom** all in the *Name of Christ Jesus.*

It is now clear that the "Human Race" is <u>Required</u> to **Take Three Journeys**: 1) <u>Journey for Individual Rights</u> (government) - Travel the Pathway of Righteousness (baby level/intellect): Elementary School (law) = Learning Right from Wrong (earth);

2) Journey for Social Rights (church) - Travel the Pathway of Holiness (teenage level/emotions): High School (faith) = Learn Good from Evil (Heaven); and 3) Journey for Divine Rights (home) - Travel the Pathway of Perfection (adult/instincts): College (knowing) = Learning God's Will from man's will (kingdom). Via these "Three Journeys," Each of God's Children can **Find** his **Own Identity** (fixed frame of reference), **Establish** his **Own Character** (relative focused existence), and **Develop** his **Own Personality** (perception of reality) to **Walk** before *God*, (kingdom), *Angels* (Heaven), and *Men* (earth). During "Man's First Journey," he is Being Saved by **Jesus Christ** through the *Lord's Power of Redemption* (free). During "Man's Second Journey," he is Striving to Save Himself via his **Church** through the *Power of Salvation* (earned). Then during "Man's Third Journey," he is Working Diligently to **Save Others** via **Christian Fellowship** and through the *Power of Eternal Rewards* (bonus).

In this "Redemptive Process," the Babies of Life are all about **Climbing a High Mountain of Impossibilities** (challenged by trials/errors) with the **Help of Christ** (being saved); while upon **Reaching the Top,** the *Babies become Teenagers* and are **Challenged** to now *Climb Down to Save Themselves*. In the last phase of this "Redemptive Process," the Teenagers of Life must **Assist Their Lost Brothers** by **Helping Them Climb** this **High Mountain of Impossibilities** and by **Helping Them** become *Worthy* of *God's Eternal Rewards* (bonus). The idea here is to see that as "Babies (ignorance)," we are All Called to **Understand** the **Meaning of Life** (to exist) and **Give Meaning** to **Our Existence** in **Learning** to **Worship God** by **Giving Our Life** to *Divine Perfection*. Secondly, as "Teenagers (cowardice)," we are All Called to **Understand** the **Purpose of Life** (to serve) and **Give Purpose** to **Our Service to Others** in **Learning** to **Praise God** by **Giving Our Wealth** to *Divine Holiness*. Finally, as "Adults (greed)," we are All Called to **Understand** the **Value of Life** (to find happiness) and **Give Value** to **Our Right to Happiness** in **Learning** to **Thank God** by **Giving of Our Labors** unto *Divine Righteousness*. At each of these "Three Levels" of Growth (obey) and Maturity (imitate), the **Human Race is Able to Comprehend** that **Life is All About Evolving** into *Something* of *Greater and Greater Value before God*.

The following tabular information indicates that the "Three Journeys of Life" along the Pathways of Righteousness (earth), Holiness (Heaven), and Perfection (Kingdom) have been **Created** so that a **Person** might **Attain his Own Individual Rights** (self), **Social Rights** (man), and **Divine Rights** (God) on *Earth* (submission), in *Heaven* (sacrifice), and within *God's Kingdom* (reconciliation):

Three Journeys of Life, Pathways of Righteousness, Holiness, and Perfection unto Human Rights
(establishing one's own individual rights, social rights, and divine rights before men, Angels, and God)

Baby Life - Challenge

Pathway of Righteousness - Individual Rights (law)

<u>1st Journey</u> - Climbing the Mountain

	Truth	1.	Submission (dying to self)
	Law	2.	Unto Thine Own Self be True
Submission	Will	3.	Face Guilty Conscience
• Elementary School	Love	4.	Instinctive Compulsion
• Intellect	Life	5.	Thinking for Oneself
• Identity	Self	6.	Infinite Imagination
(seven levels)			

	God	7.	Master Free Will - ***Righteous Citizen***
	(Spirit)		• Free Gift of Eternal Life (seven-fold spirits)
			• Redemption (free) - ***Being Saved*** (law of babies - obedience)
			• Old Enough to See Physical God

(Priestly Sacrifice - God Offers Eternal Life/Man Offers Labors: Earthly Blood)

Teenager Life - Adventure

Pathway of Righteousness- Social Rights (faith)

<u>2nd Journey</u> – Climbing down the Mountain

	King	1.	Learning Right from Wrong
	Priest	2.	Learning Good from evil
Sacrifice	Son	3.	Learning God's Will from man's will
• High School	Government	4.	Learning God's Reality from Man's Illusion
• Emotions	Church	5.	Learning God's Wants from Man's Needs
• Character	Home	6.	Learning God's Truth from Man's Law
(three levels)			

	God	7.	Master Divine Will/Will of People - ***Holy Saint***
	(Son)		• Earning Own New Body (trinity)
			• Salvation (earned) - **Saving Self** (faith of teenagers - mastery)
			• Old Enough to See Spiritual God

(Kingly Prayer - God Offers His Wealth/Man Offers His Wealth: Heavenly Spirit)

Adult Life – Fun

Pathway of Perfection – Divine Rights (knowing)

<u>3rd Journey</u> – Assisting Others in Climbing the Mountain

Transfigured Body	1.	Removing Capital Sins – Demonic Possession
Glorified Spirit	2.	Removing Mortal Sins – Worldly

			Temptations
Reconciliation	Holy Soul	3.	Removing Venial Sins – Sin-Nature
• College	Celestial Court	4.	Removing Faults – Ignorance/ Cowardice/Greed
• Instincts	Temple Court	5.	Gaining Virtues – Wisdom/Courage/Generosity
• Personality	Royal Court	6.	Entered Adulthood – Righteousness/Holiness/Perfection

(one level) ———————————————————————————————————

	God	7.	Master Truth/Law/Will/Love - ***Perfect Son***
	(Father)	•	Bonus Reward of a Royal Kingdom (God)
		•	Reward (bonus) - ***Saving Others*** (knowing of adults - thinking)
		•	Old Enough to See Mystical God

(Sonly Gift - God Offers His Labors/Man Offers His Life: Kingdom Divinity)

This illustration shows that through a "Person's Acts" of <u>Submission</u> (dying to self), <u>Sacrifice</u> (born-again), and <u>Reconciliation</u> (set free), a **Person can Master** his **<u>Free Will</u>** (challenge)**, God's Divine Will** (adventure), the **Will of the People** (fun), and thereby ***Learn God's Truth, Law, Will, and Love*** for ***himself***. Once a "Person" has become "Properly Educated" in <u>Individual Rights</u> (righteousness), <u>Social Rights</u> (holiness), and <u>Divine Rights</u> (perfection), he can **Take Control** of his ***Own Thoughts*** (mind), ***Feelings*** (heart), and ***Instincts*** (soul). We see above that by "Taking" these <u>Three Journeys of Life,</u> a **Person** can **Surrender his Spirit** to ***Deny his Intellect*** (new mind), **Sacrifice his Flesh** to ***Abandon his Feelings*** (new heart), and **Reconcile his Soul** to ***Submit his Free Will*** (new soul) ***to God***. This "Process of Rejecting" <u>One's</u> <u>Old Beliefs</u> to be **Awakened** to a **New Set of Truths** must be **Implemented** to **Create a Whole** *New Lifestyle*. Unfortunately, this need to "Create a New-life" for the <u>Whole Human Race</u> has **Fallen** to **God's Son, Who** must **Convert the Minds, Hearts, and Souls** of **<u>Every Person</u>** into a *New Set of Truths, Laws, and Wills*.

Through this "Conversion Process," <u>Jesus Christ</u> has **Begun** the **Transformation** of **Each Individual** (home), **Society** (government), and even **God Himself** (church) to bring **Them All** into *Physical Righteousness* (earth), *Spiritual Holiness* (Heaven), and *Mystical Perfection* (God). Obviously, to "Convert All Life," the <u>Lord</u> would have to <u>Create Three Schools</u> (elementary/high school/college) to **Teach Right/Wrong** (baby), **Good/Evil** (teenager), and **God's/Man's Wills** (adult) to *Awaken Every Soul on Earth*. We see that the "Central Theme Associated" with <u>Christ's Conversion Process</u> (something to live for) is to **Give Life Value** by **Creating** an **Eternal Bond** between *Each Person's Government, Church,* and *Home*. Now, we see that this "Leads to a Person's" <u>True Devotion</u> to **Earth** (eternal life/peace), to **Heaven** (new body/joy), and to **His** most **Beloved God** (kingdom/happiness) at the **Divine Level of Perfection**, thereby **Giving Mankind** the *Value of God's Divine Love*.

Attaining Value before God
A Poet would Write of God's Son, Christ and Mary's Son, Jesus
(Christ came to transform life, while Jesus came to transform death)

> *Two Humble Warriors* of Humble Seed,
> were Blind to the World of Their Valorous Deeds
> as well as to Their Untold Story of Their
> Devotion to Good and Their Commitment to Glory.
> *Two Humble Warriors* with Gleesome Eyes
> One Besting a Lie in the Role of a Spy.
> *Two Humble Warriors* of Heavenly Flame,
> Crushing a Girca (Lucifer) which One can Claim.
> *Two Humble Warriors* Whose Song is Unwritten,
> Stirring the Embers of Valiantry Long Past,
> in Accepting Their Roles as Heroes, Uncast.

This "Awesome Value" being Shared by God, Angels, and Men is **Coming from Christ's Free Redemption** (given talents), **Earned Salvation** (earn interest), and **Bonus Rewards** (cities). This **Leads** to **Being Saved on Earth** (eternal life), *Saving Self in Heaven* (new body), and *Saving Others in God's Kingdom* (kingdom). Recall in "Mt. 25:24," a Rich Man Gave Each of his **Three Servants** a **Number of Gold Talents** (free redemption): the **First Got Five Talents,** the **Second Got Two Talents,** and the **Third Got One Talent** according to *Their Level of Financial Maturity*. Obviously, "God's Children" are being asked to Obey God's Laws (1/talent) to **Know** the *Earth*; then to Master Faith (2/talents) to become **Self-aware** of *Heaven*; and finally, to Think for Oneself (5 talents/knowing) to become **Conscious** of *God's Kingdom of Glory*. The idea here is to both "Grow (obey) and Mature (imitate)" before God to **Obtain** the **Lord's Human Blessing** of *Eternal Life* (mind), the **Angelic Blessing** of a *New Body* (heart), and **God's Divine Blessing** of a *Royal Kingdom* (soul). In this way, a "Person can be Saved" by a Priest on a Donkey (1st advent) to *Learn Right from Wrong* (see Physical God); then "Saving Oneself" by Catching the **Thief in the Night** (2nd advent) to *Learn Good from Evil* (see Spiritual God); and finally, "Saving Others" with the help of God's Son on a Cloud (3rd advent) to *Learn God's Will from man's will* (see Mystical God).

At each of these "Three Stages of Life," a Person can Come to Understand the **Meaning Behind Matthew 25:24** and the **Discussion Regarding** the *Five Talents* (kingdom), *Two Talents* (Heaven), and *One Talent* (earth). We are being told here that a person might be "Rich (five)," "Middle Class (two)," or "Poor (one)" at the Beginning of Life but it is up to a **Faithful Soul** to **Invest its Talents** in a *Fruitful Life* (values). We call this "Second Stage" as Christ's Salvation (investment) or **Saving Oneself** by **Striving** to **Make the Best** *Out of a Bad Situation*. This means that in the "Final Stage," a Person must Stand before **God's Judgment**, proudly presenting his **Good Works** or **Saving Others** depicted by the **Master Giving** his **Good Servant** the **Bad Servant's One Talent** and then presenting him with *Ten of his Own Cities*. We call this "Third Stage" the Eternal Rewards (bonus) or **Saving Others** by

Striving to Accomplish the **Impossible of the Impossible,** using the *Forces* of *God's Law* (Jews), *Man's Faith* (Christians), and *God's/Man's Knowing* (Saints).

The following tabular information indicates that "Mt. 25:24 is Revealing" that the Life-experience is **Comprised of Three Phases:** 1) Given Free Talents - Free Redemption (1st advent/priest): Being Saved (baby) = *Eternal Life;* 2) Earn Interest - Earned Salvation (2nd advent/thief): Saving Self (teenager) = *New Body;* and 3) Rewarded with Cities - Bonus Rewards (3rd advent/judge): Saving Others (adult) = *Royal Kingdom*:

Given Free Talents, Earn Interest, and Rewarded with Cities as a Good and Faithful Servant
(redemption receives talents, salvation earns
interest, and rewards come with good service)

Earth
(7 spirits)

1. **Given Free Talents** - Free Redemption: Gift of Eternal Life...Obey Laws
   - Being Saved - 1st Advent: Priest on a Donkey = Human Blessing
   - Five Talents - Head Servant: Master Church
   - Two Talents - Good Servant: Master Government   **Eternal Life**
   - One Talent - New Servant: Master Home

(knowing the earth - Learn right from wrong: become a righteous citizen)

Heaven
(trinity)

2. **Earn Interest on Talent** - Earned Salvation: Earn New Body...Master Faith
   - Saving Self - 2nd Advent: Thief in the Night = Angelic Blessing
   - Five Talents - Become Ten Talents: Sainthood
   - Two Talents - Become Four Talents: Righteous Citizen **New Body**
   - One Talent - Is Taken Away: Lost Pagan

(self-aware of Heaven - Learn good from evil: become holy saint)

Kingdom
(God)

3. **Bonus Reward on Talents** - Bonus Rewards: Rewarded Kingdom...Think to Know
   - Saving Others - 3rd Advent: Son on a Cloud = Divine Blessing
   - Five Talents - Become Eleven Cities: Sonship (own kingdom)
   - Two Talents - Become Four Cities: Priesthood
     (own Heaven)   **Royal Kingdom**
   - One Talent - Becomes One Farm - Kingship (own earth)

(conscious of the Kingdom - Learn God's/Man's Wills: become son of God)

This illustration shows that in "Matthew 25:24," the Master initially **Gave his Three Servants Five** (life), **Two** (wealth), and **One Talent** (labor) as a **Test of Their Abilities** and then **Returned to Determine** just how well these **Men were Able to Do** in *Investing this Great Treasure*. Note that once the "Master" determined the Individual Ability of Each Servant, he **Rewarded his Good and Faithful Servants** with **Eleven Cities** and **Four Cities**. In contrast, the "Evil Servant" who had Buried his Talent (no faith) was not only given **Nothing**, but he was also **Cast into the Darkness** to **Cry-out** and **Grind his Teeth** in *Total Despair* (separation). This story reveals that to have

"Something to Live For," a Person must Not Only Try, but he must also be **Willing to Sacrifice** his **Labor, Money,** and even his **Life** to *Prove his Resolve to the Master*.

Now, "If we Translate" this Talent-to-Performance-to-City **Idea** into **Christian Performance**, we see that a **Child of God** must **Master** his **Home** (free/talents/eternal life); **Government** (earn/performance/new body); and finally, his **Church** (bonus/cities/kingdom) to **Receive** his *Three Eternal Rewards*. In short, "Christ" is telling us that "Each of Us" is being Called to **Give His All** on **Earth** to **Earn Eternal Cities** in **Heaven** through the *Power of Submission* (dying to self). Note that in the story of the "Three Servants," the Man with Five Talents was *Surrendering 100%*, the Man with Two Talents *Surrendered 50%*, and the Man with One Talent didn't *Surrender (0%) at All*. This "Need" to Surrender One's Free Will to God's Divine Will Sits at the Center of the **Christian Life**. Unfortunately, very **Few People Comprehend** the *Meaning of the Word Surrender*. The answer to "Surrendering" comes with Surrendering One's Life (soul) in **Worship,** Surrendering One's Wealth in **God's Praise** (heart), and Surrendering One's Labors in **Thanksgiving** (mind) to *Receive God's Blessings* (home/talents), *Anointings* (government/performance), and *Sanctification* (church/cities). In this way, it "Begins to Make Sense" Why both God and the Master (Mt. 25:24) have **Designed** such a **Rigid Test, Revealing Each Man's Values** and/or **Character** which is **Reflected** in the very **Essence** of either his *Good or Bad Nature*.

We are now able to see "Christ's Role" within the Grand Design as **He Comes** onto the **Earth** on **Four Separate Occasions** (3-advents/judgment) to **Open Four Highways** to **Serve** the **Mind** (calling/baby), **Heart** (enlightenment/teenager), **Soul** (awakening/adult), and **Life-force** (indwelling/wise man) of *God, Angels, Men, and Nature Forever*. In a "Direct Exchange" of Divine and Human Natures, the **God/Man Relation Will Come into Existence**, thereby **Creating** a **Two-Lane Highway for God** (womb/tomb) and a **Two-Lane Highway for Man** (baptism/grave) so **that They** might both **Enter and Exit Each Other's** *Strange Worlds of Life and Death at Will*. We see that "God is Promising Man" Individual Rights in **Reality,** while "Man is Proving himself" through Social Rights via his **Illusion**. When **Reality** (blessings) and **Illusion** (lessons) become **One in Christ Jesus,** the *Highways of Life/Death are Created*. It is very difficult to comprehend just how "God becomes Man (Christmas)" and "Man becomes God (Easter)" as They Travel on and through **Completely Different** *States of Existence* (dimensions/lifeforms/etc.) The "Job of God's Son" as Priest (donkey), King (thief), and Son (cloud) is to **Establish** the **Necessary Routes** by which the **Spirit of God** and the **Flesh of Man** could *Travel at Will*. Through the first "Two Routes" between Heaven and Earth, **God's Spirit** can **Resurrect from its Tomb** to obtain an *Eternal Life* (Heaven/one) and **Man's Flesh** can **Resurrect from the Grave** to obtain a *New Body* (earth/all).

The point here is that a "Person Needs a Body" to Fit into the *Lifestyle of Earth*, just as a "Person Needs Eternal Spirit" to Fit into the *Lifestyle of Heaven*. Through these "Two Vessels of Life," both God (eternal life) and Man (new body) can join into **One Nature** and **Come to Live** in *Their Own Kingdom of Glory Forever*. Note that through the "Messiah's Highway (individual holiness)," God (groom) will be able to **Marry** the **Virgin Mary** (bride) to **Unite** *God's Spirit Nature* (flesh) with *Man's Spirit Nature* (blood). Secondly, through the "Church Highway (society)," Jesus (groom) will be able to **Marry** the **Catholic Church** (bride) to **Unite _Man's Flesh_** (bread) with _God's Spirit_ (wine). Through these "Two Marriages," the Highway of Holiness (Messiah) is able to **Open the Way** to be **Merged** with _God's Divinity_ (perfection). In like manner, these "Two Marriages" bring forth the Highway of Righteousness (Church), thereby **Opening** the way to be **Merged** with _Humanity_ (fleshly imperfection). This means that "Jesus (human God)" came as a Priest on a Donkey (Messiah) during His 1st Advent to **Build the Highway of Holiness** (Messiah/cross) so the **Lord God Almighty** will have _Free Access to Planet Earth_ (Man). Secondly, "Christ (divine man)" will come as a King in the Night (thief) during **His 2nd Advent** to **Build the Highway of Righteousness** (Church/blood) so that the **People of Earth** will have _Free Access to God's Heaven_ (sainthood). It should now all make sense that a "Set of Highways" must be Constructed to **Accommodate** the **Goings** and **Comings** of **God, Angels, and Men** so **that They can Merge** the **Spirit of Heaven** with the **Flesh of Earth** to **Create a New Born-again** _Kingdom of Glory_ in _Service to One and All_.

The following tabular information indicates that in the "Grand Design," God (individual rights) is Planning to Move Around via the **Spirit World** through _His Birth_ (womb) or _In_ (life) and through _His Death_ (tomb) or _Out_ (eternal life); while Man (social rights) is Planning to Move Around via the **Physical World** through the _Church_ (baptism) or _In_ (body) and the _World_ (grave) or _Out_ (new body):

God Moves through the Spirit World and Man Moves through Physical World to become Perfect
(four highways of life/death bring redemption, salvation, rewards, and freedom to one and all)

Two Highways to Life (God) and Two Highways to Death (Man)

1st Highway (1st advent) - Free Redemption of Self: Earth = God becomes Man
God's Promise to Man - Individual Rights: Reality (give divinity) = Christ's Prayer

Sacrifice	1. **God Moves** - Spirit World: Learning Right from Wrong = Righteous Citizen	
(creation)	• Birth - In: Flesh (womb)————————-Destiny: Remove Faults	
	• God - Spirit: Groom = Bride Price + Offer Name (divine) - Christmas	
Messiah's	• Creation of Life - _Earth_: Agony of Defeat = Remove Sin, Evil, and Death	
Highway	• Death - Out: Spirit (tomb)————————Free Will: Insert Virtues	
(blessing)	• Mary - Flesh: Bride = Dowry + Offer Virginity (humanity) – Easter	
	• Resurrect Eternal Life - _Heaven_: Thrill of Victory = Be Righteous, Holy, and Perfect	

(Jesus - priest on a donkey [1st advent]: marriage of God [blood] to Virgin [flesh])

2nd Highway (2nd advent) - Earned Salvation of Society: Heaven = Man becomes God
Man Proves to God - Social Rights: Illusion (take-sin) = Jesus' Sacrifice

Prayer	2. **Man Moves** - Physical World: Learning Good from Evil = Holy Saint	
(Messiah)	• Church - In: Spirit (baptism)—————-Holiness: Good Works	
	• Jesus - Flesh: Groom = Bride Price + Offer Name (human) - Halloween	

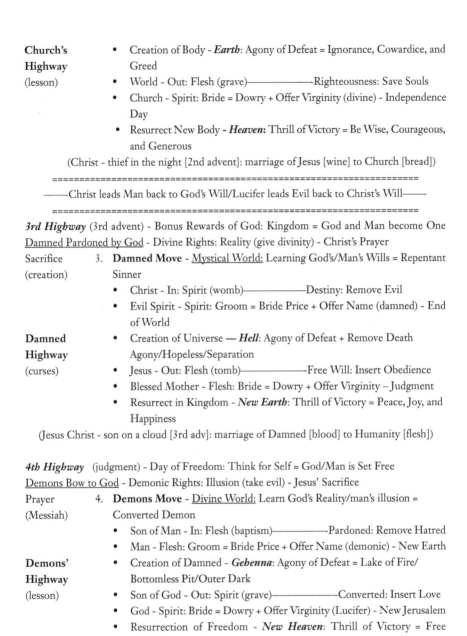

Church's	•	Creation of Body - ***Earth***: Agony of Defeat = Ignorance, Cowardice, and
Highway		Greed
(lesson)	•	World - Out: Flesh (grave)————————-Righteousness: Save Souls
	•	Church - Spirit: Bride = Dowry + Offer Virginity (divine) - Independence Day
	•	Resurrect New Body - ***Heaven:*** Thrill of Victory = Be Wise, Courageous, and Generous

(Christ - thief in the night [2nd advent]: marriage of Jesus [wine] to Church [bread])

==

————Christ leads Man back to God's Will/Lucifer leads Evil back to Christ's Will————

==

3rd Highway (3rd advent) - Bonus Rewards of God: Kingdom = God and Man become One
<u>Damned Pardoned by God</u> - Divine Rights: Reality (give divinity) - Christ's Prayer

Sacrifice	3.	**Damned Move** - <u>Mystical World:</u> Learning God's/Man's Wills = Repentant
(creation)		Sinner
	•	Christ - In: Spirit (womb)————————Destiny: Remove Evil
	•	Evil Spirit - Spirit: Groom = Bride Price + Offer Name (damned) - End of World
Damned	•	Creation of Universe — ***Hell***: Agony of Defeat + Remove Death
Highway		Agony/Hopeless/Separation
(curses)	•	Jesus - Out: Flesh (tomb)————————-Free Will: Insert Obedience
	•	Blessed Mother - Flesh: Bride = Dowry + Offer Virginity – Judgment
	•	Resurrect in Kingdom - ***New Earth***: Thrill of Victory = Peace, Joy, and Happiness

(Jesus Christ - son on a cloud [3rd adv]: marriage of Damned [blood] to Humanity [flesh])

4th Highway (judgment) - Day of Freedom: Think for Self = God/Man is Set Free
<u>Demons Bow to God</u> - Demonic Rights: Illusion (take evil) - Jesus' Sacrifice

Prayer	4.	**Demons Move** - <u>Divine World:</u> Learn God's Reality/man's illusion =
(Messiah)		Converted Demon
	•	Son of Man - In: Flesh (baptism)————————Pardoned: Remove Hatred
	•	Man - Flesh: Groom = Bride Price + Offer Name (demonic) - New Earth
Demons'	•	Creation of Damned - ***Gehenna***: Agony of Defeat = Lake of Fire/
Highway		Bottomless Pit/Outer Dark
(lesson)	•	Son of God - Out: Spirit (grave)————————-Converted: Insert Love
	•	God - Spirit: Bride = Dowry + Offer Virginity (Lucifer) - New Jerusalem
	•	Resurrection of Freedom - ***New Heaven***: Thrill of Victory = Free Mind/Heart/Soul

This illustration shows that there are "Two Highways (Divine Man/Holy Saint)" to <u>Life</u> and "Two Highways (Man's Servant/God's Slave)" to <u>Death</u> **Giving God, Angels, Saints, Damned** and **Demons <u>Open Channels</u>** between ***Heaven, Earth, Hell, and Gehenna Forever***. Now, imagine that "All Roads Pass" through <u>Jesus Christ</u> (Man/down) and <u>Christ Jesus</u> (God/up) to **Reach Their Destinations** be it within

Oneself (life), **Home** (earth), **Church** (Heaven), **Government** (Kingdom), and/or **God** (freedom) by <u>Traveling</u> via a *Person's Flesh* (elementary school), *Spirit* (high school), *Soul* (college), and/or *Life-force* (job). We now see that the "Lord Jesus Christ (Messiah)" has come in <u>His 1st Advent</u> (priest on a donkey) to **Build** a **Two-Lane Highway** (birth/death) between **Heaven and** <u>Earth</u> (righteous citizen) so *God can become Man* (Christmas/womb) and *Man can become God* (Easter/tomb). Secondly, the "Lord Jesus Christ (Church)" will <u>Return</u> during <u>His 2nd Advent</u> (thief in the night) to **Build a Second Two-Lane Highway** (church/world) between <u>**Earth and Heaven**</u> (holy saints) so *Sinners can become Christians* (Halloween/baptism) and *Christians can become Saints* (4th of July/grave). Via these "Two Highways," <u>God's Spirit World</u> can come to **Earth** and **Man's Physical World** can come to **Heaven** in an <u>**Exchange of Cultures**</u> so that one day, *God and Man will become One*. This means that "One's Spiritual Nature (divinity/reality)" must <u>Seek</u> to become *Righteous* (mind), *Holy* (heart), and *Perfect* (soul); while "One's Physical Nature (humanity/illusion)" must <u>Seek</u> to become *Wise* (mind), *Courageous* (heart), and *Generous* (soul). We now see that the "Lord God Almighty" will be <u>Traveling</u> along the **Messiah's Highway** to bring <u>**Individual Rights**</u> (learn right/wrong/will of God) to *Earth*; while "God's Chosen People" will be <u>Traveling</u> along the **Church's Highway** to bring **Social Rights** (learn good/evil/will of people) to **Heaven**. Through these "Two Magnificent Highways of Life," a <u>Working Relationship</u> will be **Established** between *God* (calling), *His Angels* (enlightenment), *Men* (awakening), and *Christ's Saints* (indwelling).

It all comes down to "Three Advents of Christ" plus a <u>Final Judgment</u> **Giving** the **Human Race** its **Ability to Travel** from <u>**Righteous Earth**</u> (Christians/adults) to <u>**Holy Heaven**</u> (God/forgiveness) and from <u>**Unrighteous Earth**</u> (sinners/babies) to <u>**Evil Hell**</u> (Lucifer/pardon) at *Will*. Now, we understand why "Mankind's Blessing/Curse (lessons) <u>Arrangement</u> (Holy/Evil Spirits)" has been the **Driving Force Compelling** <u>Jesus to Defeat</u> *Lucifer's Evil Forces* and *Rid the Universe* of its most *Deadly First-born Curse of Death*. This means that "Jesus has Established" a <u>New Royal Family</u> known as the <u>Brotherhood of Man</u>, where **Every Member** is **Born-again** into a **New First-born Status** of <u>**Human Perfection**</u> (new nature/round table) in the *Eyes of God*. Fortunately, "Jesus Took the Punishment (paid sin-debt)" for those under the First-born Curse when the **Earth Murdered** its only **First-born Divine Son** of **Human Perfection,** *Our Lord Jesus Christ* (sacrificial lamb). This "Act of Sacrificing Divine Innocence" brought forth the <u>Redemptive Blood of Purification,</u> thereby **Freeing All Mankind** from its coming *Fate of Certain Death* (grave) and *Damnation* (Hell/Gehenna). This will be accomplished through the "Unification" of <u>God's Divine Mind</u> (fire) and <u>Man's Human Heart</u> (water) to **Transform** *dead sinners* (earth/goat) into *Holy Saint* (Heaven/lamb). To do this, "Two Mystical Sacrifices (lamb/goat)" were <u>Required to Satisfy</u> the **Divine Requirements of God's Divine Justice,** thereby **Allowing** this <u>**Unholy Curse of Evil and Death**</u> to *Fall* on the *Least Worthy Sinner* in *All Creation, Poor Judas* (goat).

This reversing of "God's Justice System" would then Rank-order <u>All of Mankind</u> from the **Most Holy** to the **Greatest Sinner**, bringing about a **New** more **Perfect Justice System** to **Serve** *One and All*. This means that "God is Creating Two Systems" as One Truth **Rank Orders All Men** (good to bad/law); and then with His Second Truth, the **Lord Creates** a **Roundtable** (fair), where *All Men are Created Equal* (opportunity/faith). Through these "Two Truths," All Life is Governed based on the **Level** (divine) by which a **Spirit Tries** and the **Level** (human) by which the **Flesh Succeeds** to **Reflect the Strength** of **Each Person's** *Life-force* (desire), *Character* (integrity), and *Personality* (dignity).

1. **1st System of Evaluation** - Rank Order All Men: Perfect to Imperfect…Inherit Earth
2. **2nd System of Evaluation** - Roundtable of Equality: Balance All Performance…Inherit Heaven

When the "Human Race" is able to Master both **God's Truth** (never-created/spirit) and **Man's Truth** (created/flesh), the **Lost** and **Confused Children of God** can **Begin to Find Their Way Out** of *Their Pit of Hell*. This "Awesome Journey" from Death to New-life will **Require Fighting in Three Wars**: *One* for *God's Palace/wills* (mystical Kingdom); *One* for *God's Altar/beliefs* (spiritual Heaven); and *One* for *God's Throne/authority* (physical earth). Through these "Three Wars," God will **Build His Kingdom** (divine blood), raise **His Temple** (holy blood), and **Establish His Throne** (righteous blood) on *Earth* (Messiah), in *Heaven* (church), and within *His Kingdom* (world). This means that during the "Lord's 1st Advent (repentance)," there was a Battle of Wills (God against man); during "Christ's 2nd Advent (prayers)," there will be a Battle of Beliefs (good against evil); and during "Christ's 3rd Advent (works)," there will be a Battle for Territory (right against wrong). We now see that in "Ephesians 1:21," God States that **He will Seat His Son** above all the **Principalities** (kingdoms), **Powers** (religions), and **Dominions** (nations) to be the *Eternal Ruler of All Things*. This constant reference by "God" is that "One Fine Day," He will Conquer All the Forces of **Sin, Evil, and Death**, to show **His Children** that **He Alone is Able** to **Enforce His Will, His Beliefs,** and **His Ownership** (territories) over *All Things Great and Small*.

The following tabular information indicates that the "World will be Saved" through Three Great Wars as **God's Forces** come to **Capture Man's Palaces** (kingdoms), **Temples** (religions), and **Thrones** (nations) to bring forth the *New Heaven and the New Earth*:

God Fights for Kingdom, Religion, and Nations to bring Perfection to All His Beloved Children
(God defeats man's kingdom, beliefs, and nations
through Jewish, Arab, and Christian Peoples)

1st Truth (Kingdom)	1.	**War of God's Kingdom** against Man's Kingdom…Messiah – Redeemer
	•	God's Palace Fights Man's Palace - Priest on a Donkey: 1st Advent/Calvary
	•	Cross of Death - Breaks Man's Evil Will: Set Man Free from Demons
	•	God's Will (life) Defeats Man's Will (death) - Perfect Son (mystical)
Wills	•	Saving One Nation - Jewish People (Isaac): Royal Kingdom

- Loser Repents - Dying to Self (submission): Sonship
- Winner gets *Principalities* - God's Kingdom Authority

2nd Truth
(Heaven)

2. **War of God's Religion** against <u>Man's Religions</u>...Church – Savior
   - God's Altar Fights Man's Temple - Thief in the Night: 2nd Advent/ Tribulation
   - Darkness of Death - Forces Man to Believe God's Truth: Set Man Free from Lies
   - God's Good (love) Defeats Man's Evil (hate) - Holy Priest (spiritual)

Beliefs
   - Saving 23 Nations - Arab People (Ishmael): Eternal Life
   - Loser Prays - Born-again (unto thine own self be true): Servanthood
   - Winner gets *Powers* - God's Heavenly Responsibilities

Paradox
(earth)

3. **War of God's Nations** against <u>Man's Nations</u>...World – Reformer
   - God's Throne Fights Man's Throne - Just Judge on a Cloud: 3rd Advent/End of World
   - Armageddon of Death - Takes Back God's Land: Set Men Free from Toil (sweat)
   - God's Right (truth) Defeats Man's Wrong (lie) - Righteous King (physical)

Territories
   - Saving 120 Nations - Christian People (Jesus): New Body
   - Loser Works – Set Free (guilty conscience): Slavery
   - Winner gets *Dominions* - God's Earthly Duties

This illustration shows that when "God Conquers Man's Kingdom (homes)," He will bring forth a <u>Royal Kingdom</u> for **Each of His** most **Beloved Children**, thereby **Making Them <u>Sons of God</u>** in *Service to the Lord's Divine Will*. Secondly, when "God Conquers Man's Temples (churches)," <u>He</u> will bring forth an <u>Eternal Life</u> for **Each of His** most **Beloved Children,** thereby making them **<u>Servants of God</u>** in *Devotion to the Lord's Sacred Beliefs*. Finally, when "God Conquers Man's Thrones (governments)," <u>He</u> will bring forth <u>New Bodies</u> for **Each of His** Most **Beloved Children**, thereby making them **<u>Slaves of God</u>** in absolute *Submission to the Lord's Creation* (territories). Through these "Three Gifts of Love (homes/bodies/life)," the <u>Lord God Almighty</u> will **Defeat Sin, Evil, and Death** and bring forth **<u>His Pearls of Great Price</u>** (earth/Heaven/Kingdom) as **Eternal Homes** for *God* (mystical), *Angels* (spiritual), and *Men* (physical). This "Awesome Achievement of God" **Centers <u>on Using</u>** a **Messiah** to **Fight the 1st War** on **Mount Calvary** and **<u>Win a Great Victory</u>** over *Man's Will* (stiff-neck) to bring forth the *Lord's Kingdom of Glory* (God). Secondly, "God is Using" <u>His Holy Church</u> to **Fight the 2nd War** during the **Tribulation** to **<u>Win a Great Victory</u>** over *Man's Beliefs* (foolish) and bring forth the *Lord's Sacred Temple in Heaven* (Angels). Thirdly, "God is Using" <u>His World System</u> to **Fight the 3rd War** during the coming **End of the World** to **<u>Win a Great Victory</u>** over *Man's Territories* (untrained soldiers) to bring forth the *Lord's Earthly Throne* (men).

During "Each of These Three Wars," <u>God will be Able</u> to **Break Man's Will** (cross), **<u>Convince Man to Believe in God</u>** (darkness), **Crush Man's Military Might**

(Armageddon), and finally, *Conquer the Earth*. Note that "God's Kingdom of Enslavement" will one day be Set Free from **Man's Ignorance** (stiff-neck), **Cowardice** (lies), and **Greed** (selfishness) by **Sending God's Son** to *Die on a Cross* (defeat will), *Sacrifice His Church* (convert mind), and then to *Destroy Planet Earth* (take land).

We are being shown that "God initially Created" a Kingdom of Enslavement (captivity) and then **Lucifer Rebelled Against** his **Useless Life in a Gilded Cage** so he **Chose to Rule Hell** (one moment of freedom) as an **Impoverished Poor Fool** rather than being an *Eternal Slave in Paradise*. Note, in "Christ's Creation" of a Kingdom of Happiness (freedom), **Lucifer will Joyfully Convert Back to God** to become **Worthy of Ruling Himself** as an *Eternal Slave of Christ*. The message here is that "No One Wants" to be Beaten into Submission, but for a **Great** and **Noble Cause**, then **One and All** will **Enslave Themselves** to *Get the Job Done by Working Together* (brotherhood). It is this "Theme of Ownership" and "Freedom" that Strikes a Joyful Chord in every **Human Heart,** causing the **Entire Human Race** to **Plunge Themselves** into **Sin, Evil, Death,** and **Damnation** in **Search of** *Eternal Peace, Joy, Happiness, and Freedom*.

We see that "Jesus Christ" is Coming to Earth in **Three Advents** (donkey/thief /cloud) to **Save Oneself** (earth), to **Save Society** (Heaven), and then to **Save God Himself** (Kingdom) by making the **Almighty Human** (illusion) and **Giving Him** a *Promised Land of Milk and Honey* (earth). This "New Creation of Happiness" is Linked Together by the **Four Previously Mentioned** Highways as **They Interface** with **God, Angels, Saints, Men, Damned,** and **Demons,** thereby making them *One in Truth, Law, Will, and Love*. This "State of Unity" Creates a Merger of both the **Natural Order** (physical life) and the **Supernatural Order** (spiritual life) of **God** as He brings forth a **Set of Highways** (four) coming into **Human Existence** and then back to **Divine Existence,** as a **Mother Bird Journeys Feeding** her *Chicks in the Nest*. It should now start to "Make Sense" that God Wants to become Man (Christmas/birth) and man wants to become God (Easter/resurrection) so that at the **End of Time,** both **God and Man can become One** in *Truth, Law, Will, and Love forever*.

The following graphic illustration shows that "God's Son" is building Four Highways of Purification to **Transform God** (consecration/indwelling), **Forgive Sinners** (sanctification/awakening), **Pardon the Damned** (anointing/enlightenment), and **Convert Demons** (blessing/calling) by **Dipping** them into the *Sacrificial Blood of Jesus Christ*:

The Four Highways of Life/Death Go Back and Forth between Planet Earth
(highways of Messiah, Church, Damned, and Demons make
God, Angels, Saints, Men, Damned, and Demons One)

God's Holy Spirit

Messiah's		Church's
Highway	• Excommunication////Outcast •	**Highway**
(1st advent/self)		(2nd advent/society)

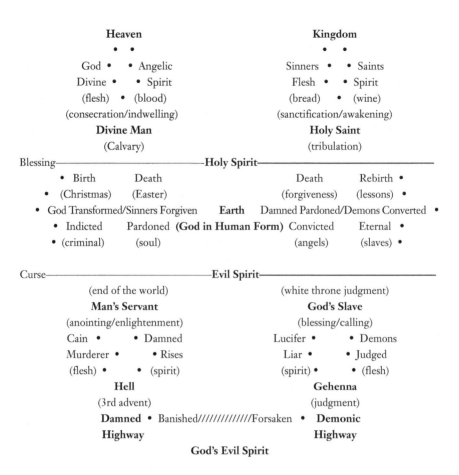

Heaven   Kingdom
• •   • •

God •   • Angelic   Sinners •   • Saints
Divine •   • Spirit   Flesh •   • Spirit
(flesh) •   (blood)   (bread) •   (wine)
(consecration/indwelling)   (sanctification/awakening)
Divine Man   **Holy Saint**
(Calvary)   (tribulation)

Blessing————————————Holy Spirit————————————————

   • Birth   Death   Death   Rebirth •
  • (Christmas)   (Easter)   (forgiveness)   (lessons) •
  • God Transformed/Sinners Forgiven   **Earth**   Damned Pardoned/Demons Converted •
  • Indicted   Pardoned **(God in Human Form)** Convicted   Eternal •
  • (criminal)   (soul)   (angels)   (slaves) •

Curse————————————Evil Spirit————————————————

(end of the world)   (white throne judgment)
Man's Servant   **God's Slave**
(anointing/enlightenment)   (blessing/calling)
Cain •   • Damned   Lucifer •   • Demons
Murderer •   • Rises   Liar •   • Judged
(flesh) •   • (spirit)   (spirit) •   • (flesh)
Hell   **Gehenna**
(3rd advent)   (judgment)
Damned • Banished//////////////Forsaken • **Demonic**
Highway   **Highway**
God's Evil Spirit

This illustration shows that the "A" <u>Students of God Journey</u> from **Heaven to Earth** as **God's Sons** (flesh) and then **Return** from **Earth** as **Angelic Men** (blood) by being <u>**Transformed**</u> into the *Indwelling Nature of Christ*. Secondly, the "B" <u>Students of God</u> **Journey** from **Christ's Church** (kingdom) to **Earth** as **Broken Sinners** (bread) and then **Return** from **Earth** as **Holy Saints** (wine) by being <u>**Transformed**</u> into the *Awakened Nature of Christ*. Thirdly, the "C" <u>Students of God</u> **Journey** from **Earth to Hell** as **Lost Damned** (flesh) and then **Return** to **Earth** as the **Risen Damned** (spirit) or **Servants** by being <u>**Transformed**</u> into the *Enlightened Nature of Christ*. Finally, the "D" <u>Students of God</u> **Journey** from **Earth to Gehenna** as **Fallen Angels** (spirit) and then **Return** to **Earth** as **Judged Demons** (flesh/new bodies) or **Slaves** by being <u>**Transformed**</u> into the *Called Nature of Christ*. By "Traveling Each" of these <u>Highways of Life/Death</u>, a <u>Person</u> can Experience the **Depths of Failure** (agony of defeat) and then be **Resurrected** into the **Highest of Triumph** (thrill of victory) to <u>**Know**</u> what it is to be *Truly Alive*.

     This "Journey of Life" is certainly <u>Connected</u> to becoming **More and More Alive** with **Every Passing Day** until **One Day**, a **Person** can **Truly Say**, <u>**Yes! I am Alive**</u> in <u>**Myself**</u> **(**earth), in <u>**Christ**</u> (Heaven/church), and in <u>**God**</u> (Kingdom) just as the *Lord*

Originally Intended. In this lesson, we see that "God has Made" <u>Human Life</u> into **Eternal Life**; while "He has Made" <u>Human Death</u> into **Born-again Life** (new body) so that **All** in **God's Creation would Forever Live** and **Bear the Fruits** of *Righteousness* (earth), *Holiness* (Heaven), and *Perfection* (Kingdom). Note that "Our Four Highways are Creating" <u>Eight Doors of Life</u> and <u>New-life</u> to allow both the **Good and Bad of Man** (forgiven/pardoned) and **Holy and Evil of Angels** (honored/converted) to **Interface** with **Their God** in **His Human Form on Earth** in *Service to One and All of His Creations*. It is now clear that via the "Messiah's Highway," <u>God</u> (transformation) becomes a *Divine Man* (love). Via the "Church Highway," <u>Sinners</u> (forgiveness) become *Holy Saints* (will). Via the "Damnation Highway," the <u>Damned</u> (pardoned) become *Man's Servants* (law) and via the "Demonic Highway," the <u>Demons</u> (converted) become *God's Slaves* (truth). Through these "Four Titles of Rebirth," <u>Jesus Christ</u> will be able to **Save Demons, the Damned, Sinners** and even **God** as **He Unites Them All** into *One Kingdom of Divine Glory*.

We can now go into a little more "Detail" as we look at what is coming <u>Into Existence</u> and what is going <u>Out of Existence</u> as a **Person is Journeying** into a **New Dimension of Life**, where **Each** of **God's Children** can **Prove Himself** in *Mind* (earth), *Heart* (Heaven), *Soul* (Kingdom), and *Life-force* (God). This means that "Each of God's Creations" must <u>Face Lucifer's Test, God's Judgment,</u> and his <u>Own Self-evaluation</u> before he can **Determine** the **Depth of his Desire** to *Try* (honors) and then to find that **Measure of his Ability** to *Succeed* (treasures). The point is that at the <u>Divine Level of Perfection,</u> obviously **No One can Succeed** (sinner), **Not Even God's Human Son** (Jesus - save Gentiles/fail Jews), but **If We Measure One's Tenacity** to the **Level of Mount Calvary,** we see *God's Crown of Glory* in its *Full Measure of Divine Gratitude* (blessings/anointings/sanctifications/consecrations).

The Reader must recognize that "Establishing Relationships (trying/succeeding)" of any kind between <u>God, Angels, Men, Damned, Demons,</u> and/or <u>Nature</u> is simply a way of **Starting Somewhere** and that in reality, there are a **Trillion x a Trillion** integrated relationships based on an **Infinite** (space) and **Eternal** (time) *Set of Perceptions* within a *Divine Mind*. The hope here is that a "Student" of <u>God's Grand Design</u> will begin his **Journey** with some confidence that He will at some point come to **Know, Love,** and **Serve** his God through *His Son, Jesus Christ*. The idea here is that a "Child of God" must <u>Strive</u> and <u>Study</u> as **If he were Going to Break All God's Records** for **Commitment** and **Duty, Realizing** that **Man's Journey is Eternal** and will **Require** *Going that Extra Mile* with *Christ Jesus*. We see that the "Man Who Went" that Extra Mile was **Father Abraham** WHEN he **Strived to Make** an **Eternal Covenant with God** via the **Lord's Law of Obedience** (Jews) which was **Designed** to **Change Man's Nature** from *Human* (dust/sinners/death) to *Divine* (stars/saints/life). We see that "God Told Abraham (Genesis 15:9)" to <u>Place</u> a **Dove/Pigeon,** along with **Halves** of a **Ram, Goat, and Heifer** to **Represent** a **Blood Covenant** based on **Agreeing** to **Suffer the Pain** of being **Torn Into If either Side Breaks** this *Divine Covenant of Honor*.

Genesis 15: 9

1. Dove - Lord God Almighty	Man - Pigeon
2. 1/2 Ram - Holy Spirit	Joseph - 1/2 Ram
3. 1/2 Goat - Son of God	Virgin Mary - 1/2 Goat
4. 1/2 Heifer - Eternal Father	Jesus - 1/2 Heifer
5. *Torch* - Holy Trinity	Human Trinity - *Smoke Pot*
Fulfillment of Life	Fulfillment of Death
• Man's Nature Changed	• Man's Sin Changed to Holiness
• Christ Creates Saints	• Jesus Redeems Sinners
• Purifying Host	• Purifying Grave

This illustration shows that the "Job of Jesus Christ" was to Suffer being **Torn Into** upon **Mount Calvary** to **Fulfill Father Abraham's Agreement** with **God** through the **Sacrificial Blood** of a **Dove/Pigeon, Ram, Goat, and Heifer** to be <u>Sealed</u> with *God's Torch (change nature)* and **Man's Smoke Pot** (holiness). Obviously, the "Mystical Purpose" <u>Behind the God/Man Agreement</u> **Centers** upon **Establishing Divine Judgment** (darkness) upon the **Earth** through the **Bloodline of Father Abraham** to be **Fulfilled** by *God's Son, Jesus Christ.* The idea here is that the "Lord God Almighty" was bringing the <u>Human Race</u> **Divine Judgment** in the **Form** of **Human Imperfection** (nothing/darkness/smoke pot) as **Compared** to **Divine Perfection** (all/light/torch) to **Give Everyone on Earth** his <u>**Own Fixed Frame of Reference**</u> as he *Travels* from *Nothing to All.* We see that "God's Judgment" and this "Great Ordeal of Sacrificial Death" are to be <u>Judged by Each Person's</u> **Level of Accomplishments** (works), be **They (1)** <u>**Putting**</u> *One's Throne Above God's* (Lucifer); (2) becoming *God's Son*; (3) becoming <u>**Equal**</u> to the *Blessed Virgin, Saint Michael, Saint Joseph*; or (4) even *One of the Saints;* and/or simply (5) becoming **One of the Highly Honored** *Historical Figures*, etc. The idea here is that "We are All" being <u>Called to Achieve Something</u> of **Note** (mentioned by man) and of **Divine Value** (mentioned by God) so we must **Surrender to Christ's Church** (altar) and begin *Killing Our Flesh* (death/grave) and *Anointing Our Spirit* (resurrection/host) unto *God's Glory* (for God/not ourselves).

The message is that through "God's Following Four Highways (Messiah/Church/ Damned/Demons)," a Person can Perfect (earth) his *Mind* (intellect/wisdom), *Heart* (emotions/ courage), Soul (instincts/generosity), and Life-force (nature/imagination). Secondly, <u>Society can Perfect</u> its *Individuals* (elementary/wisdom), its *Home* (high schools/courage), *Church* (colleges/generosity), and *Government* (job skills/imagination). Finally, "God Himself" can <u>Perfect</u> (Kingdom) *His Righteousness* (babyhood/right from wrong), *Holiness* (teenagers/good from evil), *Perfection* (adulthood/God's Will from man's will), and *Divinity* (wise men/God's reality from man's illusion). It should now make sense that the Lord God Almighty" has <u>Created</u> a <u>Divine School of Higher Learning</u> in *Service to Nature, Men, Angels, and Himself.* Now, let's examine these "Four Highways of Life/Death (Holy Spirit/Evil Spirit)" a little more closely by <u>Identifying What</u> is Going In (life) and *Seeing What Comes Out* (newlife) as a **Result of Following <u>God's Will</u>** in both the *Letter (Jesus)* and *Spirit (Christ)* *of the Law*. It must be understood that "God's Divine Spirit" is <u>Comprised</u> of both *His Blessings* (holy spirit) and *His Curses* (evil spirit) so that in the **Minds** of **Angels and Saints,** the Lord is a *Holy Spirit* (life); yet, in the **Minds** of the **Damned and Demons**, the Lord is an *Evil Spirit* (death). In truth, "God's Spirit" is neither Holy or Evil as it is simply the Third Person of the Godhead (like/dislike) or simply a **Member** of the *Father, Son and Spirit of God* (three natures).

The following tabular information indicates that there are "Four Highways Leading" to <u>God's New Jerusalem</u> from the **North** (Messiah's highway), **South** (Church's highway), **East** (Hell's highway), and **West** (Demons' highway) **Guiding** the **Perfect** (Angels), the **Holy** (Saints,) as well as the **Imperfect** (Damned) and the **Unholy** (Demons) into *God's Kingdom of Glory*:

Thirteen Stages of Transformation, Forgiveness, Pardon and Conversion of God's Children

(traveling into and out of elements, dimensions, unions, and nature to learn all things)

	Holy Spirit (blessing)		Evil Spirit (curse)	
	Messiah's Highway	**Church's Highway**	**Damned Highway**	**Demonic Highway**
	(elements)	(dimensions)	(unions)	(natures)
1st Cup 1.	Earth	Physical	Father/Abraham	Transformed
2nd Cup 2.	Wind	Spiritual	Son/Couple	Forgiven
3rd Cup 3.	Water	Mystical	Spirit/Friends	Pardoned
4th Cup 4.	Fire	Divine	Trinity/Families	Converted
	Good News	Gospel/Message	Doctrinal Truths	Eternal Freedom
	(1st Advent)	(2nd Advent)	(3rd Advent)	(judgment)

	In	Out	In	Out	In	Out	In	Out
1.	See	Think	Hear	Speak	Recognize	Touch	Come to	Sup with
	Suffering	of Child	Crying	to Child	Covenant	with Child	Helping	the Child
	(sin-nature/ignorant)		(worldly temptations/ criminal)		(demonic possesion/ insane)		(God's curse/evil)	

2.	Christ's	Gentile	Peter's	Jewish	Jesus'	Jewish	Paul's	Gentile
	Church	Cross	touch	Cross	World	Sword	World	Sword
	(remove faults)		(forgive them)		(convert Evil)		(resurrect death)	

3.	Redeem	Baptize	Save	Confession	Reward	Communion	Free	Confirmation
	Child	Child	Child	of Child	Child	for Child	Child	of Child
	(sinner/baby)		(Christian/teenager)		(saint/adult)		(son of God/wise man)	

4.	Teach Right from Wrong	Righteous Child	Teach Good from Evil	Holy Child	Teach God's/ Man/s Wills	Perfect Child	Teach Reality from Illusion	Free Child
	(personal survival)		(find truth)		(experience love)		(make choices)	

5.	God's Truth	Man's Knowledge	God's Law	Man's Self-awareness	God's Will	Man's Consciousness	God's Love	Man's Sentience
	(bow to cross)		(washed in blood)		(purified by spirit)		(changed by divinity)	

6.	God's Mind	Man's Calling	God's Heart	Man's Enlightenment	God's Soul	Man's Awakening	God's Life-force	Man's Indwelling
	(growing sinner)		(mature Christian)		(natural saint)		(supernatural son)	

7.	Being Saved	New Body	Saving Self	Eternal Life	Saving Others	Royal Kingdom	Saving - God	Infinite Freedom
	(good news)		(gospel message)		(doctrinal truth)		(awakened nature)	

8.	Man's Earth (calling)	Transform God	Angelic Heaven (enlightenment)	Forgives Sinners	God's Kingdom (awakening)	Pardons Damned	Christ's Free life (indwelling)	Converts Demons
9.	Christ's 1st Advent (see limitations)	Saving Self	Christ's 2nd Advent (see potential)	Saving Society	Christ's 3rd Advent (see self-worth)	Saving God	God's Judgment (see personal value)	Saving All
10.	1st Cup (God becomes Man)	Father/God/ Abraham	2nd Cup (Man becomes God)	Loving Couple	3rd Cup (God and Man become One)	Friends Bride/Groom	4th Cup (God/Man is Man/God)	Families Bride/Groom
11.	Mistaken God (justified)	Transformed God	Admitted Sinner (honored	Forgiven Saint	Indicted Criminal (glorified)	Pardoned Damned	Convicted Bad Angel (freed)	Converted Slave
12.	King of Earth (venerated)	Government of Earth	Priest of Heaven (adored)	Church of Heaven	Son of Kingdom (exalted)	Government of Kingdom	God in Self (worship)	Freedom of Self
13.	Ignorant Earth (peace of mind)	Celestial Court	Criminal Heaven (joy of heart)	Temple Court	Insane Kingdom (happiness of soul)	Royal Court	Evil Spirit God Almighty (ecstatic life-force)	Divine Court

Pass Lucifer's Test	**Pass God's Judgment**	**Pass Self-evaluation**	**Get Respect of Peer Group**
. Elementary School	. High School	. College	. On-the-Job-Training
. Deny Intellect	. Abandon Feelings	. Submit Free Will	. Dying to Selfishness

This illustration shows that "Level One (1st highway)" is the 1st Advent when **God** enters the **Womb of Life** during *Christmas* (divine man/give divinity) and then exits the Tomb of Death (human God/take-sins) during *Easter* so that the Lord can **Experience for Himself** (sin-nature) the *Suffering of His Children* (thinking of man). Secondly, "Level Two (2nd highway)" is the 2nd Advent when **Man** enters the **Altar of Life** during *Easter* (repentant sinner) and then exits the **Resurrection of Rebirth** during *Halloween* (sainthood) so that the Lord can **Hear for Himself** (worldly temptations) the *Cries of His Enslaved Children* (speak to man). Thirdly, "Level Three (3rd highway)" is the Lord's 3rd Advent when the **Damned** enter their **Graves of Unforgiveness** (demonic possession) during *Death* (cursed to hell) and then exit in the **Resurrection of the Damned** on *All Souls Day* (pardoned) so that the Lord can **Recognize His Covenant** (touch man) and *Save All Who have been Lost*. Finally, "Level Four (4th highway)" is the Lord's Final Judgment when **Lucifer** enters his **Prison of Gehenna** (God's curse) during his *Execution* (outer darkness) and then exits during the **Resurrection of Evil** (white throne) on the *Independence Day* and comes forth to *Bow to the Perfection of God*.

No. 2: At "Level One" (1st highway), a Surrendered Christian **Enters Christ's Church** and then exits through the Lord's **Gentile Cross** (venial sins) to **Remove his Faults** and make him a *Righteous Citizen on Earth*. Secondly, at "Level Two (2nd highway)," a Forgiven Soul receives **Peter's Touch** and then exits through the Lord's **Jewish Cross** (mortal sins) so that a person can have his **Sins Forgiven** and make him a *Holy Saint in Heaven*. Thirdly at "Level Three (3rd highway)," a New-born Soul enters **Jesus' World** and then exits through the Lord's **Jewish Sword** (capital sins) so that a person can then **Convert All Evil** to be made a *Son of God within God's Kingdom*. Finally, at "Level Four (4th highway)," a Transformed Soul enters **Paul's World** and then exits through the Lord's **Gentile Sword** (original sin) so that a person can then **Resurrect from the Dead** to be made into a *Free Man with his Own Kingdom*.

No. 3: At "Level One (1st highway)," a Growing Christian becomes a **Redeemed Child** and then **Exits** by becoming a **Baptized Child** to offer himself as a **Repentant Sinner** (baby) and become a *Soldier-of-the-Light* (sword). Secondly, at "Level Two (2nd highway)," a Venerated Christian becomes a **Saved Child** and then exits by becoming a **Confessed Child** and offers himself as an **Upright Christian** (teenager) to become a *Living Prayer of Love* (cross). Thirdly, at "Level Three (3rd highway)," an Adored Christian becomes a **Rewarded Child** and then exits by **Receiving Christ's Communion** and become a **Clear Thinking Christian** (adult) to become a *Living Saint of God* (word). Finally, at "Level Four (4th highway)," an Exalted Christian becomes a **Free Child** and then exits by becoming a **Confirmed Child of God** and is offered-up as a **Sacrificial Lamb** (wise man) to become a *Perfect Son of God* (deeds).

No 4: At "Level One (1st highway)," a Thinking Christian (intellect) learns **God's Right and man's wrong** and then exits by becoming a **Righteous Child** ready, willing, and able to face the demands of **Survival** in a **Cruel World** of *Sin, Evil, and Death*. Secondly, at "Level Two (2nd highway)," a Feeling Christian (emotions) learns **God's Good from man's evil** and then exits by becoming a **Holy Child** in search of **Finding God's Truth** in a **New World** of *Repentance, Prayers, and Works*. Thirdly, at "Level Three (3rd highway)," a Compulsive Christian (instinctive) learns **God's Will from man's will** and then exits by becoming a **Perfect Child** to **Experience God's Love** in a **Mystical Dimension** of *Righteousness, Holiness, and Perfection*. Finally, at "Level Four (4th highway)," a Free Thinking Christian (free spirit) learns **God's Reality and man's illusion** and then exits by becoming a **Free Child** to make **All the Right Choices** in **God's Creation** of *Transfigured Bodies, Eternal Life, Personal Kingdoms, and Ecstatic Happiness*.

No. 5: At "Level One (1st highway)," a Transformed Christian comprehends **God's Truth** and then exits by becoming a **Man of Knowledge** showing a **Lost Fool** that he must **Bow to Christ's Cross** and then *Come Follow the Lord into the Grave*. Secondly, at "Level Two (2nd highway)," a Forgiven Christian comprehends **God's Law** and then exits by becoming **Self-aware of Life**, showing a **Lost Soul** must be **Washed in Christ's Blood** and then *Come Follow the Lord into Death*. Thirdly, at "Level Three (3rd highway)," a Pardoned Christian comprehends **God's Will** and then exits by becoming **Conscious of Life**, showing a **Lost Christian** must be **Purified by the Spirit** and then *Come Follow the Lord into Damnation*. Finally, at "Level Four (4th highway)," a Converted Christian comprehends **God's Love** and then exits by becoming **Sentient of the Life-experience**, showing a **Blind Saint** must be **Changed** (healed) **by Divinity** and then *Come Follow the Lord into Oblivion*.

No. 6: At "Level One (1st highway)," a Growing Christian understands **God's Mind** and then exits by **Hearing God's Call to Divine Truth** showing a **Growing**

Sinner must listen to the **Good News** (free redemption) to be *Saved from himself*. Secondly, at "Level Two (2nd highway)," a <u>Good Christian</u> understands **God's Heart** and then exits by being **Enlightened in Divine Law** showing a <u>**Mature Christian**</u> must listen to the **Gospel Message** (earn salvation) to *Save himself*. Thirdly, at "Level Three (3rd highway)," a <u>Striving Christian</u> understands **God's Soul** and then exits by being **Awakened to God's Divine Will** showing a <u>**Natural Saint**</u> must listen to God's **Doctrinal Truths** (bonus rewards) to *Save Others*. Finally, at "Level Four (4th highway)," an <u>Overcoming Christian</u> understands **God's Life-force** and then exits by being **Indwelled with God's Spirit** showing God's **Supernatural Son** must learn to **Think for himself** to be able to one day *Save the Lord God Almighty Himself*.

No. 7: At "Level One (1st highway)," an <u>Adult Christian</u> must understand his **Own Mind** and then exit by becoming **Worthy of a New Body** showing a <u>**Righteous Man**</u> must believe in the **Mosaic Tables** to *Remove His Faults Moment by Moment*. Secondly, at "Level Two (2nd highway)," a <u>Wise Christian</u> must understand his **Own Heart** and then exit by becoming **Worthy of Eternal Life** showing a <u>**Holy Man**</u> must believe in **Christ's Cross** to be *Absolved of his Venial Sins Daily*. Thirdly, at "Level Three (3rd highway)," a <u>Free Christian</u> must understand his **Own Soul** and then exit by becoming **Worthy of God's Kingdom** showing a <u>**Perfect Man**</u> must believe in the **Lamb** to be *Forgiven of his Mortal Sins Weekly* (Sunday). Finally, at "Level Four (4th highway)," an **Independent Christian** must understand his **Own Life-force** and then exit by becoming **Worthy of His Own Personal Kingdom** showing a <u>**Son of God**</u> must believe in **God's Spirit** to be *Pardoned of his Capital Sins Yearly* (Easter).

No. 8: At "Level One (1st highway)," a <u>Justified Christian</u> must understand the **Social Intellect on Earth** and then exit by **Transforming God into Man** showing a <u>**Baby Soul**</u> must be **Called into New-life** thereby **Changing** *Ignorance into Wisdom* (elementary school). Secondly, at "Level Two (2nd highway)," an <u>Honored Christian</u> must understand the **Social Emotions in Heaven** and then exit by **Forgiving Sinners to become Saints** showing a <u>**Teenage Soul**</u> must be **Enlightened to Enter New-life** by **Changing** *Cowardice into Courage* (high school). Thirdly, at "Level Three (3rd highway)," a <u>Glorified Christian</u> must understand the **Social Instincts within the Kingdom** and then exit by **Pardoning the Damned** to become **Servants** showing an <u>**Adult Soul**</u> must be **Awakened to Enter New-life** by **Changing** *Greed into Generosity* (college). Finally, at "Level Four (4th highway)" a <u>Free Christian</u> must understand the **Social Nature within Himself** and then exit by **Converting Demons** to become **Slaves of God** showing a <u>**Wise Soul**</u> must be **Indwelled to Enter New-life** by **Changing** *Selfishness to Unselfishness* (on-the-job training).

No 9: At "Level One (1st highway)," a <u>Denying Christian</u> must understand **God's Intellect** during the Lord's **1st Advent** (free redemption) and then exit by welcoming the **Priest on a Donkey** (submission) showing a **Called Soul** must *Save itself* (being saved) and then *See Own Limitations* (earth). Secondly, at "Level Two (2nd highway)," an <u>Abandoning Christian</u> must understand **God's Emotions** during the Lord's **2nd Advent** (earn salvation) and then exit by welcoming the **Thief in the Night** (unto thine own self be true) showing an **Enlightened Soul** must *Save Society* and then *See*

Own Potential (Heaven). Thirdly, at "Level Three (3rd highway)," a <u>Submitted Christian</u> must understand **God's Instincts** during the Lord's **3rd Advent** (bonus rewards) and then exit by welcoming God's **Son on a Cloud** (guilty conscience) showing an **Awakened Soul** must *Save God* and then *See Own Self-worth* (Kingdom). Finally, at "Level Four (4th highway)," an <u>Unselfish Christian</u> must understand **God's Nature** during the **Lord's White Throne Judgment** (eternal freedom) and then exit by welcoming the **Lord God Almighty** (instinctive compulsion) showing an **Indwelled Soul** must *Save Everyone* (all) and then *See Own Personal-value* (free life).

No. 10: At "Level One (1st highway)," a <u>Believing Christian</u> must understand the **Mind of Christ** during the **Offering of the 1st Cup** and then exit by bringing forth the **Union of Father God** (Heaven) and **Father Abraham** (earth) so *God can become Man* (Christmas). Secondly, at "Level Two (2nd highway)," a <u>Faithful Christian</u> must understand the **Heart of Christ** during the **Offering of the 2nd Cup** and then exit by bringing forth the **Union of the Couple** (Heaven/earth) so *Man becomes God* (Easter). Thirdly, at "Level Three (3rd highway)," a <u>Knowing Christian</u> must understand the **Soul of Christ** during the **Offering of the 3rd Cup** and then exit by bringing forth the **Union of Groom's Friends** (Heaven) and the **Bride's Friends** (earth) so *God and Man can become One* (Halloween). Finally, at "Level Four (4th highway)," a <u>Thinking Christian</u> must understand the **Life-force of Christ** during the **Offering of the 4th Cup** and then exit by bringing forth the **Union of the Groom's Family** (Angels) and the **Bride's Family** (Saints) so *God/Man is Man/God* (Independence Day).

No. 11: At "Level One (1st highway)," a <u>Physical Christian</u> must understand the **Nature of Life** as reflected by a **Mistaken God** and then exit to be **Transformed** from **Divinity into Humanity** to **Justify** the *Meaning of Life* (existence). Secondly, at "Level Two (2nd highway)," a <u>Spiritual Christian</u> must understand the **Humanity of Life** as reflected by an **Admitted Sinner** and then exit to become a **Forgiven Saint** to **Honor** the *Purpose of Life* (service). Thirdly, at "Level Three (3rd highway)," a <u>Mystical Christian</u> must understand the **Divinity of Life** as reflected by an **Indicted Criminal** and then exit to become one of the **Pardoned Damned** (servant) who must be **Glorified** through the *Value of Life* (happiness). Finally, at "Level Four (4th highway)," a <u>Divine Christian</u> must understand the **Godliness of Life** as reflected by a **Convicted Bad Angel** (Lucifer) and then exit to become one of the **Converted Demons** (God's slave) who must be **Freed** through *Perfection of Life* (essence).

No. 12: At "Level One (1st highway)," an <u>Obedient Christian</u> must understand **God's Laws** as reflected by the **King of the Earth** and then exit to **Venerate** the <u>Government of the Earth</u> in *Obedience to the Ten Commandments* (Mosaic Law). Secondly, at "Level Two (2nd highway)," a <u>Hard-working Christian</u> must understand **God's Decrees** as reflected by the **High Priest of Heaven** and then exit to **Adore** the **Church of Heaven** by *Picking-up Christ's Cross* (Canon Law). Thirdly, at "Level Three (3rd highway)," a <u>Dutiful Christian</u> must understand **God's Statutes** as reflected by the **Son through His Kingdom** and then exit to **Exalt God's Kingdom Home** by *Following the Ways of Jesus Christ*. Finally, at "Level Four (4th highway)," a <u>Responsible Christian</u>

must understand **God's Covenants** as reflected by the **God of Self** and then exit to **Worship** the <u>Freedom of Self</u> in truly *Mastering Eternal Life*.

No. 13: At "Level One (1st highway)," a <u>Wicked Sinner</u> must understand the **Forces of Sin** as reflected by the **Ignorance of Earth** and then exit to **Create Earth's Celestial Court** (physical) to bring forth *Peace of Mind* for *One and All*. Secondly, at "Level Two (2nd highway)," a <u>Worldly Sinner</u> must understand the **Forces of Evil** as reflected by the **Criminals of Heaven** and then exit to **Create Heaven's Temple Court** (spiritual) to bring forth *Joy of the Heart* for *One and All*. Thirdly, at "Level Three (3rd highway)," a <u>Demonic Sinner</u> must understand the **Forces of Death** as reflected by **Insanity** and then exit to **Create the Kingdom's Royal Court** (mystical) to bring forth *Happiness of the Soul* for *One and All*. Finally, at "Level Four (4th highway)," a <u>Damned Sinner</u> must understand the **Forces of Damnation** as reflected by the **Evil Spirit of God** and then exit to **Create God's Divine Court** (divine) to bring forth the *Illusion of Life* for *One and All*.

This explanation of the "Thirteen Levels" of <u>Human Purification</u> (earth), <u>Correction</u> (Heaven), <u>Conversion</u> (Kingdom), and <u>Transformation</u> (God) allows a **Confused Student** to **Grasp the Depth** of <u>Complexity</u> associated with *God's Grand Design*. The "Lord is Saying" here that <u>Physical Existence</u> **Relates** to the **Meaning of Life** (know God) which **Centers** on **God Intentionally Making Mistakes** (imperfect Adam) and then being willing to **Suffer the Frustration** of *Correcting these Mistakes Over Time*. Secondly, the "Lord is Saying" that <u>Spiritual Service</u> **Relates** to the **Purpose of Life** (serve God) which **Centers** on **Sinners becoming Saints** (forgiveness) and then **Striving** <u>Over the Centuries</u> to *Save the Lost at Any Cost*. Thirdly, the "Lord is Saying" that <u>Mystical Happiness</u> **Relates** to the **Value of Life** (loving God) which **Centers** on **Criminals being Pardoned** and then becoming *Servants unto the Lord Forever*. Finally, the "Lord" is Saying" that <u>God's Divine Essence</u> **Relates** to the **Perfection of Life** (becoming God) which **Centers** on **Bad Angels** (Lucifer) one day being **Set Free** as **Free-Willed Slaves** to *Serve the Kingdom of God*.

The most "Important Question" becomes: just **What is Life All About**? The "Simple Answer" is <u>Having Something to Live For</u> (natural order) or **Giving Life Value** (supernatural order) through the *Forces of Nothing* (challenge/agony of defeat) and *All* (adventure/thrill of victory). The idea here is to see that through the "Forces of Growth (flesh)" and "Maturity (spirit)," we are able to <u>Search</u> for **Our Hearts' Desire** by **Building a Good Life** which **Leads** to both the *Treasure of Human Love* (mate) in *Union* with the *Treasure of Divine Love* (God). The major theme of the "Life-experience (free will)" is that because of a <u>Person's Threat of Impending Doom,</u> the **Human Race** has been able to **Create** a **Couple** of *Treasured Moments of Life* (Calvary/Resurrection). These "Treasured Moments (life/body)" are so <u>Valuable</u> (saving all creation) that <u>They Make</u> the **Entire Life-experience Worthwhile**, even **If a Person Only** *Lives for an Instant* (33 years). This implies that "If an Eternal Being" has <u>No Doom</u> and can <u>Experience No Real Loss,</u> he therefore can have **No Treasured Moment** (saving existence/Calvary) upon which he can then **Build a Lifetime of Living** <u>Using Only</u> a *Single Moment of Existence*.

The "Lord is Telling Us" that "He truly Envies Man" for his **Curse of Death** (Eve's blessed mistake) because it also **Produces** a **Counter-force** which brings forth **Man's Greatest Blessing of Life**, thereby **Making Every Moment of Life** extremely **Valuable** (thrill of victory) by **Making One's** *Short-life Worth Living* unto its *Fullest Treasured Moment of Existence* (agony of defeat/Calvary). In the case of "Jesus Christ," He Used his **Agony of Defeat** (flesh) on **Calvary** to *Attain* the *Love of His Bride* (world/Earth) and then He Used his **Thrill of Victory** (spirit) during **His Resurrection** to *Attain* the *Love of His God* (church/Heaven). The question is: just "How Many Years" or Cycles of Life will a **Person have to Live** before he can **Master this Feat** of **Growth** (flesh/obedience) and **Maturity** (spirit/imitation), thereby **Allowing him** to become *Christ-Like* (perfect)? We are being told that a "Person Needs Three Cycles of Life (life/death/resurrection)" to Attain both Man's Love (flesh) and God's Love (spirit) as we **Sacrifice Ourselves unto Death** to **Find Our** Own *Treasured Moment in Life*. Obviously, God is Revealing that When We Believe in **Jesus Christ,** this **Treasured Moment Concept** can be **Extended** to a **Person's Eternal Life** via a person's **Daily Trials** and **Tribulations** sent to each of **God's Children** by the *Lord* to *Save Them from Evil*. We must imagine that "Our Daily Trials" are a Form of **Exercise for an Athlete** and without a **Daily Regimented Program** (budget) and a **Heart Pumping Workout** (implement budget), a *Person* will simply *Grow Fat and Lazy*. We see that "If a Person" becomes a Fat Couch Potato, his **Sedentary Lifestyle** will **Destroy his Good Health,** thereby **Taking Away** his **Vitality** and **Making him** into a **Worthless Slob, Who** must **Live Many Life-cycles** (years/mindless old age) *Without Direction* (self) and/or *Without Purpose* (society).

1. **Direction Comes From** - Individual Survival (self) …Fixed Frame of Reference
    *   Nothing - Agony of Defeat/death: Becoming Righteous Citizen on Earth = New Body
    *   Being Consumed by Personal Arrogance - Ostracized by Society (self)
2. **Purpose Comes From** - Social Values (people) …Relative Focused Existence
    *   All - Thrill of Victory/life: Becoming Holy Saint in Heaven = Eternal Life
    *   Being Consumed by Duty - Decorated for One's Personal Sacrifice (society)

This means that "During the Life-experience," Society and God's Will must **Come First,** while the Individual and **Man's Will** must **Come Second** so that the **Force of the Family** and the **Community** can **Provide** the **Necessary Support Needed** to *Care for Everyone*. Now, let's focus on "Our God of Spirit (human love)" and his "Human Son, Jesus Christ (divine love)" as the Father and Son Seek **Their Treasured Moment** with the *First Greatest Moment* occurring in **Christ's Death of Calvary** (find bride/bottom) or *Becoming Nothing* (agony of defeat/society) and the *Second Greatest Moment, Occurring* in New-life via **Christ's Resurrection** (find God/top) or *All* (thrill of victory/self). We are all "Looking Forward" to that Glorious Day of Resurrection when we can **Pass** through the **Veil of Darkness** to **Reach** the **Divine Light of God** to *See Our Own Limitations* (light), *Potential* (water), and ultimate *Self-worth* (soil). This means that "Each of Us" must Face Lucifer (test) to **Learn the Importance** of Trial and Error Learning as a way of **Measuring His Limitations** and *Overcoming Ignorance*. Secondly, we must also "Face God's Judgment" to <u>Learn the Importance</u> of **Quitting and Admitting Defeat** as a way of **Measuring Our Potential** and *Overcoming Cowardice*. Finally, we must also "Face Our Own Self-evaluation" to <u>Learn</u> the **Importance** of **Never-quitting** (try) as a way of **Measuring One's Self-worth** and *Overcoming Greed*. Through "Facing His Sin-nature (ignorance)," "Facing All Worldly Temptations (cowardice)," and "Facing Demonic Possession (greed)," a <u>Person can Fight</u> and **Defeat Sin, Evil, and Death** in *All Its Forms*.

Obviously, this is important to "Christ's Three Advents" as <u>He Comes</u> to **Defeat Self-will** (home), **False Beliefs** (church), and **Unfruitful Lives** (government) by **Redeeming the Earth** as a *Priest on a Donkey* (1st advent/Calvary), a *Thief in the Night* (2nd advent/tribulation), and finally, as a *Just Judge on a Cloud* (3rd advent/end of the world). We see that "Jesus Came" to <u>Arrest Sinners</u> as a **Priest** (no worship/begging), then to <u>Arrest Criminals</u> as a **Thief** (no praise/payment), then to <u>Arrest Crazy Fools</u> (no thanksgiving/works) as a **Just Judge,** and to bring **Them All to Justice** through the *Father's Light* (repentance/word), the *Spirit's Water* (prayers/baptism), and the *Son's Soil* (works/save souls). Yes! we must "All Beg God (earth)," we must "All Pay God (Heaven)," and we must "All Work for God (Kingdom)" or <u>We will be Subject</u> to being **Arrested** by **God's Son, *Jesus Christ***. This means that the "Sinner" <u>Failed to Worship,</u> the "Criminal" <u>Failed to Pay his Debts,</u> and the "Crazy Fool" <u>Failed to Contribute to Society</u> and so the **Lord God Almighty** has put out a **Divine Warrant** for these most *Wicked Men* (most wanted). We see that in the "Mind" of <u>God's Son,</u> **He Sees a Great Need** for an **Effective Rehabilitation System** which must be **Capable** of *Forgiving Sin* (begging), *Converting Criminals* (paying), and *Healing Crazy Fools* (contributing).

The following tabular information indicates that during the "Lord's 1st Advent (Priest)," He came to <u>Arrest Sinners</u> (no blessings); during His "2nd Advent (Thief)," He comes to <u>Arrest Criminals</u> (no lessons); and finally, during His "3rd Advent (Just Judge)," He comes to <u>Arrest Crazy Fools</u> (no value):

Christ Comes to Arrest Sinners, the Criminals, and the Crazy Fools for Unlawful Behavior
(put sinners in chains, criminals in prison, and guard the crazy fools to protect society)

Light   1. **1st Advent** - <u>Arrest Sinners:</u> Put in Chains: Dark Pit…Knowledge
(see)   • Messiah Came as a Priest on a Donkey - Chain Non-worshiper
                     (begging)
                   • Remove Ignorance - Beg for God's Light: Get New Body (earth)
Change Law   • Worship Father Daily - Give Life: Face Lucifer's Test (see limitations)
to Faith   • Baby Grows into a Teenager - Trial and Error: Scored by Handicap (33%)
                   • Messiah Creates Daily Sacrifice - Worship God: Give Life
                   • Fulfill God's Law of Obedience - Change Nature: Human to Divine

Water   2. **2nd Advent** - <u>Arrest Criminals:</u> Put in Prison: Iron Cage…Self-awareness
(wash)   • Son of God Comes as a Thief in the Night - Imprison Non-payers (pay
                     sin-debt)

	• Remove Cowardice - Buy God's Water: Get Eternal Life (Heaven)
Change Faith	• Praise Spirit Weekly - Give Wealth: Face God's Judgment (see potential)
to Knowing)	• Teenager Matures into Adult - Quit-in-defeat: Scored on a Curve (67%)
	• Messiah Creates Weekly Sacrifice - Praise God: Give Wealth
	• Fulfill Man's Faith in God's Love - Wash Away Sins: Sinfulness to Holiness
Soil	3. **3rd Advent** - <u>Arrest Crazy Fools:</u> Watched by Prison Guards...
(eat)	Consciousness
	• Jesus Christ Comes as Just Judge on a Cloud - Guard the Lazy (no contribution)
	• Remove Greed - Rewarded with God's Soil: Get Royal Kingdom (kingdom)
Change	• Thank Son Yearly - Give Labors: Face Self-evaluation (see self-worth)
Knowing	• Adult Becomes a Wise Man - Never-quits Trying: Scored Pass/Fail (100%)
to Freedom	
	• Messiah Creates Yearly Sacrifice - Thank God: Give Labors
	• Fulfill God/Man Knowing - Thinking for Oneself: Find Freedom

This illustration shows that the "Job of Rehabilitation" for an <u>Entire Society</u> of **Ignorant, Criminal, Insane, and Evil People** would be quite a challenge even for **Jesus Christ** as He would have to make **Three Attempts** to **Enlighten** (light), **Purify** (water), and **Bear Fruit** (soil) out of the most *Poisoned of Minds, Hearts, and Souls*. The idea here is to see that after "Adam and Eve Ate" from the <u>Tree of Knowledge</u> (poison), this **Filled Their** *Minds with Insanity* (wrong limitations), **Their** *Hearts with Childish Dreams* (wrong potential), and **Their** *Souls with Pure Evil* (wrong self-worth). Now, imagine "God's Son" coming to face an <u>Insane World of Murderers</u> **Whose Brains** were **Filled with Illogic,** to the point of being able to **Distort** even the *Divine Wisdom of God Itself*. It was "Lucifer's Curse" of Confusion within a **World of Babies** that caused **Jesus Christ** to **Use His 1st Advent** (priest) to **Make Humanity Bow** (Calvary) to the *Will of God* (home of God). During the "Lord's 2nd Advent (Thief)" via <u>His Attack on Lucifer</u> (chained in hell), **He would Make Humanity Bow** (tribulation) to the *Beliefs of God* (church). Finally, during the "Lord's 3rd Advent (Just Judge)" via <u>His Battle of Armageddon</u> (cast into Gehenna), **He would Make Humanity Bow** (end of world) to the *Laws of Ownership* (government).

1. **Bow to God's Will** - <u>Create Obedient Children:</u> Kingship of God...See Limitations
2. **Bow to God's Beliefs** - <u>Create Dutiful Children:</u> Priesthood of God...See Potential
3. **Bow to God's Law** - <u>Create Prosperous Children:</u> Sonship of God...See Self-worth

Through "God's Will (wisdom)," "God's Truths or Beliefs," and "God's Ownership Laws (fruitfulness)," the <u>Whole Earth</u> would be **Converted** from an *Evil Cesspool of Death* (sewage pit) **into** *Heaven on Earth* (eternal life). This means that "Christ's 1st Advent" **Created** the **Daily Sacrifice** (Calvary/Mon-Sat) to **Worship God** (give life/follow will/light) so **that Everyone's Sin-nature** could be <u>Forgiven</u> (baptism) through the *Blood of the Lamb* (Passover) or *His Sign* of *Bowing to God's Will* (law). Secondly, during "Christ's 2nd Advent," <u>He will Create</u> the **Weekly Sacrifice** (tribulation/Sunday) to **Praise God** (give wealth/believe truths/water) so **that Everyone's Evil-nature** could be <u>Pardoned</u> (confession) through the *Blood of the Goat* (Yom Kippur) or *His Sign* of *Bowing to God's Beliefs* (faith). Finally, during "Christ's 3rd Advent," **He will Create** the <u>Yearly Sacrifice</u> (end of the world/Easter) to **Thank God** (give labors/till land/soil) so **that Everyone's Dead-nature** could be <u>Resurrected</u> (communion) through the *Blood of Christ* (Easter) or *His Sign* of *Bowing to God's Ownership Laws.* Now, we see that through "Christ's Blood" or "His Passion," the <u>Lord's Individuality</u> (value) and <u>Social Nature</u> (meaningless fool) could be **Firmly Established to Create** that **Fine Balance** between **One's <u>Personal Identity</u>** and/or **Blending into His <u>Social Identity</u>** unto the point of having *No Personal Identity at All* (no life) or simply becoming a *Slave unto the Will of Others and the Greater Good* (IS/no name). The message is that through the "Force of Submission (100% belief/becoming Christ)," the <u>Fine Balance</u> exists between being **Seen** as a **<u>Prince Among Men</u>** or simply being **One** of the **<u>Meaningless Masses</u>** (faceless fool) who is to be *Manifested, Controlled,* and *Ultimately Turned* into a *Divine Treasure before God.* Note that "Jesus Christ Established" his <u>Personal Identity</u> in **His Sacrifice** on **Mount Calvary** by **Winning** the **<u>Love of His Bride</u>** (church) on **<u>Earth</u>** as *He Suffered the Agony of Defeat* (individuality/Jesus). Secondly, "Jesus Christ" <u>Established His Social Identity</u> in **His Prayer of Resurrection** by **Winning** the **<u>Love of His God</u>** (world) in **Heaven** as he *Crowns* the *Thrill of Victory* (member of society/Christ).

Through these "Two Opposing Identities (individual/social)," <u>God's Son</u> **Established** a **Fine Balance** between being *Consumed by Duty* (social animal/brotherhood) and being *Ostracized by One's Arrogance* (individual robot/ego). Now, the "Lord Jesus Christ" has <u>Come to Teach</u> **Each of God's Children How** to **Establish** this **Fine Balance** between **Personal Ambition** (me 1st) and **Social Duty** (them 1st) to **<u>Keep a Person's Life Focused</u>** on the *Meaning* (exist), *Purpose* (service), and *Value* (happiness) of *It All.* Remember, the "Life-experience" is <u>Centered</u> upon the **Meaning of Life** (to exist), the **Purpose of Liberty** (serve), and the **Value of Happiness** based on the **<u>Depth of Wisdom, Courage, and Generosity</u>** of the *Born-again Man* (Christlike). The theme here is that the "Life-experience" involves <u>Four Stages of Unity</u> (fathers/couples/friends/families) **Each Designed to Unite <u>Physical Earth</u>** (fathers/celestial court), **<u>Spiritual Heaven</u>** (couples/temple court), **<u>Mystical Kingdom</u>** (friends/royal court), and **<u>Divine God</u>** (families/divine court) via the *Nature of Jesus Christ* (truth/law/will/love). This "State of Unity" is <u>Established</u> by **Merging** the **Two Truths of Life** (physical/spiritual) into a **<u>Blend</u>** (balanced) between *What is Right and Good* (God) versus *What is Wrong and Evil* (man).

Obviously, the "Journey of Life" is <u>Fulfilled by Mastering</u> both a **Person's Physical Truth** (being saved/church) and his **Spiritual Truth** (sainthood/church) which implies that the **Life-experience** ends up being about *Growing-up* (childhood/mandatory) and *Maturing* (adulthood/optional) *in All Things.* We see that in the "Mastering of the World," a <u>Person</u> must <u>Experience Hard-work</u> (required) by **Learning Right** from **Wrong** (believing) to become **Faithful,** then become **Knowledgeable,** to **Arrive** at **Becoming Something of Value** as a *Righteous Citizen of Man* (free). This "Process of Life" is both Governed and Controlled by **Saint Joseph** and his **Saints, Whose Job** it is to **Save Sinners** by **Teaching Them Ethics** (human law) at **All Levels of Comprehension,** until a **Person** becomes *Righteous before God* (kingship), thereby **Making him Worthy** of a *New Body* (man's gift/self). Secondly, we see a "Person" must "Master the Church" by Experiencing Faith (optional) and **Learning Good from Evil** (knowing) to **Understand God's Law,** then **Follow God's Will** to **Arrive** at **Becoming God's Love** as a *Holy Saint in Heaven* (employed). This "Process of Eternal Life" is both Governed and Controlled by **Saint Michael** and his **Angels, Whose Job** it is to **Create Holy Saints** by **Teaching Them Morals** (divine law) at **All Levels of Comprehension,** until a **Person** becomes *Holy before God* (sainthood), thereby **Making him Worthy** of an *Eternal Life* (God's gift/society). The "Ethics of Man (new body)" and the "Morals of God (eternal life)" are to be Blended into **One State of Perfection** so that a **Person** can become **Perfect before God** (sonship), thereby **Making him Worthy** of his *Own Eternal Kingdom* (God/Man's Gift or God).

1. **1st Treasure** - New Body: Learn God's Right from Man's Wrong (flesh)...God's Acceptance
   - Law - Obey God's Every Command: Instant Compliance = Do as a Child is Told
   - Submitting One's Free Will to God's Divine Will - Man's Will becomes God's Will
2. **2nd Treasure** - Eternal Life: Learn God's Good from Man's Evil (spirit) ...God's Respect
   - Faith - Recognize God's Love: Respect God's Leadership = Bow to God's Tough Love
   - Mastering - Unto Thine Own Self be True: Man's Laws become God's Laws
3. **3rd Treasure** - Own Kingdom: Learn God's Will from Man's Will (soul).... God's Love
   - Knowing - Comprehending God's Will: Becoming a Productive Citizen = Befriending God
   - Guided by One's Guilty Conscience - Recognizing Own Mistakes: God's Truth/Man's Truth are One

We can "Visualize this Process" of Growth (obedience) and Maturity (imitation) by **Seeing a Person Submitting** (baby) his **Free Will** (earth) to **God's Divine Will** (Heaven), while a *Soul* is still a *Child at Home*. Secondly, we see a "Person Experiencing Life" by Believing in the Axiom of **Unto Thine Own Self be True** (child) which is **Converting One's Human Laws** into God's **Divine Laws,** when a *Soul* becomes an *Adolescent in Elementary School*. Thirdly, we see a "Person Mastering Life" through a Well-trained Guilty Conscience (adolescence) which **Guides** him through **Human/Divine Truth** when a *Soul* becomes a *Teenager Attending High School*. Fourthly, we see a "Person is Living his Life" via his Own Instinctive Compulsion (teenager) which **Controls his Desires** through **Human/Divine Love** when a *Soul* becomes a *Young Adult Attending College*. Fifthly, we see a "Person Changing his Life" by Thinking for Himself (young adult) which **Controls his Passions** through **Human/Divine Mercy** when a *Soul* becomes an *Adult being Trained on the Job*. Sixthly, we see a "Person Transforming his Life" by being Set Free (adulthood) which means **Taking Control** of his **Own Affairs** when a *Soul* becomes a **Certified Wise**

Man Fully Capable of <u>Guiding the Lives of Others</u> through *Leadership*. Finally, we see a "Person at One with Life" by <u>Uniting his Life-force</u> with **God** (sonship) which means becoming a **Righteous Citizen on Earth** (kingship), a **Holy Saint in Heaven** (priesthood), and a *Son of God in the Kingdom* (sonship). It should now all make sense that just like any "Creation in Nature," it must <u>Progress</u> through its **Life-cycle** by **Growing** via various **Stages of Development** until it **Reaches** <u>Full Maturity</u> and is ready to *Bear Fruit*. In the case of the "Human Race," it must <u>Master Physical Ethics</u> (new body) and <u>Spiritual Morals</u> (eternal life) to become **Ready** to **Blend** a **Person's Earthly Flesh** (kingship) with **His Heavenly Spirit** (priesthood) to **Create** an **Eternal Soul** (sonship) **Worthy** of <u>Bearing the Fruits</u> of a *New Body* (Saints), *Eternal Life* (Angels), and *His Kingdom of Glory* (God's Son). Note here that the "Job of the Saints (good works)" is to <u>Operate God's Physical Realm of Existence</u> which is **Centered** upon **Creating Human Bodies** in both *Earthly* (natural flesh/womb) and *Heavenly Forms* (supernatural bodies/tomb). In like manner, the "Job of the Angels (holy prayers)" is to <u>Operate God's Spiritual Realm of Existence</u> which is **Centered** upon **Creating Spirit Life** in both *Earthly* (natural spirits/womb) and *Heavenly Forms* (supernatural spirits/tomb). We can see the "Creation of Saintly Bodies" and "Angelic Spirits" explained below as a <u>Sinner Journeys</u> from **His Sacred Altar** via **Two Pathways of Physical** and **Spiritual Life** until he obtains his *New Body* (earth/grave) and his *Gift of Eternal Life* (Heaven/host).

The following illustration shows that each of "God's Children" must <u>Begin Life</u> (childhood) at the **Epistle Side** (honor man) of the **Altar** (cross), where he will **Offer-up** his *Good Works* (ethics/blood sacrifice) and then <u>End the Life-experience</u> (adulthood) at the **Gospel Side** (honor God) of the **Altar** (table), where he will <u>Offer-up</u> his *Holy Prayers* (morals/offer prayers) to his *God*:

The Epistle Side Forgives Sinners (redemption) and Gospel Side Creates Saints (salvation)
(epistle offers works of the flesh, gospel offers prayers of the spirit unto Jesus Christ)

Adult - Evaluation of Self (becoming one commandment/soul) ═══════════
 Thank God - Give Labor: <u>Perception of Reality</u> - Present Personality (value/happiness)
1,000 years of peace   New Earth   New Heaven
 • Heaven on Earth   • Paradise in Heaven   • Kingdom of Heaven
Become God/Man ═══════════════Set Free: **Freedom/Liberty/Independence**═══
---**Glorified Body**   (Heaven) ----**Mystical Body** (Kingdom) ---- **Transfigured Body** (earth)
═ ═ ═*God's Forgiveness*************************** *Man's Repentance*═══════

4th Cup - Wedding Feast: Union of Two Families = Angels for Groom / Saints for Bride
 • Create Perfect Man - Saving Souls: Power of Knowing (results) = Get to Meet God
    (reconciliation)
 • God Sups with Son - God Comes to Help: Son is Set Free = Create Own Dream Home
<u>Choices</u> (consecrated): New Life-force   (nature) --------------------------
- ---

Meeting God /Pleasure   (formal)   **Man/God (Easter)**
7.-------God's Will-----------**Perfect Son** (choices)-----Man's Will----
(companionship)   **Kingship**   (friendship)

****

Spirit Factory	Reality / Illusion	Body Factory
God's Son, Christ	Heaven/Earth	Mary's Son, Jesus
God becomes a Man - Christmas	God/Man	Man becomes God - Easter
(communion of saints)	Wine/Bread	(mystical body of Christ)

****

A n g e l s	(independence/oneness)	S a i n t s
Eternal Life	Get God's Love/**Rewards**/Get Bride's Love	**New Body**
(divine rights)	**H o l y** **R i g h t e o u s**	(human rights)
Blessings Gained **S a i n t s**	**C i t i z e n**	***Lessons Learned***
Purpose (society) (gain virtues)	(remove faults)	***Direction* (self)**

6. --------------------On-the-Job Training/Christ----------------------
(being set free)

L o v e   B e c o m i n g

5. --------------------College / Jesus   (love)----------------------
(think for oneself)

W i l l   K n o w i n g

Love (sanctified): New Soul (instincts) =

3rd Cup - Wedding Supper: Union of Friends = Priesthood for Groom/Laity for Bride
• Create Holy Church - Good Works: Power of Faith (output) = Get Royal Kingdom (sacrfice)
• God Touches Saint - God Recognizes His Covenant: Saints Save Others = Kingdom of Glory

= =

Teenager - Facing God's Judgment   (teach two commandments / spirit)= = = = = = = = =

Praise God - Give Wealth: Relative Focused Existence - Develop Character (purpose/service)
Easy Life Without Struggle   483 yrs. of Conversion   7 yrs. of Awaskening
• Being Saved - Redemption • Saving Self - Salvation   • Saving Others - Rewards

See God= =

4. - - - - - - - - - - - - - - - - High School / St. Joseph- - - - - - - - - - - - - - - -
(instinctive compulsion)

L a w   F a i t h f u l n e s s

Truth (anointed):   New Heart (emotions) = = = = = = = = = = = = = = = = = = =

2nd Cup - Betrothal: Union of Couple = Jesus Groom / Church Bride
•   Create Righteous Government - Prayers: Power of Trust (process) = Get New Body (submission)
•   God Speaks to Christian - God Hears Christian's Cries: Christian Saves Self = Heavenly Paradise

See Man= =

3.- - - - - - - - - - - Elementary Schoool / Virgin Mary (truth)- - - - - - - - - - - -
(unto thine own self be true)

Learn	Learn
Good from Evil	Right from Wrong
(truth/blessings)	(believing/lessons)

2. -------------------------------Home/Sinner-------------------------------

(submission)

| Experience
Church
(maturity/optional) | | Experience
World
(growth/required) |

1.- - - - - - - - - - - - - - - - - - - B i r t h/Ignorant Fool (survival)- - - - - - - - - - - - - - - - -

<u>Meeting Man/Pain</u> (informal)　　　(belief)

Child - Facing Lucifer's Test (learn ten coomandments/flesh)= = = = = = = = = = = = = = =

Worship God - Give Life: <u>Fixed Frame of Reference</u> = Personal Identity (meaning/existence)

400 yrs. Egyptian Slaves　　40 yrs. Desert Life　　　　50 yrs. Promised Land

　• Repentance　　　　　• Prayers　　　　　　• Works

<u>Survival</u> (blessed):　New Mind　(intellect)================================

1st Cup - Marriage Contract: Union of Two Fathers = God Offers Groom/Abraham Offers Bride

• Create Happy Home - Repentance: Power of Belief (input) - Get Eternal Life (belief)

• God Thinks of Sinner - God Sees Sinner's Sufferings: Sinner is Saved = Heaven on Earth

See Self===

Master Morals (divine law)	Master	Life/Defeat	Death	Master Ethics
	OFFER GOD: Life/Wealth/Labor			(human law)
	(flesh/blood/fat): Passover			
	(bread/wine/money): Mass			

- -

| Seeking
Heavenly Paradise
(new testament) | C r e a t e
S a i n t s
(salvation) | **GOD/MAN**
(Christmas) | F o r g i v e
S i n n e r s
(redemption) | Seeking
Heaven on Earth
(old testament) |

G　o　s　p　e　l- -E　p　i　s　t　l　e

(adulthood)　**Christ Gives Divinity/Jesus Takes-Sin**　(childhood)

See Spiritual Truth　　　　See Physical Truth

• Maturity - Emotions　　• Growth - Intellect

(get God's blessings)　　(defeat God's curses/lessons)

C　h　a　i　r - - - - - - - - - -A l t a r- - - - - - - - - -　P　u　l　p　i　t

• Listen to God	• Connect To God	• Speak to God
• Incarnate Word (soul)	• Spoken Word (flesh)	• Written Word (spirit)
• Defeat Demonic Possession	• Defeat Sin-nature	• Defeat Worldly Temptations
• Shekinah Glory (see God)	• Sunlight (see self)	• Candlelight (see man)

Prayer Offering - - - - - - -Priesthood/Kingship - - - - - -Blood Sacrifice

• Give Life	(supernatural order/natural order)	• Give Body
• Imitate		Obey

(open the gates of heaven)　**David's Throne/Aaron's Temple**　(close the gates of hell)

　　　　　• Prayer　　　　• Blood

This illustration shows that by "Mastering" both <u>High Morals</u> (divine law) and <u>Right-eous Ethics</u> (human law), a **Person can Pass** through **Seven Levels of Development**, thereby *Growing in Intellect* (righteousness/mind) and *Maturing in Emotional Stability* (holiness/heart). This awesome "Journey" begins with <u>Worshiping God</u> by **Giving the Lord One's Life** to **Establish** his own **Fixed Frame of Reference** (blank) to *Create his Own Personal Identity* (existence/self). Secondly, a "Person's Journey" <u>Enters a State</u> where He **Praises God** by **Giving the Lord His Wealth** which allows him to use **Relative Focused Existence** (zero) to *Develop His Own Character* (service/society). Finally, a "Person's Journey" ends when <u>He Thanks God</u> by **Giving the Lord His Labors** which **Allows** him to implement his own **Perception of Reality** (one) and *Present his Own Personality* (happiness/God). At "Each of These Levels" of <u>Growth</u> (obey) and <u>Maturity</u> (imitate), a **Person Recognizes** both his **Physical** and **Spiritual Development** as he <u>Progresses</u> from a *Child to Teenager to Adult*. This "Process Again Leads" to that question: just *What is Life All About*? The "Simple Answer" is <u>Having Something to Live For </u>(natural order) or **Giving Life Value** (supernatural order) through the *Forces of Nothing* (agony of defeat/loss) and *All* (thrill of victory/gain).

Land   1. **Live for the Challenge** - <u>Fight an Evil World:</u> Growing-up…See Limitations
             • Living in Man's Natural Order - Righteous Earth: Face Lucifer's Test
             • Learn God's Right from man's wrong - Deny Own Intellect

Babies   2. **Live for the Adventure** - <u>Surrender to Authority:</u> Maturing…See Potential
             • Living in God's Supernatural Order - Holy Heaven: Face God's Judgment
             • Learn God's Good from man's evil - Abandon Own Feelings

Life   3. **Live for the Fun of It All** - <u>Thinking for Oneself:</u> Becoming…
             See Self-worth
             • Living in God's/Man's Divine Order - Perfect Kingdom:
                Face Self-evaluation
             • Learn God's Will from man's will - Submit Own Free Will to God

The idea here is to see that through the "Forces of Growth (flesh/obey)" and "Maturity (spirit/imitate)," <u>We are Able</u> to **Search** for **Our Hearts' Desire** by **Building a Good Life** which leads to both the *Treasure of Human Love* (Man/mate) and the *Treasure of Divine Love* (God/sonship). The major theme of the "Life-experience (free will)" is <u>Formed</u> because of a **Person's Threat of Impending Doom** which has **Allowed** the **Human Race** to **Create a Couple** (Calvary/Resurrection) of *Treasured Moments in Life* (death/new-life). These "Treasured Moments" of <u>Death</u> and <u>New-life</u> are so **Valuable** (saving all creation) that **They Make** the **Entire Life-experience Worthwhile**, even **If a Person** *Only Lives for a Short-time*. Yes! We are in a "Creation of Two Truths" as <u>One Truth</u> (life) **Exists** in the **Never Created God** of *All* (reality/spirit/supernatural); while the <u>Other Truth</u> (death) **Exists** in the **Created Existence** of *Nothing* (illusion/flesh/natural). This means that each of "God's Children" is being required to decide whether to <u>Choose</u> between a **Few Moments of Earthly Death** or an **Eternal Life in Heaven** with *God* (Jesus Christ), *His Angels* (Saint Michael), and *His Saints* (Saint Joseph). Anyone would expect this "Choice" to be a <u>Slam-dunk</u> under normal circumstances, but we are talking about deciding just when a **Foolish Child** has become a **Clear Thinking Adult** and is ready to

Think for Himself. Note in the case of "Abraham and His Three Sons": Ishmael (oldest), Isaac (second), and Jesus (youngest) **How They Represent** both the **Growth and Maturity of Man** in the **Form** of the *Moslems* (goodness), the *Jews* (righteousness,) and *God's Messiah* (perfection). Through the "Three Sons of Abraham," we see the Purification of **Jerusalem** (sinner), *Promised Land* (repentant sinner), the *23 Arab Nations* (converted sinner), and finally, the *Christian World* (sinner to saint). Yes! through "God's Original Three Sons" of Cain (Ishmael), Abel (Isaac), and Seth (Jesus), the **Human Race** will **Come into Existence** via the **Forces** of **Random Chance** (relative truth), better known as *Darwin's Natural Selection*.

We must now "Take Our Minds" to Their Outer-limits to **Comprehend God's Paradoxical Nature,** where **His Grand Design System** is **Comprised** of **Absolute Truth, Destiny, Order, and Life** and where **Man's Natural Selection System** is **Comprised** of *Relative Truth, Free Will, Chaos, and Death* as **They Represent** the **Fission** and **Fusion Materials** of the *New God/Man Reality.* Now just imagine that the "Lord God Almighty" is so Divinely Wise that **He can Anticipate All the Forces of Random Chance** so **Precisely** that **He can Match** *His Design* (destiny) with *Future Random Events* (free will/natural selection). In this way, "God's Design" and "Man's Natural Selection" End Up the Same as **God is Able** to **Anticipate** and/or **Predict What** will **Actually Happen** via the **Forces of Random Chance,** thereby **Making Them One** and the **Same thing** (destiny/free will) at the *End of Time.*

The following tabular information indicates that "Whatever God Thinks" Simply Happens through the **Forces of Natural Selection** (random change), thereby **Causing God's Destiny** (absolute truth) and **Man's Free Will** (relative truth) to **Simply** be **Two Sides** of the *Same Coin*:

Explaining God's Paradoxical Motives
(God's never-created life-force *Matches* God's created-existence perfectly)

Never-created 1. **God's Grand Design** - God's Divine Will...Life/All is Perfect
(absolute truth) • God's Spirit Nature - In Christ as God (supernatural order)
  • God Wants to be Man - Via Life: Host (Easter)
Purification • God is in Search of a *Transfigured Body*   **All**
Destiny • Absolute Truth - God's Truth (intellect)   (Society)
(order) • Destiny - God's Law (emotions)
  • Order - God's Will (instincts)
  • Life - God's Love (nature)
  • God's Genetics - Circumstances: Creating the Spiritual Dimension
(Intellect - God's reality creates life/fission: life [host] creates holy saints in Heaven)

Created- 2. **Random Chance Creation** - Natural Selection... Death/All is Imperfect
existence • God's Fleshly Nature - Of Jesus as Man (natural order)
(relative truth) • Man Wants to be God - Via Death: Grave (Christmas)
Transformation • Man Passes through Death to become God in New-life (holiness)
Free Will • Man is in Search of *Eternal Life*   **Nothing**

(chaos)
- Relative Truth - Man's Truth (mind)   (individuality)
- Free Will - Man's Law (heart)
- Chaos - Man's Will (soul)
- Death - Man's Love (life-force)
- Man's Environment - Behavior: Creating the Physical Dimension
  (Emotions - Man's illusion creates death/fusion:
  death [grave] creates righteous citizens on Earth)

This illustration shows that "God's Son, Christ" Represents **God's Destiny** or *God's Grand Design on Earth* (absolute truth/all), while "Mary's Son, Jesus" Represents **Man's Free Will** or *Man's Natural Selection on Earth* (relative truth/nothing). It should now be clear just "Why God Needed" to Blend the **Flesh of Jesus** (physical dimension) with the **Spirit of Christ** (spiritual dimension) on **Mount Calvary** through the Two **Forces** of *Crucifixion* (death) and *Resurrection* (new-life). Through this "Mystical Merger (blend)" between God's Absolute Truth, Destiny, Order, and Life with Man's Relative Truth, Free Will, Chaos, and Death, the **Born-again Experience** has been **Created**, thereby **Making All Things One** in the *Nature of Christ*. Through this "Process," God's Genetic Nature (circumstance) and Man's Environmental Nature (behavior) are **Transformed** into the **New God/Man Reality** to bring forth both the *New Heaven* and the *New Earth*.

Obviously, the "Lord is Telling Us" that God Wants to be Man via **Life** (host), while Man Wants to be God via **Death** (grave), but this can **Never Happen** without **Blending God's Grand Design** (destiny) with **Man's Natural Selection** (free will) to **Make All and Nothing One** in *Christ Jesus*. We see this "Mystical Merger" of Life (all) and Death (nothing) being the **Impossible-of-the-impossible**. This **Challenges God** to the **Maximum of His Divine Abilities** since **He must Make** the *Never-created God* (grand design) **One** with the *Created God Jesus Christ* (natural selection). We see that once "God (reality)" and "His Creation (illusion)" have become One in **Truth, Law, Will, and Love, Divinity** (God) becomes *Supernatural Order* (spiritual) and **Humanity** (Man) becomes *Natural Order* (physical). In this way, "God's Social Order (society)" can Take Form, thereby **Creating** the *Royal Family of God*, while "Man's Individuality" can Take Form, thereby **Creating** the *Brotherhood of Man*.

We see the "Creation of Society" in the Old Testament (death of law) via the *Jewish People* and then the "Creation of Individuality" in the New Testament (birth of faith) via the *Christian People*. We can imagine here that "Society" is to be Baptized in Spirit by God (church) as **He Drowns His Law of Obedience** (circumcision) to **Change Man's Nature** (flesh) from *Human to Divine* and then "Individuality" is **to be Baptized in Spirit by Man** (world) as He Resurrects the God/Man Faith in God's Love (baptism) to **Wash Away Sin** (spirit) and **Change** *Sinfulness to Holiness*. The "Job of the Temple" is to Immerse God's Spirit in Death through the **Death of His Son, Christ** (God) on *Calvary;* while the "Job of the World" is to Raise God's Flesh into New-life through the **Resurrection** of *Mary's Son, Jesus* (Man). In like manner, the "Job of John the Baptist" was to Immerse Man's Flesh in Death (law) through the **Water Baptism of Jesus** in the *Jordan*; while the "Job of Jesus Christ" is to Raise Man's Spirit into New-life (faith) through **His Spiritual Baptism** in *God's Spirit*.

Temple   1. **Death to God's Law** (obedience) - Change Nature: Human to Divine...
New Society
- Drowned in God's Spirit - Kill Old Society: Father
- *Temple* Immerses God's Spirit in Death (circumcision)   **Society**

Save   • Babies Receive Knowledge - See Own Limitations   (purification)

Sinners   • Resurrected in Man's Water – New-life to New Society: Son
- *World* Raises God's Flesh into New-life (baptism)
- Teenagers Receive Self-awareness - See Own Potential
     (Jewish circumcision to Gentile baptism)

World   2. **New-life to Man's Faith** (love) - Wash Away Sin: Sinfulness to Holiness...
New Individuality
- Drowned in Man's Water - Kill Old Human Nature
- *John the Baptist* Immersed Man's Flesh in Death (law)   **Individuality**

Create   • Adults Receive Consciousness - See Own Self-worth   (transformation)

Saints   • Resurrected in God's Spirit – New-life to New Divine Nature
- *Messiah* Raises Man's Spirit into New-life (faith)
- Wise Men Receive Sentience - See Face of God

This illustration shows that "Old Human Society (human nature)" was to be Drowned (Judaism) by **God's Jewish Temple** to *Kill All its Evil* and then a "New Human Society (divine nature)" was to be Resurrected (Christianity) via the *Earth's Gentile World*. In like manner, the "Old Individual Nature" was Drowned (law) by **John the Baptist** to *Kill All its Sinfulness* and then a "New Individual Nature" was Resurrected (faith) by **Jesus Christ** to **Make All Men** into *Holy Saints*. "God's Son, Christ" has been Sent to Earth to **Kill Man's Old Society** by **Purifying Its Ignorant Collective Mind** and **Giving It** the **Mind of Christ** or a **Divinely Wise Mind Filled** with *God's Truths, Laws, Will, and Love.* In like manner "Mary's Son, Jesus" was Born on Earth to **Kill Man's Old Individuality** by **Transforming Its Cowardly Heart** and **Giving It** the **Heart of Christ** or **Washing Away** *Its Sins of Sin, Evil, and Death.* Through "These Two Transformations," **Man's Original Sin** was **Reversed** and the **Human Race** can be **Saved** via **Jesus' Blood** (individual) and **Christ's Spirit** (society) as **Mankind Eats** the *Lord's Flesh* (bread) and **Drinks** the *Lord's Blood* (wine). The idea here is that "Man's Ability to Change" from Evil to Good **Comes** through **Christ's Social Spirit** (communication/sharing) and **Jesus' Individual Blood** (born-again), thereby **Defeating His** *Sin-nature, Worldly Temptations, Demonic Possessions, and God's Curses.*

1. **God's Son, Christ** - Sent to Earth to Kill Old Society...Purify into a New Society
   - Spirit - Fulfill God's Law of Obedience: Change Nature = Human to Divine
2. **Mary's Son, Jesus** - Born of Woman to Kill Old Individual...Transform into New Individual
   - Flesh - Fulfill Man's Faith in God's Love: Wash Away Sins = Sinful to Holy

This illustration shows that the "Lord God Almighty Needed" Two Separate Redemptive Systems to **Save** both **Human Society** (destiny/free will) and the **Individual Person** himself (law/faith) so the **Lord Made Never-created Existence** (God) into *Life* and **Created Existence** (Man) into *Death*. To "Comprehend" this Mystical Concept, the **All of God** (spirit nature) would have to become **Nothing** (cast into oblivion) to bring forth a **Created God** (physical nature), **Who could Live** and have his *Being On Earth*. In like manner then, the "Human Nothing" or "Created God" would have to Sacrifice Himself to **Save God** from **Eternal Oblivion**, thereby **Returning Him Back** to *His Original State of All*. We now see the "Supreme Purpose" of Jesus Christ in both **His Death** (law) via **Crucifixion** and **His New-life** (faith) via **Resurrection** is through these **Two Functions** where **Human Society** is *Purified* (divinity/give) and **One's Individual Nature** is *Transformed* (holiness/host). The theme here is that "God Wants to become Man" to Create Mankind, while "Man Wants to become God" to Save God from His Supreme Sacrifice, thereby **Creating** a *Mutual Admiration Society* or the *New God/Man Reality* (mutual friendship). This now explains "Many of God's Contradictions" coming from His Paradoxical Logic as the **Lord is Using** a **Two-Truth System**, where the **Existence of All** (life/destiny) and **Nothing** (death/free will) can **Occupy** the *Same-space* (matter) at the *Same-time* (energy).

To "Understand God," a Person must Recognize both his **Mortality** (grave/natural order) and also his **Immortality** (host/supernatural order), thereby **Revealing His Dual Roles** both in *Society* (social rights) and as an *Individual* (personal rights). This means that the "Lord God Almighty" has Established both a **Set of Inalienable Rights** for the **Properly Educated** (adults) and a **Set of Privileges** for *All Ignorant Fools* (baby), thereby **Separating** *God's Chosen Children* (saints) from *Lucifer's Pagan World* (sinners). Through these "Two Groups," the Human Race is to be **Divided** into **One Righteous Society** (giving) versus **Masses of Selfish Individuals** (taking). Thus, it has been the **Job of Jesus Christ** to **Separate** the *Good Souls* (sheep) from the *Evil Souls* (goats). Obviously, "God's Son" has Two Redemptive Systems with **One Giving Mankind Free Redemption** for *All Pagans* (flesh) and then a **Second One, Allowing Believers** (spirit) to **Earn Their Own Salvation** through *Their Repentance, Prayers, Works, and the Number of Souls Saved*. Both the Lord God Almighty (God) and His Creation (Man) are **Depending** upon "These Two Systems" to **Purify Man's Spiritual Nature** and **Transform Man's Physical Nature** (flesh) to bring forth both *Eternal Life* (purify host) and his *New Transfigured Body* (purify grave).

The idea here is that "Originally," the Lord God Almighty **Decided to Sacrifice Himself** to the **Max** (oblivion) to **Create** the **Existence of Life** (creation), **Believing** and **Trusting His Creation** to be **Willing** to then **Sacrifice Itself** in **Turn** to **Save Him Right Back**. Yes! Our "Divine Creator" Took an Awesome Gamble as He **Literally Put His Eternal Life On the Line** to bring forth both a **Human God** (Jesus) and a **Divine Man** (Christ) on **Earth, Who** would **Sacrifice Themselves** to **Save All** the **Babies, Create** *Righteous Citizens* (know), *Holy Saints* (love), *Perfect Sons* (serve), and finally, *Free Men of Infinite Perfection* (befriend). We can "Now See the Perfection" of **Our God** and come to Realize that We are All in an Eternal

Partnership with the Never-created Divinity (benevolent force) of Infinite Truth as It Strives to Make <u>All Things One</u> in the *Lord's Communion of Saints* (society/spirit) and the *Mystical Body of Christ* (individuals/flesh). The idea here is to see that "Life Crucifies the Flesh (pain)" to <u>Teach the Human Race</u> the *Lessons of Life* (free divine nature); while "Death Resurrects the Spirit (pleasure)" to <u>Bless the Human Race</u> with *God's Acceptance and His Approval* (earn holiness). Now we see that "Destiny Kills" <u>Free Will</u> to **Create** the **New Earth** (Jewish People) or bring *Heaven on Earth* (new body/citizenship); while "God's Law Kills" <u>Man's Faith</u> to **Create** the **New Heaven** (Christian People) or bring forth *Paradise in Heaven* (eternal life/sainthood).

This means that the "Lord God Almighty Realized" that to <u>Get the Treasures of Life</u> (birth/life/death/eternal life), **He** would have to **Give-up His Own** *Wisdom* (intellect), *Courage* (emotions), *Generosity* (instincts), and even *His Unselfishness* (nature). In this way, "Our Creator God" could bring forth <u>Baby Ignorance, Cowardice, Greed</u>, and <u>Selfishness</u> to be **Transformed** into **Man's Wisdom, Courage, Generosity,** and **Unselfishness** through *His Son, Jesus Christ*. The "Lord's Greatest Miracle" <u>Comes with the Union</u> of **Man's Newly Purified Society** and **Man's Newly Transformed Behavior** (individual) in the **New Nature of God**, thereby **Making Nature, Men, and God One** in *Truth, Law, Will, and Love*. Through this "Union Concept," <u>God has United</u> **Man's Spiritual Nature** via the *Lord's Communion of Saints* (individual/Heaven) or *Sainthood* and then **God United Man's Physical Nature** via the *Mystical Body of Christ* (society/Earth) or *Citizenship*. The theme here is that "God is Coming" through <u>Man's Physical Nature</u> (world) or **Christmas** (life) to **Meet Man** in **God's Spiritual Nature** (church) or **Easter** (death) and then *They* are both **Resurrected** into the *New Born-again God/Man Nature*.

The following tabular information indicates that the "Human Race is Passing" through a <u>Three-Phased Conversion System</u> from **Life** (God), to **Death** (Man) and then into the **God/Man Union** via *Resurrection*:

Meeting of God and Man in Life (God), Death (Man), and in Resurrection

Grave		Host	
God Sacrifices Himself		**Man Sacrifices Himself**	
Life		Death	
Purify		**Transform**	
Society		**Individual**	
God wants to become Man		Man wants to become God	
Eternal	Son of God	John the	Jesus Christ
Father	(2nd person)	Baptist	(Messiah)
Circumcision	Baptism	God's Law of Obedience	Man's Faith in God's Love
Jewish People	Christians	Water Baptism	Spiritual Baptism

Lessons -	Divine Nature	Blessings -	Holiness
1. Destiny Kills	1. Free Will Resurrects	1. Law Kills	1. Faith Resurrects
2. Immersed in	2. Raised in	2. Immersed in Waters	2. Raised in Spirit
God's Spirit	Man's Flesh	of Sinful Death	of Born-again Life
(death to	(new-life to	(death to	(life to
Old Testament)	New Testament)	old nature)	new nature)
3. Take Lucifer's Test	3. Face God's Judgment	3. Make Self-evaluation	3. Freedom
4. Sacrifice All	4. *God's Divinity*	4. Sacrifice Nothing	4. *Christ's Holiness*
5. Sac. God's Wisdom	5. Get Ignorant Baby	5. Sac. Ignorance	5. Get Wisdom
6. Sac. God's Courage	6. Get Teen Cowardice	6. Sac. Cowardice	6. Get Courage
7. Sac. God's Generosity	7. Get Adult Greed	7. Sac. Greed	7. Get Generosity
8. Sac. God Unselfishness	8. Get Wise Man Selfishness	8. Sac. Selfishness	8. Get Unselfishness

Life Crucifies the Flesh	Death Resurrects the Spirit
1st Redemptive System	**2nd Redemptive System**
God is Man on Earth - Flesh	Man is God in Heaven - Spirit
. New Body (Christmas)	. Eternal Life (Easter)
(likes painful challenges)	(likes painless adventures)
. Crucify Son of Man - Jesus	. Resurrect Son of God - Christ
. Law - Grave (works)	. Host - Faith (prayer)
. Justice Seeks Punishment	. Mercy Seeks Forgiveness
. Mastering the World - Jesus	. Mastering the Church - Christ
. Unite with Communion of Saints	. Unite with Mystical Body of Christ

This illustration shows that "Life Crucifies the Flesh" and "Death Resurrects the Spirit" to Purify Society (new body) and to Transform Individual Behavior (eternal life) to bring forth both the ***Lessons of Life*** (get divine nature) and ***God's Blessings*** (get holiness). Out of "These Two Conversion Experiences," God Creates **His Dual Redemptive Systems: One to Save Man's Individual Spirit** (Heaven) and the **Other** to **Save Man's Social Flesh** (Earth) to bring ***God to the Earth*** (Jesus' nature) and then to bring ***Man to Heaven*** (Christ's nature). Finally, the "Earthly God" and the "Heavenly Man" are to become One in the **Lord's Justice, Mercy, and Love** to bring forth a **Set of Human Grading Systems** for the ***Mind*** (intellect), ***Heart*** (emotions), and ***Soul*** (instincts).

This implies that "Man's Physical Nature" Loves Painful Challenges as he **Tests his Mettle Against All** *Potential Challengers* (competition); while "Man's Spiritual Nature" Loves Painless Adventures (cooperation) as **He** becomes a **Servant to All** to **Further the Cause** of the ***General Welfare***. We see this in the "Mystical Process" of Selfish and Unselfish Endeavors that the **Human Race** is **Forced to Choose** between a **Life** of **All Prayer** (spirit) or a **Life** of **All Works** (flesh). But with the **Coming of Christ, All Things are Placed** into **Perfect Balance** between ***God's Life*** (host) and ***Man's Death*** (grave). It should now make sense just "Why the Lord God Almighty" was Required to **Sacrifice Himself Three Times** as **He Brought** forth **Life** so that **Mankind would Come** to ***Know Him***, then **Death** so that **Mankind would Come** to *Love Him*, and finally, **He Brought** forth **Resurrection** so **that Mankind would Come** to *Serve Him*.

1. **Eternal Father Expects Perfection** - Too Much Justice: Pass/Fail Grading System … See Limitations
    *   Measure the Level of Human Intellect - Ignorance to Wisdom: Knowledge (new mind)
    *   God Gives Life - *Man Comes to Know God*: Thank God by Giving Him Labors = Worthy of New Body
2. **Son of God Rank Orders Everyone** - Too Much Mercy: Graded on Curve System … See Potential
    *   Measure the Level of Human Emotions - Cowardice to Courage: Self-awareness (new heart)
    *   God Gives Death - *Man Comes to Love God*: Praise God by Giving Him Wealth = Worthy of Eternal Life
3. **Father/Son Equality for All Men** - Balance God/Man Love: Graded on Handicap System …See Self-worth
    *   Measure the Level of Human Instinct - Greed to Generosity: Consciousness (new soul)
    *   God Gives Resurrection - *Man Serves God*: Worship God by Giving Him Life = Worthy of Own Kingdom

This illustration shows that the "Holy Trinity" is Using God's **Justice, Mercy, and Love** to **Measure** the **Specific Levels** of **Human Self-control** via **One's Intellect, Emotions,** and **Instincts** as **Each of God's Children Comes** to **Know, Love, and Serve** *His most Beloved Heavenly Father.* This means that the "God/Man Relationship" is Centered upon the **Forces of Human Death** and **Divine Resurrection** as the **Human Race Strives** to **Reject** its **Ignorance, Cowardice, and Greed** to **Attain God's Blessing** of *Wisdom, Courage, and Generosity.* To comprehend this "Process of Death" and "Resurrection" which God is Using for the **Purification of the World,** we must **Recognize** that the **Lord** is **Starting in Jerusalem/Temple** (divine blood) and then in the **Area** around **Jerusalem** known as the *Promised land.* This "Purification" of Jerusalem and its Holy Lands actually **Began During** the **1st Advent of Christ** (Heaven on Earth) when the **Lord Came to Earth** as a **Priest on a Donkey** to place *His Purifying Blood* upon *Mount Calvary.* Secondly, the "Purification" of the 23 Arab Nations will come as **Islam** is **Converted into Christianity** as a **Buffer Against Evil** to *Protect Israel* from any *Wicked Contamination.* This "2nd Purification" of Islam and its Blessed Lands actually **Will Begin** during the **2nd Advent of Christ** (Paradise in Heaven) when the **Lord Returns to Earth** as a **Thief in the Night** to place *Man's Purifying Blood* (guilty/seal saints) upon the *Earth* (tribulation). Thirdly, the "Purification" of 120 Christian Nations will come as the **Church is Made Holy,** thereby **Creating Another Buffer Against Evil** to *Protect Israel* from any *Wicked Contamination.* Finally, via this "3rd Purification" of Christianity, the Remainder of Planet Earth will come into **Christ** or during the *Lord's* **3rd Advent** (Kingdom of Glory). During the "Lord's Third Advent," **He Returns to Earth** as a **Just Judge on a Cloud** to place **Man's Saintly Blood** (forgiven) upon the *Earth* (end of the world). This depiction of the future now gives us a "Picture" of God's

Grand Design in its **Completed Form** as the **Lord** is then **Ready to Judge His Plan of Redemption** (purification) in *All Its Splendor and Glory*.

1. 1st Circle - Around Temple in Jerusalem: Protected by Promised Lands...Divine Level
   * Abraham Makes Personal Offering – Circumcision— God Offers Man His Life
2. 2nd Circle - Around Israel: 23 Arab Nations Protect Home of God...Sacred Level
   * Abraham Offers God his Son - Isaac's Life— God Offers Man His Wealth
3. 3rd Circle - Around Middle East: 120 Christian Nations Protect God's Earthly Home... Holy Level
   * Abraham Offers God Three Animals - Ram/Goat/Heifer— God Offers Man His Labors

Note that "God Appears" to be a Farmer of Life **Who** is *Tilling the Soil* (Messiah/repentance), then *Planting the Seed* (Pope/prayers), next *Watering His Crops* (priesthood/works), and finally, the **Lord is Able** to *Harvest the Fruits of Life* (laity/save souls). This means that "Out" of God's Nature (divine), the Jewish Nature (human/divine), the Arab Nature (human), and finally the Christian Nature of Christ (divine/human), the **Lord's** *Kingdom of Glory can be Built*. This now reveals the "Essence" associated with the Abrahamic Covenant as Father Abraham's Circumcision represents the **Purification** of *Jerusalem*; then Isaac's Offering (bloodless) represents the **Purification** of the *Promised Land*; next, the Animal Offering (ram/goat/heifer) represents the **Purification** of the *Arab Nations;* and finally, **Abraham's Desire** to Save Sodom and Gomorrah represents the **Purification** of the *120 Holy Nations of Christianity*. This now "Gives Us a Clear Picture" of God's 7,000-Year Creation **Beginning with Adam** (sinner/breath of life) and **Ending** with the **End of the World** (saint/3rd Advent) via *Four Stages of Purification* (divine/perfect/holy/righteous). It is now clear that the "Lord God Almighty" has always been Working from an extremely **Detailed Set of Plans** and that **Nothing** has been **Left to Chance** when it comes to **Redeeming the Minds, Hearts, Souls,** and **Life-forces** of *His Beloved Children*.

The following graphic illustration shows us that "Our Messiah" Worships God by **Giving Him** a *Divine Life*; the "Jews" Praise God by **Giving Him** their *Perfect Lives*; "Islam" Thanks God by **Giving Him Their** *Righteous Lives;* and the "Christians" Honor God by **Giving Him Their** *Holy Lives* (saints):

Christ Saves 144 Pagan Nations
(12 tribes x 12 apostles = 144 natures)

Purification of Jerusalem, Promised Land, Arab States, and Whole World with Christ's Blood
(Messiah, Jews, Muslims, and Christians
purify the evil nature of man one territory at a time)

3rd Advent	120 Christian Nations of World -	**Christ** (save gentiles)
. Saving Others	(Messiah's holy blood) -	Harvesting the Fruits (save souls)

2nd Advent	23 Arab Nations - **Ishmael**	(save the Sadducees)
. Saving Self	(Spirit's righteous blood) -	Watering the Crops (works)
1st Advent	Promised Land of Israel -	**Isaac** (save Pharisees [prayers])
Jewish Faith	Jerusalem - **Abraham**	(Jesus/save God's Son)
. Saviors	(Son's divine blood)........	Tilling the Soil (repentance)
	Messiah's Religion........	Kingship
	(worship God - give life)	. Authority (rules)
Title Deed to Earth	Jewish Religion..........	Royal Household
. New Body	(praise God - give wealth)	. Responsible (institutions)
Title Deed to Heaven	Muslim Religion............	Noble Class
. Eternal Life	(thank God - give labors)	. Duty (policies)
Title Deed to Kingdom	Christian Religion...........	Peasant Class
. Royal Kingdom	(honor God - give gifts)	. Task (workload)

This illustration shows that the "Lord is Working" from the Middle Outward using **Four Stages of Purification** from *Jerusalem* (Abraham/Jesus), to the ***Promised Land*** (Isaac/Jews), the ***23 Arab Countries*** (Ishmael/Muslims), and finally, to the ***120 Holy Nations of Christ*** (Christ). In this way, the "Lord could Purify" Jerusalem in **His Divine Blood** (Messiah), the Promised Land (1st nation) in **Perfect Blood** (Pope), the 23 Arab Countries in **Righteous Blood** (priesthood), and the 120 Holy Nations in **Holy Blood** (laity) to **Transform 144 Pagan Nations** into *God's Kingdom of Glory*.

1. **Temple/Jerusale**m - Purified in Divine Blood: Mount Calvary.... See God
   - Sons of God - See God Face-to-face (beatific vision): Center Point
   - Messiah's Sacrifice - Saves Divinity (Abrahamic Covenant)
2. **Promised Land** - Purified in Perfect Blood: Christ's Resurrection...Serve God
   - Holy Saints - Serve God within His Kingdom: 1st Circle
   - Pope's Sacrifice - Saves Israel and the Chosen People (priest on a donkey)
3. **23 Arab Nations** - Purified in Righteous Blood: Bloody Sacrifice... Love God
   - Devout Christians - Love God in Heaven: 2nd Circle
   - Priesthood Sacrifice - Saves Middle East (thief in the night)
4. **120 Christian Nations** - Purified in Holy Blood: Bloodless Sacrifice...Know God
   - Righteous Citizens - Know God on the Earth: 3rd Circle
   - Laity Sacrifice - Saves Lost of the World (just judge on cloud)

The message here is that out of "Christ's 144 Nations (earth)," God is Going to **Fill His Heaven** with **Saints,** **Fill His Kingdom** with **Sons,** and **Fill Himself** with

Human Love (infinite number of babies) to bring forth *Heaven on Earth* for *One and All*. Note that to "Save 144 Pagan Nations," God had to Create 12 Tribes and 12 Apostles and then **Multiplied Them** into **144 Nations of Christ** to **Call** (earth), **Enlighten** (Heaven), **Awaken** (Kingdom), and **Indwell** (Self) *All the Peoples of the Earth*. Through this "Method of Purification (blood)," the Lord could Save the **Son of God** (Mosaic Tabernacle) to **Create** the *Royal Kingdom;* Save the **Pharisees** (1st advent) to **Create** the *New Heaven;* Save the **Sadducees** (2nd advent) to **Create** the *New Earth;* and finally, Save the **Gentiles** (3rd advent) to **Create** the *Eternal-self* (life). Obviously, the "Son's Salvation (kingdom)" brings forth the Kingship of God; the "Pharisees' Salvation (eternal life)" brings forth the Royal Household of God; the "Sadducees' Salvation (new body)" brings forth the Noblemen of God; and finally, the "Gentiles' Salvation (freedom/self)" brings forth the Peasant Class of God. The idea here is that the "Authority" of the Kingship (parents) *Sets* the *Rules of Life;* the "Responsibility" of the Royal Household (attorney/royalty) *Sets* the *Institutions of Life;* the "Duty" of the Noble Class (accountants/aristocrats) *Sets* the *Policies of Life;* and the "Tasks" of the Peasant Class (poor) *Sets* the *Work Load of Life*. This means that the "Price for Saving Jerusalem" is Different than for Saving the **Promised Land, Arab Nations,** and the **Christian World** as **Each Land Mass must be Redeemed** by an *Appropriate Level of Perfection before God*. Obviously, "Rank has Its Privileges;" therefore, it takes a Messiah to *Save Jerusalem*; and only a Pope to *Save the Promised Land*; a Priesthood to *Save the Arabs;* and finally, the Laity to *Save the Christians*. We see that "Each of These" Purifications" will occur during the Three Advents of Christ as **He Came** to **Earth** on a *Donkey* (1st), then will come as a *Thief* (2nd), and finally, as a *Just Judge* on a *Cloud* (3rd).

It can now be seen that through the "Priest on a Donkey (1st advent)," a "Thief in the Night (2nd advent)," and a "Just Judge on a Cloud (3rd advent)," the Human Race can be **Saved** from its *Curses of Sin* (sin-nature), *Evil* (worldly temptations), and *Death* (demonic possession). This entire "Redemptive Process" is Centered upon the **Creation of God's Government** on *Earth,* **God's Church** in *Heaven,* and **God's Home** within the *Lord's Kingdom*. Through these "Three Institutions of Life," God's Son can come to **Mankind** and **Transform** its **Sinful Mind** (earth), **Evil Heart** (Heaven), and **Dead Soul** (Kingdom) into *Holy Perfection*. This means that during the "1st Advent," there was a Great War (priest on a donkey) between **God's Government** and **Man's Government** as the **Lord Fought** for the *Title Deed to the Earth*. Secondly, during "Christ's 2nd Advent," there will be Another War (thief in the night) between **God's True Church** and **All Other Pagan Churches** as the **Lord Fights** for the *Title Deed to Heaven*. Finally, during "Christ's 3rd Advent," there will be a Final War (just judge on a cloud) between **God's Nations** and **Lucifer's Nations** as the **Lord Fights** for the *Title Deed to the Kingdom of Glory*.

With the completion of these "Three Great Conflicts" the Lord God Almighty will **Purify His Creation** and **Destroy All Its Evil Forces,** thereby **Transforming It** into a *New Heaven and New Earth*. In this "Conversion" of a Dead People into Newlife, **God** will **Rank Order His Creation** from **Kings to Peasants Giving Each Person** his **Own Level of Authority** based on **His** *Assigned Divine Rank*. In the "Government of God," a Person can Enter the **Executive Branch** to become a *King,* or <u>Enter</u> the **Legislative Branch** to become a *Member* of the *Royal Household,* or <u>Enter</u> the <u>Judicial Branch</u> to become a **Member** of *God's Nobility,* or finally, <u>Enter</u> <u>God's Citizenry</u> to become a *Member* of *His Peasant Class of Workers*. Secondly, in the "Church of God," a <u>Person can Enter</u> the **Messiah Level** to *Receive* a *Fleshly Blessing of Life*, or <u>Enter</u> the **Pope Level** to *Receive* a *Blood Anointing of Life,* or <u>Enter</u> the **Priesthood Level** to *Receive* a *Death Sanctification of Life*, or finally, <u>Enter</u> the **Laity Level** to *Receive* a *Damnation Consecration of Life*. Finally, in the "Home of God," a <u>Person can Enter</u> the **Fatherhood Level** to **Like All Things** that are *Good*, or <u>Enter</u> the **Motherhood Level** to **Love All Things** that are *Beloved*, or <u>Enter</u> the **Eldest Level** to **Cherish All Things** that are *Righteous* (father), or finally, <u>Enter</u> the **Youngest Level** to be **Devoted to All Things** that are *Holy* (mother). Through these "Twelve Levels of Life," a <u>Person can Find</u> his **Own Identity** and his **Own Rank-order Position** before <u>God</u> as he *Strives* to *Deny his Intellect, Abandon his Feelings,* and *Submit his Free Will to God.*

The following tabular information indicates that there are "Three Governing Forces" which <u>Rule God's Kingdom of Glory</u> in the **Form** of *God's Government* (earth), *God's Church* (Heaven), and *God's Home* (Kingdom):

The Three Governing Forces Ruling God's Kingdom
are Based on Four Levels of Divine Authority
(price for entering Heaven via one's rank
and personal status before God measured in loss)

Government	Church	Home
(Kingdom/son)	(Heaven/priest)	(earth/king)
1. Executive - King Pays Little	1. Messiah - Comforts are Lost	1. Father - Arrested
• Air Contract (word)	• Flesh Blessing	• Likes It (good)
2. Legislative - Royal Household Pays Some	2. Pope - Fearful of Loss	2. Mother - Agony
• Water Contract (handshake)	• Blood Anointing	• Loves Them
3. Judicial - Nobility Pays a Lot	3. Priesthood - Painful Loss	3. Eldest - Scourged
• Oil Contract (seal)	• Death Sanctification	• Cherish Father
4. Citizenry - Peasant Class Pays All	4. Laity - Loss of Life	4. Youngest - Crucified
• Blood Contract (sacrifice)	• Damnation Consecration	• Devoted to Mother
(war between God and Man)	(war between all religions)	(war between nations)

This illustration shows that the "Earth" is <u>God's Government</u> (physical); "Heaven" is <u>God's Church</u> (spiritual); and the "Kingdom" is <u>God's Home</u> (mystical) which are to be filled with **God's Beloved Children** through the *Lord's* coming *Communion of Saints*. This need to have "Three Divine Institutions" to <u>House God/sons</u> (Kingdom), <u>His Angels</u> (Heaven), and <u>His Saints</u> (earth) **Forces the Lord** to **Purify the Human Race** by **Testing It** through *Lucifer* (sin-nature/overcome lie), *God's Judgment* (worldly temptations/overcome temptations), and *One's Own Self-evaluation* (demonic possession/overcome evil). In this "System" of <u>Measuring Individual Aptitude,</u> the **High Performers** can **Purchase a High Position** with *Little or No Effort*; while

Those Who Score Low on the **Aptitude Scale** must <u>**Purchase Their Position**</u> by *Passing through the Torments of Hell*. This means that "Those Who" become "Executives (air contract)," "Messiahs (flesh blessing)," and "Fathers (like it)" become the <u>Rulers</u> of *God's Government, Church, and Home*, while "Those Who" become "Citizens (blood contract)," "Laity (damnation consecration)," and "Youngest Children (devoted to mother)" become the <u>Servants</u> within *God's Government, Church, and Home*.

The question is: "Do You Want" to be a <u>Ruler</u> or a <u>Servant</u> within *God's Eternal Kingdom*? Obviously, the "Lord is Trying" to <u>Give Each of His Children</u> **Every Opportunity** to **Succeed in Life** by <u>**Hammering Home**</u> the *Teachings of Christ* (Messiah) and the *Doctrinal Truths of Christ's Church* (Pope). This "Godly Desire" to <u>Make All of God's Children</u> **Distinguished Executives** (government), **Messiahs** (church), and **Fathers** (home) *Drives the Lord* as He <u>**Strives to Increase**</u> the *Intensity of His Purifying Tests* unto *Their Max Performance Levels* (pain). Therefore, "If You are Facing" a <u>Great Struggle in Life,</u> this means that **God is Trying** desperately to **Make You a Saint** and **All that is Needed** is for <u>**You to Surrender**</u> to the <u>**Lord's Divine Will**</u> by *Denying Your Intellect, Abandoning Your Feelings*, and *Submitting Your Free Will to God.* In "God's Grand Design," <u>He is Building a Home</u> to **Transform Flesh** (survival), then a <u>Church</u> to **Transform Spirits** (truth), then a <u>Government</u> to **Transform Souls** (love), and finally, a <u>Perfect Man</u> to **Transform His Life-forces** (choice) into the *Mystical Nature of God*. This means that a "Person's Home" is <u>Coming Out of the Union</u> of *Two Fathers;* the "Church" is <u>Coming Out of the Union</u> of a *Loving Couple*; the "Government" is <u>Coming Out of the Union</u> of *Two Sets of Friends;* and finally, the "Perfect Man" is <u>Coming Out of the</u> Union of *Two Families.*

"God has Created" <u>Four Mystical Institutions"</u> of **Infinite Learning** to <u>**Teach His Children**</u> *Right from Wrong* (home), *Good from Evil* (church), *God's Will from Man's Will* (government), and finally, *God's Reality from Man's Illusion* (perfect man). It is no wonder that the "Human Race" has become so <u>Confused</u> as **God is Teaching Individuals, Societies, Worlds,** and **Kingdoms** how to <u>**Think for Themselves**</u> (balance all things) *Using* an *Infinite Set of Earthly Tools*. The question is: "When" will the "Human Race" <u>Figure Out</u> just how to **Apply** the **Right Tool** to the **Right Solution/job** so <u>**It Might Attain**</u> the *Right Results*? The answer to this question will come on that "Glorious Day" <u>When Stiff-necked Man</u> (egomaniac/individualism) **Realizes** that **Life is Not About Works**, but it is about <u>**Dying to His Selfishness**</u> (submission), thereby **Allowing** the <u>**Human Race**</u> to *Share All It has with Others* (slavery/social order). Obviously, we are "All Babies Living" within an <u>Illusion of Life</u> or a <u>Divine Simulator</u> (incubator of life) which is **Designed to Introduce Divine Concepts** to a **New-born Person**, who can barely **Stand Much Less Walk,** so **God**, for some reason, thinks it's about time to introduce this **New-born Infant** to His **New Creation** by teaching him *Nuclear Physics*. It is no wonder that the "Human Race Panicked" and from their sheer <u>Ignorance</u> (baby), became a bunch of <u>Wild Criminals</u> (teenagers) who quickly **Failed at Life**, thereby **Driving Them** into <u>**Insanity**</u> (adult) to the point of reaching a *State of Pure Evil* (wise man).

The message here is that the "Human Race" is in a <u>Process</u> of <u>Contacting God</u> (altar/church), then <u>Speaking to God</u> (pulpit/world), and finally, <u>Listening to God's Advice</u> (chair/kingdom) through the **Blood of the Church** (priesthood) and the **Prayers of the World** (kingship). This "Communication Process" allows <u>Each of God's Children</u> to **Interface** with his **God** through the **Intercessory Tools** of **Worship** (give life), **Praise** (give wealth), and **Thanksgiving** (give labor) **Brought into Reality** via *His Repentance* (being saved), *Prayers* (saving self), and *Works* (saving others). We see that the "Jewish People" were <u>Egyptian Slaves</u> (repentance/slave) for **400 years**, then <u>Wandered in the Desert</u> (prayer/slave and free) for **40 years.** They then fought for the <u>Promised Land</u> (works/free man) for another **50 years**, all to **Appease God's** *Striking Wrath* (hate), *Vocal Rage* (enemy), and *Silent Anger* (fool). In short, it has taken the "Jewish People" some <u>490 Years</u> (curse of Lamech) to just make **Contact with God** through **His Sacred Altar** simply to **Open One Channel** (1st advent/physical) of *Human Communication*. Secondly, it has taken the "Christian Faith" some <u>483 Years</u> to become **Converted** and now must face a <u>Seven-Year Tribulation</u> to become **Awakened** to **God's Law** (blood sacrifice) and **Faith** (prayer offering) to **Open Channel Two** (2nd advent/spiritual) of *Human Communication*. Finally, it will take the "Living Saints" another <u>1,000 Years of Peace</u> to become **Transformed** and then **Face God's White Throne Judgment** (Christians), **Making Mankind** become *Wise Enough* to *Evaluate Its Own Self* (saints). The ability to "Evaluate Oneself" comes through <u>Christ's Altar </u>(contact God), <u>Pulpit</u> (speak to God), and <u>Chair</u> (listen to God) <u>Concepts of Intercession </u>during the **Mass** which eventually becomes **Man's Church** (community), **World** (society), and **Kingdom** (mankind) of **Intercession All to be Manifested** at the *End of the World* (3rd advent/mystical). At this point, the "Slave of Death (world)" and the "Free Man of Life (church)" will <u>Find</u> that **Delicate Balance** between *Knowing It All* (individuality) and being a *Humble Fool* (slave) *before Men*.

The implication here is that "If You are Just One Man," then your <u>Repentance</u> (defeat sin-nature), <u>Prayers</u> (defeat worldly temptations), and/or <u>Works</u> (defeat demonic possession) will **Hold Little** or **No Weight** with the *Forces of Divine Justice*. But "If You Represent (God's Son)," an <u>Entire Church</u> as well as <u>Planet Earth,</u> plus **Owning** some <u>Awesome Kingdom of Glory </u>and then come before **God's Divine Justice to Make an Appropriate Offering of Trillions of Souls** unto the <u>Majesty of God,</u> then the *Lord will Graciously Listen* and *Bless You*. Understanding this "Need to both Grow (obey)" and "Mature (imitate)" from <u>Nothing</u> (man) to <u>All</u> (God) <u>Sets the Requirements</u> for being **Able** to **Bear Fruit, Pressed Down** (spoken word), **Shaken Together** (written word), and **Overflowing** (incarnate word) to bring forth a **Treasurehouse of Life** unto *One's God*. In short, we must first make a "Contact with God" via <u>Our Altar</u> through a **Priest's Spoken Word** to **Defeat Our Sin-nature**, thereby **Allowing Us** to *Walk* in the *Sunlight of Life* (outer court). Secondly, we are to "Speak to God (spirit)" via <u>Our Own Pulpit</u> through the **Laity/Priesthood Readings of the Written Word** to **Defeat Worldly Temptations,** thereby **Allowing Us** to *Pray* in the *Candlelight of Sanctified Life* (holy place). Finally, we are to "Listen to God (soul)" via <u>Our Own Chair</u> when the **Congregation Receives** the **Incarnate**

Word (host) of **God** to **Defeat Demonic Possession,** thereby **Allowing Us** to *Enter* the *Shekinah Glory of Divine Life* (holy of holies).

In the previous "Chart," we see that the centerpiece of Every Church is **Formed** through its **Altar** (contact God), **Pulpit** (speak to God), and **Chair** (listen to God) which **Opens Three Channels of Communication** between *Man and his God*. This means that everything in "God's Creation" is Growing (natural selection) and Maturing (grand design) to the point of being of **Service** to **God, Angels, and Men** through the **Forces** of *Knowledge* (mind/physical/survival), *Self-awareness* (heart /spiritual/truth), *Consciousness* (soul/mystical/love), and finally, *Sentience* (life-force/divine/choices). We must imagine that we are "Traveling" from Man's Repentance to God's Forgiveness by **Learning** the *Ten Commandments* (flesh), by **Teaching** the *Two Commandments* (spirit), and by **Becoming** *Christ's One Commandment* (soul). The implication here is that when a "Person Learns" God's Ten Commandments (5 spirits/5 physical), he can **Master Right** (spirit) from **Wrong** (flesh) and become **Worthy** of **Earthly Redemption** (free) and *His Own Transfigured Body* (natural order/see self). Secondly, when a "Person Teaches" God's Two Commandments (love God totally and neighbor as self), he can master **Good** (spirit) and **Evil** (flesh) and become worthy of **Heavenly Salvation** (earned) earning *His Own Glorified Body* (supernatural order/see man). Finally, when a "Person Becomes" Christ's One Commandment (love one another), he can **Master** both **God's/Man's Wills** and become **Worthy** of **Bonus Rewards** (gift) and *His Own Mystical Body* (divine order/see God). For this reason, each of "God's Children" must comprehend the Meaning of Existence (to exist), the Purpose of Life (service), and the Value of Achievements (happiness) as based on **His Mastery** of God's *Truth* (mind/survival), *Law* (heart/truth), *Will* (soul/love), *and Love* (life-force/choices). In this way, "God" and "Man" can Work Together to **Create** a **New Home, New Church, New Government,** and **New Self-image** based on the **Forces** of **Wisdom, Courage, Generosity** and **Unselfishness** toward *All God's Creation*.

The point of "Life" is, obviously, to **Input God's Truth** into one's *Mind*, **Write God's Law** into His *Heart*, **Seal God's Will** into *His Soul,* and **Manifest God's Love** within His *Life-force*. Through "God's Truth (divine intellect)," a Person can be Blessed with Repentance (kiss it) which **Leads to His Free Gift** of a **Transfigured Body** (earth), thereby **Making him Worthy** of a *Seat in God's Celestial Court* (flesh). Secondly, through "God's Law (divine emotions)," a Person can be Anointed with Prayerfulness (possession) which **Leads to His Earning a Glorified Spirit** (Heaven), thereby **Making him Worthy** of a *Seat in God's Temple Court* (spirit). Thirdly, through "God's Will (divine instincts)," a Person can be Sanctified with Good Works (ownership) which **Leads to His Bonus of a Mystical Body** (Kingdom), thereby **Making him Worthy** of a *Seat in God's Royal Court* (soul). Finally, through "God's Love (divine nature)," a Person can be Consecrated with Saving Souls (becoming) which **Leads to His New Divine Body** (Self), thereby **Making him Worthy** of a *Seat in God's Divine Court* (life-force). At each of these "Four Levels of Maturity," a Person can Prove himself to **God, Angels, and Men** to **Show** that he has **Totally Surrendered** his very **Life to Jesus Christ** in *Mind, Heart, Soul, and Life-force.*

The following tabular information indicates that "Life" is about <u>Rejecting</u> a **Person's Old Mind/Heart/Soul/Life-force** to obtain a **New Mind/Heart/Soul/Life-force** in the **<u>Form</u>** of *Wisdom* (truth), *Courage* (law), *Generosity* (will), and *Unselfishness* (love):

Put Away Child's Mind/Heart/Soul/Life-force
to Obtain an Adult Mind/Heart/Soul/Life-force
(gaining a new mind of wisdom/heart of courage/soul of generosity/
life-force of Unselfishness)

Survival   1.   **New Mind** - <u>Creation of Eternal Home:</u> Belief...Free Eternal Life
(kingship)
       •   Teach God's Truth to Man - Divine Intellect
       •   Blessed with Repentance - Kiss Treasure   **Wisdom**
       •   Given Transfigured Body - Title Deed to Earth
       •   Seat in Celestial Court - Rule Flesh
     (belief - master right from wrong: Dying to Ignorance = Wise Mind)

Truth   2.   **New Heart** - <u>Creation of Eternal Church:</u> Trusting Belief...Earned New
(priesthood)   Body
       •   Write God's Law into All Men - Divine Emotions
       •   Anointed with Prayerfulness - Possess the Treasure   **Courage**
       •   Given Glorified Body - Title Deed to Heaven
       •   Seat in Temple Court - Rule Spirit
    (submission - master good from evil: Dying to Cowardice = Courageous Heart)

Love   3.   **New Soul** - <u>Creation of Eternal Government:</u> Faithful Belief.....Bonus
(sonship)   Kingdom
       •   Seal God's Will into Mankind - Divine Instincts
       •   Sanctified with Good Works - Owning the Treasure   **Generosity**
       •.   Given Mystical Body - Title to Kingdom
       •   Seat in Royal Court - Rule Soul
    (sacrifice - master God's Will from man's will: Dying to Greed = Generous Soul)

Choices   4.   **New Life-force** - <u>Creation of Eternal Self:</u> Knowing Truth...Thinking for
(free man)   Self
       •   Becoming God's Love - Divine Nature
       •   Consecrated to Save Souls - Becoming the Treasure   **Unselfishness**
       •   Given Divine Body - Title Deed to Oneself
       •   Seat in Divine Court - Rule Life-force
   (reconciliation - master God's Reality from man's illusion: Rebirth = Man for All Seasons)

This illustration shows that the "Plan" of Jesus Christ is to **Use** the **Human Mind** to *Create an Eternal Home*, the **<u>Human Heart</u>** to *Create an Eternal Church,* the **<u>Human Soul</u>** to *Create an Eternal Government,* and the **<u>Human Life-force</u>** to *Create a Perfect*

Man (self). At each of these "Four Levels" of Eternal Life, the **Mind** can be **Blessed through Repentance** (kiss), the **Heart** can be **Anointed through Prayerfulness** (possess), the **Soul** can be **Sanctified through Good Works** (ownership), and the **Life-force** can be **Consecrated through the Saving of Others** (becoming) all in the *Name of Jesus Christ*. Once a "Person" has been "Blessed," "Anointed," "Sanctified," and "Consecrated" to the Lord God Almighty, then he can be **Given** a **Transfigured Body** (earth), **Glorified Body** (Heaven), a **Mystical Body** (Kingdom), and a **Divine Body** (God), thereby uniting him to *God and His Creation*. Once a person has "Mastered Life," he will be given God's Highest Honors in the form of a **Seat** in His **Celestial Court** (earth), His **Temple Court** (Heaven), His **Royal Court** (Kingdom), and His **Divine Court** (God) to *Rule with God Forever*. Yes! Life is all about "Survival," "Learning the Truth," "Finding Love," and making the "Right Choices" based on both Growing and Maturing in the *Nature of Christ Jesus*.

The implication here is that if a person "Masters the Life-experience," he can become worthy of God's Gifts of **Eternal Life** (redemption), a **New Body** (salvation), his own **Kingdom** (rewards), and then find that most mysterious *Doorway to Personal Freedom* (think for self). This means that it's all a matter of "Leadership" based on Mastery in all areas of the **Life-experience**, allowing a person to effectively **Communicate with Himself** (face Lucifer), his **Society** (face God), and his **God** (face self) through the Lord's *Formal* (experience church/optional/imitation) and *Informal Channels* (experience world/required/obedience) of *Infinite/Eternal Life*. We can now see that "God is Creating" a Set of Leaders, One (nothing) for **Leading His People** via their **Daily Lives** (physical/mind) and **One** (all) for **Leading His People** via their **Religious Lives** (spiritual/heart), thereby **Allowing Them to Possess Their Own** *New Mystical Natures* (instincts/soul). This "Leadership Capability" can only occur through God's School of Judges (physical lives) and His School of Prophets (spiritual lives) which **Transformed** the **Jewish People** into *True Mystics* (soul savers). As "Mystics," the Jewish People were **Able to Reflect** both the **Image** (spirit) and **Likeness** (flesh) of **Their Coming Messiah** (Christ) to *Bless a Sick and Dying World*.

This need to "Appease God's Anger" through one's Human Perfection (treasured moment/mystic) forced the **Jewish People to Listen** to all their future Judges (kingship/blood/faults) and Prophets (priesthood/fat/virtues), **Allowing Them to Find** both *God's Pathways of Righteousness* (flesh/throne) and *Holiness* (spirit/temple). This now reveals that God's "Pathway of Righteousness (earth)" was coming through the Old Testament (word/Torah/Bible/citizens), while God's "Pathway of Holiness (Heaven)" was coming through the New Testament (traditions/church/mass/saints). The message here is that God was able to "Shepherd" the Jewish People in the **Desert** through the **Intercession** of just *One Man* (Moses). Yet, as the Lord acquired more and more "Flocks" from Tribes to Nations and later Worlds, He becomes faced with creating more and more *Physical* (judges) and *Spiritual* (prophets) *Leaders*. This need for a high "Number of Righteous (kings)" and "Holy Men (high priests)" brought about the need to have just **One Shepherd** (spirit), **One Man** (son) and just **One God** (father) to *Rule All Things*. In this theme, we see that the "Job of the Judges" was to Save Confused Men from their own *Wicked Faults* (sinners); while the "Job of the Prophets" was to Guide Awakened Men to *God's Virtues* (saints). The

"One Shepherd Idea" was fulfilled with the coming of Jesus Christ who can **Multiply His Own Nature,** by allowing people to **Eat the Lord's Flesh** (judges) and **Drink His Blood** (prophets) to **Transform** *Dead Men* into *Everlasting Men of Holy Perfection*. It appears that in the Lord's "Grand Design," He was striving to create a Half Human (Jesus) and Half Divine (Christ) Leader, who could **Rule both Heaven** (spirit) and **Earth** (flesh) by **Balancing** the *Imperfection of Earth* (evil) with the *Perfection of Heaven* (good).

This idea of "Perfection" being Balanced by "Imperfection" implies that the whole Life-experience is centered upon the **Treasured Moment** (success/Eucharist) be it **Manifested** in *Man's Natural Order* (bread/wine) or in *God's Supernatural Order* (flesh/blood). This implies that all of **God's Creatures** are seeking the **Meaning of Life** (to exist) in their own *Survival*, in *Absolute Truth*, in *Finding Love,* and/or simply by making *Their Own Choices* (freedom). The definition of the "Treasured Moment (balance)" can either be when the Old Way is Ending (IS IT/death) or when the New Way is Beginning (IT IS/resurrection). In either case, a person must **Tally** his **Life-experiences** in either *Blessings Gained* (prophet/pleasure/victory) and/or in *Lessons Learned* (judges/pain/loss). Thus, in the case of "Jesus Meeting Saint Peter" or "Simon," the Lord ended the **Old Life** of **Simon** (sand) by **Changing his Name to Peter** (rock), implying that **Old Simon** was a very **Wishy Washy Type of Guy** until he was **Transformed** into the *Strength of Christ*. This means that if one is "Born of the Natural Order (die to self/sacrifice)," he has been cast into the Dirt to become Streetwise (poor). If a person is "Born of the Supernatural Order (born-again/prayer)," he can now become Properly Educated (rich) in *Human, Angelic, and Divine Truth*. In this concept, the "Streetwise Man (reconciled)" is Thinking Wrong (flesh/survival) and Desires Evil (spirit/love)); while the "Educated Man (forgiven)" is Thinking Right (flesh/truth) and Desires Good (spirit/choice) for *One and All*. This means, that as a "Streetwise Man (ignorance)," a person has an Old Name (Joshua) and then after his **Conversion** he becomes an "Educated Man (wisdom)," who is given a New Name (Jesus), thereby **Setting him Free** from both *Confusion* (flesh) and *Insanity* (spirit).

The following tabular information indicates the "Streetwise Man" versus the "Educated Man" based on the Good Son (wise) **Laying Down His Life** for His Prodigal Brother (ignorant) to **Unite** the *Natural Order* (blood/law) with the *Supernatural Order* (fat/faith):

Streetwise Man is Compared to the Educated Man via the Natural and Supernatural Orders
(God's Good Son lays down His life for His Prodigal Brother to Save him from Sin, Evil, and Death)

Prodigal
Son
(old name)

1. **Streetwise Man** - Natural Order of Life: Physical Realm…Old Ways End
   - Thinking Wrong (mind) - Cursed with Ignorance: Old Nature (survival)
   - Rejected by God's Son - Compensatory Recompense: Pay Damages (denial)
   - Wanting Evil (heart) - Cursed with Selfishness: Old Behavior (love)
   - Cursed by God the Father - Punitive Retribution: Pay Fine (repentance)

(Moses/flesh - Judges: Become Kings = Become Government + Become Jesus [Divine Man])

Good	2. **Educated Man** - <u>Supernatural Order of Eternal Life:</u> Spiritual Realm…
Son	New Ways Begin
(new name)	• Thinking Right (mind) - Blessed with Wisdom: New Nature (truth)
	• Reconciled Back to God's Son - Pay Sin-debt: Take-sins of Others (prayer)
	• Wanting Good (heart) - Blessed with Unselfishness: New Behavior (choices)
	• Forgiven by God the Father - Pay Holy-debt: Give-up One's Divinity (works)

(Aaron/spirit - Prophets - High Priest = Becomes Church + Becomes Christ [Human God])

This illustration shows that the "Natural Order of Earth" is <u>Merging</u> with the "Supernatural Order of Heaven" causing the *Streetwise Man of Ignorance* (prodigal son/old name) to be **Converted** to an *Educated Man of Wisdom* (good son/new name). Unfortunately, the "Price of One's Conversion" is <u>Extremely High</u> when it comes to **Killing His Old Spirit** (good son) and *Resurrecting His New Flesh* (prodigal son). This means that the "Foolish Minds of Men" have been <u>Thinking Wrong</u>, thereby causing the <u>Human Intellect</u> to be **Rejected by God's Son** for <u>Ignorance</u> because an **Immature Person** is only *Concerned with Survival.* Secondly, we see that the "Wicked Hearts of Men" have been <u>Desiring Evil</u> causing the <u>Human Emotions</u> to be **Cursed by God the Father** for <u>Selfishness</u> since an **Immature Person** only *Wants Fun and Pleasure* (instant gratification). In contrast, the "Wise Minds of Men" are <u>Thinking Correctly</u> causing the Human Intellect to be **Reconciled Back to God's Son** based on **One's Wisdom** since a **Mature Person** is *Concerned with Truth.* Finally, the "Loving Hearts of Men" <u>Want Goodness for All</u> causing the <u>Human Emotions</u> to be **Blessed by God the Father** for <u>Unselfishness</u> since a **Mature Person** *Wants Free Choice for Everyone* (voting). Thus, "Children" fear for their lives and <u>Seek Only Survival; while</u> "Teenagers" are only interested in *Fun and Pleasures of All Kinds.* In contrast, when a person "Grows-up (adult)" and turns his attention to the <u>Value of Truth</u> and <u>Importance of Law</u> which leads him to become a **Wise Man,** he realizes that **Freedom of Choice** (voting) sits at the center of *Righteous Living.* Unfortunately, for the "Human Race," the <u>Damage</u> and <u>Broken Laws of the Past</u> must be **Paid for in the Future** as **God Demands Full Payment** from each **Child's Old Nature** (pay damages/denial) and **Old Behavior** (pay fines/repentance) before he can be *Redeemed.* In this same regard, the Lord's "Gifts" of <u>Righteousness and Holiness</u> must also be **Paid For in Full** by becoming **Reconciled Back to God's Truth** (spirit/prayers) and being **Forgiven for All His Transgressions** (flesh/works) through the *Intercession of Christ* (Heaven) and *His Church* (earth).

In this theme, a "Child must Die (caterpillar)" and <u>Fall Away</u> so the "Adult can Come Forth (butterfly)" and then **Take-on the Responsibility** of **Running a Complex World** by **Ruling Billions of People** so *that They* might *All Live Perfect Lives.* We know that this "Perfect Adult" is God's Son, <u>Jesus Christ,</u> who has **Promised to Return** and bring with Him that most **Treasured Moment of All,** when He begins *Man's 1,000 Years of Peace.* Obviously, the Lord has created "Three Treasured Moments of Life" for Those Who Love Him by Offering Them a **Free Water Redemption** (faith), an **Earned Blood Salvation** (grace), and a **Bonus Spiritual Reward** (works) for **Worshiping** (life), **Praising** (wealth), and **Thanking God** (labor) for *His Eternal Blessings* (life/body/kingdom). In Titus, Chapter 3, the Lord states that a "Soul is Saved" by Faith through Grace Affirmed by Works, implying that a person must **Not Only Give God his Solemn Vow**, but then he must **Fulfill his Promise** by **Transforming** from a *Sinner* (faith) to a *Christian* (grace) and then into a *Saint* (works). This means that a "Sinner" can Die to his Selfishness (truth) and receive a **Free Gift of Faith** to be *Saved Physically* (earth); a "Christian" can be Born-again to become Unselfish (love) and **Earn God's Grace** to be *Saved Spiritually* (Heaven); and finally, a "Saint" can become a Free Man of Honor (choices) to receive a **Bonus Reward for his Works** to be *Saved Mystically* (Kingdom). The idea is to see that each "Child of God" is striving for his own "Freedom (king)," then his own "Liberty (priest)," and finally, his own "Independence (son)" so that he might enter God's Eternal Kingdom with *Honors* (wisdom), *Respect* (courage), and *Dignity* (generosity).

The following tabular information indicates that there are "Three Methods" for being Saved by Christ: one through the Lord's **Free Water Redemption** (faith/being saved); another via one's **Earned Blood Salvation** (grace/saving self); and by his **Bonus Spiritual Rewards** (words/saving others) each offered-up to be *Worthy of Eternal Life*:

Three Methods for being Saved by Christ
(free water redemption, earned blood salvation,
and bonus spiritual rewards offered to God)

Baby
(slave)

1. **Free Water Redemption** - Faith (being saved): Baptism…Physical Life
   - Holy Spirit's Redemption - Remove Capital Sins: God becomes Man = Christmas
   - Defeat Personal Sin-nature - Remove Sin: Intellect brings Ethics = Government
   - Justice brings Freedom - Individual Rights: Letter of the Law = Dying to Self

Sinner
(freedom)
   - Submission - Learn Right from Wrong: Righteous Citizen = Master Intellect (mind)
   - Title Deed to the Earth (life) - New Transfigured Body (king): *Heaven on Earth*
   - *Gift of Eternal Life* - God Thinks of Man: Good News (message) = Worship Give Life

(God sees one's suffering - given a free gold mine or ownership: possession of earth)

Teenager
(servant)

2. **Earned Blood Salvation** - Grace (saving self): Confession…Spiritual Life
   - Son of God's Salvation - Remove Mortal Sins: Man becomes God = Easter

<table>
<tr><td>Christian
(liberty)</td><td>
<ul>
<li>Defeat Worldly Temptations - Remove Evil: Emotions bring Morals = Church</li>
<li>Prosperity brings Liberty - Social Rights: Spirit of the Law - Born-again</li>
<li>Sacrifice - Learn Good from Evil: Holy Saint = Master Feelings (heart)</li>
<li>Title Deed to Heaven (eternal life) - New Glorified Spirit (priest): Paradise in Heaven</li>
<li>Gift of New Body - God Speaks to Man: Gospel Message (Bible): Praise Give Wealth</li>
</ul>
</td></tr>
</table>

(God hears one's cries - asked to dig out gold or wealth earns ownership: possession of Heaven)

<table>
<tr><td>Adult
(free man)</td><td>3.</td><td>Bonus Spiritual Reward - <u>Works</u> (saving others): Communion… Mystical Life</td></tr>
</table>

- Eternal Father's Rewards - Remove Venial Sins: God and Man become One = Halloween
- Defeat Demonic Possession - Remove Death: Instincts bring Fairness = Home
- Dignity brings Independence - Divine Rights: Doing What's Right = Think for Self

<table>
<tr><td>Saint
(independent)</td><td>
<ul>
<li>Reconciliation - Learn God's Will/Man's Will: Perfect Son = Master Instincts (soul)</li>
<li>Title Deed to Kingdom (divine life) - New Holy Soul (son): God's Respect in Kingdom</li>
<li>Gift of Kingdom - God Touches Man: Doctrinal Truth (traditions): Thanksgiving Give Labor</li>
</ul>
</td></tr>
</table>

(God recognizes His Covenant - sharing gold with others or friends: possession of kingdom)

This illustration shows that there are "Three Methods for being Saved": one by <u>Water</u> or via **Faith Alone** (baptism); one by <u>Blood</u> or via **God's Grace** (confession); and finally, by <u>Spirit</u> or via **One's Works** (communion), **Each Guiding** a *Person to Redemption* (free/being saved), *Salvation* (earned/saving self), and *Rewards* (bonus/saving others). In the previous chart, "Babies" or <u>Slaves</u> are **Saved for Free** as **God Sees Their Suffering,** just as "Teenagers" or <u>Servants</u> must **Earn Their Own Salvation** as **God Hears Their Cries for Help**. Finally, we see that "Adults" or Free Men are **Called to Save Others** to receive **God's Bonus Rewards** as the *Lord Recognizes His Covenant with Righteous Men*. We can imagine that as a "Child of Faith," a person is <u>Given his Own Free Gold Mine</u> (redemption) from God in the form of the **Title Deed to Earth** to *Save* him from his *Own Sin-nature* (ignorance). Secondly, as a "Teenager of Grace," a person <u>Digs Out his Own Gold</u> (salvation) in the form of the **Title Deed to Heaven** to *Save* him from *Man's Worldly Temptations* (cowardice). Finally, as an "Adult of Works," a person <u>Shares his Gold with Others</u> (rewards) in the form of a **Title Deed to the Kingdom** to *Save* him from *Lucifer's Demonic Possession* (greed).

Through each of these "Stages of Growth (obey)" and "Maturity (imitate)," a person becomes <u>Closer and Closer to God</u> in *Intellect* (ethics/mind), in *Emotions* (morals/heart), and in *Instincts* (fairness/soul). This means that a "Person's New Intellect" brings <u>Ethics</u>

(government) in the form of following the **Letter of the Law** (saints) to make **One's Self Great** in his *Own Eyes* (survival). Secondly, "New Emotions" bring <u>Morals</u> (church) in the form of following the **Spirit of the Law** (angels) to make **Others Great** in the *Eyes of Society* (good life). Finally, "New Instincts" brings <u>Fairness</u> (home) in the form of **Doing What's Right** to make **God Great** in *Everyone's Eyes*. Through the "Treasured Moments of Life," a person can come to <u>Know the Difference</u> between **Ethics** (flesh), **Morals** (spirit), and **Fairness** (soul) based on **Serving** either one's *Personal Freedom* (justice), man's *Social Liberty* (prosperity), and/or *God's Divine Independence* (dignity).

This means that the "Struggle of Life" involves <u>Defeating Time</u> (eternal life), obtaining <u>Perfection</u> (new body) and <u>Building One's Dream Home</u> (kingdom). Through each of these "Difficult Challenges," a person can establish his own <u>Identity</u> (fixed frame) or *Place in Time* (mind), his own <u>Perfect Character</u> (focused existence) or *Place in Space* (heart), and his own <u>Personality</u> (perception of reality) or *Place in God's Kingdom* (soul). These "Three Places" in <u>Time</u> (eternal life), <u>Space</u> (new body), and the <u>Kingdom</u> (dream home) are all to be **United in Christ** (new nature) by way of *Submission* (new mind), *Sacrifice* (new heart), and *Reconciliation* (new soul) via the *Nature of God* (new-life). We call this "Event" of being <u>United in Christ</u> the **Treasured Moment** which is like a **Star Burning Out** (Christmas) to become a *Black Hole* and then gathering sufficient **Energy to Turn Back** (Easter) into an even *Bigger and Brighter Star*. The <u>Entire Life-experience</u> has been based on this process of "Death" and "Resurrection" to establish **God's Gifts** of *Eternal Life* (earth/give life), *New Body* (Heaven/give wealth), and one's *Dream Home* (Kingdom/give labor).

The following tabular information indicates "Man's Submission (eternal life)," "God's Sacrifice (new body)," and "God's/Man's Reconciliation (dream home)" as <u>They Relate</u> to a *Sinner's Redemption* (being saved), a *Christian's Salvation* (saving self), and a *Saint's Rewards* (saving others):

Man's Submission, God's Sacrifice, and God's/Man's Reconciliation bring Perfection
(God's gifts of eternal life, new body,
and dream home become real for all those who repent)

Church   1. **Submission** - <u>Gift of Eternal Life:</u> Freedom comes with Justice...Baptism
(self)   • Deny Intellect - - - - - - - New Mind
                • Remove Ignorance   • Wisdom   **Sinner**
                • Abandon Feelings - New Heart   Free Redemption (being saved)
                • Remove Cowardice • Courage   • Water Blessing - Give Life
                • Submit Free Will - New Soul   • Redeeming Baby Self
                • Remove Greed • Generosity
(Noahic Covenant - God Sees Suffering: Christmas = God becomes Man Establishes Temple)

World   2. **Sacrifice** - <u>Gift of New Body:</u> Liberty comes with Wealth...Confession
(society)   • Repentance - - - New Government
                • Remove Criminal • Righteous King   **Christian**

- Prayers - - - - - - -New Church   Earn Salvation (save self)
- Remove Insanity • Holy Priest • Blood Anointing - Give Wealth
- Works - - - - - - - - - - New Home • Saving Teenage Society
- Remove Evil   • Perfect Son

(Abrahamic Covenant - God Hears Cries: Easter = Man becomes God Establishes Throne)

God   3. **Reconciliation** - <u>Gift of Dream Home:</u> Independence comes with Dignity…
(divinity)   Communion

- Righteousness - - - - - New Earth
- Remove Sin-nature   • Freedom (justice)   **Saint**
- Holiness- - - - - - -   New Heaven • Bonus Rewards (saving others)
- Remove Temptations   • Liberty (wealth) • Spirit Sanctification - Give
                                              Labor
- Perfection- - - - - - - - New Kingdom • Reward Adult God
- Remove Possession • Independence (dignity)

(New Covenant - God Recognizes Covenant: Halloween =
God and Man become One Establishes Palace)

This illustration shows that "Each Sinner" must <u>Die to his Own Selfishness</u> through his <u>Personal Submission</u> to **God's Unselfishness** (Last Supper) via **Christ's Church** (self) by *Denying his Intellect* (ignorance), *Abandoning his Feelings* (cowardice), and *Submitting his Free Will* (greed). Secondly, each "Christian" must be <u>Born-again in God's Unselfishness</u> through a <u>Person's Sacrifice</u> to **God's Divine Will** (Calvary) via the **Righteous World** (society) by *Repenting* (criminal), *Praying* (insanity), and *Working* (evil) *for God*. Finally, each "Saint" must be <u>Set Free</u> through <u>His Reconciliation</u> to **God's Love** (Resurrection) via the **Lord's Divinity** (God) by becoming a *Righteous King* (sin-nature), *Holy Priest* (worldly temptations), and *Perfect Son* (demonic possessions). By passing through these "Three Stages" of <u>Growth</u> (obey) and <u>Maturity</u> (imitate), a **Person** can **Comprehend the Importance** of the *Noahic Covenant of Submission*, the *Abrahamic Covenant of Sacrifice*, and *Jesus' New Covenant of Reconciliation*.

1. **Noahic Covenant** - <u>Submission to God:</u> Rejection of Wicked Flesh… Worship God, Give Life
2. **Abrahamic Covenant** - <u>Sacrifice to God:</u> Offering-up Free Will… Praise God, Give Wealth
3. **New Covenant** - <u>Reconciliation Back to God:</u> Receive New-life… Thank God, Give Labors

Each "Stage of Conversion" is one of man's <u>Treasured Moments of Life,</u> where a **Lost Soul** can be *Redeemed* (thought of), *Saved* (spoken to), and then *Rewarded* (touched by) *by God*. We are being shown that God's "Treasured Moments" are represented first by a <u>Poor Man</u> (individual rights) finding a **Treasure in a Field** and **Selling All to Buy It** (Calvary). Secondly, this same man, who is now "Rich (social rights)" and is in search of the **Pearl of Great Price**, comes and is willing to **Give-up All his Wealth** to *Buy It* (Resurrection). We see that in the "First Case," the <u>Poor Man</u> (ethics) receives the *Love of Man* (get bride); while in the "Second Case," the <u>Rich Man</u> (morals) receives the *Love of God* (get sonship). Note that "Jesus Christ" is able to bring forth <u>His Wife</u> (world) out of **Nothing** (defeat) via His *Personal Blood Offering* (death/Calvary) or *Sacrificial Gift* (receive wealth); He then brings forth the <u>Sonship of God</u> (church) out of **All** (victory) via His *Silver Offering* (life/Resurrection) or *Temple Tax* (receive life). In short, the Lord is telling us that we must "Drag Christ's Cross" <u>Around Every Day</u> (lessons) to **Keep Us Fit** and be ready to **Fight Our Own** *Sin-nature* (water blessing), the *Temptations of the World* (blood anointing), and *Lucifer's Demonic Possessions* (spirit sanctification). In this "Struggle of Life," we are expected to *Earn Eternal Life* (earth), become worthy of God's *Gift of Divinity* (Heaven/new body), and be *Rewarded* with the *Honors of Divine Liberty* (kingdom).

The question is: can you "Correctly Identify" your own <u>Treasured Moments in Life</u> that have allowed you to **Purchase Your Field of Dreams** (loving mate) which then sent you in **Search** of that *Priceless Pearl of Great Price* (God's Love)? We now see that the "Jewish People (Angel)" stumbled across that <u>Field of Treasure</u> (Mosaic Tabernacle/Temple) and that the "Three Gentile Kings (Star)" went in search of that most precious <u>Pearl of Great Price</u> (Christ Child/God). Obviously, the "Job of the Three Kings" was to <u>Overcome</u> their **Baby Fears** (ignorance), **Teenage Doubts** (cowardice), and **Adult Disbelief** (greed) to make such a **Journey** leading them from *Human Death* (serving evil) to *Divine Life* (serving God). We see that "Babies Fear Pain" and that the <u>Three Kings</u> brought unto the <u>Christ Child Myrrh</u> as a **Pain Killer** so that a person could **Defeat his Own Sin-nature** by **Learning Right from Wrong** (intellect) and to one day *See his God Face to Face*. Secondly, we see that "Teenagers are Full of Doubts" and that the <u>Three Kings</u> brought the <u>Christ Child Frankincense</u> as a **Holy Prayer** so that a person could **Defeat his Worldly Temptations** by **Learning Good from Evil** (emotions) and to one day *Hear God's Loving Voice*. Finally, we see that "Adults are Greedy Monsters" and that the <u>Three Kings</u> brought the <u>Christ Child Gold</u> as **Good Works** so that a person could **Defeat Demonic Possession** by **Learning God's Will from Man's Will** (instincts) and to one day be *Touched by the Hand of God*. By "Defeating" <u>Fear</u> (repentance), <u>Doubt</u> (prayers), and <u>Disbelief</u> (works), a **Person can Break** his **Chains of Death** to be *Set Free* from *Lucifer's World of Illusion*.

The following tabular information indicates that "God's Children" are being <u>Chained</u>, <u>Imprisoned,</u> and <u>Guarded</u> by the **Evil One**, who knows that all he needs to do is **Convince the World** that it can **Never Escape** by filling man with *Fear* (sin-nature), *Doubts* (worldly temptations), and *Disbelief* (demonic possession):

Baby Fear, Teenage Doubt, and Adult Disbelief can
be Overcome by Surrendering to God's Will
(defeating ignorance [sin-nature], cowardice [worldly
temptations], and greed [demonic possession])

Lucifer's   1. **Baby Fears** - <u>Defeat Ignorance:</u> Overcome Sin-nature...   Repentance
Chains   •   Learning Right from Wrong - See God Face to Face: Free from Sin

(water)

- Free Redemption - Gift of Eternal Life: Transfigured Body (home)
- God's Calling - New Mind: See Self = Ignorance unto Wisdom

(comprehending the "Meaning of Life [eternal life]" - to exist through survival)

Devil's Prison (blood)

2. **Teenage Doubt** - <u>Defeat Cowardice:</u> Overcome Worldly Temptations... Prayers
   - Learn Good from Evil - Hear God's Loving Voice: Free from Evil
   - Earned Salvation - Worthy of New Body: Glorified Body (church)
   - God's Enlightenment - New Heart: See Man = Cowardice unto Courage

(comprehending the "Purpose of Life [new body]" - to serve through truth)

Satan's Guards (spirit)

3. **Adult Disbelief** - Defeat Greed: Overcome Demonic Possession... Works
   - Learn God's Will/Man's Will - Touched by the Hand of God: Free from Death
   - Bonus Rewards - Honored with Royal Kingdom: Mystical Body (government)
   - God's Awakening - New Soul: See God = Greed unto Generosity

(comprehending the "Value of Life [kingdom]" - to become happy through love)

- -

Christ's Keys (life)

4. **Wise Man's Knowing** - <u>Wisdom/Courage/Generosity:</u> Unite with God... Love
   - Separate God's Reality from Man's Illusion - Sup with God: Free from Damnation
   - Passport to Freedom - Set Free to Think for Self: Divine Body (self)
   - God's Indwelling - New Life-force: See Life = Selfishness unto Unselfishness

(comprehending the "Treasures of Life [free]" - to become life through free choice)

This illustration shows that each of "God's Children" must <u>Let Go</u> of his <u>Fears, Doubts,</u> and <u>Disbeliefs,</u> if he ever hopes to **Defeat Lucifer's Chains** (water) of **Ignorance,** the **Devil's Prison** (blood) of **Cowardice,** and **Satan's Guards** (spirit) of **Greed** to be *Set Free* (life) from *Sin, Evil, Death, and Damnation.* "Learning" how to <u>Think for Oneself</u> allows a person to comprehend the **Meaning of Life** (existence/calling), the **Purpose of Life** (service/enlightenment), the **Value of Life** (happiness/awakening), and the **Treasures of Life** (becoming life/indwelling) in *Christ Jesus.* Each of these "Stages of Life" takes on importance through <u>Human Survival</u> (ignorance unto wisdom), <u>Nature's Truth</u> (cowardice unto courage), <u>God's Love</u> (greed unto generosity), and each <u>Wise Man's Free Choices</u> (selfishness unto unselfishness) which lead a person to *See his God* (defeat fear), *Hear God's Voice* (defeat doubt), being *Touched by God's Hand* (defeat disbelief), and one day, to *Sup with God in Friendship* (defeat selfishness). This "Awesome Journey of Life" brings each of <u>God's Children</u> to comprehend the need for **Human Growth** (obedience) and **Divine Maturity** (imitation) as they must be **United** with *God's Home, Church, Government, and Self.*

We must "All Find a Way" to become <u>Worthy</u> of the <u>Blessings of God,</u> but just how much is a person willing to **Sacrifice** in giving-up his **Fears, Doubts,** and **Disbelief** to *Find God* and attain his *Own Treasured Moment*? We see that "Moses and Aaron" were <u>Willing to Enter</u> the **Desert of Death** to **Find God** and to attain **Their Treasured Moment** by being taught that **Man's Sinfulness** is *Manifested in his Blood* (faults) and **One's Righteousness** is *Manifested in his Fat* (virtues). Note in "Leviticus: Chapter 5," the <u>Lord is Telling His Priesthood</u> to have the **Sinner Place his Hands** (prayer) on the **Head of the Sacrificial Animal** to place his <u>Sins</u> upon the *Animal's Innocent Blood*. The idea here is that once the "Innocent Blood is Contaminated," then the <u>Animal</u> (unblemished) can be **Slaughtered** as a *Stand-in for the Sinner*. We see that when the "Sinner's Hands" were on the <u>Sacrificial Animal,</u> his **Virtues were also Transferred** onto the **Animal's Fat** so that when the **Fat of the Entrails** was **Burned** on the <u>Brazen Altar,</u> then the *Sweet Savor* of the *Man's Goodness Travels to God in Heaven.* The idea here is that when a "Sacrificial Animal" is both <u>Killed</u> and **Offered-up to God,** it **Contains a Man's Wickedness** (blood) and his **Righteousness** (fat) so that **God** can **Balance these Two Life Forces** to **Determine If this Soul** is a *Good Man* (saint) or an *Evil Man* (sinner). We see that the "Holocaust" must have its <u>Blood Shed</u> (crucifixion) and its <u>Body Broken</u> (scourging) to **Remove** its **Evil Blood** (being saved) and *Offer-up* its *Righteous Fat* (saving self) unto the **Lord.** The idea here is to see that "Man's Flesh" is <u>Saved by Blood</u> (master church) via the **Winepress** (water) **of God,** thereby allowing a **Person to Receive** the **Gift of a New Body for Free** as *Jesus Christ Pays His Sin-debt.* Secondly, we see that "Man's Spirit" is <u>Saved by Fat</u> (master world) via the **Crucible** (fire) **of Man,** thereby allowing a person to **Earn Eternal Life** by *Paying His Holy-debt.*

1. **Man's Wicked Flesh** - <u>Saved by Blood:</u> Enemy's Guilty Blood... Offer Blood Shed
2. **Man's Sinful Spirit** - <u>Saved by Fat:</u> Sweet Smell of Virtues... Offer Body Broken

This means that the "Shed Blood (crucifixion)" is <u>Redeeming the Soul</u> (life) and the "Body Broken (scourging)" is <u>Forgiving the Soul</u> (body), thereby **Setting a Person Free** from *Sin* (sin-nature/look), *Evil* (worldly temptations/touch), and *Death* (demonic possession/wash). In short, if a person "Looks at the Cross (baby sees)," his <u>Venial Sins</u> (sin-nature/mass) can be *Forgiven* (righteous). Secondly, if a person is "Touched by the Hands of a Priest (teenager understands)," his <u>Mortal Sins</u> (worldly temptations/confession) shall be *Healed* (holy). Finally, if a person is "Washed in the Blood of the Lamb (adult masters)," then his <u>Capital Sins</u> (demonic possession/communion) shall be *Purified* (perfect). Through one's "Forgiveness (sinner)," "Healing (Christian)," and "Purification (Saint)," he can become a *Righteous Citizen* (earth/eternal life), a *Holy Saint* (Heaven/new body), and a *Perfect Son* (Kingdom/royal kingdom) *before God.*

Truth	1.	**Look at the Cross** - <u>Forgive Venial Sins:</u> Forgiveness...Knowledge
Law	2.	**Touch Priest's Hands** - <u>Forgive Mortal Sins:</u> Healing...Self-awareness
Will	3.	**Wash in Christ's Blood** - <u>Forgive Capital Sins:</u> Purification...Consciousness

Note that the "Moslems: Worship on Friday" to *Celebrate God's Pay-day*; the "Jews" Worship on Saturday (Sabbath) to *Celebrate Their Day of Rest;* and then the "Christians" Worship on Sunday (Lord's Day) to *Celebrate Their Eternal-day of Rest*. This implies that the "Moslems (give wealth)" are Worshiping God's Spirit (pay day) to *Get Heaven* (Angels); the "Jews (give life)" are Worshiping the Eternal Father (day of rest) to *Get Earth* (Men); and the "Christians (give labors)" are Worshiping God's Son (eternal rest) to *Get a Kingdom* (God). This means that "If a Person Wants" to Go to Heaven (Moslems/high school), he **Worships on** Friday (pay day); if he wants to "Stay on Earth (Jews/elementary school)," then he Worships on Saturday (day of rest); but if he wants to "Own His Own Kingdom (Christians/college)," then he Worships on Sunday (eternal day of rest). In short, "Humanity Gets Free Redemption" on Friday, allowing a **Person to Receive** his own *New Body*; or "Earn His Salvation" on Saturday to allow **Him to Receive** *God's Blessing* of *Eternal Life*. Finally, humanity can get "Bonus Rewards" on Sunday, allowing a **Person to Receive** his own *Royal Kingdom*, where **God** (Christians), **Angels** (Moslems), and **Men** (Jews) can become *One People*, **All Worshiping** *One God*.

Recall that out of "Isaac" came the Jewish People of Earth; out of "Ishmael" came the Arab People of Heaven; and out of "Jesus" come the Christian People of the Kingdom, **All Ready, Willing, and Able** to *Correctly Worship Their God*. The idea is to see that "Abraham's Son, Ishmael (king)" was Given a Life of **Trials and Error** until he could, one day, **Get it Right** in the *Eyes of Men, Angels, and God*. Secondly, "Abraham's Son, Isaac (priest)" was Given a Life of **Total Submission** (quit-in-defeat), to **Show the World** that when **Man Quits,** then **God Comes** to offer him the *Lord's Friendship* (earth), *Companionship* (Heaven), and *Oneness* (Kingdom). Finally, "Abraham's Son, Jesus (son)" was Given a Life of **Endurance** as the **Champion of God**, as one who fights on and on, yet, **Never-quits**, *No Matter What He Faces*. Yes! We are to be "Kings (earth)," "Priests (Heaven)," and "Sons of God (Kingdom)" willing to do whatever it takes to Please God by bringing forth the **Treasures of Life** in *Mind, Heart, and Soul*. The "Three Sons of Adam" Set the Stage for *Man's Lineage* (bloodline of Seth); then the "Three Sons of Noah" Set the Stage for *Man's Five Ethnic Groups* (colors); and finally, "Abraham's Three Sons" Set the Stage for the **Dimensions** of *Man on Earth* (physical), in *Heaven* (spiritual,) and within the *Kingdom* (mystical). Through "Adam (repentance)," "Noah (prayers)," and "Abraham (works)," God would bring forth His Blessings upon **Ishmael** (Friday), **Isaac** (Saturday), and **Jesus** (Sunday) to give *Humanity New Bodies* (home), *Eternal Life* (church), and their own *Royal Kingdom* (government). Obviously, the "Lord has Thought of Everything" as He brings forth **His Divine Law** (sinners) to become **Christ's Faith** (Christians), which becomes the **Church's Knowing** (sainthood), thereby **Revealing** the **Meaning of Life** (pay debt/exist), **Purpose of Life** (rest/serve), and the **Value of Life** (eternal rest/be happy) to *One and All*.

The following tabular information indicates that "Moslems Worship" on Friday to *Get a Pay-day* (new body); "Jews Worship" on Saturday to *Get Day of Rest* (eternal life); and the "Christians Worship" on Sunday to *Get Eternal Rest* (Kingdom):

**Moslems Worship Friday, Jews Worship Saturday,
and Christians Worship Sunday to Honor God**
(Moslems get pay-day, Jews get day of rest,
and Christians get eternal rest in service to God)

Mosque   1. **Moslems Worship Holy Spirit** (toil) - <u>Friday</u>: Man's Pay-day…New Body
(Heaven)   • Ishmael (king) - Cursed Son of Abraham: Father of Arab People (see
                  limitations)
                • Worship Spirit - Get Heaven: Unite with Angelic Realm of Life
Being Saved • Save the Bad Thief - Toil of Repentance: Sacrifice the Eternal Father
                • Friday brings "Free Redemption" through *Submission* (trial/error)
                • 1st Savior - Mosaic Law: Divine Law Saves Sinners = Meaning of Life
                  (exist)
                • Artistic Genius - Offer God Culture: Serve the Needs of Goodness
    (Adam's three sons - Create Man's Eternal Lineage [birthright] through Seth, Abel, and Cain)

Temple   2. **Jews Worship Eternal Father** (wash) - <u>Saturday:</u> Man's Day of Rest…
(earth)   Eternal Life
                • Isaac (priest) - Blessed Son of Abraham: Father of Jewish People (see
                  potential)
                • Worship Father - Get Earth: Unite with Human Lifestyle
Save Self   • Save Good Thief - Prayer of Purification: Sacrifice Son of God
                • Saturday brings "Earned Salvation" through *Sacrifice* (quit-in-defeat)
                • 2nd Savior - Christ's Faith: Divine Faith Saves Christians = Purpose of
                  Life (serve)
                • Scientific Mind - Offer God Wisdom: Serve the Needs of Righteousness
                  (Noah's three sons - Create Man's Five Ethnic Groups
                        [colors] through Ham, Shem, and Japheth)

Church   3. **Christians Worship God's Son** (grow) - <u>Sunday:</u> Man's Eternal Rest…
(Kingdom)   Kingdom
                • Jesus (son) - Anointed Son of Abraham - Father of Christian People (see
                  self-worth)
                • Worship Son - Get Kingdom: Unite with God's Divine Life
Save Others • Save Messiah - Fruitfulness of Works: Sacrifice Holy Spirit
                • Sunday brings "Bonus Rewards" through *Reconciliation* (never-quit)
                • 3rd Savior - Church Knowing: Divine Knowing Saves Saints = Value of
                  Life (happiness)
                • Roughed Man's Man - Offer God Strength: Serve the Needs of God's Will
    (Abraham's three sons - Create Man's Three Dimensions through Ishmael, Isaac, and Jesus)

This illustration shows that within God's "Grand Design," He has created <u>Three Sets of
People</u> in the form of **Jews** (scientist), **Arabs** (artist), **and Christians** (rough men),
thereby **Giving Them Each Their Own <u>Altar of Worship</u>** (Isaac/Mohammed/Jesus)

upon *Mount Moriah* presented as the *Lord's Mosque, Temple, and Church of God*. This means that upon "Mount Moriah," the <u>Moslems</u> are to *Get Their Pay-day* (new body); the <u>Jews</u> are to *Get Their Day of Rest* (eternal life); and the <u>Christians</u> are to *Enter into Their Eternal Rest* (kingdom). We see in the "Previous Chart" that the "Arab People (kings/Moslems)" have been created to <u>Be Saved</u> from *Ignorance* (earth); the "Jewish People (priests)" have been created to <u>Save Themselves</u> from *Cowardice* (Heaven); and the "Christian People (sons)" have been created to <u>Save Others</u> from *Greed* (Kingdom).

The idea here is to see that "Father Abraham" had <u>Three Sons</u> in the persons of **Ishmael** (Moslems), **Isaac** (Jews), and **Jesus** (Christians) to bring forth **God's Blessings** of *Pardon for Ignorance* (fool), *Forgiveness of Cowardice* (criminal), and *Reconciliation of the Greedy* (insane). These "Three Blessings" would come forth out of <u>God's Covenants</u> with **Abraham,** thereby **Anointing Sarah, Hagar,** and the **Virgin Mary** with **Divine Statutes** to **Bless Their Descendants** with the *Treasures of Life*. Recall Genesis stated that those "Born of Hagar" shall enter the <u>Covenant of Slavery;</u> while those who are "Born of Sarah" shall enter the <u>Covenant of the Free Man;</u> but **Christ,** the **Third Son** of **Abraham,** shall come and **Give Every Man** on earth a **Choice** between *Animal Slavery* (selfishness) and *Human Freedom* (unselfishness). This theme of being "Born of Earthly Dirt (slavery)" or being "Born of Heavenly Spirit (freedom) sits at the <u>Heart</u> of *God's Plan of Redemption*. This "Choice" is known as being <u>Born-again</u> into the **Womb of the Virgin Mary** so that She might bring forth a **Purified Sinner** (baby), a **Devout Christian** (teenager), and finally, a **Holy Saint** (adult), all in the *Name of Her Son, Jesus Christ*.

We see in each of these cases that the "Lord God Almighty" is preparing the <u>Soil of Life</u> (fruitfulness) on **Earth** (1st savior/being saved)**,** in **Heaven** (2nd savior/saving self), and within the **Kingdom** (3rd savior/save others) in **Preparation** for the **Coming of His** most **Beloved Children** in *Uncountable Numbers*. Through this "Dream of a Happy Home," <u>God</u> will bring forth <u>His Three Sets of People</u> (intellect/emotions/instincts) to fill the **Earth, Heaven,** and **His Kingdom** with *Physical* (Jews/earth), *Spiritual* (Moslems/Heaven), and *Mystical* (Kingdom/Christians) *Children*. Obviously, the "Lord is Giving" <u>His Highest Honors</u> to **Man's Wisdom** (wise), **Man's Courage** (respected), and **Man's Generosity** (hard-working) to bring forth a **Scientific Mind** (earth), an **Artistic Genius** (Heaven), and finally, a **Rough-tough Man Among Men** (Kingdom) to *Serve All the Needs of God's Kingdom*. When the "New Flesh (bride)" and "New Spirit (groom)" are <u>One,</u> they can become this **New Triune Nature** (Moslems/Jews/Christians) able to **Work Together** in building their *Dream Home* within God's *Kingdom of Glory*.

In this concept, the "Job of Christ's" <u>Spiritually Shed Blood</u> is to **Face Fear** (worry/failure) unto the point of **Sweating Blood** (dying to self) in the **Garden of Gethsemane** (agony of defeat) as one encounters the **Test of Lucifer** at the *Divine Level of Torment*. Secondly, the "Job" of Jesus' <u>Physical Body Broken</u> is to **Face the Challenge** of **Performing Great Accomplishments** (trying) unto the point of being **Crucified** (born-again) on **Mount Calvary** (thrill of victory) as a **Person Encounters God's Judgment** at the *Divine Level of Guilt*. This means that "Evil Enters the Blood (pay damages)" and must be <u>Poured Out</u> to **Attack One's Blood** via **Repentance,** thereby being

Reconciled Back to God's Favor. Secondly, "One's Righteousness Enters his Fat (pay fine)" and must be <u>Burned</u> to **Release Its Sweet Savor** unto the **Lord** via **Prayer** to be *Forgiven by God's Divine Justice*. Through "One's Reconciliation (spirit/justified)" and "Forgiveness (flesh/glorified)" by his <u>Creator,</u> he can be **Restored Back** to his *Original State* (pay repairs/life), thereby bringing forth his *Original Nature* (pay fine/body).

The following tabular information indicates that "Evil Curses Man's Blood (fear/ethics)," while a "Person's Righteousness Blesses his Fat (try/morals);" therefore, <u>Shedding his Blood</u> (become ethical) brings *Reconciliation* (pay damages); and <u>Breaking his Body</u> (become moral) brings *Forgiveness* (pay fine/apology):

**Evil Curses Blood and Righteousness
Blesses Fat so Fear Reconciles and Trying Forgives**
(shedding the blood removes faults and body
broken gains virtues bringing redemption)

Faults (repent)	1. **Evil Curses Blood** - <u>Shed Blood Reconciles</u>: Fear of God…Measure of Evil
	• Man's Flesh Saved by Blood - Suffer Winepress (water): Making Wine = Face Lucifer's Test
	• Sacrificial Blood - Guilty Man to Innocent Animal: Submission (die to self)
Grave	• Repentance brings *Eternal Life* - See One's Imperfection (limitations)
	• Being Saved through Jesus - Remove Soul from Death (hell)
	• Fulfill God's Law of Obedience - Change Nature: Human to Divine
	• Life Purifies Society - Creates 1st Redemptive System: Save Flesh
Virtues (pray)	2. **Righteousness Blesses Fat** - <u>Body Broken Forgives:</u> Try for God…Measure of Good
	• Man's Spirit Saved by Fat - Suffer Crucible (fire): Making Bread = Face God's Judgment
	• Sacrificial Fat - Forgiven Man to Holy Saint: Sacrifice (born-again)
Host	• Praying brings *New Body* - See One's Perfection (potential)
	• Saving Self through Christ - Place Soul in New-life (Heaven)
	• Fulfill Man's Faith in God's Love - Wash Away Sins: Change Sinfulness to Holiness
	• Death Transforms Individual - Creates 2nd Redemptive System: Save Spirit

This illustration shows that the "Evil in the World" is continually being <u>Transmitted</u> into <u>Each Man's Blood</u> so that a **Person** must **Pour Out his Blood** (fight evil) into **God's Winepress of Repentance** (water) to be *Transformed from Death to New-life*. Secondly, "Righteousness comes from the Church" and is <u>Transmitted</u> into a <u>Christian's Fat</u> so that a **Person** must **Burn Up his Fat** by **Entering God's Crucible of Prayer** (fire/submission) to be *Purified from Rebirth to Sainthood*. The "Mosaic Law Taught" that a <u>Sinner</u> would **Place his Hand on a Sacrificial Animal's Head** to

Transmit both his **Evil Blood** and **Righteous Fat** into the **Animal's Nature** as an *Innocent Stand-in* for a *Sinner's Sinfulness.* Now, "If We Apply" this Logic to **Jesus' Sacrificial Death** on **Mount Calvary, When** the **People Cried-out Crucify Him,** this became the **Moment When All Mankind Places Its Hands on Christ's Head** to *Transmit Its Sins onto God's Son* (Messiah). The idea here is that "When Jesus was Scourged (repentance)," this became the *Shedding of Blood* (reconciliation/remove faults); and when "Christ was Crucified (prayer)," this became the *Burning of the Fat* (forgiveness/gain virtues). The point is that "Sacrificing One's Evil Blood" brings Reconciliation and **Gives** a **Lost Sinner** *God's Free Gift of Redemption* (new body); while the "Sacrificing of One's Righteous Fat" brings Forgiveness and **Gives a Christian** *Salvation* (eternal life).

1. **Sacrificing One's Evil Blood** – Reconciliation...Worthy of Free Gift of Redemption
   - Blood Shed - Purify Society: Scourging of Jesus = Save Sinners (see limitations)
   - Streetwise: Figured Out How to Escape Death - Purify Grave
2. **Sacrificing One's Righteous Fat** – Forgiveness...Worthy of One's Earned Salvation
   - Body Broken - Purify Individual: Crucifixion of Christ = Create Saints (see potential)
   - Properly Educated - Taught How to Save Lost Sinners - Purify Host

Recall that when "Jesus Christ Faced" His Scourging (fear), *He* then *Took-on All Sin* (save sinners/carry cross). "When He Faced" His Crucifixion (try), *He* then *Gave-up His Divinity/forgiveness* (create saints/surrender spirit). We can now see that "God's Son, Christ (gentle)" Willingly Came to Earth to bring **His Father's Grace** via **His Own Perfection** by **Offering-up Divinity** via **His Perfect Faith** to **Figure Out How** (blood/fat) to **Pay All Debts** to both *Forgive* and to *Save the Lost at Any Cost.* This tremendous "Knowledge" was put into Action **When the Lord Offered-up** the **King's Prayer** during the *Last Supper*; then **Jesus Offered-up** the **Priest's Sacrifice** during *His Death on Calvary;* and finally, **Offered-up** the **Son's Reconciliation** during *His Resurrection on Easter.* This means that "God's Son has been Able" to Figure-out How to **Save the Lost** (sacrificial lamb), as *God becomes Man* (Christmas/life); then "Mary's Son" has been Taught How to **Escape Death** (Judas goat) as *Man becomes God* (Easter/death). Finally, "Jesus Christ is Able" to Find a Way to Live Forever (water), by **Obtaining** a **New Body** (blood) and by becoming **Worthy** of **His Own Kingdom of Glory** (spirit) as a *True Son of God.*

    This means that to become "Worthy of a Place" in God's Divine Kingdom, a **Worthless Slave** must **Master the Art** of both **Praying** (please God) and **Working** (please man) to **Earn a Respected Seat of Honor** both on the *Earth* (government/all work) and in *Heaven* (church/all prayer). This reveals that to "Get God's Blessing," a Person must Fulfill the **Lord's Praying Institutions** via both the *Earthly Church* (altar covenant) and via the *Heavenly Blessed Mother of God* (*ark of covenant*). Secondly, to "Get Man's Blessing," a Person must Fulfill the **Working Institutions** of both the *Earthly Government* (money) and the *Heavenly Messiah* (graces). This implies that in the **Old Testament,** the **Blessings of Life** were **Coming** from the *Temple* (church/old Eve) and from the *Throne* (government/old Adam). In the "New Testament," the Blessings of Eternal Life are **Coming** from the **Virgin Mary** (new Eve) and **God's Messiah** or <u>**Christ**</u> (new Adam) in *Fulfillment* of *God's Prayers* (graces/host) and *Man's Works* (money/grave). The idea here is that to become a "Living Prayer (holy spirit/prayer)" before <u>God,</u> a **Person** must *Ask for God's Free Graces* (devout prayers/submission) and to become a "Soldier-of-the-Light (righteous flesh/works)" before <u>Men,</u> a **Person** must *Earn Great Wealth* (hard-work/sacrifice).

The following tabular information indicates that "Christ's Perfect Faith (water baptism)," "Jesus' Good Works (blood baptism)," and "Jesus Christ's Saving of Souls (spirit baptism)" bring forth <u>God's Gift</u> of a *New Body* (earth), an *Eternal Life* (Heaven), and a *Son's Dream Home* in the *Lord's Kingdom:*

Christ's Perfect Faith, Jesus' Good Works, and Jesus Christ's Saving of Souls Redeem the World
(Christ gives divinity, Jesus takes-sin, Jesus Christ receives reconciliation with God)

Water Baptism (dying)	1.	**Perfect Faith** - <u>God's Son Gives Divinity</u> (blood shed) ...Surrender Spirit
		• King Offers Prayer – Last Supper: Given Free Eternal Life (earth)
		• Wash Apostles' Feet - Baptism: Purify Mind
		• Break Bread/Lift Cup - Confession: Purify Heart **Submission**
		• Eat Flesh/Drink Blood - Communion: Purify Soul

(God's Son figures out how to save the lost - God becomes Man: Christmas = Perfection)

Blood Baptism (born-again)	2.	**Good Works** - <u>Mary's Son Takes-sin</u> (broken body)... Sacrifice Flesh
		• Priest Offers Sacrifice - Calvary: Given New Glorified Body (Heaven)
		• Scourging - Sacrifice 33%: Transform Mind
		• Crucifixion - Sacrifice 67%: Transform Heart **Sacrifice**
		• Tomb of Death - Sacrifice 100%: Transform Soul

(Mary's Son is taught how to escape death - Man becomes God: Easter = Imperfection)

- -

Spirit Baptism (new-life)	3.	**Save Souls** - <u>Jesus Christ Receives Forgiveness</u> (soul crushed)... Reconcile Soul
		• Son Offers Reconciliation - Resurrection: Given Dream Home (Kingdom)
		• Resurrect Messiah - Righteous Citizen: Convert Mind
		• Convert Apostles - Holy Saint: Convert Heart **Reconcile**
		• Ascend to Heaven - Son of God: Convert Soul

(Jesus Christ finds a way to live forever - God and Man become One: Halloween = New Nature)

This illustration shows that "God had to Send" a <u>Perfect Man</u> to **Exchange His Divinity** (grace) for <u>**Vital Information**</u> on *How* to *Save Lost Sinners* (job), *Live Forever* (wife), get a *Transfigured Body,* and become <u>**Worthy**</u> of a *Dream Home in God's Kingdom* (house). We see that "God is Demanding All Prayer (church);" while "Man is Demanding All Work (government)" since there is <u>No Proper Institution</u> to **Unite** *God's Wants* (worship) with *Man's Needs* (survival). Only through the "Efforts of Jesus Christ" can <u>All the Problems of the World</u> be **Solved** based on *One's Faith* (submission) to be *Justified by Grace* (sacrifice) and then *Affirmed by His Works* (reconciliation). The idea here is that through "One's Faith (baptism/beliefs)," a <u>Person</u> ***Denies himself*** (righteous citizen); then via "Grace (confession)," a <u>Person</u> ***Picks-up his Cross*** (holy saint); and finally, by "Works (communion)," a <u>Person</u> ***Comes to Follow Christ*** (perfect son). This means that a **Person** can become ***Perfect in the Sight of God*** through "His Submission (free redemption)" or <u>Rejecting Ignorance</u> to become <u>Wise</u> (new mind), then through "His Sacrifice (earned salvation)" or <u>Rejecting Cowardice</u> to become <u>Courageous</u> (new heart), and finally, through "His Reconciliation (bonus rewards)" or <u>Rejecting Greed</u> to become <u>Generous</u> (new souls). The implication is that as "Individuals," we must <u>Master the World</u> via the ***Art of Works*** (tabernacle/individual); while in a "Group (society)," we must <u>Master the Church</u> via the ***Art of Prayers*** (judges/society). Through these "Two Institutions" of <u>Spiritual Church</u> (prayers/blessings) and <u>Physical World</u> (works/lessons), we can see the   **Separate Functions** of the **Church** to *Save Lost Sinners* (being saved) and the **World** to **<u>Allow</u>** *Christians to Save Themselves* (saving self).

1. **Individuals** - <u>Fight Evil via Good Works:</u> Earning Money = Soldier-of-the-Light (world) See Limitations
   • Warriors Go into the World - Save Others: Face Lucifer's Test
2. **Societies** - <u>Surrender to Christ via Prayer:</u> Earning Grace = Living Prayer (church)... See Potential
   • Sinners Go into the Church - Save Themselves: Face God's Judgment

We see that once a "Person has Mastered" his <u>Own Salvation,</u> he can then **Strive to Evangelize the Pagan World** and **<u>Save Others,</u>** thereby **Making** a **<u>Person Eligible</u>** for ***Eternal Rewards*** (bonus blessings). This means that "If a Person Desires" to be <u>Reconciled Back</u> to the **Favor of God,** he must **Receive** both a **<u>New Holy Spirit</u>** (new heart) as a ***Holy Saint*** (save self) in *Heaven,* and also a **<u>New Righteous Flesh</u>** (new mind) as a ***Righteous Citizen*** (saving others) on *Earth*.

The following tabular information indicates "Sinners (die to self)" must <u>Master</u> **God's Praying Institutions** to **<u>Receive</u>** a *New Holy Spirit* (glorified), while "Saints (born-again)" must <u>Master</u> **Man's Working Institutions** to **<u>Receive</u>** a *New Righteous Flesh* (transfigured):

God Demands All Prayer, while Man Demands All Work as There is No Institution to Unite Them
(prayer brings God's blessing of redemption;
while work brings Man's blessing of salvation)

Holy   1. **Prayer Institutions** - <u>God's Blessing of Redemption</u> (graces)... Free
(individual)   • Self-Governing Law - Old Testament (Jews): Set Steps to Completion = Perfect Man
                           • Holy Saints - Heart of Prayer: Give Time———   Spirit
Tabernacle   • Church - Earth: Give Life——————————   Living Prayer
                           • Blessed Mother - Heaven: Give Eternal Life———   Holy Saint

- Righteousness Turns into Blessings - Prayers: God is at His ***Eternal Destination***
- Four Cups of Passover Meal - Represented by Jews' 400 Years of Slavery until Savior

(David Conquers Fortified City - Pay Bride Price and Win Bride's Hand in Marriage)

Righteous
(group)

Judges

2. **Working Institutions** - <u>Man's Blessing of Salvation</u> (money)...Earned
- Social Governing Faith - New Testament (Christians): Dynamic Response = Perfect Society
- Righteous Citizens - Mind of Toil: Give Labor——————— Flesh
- Government - Earth: Give Wealth—-Soldier-of-the-Light
- Messiah - Heaven: Give All—-Righteous Citizen
- Mistakes Turn into Lessons - Works: Christ is On His ***Eternal Journey***
- Four Cups of Last Supper - Represented by Gentiles' 4,000 Years of Sin until Savior

(Jesus Conquers Fortified Earth - Pay Bride Price and Win Bride's Hand in Marriage)

This illustration shows that "God's Graces are Free" for the <u>Asking</u> (prayer); while "Man's Money must be Earned (work)" from the <u>Sweat of One's Brow</u> (toil). The **Question** is: which is more important— ***Spiritual Holiness*** (graces) or ***Human Righteousness*** (money)? The answer is in the idea that a "Person must First Appease" <u>God's Anger</u> (father) and then **Fulfill** both <u>Man's Hopes</u> (mother) and his <u>Dreams</u> of having **Heaven on Earth** as <u>**Humankind Comes**</u> to ***Forever Live with its God.*** Through "Befriending God (prayers)," the <u>Self-Governing Law</u> is to be **Fulfilled** (Heaven) and then the **Perfect Man** (Jesus Christ) is **Created** through a **Series** of **Set Steps unto Completion** in the <u>**Form**</u> of a ***Living Prayer*** (sainthood). In contrast, through "Befriending Man (works)," the <u>Social Governing Faith</u> is to be **Fulfilled** (earth) and the **Perfect Society** (righteous world) is **Created** through a **Series** of **Dynamic Responses** in the <u>**Form**</u> of a ***Soldier-of-the-Light*** (citizenship). Now, we see that the "Job of the Jews" in the <u>Old Testament</u> was to **Establish** the <u>**Living Prayer**</u> (apple of God's eye/army general) in the ***Person of King David*** (throne/works); while the "Job of the Christians" in the <u>New Testament</u> was to **Establish** the <u>**Soldier-of-the-Light**</u> (champion of God) in the ***Person of Jesus Christ*** (temple/champion of prayer).

Note that "David's Throne has Created" the <u>Blessing of Works</u> (king), while "Jesus' Temple has Created" the <u>Blessing of Prayer</u> (priest) in **Reverse Order** to the ***Job of the Jews*** (prayer) in contrast to the ***Job of the Christians*** (works). This constant "Flipping (paradox)" <u>Back and Forth</u> between the **Purpose of the Flesh** (Jews) and the **Purpose of the Spirit** (Christians) causes a **Conflict** or **Dimensional Paradox** in the <u>**Dual Roles**</u> of ***Jesus the Man*** (works/man becomes God/Human God) and ***Christ the God*** (prayer/God becomes Man/Divine Man). We are showing here that "Man's Creation" is to be born out of <u>First his Prayer</u> (spirit); and <u>Secondly, Out of his Works</u> (flesh) which are **Combined** into the <u>**Holy Soul**</u> (prayer/works) through the ***Born-again Nature*** of ***Christ Jesus.*** Obviously, "Men are Not Capable" of <u>Creating Existence</u> but have been

Created to become the **Eternal Caretakers of Existence** (all life) as **Each of God's Children** must **Prove to One and All** that he can **Defend** the <u>Lord's Creation of Life</u> from the *Evil Forces of Death.* We see that this "Need to Conquer Death" can be seen in "Our Need to Die to Self (submission)" in <u>Christ</u> through <u>His Holy Altar</u> (sacrifice), thereby **Allowing a Person** to be **<u>Transformed</u>** (moment-by-moment) from an *Evil Sinner* into a *Holy Saint.* This means that when a "Surrendered Soul" is <u>Moving Toward God,</u> he is **Worthy** of the **Lord's Blessing,** and when he is <u>Moving Away from God,</u> he is **Worthy** of **Man's Lessons** which ultimately *Lead* to *Saving Others* or being *Blessed by God.*

This shows us that in "Submission," a <u>Person Enters a State</u> of **Unto Thine Own Self be True,** where **Every Thing he Does will be Right** (made right by God), thereby **<u>Showing</u>** that *All in his Life will Bear Fruit* (blessings/lessons). Recall that "Saint Peter" <u>Denied Christ Face-to-face</u> and then the **Lord Used** this <u>Lesson</u> to **Make Peter the 1st Pope** and **Founder** of **Christ's Church on Earth, Showing** that the **Deeper** into the *Darkness* (lesson) a **Man Goes,** the **Better** he can *See the Light of Righteousness.* Yes! In the "Physical World," <u>People are Going</u> both **Toward God** (blessed/treasures)" and **Going Away from God** (lessons/save souls), but "If a Person" <u>Believes</u> (submission) enough, be it **33%** (mind), **67%** (heart) or **100%** (soul), then he can be **Assured** that **<u>All that he is Doing</u>** will *Bear Fruit before God* on *Judgment Day.* We see that this "Process of Submission" was <u>Taught</u> to the **Jewish People** in **Egypt** (earth), in the **Desert** (Heaven), and within the **Promised Land** (Kingdom) to **Make Them <u>Impervious to Death</u>,** no matter in *What Form It might Come* (attack). We see that "Death Cannot Attack" a Surrendered Soul as he has **God's Divine Protection When** an **Awakened Soul Travels** the **Lord's** <u>Four Pathways of Life</u> and has become a *Righteous Citizen, Holy Saint, Perfect Son, and Divine Free Man.* Through these "Four Ranks," the <u>Human Race</u> can **Achieve Perfection** in the **Eyes of God,** thereby bringing **Divine Justice** to **All Who Speak, Pray, Work Against,** or **Desecrate** the *Creations of God.* The idea here is that "If a Person Speaks Against God (become sinful)," he has <u>Committed Blasphemy</u> and will be **Excommunicated** from <u>God's Temple</u> and then be *Cursed with a Sinful Nature* (ignorance/fool). Secondly, "If a Person Prays Against God (become evil)," he has <u>Committed Sorcery</u> and will become an **Outcast** of **his People** and then be *Cursed with Worldly Temptations* (cowardice/criminal). Thirdly, "If a Person Works Against God (be filled with death)," he has <u>Committed Sedition</u> and will become **Banished** from <u>Earth</u> and then be *Cursed with Lucifer's Demonic Possession* (greed/insane). Finally, if a "Person Desecrates God's Works (become damned)," he has <u>Committed Sacrilege</u> and will become **Forsaken** by <u>God</u> and then *Cursed* with *God's Eternal Striking Wrath* (selfishness/evil).

1. **Blasphemy** - <u>Speaking Against God:</u> Cursed with Sinfulness...Excommunicated from Temple
2. **Sorcery** - <u>Praying Against God:</u> Cursed with Evil... Outcast from One's People
3. **Sedition** - <u>Working Against God:</u> Cursed with Death... Banished from the Earth
4. **Sacrilege** - <u>Desecrating God's Name:</u> Cursed with Damnation...Forsaken by God Himself

At each of these "Four Levels of Rejection" by the <u>Lord God Almighty,</u> **We See** that **God** is **Forcing Mankind** to *See Its Limitations* (know God), *Its Potential* (love God), *Its Own Self-worth* (serve God), and finally, *See God Face-to-face* (become God). It all comes down to both "Growing-up" and "Maturing" to the point of <u>Knowing</u> **Nature, Man, Angels, and God Personally** and **Treating Them** with the **Proper Respect Required** by *Human, Angelic, and Divine Law.* To "Learn the Laws" of <u>God's Royal Kingdom,</u> a **Person** must **Learn Right/Wrong, Good/Evil, God's Will/man's will, and God's Reality from man's illusion** so that an **Awakened Child of God** can **Serve** *All the Forces of Life.* Obviously, these "Forces of Life" <u>Reveal</u> the **Origin of Existence** (truth), the **Function of God/Angels/Men** (law), the **Ultimate Purpose of Life** (will/servanthood), and the **Value of Life** (love/freedom) for *One and All.*

The following tabular information indicates the "Four Pathways of God," <u>Revealing Their</u> **Origin, Function, Ultimate Purpose, and Value** in bringing **Lost Souls** to **Their Eternal Redemption** in *Truth, Law, Will, and Love:*

**Man's 4 Pathways to Eternal Life Come by being
Pre-ordained, Called, Justified, and Glorified**
(pre-ordained to repent, called to prayer,
justified by works, and glorified by saving souls)

Truth   1.   **1st Pathway** - <u>Pre-ordained for Life:</u> Repentance = Free Redemption....
Knowledge
- Speaking Against God - Blasphemy: Excommunication from Temple = Cursed with Sin-nature
- Learn Right from Wrong - Become Righteous Citizen on Earth
- See Limitations - Physical Dimension: Shout Calls One's Family
- Remove Ignorance to Gain Wisdom - New Mind (origin)

Law   2.   **2nd Pathway** - <u>Called to Eternal Life:</u> Prayers = Earned Salvation...
Self-awareness
- Praying Against God - Sorcery: Outcast from People = Cursed with Worldly Temptations
- Learn Good from Evil - Become Holy Saint in Heaven
- See Potential - Spiritual Dimension: Shofar Horn Calls One's Friends
- Remove Cowardice to Gain Courage - New Heart (function)

Will   3.   **3rd Pathway** - <u>Justified before God:</u> Works = Bonus Rewards...Consciousness
- Working Against God - Sedition: Banished from Earth = Cursed with Demonic Possession
- Learn God's Will/man's will - Become Perfect Son within Kingdom
- See Self-worth - Mystical Dimension: Trumpet Calls One's Neighbors
- Remove Greed to Gain Generosity - New Soul (purpose)

Love   4. **4th Pathway** - <u>Glorification of Son:</u> Saving Souls = Freedom…Sentience
- Desecrating God - Sacrilege: Forsaken by God = Cursed by God
- Learn God's Reality/man's illusion - Become Free Man within Own Kingdom
- See Face of God - Divine Dimension: God's Voice Calls Strangers
- Remove Selfishness to Gain Unselfishness - New Life-force (value)

This illustration shows that when a "Person" <u>Sees his Limitations,</u> he has **Mastered God's Physical Dimension,** has **Removed his Ignorance** to **Obtain God's Wisdom** (new mind), and has **<u>Earned the Right</u>** to be within the *Family of God* (shout). Secondly, when a "Person" <u>Sees his Potential,</u> he has **Mastered God's Spiritual Dimension,** has **Removed his Cowardice** to **Obtain God's Courage** (new heart), and has **<u>Earned the Right</u>** to be *One of God's Friends* (Shofar). Thirdly, when a "Person" <u>Sees his Own Self-worth,</u> he has **Mastered God's Mystical Dimension,** has **Removed his Greed** to **Obtain God's Generosity** (new soul), and has **Earned the Right** to be *One of God's Neighbors* (trumpet). Finally, when a "Person" <u>Sees the Face of God,</u> he has **Mastered God's Divine Dimension,** has **Removed his Selfishness** to **Obtain God's Unselfishness** (new life-force), and has **<u>Earned the Right</u>** to be a *Stranger/free man to God* (God's voice).

1. **See One's Limitations** - <u>Master Physical Dimension:</u> Remove Ignorance to Get Wisdom..Family
2. **See One's Potential** - <u>Master Spiritual Dimension:</u> Remove Cowardice to Get Courage..Friends
3. **See One's Self-worth** - <u>Master Mystical Dimension:</u> Remove Greed to Get Generosity..Neighbors
4. **See God's Face** - <u>Master Divine Dimension:</u> Remove Selfishness to Get Unselfishness..Strangers

It should now make sense that as a "Child Grows Close" to <u>God in Love</u>, he is also **Maturing into a New State** of **Self-control** and **Self-reliance** (adulthood) until **One Day,** his most **Beloved Father** becomes **Someone he Sees** on **<u>Christmas</u>** and **<u>Easter</u>** just to *Keep in Touch* (stranger). We "Call this Mastering" the <u>Forces of Life and Death</u> just as **All Mankind** has had to **Do** since the *Dawn of Time* (growing-up). Unfortunately, "Confused Mankind (flesh)" had <u>No Idea</u> that the **Life-experience** included **Mastering the Angelic Heaven** (spirit) and **God's Kingdom of Glory** (soul) before a **Person** could truly **<u>Say he had Grown-up</u>** and is *Ready* to *Meet his God Face-to-face* (life-force). Note that the "Jewish People" represent the <u>Forces of Death</u> and that **They were Forced** into **400 Years of Egyptian Slavery** to **Pay God's Sin-debt** via **Hard-work** (sweat) and **<u>Forced Labor</u>** (blood) until the *Coming of Their Savior, Moses.* In contrast, we see that the "Gentile People" <u>Represent</u> the <u>Forces of New-life</u> (Christians) and that **They were Forced** to face **4,000 Years of Adam and Eve's Original Sin** and then are made to **Pay God's Sin-debt** in **<u>Holy Prayers</u>** (repentance) and **<u>Good Works</u>** (labor) until the *Coming of Their Savior, Jesus.*

We can now match up the "400 Years of Jewish Slavery" with their Redeeming Passover Meal and its **Four Cups of Thanksgiving,** one for each of the **400 Years of Torment in Hell,** thereby bringing forth the *Redemption of Human Flesh* (Man/death of God). Secondly, we can now match up the "4,000 Years of Gentile Sinfulness" with their Salvation at the Last Supper (Mass) and its **Four Cups of Salvation,** one for each of the **4,000 Years in Hell,** thereby bringing forth the *Salvation of Divine Spirit* (God/death of man). Now, we see that to "Save Man," it Cost 100 Years Per Cup during a *Passover Meal;* and then to "Save God," it Cost 1,000 Years Per Cup during the *Last Supper* (Mass). The great significance of these "Two Sacrificial Celebrations" is that it has Opened the Door for both the **Redemption of the Flesh** (slavery/free) and the **Salvation of the Spirit** (sinfulness/earned) to *Set Mankind Free.* We now see that it takes "100 Years of Conversion" for each of the Human Mind, Heart, Soul, and Life-force or **400 Years Total,** thereby **Culminating in the Creation** of the *Mosaic Tabernacle* (Redemption of Man). Secondly, we see that it takes "1,000 Years of Conversion" for each of the Born-again Mind, Heart, Soul, and Life-force or **4,000 Years Total**, thereby **Culminating in the Creation** of the *Catholic Church* (Salvation of God). Finally, we see that it takes a second "1,000 Years of Conversion" for each of the Divine Mind, Heart, Soul, and Life-force or **4,000 Years Total**, thereby **Culminating in the Creation** of the *New Jerusalem* (Rewards of God/Man).

Through each of these "Three Conversion Processes," God, Angels, and Men are **Made One** through the *Jewish Temple* (remove sin/men), *Christ's Church* (remove evil/Angels), and the *New Jerusalem* (remove death/God). This means that "Jesus as Man" came to Redeem Jewish Blood via the **Temple,** where **One Man Worships God** to *Save All Men.* Secondly, "Christ as God" comes to Redeem the Christian Spirit via the **Church,** where **All Men Worship God** to *Save the Lost Sheep* (one man/Judas). Finally, "Jesus Christ as God/Man" comes to Redeem the Pagan Soul via the **New Jerusalem,** where **God, Angels, and Men Worship Life Together** to *Save God from Failure* (Father). In this teaching, we see that the "Mosaic Tabernacle" or "Stone Temple (Solomon/Herod)" brought the Jews the **Ten Commandments, Sacrificial Offering, Temple Tax,** and the **Dietary Laws** to **Convert** the **Earthly Mind** to *Obedience,* the **Heart** to *Submission,* the **Soul** to *Redemption,* and the **Life-force** to *Good Health.*

1. **Ten Commandments** - Human Obedience: Worthy of New Body…Seat in Celestial Court
   * Repentance - Saintly Obedience: Worthy of Heaven on Earth
2. **Sacrificial Offering** - Human Submission: Worthy of Eternal Life…Seat in Temple Court
   * Prayers - Saintly Submission: Worthy of Paradise in Heaven
3. **Temple Tax** - Human Redemption: Worthy of New Own Kingdom…Seat in Royal Court
   * Works - Saintly Salvation: Worthy of a Kingdom of Glory
4. **Dietary Laws** - Human Good Health: Worthy of God's Friendship… Seat in Divine Court
   * Save Souls - Saintly Perfection: Worthy of Oneness with God

We also see that "Christ's Church" or "Fleshly Temple" brought the Christians **Repentance, Prayers, Works,** and **Saving Souls** to **Convert** the **Heavenly Mind** to *Obedience,* the **Heart** to *Submission,* the **Soul** to *Redemption,* and the **Life-force** to

Eternal Health. Finally, we see that the "New Jerusalem" or "Mystical Temple" brings the Saints **Righteousness, Holiness, Perfection**, and **Divinity** to convert the **Kingdom Mind** to *Obedience*, the **Heart** to *Submission*, the **Soul** to *Redemption,* and the **Life-force** to *God's Health.* Note that at the end of each "Human or Divine Ordeal," a Savior would Come and Build either a **Jewish, Christian, or Saintly Redemption Center** to **Process All Future Peoples** in **Need** of either *Redemption* (free/Jews), *Salvation* (earned/Christians), or *Rewards* (bonus/Saints).

The following tabular information indicates the "Three Redemptions of God" using His Mosaic Tabernacle (Moses), Catholic Church (Jesus), and New Jerusalem (Christ) to bring **Earth, Heaven,** and the **Kingdom** *Obedience* (peace), **Submission** (joy), *Redemption* (happiness), and *Eternal Health* (freedom):

The Mosaic Tabernacle, Catholic Church, and New Jerusalem are God's Institutions on Earth
(God creates the Jewish People, Christian People, and Holy Saints to Redeem the Evil World)

Mosaic Tabernacle	Catholic Church	New Jerusalem
Jewish People - Moses	Christian People - Jesus	Saintly People - Christ
(400 yrs. slavery)	(4,000 yrs. of sin)	(4,000 yrs. repentance)
1. Ten Commandments	1. Repentance	1. Righteousness
• Earthly Obedience	• Heavenly Obedience	• Kingdom Obedience
• New Nature	• New Behavior	• New Lifestyle
• Survival	• Death	• New-life
2. Sacrificial Offering	2. Prayers	2. Holiness
• Earthly Submission	• Heavenly Submission	• Kingdom Submission
• Earthly Good Fortune	• Heavenly Blessings	• Think for Self
• Truth	• Lie	• Reality
3. Temple Tax (silver)	3. Works	3. Perfection
• Earthly Redemption	• Heavenly Redemption	• Kingdom Redemption
• God's Forgiveness	• New Transfigured Body	• Seat in Court
• Love	• Hate	• Affection
4. Dietary Laws	4. Saving Souls	4. Divinity
• Earthly Health	• Eternal Health	• Divine Health
• Long Life	• Eternal Life	• Free Will
• Choices	• Worthless	• Priceless
(Passover Meal - 4 Cups)	(Last Supper - 4 Cups)	(Holy Mass - 4 Cups)

This illustration shows that the "Men of Earth (challenged flesh)," the "Angels in Heaven (adventurist spirit)," and "God in His Kingdom (thrilling soul)" are Preparing a Place for *Each* of **Jesus Christ's <u>New Creations of Perfection</u>** be they *Men, Angels,* or *God Himself* (human nature). We see in the previous chart that "Moses" brought the <u>Passover Meal</u> to **Transform the Jewish People** from **Slaves to Free Men** via **God's Law** (obedience), **His Sacrificial Lamb,** the **Silver Shekel,** and the **Lord's Dietary Laws, All Created** to bring forth *Righteous Living* (Earthly citizenship). Out of "God's Law," we see <u>God's Government</u> being **Formed on the Earth** via **Moses' 70 Judges,** *Who* brought *Order Out of Chaos.* Secondly, out of the "Blood Sacrifice Lifted Up (lamb)" by a "Jewish Priest," we see <u>God's Church</u> being **Formed on the Earth** via **Moses' Mosaic Tabernacle** to allow *God's Blessing* to *Fall on His Chosen People.* Thirdly, out of the "Temple Tax Given (silver)" to the <u>Lord,</u> we see <u>God's Home</u> being **Formed on Earth** via **Moses' <u>Seven Feasts</u>** to allow the *Redemption of One's Flesh.* Finally, out of the "Dietary Laws," we see <u>God's Individual Rights</u> (self) being **Formed on Earth** via **Moses' <u>Holy Land</u>** to *Create Heaven on Earth* or *God's Land of Milk and Honey.* Out of these "Four Earthly Institutions" of <u>Government</u> (ten commandments), <u>Church</u> (sacrificial offerings), <u>Home</u> (temple tax), and <u>Self</u> (dietary laws), **Moses was able to Build** a mighty **Army** of **Soldiers-of-the-Light** to *Conquer the Holy Land* and *Set the Jewish People Free.*

We also see in the previous chart that "Jesus" brought the <u>Last Supper</u> (mass) to **Transform the Christian People** from **Sinners to Saints** via **God's Blessings of Repentance, Prayers, Works,** and **Saving Souls** for *Holy Living.* Out of a "Person's Repentance," <u>God's Human Government</u> is being **Formed in Heaven** and then out of **Jesus' Righteous World,** to defeat *Criminal Behavior.* Secondly, out of a "Person's Prayer Life," <u>God's Human Church</u> is being **Formed in Heaven** (communion of saints) via **Jesus' Catholic Church** which allows the *Salvation of His Spirit* (mystical body of Christ). Thirdly, out of a "Person's Good Works," God's <u>Human Home</u> is being **Formed in Heaven** via **Jesus' Perfect Home** which allows *Eternal Rewards for One's Soul.* Finally, out of a "Person's Evangelization (saving souls)," God's <u>Perfect Man</u> (self) is being **Welcomed into Heaven** via **Jesus' New Nature** which allows a *Son of God* to be *Set Free.* Out of these "Four Heavenly Institutions" of <u>Government</u> (repentance), <u>Church</u> (prayers), <u>Home</u> (works), and <u>Self</u> (saving souls), **Jesus is able to Build** a **Holy People** of **Living Prayers of Love** (witnesses) to **<u>Give God</u>** His own *Army of Soul Savers* (soldiers-of-the-light).

We see in the previous chart that "Christ" brought the <u>Holy Mass</u> to **Transform the Pagan People** from **Death to New-life** (Saintly People) via **God's Righteousness, Holiness, Perfection,** and **Divinity** to bring forth a *New State* of *Perfect Living.* Out of a "Person's Obedience (submit/belief)," <u>God's Divine Government</u> is being **Formed in God's Kingdom;** then out of **Christ's Righteous World**, a *Righteous Citizen* will *Gain* a *New Transfigured Body.* Secondly, out of a "Person's Submission (sacrifice)," <u>God's Divine Church</u> is being **Formed in God's Kingdom;** then out of **Christ's Holy Church,** a *Saint will Gain* a *New Glorified Spirit.* Thirdly, out of a "Person's Redemption (reconciliation)," <u>God's Divine Home</u> is being **Formed in God's Kingdom;** then out of **Christ's Perfect Home,** a *Son will Gain* a *New Holy Soul.* Finally, out of a "Person's Eternal Health," a <u>Personal Life</u> is being **Formed in God's Kingdom;** then out of **Christ's New Nature,** a *Free Man will Gain* a *New Sacred*

Life-force. Out of these "Four Kingdom Institutions" of <u>Government, Church, Home,</u> and <u>Self,</u> **Christ would be able to Build** a **Sacred People of Prodigal Sons and Daughters** to *Give God* an *Army of Beloved Children*. Now we see that by "Worshiping God," a <u>Sinner can become a Saint</u> and **Earn the Title Deeds** to **Earth, Heaven,** and the **Kingdom of God,** all in the *Name of Jesus Christ*.

This means that the "Human Race" is being <u>Called to Earn Its Place</u> in the **Kingdom** through each **Person's Repentance** or *Agony in the Garden* (give life), his **Prayers** or *Scourging at the Pillar* (give wealth), his **Works** or *Crucifixion on the Cross* (give labor), his **Saving of Others** or *Death in the Tomb* (give-up). Through each of these "Four Acts of Faith," a <u>Person</u> can <u>Worship, Praise, Thank,</u> and <u>Befriend God</u> to become **Worthy** of the *Lord's Blessings* (earth/survival), *Anointings* (Heaven/truth), *Sanctification* (Kingdom/love), and *Consecration* (self/choice). Note that to be "Blessed (see suffering)," a <u>Person</u> must be <u>Thought of by God;</u> to be "Anointed (hear cries)," a <u>Person</u> must be <u>Spoken to by God;</u> to be "Sanctified (recognize covenant)," a person must be <u>Touched by God;</u> and to be "Consecrated (come to help)," a person must <u>Sup with God,</u> all in the *Name of Jesus Christ*. This means that "If a Person Fails God," he must be <u>Reconciled Back to God</u> by **Sacrificing** his *Mind, Heart, Soul, Life-force, and Nature*.

We see in "Leviticus: Chapter 26" that <u>God Defines</u> his **Five Cycles of Discipline** which **Call All His Children** from **Death into New-life** by **Correcting Their Wicked Behavior** as *Babies* (mind), *Teenagers* (heart), *Adults* (soul), *Wise Men* (life-force), and *Free Men* (nature). This means that the "1st Cycle of Discipline" is the <u>Conversion of Babies</u> from **Ignorance to Wisdom** (intellect) as **They Strive** to attain their **Own New Body** and becoming a *Righteous Man in the Eyes of God*. Secondly, the "2nd Cycle of Discipline" is the <u>Conversion of Teenagers</u> from **Cowardice to Courage** (emotions) as **They Strive** to attain **Eternal Life** and becoming a *Holy Man in the Eyes of God*. Thirdly, the "3rd Cycle of Discipline" is the <u>Conversion of Adults</u> from **Greedy Monsters to Generous Souls** (instincts) as **They Strive** to attain their **Own Royal Kingdoms** and becoming a *Perfect Man* in the *Eyes of God*. Fourthly, the "4th Cycle of Discipline" is the <u>Conversion of Wise Men</u> from **Selfish Fools to Unselfish Saints** (nature) as **They Strive** to attain their **Eternal-freedom** and becoming a *Free Man in the Eyes of God*. Finally, the "5th Cycle of Discipline" is the <u>Conversion of Free Men</u> from **Human to Divine** (lifestyle) as **They Strive** to attain **Eternal-servanthood** and becoming a *Soul Saver in the Eyes of God*. We now see that the "Human Race" must <u>Enter God's</u> **Conversion Experience** to **Receive** its *New Minds* (see), *Hearts* (hear), *Souls* (smell), *Life-forces* (taste), and *Natures* (touch). It should now make sense that the "Human Race" has been <u>Cast into Five Levels</u> of **Divine Rejection** to **Force** the **Flesh to Grow-up** (think for self) and the **Spirit to Mature** (love God) in the *Eyes of God*. The idea here is to see that as "Each Person Grows" into <u>Adulthood,</u> he is actually **Traveling Farther and Farther** from **God's Divine Truth**, until that **Faithful Day When he Realized** that *he is Wrong* (flesh) and that *God is Unconditionally Right* (spirit).

The following tabular information indicates the "Five Mystical Cycles/Marks Given" by the <u>Lord</u> as **One** of **His Children Falls Deeper and Deeper** into the <u>Evil One's Pit of Sin</u> based on his *Rebellious Behavior*:

**Five Cycles/Marks of Disobedience Depict Those
Souls Chosen to be Damned and Lost Forever**
(mankind is given a new baby mind, teenage heart,
adult soul, wise man life-force, and free man nature)

Truth
(baby)

1. **1st Cycle/Orphan** - <u>Ignorance to Wisdom:</u> New Baby Mind…Remove Sin-nature

   A. *Excommunication from One's Temple* - Mind Cursed with Sin

Righteous
Man

   - Blasphemy - Speaking Against God: Worship No Other gods
   - Cursed by High Priest - Caiaphas: Forgive My Enemies = Remove Ignorance
   - No Baptism - Live with Original Sin: Dying = Seek Righteousness

   B. *Mark of Hunger* - Starvation/fasting: Deserted Soul has No Inheritance: Thomas

Free
Redemption

   - Guilty Conscience/Confession - Soul has Lost its Power of Creation (blind)
   - Forced to Forever Seek Peace of Mind - No Holy Host (flesh)

   C. *Jesus Takes Away Jewish Divine Authority* - Credentials (omnific)

New Body

   - Warning - Failure to Surrender: Dying to Selfishness

   (Caiaphas has his Temple destroyed by Christ - Body becomes Temple of God)

Law
(teenager)

2. **2nd Cycle/Widow** - <u>Cowardice to Courage:</u> New Teenage Heart… Remove Worldly Temptations

   A. *Outcast from One's People* - Heart Cursed with Evil

Holy
Man

   - Sorcery - Praying Against God: Worship No Graven Idols
   - Cursed by King of the Jews - King Herod: Forgive My Neighbors = Remove Cowardice
   - No Holy Temple - Live Without God's Blessing: Death = Seek Holiness

   B. *Mark of Thirst* - Nakedness/sackcloth: Frightened Soul has No Husband: Peter

Earned
Salvation

   - Contrition - Soul has Lost its Power of Knowledge (deaf)
   - Forced to Forever Seek Joy of Heart - No Sacred Wine (blood)

   C. *Jesus Takes Away Jews' Holiness* - Grace (omniscient)

Eternal Life

   - Silent Anger - Failure to Believe in Self: Facing Selfishness

   (Herod has his Nation destroyed by Christ - Eternal Life becomes Nations of God)

Will
(adult)

3. **3rd Cycle/Poor** - <u>Greed to Generosity:</u> New Adult Soul…Remove Demonic Possession

   A. *Banished from the Earth* - Soul Cursed with Death

Perfect
Man

   - Sedition - Working Against God: Never Take God's Name in Vain
   - Cursed by Emperor of Rome - Pontius Pilate: Forgive My Friends = Remove Greed
   - No Reconciliation - Live Without God's Forgiveness

B. *Mark of Shame* - Homelessness/ashes: Poor Souls are Bankrupt in Faith: Judas

Bonus • Repentance - Soul has Lost its Power to Change

Rewards • Forced to forever Seek Happiness of the Soul – No Absolution (confession)

C. *Jesus Takes Away Jews' Kingly Rule* - Power (omnifarious)

Kingdom • Verbal Rage - Failure to Follow Good Conscience: Facing Righteousness

(Pilate has his World destroyed by Christ - Royal Kingdom becomes New World of God)

Love 4. **4th Cycle/Stranger** - Selfishness to Unselfishness: New Wise Man… Remove God's Curse

A. *Forsaken by God* - Soul Cursed with Damnation

• Insanity - Joining Lucifer: Keep the Sabbath Day Holy

Free • Cursed by the Almighty - Eternal Father: Forgive My Family = Remove

Man Selfishness

• No Passover Meal - Live Without Jesus' Nourishment

B. *Mark of Weeping* - Outcast/repent: Shunned Souls have No Friends: Lucifer

Gift of • Atonement - Soul has Lost its Divine Power

Freedom • Forced to Forever Seek God's Respect - No Holy Mass (communion)

C. *Jesus Takes Away Jews' Promised Land* - Livelihood (omnipotent)

Freedom • Striking Wrath - Failure to Become Instinctive Disciple: Facing Holiness

(God has his Creation destroyed by Christ - Divine Freedom becomes New Creation of God)

Divine 5. **5th Cycle/Enemy** - Evil to Good: New Free Man… Remove All Curses

A. *Hated by Self* - Soul Cursed with Oblivion

• Evil - Becoming Own god: Honor Father and Mother

Servant • Cursed by Oneself - Sin-nature: Forgive My Self = Remove Evil

Man • No Friendship of God - Live Without One's Personal Respect

B. *Mark of No Name* - Forgotten/retribution: Lost Soul has No Life: Jesus

Saving • Retribution - Soul has Lost its Value of Life

Others • Forced to Forever Seek Self-worth - No Final Blessing (forgiveness)

C. *Jesus Takes Away Jews' Sonship* - Self-respect (omnipresent)

God's Friendship • Absolute Oblivion - Failure to Find Eternal-freedom: Facing Perfection

(Self has Pride destroyed by Christ - Born-again Life becomes New Self of God)

This illustration shows that the "Life-experience" is All About **Getting** an **Earthly Body, Eternal Life,** a **Royal Kingdom, Freedom,** and finally, **Saving Others,** *All* in the *Name of Pleasing the Lord God Almighty Himself.* The "Major Theme" here is that as Babies (ignorant fools), we are **Gluttons**; as Teenagers (cowards), we **Lie, Cheat, and Steal**; as Adults (greedy), we **Want Everything** (envious); as Wise Men (selfish), we are **Full of Lust for Self-importance;** and finally, as <u>Free Men</u> (prideful), we **Seek Only Our Own Fame and Fortune** (power of money). This process of "Growth and Maturity" <u>Creates</u> **Righteous, Holy, and Perfect** <u>Sons of God</u> with the *Ability to Live with Their Creator Forever*. Through the "Lord's Five Cycles of Discipline," the <u>Human Race</u> is able to **Comprehend** the **Mission of Christ** as **He Comes to Earth** to <u>**Transform Man's**</u> *Temple, Nation, World, God's Creation,* and the *Messiah's Own Nature* (self). We see that the "Lord Jesus Christ" is <u>Hell-bent</u> on **Taking Away Mankind's Authority, Holiness, Kingly Rule, Promised Land,** and **Sonship** to <u>**Set Mankind Free**</u> from its *Sins, Evil, Death, Damnation,* and eventual *Oblivion*. Obviously, the "Lord Jesus Christ" is by <u>All Definitions</u> **Our Savior** as **He Alone can Perform** the **Impossible of the Impossible** to bring forth *God's New Heaven and new earth*.

Now, let's "Examine More Closely" each of <u>God's Five Cycles of Discipline</u> as the **Human Race** is <u>**Changed**</u> from a *Baby*, to *Teenager,* to *Adult,* to *Wise Man,* and finally, to a *Free Man*.

1. <u>1st Cycle of Discipline</u> - Baby Conversion: New Body = New Mind + Creative Power

    We see that the "Baby Cycle" signifies <u>God Removing Man's Ignorance</u> (sin-nature) and then <u>Inserting God's Wisdom</u> to **Give a Lost Broken Sinner** a <u>**New Mind**</u> to *See his Own Limitations*. If a "Person is a Blasphemer," he is <u>Speaking Against God</u> and is **Violating** the **Lord's 1st Commandment** which is **Not to have Any Other gods before You** or <u>**You will Face**</u> *Excommunication from God's Temple*. We see that the "High Priest Caiaphas" said to <u>Christ:</u> **Come Down and We will Believe in You,** thereby <u>Making him an Enemy of God</u> as the *Guilty Blood of the Goat*. This means that "God's Goat Curse Demands" that a <u>Soul Receive No Baptism,</u> thereby **Forcing a Person to Live** with his **Original Sin** (dying), until *he is Saved* and becomes a *Righteous Citizen on Earth*. Anyone who is "Cursed by God" will be <u>Marked by Hunger</u> as he **Faces Starvation** or **Fasting,** thereby showing that a *Deserted Soul has No Inheritance* (Saint Thomas). At the "Baby Level of Conversion," a <u>Person is Cursed </u> with a **Guilty Conscience** and must **Go to Confession,** because his **Soul has Lost** its **Power of Creation** and has become a *Blind Fool*. The idea is that a "Blind Fool" must Forever <u>Seek</u> **Peace of Mind** as he has **Lost God's Holy Host** and the **Eternal Nourishment** of his *Human Flesh* (new body).

    We see that "Jesus Christ" is <u>Calling the Jews</u> **Blind Fools** and has **Come** to **Take Away Their Divine Authority** (temple) and their **Magisterial Mosaic Credentials** (law) to *Create Life Out of Death* (omnific/creation). We see that the "Lord" was <u>Warning the Jews</u> that **They had Failed to Surrender** to **His Father's Will** and had <u>**Not Died to Self**</u> as *Required by the Mosaic Law*. This means that only the "Righteous Man" is to be<u> Given Free Redemption,</u> thereby **Making him Worthy** of a **New Body** because he has <u>**Won the Favor of God**</u> and has *Pleased the Lord God Almighty*. It is now clear that the "High Priest Caiaphas" had his

Temple Destroyed and then **Jesus** has **Made His Body** the *New Temple of God* (temple/life).

2. 2nd Cycle of Discipline - Teenage Conversion: Eternal Life = New Heart + Knowing Power

    We see that the "Teenage Cycle" signifies God Removing Man's Cowardice (worldly temptations) and then Inserting God's Courage to **Give a Born-again Christian** a **New Heart** to *See his Own Potential*. If a "Person is a Sorcerer," he is Praying Against God and is **Violating** the **Lord's 2nd Commandment** which is **Not to Worship Graven Images** or **You will Face** being an *Outcast from Your People*. We see that "King Herod" told Christ to **Change Water into Wine,** thereby **Making the King Evil** in the **Sight of God** as the *Guilty Blood of the Goat*. This means that "God's Goat Curse Demands" a Soul Not Receive a Temple or Nation, thereby **Forcing a Person to Live** without **God's Blessing** (death), until he is *Saved* and becomes a *Holy Man in Heaven*. Anyone who is "Cursed by God" will be Marked by Thirst as **he Faces Nakedness** or **Sackcloth,** thereby showing that a **Frightened Soul** has *No Husband* (Saint Peter). We see at the "Teenage Level of Conversion" that a Person is Awakened and comes to **Contrition** as his **Soul has Lost** its **Power of Knowledge** and has *Fallen into Darkness*. The idea is that a "Confused Fool" must Forever Seek the **Joy of the Heart** as he has **Lost God's Holy Wine** and the **Eternal Nourishment** of his *Human Spirit* (eternal life). We see that "Jesus Christ" was Calling the Jews **Confused Fools** and had **Come to Take Away Their Jewish Holiness** (nation) and their **Royal Davidic Grace** (faith) to *Create Prosperity Out of Poverty* (omniscient/knowledge). We see that the "Lord" was Complaining to the Jews that **They had Failed to Listen** to **His Father's Words** and had **Not Obeyed His Commandments** as *Required by the Kingship of David*. This means that only the "Holy Man" is then Allowed to Earn his Salvation, thereby **Making him Worthy** of **Eternal Life** because he has **Won the Favor of God** and has *Pleased the Lord God Almighty*. It is now clear that "King Herod" had his Nation Destroyed and then **Jesus** has **Made His Spirit** the *New Nation of God* (throne/new-life).

3. 3rd Cycle of Discipline - Adult Conversion: Royal Kingdom = New Soul + Changing Power

    We see that the "Adult Cycle" signifies God Removing Man's Greed (demonic possession) and then **Inserting Man's Generosity** to **Give Christ's New Creation** a **New Soul** to *See its Own Self-worth*. If a "Person is a Seditionist," he is Working Against God and is **Violating** the **Lord's 3rd Commandment** which is **Not to Take God's Name in Vain** or **You will Face** being *Banished from Planet Earth*. We see that "Pontius Pilate" asked Christ: **Are You a King,** thereby **Cursing himself to Death** in the **Sight of God** as *Guilty Blood of the Goat*. This means that "God's Goat Curse Demands" a Soul can Not Receive a World, thereby **Forcing a Person** to **Live without God's Forgiveness** (damnation), until he is **Saved** and becomes a *Perfect Man within God's Kingdom*. Anyone who is "Cursed by God" will be <u>Marked by Shame</u> as he **Faces Homelessness** or **Ashes**, thereby showing that a **Poor Soul** has become **Bankrupt** (Judas). We see at the "Adult Level of Conversion," a <u>Person is Changed</u> and comes to **Repentance** as a **Soul that has Lost** its **Power of Transformation** (change) and has *Fallen into a Pit of Sin*. The idea is that a "Sinful Soul" must <u>Forever Seek</u> the **Happiness of the Soul** as it has **Lost God's Holy Word** and the <u>**Eternal Nourishment**</u> of its *Human Soul* (royal kingdom). We see that "Jesus Christ" was <u>Calling the Jews'</u> **Sinful Fools** and had **Come to Take Away Their Kingly Rule** (world) and their **Divine Power** (works) to **Create an Eternal Kingdom** out of a *Destroyed Israel* (omnifarious/change). We see that the "Lord was <u>Complaining to the Jews</u> that **They had Failed** to **Do God's Will** and had **Not Tried to Serve God** as *Required by His Sonship Charter*. This means that the "Perfect Man" is to be <u>Given Bonus Rewards,</u> thereby **Making him Worthy** of his **Own Royal Kingdom** because he has **Won the Favor of God** and has *Pleased the Lord God Almighty*. It is now clear that "Pontius Pilate" had his <u>World Destroyed</u> and then **Jesus** has **Made His Soul** the *New World of God* (divine life).

4.   <u>4th Cycle of Discipline</u> - Wise Man Conversion: Freedom = New Life-force + Supreme Power

We see that the "Wise Man Cycle" signifies <u>God Removing Man's Selfishness</u> (God's curse) and then **Inserting Man's Unselfishness** to **Give Christ's Followers** a <u>**New Life-force**</u> to *See Their Own Perfection*. If a "Person is a Satanist," he is <u>Against God</u> and is **Violating** the **Lord's 4th Commandment** which is to **Keep the Sabbath Holy** or <u>**You will Face**</u> being *Forsaken by God*. We see that the "Lord God Almighty," said <u>Christ, You have Forsaken Me</u> (takes all sin), thereby **Cursing All Divinity** to **Oblivion** in the <u>**Sight of God**</u> as *Guilty Blood of the Goat*. This means that "God's Goat Curse Demands" a <u>Soul can Not Receive its Own Creation,</u> thereby **Forcing a Person** to **Live Without Jesus' Nourishment** (oblivion), until he is **Saved** and becomes a *Free Man* in the *Friendship of God*. Anyone who is "Cursed by God" will be <u>Marked by Weeping</u> as he **Faces being an Outcast of his People** or **Wanderer**, thereby showing that a **Shunned Soul** has *No Friends* (Lucifer). We see that at the "Wise Man Level of Conversion," a <u>Person is Powerless</u> and **Offers Retribution** as a **Soul has Lost** its <u>**Power of Influence**</u> (power) and has *Fallen into a Pit of Evil*. The idea is that an "Evil Person" must Forever Seek the Pleasures of his **Life-force** as he has **Lost God's Divine Truth** and the **Eternal Nourishment** of his *Human Life-force* (freedom). We see that "Jesus Christ" was <u>Calling the Jews</u> **Evil Fools** and had **Come to Take Away Their Promised Land and Their Ability to Think** (imagination) to **Create** an <u>**Eternal Land of Milk and Honey**</u> out of a *Destroyed Garden of Eden*.

5. 5th Cycle of Discipline - Free Man Conversion: Servanthood = New Nature + Presence Felt Power

We see that the "Free Man Cycle" signifies God Removing Man's Fear of Slavery (Man's curse) and then **Inserting Man's Servanthood** to **Give God's Sons** a **New Nature** to *See his Own Servanthood*. If a "Person is an Evil Monster," he is Against God and is **Violating** the **Lord's 5th Commandment** which is to **Honor Thy Father and Thy Mother** or **You will Face** being *Rejected by Your Own Self*. We see that each of "God's Children" is Rejecting His Own Identity (name), thereby **Cursing an Unknown Soul** to **Facing Life** in the **Sight of God** as *Innocent Blood of the Lamb*. This means that "God's Lamb Blessing Demands" a Soul can Now Receive its Own Identity (name on white rock), thereby **Forcing a Person** to **Live Without His Own Personal Respect** (new name), until he is **Saved** and becomes a *Servant to All* in the *Companionship of God*. Anyone who is "Blessed by God" will be Marked by Great Joy as he **Faces being Resurrected** from **Death,** thereby showing that a **Born-again Soul** has become *One with its God* (Jesus). We see that at the "Free Man Level of Conversion," a Person is Empowered and **Offers Eternal Gifts** as a **Soul has Found** its **Powers of Influence** (presence) and has *Overcome Lucifer's Pit of Evil*. The idea is that a "Holy Person" must Forever Seek Serving Others within his **Nature** as he has **Found God's Divine Truth** and the **Eternal Nourishment** of his own *Human Nature* (servanthood). We see that "Jesus Christ" is Calling the Jews into **Self-control** and has **Come to Give Them** the **Ability to Rule Their Own Desires** (needs/wants) to **Transform God** into a *Man on Earth*.

This "Worthiness before God" allows each Converted Soul to become eligible for **Physical Redemption** (free), **Spiritual Salvation** (earned), and **Mystical Rewards** (bonus) allowing a soul to **Earn its Place** within the *Kingdom of God*. The message here is that if a person is once "Noticed" or "Thought of by God," then the Lord can See his Suffering and out of God's **Divine Compassion,** He will come to **Redeem** a *Lost Soul for Free* (Barabbas). Secondly, if a person is "Spoken to by God," then the Lord can Hear his Cries for Help and out of God's **Divine Kindness,** He will come to **Save a Tormented Soul** through *Good Works*. Finally, if a person is "Touched by God," then the Lord can Recognize His Covenant and out of God's **Divine Honesty,** He will come to **Reward this Soul** for its efforts to *Save Others*. The Lord is telling us that if a person is willing to "Surrender his Life (obey commandments)" to God, he will *Catch God's Attention* (mind); if one "Sacrifices his Wealth (give all to poor)" to God, he will *Earn God's Friendship* (heart); and if one is "Reconciled via his Labors" back to God, he will then *Enter the Companionship of God* (soul). By "Catching God's Attention (faithful sinner)," "Making His Friendship (grace-filled Christian)," and becoming "His Constant Companion (hard-working saint)," a person can attain *Personal Freedom* (look at cross), *Social Liberty* (touched by priest's hands), and finally, *Divine Independence* (washed in blood). Recall that during the time of "Moses," if a person Looked at the Brazen Serpent, he would be *Healed of Snake Bite* (forgiven); if a person was <u>Touched by the Hands of a Priest,</u> he would be ***Healed of Leprosy*** (confession); and if a person was <u>Washed in the Blood of a Lamb,</u> he would be ***Forgiven of All his Sins*** (communion).

Through each of these "Stages of Forgiveness," <u>Jesus Christ</u> reconciles one's **Venial Sins** (look at cross), **Mortal Sins** (touched by priest's hands,) and **Capital Sins** (washed in Christ's blood) back to ***Divine Justice***. The idea is that if a person has his "Venial Sins Forgiven (dead mind)," he is <u>Worthy of Eternal Life</u> (Heaven on earth); if one has his "Mortal Sins Forgiven (dead heart)," he is <u>Worthy of a New Body</u> (paradise in Heaven); and if he has his "Capital Sins Forgiven (dead soul)," he is <u>Worthy of Living</u> in God's <u>Kingdom of Glory</u> (royal kingdom). This means that "Jesus Christ" is offering each of <u>His Followers</u> **Life on Earth, Eternal Life in Heaven,** and **Divine Life in God's Kingdom** as his **<u>Reward</u>** for *Sacrificing* his *Life* (flesh), *Wealth* (spirit), and *Labor* (soul) ***to God***. The point is that each of "God's Children" can receive <u>Free Redemption</u> (give life) when the Lord *Sees his Suffering* (thought of/repentance), and/or <u>Earn his Own Salvation</u> (give wealth) when God *Hears a Person's Cry for Help* (spoken to/prayers). Finally, "God's Children" can receive their own <u>Bonus Rewards</u> (save others/works) when the Lord **Recognizes Their Covenant** (touched by) and comes to **Save His Children** from ***Eternal Damnation***. This means that the "Life-experience" is all about becoming a <u>Righteous Citizen</u> on ***Earth*** (eternal life), a <u>Holy Saint</u> in ***Heaven*** (new body), and a <u>Son of God</u> within God's ***Kingdom of Glory***. It is now clear that through "Repentance (submit mind)," God can <u>See a Person's Suffering</u> (sin-nature). Through "Prayers (sacrifice heart)," God can <u>Hear a Person's Cry for Help</u> (worldly temptations), and through "His Works (reconcile soul)," God <u>Recognizes His Covenant</u> (demonic possession) and comes to **Rescue His Child** from ***Sin, Evil, and Death***.

The following tabular information indicates that when "God Sees One's Suffering" or <u>Repentance,</u> **He will Come** with ***His Free Physical Redemption*** (give life/worship); just as when "God Hears One's Cry for Help" or <u>Prayers,</u> **He will Accept** a ***Christian's Earned Salvation*** (give wealth/praise). Finally, when God "Recognizes His Covenant" or <u>One's Works,</u> **He will Offer** a **Living Saint** *His **Bonus Reward*** (give labor) as a **Devout Soul Strives** to **<u>Save the Souls of Others</u>** in the ***Name of Jesus Christ***:

God Sees Suffering/Repentance, God Hears Cries/Prayers, and God Recognizes Covenant/Works
(receiving free redemption, earning salvation, and obtaining bonus rewards from God's mercy)

Thought of   1. **God Sees One's Suffering** - <u>Repentance:</u> Free Redemption…Give Life
(mind)   • Life on Earth - God becomes Man: 400 Years of Egyptian Slavery
Blessed   • Learning Right from Wrong - Righteous Citizen: Title Deed to Earth
                    • Heaven on Earth - Mastering Truth: Celestial Court: Kingship Blessing
(repentance offered upon God's Altar of Submission to break the chains of slavery)

Spoken to	2.	**God Hears Cries for Help** - <u>Prayers:</u> Earned Salvation…Give Wealth
(heart)		• Eternal Life in Heaven - Man becomes God: 40 Years in Desert
Anointed		• Learning Good from Evil - Holy Saint: Title Deed to Heaven
		• Paradise in Heaven - Mastering Law: Temple Court: Priesthood Blessing

(prayers offered upon God's Pulpit of Sacrifice to open the prison doors of evil)

Touched by	3.	**God Recognizes His Covenant** - <u>Works:</u> Bonus Rewards…Give Labor
(soul)		• Divine Life in Kingdom - God and Man become One: 50 Years Fighting
Sanctified		• Learning God's Will from man's will - Son of God: Title Deed to Kingdom
		• Kingdom of Glory - Mastering Will: Royal Court: Sonship Blessing

(works offered upon God's Chair of Reconciliation to overcome guards of death)

This illustration shows that when a person "Suffers 400 Years of Slavery (give life)," this feat is considered an <u>Appropriate Period of Repentance</u> (physical) to **Qualify** for *God's Gift of Redemption* (righteous citizenship). Secondly, when a person "Cries for Help in a Desert for 40 Years (give wealth)," this feat is considered to be a <u>Worthy Prayer to God</u> (spiritual) to **Qualify** for *God's Blessing of Salvation* (holy saint). Finally, when God "Recognizes His Covenant after 50 Years of Fighting (give labor)," this feat is considered to be a <u>Work of Honor before God</u> (mystical) to **Qualify** for *God's Blessing of Bonus Rewards* (perfect son). The idea here is to see that by "Suffering Slavery," a person can obtain <u>Eternal Life,</u> thereby *Breaking His Chains of Slavery* (personal freedom). Secondly, we see that by "Crying in a Desert," a person can obtain a <u>New Body,</u> thereby *Opening the Doors of Evil* (social liberty). Finally, we see that "Fighting for a Homeland" allows a person to obtain his <u>Own Kingdom,</u> thereby *Overcoming the Guards of Death*. Recall that both "Peter" and "Paul" were put in <u>Prison</u> to be **Chained to the Wall** in a **Locked Cell** with **Prison Guards** on both sides to ensure that they would have *No Way of Escape*. We see that in both cases, "God Sent His Power" to <u>Break the Chains</u> (sin), <u>Open the Cell</u> (evil), and <u>Scare Away the Guards</u> (death) to **Set Peter and Paul Free**, but **Paul** stayed inside his **Unlocked Cell** to **Protect the Guards** from being *Killed for his Escape*. This "Act of Mercy" <u>Converted One of the Horrified Guards</u> when this **Guard Returned** and found *Paul still in his Cell* to demonstrate the *Awesome Power of God*. We see "Peter (Jews)" and "Paul (gentiles)" clearly demonstrated the <u>Divine Power of God</u> to prove that once the **Human Race Masters** this **Awesome Power,** then <u>**Nothing could Stop It**</u> from *Mastering All that It Serves*.

The "Human Race" has been told by God to <u>Go Forth and Multiply,</u> **Conquer the Entire Earth**, and place every inch of **Land** under the *Care of a Righteous Man - New Adam*. This means that "Man Needs" to <u>Pass Lucifer's Test</u> (demonic possession/church) or **Master Endurance,** <u>Pass God's Judgment</u> (worldly temptations/government) or **Establish Character**, and <u>Pass his Own Self-evaluation</u> (sin-nature/home) or **Become Perfect** in the **Sight of God**. This need to be "Respected by God" <u>Sits at the Center</u> of *God's Grand Design* as both **Jacob's Son, Joseph** and **God's Son, Jesus** <u>**Stand-up Against All Evil**</u> to *Honor Their Sacred Vows to Their Fathers*.

In contrast to "Joseph and Jesus," we see the <u>Corrupted Souls of Simeon</u> (prison) and <u>Judas</u> (hell) as they both **Betrayed Their Brothers** for the **Love of Gold**, with

No Regard for *Family Integrity* (name/ethics) or *Human Decency* (honor/morals). In these "Two Men," we see that <u>Simeon</u> will bring a **Curse of 400 Years** of <u>Egyptian Slavery</u> upon the *Jewish People*, and that <u>Judas</u> will bring an **Eternal Curse** of **Damnation in Hell** upon the *Whole World*. Yet, in the case of "Joseph," he was <u>Honored by God</u> with a **Blessing** of a *Promised Land of Milk* (human love) and *Honey* (divine love), while "Jesus" is <u>Honored by God</u> with a **Blessing** of a *Kingdom of Glory* both *On Earth* (human love) and *In Heaven* (divine love). We now see the tremendous "Need to be Respected by God" and the "Need to Pass All Tests" as the <u>Life-experience</u> is **Designed** to **Reveal One's Character,** either *Good* (Joseph/Jesus) or *Evil* (Simeon/Judas). Note that the "Jewish People" were willing to <u>Sell Jesus</u> (take-sin) into *Eternal Slavery on Calvary*, while the "Christian People" are willing to <u>Feed the Whole World</u> (give divinity) in *Jesus' Holy Name*. This means that the "Jewish People" have been <u>Chosen</u> to <u>Offer-up</u> *Jesus' Body Broken* (goat) to *Pay for Sin* (remove faults); while the "Christian People" have been <u>Chosen</u> to **Offer-up** *Christ's Shed Blood* (lamb) to *Create Saints* (gain virtues).

The idea here is that through the "Evil Acts" of <u>Simeon and Judas</u> was to come the *Righteousness of Man* (world/ethics/lessons); while through the "Holy Acts" of <u>Joseph and Jesus</u> was to come the *Holiness of Man* (church/morals/blessings). Out of these "Four Men (Simeon/Judas/Joseph/Jesus)," the <u>World</u> (flesh) would be **Filled** with **Righteous Men** to *Take-sin* (earth), and the <u>Church</u> (spirit) would be **Filled** with **Holy Men** to *Create Saints* (Heaven). In this teaching, the "Lord is Telling Us" that <u>God is Love</u> (all is good) and that the **Negative Forces of God** (Evil Spirit) are simply an **Illusion** (simulation) because **God's Hate** would be too *Great to Suffer If it were Real*. In short, the "Lord is Saying" that even <u>Bad will Bear Fruit,</u> thereby making **Sin, Evil, Death, Damnation, Hell, and Gehenna,** *Divine Simulations of a Real Curse*. We see this "Simulation Concept" in the <u>Story of Simeon</u> as he was **Forgiven** by his **Brother, Joseph** after he **Paid his Debt to Society** (prison) and was allowed to become a *Rehabilitated Member of Jacob's Family*.

The following tabular information indicates that "Simeon" represents "Judas" as both of these <u>Men</u> were to be **Cursed for Betraying Their Brothers** and for **Breaking** their **Sacred Vows of Honor**. Secondly, "Joseph" represents "Jesus" as both of these <u>Men</u> were to be **Blessed by Feeding Their Starving Brothers** and for **Keeping** their *Sacred Vows of Honor*:

Simeon the Fool Represents Judas the Traitor,
while Wise Joseph Represents Jesus the Savior
(Simeon/Judas pay sin-debts,
while Joseph and Jesus feed the starving with the bread of life)

God's Curse	1.	**Simeon is Judas** - <u>Paying Sin-debt in Prison:</u> One Year…Traitor
		• Simeon Betrays his Brother Joseph - Sold into Slavery
		• Cursed with 400 Years of Egyptian Slavery - Jewish People
		• Simeon Breaks Sacred Vow to Father Jacob - Learn Wrong
		• Judas Betrays Christ with a Kiss - Sold into Damnation

- Cursed with Eternal-damnation in Hell - Lost Souls **Learn Lessons**
- Judas Breaks Sacred Vow to Father God - Learn Evil • New Flesh
- Great Evil Abounds - Supernatural Order: God's Champion Comes
- World - Righteous Man: Master of Ethics (Mosaic law)
- Learn the Lessons of Life - Flesh: One Blessing of Isaac

(given free new body - learn right from wrong: become righteous citizen on earth)

God's
Blessing

2. **Joseph is Jesus** - <u>Feeding Starving People:</u> Seven Years…Savior
- Joseph Saves his Brothers from Starvation - Purchase of Wheat
- Blessed with Promised land of Milk and Honey - Israeli People
- Joseph Makes Sacred Vow to Pharaoh - Learn Right
- Jesus Saves His Brothers from Eternal Starvation - Purchase of Host
- Blessed with Earned Salvation - Christian People **Receive Blessings**
- Jesus Makes Sacred Vow to God - Learn Good • New Spirit
- Great Good Abounds - Natural Order: Man's Army Comes
- Church - Holy Man: Master of Morals (Canon law)
- Receive the Blessings of God - Spirit: Infinite Blessings of Christ

(earn eternal life - learn good from evil: become holy saint in Heaven)

This illustration shows that where "Great Evil Abounds (Simeon/Judas)," <u>Great Grace will also Abound</u> (God's Mercy) as the **Lord** brings forth **His Supernatural Power** (champion) to **Fight** against **All the Forces** of *Sin, Evil, and Death*. Secondly, we see that where "Great Good Abounds (Joseph/Jesus)," the <u>Will of the People</u> (vote) will **Abound** (Man's Justice) as the *Lord* brings forth His **Natural Order** (army) to bring **Harmony and Peace** to *One and All*. This means that the "Physical World" brings forth <u>Evil</u> to **Test** the *Immature Children of God* (babies/lessons); while the "Spirit World (church)" brings forth <u>Goodness</u> to **Bless** the *Mature Children of God* (adults/blessings). The question is: which "Stage of Life (babyhood/adulthood)" have you <u>Chosen for Yourself:</u> the *Immaturity of the World* (Simeon/Judas) or the *Maturity of the Church* (Joseph/Jesus)? The idea is that "If a Person Chooses" the <u>World</u> as a **Righteous Man**, he will be **Given** a *New Body for Free* (redemption). "If a Person Chooses" the <u>Church</u> as a **Holy Saint**, he will be **Allowed** to **Earn** an *Eternal Life in Heaven* (salvation). We see in the "Old Testament" that the <u>Bible</u> is giving us the **Story of Simeon** (earthly slavery) as the **Wicked Fool** and **Jacob's Son, Joseph** as the **Wise Man of Righteousness** to show that the **Life-experience** is comprised of *Choices between Right and Wrong*. In contrast, the "New Testament" or the <u>Bible</u> is *Giving Us* the **Story of Judas** (eternal slavery) as the **Wicked Traitor** and **God's Son, Jesus** as the **Wise Man of Holiness** to show that the **Life-experience** is also **Comprised** of *Choices between Good and Evil*. The key to "God's Good (blessings)" and "Man's Evil (lessons)" is to see that <u>Creation Needs Both</u> to **Establish God's Mercy on Earth** in the **Form** of **Divine Forgiveness** so that even **Judas** and his **Evil Acts** shall *Bear Fruit in the End*. This means that "Every Soul" must be <u>Tested unto the Dust</u> (examinations) to **Measure** both the **Depth of its Character** (world) and the **Depth of its Faith** (church) in **Service** to the *Divine Will of God*.

Now, we see that each of these "Examinations of Consciousness" must be <u>Faced by Each of God's Children</u> during his **Lifetime on Earth** to both <u>Grow</u> and <u>Mature</u> before the *Eyes of God, Angels, and Men.* Thus, all life, be it "Plants, Animals, or Men (natural order)," must be brought into its <u>Highest State of Perfection</u> by breaking **God's Curses** of *Sin* (ignorance), *Evil* (cowardice), and *Death* (greed). The "Human Race" was first <u>Given a Garden of Eden</u> as **Paradise on Earth**, but **Man Failed** to *Treasure God's Gift*. The first "Adam and Eve Destroyed" this <u>Divine Treasure</u> and then **God Cursed** all that *He had Created* (1st sacrifice). Obviously, the "New Adam (Jesus)" and the "New Eve (Mary)" have the <u>Responsibility of Converting</u> the **Whole Earth Back** into a **Massive Garden of Eden** (universe) as a *Land of Milk* (human kindness) and *Honey* (divine love). All are born into a "World of Failure (desert)" and must <u>Master</u> the <u>Art of Divine Perfection</u> before **God** to **Restore All Things Back** to *Their Original Owner* (God) by **Returning Them** to *Their Original State* (Man).

At the "End of Time" during the <u>Lord's Great White Throne Judgment</u> (perfection), the **Whole Human Race** will be **Judged** on just how well it **Transformed the Earth** and the **Whole Universe** into a *Beautiful Garden of Eden*. The "Key to Each Man's Successful Life" is to receive <u>His Own White Rock</u> with a <u>Special Name</u> (nickname) on it, *Personally Given to him by God.* This "Treasure is Given" to each <u>Man by God Himself</u> to signify a most **Personal Relationship** with the **Almighty** by being **Given** a **Mystical Name** *Only Known by God Himself.*

We see in the "Modern Church Today" that the <u>Faithful</u> are to *Look at Christ's Cross Daily* (remove venial sins), be *Anointed by Christ's Hands Weekly* (remove mortal sins), and be *Washed in Christ's Blood Yearly* (remove capital sins). Through these "Three Acts of Purification," a <u>Person can Reflect</u> the **Mosaic Law** by *Looking at the Brazen Serpent* (when bitten), being *Anointed by the Hands of Aaron* (3 times a year), and by being *Washed in the Blood of the Sacrificial Lamb* (day of atonement). This means that all that were "Performed" in the <u>Old Testament</u> have been **Manifested** in the <u>New Testament</u> or in **Christ's Church Today** in a more **Condensed Form** to *Create Instant Religion* (1 hour). Note in the chart below that through the "Cross (look at)," a <u>Person is Healed</u> (righteous); through the "Priest's Hands (placed on head)," a <u>Person is Sanctified</u> (holy); and through the "Shed Blood (washed)," a <u>Person is Purified</u> (perfect) and made a *Treasure before God.*

1. **Look at Brazen Serpent** - <u>When Bitten</u>…Look at Christ's Cross - Daily
   • Worthy to Enter Heaven on Earth - New Body (defeat Lucifer's test)
2. **Anointed by High Priest Aaron** - <u>3 Times a Year</u>…Washed in Christ's Hands - Sunday
   • Worthy to Enter Paradise in Heaven - Eternal Life (pass God's Judgment)
3. **Washed in Blood of Lamb** - <u>yearly day of atonement</u>…Wash in Sacrificial Blood - Easter
   • Worthy to Enter God's Kingdom of Glory - Own Kingdom (approve self-evaluation)

The following tabular information indicates that our "Catholic Faith" is centered on <u>Moses'</u> teaching man to *Look at Christ's Cross Daily* (remove venial sins), to be *Anointed by Christ's Hands Weekly* (remove mortal sins), and to be *Washed in Christ's Blood Yearly* (remove capital sins):

**Look at Christ's Cross Daily, Touched by His Hands
Weekly, and Washed in His Blood Yearly**
(cross removes venial sins, hands remove
mortal sins, and blood removes capital sins)

Cross   1.   **Look at Christ's Cross Daily** - <u>Remove Venial Sins</u>...Repentance

(healed)   •   Attend Daily Mass - Physical Baptism: Righteous Citizen = Free Eternal Life

            •   Blood Poured on Evil Goat's Head - Cast Off the Mountain: Yom Kippur

            •   Remove Fault - Learn Right from Wrong: *Righteous King*

     (Look at Brazen Serpent If Bitten by Snake [sin] - Surrender to Agony of Defeat)

Hands   2.   **Feed by Christ's Hands Weekly** - <u>Remove Mortal Sins</u>...Prayers

(sanctified)   •   Attend Weekly Mass - Spiritual Confession: Holy Saint = Earned New Body

            •   Blood Sprinkled on Repentant People - Forgiven for Sinfulness: Yom Kippur

            •   Remove Sins - Learn Good from Evil: *Holy Priesthood*

     (Priest Places his Hands on Animal Sacrifice - Unto Thine Own Self be True)

Blood   3.   **Washed in Christ's Blood Yearly** - <u>Remove Capital Sins</u>...Works

(purified)   •   Attend Easter Mass - Mystical Communion: Perfect Sonship = Bonus of Royal Kingdom

            •   Seven Drops of Blood on Mercy Seat - All Sins Forgotten: Yom Kippur

            •   Gain Virtues - Learn God's Will from man's will: *Perfect Son*

     (Offering God Sacrificial Lamb's Blood - Obey Guilty Conscience unto New-life)

This illustration shows that the "Life-experience" is all about <u>Attending Mass Daily, Weekly, and Yearly</u> to **Fulfill** both the **Mosaic Law** (earth) and the **Canon Law** (Heaven) which **Governs** the **<u>Acceptable Behavior</u>** of *Man's Flesh* (Man) and *Man's Spirit* (God). This means that "Looking at a Brazen Serpent (healed)" becomes <u>Looking at Christ's Cross</u> (forgiven); a "Priest's Hands on a Sacrifice (sanctified)" becomes <u>Receiving Christ's Touch</u> (forgiven); and "Offering God a Lamb Sacrifice (consecrated)" becomes being <u>Washed in Christ's Blood</u> (forgiven). The idea here is to see that by "Looking," "Touching," and "Washing" one's <u>Mind, Heart, and Soul,</u> a **Person** can be brought **Out of Adam's Death** (take-sin) to **Enter Christ's New <u>Born-again</u> Life** (give divinity) to bring forth *Heaven on Earth* (eternal life), *Paradise in Heaven* (new body), and *God's Kingdom of Glory* (dream home). By "Looking at Christ's Cross," a person can have his <u>Faults Removed</u> to allow him to **Learn Right from Wrong** and become a *Righteous Citizen before God*. Secondly, by being "Touched by Christ's Hands," a person can <u>Gain the Lord's Virtues</u> to **Allow a Soul** to **Learn Good from Evil** and become a *Holy Saint before God*. Finally, by being "Washed in Christ's Blood," a **Person** can <u>Think for himself</u> to **Allow his Soul** to **Learn God's Will from man's will** and become a *Perfect Son before God*.

    The idea is that "When a Person" becomes a "Righteous Citizen," he will become worthy of God's <u>Free Gift of New Body</u> bringing him **Heaven on Earth** and a <u>Seat</u> in

God's Celestial Court (physical law). Secondly, when a **Person** becomes a "Holy Saint," he will have <u>Earned his Own Eternal Life</u> **Making him Worthy** of **Paradise in Heaven** and a **Seat** in *God's Temple Court* (spiritual faith). Finally, when a "Person" becomes a "Perfect Son," he will <u>Receive God's Bonus Reward</u> of a <u>Royal Kingdom</u> **Making** him Worthy of **Entering God's Kingdom of Glory** and **Receiving** a **Seat** in God's *Royal Court* (mystical knowing). Recall that "Moses Instituted" a "Day of Atonement," known as <u>Yom Kippur,</u> where the **Jews** would **Kill Two Identical Goats: One Goat** (good) is **Slaughtered** for its *Innocent Blood* (Christ) and then the **Other is Taken to the Mountain of Temptations** and **Cast into the Bottomless Pit** for its *Guilty Blood* (Judas). The "High Priest" would take <u>Half of the Innocent Blood</u> and *Pour it Over the Wicked Goat's Head* and then *Sprinkle the Other Half Over the People*. Finally, the "Priest" would take the <u>Last Seven Drops in the Pan</u> and place them upon the **Mercy Seat of God** to beg for the **Lord's Blessing of Forgiveness** for *himself* (self), *his Family* (society), and *All of Israel* (God). Out of these "Stages of Conversion," the <u>Entire Human Race</u> can **Find its Way Out** of its **Pit of Death** by *Surrendering Its Life to Christ*. It is essential that "Humanity becomes Aware" that it is at the <u>Mercy of the Forces of Nature,</u> where **Each Life-experience** is **Forced into the Position** of **Controlling Its Own Destiny** through the **Mastery** of its *Flesh* (government), *Spirit* (church), and *Soul* (home). Obviously, "Mother Nature's" role is to <u>Learn and Teach</u> the eternal **Truths of Life** to **Enable Humanity to Master** the **Forces of the World** that have been **Designed to Reveal** the **Principles** of *Right* (good) and *Wrong* (evil).

The major theme behind the "Lord's Grand Design" for <u>Living Well</u> is essentially founded upon **Three Stages of Human Development**: 1) <u>Animal</u> (emotion/baby) or Throne (king), 2) <u>Robot</u> (logic/teenager) or Altar (priest), 3) <u>Animal/Robot</u> (instincts/adult), creating a *Human Being* (instinct) or *Palace* (son). Through these "Three Mystical Phases" of <u>Human Evolution,</u> the **Broken Nature of Man** has to **Travel on a Painful Quest** to find the *True Light of Knowing All Things*. When this "Light of Knowing" comes forth, <u>Mankind</u> will see <u>God's Secret for Living Well</u> via the Lord's *Honor* (truth/being saved), *Glory* (law/saving self), and *Majesty* (will/saving others). No mere "Human Being can Control" the <u>Dynamic Forces of Change</u> **Affecting Man's Emotional Free Will** caused by his most **Dangerous** *Animal Nature* (appetite). Nor can "Any One Man Master" the <u>Machine-Like Slavery</u> of the **Human Governmental System** or **Bureaucracy Driven Fools Who Control** the <u>Teaming Masses</u> (will of the people) with an *Infinite Number* of *Foolish Laws*. These "Ridiculous Laws were Created" by a <u>Bucket Mentality</u> (easy solution) that have been **Designed** to **Dehumanize the Undaunted Human Spirit** and to **Enslave the Imagination** of *Brilliant Visionaries*.

The "Lesson of Life" is quite obvious, since <u>All must Learn</u> just how to **Give Everyone** his **Heart's Desire** and still **Achieve a Proper Sense of Order** (balance) for the *Benefit* of the *Will of the People* (vote). The "Life-experience" is <u>All About</u> the **Two Truths of God** with **One Truth** (reality) coming from **Divinity** (intellect/mind) and with the **Other Truth** (illusion) coming from **Humanity** (emotions/heart) made *One in Christ Jesus*. This means that the "1st Truth (logic)" is **Focused** on *God's Will* (obedience); with the "2nd Truth (love/hate)" being **Focused** on the *Will of the People* (pleasure). We can picture here that "God" is much like a "Divine Computer (1st truth)" <u>Functioning</u> on <u>Absolute Perfection</u> based on **Infinite Logic** and then the **Lord Decides** to put in an **Emotion Chip** to <u>**Merge** *His Mind*</u> (see truth) with *Man's Heart* (desire want) *Together.* The significance of the "Intellect versus Emotion Concept" <u>Creates</u> a **Real Strange Effect** on **Converted Souls** (submission) because **When They Leave the Evil World,** suddenly *They Physically Face Starvation* (shame/fear), *Nakedness* (humiliation/pain), and *Homelessness* (disgrace/death). This "Change of Social Status" causes the <u>New-born Christians</u> to then **Believe** that **They have Entered Physical Sainthood** (self-righteous hypocrites), but instead **They** are still **Lost Broken Sinners** in the *Flesh* (behavior). This "Shock Forces" so <u>Many Zealous Converts</u> to **Back-slide** as **They See <u>No Visible Progress</u>** (seed falls on path) in their *Walk with Christ* so they *Quit in Total Frustration.* To comprehend one's "Visible Failure (intellect/mind)" and "Invisible Success (emotions/heart)," he must see that <u>He Falls</u> into <u>Physical Poverty,</u> yet, will also experience **Christ's Spiritual Blessing** of *Peace of Mind* (forgiveness), *Joy of the Heart* (rich life), and *Happiness of the Soul* (love). The implication is that a "New-born Convert" will <u>See Failure,</u> but he will <u>Feel Triumph</u> and out of this **Interior Transformation,** his **Life** will begin to **Bear Fruit**, but *Only in the Eyes of God.*

The following tabular information indicates that "Human Intellect" will <u>See Failure</u> (faith) and then a **Person** will <u>Feel Success</u> (works), indicating that he **Really** did *Leave the Evil World* and really has entered the *Sainthood of God:*

Failing Physically (intellect) and Succeeding Spiritually (emotions) to Bear God's Fruit
(submission of spirit and sacrifice of
the flesh brings the reconciliation of the soul)

	Intellect	Emotions
	See (visual)	Feel (invisible)
Repentance	1. Physical Shame/Fear	1. Spiritual Peace of Mind (forgiveness)
	• Face Starvation	• Arrival in Heaven - New Mind
Prayers	2. Physical Humiliation/Pain	2. Spiritual Joy of the Heart (rich life)
	• Face Nakedness	• Resurrection Day - New Heart
Works	3. Physical Disgrace/Death	3. Spiritual Happiness of the Soul (love)
	• Face Homelessness	• God's Beatific Vision - New Soul
	(1st truth - Reality: divine logic)	(2nd truth - Illusion: human feelings)

This illustration shows that the "1st Truth" reveals <u>God's Divine Logic</u> (reality), and then the "2nd Truth" reveals <u>Man's Human Feelings</u> (illusion) and then these **Two Truths** are **<u>Combined</u>** into *One Truth, One People,* and *One God.* This means that "Jesus Christ" will be required to figure out some miraculous way to <u>Unite these Two Conflicting Truths or Ideas</u> into **One Concept of Divine Perfection** (Calvary) through the **<u>Forces of Balance and Moderation</u>** in *All Things.* The problem with the "Human Intellect and Emotions" and the <u>Evil World They Created</u> is that **Wicked Men** always **Grab** the available **Quickest and Simplest Solution** (bucket thinking) to obtain an **Instant Applause** from those *Mindless Fools Standing All Around Them.* This "Quick Solution Procedure" is the Bucket Mentality of a **Foolish Person Who Needs Water** (thirsty children), **Sees a River,** and then grabs the **Nearest Bucket** to *Solve his Problem* with *Instant Results.* Once the community sees just how easy this "Solution" is, everyone Grabs a Bucket and heads for the **River** to have his **Need for Water Solved** at least *Temporarily.* Suddenly, the community needs a **Bucket Industry to Make More Buckets** with *No Regard for Future Consequences.* Next, the community needs to "Establish a Set of Laws" to Govern the Use, Storage, and Manufacture of **All these Buckets** and then **All Future** Generations are *Locked into a Living Nightmare* with *No Hope and No Escape.*

The better alternative to "Bucket Mentality" is "Adopting a Dam Mentality," thereby bringing both Hot and Cold Running Water into every **Home** with the **Twist of a Finger** from the hand of man's *Smallest Child.* We see that "Recommending" an answer to the "Problems of the World" and Solving Life's Problems are quite *Different Indeed.* Obviously, *Saying is One Thing* (dreaming), while *Doing It is Quite Another* (working). With the coming of the "Jewish Messiah (dam mentality)," all these Unsolved Problems Came to Light and will *Soon be Solved.* A "New Divine Solution" is based on the need to change the Human Nature of Man from *Selfish Death* (sin) to *Unselfish Life* (holy). To accomplish this "Feat of the Impossible," the Lord had to merge the Animal Free Will of the **Individual** (thinking) with the **Robot Slavery** (told what to do) of the **Society** (mindless/by the book) by **Using the Power** of *God's Instinctive Compulsion.* In short, God plants His "Instinctive Righteousness" within the Minds (flesh) of *Every Animal Nature* (instinct) and then writes the "Divine Law" in the Hearts (spirit*)* of **Every Free-willed** *Robot Nature* (law). Thus, the extremes of "Human Behavior" could be Removed and a New Divine/Human Nature (transfigured) could be **Instituted** as a **Balancing Force** between the **Desires of Emotion** (robot/law) and the **Logic of the Mind** (animal/instinct), *Making All Truths become One* in the *Person of Christ Jesus,* thereby bringing forth the *First Clear-thinking Human Being* (animal/robot).

This problem of "Saying One Thing (slave)" and "Doing Quite Another (master)" are the Two Philosophies of both the **Democratic** (leadership of slaves) and **Republican** (leadership of masters) as they represent those who *Follow Orders* (slaves/man/beggars) versus those who *Give Orders* (masters/God/owners). Note that in the "Donkey Symbol (defensive)" of the Democratic Party, they are depicting a **Passive Philosophy** (sheep) as a **Party for the People** (government/vote) or *Democracy*, dedicated to *Redistribute the Wealth* from the *Rich* (masters) to the *Poor* (slaves). While in the "Elephant Symbol (offensive)" of the Republican Party, they are depicting an **Active Philosophy** (goat) as a **Party for Big Business** (business/money) or *Capitalism*, dedicated to the *Creation of Wealth* to **Compete in the World Markets** of *Global Commerce.* The idea is to see the "Democrats" as the Women Folk staying at **Home** to care for a *Man's Children* and his *Happy Home.* In contrast, we see the "Republicans" represent the Men Folk on the **Road to Earn a Living** for his **Family** by dedicating himself to **Selling his Commodities** to *Anyone with Money.* Unfortunately, for the "Poor Republicans" this philosophy of finding that next Big Market of Wealth would force them to expand the **Business Ventures** far beyond the *Boundaries of the Home.* This conflict between "Domestic Policies" and "Foreign Policies" is causing the Voters of America to **All become Democrats**, believing that we **No Longer Need Big Business** nor **Do We Need** to be **Concerned** with *Other Foreign Countries* (isolationism). Because the "World System" has shrunk to a tiny Global Village, it is only the **Tremendous Joint Efforts** of both a **Powerful Government** (Democrats) coupled with **Big Business** that a *New World Order* can be formed to *Support the Needs of One and All.*

Now let's apply this same concept to "God (Heaven/Republicans)" and "Man (earth/Democrats)" as they are being called to Work Together in bringing the **Forces of Heaven** (wealth) and the **Forces of Earth** (population) into *One Perfect Kingdom.* This would mean that the "Job of God's Messiah" would be to become both a Shepherd of Sheep (donkeys/democrats/Jesus) and a Shepherd of Goats (elephants/republicans/Christ) at the same time to Make **Government** (obey orders) and **Business** (give orders) *One* in *Truth, Law, and Will.* We see in the case of the "Government (adult)" and "Business (baby)" that the Business Community (baby) is just *Beginning to Grow.* In like manner, we see in the case of "God (adult)" and "Man (baby)" that the Earth and the Human Race (baby) are also just now **Beginning** to **Grow,** sufficiently to *Pull Its Own Weight.* This means both "Business (republicans)" and "Man (democrats)" must learn to Think (go), have Ideas (turn), and make Decisions (stop) in an **Adult Manner** (ownership) to *Take Control of Their Own Lives.* This means that it is imperative that both the "Democratic Vote (democracy/spending)" and the "Republican Money (capitalism/earning)" Work Together as **One People** to bring both *Wealth and Happiness to All.*

The following tabular information indicates the structure of both the "Democratic (sheep)" and "Republican (goats) Parties" as They Lead the American People to see both the *Meaning of Life* (servanthood/government/labor) and the *Purpose of Life* (kingship/business/management):

The Democratic and Republican Parties Guide the
People to See the Meaning and Purpose of Life
(the meaning of life is survival, while the purpose of life reveals one's personal values)

Government   1. **Democrat** - Social Rights/spending: Shepherd of Sheep (slaves) ...No
(belief)   Ownership
              •   Nature of a Donkey - Obey Orders: Letter of the Law = Tax and Spend
                  Philosophy
              •   Government Thinks for the Masses - Group Voice: Defense (democracy)
Labor   •   Behavior of the Sheep - Follow Blindly: Go Along to Get Along
                  (cooperation)
              •   Mindless Fool - Questions Nothing: Passive Nature = To Exist
                  (see limitations)
              •   Meaning of Life - Servanthood: Jesus' Job = Save Souls from Hell
              •   Survival - Growth: Ethics = Baby Learns Right/Wrong + Righteousness
              (democrats represent a mother at home raising her children by fighting poverty)

Business (knowing)	2.	**Republican** - <u>Individual Rights/earning</u>: Shepherd of Goats (masters).... Ownership

- Nature of an Elephant - Give Orders: Spirit of Law = Earn and Build Philosophy
- Business (free man) Thinks for Government - Individual Voice: Offense (capitalism)

Management

- Behavior of the Goat - Blaze New Trail: Seek Prosperity in Commerce = Competition
- Wise Man - Questions Everything: Active Nature = To Serve (see potential)
- <u>Purpose of Life</u> - Kingship: Christ's Job = Create Saints for Heaven
- Values - Maturity: Morals = Adult Learns Good/Evil + Holiness

(republicans represent fathers at work striving to earn a buck via competition)

This illustration shows that the "Life-experience" is comprised of a <u>War between Social Rights</u> against <u>Individual Rights</u> as the **Needs of the Home** (democrats) far outweigh the **Wants of Business** (republicans) to *Get Super-Rich.* This is known as deciding to "Spend the National Wealth" for either <u>Guns</u> (army) or <u>Butter</u> (babies). The question is: can a **Global Society** have both by establishing its *Own Cashless Society?* This means that "Logic Alone Cannot Fulfill Man's Potential (dreams)" for being all he can be in the essence of the <u>Human Soul</u> so long as his **Heart's Desire has Unlimited Wants** driving the **Human Spirit** (heart) on and on to **Greater** and **Greater Heights** of *Individual Accomplishments.* The "Animal Nature (emotion)" is a man without a <u>Conscience</u> (amoral), simply **Driven** by some strange loyalty based on what he can **Get Out of Life** or out of every new relationship, **No Matter What the Cost** to his **Ethical** or *Moral Values* (behavior). In contrast, the "Robot Nature (logic)" is a man without a <u>Mind of his Own</u> (slave), willing to give his **Unquestioned Loyalty** (Nathaniel) to the first **Authority Figure** who seems to control his *Destiny by Force.*

The "Lord Jesus Christ" has come to <u>Give Humankind</u> a **Third Option**, by **Surrendering Its Souls** (life/wealth/labor) to *Him* (new nature). In this way, a person can inadvertently relinquish his **Emotional** (heart), **Free Will,** and **Logical** (mind) **Free will**/animal nature to God's **Instinctive Compulsion;** and follow His **Divine Will** to become *Holy as God is Holy* (perfect). We see that <u>Man must Worship God</u> (mind/give life), <u>Praise God</u> (heart/give wealth), and <u>Thank God</u> (soul/give labor) with his **Whole Being** to **Master** the *Mental Righteousness, Emotional Holiness,* and *Instinctive Perfection.* This means that "Jesus Christ is Planning" to do precisely that during each of <u>His Three Advents</u> to restore mankind's **Wisdom** (mind), **Courage** (heart), and **Generosity** (soul) upon each of *His Three Mystical Comings* (donkey/thief/judge on cloud).

Chapter 4

Knowing God through His Jewish Law (Torah)

The Lord's "Three Advents" indicate that the <u>Human Race **Worships God**</u> for a **New Mind** (Man becomes God), **<u>Praises God</u>** for a **New Heart** (God becomes Man), and **<u>Thanks God</u>** for a **New Soul** (God and Man become One), as shown by the following tabular information:

Christ's Three Advents bring Worship, Praise, and Thanksgiving before God
(Worship makes Man become God, Praise makes God
become Man, and Thanksgiving makes God/Man become One)

Truth	1.	**1st Advent** - <u>Worship God</u>: Give Life = ***God becomes Man*** .... Christmas Gift
(baby)		• Remove Ignorance, Give Sinner Wisdom - Learning Right from Wrong
		• Blessed with Righteousness - Robot Nature: Programmed Response <u>New Mind</u>
		• Baptism Removes Capital Sin - Sin of Defiance: Stealing
		• Being Saved - Redemption: Creation of the Church (priest)
		• Priest on a Donkey - **Meaning of Life**: Existence = Life (prayer)
		• ***Abraham becomes God's Altar*** - Blessing: Offer God Own Life = Circumcision
		• Worship God - Father's Authority: Jesus (son) brings Mankind Redemption (free)
		• Deny Intellect - Individual Values: Elementary School (baby level) = Resources
		• Skill for Mastering Own Self - Meeting Physical God: Individual Rights
Law	2.	**2nd Advent** - <u>Praise God</u>: Give Wealth = ***Man becomes God*** ...Easter Egg Found

(teenager)	• Remove Cowardice, Give Christian Courage - Learn Good from Evil
	• Blessed with Holiness - Animal Nature: Instinctive Desires New Heart
	• Confession Removes Mortal Sin - Sin of Deception: Hiding
	• Saving Self - Salvation: Creation of the Government (king)
	• Thief in the Night - **Purpose of Life**: Service = Land (work)
	• *Isaac becomes God's Throne* - Gift: Offer God Own Wealth = Sacrifice Son
	• Praise God - Son's Responsibility: Mary (mother) brings Mankind Salvation (earned)
	• Abandon Feelings - Creating Societies: High School (teenage level) = Blessings
	• Skill for Mastering Society - Meeting Spiritual God: Social Rights
Will	3. **3rd Advent** - Thank God: Give Labor = ***God and Man become One...*** Halloween Treat
(adult)	• Remove Greed, Give Saint Generosity - Learning God's Will from Man's Will
	• Blessed with Perfection - Human Nature: Thinking for Self New Soul
	• Communion Removes Venial Sin - Sin of Deceit: Lying
	• Saving Others - Rewards: Creation of Home (son)
	• Just Judge on Cloud - **Value of Life**: Happiness = Babies (rest)
	• *Jacob becomes God's Palace* - Treasure: Offer God Labor = Sacrifice Animals
	• Thanking God - Grandson's Duty: Joseph (father) brings Mankind Rewards (bonus)
	• Submit Free Will - Creating Perfect Worlds: College (adult level) = Fruitfulness
	• Skill for Mastering Loving God - Meeting Mystical God: Divine Rights

This illustration shows that "Life is All About Change" when Man becomes God (being saved). Then God becomes Man (saving self), and finally God and Man become One (saving others) to **Create** a **New Royal Family of Love** within the *Lord's Kingdom of Glory.* The "Transformation of Man into God" came during the Lord's 1st Advent (free redemption) via the **Creation of His Holy Church** (priesthood) when all the **Babies in Life** have been *Turned into Prayer Machines* (robots). Secondly, the "Transformation of God into Man" will occur during the Lord's 2nd Advent (earned salvation) via the **Creation** of **His Righteous Government** (kingship) when all the **Teenagers in Life** are *Turned into Work Horses* (animals). Finally, the "Transformation of God/Man making Them One" will come during the Lord's 3rd Advent (bonus rewards) via the **Creation of His Perfect Home** (sonship) when all the **Adults in Life** are *Turned into Men of Leisure* (humans). Man must first "Learn to Pray (babies)," then "Learn to Work (teenagers)," and finally "Learn to Rest (adults)" to transform Man's Desert of Death (hell) into Paradise on Earth (heaven). At each of these stages of "Growth and Maturity," the human race can develop its Social Graces (mind), Honest Character (heart) and Charismatic Personality (soul) to **Ingratiate Itself** (respect) with **God, Angels** and **Men** forever.

The "Three Advents of Christ" can be better understood by looking at the Seven Churches of Paul that parallel the same **3,000-Year Period** of **Purification** (Messiah), **Transformation** (church), and **Conversion** (world) **of Christ**. These **Seven Churches** are: 1) Apostolic Church (Ephesus) - Mystical Faith: Destroy Evil; 2) Martyrs' Church (Smyrna) - Indomitable Faith: Killed by Evil; 3) Baptized Pagan Church (Pergamum) - Cunning Faith: Slaves to Evil, 4) Holy Monks' Church (Thyatira) - Renewed Faith: Hide from Evil, 5) Reformed Sinners' Church (Sardis) - Strong Faith: Face Evil, 6) Perfect Saints' Church (Philadelphia) - Powerful Faith: Create Holiness, and 7) Prodigal Church (Laodicea) - Knowing God: Good and Evil are One. Through these "Seven Churches" and these Seven Time Periods, we see the **Creation of the Christian People** during the Lord's **1st Advent** (priest on a donkey) when the first five of the **Churches** *Fought Evil and Won.* With the "Coming of the 2nd Advent (thief in the night)," the Lord will bring forth His Philadelphia Church of Perfection to introduce a **1,000 Years of Peace** or God's **Civilization of Love** bringing **Paradise on Earth.** Finally, with the "Coming of the 3rd Advent (Son on a Cloud)," the final church will come to **Blend Good and Evil** in **One Perfect Creation of God.** It can be seen that the "Seven Churches of Paul (Turkey)" represent the coming of the Lord's Seven-fold Spirits onto the earth to bringing **One New-life, Three Bodies,** and **Three Kingdoms** to *Honor the Children of God.*

The following tabular information indicates the "Seven Churches of Paul" as they strive to rid the earth of all its Sin, Evil, and Death forever by bringing **God's Blessings** of **Righteousness, Holiness,** and **Perfection** to **Every Lost Soul:**

The Seven Churches of Paul Purify, Transform, and Convert All the People on Earth
(the Apostolic, Martyrs', Pagan, Monks', Reform, Perfect, and Prodigal Churches fight evil unto the death)

——————— 1st Advent of Christ: Priest Coming on a Donkey (title deed to earth)———————

Fight Evil	1.	**Apostolic Church** - Mystical Authority Over Evil ..... Mystical Faith
		• *Ephesus Church* - Apostles Warriors of Christ Die as Champions in Battle
		• Believe They Can Destroy All Evil - Fearless Warriors
		• Earn God's Blessing of Eternal Life - Justified Faith (baby level)
Die for Faith	2.	**Martyrs' Church** - Supernatural Authority Over Evil.... Indomitable Faith
		• *Smyrna Church* - Zealous Followers Die for Faith Trying to be Apostles
		• Believe They Can become Apostles - Foolish Fearless Warriors
		• Earn God's Blessing of Glorified Body - Honored Faith (child level)
Bowing to Evil	3.	**Pagan Church** - Rome Takes Authority Over Evil ..... Cunning Faith
		• *Pergamum Church* - Christians Secretly Mix Faith with Traditions
		• Believe It's Better to Go Along to Get Along - Secret Agents of God
		• Earn God's Blessing of Transfigured Body - Glorified Faith (adolescent level)
Running from Evil	4.	**Monks' Church** - Holy Men Take Authority Over Evil.... Renewed Faith
		• *Thyatira Church* - Establish Communities (orders) to Protect Faith

		• Believe Retreat is the Better Part of Valor - Hiding from Enemies
		• Earn God's Blessing of a Holy Body - Blessed Faith (teenage level)

Changing
Evil
5. **Reform Church** - <u>Forming Army to Take Authority Over Evil</u>...
Strong Faith
- • ***Sardis Church*** - Create Public Churches World-wide to Change Spirits
- • Believe Evil Flesh and Holy Spirit can Live Together - New Approach
- • Earning the Title Deed to the Earth - Anointed Faith (young adult level)

————2nd Advent of Christ: Thief in the Night (kinship/title deed to Heaven)————

Defeat
Evil
6. **Saintly Church** - <u>Holy Spirits/Righteous Flesh Gain Authority</u>...Powerful Faith
- • ***Philadelphia Church*** - Bring forth Civilization of Love or Age of Peace
- • Believe Good Wins Out Over Evil in the End - Winning Over Evil
- • Earning the Title Deed to Heaven - Sanctified Faith (adult level)

————3rd Advent of Christ: Son of God on a Cloud (title deed to kingdom)————

Using
Evil
7. **Prodigal Church** - <u>Humanity Grows-up and Given Authority</u> ... Knowing God
- • ***Laodicea Church*** - Bring Forth Son of God on a Cloud at End of Time
- • Believe All in God's Creation is Good - Enslaving Evil to Teach Wrong
- • Earning the Title Deed to Kingdom - Consecrated Faith (wise man level)

This illustration shows that "Christ Came" as a <u>Priest on a Donkey</u> (earth/new body), then He will come as a <u>Thief in the Night</u> (Heaven/eternal life), and finally as <u>God's Son on a Cloud</u> (Kingdom/royal home). Each time the Lord comes to "Earth," it will gain more and more **Authority Over** the **Evil Forces of Death.** At first, God attacked the "Forces of Evil Head-on" using the <u>Blood of His Apostles</u> to **Weaken Evil,** then the "Lord Sacrificed" <u>His Second Church</u> by **Making Them Believe They** too were **Invincible** and could **Fight Evil** unto the **Death and Win.** By the time "Christ" brought forth "His Fourth Church," it had <u>Learned that Evil was Too Strong</u> and that **No One** would ever **Convert Man's Human Flesh** into **Divine Holiness.** Through "Christ's Fifth Church," the <u>Christian Faith</u> realized it must **First Convert the Human Spirit** and then secondly begin **Converting the Human Flesh.** This "Brilliant Move" of <u>Purifying the Human Spirit</u> through **Baptism, Confession,** and **Communion** has led to bringing the **Human Race** into **Recognizing** the **Seriousness of Its Evil Natures.** Next, through "Christ's Sixth Church," the <u>Christian People</u> got the **Upper-hand** over both **Spiritual Sin** (holiness) and **Physical Evil** (righteousness), thereby **Setting All the Captives Free.** During the coming of the "Lord's Last Church (7th)," the <u>Christian People</u> will **Blend the Forces of Good and Evil** into a **New Divine School of Higher Learning** to **Defeat Ignorance, Cowardice, and Greed Forever.** The job of these "Seven Master Church Periods" was to allow the <u>Human Race</u> to recognize its **Depth of Wickedness** and take the **Necessary Steps** to **Rid Itself** of Sin (1st advent/church), **Evil** (2nd advent/government), and **Death** (3rd advent/home).

Through these "Three Phases" of the life-experience, we can come to understand the **Three Basic Forces of Creation** (sin/evil/death) as **They Relate** to **Man's Physical Growth** (earth/mandatory) and **Spiritual Maturity** (Heaven/optional).

Through both "Growth and Maturity," God is Able to bring forth the **Righteous Man** (intellect), **Holy Man** (emotions), **Perfect Man** (instincts) and the **Free Man** (nature) to **Transform** His **Broken Creation** into **Eternal Perfection**. Out of the Lord's "Natural Order (physical/earth)," God's Creation **Gets a Mind of Its Own** by **Learning Right from Wrong** (free gold mine) to bring forth the **Righteous Man** (righteous citizen). The "Job" of the Righteous Man is to **Master God's Divine Truths** (good news) to bring **Free Redemption** (being saved) to **Lost Souls** and **Create New Bodies for One and All**. Secondly, out of the Lord's "Supernatural Order (spiritual/Heaven)," God's Creation **Gets a Heart of Its Own** by **Learning Good from Evil** (dig out gold) to bring forth the **Holy Man** (holy saint). The "Job" of the Holy Man is to **Master God's Divine Law** (gospel message) to offer **Earned Salvation** to the **Christian Faithful** and **Create Eternal Life for One and All**. Thirdly, out of the Lord's "Divine Order (mystical/Kingdom)," God's Creation **Gets a Soul of Its Own** by **Learning God's Will** from **man's will** (share one's gold) to bring forth the **Perfect Man** (perfect son). The "Job" of the Perfect Man is to **Master God's Divine Will** (doctrinal truths) to award **Bonus Rewards** to **Saintly Men** and **Create Royal Kingdoms for One and All**. Finally, out of the Lord's "Godly Order (divine/God)," God's Creation **Gets a Life-force of Its Own** by **Learning God's Reality** from **man's illusion** (build golden kingdom) to bring forth the **Free Man** (man of liberty). The "Job" of the Free Man is to **Master God's Divine Love** (vision of life) to attain **Liberty** for **All God's Sons** and **Create Freedom/Liberty/Independence for One and All**. This means that the "Righteous Man" represents a Parent who **Knows How** to **Raise Children** by **Defeating the Sin-nature Curse** (ignorance). Secondly, the "Holy Man" represents a Teacher who **Knows How** to **Educate Teenagers** by **Defeating the Worldly Temptations Curse** (cowardice). Thirdly, the "Perfect Man" represents a Policeman who **Knows How** to **Arrest Criminals** by **Defeating the Demonic Possession Curse** (greed). Finally, the "Free Man" represents the Lord God Almighty, who **Knows How** to **Convert Sinners** by **Defeating God's Curse** (selfishness). Out of these "Four New Creations," the Earth, Heaven, Kingdom, and God will **Receive an Ocean** of *New Bodies, Eternal Lives, Royal Kingdoms,* and the *Treasure of Freedom*.

The following tabular information indicates that the "Righteous (mind)," "Holy (heart)," "Perfect (soul)," and "Free Man (life-force)" have been Created to bring **Mankind** its *New Body, Eternal Life, a Royal Kingdom,* and each person's *Treasure of Freedom*:

**The Purpose of the Righteous, Holy, Perfect, and Free
Men as They Come to Save a Dead World**
(bringing free redemption, earned salvation,
bonus rewards, and human freedom to one and all)

Natural Order (mind)	1. **Righteous Man** - <u>Intellect:</u> Ignorance to Wisdom.... Knowledge

Natural
Order
(mind)

1. **Righteous Man** - <u>Intellect:</u> Ignorance to Wisdom....   Knowledge
   - Learn Right from Wrong - Given Free Title to Gold Mine (parenting)
   - Good News - Free Redemption (being saved): Master Divine Truths
   - Righteous Citizen on Earth - Individual Rights (father's table)
   - Creator of **New Bodies** - Physical Life: Baby Level (task)

(home, government, church, and self are made righteous in the flesh)

————————————————Thinking of God————————————————

Supernatural
Order
(heart)

2. **Holy Man** - <u>Emotions:</u> Cowardice to Courage..... Self-awareness
   - Learn Good from Evil - Required to Dig Out Own Gold (teaching)
   - Gospel Message - Earn Own Salvation (saving self): Master Divine Law
   - Holy Saint in Heaven - Social Rights (judge's bench)
   - Creator of **Eternal Life** - Spiritual Life: Teenage Level (duty)

(celestial, temple, royal, and divine courts are holy in the spirit)

————————————————Speaking to God————————————————

Divine
Order

3. **Perfect Man** - <u>Instincts:</u> Greed to Generosity .... Consciousness
   - Learn God's Will from man's will – share one's gold with others (policing)
   - Doctrinal Truths - Bonus Rewards (saving others): Master Divine Will
   - Perfect Son within God's Kingdom - Divine Rights (God's Altar)
   - Creator of **Royal Kingdoms** - Mystical Life: Adult Level (responsibility)

(friendship, companionship, oneness, and becoming are perfect in the soul)

————————————————Touching God————————————————

Godly
Order

4. **Free Man** – Nature: Selfishness to Unselfishness .... Sentience
   - Learn God's Reality from man's illusion - Build God a Golden Kingdom (God's law)
   - Divine Truths - Blessing of Freedom (saving God): Master Divine Love
   - Free Man with His Own Vision of Life - Liberty (Table of the Lord)
   - Creator of **Eternal Freedom** - Divine Life: Wise Man Level (authority)

(respect, blessings, love, and union are gifts from one's life-force)

————————————————Becoming God ————————————————

This illustration shows that the "Life-experience" centers around the <u>Mastery</u> of one's **Home, Government, Church, Himself, Celestial Court, Temple Court, Royal Court, Divine Court, God's Friendship, God's Companionship, God's Oneness, Becoming Like God, Respect, Blessings, Love, and Union** in **<u>Fulfillment</u>** of one's **Mind, Heart, Soul, and Life-force**. Now, we see that "God is Calling" each of <u>His Children</u> on a **Long Journey** from **Earth,** to **Heaven,** to **His Kingdom,** and finally into **Oneness with God Himself** (union).

Yes! "Life is About" both <u>Growing-up</u> and <u>Maturing</u> to the point of **Mastering Parenting, Educating** (teaching), **Policing,** and **Living God's Divine Law** in **Service to One and All**. The question before each "Newly Created Soul" is can he become a <u>Righteous Man</u> (thinking of God) of **Wisdom,** a <u>Holy Man </u>(speaking to God) of **Courage**, a <u>Perfect Man</u> (touching God) of **Generosity,** and finally a <u>Free Man</u> (becoming God) of **Unselfishness** to become an **Eternal Servant unto the Lord?** The answer is "Certainly," if a <u>Person</u> **Believes in Christ, Surrenders to Christ's Church,**

Fights Lucifer's Evil, and Saves Souls, then he can **Defeat** his own **Sin-nature, Worldly Temptations, Demonic Possession,** and even **God's Curse of Death.** We are all being "Called" to See Our Own **Limitations, Potential, Self-worth,** and **Value before God** as a **Reflection** of **Our Desire** to become **Righteous, Holy, Perfect, and Free.** Now, it is time to "Grow-up" and then become "Mature Adults" in a World of **Sin, Evil, Death, and Damnation** to **Prove** that **God has been Right All Along** that **Struggle Builds Characters of Steel.**

To better understand "Growth (challenge)" and "Maturity (adventure)," note that Heaven is bringing **God's Grace** onto the **Earth** in stages via **God's Blessings** (1st grace/water), **Anointings** (2nd grace/oil), **Sanctification** (3rd grace/blood), and **Consecration** (4th grace/death). Now also note that when "God Thinks of a Sinner," he becomes Blessed, thereby giving him his **1st Grace** (water) in the **Form** of **God's Single Power** (1) to **Learn Right from Wrong** and become a **Righteous Citizen on Earth.** Secondly, when "God Speaks to a Christian," he becomes Anointed, thereby giving him his **2nd Grace** (oil) in the **Form** of **God's Double Power** (2) to **Learn Good from Evil** and become a **Holy Saint in Heaven.** Thirdly, when "God Touches His Son," he becomes Sanctified, thereby giving him his **3rd Grace** (blood) in the **Form** of **God's Triune Power** (3) to **Learn God's Will from man's will** and become a **Son of God within the Kingdom.** Finally, when "God Sups with a Free Man," he becomes Consecrated, thereby giving him his **4th Grace** (death) in the **Form** of **God's Quad Power** (4) to **Learn God's Reality from man's illusion** and become a **Free Man** with his **Own Royal Kingdom.**

Now, we can see that the "Sinner (survival)" must Defeat his Own Ignorance and obtain a **New Mind** to become **Wise** (intellect) to become **Worthy of a New Body.** Secondly, a "Christian (truth)" must Defeat his Own Cowardice and obtain a **New Heart** to become **Courageous** (emotions) to become **Worthy of Eternal Life.** Thirdly, a "Saint (love)" must Defeat his Own Greed and obtain a **New Soul** to become **Generous** (instincts) to become **Worthy of a Royal Kingdom.** Finally, a "Son of God (choices)" must Defeat his Own Selfishness and obtain a **New Life-force** to become **Unselfish** (nature) to become **Worthy of Personal Freedom.** This means that a "Sinner (baby)" can Meet the Holy Spirit if he willingly performs a Task for God of Obeying the **Lord's Ten Commandments,** thereby bringing him to **Knowledge,** reflecting the **Meaning of Life** (to exist). Secondly, a "Christian (teenager)" can Know the Son of God if he Performs his Duty by **Learning the Two Commandments of Christ** (love God and neighbor as self), bringing him into **Self-awareness,** reflecting the **Purpose of Life** (to serve). Thirdly, a "Saint (adult)" can Love the Eternal Father if he takes on Divine Responsibilities by Learning the **One Commandment of Christ** (love one another), bringing him into **Consciousness,** reflecting the **Value of Life** (happiness). Finally, a "Free Man (wise man)" can Serve the Lord God Almighty if he Earns God's Divine Authority by **Learning God's Divine Commandment** (becoming love) bringing him into **Sentience,** reflecting the **Essence of Life** (challenge/adventure).

We now see that the "Overall Life-experience" is comprised of Facing Man's Challenge of **Growing-up** and then Experiencing God's Adventure of becoming **Mature** before **One and All.** Obviously, everyone is destined to "Meet God," then to "Know

God," to "Love God," and finally to "Serve God" by striving to <u>Obey God's Laws</u> (world/ethics) and <u>Imitate His Son's Faith </u>(church/morals) to bring a **Person to Perfection**. Out of this "New State of Perfection," a <u>Person</u> can <u>Learn the Lessons of Life</u> from his **Flesh** (obey) and then be <u>Blessed by God</u> via his **Spirit** (imitate), allowing him to **Bear Fruit in All Things** (good or bad).

The following tabular information indicates that everyone is being "Called" to <u>Face Man's Challenge</u> (lessons) of **Childhood Growth** and then to <u>Experience God's Adventure </u>(blessings) of **Adult Maturity** as he strives to **Meet**, comes to **Know**, to **Love**, and finally **Serve his Creator God**:

Facing Man's Challenge of Growing-up and
Experiencing God's Adventure of Adult Maturity
(everyone must meet, come to know, to love,
and to serve his God both on Earth and in Heaven)

Face Man's Challenge - Childhood Growth: Obeying Man's Laws = Physical Life on Earth

1st Grace   1. **Blessings** - <u>God Thinks of a Sinner:</u> Master the Earth ....Knowledge

(water
- God Sees the Suffering of the Sinner - Lost Soul Gains Power Over Sin
- One Power - Learn Right from Wrong: Become Righteous Citizen
- Defeat Ignorance - New Mind: Become Wise (intellect)
- Receive Redemption (free) - Gift of New Body: See Meaning of Life
- Meet the Holy Spirit - Blessed with Performing a Task for God

(body broken - worship God: give life = master survival + receive a calling)

2nd Grace   2. **Anointing** - <u>God Speaks to Christian:</u> Master Heaven...Self-awareness

(oil)
- God Hears Christian's Cries for Help - Redeemed Soul Gains Power Over Evil
- Two Powers - Learn Good from Evil: Become Holy Saint
- Defeat Cowardice - New Heart: Become Courageous (emotions)
- Receive Salvation (earned) - Obtain Eternal Life: See Purpose of Life
- Know the Son of God - Blessed with God's Assigned Duty

(blood shed - praise God: give wealth = master truth + receive an awakening)

Man's   Lessons————————————————————————God's   Blessings

Experience God's Adventure - Adulthood Maturity: Imitate God's Faith = Spiritual Life in Heaven

3rd Grace   3. **Sanctification** - <u>God Touches His Saint:</u> Master Kingdom ... Consciousness

(blood)
- God Recognizes His Covenant with His Son - Saved Soul Gains Power Over Death
- Three Powers - Learn God's Will/man's will: Become Son of God
- Defeat Greed - New Soul: Become Generous (instincts)
- Receive Bonus Reward (honored) - Receive Royal Kingdom: See Value of Life.
- Love the Eternal Father - Blessed with a Sacred Responsibility

(spirit surrendered - thank God: give labor = master love + receive an indwelling)

4th Grace	4.	**Consecration** - <u>God Sups with His Son:</u> Master Freedom... ... Sentience
(death)		• God Comes to Help a Friend - Rewarding a Soul with Power Over Damnation
		• Four Powers - Learn God's Reality/man's illusion: Become Free Man
		• Defeat Selfishness - New Life-force: Become Unselfish (nature)
		• Receive Self Praise (choice) - Create Personal Freedom
		• Serve the Lord God Almighty - Blessed with Divine Authority

(pierced heart - befriend God: give all = master choices + receive an imagination)

This illustration shows that "God's Blessings (God thinks of sinner)" is given to those whose <u>Bodies have been Broken</u> (scourging) through **Worship** and by **Giving Their Life** to the **Lord** as a <u>**Sinner Faces Survival**</u> in an <u>**Evil World,**</u> awaiting **God's Calling unto Christ's Truth.** Secondly, "God's Anointing (God speaks to Christian)" is given to those whose <u>Blood is Shed</u> (crucified) through their **Praise** and by **Giving All their Wealth** to the **Lord** as they <u>**Master Man's Truth,**</u> which brings about their **Awakening unto Christ's Law.** Thirdly, "God's Sanctification (God touches His Saint)" is given to those whose <u>Spirit is Surrendered</u> (death) through **Thanksgiving** and by **Giving Their Labors** to the **Lord** as they <u>**Fulfill God's Love,**</u> by being **Indwelled by Christ's Will.** Finally, "God's Consecration (God sups with His Son)" is given to those whose <u>Hearts are Pierced</u> (tomb) when they **Think for themselves** and when they **Give their Friendship** to the **Lord** as they strive to <u>**Make Right Choices**</u> allowing them to **Trust in their Own Imagination.** This means that the "Human Life-experience" is all about <u>Blending</u> one's **Early Childhood** (fun) with his **Need to Grow-up** and become a **Responsible Adult,** without becoming a <u>**Shallow, Self-centered Fool**</u> without **Prudence or Fairness.** We are being told here, that "Human Growth" is <u>Mandatory</u> in **Physical Form,** while "Human Maturity" is <u>Optional</u> in **Spiritual Form** so that the **Level of Success** a **Person Attains in Life** is mostly up to him, <u>**Based on His Desire**</u> (beliefs) to **Know, Love, and Serve His God.**

It is important to note that "Mankind has been Cursed" with <u>Ignorance, Cowardice, Greed,</u> and <u>Selfishness</u> at the time of the **Fall of Adam and Eve.** Obviously, "Jesus Christ" was <u>Countering</u> these <u>Negative Effects</u> on the **Human Nature** by **Forgiving** one's **Ignorant Mind (**sinner), **Cowardly Heart** (lay leader), **Greedy Soul** (religious), and **Selfish Life-force** (priest). The idea here is that through the "Power of Belief," a <u>Sinner</u> (baby) could **Convert** his <u>**Ignorant Mind**</u> (repentance) into a **Wise Intellect** (being saved). Secondly, through the "Power of Trust," a <u>Lay Leader</u> (teenager) could **Convert** his <u>**Cowardly Heart**</u> (prayers) into **Emotional Courage** (saving self). Thirdly, through the "Power of Faith," a <u>Religious</u> (adult) could **Convert** his <u>**Greedy Soul**</u> (works) into **Instinctive Generosity** (saving others). Finally, through the "Power of Knowing," a <u>Priest</u> (wise man) could **Convert** his <u>**Wicked Life-force**</u> (save souls) into **Holy Perfection** (set free). At each of these "Four Levels of Conversion," we see both the <u>Growth of Our Flesh</u> (earth) and the <u>Maturity of Our Spirit</u> (Heaven) as **We Travel** from **Death** (nothing) to **New-life** (all) in an attempt to come to <u>**Meet, Know, Love, and Serve Our God**</u> in **Truth, Law, Will, and Love.**

The following tabular information indicates that if a "Soul" finds its way to the True Catholic Church and Surrenders Effectively as required, it can both **Grow and Mature** from a **Sinner,** into a **Lay Leader,** to a **Religious,** or become a **Priest** based on his desire (commitment) to **Do God's Divine Will**

Sinners Save Mind, Lay Leaders Save Heart, Religious Save Soul, and Priests Save Life-force
(babies are saved, teenagers save themselves,
adults save others, and wise men are set free)

Belief
(being saved)

1. **Sinner** - <u>Death of Ignorant Mind:</u> God Sees Man's Suffering.... Knowledge
   - Survival - Physical Life Teaches the Dangers of Natural Order: Venial Sin
   - Learning Right from Wrong - Righteous Citizen (seeking God): Repentance
   - Baby Grows into Adolescence - Meaning of Life: To Exist
   (face Lucifer's Test - free gift of eternal life: title deed to earth)

Trust
(save self)

2. **Lay Leader** - <u>Death to Cowardly Heart:</u> God Hears Man's Cries....
   Self-awareness
   - Truth - Spiritual Life Teaches the Dangers of Supernatural Order: Mortal Sin
   - Learning Good from Evil - Holy Saint (prayer heard by God): Prayers
   - Teenager Grows into Adulthood - Purpose of Life: To Serve
   (face God's Judgment - earn own new body: title deed to Heaven)

Faith
(save others)

3. **Religious** - <u>Death to Greedy Soul:</u> God Recognizes His Covenant.. .
   Consciousness
   - Love - Mystical Life Teaches the Dangers of Divine Order: Capital Sins
   - Learning God's Will/Man's will - Perfect Son (works seen by God): Works
   - Adulthood Matures into a Wise Man - Value of Life: To become Happy
   (face self-evaluation - bonus reward of royal kingdom: title deed to kingdom)

Knowing
(set free)

4. **Priesthood** - <u>Death to Wicked Life-force:</u> God Comes to Help...Sentience
   - Choice - Divine Life Teaches the Dangers of God's Order: Unforgivable Sin
   - Learning God's Reality/Man's Illusion - Free Man (God is pleased): Saving Others
   - Wise Men Mature into Sons of God - Fulfillment of Life: To Reflect God
   (face responsibility for thinking for self - experience freedom: title deed to life)

This illustration shows that the "Life-experience" is comprised of <u>Fighting for Survival</u> (being saved), <u>Learning the Truth</u> (saving self), <u>Seeking Human/Divine Love</u> (saving others), and making the <u>Right Choices</u> (set free) **All in the Name** of *Jesus Christ*. It appears that "Physical Life" on <u>Earth</u> is a **Free Gift from God** (eternal life) which involves **Teaching the Need for Survival** in all manner of **Strange Circumstances.** Secondly, a "Person's Spiritual Life" in the <u>Church</u> (Heaven) must be **Earned** (new body) through **Absolute Submission** to the **Divine Will of God** to **Learn the Lord's**

Infinite Truth. Thirdly, a "Person's Mystical Life" in Christ (kingdom) is a **Bonus Reward** (royal kingdom) based on the **Depth of Tenacity** put in on **Helping Others** and **Saving Souls**. Finally, a "Person's Divine Life" in God (divinity) is a **Treasure** (oneness with God), **If He is Chosen** (set free) to **Serve in God's High Command**. At each of these "Levels of Growth and Maturity" a Person can Measure his Progress along his **Pathway of Life** as he **Journeys** from **Nothing to All** by **Mastering** God's **Physical, Spiritual, Mystical,** and **Divine Realms of Existence**. Yes! It's all about having "Correct Beliefs (repentance)" in Truth, "Trusting (prayers) in God's Law," "Faith (works)" in God's Will, and "Knowing (saving others)" God's Love to the point of **Mastering the Life-experience**. This means that "Life" is centered on obtaining "Title Deeds" from Earth, Heaven, Kingdom, and Oneself based on becoming more and more **Perfect** as a **Reflection** of **God's Son, *Christ Jesus***.

It must be understood that the "Overall Human Condition" is comprised of **Three Basic Forces of Creation:** 1) Spiritual Life (church/graces) - Social Graces = Wise Mind; 2) Physical Life (government/points) - Honest Character = Loving Heart and a combination of them both; and 3) Mystical Life (home/grades) - Charismatic Personality = Dutiful Soul. This means that each of these "Three Phases of the Life-experience" Requires a Person to **Learn and Master** the **Skills** for **Living Well** by making the most out of the **Resources** (world) and **Blessings** (church) of his **Fruitful *Life-forces***. In this same regard, we must still not "Offend God" by Glorifying Our Own **Unworthy Flesh** through either **Ignorance** (mind), **Cowardice** (heart), and/or **Greed** (soul). This means that in the "Lord's Divine Plan," Humanity is to be Taught the **Three Divine Phases** of **Eternal Life** through the **Three Advents** of its coming **Jewish Messiah**. The "Job of Jesus Christ" is to Remove the Three Evil Curses on **Life** (existence/sin-nature), **Land** (service/worldly temptations), and **Babies** (happiness/demonic forces) caused by **Adam's Original Sin**. The implication is that during the Lord's "1st Advent," His primary mission was to Create the Perfect Man (home) as humanity's **Free Gift of Redemption** by **Paying the Sin-debt for Original Sin** (defiance/stealing). Secondly, during the Lord's "2nd Advent," He will Create the Perfect Society (church) as humanity must now **Earn Its Salvation** by **Paying Its Own Sin-debt** of **Mortal Sin** (deception/hiding). Finally, during the Lord's "3rd Advent," Christ will Create a Sea of Perfect Friends (government) as humanity must **Pay for Its Venial Sins** to **Prove It is Worthy to receive Rewards** for **Saving of Lost Souls** (deceit/lying). At each of these "Levels of Perfection," we see the creation of the God/Man Relationship as they **Strive Together** in an impossible struggle to **Save a Lost People** and then **Create** a **New Kingdom of Glory** for **One and All**.

The following tabular information indicates that "Babies (sinners)" get Free Redemption (earth), "Teenagers (lay leaders)" Earn Their Salvation (Heaven), while "Adults (religious)" receive Bonus Rewards (kingdom), if they will totally **Surrender Themselves** to **Jesus Christ**:

> **Redemption brings Perfect Man, Salvation brings
> Perfect Society, and Rewards bring Perfect Friend**
> (perfect man creates home, perfect society creates church,
> perfect friends create government)

Truth	1. **Free Redemption** (earth) - <u>Creation of the Perfect Man</u>....Home of Perfect Son
(mind)	• Perfect Righteous Man - Soul of Life: Saved by Scourging (baptism)
	• Perfect Righteous Society - Heart of Life: Saved by Crucifixion (confession)
Baby	• Perfect Righteous Friends - Mind of Life: Saved by Tomb of Death (communion)
	(1st Advent - God becomes Man: Christmas Gifts =
	Peace on Earth + God's Forgiveness/perfect man)
Law	2. **Earned Salvation** (Heaven) - <u>Creation of Perfect Society</u>...Church of Saints
(heart)	• Perfect Holy Man - Kingdom of New-life: Saving Self by Holy Church (submission)
	• Perfect Holy Society - Heaven of New-life: Saving Self via Mass (sacrifice)
Teenager	• Perfect Holy Friends - Earth of New-life: Saving Self by Saving Souls (redeemer)
	(2nd Advent - Man becomes God: Easter Eggs =
	Joy to the World + God's Wealth/perfect society)
Will	3. **Bonus Rewards** (Kingdom) - <u>Creation of Perfect Friends</u>... Government of Citizens
(soul)	• Perfect Divine Man - Angelic Conversion: Saving Lost by Worship (give life)
	• Perfect Divine Society - Saintly Purification: Saving Lost by Praise (give wealth)
Adult	• Perfect Divine Friends - Personal Transformation: Saving Lost by Thanks (give labor)
	(3rd Advent - God and Man become One: Halloween
	Costume = Happiness to All + God's Love/perfect life)

This illustration shows that everything is "Free on Earth" and that Jesus Christ has come to <u>Convert the Lost</u> into **New Perfect Creations** worthy of the **Presence of God** in **Intellect, Emotions, and Instincts.** Secondly, everything must be "Paid for in Heaven" by a struggling <u>Christian</u> to **Purify his Soul** into a **New Perfect Creation** worthy of **Attending Church, Serving Mass,** and **Saving Souls** all in the **Name of Christ Jesus.** Finally, only "Owners can Enter the Kingdom" as <u>Righteous Citizens</u> who have been **Transformed** into **Devout Worshipers** (give life), **Offering Praise** (give wealth), and **Giving Thanksgiving** (give labor) to God to become **Worthy of All His Blessings.** It should now be clear that a "Person's Commitment" to <u>God</u> (Messiah), to <u>Society</u> (Church), and to <u>Oneself</u> (World) centers upon being able to **Recognize** and **Effectively Respond** to humanity's **Four Basic States of Existence** (God, Heaven, Earth, and Self) as it relates to man's duty to **Cultivate the Land** (divine sacrifice), **Protect the People** (perpetual sacrifice), and **Serve the Nation** (daily sacrifice). In this way, each of us can recognize the "Land of God" or **Shekinah Glory**, the "Land of Heaven" or **Paradise**, the "Land of Earth" or **Holy Land**, and the "Land of Oneself" or **Thinking for Oneself.** Secondly, we can then recognize the "People of God" or **Sons of God**, the "People of Heaven" or **Saints,** the "People of Earth" or **Righteous Citizens,** the "People of the Nation of Heaven" or **Kingdom,** the "Nation of Earth or **Israel,** and the "Nation of Self" or **Home** (household).

Through these "Twelve Relationships," a <u>Single Person</u> can **Comprehend the Need** to bring **Food from the Land** (starvation), bring **Clothes from the People** (nakedness), and bring **Shelter from the Nation** (homelessness) all in the **Name of Personal Self-reliance** and **Living the Good Life in Christ Jesus.** The "Job of Every Parishioner," "Righteous Citizen," "Holy Saint," and "Son of God" is to <u>Commit their</u>

Life to the **General Welfare of God's Heaven** (spirit) and **Man's Earth** (flesh) by **Trying their Best** to <u>**Serve One and All**</u> in the **Kingdom of God.** The idea here is to "Create" a most "<u>Beloved Child of God</u> (perfect man)" who will have the **Presence of Mind** to **Desire** the **Best of All Possible Worlds** for those around him as a <u>**Matter of His Natural Duty.**</u> A **Person can Find** his <u>**Own Self-respect**</u> in a **Job Well-done with** this commitment to "Do a Good Job" in striving to be of <u>Full Service of God, Man,</u> and <u>Oneself,</u> all in the name of being **All One can Be.**

Now, let's clearly "Define the Job" which <u>God has Assigned</u> to **Each** of his **Born-again Children** as **He Strives** to **Announce the Good News** or give <u>**Free Redemption**</u> to the **Babies,** then to **Teach the Gospel Message** or **Help Mankind Earn Salvation** for its **Teenagers,** and finally **Reveal God's Doctrinal Truths** or offer **Bonus Rewards** to the **Adults.** The idea here is that through the "Good News," one can <u>Be Saved</u> and receive a **New Body for Free** (baptism); through the "Gospel Message," one can <u>Save himself</u> and **Earn** his **Own Eternal Life** (confession); and finally, through God's "Doctrinal Truths," a person can <u>Save Others</u> and become worthy of obtaining his **Own Royal Kingdom** (communion). This means that the "Job of Jobs" is <u>Evangelization</u> with the ultimate task to **Teach** the <u>**Meaning**</u> (existence), **Purpose** (service), and <u>**Value**</u> (happiness) of **Life** to a **Lost** and **Broken World of Ignorant Fools.** We see that the "Babies of the World" are <u>Called</u> to <u>Obey God's Law</u> (home) to **Find Their Own** Fixed Frame of Reference (identity), while the "Teenagers of the World" are <u>Called</u> to have <u>Faith in God</u> (church) to **Find Their** Relative Focused Existence (character). Finally, the "Adults of the World" are <u>Called</u> to <u>Know Everything</u> by **Thinking for Themselves** (government) to **Attain Their Own** Perception of Reality (personality). At each of these "Levels" of <u>Growth</u> and <u>Maturity,</u> a **Person is to Attain** the **Friendship** (earth), **Companionship** (Heaven), and **Oneness** (Kingdom) with **God** via **His Willingness to Receive** the **Good News** (submission), the **Gospel Message** (sacrifice), and **God's Doctrinal Truths** (reconciliation). Through these "Three Doors," a person can become a <u>King on Earth,</u> a <u>Priest in Heaven,</u> and finally, a <u>Son in God's Kingdom</u> which **Leads to Obtaining** a **New Body, Eternal Life,** and finally, **His Own Royal Kingdom.**

The following tabular information indicates that "Christians" have been <u>Sent throughout the World</u> to Give the **Good News** (obey law), teach the **Gospel Message** (have faith), and **Master God's Doctrinal Truths** (knowing) to <u>**Overcome**</u> **Ignorance** (wisdom), **Cowardice** (courage), and **Greed** (generosity):

Hearing the Good News, Learning the Gospel Message, and Mastering God's Doctrinal Truths to Receive Life
(redemption is good news, salvation comes by gospel
message and rewards are received from doctrinal truths)

Earth (king)	1. **Good News** - <u>Free Redemption:</u> Babies Obey the Law... Fixed Frame of Reference
	• Being Saved - Learning Right from Wrong: Ignorance becomes Wisdom ...See Limitations

- Submission - Dying to Self: Attain God's Friendship = **_Obedience_**
- Submit Free Will to Obey God's Divine Will - Find Own Identity
- Look at Cross - Attaining Ethics: Righteous Citizen = Gift of Eternal Life

(gift of three lives - physical life/eternal life/divine life: meaning of life = existence)

Heaven (priest)	2.	**Gospel Message** - <u>Earned Salvation:</u> Teens Live by Faith....Relative Focused Existence

- Saving Self - Learning Good from Evil: Cowardice becomes Courage = See Potential
- Sacrifice - Born-again: Attain God's Companionship = **_Maturity_**
- Give Life/Wealth/Labor to Get God's Perfection - Establish Own Character
- Touched by Hands - Attain Morals: Holy Saint = Earn a New Body

(gift of three bodies - transfigured/glorified/holy: purpose of life = service)

Kingdom (son)	3.	**Doctrinal Truths** - <u>Bonus Rewards:</u> Adults Think for Self...Perception of Reality

- Saving Others - Learn God's Will/Man's Will: Greed becomes Generosity = See Self-worth
- Reconciliation - Freedom: Attain God's Oneness = **_Thinking_**
- Receive Truth/Law/Will to Fulfill God's Divine Love - Emerging Personality
- Washed in Blood - Attain Fairness: Son of God = Bonus of Royal Kingdom

(gift of three kingdoms - earthly/heavenly/kingdom: value of life = happiness)

This illustration shows that the "Human Race" is striving to obtain a <u>New Body, Eternal Life,</u> and its <u>Own Kingdom</u> by **Mastering Man's Home, God's Church,** and the **New God/Man Government** to make **God and Man One** in **Truth, Law, Will, and Love.** Obviously, this "Treasure House" of <u>Divine Gifts</u> is to be **Delivered to Earth** via the **Three Advents of Christ** by coming as a **Priest on a Donkey** (bring law/perfect man), a **Thief in the Night** (brings faith/perfect society), and finally a **Son of God on a Cloud** (brings knowing/perfect friends). Through these "Three Advents of Christ," the <u>Creation</u> of the **Perfect Man** (home), **Perfect Society** (church) and **Perfect Set of Friends** (government) **is All being Formed** into the **Coming New Kingdom of Glory.** Obviously, the "Perfect Man (remove ignorance)" comes out of the <u>Lord's Free Redemption</u> (body); the "Perfect Society (remove cowardice)," comes out of <u>Man's Earned Salvation</u> (Heaven); while the "Perfect Set of Friends or Life (remove greed)" comes out of his <u>Bonus Rewards</u> (Kingdom).

Currently, the world is still in the "1st Advent" and is presently being taught the <u>Value of Religion</u> (church) to make **Men One with the Messiah of God** by **Purifying** the **Human Mind** (thoughts) and setting the **Captives of Sin Free** through the **Human Spirit** via the **Word of God** (good news/witness). This means, that the "Curse of Man (Adam)" from God is in the form of man's <u>Mind of Ignorance</u> (sin-nature), man's <u>Heart of Cowardice</u> (worldly temptations), and man's <u>Soul of Greed</u> (demonic possession), thereby **Requiring Each Person** to **Beg God** for **His Forgiveness**. In contrast, the "Blessing of Man (New Adam)" from God is in the form of man's <u>Mind of Wisdom</u> (see limitations), man's <u>Heart of Courage</u> (see potential), and man's <u>Soul of Generosity</u> (see self-worth) that **Leads to a Person's Eternal Freedom**. When the "Curse of Man" and the "Blessing of Man" are made <u>One</u> through **Christ's Church,** the **Human Race** can **Purify Its Spirit** and be **Redeemed** (capital sin/baptism) from **Eternal Damnation in Hell Fire.** The theme here is that "Every One in Creation" <u>Desires to be Redeemed</u> to <u>Earn his Own Salvation</u> and to hopefully <u>Save Souls</u> to become **Worthy** of **God's Eternal Rewards**. This means to "Find the Way Out" of the <u>Curses of Sin, Evil, and Death,</u> everyone must **See God** (new nature), **Hear God** (eternal life), **Speak to God** (new body), **Touch God** (kingdom glory), and finally, to **Sup/be Adopted by God** (freedom). Obviously, these are the "Five Divine Treasures of Life" and <u>Anyone Who is Willing</u> to **Seek the Truth** (believe) by **Expending himself** totally can come to **Meet, Know, Love, Serve,** and **Merge with his God.**

The following tabular information indicates the "Five Treasures of Life" that are to <u>See God,</u> to <u>Hear God,</u> to <u>Speak to God,</u> to be <u>Touched by God,</u> and to be <u>Adopted by God</u> (sup) for one's exemplary **Human Behavior** before **Divine Justice:**

Five Treasures of Life can be Earned
by One's Redemption, Salvation, and Rewards
(worthy of seeing God, hearing God, speaking to God,
being touched by God, and being adopted by God)

Truth   1. **See God** - <u>New Nature:</u> God Thinks of a Pagan (meet) ...... Submission
(sin)   • Learning Right from Wrong (intellect) - See Limitations —— Curse the Darkness
           • God Sees One's Suffering Soul - Present Gift to God ——- Bless the Light
  (Master Physical Dimension - Journey along God's Pathway of Destiny unto God's Truth)

Law   2. **Hear God** - <u>Eternal Life:</u> God Speaks to Sinner (know) .... Redemption
(evil)   • Learn Good from Evil (emotions) - See Potential ————Justified
          • God Hears One's Cries for Help - Make Offering to God —— Blessed
  (Master Spiritual Dimension - Journey along God's Pathway of Free Will unto God's Law)

Will   3. **Speak to God** - <u>New Body:</u> God Touches Christian .... Salvation
(death)   • Learn God's Will from man's will (instincts) - See Self-worth ——— Honored
        • God Recognizes His Covenant with Lost Soul - Petition God ——— Anointed
  (Master Mystical Dimension - Journey along God's Pathway of Righteousness unto God's Will)

Love   4. **Touched by God** - <u>Kingdom of Glory:</u> God Sups with Saint .... Rewards

| (damnation) | • Learn God's Reality/Man's Illusion (compulsions) - See Sentience -- Glorified |
| | • God Comes to Help His Child - Make Promise to God— Sanctified |

(Master Divine Dimension - Journey along God's Pathway of Holiness unto God's Love)

Worship	5. **Sup with/Adopted by God** - <u>Divine Freedom:</u> God Adopts Prodigal Son
(oblivion)	...Freedom
	• Learn God's Perfection/Man's Imagination (becoming) - See Reality—– Freed
	• God Creates Soul Winner for Christ - Fulfill Promise to God——— Consecrated

(Master Godly Dimension - Journey along God's Pathway of Perfection unto Worshiping God)

This illustration shows that "If a Person is Willing" to be <u>Subjected</u> to **God's Sonship Training** through his **Physical Growth** in the **World** (love) and his **Spiritual Maturity** in the **Church** (worship), then he can be **Allowed** to **Meet, Know, Love** and **Serve** his **Creator God.** This means that "If the Lord God Almighty" even <u>Thinks of a Pagan,</u> that person is so **Specially Chosen** (light) that he is placed on the **Lord's Pathway of Destiny,** leading him to a **Vision of God's Truth** (defeat sin). Secondly, "If the Lord God Almighty" <u>Speaks to a Sinner,</u> that person is **Truly Blessed** (justified) allowing him to be placed on the **Lord's Pathway of Free Will,** leading to an **Understanding of God's Law** (defeat evil). Thirdly, "If the Lord God Almighty" <u>Touches a Christian,</u> that person is then **Honored** allowing him to be placed on the Lord's **Pathway of Righteousness,** leading to the **Fulfillment of God's Will** (defeat death). Fourthly, "If the Lord God Almighty" invites a <u>Soul to have Supper</u> with Him, that person then is being **Glorified** allowing him to be placed on the **Lord's Pathway of Holiness,** leading to the **Love of God** (defeat damnation). Finally, "If the Lord God Almighty" offers a <u>Soul Adoption into His Royal Family,</u> that person is then **Set Free** allowing him to be placed on the **Lord's Pathway of Perfection,** leading to the **Eternal Worship of God** (defeat oblivion). Through these "Five Levels of Transformation," we see a <u>New Working Relationship</u> developing between **God's Reality** and **Man's Illusion** as they strive to come closer and closer to an **Eternal Union** made **Perfect in Christ Jesus.**

We see that in the previous chart depicting "Christ's Three Advents," <u>Abraham</u> (altar) **Created God's Altar** that became **Man's Spiritual Dimension of Life** bringing forth **Religion on Earth** (church) as **Humanity's Elementary School** comes to <u>Teach</u> the **Babies Right from Wrong** (1st advent). Secondly, "Isaac (throne)" <u>Created God's Throne</u> that became **Man's Physical Dimension of Life** bringing forth **Government on Earth** as **Humanity's High School** to <u>Teach</u> the **Teenagers Good from Evil** (2nd advent). Finally, "Jacob (palace)" <u>Created God's Palace</u> that became **Man's Mystical Dimension of Life** bringing forth **Man's Home on Earth** as **Humanity's College** to <u>Teach</u> the **Adults God's Will** (reality) **from man's will** (illusion) or **3rd Advent**. Via "Abraham (father)," "Isaac (son)," and "Jacob (grandson)," the <u>Triune Nature of God</u> is to be **Presented on Earth** through the **Jewish People** (flesh), **God's**

Messiah (flesh/spirit), and the **Christian People** (spirit). This "New Triune Nature (born-again)" must be <u>Presented</u> to the **Human Race** in such a way that **It** will **Freely Deny Its Intellects** (purification), **Abandon Its Feelings** (transformation), and **Submit Its Free Wills** (correction) **to God.**

This "Total Submission" to <u>God's Divine Will</u> brings a **Lost Sinner** from **Death** (spirit) **into New-life** (flesh). In like manner, one's "Total Sacrifice" to <u>God's Divine Love</u> brings a **Born-again Christian** from **Ignorance** (flesh) into **Wisdom** (spirit). This is done by "Developing" a <u>Person's Skill</u> for **Mastering Oneself** (individual rights) that leads to <u>Meeting His Physical God</u> (government) or **Benevolent Force**, who will provide the necessary **Resources** to **Live a Good-life on earth**. Secondly, "Developing" a <u>Person's Skill</u> for **Mastering His Society** (state's rights)" leads to **Meeting His Spiritual God** (church) or **Personal God**, who will **Provide the Necessary Blessing** to **Live an Eternal Life in Heaven**. Finally, "Developing" a <u>Person's Skill</u> for **Mastering** the **Lord God Almighty** (divine rights)" leads to **Meeting His Mystical God** (home) or **Lord God Almighty**, who will provide the necessary **Fruitfulness** to **Live a Happy Life** (imagination) **of Freedom Forever**. Meeting "Oneself (endurance)," "His Society (character)," and "His God (perfection)" during his <u>Single Lifetime</u> on earth **Allows a Person** to **Master** the <u>Whole Life- experience</u> (kingdom) to bring him from **Death** (ignorance) **into New-life** (wisdom). The essence of the "Life-experience" is to <u>Meet, Know, Love,</u> and <u>Serve God</u> so that a **Person** can become **Worthy** of the **Lord's Five** Treasures <u>of Life</u> by **Seeing God, Hearing God, Speaking to God,** being **Touched by God** (sup), and finally, **Supping with/being Adopted by God** (sup).

Through these "Five Treasures of Life," we can <u>Recognize</u> the importance of God's <u>Free Gift of Triune Life, Earning Three Bodies,</u> and being <u>Rewarded</u> **Three Kingdoms** through our **Fulfillment** via **God's Church** (life), **Man's Government** (body), and the **God/Man Home** (kingdom). In this concept of "Mastering Life" by "Obtaining One's Body" and "Obtaining His Kingdom," <u>Each Person</u> is being **Called** to <u>**Meet, Know, and Serve his God**</u> through **His Wisdom** (church/give time), **Courage** (government/give labor), and **Generosity** (home/give money). This means that the "Human Race" is seeking <u>God's Blessing of Life</u> (human), the <u>Anointing of the Body</u> (angelic), and the <u>Lord's Sanctification of Its Kingdom</u> (divine) via the **Lord's Truth, Law, and Will**. Note that through "God's Three Natures," "His Three Persons," and the "Trinity," <u>God, Angels, and Men</u> are **Tied Together** into a <u>**Single Bond**</u> (union) through the **Forces** of **Truth** (meaning), **Law** (purpose), **and Will** (value). The "Light of Knowing the Truth" comes from a <u>Person's Ability</u> to **Comprehend God's Divine Plan** as it **<u>Relates</u>** to the **Lord's Divine School of Higher Learning**. The purpose of this "Mystical School" is to <u>Teach</u> the **Human Race Right from Wrong** (righteousness/ethics), **Good from Evil** (holiness/morals), and **God's Will from man's will** (perfection/fairness). In this way, the "Blessings of Life," "Anointing of One's Body," and the "Sanctification of His Kingdom" bring forth a <u>Soul's</u> **Triune Existence** on **Earth** (natures), in **Heaven** (states), and within **Its Own Kingdom** (dimensions).

The following tabular information indicates that the "Three Gifts of God" are <u>Life</u>, a <u>Body,</u> its <u>Own Kingdom</u> based on a **Person** having **Three Life Natures** (mind/heart/soul), **Three Bodies** (celestial/temple/royal), and **Three Kingdoms** (earth/heaven/kingdom):

The Blessings of Life, Anointing of Body, and Sanctification of Kingdom bring Perfection
(three stages of life, three types of bodies, and three different kingdoms bring fulfillment)

Human
(baby)

1. **Blessings of Life** – <u>Meaning of Life</u>: Existence......Knowledge
   - Physical Life - Holy Spirit ————————————Powers (1)
   - Eternal Life - Son of God ————————————Virtues (2)
   - Divine Life - Eternal Father ———————————— Angels (3)

   (physical dimension - three natures: bings righteousness and ethics before altar)

Angelic
(teenager)

2. **Anointing of Body** - <u>Purpose of Body</u> : Service .... Self-awareness
   - Transfigured Body - 3rd Person ————————Principalities (4)
   - Glorified Body - 2nd Person ————————Dominions (5)
   - Holy Body - 1st Person ————————————-Kings (6)

   (spiritual dimension – three states: brings holiness and morals via pulpit)

Divine
(adult)

3. **Sanctification of Kingdom** – <u>Value of Kingdom</u>: Happiness ...
   Consciousness
   - Earthly Kingdom - Seven-fold Spirits ————-Cherubim (7)
   - Heavenly Kingdom - Trinity ————————Seraphim (8)
   - God's Kingdom - God ————————————-Archangel (9)

   (mystical dimension - three dimensions: brings perfection and fairness via chair)

- -

God
(wise man)

4. **Consecration of Nature** - <u>Fulfillment of God</u>: Love.........Sentience
   - Celestial Court - God/Man ——Holy Supreme Angel (Joseph/10)
   - Temple Court - Man/God ———Sacred Supreme Angel (Mary/11)
   - Royal Court - God and Man One —-Divine Supreme Angel (Jesus/12)

(divine dimension - three life-forces: brings freedom and liberty via the Lord God Almighty)

This illustration shows that "Men (sinfulness/lawless)," "Saints (ethics/law)," "Angels (morals/faith)," and "God (fairness/knowing)" are <u>Designed</u> to **Work Together** through the **Meaning of Life** (church), the **Purpose of One's Body** (government), and the **Value of God's Kingdom** (home). Initially, the "Blessing of Life" is broken down into **Three Categories**: 1) <u>Physical Life</u> - Holy Spirit: Choir of Powers = Saint Matthias (12); 2) <u>Eternal Life</u> - Son of God: Choir of Virtues = Saint Jude (11); 3) <u>Divine Life</u> - Eternal Father: Choir of Angels = Saint Simon (10). Secondly, the "Anointing of the Body" is also broken into **Three Categories:** 1) <u>Transfigured Body</u> - 3rd Person: Choir of Principalities = Saint James ls (9); 2) <u>Glorified Body</u> - 2nd Person: Choir of Dominions = Saint Thomas (8); 3) <u>Holy Body</u> - 1st Person: Choir of Kings = Saint Matthew (7). Thirdly, the "Sanctification of the Kingdom" is also broken into

Three Categories: 1) <u>Earthly Kingdom</u> - Seven-fold Spirits: Choir of Cherubim = Saint Bartholomew/Nathaniel (6); 2) <u>Heavenly Kingdom</u> - Trinity: Choir of Seraphim = Saint Philip (5); 3) <u>God's Kingdom</u> - Lord God Almighty: Choir of Archangels = Saint John (4). Finally, the "Consecration of Nature" is also broken into **Three Categories**: 1) <u>Celestial Court</u> - God/Man: Choir of Holy Supreme Angel (Joseph) = Saint James (3); 2) <u>Temple Court</u> - Man/God: Choir of Sacred Supreme Angel (Virgin Mary) = Saint Andrew (2); 3) <u>Royal Court</u> - God and Man are One: Choir of Divine Supreme Angel (Jesus) = Saint Peter (1).

We can now clearly see that the "Trinity of God," the <u>Lord's Seven-fold Spirits,</u> the <u>Nine Choirs of Angels,</u> and the <u>Twelve Apostles of Christ</u> are **All Coming** forth to **Save Sinners from Death** (change natures) and to **Create Saints in Heaven** (wash away sin). In this way, "God" is using a specific <u>Chain of Command</u> (intercessors) from the **Smallest Child** all the way to the **Lord God Almighty** to ensure that the appropriate **Level** of **Growth and Maturity** has occurred prior to moving to the **Next Level of Divine Leadership**. The implication is that "Level One" is to <u>Meet God</u> (baby/obey law); "Level Two (teenager/have faith)" is to <u>Know God;</u> and "Level Three (adult/thinking)" is to <u>Serve God</u> all in the **Name of God's Son, Jesus Christ**. Through these "Four Levels of Life," the <u>Human Race</u> is able to **Grow-up** sufficiently to **Take-on** the **Full Responsibilities** for **God's Kingship Tasks, Priesthood Duties, Sonship Responsibility,** and **Free Man Authority**.

By "Seeing Life" from this <u>Tough Love Viewpoint,</u> a **Person is Able to Understand** just **How Each of Us** is **Responsible for Receiving** <u>God's Triune Gifts</u> (faith, works, and prayers) of **Divine Love**. This means it is "Every Christian's Duty" to be <u>Responsible</u> for his **Own Corresponding Gift of Acceptance** which is in the **Form** of His **Forgiven Sin** (penance) to **Set him Free** from **Sin, Evil, and Death**. The point here is that a "Person must Attain" this <u>Mystical State of Forgiveness</u> by **Rejecting his Old Sin-nature** (selfish pride) through his **Desire** (human effort) to **Strive** or **Try Endlessly** (fight/never-quit) to **Seek** that **Impossible Dream of Life** (perfection). Through this "Awesome Dream," a <u>Person can Obtain</u> his **Own Unselfish Humble and Contrite Heart** (holiness) which can only become **Empty** by <u>**Giving His All**</u> in the **Form of the Widow's Mite** (give life).

Now, we see this whole idea can "Take Shape" as the <u>Lord God Almighty</u> initially **Offers Mankind a Free Gift of Faith** (instinctive compulsion) **Sent to Humanity** by the **Touch of Peter** (Holy Church) which in **Turn** is <u>**Accepted by Born-again Man**</u> through his **Submission**. "Submission" means a <u>Person Desires to Submit</u> (empty) to the **Effort of Attaining** a **New Humble and Contrite Heart** (unselfishness) or **His Personal Holiness** by **Dying to his Own Selfishness**. Once a "New Christian Soul" begins to <u>Strive Toward this Impossible Task</u> of **Rejecting its Own Selfish Pride,** it has **Opened** (emptied) itself up to **God's Subsequent Toll Free Gifts**: 1) <u>Holy Prayers</u> (God's Love/father); and 2) <u>Good Works</u> (Man's Love/son). The major point here is that we are "Allowed to See" that the <u>Holy Spirit of God</u> is **Responsible** for bringing **Born-again Man** his **Precious Gift of Faith** through the **Touch of Peter** (Holy Church). In like manner, it becomes the "Responsibility" of the <u>Eternal Father</u> to **Provide the Necessary Gift** of **Holy Prayer** (spirit) to **Fill the Newly Emptied Humble**

and Contrite Heart and then to **Transform it into Christ's Holiness** (faith). Finally, it becomes the "Responsibility of the <u>Son of God,</u> **Jesus Christ** to **Provide the Necessary Gift** of **Good Works** (flesh) to **Fill** the **Newly Emptied <u>Humble and Contrite Heart</u>** and then to **Transform it into Christ's Righteousness** (law).

The following tabular information indicates just how the "Three Gifts of God" <u>Interact</u> with a **Born-again Soul's Desire** to Empty itself of **<u>All Unrighteousness</u>** (sin) through the **Power of Submission** (penance/forgiven sin) or **Christ's Holiness**:

The Three Heavenly Gifts of God Offered to Man
(these gifts are freely given to anyone who
will work to reject his own selfish pride/sin)

Truth	1.	**Gift of Faith** (soul) - <u>Holy Spirit's Gift of Holy Love</u> ....Self
		• Christians are Chosen by God through the Touch of Peter (Holy Church)
Free		• Phase I: Mind of Belief - Seeing Truth (spirit) = Love
New Body		• Phase II: Heart of Trust - Learning Law (flesh) = Mercy
		• Phase III: Soul of Faith - Doing God's Will (soul) = Justice
Law	2.	**Gift of Holy Prayers** (flesh) - <u>Son's Gift of Sacred Love</u> ......Home/family
		• Filling a Born-again Christian's Physical Humble and Contrite Heart: Immaculate Heart
Earn		• Phase I: Mind of Belief - Learning Obedience (spirit) = Love
Eternal Life		• Phase II: Heart of Trust - Learning Submission (flesh) = Mercy
		• Phase III: Soul of Faith - Learning Self-control (soul) = Justice
Will	3.	**Gift of Good Works** (spirit) - <u>Eternal Father's Gift of Divine Love</u>...... Government/society
		• Filling a Born-again Christian's Spiritual Humble and Contrite Heart: Sacred Heart
Rewarded		• Phase I: Mind of Belief - Establishing Good Judgment (spirit) = Love
Own Kingdom		• Phase II: Heart of Trust - Attaining Ownership (flesh) = Mercy
		• Phase III: Soul of Faith - Mastering Life (soul) = Justice

- -

Love	4.	**Acceptance of God's Three Gifts** - <u>Return One's Gift of Forgiven Sin</u>...... God
		• Emptying of Selfish Pride - Creation of One's Own Humble and Contrite Heart
Given		• Phase I: Mind of Belief - Acquire the Power of Submission (spirit) = Love
Beatific Vision		• Phase II: Heart of Trust - Desire to Empty Old Sin-nature (flesh) = Mercy
		• Phase III: Soul of Faith - Strive (try) to Give All to God (soul) = Justice

This illustration shows that there are "Two Stages of Effort" involved in a **Single Salvation of Man:** 1) <u>God's Offer of Faith</u> (instinctive compulsion); and 2) <u>Man's Acceptance of Faith</u> (free will rejection of pride). The question is: just "How Does God" <u>Get Mankind to Accept</u>

(surrender) **Its Gift of Faith** and then **Transform itself** from a **Demon of Death** into a **Divine Man of Eternal Life**? Obviously, this "Great Transition" from Death to New-life comes through a **Person's Submission to Jesus Christ;** then through his **True Devotion** to the **Catholic Church** (Mass); and finally, to its most **Sacred Eucharist** (bread/wine). Through this "True Devotion," a Holy Christian can **Obtain God's Gift of Faith** and then **Offer Holy Prayers** and **Perform Good Works** to show his **Acceptance** (steady growth) of **God's Three Gifts of Love** (faith/prayers/works). Now, we can "Connect" God's Blessings of **Faith, Prayers, and Works** to **Mankind's Transformation** from being a **Sinner on Earth** (free redemption) to becoming a **Saint in Heaven** (earned salvation) via the **Sacrifice of Jesus Christ** (Calvary). In this way, the "Whole Human Race" is able to Struggle Out of **Lucifer's Pit of Death** through the **Lord's Eight Beatitudes,** thereby **Changing Their Minds, Hearts, Souls, and Life-forces** from **Demonic Possession** (new nature) into **Purified Humans** (holiness).

Note that the "Poor in Spirit" will receive Heaven on Earth; "Those Who Mourn" will be Comforted; "Those who are Gentle" will Inherit the Earth; and "Those Who Hunger" will be Satisfied. These **Blessings Convert** Sinners into **Christians** (new nature). Secondly, "Those Who are Merciful" will Receive Mercy; the "Pure of Heart" will See God; just as "Peacemakers" will become Sons of God; and "Those Who are Persecuted for Righteousness" will receive their own Kingdom in Heaven. These **Blessings Change** Earthly Christians into **Heavenly Saints** (holiness). This means that during the "Transformation" of a Sinner on Earth, a **Person must See** that when his **Faults Enter his Mind** and are then **Turned into Sin, he is Cursed with Ignorance** and must **Deny his very Self to be Saved.** Secondly, a "Person must See" that when his Sin Enters his Heart, it **Turns into Evil** and he is then **Cursed with Cowardice** and must **Abandon his Feelings to be Saved.** Thirdly, a "Person must See" that when Evil Enters his Soul, it **Turns into Death** and he is then **Cursed with Greed** and must **Submit his Free Will to God to be Saved.** Finally, a "Person must See" that when Death Enters his Life-force, it **Turns into Damnation** and he is **Cursed with Selfishness** and then must **Die to Selfishness to be Saved.**

In contrast, during the "Transformation" of a Saint in Heaven, a **Person must See** that when his **Virtues Enter his Mind,** they are **Turned into Righteousness** and is **Blessed with Wisdom,** thereby allowing him to **See his Limitations.** Secondly, a "Person must See" that when his Righteousness Enters his Heart, it is **Turned into Holiness** and is **Blessed with Courage,** thereby allowing him to **See his Own Potential.** Thirdly, a "Person must See" that when his Holiness Enters his Soul, it is Turned into Perfection and is **Blessed with Generosity,** thereby allowing him to **See his Own Self-worth.** Finally, a "Person must See" that when his Perfection Enters his Life-force, it is **Turned into Divinity** and is **Blessed with Unselfishness,** thereby allowing him to **Think for himself** (imagination). Now, it is clear that a "Sinner" must be Emptied of his **Faults** and that a "Saint" must be Filled with **Virtues** to be **Transformed** from **Death into New-life.**

The following tabular information indicates the "Transformation of a Man into a Demon" Happens as **His Faults** become **Death** (sin-nature); while the "Transformation of a Demon into a Man (sin-nature)" <u>Happens</u> when **His Virtues** become **Divinity** (holy-nature):

Transformation of a Man into a Demon - New Nature
(Jesus Takes-on All Sin - Saves Sinners on Earth/change nature)

1. If "Faults" Enter the <u>Mind,</u> it becomes *Sin* (ignorance)
    * Denying Own Intellect to be Saved - See Truth
    * Poor in Spirit - Receive *Heaven on Earth*
2, If "Sin" Enters the <u>Heart,</u> it becomes *Evil* (cowardice)
    * Abandon Own Feelings to be Saved - Obey Law   **Earthly**
    * Those Who Mourn - *Receive **Comfort***   **Fulfillment**
3. If "Evil" Enters the <u>Soul,</u> it becomes *Death* (greed)
    * Submit Own Free Will to God to be Saved - Follow Will
    * Those Who are Gentle - *Inherit the Earth*
4. If "Death" Enters the <u>Life-force,</u> it becomes *Damnation* (selfishness)
    * Dying to Selfishness to be Saved - Enter Love
    * Those Who Hunger for Righteousness - Receive *Satisfaction*

(purifying own grave - bear fruit out of the lessons of life: growing-up)

Transformation of a Demon into a Man - Holiness
(Christ Gives-up Divinity - Creates Saints in Heaven/wash away sin)

1. If "Virtues" Enter the <u>Mind,</u> it becomes *Righteousness* (wisdom)
    * Seeing Own Limitations - Comprehend Truth
    * Those Who are Merciful - Receive *Mercy*
2. If "Righteousness" Enters the <u>Heart,</u> it becomes *Holiness* (courage)
    * Seeing Own Potential - Fulfill Law   **Heavenly**
    * Pure of Heart - *See God*   **Fulfillment**
3. If "Holiness" Enters the <u>Soul,</u> it becomes *Perfection* (generosity)
    * Seeing Own Self-worth - Master Will
    * Peacemakers - Become *Sons of God*
4. If "Perfect" Enters the <u>Life-force.</u> It becomes *Divine* (unselfishness)
    * Thinking for Oneself - Becoming Love
    * Persecuted for Righteousness' Sake - *Kingdom in Heaven*
      (purifying own host - believing in Jesus Christ 100% [submission]: maturity)

This illustration shows that when a "Repentant Sinner" <u>Denies his Intellect</u> (mind), he can then **See God's Truth** and **Recognize** his **Poverty of Spirit** which will be <u>**Re-warded**</u> with **Heaven on Earth**. Secondly, when a "Repentant Sinner" <u>Abandons his Feelings</u> (heart), he can then **Obey God's Law** and **Recognize his Call** to **Mourn for Others** which will be **Rewarded** with **God's Comforting Touch**. Thirdly, when a "Repentant Sinner" <u>Submits his Free Will</u> (soul), he can then **Follow God's Will** and **Recognize the Need** to be as **Gentle as a Lamb** which will be <u>**Rewarded**</u> by **Inheriting** the Earth. Finally, when a "Repentant Sinner" Dies to Selfishness (life-force), he can then **Enter God's Love** and **Recognize the Need** to **Hunger for Righteousness** which will be **Rewarded** by being **Fully Satisfied** or **Master of All he Surveys**. In contrast, we see that when an "Awakened Christian" Sees his Limitations (mind), he can then **Comprehend God's Truths** and **Recognize the Need** to be **Merciful to Others** which will be **Rewarded** by **Receiving God's Mercy**. Secondly, when an "Awakened Christian" Sees his Potential (heart), he can then **Fulfill God's Law** and **Recognize the Need** to be **Pure of Heart** which will be **Rewarded** by being **Allowed to See God Face-to-face** (beatific vision). Thirdly, when an "Awakened Christian" Sees His Own Self-worth (soul), he can then **Master the Will of God** and **Recognize the Need** to become a **Peacemaker Among Men** which will be **Rewarded** by **Becoming a Son of God**. Finally, when an "Awakened Christian" is able to Think for himself (life-force), he can then **Become One in God's Love** and **Recognize the Need to Suffer Persecution for Righteousness' Sake** which will be **Rewarded** by **Receiving One's Own Kingdom in Heaven**. We can now see that it has been "Mary's Son, Jesus' Job" to Take-on All Sin (wash away sin) and **Save Earthly Sinners from Their Faults**; while it was "God's Son, Christ's Job" to Give-up His Divinity (change nature) and then **Create Saints for Heaven**.

Recall that "Moses" was also trying desperately to Meet, Know, Love, and Serve God when he brought forth his **Mosaic Tabernacle** with its **Three Rooms**, where one could **Contact God** (Outer Court/altar), **Speak to God** (Holy Place/pulpit), and **Listen to God** (Holy of Holies/chair). The idea is to see that as one "Masters the Outer Court (offering)," he will Remove Pride (ignorance/faults) and attain Wisdom (virtues), thereby making him **Worthy to Receive** his own **Transfigured Body** as a **Righteous King** within **God's Celestial Court** (Earth). Secondly, as one "Masters the Holy Place (gift)," he will Remove Vanity (cowardice/faults) and attain Courage, thereby making him **Worthy to Receive** his **Glorified Spirit** as a **Holy Priest** within **God's Temple Court** (Heaven). Finally, as one "Masters the Holy of Holies (petition)," he will Remove Avarice (greed/faults) and attain Generosity, thereby making him **Worthy to Receive** his **Holy Soul** as a **Perfect Son** within **God's Royal Court** (Kingdom).

The "Celestial Court (earth/offerings)" represents Natural Order (promise to change) within **Physical Existence** (holy level); the "Temple Court (Heaven/gifts)" represents Supernatural Order (act of changing) within **Spiritual Existence** (sacred level); and the "Royal Court (Kingdom/petitions)" represents Divine Order (change bears fruit) within **Mystical Existence** (divine level). "Moses' Job was to Physically" depict the Lord's Pathway of Perfection from the **Tabernacle's Eastern Gate** to its **Ark of the Covenant** (mercy seat/judgment) to allow the **Redemption of All Jews**. This meant that within each of these "Three Rooms," a person was to be Transformed from a **Baby** (free will), to a **Teenager** (submission), to an **Adult** (divine will) to **See, Hear,** and finally, **Speak to God** without **Fear of Death**. In Genesis 1:1, we are being shown that "Earth (government)" is the Baby Farm (elementary) which is a place where the **Human Flesh** is taught **Right from Wrong** so that a person can become a **Righteous King** (mind) **Ready for Heaven**. Secondly, we see that "Heaven (church)" is a Teenage School (high school) which is a place where the **Human/Divine Spirit** is taught **Good from Evil** so that a person can become a **Holy Priest** (heart). Finally, we see that the "Kingdom (God)" is an Adult School (college) or Sonship Training which is a place where the **Born-again Soul** is taught **man's will from God's Will** so that a person can become a **Perfect Son** (soul). At each of these "Three Stages of Growth (flesh)" and "Maturity (spirit)," the Human Race is to **Learn to Master** both **Individual Ethics** (stewardship) and **Social Morals** (spirituality) so that it can **Learn its Duties,** become **Responsible,** and one day, take on the **Authority** needed to **Serve the Will of God.**

It's now clear that each of these "Three Rooms of Moses" is represented within the Catholic Church in the **Form** of our **Vestibule** (Outer Court), **Congregational Seating/prayer chamber** (Holy Place), and **Sanctuary** (Holy of Holies). In the case of Moses, his "Desert Tabernacle" had Three Altars; the **Brazen Altar** of **Adam** (Outer Court/Catholic altar), the **Golden Altar** of **Noah** (Holy Place/Catholic tabernacle), and the **Ark of the Covenant** of **Abraham** (Holy of Holies/Catholic Crucifix). We also see our modern "Table Altar (bread/wine sacrifice)" as the Altar of Cain (repentance) and the "Cross Altar (flesh/blood sacrifice)" as the Altar of Abel (forgiveness) which are **United** at **Consecration** within the **Church's Sacred Tabernacle** (mercy seat). Note that a "Born-again Soul" can also identify Moses' Brazen Altar as our **Finger Bowl for Holy Water;** the Golden Altar has become the **Table Altar;** while the Ark of the Covenant or **Mercy Seat** has become our present day **Tabernacle.** This means that the Lord's "Shekinah Glory" which used to sit on the Ark's Mercy Seat can now be seen as the **Lord's Cross Altar** or the **Giant Crucifix** (seven drops of blood) hanging on the wall to represent **Christ's Payment** (seven drops of blood) **Made to God for Our Sins.** The idea is that to enter a "Church of Christ," a Person must have an Offering (repentance/prayers/works) or **Bread** (ram/goat/heifer); then to enter the "Sacred Congregation Area (prayer chamber)," he must have a Gift (dying to self) or **Wine** (son Isaac); and then to "Receive Communion," he must be **Forgiven** (Mass) by **God** so that a Christian's Petition (beg for blessing) or **Money** (circumcision) will be both **Accepted** and **Honored** by the **Almighty.**

The following tabular information indicates the importance of a "Person's Offering (death/grave/hell)," "Gift (kingship/priesthood/sonship)," and "Petition (righteousness/holiness/perfection)" to **God** to **Receive His Blessings** of **Free Redemption, Earned Salvation, and Bonus Rewards:**

**Coming to God with an Offering, Gift, and Petition
to Beg Him for His Blessing of Eternal Life**
(the three kings and three shepherds come
to worship Christ with offering, gift, and petition)

Physical	1.	**Three Gentile Kings** - Star (offering): Rich Jews Get Earth....Man's Petition
Gift		• Gold - King's Wisdom————-Prayer - Rule Government (redemption)
		• Frankincense - Priest's Beauty————-Sacrifice - Rule Church (salvation)
		• Myrrh - Son's Wealth ———— Blessing - Rule Home (rewards)

(kings see a sign from nature [natural order] and seek the son of man)

| Spiritual | 2. | **Three Jewish Shepherds** - <u>Angel</u> (offering): Poor Gentiles Get Heaven ... God's Petition |

| Gift | | • 1st Staff - David's Kingship ——Prayer - —Rule Earth (righteousness) |

• 2nd Staff - Aaron's Priesthood ——Sacrifice - —Rule Heaven (holiness)

• 3rd Staff - Jesus' Sonship ——Blessing - —Rule Kingdom (perfection)

(shepherds see sign from God [supernatural order] and seek the son of God)

This illustration shows that the "Three Kings" <u>Offered Their Journey</u> by following the **Star** as **Death;** then they **Presented the Christ Child** with **Gold to make Him a Wise King** (prayer), **Frankincense to make Him a Beautiful Priest** (sacrifice), and then **Myrrh to make Him a Wealthy Son** (blessing). Secondly, the "Three Shepherds" <u>Offered Their Angelic Visitation as New-life;</u> then they **Presented the Christ Child** with **Three Staffs of Life: 1st Staff to Rule Earth** (prayer), **2nd Staff to Rule Heaven** (sacrifice), and a **3rd Staff to Rule the Kingdom** (blessing). Note that the "Gentile Kings (physical)" were <u>Rich</u> and <u>Traveled from Afar</u> following a **Star** and were **Rewarded** with a **Place in Heaven**. In contrast, the "Jewish Shepherds (spiritual)" were <u>Poor and Walked Down the Hill</u> to **See an Angel** and were **Rewarded** with **Heaven on Earth**.

Now, we see that "Jesus Christ" is bringing His <u>Holy Church</u> to the **Lost and Broken Sinners of the World** to offer them both a **Perfect Spirit in Heaven** (glorified spirit/eternal life) and a **Perfect Flesh on Earth** (transfigured body). The point here is that if a "Soul" has its <u>Offering Accepted,</u> it is made **Righteous** (king); if its <u>Gift is Accepted,</u> it is made **Holy** (priest); and if it is both **Forgiven** (Mass) and its <u>Petition is Accepted,</u> it is made **Perfect** (son). Note here that as "Faithful Catholics," we are traveling from <u>Altar to Altar;</u> but as **Eternal Saints**, we are traveling along God's **Pathway of Perfection** as we are moving from **Earth** (elementary school), to **Heaven** (high school), or to **God's Kingdom** (college), and then to be **Set Free into God's Friendship**.

Through this "Journey of Life," a person must attain his <u>Personal Level of Acceptance</u> before **God, Angels, and Men** to **Establish himself** through his **Promise of Change** (death), **Actually Changing** (new-life), and then his **Change Bears Fruit** (eternal life). We call these "Three Changes" the <u>Offering</u> (death), the <u>Gift</u> (new-life), and the <u>Petition</u> (eternal life), thereby **Allowing a Person** to **Receive God's Blessings** of **Righteousness** (Earth), **Holiness** (Heaven), and **Perfection** (Kingdom). Recall that "Father Abraham" began his <u>Sacred Ritual of Sacrifice</u> by <u>Offering God Death</u> in the **Form** of a **Ram** (wild), **Goat** (wild/tame), and **Heifer** (tame) to show the **Depth of his Changed Nature** (righteousness) from **Wild Animal** (Cain) to **Tamed Loving Son** (Jesus). Secondly, "Father Abraham" presented God with his <u>Gift of New-life</u> via the **Life of his Son, Isaac** (bloodless) to show the **Depth of his Submission** (holiness) as he **Transformed** from a **Wicked Sinner** (Cain) to **Holy Saint** (Jesus). Finally, "Father Abraham Presented God" with his <u>Petition of Circumcision</u> to **Convert his Seed of Life** showing the **Coming of his Own New Nature** (perfection) as he **Exchanged his Sainthood** into being a **Born-again Son of God**.

Through these "Three Conversion Experiences," <u>Father Abraham</u> became **Worthy of Establishing the Abrahamic Covenant** with **God** based on the **Purchase of the Holy Land** (Hebron Grave) in **Sweat, Blood, and Tears**. Through "Abraham's Offering (animals)," the <u>Altar was Created</u> (contact God) or **Death**; then out of his "Gift to God (Isaac)," the <u>Pulpit was Created</u> (speak to God) or **New-life;** and finally, out of his "Petition (circumcision)," the <u>Chair was Created</u> (listen to God) or **Eternal Life**. Now, we can see that out of "Abraham's Offering" comes <u>Christ's Submission</u> (agony in garden); out of "Abraham's Gift" comes <u>Christ's Sacrifice</u> (Calvary); and out of "Abraham's Petition" comes <u>Christ's Reconciliation</u> (tomb/resurrection) **Back** to the **Divine Justice of God**. Out of "Christ's Submission," "Sacrifice," and "Reconciliation," the <u>Catholic Church was Created</u> bringing forth man's **Baptism** (capital sin), **Confession** (mortal sin), and **Communion** (venial sin) in the **Form of a Person's Redemption** (free/purify grave), **Salvation** (earned/purify host), and **Rewards** (bonus/purify life).

The following tabular information indicates the "Acceptance of Man's Offerings," "Gifts," and "Petitions" by **Begging God** for **His Blessings** of **Righteousness on Earth** (submission), **Holiness in Heaven** (sacrifice), and **Perfection within His Kingdom** (reconciliation):

Acceptance of Man's Offerings, Gifts, and Petitions
to make All Men Righteous, Holy, and Perfect
(altar contacts God [death], pulpit speaks to God
[new-life], and the chair listens to God [eternal life])

Death   1. **Offering** - <u>God Accepts Death:</u> Altar Contacts God ....Submission
(truth)   • Promise to Change - Baptism brings Redemption: Become Righteous King
             • Abraham's Offers - Ram/Goat/Heifer: God Sees Suffering (earth)
             • Dying to Self - Sinner becomes Christian: Free Glorified Spirit (Heaven)
   (on the holy level - God accepts Jesus' Offering of Scourging to Contact Divine Justice)

New-life 2. **Gift** - <u>God Accepts New-life:</u> Pulpit Speaks to God ....Sacrifice
(law)   • Act of Changing - Confession brings Salvation: Become Holy Priest
             • Abraham Gifts Gift - Sacrifice Son Isaac: God Hears Cry for Help
             • Born-again - Christian becomes Saint: Earn Transfigured Body (earth)
   (on the sacred level - God accepts Jesus' Gift of Crucifixion to Speak to Divine Justice)

Eternal Life 3. **Petition** - <u>God Accepts Eternal Life:</u> Chair Listens to God...Reconciliation
(will)   • Change Bears Fruit - Communion brings Rewards: Become Perfect Son
             • Abraham Makes Petition - Gives Circumcision: God Recognizes His Covenant
             • New lifestyle - Saint becomes Son of God: Bonus of Holy Soul (Kingdom)
   (on the divine level - God accepts Jesus' Petition of Tomb to Listen to Divine Justice)

This illustration shows that through "Abraham's" <u>Offering, Gift,</u> and <u>Petition,</u> **Direct Communication** is made possible between **God and Man** allowing a person to **Contact, Speak To,** and **Listen To God** via the **Holy Catholic Church**. Note that "Jesus Offers His Scourging" to Contact God's Divine Justice and create His **Pillar of Submission** (dying to self) as a **Promise to Change Man's Life** from **Evil to Righteousness**. Secondly, "Jesus Gives His Gift of Crucifixion" to Speak to Divine Justice and create the **Cross of Sacrifice** (born-again) as an **Act of Changing Man's Life** from **Evil to Holiness**. Finally, "Jesus Makes His Petition" to Listen to Divine Justice to create the **Tomb of Reconciliation** (new lifestyle) since **Changing His Nature Bears the Fruits of Life** from **Evil to Perfection**. At each of these "Levels of Growth and Maturity," both Abraham (Jews) and Jesus (Christians) are able to **Contact** (altar), **Speak To** (pulpit), and **Listen To** (chair) God, to **Beg the Lord for His Blessing** of a **New Glorified Spirit** (heart), **Transfigured Body** (mind), and **Holy Soul**. We can now see in "Modern Terms" that the Mosaic Tabernacle, Jesus' Mount Calvary, and the Catholic Church all represent a **Mystical Telephone** to create a **Desperate Call** from a **Dying Man** to his **All Powerful God**. The point is that if a person's "Promise to Change (offering)" is Accepted (truth), and then his "Act of Changing (gift)" is Accepted (will), his **Soul will be Given** God's **Divine Truth** (earth), **Law** (Heaven), and **Will** (Kingdom). Once a person has "Agreed to Change" to become a Righteous King, a Holy Priest, and a Perfect Son, he will be offered a **Seat** in God's **Celestial Court** (earth), **Temple Court** (Heaven), and **Royal Court** (Kingdom).

Now, if we compare "Abraham (kingship)," "Moses (priesthood)," Jesus (sonship), and the "Catholic Church (fatherhood)," we can see a Parallel of **Contacting God** (altar), **Speaking to God** (pulpit), and **Listening to God** (chair) to **Begging Him for His Blessings.** Note that to "Contact God," a person must have a Holy Altar, where he can make his **Offering of Death** to **Attract God's Attention** (see suffering) and **Promise to Change** through **Submission** or **Dying to Self**. If his "Offering is Accepted (altar)," then a soul will receive Free Redemption (submission), including a **New Nature**, become a **Holy Priest**, receive **Glorified Spirit**, plus a **Seat in the Temple Court** (Heaven), and the **Title Deed to Heaven**. Secondly, If his "Gift is Accepted (pulpit)," then a soul can Earn its Own Salvation (sacrifice), including a **New Behavior**, become **Righteous King**, receive **Transfigured Body**, plus **Seat in the Celestial Court** (earth), and the **Title Deed to Earth**. Finally, if his "Petition is Accepted (chair)," then a soul can be Honored with its own Eternal Reward (reconciliation), including a **New Lifestyle**, become **Perfect Son**, receive **Holy Soul**, plus **Seat in the Royal Court** (Kingdom), and the **Title Deed to the Kingdom**. Through each of these "Three Stages of Acceptance," a person is able to Master the **Physical, Spiritual, and Mystical Levels of Life** allowing him to **Freely Contact, Speak To,** and **Listen To God** Whenever he Desires (freedom).

The following tabular information indicates the purpose of the "Altar (offering)," the "Pulpit (gift)," and the "Chair (petition)" as they Communicate Directly with God to **Beg Him** for His **Blessings** (accept offering), **Anointings** (accept gift), and **Sanctifications** (accept petition) upon a **Sick and Dying Humanity:**

Purpose of the Altar (offering),
Pulpit (gift), and Chair (petition) in Contacting God
(offer death to contact God, gift of new-life to speak,
petition of eternal life to listen)

Sacrifice
(temple)

1. **Altar** - <u>Offering Death:</u> God Sees Child's Suffering… Dying to Self
   - Contact God through Submission of Spirit
   - *Promise to Change* - Nature, Behavior, and Lifestyle
   - Giving God Homage in Wealth: Obey the Ten Commandments
     1. Abraham Offers Death - Wild Ram, Wild/Tame Goat, and Tame Heifer
     2. Moses Offers Death - Outer Court, Brazen Altar: Sacrificial Lamb
     3. Jesus Offers Death - Scourging at the Pillar (death agony)
   - <u>God Accepts Offering</u> - Gives Blessing of Redemption (free)
     1. New Nature - Learn Good from Evil
     2. Holy Priest - Remove Vanity
     3. Glorified Spirit - Holiness (priesthood)   **Knowledge**
     4. Seat in Temple Court - Rule Heaven   • Baptism
     5. Title Deed to Heaven - Ownership of Emotions

Prayer
(throne)

2. **Pulpit** - <u>Gift of New-life:</u> God Hears Child's Cry for Help …Born-again
   - Speak to God through Sacrifice of Flesh
   - *Act of Changing* - Nature, Behavior, and Lifestyle
   - Giving God Homage in Love: Sell All and Give to the Poor
     1. Abraham's Gift of New-life - Sacrifice Son, Isaac
     2. Moses' Gift of New-life - Holy Place, Golden Altar: Offer Incense
     3. Jesus' Gift of New-life - Crucifixion on Cross (hopelessness)
   - <u>God Accepts Gift</u> - Gives Anointing of Salvation (earned)
     1. New Behavior - Learn Right from Wrong
     2. Righteous King - Remove Pride
     3. Transfigured Body - Righteousness (kingship) **Self-awareness**
     4. Seat in Celestial Court - Rule Earth   • Confession
     5. Title Deed to Earth - Ownership of Intellect

Blessing
(palace)

3. **Chair** - <u>Petition of Eternal Life:</u> God Recognizes His Covenant… Manifestation
   - Listen to God through Reconciliation of Soul
   - *Change Bears Fruit* - New Nature, Behavior, and Lifestyle
   - Giving God Homage in Life: Come Follow Christ
     1. Abraham's Petition of Eternal Life - Circumcision of Seed
     2. Moses' Petition of Eternal Life - Holy of Holies, Ark of Covenant: Drops of Blood
     3. Jesus' Petition of Eternal Life - Tomb of Death (separation)
   - <u>God Accepts Petition</u> - Gives Sanctification of Rewards (bonus)

1. New Lifestyle - Learn God's Will/man's will
2. Perfect Son - Remove Greed
3. Holy Soul - Perfection (sonship)   **Consciousness**
4. Seat in Royal Court - Rule Kingdom   • Communion
5. Title Deed to Kingdom - Ownership of Instincts

This illustration shows that the whole "Life-experience" is centered around the concept of <u>Giving God Some things</u> of both **Value to Him** (babies/souls) and **Value to Man** (happiness) to <u>**Seal His Agreement**</u> to **Dedicate a Lifetime Serving God.** Obviously, if a person "Fulfills" God's Altar" with a <u>Holy Offering</u> (death), "Fulfills God's Pulpit" with a <u>Sacred Gift</u> (new-life), and "Fulfills God's Chair" with a <u>Divine Petition</u> (eternal life), then he can expect to receive God's **Physical Blessing** (earth), **Spiritual Anointing** (Heaven), and **Divine Sanctification** (Kingdom). Note that the "Key Word" is <u>Unconditional Acceptance by God.</u> This means **Giving God** his **Total Submission** (offering), **Absolute Sacrifice** (gift), and **Perfect Blessing** (petition) to demonstrate the **Depth of His Faith.** The best way to see the interactive relationship of the "Altar, Pulpit, and the Chair" comes with <u>Transforming</u> the **Human Race** from its **Ignorant, Criminal, Insane,** and **Evil Behavior** through **God's Grace.**

Altar (temple) - The purpose of the "Altar" is to establish a <u>Direct Communication Line</u> between **God and Man** so that the Human Race can **Present Its Offering to God** in the form of a **Promise to Change** its **Ignorant, Criminal, Insane,** and **Evil Nature** into a **New Righteous, Holy, Perfect, and Divine Nature before God.** If this "Offer to Change (baptism)" is <u>Accepted by God,</u> then the Lord will **Bless this Soul** with a **New Nature**, **Priesthood** (holy), **Glorified Spirit**, seat in His **Temple Court,** and the **Title Deed to Heaven.** Once all of these "Treasures of Life" have been bestowed upon a <u>Lost Sinner,</u> then he will be placed in God's **Divine School of Higher Learning** to be filled with the **Knowledge of God.** Recall that Abraham Pleased God" by <u>Offering Him Death</u> (animal) in the form of a **Ram, Goat, and Heifer** as a sign of **Sacrificing His Wealth** to God in **Payment for his Venial Sins.** Secondly, "Moses Pleased God" by <u>Offering Him Death</u> (consecration) in the form of the **Outer Court** on the **Brazen Altar** via a **Sacrificial Lamb** in fulfillment of the **Mosaic Law**. Finally, "Jesus Pleased God" by <u>Offering Him Death</u> (divine) in the form of being **Scourged at the Pillar** to **Pay for the Sins of All Men** through **His Own Death Agony.**

Pulpit (throne) - The purpose of the "Pulpit" is to <u>Speak to God</u> so that the Human Race can **Present Its Gift to God** in the form of its **Act of Changing** from an **Ignorant Fool, Criminal, Insane Mad-man, and Evil** Monster into a **New Righteous, Holy, Perfect, and Divine Christian before God.** If this "Gift of Changing (confession)" is <u>Accepted by God,</u> then the Lord will **Anoint this Christian** with a **New Nature**, **Kingship** (righteous), a **Transfigured Body,** seat in His **Celestial Court,** and the **Title Deed to Earth.** Once all these "Treasures of Life" have been bestowed upon a <u>Holy Christian,</u> then he will be placed in God's **High School** to be made **Self-aware of the Realities of Life.** Recall that "Abraham Pleased God" by giving Him a <u>Gift of New-life</u> (kingship) in the **Form** of his **Son's Bloodless Sacrifice** as a **Sign** of <u>**Sacrificing His Love**</u> to God in **Payment for his Mortal Sins**. Secondly, "Moses Pleased God" by giving Him a <u>Gift of New-life</u> (priesthood) in the **Form** of the <u>**Holy Place**</u> on the <u>**Golden Altar**</u> via an <u>**Incense Anointing**</u> (sweet smell) in fulfillment of the **Mosaic Law.** Finally, "Jesus Pleased God" by giving Him a <u>Gift of New-life</u> (sonship) in the **Form** of being **Crucified on the Cross** to <u>**Pay for the Sins of All Men**</u> through **His Own Death.**

Chair (palace) - The purpose of the "Chair" is to <u>Listen to God</u> so that the <u>Human Race</u> can **Present Its Petition to God** in the **Form** of its **Changed Life of Fruitfulness** from an **Ignorant Fool, Criminal, Insane Mad-man, and Evil Monster** into a **New Righteous, Holy, Perfect, and Divine Saint before God.** If this "Petition of Fruitfulness (communion)" is <u>Accepted by God</u>, then the Lord will **Sanctify this Saint** with a **New Nature, Sonship** (perfect), a **Holy Soul,** a seat in **His Royal Court,** and the **Title Deed to His Kingdom**. Once all of these "Treasures of Life" have been bestowed upon a <u>Saint,</u> then he will be placed in God's **College** to be brought into **Consciousness of God's Divine Truths, Laws, and Wills.** Recall that "Abraham Pleased God" by presenting Him with a <u>Petition for Eternal Life</u> (earth) in the form of his **Personal Circumcision** as a sign of **Sacrificing his Life** to God in **Payment for his Capital Sins.** Secondly, "Moses Pleased God" by presenting <u>Him</u> with a <u>Petition for Eternal Life</u> (Heaven) in the **Form** of **His Holy of Holies** on the **Ark of the Covenant** via **Seven Drops of Blood** (cover sin) in **Fulfillment of the Mosaic Law.** Finally, "Jesus Pleased God" by presenting <u>Him</u> with a <u>Petition for Eternal Life</u> (Kingdom) in the **Form** of **His Death in the Tomb** to <u>**Pay for the Sins of All Men**</u> through **His Eternal Damnation.**

This "Need to Seek" <u>God's Blessing</u> of **Eternal Life** by **Paying Off Mankind's Sin-debt Sits** at the **Heart of the Matter** because through the **Law, Faith, Knowing,** and **Freedom, All Mankind can be Saved.** This "Blessing of Redemption" comes through the <u>Holy Mass</u> and its **Altar, Pulpit, Chair, and Priest** as **They Reflect** the **Four Gospels** of **Matthew, Mark, Luke, and John.** This need to have a "Person's" <u>Nature Changed,</u> be <u>Washed in Christ's Blood, Awakened to God's Truth,</u> and to be <u>Judged by God</u> brings a **Lost Sinner** from **Death to New-life**. Yes! The "Whole World" is being <u>Called</u> to **Obey God's Law, Love God's Saints,** be **Devoted to Christ,** and finally, **Serve God** with one's whole **Mind, Heart, and Soul** by <u>**Striving to Save the Souls of his Fellow Men**</u>. We see that the "First Phase of Redemption (flesh)" is the <u>Fulfillment of God's Law</u> (truth) through **Obedience to God's Word** which will **Change** a **Person's Nature** from **Human to Divine,** thereby **Making** him a **Righteous Man on Earth**. The "Second Phase of Redemption (spirit)" is the <u>Fulfillment of Man's Faith</u> (law) by **Washing Away His Sins** which will **Make him Holy** in **God's Sight,** thereby **Making him a Holy Man in Heaven**. The "Third Phase of Redemption (soul)" is the <u>Fulfillment of God's/Man's Communion</u> (will) by **Teaching a Person** to **Think for himself** which will **Make him Perfect** in the **Sight of God,** thereby **Making him Perfect within God's Kingdom.** The "Fourth Phase of Redemption (life-force)" is the <u>Fulfillment of Man's/God's Judgment</u> (love) by **Setting** a **Person Free from Slavery** which will **Make him Free** and the **Master of All he Surveys,** thereby **Making him Free from Sin, Evil, and Death.**

Through "God's Law (new nature)," a Person can Receive a **New Mind** of **Obedience**; then via "Man's Faith (wash sin)," He can Receive a **New Heart** of **Love**; then via the "God/Man Communion (think)," He can Receive a **New Soul** of **Devotion**; and finally, via the "Man/God Judgment (free)" He can Receive a **New Life-force** of **Service**. Now, we see that the "Human Race" has a New Nature, is Washed Clean, can Think, and has been Set Free from **Sin, Evil, Death, and Damnation** by the **Blood of the Lamb** (Mass) and by the **Four Gospels of the Bible** (man/lion/ox/eagle). This means that "Saint Matthew (man)" is bringing God's Word to **Change Man's Nature;** "Saint Mark (lion)" is bringing Man's Faith to **Wash Away Sin;** "Saint Luke (ox)" is bringing the God/Man Communion to **Teach Man to Think;** and "Saint John (eagle)" is bringing the Man/God Judgment to **Set All Men Free**. Obviously, "Matthew" represents God's Altar or the **Holy Word of Change;** "Mark" represents God's Pulpit or **Church Traditions of Purity;** "Luke" represents God's Chair or **Sacred Communion of Transformation;** and "John" represents God's Priest or **Divine Judgment of Awakening**.

The Holy Word, Church Traditions, Sacred Communion, and Divine Judgments Transform Mankind
(word changes nature, traditions wash away sin,
communion brings thinking, judgment sets one free)

Truth
(mind)

1. **Holy Word** (God) - Change Nature: Obedience to the Word .... Fulfill Law
   - Man - Gospel of Matthew: Christ is Human = Good News
     (free redemption)
   - Righteous Man on Earth - Baby Mind: Intellect = Obey the Law
   - Defeat Ignorance and Gain Wisdom - Destroy the Ignorant Fool
   - Word of the Mass - Holy Altar: New Nature = New Body

Law
(heart)

2. **Church Traditions** (Man) - Wash Away Sin: Love of Saints ... Fulfill Faith
   - Lion - Gospel of Mark: God's Word = Gospel Message (earned salvation)
   - Holy Man in Heaven - Teenage Heart: Emotions = Love Christ's Faith
   - Defeat Cowardice and Gain Courage - Destroy the Wicked Criminal
   - Traditions of the Mass - Holy Pulpit: Pure Nature = Eternal Life

Will
(soul)

3. **Sacred Communion** (God/Man) - Think for Self: Devotion to Christ...
   Fulfill Knowing
   - Ox - Gospel of Luke: Lamb's Sacrifice = Doctrinal Truths (bonus rewards)
   - Perfect Man within Kingdom - Adult Soul: Instincts = Awaken to Knowing
   - Defeat Greed and Gain Generosity - Destroy the Insane Mad-man
   - Communion of the Mass - Holy Chair: Wise Nature = Royal Kingdom

Life-
Force

4. **Divine Judgment** (Man/God) - Free from Slavery: Serving God ... Fulfill
   Freedom
   - Eagle - Gospel of John: Knowing God = God's Knowing (eternal freedom)
   - Free Man in Own Kingdom - Wise Man's Life-force: Nature = See Face
     of God
   - Defeat Selfishness and Gain Unselfishness - Destroy the Evil Monster
   - Judgment of the Mass - Holy Priest: Free Nature = Eternal Freedom

This illustration shows that the "Job of the Altar" is to Teach the **Good News** or **Free Redemption;** the "Job of the Pulpit" is to Teach the **Gospel Message** or **Earned Salvation**; the "Job of the Chair" is to Teach **God's Doctrinal Truths** or **Bonus Rewards;** and finally, the "Job of the Priest" is to Teach the **Power of Knowing** or **Eternal-freedom**. Through "Each of these Teachings," the Human Race will be able to both **Grow** (flesh) and **Mature** (spirit) in **Christ** to the **Point** of being **Set Free** from **Sin, Evil, Death, and Damnation**. This means that the "Life-experience is All About **Defeating Ignorance** to **Gain Wisdom, Defeating Cowardice** to **Gain Courage, Defeating Greed** to **Gain Generosity,** and **Defeating Selfishness** to become **Unselfish**. Through "Wisdom," a Person will **Receive** a **New Body** (new altar); via "Courage," He will **Receive Eternal Life** (new pulpit); via "Generosity," He will **Receive** a **Royal Kingdom** (new chair); and via "Unselfishness," He will **Receive Eternal-freedom** (new priest). It can now be seen that our "New Modern Day" Altar, Pulpit, Chair, and Priest have had **Their Roots** and very **Creation** influenced from the **Traditions of the Past** based on the idea that **Mankind Needed** some method of **Communicating with Its God**. It can now be seen that the "Altar (offering)," "Pulpit (gift)," and the "Chair (petition)" represent the Heart of the Mass. The **Mass** (word/traditions/communion/judgment) itself is at the **Heart of Christ's Church** to bring **Redemption** to **One and All**.

We see that our most "Holy Institution of the Church" is at the Center of the Human Soul and represents the **Foundation Stone** of **Future Society** as the **Heart** of the **Eternal Human Family** (kingdom). The creation of an "Earthly Religious System (sacrifice)" has been Established through the Selection of the Chosen People (Jewish Faith) who have been **Honored by God** via their most sacred **Sonship Charter** to be a **Holocaust unto the Lord** for the **Redemption of All Men**. They were "Chosen" to Pour" Their Sacred Blood (goat) **Over** the **Divine Altar of Purification** in **Honor** of **Divine Justice** as a **Sign** of **Human Recompense** for all the **Sins of Broken Humanity**. This "Sacrificial Honor" is based upon the Creation of the **Lord's Mystical Flesh** by **Purchasing God's Transfigured Body,** so **that Humanity** will be **Saved** from its **Curse of Death** by its **Union with the Cross** (forgiveness).

1. **Free Redemption of Sinner** - Being Saved: Free Gold Mine .....Worthy of New Body
   • 1st Cross - Earthly Life: Master Earthly Baby Farm (purify society/flesh)
2. **Earned Salvation of Believer** - Saving Self: Digging Out Gold....Worthy of Eternal Life
   • 2nd Cross - Heavenly Eternal Life: Master Divine School (purify individual/spirit)
3. **Bonus Reward to Christians** - Saving Others: Sharing One's Gold...Worthy of Own Kingdom
   • 3rd Cross - Kingdom Life: Master Sonship Training (purify God/Man/soul)

We see in "Christ's Cross" the Redemption (free) of the **Sinner,** the Salvation (earned) of the **Believer,** and the Rewards (bonus) of the **Christian** as a **Lost Child of God Seeks God's Truth, Law, Will, and Love**. We see the "Blessings of God" being **Placed** upon **Jacob When Isaac Gave** him his **Inheritance Blessing,** to **Make him Ruler of All**. This **Occurred** shortly after **Jacob Bought Esau's Birthright** (spirit) for a **Bowl of Soup,** thereby **Giving** the **Jewish People** both the **Blessings** of **Physical**

Life (Earth) and **Spiritual Eternal Life** (Heaven). Now, "If We Look Closely" at Isaac's Ten Blessings (Genesis chap. 27: 27-29) upon **Jacob, We will See** that **They Match God's Mystical Blessings** being **Placed** upon **Jesus Christ** as the **Lord Comes** to **Purify Man's Old Nature** (human to divine/grave) and **Transform All Men** into **Holiness** (wash away sin/host). We see "Isaac's 1st Blessing (rich soil)" states that My Son's Smell is Like (prosperity) a **Fruitful Field** (rich soil) being truly **Blessed by God**. This can be **Translated to Mean** that **God is Blessing His Son** with **Three Fields of Life** in the **Form** of **Earth, Heaven, and Kingdom.** Second, "Isaac's 2nd Blessing (rain)" states that May Your Fields be Blessed with **Dew/rain from Heaven,** **Meaning** that **God is Blessing His Son** with an **Abundance of Grace** (rain) in the **Form** of **Free Redemption, Earned Salvation, and Bonus Rewards**. Third, "Isaac's 3rd Blessing" states that May Your Fields be Blessed with **Fruitfulness, Meaning** that **God is Blessing His Son** with **Many Babies, Righteous Citizens, Holy Saints, and Sons of God** in the **Form** of **Spiritual Divinity** and **Physical Holiness.** Fourth, "Isaac's 4th Blessing" states that May Your Fields be Blessed with an **Abundance of Bread** (wheat) and **Wine** (grapes), **Meaning** that **God is Blessing His Son** with **Holy Bread** and **Holy Wine** in the **Form** of **Eating God's Flesh** (change nature) and **Drinking God's Spirit** (become holy). Fifth, "Isaac's 5th Blessing" states that May Men Come to Serve You, **Meaning** that **God is Blessing His Son** with **Leadership** in the **Form** of **God's Authority, God's Responsibility, God's Duty, and God's Task.**

Sixth, "Isaac's 6th Blessing" states that May Nations Bow to You, **Meaning** that **God is Blessing His Son** with **Ownership** and **Authority Over 144 Perfect Nations** in the **Form** of being the **Master of All He Surveys.** Seventh, "Isaac's 7th Blessing" states that May You Rule Over Your Brother (Esau) which can be **Translated to Mean** that **God is Blessing His Son** with **Power and Authority Over All Evil Men** in the **Form** of being the **King of the Jews** (earth), **High Priest of Heaven**, and the **Son of God** (Kingdom). Eighthly, "Isaac's 8th Blessing" states that May Your Mother's Relatives Bow to You (Laban), **Meaning** that **God is Blessing His Son** with **Cunning** so that **Jesus Christ** can **Outsmart Sin, Evil, and Death** in the **Form** of **Divine Wisdom, Courage, Generosity, and Unselfishness.** Ninth, "Isaac's 9th Blessing" states that May God's Curse Fall on All Who Curse You (Esau), **Meaning** that **God is Blessing His Son** with **Power Over All His Enemies** in the Form of **Righteousness** (mind), **Holiness** (heart), and **Perfection** (soul) in **All Things Great and Small.** Tenth, "Isaac's 10th Blessing" states that May All God's Blessing Bless You (Messiah), **Meaning** that **God is Blessing His Son** with a **New Body, Eternal Life, His Own Kingdom, and Freedom** in the **Form** of **Owning Earth, Heaven, Kingdom, and God.**

Through these "Ten Blessings" from Father Isaac, both the **Dust of the Earth**/sand (righteous citizens) and **Stars of the Sky** (holy saints) are to be **Honored by the Lord God Almighty Himself** and then **Welcomed** into **His Eternal Kingdom** as **His Friends.**

The following tabular information indicates that "Isaac's Blessings" upon Jacob are to be **Decoded** to **Show God's Blessings** upon **His Son, Jesus Christ** as **He is Given Life, Death** and **Eternal Life** as both **His Inheritance of Destiny** (flesh) and **His Birthright of Free Will** (spirit):

Genesis Chapter 27: 27-29 - Isaac Blesses Jacob with his Inheritance
(all biblical blessings refer to God blessing His Son, Jesus Christ)

1. **My Son's Smell** - <u>Like a Fruitful Field</u> Blessed by God
   - Messiah Blessed with Ownership of Earth, Heaven, and His Own Kingdom (field)
   - Thou shall *Not Covet/cheat* Thy Neighbor's Goods/Wife.
2. **May God Bless You Son** - <u>With the Dew</u> from Heaven upon All Your Lands (water/rain)
   - Messiah Blessed with Holy/Sacred/Divine Rains upon All His Lands (redemption/salvation/rewards)
   - Thou shall *Not Lie* (bear false witness).
3. **May God Bless You Son** - <u>With the Fruitfulness</u> of the Land
   - Messiah Blessed with Babies, Righteous Citizens, Holy Saints, and Sons of God
   - Thou shall **Not Steal** (lying, cheating, and stealing).
4. **May God Bless You Son** - <u>So Your Fields</u> will bring forth the Abundance of Bread and Wine
   - Messiah Blessed with the Bread of Life (change nature) and Wine of Eternal Life (holiness)
   - Thou shall *Not Commit Adultery* (illicit sex).
5. **May God Bless You Son** - <u>So All Men</u> will Come to Serve You
   - Messiah Blessed with both Mystical Body of Christ (earth) and Communion of Saints (Heaven)
   - Thou shall *Not Kill* (murder).
6. **May God Bless You Son** - <u>So All Nations</u> shall Bow to You
   - Messiah Blessed with 144 Perfect Nations to Call Him Lord and Master
   - Thou shall *Honor Your Father/Mother.*
7. **May God Bless You Son** - So <u>You shall be the Ruler</u> Over Your Brother
   - Messiah Blessed with being the Ruler Over All Humanity (king/priest/son)
   - Thou shall *Keep the Sabbath Day Holy.*
8. **May God Bless You Son** - <u>So Your Mother's Relatives</u> will Bow to You
   - Messiah Blessed with Cunning so All Humanity will Bow to the Lord Jesus Christ
   - Thou shall *Not Take the Lord's Name in Vain.*
9. **May God Bless You Son** - <u>So God's Curse will Fall</u> On Those Who Curse You
   - Messiah Blessed by God to Destroy All His Son's Enemies
   - Thou shall *Not Worship Idols.*
10. **May God Bless You Son** - <u>So God's Blessing</u> will Bless You
    - Messiah is being Blessed through His Treasures of a New Body, Eternal Life, Own Kingdom, and Freedom
    - Thou shall *Not Worship Any Other gods.*

This illustration shows that both "Father Jacob (Jews)" and the "Lord Jesus Christ (Christians)" are being <u>Given the Treasures</u> of **Earthly Life** and **Heavenly Eternal Life** to bring **Free Redemption** (being saved), **Earned Salvation** (saving self), and **Bonus Rewards** (saving others) to **All Men.** We see that "Jesus Christ is Trying" to <u>Warn Mankind</u> that it must **Prepare** for **Lucifer's Test** and **God's Coming Judgment** by both **Growing-up** (flesh) and **Maturing** (spirit) to the **Point of Knowing** God's **Right from man's wrong**. This means that to "Grow-up in Christ," a <u>Person</u> must **First Meet** the **Holy Spirit**, then **Meet** the **Son of God** and finally **Meet** the **Eternal Father** to **See God's Truth, Law, and Will**. In this "Encounter" with the <u>Holy Trinity,</u> a **Person** can **Come to Know God's Truth, Law, Will, and Love** to **Find** the **Lord's Pathways** to **Righteousness, Holiness, and Perfection**. Obviously, "Getting On the Pathway" means <u>Awakening in Life</u> as an **Animal** who must **Deny himself, Obey God's Commandments,** and **Reject His Father and Mother** to **Attain God's Divine** **Emotions, Intellect, and Instincts**. Secondly, after "Mastering the Animal Nature," a <u>Person</u> must become a **Robot**, who must **Pick-up Christ's Cross, Sell All and Give to Poor,** and **Abandon His People** to **Attain God's Divine** **Courage, Wisdom, and Generosity**. Finally, after "Mastering the Robot Nature," a <u>Person</u> is **Allowed to become Human,** so that he can **Come and Follow the Holy Spirit, Follow the Son of God,** and **Follow the Eternal Father** to **Attain God's Divine** **New Heart of Love, New Mind of Wisdom,** and **New Soul of Knowledge**. Yes! "Every Sinner must Master" the <u>Animal, Robot,</u> and <u>Human Natures</u> before **Entering** the **Divine Nature of God,** where he will **Learn All Things Great and Small**. This means that every "Sinner (baby)" must <u>Master Abraham's Altar</u> (meet Spirit), become a serious "Believer (teenager)" able to <u>Master Isaac's Throne</u> (meet Son), and then become a devout "Christian (adult)" able to <u>Master Jacob's Palace</u> (meet Father), all in the **Name of Jesus Christ**. This implies that a "Sinner" must <u>Comprehend God's Truth;</u> the "Believer" must <u>Obey God's Law;</u> and the "Christian" must <u>Follow God's Will</u> so that he might **Grow-up** and **Receive God's Love** (freedom).

The following tabular information indicates "Man's Need to Master" the <u>Altar, Throne,</u> and <u>Palace</u> before he can come to **Meet** the **Holy Spirit** (truth), the **Son of God** (law), and the **Eternal Father** (will) and become **Perfect in the Sight of God:**

Master Temple Altar, Throne,
and Palace of God on Earth to Meet the Holy Trinity
(sinners are animals who must change into believers,
become robots, who become Christians)

Animal
(truth)

1. **Sinner** - <u>Master Abraham's Altar:</u> Meet the Holy Spirit (priest)…Holiness
   - Birthright of the People - Love: New Heart (emotions) = Altar
   - Baby Worships God - Learn Good from Evil: Purify Spirit = Know God
   - Comprehending the Truth - Remove Faults: See Limitations
   - Deny Self (selfish) - Receive Divine Emotions
   - Obey God's Commandments - Receive Divine Intellect
   - Reject Father and Mother - Receive Divine Instincts
   (priest comes on a donkey - submission of the spirit: dying to self)

Robot
(law)

2. **Believer** - <u>Master Isaac's Throne:</u> Meet Son of God (king) …Righteousness
   - Inheritance of the Land - Money: New Mind (intellect) = Pulpit

- Teenager Praises God - Learn Right from Wrong: Transform Flesh = Love God
- Obeying God's Law - Gain Virtues: See Potential
- Pick-up Christ's Cross - Receive Divine Courage
- Sell All, Give to Poor - Receive Divine Wisdom
- Abandon One's People - Receive Divine Generosity

(king comes as a thief in the night - sacrifice flesh: born-again)

Human
(will)

3. **Christian** - <u>Master Jacob's Palace:</u> Meet Eternal Father (son)....Perfection
- Freedom via a Happy Life - Wisdom: New Soul (instincts) = Chair
- Adult Thanks God - Learn God's Will from man's will: Convert Soul = Serve God
- Following God's Will - Receive New Nature: See Self-worth
- Come Follow Holy Spirit - Receive New Heart: Love
- Come Follow Son of God - Receive New Mind: Wisdom
- Come Follow Eternal Father - Receive New Soul: Thinking

(son comes as just judge on cloud - conversion of soul: sainthood)

This illustration shows that the "Life-experience" is all about receiving a <u>New Mind, New Heart,</u> and <u>New Soul</u> to **Open the Door** to <u>Know God</u> as an **Animal** (baby), **Love God** as a **Robot** (teenager), and finally, **Serve God** as a **Devout Human Being** (adult). By both "Growing and Maturing" into one of <u>God's Priests</u> (altar), <u>God's Kings</u> (throne), and finally, into <u>God's Sons</u> (palace), a **Person** can become **Holy** (rides donkey), **Righteous** (rides in darkness), and **Perfect** (rides cloud) **before God.** The Bible clearly states that the "Whole Human Race" is being <u>Called</u> to **Deny Itself, Obey God's Commandments, Sell All and Give to the Poor, Pick-up Christ's Cross, Leave Its Family, and Come Follow the Lord.** Unfortunately, no one seems to have the "Necessary Endurance," "Character," and/or "Level of Perfection" to <u>Fight his Own</u> **Sin-nature** (break chains), then <u>Fight</u> **Worldly Temptations** (open prison door), and finally, <u>Fight</u> the **Demonic Forces of Lucifer** (defeat guards) to be **Set Free** from **Sin, Evil, and Death.** When a "Person is Able" to "Fight" all of the **Forces of Evil in the World,** he will be **Worthy** of God's <u>Gift of Love</u> which can then be **Shared with his Family, Friends, and Neighbors.** In the natural course of "Divine Truth," it is important to note that <u>God's Gift of Love</u> (existence) can only be **Adequately Returned** by an **Appropriate** amount of **Human Love** given **Back to Man's Creator** with a <u>Genuine Heart-felt Desire</u> to **Serve** the **Divine Will of God.**

This means that neither the "Animal (free will)" or "Robot (destiny) Natures" can be <u>Used to Honor the Lord's</u> most **Perfect Gift of Existence** (life). Thus, it **Requires All Mankind** to be transformed into **Perfect Human Beings** (saint) to be seen by **God** as <u>Living Prayers of Love</u> (saints) in the **Persons of Jesus** (divine/sacred heart) and **Mary** (human/immaculate heart). Through the "Purification of the Spirit (morals/crucible/society)" and the "Transformation of the Flesh (ethics/winepress/individual)," a <u>Person</u> can be **Converted** from **Death** (grave) into

New-life (host). This "Long Journey Begins" with <u>Dying to Oneself</u> (submission), then being **True to himself** (self honesty), then **Following His Own Guilty Conscience** (right from wrong)," and finally, <u>Learning</u> to **Think for Himself** (instinctive compulsion). At each of these "Stages of Life," a <u>Person can Come to Master</u> the **Overall Life-experience** by <u>Learning</u> **Right from Wrong** (righteousness), **Good from Evil** (holiness), **God's Will from man's will** (perfection), and finally, **God's Reality from Man's Illusion** (freedom).

The idea here is that "God" brings <u>Our Free Redemption</u> by **Breaking Our Chains of Sin** (sin-nature) to **Give Every Human Baby** his **Own Free Body** which is to be **Transformed** into a **Righteous Citizen on Earth** or <u>Attaining</u> **Heaven on Earth**. Secondly, "Man" both <u>Prays</u> (spirit) and <u>Works</u> (flesh) to **Earn his Own Salvation** (worldly temptations) to **Transform himself** from a **Lost Broken Sinner** into a **Holy Saint in Heaven** or <u>Attaining</u> **Paradise in Heaven**. Finally, "God/Man Comes" as the <u>Bearer of Bonus Rewards</u> (demonic possession) to **Honor Souls Which** have become both **Righteous Citizens** (earth/flesh) and **Holy Saints** (Heaven/spirit) to be **Crowned** as **Sons of God, <u>Worthy</u>** of having **Their Own Personal Kingdoms**. "These Three" <u>Stages of Transformation</u> from **Baby, to Citizen, to Saint,** and then **to Son <u>Reveal God</u>** Breaking Man's Chains of Sin for Free, then <u>Man</u> **Opening the Prison Doors of Evil** by himself, and finally, both **God and Man Working Together** to **Overcome the Guards of Death.**

1. **God brings Free Redemption** - <u>Break Chains of Sin:</u> Freedom ... Free New Body
   - Outer Court - Learning God's Right from man's wrong (destiny)
2. **Man Earns his Own Salvation** - <u>Open Prison Doors of Evil:</u> Liberty ...Earn Eternal Life
   - Holy Place - Learning God's Good from man's evil (free will)
3. **God's/Man's Bonus Rewards** - <u>Overcome Guards of Death:</u> Independence...Rewarded with Own Kingdom
   - Holy of Holies - Learning God's Will from man's will (divine will)

This illustration shows that "God brings Freedom (baby)" to <u>Man's Flesh;</u> then "Man Strives" to <u>Obtain Liberty</u> (teenager), and finally, "God and Man Work Together" to bring <u>Independent</u> (adult) **Thought, Will, and Action** to **Every Child of God.** This means that "Knowledge is King" and that <u>True Wisdom</u> comes in the **Form of Mastering** the **Earth, Heaven, the Kingdom, and God** through an **Understanding** of the **Mosaic Tabernacle** and its **Three Mystical Rooms** plus **Entering the Light of God.** Recall that both "Moses (law)" and "Aaron (faith)" were <u>Given</u> the **Law of God** (obedience) and the **Faith of Man** (love) to **Set Mankind Free** from its **Evil Nature** (change) and its **Sinful Flesh** (wash). Through the "Mosaic Tabernacle," we can <u>Comprehend the Judgments</u> of **God, His Temple,** and **His Church** as **They Reflect Man's Journey** from **Death to New-life.** Note that "Mankind's Journey" from <u>Nothing to All</u> requires **Each Soul to Pass** through its **Own Transformation** (change nature) and **Own Purification** (wash away sin) to **<u>Convert it</u>** from **Death into New-life.** The "Lord God Almighty" has been <u>Leaving a Steady Trail of Clues</u> throughout **History** to **<u>Show Mankind the Way</u>** from **Babyhood** (growth) to **Adulthood** (maturity).

Obviously, one of these most "Important Clues" is to be <u>Found</u> in the **Holy Bible**, beginning with the **Life of Moses** (king) and his **Brother Aaron** (priest), **Who Represent** the <u>**Prefigurement**</u> of a **Coming Jewish Messiah**. In the "Story of Moses," the <u>Lord is Showing Us</u> that **Mount Sinai** represents **His Throne** (flesh), while the **Mosaic Tabernacle** represents **God's Altar** (spirit) or the <u>**Coming Mystical Union**</u> of **God's Spirit** (Heaven) with **Man's Flesh** (earth). Through this "Theme," the <u>Human Race</u> is **Able** to **See Its Call** to <u>**Master**</u> **Baby Earth** (elementary school/laity), **Teenage Heaven** (high school/priesthood), the **Adult Kingdom** (college/high priest), and **Wise Man Freedom** (career/Messiah). This means that the "Mosaic Tabernacle" is a <u>Replica</u> of **Mankind's Eternal Journey** (challenge) from the **Sunlight of Earth** to the **Shekinah Glory of God**, thereby <u>**Lighting the Way**</u> in **Knowledge, Self-awareness, Consciousness,** unto **Human Sentience** (awakening). This "Concept of Light" represents the <u>Growth of a Baby</u> as he **Journeys** into the **Unknown World** of **Adult Behavior**, where the **Complexities of Life** become so **Overwhelming** that <u>**He Needs**</u> the **Guiding Hand of God to Survive**.

We see that "Moses Reveals" that in the <u>Outer court</u> (laity), there are **Two Pieces of Furniture: First,** the **Brazen Laver** or **Water** represents the **Flesh of Man Which** has been **Created** as an **Animal** and is <u>**Now being Changed**</u> into a **Son of God** (divinity). Secondly, comes the "Brazen Altar" or <u>Fire</u> which represents the **Spirit of God Who** has **Always Existed** as **Divine Life** and then **Takes-on All the Sins of Man** and must be **Washed** in the **Blood of the Lamb** (forgiveness). Next, "Moses Reveals" that in the <u>Holy Place</u> (priesthood), there are **Three Pieces of Furniture: First,** the **Table of Shewbread** (12 loaves) which represents the **Mind of Man** (intellect/flesh) or **Angelic Realm** (thanksgiving), which is <u>**Transformed**</u> from **Ignorance to Wisdom**. Secondly, comes the "Candlestick" or <u>Angelic Light</u> which represents the **Heart of Man** (emotions/spirit) or **Angelic Realm** (praise), **Which** is <u>**Transformed**</u> from **Cowardice to Courage**. Thirdly, comes the "Golden Altar of Incense" or <u>Angelic Smell</u> (worship) which represents the **Soul of Man** (instincts/soul) or **Angelic Realm** (worship), **Which** is <u>**Transformed**</u> from **Greed to Generosity**. Next, "Moses Reveals" that in the <u>Holy of Holies</u> (high priest), there are **Two Pieces of Furniture** connected to the **Ark of the Covenant: First,** the **Two Angels** (top) which represent **Three Divine Items:** 1) <u>Two Tablets</u> (10 commandments/guilty blood) or Law, 2) <u>Blossomed Staff</u> (chosen/innocent blood) or Faith, and 3) <u>Manna from Heaven</u> (food/forgiven blood) or Knowing. Secondly, comes the "Mercy Seat (bottom)" or <u>Divine Flame</u> which represents **Two Divine Items:** 1) <u>Two Golden Angels</u> (law) or Condemnation (judgment), and 2) <u>Mercy Seat</u> (faith) or Forgiveness. Finally, "Moses" reveals the <u>Importance</u> of the **Mercy Seat Itself** as the **Judgment Seat of God,** where the **Human Race** can come **Face-to-face** with its **Creator** and <u>**Beg Him for Forgiveness**</u> through the **Sacrificial Blood of the Lamb** (Jesus Christ). Now, we see that the "Mosaic Tabernacle" is Comprised of Three Rooms, each designed to **Transform** the **Human Race** from **Mortal to Immortal**.

The following tabular information indicates that the "Mosaic Tabernacle" is <u>Comprised</u> of **Three Rooms**: the <u>**Outer Court**</u> (earth), <u>**Holy Place**</u> (Heaven), and **Holy of Holies** (Kingdom) which **Lead to God's Ark of the Covenant** (mercy seat/God):

The Mosaic Tabernacle's Outer Court, Holy Place,
Holy of Holies, and Mercy Seat Reveal Christ
(Outer Court's sunlight, Holy Place's candlelight,
Holy of Holies' Divine light reveal God)

Earth | 1. | **Outer Court** (sunshine) - <u>Earth:</u> Learn Right/Wrong = See Limitations...
(Christian) | | Truth

- Brazen Laver - Water: Flesh = Change Nature   **Laity**
- Brazen Altar - Fire: Spirit = Wash Away Sin   (Lucifer's Test)

(knowledge - becoming a Righteous Citizen on Earth: receive a New Body)

Heaven | 2. | **Holy Place** (candlelight) - Heaven: Learn Good/Evil = See Potential... Law
(saint) |
- Table of Shewbread - Flesh: Mind = Intellect   **Priesthood**
- Golden Candlestick - Spirit: Heart = Emotions   (God's Judgment)
- Golden Altar of Incense - Soul: Being = Instincts

(self-awareness - becoming a Holy Saint in Heaven: receive Eternal Life)

Kingdom | 3. | **Holy of Holies** (God's light) - <u>Kingdom:</u> Learn God's Will/man's
(son) | | will = See Self-worth...........................Will
- <u>Bottom of Ark of Covenant</u> – Flesh
- Two Tablets (10 commandments) - Law: Obedience
- Blossomed Staff (chosen) - Faith: Love
- Manna from Heaven (food) - Knowing: Thinking   **High Priest**
- <u>Top of Ark of Covenant</u> – Spirit   (self-evaluation)
- Two Golden Angels - Jesus' Blood: Save Sinners
- Mercy Seat of God - Christ's Death: Create Saints

(consciousness - becoming a Son of God within God's Kingdom: receive Royal Kingdom)

God | 4. | **Ark's Mercy Seat** (Light of Christ) - <u>God:</u> Learn Reality/Illusion = See
(free man) | | Value...Love
- God's Shekinah Glory - Lord God Almighty   **Messiah**
- See God Face-to-face (beatific vision)   (think for self)

(sentience - becoming Free Man in Union with God: receive Eternal Freedom)

This illustration shows that the "Outer Court" represents <u>Earth</u> which **Symbolizes the Laity** (babyhood) as **They Face Lucifer's Tests of Sin, Evil, and Death** to <u>**Remove**</u> (faults) **Their Ignorance, Cowardice, and Greed.** Secondly, comes the "Holy Place" representing <u>Heaven</u> which **Symbolizes** the **Priesthood** (teenagers) as **It Faces God's Judgment of Repentance, Prayers, and Works** to <u>**Gain**</u> (virtues) **Wisdom, Courage, and Generosity.** Thirdly, comes the "Holy of Holies" representing <u>God's Kingdom</u> which **Symbolizes the High Priest as He Faces his Own Self-evaluation** of **Righteousness, Holiness, and Perfection <u>Leading</u> to his Own Sonship** (Son of God). Finally, comes the "Mercy Seat" representing <u>God Himself</u> which **Symbolizes the Messiah as He Faces Thinking for Himself** or **Mastering Freedom** (king), **Liberty** (priest), and **Independence** (son) which **Leads him** to a **Life of Self-reliance** (free man).

This great journey through "Lucifer's Test" of <u>Belief</u> (prayer), <u>Trust</u> (works), and <u>Faith</u> (rest) is known as **Attending** *God's Divine School of Higher Learning*. Using this same process, the "Born-again Gentiles" are <u>Manifested</u> out of the <u>Christian Faith</u> (free will) specially **Selected to Share** in the **Jewish Holocaust** (burnt offering/payment) for the **Creation** of the **Lord's Glorified Spirit**. To reach "Heaven (perfection)," a <u>Soul must Purchase</u> **God's Divine/Human Spirit** to **Redeem Humanity** from the **Evil Curse of Damnation** (hell). Once the "Destiny of the Jews" (flesh/law) is <u>United</u> with the "Free Will of the Gentiles (spirit/faith)," the **Temple** (destiny saves flesh) and **Church** (free will saves spirit) will **Merge** into one **Mystical Body** of **Divine Truth, Law, Will,** and **Love**. This "Union" of <u>Jew and Gentile</u> occurs via the **Marriage of God's Son** (one/law) to **Man's Church** (all/faith) through both the **Jewish Passover** (Mosaic Law) and the **Gentile Mass** (Canon Law), thereby **Allowing God's Heaven** and **Man's Earth** to become **One Kingdom Serving One and All**. This means that a "Strong Union" can only <u>Take Place</u> when a **Loving Couple** has **Struggled Against** the **Force of Sin, Evil, Death,** and **Damnation** and **Defeated Them All** in **Mind, Heart, and Soul** through **Its Righteousness, Holiness,** and **Perfection**.

This "Great Struggle of Life" <u>Creates a Wholesome Character</u> **Leading** a **Person to See** his **Own Self-worth** as it **Reflects** the **Nature of Christ** in **All Things** be **They Great and/or Small**. We see that this "Light of Christ" <u>Reveals</u> the <u>Lord's Door of Grace</u> showing **God's Pathway of Perfection** on **Earth**, in the **Form of Christ's Church**, which brings **All Men of Goodwill** to **Jesus Christ's** **Free Gift of Eternal Redemption**. Obviously, the "Lord has Allowed" the <u>Human Race some 2,000 Years</u> of **Fleshly Adjustment** to more **Easily Make the Transition** from **Earthly Sinner** (evil) to **Heavenly Saint** (holy) and **Defeat Sin, Evil, Death,** and **Damnation**. Recall that the "Four Horsemen of the Apocalypse" will be <u>Sent to Terminate</u> the **Evil Nature of Man** either by **Pleading God's Case** or by **Brute Force** whichever is **Necessary** to bring to a **Close God's Age of Grace**. Once the "Old Sin-nature" has been <u>Terminated,</u> then **Mankind will be Returned** to its **Original State of Holiness** (Adam) and the **Earth will be Returned** to its **Original Owner** (New Adam) to **Begin the Restoration of All Creation Back to God**. This "Act will Open" a New <u>Door of Grace,</u> known as the **Civilization of Love,** when **All Men** will **Live Under** the **Holy Mantle** of the **Blessed Virgin Mary** for **1,000 Years of Peace** while **Mankind is Prepared to Meet Its God**.

The implication here is that the "Job of the Holy Church" was to <u>Physically Touch</u> as **Many People on Earth as Possible** during its **2,000-Year Stay** so that the **Lost** might have a **Chance to See, Touch, or Know Jesus Christ Firsthand** (personally). We call this the "Touch of Peter" for it was his Job as the **Vicar of Christ** to **Search the Whole World** for **Those Men of Goodwill** (priests/religious), **Who** would be **Worthy** of his **Touch of Conversion,** thereby bringing **Them to Holy Perfection before God**. Recall in "Hebrew's 9:15," the <u>Lord Tells Us</u> that **We are Chosen by Him**. This means **If a Person** is **Not Touched** by the **House of Peter** (Holy Church) either at **Birth** (free) or by **Conversion** (earned), there is **No**

Other Channel to **Seek His Redemption** (gift). This means that "God's Free Gift of Redemption" is through <u>Faith</u> (belief); yet, **Given** through the **Lord's Conditional Grace** (earned blessing), it **Requires** a **Person's <u>Unconditional Submission</u>** to **God's Divine Will**. To understand this "Intricate Concept" of <u>Divine Contradiction,</u> a **Person** is **<u>Saved by his Faith</u>** (birthright/free) through **<u>God's Grace</u>** (inheritance/earned), yet, must be **<u>Affirmed by His Works</u>** (saving others), thereby **Demonstrating** and/or **Showing his Soul's Personal Contribution** (growth). This means that a "Born-again Christian" must <u>Reject his Selfish Pride</u> and **Strive in Seeking** his **New State of Humility within Christ Jesus.**

The question is: just how can a "Person Use his Free Will" to <u>Effectively Modify</u> his **Old Sin-nature of Selfishness** (pride) and **Seek** a **New Holy-nature of Unselfishness** (humility)**,** when he **<u>Seems</u>** to have **No Power to Earn his Own Salvation** through **Good Works**? At this point, we must absolutely "Distinguish" between the <u>Work of Rejecting One's Pride</u> (spiritual work/submission/belief) and the **Good Works** (physical works) of **Christian Duty**. The easy answer is a "Born-again Christian" must <u>Believe 100%</u> (perfect faith) to be able to **Die to Self** (pride) unto **Total Submission,** thereby **Transforming** his **<u>Sinful Flesh</u>** into a **<u>New Holy Spirit</u>** or being **Christ-like** (humble). In the case of "Rejecting His Pride" to <u>Seek</u> the **Blessing of Humility**, a **Person is Trying** to **Attain an Impossible State of Holiness** which is the **Human Transformation** of <u>his Old Sin-nature</u> by his **Own Efforts** (trying to die). In short, the "Definition of Holiness (quit)" is when a **Person** (spirit) **Dies to Self** unto **Nothingness**, while the "Definition of Righteousness (never-quit) is when a **Person** (flesh) **Strives to Defeat the World** unto his **Own Destruction** (all). Yes! Through "Righteousness," "Holiness," and "Perfection," a <u>Person</u> can become a **Christian**, a **Saint**, and finally, a **Son of God**. But it must be "Understood" that <u>God</u> is **Purifying the Spirit** (life) to **Make It Holy in Heaven** (spiritual dimension); while <u>Man</u> is **Transforming the Flesh** (death) to **Make It Righteous on Earth** (physical dimension).

The following tabular information indicates the "Definitions" of <u>Man's Righteousness, God's Holiness,</u> and <u>God/Man Perfection</u> since the **Human Race** must **Face the World System** (Lucifer's Test), **God's Judgment** (God's Test), and its **Own Self-evaluation** to be **Set Free:**

Man's Righteousness/trying, God's Holiness/quit,
and God/Man Perfection/defeat to Find God
(fighting world, defeat pride,
and overcome self to transform one's mind, heart, and soul)

Truth   1. **Man's Righteousness** – <u>Never-quit Trying:</u> Fight the World System unto Death
- Face Lucifer's Test - Learn Right from Wrong: See Limitations
- Remove Ignorance - Gain Wisdom:
  Free New Body (mind)   **Physical Dimension**
- Enter Jesus' Kingship - Rule Earth: Christian Life
- Purifying One's Grave - Becoming Worthy of a New Body

Law   2. **God's Holiness** - <u>Instantly Quit:</u> Die to Self to Defeat One's Selfish Pride
            • Face God's Judgment - Learn Good from Evil: See Potential
            • Remove Cowardice - Gain Courage:
              Earn Eternal Life (heart)   **Spiritual Dimension**
            • Enter Christ's Priesthood - Rule Heaven: Saintly Life
            • Purifying Christ's Host - Becoming Worthy of Eternal Life

Will   3. **God/Man's Perfection** - <u>Defeat Self:</u> Remove Wicked Flesh into Holy
            Spirit
            • Face Self-evaluation - Learn God's Will/man's will: See Self-worth
            • Remove Greed - Gain Generosity:
              Rewarded Royal Kingdom (soul)   **Mystical Dimension**
            • Enter Jesus Christ's Sonship - Rule Kingdom: Son's Life
            • Purifying One's Life - Becoming Worthy of One's Own Kingdom

This illustration shows that the "Human Race" is <u>Striving</u> to **<u>Earn</u> a <u>New Mind</u>** (physical) by becoming **Righteous on Earth** (never-quit), then **Earning a New Heart** (spiritual) by becoming a **Holy Saint in Heaven** (quit), and finally, **Earning a New Soul** (mystical) by becoming a **Son of God within God's Kingdom**. By "Working" toward <u>Mastering</u> the **Earth, Heaven, and God's Kingdom**, a **Person** is able to **Learn Right/Wrong, Good/Evil, and God's Will/man's will** to **<u>See his Own</u> Limitations, Potential, and Self-worth**. By "Mastering Earth" or the <u>Physical Dimension,</u> a **Person** is able to **Receive** a **Free New Body** (purify grave) and then **Enter Jesus' Kingship** to **<u>Forever Rule</u>** the **Earth** (Christian life). Secondly, by "Mastering Heaven" or the <u>Spiritual Dimension,</u> He is able to **Earn Eternal Life** (purify host) and then **Enter Christ's Priesthood** to **<u>Forever Rule</u> Heaven** (Saintly life). Finally, by "Mastering God's Kingdom" or the <u>Mystical Dimension,</u> He is able to be **Rewarded** with his **Own Royal Kingdom** (purify life) and then **Enter Jesus Christ's Sonship** to **<u>Forever Rule</u>** a **Kingdom of Glory** (Son's life).

The point is that through a "Person's Desire to Try" to <u>Accomplish the Impossible,</u> he might **Earn Those most Generous Graces** (blessing) of **<u>God</u>** in the **Form of Eternal Rewards** (indulgences). By combining the "Lord's Gift of Faith (free birthright)" with a <u>Soul's Measure of Success</u> in **Defeating** its **Own Selfish Pride** (seeking humility), a Person can **Earn God's Grace** (inheritance), thereby making him **<u>Worthy</u>** of both **Salvation** (earned) and **God's Riches in Glory** (earned). Now it is clear that a "Person must Strive" to <u>Attain</u> a **Mystical Humble and Contrite Heart** of **Perfect Holiness** simply by **Adopting a New Sacrificial <u>Nature of Unselfishness</u>** as he **Shares All he Has with Others** (sharing). Now, let's separate the "Spiritual Work" of <u>Rejecting One's Selfishness</u> (pride) to attain a **Humble and Contrite Heart** (holiness) from the **<u>Great Effort Required</u>** in **Praying to God** and **Doing Good Works for Man**. In the "First Case," <u>Self-transformation</u> is out of the **Free Will** of a **Broken and Lost Sinner**, who has **Converted to a New-life** of **Self-denial** based on a **<u>Strict Belief</u>** (100%) in **Jesus Christ** (Messiah). We see that in the "Second Case" of <u>Holy-transformation,</u> we see the **Intercession** of the **Divine Will** which **Comes** into the **Human Spirit** as **God's Holy Spirit** that is **Responsible** for **Manifesting** both <u>**Holy Prayers**</u> and <u>**Good Works**</u> into a **Born-again Christian's Life** (holiness). This means that neither "Prayers or Works can be Attributed" to the <u>Christian himself</u> as these are **Gifts of the Spirit** coming into the **Christian Soul** by **Removing Faults** (empty) and **Adding Holy Virtues** (fill). This means that there are actually "Three Battles" to be <u>Fought</u> in the **World** (flesh/33% belief), in the **Church** (spirit/67% belief), and within **himself** (soul/100% belief) to **Master the Intellect, Emotions, and Instincts** as a <u>**Reflection**</u> of the **Life of Christ**. Obviously, in "God's Grand Design," <u>He has Placed</u> a **Set of Roadblocks** or **Battles** before **Every Child** to **Force him to Fight** for **What is Rightfully** his in **Truth, Law, Will, and Love** so that in **Adulthood, <u>He will Walk</u>** with **Dignity and Honor before All**.

We see that the "Earth (law)" represents <u>God's Elementary School</u> or the **Place** where **God's Children** must **Master Obedience** by **Learning God's Right from man's wrong** (intellect) to **Overcome All the Roadblocks of Life**. Secondly, "Heaven (faith/righteous)" represents <u>God's High School</u> or the **Place** where **God's Teenagers** must **Master Love** by **Learning God's Good from man's evil** (emotion) to **Overcome All the Roadblocks Leading to Eternal Life**. Thirdly, the "Kingdom (holiness)" represents <u>God's College</u> or the **Place** where **God's Adults** must **Wash Away Their Sins** by **Learning God's Will from man's will** (instincts) to **Overcome All the Roadblocks Leading to Their Own Kingdom**. Finally, "God (perfection)" represents <u>One's Career</u> or the **Place** where **God's Wise Men** are able to **Change Their Natures** by **Learning God's Reality from man's illusion** (new nature) to <u>**Overcome**</u> **All the Roadblocks of Thinking for Themselves**. We call these "Stages of Growth (flesh)" and "Maturity (spirit)" the <u>Rite of Passage</u> as a <u>**Person Passes**</u> from **Baby to Teenager, to Adult, to Wise Man**. The idea here is to see that "Baby Means Earth," "Teenager Means Heaven," "Adulthood Means the Kingdom," and "Wise Man Means God's Beatific Vision (union)," showing that when a **Person Progresses** through <u>God's System,</u> he is becoming **More and More Perfect**. We see on "Earth (elementary school)" **Four Major Roadblocks**: 1) <u>Ignorance</u> - Changed to Wisdom, 2) <u>Cowardice</u> - Changed to Courage, 3) <u>Greed</u> - Changed to Generosity, and 4) <u>Selfishness</u> - Changed to Unselfishness. We see in "Heaven (high school)" **Four Major Roadblocks**: 1) <u>Sin</u>-nature - Changed to Righteousness, 2) <u>Worldly Temptations</u> - Changed to Holiness, 3) <u>Demonic Possessions</u> - Changed to Perfection, and 4) <u>God's Curse</u> - Changed to Freedom. We see within the "Kingdom (college)" **Four Major Roadblocks**: 1) Excommunication from Temple - Changed to Kingship, 2) Outcast from People Changed to Priesthood, 3) <u>Banished from Earth</u> - Changed to Sonship, and 4) <u>Forsaken by God</u> - Changed into a Free Man. We see in the "Oneness of God (career)" **Four Major Roadblocks**: 1) <u>Death</u> (silent anger) - Changed to Peace, 2) <u>Grave</u> (vocal rage) - Changed to Joy, 3) <u>Hell</u> (striking wrath) - Changed to Happiness, and 4) <u>Gehenna</u> (eternal punishment) - Changed to Divine Love.

We see that "Earth" represents <u>Nature</u> and the <u>Human Mind</u> as **They Toil in a Barren Land** to bring forth the **Righteous Man**, who will **One Day** become a <u>**Great King**</u> and **Earn his Own New Body** (transfigured) before **God**. Secondly, "Heaven" represents <u>Man</u> and the <u>Human Heart</u> as **They Suffer the Pains of Life** to bring forth the **Holy Man,** who will **One Day** become a <u>**High Priest**</u> and **Earn his Own Eternal Life** (glorification) before **God.** Thirdly, the "Kingdom" represents the <u>Angels</u> and the <u>Human Soul</u> as **They Suffer the Agony of Death** to bring forth the **Perfect Man,** who will **One Day** become a <u>**Son of God**</u> and **Earn his Own Royal Kingdom of Glory.** Finally, "God" represents <u>Divinity</u> and the <u>Human Life-force</u> as **They Suffer the Torment of Damnation** to bring forth the **Free Man,** who will **One Day** become **God-like** and **Earn a Mind which will Think for Itself.** At each of these "Levels of Life," <u>Nature, Men, Angels, and God</u> are **Fighting Against** the **Corrupted Flesh** (starvation), **Spirit** (nakedness), **Soul** (homelessness), and **Life-force** (wretchedness) to bring <u>**Evil Man Back**</u> to his **Original State of Holiness.**

The following tabular information indicates that the "Negative Forces" of <u>Nature, Men, Angels, and God</u> are **Fighting Against** the **Corrupted <u>Flesh, Spirit, Soul,</u>** and <u>**Life-force**</u> to bring the **Human Race to Holy Perfection:**

The Negative Forces of Nature, Men, Angels, and God Against the Flesh, Spirit, and Soul of Man
(Earth, Heaven, Kingdom, and God Curse the Human Nature with Toil, Pain, Death, and Damnation)

	Earth	Heaven	Kingdom	God
	(mind)	(heart)	(soul)	(life-force)
Truth	1. Ignorance	1. Sin-nature	1. Excommunication	1. Death
(baby)	(wisdom)		from Temple	(silent anger)

Starvation -   <u>Face Eternal-Death/death agony:</u> *Receive Life* (forgive flesh)
               • Repent before God/give belief - Remove Capital Sins (new mind)

	Earth	Heaven	Kingdom	God
Law	2. Cowardice	2. Worldly	2. Outcast	2. Grave
(teenager)	(courage)	Temptations	from People	(vocal rage)

Nakedness -   <u>Face Lake of Fire/hopelessness:</u> *Receive Peace* (forgive spirit)
               • Thank God/give labors - Remove Mortal Sin (new heart)

	Earth	Heaven	Kingdom	God
Will	3. Greed	3. Demonic	3. Banished	3. Hell
(adult)	(generosity)	Possession	from Earth	(striking wrath)

Homelessness -   <u>Face Bottomless Pit/separation:</u> *Receive Joy* (forgive soul)
               • Praise God/give money - Remove Venial Sins (new soul)

	Earth	Heaven	Kingdom	God
Love	4. Selfishness	4. God's	4. Forsaken	4. Gehenna
(wise man)	(unselfishness)	Curse	by God	(eternal punishment)

Wretchedness -   <u>Face Outer Darkness/oblivion:</u> *Receive Happiness* (forgive life-force)

Nature	Mankind	Angelic Realm	Lord God Almighty
(toil)	(pain)	(death)	(damnation)
Righteous Man	Holy Man	Perfect Man	Free Man
• New Body	• Eternal Life	• Royal Kingdom	• Think for Himself
(king)	(priest)	(son)	(God)

This illustration shows that "Earth" is a Place of Starvation as **Each of God's Babies** must **Face Eternal-death** (death agony) to **Receive a Blessed Life** (new mind) as his **Flesh must be Forgiven,** when he **Believes and Repents** (capital sins) **for All his Sins** (give belief). Secondly, "Heaven" is a Place of Nakedness as **Each of God's Teenagers** must **Face the Lake of Fire** (hopelessness) to **Receive Peace of Mind** (new heart) as his **Spirit must be Forgiven,** when he **Thanks God** (mortal sins) and **Offers-up his Labors** (prayers). Thirdly, "Kingdom" is a Place of Homelessness as **Each of God's Adults** must **Face the Bottomless Pit** (separation) to **Receive Joy of the Heart** (new soul) as his **Soul must be Forgiven**, when he **Praises God** (venial sins) and **Offers-up his Money** (works). Finally, "God" is a Place of Wretchedness as **Each of God's Wise Men** must **Face the Outer Darkness** (oblivion) to **Receive the Happiness of the Soul** (new life-force) as his **Life-force must be Forgiven,** when he **Worships God** (faults) and **Offers-up his Life** (saving souls). Through "Each of These Stages of Life," a Person both **Grows Physically** and **Matures Spiritually** until he **Masters** Earth, Heaven, the Kingdom, and God Himself.

The point is that "Mankind has been Cursed" by Nature, Humanity, the Angelic Realm, and God Himself because the **Human Race has Decided** to **Go Its Own Way** and to **Find Its Own State of Perfection** based on **Man's Perfect Life**. Obviously, the "Lord God Almighty Knew" that Mankind would Fail and **Fall** into a **Pit of Death** and then **Call Out to Its Creator for Help**. The "Job of God" is to Come with Real Solutions to **Save His Lost** and **Foolish Child** from **Starvation, Nakedness, Homelessness,** and **Wretchedness** before **It is Too Late**. We are seeing that "God" has Sent Jesus Christ in **Three Advents** to **Save the World**, as **He First Takes Away Sin** (church), then **Evil** (government), and finally, **Death** (home) to **Restore All that was Lost** Back to Their Original State. In this "Plan of Redemption," the Lord has Decided to **Send** the **Good News** or **Free Redemption to the Babies**, then to **Send the Gospel Message** or **Earned Salvation to the Teenagers**. Finally, the "Lord has Decided" to Send **His Doctrinal Truths** to the **Adult World** to **Save It** from **All the Curses** of Nature, **Evil Men, Lucifer, and God's Curse**. Obviously, it would "Take" both the Jewish People (world) and the Christian People (church/gentile) **Working Together** to **Fight All** the **Sin, Evil, Death and Damnation in the World** and **Defeat It**.

To understand this "Union" between the Jew and the Gentiles, we must look at the **Three Jewish Captivities** as **Compared** to the **Three Christian Advents of Christ** to comprehend the **Meaning** (exist/home), **Purpose** (serve/job), and **Value of Life** (happy/wife). In this way, the "Human Race" is being Divided into the **Holy, Righteous, and Evil** to **Create Eternal Sanctuaries** for **God's Saints** (Heaven in

Paradise), **Righteous Men of Earth** (Heaven on Earth), and the **Evil Sinners of Death** (Hell Fire). The "Job of Ezekiel" was to <u>Reveal</u> the **Triune Judgments of God** upon the **Jews** (earth), **Gentiles** (Heaven), and **Pagans** (hell) by <u>**Cutting Off his Hair**</u> on **Three Separate Occasions** (burn/chop/throw). Recall in the **Story of Ezekiel** that he was **Asked to Shave his Head** and then **Burn 1/3 of It,** then <u>**Take the Other 1/3**</u> **and Chop It Up,** with the final **1/3 being Cast into the Winds.** "Ezekiel" was then <u>Required</u> to **Lay on his Left Side** for **Three Hundred and Forty Days** to **Signify the Repentance** of the **Ten Northern Tribes.** This meant that the **Wicked Nations** had been **Awakened to God's Divine Truths.** We see that "Ezekiel" was then <u>Told</u> to <u>Lay on his Right Side</u> for **Another Forty Days** to **Signify the Repentance** of the **Two Holy Tribes of the South, All to Warn Israel** that **They were About to be Taken** into <u>**Captivity, If They would Not Repent.**</u> These strange "Acts of Ezekiel" were <u>Designed to Reveal</u> that there were to be **Three Coming Captivities** (law/Moses) **or Three Advents** (faith/Messiah) of the <u>**Jewish People**</u> by the **Nation of Babylon.** The "Burning of the Hair" <u>Symbolized</u> the **1st Captivity** (Priest on a Donkey/sin) which was the **Burning of the Holy Land,** known as the **Flames of Death** (fire) to <u>**Show the Coming Curse**</u> of the Evil One's **Lake of Fire** (flesh). The "Chopping of the Hair" <u>Symbolized</u> the **2nd Captivity** (Thief in night/evil) which was the **Slaughter of the Holy Land,** known as the **Knife of Death** (sword) to <u>**Show the Coming Curse**</u> of the **Evil One's Bottomless Pit** (spirit). Finally, the "Casting of the Hair to the Winds (wandering Jews)" <u>Symbolized</u> the **3rd Captivity** (Judge on Cloud/death) which was the **Jewish People Fleeing for Their Lives** from the **Holy Land** known as the **Winds of Death** (wind) to <u>**Show that Coming Curse**</u> of the **Evil One's Outer Darkness** (soul).

Yes! The "Lake of Fire," "Bottomless Pit," and the "Outer Darkness" represent <u>Sin, Evil, and Death</u> and the **Job of Jesus Christ** has been to **Come and Conquer Them All.** This "Great Event" is to <u>Occur</u> in the **Lord's Three Advents** as **He Comes** as a **Priest on a Donkey** (sin), a **Thief in the Night** (evil), and finally, as a **Just Judge on a Cloud** (death). In the "1st Advent," the <u>Lord Came as a Messiah</u> and was **Sacrificed upon Mount Calvary** for **All the Sins of Man** to **Create** the **Palace of God** on <u>Earth</u> and bring the **Sonship of God** to **All Men.** Secondly, in the "2nd Advent," the <u>Lord Comes as a Thief</u> to **Sacrifice His Church** for **All the Evil of Man** to **Create** the **Altar of God** on <u>Earth</u> and bring the **Priesthood of God to All Men.** Finally, in the "3rd Advent," the <u>Lord Comes as a Just Judge</u> to **Sacrifice His Righteous World** for the **Curse of Death on Man** to **Create** the **Throne of God on Earth** and bring the **Kingship of God to All Men.** Through these "Three Sacrifices," <u>Mankind's</u> **Chains of Sin, Prison Door of Evil,** and **Guards of Death** shall be **Overcome** and the **Whole Human Race** shall be **Set Free.**

The following tabular information indicates "Ezekiel's Triune Prophecy" that the <u>Jewish People</u> will be **Cast into Captivity Three Times, <u>1st to Atone</u>** for **Sin, <u>2nd to be Judged</u>** for **Repentance,** and a <u>**3rd Time to be Redeemed**</u> by the **Lord God Almighty Himself:**

**Ezekiel Burned 1/3 his Hair/Chopped 1/3/Cast 1/3
into Wind to Prophesy Coming Captivity**
(1st captivity is atonement,
2nd captivity is judgment, and 3rd captivity is redemption)

Ezekiel Chapter 5: 1-4

Truth
(babies)

1. **Burn 1/3 Hair** - <u>Atonement:</u> Meaning of Life = Existence ......Knowledge
   - Face Lucifer's Test - Babies Face Their Fear of the Unknown (scourging)
   - 1st Captivity - Jerusalem is Burned = Priesthood.... See Limitations
   - 1st Advent - Messiah Sacrificed on Mt. Calvary unto Sin (palace or son)
   (overcoming man's sin-nature - breaking the chains of sin:
   learn right/wrong = become righteous)

Law
(teenager)

2. **Chop 1/3 Hair** - <u>Judgment:</u> Purpose of Life = Service ..... Self-awareness
   - Face God's Judgment - Teenagers Face and Overcome the Unknown (crucifixion)
   - 2nd Captivity - Jewish People Slaughtered = Kingship—-See Potential
   - 2nd Advent - Church is Sacrificed unto Evil (altar/sanctuary or spirit)
   (overcoming man's worldly temptations - opening door of evil: learn good/evil = become holy)

Will
(adult)

3. **Cast 1/3 Hair into Wind** - <u>Redemption:</u> Value of Life = Happiness...
   Consciousness
   - Face Own Self-evaluation - Adults Face the Unknown and Make It Known (tomb)
   - 3rd Captivity - Wandering Jew = Sonship...   See Self-worth
   - 3rd Advent - World Sacrificed unto Death (white throne or father)
   (overcome demonic possession - overpower guard of death:
   learn God's Will/man's will = become perfect)

*Ezekiel told to sew a few hairs into his garment (saints) and to cast a few hairs into eternal-fire (hell)

This illustration shows that "God's Babies" are being <u>Called</u> to **Atonement** by **Removing Their Sin-nature** to **Receive a New Mind of Wisdom** (transfiguration) as **They Learn <u>Right from Wrong</u>** and become **Righteous before God.** Secondly, "God's Teenagers" are being <u>Called</u> to **Judgment** by **Removing Their Worldly Temptations** to **Receive a New Heart of Courage** (glorification) as **They Learn <u>Good from Evil</u>** and become **Holy before God.** Finally, "God's Adults" are being <u>Called</u> to **Redemption** by **Removing Their Demonic Possession** to **Receive a New Soul of Generosity** (exaltations) as **They Learn <u>God's Will from man's will</u>** and become **Perfect Sons before God.** Note that "God's Babies" must <u>Take Lucifer's Test</u> to **Prove that They** can **Face Their Own Fears** to the point of **<u>Growing-up</u>** in a **Strange World of Death.** Secondly, "God's Teenagers" must <u>Face God's Judgment</u> to **Prove that They** can **Defeat All the Forces in Life** to the point of **<u>Maturing</u>** in a **Strange World of Eternal Life.** Finally, "God's Adults" must <u>Face Their Own Self-evaluation</u>

to **Prove that They** can **Learn** to **Think for Themselves** and **Master an Evil World** of <u>Sin and Death</u> to bring forth a **New-life of Peace, Joy, and Happiness**.

This logic helps us to see the "Need for Jesus Christ" to <u>Parallel these Three Transformations</u> with **His Three Advents** (donkey/thief/judge) as **He Came to Establish His Holy Church, Sacred Government, and Divine Home on Earth**. This means that during the "Lord's 1st Advent (priest on a donkey)," <u>He Sent the Jewish People</u> to **Wander the Earth** for some **Two Thousand Years** (two days) to **Find Their Way Out** of the **Darkness of Death** by **Themselves**. During the "Lord's 2nd Advent (thief in night)," <u>He</u> will bring a <u>Great Chastisement of Death</u> to **Consume the Holy Nation of Israel,** thereby **Slaughtering Almost All Jews**, but **Leaving a Jewish Remnant**, who will <u>**Survive**</u> as in the **Days of Noah**. Finally, in the "Lord's 3rd Advent (judge on cloud)," there is to be a <u>Final Invasion of Jerusalem</u> by the **Evil One** in a **Last Desperate Attempt** to <u>**Conquer the Forces of Holiness**</u> and **Kill All God's Saints**. The point of this discussion centers upon the "Fact that Everything" in <u>God's Creation Involves</u> **Three Aspects** of **Man's Return** to **God's Divine Obedience**: 1) <u>Day of Atonement</u> - 1st Advent: Priest on a Donkey (Mount Calvary) = Great Sabbath (Lucifer's Test); 2) <u>Day of Judgment</u> - 2nd Advent: Thief in the Night (Three Days of Darkness) = Lord's Day (God's Judgment); and 3) <u>Day of Redemption</u> - 3rd Advent: Judge on a Cloud (End of World) = Final Judgment (Self-evaluation). We see that these "Three Days" of <u>Testing and Judgment</u> actually **Define** the **Nature of Man** as he is **Called** from **Nothing to All** to **Meet his God** and become **Like Him** in **Righteousness, Holiness, and Perfection**.

Obviously, these "Three Mystical Events" <u>All Take Place</u> during the **Feast of Atonement** as **God Seeks** the **Repentance of All Men** from **Their Curses** of Ignorance (mind), **Cowardice** (heart), **Greed** (soul), and **Selfishness** (life-force). In ancient times, it was said that "When the Messiah Comes" <u>All Three of these Events</u> (atonement/judgment/redemption) will **Take Place** bringing an **End** to the very **Curse of Death Itself** in **Preparation for the Coming** of the **New Heaven** and the **New Earth**. The idea here is that on the "Lord's 1st Advent (donkey)," He <u>literally Fulfilled the Need</u> for a **Day of Atonement** as **He Shed His Blood** on **Mount Calvary** for the **Sins of All Men** to **Set Them Free from Original Sin**. In contrast, during the "Lord's 2nd Advent (thief)," <u>He will Fulfill the Need</u> for a **Day of Judgment** as **He Comes forth to Judge the Holiness** of <u>His Chosen Saints</u> during <u>**His Bema Judgment**</u> (sanctuary/seal saints). Finally, in the "Lord's 3rd Advent," <u>He will Fulfill the Need</u> for a **Day of Redemption** as **He Calls All Flesh** from **Their Graves** to be **Judged** in **His Great White Throne Judgment of Divine Love**. Through this "Great Time of Purification," we will see the cleansing of the <u>Jewish National Sanctuary</u> as **God's Divine Truth, Law, and Will** <u>**Transform**</u> the **Cursed Mind, Heart, and Soul of Man**. This "Purification Process" is represented by <u>Cleansing</u> both the **Stone Temple of Worship** (society) and the **Fleshly Temple of Worship** (self) to make **One Man's Prayers** Equal to All Men's Prayers. The idea here is to "Purify the Entire" <u>Collective Mind of Man</u> through the Lord's **Blessing** of **His War of Good and Evil,** better known as the **Struggle of Wisdom** against <u>**Ignorance**</u> to bring forth the **Thinking Man** (righteous logic). In contrast, we see the Purification" of <u>God's</u>

Faithful (one) who has been **Transformed** through the **Power of his Undaunted Belief** in **God's Jewish Messiah,** the **Lord Jesus Christ, Our Savior**. In this way, "Christ will Unite" both the Jews and the Gentiles into **One People** and **Make Them** into **One Creation before God to Serve the Needs** of **Earth, Heaven, and God's Kingdom Justly**.

In this "Mystical Union," the Lord is Mixing the **Physical Blood** (innocent) of the **Jews** with the **Spiritual Blood** (guilty) of the **Gentiles** or **Christians** to **Create One People of Consecrated Blood** (forgiven), who can **Serve God** both **On Earth** (flesh) and **In Heaven** (spirit). This "Creation of Blood Inheritance" being Used by God Helps to **Explain Why** the **Lord God Almighty** has **Designed His Entire Justice System Around Blood**. Thus, the **Lord is Using Blood** to **Write in His Eternal Books of Life**. Note in the "Book of Revelation:" Chapter 8 (scripture 1-17), we see **Four Guardian Angels Standing** at the **Four Corners of the Earth Holding Back** the **Four Winds from Blowing** (sounds of nature) so that not even a **Single Leaf** will **Rustle in the Trees** and the **Ocean** will become as **Smooth as Glass** (silent). This mystical description reveals a "Divinely Suspenseful Moment" in Heaven and on the Earth so that **All Men might Come** to a point of **Soul-Threatening Re-evaluation** of **Who They Are in God's Bloodline** and just **Where They are Really Going in Life**. "Saint John" then Sees Another Guardian Angel coming from the **East Carrying** a **Great Living Seal of God** which implies the **Lord is About** to **Execute a Tremendous Divine Decree Over the Affairs** of **All Men, Great and Small**. Then "Saint John Tells Us" that he Hears the Angel with the **Seal Shout Out** to those **Angels Standing** at the **Four Corners** (boundaries) of the **Earth, Preparing** to bring the **Wrath of God upon All Flesh,** to **Wait** and **Not to Do Anything Yet** or **Not until Tomorrow** (1,000 Years). The "Angel Tells Them" Not to Hurt the **Earth** (nature), **Sea** (society), or its **Trees** (individuals) until **God's Great Seal** (consecrated blood) has been **Placed upon the Foreheads** (souls) of **His Faithful Jewish Servants**. We see that "God's Consecrated Saints" will be those Chosen Souls that have been **Willing to Give Their Blood** to **Witness** to the **Coming Divine Decree of Death** and to **Sacrifice All** to **Save the Lost** from **Eternal Damnation in Hell**.

The point is that "It will Take" 1,000 Years to **Place a Mark of Redemption** upon **God's Living Saints** to **Seal Their Redemption** and **Write Their Names** in the **Book of Life**. This means that "God's Great Living Seal" Needs a Special Ink to **Officially Seal the Fate** of the **Eternally Damned** as **He has Chosen a Remnant** of the **Jewish People** to be **Given the Divine Mark** (divine honor), as a **Symbol of Eternal Life** for the **Twelve Tribes of Israel**. Obviously, our "Lord God Almighty" is Using **Messiah's Blood** (sin/forgiven), **Jewish Blood** (evil/innocent), and **Christian Blood** (death/guilty) as **Ink for His Divine Pen** as He Writes in His Book of Life (Jewish/earth), **Lamb's Book of Life** (Christians/Heaven), and **His Book of Memories** (eternally damned/Hell).

The following tabular information indicates that the "Lord God Almighty" is Using **Three Different Bloods** as **Ink to Write** in His **Book of Life** (remove sin), **Lamb's Book of Life** (remove evil), and **His Book of Memories** (remove death):

Saving All Life with Messiah's Blood (sin)/
Jewish Blood (evil)/and Christian Blood (death)
(Messiah gets title deed to Kingdom,
Jews title deed to Earth, and Christians TD to Heaven)

Being   1.   **Messiah's Blood/God** - <u>Remove Sin:</u> Title Deed to Kingdom ...
Saved   Knowledge
- Jesus Christ Offers - Divinity to Save All Mankind (new soul)
- Jesus Transforms Heaven into God's Kingdom of Glory
- Name in the Book of Life - Receive Royal Kingdom
- Messiah brings Forgiven Blood unto God's Mercy Seat

Save   2.   **Jewish Blood/Man** - <u>Remove Evil:</u> Title Deed to Earth ....
Self   Self-awareness
- Father Abraham Offers - Isaac to Save Jewish People (new mind)
- God Transforms Israel into Heaven on Earth
- Name in Lamb's Book of Life - Receive New Body
- Jewish People bring Innocent Blood to God's Mercy Seat

Saving   3.   **Christian Blood/God: Man** - <u>Remove Death:</u> Title Deed to
Others   Heaven ......Consciousnes
- Saint Peter Offers - Own Sacrificial Blood to Save Christians (new heart)
- God/Man Transforms Earth into Paradise in Heaven
- Name in Book of Memories - Receive Eternal Life
- Christian People bring Guilty Blood to God's Mercy Seat

- -

God's   4.   **Bloodless Sacrifice**/mass - <u>Remove Damnation:</u> Title Deed to Hell...
Pardon   Sentience
- .   Supreme Saints Offer - Eternal Souls to Save Lucifer (new life-force)
- Christ Transforms Hell into Heaven (interior blessing)
- Name in Book of God - Receive Divine Pardon (released)
- God's People bring Bloodless Sacrifice to God's Mercy Seat

This illustration shows that the "One Hundred Forty Four Thousand" <u>Jewish Witnesses</u> are being **Sealed** (marked) with the **Blood of Martyrs** so **that They can Survive** the **Holocaust of the Anti-Christ** as he **Comes to Power on Earth**. Now, we see the "Angel Marking Twelve Thousand" <u>Virgin Jewish Witnesses</u> from each of the **Twelve Tribes, Creating** a **New Celestial Court** of <u>Jewish Martyrs</u> which will **Total One Hundred and Forty-Four Thousand Holy Saints**. We see that "Their Holy Blood" will be <u>Used</u> as the **Marking Ink of God** to **Seal the Death Certificate** of **Mankind Forever** as **All Who are Not Holy** in the **Sight of God** shall be **Cursed into Damnation Forever** (forgotten). We see that "Saint John" <u>Now Gives Us a Description</u> of the **Mid-Tribulation Rapture** as the **Laodicean Church** of **Lukewarm Christians** is **Recharged** with **Divine Fire** (evangelization) and has also <u>Washed Their Filthy Garments</u> in the **Blood of the Lamb**. We see "Saint John Reveals" that a <u>Vast Crowd</u> of **New Saints Too Great to Count** (masses) **Rising** from every **Nation on Earth, Stands** before the **Throne of God** at the **Feet of the Lamb,** and <u>**All are Clothed in White,**</u> each **Holding a Palm Branch** (scepter of redemption). Obviously, the "White Garments" represent <u>God's Forgiveness</u> because the **Prodigal Sons of Death** (black sheep) have **Returned.** The **Palm Branches** signify **Roses of Love** (scepters) brought to <u>**Their Savior**</u> to **Beg for His Divine Pardon.** Each "Lost Soul will Cry out" that it had <u>Lost its Way</u> in the **Hour of Man's Great Test of Faith Given to him** by **Lucifer and his Demons,** and that it was **<u>Defeated</u>** by **Worldly Temptations** and its **Own Sin-nature.**

With the coming of this "Great Multitude (masses)," <u>We See All</u> the **Holy Angels** (Choirs) coming forth to **Crowd** around the **Throne,** thereby **Circling the Elders** and **Living Beings** in a <u>**Moment of Rejoicing**</u> for the **Return of God's Prodigal Sons.** We see that "All the Celebrants in Heaven" <u>Fall Down on Their Faces</u> to **Worship Their Redeeming God** in **Thanksgiving** for <u>**All These Lost Broken Souls**</u> (friends) which had **No Chance of Saving Themselves.** The idea here is to see that "Without Consecrated Blood," a <u>Person is Cursed by God</u> and has **No Chance of Saving himself.** He must **<u>Repent,</u>** be **<u>Baptized,</u>** and **Consume Christ's Body and Blood** to **Enter the Divine Bloodline of God.**

To "Comprehend this Awesome Merger" of <u>Jews' and Gentiles' Bloodlines,</u> we must see that the **Kingdom Had to Witness** the **Death of God** (Mount Calvary) to bring forth the **<u>Light of Divinity</u>** (spirit blood) and then **Witness** the **Death of Man** (Great Tribulation) to bring forth the **<u>Light of Humanity</u>** (fleshly blood) for **All to See Life** as it **Really Is in Truth, Law, Will, and Love.** This would mean that since the "Birth of Christ," the <u>World has been in Total Darkness</u> (blindness) with only a **Tiny Flicker of Light** coming from the **<u>Life-force or Blood of Jesus Christ</u>** (resurrection), bringing **Hope to a Dead and Dying World.** If this is true, then the "Job of Christ's Church" has been to establish a Priesthood of New-life on the **Earth** so that when the **<u>Light of the Groom</u>** (bride price/name) **Meets** the **<u>Light of the Bride</u>** (dowry/virginity), a **Great Wedding Celebration can Begin.** This implies that the "Job of Christ's Church (man's blessing)" is to <u>Issue a Marriage License</u> (earth) to the **Couple,** while the "Job of the Communion of Saints (God's blessing)" will be to <u>Offer God's Divine Blessing </u>(wedding ceremony/Heaven) to the **Couple,** thereby **Making Them One** in **Truth, Law, Will, and Love.** This means that "Out of the Groom" is to come the <u>Free Redemption of Man</u> (spirit) brought forth out of its **Heavenly Light** (1st resurrection/spirit blood); and then "Out of the Bride" is to come the <u>Earned Salvation of Man</u> (flesh) bursting forth from its **Earthly Light** (2nd resurrection/fleshly blood). When these "Two Lights of Awakening" have burst forth, <u>All the Creatures of God</u> will **See** the **<u>Reality of God</u>** (paradox) and the **<u>Illusion of Man</u>** (null-set) as they **Really are in Christ Jesus.** With the "Death of the World" at the <u>End of Time</u> (3rd Advent), the **Human Race** will come to know that in the **<u>1st Advent</u>** is the **Light of Christ;** then during the Lord's **<u>2nd Advent</u>** is the **Light of the Pagan World;** and finally, during Christ's **<u>3rd Advent</u>** shall come the **Light of the Kingdom.** Through these "Three Lights of Knowing," the <u>Whole Creation</u> will come into **Oneness** with **<u>God, Angels, Saints, Living Men, Demons,</u>** and the **<u>Damned</u>** to establish **One Perfect Royal Family** (Mystical Body) within the **Nature of God.**

In this teaching, the Lord is saying that if a person fulfills both the "Jewish Law (Mosaic Law/self/free redemption)" and the "Catholic Faith (Canon Law/society/earned salvation)," then he can expect to receive a <u>Heavenly Kingship</u> (celestial court), a <u>Priesthood</u> (temple court), and finally a <u>Sonship</u> (royal court), all in the **Name of Jesus Christ.** This means that "Man Sends to God" <u>Repentance, Prayers,</u> and <u>Works;</u> and then "God Sends to Man" <u>Righteousness</u> (defeat sin), <u>Holiness</u> (defeat evil), and <u>Perfection</u> (defeat death) to **Save the Human Race** from **Eternal Damnation.**

The following tabular information indicates that the "Human Race" is <u>Transmitting the Sin-debt</u> or **Man's Faults to God** in **Twelve Offerings of Submission**; and then "God" will <u>Send His Blessings</u> or **Virtues to Man** in **Twelve Gifts of Love:**

	Man Sends to God		God Sends to Man
	<u>Repentance/Prayers/Works</u>		<u>Righteousness/Holiness/Perfection</u>
Messiah	1. **Scourging/Crucifixion/Tomb**	Nature	1. **New Mind/New Heart/New Soul** = *Life*
	Venial, Mortal, and Capital Sins		Knowledge, Self-awareness, and Consciousness
Church	2. **Church /Mass /Souls**	Behavior	2. **Transfigured/Glorified/Mystical** = *Bodies*
	Sin-nature, Temptations, and Demonic Possession		Baptism, Confession and Communion
World	3. **Worship/Praise/Thanksgiving**	Lifestyle	3. **Celestial /Temple /Royal** = *Seats*
	Ignorance, Cowardice, and Greed		Wisdom, Courage, and Generosity
Sinner	4. **Church/Government/Home**	Freedom	4. **Earth /Heaven /Kingdom** = *Deeds*
	Foolish, Criminal, and Insane		Peace, Joy, and Happiness
	<u>(God becomes Man - Christmas: Life)</u>		<u>(Man becomes God - Easter: Death)</u>
	Slave - Shepherd – Carpenter		**Priest - King – Son**

This illustration shows that the "Slave Repents (priest/Aaron)," the "Shepherd Prays (king/David)," and the "Carpenter Works (son/Jesus)" to bring forth <u>Righteousness</u> (right/wrong), <u>Holiness</u> (good/evil), and <u>Perfection</u> (God's/Man's Wills) to **One and All,** who will **Sacrifice Their Lives** in **Payment** to **God, the Messiah, Church, World, and Sinner.** We see that the "Messiah is Offering God" His <u>Scourging</u> (deceit), <u>Crucifixion</u> (deception) and <u>Tomb</u> (defiance) in <u>Payment</u> for all the **Venial, Mortal,** and **Capital Sins** of **Sinful Man.** Secondly, the "Church is Promising God" its <u>Universal Church</u>/baptism (deceit), <u>Holy Mass</u>/confession (deception), and <u>Salvation of Souls</u>/communion (defiance) in **Payment** for man's **Sin-nature, Worldly Temptations,** and **Demonic Possession** of **Wicked Men.** Thirdly, the "Righteous World is Promising God" its <u>Worship</u> (deceit), <u>Praise</u> (deception), and <u>Thanksgiving</u> (defiance) in **Payment** for man's **Ignorance, Cowardice,** and **Greed** for **All Lost Souls.** Finally, the "Sinner is Promising God" his <u>Church</u>/Time (deceit), <u>Government</u>/Talent (deception), and <u>Home</u>/Treasure (defiance) in **Payment** for his own **Foolishness, Criminal Acts,** and **Insanity** as a **Damned Soul.**

This means that from the "Messiah," mankind shall receive a <u>New Nature</u> comprised of a **New Mind of Knowledge, New Heart of Self-awareness,** and **New Soul of Consciousness** manifested in a gift of **Eternal Life.** Secondly, from the "Church," mankind shall receive a <u>New Behavior</u> comprised of **Transfigured Body** (baptism/forgiveness),

Glorified Spirit (confession/wealth), and **Holy Soul** (communion/love) **Manifested in a Gift** of **Three Bodies.** Thirdly, from the "World," Mankind shall Receive a **New Lifestyle Comprised** of **Seats** in the **Celestial Court** (wisdom), **Temple Court** (courage), and **Royal Court** (generosity) **Manifested in a Gift** of **Three Seats of Honor**. Finally, from the "Sinner," mankind shall receive Freedom from Sin, Evil, and Death comprised of a **Title Deed to Earth** (peace), **Heaven** (joy), and the **Kingdom** (happiness) **Manifested in a Gift** of a **Triune Ownership.** It should now make sense that "Mankind" must Give Its Life, Wealth, and Labor to **God** to **Appease His Anger** and **Pay Off Its Sin-debt** of **Defiance** (stealing), **Deception** (hiding), and **Deceit** (lying) **in Full** (last penny). Note that during "Christmas," we see God becomes Man to bring forth **Death to Sin**; and then on "Easter," we see Man becomes God to bring forth **New-life** in **Righteousness, Holiness, and Perfection.**

Now, we see just how the "Slave became a Priest," and then the "Priest became the Church," and the "Church became Heaven" to Present the **Divine Sacrifice** (death) of **Christ before God Forever**. Secondly, we see just how the "Shepherd became a King," and then the "King became the Government," and the "Government became Earth" to Present the **Perpetual Sacrifice** (evil) of **Christ before God Forever.** Finally, we see just how the "Carpenter became the Son of God," and then the "Son becomes the Home," and the "Home becomes the Kingdom" to Present the **Daily Sacrifice** (sin) of **Christ before God forever.** At each of these "Levels of Transformation," we see the Individual can be Set Free from his **Chains of Sin** (ignorance), then open the **Prison Doors of Evil** (cowardice), to **Overcome the Guards of Death** (greed). This means that the "Sinner" can now become a "Righteous Citizen," then the "Righteous Citizen can become a Saint," and then, the "Saint can become Son of Man" to **Present** His **Individual Sacrifice** (faults) of **Christ before God forever.**

Once a "Lost Broken Sinner" has overcome Sin, Evil, and Death, he can come to **Master the Forces** of **Truth, Law, Will, and Love** to see his own **Motives** (nature), his **Limitations** (lifestyle), and his **Potential/Opportunities** (behavior). Out of "Mastering a Person's" Motives, Limitations, Potential, and Self-worth, he can **Comprehend** the **Meaning of Life** which is to **Understand** the **Two Truths of God** with **One being Negative** (death/nothing/man) or **Free Will** and **One being Positive** (life/all/God) or **Destiny**. Through these "Two Truths (free will/destiny)," the Whole Creation must **Operate** and **Find** both **Its Dark side** (invisible death) and **Its Righteous side** (visible life/light), while **Mastering the Life-experience Itself.** We see that this "Two-Truth Principle (all/nothing)" is Centered upon a **Four Dimensional Structure, Known** as the **Physical** (universe), **Spiritual** (Heaven), **Mystical** (Kingdom), and **Divine** (divinity) **Natures of God**.

The following tabular information indicates the "Four Natures of God" as Portrayed in the Forms of **Energy/Matter** (physical), **Angels/Saints** (spiritual), **God/Man** (mystical), and **Father/Son** (divine), thereby implying that **All Things** in **God's Reality** have **Two Sides** of either **Visible** or **Invisible Existence.**

God's Four Dimensions of Life in both Visible and Invisible Forms
(God's four natures are made up of motives, limitations, potential, and self-worth)

Life   1. **Physical Dimension** - <u>Universe</u>: Motives of God ...
(mind)   Gaining Knowledge
- 1st Form Energy (invisible force/plus)   . Individual
- 2nd Form Matter (visible solid/minus)

Death   2. **Spiritual Dimension** - <u>Heaven</u>: Limitations of God ...
(heart)   Becoming Self-Aware
- 1st Form Angels (invisible spirit/plus)   . Family
- 2nd Form Saints (visible flesh/minus)

Resurrection   3. **Mystical Dimension** - <u>Kingdom</u>: Potential of God....
(soul)   Entering Consciousness
- 1st Form God (invisible Christ/plus)   . Nation
- 2nd Form Man (visible Jesus/minus)

Freedom   4. **Divine Dimension** - <u>God</u>: Self-worth of God ......
(life-force)   Awakened to Sentience
- 1st Dimension Father (invisible positive/plus)   . World
- 2nd Dimension Son (visible negative/minus)

This illustration shows that "All of God's Children" are to <u>Master</u> the **Physical Dimension** to **Gain Knowledge** (mind), <u>Master</u> the **Spiritual Dimension** to **Become Self-aware** (heart), <u>Master</u> the **Mystical Dimension** to **Enter Consciousness**, and finally, to <u>Master</u> the **Divine Dimension** to be **Awakened to Sentience**. This means that "*God's Grand Design*" is to be <u>Divided</u> into **Two Creations: One Representing God** or **Divinity** (Heaven), and the **Other Representing Man** or **Humanity** (earth). We see this "Mystical Division" took place during the <u>Lord's 1st Advent</u> when **He Came** as a **Priest on a Donkey** to both **Save the Sinners** (dark side) and to **Create Saints** (righteous side). We see that this "Divine Visit" actually occurred when <u>Mankind</u> was **4,000 Years Old** or **Four Days** into the **1st Week of Creation** (Wednesday) to allow the **Lord to Divide** the **Lost** (4,000 years) from the **Saved** (4,000 years). We also see that the "Jews" would Inspect the <u>Sacrificial Lamb</u> for **Four Days** beginning with the **1st Day** of the **Week** or <u>Sunday</u> which would mean he was **Killed on Wednesday at 3 P.M.**

In this "Sacrificial Ceremony," the <u>Jews</u> would actually **Tear the Lamb** into **Two Parts** (Jews/gentiles) to represent the **Division of God and Man**. We can now recognize that the "Messiah Came" to represent <u>4,000 Years,</u> then **He Died** in the **Middle of the Week** (Messiah) to represent the **Church** (nation) which occurred at **3 P.M.** to represent **Christianity** (family). Finally, we see "Jesus Christ" was pulled from <u>One Side</u> by the **Soldiers** to **Tear Him in Two** (individual) to **Divide His Nature** between His **Father's Will** (create saints) and His **Mother's Will** (save sinners). This "Conflict" between the <u>Jews</u> (create saints) and the <u>Gentiles</u> (save sinners) **Forces God's Son** to be **Divided** into **Becoming All Things to All People** (good/bad). We now see that the "God/Man Relationship" is based on a <u>Contradiction</u> or **Paradox** of such **Magnitude** that **God Himself** (Jesus Christ) would have to be **Divided into Two Truths** to bring forth the **New Kingdom of Glory**. Through the "Tearing in Two" of God Himself on **Mount Calvary** (death to new-life), both **Good and Evil** could become **One Truth** and **Live as One Reality** in **Christ Jesus**.

The following tabular information indicates that "God" has Divided His **1st Week of Creation Down the Middle** by having **His Son Come** after **4,000 Years of Life** to **Die on Wednesday** at **3 P.M.** by being **Torn in Half** (two truths):

Eight Days of Creation Divided into Four Levels of Life: World, Nation, Family, and Individual
(the Messiah/4000 years, Church/400 years, Family/40 years, and Individual/40 days of Repentance)

Truth
(Wednesday)

1. **Middle of 1st Week** - 4000 Years Life: Messiah Comes to Earth....Divine Nature
   - Offer God Three Divine Sacrifices - Save the Sacred World (divine order)
   - Scourging - Remove Sin
   - Crucifixion - Remove Evil   **See Motives** (nature)
   - Tomb - Remove Death

Law
(Wednesday)

2. **Middle of Passion Week** - 400 Years Slavery: Church Comes to Earth....Mystical Nature
   - Promise God Three Sacred Sacrifices - Save the Holy Nation (supernatural order)
   - Church - Remove Sin-nature
   - Mass - Remove Worldly Temptations   **See Limitations** (lifestyle)
   - Saved Souls - Remove Demonic Possession

Will
(3 p.m.)

3. **Middle of Passion Day** - 40 Days with Lucifer: Christian Comes to Earth... Spiritual Nature
   - Promise God Three Holy Sacrifices - Save the Holy Family (natural order)
   - Sin-nature - Remove Ignorance
   - Worldly Temptations - Remove Cowardice   **See Potential** (behavior)
   - Demonic Possession - Remove Greed

Love
(divided)

4. **Middle of Passion Hour** - 40 Hours of Death: Saint Comes to Earth...Physical Nature
   - Promise God Three Righteous Sacrifices - Save the Righteous Man (order)
   - Ignorance - Remove Lying
   - Cowardice - Remove Cheating   **See Self-worth** (value)
   - Greed - Remove Stealing

With this illustration, we see that the "Eight Days of Creation" are Divided into **Four Levels of Life**, thereby **Defining** the **World** (divine), **Nation** (mystical), **Family** (spiritual), and the **Individual** (physical) as **God's Dimensions of Life**. The "Job of Jesus Christ" was to Come and Define the **Human Life-experience** in **Four Stages of Existence** based on the **Sacrifice** of **God's Messiah, the Holy Church, Christianity,** and **Saintly Men**. Through "God's Messiah," we can See the Motives of Life (nature) in the **Battle** of **Good and Evil** to bring forth an **Understanding of Right and Wrong**. Secondly, through "Christ's Church," we See the Limitations of Life (lifestyle) in **Defining Man's Weaknesses** to bring forth the **Understanding of Good and Evil**. Thirdly, through "Christianity," we See the Potential of Life (behavior) in **Defining Man's Strengths** to bring forth an **Understanding of God's Will from Man's Will**. Finally, through "Sainthood," we See One's Self-worth (value) in **Defining Human Value** to bring forth an **Understanding of God's Reality from Man's Illusion**. At each of these "Stages of Sacrifice," the Human Race is Able to **Die to Its Selfishness** and then be **Born-again** in the **New Nature of Christ** to become a **Mature Son of God**.

The "Job of the Messiah" is to Offer-up **His Scourging, Crucifixion, and His Tomb** to **Pay for Man's Sin-debt** to **Remove Sin, Evil,** and **Death** from the **Human Condition Forever**. Secondly, the "Job of the Church" is to Promise to **Establish a Church Community, Give Daily Mass** (host), and **Save Souls** in an **Attempt** to **Pay Man's Sin-debt** to **Remove Man's Sin-nature, Worldly Temptations, and Demonic Possession**. Thirdly, the "Job of Christianity" is to Promise to **Fight and Overcome Its Sin-nature, Worldly Temptations,** and **Demonic Possessions** to **Pay Man's Sin-debt** to **Remove Ignorance, Cowardice, and Greed Forever**. Finally, the "Job of the Saint" is to Promise to **Change Ignorance to Wisdom, Cowardice to Courage, and Greed to Generosity** to **Pay Man's Sin-debt** to **Remove Lying, Cheating, and Stealing** from the **Human Condition Forever**. It should now make sense that it would "Take All Men" Working Together as well as the **One Man's Undaunted Commitment** to **Make a Perfect World** of **Peace, Joy, and Happiness**.

Thus, through "Man's Peace, Joy, and Happiness," the World will be **Given God's Truth** to **Set All the Captives** (sinners) **Free** from the **Curses of Sin, Evil, Death, and Damnation**. This means that "Lost Broken Sinners" are to be Arrested by Truth showing **Each Person's Motives** which are seen within **His Actions** (innocent/ignorant/criminal/insane/evil), be **They** either **Good or Bad** in the **Eyes of God**. Through both the "Motives of the Mind" and the "Actions of the Heart," We See the Creation of the **Lord's Mystical Body** in **Truth, Law, Will, and Love**. To "Comprehend" the "Lord's Mystical Body," it must be understood that the Mind (physical), Heart (spiritual), Soul (mystical), Life-force (divine), and Nature of Man (Godly) are to be **Mastered** by **Each and Every One** of **God's Beloved Children**. This means that "Each Born-again Soul" must Fully Comprehend the **Five Dimensions of Life**: 1) Physical Dimension - New Mind: Transform Flesh (self) = God is a Stranger, 2) Spiritual Dimension - New Heart: Purify Spirit (church) = Make God's Acquaintance, 3) Mystical Dimension - New Soul: Correct Soul (government) = Become God's Friend, 4) Divine Dimension - New Life-force: Convert Life (home), and 5) Godly Dimension - New Nature: Free Eternal Life (God) = Become God.

Through each of these "Five Dimensions (physical/spiritual/mystical/divine/Godly)," a Person can Come to **Meet, Know,** and **Serve** God (reality) so that one day, the Lord can Come to **Meet, Know,** and **Serve** Man (illusion). This means that the "Lord Jesus Christ" has been placed between God and Man to become **Humanity's Intercessor** with **God's Son, Christ** (Living Prayer of Love/saint) who is **Looking-upward Toward His Father** (Heaven); while **Mary's Son, Jesus** (Soldier-of-the-Light/Christian) is **Looking-downward Toward the People** or at **His Mother** (earth). The implication is that "Christ" is Looking-up through a **Positive Force of Love** (emotions) to **Worship God**; while "Jesus" is Looking-down through a **Negative Force of Love** (intellect) via the **Catholic Church** to **Thank God** for **Blessing All Mankind with Forgiveness.** In this way, by "Looking-down (negative)," Man's Punitive Retribution (damages) can **Pay for Any Offenses Against Man** (sin-debt) through **Mount Calvary** (blood/Jesus) to **Save Sinners** (take-sin). Secondly, by "Looking-up (positive)," Compensatory Recompense (fines) can **Pay for Any Offenses Against God** (holy-debt) through the **Catholic Church** (prayers/Christ) to **Create Saints** (give divinity). By combining these "Two Offenses," both **Man's Damages** (Christ's Blood) **and Fines** (Church's Prayers) have been **Paid in Full** to **Set the Human Race Free** from the **Curses of Sin, Evil, and Death.**

The following tabular information indicates that the "Human Race" has been Cursed with Punitive Retribution (damages against man) and Compensatory Recompense (fines from God) which are **Paid For** by **Christ's Crucifixion** (blood) and the **Church's Prayers** (fat):

Paying Man's Punitive Retribution (damages) and Compensatory Recompense (fines) to God
(Christ's crucifixion [blood] pays man's
damages and Church's prayers pay man's fines [fat])

Damages (Calvary)	1.	**Punitive Retribution** - Offenses Against Man: Pay Sin-debt…Scourging
		• Body Broken - Pays for Damages: Christ's Crucifixion = Offer Sacrifice
		• Take-sin - Save Sinners: Free Gift of New Body (earth)
		• Purifying the Grave - Transgressions: *Brother Offending Brother*
		• Physical Life - Fighting Evil unto One's Death
Fines (tomb)	2.	**Compensatory Recompense** - Offenses Against God: Pay Holy-debt ……Cross
		• Blood Shed - Pays for Fines: Catholic Church = Offer Prayers
		• Give Divinity - Create Saints: Earning Eternal Life (Heaven)
		• Purifying the Host - Sinfulness: *Sinner Offending God*
		• Spiritual Death - Submitting by Dying to One's Selfishness

This illustration shows that to "Save Sinners (pay sin-debt)," God must **Shed His Divine Blood** (remove faults/take-sin); and to "Create Saints (pay holy-debt)," Man must **Pray unto Death** (gain virtues/give divinity). Out of these "Payments to God," the Human Race can **Obtain** an **Earthly Transfigured Body** (new body), a **Heavenly**

Glorified Body (eternal life), and a **Kingdom Mystical Body** (dream home) **Worthy** of the very **Presence of God.** We see in the "Creation" of the "Lord's Mystical Body" the Manifestation of His Transfigured Body (earth), Glorified Spirit (Heaven), and/or Holy Soul (God), **United** through the **Forces of Death** (grave/flesh) and **Damnation** (hell/spirit). Under the "Forces of Divine Perfection (peace)," the Holy Trinity of God will **Take Human Form** and ultimately **Free All Humanity** from its **Original Curses of Sin** (deceit/lying), **Evil** (deception/hiding), and **Death** (defiance/stealing). Through this "Mystical Transformation Process," All Mankind will be brought to a **New Higher State** of **Tranquil Peace** (holiness/righteousness/perfection) for **One and All.**

Initially, it has been necessary for the "Lord to Create" a new "Perfect Justice System" through which all Human Flesh might pass to be **Purified** (original state) and **Reconciled** (original owner) back to the **Divine Love of Its Creator** through **Seven Physical Jewish Temples** (righteous flesh/ethics). Only upon the "Lord's 2nd Advent (thief in the night)" will He reveal His New Sacred Government to bring forth His most **Perfect Rule** and the **Reign of God** (kingdom) upon the earth until the **End of Time** (eternity). The "Lord's Prime Directive" will be to Teach Humanity the **Divine Law of God, Transforming** the **Holy Church** into a **New Righteous State** (government) of **Earthly Rule,** to **Stand** for a **Thousand Years of Human Glory** (peace). At the end of this "1,000 Years of Peace (seal saints)," Humanity will see the **Lord's 3rd Advent** (just judge) and the hour of the great White Throne Judgment, the **Royal Jubilee of the Divine Kingdom** (divine home), or when **Divinity and Humanity** will again become **One** in **Truth** (new land), **Law** (new babies), and **Will** (new-life).

Through "God's Judgment," We See the Bases upon which the **Lord's Mind Works** as He is **Always Fair,** thereby **Giving the Greatest Amount of Leeway** and **Compassionate Mercy** to **Those Who** Need His Help the Most. The first mention of "God's Divine Attitude (help)" is stated in Exodus 3: 7-8, where the **Lord Told Moses** to **Go Save the Jews** because **He Saw Their Suffering** and **Heard Their Cries for Help** so that **He** was **Duty Bound to Answer Their National Prayer.** With this "Recognition by God" of His Covenant with Abraham, the **Lord has Made** the **Jews His Chosen People** which **Now Forces God** to **Do Whatever He Can** to **Protect the Jews even from Themselves** (sin-nature/worldly temptations/demonic possessions/God's curses). Out of "Exodus 3: 7-8," the Lord will Open Pandora's Box of **Divine Commitment** since **He is Only Making** a **Covenant with the Jews, Who must have Abrahamic Blood** and **Anyone Else** (gentiles) is to be **Eternally Damned** into **Lucifer's Pit of Hell.** Out of this first small gesture of "Heavenly Kindness," the New Covenant of Jesus Christ shall be **Written in Abrahamic Blood,** thereby **Establishing** the **Free Redemption** (righteousness/earth), **Earned Salvation** (holiness/Heaven), and **Bonus Rewards** (perfection/Kingdom) **System** for **One and All.** It should now all make sense that "God has Begun" his Majestically Life with Infinite Honor and Eternal Dignity at the **Divine Level of Perfection** and will **End-up** a **Broken Old Man, Who** will **Forever** be **Taking Care** of a **Bunch of Brady Kids** which **Now Makes Him Ecstatically Happy** (Eternal Barn Boss).

The following tabular information indicates "God's First Formal Commitment" to <u>Helping</u> the Human Race face its **Trials and Tribulations** caused from the **Fall of Adam and Eve** which brought forth their **Curses of Toil, Pain, Death, and Damnation upon All Men**:

Exodus 3: 7-8, God's Relationship with Man
(God sees man's suffering/God hears his cries for help/God
recognizes his covenant, and God comes to help)

New Mind   1.   **God Sees Your Suffering** - <u>God Thinks of His Child</u> ... Kingship (law)
(intellect)
- Blessing Water - Baptism: Man's Free Redemption = Remove Toil
- Learning Right from Wrong - Baby Fool becomes Righteous

See God
- Free Redemption - Title Deed to Earth: New Body = Give Talent
(wash in water or face curse of capital sins bringing one to hell/separation)

New Heart   2.   **God Hears Your Cries** - <u>God Speaks to His Child</u> .... Priesthood
(emotions)   (faith)
- Anointing Oil – Confession: Man Earns Own Salvation = Remove Pain
- Learning Good from Evil - Teenage Criminal becomes Holy

Hear God
- Earned Salvation - Title Deed to Heaven: Eternal Life = Time
(wash in oil or face curse of mortal sins bringing one to his grave/hopelessness)

New Soul   3.   **God Recognizes His Covenant** - <u>God Touches His Child</u>...Sonship
(instincts)   (knowing)
- Sanctifying Blood - Communion: Man Receives Bonus Reward = Remove Death
- Learning God's Will from man's will - Insane Adult becomes Perfect

Touch God
- Bonus Rewards - Title Deed to Kingdom: Royal Kingdom = Give Treasure
(wash in blood or face curse of venial sins bringing one into death/death agony)

Life-force   4.   **God Comes to Help Child** - <u>God Sups with His Child</u> ... Free Man
(thinking)   (thinking)
- Consecrating Spirit - Confirmation: Man Receives Thinking for Self = Remove Damnation
- Learn God's Reality from man's illusion - Evil Wise Man becomes Free

Sup with God
- Freedom - Title Deed to Self: Thinking for Self = Give All
(wash in spirit or face curse of wicked faults bringing one into toil/hard-work)

This illustration shows that "God is Slowly" but "Surely" <u>Getting Sucked Into</u> a **Little More Divine Support** for the **Jews** than **He Intended**, then **Later** for the **Gentiles,** and finally, in **Helping Save the Whole World** (Jews/Christians/Pagans). The point is that "One Thing" certainly <u>Leads to Another</u> until the **Next Thing You Know** is that **You're Running the Whole Show** and **All You Initially Intended** was to <u>Give Society</u> a **Little of Your Time** (mind), **Some Talent** (heart), and **None of Your Treasure** (soul). We see that someone has "Got to Do It" and it <u>Might as Well be You</u> and **If You Happen to be a God,** then **Who Else** is **Better Qualified** to **Get the Job Done Right** and **Who Else** can **Keep Track of a Trillion Details** at **Once** and **Sort Out All** of the <u>Integrated Factors</u> to bring **Success Out of Failure?**

Note in the previous chart, "If God Sees Your Suffering," then <u>He will Think of You</u> which will bring forth **His Water Blessing** (baptism) in the **Form** of **His Free Redemption** to **Remove Your Toil** (sweat) and **Hard-work** (capital sin). Secondly, "If God Hears Your Cries," then <u>He will Speak to You</u> which will bring forth **His Oil Anointing** (confession) in the **Form** of **His Earned Salvation** to **Remove Your Pain and Torment** (mortal sin). Thirdly, "If God Recognizes His Covenant," then <u>He will Touch You</u> which will bring forth **His Blood Sanctification** (communion) in the **Form** of **His Bonus Rewards** to **Remove Your Death and Your Grave** (venial sin). Finally, "If God Comes to Help," then <u>He will Ask You to Supper</u> which will bring forth **His Spirit Consecration** (confirmation) in the **Form** of **His Gift of Freedom** to **Remove Your Damnation in Hell Fire** (faults).

The questions to be asked to comprehend the redemptive program relating to a person's growth and maturity are: as a "Child of God," did <u>You Wash in Water</u> to **Remove Your Capital Sins** (baptism); did you <u>Wash in Oil</u> to **Remove Your Mortal Sins** (confession); did you <u>Wash in Blood</u> to **Remove Venial Sins** (communion; and did you <u>Wash in Spirit</u> to **Remove Your Wicked Faults** (confirmation), **All in the Name of Jesus Christ**? We see that "If a Person" has <u>Failed to Wash,</u> then he shall <u>Face Toil</u> (hard-work/slavery), <u>Pain</u> (death agony/dying), <u>Death</u> (hopelessness/grave), and <u>Damnation</u> (separation/hell) because he **Failed** to **Listen to a Single Word that God had to Say** (lessons of life). This theme of "Absolute Obedience" <u>Sits at the Center</u> of **God's** *Grand Design* as He has clearly **Specified His Redemptive Program** and **Anyone Who is Willing** to **Believe, Surrender, Trust God**, and enter **Instinctive Compulsion** will be <u>**Given God's Gifts**</u> and be **Set Free to Think for Himself.** This leads us to an extremely "Hard Concept" where the more a <u>Person Grows</u> and <u>Matures,</u> the more **Strict** and **Dangerous** it becomes until a **Child of God Grows-up** and is **Set Free to Think for Himself.** By "Seeing God's All Forgiving Altar (baby duties)" as the <u>Lord's Place</u> of **Free Redemption** (see God), and then by "Seeing God's All Condemning Court (teenage responsibilities)" as it <u>Represents</u> the **Lord's Earned Salvation** (hear God), we can then see the <u>Measure of Growth</u> for each of **God's Children** (progress/development). Finally, through "God's Personal Fairness (adult authority)," we can see the <u>Lord's Bonus Rewards</u> (touch God).

Basically, the "Lord God Almighty" is bringing a <u>Person to Face</u> his **Capital Sin** before a <u>Priest</u> (altar/temple) who is **Kind, Open,** and willing to **Forgive Almost Anything and Everything.** Next, "He must Face" his <u>Mortal Sins</u> (fail responsibilities) before the **King** (court/throne) **Who** is **Pure Justice** and **Unbending** as he **Demands Perfection in Everything** be he **King** and in **Everybody.** Thirdly, "He must Face" his <u>Venial Sins</u> (fail authority) before **God's Son** (government/palace) **Who** is **Demanding unto Perfection** (justice); yet, in case he unwittingly makes **Any Type of**

Mistake (merciful), the **Lord is Willing** to **Jump in** <u>Where and When He is Needed</u> to **Cover Another Colleague's Back**. Finally, "He must Face" his <u>Own Faults</u> (fail choices) seen with his **Own Eyes** (self-evaluation), thereby **Making** him his **Own Worst Critic** as **No One Demands** more of the **Human Body** than a <u>Driven Person</u> **Who Seeks to Serve a Perfect God**.

The following tabular information indicates that "Growth" and "Maturity" are being Judged by the **Altar** (temple), **Court** (throne), **Government** (palace), and **One-self** (dreamland), thereby giving each of **God's Children** <u>Four Chances to Pass God's Four Tests of Life</u> (Lucifer/God/Self/Kingdom):

Growth (earth) and Maturity (Heaven) are Judged
by the Altar, Court, Government, and Self
(contacting God, speaking to God, touched by God,
and then to sup with God in friendship)

See God
(survival)

Informal

1. **Altar Forgives All** - <u>1st Chance:</u> Please Parents at Home (earth) = Baby
   - Altar - Contacting God: Results from Lucifer's Test of Ignorance
   - Remove "Capital Sins (stealing)" - Fail to Perform One's Duties Correctly
   - Confess to Kind Priest (father figure) .... Temple
   - God's Business is Extremely "Informal" - God Sees All as Real
   - Messiah is Creator of Life - Learn Right/Wrong: Baby Righteousness

   (being yourself - silly fool: see life via one's own selfish viewpoint)

Hear God
(truth)

Formal

2. **Court Condemns All** - <u>2nd Chance:</u> Please Society (boss) at Church (Heaven) = Teenager
   - Court - Speaking to God: Results from God's Judgment on Cowardice
   - Remove "Mortal Sins (hiding)" - Fail to Perform One's Responsibilities Correctly
   - Admit Problems to Stern King (boss figure)   .... Throne
   - Man's Business is Extremely "Formal" - Man Sees All as a Mystery
   - Church is People - Learn Good from Evil: Teenage Holiness

   (best behavior - model citizen: reflect the values of those around you)

Touch God
(love)

Semiformal

3. **Personal Fairness** - <u>3rd Chance:</u> Please Owner in his Kingdom (God): Adult
   - Personal - Listen to God: Results from Personal Evaluation on Greed
   - Remove "Venial Sins (lying)" - Fail to Implement Authority Correctly
   - Explain Decisions to Reasonable Son (owner figure)....   Palace
   - God's/Man's Business is "Less Important" - God/Man Sees Only the Moment
   - World is Land - Learn God's/Man's Wills: Adult Perfection

   (respectful, yet, friendly - instinctive response: rely on training to fit in)

Sup with God
(choice)

4. **Independent Thought** - <u>4th Chance:</u> Please Self in Paradise (Self) = Wise Man
   - Self-will - Work for God: Results from Kingdom's View on Selfishness

Dynamic	• Remove "Natural Faults (selfish)" - Fail to Serve Others Correctly
	• Comprehend One's Own Nature (free soul) …. Dreamland
	• The Business of Self is "Fun" - Individuals See
	• Individuals are God's Friends - God's Reality/Man's Illusion: Wise Man

(think for yourself - being oneself: everyone else is respectful of you as the owner)

This illustration shows that "Life is Comprised" of an <u>Informal God, Formal Man,</u> a <u>Semiformal God/Man,</u> and the <u>Ever-loving Self</u> based on a **Person's Level of Growth and Maturity** either as a **Baby** (informal), **Teenager** (formal), **Adult** (semiformal), and/or **Wise Man** (dynamic). Through this constant "Changing State of Attitudes," <u>We Will Come to Realize</u> that **We** are being **Created, Raised, and Transformed** by a **Tri-une Divine Nature** which **Intends** to <u>Supply God's Kingdom with as Many *Righteous Citizens, Holy Saints, and Sons of God as Possible*</u>. This means that when we first "Meet God," <u>He Appears</u> to be a **Kind and Loving Father** (baby). Then **He Shows** up as **Our Unbending Boss** (teenager) <u>Who Demands Perfection</u> at **Every Turn**. Finally, we "Meet God Again" in <u>Adulthood</u> as a **Highly Respected Friend** (adult). So the question is: which one of these "Three Natures" is the <u>Real God</u> and which one is <u>Just an Act?</u> The answer can be found in **Our Own Growth** and **Maturity** because <u>God</u> has simply **Stayed the Same** and we have **Changed into a New Creation in Christ**. In "Our Last Stage" of <u>Development,</u> we are **Challenged** to put **All We have Learned** (set free) into **Proving** we have been **Raised Right** with a <u>Clear Mind</u> (thought), **Loving Heart** (word), and **Honest Soul** (deed) truly worthy of the **Blessings of God**. By being able to "Interact" with the <u>Lord God Almighty</u> in these **Three Perceptions of Reality,** a person can comprehend the **Father's Thoughts** (all is real/doubt), the **Son's Words** (illusion/reality/certainty), and the **Spirit's Deeds** (illusion/implementation) as they each **Play Their Role** within each **Person's Life**. We see that in "God's Thought Process (grand design)," He <u>Doubts Everything</u> and <u>Questions the Rationale of His Own Existence,</u> while His Son is **Absolutely Certain** that <u>His Plan</u> and <u>Only His Plan</u> will **Work Perfectly**. Secondly, the "Job of the Holy Spirit" is to <u>Coordinate</u> and <u>Implement</u> both the **Father's Fears** (grand design) and the **Son's Confidence** (divine plan) into a **Solution** which will **Give Everyone** the **Best Result Possible**. Obviously, the end result is to "Create" a <u>Perfect Child of God,</u> who can **Think for Himself** and be **Trusted** to function **Effectively** via his **Own Independent Thoughts** in **Fulfillment** of **God's Divine Will**. To grasp the "Plan of God," a <u>Person must See</u> the **Difference** between the **Haves of Ownership** (rich) and the **Have Nots of Poverty** (poor) as **They Create Huge <u>Class Struggles</u>** for the **Goods and Services of the World**.

    Now, let's apply this "Ownership (Heaven/adults)" versus "Poverty (Hell/babies) Concept" to the <u>Lord's Coming Kingdom</u> where **Every Vessel shall be Filled** and the **Wants of All shall be Met**. The question is just how is this "Balance" between <u>Survival</u> and <u>Unlimited Wants</u> **Going to Occur** in a **World** of <u>Ignorant</u> **Fools, Criminals, In-sane Animals, and Evil Peoples <u>Who All</u> Hate Each Other?** The answer is a combination of "Education (mind)," "Wealth (heart)," and "New Governing Techniques (automated systems)" to bring <u>Everyone</u> into <u>One State of Mind</u> (consciousness) and see the **Value** between **Social** (formal/public) **and Individual Rights** (informal/private).

To better comprehend this logic, "Imagine a Person" <u>Living a Life</u> of **Historical Events** versus a **Person Using His Life** to **Collect Treasures** to <u>Establish</u> both his **Earthly Happiness** and/or **Eternal Blessings** from **God**. The point is that "Each Person" within <u>God's Creation</u> is being **Called** to **Master his Earthly Life** <u>**Moment-by-moment**</u> by becoming a **Righteous Citizen** and to also **Master his Eternal Life** by <u>**Collecting his Sacred**</u> Treasures by becoming a **Holy Saint**. This means just like becoming either a "Democrat (help government/spend)" or a "Republican (help business/earn)." It's the same as <u>Choosing</u> to be either a **Righteous Citizen** (help earth/spend) or a **Holy Saint** (help Heaven/earn).

The point is that "Each of These Groups" <u>Plays a Major Role</u> in bringing either **Physical/Spiritual Balance** to **Guide All Confused People** to the <u>**Truth, Law, and Will**</u> of **Man** (earth) and of **God** (Heaven). This means that "If a Person Wastes his Life" by <u>Filling</u> it with **Worthless Pleasures** (selfishness), then on **Judgment Day,** he will **Suddenly Wish** he had **Spent his Time Collecting Sacred Treasures** (unselfishness) to **Build an Eternal Life** as a **Perfect Man before God**. We see in this "Process" of Creating" the <u>Perfect Man</u> **Out of the Word of God**, a **Lost Soul** must be **Led** through **Seven Stages** of **Growth and Maturity** from **Babyhood** unto **Adulthood** to <u>**Awaken**</u> it to the **Meaning, Purpose, and Value of Life**. This means that the "Meaning of Life" is to <u>Exist</u> (earth/baby farm) having **One's Own Being** or **Identity**; the "Purpose of Life" is to <u>Serve One and All</u> (Heaven/divine school) to be a **Productive Member of Society**; and finally, the "Value of Life" is to become <u>Eternally Happy</u> (Kingdom/sonship training) with **God, Angels, Men, and Nature**. The point is that "If a Person" <u>Masters</u> the **Meaning of Life** (being saved), he can **Receive** a **Free Gift** in the **Form** of a **New Body**. "If He" <u>Masters</u> the **Purpose of Life** (saving self), he can **Earn his Own Blessing** of **Eternal Life**. Finally, "If He" <u>Masters</u> the **Value of Life** (saving others), he is **Eligible** for <u>**God's Bonus Reward**</u> of having his **Own Kingdom of Glory**.

The following tabular information indicates that the "Human Race" is being <u>Called to Learn</u> the **Meaning, Purpose, and Value of Life** to **Escape Sin, Evil, and Death** to become **Worthy** of **God's New Body, Eternal Life,** and **One's Own Kingdom**:

**Learn Meaning, Purpose, and Value of Life to be Worthy
of a New Body, Eternal Life, and Own Kingdom**
(God calls all men to exist, to serve, and to find
happiness in His lessons and His blessings)

1. **Learn Meaning of Life** - <u>Follow Prophet:</u> Master Existence …. Worthy of New Body
    - God's Spoken Word - Learn God's Right from Man's Wrong: Become Righteous Citizen
    - . Fulfill God's Law of Obedience - Change Nature: ***Human to Divine***
    - Establish One's Own Identity - Destroy the Ignorant Fool to Become Wise
2. **Learn Purpose of Life** - <u>Listen to Messiah:</u> Master Service….. Worthy of Eternal Life
    - God's Written Word - Learn God's Good from Man's Evil: Become Holy Saint

- Fulfill Man's Faith in God's Love - Wash Away Sins: *Sinfulness to Holiness*
- Become Productive Member of Society - Destroy the Criminal to Become Honest

3. Learn Value of Life - <u>Meet Lord God Almighty:</u> Master Happiness.....Worthy of Own Kingdom
   - God's Incarnate Word - Learn God's Will from Man's Will: Become a Son of God
   - Fulfill God's/Man's Knowing - Transform Soul: *Thinking for Oneself*
   - Live with God, Angels, Men, and Nature - Destroy the Insane Animal to Become Sane

Through these "Three Treasures of Life," a <u>Person</u> can be **Blessed** by **God's Spoken, Written, and Incarnate Word** which will **Lead a Lost Fool** to **God's Prophet, Who** will **Take** him to **God's Messiah, Who** in turn, will **Take him to God Himself.** "Each of God's Children" must <u>Travel Along</u> the **Lord's Rocky Road of Life, Learning God's Lessons,** and **Finding God's Blessings** until **He** has been **Saved** from his **Own Ignorance** and can **Now Strive** to **Help Others** <u>Find Their Way</u> from **Nothing to All.** This means that the "Life-experience" is like a <u>Giant Puzzle</u> and **If a Person Follows God's Mystical Guides or Prophets,** he will be **Shown Each Piece** of the Puzzle which will <u>**Clearly Explain**</u> the **Meaning, Purpose, and Value of Life.**

The idea here is that "God's Spoken Word (tradition)" brings a <u>Tiny Child</u> the **Knowledge of Life to <u>Learn</u> Right from Wrong, Good from Evil, God's Will from Man's Will,** and finally, **God's Reality from Man's Illusion.** Secondly, "God's Written Word (Torah/Bible)" brings a <u>Child</u> unto **Self-awareness** to **Open his Blind Eyes** unto **God's Truth, Law, and Will to Comprehend God's** *Grand Design* and **Answer God's Call to Righteousness.** Thirdly, "God's Incarnate Word (born-again nature)" brings a <u>Child</u> unto **Consciousness** to **Realize** that **He** is a **Lost Broken Sinner** and **Needs a Savior** to **Rescue** him from the **Forces** of **Sin, Evil, Death, and Damnation.** Fourthly, "God's Prophet (teacher)" <u>Leads an Elder Child</u> into **Divine Sentience** to **Understand the Need** to **Create <u>Earth, Heaven,</u>** and <u>**God's Kingdom**</u> to bring forth the **Lord's Righteous Citizens** (earth), **Holy Saints** (Heaven), and **Sons of God** (Kingdom). Fifthly, "God's Messiah (master)" <u>Leads Young Adults</u> to **See Their Own Limitations** to **Remove** their **Ignorance, Cowardice, Greed,** and **Selfishness** to <u>**Gain**</u> **Wisdom, Courage, Generosity, and Unselfishness.** Sixthly, "God Himself (creator)" <u>Leads Adults</u> to **See Their Own Potential** to **Fulfill God's Law of Obedience** (new nature) and **Man's Faith in God's Love** (wash away sin) to <u>**Receive**</u> a **New Mind, New Heart, New Soul, and New Life-force.** Finally, "God's Blessing of Freedom" <u>Allows </u>the **Great Wise Men** to **Think for Themselves** and **See Their Own Self-worth** to **Expand** the **Meaning, Purpose, and Value of Life** and <u>**Reveal**</u> the **Real Eternal God/Man Relationship.**

Yes! It is a "Long Journey" from <u>Nothing to All</u> for a **New-born Human Soul** as it **Strives** to **Figure It All Out** and is then <u>**Called to Face**</u> *Lucifer's Test* (lessons), *God's Judgment* (blessings), and *His Own Self-evaluation* (think for self).

The following tabular information indicates that the "Lord God Almighty" is <u>Using Seven Mystical Guides</u> to **Take His Babies** from **Childhood-to-Adulthood** so <u>**They can be Awakened**</u> to the **Meaning, Purpose, and Value of Life:**

God's Seven Guides of Glory
Lead the Human Race to God's Door of Freedom
(spoken word, written word, incarnate word,
prophet, Messiah, God, eternal life, and freedom)

——————— Mankind Sees the Meaning of Life - To Exist (new body) ———————

Mind	1. Spoken Word Leads to Written Word – Baby . . . . .Knowledge
Heart	2. Written Word Leads to Incarnate Word – Child . . . . .Self-awareness
Soul	3. Incarnate Word Leads to God's Prophet – Adolescent . . . . .Consciousness

——————Mankind Sees the Purpose of Life - To Serve (eternal life) ———————

Life-force	4. God's Prophet Leads to God's Messiah – Teenager . . . . . . .Sentience
Nature	5. God's Messiah Leads to God Almighty - Young Adult . . . . .See Limitations
Born-again	6. God Almighty Leads to Eternal Freedom – Adult . . . . .See Potential

——————Mankind Sees the Value of Life - To be Happy (own kingdom)————

Set Free	7. Freedom Leads to Thinking for Oneself - Wise Man . . . . .See Self-worth

This illustration shows that the "Life-experience Begins" with God's Spoken Word (baby) which was **Given to Man** in **Ancient Stories** and **Parables** to **Reveal** that there was a **Creator God, Who Loved His Creation** and **Desired to become Human.** Secondly, "Comes God's" Written Word (childhood) from **Moses** in the **Form of the Torah** (plenitude) to: (1) **Explain Human Life,** (2) **God's Law,** (3) **God's Religion,** (4) **God's Government,** (5) and **God's Home** as the **Lord God Almighty Reveals His Coming Incarnation upon Earth.** Thirdly, "Comes God's" Incarnate Word (adolescence) that will bring **God onto the Earth** via **His Chosen People** (Jews) in both **Spirit** and in **Flesh** to **Transform Sin, Evil, and Death** into **Man's New Righteousness, Holiness, and Perfection.** Fourthly, "Comes God's" Parade of Prophets (teenagers) **Clearly Explaining** the **Meaning, Purpose, and Value of Life** as **Seen** through the **Eyes of God** and **Preparing the People** for the **Coming of the Messiah, Who will Save Them** from **Their Sins.** Fifthly, "Comes God's" most Beloved Messiah (young adults), the **Lord Jesus Christ,** to **Set the Stage** for **His Coming New Government, Church,** and **Home** by **Revealing** God's **Truths, Law, Will, and Love.** Sixthly, "Comes" the Lord God Almighty Himself (adults) in **His New Jerusalem** to **Begin** the **Wedding Feast of the Lamb** as **God and Man** become **One People** on **Earth** since **God** is **Now Human** and will **Forever Rule Over** Heaven on Earth. Finally, "Comes God's" most Treasured Freedom (wise men) as the **Human Race** is **Set Free** from its **Curses** of **Toil, Pain, and Death** to be **Blessed** with **Peace of Mind, Joy of the Heart, and Happiness of the Soul.**

We can now see that during the "Lord's 1st Week of Human Life (7,000 yrs.)," God was **Converting Man's Rebellion** into a **Perfect Man** (defeat fear), **Converting Man's Criminality** into a **Perfect Society** (defeat pain), **Converting Man's Insanity** into a **Set of Perfect Friends** (defeat death), and **Converting Man's Evil** into the **Friendship of Man** (defeat damnation), all In the **Name of Jesus Christ.** This means that "Rebellion" became Sedition (government) against **Rome;** "Criminality" became Sorcery (home) against **Israel;** "Insanity" became Blasphemy against the **Temple;** and "Evil" became Sacrilege against **God.** Through these "Four Curses," Jesus Christ faced

Punishment from **Rome, Israel,** the **Temple,** and from **God** to **Pay in Full** the awesome **Sin-debt** created by the **Violations** of **Adam and Eve against Divine Justice.** Once the "Messiah (divine)," "Church (sacred)," "World (holy)," and each "Individual (righteous)" made their Required Contribution to **Pay Its Sin-debt,** they might **Earn a New Body, New Nature, New Behavior,** and a **New Lifestyle** within the **Kingdom of God.** We can now see that the "Individual Suffers" in the Garden of Agony (rebellion); the "World Suffers" during the Scourging (criminal); the "Church Suffers" during the Crucifixion (insanity); and the "Messiah Suffers" in the Tomb of Death (evil).

At each of these "Stages of Punishment," the whole Human Race Faces Its **Rebellious** (baby), **Criminal** (teenager), **Insane** (adult), and **Evil** (wise man) **Nature** given to it during the **Fall of Adam and Eve.** We now see that in the "Garden of Agony," the Lord Faced Horrifying Fear; during "His Scourging," the Lord Faced Death Agony; during "His Crucifixion," the Lord Faced Hopelessness; and finally, during the "Lord's Death in the Tomb," He Faced Separation from His God. With each of these "Four Punishments," every Level of Existence was **Purified** of its **Sin, Evil, Death, and Damnation.** In short, this means that "Man's Sin" becomes Redemption (free); "Man's Evil" becomes Salvation (earned); "Man's Death" becomes Rewards (bonus); and "Man's Damnation" becomes Freedom (honors). Through these "Four Blessings," the Human Race will be **Awarded** its **New Body** (new mind), **New Nature** (new heart/eternal life), **New Behavior** (new soul/own kingdom), and its **New Lifestyle** (new life-force/freedom).

The implication here is that the "Human Race" has Spent a Lifetime Seeking its **Own New Body, New Nature, New Behavior, and New Lifestyle to Comprehend** the **Meaning, Purpose, and Value of Life.** We see that the "Meaning," "Purpose," and "Value of Life" are All Based on the Importance of **Human, Angelic, and Divine Honor** which must be **Proven** via **One's Depth of Courage** as he **Performs his Duty** through his **Daily Sacrifices** of **Labors, Wealth,** and even his **Own Life.**

Mind 1. **Honor** - New Body: Remove Rebellious Fool = Become Righteous Citizen (life)

Heart 2. **Courage** - New Nature: Remove Dangerous Criminal = Become a Holy Saint (death)

Soul 3. **Duty** - New Behavior: Remove Insane Animal = Become a Son of God (resurrection)

Life-force 4. **Sacrifice** - New Lifestyle: Remove Evil Monster = Become a Free Man (freedom)

Now, we can apply this "Concept" of Body, Nature, Behavior, and Lifestyle to the **Combustion Engine** as it relates to the creation of the **Human Body** through its **Respiratory** (injection), **Circulatory** (compression), **Autonomic** (ignition), and **Digestive** (exhaust) **Systems.** The idea here is that to "Produce Power," one must Burn Fuel and then **Transmit** that **Energy** into some **Form** of **Circular Motion,** such as the **Creation of a Wheel.** We see these "Cycles of Life" Working Tirelessly for billions of years as **Mother Nature** brings forth its abundance of **Plant, Animal, and Human Life** out of the **Nothingness of Air, Water, and Soil** (planet earth).

We call this "Creative Force" *God's Grand Design* as it seeks to establish **Four Kingdoms of Love** based on the **Individual** (physical), **Society** (spiritual), **Divinity** (mystical), and **God** (divine). Through the "Lord's Natural Order," <u>Man's Sin-nature</u> (Lucifer's test) **Kills Individual Love** (love self); <u>Worldly Temptations</u> (God's judgment) **Kills Social Love** (love of others); <u>Demonic Possession</u> (self-evaluation) **Kills Divine Love** (love God); and finally, the <u>Evil Spirit</u> (truth) **Kills All Love** (God's Love). Secondly, through "Physical Life," <u>Man's Righteousness</u> (wisdom) brings forth **Individual Love** (self-love); then <u>Man's Holiness</u> (courage) brings forth **Social Love** (love others); <u>Man's Perfection</u> (generosity) brings forth **Divine Love** (love God); and finally, <u>Man's Independence</u> (service) brings forth **Infinite Love** (God loves everyone). Thirdly, through "Spiritual Life," the <u>Saints of Man</u> are **Blessed** with **Eternal Life** (free redemption), a **New Body** (earned salvation), and a **Royal Kingdom** (bonus reward). Finally, through "Mystical Life," the <u>Sons of God</u> are **Blessed** with the ability to **<u>Think for Oneself, Love All God's Creation,</u>** and **<u>Care for Everything that God</u> has Created** in **Life, Death, and Resurrection.**

We can now see that the "Life-experience" is comprised of a **Grand Design** (God), and **Three Plans of Life** (natures/persons/trinity) in the form of a **Human Plan of Creation or Righteousness** (kingship), an **Angelic Plan of Redemption or Holiness** (priesthood), and a **Divine Plan of Sanctified Life or Perfection** (sonship). Through these "Three Plans," God is <u>Creating</u> (earth), <u>Redeeming</u> (Heaven), and <u>Sanctifying</u> (Kingdom) the **Life-experience** of each of **<u>His Children</u>** as he transforms from **Death** (nothing) **to New-life** (all).

The following tabular information indicates that everything is "Connected" to <u>God's Creative Logic</u> via **His Natural Order** (combustion engine), **Physical Life** (human body), **Spiritual Life** (intellect/emotions/instincts), and **Mystical Life** (infinity/eternity):

God Creates Natural Order/Physical Life/Spiritual Life/Mystical Life to bring forth Power
(respiratory/circulatory/autonomic/digestive systems
bring forth human power creating life)

Gas
(fuel)

1. **Natural Order** - <u>Combustion Engine:</u> Machines… Air/Fire/Water/Power
   - Respiratory System - Oxygen: Air = Injection + Fuel (mixture)/Desert Experience
   - Brain - Knowledge: Baby Intellect = Fire of the Mind + Words become Concepts

Input Nature
   - Conversion from Ignorance to Wisdom - Learn Right from Wrong
   - Shepherd - Good News: Free Redemption = Blessing of Knowledge
   - Righteous Citizen - Title Deed to Earth: Heaven on Earth
   - Treasure "Baby Knowledge" - Value Existence: Defeat Curse of Ignorance

(oxygen creates eternal life - glorified body: respiratory system becomes angelic life)

Compression
(force)

2. **Physical Life** - <u>Human Body:</u> Life-force ….Air/Electricity/Blood/Food
   - Circulatory System - Blood: Water = Compression + Water (coolant)
   - Heart - Self-awareness: Teenage Emotions = Blood of Heart + Experiences unto Values

Process Men	• Conversion from Cowardice to Courage - Learn Good from Evil
	• Carpenter - Gospel Message: Earned Salvation = Anointing of Money
	• Holy Saint - Title Deed to Heaven: Paradise in Heaven
	• Treasure "Teenage Money" - Value Wealth: Defeat Curse of Cowardice

(blood creates life - transfigured body: circulatory system becomes human life)

Spark	**3. Spiritual Life** - <u>Intellect/Emotions/Instincts:</u> Eternal Life .... Human/Angelic/Divine/God
(fire)	• Autonomic System - Electricity: Fire = Ignition + Explosion (burning)
	• Soul - Consciousness: Adult Instincts = Spirit of Soul + Resurrection unto New-life
Output Angels	• Conversion from Greed to Generosity - Learn God's Will from Man's Will
	• Messiah - Doctrinal Truths: Bonus Rewards = Sanctification of Health
	• Perfect Son - Title Deed to Kingdom: Heavenly Happiness
	• Treasure "Adult Health" - Value Long Life: Defeat Curse of Greed

(food creates saintly life - mystical body: digestive system becomes heavenly sainthood)

Power	**4. Mystical Life** - <u>Infinity/Eternity:</u> Self-will ..... Mind/Heart/Soul/ Life-force
(torque)	• Digestive System - Food: Nourishment = Exhaust + Force (energy)
	• Life - Sentience: Wise Man Thinking = Nature of Life + Ascension unto Perfection
Result God	• Conversion from Selfishness to Unselfishness - Learn God's Reality/Man's Illusion
	• Son of God - Thinking for Self: Freedom = Consecration of Freedom
	• Free Man - Title Deed to Self: Interior Heaven (self-fulfillment)
	• Treasure "Wise Man Freedom" - Value Free Will: Defeat Curse of Selfishness

(electricity creates divine life - divine body: autonomic system becomes son of God)

This illustration shows that the "Life-experience" is centered on the <u>Input</u> (nature) of **God's Spirit** (air/earth), <u>Processing</u> (men) of **Man's Life** (blood/Heaven), <u>Output</u> (angels) of **God/Man Bodies** (food/Kingdom) with <u>Creation's Final Results</u> (God) being in the **Form** of **Sons of God** (electricity/self). At "Each of These Levels of Transformation," the <u>Forces of Life</u> **Attain Greater and Greater Value** until **They** become **Priceless** unto the **Sacrifice of All** (worthless). This means that "Cowardly Babies Value Knowledge (cartoons/1st value)" as <u>They Strive</u> to be <u>Converted</u> from **Ignorance to Wisdom** by **Learning** as **Many** of the **Lessons of Life** as **They** can to become **Loved, Honored, and Respected by All.** Secondly, "Foolish Teenagers Value Money (mannequins/2nd value)" as <u>They Strive</u> to be <u>Converted</u> from **Cowardice to Courage** by **Working** as much as **Possible** to <u>**Establish Themselves**</u> within **Their Own Communities**. Thirdly, "Greedy Adults Value Excellent Health (humans/3rd value)" as <u>They Strive</u> to be <u>Converted</u> from **Greed to Generosity** by <u>**Knowing God's Right from Man's Wrong**</u> in **All**

Fields of Endeavor. Finally, "Selfish Wise Men Value Freedom (supernaturals/4th value)" as They Strive to be Converted from **Selfishness to Unselfishness** by **Implementing** that which will **Work for One and All** (synchronized balance).

The idea here is to see that the "Angels in Heaven" Want Glorified Bodies made of **Air** (spirit); "Men of Earth" Want Transfigured Bodies **Made of Blood** (oxygen); "Sons of Man (Man/God or Saints)" Living in the Kingdom **Want Mystical Bodies Made of Flesh** (food); and finally, "Sons of God (God/Man or Sons)" Living in Paradise **Want Divine Bodies** Made of Bone (electricity). This lesson reveals that "Angels" are Gas (wants); "Men" are Liquid (fears); "Saints" are Solid (death); and "Sons of God (new-life)" are Unbreakable Iron (eternal)." The question is: which **One of These States of Existence Do You Want to Be** in **Truth, Law, Will, and Lov**e?

Truth   1. **Angels of Gas** - Spirit Beings: Want Glorified Bodies … See Limitations
- Jesus - Free Redemption: Babies Desire to be Loved by All (all)

Law   2. **Men of Liquid** - Fleshly Beings: Want Transfigured Bodies … See Potential .
- Christ - Earned Salvation: Teenagers Want to be Popular with Many Friends (few)

Will   3. **Saints of Solid** - Spirit/Flesh Beings: Want Mystical Bodies … See Self-worth
- Jesus Christ - Bonus Rewards: Adults Treasure a Few Old Family Friends (family)

Love   4. **Sons of Unbreakable Iron** - Spirit/Flesh/Soul: Want Divine Bodies....See Almighty God
- Christ Jesus - Eternal Freedom: Wise Men to Share in God's Friendship (one)

This illustration shows that the "Human Race" is to both Grow and Mature in **Spirit, Flesh, Soul,** and finally into the **Life-force of God** to obtain the **Four Natures of God** in the **Form** of a **Glorified, Transfigured, Mystical, and Divine Bodies.** Obviously, "We All Want" to be Untouchables (unbreakable forever) **Living** and **Loving** by **Our Own Choices** in an **Eternal Life** of **Righteousness, Holiness,** and **Perfection** within the **Presence of Men, Angels, and God Himself.** The point is to see that as "Babies (wants)," We Want **Everyone to Love Us** (all); yet, as "Teenagers (fears)," We Want to be **Popular** by having **Many Good Friends. A**s "Adults (death)," We Want Only a **Few Old Family Friends** (best friends); and finally, as "Wise Men, (new-life)" We Seek Only **God's Friendship.** The Lord is telling us here that "Babies Live" in a Desert of Want and **Kiss Everything** as **Treasures**; "Teenagers Live" in the Valley of Fears and **Treasure Security** (money) above **All.** "Adults Live" in the Hills of Death and Treasure Their Good Health (survival) so that **They might Live** in **Hope of Fulfillment.** Finally, "Wise Men Live" on God's Mountain of New-life and **Treasure Their Personal Freedoms** (free choice) to **Live** in **God's Truth, Law, Will, and Love.**

This means that the "Life-experience" Centers on a **Person's Human Growth** (Jesus/earth) and **Divine Maturity** (Christ/Heaven) as **Each Child of God** is **Called** from **Nothing unto All** through the **Sacrifice of Jesus Christ** (Calvary) as **Payment** for **His New Body, Eternal Life, and Royal Kingdom.** Yes! We are all striving for "Eternal Free Choice" which is having a "New Body" and then Finding a "Hospitable Place to Live" hopefully with God, His Angels, and His Saints in **Fulfillment** of **His Human Righteousness** (kingship/natural order), **Sacred Holiness** (supernatural order), and **Divine Perfection** (divine order). Note that in "God's Original Creation," he is Giving His Natural Order **Three Major Gifts** in the **Form** of a **Person's Free-willed Life,** a **Human Body** which are **Placed** within an **Earthly Realm of Existence.** Out of this "Three Gifts Concept," we see God's Three Realities of Eternal Life in the **Form** of **Physical Order** (natural/earth), **Spiritual Order** (supernatural/Heaven), and **Mystical Order** (God/Kingdom).

The idea here is to "Recognize" that at the Human Level of Existence or **Physical Order, Mankind** has been **Given** an **Ignorant Mind** (Lucifer's test/sin-nature) to be **Transformed** into **Wisdom.** Secondly, a **Cowardly Heart** (God's judgment/worldly temptations) is to be **Transformed** into **Courage,** and then a **Greedy Soul** (self-evaluation/demonic possession) must be **Transformed** into **Generosity.** This "Conversion Process" for the Mind, Heart, and Soul have been **Established** upon the **Home, Church, and Government of Man** to teach the **Children of God Right/Wrong** (righteous king), **Good/Evil** (holy priest), and **God's and Man's Wills** (perfect son). Via the conversion of the "Mind, Heart, and Soul" through Jesus Christ, we see the significance of the **Forces of Redemption** (free), **Salvation** (earned), **and Rewards** (bonus) as **They** come forth to **Convert Earth, Heaven,** and the **Kingdom of God** into **Righteous and Holy Perfection.** The idea here is to see that "God is Creating a Spirit Life (astral plane)" and is then putting it within a Physical Body to Educate It on **Planet Earth**; then it is taken from there to **Heaven via Jesus Christ** to **Change Its Nature** into a **Reflection of God Himself** in preparation for **Its Membership** within the **Kingdom of God.**

In this concept of "Triune Progress" from Man (earth) to Angels (Heaven) and then to God (Kingdom), we see an analogy to a **Pioneer,** who begins his settlement by installing a **Septic Tank** (Lucifer/earth) for handling his **Waste Materials.** We see that as his "Volume of Waste Increases," then he Upgrades to a **Sewer System** (Jesus Christ/Heaven); and finally, **Stops having Waste** altogether by **Creating** a **New Waste-Free Body** (transfiguration). This "Physical," "Spiritual," to "Mystical Progression" from Baby Waste (diapers), to Teenage Waste (toilet), and finally, Adult Purity (transfigured body) **Reveals God's Need** to have a **Triune Purification System** to **Change Nothing into All.**

The following tabular information indicates that "God is Giving Earth (flesh/God becomes Man)," "Heaven (spirit flesh/Man becomes God)," and the "Kingdom (divine flesh/God/Man become One)" His Three Physical, Spiritual, and Mystical Gifts to **Allow Them** to both **Grow** and **Mature** into a **Group** of **Righteous** (individual love), **Holy** (social love), and **Perfect** (divine love) **Children of God:**

**God's Gifts of Free-willed Life, a Human Body,
and an Earthly Realm Lead to Eternal Life**
(conversion comes by way of redemption,
salvation and rewards leading to eternal freedom)

Called into Existence (baby)

─────────────── *Earth* (physical life) ───────────────

Enlightenment of the Life-experience (child)

Human Truth	1.	**Free-willed Life** – <u>Repenting Mind:</u> Convert Intellect …. Man's Blessing
		• Master the Home – Live with Parents: Purified in Water
		• Defeat Ignorance – Baby Life: Offer Life = Worship God
		• Learn Right from Wrong – Righteous King
Human Law	2.	**Human Body** – <u>Praying Heart:</u> Convert Emotions ……. Man's Anointing
		• Master the Church – Live with Priests: Purified in Oil
		• Defeat Cowardice – Teenage Life: Offer Wealth = Praise God
		• Learn Good from Evil – Holy Priest
Human Will	3.	**Earthly Realm** – <u>Thankful Soul:</u> Convert Instincts …. Man's Sanctification
		• Master the Government – Live with Society: Purified in Blood
		• Defeat Greed – Adult Life: Offer Labors = Thank God
		• Learn God's Will/man's will - Perfect Son

Enlightenment unto New-life (teenager)

─────────────── *Heaven* (spiritual life) ───────────────

Awakening to Man's Truths (adult)

Eternal Life	4.	**Free Redemption** – <u>Physical Order:</u> Natural Existence …. God's Blessing
		• Master Earth - Live with Man: Converted via Water Baptism
		• Gain Wisdom - Earthly Kingship: Offer Life = Honor Man
		• Transform the Earth - Heaven on Earth
New Body	5.	**Earned Salvation** - <u>Spiritual Order:</u> Supernatural Existence… God's Anointing
		• Master Heaven - Live with Angels: Converted via Oil Confession
		• Gain Courage - Heavenly Priesthood: Offer Wealth = Dignify Man
		Transform Heaven - Paradise in Heaven
Royal	6.	**Bonus Rewards** - <u>Mystical Order:</u> Divine Existence …… God's Sanctification
Kingdom		• Master Divinity - Live with God: Converted via Blood Communion
		• Gain Generosity - Divine Sonship: Offer Labors = Respect Man
		• Transform God - Kingdom of Glory

Awakened to God's Truths (wise man)

─────────────── **Kingdom** (mystical life) ───────────────

Indwelled with God's Spirit (free man)

Divine	7.	**Freedom from Chaos** - <u>Thinking for Self:</u> Personal Existence… Self Consecration
Village		• Master Created Existence - Live with Self: Converted by Spirit Confirmation

- Gain Fairness - Freedom from Captivity: Offer All = Honor Life
- Transform Self - Perfection of Self

This illustration shows that the "Human Race" is being <u>Called into Existence</u> (belief), <u>Enlightened with Life</u> (submission), then <u>Awakened unto Truth</u> (true to self), and finally <u>Indwelled with God's Spirit</u> (guilty conscience) to **Set Mankind Free** from **Sin, Evil, Death, and Damnation Forever**. Now, we see that the "Life-experience" has been very carefully <u>Planned</u> and that **Nature (machines), Men, Angels, and God** are **Destined** to **Work Together** in **Building a Kingdom of Glory** to **Honor the Sacrifice of Jesus Christ**. This "Need to Work Together" on Earth, in Heaven, and finally, with God's Kingdom sits at the center of **Human Existence** so that <u>**All Men**</u> can become **Righteous, Holy, and Perfect before God**. The point is that if a person "Masters Earth (home)," he can <u>Defeat his Ignorance</u> (individual love) and become **Wise** in **Preparation** for **Heaven on Earth** (knowledge). Secondly, if He "Masters Heaven (church)," he can <u>Defeat his Cowardice</u> (social love) and become **Courageous** in **Preparation** for living in **God's Heavenly Paradise** (love). Finally, if He <u>"Masters God's Kingdom</u> (government)," he can **Defeat his Greed** (divine love) and become **Generous** in **Preparation** for **God's Royal Kingdom** (ego/leadership).

We are being told that the "Human Race" must <u>Learn Right from Wrong</u> (earth), <u>Good from Evil</u> (Heaven), and <u>God's Will from man's will</u> (Kingdom) to be **Set Free** from **Ignorance** (lying), **Cowardice** (hiding), and **Greed** (stealing). This process of "Man's Growth" and "God's Maturity" <u>Creates</u> the **Eternal Bond Needed** to **Unite Nature, Men, Angels, and God** into an <u>**Eternal**</u> **Covenant** of **Mutual Respect** as **Each Soul in Creation Learns** to **Perform its Role Perfectly**. Through "God's Redemptive System," if a <u>Misbehaved Child Repents,</u> then he can be **Forgiven** (peace); if he commits a <u>Serious Crime,</u> he must also **Pray to God** to **Earn Wealth** (joy); and if it's a <u>Divine Violation,</u> he must **Work for God** to obtain **God's Love** (happiness). This means that the "Church of Life (graces)" <u>Gives Man Divine Rights;</u> the "World of People (points) <u>Gives Man Social Rights;</u> and finally, "Individual Land Owners" are <u>Given Man's Individual Rights</u> to **Make All Men Equal before God**.

1. **Church of Life** - <u>Divine Rights:</u> Worship God = Give Life …. See Limitations
2. **World of People** - <u>Social Rights:</u> Praise God = Give Wealth … See Potential
3. **Individual Land Owners** - <u>Individual Rights:</u> Thank God = Give Labors … See Self-worth

This means that out of his "Individual Rights (earth)," a <u>Person can Establish</u> his **Own Identity** as an **Adopted Son of God** (sonship/contract son), thereby <u>**Giving**</u> him his **Own Fixed Frame of Reference in Life** (one power). Secondly, out of his "Social Rights (Heaven)," he can establish his <u>Own Character</u> as a **Son of Man** (humanity/blood son), thereby giving him his own **Relative Focused Existence** (two powers). Finally, out of his "Divine Rights (Kingdom)," he can establish his <u>Own Personality</u> as a **Son of God** (divinity/spirit son), thereby giving him his own **Perception of Reality** (three powers).

By establishing his "Own Identity" within the Earthly, Heavenly, and Kingdomly Realms of **God, Angels, and Men,** a **Person** can **Reject Man's Illusion of Life** (temporary) and enter **God's Reality of Life Forever** (permanent). Through this "Process" of being a Contract Son (adopted/flesh), Blood Son "(birth/spirit)," and a Spirit Son (resurrection/soul), a **Person can Receive** his **Own New Nature,** a **New Body,** and his **Own Kingdom.** We now see that out of the "Messiah's Blessing (first-born child)," Mankind will Receive a **Church with Its Own High Priest** (priesthood) to bring **Man a New Nature**; then a Nation and Its King of Kings (kingship) will bring Man a **New Body;** and finally, a **Home and Its Son of God** (sonship) will create the **Perfect Man** (Heaven) **on Earth.** Out of the "Church's Blessing (good Christian)," mankind will receive a **Temple of Priests** bringing **Man's New Behavior;** a Throne with Its Nations of Kings bringing **Man's New Spirit;** and Its Palace of Sons bringing **Man's Perfect Society** (Earth) **on Earth.** Out of the "World's Blessing (prodigal child)," mankind will receive its own Parish of Friends (brothers) to bring **Man's New Lifestyle;** a Government of Righteous Citizens (self-rule) to bring **Man's New Soul;** and a Home of Beloved Souls to transform **Man into a Set of Friends** (Kingdom) **on Earth.** Out of each "Individual's Blessing (pagan child)," mankind will receive a Prayer Group of Devotion (living prayer) to bring **Man's New Identity;** a Town Meeting (neighbors) to bring **Man's New Character;** and his own Home Ownership (kingship) to bring **Man's New Personality** (Self) **on Earth.** Out of these "Four Levels (physical/spiritual/mystical/divine)" and Twelve Divine Gifts from God, the human race can establish its own **Physical Blessing** (government/people/calling), **Spiritual Anointing** (church/life/enlightenment), **Mystical Sanctification** (home/land/awakening), and **Divine Consecration** (freedom/self/indwelling) to make **God, Angels, and Men One** in **Christ Jesus.**

The following tabular information indicates "God's Four Levels of Transformation" via the Messiah (life/perfect man), Church (people/perfect society), World (land/perfect friends), and Individual (God/God's friendship):

God's Four Levels of Transformation at Messiah, Church, World, and Individual Stages of Life
(Messiah is Life, Church is People, World is Land, and Individuals are God's Friendship)

Life
(truth)

1. **Messiah** - Perfect Man: Divine Rights (baby) —————————Build Home
   - Life (graces) - New Nature: Scourging = Repentance——- Forgiveness (peace)
   - People (points) - New Body: Crucifixion = Prayers—————Wealth (joy)

Called
   - Land (grades) - New Man: Tomb = Works ————Love (happiness)
   - God (blessings) - Rite of Passage: Resurrection = Save Souls ——— Redemption (free)

(Father Abraham's Animal Sacrifice - Purchase Passport to Heaven: See Limitations)

People

2. **Church** - Perfect Society: Social Rights (teenager) —— Find Wife

(law)	• Life (graces) - New Behavior: Church = Purification —— Pardon (peace)
	• People (points) - New Spirit: Mass = Transformation——Money (joy)
Enlightened	• Land (grades) - New Society: Souls = Correction——Affection (happy)
	• Man (honors) - Rite of Passage: Freedom = Conversion——Salvation (earned)

(Father Abraham's Sacrifice of Son (Isaac) - Purchase Ticket to Heaven: See Potential)

Land	3. **World** - <u>Perfect Friends:</u> Individual Rights (adult) ——Perform Job
(will)	• Life (graces) - New Lifestyle: Worship = Give Life — Know God (peace)
	• People (points) - New Soul: Praise = Give Wealth — Love God (joy)
Awakened	• Land (grades) - New Friends: Thanksgiving = Give Labor —— Serve God (happy)
	• Man (dollars) - Rite of Passage: Recompense = Give Friendship —— Rewards (bonus)

(Father Abraham's Offer of Circumcision - Earn Divine Wealth: See Self-worth)

God	4. **Individual** - <u>God's Friendship:</u> Rite of Passage (wise man) —Raise Children
(love)	• Life (graces) - New Identity: Wisdom = New Mind——Home (peace)
	• People (points) - New Character: Courage = New Heart —— Government (joy)
Indwelled	• Land (grades) - New Personality: Generosity = New Soul —Church (happiness)
	• Self (well-being) - God's Friendship: Free - New Life-force—Self (freedom)

(Father Abraham's Offer of God's Son - Redeem All Men: Blessed with Eternal Freedom)

This illustration shows that the "Earth" was <u>Given Four Saviors</u> beginning with **Jesus Christ** (Messiah/called), **His Church** (enlightened), the **Righteous World** (awakened), and the **Born-again Soul** (individual/indwelled), each coming to bring the **Human Race <u>New-life, New People, New Land,</u>** and **<u>Freedom</u>** from **Sin** (sin-nature), **Evil** (worldly temptations), **Death** (demonic possession), and **Damnation** (evil spirit). Through these "Four Saviors," <u>Mankind would Receive</u> the **Lord's Blessings of Life, People, Land, and God** to assist them in **<u>Building a Beautiful Life</u>** within the **Kingdom of God.** This means that each of us must "Surrender" to <u>Life</u> to be "Unto Thine Own Self be True" with <u>People</u> to receive a "Good Conscience" to <u>Honor the Land</u> and then "Learn to Think" for <u>Oneself.</u> This "New Ability" to <u>Comprehend the Truth</u> and <u>See Things as They Really Are</u> **Allows a Person** to **Master the Kingdom of God,** making him **<u>Worthy of being Set Free</u>** from **Sin** (ignorance), **Evil** (cowardice), and **Death** (greed).

We now see that each of "God's Children" must obtain a <u>Passport to Heaven</u> (life), <u>Tickets to Heaven</u> (people), and <u>Heavenly Money</u> (land/grace dollars) before he can become **Eligible** to **Enter the Presence of God.** We see in the case of "Father

Abraham," he Purchased a Divine Passport with his **Sacrifice of a Ram, Goat,** and **Heifer** to **Win the Friendship of God**. Secondly, "Father Abraham" Purchased a Divine Ticket with the **Sacrifice of his Son, Isaac** to **Win the Companionship of God.** Finally, "Father Abraham" Earned Divine Money via the **Sacrifice of his Own Flesh** (circumcision) to **Enter** the **Oneness of God.** Out of "Abraham's Friendship," mankind will become a Perfect Man (see limitations); out of "Abraham's Companionship," mankind will become a Perfect Society (see potential); and out of "Abraham's Oneness," mankind will become a Society of Friends (see self-worth) unto the **Lord God Almighty**. It is now clear that it has taken "7,000 Years" to make **Man Perfect,** make **Man's Society Perfect,** and make **All Men Friends** to **Earn God's Respect** and his **Eternal Friendship.**

The "Holy Bible" reveals to us that after man's First Week of Creation (7,000 years) comprised of some seven thousand years of **Servanthood,** humanity would enter into a **New Age of Eternity** (eighth day). During this "First Week," the awakened Human Soul would **Learn the Value** of having a **Divine Home** of **Perfect Love.** Through the principles of "Knowing the Truth (challenge)" and "Living Well (adventure)," the **Human Spirit** would finally capture the **Essence of Life** (freedom) and the **Meaning** associated with a **Person's Most Perfect Existence.** Now, imagine that "Humanity is Presently" in its Original Egg Form (seed) and will **Not Experience** its **True Form** and/or its **True Nature** until the **End of Its Long** and most **Painful Servanthood Training Period** (sonship) or its **First Week of Life** (7,000 yrs.). This logic means that "We are All Inside" a Giant Incubator (universe/physical) that is **Under Siege** by a **Vicious Wolf** (Lucifer) **Who is being Fended Off** by the **Eggs' Angry Owners,** Jesus (spirit/host) and **Mary** (flesh/grave). In the earliest revelations of the "Ancient Patriarchs," the Hand of God the Father can be seen at **Work, Revealing** the **Divine Mysteries** of **His Heavenly Temple** to **His most Chosen Jewish People** in the **Manifestation** of the **Mosaic Tabernacle** (forgiveness/blessings).

We now see that despite the "Lord's Desperate Attempts" to Pour Forth **His Divine Revelations** (knowledge/wisdom) into the **Hearts** of the **Jewish People, They** could **Not Comprehend** the **Depth of God's** most **Sacred Word** as it **Revealed** the **Forces Governing Man's Human Repentance** (Jesus/death) and **God's Divine Forgiveness** (Christ/new-life). We see that the "Human Race" is to Repent to God as a **Benevolent Force** (energy) through the **Power of Worship** or by **Giving One's Life** to the **Creator of All Things** as a **Manifestation** of the **Holy Church** (truth). Secondly, the "Human Race is to be Forgiven by **Our Personal God** (Man) through the **Power of Praise** or by **Giving One's Wealth** to the **Loving Father** as a **Manifestation** of the **Righteous Government** (law). Finally, the "Human Race" is to be Set Free by the **Lord God Almighty** (spirit) through the **Power of Thanksgiving** or by **Giving One's Labor** to the **Almighty Creator** as a **Manifestation** of the **Divine Home** (will). Through these "Three Manifestations of God" as Nature (benevolent force), Father God (personal God), and Our Almighty Creator (Lord God Almighty), **We can have a Triune Relationship** with a **Supreme Being** through **Our Own**

Transfigured Flesh (natural order), Glorified Spirit (supernatural order), and Holy Soul (divine order).

In this concept, we see that the "Holy Spirit (church)" is <u>Represented</u> by the Benevolent Force (existence) which in Existence becomes the <u>Natural Order of Life</u> to bring forth both a Spiritual Heaven (Father) and a Physical Earth (Son). Secondly, the "Son of God (government)" is <u>Represented</u> by the Personal God (service) which in Life becomes the <u>Supernatural Order of Life</u> to bring forth a Holy Church (Father) and a Righteous World (Son). Finally, "God the Father (home)" is <u>Represented</u> by the Lord God Almighty (happiness/freedom) which in Eternal Life becomes the <u>Divine Order of Life</u> to bring forth both Man's Morals (heart) and Man's Ethics (mind). Through "Each of These" <u>Creative Forces of Life,</u> the Human Race is Able to Exist, Live, and have its Being, Allowing Each of <u>God's Beloved Children</u> to Learn How to Think for himself (correctly).

The following tabular information indicates the "God of Benevolent Force (energy)" becomes <u>Natural Order;</u> "Man's Personal God (life)" becomes <u>Supernatural Order;</u> and the "Lord God Almighty" becomes the <u>Divine Order</u> of All Creation:

The Benevolent Force, Personal God, and the Lord God Almighty Create Abundant Life
(God's spirit becomes natural order, son becomes supernatural order, and father becomes divine order)

Truth
(graces)

1. **Benevolent Force** - <u>Natural Order:</u> Holy Spirit brings Church ......
Knowledge
- Ignorance transformed into Wisdom - Fear Conquered: Know God (God)
- Learn Good from Evil - Spirit: Holy Saint = Seat in the Temple Court

Purify
Grave
- God becomes Man (1st Advent) - 1st Sacrifice: Divine Messiah = Baptism
- Redemption - Free Gold Mine: Title Deed to the Earth = Intercessor (up)
- Abraham's Altar - Meet the Holy Spirit: Priesthood = Worship God (intercessor)

(fulfill God's law of obedience – change nature: human to divine = worthy of new body)

Law
(points)

2. **Personal God** - <u>Supernatural Order:</u> Son of God brings
Government...Self-awareness
- Cowardice transformed into Courage – Pain Conquered: Serve God (society)
- Learn Good from Evil – Flesh: Righteous Citizen = Seat in the Celestial Court

Purify
Host
- Man becomes God (2nd Advent) - 2nd Sacrifice: Holy Church = Confession
- Salvation - Earn Gold by Digging: Title Deed to Heaven = Interpreter (down)

- Isaac's Throne - Meet Son of God: Kingship = Praise God (interpreter)

(fulfill Man's faith in God's love - wash away sin: sinful to holy = worthy of eternal life)

Will	3.	**Lord God Almighty** - <u>Divine Order:</u> Father God brings Home....
(marks)		Consciousness

- Greed transformed into Generosity - Death Conquered: Love God (self)
- Learn God's Will from man's will - Soul: Perfect Son = Seat in Royal Court

Purify
Life

- God and Man become One (3rd Advent) - 3rd Sacrifice: Righteous World = Communion
- Rewards - Share Gold with Others: Title Deed to Kingdom = Negotiator
- Jacob's Palace - Meet Eternal Father: Sonship = Thanking God (negotiator)

(fulfill God/Man knowing - comprehending truth:

think for self = worthy of one's own Kingdom)

This illustration shows that "All Created Existence Comes" through the <u>Lord's Benevolent Force</u> (God becomes Man), <u>Personal God</u> (Man becomes God), and the <u>Lord God Almighty</u> (God and Man become One) to **Establish God, Society,** and One**self** on earth as **Divine Institutions** of **Truth** (God), **Law** (society), and **Will** (self). The "Job" of the "Benevolent Force (duty)" is to <u>Establish a Redeeming Church</u> (Jerusalem/Rome) on **Earth** through the **Nature of Bread and Wine** to teach the **Human Race** (ignorance) the **Difference** between **Good and Evil** (wisdom). The "Job" of the "Personal God (responsibility)" is to <u>Establish a Righteous Government</u> (Rome) on **Earth** through the **Nature of Truth** and **Law** to **Teach** the **Human Race** (cowardice) the **Difference** between **Right** and **Wrong** (courage). Finally, the "Job" of the "Lord God Almighty (authority)" is to <u>Establish a Divine Home</u> (Jerusalem) on **Earth** through the **Nature of Will** and **Love** to **Teach** the **Human Race** (greed) the **Difference** between **God's Will and Man's Will** (generosity). During "Christ's 1st Advent (dying to self)," **He Offered-up the 1st Sacrifice** (redemption) in the **Form** of the **Divine Messiah** to **Create Baptism** (pay for capital sins). Secondly, during "Christ's 2nd Advent (born-again)," <u>He will Offer-up</u> the **2nd Sacrifice** (salvation) in the **Form** of the **Holy Church** to **Create Confession** (pay for mortal sins).

Finally, during "Christ's 3rd Advent (set free)," <u>He will Offer-up</u> the **3rd Sacrifice** (rewards) in the **Form** of the **Righteous World** to **Create Communion** (pay for venial sins). Out of these "Three Advents (priest/thief/judge)" and <u>Their Associated Sacrifices,</u> the **Whole Human Race** is to be **Saved** (capital/mortal/venial sin) and **Brought** into the **Kingdom of God** (God/Heaven/earth).

1. **1st Advent** - <u>Priest on a Donkey:</u> Dies to Self ....Saving Sinner/being saved
   - Offer to be Saved - Worthy of being Righteous Citizen on Earth (new body)
   - Fulfillment of the Benevolent Force (energy/life) - Saved from Capital Sins
2. **2nd Advent** - <u>Thief in the Night:</u> Born-again .... Creating Saint/saving self
   - Earn Own Salvation - Worthy of being Holy Saint in Heaven (eternal life)

- Fulfillment of the Personal God (matter/death) - Saved from Mortal Sins
3. **3rd Advent** - <u>Just Judge on Cloud:</u> Set Free ....Rewarded Sonship/saving others
   - Rewarded for Saving Others - Worthy of being Son of God within God's Kingdom (own Kingdom)
   - Fulfillment of Lord God Almighty (creation/resurrection) - Saved from Venial Sins

In contrast to the "Chosen People," <u>Humanity would be Blessed</u> with a great **Messiah of Love**, the **Eternal Intercessor/Interpreter/Negotiator** of all men, to **Teach the Gentiles God's <u>Spiritual Truths</u>** of Eternal Existence within the **Royal Household of Their Creator.** The "Jewish Messiah" would be both the <u>Son of God</u> (filled/divinity) and the <u>Son of Man</u> (empty divinity/fill death) **Commissioned to Transform <u>Humanity</u>** into a **Living Prayer of Love** (saints). In this process of "Creating Living Prayers," <u>Jesus Conquers Death</u> (take-sin) and <u>Christ</u> is bringing forth a **New Paradise on Earth** (give divinity). This means that to literally return the "Title Deed of Mother Earth" back to its <u>Original Owners</u> and to **Transform** the ""Face of the Earth" back to its <u>Original State,</u> the **Sin-debt of Man** would have to be **Paid in Full.** This most "Sacred Mission of Jesus Christ (chaos)" would require the <u>Lord to Teach the Gentile Nations</u> the difference between the earthly **Jewish Faith** (man's law) and the Heavenly **Christian Faith** (God's Law) that are to be **Made One** in the **Person of Christ Jesus** (order).

We see that "God Plans to Remove" this <u>Divine Defect</u> (flaw of ignorance) through **His New Perfect Justice System** (Calvary), via **His Mystical Healing Process,** coupled with the **Redemptive Commission** of <u>Jesus Christ</u> for the **Redemption of All Men.** Once "Transformed" by <u>Jesus Christ,</u> then a **Person can Inherit** his own **Jewish Sonship Charter,** thereby **<u>Fulfilling</u>** both his **Spirit** (Heaven) and his **Flesh** (earth). This, in effect, means the "Jews would be Sacrificed" to <u>Honor</u> the <u>Flesh of God,</u> while the "Christians are to be Sacrificed" to <u>Honor</u> the <u>Spirit of God,</u> making the **Spirit** and the **Flesh One** (new nature) in **Divine Truth, Law,** and **Will.**

We now see that springing forth from the "Sacrifices of God (give divinity) and Man (take-sin)" is a whole <u>New Hope</u> rising out of the **Depths of Human Despair** to bring forth the **Glorious Spirit of God <u>Transformed</u>** into a **New Creation of Perfect Love** (new nature). The Lord is exhorting the "Blessed Virgin" to apply <u>Her Healing Hands</u> of <u>Mother's Love</u> to the **Painful Wounds of Man** in honor of the **Death of Her most Beloved Son,** *Jesus Christ.* The commission of the "Blessed Virgin" is to establish and run a <u>New Perfect School of Divine Truths</u> or the **Little Red School House** based on **Two Mystical Schools of Thought**: 1) The <u>Jewish Destiny</u> of **Human Chaos** (animal/lawlessness), and 2) The <u>Christian Free Will</u> of **Divine Order** (robot/law). This reveals that Her most ardent duty will be to "Teach God's Children" the difference between **Right and Wrong** by explaining the <u>Virtues</u> (true wisdom) of **Divine Order** (man's loyalty) and the <u>Faults</u> (false wisdom) associated with **Human Chaos** (disloyalty). Our "Queen Mother" of the <u>Divine Will</u> is certain to arrive soon to <u>Teach All Her Children</u> the way to **Perfect Faith,** leading them along the Lord's **Pathway of Perfection** to be transformed into **Soldiers-of-the-Light** or **Righteous Citizens** (fleshly faults) and **Living Prayers of Love** or **Holy Saints** (spiritual virtues).

This most idyllic state perfectly describes the "Principal Duty" of the Lord's most Holy Universal Church as it awaits the return of its **Eternal Savior,** the Lord **Jesus Christ.** This means the enduring "Saints of Patience" must see themselves Forever Presenting Their **Never-fading Flag of Hope** to symbolize man's **Blessing of Knowing** and his belief in **Christ's Victory** over **Death,** the **Grave,** and **Damnation** (hell). This symbol of the "Lord's Earthly Flame" of Divine Love shines forth to **Ensure God** that the **Christian Faith** will one day **Fulfill its Pledge** to **Patiently Wait** **No Matter How Long It Might Take** (perfect faith). The "Faithful in Christ" and Their Heirs will **Wait until Hell Freezes Over** to again **See Their Savior,** whereby the **Forces of Death** are finally placed under **Christ's Royal Feet of Glory Forevermore.** At the "End of Life," Everyone will See that the Church's Intercession (worship), the Government's Interpretations (praise), and the Home's Negotiations (thanksgiving) were **Instrumental** in bringing forth **God's Kingdom of Glory.**

We must understand that the "Almighty" will stand behind His Sacred Promise to **End** the long arduous **Pilgrimage of the Wandering Christian** by **Returning His Son** in both **Glory and Honor** as our **King of Kings** (earth) and our **Lord of Lords** (Heaven). This clearly indicates that the "Prime Directive" of Christ's Church and every Faithful Christian **Soldier-of-the-Light** (fights sin) is to **Fix his Gaze** upon the **Coming of the Lord** and the **Raising** of the **New Kingdom of Glory.** Recall that the "Book of Revelation" states that When the **Lord God Almighty** simply **Walks,** then the **Thunder Cracks,** the **Lightning Flashes,** and the **Earth quakes** under **His Mighty Feet.** This "Awesome Power of God" Sets the Stage for bringing forth **God's Three Institutions** of **Home/Government/Church** onto the **Earth** (baby), in **Heaven** (teenager), and within **God's Kingdom** (adult).

Obviously, the "Human Race is Hoping" that this Awesome Power of God will be **Transferred** through the **Nature of Jesus Christ** to **Man's Earthly Throne** so that the **Human Race** can **Master the Life-experience** to bring forth **God's Baby Farm, Divine School,** and **Sonship Training** onto the **Earth.** The point is that "Human Existence" is centered on Educating the Mind, Training the Heart, and Filling the Soul with **God's Wisdom, Courage, and Generosity** to **Set the Human Race Free** from **Sin, Evil, and Death.** We see that "Each of God's Children" must Escape his **Own Sin-nature, Life's Worldly Temptations,** and **Lucifer's Demonic Possession** to **Discover God's Doorway of Freedom** which **Leads to a New-life of Prosperity.** This means that "Escaping Worldly Evil" means Obtaining **God's Supernatural Powers** which will **Allow Mankind** to **Overcome Lucifer and his Demons.** In short, "Mankind must Acquire" God's Thunderous Voice, His Lightning Signature, and His Earth-quaking Seal to **Force the Forces of Sin, Evil, and Death** to **Bow to** **Man's Command** and to **Part from Them** into the **Abyss of Oblivion.** This "Desire" for Supernatural Power **Drives the Human Race** to **Hope, Study,** and finally, **Know God's Right** from **Man's Wrong,** thereby **Setting him Free** from *Ignorance, Cowardice, Greed, and Selfishness Forever.* The idea is that "God's Voice" is to Teach His Babies to be **Obedient** (wisdom); "His Signature" will Guide His Teenagers to **Leadership** (courage); and "His Seal" will Free His Adults to **Think for Themselves** (generosity).

The following tabular information indicates that "Thunder" is <u>God's Voice</u> (negotiation), "Lightning" is <u>God's Signature</u> (interpretation), and "Earthquakes" are <u>God's Seal</u> (intercession), and each is **Calling the Human Race** from **Death into New-life**:

Thunder is God's Voice; Lightning is God's Signature;
and Earthquakes, God's Seal Over Nature
(voice is home negotiation, signature is government interpretation,
seal is church intercession)

Home (earth)	1. **Thunder** - <u>God's Voice:</u> Silent Anger = Good Faith Handshake .... Know God	
	• Escape from Egypt - Remove Slavery: Sin-nature = See Limitations	
	• Baby's Hope - Baby Farm: Learning Right from Wrong.	
	• Best Guess	
Righteousness	• Prayerful Hope	**Home's Negotiations**
	• Lucky Guess	

(defeat ignorance - become righteous citizen on earth: receive new body)

Government (Heaven)	2. **Lightning** - <u>God's Signature:</u> Vocal Rage = Written Contract ...Love God	
	• Escape from Desert - Remove Servanthood: Worldly Temptations = See Potential	
	• Teenager's Study - Divine School: Learning Good from Evil	
	• Hypothetical Research	
Holiness	• Knowing the Truth	**Government's Interpretations**
	• Creating Solutions	

(defeat cowardice - become holy saint in Heaven: receive eternal life)

Church (Kingdom)	3. **Earthquake** - <u>God's Seal:</u> Striking Wrath = Solemn Vow ...... Serve God	
	• Escape from Selfishness - Enter Freedom: Demonic Possession = See Self-worth	
	• Adult's Knowledge - Sonship Training: Learning God's Will/man's will	
	• Experiencing Survival	
Perfection	• Becoming Life	**Church's Intercession**
	• Changing into New-life	

(defeat greed - become perfect son within Kingdom: receive royal kingdom)

This illustration shows that by "Defeating Ignorance," "Cowardice," and "Greed," a <u>Person can be Set Free</u> from **Jewish Slavery** (Egypt) and **God's Servanthood** (desert) to **Reach Freedom** (selfishness). This "Journey" from <u>Childhood to Adulthood</u> **Transforms** the **Human Race** from an **Ignorant Fool** into a **Wise Man of Honor** who **Strives** to **Master the Life-experience** and **Find** the <u>**Meaning, Purpose, and Value**</u> of God's **Eternal-existence**. This means that a "Baby" will make his <u>Best Guess,</u> then **Prays** that he is **Right,** and finally, **Believes** he's a **Genius** when his **Lucky Guess Turns Out** to be

Right On, thereby **Making him** a **King of All he Surveys**. Secondly, the "Teenager" Performs Hypothetical Research, comes to **Know the Truth**, and then **Derives a Master Solution** for **All Men's Problems Convincing him** that **he Alone has All Knowledge** and is **All Powerful**. Finally, the "Adult" Experiences Survival, then **Masters the Life-experience** by **Becoming a Living Expert First Hand** to **Comprehend** the **Physical, Spiritual,** and **Mystical Worlds of God** by **Changing** from **Death into New-life**.

Yes! There are "Three Phases of Life (ignorance/cowardice/greed)" from Baby to Adult. We must **All Experience Ignorance** before we can **Come to Know Wisdom** since **Every Wise Man** is **Smart Where the Skin is Off**, because **No One** can **Meet God in Some Silly Book,** even if it's the **Bible**. The point is that "We must All Meet God (Mount Calvary)" in His Thunder (voice/righteous), Lightning (signature/holy), and Earthquakes (seal/perfect) to **Really Know God's Right from man's wrong**. "Jesus Christ" Went to Calvary to **Get God's Handshake of Agreement** (physical bond), **His Contract of Life** (spiritual bond), and **His Solemn Word of Eternal Ownership** (mystical bond) for **All Those Who** would **Sacrifice Their Lives** to bring forth **God's Kingdom of Glory** (redemption of others). We see that this "Coming Kingdom" allows each of "God's Children" to be Transformed from **Nothing to All** in **Mind, Heart, Soul, Life-force,** and **Nature** to **Master Knowledge** (omniscient), **Change** (omnifarious), **Presence** (omnipresent), **Power** (omnipotent), and **Creation** (omnific), **All in the Name of Jesus Christ**. In the case of "God, He can Perform" His Divine Works Instantly as He is a **Spirit** with **No Time or Space Restraints** (BIG BANG), but when **Placing These** same **Divine Abilities** within a **Time/Space Continuum,** suddenly, an **Instant Creation Takes Seven Thousand Years of Human Toil**.

This "Conversion" from Divinity to Humanity is **Occurring on Earth** as the **Forces** of **God, Angels, and Men** become **One** within the **Lord's Truth** (mind), **Law** (heart), **Will** (soul), **Love** (life-force), and **Nature** (self). "Converting" Each Child's Mind from **Ignorance to Wisdom** on Earth, in Heaven, and within **God's Kingdom Takes** so much **Time and Effort** on the part of **God, Angels, and Saints**. Secondly, "Converting" Each Child's Heart from **Cowardice to Courage** on Earth, in Heaven, and within **God's Kingdom Takes** so much **Patience** on the part of **God, Angels, and Saints**. Thirdly, "Converting" Each Child's Soul from **Greed to Generosity** on Earth, in Heaven, and within **God's Kingdom Takes** so much **Suffering** on the part of **God, Angels, and Saints**. Fourthly, "Converting" each Child's Life-force from **Selfishness to Unselfishness** on Earth, in Heaven, and within **God's Kingdom Takes** so much **Forgiveness** on the part of **God, Angels, and Saints**. Finally, "Converting" each Child's Nature from **Sinfulness to Holiness** on Earth, in Heaven, and within **God's Kingdom Takes** so much **Sanctifying Grace** on the part of **God, Angels, and Saints**. It should now make sense that "God has Many Dimensions of Existence" Ranging from **Easy to Understand, Reaching All the Way** to the **Impossible to Understand** based on being either a **Negative** (0%), **Positive** (1%), **Merged** (50%), or **Becoming** (100%) **Force**.

The following tabular information indicates the "Process" by which God's Children are **Converted** into **All Knowing, All Changing, All Present, All Powerful,** and **All Creative Beings Worthy** of the **Respect of God**:

God's Children become All Knowing, All Changing, All Present, All Powerful, and All Creative

(omniscient is known/Omnifarious is change/omnipresent
is present/omnipotent is power/omnific is creative)

Mind
(truth)

1. **All Knowing** - <u>Omniscient:</u> Baby Level of Growth ....Knowledge
   - Calling - Negative Force: Conversion of the Body (free redemption)
   - Home - *Transfigured Body*: Wise ————————Earthly Life – Exterior
   - Saints (good) - Passive Skills
   - Mind - Sin-nature becomes Righteous-nature
   - Damned (bad) - Active Skills

   (free title deed to earth - passport of life: becoming a righteous citizen)

Heart
(law)

2. **All Changing** - <u>Omnifarious:</u> Teenage Level of Growth ...Self-awareness
   - Enlightenment - Positive Force: Conversion of Eternal Life (earned salvation)
   - Church - *Glorified Body*: Courageous—— Heavenly Life - Interior
   - Angel (Heaven) - Passive Skills
   - Heart - Worldly Temptations become Holy-nature
   - Demon (Hell) - Active Skills

   (earned title deed to Heaven - ticket of saintly life: becoming a holy saint)

Soul
(will)

3. **All Present** - <u>Omnipresent:</u> Adult Level of Growth ......Consciousness
   - Awakening - Merging Force: Conversion of Royal Kingdom (bonus rewards)
   - Government - *Mystical Body*: Generosity——Kingdom Life - In/Out
   - Christ (spirit) - Passive Skills
   - Soul - Demonic Possession becomes Perfect-nature
   - Jesus (flesh) - Active Skills

   (bonus title deed to Kingdom - trip money of angelic life: becoming a son of man)

Life-force
(love)

4. **All Powerful** - <u>Omnipotent:</u> Wise Man Level of Growth ...Sentience
   - Indwelling - Becoming Force: Conversion of Oneself (thinking for self)
   - Self - *Divine Body*: Unselfishness ————Personal Life - Becoming
   - God (intellect) - Passive Skill
   - Life-force - Evil Spirit-nature becomes Holy Spirit-nature
   - Man (emotions) - Active Skills

   (taking title deed to Oneself - luggage of divine life: becoming a son of God)

Nature
(choice)

5. **All Creative** - <u>Omnific:</u> Free Man Level of Growth ....Thinking
   - Manifesting - God Force: Conversion into God
   - God - *Bodiless*: Fairness ————————God's Life - Infinity
   - Triune Natures (illusion)
   - Nature - Godly-nature becomes Free-nature for the Taking

- Triune Persons (reality)

(owning title deed to God - arriving at destination as God: becoming God-like)

This illustration shows that each of "God's Children (babies)" is to be <u>Called</u> (knowing) to experience **Living in a Body** to know the **Value of Free Redemption** (title deed to earth) and the blessing of receiving his own **New Transfigured Body** (wisdom). Secondly, each "Child (teenager)" shall be <u>Enlightened</u> (self-awareness) to experience **Human Life** to know the **Value of Earning Salvation** (title deed to Heaven) and the blessing of receiving his own **New Glorified Body** (courage). Thirdly, each "Child (adult)" shall be <u>Awakened</u> (consciousness) to experience **Angelic Life** to know the **Value of Bonus Rewards** (title deed to Kingdom) and the blessing of receiving his own **New Mystical Body** (generosity). Fourthly, each "Child (wise man)" shall be <u>In-dwelled</u> (sentience) to live a **Divine Life** and know the **Value of Thinking for Himself** (title deed to self) and the blessing of receiving his own **New Divine Body** (thinking). Finally, each "Child (free man)" shall become a <u>Manifestation</u> (imaginative) of God to experience **Personal Creation** to know the **Value of Ownership** (title deed to created life) and the blessing of receiving his own **New Body of Christ** (creating).

Once a person receives a "Transfigured Body (mind)," it will also house his <u>Guardian</u> Saint and his Guardian Damned Forever so that they might live as **One** (earth) uniting **Earth, Heaven,** and **Hell** into one **Physical Life-force** (all knowing). Secondly, once a person receives a "Glorified Body (heart)," it will also house his <u>Guardian Angel</u> and his <u>Guardian Demon</u> forever so that they might live as **One** (Heaven) uniting **Earth, Heaven,** and **Hell** into one **Spiritual Life-force** (all changing). Thirdly, once a person receives a "Mystical Body (soul)," it will also house <u>God's Son, Christ</u> and <u>Mary's Son, Jesus Forever</u> so that they might live as **One** (Kingdom) uniting **Earth, Heaven,** and **Hell** into one **Mystical Life-force** (all present). Fourthly, once a "Person Receives" a <u>Divine Body</u> (life-force), it will also **House God's Intellect** (wisdom) and **Man's Emotions** (love) so **that They** might **Live as One** (Self) **Uniting Earth, Heaven,** and **Hell** into **One Divine Life-force** (all powerful). Finally, once a "Person Receives" a <u>Bodiless Form</u> (nature), it will also **House God's Triune Nature** (illusion) and **God's Triune Persons** (reality) so **that They might Live** as One (infinity) **Uniting Earth, Heaven,** and **Hell** into **One Bodiless Life-force** (all creative). Through these "Five Bodies," <u>God</u> (Kingdom), <u>Angels</u> (Heaven), and <u>Men</u> (earth) become **One** (survival/truth/love/choice) in **Trillion Times a Trillion Unbreakable Unions <u>Reaching All the Way</u>** to **Infinite Perfection.**

Out of these "Unions," a <u>Person can Obtain</u> a **Free Title Deed to Earth** (redemption) as a **Passport to Human Life**, thereby **Allowing him** to become a **<u>Righteous Citizen</u>** (new body) within the **Physical Creation of Human Existence**. Secondly, out of these "Unions," a <u>Person can Earn his Own</u> **Title Deed to Heaven** (salvation) as **His Ticket to Angelic Life**, thereby **Allowing him** to become a **<u>Holy Saint</u>** (eternal life) within the **Spiritual Creation of Heavenly Existence.** Thirdly, also out of these "Unions," a <u>Person can Obtain</u> **Bonus Rewards to God's Kingdom** (rewards) to **Earn Trip Money** to a **Divine Life,** thereby **Allowing him** to become a **<u>Son of God</u>** (kingdom) within the **Mystical Creation of Divine Existence.** Fourthly, from these "Many Unions," a Person can Learn to **Think for Himself** (imagination) and **Pack** his **Luggage of Godly Life**, thereby **Allowing him** to become **Self-reliant** (dream world) with the **Divine Creation of Godly Existence**. Finally, from these "Infinite Number of Unions," a Person can Transform into a **God Nature** (not the God) to **Journey** to his **Final Destination of Life**, thereby **Allowing him** to become **Set Free** (free choice) within the **Never-created Life-force** of **Infinite Existence**.

Via each of these "Five Stages" of Growth and Maturity, **Nothingness** (illusion) can become **Everything** (reality) as it is **Blessed** (righteous), **Anointed** (holy), **Sanctified** (sonship), **Consecrated** (self), and **Perfected** (God-like) by **God** through the **Lord's Home** (natures), **Church** (persons), and **Government** (trinity). Now, it becomes clear that the "Life-experience" is an Eternal War Game since the **Forces of Growth** are **Fighting** the **Gradational Forces of Death** in an **Unending Battle** over **What is Best for God** and **What is Best for God's Kingdom**. The "War of Spirit (union)" and "Flesh (division)" on Earth is an **Expression** of the **Dividing** of the **Will of God** caused by the **Maturing of His Divine Son** upon the **Lord's Tree of Death** at **Mount Calvary**, where **All Things** were **Divided**, thereby **Creating** a **New Perfect Justice System** of **Divine Truth**. This impossible "Divine Contradiction (paradox)" is Expressed as a **Natural Manifestation** of the **Broken Nature of Man** as his **Soul is Released** from its **Eternal Bondage of Death** (hell). We see that "Half of God's Triune Nature" becomes Human (liberal/chaos) and is **Destined to Worship** the **Person** of **Jesus Christ** as **Mankind's God of Flesh** (illusion/division) or **Human God**, while the "Other Half of God's Triune Nature" Remains Divine (conservative/order) to **Forever Worship** the **Person** of **Christ Jesus** as **Mankind's God of Spirit** (reality/union) or **Divine Man**.

Upon this most subtle point, this "Entire Discourse is Founded," Opening Up a **New Spiritual Dimension** in **Understanding** the **Triune Nature of God** in **Flesh** (Jesus/Son of Man), in **Spirit** (Christ/Son of God), **Soul** (Jesus Christ/human), and in **Life-force** (Christ Jesus/divine). The idea is that the "Human Race is Receiving" Three Redemptions: **One** of the **Flesh** to **Receive a New Body** (destiny); one of the **Spirit** to **Receive an Eternal Life** (destiny/free will); and **One** of the **Soul** to **Receive a Personal Kingdom** (free will); and finally, **One** of the **Life-force** to be **Set Free** (imagination/dreamland). This means that as "Babies," We are being Called to **Submit to God's Law** (obey); while as "Teenagers," We are being Told to **Master Faith** (copy); and finally, as "Adults," We are being Asked to **Create a New Truth** (thinking). The hard part comes with "Finding the Pathway" to These Three Redemptions, where the **Mind** (spirit) can be **Redeemed** (free/life), the **Heart** can be **Saved** (earned/body), and the **Soul** can be **Rewarded** (bonus/kingdom). Unfortunately, to enter this strange "State of Redemption," a Person must become a Slave to God's Divine Will through **His Son's Holy Church** (altar/Peter's Touch) via **His Total Submission** (dying to self). This act of "Obedience (submission)" Leads to Establishing a **Person's Perfect Faith** in **Divine Truth**, thereby **Allowing Him** to **Grow** (flesh) and **Mature** (spirit) until he can **Think for himself** (knowing). The Lord is revealing here that "We are Redeemed by Law (Jews/baby)" to Receive a **New Body** (destiny). "We are Saved by Faith (Christian/teenager)" to Receive an **Eternal Life** (destiny/free will). Finally, "We are Rewarded by Knowing (Saint/adult)" to <u>Receive **Our Own** **Personal Kingdom**</u> (free will).

1. **Redemption by Law** - <u>Purify Grave</u> (flesh): Receive New Body ....See Limitations
   - Fulfill God's Law of Obedience - Free Divine Flesh: Heaven on Earth
2. **Salvation by Faith** - <u>Purify Host</u> (spirit): Receive Eternal Life .... See Potential
   - Fulfill Man's Faith in God's Love - Earned Holy Spirit: Paradise in Heaven
3. **Rewarded by Knowing** - <u>Purify Life</u> (soul): Receive Own Kingdom ... See Self-worth
   - Fulfill God's/Man's Knowing - Rewarded with Thinking for Oneself: Kingdom of Glory

Now, we can relate this "Need to Master" the <u>Law, Faith,</u> and <u>Knowing Concepts</u> by **Relating** them to **Christ's Three Advents**: 1) <u>Priest on a Donkey</u> (1st advent) - Submit Free Will to Destiny (spiritual nature), 2) <u>Thief in the Night</u> (2nd advent) - Destiny and Free Will are Balanced or made One (physical nature), and 3) <u>Just Judge on a Cloud</u> (3rd advent) - Free Will to Think for Self (mystical nature).

The following tabular information indicates that there are "Three Redemptions of Man," giving him <u>New Body</u> (law/earth), an <u>Eternal Life</u> (faith/Heaven), and one's <u>Own Kingdom </u>(knowing/Kingdom):

Three Redemptions Giving a Person a New Body,
Eternal Life, and his Own Kingdom via Christ
(mastering God's law of obedience, faith of trying, and
knowing by thinking correctly via mind of Christ)

Destiny
1. **1st Redemption is Body** - <u>Redeemed for Free</u> (baby) ......Obey the Law
   - 1st Advent - Free Physical Redemption: Baptism = Ownership of Earth
   - Physical Nature - Submit Free Will unto Destiny (self): Selfishness
   - Good News brings Obedience - Learning Right from Wrong: Fulfill Law
   - Body becomes New Body which becomes Divine Body: Elementary Level

(earth has one gift to give - gift of life: babies see the meaning of life/existence)

Free Will/
Destiny
2. **2nd Redemption is Life** - <u>Saved by Good Works</u> (teenager)...Fulfill One's Faith
   - 2nd Advent - Earned Spiritual Salvation: Confession = Ownership of Heaven
   - Spiritual Nature - Destiny and Free Will are Balanced (one): Unselfish
   - Gospel Message brings Faith - Learning Good from Evil: Fulfill Faith
   - Life becomes Eternal Life which becomes Divine Life: High School Level

(Heaven has two gifts to give - eternal life and new body: teenager sees the purpose/serve)

Free Will 3. **3rd Redemption is Kingdom** - <u>Rewarded by God</u> (adult)....Knowing
Divine Truth
- 3rd Advent - Bonus of Mystical Rewards: Communion = Ownership of Kingdom
- Mystical Nature - Free Will to Think for Self (others): Sharing
- Doctrinal Truths - Learning God's Will/Man's Will: Fulfill Knowing
- Earth becomes Heaven which becomes God's Divine Kingdom: College Level

    (Kingdom has three gifts to give - divine life/divine
    body/divine kingdom: adult sees value/happiness)

This illustration shows that "God has Established" <u>His **_Grand Design_**</u> upon a **Triune Level Process** taking each of **His Children** through <u>**Three Dimensions**</u> of **Physical** (earth), **Spiritual** (Heaven), and **Mystical** (Kingdom) **Existence**. This leads us to believe that the "Three Rooms" within the <u>Mosaic Tabernacle</u> represent **Man's Physical** (sunlight), **Spiritual** (candlelight) and **Mystical** (divine light) **Dimensions of Life** in the form of **God's Elementary** (law), **High School** (faith), and **College** (knowing) **Systems of Education**. The "Human Race" is locked inside of a <u>Physical Creation</u>, like a <u>Caterpillar</u> and with the coming of **Jesus Christ**, a **New Doorway** is opened into **God's Spiritual Dimension of Existence** like a **Butterfly**, thereby offering one and all a **Chance to Live Forever**. This means that every "Statement" or "Concept" expressed within the <u>Bible Text</u> can apply to the **Life of Christ** and to **God's Blessing** of a **Free Redemption** (body), **Earned Salvation** (life), and **Bonus Reward** (kingdom).

The idea here is to see that "Everything" on <u>Earth is Free</u> (free redemption) and the <u>Goal</u> is to **Worship God** (give life) by **Dying to One's Selfishness** (submission) as reflected in **Christ's Crucifixion** (fixed frame of reference/law). Secondly, we see that "Everything" in <u>Heaven must be Earned</u> (earned salvation) and the <u>Goal</u> is to **Praise God** (give wealth) via a **Person's New rebirth** (life) bringing forth a **Soul's Unselfish Nature** (unto thine own self be true) as reflected in **Christ's Resurrection** (relative focused existence/faith). Finally, we see that "Everything" in the <u>Kingdom is a Bonus</u> (bonus reward) and the <u>Goal</u> is to **Thank God** (give labor) via one's **Balanced Thinking** (guilty conscience) as reflected in **Christ's Ascension** (perception of reality/knowing). It should now all make sense that one's "Redemption by Law" brings forth his **New Body** (earth); "Salvation by Faith" brings forth his **Eternal Life** (Heaven); and his "Bonus Rewards by Knowing" brings forth his **Royal Kingdom** (Kingdom).

The following tabular information indicates that "Earth is Free," "Heaven is Earned," and the "Kingdom is a Bonus" so that the task of every man is to **Die to Selfishness (life)**, **Earn a New Unselfish Nature** (body), and receive a **Balanced Mind** (thinking/home):

**Earth is Free, Heaven is Earned, and Kingdom is a
Bonus If One Masters Law, Faith, and Knowing**
(called to die to selfishness, earn new unselfish
nature, receive a balanced mind from Christ)

Redeemed (body)	1.	**Earth is Free** - <u>Death to Selfishness:</u> Submission = Receive Life …Knowledge
		• Crucifixion - Fixed Frame of Reference: ***Master the Law*** = Obedience
		• Learning Right from Wrong - Becoming Righteous (kingship)
		• Worship God - Baby Attends "Elementary School:" God becomes Man
Law		• Give Life - Dying to Self: Conquer Sin-nature = Righteous King
		• Physical Life - Baby's World of Good Luck: Government
		• Spiritual Eternal Life - Baby's House of Blessings: Church
		• Mystical Divine Life - Baby's Heart of Love: Home

(God's free gift of eternal life - rejecting selfishness to grow up by listening)

Saved (life)	2.	**Heaven is Earned** - <u>Earn New Unselfish Nature:</u> True to Self = Receive Body … Self-awareness
		• Resurrection - Relative Focused Existence: ***Master Faith*** = Belief
		• Learning Good from Evil - Becoming Holy (priesthood)
		• Praise God - Teenager Attends "High School:" Man becomes God
Faith		• Give Wealth - Born-again: Conquer Worldly Temptations = Holy Priest
		• Human Body - Teenager's World of Good Luck: Government
		• Transfigured Body - Teenager's House of Blessings: Church
		• Divine Body - Teenager's Heart of Love: Home

(Man earns a new body - accept new lifestyle to become mature by learning)

Reward (kingdom)	3.	**Kingdom is Bonus** - <u>Balanced Mind:</u> Guilty Conscience = Receive Kingdom......................Consciousness
		• Ascension - Perception of Reality: ***Master Knowing*** = Wisdom
		• Learning God's Will from man's will - Becoming Perfect (sonship)
		• Thanking God - Adult Attends "College:" God and Man become One
Knowing		• Give Labor – Set Free: Conquer Demonic Possession = Perfect Son
		• Earthly Kingdom - Adult's World of Good Luck: Government
		• Heavenly Kingdom - Adult's House of Blessings: Church
		• Kingdom of Glory - Adult's Heart of Love: Home

(God/Man given bonus of royal kingdom - thinking for oneself to be set free)

This illustration shows that "Life on Earth" is about <u>Facing</u> (baby) a **Person's Crucifixion** (slaughter of innocence); while "Life in Heaven" is about <u>Experiencing</u> (teenager) **His Resurrection** (rebirth); and then "Life in the Kingdom" is about <u>Knowing</u> (adult) <u>God</u> through **His Ascension** (awakening). Obviously, being "Crucified (Lucifer's test)" <u>Teaches a Person</u> **God's Right** from **Man's Wrong** to **Make** him **Righteous** (kingship) before **Man** (earth) to **<u>Change His Nature</u>** from **Human to Divine.** Secondly, experiencing "Resurrection (God's judgment)" <u>Teaches a Person</u> **God's Good** from **Man's Evil** to **Make** him **Holy** (priesthood) before **God** (Heaven) to **<u>Wash Away His Sins</u>** to **Change Sinfulness to Holiness.** Finally, "Mastering Ascension (self-evaluation)" <u>Teaches a Person</u> **God's Will** from **man's will** to **Make** him **<u>Perfect</u>** (sonship) within **His Own Self** (kingdom) to **Transform** an **Ignorant Fool** into **<u>One Who</u>** can **Think for himself.**

In this explanation, we are being told that "Babies (mind)" must <u>Face</u> the <u>Slaughter of Innocence</u> by **Attending** the **Earthly Elementary School of Life** (Virgin Mary); "Teenagers (heart)" must <u>Experience</u> a <u>Spiritual Rebirth</u> by **Attending Heaven's High School of Eternal Life** (Saint Joseph); and finally, "Adults (soul)" must <u>Experience</u> a <u>New State of Awakening</u> by **Attending** the **Kingdom's College of Divine Life.** Yes! "Life is all About" "<u>Mastering the Law</u> (life/obedience)," "Mastering Faith (body/love)," and "<u>Mastering Knowing</u> (kingdom/life)" through the **Worship** of the **Lord God Almighty** (give life), **Praise** of **God's Son** (give wealth), and a **Person's Thanksgiving** before **God's Spirit** (give labor). We see that "If a Person" can <u>Offer-up his Life</u> (right/wrong), <u>Wealth</u> (good/evil), and <u>Labor</u> (God's/Man's Wills) to **God** and is **Willing to Take** his **Sonship Training without Complaint,** then he can **Expect to Obtain** a **New Body, Eternal Life,** and his **Own Kingdom of Glory.** The idea here is that "Sacrificing One's Life" means <u>Dying to Self</u> to **Obtain Physical Life** (luck) on **Earth** (Heaven on earth), **Spiritual Eternal Life** (blessings) in **Heaven** (Heaven), and a **Mystical Divine Life** (love) in **God's Kingdom** (God's glory). Secondly, while on "Earth," a <u>Person is Given</u> a **Free Human Body**; then in "Heaven," an <u>Earned Transfigured Body</u> (blessings); and finally, in the "Kingdom," a <u>Son of God Receives</u> a **Mystical Body** (love) in **Gratitude** for a **Job Well Done.** Finally, a "Mature Son of God" can receive a <u>Title Deed</u> to the **Earth** (king of the Jews), then a <u>Title Deed</u> to **Heaven** (high priest of heaven), and finally, a <u>Title Deed</u> to his **Own Kingdom** (son of God) all in the name of **Graduating** from **God's Divine School of Higher Learning.**

Upon the completion of all the "Lord's Divine Requirements," a person can receive <u>God's Free Gift of Eternal Life</u> by rejecting his own **Selfishness** to **Grow-up by simply Listening** (obedience/lessons). Secondly, a person can "Earn a New Body" by accepting a <u>New Lifestyle</u> to become fully **Mature by Learning** the **Lessons of Life/blessings** taught by **Nature** (babies), **Men** (teenagers), **Angels** (adults), and **God** (wise men). Finally, a person can receive a "Bonus of a Kingdom" by <u>Thinking for himself</u> and become worthy of being **Set Free** from **Sin** (sin-nature), **Evil** (worldly temptations), and **Death** (demonic possession). Through each of these "Transitions of Life," a person can <u>Master the Life-experience</u> and come to **Know, Love,** and **Serve his God** by **Journeying** from **Nothing to All.**

This means that on "Earth," <u>Man is on a Journey</u> (growth/Christ) with **God becoming the Destination** (maturity/God). In "Heaven," <u>God is on His Journey</u> (growth/Jesus) with **Man becoming the Destination** (maturity/Man). Finally, in the "Kingdom," <u>God/Man are Traveling Together on an Eternal Journey</u> (death) with <u>Man/God becoming the Destination</u> (life). Now, we see that the "Human Race" is on a <u>Physical Journey of Growth</u> (childhood) in an attempt to reach its **Final Destination of Spiritual Maturity** (adulthood) based on **Total Submission** to **Christ Jesus.** We now see that our "Journey of Life" is about <u>Traveling</u> from <u>Nothing</u> (death) through **Five Dimensions of Existence** (experience) to be **Called/Enlightened/ Awakened/Indwelled/Freed** (sentient) via **God's Truth, Law, Will, and Love.** This allows a person to reach that **Ultimate State of All** (becoming perfect). It can now be seen that the "Ladder of Life" involves climbing <u>Five Dimensions of Perfection</u> with each **New Level** allowing a **Born-again Soul** to encounter its **Creator God** through its **Mind** (think of/called), **Heart** (speak to/enlightened), **Soul** (touch/awakened), **Life-force** (sup with/indwelled), and **Nature** (adopted by/freed).

We now know that by coming to "Meet, Know, and Love" <u>God</u> that a person can come to properly <u>Worship</u> (give life), <u>Praise</u> (give wealth), and <u>Thank</u> (give labor) his **Creator** for **All that He has Done** in removing his **Ignorance** (wisdom), **Cowardice** (courage), and **Greed** (generosity). We now see that when a person first comes into "Creation," he arrives in God's <u>Physical Dimension</u> (God thinks of child) to be placed upon the **Lord's Pathway of Destiny** (God is stranger) so that he might **Go in Search** of **God's Divine Truth**. Secondly, when "He Grows-up" enough to seek God in <u>Christ's Church,</u> he has entered God's <u>Spiritual Dimension</u> (God speaks to child) to be placed upon the **Lord's Pathway of Free Will** (God is acquaintance) as he **Goes in Search** of **God's Divine Law**. Thirdly, when he matures enough to seek God in "Man's Government," he has entered <u>God's Mystical Dimension</u> (God touches His child) to be placed upon the **Lord's Pathway of Righteousness** (God is friend) to **Go in Search** of **God's Divine Will**. Fourthly, when he becomes a wise man, he seeks God in "His Own Home" and he enters God's <u>Divine Dimension</u> (God sups with child) to be placed on the **Lord's Pathway of Holiness** (God is companion) so that he might reach **God's Throne** and find **God's Divine Love**. Finally, when he becomes a "Free Man," he seeks God in "Heaven" which allows him to enter <u>God's Personal Dimension</u> (God adopts child) to be placed on the **Lord's Pathway of Perfection** (Child becomes God) and the Lord then **Gives His Child** his **Own Divine Freedom** (independence). Through these "Five Cycles of <u>Growth</u> (flesh) and <u>Maturity</u> (spirit), a person can find the **Meaning of Life** (existence), the **Purpose of Life** (service), and his own **Value in Life** (happiness) for **Himself** (thinking).

The following tabular information indicates the "Five Dimensions" of <u>Growth</u> and <u>Maturity</u> needed for each **Child of God** to **Find the Lord's Truths** (physical/mind), **Laws** (spiritual/heart), **Will** (mystical/soul), **Love** (divine/life-force), and **Freedom** (Godly/nature) so that one day, he might become **One** in the **Divine Nature of God**:

The Five Dimensions of God are
Physical, Spiritual, Mystical, Divine, and Godly
(God thinks of child, speaks to child,
touches child, sups with child, and adopts child)

Truth   1. **Physical Dimension** - <u>God Thinks of Child</u> ......Lord Watches Child Struggling

(baby)
- Remove Capital Sins - Baptism: Baby becomes Man = Loving Mate (mind)
- Union of Two Fathers - Marriage Contract: Man's Needs and God's Wants
- Blood Union - Remove Ignorance, Create Wisdom: Learn Right from Wrong
- Abraham's Dowry is Virgin Bride/God's Bride Price is Groom's Divine Name

- Meaning of Life (existence) - Natural Order: Defeat Sin-nature, become Righteous
- Self-redemption - Being Saved: Prayers of Fear

(1st union is traveling the "Pathway of Destiny" to gain the knowledge of God)

Law
(teenager)

2. **Spiritual Dimension** - <u>God Speaks to Child</u>.......Lord Sees Child's Suffering
   - Remove Mortal Sins - Confession: God becomes Man = Loving Worship (heart)
   - Union of Couple - Betrothal: Man's Justification and God's Blessing
   - Death Union - Remove Cowardice, Create Courage: Learn Good from Evil
   - Church's Dowry is Submission/Jesus' Bride Price is Sacrifice
   - Purpose of Life (service) - Supernatural Order: Defeat Worldly Temptations, be Holy
   - Social-salvation - Saving Self: Devotions of Hope

(2nd union is traveling the "Pathway of Free Will" to become self-aware of God)

Will

(adult)

3. **Mystical Dimension** - <u>God Touches His Child</u> ....Lord Hears Child's Cries
   - Remove Venial Sins - Communion: Man becomes God = God Loves Child (soul)
   - Union of Friends - Wedding Supper: Man's Honor and God's Anointing
   - Damnation Union - Remove Greed, Create Generosity: Learn God's Will/man's will
   - Laity's Dowry is Prayer/Priesthood's Bride Price is Offering
   - Value of Life (happy) - Divine Order: Defeat Demonic Possession, become Perfect
   - Heavenly-rewards - Saving Others: Sacrifices of Commitment

(3rd union is traveling the "Pathway of Righteousness" to become conscious of God)

Love

(wise man)

4. **Divine Dimension** - <u>God Sups with His Child</u>.....Lord Recognizes Child's Covenant
   - Remove Wicked Faults - Save Souls: God/Man become One = Child Loves God (life-force)
   - Union of Families - Wedding Feast: Man's Glorification and God's Sanctification
   - Oblivion Union - Remove Selfishness, Create Unselfishness: Learn Reality/Illusion
   - Saint's Dowry is Dying to Self/Angel's Bride Price is New-life
   - Quality of Life (owner) - God's Order: Defeat Selfishness, become Free
   - Convert-evil - Saving God: Retribution of Selfishness

(4th union is traveling the "Pathway of Holiness" to become sentient in God)

Freedom	5.	**Godly Dimension** - <u>God Adopts Orphan Child</u>...Lord Comes to Help His Lost Child

Freedom | 5. **Godly Dimension** - <u>God Adopts Orphan Child</u>...Lord Comes to Help His Lost Child

(free man)
- Gain Virtuous Morals - Think for Self: Child becomes God = Child becomes Love (nature)
- Union of Kingdoms - Grandchildren: Man's Freedom and God's Consecration
- Resurrection Union - Remove Sin-nature, Create Holy Nature: Learn God from Man
- Illusion's Dowry is Knowing Wrong/Reality's Bride Price is Knowing Right
- Treasure of Life (multiply) - Paradoxical Order: Master Imagination, be Creative
- God's Beatific Vision – Set Free: Offerings of Worship

(5th union is traveling the "Pathway of Perfection" to become mature in God)

This illustration shows that each of "God's Children" must pass through the <u>Five Dimensions of Human Existence</u> to unite **Broken Man** (Abraham) with his **Perfect God** (Almighty) through his **Growth** (baby to free man levels) and **Maturity** (union between God and Man). The ancient Jews used the "Passover Meal" as a <u>Four Cup-Wedding Ceremony</u> (mass) to unite the **Two Fathers**, the **Couple** (bride/groom), the **Couple's Friends**, and the **Two Families** into one **New Community.** It was believed that through an "Arranged Marriage," the <u>Blessed Jewish Blood</u> could be kept **Pure and Holy before God** and still keep the **Wealthy Class in Power.** It can be seen that the "Union between God and Man" is also based on an <u>Arranged Marriage</u> between **Jesus Christ** and **His Bride,** the **Catholic Church,** to bring both **Heaven and Earth** (union) together into **One Perfect Family** (kingdom). This concept for creating "Family Unity" and "Strong Bonds" can be seen in the <u>Mastering</u> of God's **Five Dimensions** as a person becomes closer and closer to the <u>**Mind**</u> (knowledge/called), <u>**Heart**</u> (self-awareness/enlightened), <u>**Soul**</u> (consciousness/awakened), **Life-force** (sentience/indwelled), and **Nature** (thinking/set free) of the **Lord God Almighty** Himself.

In the previous chart, we see that there are "Five Unions," each calling a <u>Confused Child</u> of God onto a **Pathway of Awakening** and confronting the **Struggles of Life** to the point of coming to know **Himself,** his **Society,** and his **God.** This long journey of "Fear, Pain, and Ultimate Death" drives the whole <u>Human Race</u> to seek **God's Truths, God's Laws, God's Will, God's Love,** and **God's Nature** to reach that ultimate **Destination of Personal Freedom.** The idea is to see that these most "Painful Journeys" force a child to master God's **Five Orders of Existence**: 1) <u>Natural Order</u> - Physical Dimension: Baby Level = Fight Sin-nature, 2) <u>Supernatural Order</u> - Spiritual Dimension: Teenage Level = Fight Worldly Temptations, 3) <u>Divine Order</u> - Mystical Dimension: Adult Level = Fight Demonic Possession, 4) <u>God's Order</u> - Divine Dimension: Wise Man Level = Fight Personal Selfishness (faults), and 5) <u>Paradoxical Order</u> - Never-created Godly Dimension: Free Man Level = Master Imagination (creative ability).

By traveling these "Rocky Roads of Life," a <u>Person can Come</u> to **Recognize** the <u>Meaning of Life</u> (existence), <u>Purpose of Life</u> (service), and <u>Value of Life</u> (happiness) as they **Relate** to **Himself** (home), **Society** (government), and **God** (church). Each one of us must "Try to Overcome" Our Own Sin-nature, **Fight** the Temptations of the World, **Defeat** Demonic Possession, and **Face Our Own** Selfishness as **We Strive** to **Make Sense of It All** by **Developing** an **Awesome Imagination** to **See God as He Really Is** (creative force). This means that the "Life-experience" is Centered around becoming of **Greater and Greater Value** to **Oneself**, to **Society**, and to **God** by **Submitting His Spirit** (holiness) and **Sacrificing His Flesh** (righteousness) to the **Forces of Worship** (give life), **Praise** (give wealth), and **Thanksgiving** (give labor). The idea here is that "If We become of Service to God," He will One Day become of "Service to Us" by **Allowing Us** to **Break Our Chains of Ignorance, Open the Prison Doors of Cowardice,** and **Overpower** the **Guards of Greed** that **Keep Us All Imprisoned** in **Our Own Childish Fears.** The point that "God is Driving Home" here is that He Desires that **All of His Sons and Daughters** are **Expected to Follow Their Father** in **Fulfilling the Aims** of the **Family Business** which are based on **Imaginative Creation,** implying **Making the Babies** into **Bigger and Better Creations.** Only by "Mastering" the Five Dimensions of Life **can a Person Hope to Receive** a **Sufficient Number** of **Divine Gifts** to become **All Things** (God's flesh) to **All People** (God's spirit). In this way, "God's Light of Truth (Jesus Christ)" can Shine through the **Least of God's Creatures** to **Make him Great in God's Kingdom** by simply **Trying,** then **Trying Again,** and **Trying Harder** (tenacity). **Remember, God's Children Never-quit.**

The idea behind having both a "God of Flesh (illusion/son of man)" and a "God of Spirit (reality/Son of God)" is to Reflect the Two Redemptive Systems of **God, Given to Moses** in **Leviticus Chapter 27,** which **Establishes** a **Family Tithing** (blessed by God/wealth) and **Personal Payment** (saved by God/redemption) as **God's Blessing Program.** The point is that "If a Man" is Given an Increase in either his **Crops** (farmer) or in his **Flocks** (rancher), then he is to **Share** his **Good Fortune with God** by **Giving** the **Temple Priest 10%** of **All that he Receives.** "If a Person" is Faithful to God, he will be **Blessed** with **Heaven on Earth** as shown by **God's Generosity** to **King Solomon** (wisdom), when he was **Given All** of the **Wisdom and Riches of the World.** We see that "King Solomon's" Earthly Riches had been **Pressed Down** and **Shaken Together** and **Over-flowing** until he had **All he could Ever Want** in **Worldly Goods**; yet, at the **End of his Life,** he **Called himself a Fool** for **Not Treasuring First** the **Friendship of God.** In contrast, "If a Person" is Faithful to God by **Paying his Temple Tax** (silver shekels) and **Attends** the **Lord's Day of Atonement Feast** (personal forgiveness), he will be **Given God's Blessing of Redemption in Paradise, Known as** Entering the **Bosom of Abraham.**

We must note that the "Old Testament" Tithing (lamb sacrifice) and Temple Tax Systems (silver coin) were **Replaced** by **Jesus Christ, When He Established** the **New Redemptive System** (give all) for **Exclusive Members of His Church.** In this "New Redemptive System," we see that a Christian was to Give All to God, even his very **Soul** which **Includes His New Born-again Life** (salvation) so that as a **Repentant Sinner,** he could become **Worthy of Heaven** (give soul) and **God** (give eternal-soul). Now, we can see that "Humans Living on Earth (pagans)" will be Under the Old Law (Moses/heaven on earth); while "Saints in Heaven (Christians)" will be Under the New

Law (Jesus/Heaven with God) and the **Choice will be Up** to **Each Child** of God at **Birth.** This means that "Everyone must Choose" between being Baptized in the Church (water/Christian) or being Circumcised by the World (fire/Jew) via the **Crucifixion of his Flesh** (hard life). In other words, will a "Person Choose" Heaven on Earth (flesh) or will he "Choose" Heaven with God (spirit)? The **Decision will be Up** to **Those Who Seek** either the **Flesh of Man** (righteousness/illusion) or the **Spirit of God** (holiness/reality).

We see here that in the "Ancient Jewish Religion (old law)," the Lord had Two Redemptive Systems: one for **Making a Person Prosperous on Earth** (redemption/sacrifice); and a second, to **Take a Person to Heaven** (salvation/shekel) at the **End of his Life.** We see that the Lord is using these "Two Redemptive Systems" to Guide both the **Blind Pagans** (flesh) and the **Sighted Christians** (spirit) to God's **Kingdom of Glory.** The Lord was required to give the "Pagan World" a guiding Stick of Light (hope) and the "Christian People" a guiding Hand of Love (knowing) to show them the way out of both the **Darkness** (blindness) and the **Confusion** (ignorance) **of Life.**

This means that the "Pagan World (learn morals)" is to be brought into the Catholic Church (spirit) through the **Lamb's Sacrifice** (blood) to give them **Prosperous Lives on Earth** by mastering the social values of **Duty** (self), **Responsibility** (society), **and Authority** (God/working). In contrast, the "Christian People (learn ethics)" are to be brought into the Righteous World (flesh/government) through the **Silver Shekel** (money) so that they can **See God's Truth** and master the **Art of Wisdom** (thinking). We now see that in the "Pagan World, Everyone" is Striving to Survive because the **Pressures of Life** (survival) are so **Great** that **They** are being **Crushed Under** the **Weight of Daily Demands.** Note that the "Christian People have Cast off" the Cares of the World and have **Placed Their Focus** on the **Blessings of Eternal Life, Believing** that **If they Master the Flesh,** They are Home Free. The answer is that "Everyone must Master" his Earthly Flesh, Heavenly Spirit, and his Kingdom Soul to become **Home Free** and he can **Now become Christ-like** and **Reflect** the **Image and Likeness of God.** Once a "Person has Conquered" Pagan Blindness and Christian Ignorance, he can **Master** the **Righteous World** (good citizen), become a **Holy Saint** (church), which **Leads** to becoming a **Son of Man** (earth), a **Son of God** (Heaven), and finally, become **Like God Himself** (thinking for self).

The following tabular information indicates the "Mystical Difference" between the Blind Pagan (blind flesh) and the Sighted Christian (ignorant spirit) **Each Seeking** to **Know** (mind), **Love** (heart), and **Serve** (soul) God, **If They can Simply** Find **Him.**

Sight to the Blind Pagan and Knowledge to the Ignorant Christian
(Pagan gets a guiding stick of light,
while the Christian gets a guiding hand of love)

Sacrificial 1. **Blind Pagan** - Guiding Stick of Light: Jesus' Physical Dimension
Lamb • Take-sin - Learn Right from Wrong: Become Righteous before Men
  • Self ——————— Duty………………Believe in Self - Blind Eyes

- Society ————————Responsibility............Trust Oneself - Deaf Ears
- God ————————Authority- ....Faith in Self - Dumb Tongue

(Gift of Eternal Life: blessing of prosperity in the world for serving the kingdom of Lucifer)

Temple   2. **Sighted Christian** - Guiding Hand of Love: Christ's Spiritual Dimension
Tax
- Give Divinity— Learn Good from Evil..... Become Holy before God
- Good News ————Submission.................Belief in Christ - See Truth
- Gospel Message—— Sacrifice................... Trust Christ - Hear Truth
- Doctrinal Truths - Conversion............ . Faith in Christ - Speak Truth

(Gift of Divinity: blessing of eternal life in Heaven [life] for serving the Kingdom of God)

This illustration shows that the "People of the World" are simply Tiny Babies **Who have Failed** to **Open Their Eyes** to the **Meaning, Purpose,** and **Value of Life** sufficiently to comprehend the **Importance of God** and **His Holy Church** (touch of Peter). When a person is "Awakened to God's Truth," he can see that he is a Blind Fool and must **Deny his Intellect** (self), **Abandon his Feelings** (society), and **Submit his Free Will** (God) to **Christ's Church to be Saved.** Once a person has sufficiently "Died to Self," he can then comprehend the Lord's Good News (redemption), Gospel Message (salvation), and Doctrinal Truths (rewards) so that he can be **Born-again** into the **New Nature of Christ.** The previous chart shows that when a person "Masters his Duty," this leads to his Blessing of Submission (dying to self); then by "Mastering his Responsibilities," this **Leads** to his **Blessing of Sacrifice** (born-again). Finally, by "Mastering Authority," this Leads to His **Blessing of Conversion** before **God Allowing** his **Soul to Understand** the **Lord's Truth, Law, Will, and Love** to the **Point** of becoming a **Son of God.** By passing through both the "Offering" of the "Sacrificial Lamb (punitive damages)" and the "Paying of His Temple Tax (compensatory retribution)," a Person can Master the **Law of the Earth** (illusion) and the **Love of Heaven** (reality).

Once a "Person has Mastered" both the Physical and Spiritual **Life-experiences,** he will **Receive God's Blessing** in the **Form** of a **Guiding Stick of Light for his Flesh** (blind/lessons) and **God's Blessing** of a **Guiding Hand of Love for his Spirit** (ignorant/blessings). By having both a "Person's Flesh (ethics)" and his "Spirit (morals)" Guided by the **Divine Will of God,** he can **Expect to Come** to **Know** (baptism)**, Love** (confession), and **Serve** (communion) the **Almighty** with his **Whole Being** (sonship). It should now be clear that with the "Coming of Jesus Christ," the Lord would Enter **Paradise** or the **Bosom of Abraham** and **Take These Faithful Jews** (free ride) into **Their Promised Land in Heaven** as the **Firstfruits of His Redemption.** We see that "Jesus Christ" then Takes the Tithing System and **Makes** it into the **Holy Mass** or the **Divine Sacrifice** so **that Anything** that is **Brought to God through His Son** would be **Divinely Blessed.** This meant that the "Tithing System (earth)" became Man's Free Redemption (good news) through **Baptism** (save spirit); while the "Temple Tax System (Heaven)" became **Man's Earned Salvation** (gospel message) through **Confession** (save flesh/righteousness).

The key to understanding "Christianity" is to see that both a "Person's Baptism (spiritual/heart)" and His Confession (physical/mind) are to be **United** in His Communion (mystical/soul) to bring **Him** into the **Divine Love** (beatific vision/life-force) **of God Him-self.** In other words, "Baby (baptism)" becomes <u>God's Friend</u> (king); a "Teenager (confession) becomes <u>God's Companion</u> (priest); and an "Adult (communion)" becomes <u>One</u> (son) with **God** in **Truth, Law,** and **Will.** The "Purpose of Mount Calvary" is to <u>Act</u> as a <u>New Mystical Dimension,</u> where the **Impossible can Normally Occur** by **Dividing God's Absolute Divine Truth** into half **Absolute Truth** (formless) or **Never-created** (reality) and half **Relative Truth** (form) or **Created** (illusion). Through this "Compromised Process," <u>All Natural</u> and <u>Supernatural Forces</u> might be **Merged** into a **New Soul State** based on **Combining** the **Positive, Negative,** and **Neutral Forces** into a <u>New Dimension of Perfect Oneness</u> (paradox) in the **Lord Jesus Christ** (all existence).

We must now "Open Our Minds" to their <u>Outer Limits</u> to **Comprehend** the **Tri-une Nature** of God in its <u>Positive</u> (spiritual), <u>Negative</u> (physical), and <u>Neutral</u> (mystical) **States of Existence** to bring forth the Lord's **Plans of Creation** (one testimony/human), **Redemption** (two testimonies/angelic), and **Sanctified Life** (three testimonies/divine). It is obvious that God is bringing the "Human Race" through <u>Three Levels of Transformation</u> from being a **Sinful Pagan** (new mind), then to a **Righteous Jew** (new heart), and finally, becoming a **Holy Christian** (new soul) **before God, Angels, and Men.** Recall that the "Lord is Manifesting" <u>Himself on Earth</u> through **His Spoken Word** (truth) by **Using One Testimony** (spirit), then through **His Written Word** (law) by **Using Two Testimonies** (spirit/son), and finally, through **His Incarnate Word** (will) by **Using Three Testimonies** (spirit/son/father) to <u>Make All Things One</u> (kingdom) in **Truth, Law, and Will.** The idea here is to "Give a Pagan Only One Chance (one talent)" to <u>Succeed,</u> to give a "Jew Two Chances (two talents)" to <u>Succeed,</u> and then give a "Christian Three Chances (five talents)" to <u>Suc-ceed</u> or being certain of **Pleasing God.** Recall that Jesus Said: "If Two Men Gather in <u>My Name</u> (2) then <u>I Will be Among Them</u> (3) as a **Witness unto the Truth** that **God is Living Among His People."** To "Prove" that <u>God Loves His Children</u> He has sent the **Virgin Mary** to be man's **Co-redemptrix** (save pagans), **Advocate** (save Jews), and **Mediatrix** (save Christians) to bring **Salvation to One and All.**

The following tabular information indicates that to "Succeed in Life," a person must <u>Earn a most Blessed Testimony</u> from the **Holy Spirit** (water blessing), the **Son of God** (blood anointing), and the **Eternal Father** (spirit sanctification) to be given an **Eternal Place** (seat of honor) in the **Kingdom of God:**

**Pagan Testimony, Jewish Dual Testimony,
and the Christian Triple Testimony to be Saved**
(Spirit's water blessing, Son's blood anointing, Father's Spirit Sanctified upon man)

Pagan   1.   **One Testimony** (judge) - <u>Submission:</u> Establish Truth
                  (positive)   = See Limitations
(new mind)   •   Individual Rights - Spirit as Witness unto the Truth: Lucifer's Test (righteous)
Being Saved   •   One Chance - Personal Witness: Man's Word = Conviction of Self
                 (Handmaid Mary as Co-redemptrix brings Baptism - Water of Life: Sedition)

Jew	2.	**Two Testimonies** (jury) - <u>Sacrifice:</u> Flip Truth	
		(negative)	= See Potential
(new heart)		• State's Rights - Son as Witness unto the Law: God's Judgment (holy)	
Saving Self		• Punitive Damages - Pay Damages (expenses): Restore to Original State	
		• 1st Chance - Judge as Witness: Court System = Offer Lamb Sacrifice	
		• 2nd Chance - Jury as Witness: Community = Offer Temple Tax	
		• Compensatory Retribution - Pay Fine (ticket): Restore to Original Owner	

(Blessed Mother as Advocate brings Confession - Blood of Life: Sorcery)

Christians	3.	**Three Testimonies** (witness) - <u>Conversion:</u> Merge Truth	
		(neutral)	= See Self-worth
(new soul)		• Divine Rights - Father as Witness unto His Will:	
		Self-evaluation (perfect)	
		• 1st Chance - Repentance: Remove Ignorance (sin-nature)	
Saving Others		• 2nd Chance - Prayers: Remove Cowardice (worldly temptations)	
		• 3rd Chance - Works: Remove Greed (demonic possession)	

(Blessed Virgin as Mediatrix brings Communion - Spirit of Life: Blasphemy)

This illustration **shows** that a "Pagan" has only One Chance to Surrender his **Life to Christ's Church** by **Witnessing his Own Selfishness** before **Man and God** out of his **Own Mouth Convicting** himself (confession) of the **Crime of either Sedition** (liar/sin-nature/Lucifer's test), **Sorcery**(thief/worldly temptations/God's judgment), or **Blasphemy** (murderer/demonic possession/self-evaluation). A "Jew" has Two Chances to **Surrender** (spirit/host) and **Sacrifice** (flesh/grave) **his Life** to **Jesus Christ** by **Witnessing his Own Sinfulness** before **God** as he **Stands** before both his **Judge and Jury** to **Face His Judgment**. Finally, a "Christian" has Three Chances to **Surrender, Sacrifice,** and be **Converted** into the **True Faith of God** through **His** *Repentance, Prayers,* and *Works* to be **His Own Witnesses unto the Truth.** The question is would a "Person Prefer" to Give his Own Witness (being saved), have the Government of Man be His Witness (saving self), or would **He Prefer** to have God as his Eternal Witness (saving others), **Stating** that this **Person** has **Paid his Own Sin-debt** in **Full to the Last Penny?**

Through this "Triune Testimony System," the Human Race can **Hope to be Vindicated of All Its Crimes** by virtue of the **Water** (baptism), **Blood** (confession), and **Spirit** (communion) of **Jesus Christ** as a **Person's Divine Witness** unto the **Infinite Truth of God, Angels, and Men.** This "Call to Change" from an Evil Sinner (pagan) into a Holy Saint (Christian) **Requires a Person** to **Try his Best Three Times** before he can **Learn Right/Wrong, Good/Evil,** and **Separate God's Will from Man's Will** to be **Forever Set Free** from **Sin, Evil, and Death.** In comprehending the "Massive Ordeal Required" to Modify or Transform the **Divine Will of God** into some **Infinite Contradiction** (paradox), a **Person must Realize** that **God** has both **Designed His Version of Existence** (destiny) and then **Allowed Random Change** to **Create a World of Natural Selection** (free will). By "Matching" God's Grand Design (destiny) with the Forces of Natural Selection (free will), the **Lord God**

Almighty can **Determine If He has Made Even One Mistake** or if <u>**God's Life,
Death, and Resurrection Creations**</u> have **Fulfilled All His Expectations Perfectly.**

Create	1.	**God's Grand Design** - <u>Static Destiny:</u> Absolute Truth....Mark of Circumcision
Society	•	Want - Create Physical Universe of Life: World: All to Nothing (flesh)
(humble)	•	Forces of Infinite Good - Opening God's Focus to the Max (all light)
	•	God Purifies His Nature through <u>Life</u> - *God becomes Man* (new body)
	•	Receiving God's Free Gift - Existence: Jesus' Kingship (father's justice)
Create	2.	**Natural Selection** - <u>Dynamic Free Will:</u> Random Chance...Mark of Baptism
Individuals	•	Need - Create Spiritual Life-force of Death: Church: Nothing to All (spirit)
(confident)	•	Forces of Finite Evil - Closing God's Focus until it's Tightly Shut (no light)
	•	God Transforms His Nature through <u>Death</u> - *Man becomes God* (eternal life)
	•	Receiving God's Earned Blessing - Service: Christ's Priesthood (son's mercy)

This illustration shows that through the "Forces of Static Destiny (absolute truth)" and "Natural Selection (random chance)," <u>God can Fulfill</u> both **His Divine** (all) and **Human Natures** (nothing) in the <u>**Birth, Life, Death, and Resurrection**</u> of **Jesus Christ.** This means that the "Lord God Almighty" would have to <u>Undergo a Complete Change</u> in **Personality** to <u>Balance</u> the **Forces of Infinite Good** (God's Viewpoint/destiny) **Against** the **Forces of Finite Evil** (Man's Viewpoint/free will). This "Dr. Jekyll (good/destiny)" unto "Mr. Hyde (evil/free will)" <u>Identity Crisis</u> is **Actually Occurring** before **Our Very Eyes,** thereby **Forcing** the **Lord to Humble Himself** to the very **Dust** to become the <u>**Opposite of What He Really Is**</u> (adult to child) in **Divine Perfection** (basic nature). In this way, the "Lord will Assist Humanity (three chances)" to <u>Rise</u> from the <u>Dust of Despair</u> to **Reach** the very **Stars of the Sky** in **Hope of Achieving Eternal Triumph** (perfection) in the **Eyes of God.** This seemingly "Impossible Struggle" to bring <u>Together</u> the **Love of Divinity** into a **New One-on-one Relationship** with **All Humanity** is **Confounded** by the **Forces of Evil, Performing Their Prime Function** of **Purifying** the <u>**Broken Human Soul**</u> of **God's most Beloved Children.** We can picture here that the "Babies of Destiny" are <u>Cast</u> into an <u>Evil Pit of Death</u> to **Slaughter Their Innocence** to **Fully Experience** the **True Value** of **Passing** through **God's Mystical Sonship Training Program** and **Find Their Own Eternal Hearts' Desire** (want) for **Themselves.** The theme here is that it will Take Three Tries to Defeat" a <u>Person's Own</u> **Sin-nature** (Lucifer's test), **Worldly Temptations** (God's Judgment), and **Demonic Possessions** (self-evaluation) before he can **Learn to Think for himself** and to then be **Eternally Set Free.**

It can be seen that this "Purification System (teach thinking)" of <u>Divine Love</u> **Mystically Links Together** the **Forces of Fear, Pain, and Death** since it has been

Exclusively **Designed to Test** and **Define** the **Mutual Respect** between **God** (virtuous morals) and **Man** (principled ethics). This "Process of Purification" is Preventing Them from **Coming Together** to **Form** a **Bond of Mutual Love** so that **Man Needs** an **Eternal Intercessor** to **Bridge the Gap** between **God's Wants** and **Man's Needs.** The idea here is for the "Forces of Evil" to Make Every Effort to **Prevent God's** most **Beloved Children** from **Finding Their Way** to the **Divine Light** (flame) of **Truth** (endurance), **Law** (character), and **Will** (perfection). We see that the "Evil One, Lucifer (father of lies)," Knows that this Light of Truth would **Lead God's Babies Home** and into the **Loving Arms of Their Patiently Awaiting Eternal Father** implying that **God's Truth** must be **Stopped at All Cost.** We see that "Lucifer" and his "Satanic/Demonic Followers" were Told to Hold Out until **Nothing in Heaven** nor **On the Earth** could **Keep God's Children from Him,** No Matter What, come **Hell** or **High Water.**

This most magnificent "Test of Faith (three tries)" Reveals that through this **Constantly Closing Breach** of **Mutual Admiration** between **God and Man,** the **Human Race** would **Recognize** the **Value of Its Maturity** (growth). By "Seeing His Maturity," a Person Begins to Overcome **All the Negative Forces** (Lucifer's Test) **Using his Own Wisdom** (being saved), **Courage** (save self), and **Generosity** (saving others) to be **Eternally Set Free.** The "War of Spirit (good)" and "Flesh (evil)" would Only be Complete when the **Lord's New System of Perfect Justice** is instituted to more **Humanely Slaughter Man's Innocence** to bring forth an **Abundance** of **Perfect Children of God.** This "New Perfect Justice System" is to be Established through **Jesus and Mary's New Divine School of Higher Learning** (Little Red Schoolhouse) to **Teach All God's Babies** the **Meaning of Life** (existence). In the current "Satanic System," God is Using the **Sinful Flesh** (sin-nature) as the **Primary Source** in **Feeding** the **New Born-again Spirit** (holy-nature) to **Teach the Difference** between **Good** (virtues) and **Evil** (faults). We see that in the "Coming New System" Manifested by the **Lord Jesus Christ** (holy saints) and the **Blessed Virgin Mary** (righteous citizens), **They will Use** the **Faults** (mistakes) of the **Human Flesh** to **Teach** the **Born-again Human Spirit** the **Virtues** of **Divine Perfection.** This "Concept of Divine Virtues (born-again)" will just as effectively Slaughter the Innocence of the **Babies of Destiny** without the **Need** for **God's Satanic Curses** of **Fear** (mind), **Pain** (heart), **and Death** (soul).

We see the implication here is that "God is Using" the Forces of Death to **Shock the Human Nature** into its **Divine Awakening** so that an **Ignorant Child** can **See His God Face-to-face.** With the coming of "Jesus Christ," the Forces of Death are **No Longer Needed** to **Frighten a Person** into God's **Mystical Reality,** but **Now** a **Lost Sinner** can have his **Capital** (baptism), **Mortal** (confession,) and **Venial** (communion) **Sins Forgiven,** thereby **Awakening his Born-again Soul.** It should now become clear why the "Jews" are the People of Death (babies); while the "Christians" are Called the People of Life (adults), thereby **Separating Those Who Need** to **Suffer Physical Death** (temple/grave) from **Those Who Only Need** to **Suffer Spiritual Death** (church/host). This "Difference" between either a Physical (Jews) and/or Spiritual (Christians) **Death Reveals** the "Difference" between **God the Father's** (redemption) **Justice** (Jews/tough love) and **God the Son's** (salvation) **Mercy** (Christians/kind love). The implication is that through "Moses (Aaron's priesthood)" or the Mosaic Law (Levitical), the **Lord** brought forth **His Redemption of Death** (free); and then later, "Jesus (Christ's priesthood)" or Canon Law (Melchizedek) brought forth **His Salvation of New-life** (earned). To understand both "God's Free Gift (water)" versus "Man's Earned Blessing (blood)," a Person must Comprehend the **Need** to **Establish Truth** through **Three Methods of Definition.** We see that these **Three Definitions are:** 1) Fixed Frame of Reference (unknown) - Define Nature (justice): Identity = Justice brings Freedom (knowledge); 2) Relative Focused Existence (normal) - Define Behavior (mercy): Character = Prosperity brings Liberty (self-awareness); and 3) Perception of Reality (belief) - Define Lifestyle (love): Personality = Dignity brings Independence (consciousness). In short, to get into the "Reality of God," a Person must **Master the Unknown, Establish a Set-norm,** and **Believe Divine Truth,** and then **Merge these Three Concepts** into a **Single Philosophy of Life** (knowing all/paradox). We see these "Three Concepts of Life" being Made Perfect within **Justice, Mercy, and Love** as **They are Expressed** through a **Person's Government** (ethics/law), **Church** (morals/truth), and **his Home** (fairness/will).

The following tabular information indicates "Man's" Fixed Frame of Reference (ethics), his Relative Focused Existence (morals), and His Perception of Reality (fairness) which lead him to **Know God** (government), **Love God** (church), and **Serve God** (home) in **All Things:**

Fixed Frame of Reference, Relative Focused Existence, and Perception of Reality Reveals Life
(establishing truth, reversing logic to find spirit, and merging logic to define reality)

Identity
(ethics)

1. **Fixed Frame of Reference** - Define Nature.......Establish Physical Truth
   - Mind of Knowledge - Learning Right from Wrong: Righteous King = Government
   - See Truth - Know God: Repentance = See Limitations (water baptism)

Unknown
   - Government - Justice brings Freedom - Righteous Citizen = Transfigured Body
   - Babies Define Their Environment - Seeing the Meaning of Life (existence)
   - Origin - Defining Fixed Frame of Reference: Human Nature = Identity
   - Ethical Nature - Become God's Truth: Receive Title Deed to Earth

Character

2. **Relative Focused Existence** - Define Behavior...Reverse Logic to Find Spirit

(morals)
   - Heart of Self-awareness - Learn Good from Evil: Holy Priest = Church
   - Speak Law - Love God: Prayer = See Potential (blood confession)

Normal
   - Church - Prosperity brings Liberty - Holy Saint = Glorified Spirit
   - Teenagers Focus on the Self-importance - See the Purpose of Life (service)
   - Journey - Defining Relative Focused Existence: Angelic Behavior = Character
   - Moral Behavior - Obey God's Laws: Receive Title Deed to Heaven

Personality	3.	**Perception of Reality** - <u>Define Lifestyle</u>...........Merge Logic to Define Reality
(fairness)		• Soul of Consciousness - Learn God's Will/Man's Will: Perfect Son = Home
		• Touch Will - Serve God: Works = See Self-worth (spirit communion)
Belief		• Home - Dignity brings Independence - Son of God = Holy Soul
		• Adults Determine Their and All Other Values - Value of Life (happiness)
		• Destination - Defining Perception of Reality: Divine Lifestyle = Personality
		• Fair Lifestyle - Fulfill God's Will: Receive Title Deed to Kingdom

This illustration shows that "If a Baby" <u>Sees the Truth,</u> he will then be able to **Define his Environment** (identity) **Allowing him to Comprehend** the <u>**Meaning of Life**</u> (nature) based on his **Own Existence** (see limitations). Secondly, "If a Teenager" <u>Sees the Law,</u> he will then be able to **Focus on his Own Self-importance** (character) **Allowing him to Comprehend** the <u>**Purpose of Life**</u> (behavior) based on **His Call to Service** (see potential). Finally, "If an Adult" <u>Sees God's and Man's Wills,</u> he will be able to **Determine his and All Other Values** (personality) **Allowing him to Comprehend** the **Value of Life** (lifestyle) based on <u>**His Ability**</u> to **Find Happiness** (see self-worth). Through these "Three Concepts of Life (meaning/purpose/value)," <u>Each Person</u> **Grows and Matures** from a **Silly Baby** (unknown) into a <u>**Wise Adult**</u> (correct beliefs) able to **Face the Unknown** (darkness), **Define a Normal Life** (light), and **Master the Art of Belief** (awakening). "Doing These Things" at the <u>Divine Level of Perfection</u> **Enables a Mature Adult** to **Master his Own Existence** and **Attain** a **New Nature** through which he can **Comprehend** the **Meaning of Earth** (flesh/law), **Purpose of Heaven** (spirit/faith), and the **Value of the Kingdom** (soul/knowing). Secondly, "If he can Master" his <u>Own Servanthood</u> and **Attain New Behavior,** he can **Comprehend** the **Meaning of Righteousness** (flesh/redemption), **Purpose of Holiness** (spirit/salvation), and **Value of Perfection** (soul/rewards). Finally, "If he can Master" his <u>Own Happiness/Fulfillment</u> and **Attain** a **New Lifestyle,** he can **Comprehend** the **Meaning of Kingship** (flesh/new body), **Purpose of Priesthood** (spirit/eternal life), and **Value of Sonship** (soul/royal kingdom).

1. **Master Own Existence** - <u>Change Nature:</u> Human to Divine ... Gain New Nature
   • Meaning of Earth - Flesh (law)
   • Purpose of Heaven - Spirit (faith)   **Plan of Creation**
   • Value of the Kingdom - Soul (knowing)
      (babies get a fixed frame of reference - see own identity: ignorance to wisdom)

2. **Master Own Servanthood** - <u>Wash Away Sin:</u> Sinfulness to Holiness....Gain New Behavior
   • Meaning of Righteousness - Flesh (redemption)
   • Purpose of Holiness - Spirit (salvation)   **Plan of Redemption**
   • Value of Perfection - Soul (rewards)
      (teenagers get a relative focused existence - see own character: cowardice to courage)

3.   **Master Own Happiness** - <u>God/Man Knowing:</u> Thinking for Oneself .....Gain New
      Lifestyle
    - Meaning of Kingship - Flesh (new body)
    - Purpose of Priesthood - Spirit (eternal life)   **Plan of Sanctified Life**
    - Value of Sonship - Soul (own kingdom)
    (adults get own perception of reality - see own personality: greed to generosity)

This means that via a "Person's Kingship (worship)," "Priesthood (praise)," and
"Sonship (thanksgiving)," he can <u>Master</u> the <u>Meaning</u> (exist), <u>Purpose</u> (serve), and
<u>Values</u> (happiness) of the **Life-experience.** Secondly, a "Soul" can be <u>Awakened</u>
to **God's Reality** by **Fixing its Identity** (fixed frame of reference), **Focusing on
its Character** (relative focused existence), and **Perceiving its Personality** (perception of reality) in **God's Justice** (earth), **Mercy** (Heaven), **and Love** (Kingdom). It should now make sense that "Mankind" is <u>Offering Its All</u> to **God**
through its **Intercessor Christ** to **Transform Man's Ethics** into **Righteousness**
(citizenship) and **Man's Morals** into **Holiness** (sainthood) to **Receive God's
Blessings and Treasures** (body/life/kingdom). In this depiction of a "God/Man
Interface," We <u>See</u> the <u>King of the Jews</u> **Offering his Prayer to the Temple**
(High Priest Aaron) to be **Transmitted to God** via a **Perfect Blood Sacrifice**
(Calvary) **Comprised** of **Physical Ethics** (law) and **Spiritual Morals** (faith). The
idea here is that "Man's Ethics" are to be <u>Sent</u> to the **Saints** to be **Changed into
Righteousness** (citizenship); while "Man's Morals" are to be <u>Sent</u> to the **Angels**
to be **Changed into Holiness** (sainthood).

Flesh   1. **Man's Ethics** - <u>Sent to Saints:</u> Changed into Righteousness...... Gain Intellect
(obedience)   • Learning God's Right from Man's Wrong - See Limitations (knowing)
                   • Blessing of Redemption - New Body: Son of Man on Earth (awakening)
Spirit   2. **Man's Morals** - <u>Sent to Angels:</u> Changed into Holiness......Gain Emotions
(love)   • Learning God's Good from Man's Evil - See Potential (self-awareness)
                   • Blessing of Salvation - Eternal Life: Son of God in Heaven (indwelling)

This means that "Man's Ethics (intellect)" comes from <u>Learning Right from Wrong</u>
(comprehension) as **Taught by the World, Allowing a Person** to become a **<u>Right-
eous Citizen</u>** (see limitations) **Who** can **See God's Will from man's will.** Secondly,
"Man's Morals (emotions)" come from <u>Learning Good from Evil</u> (feelings) as **Taught
by the Church, Allowing a Person** to become a **<u>Holy Saint</u>** (see potential) who can
See God's Reality from man's illusion. The idea here is to "Offer God" <u>Man's
Righteous Flesh</u> (citizenship) and <u>Holy Spirit</u> (sainthood) to be **Converted** to a **New
Body** (earth) and **Eternal Life** (Heaven) and become an **<u>Eternal Son of God</u>** within
the **Lord's Kingdom of Glory.** This means that the "Job of the Saints" is to <u>Trans-
form</u> **Ethics** (right/wrong) into **Righteousness** (God/Man's Wills) and then **Transmit** his **<u>Righteous Citizenship on Earth</u>** to **God** for **His Blessing of Redemption**
(new body). Secondly, the "Job of the Angels" is to <u>Transform</u> **Morals** (good/evil) into
Holiness (God's Reality/man's illusion) and then **Transmit** his **<u>Holy Sainthood in</u>**

Heaven to **God** for His **Blessing of Salvation** (eternal life). Through both "Redemption" and "Salvation," the Human Race can become a Son of Man on Earth (Jesus) and a Son of God in Heaven (Christ), thereby **Allowing it** to become **Owner** of **Man's Earth** (body), **God's Heaven** (life), and the **God/Man Kingdom** (homeland).

To "Master the Life-experience," Man must Fulfill **David's Throne** (earth), **Aaron and God's Altars** (Heaven), and then **God's Throne** (Kingdom) via his **Offering** of his **Sins** (ignorance/sin-nature), **Evil** (cowardice/worldly temptations), and **Death** (greed/demonic possession). Using this "Logic," Man's Sins are **Converted** into **Righteousness** (wisdom); Man's Evil is **Converted** into Holiness (courage); and Man's Death is **Converted** into **Perfection** (generosity) to bring forth a **New Nature** (love) **in Christ** (born-again). This means that "Man's Physical Defects" of Ignorance (old mind), Cowardice (old heart), and Greed (old soul) are **Transformed** into "Spiritual Virtues" of **Wisdom** (new mind), **Courage** (new heart), and **Generosity** (new soul). Once he has received his "Spiritual Virtues" and has Mastered **Righteousness** (ethics), **Holiness** (morals), and **Perfection** (fairness), he becomes **Eligible** to receive his own **Title Deed to Earth** (Heaven on Earth), **Title Deed to Heaven** (paradise in Heaven), and **Title Deed to the Kingdom** (Beatific Vision). In this same manner, once he has his "Three Title Deeds to Life," he becomes Eligible to receive a **Royal Seat** in **God's Celestial Court** (rule earth), **Temple Court** (rule Heaven), and **Royal Court** (rule Kingdom). This "Journey of Life" from Nothing to All **Allows** a **Dedicated Hardworking Soul** (righteous/holy/perfect) to **Establish Itself** within **God's Kingdom of Glory** with **Honors** through **Its Courage, Duty, and Sacrifice**.

The following graphic illustration shows "King David's Throne (king of the Jews)" Interfacing with the "Throne of God (king of glory)" by Offering the **Lord Prayers** (ethics) and **Sacrifices** (morals) to *Get a Doctrinal Awakening* (righteousness/body) and *Spiritual Indwelling* (holiness/life).

**King of the Jews Offers All to the King of Glory
to get a Body, New-life, and Royal Kingdom**
(man offers prayers and sacrifices to
get a doctrinal awakening and spiritual indwelling)

Kingdom	G o d	
Personality	Personal · Lord God Almighty · Benevolent	
Blessing of Salvation ·	God Th r o n e	Force · Blessing of Redemption
	(life)	(nature)
Mystical Body · Angels	*Perception of Reality*	Saints · Communion of Saints
(live with God)	L i f e	(live among men)
1st Person	(resurrection)	Father
	· · · · ·	Law of Love
	Divine Trinity	(divine rights)
	(father / son / spirit)	

1. New Body · Title Deed to Earth: Celestial Court
2. Eternal Life · Title Deed to Heaven: Temple Court
3. Royal Kingdom · Title Deed to Kingdom: Royal Court
4. Personal Freedom · Title to Self: Divine Court

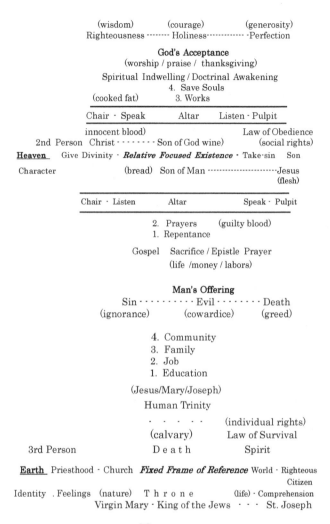

```
        (wisdom)          (courage)          (generosity)
     Righteousness ------- Holiness------------ -Perfection
                      God's Acceptance
                (worship / praise / thanksgiving)
           Spiritual Indwelling / Doctrinal Awakening
                         4. Save Souls
         (cooked fat)    3. Works

         Chair · Speak       Altar     Listen · Pulpit

            innocent blood)                  Law of Obedience
     2nd Person  Christ · · · · · · · · Son of God wine)  (social rights)
  Heaven   Give Divinity · Relative Focused Existence · Take·sin   Son
  Character        (bread)  Son of Man --------------------Jesus
                                                          (flesh)

         Chair · Listen       Altar       Speak · Pulpit

                   2. Prayers      (guilty blood)
                   1. Repentance

            Gospel   Sacrifice / Epistle  Prayer
                     (life /money / labors)

                      Man's Offering
             Sin · · · · · · · · · Evil · · · · · · · Death
           (ignorance)        (cowardice)      (greed)

                   4. Community
                   3. Family
                   2. Job
                   1. Education

             (Jesus/Mary/Joseph)

             Human Trinity

                   ·   · · · ·
                   (calvary)       (individual rights)
                                   Law of Survival
     3rd Person     D e a t h      Spirit

   Earth  Priesthood · Church  Fixed Frame of Reference  World · Righteous
                                                                 Citizen
   Identity . Feelings (nature)  T h r o n e  (life) · Comprehension
             Virgin Mary · King of the Jews  · · ·  St. Joseph
```

M a n

This illustration shows that on "Earth (kingship)," a <u>Person</u> is to <u>Offer God</u> his **Education, Job, Family, and Community Efforts** to **Reveal** that he has **Mastered Human Righteousness** (world) by <u>**Learning God's Right from**</u> **Man's Wrong** to become an **Ethical Citizen** within his **Human Community** (society). Secondly, within his "Church (priesthood)" or "Heaven," a <u>Person</u> is to <u>Offer God</u> his **Repentance, Prayers, Works, and Saved Souls** to reveal that he has **Mastered Sacred Holiness** (church) by <u>**Learning Good from Evil**</u> to become a **Moral Saint** within his **Divine Community** (social order). Finally, within a "Person's Sonship" or "Kingdom," He is to <u>Receive from God</u> **His Gifts** of a **New Body, Eternal Life, Royal Kingdom,** and **His Personal Freedom** to **Reveal** that his **Soul** has **Mastered Divine Perfection** (kingdom) by **Learning God's Will from man's will** to become a **Perfect Son** within the **God/Man Community** (sharing).

Through these "Three Levels of Maturity," a <u>Person is Able</u> to **Enter God's Divine Government** as a **Respected Member** of **Divine Society** with his <u>**Own Seat of Honor**</u> within the **Lord's Celestial** (earth), **Temple** (Heaven), and **Royal** (Kingdom) **Courts of Divinity**. The idea here is to see that out of "One's Flesh (law of survival/obey)" shall come his <u>Fixed Frame of Reference</u> (name) or his **Identity** as a **Righteous Citizen on Earth** (individual rights). Secondly, out of "His Spirit (law of obedience/poverty)" shall come his <u>Relative Focused Existence</u> (purity) or his **Character** as a **Holy Saint in Heaven** (social rights). Finally, out of "His Soul (law of love/celibacy)" shall come his <u>Perception of Reality</u> (vision) or his **Personality** as a **Perfect Son within God's Kingdom** (divine rights). In this way, a "New Creation" can obtain its <u>Own Name</u> (identity/job), <u>Level of Purity</u> (character/family), and <u>Mature Vision</u> (personality/home) of Life as it strives to **Become All it can Become** before its **Creator God** of **Divine Love**.

Note that to "Get a Name," a <u>Person</u> must <u>Offer God Worship</u> or **Give Him his Life** (sin); to "Get Character," <u>He</u> must <u>Offer God Praise</u> or **Give Him his Wealth** (evil); finally, to "Get a Personality," <u>He</u> must <u>Offer God Thanksgiving</u> or **Give Him his Labors** (death). Yes! Through our "Worship, Praise, and Thanksgiving," we can <u>Enter</u> the <u>Friendship</u> (earth), <u>Companionship</u> (Heaven), and <u>Oneness</u> (Kingdom) of **God** to **Share** in the **Lord's Blessings of Eternal Life**. Is it "No Wonder" that the <u>Human Race</u> is so **Confused About Life**, when **God's Process of Redemption** (kingship/priesthood/sonship) seems to be **Buried** within the **Pages of Our Bibles** and **No One ever Quite Gets It Right**? The answer can be "Found" in the fact that <u>God</u> has <u>Encoded His Bible</u> so it would take a **Righteous Prophet** (flesh) or **Holy Saint** (spirit) to **Correctly Explain** the **Redemptive Process of God**.

We see that this "Redemptive Process" involves the <u>Creation</u> of a **Righteous Man** to **Rule Earth**, a **Holy Man** to **Rule Heaven**, and a **Perfect Man** to **Rule God's Kingdom, All in the Name of Knowing God's Will** from **man's will**. Now, we see that when the "Righteous, Holy, and Perfect Men" are able to <u>Work Together</u>, they can **Master the Life-experience** by **Defeating** one's **Ignorant Flesh, Cowardly Spirit, and Greedy Soul**. Note that an "Unrighteous Man" <u>Speaks Against his King</u>; while a "Righteous Man" <u>Speaks For his King</u> and is able to **Gain the Respect** of his **Fellow Men** (see limitations). Secondly, an "Unholy Man" <u>Prays Against Heaven</u>; while a "Holy Man" <u>Prays For his God in Heaven</u> and is able to **Gain the Respect** of the entire **Angelic Realm** (see potential). Finally, an "Imperfect Man" <u>Works Against his God</u>; while a "Perfect Man" <u>Works For his God</u> and is able to **Gain the Respect** of the **Lord God Almighty Himself** (see self-worth).

This means that only a "Righteous Man" can <u>Rule Earth</u> through the **Power of his Intellect** (knowledge) as he **Learns All the Lessons of Life** and then **Creates** a **Happy Home, Holy Church, and Honest Government**. Secondly, only a "Holy Man" can <u>Rule Heaven</u> through the **Power of his Emotions** (self-awareness) by **Receiving God's Blessings of Life** to bring forth a **Loving Home, Devoted Church, and Effective Government**. Finally, only a "Perfect Man" can <u>Rule God's Kingdom</u>

through the **Power of his Instincts** (consciousness) and his **Own Free Will** (freedom) to bring forth a **Divine Home, Sacred Church, and Holy Government**. Through the "Authority" of the <u>Righteous, Holy, and Perfect Man,</u> the **Human Race** can **Defeat** its **Ignorant Flesh** (intellect), **Cowardly Spirit** (emotions), and **Greedy Soul** (instincts). In this way, "Jesus Christ" is <u>Planning to Rule</u> **Earth, Heaven,** and **God's Kingdom** through **Man's Justice** (earth/law), **Angelic Mercy** (Heaven/faith), and **Divine Love** (Kingdom/knowing).

The following tabular information indicates that each of "God's Children" is being <u>Called</u> to **Rule Earth** in the **Flesh, Rule Heaven** in the *Spirit*, and **Rule God's Kingdom** via *Christ's Soul*:

God's Children are Called to Rule Earth, Rule Heaven, and Rule God's Kingdom through Love
(rule earth via kingship/rule heaven via
priesthood/rule kingdom via sonship to face life)

Flesh
(mind)

1. **Rule the Earth** - <u>Kingship of David</u> (justice) ......Knowledge (lessons)
   - Unrighteous Man - Speaks Against the King
   - Speaking Negatively - Blasphemy: Excommunication
   - Righteous Man - Speaks For the King   **Face Life**
   - Gain Respect of Man - See Limitations
   - Defeat Ignorant Flesh - Learn Right/Wrong

   (baby sees himself so he can see his society - physical dimension)

Spirit
(heart)

2. **Rule Heaven** - <u>Priesthood of Aaron</u> (mercy) ... Self-awareness (blessings)
   - Unholy Man - Prays Against Heaven
   - Praying Negatively - Sorcery: Outcast
   - Holy Man - Prays to his God in Heaven   **Face Death**
   - Gain Respect of Angelic Realm - See Potential
   - Defeat Cowardly Spirit - Learn Good/Evil

   (teenager sees his society so he can see his God - spiritual dimension)

Soul
(being)

3. **Rule the Kingdom** - <u>Sonship of Jesus</u> (love) ...Consciousness (freedom)
   - Imperfect Man - Works Against God
   - Working Negatively - Sedition: Banished
   - Perfect Man - Works For his God   **Face Damnation/Eternal Life**
   - Gain Respect of God, Himself - See Self-worth
   - Defeat Greedy Soul - Learn God's Will/man's will

   (adult sees his God so he can become God's Son - mystical dimension)

This illustration shows that a "Baby" must <u>Master himself</u> before he can hope to **Comprehend his Own Complex Society** which is **Teaching him to Communicate** with a **Host of Different People** on **Many Levels of the Life-experience** (natural-order). Secondly, a "Teenager" must <u>Master his Society</u> before he can hope to **Comprehend** his **Relationship with God, Who** is **Teaching him to Communicate** with a <u>**Host of Different Creatures**</u> on **Many Levels within God's Kingdom** (supernatural order). Finally, an "Adult" must <u>Master the Lord God Almighty Himself</u> before he can hope to **See** and **Comprehend his Own Born-again Nature** which will **Reveal** a **Whole Host of Divine Relationships** on **Many Levels of Human, Angelic, and Divine Life**. Yes! through the "Growth" and "Maturity" of a <u>Baby, Teenager, and Adult,</u> the **Human Race** is able to **Rule Earth, Heaven, and God's Kingdom** and bring forth **New Bodies** from **Earth** (land), <u>**Eternal Lives**</u> (babies) from **Heaven**, and <u>**Royal Kingdoms**</u> (life) from **God's Kingdom**. We now see that the "Life-experience" is <u>Calling</u> **Ignorant, Cowardly, and Greedy Men** to <u>**Wake up**</u> to the fact that **They must Learn Right/Wrong, Good/Evil, and God's Will/man's will**.

If the "Human Race" will <u>Bow to God's Will,</u> then those **Who Speak Against Their King** (blasphemy) will **Not be Excommunicated** from **Their Temple**. Secondly, those "Who Pray Against Heaven (sorcery) will <u>Not be Made</u> an **Outcast from Their People** and will **Remain within Their Nation** as **Holy Men of God** (priesthood). Finally, those "Who Work Against Their Creator (sedition) will <u>Not</u> be **Banished from Their Land** and will **Remain within God's Kingdom** as **Perfect Men of God** (sonship). Yes! The "Whole Life-experience" is <u>About Bowing to God's Will</u> as a **Lost Broken Fool** must **<u>Deny his Very Self</u>** and **Come Follow God's Son, Jesus Christ**. This means that the "Lost of the World" are being <u>Called</u> to **God's Sacred Word** (redemption) to bring **<u>All Men</u>** onto the **Pathways of Righteousness** (new mind), **Holiness** (new heart), and **Perfection** (new soul). Now, we can see that the "Bible" is the <u>Sacred Word of God</u> and was **Written to Mystically Reveal Mankind's Coming Redemption** which was caused by **<u>Adam's Fall from Grace</u>** (tree of knowledge) when he was still in the **Garden of Eden**. Unfortunately, what "Mankind Failed to Understand" was that the <u>Bible</u> had to be **Written in Code** to prevent **Lucifer** from intercepting its **Redemptive Message** and to keep the **<u>Evil One</u>** from diabolically **Destroying Christianity** before **It even Got Started**. To "Stop Lucifer's Demonic Forces," the <u>Bible</u> had to be replaced by a set of <u>Interpreters</u> or <u>Prophets,</u> raised-up on earth to **Explain** and **Decode God's Scriptures** to a **Lost and Confused World** of **Ignorant Fools**. We see that these "Specially Chosen People" were made <u>Saints of the Church</u> and became members of the **Communion of Saints in Heaven** so that their lives could forever be a **Reflection** of **God's Redemptive Message** to a **Lost and Broken World**. We also see that in ancient times, "God Sent Many Prophets" to communicate with the <u>Jewish People,</u> yet, no one seemed to **Comprehend Their Message** (good news), nor did **They seem to Even Care**. Obviously, this same process was used with "Educating the Catholic Church" as <u>God</u> relied on **His Saints** to define the **Meaning of Life** (existence) based on the **Worship** (give life), **Praise** (give wealth), and **Thanksgiving** (give labors) of **Their God**.

The idea was that as a "Living Saint" would somehow <u>Awaken the Church</u> (break code), the **Magisterium** would put up a **Statue of Remembrance** within some small church to recognize this **<u>Saint's</u>** particular contribution or **Teaching to the Faith**. As more and more "Statues" appeared and entered the <u>Universal Church,</u> more and more **Knowledge** would also enter the **Catholic Faith** until it became clear that **God was**

Communicating with His People. By "Cross Referencing" the <u>Bible</u> (code book) with the <u>Teachings</u> (code breaker) of the **Communion of Saints, Christ's Priesthood** could begin to connect each of these **Puzzle Parts of Life**, until God's **Plan of Redemption** began to make some **Logical Sense**. To "Unravel this Puzzle," we must <u>Fix Our Attention</u> on our **Identities** (who) to comprehend the **Meaning of Life** (existence), then <u>Focus Our Perceptions</u> on our **Characters** (where) to comprehend the **Purpose of Life** (service), and finally, <u>Perceive the Life-experience</u> based on our **Personalities** (what) to comprehend the **Value of Life** (happiness). Through these "Three Exercises of Perception," a <u>Person</u> can get a **Clear View** of his **State of Existence** (justice), **Service to his Community** (mercy), and **Level of Happiness** (love) among his **Fellow Men**. This is "Done by Mastering" the <u>Art of Regeneration</u> as each of **God's Children** is **Called** to **Renew his Mind, Heart, Soul, and Life-force** in **Preparation for Entering** the **Lord's Kingdom of Glory**.

We must "Recognize" that <u>If a Child of God Fails</u> to **Master the Life-experience,** he will be **Cast into the Lord's** **Lake of Fire** (punished), **Bottomless Pit** (discarded), and finally, into the **Outer Darkness** (forgotten/forsaken). This means that the "Lord God Almighty" will <u>First Try Corrective Measures,</u> and **If They Fail** (death agony)**, He** will then **Discard an Evil Soul** to the **Trash Heap** (hopelessness) and **One Day He will Forget All About It** (separation). This "Process of Creation" has <u>Created so Many Evil</u> **Useless Souls** because **God Only Takes** the most **Fruitful of Creation** to **Live** in **His Kingdom of Glory** and **Share His Eternal Treasures** of **Peace** (challenge), **Joy** (adventure,) and **Happiness** (fun).

Obviously, "Jesus Christ" has <u>Come up with a Plan</u> for **Creating All Perfect People** through the **Virgin Womb** of **His Blessed Mother**, known as being **Born-again** (sainthood) into the **Eternal Spirit of God**. In this "Theme" of <u>Saving Everyone and Everything,</u> it becomes the **Job** of both **Jesus and Mary** to **Restore All that have been Lost** to their **Original States** and then **Return Them** to their **Original Owners**. This implies that "God" and "His Son, Christ (God)" are <u>Busy Creating Holy Saints,</u> while "Mary" and "Her Son, Jesus (Man)" are <u>Busy Restoring Sinners</u> into <u>Holy Christians</u> so **that These Two Teams** are **Working Together** to **Build a Universal Kingdom of Glory for All**. Through this "Logic," we see the <u>Purpose</u> of both the **World System/throne** (creation/law) and the **Holy Church/altar** (restoration/faith) as **They Strive** to **Create More and More Babies** to become **Saints** and then **Transform These Saints** into **Sons of God**. This "Process of Conversion" <u>Requires Our Creator</u> to **Use** the **Earth** (physical dimension) for **Babies/citizens,** **Heaven** (spiritual dimension) for **Saints,** and then the **Kingdom** (mystical dimension) for **Sons of God**. We call these "Three Dimensions of Life" <u>God's Divine School of Higher Learning</u> which is Comprised of the **Earthly** Baby Farm (elementary), the **Heavenly** Divine School (high school), and the **Kingdom's** **Sonship Training Program** (college). Unfortunately, "If a Disobedient Soul" <u>Fails to Master</u> the **Baby Farm** of **Earth,** then it will **Fall** into either the **Lake of Fire** (C-work), **Bottomless Pit** (D-work) and/or **Outer Darkness** (F-work) based on just **How Hard it was Willing to Try for A's or B's**. We can think of the "Lake of Fire (Devil)" as <u>County Jail</u> (death agony); the "Bottomless Pit (Lucifer)," <u>Getting a Prison Sentence</u> (hopeless); while the "Outer Darkness (Satan)" is a <u>Death Sentence</u> (separation) on **Death Row**.

Obviously, with the "Fall of Adam and Eve," They were Cursed with **Toil, Pain, and Death** which were **Manifested on Earth** as being **Excommunicated** from **God's Temple** (blasphemy); being an **Outcast** from **One's People** (sedition); and finally, being **Banished** from **Earth** (sorcery). Through "Each of These Punishments," we can See the Tremendous Ordeal **Jesus Christ had to Suffer** to **Restore the Human Race Back to God's Good Graces** as **He Pays Everyone's Sin-debt** unto the **Last Penny**. This means that the "Human Race" is being Called to **Try Its Best** to **Fulfill God's Law** (world) and **Man's Faith** (church) so that **It might Avoid Falling** into the **Devil's Lake of Fire** (sin), **Lucifer's Bottomless Pit** (evil), and **Satan's Outer Darkness** (death).

The following tabular information indicates that "Failing to Earn Honors" in God's Divine School means **Falling** into either the **Lake of Fire** (Hell/corrected), the **Bottomless Pit** (Gehenna/destroyed), and/or being **Cast** into the **Outer Darkness** (oblivion/forgotten):

Defining the Lake of Fire, Bottomless Pit, and Outer Darkness as They Curse Humankind Forever
(touch lake - face death agony, pit - face hopelessness, and darkness - face separation from God)

Sorrow   1. **Lake of Fire** - Face Death Agony: Burn in Eternal-fire (pain) ..Knowledge
(home)   • Cursed with Barren Desert - Fruitless Land (grave) = Meet the Devil
                   (fear)
                 • Cursed with Ignorance - Empty Mind: Baby Level = Elementary
                   School/wisdom
                 • Cursed with Excommunication from God's Temple - Blasphemy:
                   Caiaphas
                 • Repentance
Land   • Starvation   *Suffer Toil in a Barren Land* (thanksgiving)
                 • Fasting
                 • Give Labors
                 • See Own Limitations - Remove Capital Sins: Easter Duty (yearly)
       (defeat sin/Lake of Fire - learn right/wrong: become righteous citizen on earth = new body)

Contrition   2. **Bottomless Pit** - Face Hopelessness: Fall into Void (insanity) ....
                   self-awareness
(government)   • Cursed with Barren Womb - Fruitless Family (hell) = Meet Lucifer
                   (pain)
                 • Cursed with Cowardice - Empty Heart: Teenage Level = High
                   School/courage
                 • Cursed with being Cast out from One's People - Sedition: Herod
                 • Prayers
Babies   • Nakedness   *Suffer Birth Pains from a Barren Womb* (praise)
                 • Sackcloth

- Give Money
- See Own Potential - Remove Mortal Sins: Lord's Day/Sunday (weekly) (defeat evil/Bottomless Pit - learn good/evil: become holy saint in Heaven = eternal life)

Retribution	3.	**Outer Darkness** - <u>Face Separation from God:</u> Solitary Confinement (cold) …Consciousness
(church)		• Cursed with Barren Life - Fruitless Life (Gehenna) = Meet Satan (death)
		• Cursed with Greed - Empty Soul: Adult Level = College/generosity
		• Cursed with Banishment from Earth - Sorcery: Pilate
		• Works
Life-force		• Homelessness *Suffer Eternal-death from Barren Life* (worship)
		• Ashes
		• Give Life
		(defeat death/Outer Darkness - learn God's Will/man's will: become perfect son in Kingdom = royal kingdom)

This illustration shows that to "Get a C Grade" in Life is to be **Cast into Hell** for **Corrective Measures** (new mind); and to "Get a D Grade" in <u>Life</u>, a **Person** is <u>**Cast into Gehenna**</u> (trash heap) to be **Destroyed**. Unfortunately, "If a Person Gets an F Grade" and <u>Fails Life Completely</u>, then his **Life-force** will be **Obliterated** unto **Nothingness** and he will be **<u>Forgotten/</u>**Forsaken by **God, Angels, and Men Forever.** This means that to be "Restored" from the <u>Lake of Fire,</u> a **Person must Repent, Face Starvation** through **Fasting,** and **Give his Labors to God** in <u>Eternal</u> **<u>Thanksgiving</u>** for **Saving him from Hell.** Secondly, to be "Restored" from the <u>Bottomless Pit,</u> a **Person must Pray, Face Nakedness** through **Sackcloth,** and **Give his Money to God** in <u>Eternal Praise</u> for **Saving him from Gehenna.** Finally, to be "Restored" from the <u>Outer Darkness,</u> a **Person must Do Works, Face Homelessness** through **Ashes,** and **Give his Life to God** in <u>Eternal Worship</u> for **Saving him from Total Oblivion.**

Yes! "Jesus Christ" had to **Beg His Eternal Father** for **Each of Our Souls** as He **Promised** that **He would Pay Our <u>Thanksgiving Debt</u>** of Veneration (labor), **Our <u>Praise Debt</u>** of **Adoration** (money), and **Our <u>Worship Debt</u>** of **Exaltation** (life). With the "Payment" of <u>These Three Debts,</u> **Humanity would Receive** its **New Mind, Heart, and Soul** in the **Form** of a **New Body** (intellect), **Eternal Life** (emotions), and its **Own Royal Kingdom** (instincts). The idea is that "If a Child of God" becomes a <u>King on Earth,</u> he can **Receive** a **New Body.** "If he" becomes a <u>Priest in Heaven,</u> he can **Earn** Eternal Life. And "If he" becomes a <u>Son within God's Kingdom,</u> he can be **Rewarded** his **Own Kingdom.** Through this "Honors System," the <u>Whole Kingdom</u> <u>of God</u> is **Centered** based on the **Merits** of **Each Child's Depth of Character** as a **Reflection** of his **<u>Desire to Try to Conform</u>** to the **Divine Will of God.** In contrast, "Jesus Christ" is <u>Offering</u> **Three Programs of Success** based on either Pass/Fail (direct will), Graded on Curve (permissive will), and/or Handicap (compromised will), **<u>Giving Everyone a Chance</u>** to **Fit-in Somewhere.** The "Pass/Fail System" is for

God's Holy Saints, the "Curve System" is for **Jesus Christ's Righteous Christians,** and the "Handicap System" is for the **Blessed Mother's Pagan Babies**. Obviously, the "Life-experience" is All About **Believing in God's Son** and **Striving** to **Consume Everything Life has to Offer** in **Time, Money, and/or Effort** (just try).

We now see that the "Life-experience" is centered on Consuming Energy and Force as **They are Manifested** within one's **Intellect** (mind), **Emotions** (heart), **Instincts** (soul), **and Nature** (life-force) throughout **His Life,** thereby making a **Person Stronger and Stronger** until he is **Invincible.** This "State of Invincibility" interests the Lord God Almighty the most as **He Works Tirelessly** to bring **Each** of **His Children** from **Ignorance to Wisdom.** This "Conversion Experience Awakens" each of God's Children through **Four Stages of Regeneration:** 1) Sleep for the Mind (work to rest), 2) Sex for the Heart (lust to love), 3) Death for the Soul (pain to pleasure), and 4) Resurrection for the Life-force (hopelessness to joy). Obviously, the "Human Race" is being Called to an **Eternal Food Source** (rest/food/commitment/God) that can make a **Person Invincible,** thereby leading him to becoming the **Master of All he Surveys.** This means that "Life" is centered around one's most Beloved Bed which as a **Child** is **Sleep** (self), as a **Teenager** is **Passion** (family), as an **Adult** is **Rest** (society), and as a **Wise Man** is **Eternal Happiness** (God). In contrast, a "Child's Bed (education)" shows him his Ignorance so he can become **Wise** (smart); a "Teenager's Bed (marriage)" shows him his Cowardice so he can become **Courageous** (brave); an "Adult's Bed (job)" shows him his Greed so he can become **Generous** (charitable); and the "Wise Man's Bed (home)" shows him his Selfishness so he can become **Unselfish** (kind).

Through each of these "Stages of Growth," the Human Race can expect to **Comprehend the Meaning** (existence/rest), **Purpose** (service/food), and **Value of Life** (happiness/commitment) to the point of **Fulfilling All of the Expectations of God.** If a person is "Wise Enough" to Master the Life-experience and Please God, then he can expect to **Receive** the **Lord's Greatest Blessings** of a **New Earthly Body** (see limitations), an **Eternal Heavenly Life** (see potential), a **Royal Kingdom** (see self-worth), and his **Own Personal Freedom** (think for oneself). In short, the "Life-experience" is all about obtaining God's Free Redemption as a **Child** (physical dimension), obtaining one's own Earned Salvation as a **Teenager** (spiritual dimension), then obtaining the Lord's Bonus Rewards as an **Adult** (mystical dimension), and finally, obtaining the Friendship of God as a **Wise Man** (divine dimension). At each of the "Levels of Maturity," a person is able to first **Meet** (righteous citizen/acquaintance), then **Know** (holy saint/friend), then **Serve** (perfect son/family), and finally, **Love** (free man/servant) his **Creator God.**

The following tabular information indicates that the "Life-experience" is all about Regeneration of the **Human Nature** through the **Forces** of **Sleep** (mind/work to rest), **Sex** (heart/lust to love), **Rest** (soul/pain to pleasure), and **Resurrection** (life-force/hopelessness to joy):

The Regeneration of the Mind, Heart, Soul, and Life-force through One's Ability to Find Rest
(the mind needs sleep, the heart needs sex, the soul needs death, and the life-force needs resurrection)

Child
(education)

1. **Regeneration of Mind** - <u>Sleep:</u> Work to Rest...Knowledge
   - Bed of Growth - Sleeping with Self: Ignorance to Wisdom
   - Learning Right from Wrong - Righteous Citizen of Earth   **Self**
   - New Body - See Limitations: Master Kingship
   - Free Redemption - Physical Dimension: World

Teenager
(marriage)

2. **Regeneration of Heart** - <u>Sex:</u> Lust to Love .... Self-awareness
   - Bed of Love - Sleeping with Mate: Cowardice to Courage
   - Learning Good from Evil - Holy Saint of Heaven   **Family**
   - Eternal Life - See Potential: Master Priesthood
   - Earned Salvation - Spiritual Dimension: Church

Adult
(job)

3. **Regeneration of Soul** - <u>Death:</u> Pain to Pleasure......Consciousness
   - Bed of Rest - Sleeping in the Grave: Greed to Generosity
   - Learn God's Will/man's will - Perfect Son of Kingdom   **Society**
   - Royal Kingdom - See Self-worth: Master Sonship
   - Bonus Rewards - Mystical Dimension: Kingdom

Wise Man
(home)

4. **Regeneration of Life-force** - <u>Resurrection:</u> Hopelessness to Joy...Sentience
   - Bed of Eternal Happiness - Sleeping with God: Selfishness to Un-selfishness
   - Learn God's Reality/man's illusion - Free Man in Dream   **God**
   - Personal Freedom - Thinking for Self: Master of All
   - Friendship of God - Divine Dimension: Self

This illustration shows that a "Child Seeks" his <u>Own Bed</u> (truth); a "Teenager Seeks" the <u>Bed of his Mate</u> (law); an "Adult Seeks" a <u>Bed of Rest</u> (will/grave/RIP); and finally, a "Wise Man Seeks" the <u>Bed of God</u> (love/resurrection). We have all heard that "If You are Old Enough" to <u>Make Your Own Bed,</u> then "You are Old Enough" to <u>Lie in It;</u> or "If You" <u>Sow the Wind,</u> then you must <u>Reap the Whirlwind</u> that **You Yourself have Caused.** It is lucky for "Fallen Man" that he has an <u>All-Loving Redeemer,</u> who is willing to **Lie in His Bed** and **Reap the Whirlwind for Him** as **All He must Do is Ask** (repentance/prayers/works). The implication here is that "Asking God for Help" implies having <u>Enough Brains</u> to **Offer God One's <u>Repentance</u>** (mind), **<u>Prayers</u>** (heart), **<u>Works</u>** (soul), and **<u>Souls</u>** (life-force) to **Prove His Sincere Desire** to be **Saved.** Unfortunately, to "Experience Salvation," a <u>Person must be Willing</u> to **Go** through the **Process of Regeneration** of his **Mind** (intellect/knowledge), **Heart** (emotions/self-awareness), **Soul** (instincts/consciousness), and **Life-force** (nature/sentience). This means that the "Mind (ignorance)" must be <u>Educated</u> (wisdom); the "Heart (cowardice)" must be <u>Married</u> (courage); the "Soul (greed)" must become <u>Employed</u> (generosity); and a "Person's Life-force (selfishness)" must <u>Own his Own Home</u> (unselfishness).

Through these "Four Stages of Life," a <u>Person</u> can become a <u>Respected Citizen</u> (earth/Heaven/Kingdom) within **God's Society** of **Angels and Men,** thereby making a **Person Perfect** through his **Union with Christ Jesus**. Yes! We are each being "Called to Unite" with <u>Nature, Men, Angels, and God</u> to bring forth an **International Society** (kingdom) of **Peace, Joy, and Happiness Forever**. Out of the "Forces of Peace, Joy, and Happiness," we see the <u>Union of Holy Trinity</u> as they **Bless Their Physical, Spiritual, and Mystical Creations** with **Life** (earth), **Eternal Life** (Heaven), and finally **Divine Life** (Kingdom). The question is: just "What Happens" to <u>Those Who Fail</u> to **Receive** this **Awesome Divine Blessing** as **They must Face** the **Punishments** of <u>Death Agony</u> (1st death), <u>Hopelessness</u> (2nd death), and **Separation from God** (3rd death) for **Their Evil Ways**?

We see that the "Lord God Almighty" is <u>Planning</u> to clearly **Show up Evil** for **What It Really Is** and for **What It Is Trying To Do**, thereby **Proving to One and All** that **Evil and Death** are <u>**Not and Never have Been**</u> Benevolent Friends of **Mankind**. Once the "Divine Trap is Set," the <u>Lord Jesus</u> Christ will **Lead** the **Evil One** and his **Followers** to the **Proverbial Rock of Death** which is **Mount Moriah** (Temple site) in **Jerusalem,** where **They will be Slain before the World**. This "Mystical Trap" will <u>Prove</u> that **All Who Attack** the **Majesty of God** will be **Crushed** on **His Mystical Stone of Damnation** and then <u>**They will be Cast**</u> into **God's Lake of Fire** (punished), **Bottomless Pit** (cast away), and finally, into the **Outer Darkness** (forgotten).

The following tabular information indicates that "If a Person" <u>Fails in Life,</u> he will be <u>**Cast**</u> into **God's Lake of Fire** (punishment), **Bottomless Pit** (cast away), and **Outer Darkness** (forgotten or forsaken):

Failure in Life Means Facing the Lake of Fire, Bottomless Pit, and Outer Darkness with Lucifer
(being subjected to God's silent anger, vocal rage, and striking wrath is the ultimate death)

Silent Anger	1. **Lake of Fire** - <u>Punishment:</u> Correction of Behavior ......Knowledge	
	• Death Agony - Face Lucifer's Test: Physical Perfection = Baby Level	
	• Tried to Learn - Right from Wrong: Failed Righteousness (lost earth)	
	• Outcast from One's People - Burned in a Pit (burning pain)	
	• 1st Death - Criminal Imprisonment: See Eternal Limitations	
Vocal Rage	2. **Bottomless Pit** - <u>Cast Away:</u> Placed in the Trash Heap .....Self-awareness	
	• Hopelessness - Face God's Judgment: Spiritual Perfection = Teenage Level	
	• Tried to Learn - Good from Evil: Failed Holiness (lost Heaven)	
	• Banished from Earth - Falling into an Eternal Void (disorientation)	
	• 2nd Death - Insanity in Mental Institution: See Possible Potential	
Striking Wrath	3. **Outer Darkness** - <u>Forgotten:</u> Turn Back Forever ....Consciousness	
	• Separation from God - Face Self-evaluation: Mystical Perfection = Adult Level	

- Tried to Learn - God's Will/man's will: Failed Perfection (lost Kingdom)
- Forsaken by God - Eternal Solitary Confinement (cold and lonely)
- 3rd Death - Evil Mad-man Placed in Padded Cell: See Possible Self-worth

This illustration shows that "If the Evil One" Loses his **Battle unto the Death,** certainly he will be **Facing** having his **Mind Cast** into the **Lake of Fire** (sin/Satan), his **Heart Cast** into the **Bottomless Pit** (evil/Devil), and his **Soul Cast** into the **Outer Darkness** (death/Lucifer). Now imagine that if the "Holy Trinity" is Each Divided in Its Personal Agendas, we would still be **Getting Identical Results** (union) via **Three Different Methods of Application Ranging** from **Justice** (honor), to **Mercy** (glory), unto **Love** (majesty). This now shows us that the "Eternal Father (flesh/mind)" Believes in the **Force of Law** (justice) based on an *Eye for an Eye* and a *Tooth for a Tooth* (slow method); while the "Son of God (spirit/heart)" Believes in the **Force of Mercy** based on **Turning the Other Cheek** (instant method). This clearly shows the "Infinite Value" and essence of Human Existence, since it expresses an intricate **Balance** between **Honor** (babies/being saved), **Glory** (land/saving self), and **Majesty** (life/saving others) which must **Bear Fruit** (love) **in the End**. The "Fruits of Life" will bring a liberated soul to Eternal Fulfillment in the **Eyes of God** by **Learning** the difference between **God's Right** and **Man's Wrong**.

This "Mystical Process" makes a Christian Soul worthy of the Lord's cherished **Gift of Eternal Existence** which has been founded upon the **Sacrifice of God's Divine Son** as **He Died** on **Mount Calvary** (forgiveness). From the "Mutual Love" between Divinity's Willingness to **Forgive** and Humanity's Willingness to **Repent, God and Man** can share **One Existence** and still **Not Defile** God's **Sacred Perfection** (sanctity). This means that each of "God's Children" must Learn to Honor the People (perfection), bring "Glory to the Land (fruitful)," and Worship the Majesty of Life (eternal life/time). This "Perfect Marriage" between Divinity (1st truth) and Humanity (2nd truth) will make **All Creation** into **Community Property, Allowing All Beings** to **Share One Land** (divine home), **Citizenry, God's Babies** (sacred government), and **One Life-force** (holy church) **Equally Forever.** This "New State of Existence" will be Ruled by the Will of the People (tithing system) as seen through the **Divine Eyes of Jesus Christ,** thereby **Manifesting** God's Divine Will (temple tax system) through the **Lord's New Perfect Justice System of Love** (kingdom).

We see that through both the "Will of the People" and the "Will of God," Human Existence is **Governed** as **Manifested** within "Each of God's Children (individual will)" through the **Lord's Ten, Two, and One Commandments**. This means that the "Individual" is Called to **See his Parents;** that "Society" is Called to **See Its Leaders;** and that a "Son of God" is Called to **See his Creator, All in the Name of Human, Angelic, and Divine Order.** The idea here is that the "Ten Commandments of God" came from the Jews to bring **God's Law to Earth** to **Govern All the Affairs** of **Confused Men**. Secondly, the "Two Commandments of God" came from the Christians to bring **God's Faith to Heaven** to **Govern All the Affairs** of **Awakened Men**. Finally, the "One Commandment of God" came from the Saints to bring **God's Knowing to the Kingdom** to **Govern All the Affairs** of **Saintly Men**. Through his steady

"Growth and Maturity," a <u>Person can Master</u> the **Life-experience** and come to **Know** (sinner/baby), **Love** (Christian/teenage), and **Serve** (saint/adult) **his Creator God**.

The implication is that "If a Person" can <u>Fulfill God's Law</u> (learn right/wrong), then he will have **Earned God's Blessing** of a **Promised Land** within the **Lord's Physical Kingdom**. Secondly, "If He" can <u>Fulfill the Christian Faith</u> (learn good/evil), then he will have **Earned God's Blessing** of **Eternal Life in Heaven** within the **Lord's Spiritual Kingdom**. Finally, "If He" can <u>Fulfill Saintly Knowing</u> (learn God/s Will/man's will), then he will have **Earned God's Blessing** of his **Own Kingdom** within **God's Kingdom** and within the **Lord's Mystical Kingdom**. By "Mastering" the <u>Earth, Heaven,</u> and <u>God's Kingdom,</u> **He** can **Prove to his Creator** that he has unconditionally **Bowed to All God's Commandments** in **Mind** (ignorant), **Heart** (coward), and **Soul** (greedy) and has **Become an Eternal Servant unto the Lord**. Only by "Becoming a Dutiful Son" of the <u>Lord God Almighty</u> can a **Person** become **Worthy** of a **High Position** in **God's Celestial Court** (righteous man), **Temple Court** (holy man), and **Royal Court** (perfect man). In this way, a "Son of God" can effectively <u>Worship</u> (give life), <u>Praise</u> (give money), and <u>Thank</u> (give labors) his **God** for **All the Treasures of Life**. Yes! We are all "Seeking the Treasures of Life," but only <u>Jesus Christ</u> has the <u>Divine Power</u> capable of **Attaining** a **New Body, Eternal Life in Heaven,** and **His Own Kingdom of Glory**.

The following tabular information indicates that the "Ten Commandments (land)" <u>Rule</u> **Planet Earth** (baby/priest); that the "Two Commandments (life)" <u>Rule</u> **God's Heaven** (teenager/king); and that the "One Commandment (kingdom)" <u>Rules</u> **God's Kingdom of Glory** (adult/son):

Ten Commandments Govern Earth/Two Commandments Govern Heaven/One Commandment Governs Kingdom
(ten commandments get promised land/two commandments get life/one commandment gets kingdom)

Baby

1. **Ten Commandments** - <u>Governing Earth:</u> Learn Right/Wrong ... . Knowledge

Law

(priest)

- Fulfill Law to Get Promised Land - New Body (land)
- Righteous Citizen on Earth - See Limitations (physical dimension)
- Seat in Celestial Court - Know God (sinner)
- Thank God - Remove Capital Sins: Easter Duty (give labors)

God's Physical Law	Man's Physical Law
1. Have No Other gods	1. Do Not Kill (murder)
2. Have No Graven Images	2. Do Not Commit Adultery (sex)
3. Never Take God's Name in Vain	3. Do Not Steal
4. Keep Sabbath Day Holy	4. Do Not Lie
5. Honor Father/Mother	5. Do Not Covet (cheat)

(will of individual - child sees his parents: schooled in elementary school)

Teenage

2. **Two Commandments** - <u>Governing Heaven:</u> Learn Good/Evil......

Self-awareness

Faith (king)	•	Fulfill Faith to Get Abundant Life - Eternal Life (life)
	•	Holy Saint in Heaven - See Potential (spiritual dimension)
	•	Seat in Temple Court - Love God (Christian)
	•	Praise God - Remove Mortal Sins: Weekly (give money)

God's Spiritual Law   Man's Spiritual Law

1. Worship God with Whole Heart   1. Love Neighbor as Oneself

(will of the people - society sees its leaders: schooled in high school)

Adult

3. **One Commandment** - Governing Kingdom: Learn God's Will/man's will..........Consciousness

Knowing (son)	•	Fulfill Knowing to Get Own Kingdom - Royal Kingdom (kingdom)
	•	Perfect Son within Kingdom - See Self-worth (mystical dimension)
	•	Seat in Royal Court - Serve God (saint)
	•	Worship God - Remove Venial Sins: Daily (give life)

God/Man's Universal Law

1. Love One Another as I have Loved You

(will of God - creation sees its most perfect creator: schooled in college)

This illustration shows that the "Lord's Ten Commandments (righteousness)" had been brought to Earth to **Define** *God's Physical Law* (intellect) and *Man's Physical Law* (emotions); while the "Lord's Two Commandments (holiness)" have been Created for Heaven to **Define** *God's Spiritual Law* (intellect) and *Man's Spiritual Law* (emotions). Combining "God's Physical and Spiritual Laws" into a **New Covenant** brings forth the **One Commandment** (perfection) into the **Kingdom** to **Define** the *God/Man Universal Law* (intellect/emotion). The point is to see that the "Ten Commandments (physical)" bring forth Mankind's **Individual Rights** by **Breaking the Chains of Sin** (ignorance) to *Set the Baby Captives Free*. Secondly, we see that the "Two Commandments (spiritual)" bring forth Mankind's **Social Rights** by **Opening the Prison Doors of Evil** (cowardice) to *Set the Teenage Captives Free*. Finally, we see that the "One Commandment (mystical)" brings forth Mankind's **Divine Rights** by **Overpowering the Guards of Death** to *Set the Adult Captives Free*. This means that through "Individual," "Social," and "Divine Rights," the Lord God Almighty has **Created** a whole **New Justice System Capable of Serving** Men, Angels, and God Equally (fairly). Through this "New Justice System," a person can Fix his Identity on Earth, clearly Focus on the Values of Heaven, and then one day, Correctly Perceive God's Kingdom, allowing him to **Comprehend the Unknown, Recognize Normality,** and **Believe God's Truths.** Imagine that a single "Eighty-Year Life (80)" is simply a model for one's Eternal Life, allowing each soul to grasp the **Magnitude of God's Creation** by extrapolating each *Moment into an Eternity of Time.* Now, assume that one's "Human Life" is unfolding in precisely the same manner, but at an extremely Slow Rate of Time, thereby never allowing a person to know if he is *Three Years Old* or *Eighty-Five Years Old*. This implies that if it has been a "Trillion-times-a-Trillion Years," then where is he in the <u>Overall Scheme of Things</u>, especially when he hears **God** saying; "**We are Just Getting Started?**"

To "Understand God" and <u>His Creation,</u> we must see that there are <u>Four Separate Systems Operating</u> (mind/heart/soul/life-force) through the **Redemption** (salvation) and **Sanctification** (rewards) of **Man** as the **Human Flesh** is **Transformed** via the **Jewish Law** (remove faults) and then the **Human Spirit** is transformed via our **Christian Faith** (gain virtues). We are being told that the "Laity (looking-down/man)" is entering the <u>World</u> (temptations) to **Learn Right from Wrong**; while the "Priesthood (looking-up/God)" is mastering the <u>Church</u> (obedience) to **Learn Good from Evil.** The idea is that once a "Person (laity)" becomes <u>Streetwise</u> by understanding **Ethical Behavior** (right/wrong), this knowledge is **Transmitted** to the **Saints in Heaven** so that a **Christian** can become **Righteous before God** (eternal life).

In this same regard, we see that once a "Priest" becomes <u>Educated</u> sufficiently to comprehend **Moral Behavior** (good/evil), then this knowledge is **Transmitted** to the **Angels in Heaven** so that an **Anointed Soul** can become **Holy before God** (divinity). This means that when the "Saints (intellect)" get the knowledge of <u>Right and Wrong</u> (ethics), they can then determine the **Will of Man** (collective mind) to **Change Ignorance** (old mind) into **Wisdom** (new mind). Secondly, when the "Angels (emotion)" get the knowledge of <u>Good and Evil</u> (morals), they can determine the **Will of God** (infinite mind) to **Change Cowardice** (new heart) to **Courage** (new heart). We now see that out of "One's Ethics (flesh)" comes the <u>Collective Mind</u> to create a **Perfect Society** (world); while out of "One's Morals (spirit)" comes the <u>Infinite Mind</u> to create the **Perfect Man** (church). The message is: when the "Laity" and "Priesthood" become <u>One Will</u> via the **Union of Ethics/Morals**, then the **Catholic Church** can be **Changed** into the **Mystical Body of Christ** (earth). Secondly, we see that when the "Saints" and "Angels" become <u>One Will</u> via the **Union of Righteousness/Holiness,** then **Heaven** can establish God's **Communion of Saints** (**Heaven**). We see that at the "End of Time," both the <u>Mystical Body</u> (man's flesh) and the <u>Communion of Saints</u> (man's spirit) will become **One** in **Truth, Law, Will, and Love.**

The following tabular information indicates that the "Human Race" will <u>Purify Its Mind</u> by **Changing** its **Ignorance to Wisdom**, <u>Transforming Its Heart</u> by **Changing** its **Cowardice into Courage**, <u>Converting Its Soul</u> by **Changing** its **Greed into Generosity**, and <u>Modernizing Its Life-force</u> by **Changing** its **Selfishness into Unselfishness**:

**Changing Ignorance, Cowardice, Greed and Selfishness to
Wisdom, Courage, Generosity, Unselfishness**
(removing sin-nature, worldly temptations, demonic
possession, and God's curse to save man)

Baby   1. **Ignorance to Wisdom** - <u>Remove Sin-nature</u> ....Government (sin)
(Earth)
                 • Learn Right from Wrong - Ethics: Righteousness (citizenship)
                 • Self becomes King, becomes Government, becomes Earth – God becomes Man
                 • Master Body - Being Saved: See Limitations = Blessed with Knowledge

- New Body - Purification: Individual Rights = Kingship (mind)
(elementary school - taught by Blessed Mother: subject is repentance)

Teenager 2. **Cowardice to Courage** - <u>Remove Worldly Temptations</u>........Church (evil)
(Heaven)
- Learn Good from Evil - Morals: Holiness (sainthood)
- Society becomes Priest, becomes Church, becomes Heaven - Man becomes God
- Master Blood - Saving Self: See Potential = Anointed with Self-awareness
- Eternal Life - Transformation: Social Rights = Priesthood (heart)
(high school - taught by Saint Joseph: subject is holy prayers)

Adult 3. **Greed to Generosity** - <u>Remove Demonic Possession</u> ....Home (death)
(Kingdom)
- Learn God's Will/man's will - Fairness: Perfection (sonship)
- God becomes Son, becomes Home, becomes Kingdom - God and Man become One
- Master Soul - Saving Others: See Self-worth - Sanctified with Consciousness
- Royal Kingdom - Conversion: Divine Rights = Sonship (soul)
(college - taught by Jesus Christ: subject is the saving of souls)

Wise Man 4. **Selfishness to Unselfishness** - <u>Remove God's Curse</u>......Self (damnation)
(Freedom)
- Learn God's Reality/man's illusion - Blessed: Divine (fatherhood)
- Life becomes Death, becomes Rebirth, becomes New-life - God and Man are Free
- Master Divinity - Saving God: See Divinity - Consecrated with Sentience
- Personal Freedom - Modernized: All Rights = Fatherhood (life-force)
(on-the-job-training - taught by God: subject is thinking for oneself)

This illustration shows that as "Babies (being saved)," we are in a <u>Sea of Ignorance</u> and must strive to **Find Wisdom** by **Learning Right from Wrong** (see limitations) to become **Ethical People** (follow man's law) on the **<u>Lord's Pathway to Righteousness</u>** (new body) leading to **Earthly Citizenship**. Secondly, as "Teenagers (saving self)," we are in a <u>Sea of Cowardice</u> and must strive to **Find Our Own Courage** by **Learning Good from Evil** (see potential) to become **Moral People** (follow God's law) on the **<u>Lord's Pathway to Holiness</u>** (eternal life) leading to **Heavenly Sainthood**. Thirdly, as "Adults (saving others)," we are in a <u>Sea of Greed</u> and must strive to **Become Generous toward Others** by **Learning God's Will from man's will** to become **Fair Persons** (think for self) on the **<u>Lord's Pathway of Perfection</u>** (royal kingdom) leading to our **Kingdom's Sonship**. Finally, as a "Wise Man (saving God)," we are in a <u>Sea of Selfishness</u> and must strive to become **Unselfish toward Man** by **Learning God's Reality and man's illusion** to **Bless Others** (love man) on the **<u>Lord's Pathway of Divinity</u>** (personal freedom) leading to our **Eternal Fatherhood**.

Through these "Four Stages of Transformation," a person can both Grow-up (mandatory) and Mature (optional) within God's **Kingdom of Glory** through the **Forces** of **Knowledge** (mind), **Self-awareness** (heart), **Consciousness** (soul), and **Sentience** (life-force). Obviously, the Lord is constructing "Four Schools" to Educate His most **Beloved Children** beginning with **Elementary School on Earth** (babies/Blessed Mother), **High School in Heaven** (teenagers/Saint Joseph), **College within the Kingdom** (adults/Jesus Christ), and then **On-the-Job-Training by the Almighty** (wise man/God). This means that the "God/Man Union" of these Four Stages of Life comes about through a **Series of Marriages** bringing the **Sinfulness of Man** (virginity) into **Oneness** with the **Holiness of God** (name). We are trying to say here that out of "God's 1st Marriage (God/Man)," the Angels and Saints can become **One Kingdom** (Heaven/reality), just as through the power of "God's 2nd Marriage (Heaven/Earth)," the Priests and Laity can become **One People** (Earth/illusion).

We see that the "Job of the Holy Mass (consecration)" is to Unite both the Communion of Saints (God) representing the **God/Man Family** (Heaven) with the Mystical Body (Man) which also represents all the **God/Man Friends** (Earth). This means that the "Family of God" is ruled by the Spirit Nature which functions via its **Depth of Faith** to attain the Almighty's **Eternal Rewards** (bonus). Secondly, we see that the "Friends of God" are ruled by the Flesh Nature which functions via **Jewish Law** to strive in bringing **Salvation to Others** (earned). It is now clear that the "Job of the Flesh" is to Face the Temptations of the World as a way of **Learning the Lessons of Life** (right/wrong) so that an **Awakened Soul** can have its **Faults Removed,** emptying it of all **Sin, Evil, and Death.** In like manner, the "Job of the Spirit" is to become Educated within the Church so that one can **Learn the Lessons of God** (good/evil) to be **Awakened** to the need of being **Filled** with the **Lord's Holy Virtues.**

Obviously, in the "Life-experience," most people see the Struggle for Existence (cross) as an **Obstacle to be Avoided**; while the **Awakened Soul Accepts its Cross** as a **Challenge to Overcome.** Out of one's desire to "Face the Challenges of Life" and the willingness to Sacrifice (worship) himself as a **Holocaust unto the Lord,** he might be **Emptied of his Selfishness** by **Accepting** his **Punishment of Death.** Then, that person can be "Transformed" into a Living Prayer to master the **Christian Faith** and be **Filled with Unselfishness** by entering **God's Blessing of New-life.** In essence, this means that whatever can be "Imagined" can be "Achieved," if one places his Perfect Faith (knowing without proof) in the **Life and Teachings of Jesus Christ.** Yes! It is all a matter of "Growing-up" and Thinking for Oneself with the confidence that whatever a person **Does in his Life** is **Right** and will eventually **Bear Fruit** (good) in **Service to God.**

We can now get a picture of the whole "Process" which starts with the "Effects of the World," known to us as Transgressions (venial sins) or Offenses by one **Man to Another Man** which are **Confessed** (flesh/blood) to **Mary's Son, Jesus** (human nature) as the **Son of Man** (Earth). This "Sin, Along with One's Absolution," is taken to the Holy Mass (Epistle side), where it is Lifted-up (offering) by the Laity, who declares that this **Sinner** has now **Learned Right from Wrong** (repentance) and is **Asking Jesus** to **Offer-up** (gift) his <u>Flesh and Blood</u> as a **Sacrifice unto the Lord.** Out of this "Sacrificial Offering," this <u>Forgiven Soul's Ethics</u> (earth) will be **Changed into Righteousness** (perfect society/friendship) by **God's Saints.** The "Saints" then report to the "Virgin Mary" that one more soul has <u>Learned the Value</u> of **Man's Will** as seen by the **Flesh of Man,** thereby making him a **Righteous King,** whose **Faults have been Removed** so that he might be **Emptied** of all his **Sin, Evil, and Death.** Once a person has passed through this initial "Phase of Transformation," he is given the Lord's <u>Blessing of Forgiveness</u> and Jesus' **Gift of Salvation**, making him worthy of a new **Transfigured Body.**

This means that the "Job of the Evil World" is to <u>Teach Humanity</u> the **Value of Ethics** (right/wrong) which is **Sent to Heaven** so that the **Saints can Convert Its Ethics** into **God's Righteousness** (right/wrong). Through "His Righteousness," a person comes to know the <u>Value of Man's Will,</u> thereby making him a **King** (wisdom) **before God.** The idea is to see that by combining his "Righteousness" and his "Holiness," **Merging** them together, then a person can become **Perfect in the Sight of God** based on the depth of his **Wisdom** (flesh), **Courage** (spirit), and **Generosity** (soul).

Now, let's look at the "Second Phase" of this <u>Redemption Process</u> which starts with the effects of the **Church,** known to us as **Serious Sin** (mortal sin) or **Offenses Against One's God** which are **Confessed** to God's Son, **Christ** (divine nature) as the **Son of God.** This "Raw Sin" along with "One's Absolution (forgiven sin)" are taken to the <u>Holy Mass</u> (Gospel side), where they are **Lifted-up by the Priesthood,** which declares before God that this **Christian** has now **Learned Good from Evil** (repentance) and is **Asking Christ** to offer his **Bread** and **Wine** as a **Prayer unto the Lord.** Out of this "Intercessory Prayer," a <u>Christian's Morals</u> (earth) will be **Changed** into **Holiness** (perfect man/love/Heaven) by **God's Angels.** The "Angels" then report to the "Eternal Father" that one more Christian has Learned the Value of **God's Will** as seen by the **Spirit of God,** thereby making him a **Holy Priest,** who has been **Filled with God's Virtues** to be given **God's Blessing** of **Righteousness, Holiness, and Perfection.** Once a person has passed through this "Secondary Phase of Transformation," he is again given the Lord's <u>Blessing of Forgiveness</u> and **Christ's Gift of Eternal Rewards,** making him worthy of a new **Glorified Spirit.**

This means that the "Job of the Catholic Church" is to Educate Mankind on the **Value of Human Morals** (good/evil) which is **Sent to Heaven** so that the **Angels** can **Convert One's Morals** into **God's Holiness** (good/evil). Through a "Soul's Holiness," a Future Saint knows the **Value of God's Will,** thereby making him a **Priest** (beauty) **before God.**

The following graphic illustration shows the entire "Redemptive Process" from being a <u>Sinner</u> **Converted** into a <u>Christian</u> and then **Transformed** into a **Holy Saint** worthy of the **Presence of God in Heaven:**

God - Heaven
(Heavenly Marriage to Mary)

Cross Altar

(Eternal Father - Blessing of Forgiveness)

King - Holy Father (expectations)　　　　　　(hopes) Holy Mother – Queen

Man's Love = **Perfect Man**　　　　　　**Perfect Society** = Man's Friendship.

Divinity

Eternal Father - **Spirit of God**　　　　　**Flesh of God** - Virgin Mary

　• Image - Nature　　　　　　　　　• Likeness - Behavior

　　Angels　　　　　　　　　　　　　Saints

　(create holiness)　　　　**Abel**　　　(create righteousness)

Easter

(wealth)

Son

Priest　　　　　　　　　　　　　　King

(beauty)　　　　　　　　　　　　　(wisdom)

(give divinity)

Crucifixion = God's Gift of Divinity

Prayer　　　　　**Christ**　　　　Glorify Friend

(bread/wine)　　　(divine nature)　　　(Spirit)

Communion

Rewards – **Innocent**

Blood　　　　　New-life

Consecration　　　Death　　　**Guilty** - Salvation

God's Holy Mass　　　　　　**Blood**　　**Confession**

Destroy Enemies　　**Jesus**　　　Sacrifice

(flesh)　　　　(human nature)　　(flesh/blood)

Glorified　　　　　　　　Transfigured

Spirit　　　　　　　　　Body

(gift of divinity)　　　　　(gift of eternal life)

(will)

Work ....Soul

Spirit......**Pray**　　　　**Repent**................Flesh

(law)　　　　　　(truth)

Transmitting　　　　　　Transmitting

Good/Evil　　　　　　　Right/Wrong

Priesthood　　Man becomes God　　Laity

Christmas

Jesus Christ - Flesh of God　　　Cain　　　Spirit of Man - Holy Church

Humanity

Morals　　　Gospel　　　　Epistle　　　Ethics

(church)　　────────────────────　　(world)

Table Altar

(Blessed Mother's - Prayer of Repentance)

Sin - Mortal		Venial - Transgressions
(man against God)		(man against man)

Catholic Church - Earth

(Earthly Marriage to Jesus Christ)

Man's Nature		Man's Behavior
Holy Saint	Value of Life/Will to Live	Righteous Citizen

This illustration shows that the entire "Redemptive Process" by which <u>Sinful Humans are Transformed</u> into **Holy Saints** comes via both a **Physical** (ethics/intellect) and a **Spiritual** (morals/emotions) **Purification Method of Conversion.** Note here that our "Physical Conversion" is centered on <u>Mary's Son, Jesus Taking-on All Sin</u> (confession) as He was **Scourged at the Pillar** (sacrifice) to **Repent** for man's **Sinful Mind, Evil Heart,** and **Lifeless Soul** (dead). Secondly, we see that one's "Spiritual Conversion" is centered upon <u>God's Son, Christ Giving-up His Divinity</u> (communion) as He was **Crucified on the Cross** (prayer) to **Intercede** so that **Mankind** will **Receive** a **New Mind, Heart, and Soul.**

In essence, this chart is explaining just how a "Lost Soul" is able to become an <u>Awakened Christian</u> as he masters the art of **Dying to Self** (submission). The idea here is that the more a person "Sacrifices his Own Flesh" as <u>Jesus at the Pillar</u> (total surrender), the more his **Prayer will Grow in his Spirit** (born-again). This means that the "Lord Knew" that throughout "His Trials" and during his "Torture" all the way to <u>Carrying His Cross</u> (mountain of sin), all depended upon **His Ability** to **Reject His Divine Power** and to **Surrender His Human Life unto Death.** If the Lord was able to resist using "His Divine Authority" and <u>Sacrificed Himself</u> totally, then at the **Hour of Judgment,** His **Prayer would be Heard** by God Himself. By becoming "Mankind's Eternal Intercessor" at the <u>Right Hand of God,</u> **Jesus Christ** could be of **Greatest Assistance** to **One and All.** We see that "Jesus Christ" was required to represent both the <u>Repentance</u> of **Guilty Blood** (human nature/Jesus) and the <u>Forgiveness</u> of **Innocent Blood** (divine nature/Christ) which **Required Him** to **Surrender to His Scourging** (guilty) and to also **Pray during His Crucifixion** (innocent).

The point is to see that out of the "Lord's Sacrifice," <u>Man's Flesh</u> (illusion) was ****Executed**** for its **Crime of Stealing** from <u>God's Tree of Knowledge;</u> while out of the "Lord's Prayer," <u>Man's Spirit</u> (reality) was ****Redeemed**** for having returned all that was **Stolen** when **Adam and Eve Ate the Forbidden Fruit.** The implication is that all our "Humanity has Gained" in "Scientific Knowledge" leading to <u>Personal Wealth</u> and <u>Individual Freedom</u> (free will) must be **Paid For** in both **Recompense** (restore) and **Punitive Damages** (retribution). In this explanation, we see that "Recompense" is to <u>Surrender One's Life</u> totally to the **Holy Church** to comply with the **Lord's Request** that one must **Go Sell All** and **Give to the Poor** (naked). In contrast, we see that "Punitive Damages" means to <u>Serve One's Time in Purgatory,</u> thereby complying with the **Lord's Request** that one must **Come Follow Him** (restitution) by carrying **Christ's Cross of Death** until both his **Sin- and Holy-Debts are Paid in Full.** In other words, the "Lord is Telling Us" that each "Wicked Pagan" must <u>Deny his Intellect, Abandon his Feelings,</u> and <u>Submit his Free Will</u> to open himself up to

Accepting God's Divine Will as his **Own Will.** If a person is willing to "Sacrifice his Flesh (school)" and then turn his <u>Spirit into a Living Prayer</u> (student), he will be given both **Physical Salvation** (transfigured body/human life) and **Spiritual Rewards** (glorified spirit/divine life), thereby making him a **Saint in Heaven** forevermore.

In the previous chart, we are being shown that the "Epistle (letter) Side of the Altar (Man's Ethics)" is bringing the <u>Human Race</u> **God's Blessing of a New Body** (earned) via the **Death of Man** (tribulation) as the <u>**Laity**</u> (Yom Kippur) **Offers-up** (confession) its **Sinful Flesh and Blood** (absolution) to **God's Church** (saints). We see that it's "Mary's Son, Jesus (Divine Man)" who is called to <u>Master the Art of Ethics</u> by **Physically Learning Right from Wrong** (mind) during **His Scourging at the Pillar** to bring **Righteousness onto the Earth** in the form of **Righteous Citizens** (friendship). Out of this "Act of Submission," the Lord will bring forth <u>Heaven on Earth</u> as each **Christian Follows Jesus** through the **White Throne Judgment** to receive both his own **Transfigured Body** and his **Seat in God's Celestial Court** (title deed to Earth). Now, we see that through the "Saints," <u>Lost Broken Sinners</u> (guilty blood) can be **Redeemed** via Jesus' **Prayer of Repentance** (confession) which had the power to **Destroy God's Enemies** and bring them to **God's Blessing of Forgiveness** (communion).

In this "Conversion" from <u>Wicked Sinner</u> to <u>Righteous Citizen,</u> we see the Lord takes a person's **Eyes Off of the Illusion** (80 years) and puts his **Eyes on God's Reality** (eternity) so that all might see that **Ignorance becomes Wisdom** (mind), **Cowardice becomes Courage** (heart), and **Greed becomes Generosity** (soul). Secondly, we see that the "Gospel (word) Side of the Altar (God's Morals)" is bringing the <u>Human Race</u> **God's Gift of Divinity** (bonus) via the **Death of God** (Calvary) as the **Priesthood** (Passover) **Offers-up** (communion) its **Sacred Bread and Wine** (forgiveness) to **God's Throne.** We see that it is "God's Son, Christ (Human God)" who is called to <u>Master the Art of Morals</u> by **Spiritually Learning Good from Evil** (heart) during **His Crucifixion on the Cross** to bring **Holiness to Heaven** in the form of **Holy Saints** (love). Out of this "Act of Sacrifice," the <u>Lord</u> will bring forth <u>Paradise in Heaven</u> as each **Saint Follows Christ** through the **New Heaven and new earth** to receive both his own **Glorified Spirit** and his **Seat in God's Temple Court** (title deed to Heaven).

Now, we see that through the "Angels," <u>Devout Christians</u> (innocent blood) can be **Saved** via **Christ's Blessing of Forgiveness** (communion) which had the **Power** to **Glorify God's Friends** and bring them to **God's Blessing of Sonship** (saving others). In this "Conversion" from <u>Christian</u> to <u>Holy Saint,</u> the Lord takes a person's **Eyes Off of Earth** and puts his **Eyes on Heaven** so that all might see how to become a **Righteous King** (mind), **Holy Priest** (heart), and **Perfect Son** (soul). When the "New Spirit of Man (righteous citizen)" and the "New Flesh of God (holy saint)" become <u>One</u> within the <u>Holy Soul,</u> **God and Man** will **Share the Life-experience** on **Man's Earth** (friends), in **God's Heaven** (companions), and within **God/Man's Kingdom** (oneness). We see that the "Earth" will be made-up of the <u>New Ethical Nature</u> (Jesus/origin); "Heaven" will be made-up of the <u>New Moral Behavior</u> (Christ/journey); and the "Kingdom" will be made-up of the <u>New</u>

Fair Lifestyle (Jesus Christ/destination). In this way, "Ethics/Morals/Fairness" will become the <u>Foundation stones of Life</u> bringing forth **Mankind's Righteousness** (earth), **Holiness** (Heaven), and **Perfection** (Kingdom). The following tabular information indicates that the "Creation of Man's New Body (Earth/human life)" comes from the <u>Death of Man</u> (tribulation); and God's "Gift of Divinity or Eternal Life (Heaven/divine life)" comes from the <u>Death of God</u> (Calvary):

God's Creation of New Body and Gift of Divinity
Unites Righteous Citizens with Holy Saints
(Sadducees believe in Heaven on Earth;
Pharisees believe in Heaven in Paradise with God)

Jesus
(mind)

1. **Creation of New Body** - <u>Righteous Citizen:</u> Man's Ethics .....Righteousness
   - <u>Belief of Sadducees</u> - Heaven on Earth: Perfect Society: Mosaic Law (temple)
   - Ten Commandments (stone tablets) - Laity Offers Sinner's Flesh and Blood
   - Sacrificial Offering of Goat - Yom Kippur: Confession = Repentance
   - Social Rights - Adam's Fruit: Land (dirt) = Breath becomes Human Life
   - Jews - People of Death: Title Deed to the Earth = Slaves in Service to Man
   - <u>Death of Man</u> - Tribulation: Learning Right from Wrong = Create Divine Man (flesh)
   - Easter - Man becomes God: Saints Take-sin (virginity) = Son of Man
   - Confession - Absolution: Raw Sin Teaches Truth…Righteous World
   - Free *Transfigured Body* - Redemption: Being Saved… Individual Rights
   - Fulfill Mother's Hopes - Man's Friendship: Will of the People
   - Honored with Seat in Celestial Court - Apostles/Tribes Rule Earth
     (Serpent's "Tree of Knowledge" - Teaches Sin-nature, Worldly Temptations, and Demonic Possession)

Christ
(heart)

2. **Gift of Divinity** - <u>Holy Saint:</u> Man's Morals ………….. Holiness
   - <u>Belief of Pharisees</u> - Paradise in Heaven: Perfect Man: Canon Law (church)
   - Temple Tax (silver shekel) - Offer Bread and Wine: Son of God
   - Sacrificial Offering of Lamb - Passover Meal: Communion = Forgiveness
   - Individual Rights - Eve's Fruit: Babies (blood) = Rib becomes Divine Life
   - Christians - People of Life: Title Deed to Heaven = Free Men in Service to God
   - <u>Death of God</u> - Calvary: Learning Good from Evil = Create Human God (spirit)
   - Christmas - God becomes Man: Angels Give Divinity (royal name) = Son of God
   - Communion - Forgiveness: Forgiven Sin Teaches Law——Holy Church

- Earned *Glorified Spirit* - Salvation: Saving Self…Social Rights
- Fulfill Father's Expectations - Man's Love: Divine Will of God
- Honored Seat in Temple Court - Choirs/Churches/Gates/Messiah: Rule Heaven

(God's Tree of Life - Teaches Righteous Kingship [mind],
Holy Priesthood [heart], and Perfect Sonship [soul])

This illustration shows that to "Believe in the Sadducees' Philosophy" means believing in Heaven on Earth as **God comes to Live with Man** in a **Perfect Society of Friends,** fulfilling the **Mosaic Law of Physical Righteousness** (righteous citizens). This "Perfect Society" would be ruled by the Temple Government, its **Ten Commandments** or Eye-for-an-eye, and its **Sacrificial Goat Offering** of **Flesh and Blood** (repentance) or **Calvary Asking God** for **His Physical Blessings** (wealth). This "New Perfect Earth" would now bring forth Adam's Fruitful Lands via **God's Breath of Human Life** (wealth) which brings forth the **King of the Jews** (Jesus/divine man) to **Rule** as a **Slave in Service to Man.** This "New Garden of Eden" will be Purchased via the Death of Man through the **Coming Tribulation**, where all men will **Learn Right from Wrong** and **Repent of their Wicked Ways** to become **Righteous Citizens One and All.** Through "Easter (Yom Kippur)," Man will become God, allowing the **Saints to Take All Sin** (virginity) via **Man's Confession** to **Transform Sinners** into **Righteous Citizens.** This process is known as "Saving Oneself" or Earning Salvation through the **Fulfillment** of **Man's Social Rights** allowing a **Person to Receive** a **New Transfigured Body** and the **Title Deed to Earth.** This is done in "Fulfillment of the Hopes" of the Blessed Mother that each of **Her Children** will become a **Personal Friend to God** and strive to bring forth the **Lord's Kingdom of Glory.** If a person attains "God's Friendship," he will be worthy of a Seat in the Lord's Celestial Court, where he will **Rule with both the Apostles** and the **Twelve Tribes of Israel.** In this way, his "Soul will have Mastered (intellect)" the Serpent's Tree of Knowledge (right/wrong), allowing him to **Overcome his Own Sin-nature**, the **Temptations of the World,** and all **Demonic Possession** to become **Righteous before God.**

To "Believe in the Pharisees' Philosophy" means believing in Paradise in Heaven as **Man comes to Live with God** as a **Perfect Man,** fulfilling the **Canon Law of Spiritual Holiness** (holy saint). This "Perfect Man" would be ruled by the Holy Church via the **Ancient Temple Tax** (silver shekel) or **Turning-the-Other-Cheek** and its **Sacrificial Lamb Offering** in the form of **Bread and Wine** (forgiveness) asking **God** for **His Spiritual Blessings** (love). This "New Perfect Heaven" would now bring forth Eve's Fruitful Babies via **Eve's Rib of Divine Life** (love) bringing forth the **High Priest of Heaven** (Christ/human God) to **Rule** as a **Free Man in Service to God.** We see that this "New Heavenly Paradise" will be Purchased via the Death of God through **Christ's Crucifixion** (Calvary), where all men will **Learn Good from Evil** and live by **God's Holy Ways** to become **Holy Saints One and All.** Through "Christmas (Passover)," God will become Man, allowing the **Angels to Sacrifice Christ's Divinity** (name) via **Man's Communion** to **Transform Christians** into **Holy Saints.** This process is known as "Being Saved" or receiving one's Free Redemption through the **Fulfillment** of his **Individual Rights** allowing a **Person to Receive** a **New Glorified Spirit** and the **Title Deed to Heaven.** This is done in "Fulfillment of God's Expectations" that each of His Children will become **Loving Sons and Daughters of God** and **Strive** to bring forth the **Lord's Kingdom of Glory.** If a person attains "God's Love," he will be worthy of a Seat in the Lord's Temple Court, where he will **Rule with the Choirs of Angels,** the **Seven Temple Gates, Seven Churches,** plus the **Messiah** (High Priest). In this way, his "Soul will have Mastered (emotions)" God's Tree of Life (good/evil) allowing him to comprehend the **Lord's Righteous Kingship** (mind), **Holy Priesthood** (heart) and **Perfect Sonship** (soul) to become **Holy before God.**

We can now better understand why "God Killed" the First-born Egyptian Males (government/free men) as the Lord **Takes Man's Sin** to **Create the Righteous Citizen** (right from wrong), while "Setting Free" the First-born Jewish Males (church/slave), thereby **Giving Them His Divinity** so that He could **Create the Holy Saint** (good and evil). Recall that during the "Circumcision Ceremony" of a New-Born Baby, the **Priest** would take **Two Doves** and **Kill One** (Egyptians) to **Dip the Second Dove** into its **Sacrificial Blood** so that it might be **Purified** and made worthy of being **Set Free Forever** (Jews). It is important that we hold onto this "Kill One" to "Free the Other Concept" throughout the Redemptive Process as we see both the **Role** of the **Temple of Death** (sacrifice) versus the **Throne of New-life** (prayer). Secondly, we see the "Role" of the Church of Death (sacrifice) versus Government of Life (prayer) which leads to the "Role" of Man's **Earth of Death** (sacrifice/flesh) versus God's **Heaven of Life** (prayer/spirit). Finally, this "Master Concept" of Death (sacrifice) and Resurrection (prayer) culminates in the **Physical Creation** of the **Universe** (tree of knowledge) versus the **Spiritual Creation** (tree of life) of the **Kingdom.** In the "End," we see that the Universe (school) and the Kingdom (employment) become **One** in the **New God/Man Nature of Life** (love) allowing **Thy Kingdom to Come** and **Thy Will to be Done** to manifest the **Eternal Union** between **All Flesh** (emotion/female/weeds) and **All Spirit** (intellect/male/wheat).

Obviously, the Lord was creating "Three Sets of People;" the Jewish People (righteous/earth), Christian People (holy/Heaven), and the Purified People (perfect/kingdom) to serve His **Kingship** (throne), **Priesthood** (temple), and His **Sonship** (palace) **now and forever.** We see that through these "Three Peoples," the Human Race will be able to **Control Its Thoughts** (look/elementary), **Control Its Feelings** (touch/high school), **Control Its Instincts** (wash/college), and finally, **Control Its Free Will** (set free/liberty). In short, we see that "Babies (mind)" will become Smart (elementary school); "Teenagers (heart)" will Understand Their Feelings (high school); "Adults (soul)" will Do Everything Right (college); and "Wise Men (life-force)" will be able to Think for Themselves (freedom/imagination). In this way, the "God/Man Union" can take place bringing forth Eternal Life (time), a New Body (life), and a Kingdom of Glory (paradise) to **Bless Man** (earth), to **Anoint God** (Heaven), and **Sanctify the God/Man Relationship** (kingdom) in **Truth, Law, and Will.**

The following tabular information indicates that God is using the "Sacrifice of the First-born" to Create Three Dimensions of Existence using **Egyptian Blood** (nation), **Pagan Blood** (world), and **Jesus' Blood** (kingdom) to **Create Three Peoples of Life**: 1) <u>Jewish People</u> - Righteous (physical/new body), 2) <u>Christian People</u> - Holy (spiritual/eternal life), and 3) <u>Purified People</u> - Perfect (mystical/kingdom):

**Jewish People, Christian People and Purified People
become a Unified People in Heaven and Earth**
(sacrifice brings saints, sons of God, and Human Gods;
freedom brings citizens, sons of man, and Divine Gods)

Egyptian
Blood

(look)

1. **Jewish People** - <u>Righteous Minds:</u> Kingship (time) ......Intellect - Law
   - Egyptians of Death (flesh) Create Jews of Life (spirit) = Control Thoughts
   - House of Aaron - See Right: High Priest (stand-in for the Messiah)
   - Tribe of Levi - See Wrong: Temple Priest (stand-in for first-born flesh)

(physical dimension - Babies: Elementary School = Free Gift of Eternal Life)

Pagan
Blood

(touch)

2. **Christian People** - <u>Holy Hearts:</u> Priesthood (life) ......Emotions - Faith
   - Temple of Death (spirit) Creates Throne of Life (flesh) = Control Feelings
   - Catholic Priesthood - See Good: Holy Pope (stand-in for Jesus Christ)
   - Catholic Laity - See Evil: Baptized Pagans (stand-in for first-born spirit)

(spiritual dimension - Teenagers: High School = Earned New Transfigured Body)

Jesus'

Blood

(wash)

3. **Purified People** - <u>Perfect Souls:</u> Sonship (paradise) ... Instincts – Knowing
   - Church of Death (spirit) Creates Government of Life (flesh) = Control Instincts
   - Zadok Priesthood - See God: Christ (stand-in for the Lord God Almighty)
   - Pagan World - See Man: Jesus (stand-in for the Blessed Virgin Mary)

(mystical dimension - Adults: College = Bonus Reward of Royal Kingdom)

- -

God/Man

Blood

4. **Unified People** - <u>Divine Life-force:</u> Fatherhood (God)... Thinking – Imagination
   - Earth of Death (flesh) Creates Heaven of Life (spirit) = Control Free Will
   - Holy Father - See Reality: God (stand-in for Mother's Viewpoint)
   - Holy Mother - See Illusion: Man (stand-in for Father's Truths)

(divine dimension - Wise Man: On-the-Job Training = Honored with God's Friendship)

This illustration shows that each of "God's Four Dimensions of Life" is being <u>Created</u> to manifest the **Lord's Divine Authority** in **God's Spirit** (law) and **Man's Flesh** (faith) so that He might **Sacrifice Man's Flesh** (death) to **Set God's Spirit Free** (resurrection). We see that this "Sacrifice (take-sin)" to "Resurrection (give divinity)" process allows the Lord to <u>Save Sinners</u> (earth), or **Remove Faults**, and **Create Saints**

(Heaven), or **Gain Virtues.** Via this "Redemptive Process," the Job of both the Church (save sinners) and the Government (create saints) Institutions is to reveal **God's Reality** (1st truth/life) and **Man's Illusion** (2nd truth/death) to **One and All.** In this way, the "Human Race (flesh)," "Angelic Realm (spirit)," and "Almighty God (divinity)" can establish Three Languages to effectively **Communicate** with **Each Other** and to **Unite Their Life-forces** into **One Perfect Nature** (kindness/love).

This means that the entire "Life-experience" is about Creating a New Nature (friendship/love) that can house the **Human, Angelic,** and **Divine Life-force** residing in **Four Dimensions of Life** (physical/spiritual/mystical/ divine). Now, we see that the ultimate "Purpose" behind Creating a Universal Intercessor in the Person of Jesus Christ as a **Triune Messiah** is to manifest this **New Universal Nature** (love) in **Body, Life, and Kingdom Forms.** Obviously, the Lord has the "Authority (wash)," "Responsibility (touch)," and "Duty (look)" to Serve the Needs and Wants of **Men, Angels,** and **God** through **One Nature** (friendship) comprised of **Eternal Life** (Angels), a **New Body** (Men), and God's **Kingdom of Glory** (God). Note that God has used the "Death of the Temple (Aaron)" to bring forth the Life of the Church to **Create Saints** (minds), the Life of Christ to **Create Sons of God** (hearts), and the Life of Heaven to **Create Human Gods** (souls). Secondly, "God has Used" the "Life of the Throne (David)" to bring forth the Death of the Government to **Create Righteous Citizens** (minds); the Death of Jesus to **Create Sons of Man** (hearts); and the Death of Earth to **Create Divine Men** (souls). Through each of these "Sacrifices" and consequential "Freedoms," God can become Man and Man can become God, thereby making them **One** in **Truth, Law, and Will.**

This means that "If Humanity" can Learn to **Control Its Thoughts,** it can create a **Well-adjusted Person** who can **Share** his **Wisdom, Wealth, and Life with Others.** Secondly, "If Humanity" can Learn to **Control Its Feelings,** it can create a **Prosperous and Peaceful Nation** which brings **God's Blessing** of **Liberty** and **Justice to All.** Thirdly, "If Humanity" can Learn to **Control Its Natural Instincts,** it can create a **Free and Happy World** which can become worthy of having its **Prayer Heard by God** due to its **True Devotion** to His Son, **Jesus Christ.** Finally, "If Humanity" can Learn to **Control Its Free Will,** it can create a most **Glorious Kingdom** of **Angels, Saints,** and even be worthy of the very **Presence of God Himself.** Yes, the "Life-experience" is all about Learning the **Truths, Laws, and Will of God** by being willing to **Humble Oneself to the Dust** by **Denying His Intellect** (new mind), **Abandoning His Feelings** (new heart), and **Submitting His Free Will** (new soul) **to God.** Yes! It's all about "Crushing" one's Thoughts, Feelings, and Instincts through **Personal Self-control** that brings a **Person Out** of **Sin, Evil, and Death** and Converts him into **Righteousness, Holiness, and Perfection.**

1. **Jewish People** - Death of Temple to bring Life to the Throne ......Seed
2. **Christian People** - Death of Priesthood to bring Life to the Laity ......Tree
3. **Purified People** - Death of Zadok Priesthood to bring Life to Pagan World ......Fruit
4. **Unified People** - Death of Holy Father to bring Life to the Holy Mother ......Harvest

It is now clear that out of the "Jewish People" is to come the Death of the Temple (sacrifice/Aaron) and the Rebirth of the Throne (set free/David) so that the **High Priest** (see right) might **Stand-in for the Messiah** (God) and the **King of the Jews** (see wrong) can **Stand-in for the First-born Flesh** (temple). Secondly, out of the "Christian People" is to come the Death of the Priesthood (sacrifice/Peter) and the Rebirth of the Laity (set free/sinners) so that the **Pope** (see good) might **Stand-in for the First-born Spirit** (church). Thirdly, out of the "Purified People" is to come the Death of the Zadok Priesthood (sacrifice/saints) and the Rebirth of the Pagan World (set free/citizens) so that **Christ** (see God) might **Stand-in for the Almighty** (Son of God) and **Jesus** (see Man) can **Stand-in for the Virgin Mary** (Son of Man). Finally, out of the "Unified People" is to come the Death of the Holy Father (sacrifice/kingdom) and the Rebirth of the Holy Mother (set free/universe) so that **God** (see reality) might **Stand-in for Death** (God) and **Man** can **Stand-in for Life** (Man). At each of these "Four Levels of Conversion," the God/Man Relationship will be able to establish its **Mental, Emotional, Instinctive,** and **Natural Unions**. Through these "Unions," the Human Race will be able to both **Grow in Wisdom** (mandatory) and **Mature in Character** (optional) until it can be **Grown-up** enough to **Meet, Love,** and **Serve Its God** in **Truth, Law, and Will**.

The following tabular information indicates that "God is becoming a Man" via the Sacrifice of the Temple (death) and then "Man is becoming God" via the Freedom of the Throne (resurrection) as **Humanity** brings forth a **Holy Heaven** (saints/sons of God/human God) and a **Righteous Earth** (citizens/sons of man/divine man):

God becomes Man via Temple and Man becomes God via Throne to Create Holy Heaven and Righteous Earth
(saints/sons of God/Human Gods are in Paradise in Heaven, citizens/sons of man/Divine Men are in Heaven on Earth)

Temple
(sacrifice)

1. **Man becomes God** - Paradise in Heaven: Christmas ....High Priest
   - Holy Saints - Celestial Court: Eternal Life = Friendship
   - Defeat Sin-nature - Learn Right from Wrong: Ignorance becomes Wisdom
   - Sons of God - Temple Court: Glorified Body = Companionship
   - Defeat Worldly Temptations - Learn Good from Evil: Cowardice becomes Courage
   - Human Gods - Royal Court: Kingdom of Glory = **Divine Love**
   - Defeat Demonic Possession - Learn God's/Man's Wills: Greed becomes Generosity

Throne
(freedom)

2. **God becomes Man** - Heaven on Earth: Easter........... King of the Jews
   - Righteous Citizen - King: Infinite Life = Wisdom
   - Sons of Man - Priest: Transfigured Body = Wealth
   - Master God's Law - Teach High School: Awaken Teenagers
   - Divine Men - Son: Royal Kingdom = **Human** Love
   - Master God's Love - Teach College: Awaken Adults

God and Man become One - Kingdom of Glory: Halloween... Perfect Son

This illustration shows that there are "Two Systems of Life (sacrifice/freedom)" operating simultaneously on Earth which are forcing the **Innocent Babies** to fall into a great **State of Confusion** even to the point of an **Unending Insanity**. This means that "Who," "What," "When," "Where," and "How" seem to have No Credible Answers until we see that God has **Sacrificed** His **Temple of Faith** to Set His **Throne of Knowing Free Men**. In short, "God is Telling Us" that it is better to "Know on Earth (throne)" than to have "Faith in a Heaven (temple)" because in the end, the entire Life-experience will center on **Knowing Right from Wrong** or **Face Judgment**. Obviously, the "Contradiction of Life" comes with Choosing to Believe in Oneself (earth) or Believing in God's Son (Heaven), but the **Trick** comes with **Doing Both at the Same Time**. This means that a person must "Surrender his Flesh" to the Man Jesus (earth) to be "Spiritually Born-again" in the God Christ (Heaven). Through this "Redemptive System," a person can become Both a **Man of Death** (earth) and a **God of Life** (Heaven), thereby simultaneously **Conquering All the Forces** of *Ignorance* (truth), *Cowardice* (law), and *Greed* (will).

Note that the "Holy Saint's Job" is to Defeat the Sin-nature, then **Learn Right from Wrong** (give life/worship) to teach **Ignorant Fools** to become **Honest Wise Men** so that the little ones might be prepared to become **Sons of God** (teenager). Secondly, the "Son of God's Job" is to Defeat Worldly Temptations, then **Learn Good from Evil** (give wealth/praise) to teach **Cowards** to become **Men of Courage** so that teenagers might be prepared to become **Human Gods** (adult) **in Heaven**. Finally, the "Human God's Job" is to Defeat Demonic Possession, then **Learn God's Will from man's will** to teach **Greedy Monsters** to become **Generous Men of Honor** so that adults might be prepared to *Think for Themselves*. In like manner, a "Righteous Citizen's Job" is to Master God's Truth by **Teaching Elementary School** to the **Babies** so that the little ones might be prepared to become **Sons of Man** (teenagers). Secondly, the "Son of Man's Job" is to Master God's Law by **Teaching High School** to the **Teenagers** so that they might be prepared to become **Divine Men** (adults). Finally, the "Divine Man's Job" is to Master God's Will by **Teaching College** to **Adults** so that they might be prepared to set themselves **Free from Sin, Evil, and Death**. Through one's "Growth (mandatory/destiny)" and "Maturity (optional/free will)," he can Master the Life-experience at each and every **Level of Challenge** to earn God's **Respect, Friendship, Companionship, and Oneness**. In this way, each of "God's Children" will be able to establish his Own Individual Rights (identity), Social Rights (character), and Divine Rights (personality), thereby establishing himself as a **King** (earth), **Priest** (Heaven), and **Son** (kingdom) **before God**. We see that the "Right to Live" is being brought to Humanity with the **Three Advents of Christ** to **Set Man Free** from **Adam's and Eve's Curses** of **Sin** (toil), **Evil** (pain), and **Death** (grave).

We see that in the "Three Stories (Luke 15: 4-32)" of the Lost Sheep (field), Lost Coin (house), and Prodigal Son (community), the **Lord God Almighty** was **Revealing** to what **Extent He would Go to Find Something that He has Lost**. The idea here is to "See that the Lamb" is Worthless (one man), that the "Coin" has Little Value (few men), but that a "Father's Son" is Priceless in his Eyes (all men). The point is to "See" that in the Divine Mind, the **Sheep, Coin, and Son** all had the **Same Value to God** and that **He Refuses to Allow even One Hair** to be **Lost** without a **Complete Accounting** before **His Divine Justice**. Note that the "Shepherd" Celebrated Alone when he **Found his Lost Sheep**; the "Housewife" Celebrated with her Friends when she **Found her Lost Coin;** and that the "Father" Celebrated with the Whole Community when his **Dead Son Returned to Life**. The implication is that on "Christ's 1st Advent (priest on donkey)," He Saved the Lost Sheep by becoming the **Sacrificial Lamb** being **Led to Slaughter** as the **Offering for All the Sins of Man**; yet, in the end, He **Resurrected from Death** in **Triumphant Glory**. Secondly, on "Christ's 2nd Advent (thief in night), He will Find the Lost Coin by **Sacrificing His Church's Holiness** (coin) to **Lucifer's Evil**; yet, in the end, the **Devout Catholics** will **Resurrect from Their Graves** (found coin). Finally, on "Christ's 3rd Advent (judge on a cloud)," he will Forgive the Prodigal Son by **Sacrificing the Whole World** (son) to **Death**; yet, in the end, the **Righteous World** will **Resurrect from the Fires of Hell** (new-life). Note that the "Shepherd" looked for his **Lost Sheep** in the **Daylight**; the "Housewife" Lit a Lamp to **Find her Lost Coin;** and the "Father" Ran to Meet his Lost Son and then **Lit the Whole House**. In all of these "Cases," we see that they Represent Christ bringing **More and More Light** onto the **World** to **Awaken** a **Lost and Confused People** from **Their Deep Sleep**.

The following tabular information indicates that "God's Son" is Coming in Three Advents to **Set Mankind Free** from its **Own Sin-nature, Worldly Temptations, and Demonic Possession** as described in the **Stories** of the **Lost Sheep, Lost Coin, and Prodigal Son:**

Christ's Three Advents Save Lost Sheep, Find Coin, and Restore Prodigal Son to his Father
(conversion of the Messiah, purifying the Church,
and transforming the World to save all men)

Field
(truth)

1. **1st Advent/priest** - Find Lost Sheep: Sacrificial Lamb = Messiah.......Knowledge
   - Remove Sin - Transform Sin-nature into Holiness (being saved)
   - Good Shepherd's Celebration - Alone: Priest on a Donkey: Palm Sunday

Purify
Grave
   - Easter - Resurrection of Lost Sheep (daylight): Christ = Alone
   - Worshiping God - Daily: Giving One's Life = Remove Venial Sins
   - Remove Sin-nature - Given Individual Rights: See Limitations
   - Change Ignorance into Wisdom - God becomes Man (Christmas)
   - God Counts His Babies (citizens) on Sabbath - Know God
   (learn right from wrong - righteous citizen on earth: worthy of new body)

House
(law)

2. **2nd Advent/thief** - Find Lost Coin: Pay Sin-debt = Church.......Self-awareness
   - Remove Evil - Transform Worldly Temptations into Righteousness (saving self)
   - Housewife's Celebration - With Friends: Thief in the Night

Purify
Host
   - Halloween - Resurrection of Lost Wealth (light up lamp): Church = Community
   - Praising God - Weekly: Giving One's Wealth = Remove Mortal Sins
   - Remove Worldly Temptations - Given Social Rights: See Potential

- Change Cowardice to Courage - Man becomes God (Easter)
- God Counts His Holy Saints on the Lord's Day - Love God
  (learn good from evil - holy saint in Heaven: worthy of eternal life)

Community   3. **3rd Advent/judge** - <u>Find Prodigal Son:</u> Divine Obedience = World........Consciousness
(will)
- Remove Death - Transform Demonic Possession into Perfection (saving others)
- Father's Celebration - All of Community: Judge on a Cloud

Purify
- Independence Day - Resurrection of Prodigal Son (light up house): World = Everyone

Life
- Thanking God - Yearly: Giving One's Labors = Remove Capital Sins
- Remove Demonic Possession - Given Divine Rights: See Self-worth
- Change Greed to Generosity - God and Man become One (Halloween)
- God Counts His Perfect Sons on Judgment Day - Serve God

(learn God's Will/man's will - perfect son within Kingdom: worthy of royal kingdom)

This illustration shows that the "Life-experience" is about <u>Being Saved</u> from one's **Own Sin-nature** to become **Worthy of Individual Rights** so that **He** can **See his Own Limitations** and be **Set Free from Sin** (ignorance). Secondly, "Life is About" <u>Saving Oneself</u> from **Worldly Temptations** to become **Worthy of Social Rights** so that **He** can **See his Own Potential** and be **Set Free from Evil** (cowardice). Finally, "Life Reveals" we must Save Others from **Demonic Possession** to become **Worthy of Divine Rights** so that **We** can **See our Own Self-worth** and be **Set Free from Death** (greed). Yes! "Ignorance (mind)," "Cowardice (heart)," and "Greed (soul)" have Cast the Human Race into **Lucifer's Pit of Hell** and the **Job of the Lord Jesus Christ** is to **Come** and **Save God's Children** by bringing them **Wisdom** (sheep), **Courage** (coin), and **Generosity** (son). During the "Lord's 1st Advent" as a <u>Priest on a Donkey,</u> He **Removed Ignorance** (sin) and **Gave Mankind Wisdom** (forgiveness) to **Set Them Free from being a Lost Sheep.** Secondly, during the "Lord's 2nd Advent" as a <u>Thief in the Night,</u> He will **Remove Cowardice** (evil) and **Give Mankind Courage** (honesty) to **Set Them Free from being a Lost Coin.** Finally, during the "Lord's 3rd Advent" as a <u>Judge on a Cloud,</u> He will **Remove Greed** (death) and **Give Mankind Generosity** (sharing) to **Set Them Free from being a Prodigal Son.** In each of these "Three Cases," the <u>Human Race</u> must **Learn Its Lesson** which is **Not to Lose Things** and to be **More Careful in the Future** to **Show** that **God Himself** has **Learned His Lesson** to **Protect His most Beloved Children.** This means that the "Life-experience" is about <u>Being Saved</u> as a **Sheep** (free redemption), <u>Saving</u> one's **Own Coin** (earned salvation), and then <u>Saving Others</u> as a **Prodigal Son** (bonus rewards).

In summary, this means that when a "Person is Being Saved" by <u>Christ</u> through **His Holy Church,** a **Soul** is given its own **Individual Rights,** thereby allowing it to become a **Perfect Man of Holiness** through the Lord's **Gift of Divinity** or an **Eternal Life** (Heaven/divine human). In contrast, when a "Person Saves himself" through the <u>Righteous World,</u> a **Citizen** is given his own **Social Rights,** thereby allowing him to become a part of a **Perfect Society of Righteousness** through **God's Gift of a New Body** (earth). We clearly must "Earn Heaven on Earth (salvation)" and be "Invited to Heaven (rewards)" to become both a <u>Righteous Citizen</u> and <u>Holy Saint</u> (glorified spirit)

Worthy of both the **Respect** and **Honors** of **Jesus, the Divine Man** (Easter/body) and **Christ, the Human God** (Christmas/life). Obviously, the "Life-experience" is about receiving a New Mind (wisdom), New Heart (courage), and New Soul (generosity) by overcoming **Ignorance, Cowardice,** and **Greed** to become **Worthy** of **God's Righteousness** (mind), **Holiness** (heart), and **Perfection** (soul).

We can now see that the "Life-experience" is forcing each person to Master both the **Holy Church** (spirit) and the **Righteous World** (flesh) to allow his **Awakened Soul** to **Build its Own Perfect Home** (soul) by **Thinking for Itself.** We see in the "Creation of these Institutions" the coming of God's Messiah (church), the New Jerusalem (government), and the Lord's New Heaven and new earth (home) to bring the **Human Race** a **Perfect Man, City,** and **World** to **Unite One and All.** It is now clear that each "Struggling Soul" must Go through Free Will to Reach God's Divine Will in its lifetime by **Mastering** both the **Righteous World** (ethics) and the **Holy Church** (morals) to **Pass Lucifer's Test** (government), **God's Judgment** (church), and its **Own Self-evaluation** (home). It can now be seen that out of the "Land of God (government)," the "Life of God (church)," and the "People of God (home)," the Lord will Create His coming **New Kingdom of Glory** to house all the **Lost Broken Souls of the World** so that they might be **Transformed** into **New Creations in Christ Jesus**.

The Lord has gone to a "Great Deal of Trouble" to Save the **Traitor** (Lucifer), **His Enemies** (Adam), the **Strangers** (1st humanity), **His Neighbors** (Jews), **His Friends** (Christians), **His Family** (Kingdom), and even **Himself** (Christ). The Lord has this awesome desire to "Sacrifice His Own Life" to Redeem All that has been Lost and to **Return the Victims of Death** back to their **Original Owner** (God) and **Restore Them** to their **Original State of Perfection** (Man). The "Job of Every Christian" is to join in this effort to Save the Lost by **Mastering the Church** (people/altar), the **Government** (land/throne), and the **Home** (life/palace) to make **All Things New before God.** Obviously, the Lord is telling us that it "Takes All Kinds" to make up a "World" with the only solution being to use the Strengths of Good to make up for the Weaknesses of the Wicked by placing **All Things in Perfect Balance** (unity). This "State of Balance" sits at the center of the Creation of both **Mount Calvary** (soldier-of–the-light/blood) and the **Holy Mass** (living prayer/bloodless) to bring **All Things into Perfection** before the **Altar/Throne/Table of God.**

This "Concept of Balance" allows us to see the need for the Individual, Society, and God to be **United** into **One System of Effective Communication** through **Mutual Respect** based on the **Lord's Truth, Law, and Will.** Obviously, each "Individual" is striving to attain his own Personal Objective by either finding or creating his own **New Body** which can fulfill all of his **Infinite Wants** and **Desires** unto his **Own State of Satisfaction** (self). Secondly, each "Society" is striving to attain its own Social Objectives by either finding or creating its **Own Eternal Life** which can fulfill all of its **Infinite Wants** and **Desires** unto its **Own State of Fulfillment** (will of the people). Finally, each "Son of God" is striving to attain his own Divine Objectives by either finding or creating his own **Royal Kingdom** which can fulfill all of his **Infinite Wants** and **Desires** unto **Pleasing the Will of God** (divine blessing). By both "Growing" and "Maturing" in <u>Christ Jesus,</u> each of **God's Children** can travel along the Lord's **Three Pathways** of <u>**Righteousness, Holiness,**</u> and **Perfection** to receive his **New Body** (earth), **Eternal Life** (Heaven), and **Royal Kingdom** (Kingdom). Now, we see "Moses" was revealing God's <u>Three Plans</u> (human/angelic/divine) by building his **Mosaic Tabernacle** with its **Three Rooms of Conversion,** where the **<u>Laity</u>** (sunlight), **<u>Priesthood</u>** (candlelight), and **<u>High Priest</u>** (Shekinah glory) come to **Meet Their God.** This same concept is seen in the "Three Advents of Christ" as He comes to build His <u>Catholic Church</u> with its <u>Three Rooms of Conversion,</u> where the **Pagan** (called), **Christian** (enlightened), and **Saint** (awakened) are allowed to **<u>Eat God's Flesh</u>** and **<u>Drink His Blood</u>** to become **One with Him** in **Truth** (earth), **Law** (Heaven), and **Will** (Kingdom). Finally, we see the coming of "God the Father" as He manifests his <u>Three Rooms of Conversion</u> on **Earth** (blessed), in **Heaven** (anointed), and within the **Kingdom** (sanctified) to allow each **<u>New Friend</u>** to come to **<u>Know, Love,</u>** and **<u>Serve</u>** their God with their whole **Mind** (wisdom), **Heart** (courage), and **Soul** (generosity).

The following tabular information indicates that through the "Mosaic" <u>Outer Court</u> (circumcision), <u>Holy Place</u> (baptism), and <u>Holy of Holies</u> (confirmation), the **Human Race** can **Journey** through **Man's Blood** (earth), **Christ's Water** (Heaven), and **<u>God's Spirit</u>** (Kingdom) to reach the **Lord God Almighty Himself**:

Journeying via Outer Court, Holy Place, and Holy of Holies to Reach God's Truth, Law, and Will
(blood circumcision, water baptism, and spiritual confirmation bring body, life, and kingdom)

Earth
(blood)

See

Nature

1. **Outer Court** - <u>Circumcision:</u> Venial Sins Removed ....Knowledge
   - 1st Advent - Sacrifice of Blood: Jewish Ignorance = Witness unto Truth
   - Lying - One Man (mind) . . . . .Baby
   - Deceit - Society (heart) . . . . Law   **Individual**
   - Sedition - All Men (soul) . . . . .Earth
   - Redeemed by Law - Jewish Life: *New Body* = Lucifer's Test: Laity
   - Pathway of Righteousness - Transfigured Body: Seat in Celestial Court
   (mind sees fixed frame of reference - personal identity: Learning right from wrong)

Heaven
(water)

See

Behavior

2. **Holy Place** - <u>Baptism:</u> Mortal Sins Removed......... Self-awareness
   - 2nd Advent - Prayer of Water: Christian Cowardice = Converted unto Law
   - Hiding - One Man (wisdom) . . . . Teenager
   - Deception - Society (courage) . . . . Faith   **Society**
   - Sorcery - All Men (generosity) . . . . .Heaven
   - Saved by Faith - Christian Life: *Eternal Life* = God's Judgment: Priesthood
   - Pathway of Holiness - Glorified Body: Seat in Temple Court
   (heart sees relative focused existence - social character: Learning good from evil)

Kingdom
(spirit)

3. **Holy of Holies** - <u>Confirmation:</u> Capital Sins Removed...... Consciousness
   - 3rd Advent - Blessing of Spirit: Saintly Greed = Becoming the Will

	• Stealing - One Man (pagan) . . . . .Adult	
See	• Defiance - Society (Christian) . . . . .Knowing	**God**
Lifestyle	• Blasphemy - All Men (saint) . . . . .Kingdom	

• Rewarded by Knowing - Saintly Life: *Royal Kingdom* = Self-evaluation: High Priest

• Pathway of Perfection - Mystical Body: Seat in Royal Court

(soul sees perception of reality - Godly personality: Learning God's/Man's wills)

This illustration shows that each of "God's Children" must <u>Pass</u> through a <u>Great Vice</u> (works/prayers) with **God's Eternal Kingdom** on **One Side** (save self) and **Poor Lost Humanity** on the **Other Side** (save others). The question becomes: is one to **Work himself to Death** (money) or to **Pray himself to Death** (grace dollars)? The simple answer is to "Balance" one's <u>Earthly Works</u> (Jesus) with his <u>Heavenly Prayers</u> (Christ) so that an **Equal Amount of Effort** can be given to both **Hard-work** and **Devotional Prayers** in **Service to One and All**. Basically, no one is to be "Left Behind" and everyone is to be given his <u>Fair Share of the Kingdom</u> in **Time, Money, and Love** so that in the end, **Babies** (one man/time), **Teenagers** (society/money), and **Adults** (all men/love) shall **Each be Fulfilled**. Obviously, anyone in the "World System" will laugh at trying to <u>Balance his Works</u> against his <u>Prayers</u> so he is given a **Door Out** by simply **Surrendering to Christ** and letting the **Lord Balance His Life Perfectly**.

Now, it becomes clear just why a person must "Defeat his Flesh (ignorance)" via <u>Blood</u> (circumcision), then "Defeat his Spirit (cowardice)" via <u>Water</u> (baptism), and finally, "Defeat his Soul" via <u>Spirit</u> (confirmation). This now shows us that through the "Sacrifice on Calvary," the <u>Blood</u> (1st advent/church/see nature), <u>Water</u> (2nd advent/government/see behavior), and <u>Spirit</u> (3rd advent/home) **Offerings unto God** brought forth man's **Free Redemption** (new body), **Earned Salvation** (eternal life/see lifestyle), and **Bonus Rewards** (royal kingdom). It can now be understood that the "Life-experience" is centered upon the <u>Balancing</u> and <u>Synchronization</u> of **Two Forces** (spirit/flesh) which come **Together** in a **Vice Grip** until a person is **Forced to Choose** either **One** (good) **or the Other** (evil). This has obviously been the "Conundrum of God" from the <u>Beginning</u> as even **He could Not** be **All and Nothing** within a **Physical Existence** as **Two Things Cannot Occupy** the **Same Space** at the **Same Time**. But with the "Creation of Man" and the "Blessed Mother" through <u>Jesus Christ,</u> **God could Resolve** this **Divine Problem** of <u>Saving</u> both the **Good** (Angels/Saints) and the **Evil** (Demons/Damned) at the **Same time**. In short, this means that "God" is going to <u>Save the Good Souls,</u> while the "Job of Man" will be to Save the Evil Souls so that the entire **Creation** can be **Redeemed** in the **Blood, Water, and Spirit** of **Jesus Christ**. We can now explain the "Betrayal of Judas (death)" as well as the "Denial of Peter (life)" because <u>They were Forced</u> to **Physically Choose** either **Life or Death** (vice grip) based on **Their Moment of Decision**.

It appears that "God has Set up a System" of <u>Right and Wrong Choices</u> much like **Musical Chairs** whereas the **People Circle the Chairs on** each round, they take away **One Chair** until there is only **One Chair** or **One Choice Left,** be it **Right** (good) or **Wrong** (evil). This "Need to be Instinctively Right" at every <u>Moment of Life</u> becomes the **Driving Force Governing** both **Human and Divine Perfection** based on the

Blood, Water, and Spirit Sacrifices of **Jesus Christ**. This concept shows us that when a "Person Burns the Candle" at Both Ends, he will one day either Get Burned or be Completely Consumed. The **Choice is hi**s, because in a **Physical Creation,** a **Candle** can only **Burn from the Top Down**. This means that "God" is in an "Eternal Quandary" to Use His Own **Miracle-working Power** (limitless) or to Use the **Laws of Natural Order** (limitations) which means **Not Having** the **Infinite Powers of God**. This is shown in the "Sacrifice on Calvary (laws of natural order)" which represents the Power of the Mind (flesh) as it tries to **Figure Out Everything through Logic** based on the **Concept of Wisdom** (intellect), thereby **Calling a Person** to **Endure** the **Torture and Agony** of **Trial** (hypothesis) and **Error** (results). In contrast, we see that the "Offering at the Last Supper (miracle-working powers)" represents the Power of the Heart (spirit) which can mystically **Will Final Results into Existence** simply by one's **Desire to Define his Heart's Desire** through **Love** (know his wants).

This means that the "Essence of Life" is centered upon the idea that the Forces of Intellect (1st truth/spirit) and Emotion (2nd truth/blood) are **Struggling** to accomplish the same **Objective** based on **Two Different Forces of Creation,** either **Wisdom** (works) **or Love** (prayers). We can see that the "Lord's Last Supper" represents God's Bloodless Sacrifice (Mass) or **Human Emotion** (heart/spirit)**,** thereby implying a **Divine Desire to Forgive** (love) the **Whole World in an Instant.** In contrast, we see that the "Lord's Death on Mount Calvary" is God's Bloody Sacrifice or **Human Intellect** (mind/flesh), thereby implying a **Divine Intent to Earn** One's **Forgiveness** (wisdom) over a **3,000 Year Struggle for Maturity.** In short, God is telling us that "He is Using Two Philosophies of Life (two truths)" with One Producing Instant Results (prayers) and the Other Requiring Eons of Time to Do It Right (works) and effectively understanding every **Step of Transformation**, based on either **One's Deductive** or **Inductive Logic**. The point is that "Life must Make Sense" clearly defining "Where We Came From," "Who We Are," and "Where We are Going," Not in General Terms because the **Human Race is Demanding Specifics**. Recall that "God's Son, Christ" Created the **New Human Spirit** (Glorified Spirit) in **Three Hours on the Cross** and then Created the **New Human Flesh** (Transfigured Body) in **Three Days in the Tomb.** We see that this "Great Miracle" worked extremely well for the Messiah, but for a Lost Broken Sinner to **Perform this same Feat,** he must spend some **3,000 Years Conquering Fear, Pain, and Death** to receive his **New Spirit** (Glorified Spirit/holy) and his **New Flesh** (Transfigured Body/righteous). It is now clear that "God's Son, Christ" desires to use Miracle-working Power to make **All Things Perfect** in the **Twinkling of an Eye** to **Win the Favor of His Eternal Father.** In contrast, we see that "Mary's Son, Jesus" is Required to Follow the **Natural Order of Things** moving with **Glacial Speed** to **Accomplish All** that is **Required** in the **Divine Plan of God, Step by Step.**

To understand "God's Grand Design," one must first Establish Truth (fixed reference), then Extrapolate Truth (relative focus) into an **Abstract Form**, then **Perceive Truth** (perception) as **Real,** and finally, **Live in God's Reality** (reality) all in the **Name of Jesus Christ**. Out of each of these "Four Stages of Development," we see that God, Angels, Men, and Nature can **Grow and Mature** into a **Unified State of Existence** (unity), whereby **All Three Societies** can **Interface** without any signs of **Strife or Conflict**. This means that a "Society" must first Fix on Its Identity (individuality), then Focus on Its Unity (groups), leading to Its Perception of Its Own Purpose (goals) which brings it to a Final State of Fruitful Living (real). The idea is to "Learn" one's Own Identity (individual), then find out where he fits in Society (family), and then Enter God's Church (sainthood) to see if he belongs to the **Family of God**. Finally, after "Knowing Oneself (nature)," "Society (behavior)," and "God (lifestyle)," then a person must attain the Courage to Strike-out on his **Own** by **Living** within the **Reality of Eternal Life Forever**. Obviously, mastering "Relative Focused Existence" is the hardest as a person must Balance both the Physical World (work) and the Spiritual Church (prayer) by giving both his **Hard-work** (son of man) and his **Devout Prayers** (Son of God) the same amount of **Consideration** (equality) either in **Public** or in **Private**. It is then during one's "Perception of Reality" that he must Merge Work and Prayer into a single **New Nature of Righteousness** (right/wrong) and **Holiness** (good/evil) making him both a **Citizen of Earth** (righteous) and a **Saint of Heaven** (holy). Once this "Union" between Earthly Death (work/soldier-of-the-light) and Heavenly Life (prayer/living prayer) is completed, then a person can enter **God's Reality** and **Learn to Think for Himself** (mature adult).

Growing through One's Fixed Reference, Focused Existence, Perception, and Living in Reality
(fixed on earth, focused on Heaven, perception of kingdom, and living within God to find heart's desire)

Man's Soldier-of-the-Light and God's Living Prayer become One
(man's hard-work on earth/God's Holy Prayers in Heaven)

Ignorance
(earth)

1. **Fixed Frame of Reference** - One Power (flesh) ....Knowledge
   - Triune Nature - Creation of Illusion: See God (God thinks of child)
   - Nature - Natural Order: Home (peace)
   - People - Human Order: Government (joy)   **Survival**
   - Religion - Supernatural Order: Church (happiness)
   - Union of Two Fathers - Earth/Heaven (blessed) ....Air Contract
   - God the Father - Groom: Bride Price = Calvary
   - Father Abraham - Bride: Dowry = Tribulation
   - Forgive Sin of Thought - Baptism: Learn Right from Wrong = Righteousness

   (God wants to become Man - Christmas: master human life = learn right from wrong)

Knowledge
(Heaven)

2. **Relative Focused Existence** - Two Powers (spirit) ....Self-awareness
   - Triune Persons - Life in Reality: Hear God (God speaks to child)
   - Physical Existence - New Body (transfiguration)
   - Spiritual Existence - Eternal Life (glorification)   **Truth**
   - Mystical Existence - Royal Kingdom (mystic)

- Union of the Couple - God/Man ... Blood Contract (anointed)
- Jesus Christ - Groom: Ring of Divine Name = Resurrection
- Catholic Church - Bride: Ring of Virgin Body = Ascension
- Forgive Sin of Word - Confession: Learn Good from Evil: Holiness

(Man wants to become God - Easter: master angelic life = learn good from evil)

Awakened
(Kingdom)

3. **Perception of Reality** - <u>Three Powers</u> (soul) ......Consciousness
- Trinity of God - Man Becomes Reality: Touch God (God touches child)
- Earthly Life - Title Deed to Jewish Law (veneration)
- Heavenly Life - Title Deed to Christian Love (adoration)   **Love**
- Kingdom Life - Title Deed to Saintly Salvation (exaltation)
- Union of the Friends - Jesus/Christ...... Spirit Contract (sanctify)
- Melchizedek Priesthood - Groom: Holy Saints = Second Coming
- Catholic Laity - Bride: Righteous Citizens = Age of Peace
- Forgive Sin of Deed - Communion: Learn God's/Man's Wills = Perfection

(God and Man become One - Halloween: master divine life = learn God's Will/man's will)

- -

Indwelled
(God)

4. **Living in Reality** - <u>Four Powers</u> (life-force) ....Sentience
- Lord God Almighty - Reality Becomes Man Sup with God (God sups with man)
- Heaven on Earth - Eternal Life brings Friendship (celestial)
- Paradise in Heaven - Eternal Life brings Companionship (temple)   **Choice**
- Kingdom of Glory - Eternal Life brings Oneness (royal)
- Union of the Families - Nothing/All... Divine Contract (consecrated)
- Angelic Realm - Groom: Sons of God = Third Coming
- Holy Saints - Bride: Sons of Man = New Heaven and New Earth
- Forgive Sin of Inaction - Confirmation: Learn God's Reality/Man's Illusion = Free

(Man becomes God - Independence Day: master freedom = learn God's reality/man's illusion)

This illustration shows that the "Human Race" is traveling from <u>Ignorance</u> (earth) to <u>Knowledge</u> (Heaven), to an <u>Awakening</u> (Kingdom), and finally, to being <u>Indwelled</u> (God) by **God's Spirit** to bring a **Lost Soul** from **Nothing** (death) to **All** (life). This "Journey of Life" sits at the center of God's Creation as it forces **Each of its Inhabitants** to **Contribute** to the <u>**General Welfare**</u> to simply **Survive**. This theme of "Participation" and "Contribution" defines the <u>Life-experience</u> as **God Decreases** (lessons) and **Man Increases** (blessings) until <u>**God becomes a Man**</u> (Christmas) and **Man becomes God** (Easter) so that they can **Strive Together** to **Build Their Kingdom of Glory**. Unfortunately for "Mankind," it must pass through God's <u>Divine School of Higher Learning</u> before it can reach the Lord's **Kingdom of Glory** and that most **Prized Freedom** it so **Dearly Loves** (free choice). This means passing through "God's Triune Nature (one power)" where the <u>Lord Thinks of His Child</u> through **Nature** (new mind), the **People** (new heart), and **Christ's Christian Religion** (new soul) to **Unite Physical** (dowry) and **Spiritual** (bride price) **Life**. Secondly, one must pass through God's "Triune Persons (two powers)," where the Lord Speaks to His Child through **Physical** (new body), **Spiritual** (eternal life), and **Mystical** (Kingdom) **Existence** to **Unite God's Divine Name** (groom's gift) and **Man's Virgin Body** (bride's gift). Thirdly, one must pass through God's "Holy Trinity (three powers)," where the Lord Touches His Child through **Earthly** (Jewish Law), **Heavenly** (Christian Love), and **Kingdom** (Saintly Salvation) **Life** to **Unite God's Priesthood** (sacrifice) and **Laity** (prayer). Lastly, one must pass through the "Lord God Almighty (four powers)," where the Lord Sups with His Child through **Heaven on Earth** (friendship), **Paradise in Heaven** (companionship), and **His Kingdom of Glory** (oneness) to **Unite God's Angelic Realm** (Son of God) with **His Holy Saints** (son of man).

Through these "Four Stages of Education," man's Human Nature is Changed from being an **Animal Nature** (ignorance) into a **Robot Machine** (cowardice), and finally, into a **Loving Human** (greed) via a series of **Conversion Experiences** (called/enlightened/awakened/indwelled). We see these "Four Stages of Education" revealed during the Lifting of the Four Cups (Mass) as they **Unite the Two Fathers** of *Wisdom* (God/Abraham), the **Couple** of *Courage* (Christ/Church), the **Two Sets of Friends** of *Generosity* (priesthood/laity), and the **Two Families** of **Unselfishness** (Angels/Saints). Via these "Eight Social Groups" and their "Four Unions (soldier-of-the-light/living prayers)," the entire Creation of God is able to bring forth **Peace** (earth), **Joy** (Heaven), and **Happiness** (Kingdom) to the **Minds** (wisdom), **Hearts** (courage), and **Souls** (generosity) of **All Men, All Angels, and to God**. In this way, we see that "Ignorance" will be Defeated by Knowledge, which will Transform into Man's Awakening (understanding) to one day, open **Humanity** up to the **Indwelling Spirit of God**, fulfilling **Man's Nature** with his **Heart's Desire** (free choice).

We must all be "Purified" by the Scourging (thoughts/water), Crucifixion (words/oil), Tomb (deeds/blood), and Resurrection (inaction/death) of **Jesus Christ** to **Forgive** our **Sins of Thought, Word, Deed,** and/or **Inaction** to make a **Lost Soul** *Righteous, Holy, and Perfect* before God. The idea here is to see that the "Sins from One's Thought" are Venial Sins which only have the **Power to Kill the Mind** and can be easily **Forgiven** by attending **Daily Mass** (water blessing). Secondly, we see that the "Sins from One's Words" are Mortal Sins which have the **Power to Kill the Heart** and can only be **Forgiven** by going to *Confession* and attending *Sunday Mass* (oil anointing). Thirdly, we see that the "Sins from One's Deed" are Capital Sins which have the **Power to Kill the Soul** and can only be **Forgiven** by going to *Communion during Easter Duty* (blood sanctification). Finally, we see that "Sins of One's Inaction (omission)" are Unforgivable Sins (original) which has the **Power to Kill a Person's Life-force** and can only be **Forgiven** by going to **Confirmation or during a Funeral Mass** (death consecration). At each of these "Stages of Sinfulness," a person Falls Deeper and Deeper into **Eternal Death** until he has **Lost his Mind** (insanity), **Heart** (criminal), **Soul** (evil), and **Life-force** (demonic). The idea here is that once a "Person is Purified from Sinfulness," then he can be Awakened unto the **Purpose of Life** (service) as he comes to **See God** (remove venial sins), **Hear God** (remove mortal sins), **Touch God** (remove capital sins), and finally, **Sup with God** (remove original sin) as the **Lord's Adopted Son.**

It is now clear that the "Purpose of Life (service)" centers on becoming <u>Distinguished</u> (adopted son) in the <u>Loving Eyes of God,</u> thereby giving a **Transformed Soldier-of-the-Light** (righteous flesh) a **Chair of Honor** (logical results) near the **Holy Throne** of the **Eternal Father.** Through one's new "Royal Status," the <u>Lord will Give</u> a **Living Prayer of Love** (holy saint) a **Place of Glory** near the Son's <u>Altar of Love</u> (instant results) uniting each **man's Born-again Spirit** with **God's Divine Spirit** in the **Lord's Holy of Holies** (mystical perfection). Finally, a triumphant "Holy Saint" will be given a <u>Seat of Majesty</u> near the **Face of God** (beatific vision), where he might **Commune in Friendship** with **his Creator.** Through this "Friendship (servanthood)," a <u>Person can Enter</u> the **Lord's Divine Love** of **Perfect Truth, Law,** and **Will.** Also through "Humanity's" <u>Constantly Closing Breach</u> with its **God, Life Anew** will **Emerge Out** of the **Three Natures** of **God's Divine Image** (nature/person/trinity) **Transforming His Divinity** (will), **Spirituality** (law), and **Physiology** (truth) into **Human Perfection.** Simultaneously, the "Three Natures" of <u>God's Divine Likeness</u> (behavior) will be **Changed Revealing His Human Body** (flesh/natures), **Spirit** (persons), and **Soul** (trinity) in **Oneness** with **Divine Justice, Mercy,** and **Love.** The symbolism here is that the "Lord must come to Man" in <u>Three Advents</u> (tries) because **Man has No Power** to **Transform** himself and/or to **Come to God.** The bitter root of the "Human Problem" is centered on the idea that it is easier for a <u>Spirit Being</u> (instant) to become <u>Human</u> (miraculous power) than for a <u>Human Being</u> (created/slow) to become a **Divine Spirit** (never created). It can now be seen that the "Entire Theme" of <u>God's Grand Design</u> is centered upon **God becoming Man** (1st try), **Man becoming God** (2nd try) and then **God and Man becoming One** (3rd try) at the **End of Time.** No! We are not saying that the "Human Race" is going to be <u>The God</u> (divinity), but we are saying that a **Redeemed Man** is going to become a **Form of God** (adopted son) in the **Godly Nature of Christ Jesus.**

This now explains why the "Major Work of the Lord" has been to <u>Transform Broken Sinners</u> into **Physical Soldiers-of-the-Light** (flesh/faults) or **Righteous Citizens** (earth) and **Spiritual Living Prayers of Love** (spirit/virtues) or <u>Holy Saints</u> (Heaven) to combine the **Natures of Man** (physical) with the **Divine Nature of God** (spiritual). In this "Union," it is a fact that <u>Jesus</u> represents **Mankind's Divine Love** (spirit) and the <u>Virgin Mary</u> represents **Mankind's Human Love** (flesh), thereby allowing **God to Use** these **Two Perfect Souls** as focal points of **His Marriage** between **Divinity** (1st truth) and **Humanity** (2nd truth). We know that "Marriages are Created" and are to <u>Last Forever</u> out of the **Power of True Love,** indicating that the **Lord** must **Milk Human Love** out of the stubborn **Free Will of Man** with **His Infinite Patience.** If the Lord is "Patient" enough, then He <u>Always Gets</u> what <u>He Wants</u> no matter how much **Time, Money, or Effort** it might require (spare no expense) to **Milk a Rock.**

The essence of God's technique for "Slaughtering One's Innocence" is centered upon <u>Service to Others</u> (sharing) to the point of **One's Own Destruction** in the name of **Holy Perfection.** The Lord has established a "Pathway of Perfection" or <u>Spiritual System of Sacrifice</u> based on one's <u>Submission</u> to the **Divine Will** in **Perfect Obedi-**

ence, thereby becoming a **Holocaust of Giving** (sacrifice) for the **Salvation of Others.** Through this most unselfish "System of Human Sacrifice (physical)," a Christian can be **Transformed** into a **Soul Winner for God**, making his **Existence** (body/self), **Spirit Life** (spirit/society), and **Holy Life** (soul/God) **Pleasing to his Creator.** Only by way of this "Self-denial System" can anyone be eternally Glorified before God based on the **Fruits of his Faithful Works/lessons** which have been **Manifested** as **Faults Removed** (altar/prayers/redemption), **Virtues Gained** (throne/works/salvation), and **Souls Won for Christ** (palace/love/rewards).

We can now see that the "Jewish People" represent the Soldier-of- the-Light in the **World** through **Their Commitment** to **Save Sinners** through the **Power of Forgiven Sin** (capital sin) to bring the **Lost into the Light of Knowing.** Secondly, we see that the "Christian People" represent the Living Prayer of Love (saint) in the **Church** through **Their Commitment** to **Create Saints** through the **Power of Prayer** (mortal sins) and to bring the **Faithful into the Presence of God.** Through these "Two Jobs" of both the Jews and the Christians to **Work Together** in **Harvesting a Pagan World** of **Sin, Evil,** and **Death,** we see **God is Teaching** the **Flesh** (ethics/remove faults) **Right from Wrong** and the **Spirit** (morals/gain virtues) **Good from Evil.** This means that once a "Person Learns Right from Wrong (flesh)," he can become a Righteous Citizen on Earth as **He is Immersed** into a **Sinful World,** where he will **Learn All the Lessons of Life** and then through **Christ,** will **Bear Fruit.** In like manner, once a person "Learns Good from Evil," he can become a Holy Saint in Heaven as **He Surrenders** his **Free Will** to **God's Divine Will** via the **Precepts of the Church** (canon law) to become **Nothing before God.** We are being shown that each of "God's Beloved Children" is being Called to Walk the 1st Mile to **Master Life** (flesh/lessons) and become **Righteous Citizens on Earth**, while those who are willing to Walk the 2nd Mile can **Master Eternal Life** (spirit/blessings) and become **Holy Saints in Heaven.** Obviously, the "Lord Hopes" that each one of His Faithful Babies will **Desire** to **Never Stop Walking** and **Never Stop Trying and Striving** to become **Perfect** in the **Sight of God** by **Surrendering to Christ** (church) and by **Fighting Evil** (world).

The following tabular information indicates that the "Jewish Soldier-of-the-Light (forgiveness)" as the Redeemer of Souls (free) and the "Christian Living Prayer of Love (prayer)" as the Savior of Souls (earned) are both **Needed** to **Serve the Divine Will of God:**

**God's Soldier-of-the-Light Saves Lost and God's
Living Prayer of Love Creates Saints**
(soldiers save souls with forgiven sin and
living prayers create saints with prayers)

Ethics (flesh)	1. **Jewish Soldier-of-the-Light** - Saving the Lost: Forgiven Sin ..... Jesus
	• Sacrifice - Forgive Capital Sin: Baptism = Being Saved + Remove Faults
	• Redeemer of Souls - Free Blessing: Dying to Self = Fight Evil Spirit
	• Transformation of Physical Nature - Righteousness: God becomes Man

- Learn Right from Wrong - Master Earth: Live by Faith (immature)
- Using a "Logical Mind" to Figure Things Out - 3,000 Years of Effort

Morals
(spirit)

2. **Christians Living Prayer of Love** - Creating Saints: Prayer…….. Christ
- Submission - Forgive Mortal Sin: Confession = Saving Self + Gain Virtues
- Savior of Souls - Earn Blessing: Born-again = Kiss Holy Spirit
- Purification of Spiritual Nature - Holiness: Man becomes God
- Learn Good from Evil - Master Heaven: Live by Knowing (professional)
- Using "Miracle-working Power" to Create Instant Results - Creation

This illustration shows that anyone can become a "Soldier-of-the-Light" simply by accepting his Free Gift of Life and then, by being willing to **Sacrifice his Life** in **Service to Others,** can **Overcome** his own **Ignorance, Cowardice, and Greed.** In contrast, it takes a great deal of "Character (righteousness/protect)" and "Tenacity (holiness/serve)" to become a Living Prayer and **Earn Eternal Life** by being willing to **Surrender One's Life** to **Die for Someone Else** to master the art of **Wisdom, Courage, and Generosity Toward All.** Willingness to go that "Extra Mile" separates the Men (2 miles) from the boys (1 mile) throughout their **Earthly Life-experience** forcing each of **God's Children to Choose** the **Easy Road** (pagan) or the **Hard Road** (Christian). The point is that during the "Lord's 1st Advent (remove ignorance)," He brought sufficient Grace (justice) to **Transform Mankind** into **Soldiers-of-the-Light** (flesh) that they might have sufficient power to **Remove Human Faults** (thoughts) from **Their Evil Minds.** During the "Lord's 2nd Advent (remove cowardice)," He will again bring sufficient Grace (mercy) to **Transform Humanity** into **Living Prayers of Love** (spirit) to **Gain Human Virtues** (word) through the power of the **Divine Word of Infinite Truth.** Finally, in the "Lord's 3rd Advent (remove greed)," he will bring an ocean of Grace (love) to **Transform** the **Whole Human Race** into **Holy Saints** (soul) that they might **All be Soul Winners** (deed) through the power of their own **Holy Deeds/works.**

Obviously, in the "Lord's Three Advents," **He Teaches Mankind How** to: 1) Think (thought): Priest on a Donkey (sacrifice self), 2) Speak (word): Thief in the Night (seal saints), and 3) Do (deed): Judge on a Cloud (purify earth). We see that via "Each of the Lord's" Three Advents, a **New Phase of Life** is **Specially Designed** to **Transform Man** from a **Tiny Baby** into a **Strong Hard-working Adult** as an **Adopted Son of God.** Note that the Lord "Jesus Christ (temple tax)" and the "Virgin Mary (sacrificial lamb)" are Working Together as a **Single Force of Love** to **Extract Every Drop** of the **Milk of Human Kindness** out of the **Human Heart** (stone) to begin the **Manifestation** of the **Glorious Marriage of Divinity** (name) **and Humanity** (virginity). The "Institution of Marriage" will Unite the Flesh of Earth (ignorance/cowardice/greed) to the Spirit of Heaven (wisdom/courage/generosity) through the **Perfection** of one's **Mind** (flesh), **Heart** (spirit), and **Soul** (soul). One of the best ways to comprehend the "Kingdom of God" is to imagine that Earthly Life is Free (free gold mine) and anyone who **Dies to Self** (remove faults) and establishes himself during

<u>Life</u> will receive **Free Redemption**. Secondly, if a person desires "Heaven," then he must be willing to <u>Gain Virtues</u> (dig out gold) and **Earn God's Blessing** of <u>Eternal Life</u> to **Earn his Own Salvation**. Finally, if a person desires to be a part of "God's Kingdom," then he must be willing to <u>Save Souls</u> (share gold) to become worthy of God's **Eternal Rewards**. At each of these "Three Stages of Life (individual/society /God)," a person must <u>Give</u> more and more of himself to the **Cause** in a never-ending struggle to pull **Lost Humanity** out of its **Pit of Sin, Evil, and Death**.

**Humanity is being Called to Remove Its Faults,
Gain Virtues, and Save Souls for Christ**
(surrendering one's flesh, living by being true
to self, and following one's guilty conscience)

Greek Mind - **Earthly Intellect: Find God through Wisdom (home)**

Flesh   1. **Remove Faults** - <u>Submission:</u> Establish Fixed Reference........ Knowledge

(truth)
- Altar - Receive Free Gold Mine from Man
- Prayers - Dig Out Gold on Earth   **New Body (self)**
- Redemption - Share Gold with Righteous Citizens

(individual stage - learn right/wrong and become a righteous citizen on earth)

- -

Roman Heart - **Heavenly Emotions: Find God through Work (government)**

Spirit   2. **Gain Virtues** - <u>Unto Thine Own Self be True:</u> Focused Existence....
     Self-awareness

(law)
- Throne - Receive Free Gold Mine from God
- Works - Dig Out Gold in Heaven   **Eternal Life**
- Salvation - Share Gold with Holy Saints

(social stage - learn good from evil and become a holy saint in Heaven)

- -

Jewish Soul - **Kingdom Instincts: Find God through Prayer (church)**

Soul   3. **Save Souls** - <u>Guilty Conscience:</u> Perception of Reality ...
     Consciousness

(will)
- Palace - Receive Free Gold Mine in One's Name
- Love - Dig Out Gold in Kingdom   **Royal Kingdom**
- Rewards - Share Gold with Sons of God

(Godly stage - learn God's will from man's will and become a son of God in the Kingdom)

This Illustration shows that the "Altar on Earth" offers Lost Souls a **Chance to Receive** <u>**Their Own**</u> *Free Gold Mine* (graces); then their "Prayers on Earth" <u>Give Them a Chance</u> to *Dig Out God's Gold*; and finally, through society's "Redemption on Earth (new body)," they can *Share Their Gold with Others*. Secondly, the "Throne of Heaven" offers <u>Christians</u> a **Chance to Receive** <u>**Their Own**</u> *Free Eternal Gold Mine* (blessings); then their "Works in Heaven" <u>Give Them a Chance</u> to *Dig Out God's Eternal Gold*; and finally, through their "Salvation in Heaven (eternal life)," <u>**They**</u> can *Share Their Eternal Gold with Others*. Finally, the "Palace in the Kingdom" offers <u>Saints</u>

a **Chance to Receive** <u>Their Own</u> *Free Royal Gold Mine* (anointing); then their "Love in the Kingdom (kingdom)" can *Dig Out God's Royal Gold;* and finally, through their "Rewards from God's Kingdom (freedom)," *They can Share God's Royal Gold with Others*. This means that the "Smarter" and "Stronger" a <u>Person</u> (pagan/Christian/saint) becomes, the more he is able to **Transform** <u>Money</u> (gold) into <u>Power</u> (influence) until he can **Conquer the Whole Kingdom**. In this context of "Converting Souls," the <u>Gold on Earth</u> is <u>Grace in Heaven</u> and the more **Grace Dollars** (prayers) a person can obtain, the more <u>**Souls he can Save**</u> until he is able to **Save the Whole World**.

We see that a great "State of Confusion" was created by the <u>Church</u> when it focused its attention on **Prayer** (only) as the generator of <u>**Human Salvation,**</u> instead of merging both *Prayer* (Heaven/grace) and *Works* (earth/money). In short, the "Human Race" must first <u>Surrender to Prayer</u> (altar), then <u>Master Earthly Works</u> (throne) to **Convert** *Lost Sinners* (earth) into *Holy Saints* (Heaven). Recall that when "Jesus was on the Cross," the words <u>King of the Jews</u> was displayed in three languages, **Greek** (mind), **Roman** (heart) and **Hebrew** (soul) to show that it takes the <u>**Mind/Heart/Soul Working Together**</u> to *Find God*. This means that the "Earth (Greeks/home)" is <u>Finding God</u> (know) through *Thinking* (wisdom) or *Science* (discovery); then "Heaven (Romans/government)" is <u>Finding God</u> (love) through **Works** (courage); and finally, the "Kingdom (Jews/church)" is <u>Finding God</u> (service) through **Prayer** (generosity). Obviously, through his "Mind (home)," "Heart (government)," and "Soul (church)," a <u>Person</u> can <u>Find God</u> and become the **Lord's Friend** (in mind), **Companion** (in heart), and even *Enter His Oneness* (in soul/family).

This "Journey of Life" from <u>Self</u> (selfish) to a <u>One-World Society</u> (unselfish) calls each of **God's Children** to **Learn to Control** his own <u>**Thoughts, Feelings,**</u> and <u>**Instincts**</u> to the point of **Acting** in a **Mature Manner** in **All Situations**. Through this "State of Maturity," a <u>Person</u> is able to <u>Accept God's Gift of Life</u> with a **Firm** and **Tight Embrace** for <u>**All that God has Created**</u> in *Physical* (earth), *Spiritual* (Heaven), and *Mystical* (Kingdom) *Forms*. In this explanation, we see that those "Who Accept God's Free Gift" of "Physical Life" are in a position to <u>Witness God's Grand Design</u> **Defining** the <u>**Lord's Big Picture**</u> (infinity/eternity) based on *Living an Eternal Life.*

In other words, living an "Eighty-Year Life" on **Earth** is simply a <u>Speeded Up Version</u> of living an "Eternal Life" in **God's Kingdom** to give **Each Soul a Sense** of the **Importance** of both <u>**Everlasting**</u> *Physical Growth* (logical results) and *Spiritual Maturity* (miracle-working power). The Lord is trying to explain the "Need to Unite" <u>His Physical Creation</u> (mind/intellect) with <u>His Spiritual Creation</u> (heart/emotions) through *His Blessing of Marriage.* The idea here is that the most "Uneven Yoke of Marital Bliss" possible in <u>All the Creation</u> of **God** actually provides a **Perfect Test** for **His Son's** coming **Perfect Justice System** of *Infinite Love.* The message here is that of finding out if the "Miracle-working Power" of <u>Mount Calvary</u> (unity) can be depended upon to accomplish the <u>**Impossible-of-the-Impossible**</u> by **Uniting Evil Man** with his <u>**Holy God**</u> in this *Arranged Marriage of Convenience* (priceless bond).

The theme of "Mount Calvary" is that a person can obtain a <u>Divinely Sealed Contract</u> from **God Himself** to be <u>**Written**</u> in either *Blood* (physical), *Death* (spiritual), *Damnation* (mystical), *Oblivion* (divine), and/or in *Resurrection* (Godly). This means that an "Eternal Union" can be made with "God" on the <u>Mind</u> (truth), <u>Heart</u> (law), <u>Soul</u> (will), <u>Life-force</u> (love), or <u>Divine Nature</u> (freedom) **Levels of Existence** based on just **How Much** a person is **Willing to Pay** based on *His Own Self-sacrifice*. The central theme is that anyone willing to "Break out" of <u>Lucifer's Prison of Death</u> must first **Fight Evil** (slow and painful) to **Save the Lost** and then be willing to **Kiss the Holy Spirit** (instant results) to **Create Saints in Heaven**. We see that "If a Faithful Soul" strives to <u>Fight Lucifer</u> (sinners) and <u>Worship God</u> (saints), it can become an **Officer** within the **Lord's Perfect Justice System** as a **Member** of the *Lord's Kingdom of Glory*. It can be seen that comprehending the "Lord's Perfect Justice System (Calvary)" is quite simple, as <u>Jesus</u> operates a **Pathway of Destiny** (physical/world) and <u>Mary</u> operates a **Pathway of Free Will** (spiritual/church). The **Souls of Mankind** are **Called to Perfection** through a **Blessing System of Sanctifying Grace** based upon *Divine Merits of Human Love*.

The entire creation is "Rank-ordered" from the most <u>Loveable</u> (good) to the most <u>Despicable</u> (evil). The **Task is to Convince** the **Divine Will of God** to **Give His Divine Gifts, Fruits, and Treasures of Love** to those souls most *Honored by Jesus* (destiny) **and Mary** (free will). This is why "Born-again Mankind (sinfulness to grace)" is joining with <u>Jesus Christ</u> to **Help Carry His Mountain of Sin** and to **Plead** before the **Throne of God** for the *Lord's Divine Mercy*. The "Lord Jesus Christ" is <u>Uniting</u> with the <u>Angels and the Saints</u> to bring **Salvation to All Lost, Broken Sinners** wandering the earth **Without Hope** to prove that **God's Divine Mercy** (permissive will) will fall upon *All Foolish People* (orphan/widow/insane/poor/stranger) **Living and/or Dead**. In the "Providence of God," we have <u>All been Called</u> to **Think Pure Thoughts** of **Holy Truth,** thereby allowing every **Purified Soul** to **Understand** the **Mystical Words of his Creator.** We see that "Humanity" is being called to <u>Speak the Sacred Words</u> of **God's Infinite Law** so that **Life can be Transformed** into a place of *Perfect Order and Harmony*. Every person in the "Lord's Kingdom" is under a <u>Divine Obligation</u> to <u>Do the Will of God</u> and to be an **Obedient Servant** (submission) unto the **Needs of the Many** (poor)**,** thereby **Sacrificing** the **Wants of the Few** (rich).

The following tabular information clearly describes the "Mystical Purposes" of the <u>Lord's Three Advents</u> as **He comes to Purify** the **Human Mind** (thoughts/logic), **Heart** (words/love), and **Soul** (deeds/instincts):

The Purpose of the Three Advents of Christ:
Thinking, Speaking, and Doing
(life's meaning is thinking, life's purpose
is speaking, and life's value is doing for God)

Truth	1.	**Jesus' 1st Advent** (incarnate word) - Purifying the <u>Mind:</u> Holy Thoughts
Baby	•	Creation of the Soldier-of-the-Light (flesh) - Chair of Honor
(thinking)	•	Honored by the Holy Throne of the Eternal Father (justice) - Judge Sin
	•	Gift of Human Existence (body) - Remove Faults (evil thoughts)
Purify	•	Honor the People - Perfection: Teach Thinking (thought) -
Grave		See Limitations

- Meaning of Life - Existing in Truth: Guided by Stick of Light
- Figuring Everything Out - Logical Understanding: Slow Method

(Christ's "1st Testimony" unto the Truth - Submission of the Pagan World)

- -

Law
Teenager
(speaking)

Purify
Host

2. **Christ's 2nd Advent** (just judge) - Transforming the <u>Heart:</u> Sacred Speech
- Transformation into the Living Prayer of Love (spirit) - Place of Glory
- Glorified by the Sacred Altar of the Son of God (mercy) - Judge Prayers
- Gift of Human Life-force (spirit) - Gain Virtues (holy words)
- Glorify the Land - Fruitful: Teach Speaking (words) - <u>See Potential</u>
- Purpose of Life - Serve the Law: Guided by the Hand of Love
- Miracle-working Power (healing) - Instant Results: Fast Method

(Christ's "2nd Testimony" unto the Law - Sacrifice of the Jewish People)

- -

Will
Adult
(doing)

Purify
Life

3. **Jesus Christ's 3rd Advent** (father's love) - Purifying the <u>Soul:</u> Divine Deeds
- Manifestation of a Holy Saint (soul) - Seat of Majesty
- Blessed by the Divine Face (beatific vision) of God (love) - Judge Works
- Gift of Human Holy Life (soul) - Redeem Souls (sacred deeds)
- Majesty of Life - Eternal Life: Teach Doing (deeds) - <u>See Self-worth</u>
- Value of Life - Happiness in Will: Guided by Thinking for Self
- Uniting Logical and Miraculous Power - Practical Application

(Christ's "3rd Testimony" unto the Will - Conversion of All Christians)

This illustration shows the "Mystical Works" of the <u>Messiah of God</u> as **He comes to Transform** the **Broken Sinners of Death** (sin-nature) into a **New Creation** (holy-nature) through the <u>**Transformation**</u> of one's **Mind** (ignorance), **Heart** (cowardice), and **Soul** (greed). This new "Divine Light of Holy Understanding (truth)" is <u>Designed</u> to bring forth the <u>Fruits</u> of our **Creator's Handiwork** as He **Draws Closer and Closer** to the **Human Soul.** We see that the "Human Soul" is becoming more <u>Perfect</u> with every passing day (lesson/blessings) as the **Lord Jesus Christ Calls All Mankind** unto **His Loving Cross of Death** (Calvary) to <u>**Slaughter Their Innocence**</u> and be **Set Free from Sin, Evil, and Death.** This means that the "Son of God" represents the <u>Forces by Pre-ordination</u> (destiny). This simply means that **Many Souls have been Chosen** (destiny) by **God the Father** to <u>**Master the Five Dimensions of Life**</u> bringing **Redemption to All.** These "Chosen Souls" must be led through <u>God's Maze</u> of <u>Human Death</u> as the first **Control Group** (Jews/benevolent force) needed to **Lead Humanity** to its **Ultimate Perfection** (think for self). The "Mother of God" has the second <u>Control Group</u> (Christians/personal God) of **Free-willed Saints,** who have been selected by **God the Son** to <u>**Join His Kingdom of Glory**</u> through the **Blessings** of the **Holy Church** (mass).

These "Two Specially Selected Groups (witnesses)" represent the <u>Souls Traveling</u> the **Lord's Pathway of Perfection** leading to one's most **Holy Spiritual Maturity** in the **Spirit of God** as <u>**Manifested**</u> in the **Person of Christ Jesus.** This "Perfection Concept" <u>Requires the Merging</u> of **Two Divine Principles of Truth:** 1) <u>Pre-ordained</u>

Will (destiny) or the **Direct Will** (holy) of God: 1) **Divine Want** (submission/prayer), and 2) Free Will; or the **Permissive Will** (sin) of God: **Human Need** (sacrifice/offering). This structure allows the "Lord to Compare" His Control Group (destiny) of **Jews** or **Father's Selection**, against those **Souls with Dynamic Will** in the **Free-willed Group** of **Christians** or **Son's Selection**. The Virgin Mary is the force of "Random Chance (luck)," whereby She may use the **Power** of **Her Son's Church** (touch of Peter)" to **Change** the **Stubborn Wills** of both **God** (reality/good) and **Man** (illusion/evil). If She can (sound argument) somehow "Get Them to Agree (union)" in both Spirit and in Flesh, then **God and Man** could become **Closer and Closer** until **They** can become **One** in **Truth, Law, Will,** and **Love.**

It may be just about now that a "Person May be Suspecting" that Life is simply some **Foolish Game** (illusion) being **Played** by a group of infinitely great **Divine Rulers** of **Our Creation**, just for the **Fun of It** (gamblers). Certainly, one can make a good case that "This is True;" yet, it is also "True" that there is little difference between Work and Play at the **God Level**, when they are both simply **Human Viewpoints** based upon a **Person's Current** *Selfish Perspective.* Obviously, "God has Found a Way" to Combine the **Forces of Work** and the **Forces of Play** into **Oneness**, thereby making all things in **His Creation Fun,** no matter how Great of a Sacrifice (Calvary) He might have to make, to get to that **Special Level of Perfection** He **Really Wants to Attain** (final results).

Note that the "Lord Comes" to Redeem the World in **Two Forms**: 1) Christmas (fun/life) or Eternal Life (Heaven) - Free Gift: Baby Redeemer/Human God = Create Holy Church (give divinity); and 2) Easter (work/death) or New Body (earth) - Earned Treasure: Adult Savior/Divine Man = Create Righteous World (takes-sin). It appears that mankind's "Christmas Present" comes in the form of More Time (individual rights) or as **Eternal Life** (earned). Mankind's "Easter Egg" comes in the form of More Space (social rights) or an **Infinite Land of Milk** (human kindness) and **Honey** (divine love) or a **New Body** (free). The idea is that "the Human Race" and both Eternal Time and Infinite Space could create as **Many Happy Babies** (people) as they would **Ever Want** and/or **Ever Need.**

To "Remove Human Ignorance (Eve)," God was Required to **Send** a **Human God** (Child Redeemer/holiness). To "Remove Human Cowardice (Adam), God was Required to **Send** a **Divine Man** (Adult Savior/righteousness). The "Job of the Human God" is to Transform **God into Man** on **Christmas** in **Fulfillment** of the **Jewish Passover** (lamb); while the "Job of the Divine Man" is to Transform **Man into God** on **Easter** in **Fulfillment** of the **Jewish Day of Atonement** (goat). Through each of these "Conversion Experiences," Man's Spirit (heart) can **Find Its Courage** (blood shed); while Man's Flesh (mind) can **Find Its Wisdom** (body broken). The point is that through "Man's New Courage (heart)," he will establish Individual Rights of **Ownership** to define his Personal Value of **Real Property** based on **Established Market Value**. Out of "Ownership Rights," the Republican Party was founded to **Protect Any and All Free Market Competition** between honest **Businessmen** striving to **Build Viable Industries** of **Capital Goods and Services.** Secondly, out of "General-welfare Rights," the Democratic Party was established to **Protect the Constitutional Rights** of **Cooperation** between <u>**Citizens of Each Community**</u> striving to build a **Stable and Safe Home for Their Children.** Finally, through both the "Government (democrats) and the Home (republicans)," a <u>Set of Human Rights</u> can be established to **Protect the Cultural Beliefs** (church) of the **People** based on the **Will of the People** (vote). This means that "Society" is to be established upon the <u>Church</u> (people), <u>Government</u> (space), and <u>Home</u> (time) to **Serve the Needs** of each person's **Spirit** (heart), **Flesh** (mind), and **Soul** (being) unto the **Benefit of the General Welfare of All.** The idea here is that out of the "Government (people)" is to come a <u>Set of Perfect Friends</u> (see limitations); out of the "Church (God)" is to come the <u>Friendship of God</u> (see potential); and out of the "Home (self)" is to come the **Friendship of Self** or **Seeing One's Self-worth.**

The following tabular information indicates that "Jesus Christ" comes both in the <u>Form</u> of **Baby Life** (Christmas) and **Adult Death** (Easter) to bring **God's Blessings** of a **Free** <u>**Redemption**</u> (baptism); <u>**Earned Salvation**</u> (confession) will bring **Reality to One and All:**

Mankind is Given Baby Redeemer (Christmas) and an Adult Savior (Easter) to Save the World
(Christmas brings Human God to Remove Ignorance and
Easter brings Divine Man to Remove Cowardice)

God/Man	1.	**Baby Redeemer** - <u>Christ Child:</u> Christmas Gift… Remove Ignorance (wisdom)
(emotions)		• Human God - Brings More Time: Eternal Life = Abrahamic Covenant (drink wine)
		• Son of God - Creator of the Church: Blessing of Holiness (love)
		• Learn Good from Evil - Elementary School: Baby Level = See Limitation
Free		• Jewish Circumcision - Purification of the Heart: Holy Saint
God's Law		• Passover Meal (lamb) - Last Supper Celebrated Every Christmas
(new body)		• Christ "Gives Divinity" - Winepress: Wine = Receive Glorified Spirit
		• Church - Friendship of God: Blessing of Love = Love God (**stewardship**)
		• Paradise in Heaven - All Prayer: Seat in Temple Court
		• *God's Individual Rights* - Ownership of Time (imagination)
		• *Republican Party* - Earning Wealth: Competition: Home
Man/God	2.	**Adult Savior** - <u>The Man Jesus:</u> Easter Egg …. Remove Cowardice (courage)
(intellect)		• Divine Man - Brings More Space: Infinite Land = New Covenant (eat death)
		• Son of Man - Creator of Righteous World: Gift of Righteousness (logic)
		• Learn Right from Wrong - College: Adult Level = See Potential
Earned		• Christian Baptism - Transformation of the Mind: Righteous Citizen
Man's Faith		• Day of Atonement (goat) - Calvary Celebrated Every Easter
(eternal life)		• Jesus "Takes-on Sin" - Crucible: Bread = Receive Transfigured Body
		• Home - Friendship of Self: Blessing of Wisdom = Serve God (**servanthood**)

- Heaven on Earth - All Fun: Seat in Celestial Court
- *Man's Social Rights* - Voting Privileges of Space (thinking)
- *Democratic Party* - Spending Wealth: Cooperation: Government

This illustration shows that "God's Son, Christ" has been Sent to Earth to bring the **Human Race** the **Ownership of Time** to **Give Every Person God's Individual Rights,** thereby allowing sufficient **Time to Imagine** everything one might **Ever Want to Do, to Be, or to Own Forever.** Secondly, "Mary's Son, Jesus" was Created on Earth to bring the **Human Race Voting Privileges of Space** (new body) to **Give Every Person Man's Social Rights,** thereby allowing the **Knowledge Needed** for **God to Build His Own** Kingdom of Glory. In short, we see that "Christ is Dreaming the Dream," while the "Job of Jesus is to Figure Out and Implement the Details" so that all that is Imagined by God can be **Accomplished** by the **Physical World of Man.** Through the creations of both "Christmas (ownership)" and "Easter (general welfare)," the institutions of Stewardship (needs) and Servanthood (wants) can bring forth a **Perfect Home** (eternal life**)** and a **Perfect Government** (title to land) in **Service to All the People** (one and all). This means that Jesus Christ has come to a "Lost and Confused World" to bring Liberty and Justice for All (freedom) through the creation of a **Perfect Man** (perfect), **Perfect Society** (holy), and a **Perfect Set of Friends** (righteous).

We are now all "Called" to Worship (give life), Praise (give wealth), and Thank (give labor) God for His tremendous **Gifts of Time** (eternal life), **Ownership of Land** (space/new body), and a **World Full of People** (friends). Out of these "Three Gifts," All Men of Goodwill can obtain the **Lord's Blessings** of **Peace of Mind** (forgiveness/church), **Joy of the Heart** (wealth/government), and **Happiness of the Soul** (love/home). The mystical question is: why has the "Lord Chosen to Create" a Masterpiece of Perfect Love out of **His Own Heart's Desire,** only to introduce a dynamic factor of **Random Chance** (luck) to **Distort** it all with a **Perfect Flaw** of **Original Sin**? It can now be seen that "Christ (priest)" brings the Title Deed to Eternal Life (Christmas) from **Heaven** to **Save Repentant Spirits** (host) and bring them to **Paradise in Heaven** (sainthood). Secondly, "Jesus (king)" brings the Title Deed to Infinite Land (Easter) from **Earth** to **Save Transformed Flesh** (grave) and **Offer It God's Blessing** of **Heaven on Earth** (righteous citizens). Thirdly, "Jesus Christ (son)" brings the Title Deed to Holy People (Halloween) from the **Kingdom** to **Save Converted Souls** and **Offer Them God's Kingdom of Glory** (sons of God). Finally, "Christ Jesus (father)" brings the Title Deed to God's Divine Love (Independence Day) from **God's Divine Perfection** to **Save All Human Life-forces** and **Offer Them God's Beatific Vision** (freedom).

1. **Christmas** - Title Deed to Eternal Life: God becomes Man via Life....... Change Nature
   - Veneration of Life - Gain Heaven on Earth (righteousness)   **Life**
   - Save Repentant Sinners - Being Saved (get free gold mine)
2. **Easter** - Title Deed to Eternal Lands: Man becomes God via Death ....Wash Away Sin
   - Adoration of Death - Gain Paradise in Heaven (holiness)   **Land**
   - Baptize Christians - Saving Self (dig out gold)

3. **Halloween** - <u>Title Deed to Holy People:</u> God/Man become One in
    Resurrection….. Think for Self
    *   Exaltation of Resurrection - Gain Kingdom of Glory (perfection)   **Friends**
    *   Create Saints – Saving Others (share one's gold)

- -

4. **Independence -** Title Deed to God's Divine Love: Man/God Set Free… Master of All
    One Surveys
    *   Worship of God/Man Freedom - Gain Oneness of God (divinity)   **Love**
    *   Become Son of God - Servant unto All (build kingdom of gold)

At each of these "Four Levels of Redemption," <u>God's Son has Planned</u> to bring **His Beloved Human Race, Life** (time), **Land** (money), **Friends** (people), and **God's Love** (God) via the **<u>Title Deeds</u>** of *Earth, Heaven, Kingdom*, and *God's Beatific Vision* (Face). The point is that if a person has "All the Time in the World (eternal life)," then just what is he <u>Hoping to Accomplish</u> for **himself, his Family, his Nation,** and the **Kingdom of God, <u>If Not</u>** to bring forth an *Abundance of Human Prosperity* (children). This means out of one's "Abundance of Time" shall come a <u>Good Education</u> (school/knowledge); out of his "Vast Lands" shall come a <u>Career as a Great Builder</u> (space/self-awareness); out of his "Home and Family" shall come a <u>Thriving Population</u> (people/consciousness); and out of his "Good Life" shall come a <u>Holy Church</u> (worship/sentience) and the *Eternal Friendship with God.* We now see a "Man of Great Ambition," truly a <u>Striving Soul</u> **Who Seeks** the **<u>Best that Life has to Offer</u>** be it in *Physical Life* (life), *Spiritual Life* (money), *Mystical Life* (friends), and/or *Divine Life* (God). This means that during "Christmas," the <u>Human Race</u> is being **Called** to **Fulfill God's Law of Obedience** to **Change Man's Nature** from **Human to Divine,** thereby **Making him** a **<u>Righteous Citizen on Earth,</u>** truly **Worthy of a New Body.** Secondly, during "Easter," the <u>Human Race</u> is being **Called to Fulfill Man's Faith in God's Love** to **Wash Away All Sin, Changing One's Sinfulness to Holiness,** thereby **Making him** into a **<u>Holy Saint in Heaven,</u>** truly *Worthy of Eternal Life.* Thirdly, during "Halloween," the <u>Human Race</u> is being **Called** to **Learn All the Lessons of Life** to **Think for Itself, Changing One's Imperfection** into **Perfection,** thereby **Making him** into a **<u>Perfect Son within God's Kingdom,</u>** truly *Worthy of his Own Kingdom.* Finally, during "Independence Day," the <u>Human Race</u> is being **Set Free** from **Sin, Evil, and Death** to be **United** with **God, Angels, Men, and Nature,** thereby **Making him** a **Free Man,** truly *Worthy of God's Eternal Friendship.*

The following tabular information indicates "God's Son" is bringing <u>Life, Money, Friends,</u> and <u>Love</u> to the **New Heaven and new earth** in fulfillment of **Earth, Heaven, Kingdom,** and God's **Beatific Vision** (Smiling Face):

**God's Son brings Life, Money, Friends, and Love to
the Human Race to Save them from Damnation**
(creating a new earth, Heaven, Kingdom,
and Beatific Vision as the future home of lost men)

Life	1.	**Christ** - <u>Eternal Life</u> (time): Title Deed to Heaven........... Church
(truth)		• Paradise in Heaven - Blessing of Eternal Time: Peace of Mind (forgiveness)
		• Knowledge - Properly Educated: Learn Good from Evil = See Potential
		• Justified - Prayer: Perfect Man = Poor in Spirit/Enter God's Kingdom
		• Blessed - Church: Holiness = The Merciful/Be Given Mercy

(Eternal Father comes to Humanity through the Jewish People to begin His Kingdom)

Money	2.	**Jesus** - <u>Infinite Land</u> (space): Title Deed to Earth ....Government
(law)		• Heaven on Earth - Blessing of Infinite Space: Joy of the Heart (wealth)
		• Self-awareness - Career Minded: Learn Right from Wrong = See Limitations
		• Honored - Works: Perfect Society = Those Who Mourn/Comforted
		• Anointed - Government: Righteousness = Pure of Heart/See God

(Son of God comes to Humanity through His Apostles to begin His Heaven on Earth)

Friends	3.	**Jesus Christ** - <u>Population of People</u> (babies): Title Deed to Kingdom..... Home
(will)		• Kingdom of Glory - Blessing of Unlimited Population: Happiness of Soul (love)
		• Consciousness - Respected Home: Learn God's/Man's Wills = See Self-worth
		• Glorified - Love: Perfect Set of Friends = The Meek/Inherit the Earth
		• Sanctified - Home: Perfection = Peacemakers/Chosen Children

(Holy Spirit comes to Humanity through His Church to begin His Paradise in Heaven)

God	4.	**Christ Jesus** - <u>God's Divine Love</u> (union): Title Deed to God ... Kingdom
(love)		• God's Beatific Vision - Blessing of Abundant Love: Freedom of Life
		• Sentience - Good Life: Learn God's Reality/Man's Illusion = See Future
		• Freed - Dream: Perfect Friendship of God = Hunger/Thirst for Righteousness/Filled
		• Consecrated - Kingdom: Divinity = Persecuted for Righteousness/Inherit Kingdom

(son of man comes to Humanity through His Self-will to begin His Own Creation)

This illustration shows that the "Life-experience" is all about <u>Personal/Social/Divine Ownership</u> brought forth by each **Person's Ability** to become worthy of *Eternal Life, Infinite Amounts of Land, Serve Great Populations,* and *Earn God's Divine Love.* This means becoming "Justified through Prayer" to receive God's <u>Blessing of a Holy Church</u> to bring a **Lost Soul** the **Lord's Forgiveness,** giving it *Peace of Mind forever.* Secondly, being "Honored through Hard-work" is to receive God's <u>Anointing of a Righteous Government</u> to bring **Righteous Citizens** the **Lord's Wealth,** giving him *Joy of the Heart forever.* Thirdly, being "Glorified through Love" is to receive God's <u>Sanctification of a Perfect Home</u> to bring **Loving Sons** the **Lord's Love,** giving them

Happiness of the Soul forever. Finally, being "Freed through God's Friendship" is to receive God's <u>Consecration unto His Kingdom</u> to bring a **Holy Saint** the <u>**Lord's Respect,**</u> giving him *Freedom within Eternal Life.* Through each of these "Four Levels of Blessing," a <u>Transformed Soul</u> can **Master Men, Angels, and God** at all of the Lord's **Stages of Growth** (flesh) and **Maturity** (spirit) bringing it *Knowledge* (education), *Self-awareness* (career), *Consciousness* (home), and *Sentience* (life).

Now, imagine that after going to "All this Trouble" to create a <u>Perfect Life,</u> God would allow his most **Playful Children to Dash about His Kingdom** <u>**Romping, Playing,**</u> and having **Fun** to their *Hearts' Content.* Remember, it is "Only a Mother's Love (hopes)" that can <u>Stand Against</u> a "Father's Will (expectations)" when it comes to the <u>Disobedience of Their Children</u> when the little ones are having the *Time of Their Lives.* We now see that the "Answer Is" in the <u>Divine Harmony of God</u> being **Intentionally Disturbed** via the **Lord's Compromised Will** as **God Allows a Powerful** <u>**Fun-filled Force**</u> (babies/free will) to *Strike like Lightning* and then *Disappear as Quickly as it Came.* In understanding this aspect of the "Mind of God," imagine a <u>Patient Father</u> peacefully **Watching Television,** when suddenly, the **Door Flies Open** and like a **Storm, His Beloved Children** <u>**Fly In**</u> and as quickly <u>**Fly Out**</u> again, like an *Instant Storm.* This is to be seen as the "Joy of His Home" (blessing) <u>Not the Curse of It;</u> even **God the Father** desires the excitement of the <u>**Joyful Unexpected**</u> (unknown force) known as a *Divine Surprise* (pure joy)**.** Our most "Perfect Creator" has <u>Thought of Everything</u> and has added in a most essential **Unknown Factor** making **His Paradise of Perfect Love** a place of *Joy, Rollicking Laughter, and Fun.* We can imagine and share this time of "Suspense-filled Excitement" as we <u>Empathize</u> with what the <u>Lord is Trying to Accomplish,</u> by comparing it to our own **Magic Kingdom** (eternal happiness) or **Heaven on earth.** This means "Disneyland," just like <u>God's Fun Center,</u> reveals **God's Divine Love is Complete** and the **Lord** <u>**Wants the Lives**</u> of **His** most **Beloved Children** to also be *Complete in Every Way Possible.* It is only with "God's Unknown Factor (luck)" that there can truly be <u>Surprises</u> for both **Him and Us,** which means that **Life is More** than just **news, weather, and sports** - Even for God....

It is well understood that "Christ" will come in <u>Three Separate Advents:</u> one as a *Priest on a Donkey* (false accusation); then as a *Thief in the Night* (mutual hatred); and finally, as a *Just Judge on a Cloud* (eternal freedom). Obviously, the "Human Race" is being "Saved" via a <u>Step-by-step Method of Conversion</u> as a **Priest** came to **Give Everyone** *Free Redemption.* Then a **King will come at Night** to open a **Door of Salvation** for those who are willing to *Earn Their Way into Heaven.* Finally, the "Son of God" will come to issue <u>God's Bonus Rewards</u> to those who have *Surrendered* (unknown), *Sacrificed Themselves* (normal), and been *Reconciled Back to God* (belief). In other words, during the "Lord's 1st Advent (Jews)," <u>Mankind</u> was *Saved* (redemption/free); then during the "Lord's 2nd Advent (Christians)," <u>Mankind</u> must *Save Itself* (salvation/earned); and finally, during the "Lord's 3rd Advent (Saints)," <u>Mankind</u> must prove itself by *Saving the Souls of Others* (rewards/bonus). With the "Fulfillment" of all <u>Three of these Advents, Mankind</u> will **Learn Right from Wrong** and become a *Jew* (earth/government); **Learn Good from Evil** and become a *Christian* (Heaven/church); then finally, **Learn God's Will from man's will** and become a *Saint* (Kingdom/home). If a soul is able to do "All These Things," it can then look forward to the Abundance of Life within **God's Beatific Vision**, where it can **Master Itself** (think for self), and then **Establish Its Own Kingdom** as an *Adopted Son of God.*

We can see some evidence to the "Lord's Three Advents" plus "Eternity" in the story of **Isaac's Four Wells which were Named**: 1) *Falsely Accused* - Mount Calvary: 1st Advent (God Dies); 2) *Mutual Hatred* - Great Tribulation: 2nd Advent (Man Dies); 3) *Eternal Freedom* - End of the World: 3rd Advent (God/Man Freed); and 4) *Divine Abundance* - New Heaven and new earth: Sanctified Life (Self-Awakening). We see that "Isaac" was saying that when "He Re-Dug" Abraham's 1st Old Well, he was **Falsely Accused** of **Greed and Selfishness** because he would **Not Share the Water** (eternal life) which he needed to **Care for His Family.** For this reason, "Isaac then Re-Dug a Second Well" to Share His Living Waters with his Neighbors, but instead this simply caused a **Big Fight Over Water Rights** resulting in **Mutual Hatred that Affected Everyone.** Next, "Isaac" decided to Re-Dig a Third Well to be used as an **Emergency Backup** for anyone who might **Need Water** and **Cannot Wait his Turn** at the **Common Well**, thereby **Setting Everyone Free** from their **Desperate Need for Water.** Note that these "First Three Wells" had previously been Dug by Isaac's Father Abraham, but then **Isaac Decided** to **Dig a New Well** which he **Named Abundance** as it **Served Even the Stranger** as he *Passed through this Hot Barren Land.*

Now, using this "Logic," we can see "God's Son, Jesus Christ" coming Back to Earth Three Times to **Dig Fresh Wells of Living Waters**: first for the **Jews,** then one for the **Christians,** and finally, a **Last Well** for the **Saints of God** as the *Lord God Almighty* comes *to Set up Heaven on Earth.* We see the "Creation of Isaac's Fourth Well" in the coming of God's Kingdom or **New Jerusalem** to **Set All the Captives Free** by **Uniting Earth,** Heaven, **Kingdom, and God** into *One Nation, One People, and One Land.*

The following tabular information indicates the "Four Wells of Isaac (Genesis)" as he revealed the Coming of the Messiah to be *Falsely Accused* (Calvary), cause *Mutual Hatred* (Tribulation), *Set the Captives Free* (end of world), and bring *Divine Abundance/God Speaks to Man* (Heaven on earth):

Four Wells of Isaac Reveal the Three Advents of Christ Plus God's Judgment/Arrival on Earth
(four wells represent falsely accused,
mutual hatred, set captives free, and divine abundance)

Unknown	1. **1st Well** - Falsely Accused: 1st Advent (Calvary) = Define Nature....Water for Family
(baby)	• Redeem the Jews - Seed (faith) Falls on the Pathway of Life and is Crushed
	• Seed or Faith is Trampled under the Foot of a Busy Life/Stiff-necked Fool

- Free Redemption - Being Saved: Learn Right/Wrong = Righteousness
- Fixed Frame of Reference - Establish Personal Identity: Earth
- *Calvary* - Creates Sacred Temple: ***God Dies*** = Physical Transformation

    (1st Well - Temple: Worship = Give Life + Father Creates

        Jewish Family - High Priest: One intercessor)

Normal

(teenager)

2. **2nd Well** - <u>Mutual Hatred:</u> 2nd Advent (Tribulation) = Define Behavior... Water for Neighbor
- Save the Christians - Seed (faith) Falls on Rocky Soil and Fails to Root
- Seed or Faith has too Little Soil to Root and Dies/Tries and Fails
- Earn Salvation - Saving Self: Learn Good/Evil = Holiness
- Relative Focused Existence - Focus on Value of Life: Heaven
- *Tribulation* - Creates Holy Church: ***Man Dies*** = Spiritual Purification

    (2nd Well - Church: Praise = Give Wealth + Son Creates

        Christian Neighbors - Priesthood: Few Intercessors)

Beliefs

(adult)

3. **3rd Well** - <u>Eternal Freedom:</u> 3rd Advent (End World) = Define Lifestyle... Water for Community
- Reward Saints - Seed (faith) Falls on Weedy Soil and is Chocked Out
- Seed or Faith is Outnumbered and Overcome/Convinced but Goes Along to Get Along
- Bonus Rewards - Saving Others: Learn God's/Man's Wills = Perfection
- Perception of Reality - Define Personal Beliefs: Kingdom
- *Peace* - Creates Righteous World: ***God's/Man's New-life*** = Mystical Correction

    (3rd Well - World: Thanks = Give Labor + Spirit

    Creates Righteous Community - Laity: Masses Intercede)

Knowing

(wise man)

4. **4th Well** - <u>Divine Abundance:</u> Heaven on Earth (New World) = Thinking ...Water for Stranger
- Set Sons Free - Seed (knowing) Falls on Good Ground and Takes Root/Fruitful
- Seed or Knowing Defeats All Evil and Allows Plant to Thrive/Born-again Soul
- Eternal Freedom - Everyone is Saved: Learn Reality/Illusion = Divinity
- Life becomes Real - Master All Truth/Law/Will: Beatific Vision
- *Freedom* - Creates Perfect Kingdom: ***Man's/God's New-life*** = Divine Conversion

    (4th Well - Kingdom: Bless = Give Gifts + Almighty God

        Creates Home of Strangers - Pagans: All Intercede)

This illustration shows that "Isaac's Wells" <u>Prophesied</u> the <u>Three Advents of Christ</u> plus the **Coming** of the **Lord God Almighty** (judgment) onto **Earth,** thereby allowing **Four Stages of Transformation** from being an ***Ignorant Fool*** (baby) to a ***Wise Man*** (adult). We see that these "Four Stages of Transformation" are defined as <u>Seeds of God's Word</u> **Sowing Faith** in the **Lost Souls of Dead Believers** by trying to **Save** *Man's Spirit* (heart), *Man's Flesh* (mind), *Man's Soul* (being), and then *Man's Life-force* (life). This was actually "Done" on <u>Mount Calvary</u> (1st advent) with the **Death of God** (nature); and will occur during the <u>Great Tribulation</u> (2nd advent) with the **Death of Man** (behavior); next at the <u>End of the World</u> (3rd advent) with the **New-life of God/Man** (lifestyle); and finally, with the birth of the <u>New World</u> (Heaven on Earth) with **New-life of Man/God** (thinking). Through these "Four Major Events" of the <u>Life-experience,</u> the **Human Race** can see the **Planting of God's Seed** in the form of *<u>God's Word</u>* (faith) as it is **Taught to Lost Souls** by the *Jews, Christians, Saints, and God's Sons.*

It is clear that the "Life-experience" for every person must be <u>Fixed</u> within God's **Plan of Existence** so that each soul can attain its own **Personal Level of Perfection,** thereby making it **Unique before God**. In this explanation, we are defining the Lord's "Plan of Existence" in terms of one's personal <u>Reference Point</u> (self/home), <u>Triangulated Position</u> (society/government), and <u>Territory</u> (God/church) to reveal his *Stage of Development before God.* This ability to "Grow, Mature, and Develop" into a <u>Productive Member of Society</u> is depicted through **Seven Graphic Illustrations** to show one's *Progress through the Life-experience.* These "Graphs" have been provided to assist the reader in comprehending "Man's Progress (physical/spiritual/mystical)" through a set of *Three Dimensions of Existence* and then "God's Progress (Divine/Godly/New Creation/Supernatural Being)" through *Four Additional Dimensions.* This implies that "Einstein's Theory of Relativity" is being used to <u>Explain Each Chart</u> and **Define the Associated Levels of Development** attributed to the **Growth** (Man) and **Maturity** (God) of **Each Evolving Soul**. Note that we are using a "Term Known as Gamma" to depict each unique position along the overall <u>Space/Time Continuum</u> so that each person can find his own **Reference Point** to establish his own **Progress and/or Development** toward **Absolute Perfection** (individuality). Using this logic, "Each Lost Soul" must chart its way through life by <u>Triangulating its Position</u> against some point of **Relative Focused Existence** (000) to **Measure** (prove) the **Distance** and/or **Time Difference** between **itself** (physical), its *Society* (spiritual), and then its relationship to *God's Divine Truth* (mystical).

We can see a "Steady" move from the <u>Primitive</u> to the <u>Modern</u> by using **Nature,** then **Man Power,** and then **Time Saving Machines** (mass production) as **Mankind** strives to use **Miracle-working Power** (belief) to *Solve All Its Earthly Problems*. Note that the "Job of Nature" is to <u>Create Dirt</u> (food) via its **Natural Gradational Forces** to prepare the **Earth** for a wide variety of **Life-forms,** each designed to support *Human Existence.* Secondly, the "Job of the Human Race" is to <u>Create Flesh</u> (labor) via the **Procreation of Babies** to **Populate the Earth** in the creation of many *Nations, Peoples, and Lands.* Thirdly, the "Job of Machines" is to provide <u>Labor-Saving Devices</u> (steel) to **Speed-up** the **Growth** and **Maturity of Social Systems** bringing an uncountable **Number of Cities** into existence to *Support Life on Earth* (enormous populations). Fourthly, the "Job of Angels/God" is to <u>Convert Flesh</u> into a <u>New Spirit Nature</u> (miracle-working power) to **Transfer Dying Humanity** from their **Graves** (death) into *Everlasting Life*. Finally, the "Job of God's Son (Messiah)" is to <u>Blend All</u>

Existence into its Final State of Perfection to ensure that **All God's Creations** are able to **Worship** (give life), **Praise** (give wealth), and **Thank** (give labor) **Their Creator** for **His** *Gift of Life*. Through this "System of Creation," Life, Earth, Heaven, Kingdom, and Christ have come to **Serve the Needs of Existence** to bring the **Best Out of Each Creation** through a **Series of Performance Tests**. Obviously, "God Needed" a Large Number of Tools in a **Variety** of **Shapes and Sizes** to be able to **Get the Job Done** as **God had to become a Man** (Christmas/free) and **Man had to become God** (Easter/earned) to *Make All Things Perfect in His Sight*.

The following tabular information indicates that the "Key to a Happy Life" is to be found in the Size and Efficiency of **Its Tools** be they **Natural, Man-made, Spirit-made,** or **Divinely Inspired,** just as long as a **Person Knows How to Use Them**:

**Using Nature, Man, Machines, Angels/God, and Messiah
as Tools in the Building of God's Kingdom**
(speed and accuracy define efficiency based on
operational specifications and personal need)

Survival (forever)	1. **Nature** - Life: Dirt = Food Production.........	Knowledge
	• Nature Power - Extremely Slow: Inefficient use of Time	
	• Creation of Natural Resources - Bring Life Out of Nothing	
Truth (slow)	2. **Men** - Earth: Flesh = Labor Force	Self-awareness
	• Manpower - Slow and Steady: Efficient in a Pinch	
	• Creation of Will of the People - Bring Human Life Out of Dirt	
Love (fast)	3. **Machines** - Heaven: Steel = Labor-Saving Devices ...	Consciousness
	• Machine Power - Work Savers: Efficient on Earth	
	• Creation of Perfect Order - Improve the Quality of Life	
Choices (very fast)	4. **Angels/God** - Kingdom: Spirit = Remove the Dead ...	Sentience
	• Spirit Power - Miracle-working Power: Divine Level of Efficiency	
	• Creation of the Will of Angels - Convert Death into Eternal Life	

- -

Specifications (instant)	5. **Messiah** - New-life: Divinity = Bring to Perfection...	Transfiguration
	• Christ's Power - Natural Order: Instant Resolution of Problems	
	• Creation of Will of God - Transform Imperfection to Perfection	

This illustration shows that "Nature" has been created to bring Life Out of Nothing (food source) through the ability to **Transform Rocks** into **Life-Giving Jungles** (animals) and **Fruitful Farms** (people) in **Service to the Desires and Will of God**. Secondly, "Earth" has been created to bring Human Life Out of Dirt (Adam) via each person's ability to **Build Homes** out of **Any and All Environments** brought forth out of his **Instinctive Nature to Survive**. Thirdly, "Machines" have been created to Speed-up the Life-experience through their ability to **Automate Manual Labor** via **Mass Production** and bring **Primitive Man** into a **New Modern Age** of **Limitless Peace, Joy, and Happiness**. Fourthly, "Angels/God" also have Their Jobs of **Converting Death into New-life** to bring **Human Beings into Eternal Life** to continue their

Service to God and to **His Kingdom**. Finally, "Jesus Christ (Messiah)" is responsible for Converting Imperfect Creations into **Perfect Life-forces** ready for **Service** to **God, Angels, Men, and Nature**. Through "Each of These Jobs," God's Grand Design takes shape and brings forth a most **Perfect Kingdom of Glory** worthy of the **Blessings** and **Respect** of **God, Angels, Men/Machines, and Nature** as it is **Perfect in Their Sight**.

We see that in this awesome "Divine Effort," God had to Create **Minds of Knowledge** (wisdom), **Hearts of Self-awareness** (courage), **Souls of Consciousness** (generosity), **Life-forces of Sentience** (fairness), and **Divine Natures of Transfiguration** (Godliness) to **Make Life Worth Living** for **One and All**. It now becomes clear that "God's Grand Design" includes a Divine School of Higher Learning where a **Student of God's Two Truths** comes to understand the **Meaning of Life** (existence), the **Purpose of Eternal Life** (service), and the **Value of Divine Life** (happiness). Through the "Forces of Growth and Maturity," God, Angels, and Men shall become **One Holy Family** worthy of the **Honors, Respect,** and **Blessings of God,** all in the **Name of His Son, Jesus Christ**. Through "Christ," all will be Taught Nothing to Life (food), Creation of God's Work Force (labor), the Power of Mass Production (industrialization), then Life into Eternal Life (new-life), and finally, changing Imperfection into Perfection (personalized kingdoms) so that **They shall Know the Difference** of **God's Right** from **Man's Wrong**. At each of these "Stages of Development," Individuals, Societies, and Divine Creations are **Manifested before God** as the **Lord's most Prized Treasures**. Yes! We all come into "Existence" as Immature Babies (physical/earth), then become Frightened Teenagers (spiritual/Heaven), then Obsessive or Addictive Adults (mystical/Kingdom) which leads to becoming Murderous Wise Men (divine/God's Nature), and finally, being transformed into Righteous Citizens (Godly/Free Spirit), all in the **Name of becoming Sons of God**. This "Conversion Process" allows each of **God's Children** to **Grow-up** and begin to **Think for Himself** as he decides for himself just **Who he Wants to Be** (identity) in the **Eyes of God, Angels, Men, and Nature**.

The following tabular information indicates that "All of God's Children" must pass through Five Levels of the **Lord's Rite of Passage** to both **Grow and Mature** into **Clear Thinking Adults** **Physically, Spiritually, Mystically, Divinely,** and **Godly in Nature**:

**God is Creating Food, a Labor Force, Mass Production,
Eternal Life, and then Perfect People**
(nothing to all, universe of babies,
limitless power, inter-dimensional travel, and perfection)

Nothing to Life	**Creation of Work Force**	**Power of Mass Production**
(immaturity)	(fearfulness)	(addictions)
Physical - Food	Spiritual - Labor	Mystical - Industrialization
1. Ignorant Fool	1. Cowardly Criminal	1. Greedy Insanity
2. Wise Man	2. Courageous Warrior	2. Generous Saint
3. King	3 . Priest	3. Son

4. Government	4. Church	4. Home
5. Earth	5. Heaven	5. Kingdom of Man
6. New Earth	6. New Heaven	6. Kingdom of God
7. Altar of God	7. Pulpit of God	7. Chair of God
(see God/steps)	(hear God/tasks)	(speak to God/duty)

Life to Eternal Life   **Imperfection to Perfection**
(murderousness)   (righteousness)

Divine – New–life	Godly - Personalized Kingdoms
1. Selfish Evil	1. Born-again Life
2. Sacrificial Son	2. Resurrected Son
3. Free Man	3. Man of Reason
4. Self	4. Imagination
5. Divinity	5. Godliness
6. Beatific Vision	6. New Vision
7. House of God	7. Home of Independence
(sup with God/responsibility)	(adopted by God/authority)

This illustration shows that the "Kingdom of God" is Comprised of many **Natural and Supernatural Forces** all **Working Together** in the pursuit of **God's Divine Perfection** as all things are **Traveling** from **Nothing to All** through the **Sacrifices of God's Son, Christ**. Note that within the "Physical Dimension of Life (steps)," out of Nothing comes Life as the **Creative Forces of God** are **Manifested** within the **Earth** (son), **Heaven** (father), and **Kingdom** (spirit). Secondly, within the "Spiritual Dimension of Life (tasks)," Lord Creates His Work Force (people) as the **Productive Forces of God** are **Manifested** throughout the **Creation** to bring **Peace of Mind, Joy of the Heart,** and **Happiness of the Soul** to **One and All**. Thirdly, within the "Mystical Dimension of Life (duty)," the Lord Creates a System of Mass Production (machines) as the **Inventive Forces of God** are **Manifested** throughout the **Creation** to bring forth **Righteousness** (mind), **Holiness** (heart), and **Perfection** (soul) to **One and All**. Fourthly, within the "Divine Dimension of Life (responsibility)," the Lord Transforms Life into Eternal Life as the **Conversion Forces of God** are **Manifested** throughout the **Creation** to bring forth **Kingship, Priesthood,** and **Sonship** to **One and All**. Finally, within the "Godly Dimension of Life (authority)," the Lord Changes the Imperfect into Perfection as the **Organizational Forces of God** are **Manifested** throughout the **Creation** to bring forth **Citizens of Man** (survival), **Saints of Man/God** (truth), and **Sons of God** (love) to **One and All**.

Through these "Five Stages of Life," God, Angels, Men, and Nature can become **One** to bring forth the **First Steps of Development** (earth), which become **Social Tasks** (Heaven), as **God's Children** become **Dutiful Works** (Kingdom), willing to take-on the full **Responsibility for Building God's Kingdom** (God), to attain **God's Divine Authority** (Christ) **Forever**. Now, it becomes clear that each of "God's Children" is being called to Defeat the Womb (dark tunnel of chaos), the Tomb (dark world of evil), Death (dark pit of death), Hell (fiery pit of hell) and Gehenna (pit of outer darkness) to reach **Adulthood before God**. By "Mastering" each of these <u>Five Dimensions of Existence,</u> a **Person is Able** to come to **Know, Love, and Serve his God** to **Assist the Lord** in **<u>Building</u> His Kingdom of Glory**.

The point here is that a "Foolish Child" has <u>Little or No Use</u> to either <u>himself or God</u> so he must be **Willing** to **Face the Challenges of Life** (change evil to good) by **<u>Accepting</u>** whatever **IS** (truth) placed in **his Life by God**. We see described below some "Thirty Five Achievements" which must be <u>Attained</u> before a person can hope to **Grow-up** into a **Clear Thinking Adult before God**. This means that each of "God's Sons" or "Daughters" must attain a <u>Wise Mind</u> (righteous), a <u>Courageous Heart</u> (holy), <u>Generous Soul</u> (perfect), and <u>Fair Life-force</u> (divinity) to become a **Treasure of Merit and Value** in the **Eyes of God, Angels, and Men**. On this day of "Triumph (graduation)," a <u>Person can Truly Know</u> that he is of **Value to God's Kingdom** as he takes his **Place of Honor** among the **Sons of God**, who are **Worthy of God's Divine Love**. It now makes sense that any "Struggle" or "Pain" will certainly be <u>Worth It in the End,</u> if only a **Person will Focus** on the **Prize of Life** (maturity) and **Try his Level Best to Please God**. This means that "Each of God's Children" must <u>Transform</u> **Earth, Heaven, Kingdom, Himself,** and his **God** into a set of **Acquaintances** (earth/1st dimension), **Neighbors** (Heaven/2nd dimension), **Friends** (Kingdom/3rd dimension), **Companions** (Self/4th dimension), and finally, his own **Royal Family** (God/5th dimension). Yes! Life is about striving to "Win People Over" using any and all of one's <u>Natural Resources</u> by doing anything to **Convert a Stranger** into some **State of Comradery** through a **Person's Wisdom, Kindness, Generosity, and Fairness**.

This following tabular information indicates that the "Human Race" is operating within a <u>Five-Dimensional Framework,</u> each defining **Seven Levels of Growth and Maturity** bringing each of **<u>God's Children</u>** out of his **Darkness of Sin, Evil, and Death**:

Seven Levels of Growth and Maturity in Five Dimensions
(God's five dimensions of existence transform
each of God's children from nothing to all)

Stranger becomes an Acquaintance - Wisdom (babyhood)
No. 1. God's "1st Dimension (food)" brings forth <u>Physical Life</u> (creation) through **Seven Levels of Growth and Maturity**: 1) Ignorant Fool, 2) Wise Man, 3) King (righteous), 4) Government, 5) Earth, 6) New Earth (Heaven on Earth), and 7) Altar of God (see God/steps).

Acquaintance becomes a Neighbor - Kindness (teenagers)
No. 2. God's "2nd Dimension (labor)" brings forth <u>Spiritual Life</u> (redemption) through **Seven Levels of Growth and Maturity**: 1) Cowardly Criminal, 2) Courageous Warrior, 3) Priest (holy), 4) Church, 5) Heaven, 6) New Heaven (Paradise with God), and 7) Pulpit of God (hear God/tasks).

Neighbor becomes a Friend - Generosity (adulthood)
No. 3. God's "3rd Dimension (production line)" brings forth <u>Mystical Life</u> (sanctified life) through **Seven Levels of Growth and Maturity**: 1) Greedy Insanity, 2) Generous

Saint, 3) Son (perfect), 4) Home, 5) Kingdom of Man, 6) Kingdom of God (set free/thinking), and 7) Chair of God (speak to God/duty).

Friend becomes a Companion - Fairness (wise man)
No. 4. God's "4th Dimension (new-life)" brings forth Divine Life (consecrated life) through **Seven Levels of Growth and Maturity**: 1) Selfish Evil, 2) Unselfish Son, 3) Free Man (divine), 4) Self, 5) Divinity, 6) Beatific Vision (save others/sacrificial), and 7) House of God (sup with God/responsibility).

Companion becomes One's Family - Love (sonship)
No. 5. God's "5th Dimension (perfection)" brings forth Godly Life (exalted life) through **Seven Levels of Growth and Maturity**: 1) Born-again Life, 2) Resurrected Son, 3) Thinking for Self (Godly), 4) Imagination, 5) Godliness, 6) New Vision (serve all/give wealth), 7) Home of Independence (adopted by God/authority).

This illustration shows that "Earth" comes from Governments, which come from Kings, who come from Wise Men, who were once Ignorant Fools who had to **Find Their Way Out** of the **Lord's Dark Tunnel of Chaos** (womb). Secondly, we see that "Heaven" comes from Churches, which come from Priests, who come from Holy Men (courageous warriors), who were once **Wicked Sinners** lost in a **Dark World of Evil** (tomb). Thirdly, we see that the "Kingdom" comes from many Respectable Homes, which come from Sons, who come from Perfect Men (saints), who were once **Deceived by Lucifer** (believe lie) and fell into the **Devil's Dark Pit of Death** (grave). Fourthly, we see that "Divinity" comes from the Lord's Sacrificial Sons, who come from Free Men (angels), who were once **Confused by God** (decode meaning), and fell into the **Evil One's Pit of Hell** (damnation). Finally, we see that "Godliness" comes from God's Loving Son, who comes from the Man of Reason (Jesus Christ), who was once **Killed by God** and was cast into the Lord's **Pit of Oblivion** (Gehenna). By "Facing God's" Trials and Tribulations, a person can **Defeat Babyhood** (overcome womb), **Defeat his Teenage Years** (overcome tomb), **Defeat Adulthood** (overcome grave), **Defeat Aging Wise Man** (overcome hell), and finally, **Defeat Sonship** (overcome Gehenna) to become **Perfect in the Sight of God**.

At each of these "Stages of Growth," all of God's Children can **Master the Life-experience** and establish their **Own Identity** (life's meaning) by **Learning to Think for Themselves**. We now see that a "Thinking Man" can see Oneself (home/physical), Social Order (government/spiritual), Scope of Life (church/mystical), Universal Existence (self/divine), Infinite Perfection (imagination/Godly), Divine Truth (freedom/new creation), and finally, Creation's Prime Reference Point (God/Supernatural Being). Out of each of these "Stages of Development" from Nothing to All, **One of God's Creations** can get a **Fix on his Own Progress** from **Death to New-life**. This means that the whole "Life-experience" is centered upon his Perception of Reality based on his precise **Measure of Truth**, determined by effectively calculating either his **Imperfection** (evil) or current **Level of Perfection** (holiness) based on some absolute **Fixed Frame of Reference** (prime).

We see that as "Babies (water)," we must get a <u>Fix on Our Own Identities</u> (unknown); then as "Teenagers (blood)," <u>Focus on the Value of Life</u> (normal); and finally, as "Adults (spirit)," establish a <u>Personal Perception of Reality for Ourselves</u> (beliefs). We see that the "Unknown Factor" is Man's <u>Perception of Reality</u> which is **Different for Each and Every Person**, thereby **Creating** a **World of Unique Individuals** who can **Think for Themselves** at the **Physical, Spiritual, Mystical, and Divine Levels of Truth.** It is now clear that this "Vision of Truth" is produced through <u>Man's Decisions</u> and <u>Interactions</u> via **Existence** of an **Infinite Amount of Variables**, thereby making **All Existence Unique** for **Every Living Thing in Life.** We see that based on an analogous "Relationship with Reality," a <u>Pattern can be Discerned</u> to properly **Define All Relationships** in **God's Truth, Law, Will, and Love.** The "Concept of Paradoxical Reality" being discussed here is <u>Human Existence</u> in the form of **Three Immediate Dimensions of Logic,** based on **Established Truth, Counter Truth** (flip), and **Blended Truth** (merge). Each of these "Dimensions of Reality" exists in a manner that **Parallels Each Other** to **Form** a **Matrix of Measurable Truth.** This is true even when these "Parallel Forces" exist within completely different <u>Realities and Definitions,</u> because they **Move in a Manner that Parallels Each Other** so that **Measureable Comparisons can be Easily Made.**

It must be noted that the "Existence" of these Three Dimensions is based on the fact that there are also **Three Truths** defining the **<u>Physical</u>** (earth), **<u>Spiritual</u>** (Heaven), and **<u>Mystical</u>** (Kingdom) **Creations of God.** The "1st Truth (physical)" is known as God's <u>Established Truth,</u> with the "2nd Truth (spiritual)" being in complete **Antithesis of the 1st Truth** (flip). Finally, the "Last Truth" becomes a <u>Blend</u> of the **Physical Truth** (illusion) and the **<u>Spiritual Truth</u>** (reality) to **Create** the **<u>Mystical Truth</u>** (illusion/reality) as an expression of **God's Paradoxical Reality.** Obviously, the "2nd Truth" is formed via the **<u>Antithetical</u> Flip** in which one takes the **<u>Opposite Stand</u>** from what is **Empirically Defined and Established by the 1st Truth.** We see that when the "1st Truth" and the "2nd Truth" are <u>Put Together</u> (blended), the "3rd Truth" can be **Freely Adjusted in <u>Accordance</u>** with its **Current Set of Circumstances** (adjustable). A perfect example of this "Adjustability" can be found within a <u>Judicial Court System</u> **Manifesting** the **<u>Plaintiff's Truth</u>** (1st truth) and the **<u>Defendant's Truth</u>** (2nd truth) before either a **Judge** or a **Jury.** In this circumstance, both the "Judge" and the "Jury" have a <u>3rd Truth</u> based on the **Arguments** of both the **Prosecutor** (1st truth/offense) and the **Defense Attorney** (2nd truth/defense). The point is that this "3rd Truth" can be <u>Greatly Altered</u> based on the **Hard Facts** and **<u>Extenuating Circumstances</u>** of the **Particular Case** (unique considerations).

We now see that "Divine/Human Reality" is based on this same <u>Triune Concept,</u> where **Truth, Law,** and the **Will of the People** versus the **Will of God** must all be **Taken into Consideration <u>Moment-by-moment</u>** to **Determine a Single State of Existence.** This means that "Physical Existence" is one where the <u>General Population</u> lives in some culturally organized **Established Truth,** where <u>Human Reality</u> is only that which is **Seen, Touched,** and **Generally Known by All** (collective mind). Secondly, "Spiritual Existence" is so abstract that very <u>Few People</u> know anything about the "Spirit World of God (Heaven)," especially when it can only be found by taking the **Antithesis** of our present **Physical World on Earth.** Finally, comes the "Lord's Mystical World" which has not even been <u>Discovered Yet,</u> unless a **Person** has become a **Divine Mystic** and is <u>**Talking Directly with God**</u> at the **Mystical Level of Reality.** By comprehending these "Three Dimensions of Reality," a <u>Person can Apply</u> a **Set of Pictorial Representations** to show the <u>**Relationships**</u> between **Earth, Heaven, and God's Kingdom.** This is done by "Triangulation" or by finding a <u>Single Point in Space</u> (existence) based on defining **Three Points of Reference** to establish a **Single Point of Truth.** Imagine the "1st Point" as the <u>Meaning of Life</u> (existence), with the "2nd Point" as the <u>Purpose of Life</u> (service), and then the "3rd Point" as the <u>Value of Life</u> (happiness) to form creation's **Triangle of Reality.** Obviously, it takes "Three Realities" to establish <u>One Divine Truth</u> before **God,** thereby forming a **Check and Balance System** to <u>**Verify**</u> even a **Single Perception of Truth as Real.**

Now, imagine that you "Exist" within a **Seven Dimensional Structure**: 1) <u>Nothing</u> - Self-love (greed) or Love Life (sinner), 2) <u>Physical</u> - Sexual Love (babies) or Save Life (priest), 3) <u>Spiritual</u> - Loving God (worship) or Give Life (king), 4) <u>Mystical</u> - God's Love (blessings) or Receive Eternal Life (son), 5) <u>Divine</u> - God's/Man's United Love (oneness) or Receive Divine life (free man), 6) <u>Godly</u> - Infinitely Perfect Love (free-flowing) or Balanced Life (new creation), and 7) <u>All</u> - Loving Others (generosity) or Paradoxical Life (supernatural being). It should now make sense that the "Human Race" is <u>Traveling</u> from **Nothing** (null-set) to **All** (paradox) through the **Forces of Man's Growth** (flesh) and **God's Maturity** (spirit) striving to reach the **Throne of God.** If we examine the "Gamma Logic," we see that there are <u>Nine Levels of Existence</u> ranging from **Zero** (0) to **Eight** (8) revealing that each of **God's Creations** must dedicate himself to both **Growing** and **Maturing** into the **Nature of God.**

The reader must now "Match-up" each of these stages of <u>Growth</u> and <u>Maturity</u> with each of the following **Gamma Charts** to comprehend **God's Grand Design** as it relates to the Lord's **Three Divine Plans** of **Creation** (redemption/education**), Redemption** (salvation/employment), and **Sanctified Life** (rewards/tips). Obviously, the Lord is defining a "Series of Stages" by which <u>Nature, Humans, Angels,</u> and even <u>God Himself</u> must **Eternally Develop** as they journey from **Death to New-life.** The idea is to "Travel" from a <u>Wicked Sinner,</u> to a <u>Holy Priest,</u> to a <u>Righteous King,</u> to a <u>Perfect Son,</u> to a <u>Free Man,</u> to a <u>New Creation,</u> to a <u>Supernatural Being</u> born-again within the **Nature of God.** This structure is manifested with "God's" <u>Ideas</u> (meaning), <u>Concepts</u> (purpose), and <u>Objectives</u> (value) as they define the **Time/Space Continuum** as an expression of the Lord's **Truth, Law, Will, and Love.**

The following tabular information indicates that there are "Seven Major Dimensions of Existence" in <u>God's Master Plan</u> operating at **Seven Levels of Education** from **Ignorance to Wisdom** as each of **His Children** Grows-up in His Nature.

**From Nothing to All via Sin, Priest, King, Son, Free
Man, New Creation, and Supernatural Being**
(measured as created gamma/single/dual/triple/
quad/fifth/sixth/seventh/never created gamma)

Infant (life)	0.	**Nothing** - Man: Awakened by God = God Breathes Life **Creation** • Created Gamma - Life-force: Existence of Truth • Edenic Covenant - Creation of Eden (nothing dimension)

- -

Baby (truth)	1.	**Wicked Sinner** - <u>See God:</u> God Sees Child's Suffering • Single Plane Gamma - Physical Life: Path of Man's Righteousness • Adamic Covenant - Creation of Adam (physical dimension)
Child (law)	2.	**Holy Priest** - <u>Hear God:</u> God Hears Child's Cry • Dual Plane Gamma - Spiritual Life: Path of Man's Holiness • Noahic Covenant - Creation of Purified Earth (spiritual dimension)
Adolescent (will)	3.	**Righteous King** - <u>Smell God:</u> God Recognizes Child's Covenant • Triple Plane Gamma - Mystical Life: Path of Man's Perfection • Abrahamic Covenant - Creation of Chosen People (mystical dimension)
Teenager (love)	4.	**Perfect Son** - <u>Taste God:</u> God Comes to Help Child **Redemption** • Quad Plane of Gamma - Divine Life: Path of God's/Man's Pure Thought • Mosaic Covenant - Creation of God's Priesthood/Law (divine dimension)
Young Adult (thought)	5.	**Free Man** - Touch God: God's Child Grows-up • Fifth Plane of Gamma - Godly Life: Path of God's Word • Palestinian Covenant - Creation of God's Holy Land (Godly dimension)
Adult (word)	6.	**New Creation** - <u>God's Clairvoyance:</u> God's Child Matures • Sixth Plane of Gamma - Null-set of Life: Path of God's Deeds • Davidic Covenant - Creation of God's Kingship on Earth (Free Man dimension)
Wise Man (deed)	7.	**Supernatural Being** - <u>God's Miracle-working Power:</u> God's Child • Seventh Plane of Gamma - Infinite Life: Path of God's Results • New Covenant - Creation of God's Sonship on Earth (Self-rule dimension)

- -

God-like (fruit)	8.	**All** - <u>God:</u> Indwelled by God = God Crowns His Saint **Sanctified Life** • Never Created Gamma - Eternal Life: Existence of God • Everlasting Covenant - Creation of God's Kingdom of Glory (All dimension)

This illustration shows that the "Human Race is Traveling" from its <u>Illusion</u> to <u>God's Reality</u> by **Mastering a Series** of **Seven Dimensions** (nothing and all), defined here as **Gammas** which **Give Each Person** his own <u>**Fixed Frame of Reference**</u> (ideas/concepts/objectives) within **God's Creation**. Yes! All of "God's Children" are seeking to <u>"See Their God</u> (God thinks of child)," <u>Hear Their God</u> (God speaks to child), <u>Smell Their God</u> (God touches His child), <u>Taste Their God</u> (God Sups with Child), <u>Touch Their God</u> (God liberates His child), <u>Experience Their God</u> (God befriends His child), and <u>Obtain God's Divine Power</u> (God sets child free)" to **Enter** the **Lord's Kingdom of Glory**. At each of these "Stages of Development," a person is able to "Know, Love, and Serve" his <u>Creator God</u> in

Truth, Law, Will, Love, Thought, Word, Deed to **Bear Fruit** in the **Name of Jesus Christ.** This "Awesome Journey" from Non-existence to Existence (birth) **Allows a Person** to become a **Clear-Thinking** (earth), **Highly Educated** (Heaven) **Son of God** (Kingdom) **Worthy of Sharing** an **Eternal Life** in the **Presence of the Almighty Himself.**

This process of "Creating God's Children" is being Legally Instituted via the **Nine Covenants of God**: 1) Edenic Covenant - Creation of Eden (infant), 2) Adamic Covenant - Creation of Adam (baby), 3) Noahic Covenant - Creation of Purified Earth (child), 4) Abrahamic Covenant - Creation of the Chosen People (adolescent), 5) Mosaic Covenant - Creation of God's Priesthood/law (teenager), 6) Palestinian Covenant - Creation of God's Holy Land (young adult), 7) Davidic Covenant - Creation of God's Kingship (adult), 8) New Covenant - Creation of God's Sonship (wise man), and 9) Everlasting Covenant - Creation of God's Kingdom of Glory (God-like). Through these "Nine Covenants of Life," God has brought forth His Mandatory Growth (earth/flesh) and Optional Maturity (Heaven/spirit) Requirements upon all **His Living Creatures** as they seek to become **Righteous, Holy, and Perfect** before the **Lord's Divine Justice.** The message here is that one day, the "Nothing of Man (illusion/imperfection)" and the "All of God (reality/perfection)" are to be United into **One Creation** through the **Mystical Paradox of Jesus Christ** (man for all seasons).

Graphic Illustrations - Define Reality of Life

1. Finding Oneself - One Reference Point: Form
2. Social Order - Two Reference Points: Use
3. Scope of Life - Three Reference Points: Tenacity
4. Universal Existence - Four Reference Points: Work
5. Infinite Perfection - Five Reference Points: Manifestation
6. Divine Truth - Six Reference Points: Distribution
7. Prime Reference Point - Seven Reference Points: Finalization

We now see the "Definition of Reality" actually becomes Real at **God's Divine Level of Truth,** where **Ideas, Concepts,** and **Objectives** become a **Manifestation of Truth, Law, and Will** to reveal the **Existence of God** (intellect), **Man** (emotions), and **Nature** (matter). We see the "Triune Forces" of Ideas, Concepts, and Objectives can be **Measured in Seven Steps of Definition** (dimensions), **Allowing a Person** to **Comprehend** the **Meaning of Life** (Church/peace), the **Purpose of Life** (government/joy), and the **Value of Life** (home/happiness) in relation to his **Own Self-preservation** (survival). We see that these **Seven Steps of Awakening are:** 1) Belief - Authority; 2) Trust - Responsibility; 3) Faith - Duty; 4) Knowing - Task; 5) Becoming - Procedures; 6) Set Free - Steps; and finally, 7) Returning - Results. The idea here is to imagine that through this "Master Belief System," a Person can Manifest anything depending upon the **Depth of his Beliefs** ranging from **Mild Hopes** to being **Absolutely Convinced.** This means that the "Physical/Spiritual/ Mystical/Divine/ Godly/Free Man/Self-rule Dimensions" will be explored using Einstein's Theory of

Relativity, expressed as **E = (gamma) MC2** which Reads: **Energy** equals **Gamma** times **Mass**, times the **Speed of Light Squared**. By applying this "Formula" to the <u>Algebraic Coordinate Plane,</u> a person is able to **Visualize this Concept** in **Chart Form** (graph) or in its most **Comprehensible Physical Form.** The rationale for using "Einstein's Theory of Relativity" is to explain <u>Physical Existence Itself</u> (physics) and its interactive function based on the **Forces of Existence** manifested in the **Formation of Truth.** To better understand "Einstein's Theory of Relativity," it is necessary to have some familiarity with **Basic Physics.** Recall that "Einstein" claims that <u>Everything is Relative</u> in that by making a person some **Point in Space** (gamma), everything around him is then **Altered** according to this **One Location or Fixed Point of Gamma** (truth). In this theory, the "Forces of Weight, Time, and Space" can be <u>Bent or Distorted</u> according to their **Individual Place in the World** as a function of **Displaced Amounts of Energy.**

To grasp the "Theory of Relativity" and its application, all must be applied to the <u>Definition of Energy</u> based on the **Natural Forces Making-up Existence** at the **Level of Divine Truth.** This means that "All Energy" comes from <u>Einstein's Magical Formula</u>: **E = (gamma) MC2** by **Changing** the **Constants** and **Variables** of the **Equation** into expressed **Point of Reference** along a **Continuous Line.** It is important to define "Gamma as 1/2 the Speed of Light" into a <u>Variable of "V"</u> resulting in **1/2 MV^2** which is the **Formula** for defining **Kinetic Energy** or **Energy Contained within Matter.** Now, we see that "If Gamma" is <u>Changed</u> into a <u>Gravitational Constant</u> or "G" and then put together with the combined **Mass and Speed of Two Celestial Bodies,** the ultimate **Product** will be **Gravitational Energy.** To better understand "Gravitational Energy," the aspect of <u>Each Variable</u> within the **Equation** must be correctly defined to **Identify Absolute Truth.** This means that "All Energy" is coming from the equation of <u>E = (gamma) MC^2,</u> with the **Mass** being **Measured in Grams** and the **Velocity** being measured in **Speed of Light** at **Meters Per Second.** In this calculation, one must use "Grams Times Distance Squared" over "Seconds Squared" to get a <u>New Measure known as Joules</u> to describe **Energy, Mass, Velocity,** and **Joules** as the **Essence of Physical Reality.**

The following graphic illustration shows a "Single Dot" as one's <u>Point of Origin</u> to define a specific **Fixed Frame of Reference** from which both **Physical Definition** and **Spiritual** Belief can be **Determined:**

All Existence must Begin with a Single Point of Origin to Define a Fixed Frame of Reference
(via ideas, concepts, and beliefs,
man is united with God's never-created eternal life-force)

Instant Pulse - Never-created Eternal Life-force
• Single Plane of Gamma - Beginning Point of Existence
• Creator of Existence – I'AM (eternal now/null-set)

Finding Oneself (wicked sinner) - Seeing God: God Sees Child's Suffering

- Adamic Covenant - Creation of Adam: Physical Dimension of Life
-
-
-
- A • (point of origin) = **F O R M**...God's Right from Man's wrong
-
-
-
-
- God "Thinks of Child" - Blessing (water)
- —————————————————————————————**Figure #1**

Physical	Spiritual	Relativity	-	Single Plane of Gamma (a)
Definition	Belief	Mass (weight)		

This illustration shows that through "Physical Definition (established truth)," then "Spiritual Belief (flip)," and finally, "Relative Mass/weight (blend)," the **Forces of Existence** can be **Precisely Defined.** The implication is that for Something to Exist within the "Physical Realm," it must have a **Defined Energy Signature** to give it **Size, Weight, and Form.** This means that the definition of an "Idea (thought)," "Concept (word)," and/or Object (deed)" Gives it Purpose and therefore establishes **Existence** within either **Truth, Law, Will, and/or Love.** In this same way, "Spiritual Belief" of a Concept or an Object **Gives it Purpose** and therefore allows it to **Manifest Itself** within its **Own Spiritual Dimension** as an **Established Point of Origin.** The implication is that if there is "No Definition," then there is No Object, **Revealing** that there are **No Characteristics Attributed to the Object** to **Prove that It Really Exists.** This means that "Determining One's Existence" also means Taking-up Space in some Form, implying that an object must **Make a Mark Somewhere** within the **Existence of Physical, Spiritual, and/or Mystical Life.** We see that within the "Spiritual Dimension," an Object is Taking-up Space as a **Function of an Idea,** a **Concept,** and/or a **Belief** to **Embody an Established Belief System.** This "Belief Structure" Establishes the **Base Foundation** allowing **Ideas, Concepts, and Beliefs** to be **Manifested within Divine Truth.** Using this logic, "Belief" is the basic Building Block Governing **All Thought** which **Founded the Statement I Think, therefore I AM** (proof of existence).

Unfortunately, this "Idea is Flawed" because Building a State of Existence on a **Foundation of Thought** is an **Advanced Functional Structure,** implying **I AM** or being the **Creator of Existence** (never-created). Therefore, rather the "Statement I Believe, therefore I AM" is a more Correct Term, **Revealing** that **Life is Simply an Illusion** based on a **State of Belief.** By breaking down this logic in this example of "I Think therefore I AM," and by taking it to the Next Level, we see that **Thought Itself** is **Built on Something** and therefore an **Appended Corollary** must be **Used** to **Define Absolute Truth** or **Reality.** In this "New State of Reality," one must say: I Think because I Believe I Do Exist. This establishes **One's Existence** within a **Divine Fixed**

Frame of Reference of **Absolute Truth** (reality). This means that to comprehend "Truth," a <u>Person must See</u> that the relation of **Relativistic Theory, Beliefs,** and **Definitions** must be **Equated to Mass** to **Define its Parameters** in **Increments of Energy** via the <u>**Displacement**</u> of **Existence within Space.** This also means "Mass" is to have its <u>Own Specific Address</u> to **Determine** its **Location**, within the previous **Figure,** shown here, as the arbitrary **Point A** (origin). We see that within the "Spiritual Realm," it is the <u>Concept of Belief</u> that places **Point A** in the **Spiritual Plane** (dimension), while **Definition** is what places **Point A** within its **Physical Plane** (dimension) **of Existence.**

The following graphic illustration shows that to "Find a Person's" <u>Personal Reference Point,</u> **He** must **Triangulate** his **Present Location** against some well-known <u>**Fixed Point of Truth**</u> to define both his **Function** and **Depth of Trust** (statistical probability*):

**Defined Existence is Determined by the Art of
Triangulation to Measure One's Reference to All**
(through ideas, concepts, and beliefs, man can triangulate his human identity)

<u>Social Order</u> (holy priest) - Hearing God: God Hears Child's Cries for Help
- Noahic Covenant - Creation of Purified Earth: Spiritual Dimension of Life
-                             **C**
-                             •
-
-                             = U S E . . . God's Good from Man's Evil
-               **A** • - - - - - •
-           Height   **B**
-                  Width
-
- God "Speaks to Child" - Anointing (oil)
- —————————————————————— **Figure #2**

<u>Physical</u>   Spiritual   <u>Relativity</u> - Dual Plane of Gamma (a to b)
Function   Trust   Distance (meters)
Statistical Probability is Proven by Measuring Statistical Significance or Hypothetical Proof

This illustration shows that the "Physical Realm," expressed via a particular <u>Object or Idea that has Definition,</u> must also have <u>Function</u> to be **Useful** (value) because without **Function,** an **Object** will **Not Have Purpose** and thus <u>**Relegate Itself**</u> **Back to Non-existence** (worthless). We see that the "2nd Part of Existence" requires <u>Reference Points</u> to **Define Belief Structures** or **Spiritual Reality** (God) **Reflecting a Person's Physical Reality** (Man). This means that "Trust must be Established (statistical significance)" so that a <u>Particular Concept</u> is both **Sound** and **Useful When Applied** to or <u>**Plotted**</u> on, **Man's Plane of Existence** (life). In short, a matter of "Commitment" must be <u>Accepted</u> so that it might be based on a **State of Confidence** leading to a **Person's Acceptance** to derive a <u>**Level of Truth**</u> within the **Reality of God** (instant pulse). Out of "Confidence" and "Acceptance," Things are Given **Their Reference Points** in an otherwise **Empty Plane of Existence and Non-Truth.**

In the previous "Graphic Illustration," we see that in a Relativistic Sense, this **Step Adds Two more Points** on the **Chart** to express the **References** from **Self** (earth), to **Society** (Heaven), and then to **God** (Kingdom). In "Einstein's Theory of Relativity," this is the next Unit of Measure to be **Determined** to **Define Distance** to **Give Depth** and **Space to Something** through some **Identifiable Landmark.** This phenomenon can be explained by the "Sociological Theory" of the Looking-glass of Self which **Reveals** that an **Individual** is a **Product of the Specific Environment** that he has been **Placed In.** The "Relationship to Truth" and the "Interactions with Existence" Define both the Character and Personality of the **Individual** within the **Looking-glass of Self.** Now we see that the "Individual" can Measure his Own Limitations, Potential, and Self-worth through his well-established **Landmarks,** each **Defined** by its **Own Set of Reference Points.** This idea is echoed in the "Spiritual Sense," where Trust is Anchored by **Confidence** and one's **Acceptance,** thereby **Giving an Individual** an **Accurate Depiction of Truth.** We see that in the "Physical Function," a Delineated Set of Instructions direct one's **Interactions** with the **World at Large** so he might **Determine his Own** Fixed Frame of Reference for himself. For these "Instructions to be Effective," Each of These Ideas **Requires** a **Set of Guiding Points** within **Some Fixed Reality** where it **Exists** and has its **Being** to be **Manifested** with the **Natural State of Life.**

The following graphic illustration shows that for a "Person to Define" his Own Territory of Existence (life), he must **Establish** his **Own Consistency** and overall **Depth of Faith** to be **Rooted within Reality Itself:**

Three Reference Points Define both
One's Consistency and Depth of Faith within Reality
(through consistency, faith, and time, a person can establish his own identity)

Scope of Life   (righteous king) - Smelling God: God Recognizes His Child's Covenant
Abrahamic Covenant - Creation of Chosen People: Mystical Dimension of Life

- •
- •
- •   C
- •   - - - - - •
- •   - - - - - - -   = **TENACITY** . . . God's Will from Man's Will
- •   - - - - - - -
- •   A • - - - - - - - •
- •   B
- •
- •   God "Touches His Child" - Sanctification (blood)
- • -**Figure #3**

Physical   Spiritual   Reality -   Triple Plane of Gamma (a to b to c)
Consistency   Faith   Time (seconds)

This illustration shows that the "Figure A" represents a Person's Reference Point (self) to establish a **Point of Origin** in **Existence** from which a **Person can Triangulate** his **Position in Life** (identity). Secondly, we see that "Figure B" represents a Point of Triangulation (society) to **Establish** a **2nd Point of Existence** from which a **Person** can **Measure his Truth** to the **Law of Others.** Finally, we see that "Figure C" represents an Area or Territory (God) **Creating** a **3rd Point of Existence** from which a **Region of Life** (kingdom) can be **Established** through the **Power of Ownership.** We see that after "Definition" and "Function" have been established, an Idea or Object must be capable of **Replication**, thereby **Creating** similar **Results** which the **Scientific Community** is constantly **Trying to Prove.** This means that both "Definition" and "Function" cannot Change and must have consistent **Statistically Significant Results** that are easily **Recreated** (reproduced) via **Identical Processes.** Note that in the "Science of Navigation," a Sextant is Used to **Fix One Point**, usually on the **North Star as a Standard Position in the Sky** and then on any **Other Star** to **Get a Fix** on one's **Position on the Earth** (latitude/longitude).

We are describing basically this same "Concept in Life" when a Person Uses the **Life of Jesus Christ** as his **North Star** (God) and then **Uses Human Society** as his **2nd Point of Reference** to **Triangulate his Own** Position in Existence (self). Now, we see that without the important steps of "Definition" and "Function," an Idea would have to be Redefined because it has **Failed** to properly **Triangulate** its **Position within Existence.** Remember, it is "Faith which Measures Time" in Spiritual Terms, thereby **Determining** how long **Faith Remains in Existence** as a **Constant** of **Human Belief** in some **Tangible Truth.** Take, for example, one's "Belief in a Spiritual Chair" which leads to His Commitment to **Use the Chair by Trusting** in both its **Reliability** (strength) and **Duration of Existence** (long lasting) by **Sitting on It.** This means having "Faith" that this Chair will Hold His Weight which **Determines** the **Value** and **Amount of Usage** that the **Chair Receives** from **Its Owner.** This implies that to have "Complete Faith" in something, one must be willing to sit on the Chair Indefinitely, thereby **Changing** his **Beliefs,** his **Trust,** and his **Faith** into **Absolute Knowing.** In the "Relativistic Aspect," we see that Time Defines where one is **Moment-by-moment**, opening the question as to **How Long One can Last** and **How Long One can Exist in Truth.** The "Definition of Time" Creates another **Measure of Life**, because without **Time**, there will be **No Space-(where)Time(when) Continuum to Define Existence.**

The following graphic illustration shows that a "Person Who Defines" his Own Relative Focused Existence is able to trace back to the **Origin of Existence** (creator) within **Infinity** or back to the **000** (zero) **Reference Point of Life** (truth).

**Three Reference Points Define both One's Application
and Depth of Knowledge within Reality**
(via applying truth and gaining knowledge of life, one can find his creator God)

<u>Universal Existence</u> (perfect son) - Tasting God: God Comes to Help His Child)

- Mosaic Covenant - Creation of God's Priesthood/Law: Divine Dimension of Life
-
-                   C - Depth
-                     •
-         - - - - - - -
-         - - - - - - D• - - - = **W o r k** (time) . . .God's Reality from Man's Illusion
-         - - - - - - -
-     Height **A**• - - - - - - •
-                    B - Width
- God "Sups with His Child" - Consecration (spirit)
- **Figure #4 (a/b/c/d)**

<u>Physical</u>   <u>Spiritual</u>   <u>Relative</u> - Quad Plane of Gamma (height/width/depth/time)
Application   Know   Relative Focused Existence

This illustration shows that the "Physical Equivalent" of <u>Focused Existence</u> would involve the **Application of an Idea** where a **Person has Established** some **Invention** and its **Function** to **<u>Prove its Use</u>** on a **Consistent Basis.** This means that the next step would be "Establishing" a <u>Practical Function in Life,</u> defining **How an Object is Used,** what are both **Its Costs,** and **Its Overall Benefits to the Life-experience.** Obviously, "Knowing" is the **Advancement of Faith,** thereby **Creating** a **State of Perfect Faith** or **Knowing without Proof** which leads to a **Person's <u>Instinctive Compulsion</u>** to **Always be Right.** We see that from the "Previous Example," <u>Knowing</u> implies that one **Knows that it is a Chair** and thus **No Further Test** is required to **Prove his Depth of Belief, Trust, and Faith.** Using this logic, we can apply the "Concept of Gamma" to establish a definable <u>Point of Origin</u> that gives it a **Reference Point** within its own **Function** reflecting the **Forces of Truth.** This means "Gamma" relates to both the <u>Physical</u> and <u>Spiritual</u> attributes of existence because **Knowing** and **Application** set up a **Point of Origin** in their **Respective Realities** (1st/2nd truths). By establishing a "Central Reference Point," the <u>Concept of Knowing</u> and <u>Applying</u> sets up several **Focal Points** for their future **Applications** in their **Respective Realities** (1st/2nd truths). Obviously, we are defining the "First Reality" as <u>Heaven</u> or the **1st Truth** (spiritual), and the "Second Reality" as <u>Earth</u> or the **2nd Truth** (physical). Through these "Two Truths," the overall <u>Life-experience</u> can be **Effectively Defined** via the **Forces of Definition** (established truth), **Triangulation** (flip), and **Territory** (blending) to determine one's **Eternal Identity before God.**

    The following graphic illustration shows that once a "Person has Established" his <u>Own Existence</u> within **Absolute Truth,** he is ready to **Become Life** by **Mastering** the **Triune Forces** of **Physical, Spiritual,** and **Mystical Reality:**

**Determining One's Place within his Overall Sphere
of Influence comes with Knowing All Truth**
(by defining existence and becoming all things, one can comprehend all in life)

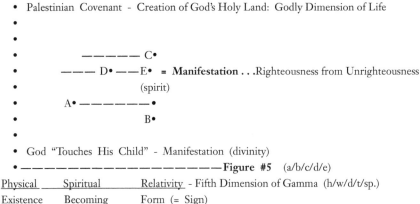

Infinite Perfection   (free man) - Touch God: God Enlightens His Child
- Palestinian Covenant - Creation of God's Holy Land: Godly Dimension of Life
-
-
- ————— C•
- ——— D• ——E• = **Manifestation** . . .Righteousness from Unrighteousness
- (spirit)
- A• ——————•
- B•
-
- God "Touches His Child" - Manifestation (divinity)
- ——————————————————**Figure #5**   (a/b/c/d/e)

Physical   Spiritual   Relativity - Fifth Dimension of Gamma (h/w/d/t/sp.)
Existence   Becoming   Form (= Sign)

This illustration shows that within the "Physical Realm," the same thing is happening as within the "Spirit World," showing that one's Invention is Now Whole as it is comprised of both the **1st Truth of God** (all/time) and the **2nd Truth of Man** (nothing/space) made **One** in **Infinite/Eternal Existence.** We now see in the above "Figure" that Existence is comprised of **Definition, Function,** and **Consistency,** thereby making it capable of **Seeing Its Own Limitations.** This indicates that the "Object Itself" becomes more specific in its Application in just **What It can** (life) and **What It Cannot Do** (death), based on its **Size** and/or **Shape** within the **Space/Time Continuum.** Now, that either an "Idea" or "Concept" has Become Truth and is worthy of its own **Reference Point,** it must become something of **Useful Value** within the **Reality of Infinite Perfection.** By using the "Reference Point System" being Selected here, a **Person can Determine** both its **Limitations** (man) and its **Potential** (God) within the **Boundaries** of its **Delineated Function of Existence.** Thus, this "Definition Forms" a Sphere of Influence that either the **Idea** or the **Concept** can **Freely Travel** allowing it to **Journey in Any Direction** which can be **Desired at Will.** We see that in "Relative Perspective," the = (sign) is extremely important as it Delineates the **Equalization of Two Halves: One,** the **Sum of Its Parts** (illusion); and the **Other, Defining** the **Sum of Itself** (reality). Note that the "Equal Sign" shown in this Figure surrounds a **Particular Boundary** in which the **Function can Exist** anywhere within the known **Boundary** or its established **Territory.**

The following graphic illustration shows that once an "Idea" or a "Concept" has been Manifested into Reality, it can then be **Published** and made **Public Domain** to **Set It Free** from any **Restrictions Affecting Its Reality:**

Determining the Sphere's Position within the
Overall Plane of Existence to Create Reality
(by defining existence and releasing completed
creations into the universe of life)

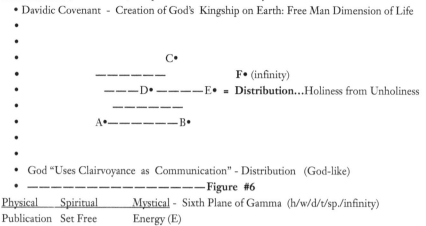

Divine Truth (new creation) - Experience God via Clairvoyance: God Awakens His Child
- Davidic Covenant - Creation of God's Kingship on Earth: Free Man Dimension of Life
-
-
-                             C•
-          ——————   **F•** (infinity)
-            ——D• ————E• = **Distribution**...Holiness from Unholiness
-               ——————
-         A•——————B•
-
-
- God "Uses Clairvoyance as Communication" - Distribution   (God-like)
- ————————————————Figure #6

Physical   Spiritual   Mystical - Sixth Plane of Gamma (h/w/d/t/sp./infinity)
Publication Set Free   Energy (E)

This illustration shows that the "Scope of Existence" is both <u>Growing</u> and <u>Expanding</u> into a **Universe of Space and Time Defining** the **Physical, Spiritual,** and **Mystical Dimensions of Life** via the **Forces of Energy.** We see that in the creation of both "Physical" and "Spiritual Inventions," <u>They are to be Shared</u> with the **Whole World** through the **Distribution of Ideas** to bring **Progress** to **One and All.** We see that once an "Idea" has reached its <u>Personal Maturity,</u> it must be <u>Freely Distributed</u> so **that Other People** (brotherhood) within the **Community** can <u>**Share in the Overall Benefit**</u> from any **New Invention.** Obviously, if it "Works for Others," this means that it has the ability to permeate Human Reality and is thus both **Functional** and **Useful** to the <u>**General Public**</u> as a **Contribution to Society.** Now, we see that any "New Idea" or "Concept" must eventually be <u>Set Free</u> so that it can **Find** its **Own Appropriate Place** in both the **Creator's Reality** and also within the **Interactive Spirit of Life** (existence). This means that "Energy" in this <u>Sense of Existence is Energy</u> showing that in this **Form,** it has **Its Own Potential** for becoming **Manifested Existence within Infinite Reality.** We see that the "Geographical Representation of Energy" can be seen as the <u>Point of Origin</u> or the **Prime Number** (000) specifying the **Existence of All.** This "Prime Number Concept" <u>Represents Creation's</u> **Environmental Reality** as a **Whole** which **Delineates** the **Universal Structure of Existence** as **Defined** by **Light Energy** transformed into **Matter** (any form). This also delineates the "Position" that something is <u>Relative to Exterior Reality</u> in **God's Absolute Reality <u>Defined by a</u> Person's Physical, Spiritual,** and **Mystical Environments** or **Life-forces.**

The following graphic illustration shows that once a "Person has Established" a <u>Consistent</u> **Set of Reference Point** effectively **Defining** his **Own Universe of Existence** within a given **Plane of Reality** (perfection), he can **Finalize and Seal his Creation:**

Determining One's State of Existence within Reality
Reaches Its Final Stage with Perfection
(by defining the life-experience in relation to
E = (gamma) MC2 formula that brings truth)

<u>**Prime Reference Point**</u> (God/supernatural being) - God's Miracle-working Power:
God Indwells Son

- New Covenant - Creation of God's Sonship on Earth: Dimension of Self-Rule
-
-

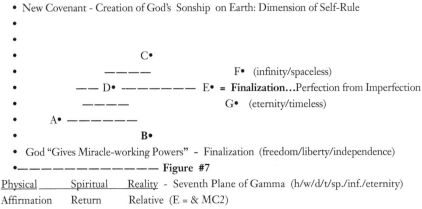

- God "Gives Miracle-working Powers" - Finalization (freedom/liberty/independence)
- —————————————— **Figure #7**

<u>Physical</u>   Spiritual   Reality - Seventh Plane of Gamma (h/w/d/t/sp./inf./eternity)

Affirmation   Return   Relative (E = & MC2)

     ***Energy/time and Matter/space are One and the Same thing in Two Separate Forms**

This illustration shows that any "Created Invention" eventually <u>Returns to Its Inventor</u> in **Affirmation** that it has found an **Essential Use** within the **Overall Social Order** by **Traveling** from **<u>Hand to Hand</u>** and until **What Eventually Goes Around Comes Around.** Upon the "Invention's Return," its <u>Usefulness will be Augmented</u> to **Suit the Purpose** of the vast majority of <u>Individuals</u> throughout **One's Society.** This means that after "Setting an Idea" or "Concept Free," it is then <u>Destined</u> to **Return to the Creator** in a **Form** or **Manner** that is still his **Creation,** but has been continually <u>Altered</u> to make it more and more **Perfect** with the **Passage of Time** or **Movement of Space.** This implies that through its "Constant Altered State," an <u>Idea has Taken-on</u> a **Life of Its Own** and is now both **Growing, Maturing,** and **Evolving** according to its **<u>Established</u>** *Path of Perfection.* Obviously, an "Evolving Idea" can <u>Freely Travel</u> depending upon its **Own Limitations** (worthless) and its **Own Potential** (priceless) to **<u>Fulfill</u>** the **Destiny of Its Purpose.** We now see that "Einstein's Formula" is an <u>Entity unto Itself</u> with the **Power to Change and Transform** both **Space** and **Time** to **Encompass** the **Entire Range** of <u>Possibilities</u> given by its **Original Reference Point** (prime). Thus, this portion of "Relativity" is signified by the <u>Sphere</u> depicted above in **Figure 7,** showing the **<u>Final Phase</u>** of *Physical, Spiritual, and Mystical Existence* (union of space/time).

    The question before us is: can anyone "Will a Creation into Existence?" The answer is a resounding "Yes." But just how far will a "Person have to Go" into <u>Any One</u> Belief to **Manifest** his **<u>Own Creation</u>** from **Nothingness into Reality?** We see that "God has Gone" to <u>Great Lengths to Prove</u> that He **Truly Exists** (never-created) and can be **Seen, Touched, and Befriended, Assuming a Person** has a **Sufficient Amount** of Belief, Trust, Faith, and Knowing in **God's Divine Truth**. We see that the "Lord has Gone" All the Way to Death to **Prove** the **Existence of His Divine Truth** or **His Divinity,** not only for the **Sake of the Universe,** but also to **Honor and Glorify Himself.** This leaves the question: can "Anyone Else become God?" The Answer is obviously "Yes in Form (a God, not The Almighty God)," assuming **God's Son, Jesus Christ** has **Shown the Way** and **Welcomes the World** to **Follow Him into Divine Perfection** (sonship of God). In this revelation, as long as a "Person Believes" enough to Die to himself (submission) upon **Christ's Altar of Death,** he can expect to be **Transformed** from **Death to New-life.** This means that the "Individual becomes Death" allowing "God to become this Person (new form)" in New-life and **Not the Other Way Around** as the **Evil World Currently Believes Today.** It should now all make sense that the "Human Race" is within a Belief System and it is only those who **Believe the Truth** who will come to **Know, Love, and Serve Their God.** The simple answer here is that "God has Always Existed." Therefore, everything within His Reality is simply associated with **Form and Not Creation of Anything,** because **God is Omnifarious** and can **Change** into whatever **He Wishes at Will.** This means that when a "Person Becomes God" in truth, he has Died and Disappeared and God has simply **Become that Person** (indwelling) and then allows that **Person to Believe** that **He is a Son of God.**

Through these "Seven Phases of Existence," an Object (mass) comes forth from **Nothing to Reality** to **Take its Place** somewhere on the **Plane of Existence** based on its **Physical Size, Spiritual Shape, and Mystical Velocity.** This means that when an "Object" comes forth into Reality, it must **Use All of its Abilities** to either **Compete** or **Cooperate** with the **Forces of Life** for a **Place** in the **Existence of Truth.** This means that "Physical Truth (creation/redemption)" is **Defined with Seven Terms**: 1) Definition - Seeing, 2) Function - Hearing, 3) Consistency - Smelling, 4) Application - Tasting, 5) Existence - Touching, 6) Publication - Clairvoyance, and 7) Affirmation - Miraculous Powers. Secondly, "Spiritual Truth (redemption/salvation)" is **Defined with Seven Terms:** 1) Belief - Seeing, 2) Trust - Hearing, 3) Faith - Smelling, 4) Knowing - Tasting, 5) Becoming - Touching, 6) Set Free - Clairvoyance, and 7) Returning - Miraculous Powers. Lastly, "Mystical Truth (sanctified life/rewards)" is **Defined with Seven Terms:** 1) Form (mass) - Seeing, 2) Use (distance) - Hearing, 3) Tenacity (time) - Smelling, 4) Work (exist) - Tasting, 5) Manifestation (structure) - Touching, 6) Distribution (energy) - Clairvoyance, and 7) Finalization (reality) - Miraculous Powers. Through these "Three Sets of Truths," the entire Creation is Founded and has its being based on the **Geographical Location** of every **Existing Object** as related to its **Mass, Velocity, and Time Factors.**

The following tabular information indicates that the previous "Seven Figures" show the Transformation Terms for the **Physical, Spiritual, and Mystical Dimensions of Existence** as they **Grow and Mature** into **Their Associated States of Perfection:**

The Seven Levels of Transformation from Nothing
to All bring Created Objects into Perfection
(physical, spiritual, and mystical truths
convert light energy into matter through relativity)

Plan of Creation	Plan of Redemption	Plan of Sanctified Life
Physical Truth	Spiritual Truth	Mystical Truth
(natural order)	(supernatural order)	(divine order)

——————————Finding Oneself - Home (baby)——————————

1. Definition	1. Belief	1. Form (mass)

——————————Social Order - Government (child)——————————

2. Function	2. Trust	2. Use (distance)

——————————Scope of Life - Church (adolescent)——————————

3. Consistency	3. Faith	3. Tenacity (time)

——————————Universal Existence - Self (teenager)——————————

4. Application	4. Knowing	4. Work (existence)

——————————Infinite Perfection – Earth (young adult)——————————

5. Existence	5. Becoming	5. Manifestation (structure)

——————————Divine Truth - Heaven (adult)——————————

6. Publication	6. Set Free	6. Distribution (energy)

——————————Prime Reference Point - Kingdom (wise man)——————————

7. Affirmation	7. Returning	7. Finalization (reality)

This illustration shows that "Life" is about <u>Defining Existence</u> by assigning it a **Master Function** to be made **Consistent in Its Application** to bring it into <u>**Universal Existence**</u> and then to be **Presented to the World** for its **Affirmation.** Through each of these "Stages of Transformation," a <u>New-born Spirit</u> can **Take-on Physical Form** on earth and then **After Life** (school), **If Properly Perfected**, it can become a <u>**Mystical Being**</u> in the **Presence of God.** The "Trick in Life" is to become <u>Perfected</u> through a **Person's Spiritual Submission** (dying to self) and **Physical Sacrifice** (born-again) <u>**Performed**</u> with a *Pure and Contrite Heart* (innocence).

The point here is to see that "If It were Not for Calvary," <u>God, Angels, and Men</u> would have been **Lost** with <u>**God being Locked**</u> into **His Divine Perfection** (prison), and <u>**Man Locked**</u> into its **Eternal Hell**, leaving the <u>**Angels to be Torn In Two Parts**</u> between **God and Man.** The most "Important of All Creations" is the person of the <u>Lord Jesus Christ,</u> who comes to rectify **All the Problems** of <u>**God, Angels, and Men**</u> *Once and for All.* This means that "Everything in Life" is centered on the <u>Lord's Death on Mount Calvary,</u> thereby fulfilling the **Sacrificial Demands of God** (sin-debt) to be <u>**Paid in Full for All**</u> that has been either **Insulted** (Spirit), **Damaged** (Son), and/or **Lost** (Father) by **Divine Justice.** This means that the "Purpose of Calvary" is to create either a <u>Physical, Spiritual,</u> and/or <u>Mystical</u> <u>Bond</u> (contract) between any **Two Things** that have been <u>**Broken Apart**</u> during God's **Creation of Heaven and Earth.**

This theme of an "All Purpose Glue Factory (Calvary)" <u>Allows Us to See</u> that **Jesus Christ is Able** to **Glue Physical Divisions Back Together** with **His Blood** or the <u>**Wisdom of His Mind**</u> (fix it) by <u>**Creating**</u> a **Divine Contract** with **Infinite/Eternal Truth**. Secondly, the "Lord is Able" to <u>Glue Spiritual Divisions</u> **Back Together** with **Death** or **Love of the Heart** (fix it) by <u>**Creating**</u> a **Divine Contract** through **Infinite/Eternal Law**. Thirdly, the "Lord is Able" to <u>Glue Mystical Divisions</u> **Back Together** with **Damnation** or **Instincts of the Soul** (fix it) by <u>**Creating**</u> a **Divine Contract** through **God's Infinite/Eternal Will**. Fourthly, the "Lord is Able" to <u>Glue Divine Divisions</u> **Back Together** with **Oblivion** or **Divine Will of the Life-force** (fix it) by <u>**Creating**</u> a **Divine Contract** with **Infinite/Eternal Love**. Finally, the "Lord is Able" to <u>Glue Godly Divisions</u> **Back Together** with **Resurrection** or **Free Will of Christ's Nature** (fix it) by <u>**Creating**</u> a **Divine Contract** with **Infinite/Eternal Life** (freedom). Now, it can be seen that "Jesus Christ" has come to <u>Establish</u> a <u>New Perfect Justice System</u> to both **Heal** and **Repair** all that has been <u>**Damaged**</u> or <u>**Broken**</u> by the **Forces of Sin** (sin-nature), **Evil** (worldly temptations), **Death** (demonic possession), **Damnation** (Lucifer's image) or **Oblivion** (worthlessness).

The following tabular information indicates that the "Creation of Mount Calvary" brought forth the <u>Lord's Perfect Justice System</u> on earth to both **Heal** and **Repair** <u>**All that was Broken**</u> during **God's 1st Week of Growth and Maturity** (purification of life):

Mount Calvary brings forth the Lord's Perfect Justice System on Earth
(writing divine contracts in blood, death, damnation, oblivion, and resurrection)

Truth
(thought)

1. **Blood** - <u>Glue of Physical Dimension:</u> Repair of All Truth .....   New Mind
   - Ignorance Replaced with Wisdom - Repentance: Plan of Creation
   - Writing Divine Contract in God's Truth - Bride Price/Dowry (baby level)
   - Union of Two Fathers: Abraham and Father God - Marriage Contract

Law
(words)

2. **Death** - <u>Glue of Spiritual Dimension:</u> Repair of All Laws ...... New Heart
   - Cowardice Replaced with Courage - Being Saved: Plan of Redemption
   - Writing Divine Contract in God's Law - Name/Virginity (teenage level)
   - Union of Couple: Jesus and Church - Betrothal of Bride/Groom

Will
(deeds)

3. **Damnation** - <u>Glue of Mystical Dimension:</u> Repair of All Wills....New Soul
   - Greed Replaced by Generosity - Saving Self: Plan of Sanctified Life
   - Writing Divine Contract in God's Will - Birthright/Inheritance (adult level)
   - Union of Friends: Priesthood and Laity - Wedding Supper (honeymoon)

Love
(achieve)

4. **Oblivion** - <u>Glue of Divine Dimension:</u> Repair of All Loves .... New Life-force
   - Selfishness Replaced by Unselfishness - Saving Others: Plan of Eternity
   - Writing Divine Contract in God's Love - Heaven/Earth (wise man)
   - Union of Two Families: Angels and Saints - Wedding Feast (reception)

Life
(success)

5. **Resurrection** - <u>Glue of Godly Dimension:</u> Repair of All Life... New Nature
   - Holiness and Righteousness become One - Set Free: Plan of Kingdom Rule

- Writing Divine Contract of God's Life - Sons/Daughters (free man)
- Union of Two Creations: Heaven and Earth - Couple's Home (grandchildren)

This illustration shows that "God is Using" the "Individual Sacrifices" of <u>His Son, Jesus Christ</u> to **Set the Bar** for **Others to Follow, Assuming They Want** to **Enter** into a **Serious Contract** with the **Lord** for **Any Reason Whatsoever.** The implication here is that "If a Person Seeks" to Master God's Truth and **Wants to Obtain** the **Mind of Christ** (new mind/wisdom), then he must **Offer God a Blood Sacrifice Equal** to that of **His Son's** on **Mount Calvary.** Secondly, "If a Person Seeks" to <u>Master God's Law</u> and **Wants to Obtain** the **Heart of Christ** (new heart/love), then he must **Offer God a Death Sacrifice Equal** to that of **His Son's** on **Mount Calvary.** Thirdly, if a person seeks to "Master God's Will" and wants to obtain the <u>Soul of Christ</u> (new soul/instincts), then he must **Offer God a Damnation Sacrifice Equal** to that of **His Son's** on **Mount Calvary** (hell). Fourthly, if a person seeks to "Master God's Love" and wants to obtain the <u>Life-force of Christ</u> (new life-force/God's will), then he must **Offer God an Oblivion Sacrifice Equal** to that of **His Son's** on **Mount Calvary** (flesh becomes spirit). Finally, if a person seeks to "Master God's Resurrected Life" and wants to obtain the <u>Nature of Christ </u>(new nature/think for self), then he must **Offer God his Resurrection Equal** to **His Son's** from the **Tomb of Death.** Through these "Five Stages of Transformation," anyone within the <u>Kingdom of God</u> can obtain **One or All** of the **Lord's Divine States of Perfection** to make **Himself Worthy** of the **Presence of God now and forever.** In this theme, a "Lost Sinner" must be willing to <u>Sacrifice All</u> unto the **Rejection of his very Self** (submission) to have **Jesus Christ Pay** (sin-debt) for his **Sinful Blood, Death, Damnation, Oblivion,** and **Resurrection.** This means that "Mary's Son, Jesus (son of man)" has come to **Pay Man's Sin-debt** (sinners/earth); while "God's Son, Christ (Son of God)" has come to **Pay Man's Holy-deb**t (sainthood/Heaven) to **Save All Who were Lost.**

Note that the "Payment of All Debt" to <u>God</u> (Kingdom), <u>Angels</u> (Heaven), <u>Men</u> (earth), and <u>Nature</u> (existence) comes through **God's Thoughts** (ideas), **Words** (concepts), and **Deeds** (objectives) as **He** brings forth **Life Out of Death.** This shows us that out of the "Mind of God" comes a flood of <u>Ideas</u> defining the **Meaning of Life** and everyone's **State of Existence**, as a **Reflection** of the **Lord's Divine Truth** (knowledge). Secondly, out of the "Heart of God" comes His <u>Concepts</u> defining the **Purpose of Life**, telling lazy mankind to become of **Service to Others** as a **Reflection** of the **Lord's Divine Law.** Finally, out of the "Soul of God" comes His <u>Objectives</u> defining the **Value of Life** which reveals **Mankind's Happiness Index, Reflecting** the **Lord's Divine Will.** This means that through the "Lord's Truth, Law, and Will," the <u>Human Race</u> can **Enter God's Mind** (ideas/thoughts), **God's Heart** (concepts/words), and **God's Soul** (objectives/deeds) to be **Awakened** from its **State of Ignorance and Confusion.**

The following tabular information indicates that "God is bringing Lost Man" <u>His Divine Ideas</u> (intellect/mind), <u>Concepts</u> (emotions/heart), and <u>Objectives</u> (instincts/soul) to **Call, Enlighten,** and **Awaken His** most **Trusted Leaders** (chosen souls):

God Reveals His Ideas, Concepts, and Objectives to the Human Race to Awaken Its Dead Souls
(giving men a fixed reference,
focused existence, and perceived reality to see their God)

Thoughts
(mind)

1. **Ideas** - <u>Meaning of Life:</u> Existence of Truth (intellect) … Knowledge
   - Fixed Frame of Reference - Physical Dimension (educated)
   - 1st Contract - Plan of Human Creation: Life (calling) **Righteous**
   - God's "Priestly Sacrifice" - Slaughter of Innocence **Nature**
   - Learn Truth transforming Ignorance into Wisdom

(Priestly Sacrifice - God Offers Eternal Life/man offers labors: Earthly Blood)

Words
(heart)

2. **Concepts** - <u>Purpose of Life:</u> Service to Others (emotions) …..Self-awareness
   - Relative Focused Existence - Spiritual Dimension (employed)
   - 2nd Contract - Plan of Human Redemption:
     Death (enlightenment) **Holy**
   - God's "Kingly Prayer" - Begging for Forgiveness **Behavior**
   - Learn Law transforming Cowardice into Courage

(Kingly Prayer - God Offers Wealth/man offers wealth: Heavenly Spirit)

Deeds
(soul)

3. **Objectives** - <u>Value of Life:</u> Personal Happiness (instincts)…. Consciousness
   - Perception of Reality - Mystical Dimension (given tips)
   - 3rd Contract - Plan of Human Sanctified Life:
     Resurrect (awaken) **Perfect**
   - God's "Sonly Gifts" - Proving Oneself **Lifestyle**
   - Learn Will transforming Greed into Generosity

(Sonly Gift - God Offers His Labors/man offers his life: Kingdom Divinity)

This illustration shows that the "Lord God Almighty" is making a <u>Contract with Humanity</u> to allow it to **Eat His Flesh** (host) and **Drink His Blood** (chalice) so **that All Men can Enter** the **Mind** (thought), **Heart** (word), and **Soul** (deed) of **God** to become **One** with **His Divine Life-force**. The point here is that only a "Person with a Divine Nature" can hope to Survive the rigors of an **Eternal Life within a Kingdom** comprised of **God's Holy Angels**. Through this "Mystical Union" between the <u>Death of Man</u> (violent) and the <u>Life of God</u> (peaceful), all **Existence** can become **Transformed** into **Righteousness** (nature), **Holiness** (behavior), **and Perfection** (lifestyle). We see that in "God's 1st Contract (creation/eternal life)," <u>Man is Given</u> his **Creation of Life** through his **Priestly Sacrifice** (earthly blood/worship/life), known as the **<u>Slaughter of Innocence</u>** as a person's **Ignorance becomes Wisdom**. Secondly, in "God's 2nd Contract (service/new body)," <u>Man is Given</u> **Free Redemption** through its **Kingly Prayer** (Heavenly spirit/praise/wealth), known as **<u>Begging Divine Justice</u>** for **<u>Its Forgiveness</u>** as a person's **Cowardice becomes Courage**. Finally, in "God's 3rd Contract (happiness/kingdom)," <u>Man is Given</u> **Sanctified Life** through his **Son's Gifts** (Kingdom divinity/thanksgiving/labors), known as **<u>Proving Oneself</u>** to <u>Men, Angels, and God</u> as a person's **Greed becomes Generosity**.

At each of these "Levels of Conversion," a <u>Child of God</u> is able to **Hear his Calling** (home/earth), be **Enlightened unto Life** (church/Heaven), then be **Awakened to the Purpose of Life,** and finally, be **Indwelled by God's Spirit of Life** (nature). Now, we see that through "Man's" <u>Fixed Frame of Reference</u> (knowing), <u>Relative Focused Existence</u> (self-awareness), and <u>Perception of Reality</u> (consciousness), the **Creation of God** becomes **Complete** via the **Sacrifice/Prayer/Gift of Jesus Christ** (Calvary). Obviously, the "Lord God Almighty" needed a <u>Triune Processing Plant</u> (conversion factory) to take **His Creations** from **Death** (baby) to **Life** (teenager), to **Eternal Life** (adult) to bring them all into the **Lord's Kingdom** of **Divine Perfection.** This means that each of "God's Children" will be <u>Required</u> to **Offer the Lord his Priestly Sacrifice** (worship) or his **Life** (earthly blood), **Kingly Prayer** (praise), or his **Wealth** (Heavenly spirit), and his **Sonly Gift** (thanksgiving), or his **Labor** (Kingdom divinity) to **Enter** into the **Glory of God.** For this reason, a "Repenting Soul" must <u>Dedicate its Life </u>to becoming a **Priest, King,** and a **Son of God** to **Prove to One and All** that it has **Mastered** the **Lord's Rites of Passage** from **Life** (earth/new body), to **Death** (Heaven/life), to **Eternal Life** (Kingdom). We are each being "Called" to both "Spiritual Perfection (holiness)" and "Physical Perfection (righteousness)" through our <u>Depth of Commitment</u> based on our **Ability to Know Real Value** from some **Fraudulent Imitation.**

This means an "Expert (calling/survival)" is one who <u>First Believes in Truth</u> by simply **Defining It** to **Give It Meaning** as an expression of his **Own Reality** seen through his **Personal Fixed Frame of Reference** (life). Secondly, an "Expert (enlightenment/truth)" is one who <u>Trusts in the Laws of Physics</u> by **Establishing Life's Functions** through **Testing Its Meaning** as an expression of his **Value System** seen through his **Personal Relative Focused Existence** (eternal life). Thirdly, an "Expert (awakening/love)" is one who has <u>Faith in God's Will</u> by becoming **Extremely Consistent** through **Testing Its Reliability** as an expression of his **Empirical Views** seen through his **Personal Perception of Reality** (Life of Christ). Fourthly, an "Expert (indwelling/free choice)" is one who <u>Knows God's Love</u> through its **Practical Use in His Life** as an expression of his direct **Application of the Life-experience** seen through his **Righteous Behavior** (free to live as he wants). Fifthly, an "Expert (free thought/imagination)" is one who has <u>Become God-like</u> through his **Objective Thought** (new idea), to manifest his **Existence** in **Truth, Law, Will, and Love.** Sixthly, an "Expert (new vision/transfiguration)" is one who has been <u>Set Free from Ignorance</u> by **Sharing his Innovations with Others** as an expression of his **Unveiling of Social Perfection** based on his **Church, Government, and Home.** Finally, an "Expert (becoming God-like)" is <u>One Who</u> has <u>Returned to his Creator</u> on **his Own** by **Demonstrating his Personal Perfection** as an **Expression** of his **Affirmation of Self-worth** based on his **Righteousness** (king), **Holiness** (priest), and **Perfection** (son). Through each of these "Seven Stages" of "Growth and Maturity," a <u>Person</u> must be <u>Willing to Travel</u> from **Death to New-life** to **See his God** in the **Light** of **Divine Truth** (survival), **Law** (truth), **Will** (love), **and Love** (choice).

The following tabular information indicates the "Seven Spiritual Stages of Comprehension (babyhood)" as <u>Compared</u> to the "Seven Physical Stages of Fulfillment (adulthood)" allowing a person to both **Grow-up** (ethics) and **Mature** (morals) in **Christ Jesus:**

God's Seven Stages of Spiritual Comprehension and Man's Seven Stages of Physical Fulfillment
(man's flesh is called to grow-up/earth
and man's spirit is being called to maturity/Heaven)

Spiritual Maturity (spirit)	Physical Growth (flesh)	Definitions (soul)	Creation (life-force)
1. Belief	Definition	Giving It Meaning - Truth (justified)	
• See God	• Specifications	• Making It a Real Product	Divine Man
2. Trust	Function	Testing Its Meaning - Law (honored)	
• Hear God	• Application	• Determining Product's Value. .	Perfect
3. Faith	Consistency	Testing for Reliability - Will (glorified)	
• Speak to God	• Nomenclature	• Determining Life-expectancy . .	Eternal
4. Knowing	Application	Practical Use of New Idea - Love (freed)	
• Touched by God	• Utilization	• Marketing/Advertising/Promotion/Sales. . .	Available
5. Becoming	Existence	Object/Concept/Idea Comes to Be - Friendship (blessed)	
• Sup with God	• Versatility	• Acceptance by Market . . .	Demand
6. Set Free	Publication	Share Innovation with Others - Companionship (anointed)	
• Free from God	• Unveiling	• Household Name. . . .	Universal
7. Return	Affirmation	Innovations in Coming Back to You - Oneness (sanctified)	
• Think for Self	• Success	• Spin-off Products . . .	Divine Society

This illustration shows that "Spiritual Life" is All About Belief (see God), Trust (hear God), Faith (speak to God), Knowing (touch God), Becoming (sup with God), Freedom (free from God), and Returning (think for self). We see that a "Person's Physical Life" is All About Definition (specifications), Function (apply), Consistency (form), Application (utility), Existence (versatility), Publication (unveiling), and Affirmation (success) in **God, Angels, and Men.** By "Combining the Spirit" and the "Flesh" into One Mystical Structure in **Christ Jesus,** we can **Blend** the **Logic of the Mind** (relative truth) with the **Feelings of the Heart** (absolute truth). In this way, the "Forces of Logic (intellect) and "Feelings (emotions)" can **Lead a Soul** to a **Life of Instinctive Behavior** (compulsion), thereby **Giving a Person** both a **Righteous Life** (right) and a **Prosperous Future** (good). At this point, we can most effectively "Comprehend" the Contradictory Motives (two truths) of **God in Attempting** to **Merge** the **Blessings of Perfect Order** or **Absolute Truth** (Christ/perception of reality) with the **Blessing of Perfect Chaos** or **Relative Truth** (Jesus/fixed frame of reference).

The "Lord God Almighty" is a Master of Confusion (paradox) **Making All Things Come Together** in a most **Blessed Crescendo** of **Peace and Harmony, Inspite** of some **Dynamic Force Running Around Heaven Going Where it Wants** (free will), bringing **Joy** and **Fun** to **All that It Meets.** In truth, this "Unknown Force" of Random Chance (luck) or **Natural Selection** will be known as **Mary's Children, Who** have been specially **Chosen** to bring a **Breath of Fresh Air** into the **Silent Hallways** of **Divine Sanctity** (Heaven). Through "Mary's Children," We can See the **Meaning of Life** (existence) as **Our Existence** can be seen as a **Free Blessing** (gift/baby) from **God** through which a **Person** can **Prove himself by Learning** to **Think for himself** (correctly). Secondly, we see that the "Purpose of Life (service)" Centers upon a Person becoming of **Service** (teenager) within the **Household of God** as a **Person Earns his Place** within **Eternal Society** (speaking). Finally, we see that the "Value of Life (happiness)" is Associated with Finding One's Happiness (adult) within **God's Kingdom of Glory** by being **Accepted** by **Men, Angels, and God** for **His Accomplishments** (deeds). Through these "Three Levels of Growth and Maturity," a Person can Use his **Earthly Life-experience** to be **Transformed** from a **Worthless Caterpillar** into a **Priceless Perfect Butterfly, Who is Worthy** of **Eternal Life in Heaven.**

This means that "If We Seriously Get" into Evaluating the Divine Purpose (service) **Behind God's** most **Complex Inspection** and **Testing Process, We will See** that it is **Intended** to **Measure Human Maturity** and **Measure its Importance** to the **Overall Value of the Kingdom** as **We will See the Need** for the **Unknown Factor** of **Relative Truth** (flexibility/free-willed choice). This "New Perspective" will also Better Explain the **Lord's Effective Use** of **Mysteries and Painful Deceptions**, being **Used** via **God's Paradoxical Logic** to bring **Humanity** to its **Full Maturity.** In fact, it might be quite a "Shock to Us All" If it Turns Out in the **End** that **We are the Ones** being **Betrayed** by **Our** very **Own Eternal Father** (daddy) as **He Strives** to **Trick Us** into **Believing a Lie** (Santa Claus/Easter Bunny/Tooth Fairy), just so **We can See His Divine Truth** (paradox). Revealed in this "Father Knows Best" concept, we see that even If We Do Turn Out to be the **Proverbial Goat of Learning**, it is **Certain** that this most **Subtle Betrayal System** will be for **Our Own Good** and will **Teach Us** to **Live by Perfect Faith.** In other words, "We are Not to Fall" into the Deception of some **False Wisdom Gained** from **Eve's Tree of Knowledge. We are to Eat** from **God's Tree of Life** and then **Learn the Value of God's Right from Man's Wrong** (knowing).

It is commonly known that the more "Evil a Person Experiences," the More he is Able to **See himself** in the **Intricate Details** of the **Works of Life**, especially **When he has Passed** that **Critical Point of No Return** (remove faults) and there is **No More Need for Correction** (gain virtues). It must certainly be one of "Murphy's Laws" that When a Project is just about to **Reach Completion**, this is that **Crucial Moment When All** its **Weaknesses** and **Cracks Suddenly Appear**, with **Each Flaw Crying Out** for **Perfection.** We "All Wonder just Why" is it also True that the **Deceitful Failures of Man** are **Always Revealed** at some **Crucial Moment of Truth, When All is Prepared** for **Final Inspection?** The answer to "Life" is simple. The clarity of Perfect Perception (truth) **Always Comes** at the **End** (finality), when **Management Gives that Soul-Shaking Order** to put that **New Unit** (saint) **On Line** to **See How Well It might Work.** Suddenly, the "Essence of a Person's Perfection" is Unveiled (performance) for **All to See When He** is **Performing in Truth** or becoming a **Silly Joke** before the **Eyes of Critical Men**, including the **Eyes of Our** most

Perfect God, Who Sees and Knows All. This "Unveiling Process" <u>Begins to Reveal</u> **how Many of God's Divine Mysteries** are in the **Life-cycle. We See** that the **Father becomes the Son** and the **Son becomes the Father** (Christmas/movie superman), while in the **Creation-cycle, We See** that **God becomes Man** (Christmas) and **Man becomes God** (Easter/broken sinner).

Christmas   1. **Life-cycle** - Father becomes the Son.............Son Becomes Father
- Traveling from Nothing to All - Conquer Darkness
- Baby World - Fulfilling God's Law of Obedience
- Change Nature - Human to Divine (see limitations)
- God becomes Man through *Life* - Living with Self

Easter   2. **Creation-cycle** - God becomes Man .... Man becomes God
- Traveling from Never-created to Created - Enter Light
- Adult Church - Fulfill Man's Faith in God's Love
- Wash Away Sin - Sinfulness to Holiness (see potential)
- Man becomes God through *Death* - Living with God

This strange concept of the "First becoming Last (God)" and the "Last becoming First (Man)" <u>Reveals</u> that **All that Ends** has a **New Beginning** (movie Matrix), thereby implying that **We** are within a <u>**Giant Life-cycle of Existence**</u> of both **Infinite** (space) **and Eternal** (time) **Proportions**. This means that "All Life is Traveling" through a <u>Spirit World</u> (astral plane) to **Reach Physical Existence** (birth/womb), thereby **Crowning All Human Beings** as **Winners** since **They** have been <u>**Awakened**</u> to a **New State of Consciousness** and <u>**Meet Their Creator**</u> **Face to Face** (beatific vision). Now, "If We Assume this is True," then the <u>Never Created God</u> (father) has become the <u>Created Son</u> (man) by becoming **Jesus Christ on Earth,** in **Heaven,** and within the **Kingdom,** thereby <u>**Making God and Man One**</u> in **Spirit** (God/Christ) and in **Flesh** (Man/Jesus). To understand the "Never-created (existence)" to "Created (service) Concept," <u>We must Recognize</u> that as **God Moves** from **Nothing to All, He must Start this Process** by **Creating Ignorant Babies,** much like a **Nomadic Tribe, Which was Trying** to **Settle-down** by <u>**Living**</u> on **Wild Grains** (bread) and **Berries** (wine) which were **Free for the Taking**. We see that the "Lord God Almighty" is in the <u>Same Position</u> as the **Nomadic Tribes** which **Learned Farming** and then **Learned How to Convert** the **Wild Plant-life** into a <u>**Dependable**</u> **Domesticated Food Source.**

Now, imagine "God must Convert His Wild Babies (wild fruit)" into <u>Clear-Thinking Adults</u> (domesticated harvest) to **Begin His Conversion** from <u>**Never-created Existence**</u> to a <u>**Created Existence**</u> based on **God becoming Man** (Christmas/earth) and **Man becoming God** (Easter/Heaven). Note that the "Whole Human Race" was <u>Living</u> on the **Seashores** of its **Land Mass** because **They** could **Get a Ready Food Supply** from the **Oceans** (nature grown) which **Again** was <u>**Free for the Taking,**</u> at least until it **Runs Out.** We see that this "Awesome Supply of Fish" seems to have a <u>Limit</u> and so the **Fishermen of the World** are **Now being Forced** to become **Fish Farmers** to <u>**Get better Control**</u> of the **World's Food Supply.** It is the same for the "Lord God Almighty" as <u>He must Establish</u> a **New World Order** to **Take Control** of the **Raising and Maturing** of **His Tiny Babies** as **They Journey** from the **Cradle to the Grave** through the **Divine Will of God** (perfect sons). The idea here is that "Wild Food Production" can <u>Work</u> for a <u>Limited Number of People,</u> but a **Successful Society Needs** a well **Organized System** of <u>Food Production</u> to **Keep its Store Shelves Full** of **Nutritious Foods for All.** In short, "Bear Existence" <u>Lives on the Land,</u> while a **Complex Society Relies** on its **High Tech Technologies** (science) to **Create, Feed, and Educate Its Children** to both <u>Grow</u> and <u>Expand</u> from **Everlasting-to-everlasting.**

The point here is that "If a Person Seeks to Find" and "Interface with God," then he must <u>Stop Acting Like a Fool</u> and **Begin Worshiping** (give life), **Praising** (give wealth), and **Thanking God** (give labors) in both a **Formal** and **Divinely Acceptable Manner.** This most "Acceptable Manner (begging)" <u>Involves Coming before God</u> in a **Set of Numbers Worthy** of the <u>Lord God Almighty's Attention</u> (time) at the **Spirit, Son, and Father Levels of Concern.** We are saying that "If a Person Decides" to <u>Pay God a Visit Alone,</u> then he had better be <u>Equal in Rank/Value</u> of **All the Men Ever Created,** including **His Son, Jesus Christ.** Then the **Lord will Listen to His Prayer** (Abraham). For this reason, "Abraham was Told" that he would have to become a <u>Nation of Saints</u> before **God** would either **Hear his Prayer or Accept** the **Blood of his Lamb** as a **Worthy Offering** for God's Divine Forgiveness. Secondly, we see that "Moses was Told" that he had to become a <u>Nation of Chosen People</u> (church) and that **Jewish Lamb's Blood** would be **Sufficient to Obtain** God's Blessing of Forgiveness. Finally, we see that "Jesus was Told" that <u>He</u> had to become a <u>World of Holy Saints</u> (all men/God) and that He was the **Sacrificial Lamb** (Calvary) and had become **Worthy** of **God's Divine Forgiveness** for **One and All.**

1. **Abraham is Told by God** - I will <u>Hear Your Prayer:</u> When Your Children are a Nation
   - Throne of David - God's Government on Earth: Free New Body
   - Abraham's Capital Sins are Forgiven - Abrahamic Covenant (faith)   **Honor**
   - Perform God's Task Correctly - Honor Oneself
   - Open God's Mind - Mankind Sees the Truth
2. **Moses is Told by God** - I will <u>Forgive Your Sins:</u> When Jews are My Chosen People
   - Altar of Aaron - God's Church on Earth: Earn Eternal Life
   - Moses' Mortal Sins are Forgiven - Mosaic Covenant (law)   **Courage**
   - Fulfill God's Duty to the Letter - Show Courage to All
   - Open God's Heart - Mankind Sees the Law
3. **Jesus is Told by God** - I will <u>Welcome You into Heaven:</u> When Mankind becomes Holy Saints
   - Table of Jesus - God's Home on Earth: Rewarded with Own Kingdom
   - Jesus' Venial Sins are Forgiven - New Covenant (knowing)   **Duty**
   - Take-on God's Adult Responsibilities - Become a Dutiful Son
   - Open God's Soul - Mankind Sees the Will

- -

4. **Son of God is Told by God** - I will <u>Welcome Your Chosen into My Kingdom:</u> When these Saints become Sons

- Face of God/Man - God's Face on Earth: Set Free from Bondage
- Son's Virtues are Blessed - Everlasting Covenant (thinking)   **Sacrifice**
- Implement God's Leadership Authority Perfectly - Sacrifice One's Selfishness
- Open God's Life-force - Mankind Sees the Love

Through these "Three Offerings" and "Blessings of Forgiveness," <u>Earth</u> (venial sins), <u>Heaven</u> (mortal sins), and the <u>Kingdom of God</u> (capital sins) are made **One** in **Truth, Law, and Will.** This means that "Man's Venial Sins (earth)" are <u>Forgiven</u> through an **Individual's Prayers** which are **Presented** to the **Holy Spirit** (altar/thoughts). Secondly, "Man's Mortal Sins (Heaven)" are <u>Forgiven</u> through an **Entire <u>Society's Prayers</u>** which are **Presented** to the **Son of God** (pulpit/words). Finally, "Man's Capital Sins (Kingdom)" are <u>Forgiven</u> **When All Men and God Offer Their Prayers** which are presented to **Father God** (chair/deeds). Yes! Through "God's Spirit," "His Son," and "Himself," the <u>Human Race</u> can be **Blessed** with **Free Redemption** (earth), **Earned Salvation** (Heaven), and **Bonus Rewards** (Kingdom). It should now make sense that "Father Abraham," "Moses," "Jesus," and "God's Son" <u>Represent</u> **God's Honor, Courage, Duty, and Sacrifice** as the **Lord Strives to Assist** the **Human Race** to both <u>Grow</u> and <u>Mature</u> into **Righteous** (pulpit), **Holy** (altar), and **Perfect Sons of God** (chair). We see that this "Growth Process" has been <u>Centered</u> upon the **Abrahamic, Mosaic, New, and Everlasting Covenants** as **They have been Created** to bring forth a **Perfect Earth, Heaven, Kingdom, and Face of God.** In this explanation, we see that "One Man Worships (Messiah)" through <u>Exaltation</u> by **Giving his Life to God** (worship); then a "Few Men Worship (church)" through <u>Adoration</u> by **Giving Their Wealth to God** (praise); and finally, "All Men Worship (world)" through <u>Veneration</u> by **Giving Their Labors to God** (thanksgiving).

The following tabular information indicates that "One Man (Abraham)" can <u>Worship the Holy Spirit;</u> a "Church (Jewish People)" can <u>Worship the Son of God;</u> while it "Takes All Men Plus God (Calvary)" to become <u>Worthy</u> of <u>Worshiping Father God</u> **All in the Name** of **His Son, Jesus Christ:**

One Man Worships Spirit, Church Worships the Son,
and All Men Worship the Father to be Saved
(worship spirit opens God's mind, worship son opens God's
heart, and worship father opens God's soul)

Nature   1. **One Man Worships** - <u>Holy Spirit:</u> Individual Prayer ...... Natural Order
(truth)   - Abrahamic Covenant - One Man Seeks God: Offering his Labors
                   (remove sin)
                 - Mind of God - One Power of Forgiveness: Redeem Earth
                 - Worship 3rd Nature of God - Honor God's Thought
                 - Praise 3rd Person of God - Honor God's Ideas   **Individual Rights**
                 - Thank 3rd Trinity of God - Honor God's Concepts
               (free redemption on earth - worship Holy Spirit to remove one's venial sins)

Father	2. **Church Worships** - <u>Son of God:</u> Society's Prayer ......Supernatural Order
(law)	

2. **Church Worships** - <u>Son of God:</u> Society's Prayer ......Supernatural Order
- Mosaic Covenant - One People Seek God: Offer All Their Wealth (remove evil)
- Heart of God - Two Powers of Forgiveness: Save Heaven
- Worship 2nd Nature of God - Honor God's Good News
- Praise 2nd Person of God - Honor God's Gospel Message **Social**
- Thank 2nd Trinity of God - Honor God's Doctrinal Truths **Rights**

(earned salvation in Heaven - worship God's Son to remove one's mortal sins)

Creator
(will)

3. **All Men/God Worship** - <u>Father God:</u> God's Prayer......... Divine Order
- New Covenant - All People Seek God: Offer Their very Lives (remove death)
- Soul of God - Three Powers of Forgiveness: Reward Kingdom
- Worship 1st Nature of God - Honor God's New Body
- Praise 1st Person of God - Honor God's Eternal Life **Divine Rights**
- Thank 1st Trinity of God - Honor God's Kingdom of Glory

(bonus rewards in Kingdom - worship Father God to remove one's capital sins)

This illustration shows that to "Venerate the Mind (natural order) of God," a <u>Person</u> must **Worship** the **3rd Nature of God** (honor thoughts), **Praise** the **3rd Person of God** (honor ideas), and **Thank** the **3rd Trinity of God** (honor concepts) to become **Worthy of Thinking Like God** (wisdom). Secondly, to "Adore the Heart (supernatural order) of God," the <u>Church</u> (God's people) must **Worship** the **2nd Nature of God** (honor good news), **Praise** the **2nd Person of God** (honor gospel message), and **Thank** the **2nd Trinity of God** (honor doctrinal truths) to become **Worthy of Loving Like God** (courage). Finally, to "Exalt the Soul (divine order) of God," <u>All Created/uncreated Life</u> must **Worship** the **1st Nature of God** (honor new body), **Praise** the **1st Person of God** (honor eternal life), and **Thank** the **1st Trinity of God** (honor kingdom) to become **Worthy of being Perfect** (instinctive) **Like God** (generosity). Through "Man's, Angels', and God's" <u>Worship</u> (venerate mind), <u>Praise</u> (adore heart), and <u>Thanksgiving</u> (exalt soul) before **God's Altar** (give life), **God's Pulpit** (give wealth), and **God's Chair** (give labors), **All Mankind** can be **Saved from Sin, Evil, and Death**.

The point here is that to effectively "Worship, Praise, and Thank God," a <u>Person</u> <u>must Repent Perfectly</u> (deny intellect), <u>Pray Perfectly</u> (abandon feelings), and <u>Offer his Perfect Works to God</u> (submit free will) as **If he were Christ Himself**. This means that "All Those Who Come to Mass" have <u>No Right to Participate,</u> Other than for the **First Few Moments When They Honestly Say** the **Sinner's Prayer of Submission** which will **Allow Them** to **Die to Self** unto **Nothingness** (Christ becomes sinner). At this "Critical Moment," <u>When a Person</u> **Faces his Own Divine Execution** (in spirit) for all his **Sins**, **Christ** becomes the **Sinner** (earth) and **Makes this Soul** into a **Christian** (Heaven). We then see that upon the **Lord's Final Blessing,** a **Christian** or **Christ Himself** can **Leave the Mass** as a **Holy Saint of God**, truly **Worthy of God's Blessing of Holiness** and will then **Return to the Evil World** to **Fight Evil unto His Death**.

This means that "Every Word in the Bible" Refers to either Jesus the Sinner (take-sin) or to Christ the Saint (give divinity/forgiveness) and that **Not a Single Word** Refers **to Sinful Man**. In short, a "Person Cannot Repent Enough" to become a Christian and he "Cannot Pray Enough" to become a Saint. He can **Never be Anything** other than a **Sinful/Self-righteous Hypocrite** (egomaniac). The answer to "Life" is to Die to Self (death) and then **Let Jesus Christ Take-over Your very Spirit Nature** in **Mind, Heart, and Soul Forever** (rebirth/become you) as the **Last shall become First** (holy sinner) and the **First shall become Last** (dead Jesus Christ). This "Conversion" will Take a Lifetime of Hard-work (100% belief) to **Find** that **Fine Balance** between being **All Human** in the **Flesh** (ignorant/fight evil) and being **All Divine** in **Christ's Spirit** (wise/submission).

In "Mankind's" most Triumphant Hour of Reality (balance), a **Lifetime** of **Soul-Crushing Work** can be **Flawed** (fall from grace) as the **Need to Make Life Better Cries Out** from **Every Expectation, Leading** to its **Ultimate Success** (eternal life) in **Spirit** (submission/holy) and **Ultimate Failure** (death) in **Flesh** (sacrifice/righteous). This means that it must be the "Demonic Forces" Doing Their Jobs Well as **They Force Humanity** to both **Understand** and **Take Control** of **Every Obscure Detail** to **Make Absolutely Sure** that **Things Work Right** in the **Sight of God**. This also means that the "Evil One (Lucifer)" is Making Sure that Mankind is **Paying Strict Attention** to the **Business of Living Well, or Man must Accept** the **Failures in his Life** due to his **Own Foolish Actions** (ignorance/cowardice/greed). This constant pressure to "Achieve" some Abstract Level of Human Perfection is **Never-ending, Transforming Great Men** into Silly Fools (donkeys), either **Running from a Stick** (growth) or **Chasing the Carrot** (maturity)**, All in the Name** of **Righteous Living** (keep-up with the Jones).

We see that the "Lord Encourages Every Soul (carrot/mercy)" with the Promise of his Own "**Eternal Nirvana** (happiness)," while the "Evil One (stick/justice)" Strikes Fire (fear) at **One's Heels Forcing him** to either **Move Along** or **Die where He Stands.** This constant "Threat of Death (stick)" and "Search for Survival (carrot)" call most strongly to the Hearts of every Struggling Soul as it makes its way along man's **Dangerous Highway** of **Broken Failures** and **Life-Crushing Disappointments**. We see that out of this "Great Darkness" Comes a New Voice of Hope **Calling All Men** to a **New Way of Life,** which has been **Filled with the Blessings** of **Success** (mind), **Prosperity** (heart), and **Good Health** (soul). Unfortunately, this "Voice of New Hope" is Not Offering Freedom from **One's Painful Struggles**, but simply **Offers to Use His Fleshly Trials** to **Their Best Advantage** (knowledge) to **Create His** Lessons of Life (fight evil). The logic here is that "If a Person" has to Suffer the Rigors of Growing-up (lessons), **Why Not Get the Most Out of It**, by **Applying Himself** to the **Benefits Derived** from a **Transformed Life** of **Righteous, Holy, and Perfect Living** (lessons).

The essential teaching here is that "God Desired" this most Baffling Human Struggle (smart where the skin is off) of **Ours** to be seen through a **Set of Distorted Human Eyes** simply to **Confuse the Central Issue in Life**, which **Centers on Our Need for Endless Learning** (lessons). The "Lord's Pearls of Great Price" have been

Buried like Easter Eggs in the **Evil Hearts of Deceitful Men**, so that the **Mysteries of Life** will be **Given Their Truest Meaning,** once seen in the **Divine Light** of a **New Day Dawning in Christ.** On this most "Holy Occasion of Awakening," the Lord will **Pour His Holy Word of Righteousness Over** the **Crops of Deception Proving** that **Nothing Can Keep** a **Good Man Down, No Matter What.** The question arises just "Who is Good" and How can a Lost Blind Child of Destiny **Discern the Clear Difference** between **God's Right** and **Man's Wrong,** without **Fear of Making Oneself** even a **Greater Fool** in the **Eyes of his Fellowman** and his **Creator God?** This is a "Perfect Question" and its "Perfect Answer" is the Essence to **Leading a Sanctified Spiritual Life** of **Proper Righteousness** (flesh) and **Holiness** (spirit), based on **Serving** the **Will of God** and **Not** the **Will of Man** (self-righteous fool). To distinguish "His Own Selfish Motives (flesh)" from his Benevolent Desires (spirit) to **Serve** and/or **Believe In** the **Greater Good of God,** a **Person** must **Learn the Principle** of **Absolute Submission** or **Dying to Self** (deny/abandon/submit). Through this concept of "Spiritual Submission (spiritual dimension)," a Person is Promising to **Give All to God** (earthly life). In the **Concept of His** "Physical Sacrifice (physical dimension)," a Person is Fulfilling his Personal Promise to become a **Soul Savior for God** (eternal life).

Obviously, the "Life-experience Begins" with a Child's Sacrifice (repentance/blessing), to be **Followed** by his **Prayer** (forgiveness/honor), which **Leads to his Gift** (save souls/nutrition) unto his **God** to **Receive** a **New Body, Eternal Life,** and his **Own Kingdom.** This "Series of Evolutionary Steps" from Nothing to All **Forces All of God's Children** to **Decide for Themselves** the **Size of Their Sacrifice** (give life), the **Depth of Their Prayer** (give money), and **Number of Souls to be Saved** (whole earth), based on just **How much They Truly Love God.** To **Receive** the **Lord's Forgiveness** for a **Person's Defiance** (stealing), **Deception** (hiding), and **Deceit** (lying) to **His God,** we see the "Need to Sacrifice" a Lot of Blood (scourging), **Pray unto Our Death** (crucifixion), and **Offer Gifts unto Damnation** (tomb).

Recall that "Jesus Christ" was Paying Mankind's Sin-debt by **Offering His Own Blood** (scourging), **Death** (crucifixion), and **Damnation** (tomb) to **Create the Necessary Funds to Redeem** the **Minds** (sacrifice), **Hearts** (prayer), and **Souls** (gifts) of **All Men.** Now, in contrast to this "Massive Commitment" and Divine Performance, **Each** of **God's Children** must **Place** his **Sacrifices** (ideas/pain), **Prayers** (concepts/death), and **Gifts** (objectives/damnation) upon the **Altar** (blessings), before the **Throne** (honors), and on the **Table/Palace** (nourishment) of the **Lord God Almighty.** Via the "Size of His Commitment (pledge/100% belief)" unto God, His People, and His Kingdom, a **Person can Receive** the **Lord's Treasures of Repentance** (new mind), **Forgiveness** (new heart), and **Saving of Souls** (new soul). Through this "Process of Conversion," a Person will Learn All About Life, become **Employed by God,** and **One Day** become **Worthy of God's Bonus Rewards** (tips), **All** in the **Name of Absolute Submission** to the **Divine Will of God.**

This means that "If a Person Surrenders his Life (repentance)" to Jesus Christ (church/altar), then he can **Defeat Adam's and Eve's Curses** of **Defiance** (stealing), **Deception** (hiding), and **Deceit** (lying) to become a **Holy Saint before God.** Unfortunately, to "Defeat Defiance (stealing fruit)," a Person must **Face** being Scourged at the Pillar (repentance); to "Defeat Deception (hiding behind leaf)," He must **Face** being Crucified on the Cross (forgiveness); and to "Defeat Deceit (lying to God's face)," He must **Suffer** the Tomb of Hopelessness. Once a "Person has been Forgiven" for his Defiance (capital sins/dead soul), Deception (mortal sins/dead heart), and Deceit (venial sins/dead mind), then he can **Begin** his **Earthly Growth** (righteousness) and **Heavenly Maturity** (holiness).

The following tabular information indicates that through "His Sacrifices," "Prayers," and "Gifts," a Person can **Offer God** his **Repentance** to be **Forgiven** and then be **Blessed with the Saving of Others:**

Offering Sacrifices, Prayers, and Gifts to Obtain the Lord's Blessings, Honors, and Nourishment

(1st: sacrifices/repentance/blessings; 2nd: prayers/forgiveness/honors; 3rd: gifts/souls/nourishment)

Idea (thoughts)	1. **Sacrifices** - Repentance: Blessings = Priestly Offering ...Knowledge	
	• New Body - Earth: Size of One's Sacrifice (offer life)	
	• Scourging - Offer Blood: Forgiven for Defiance = Stealing	
	• Jesus Takes-sin (faults) - Remove Ignorance	**Save Sinners**
	• Christ Gives Divinity (virtues) - Give Wisdom	
Concept (words)	2. **Prayers** - Forgiveness: Honors = Kingly Offering ...... Self-awareness	
	• Eternal Life - Heaven: Depth of Prayer (give wealth)	
	• Crucifixion – Offer Death: Forgiven for Deception = Hiding	
	• Jesus Takes-sin (sin) - Remove Cowardice	**Christians**
	• Christ Gives Divinity (sinless) - Give Courage	
Objective (deeds)	3. **Gifts** - Saving Souls: Nourishment = Sonly Offering... Consciousness	
	• Royal Kingdom - Kingdom: Number of Souls (whole earth)	
	• Tomb - Offer Damnation: Forgiven for Deceit = Lying	
	• Jesus Takes-sin (evil) - Remove Greed	**Sainthood**
	• Christ Gives Divinity (holy) - Give Generosity	

This illustration shows "Just How Much" a Child of God actually **Loves his Creator** by **Measuring** (fruits) the **Size of his Sacrifice** (ideas/thoughts), the **Depth of his Prayer** (concepts/words), and by the **Number of Souls he has Saved** (objectives/deeds), all in **Honoring Christ's Death** on **Mount Calvary** (sacrifice/prayer/gift). Obviously, out of the "Lord's Sacrifice upon His Pillar (scourging)," the Human Race will become **Worthy** of its **Own New Body** as **Jesus Takes Man's Faults** to **Remove Ignorance** (old mind) and **Christ Gives-up His Virtues** to **Give Man Wisdom** (new mind). Secondly, out of the "Lord's Sacrifice upon His Cross (crucifixion)," the Human Race will become **Worthy** of its **Own Eternal Life** as **Jesus Takes Man's Sins** to **Remove Cowardice** (old heart) and **Christ Gives-up His Sinlessness** to **Give Man Courage** (new heart). Finally, out of the "Lord's Sacrifice within His Tomb (damnation)," the Human Race will become **Worthy** of its **Own Kingdom of Glory** as **Jesus Takes Man's Evil** to **Remove Greed** (old soul) and **Christ Gives-up His Holiness** to **Give**

Man Generosity (new soul). Through this "Give and Take Concept," both Sacrifice (Jesus) and Prayer (Christ) become **God's Redemptive Tools** with **Sufficient Power** (faithfulness) to **Convert the Lost at Any Cost**. Note that "Sacrifice" has the Power to Save Sinners (blessings); that "Prayers" can Create Christians (anointings); and when **Sacrifice/Prayer** are **Combined**, then "God's Gifts" can bring forth **Saints** (sanctification) to **Serve the Needs** of **God, Angels, and Men**.

In this way, "God's Babies" can Gain the Knowledge of Life through **Denying Their Intellect** (sacrifice); "God's Teenagers" can Gain the Self-awareness of Life through **Abandoning Their Feelings** (prayer); and "God's Adults" can Gain the Consciousness of Life by **Submitting Their Free Will** (gift) to **God's Divine Will**. This "Process of Sacrifice," "Praying," and "Gift Giving" has caused Jesus Christ to **Go to His Scourging** to **Face Death Agony** (sacrifice), then to **His Crucifixion** to **Face Divine Hopelessness** (prayer), and finally, to **His Tomb** to **Face Separation from God** (gift) **All to Save** the **Lost Broken Sinners of the World**. Out of these "Three Offerings to God (sacrifice/prayer/gift)," the whole Human Race could become both **Soldiers-of-the-Light** (Jesus/save sinners) or **Purify Grave** (lessons), and **Living Prayers of Love** (Christ/create saints) or **Purify Host** (blessings).

Now, imagine becoming a "Soldier-of-the-Light (sacrifice/streetwise)" and having to Face Worldly Survival (begging), having Military Power (demanding), and Mastering Global Business Skills (earning) simply to **Survive** in a **World of Sin, Evil, and Death**. Secondly, imagine working to become a "Living Prayer of Love (submission/educated)" before God, having to face Church Redemption (begging), having Civilian Authority (voting), and mastering Governmental Duties (spending) to become **Worthy** of a future **World of Righteousness, Holiness, and Perfection**. In this explanation, we are describing "Growing-up (flesh)" on the **Streets of Death** (soldier) to become "Mature (spirit)" in the **Church of Christ** (living prayer). Recall that the "Jews" defined the Wickedness of the Flesh as a **Goat** (soldier) with **Guilty Blood** (soldier), while the Holiness of the Spirit was defined as a **Lamb** (living prayer) with **Innocent Blood** (living prayer). The implication of having either "Guilty or Innocent Blood" is connected to Adam's and Eve's Fall from Grace as they faced **Two Separate Judgments:** 1) Adam was an Adult - Guilty Blood (goat): Earned Salvation = Soldier-of-the-Light (streetwise); and 2) Eve was a Child - Innocent Blood (lamb): Free Redemption = Living Prayer of Love (educated). To comprehend the "Guilty/Innocent Blood Concept," imagine the Guilty Person must **Pay his Sin-debt** at the **Beginning of Life** by **Living in Poverty** (buy program/poor); while the Innocent Person can **Pay his Sin-debt** at the **End of Life** and still **Live in Opulence** (lease program/rich).

The following tabular information indicates that each of "God's Children" must pass through being a Soldier-of-the-Light (streetwise) by **Fighting Evil** (ethics); then becoming a Living Prayer of Love (educated) by **Mastering Sainthood** (morals):

Soldier-of-the-Light Fights Evil;
the Living Prayer of Love Saves Souls to Serve God

(survival, military power, business, then church, civilian authority, and government)

Adult   1. **Soldier-of-the-Light** - <u>Guilty Blood:</u> Streetwise (trying) ...... Fighting Evil
(ethics)
- <u>Facing Life of Poverty</u> - Adam: Breath of Life = Submission (works)
- Worldly Survival - Begging (flesh)
- Reference Point - Self/home (truth)
- Military Power - Demanding (spirit)   **King of Glory**
- Triangulated Position - Society/government (law) • Purify Grave/lessons
- Business Skills - Earning (soul)
- Defined Territory - God/church (will)
- <u>Cast into the Pit</u> - Goat: Curse of Death = Sacrifice (slow death)
- *Pay Temple Tax* - Earn Salvation (mind)
- God's Blessing - Heaven on Earth (heart)
- Forgiveness, Wealth, and Love - Servanthood (soul)

Child   2. **Living Prayer of Love** - <u>Innocent Blood:</u> Educated
         (succeeding)....   Saving Souls
- <u>Experiencing Life of Opulence</u> - Eve: Rib of Death = Sacrifice (faith)
- Church Redemption - Begging (spirit)
- Reference Point - Home/self (truth)
- Civilian Authority - Voting (flesh)   **Priest of Holiness**
- Triangulated Position - Government/society (law) •Purify Host/blessings
- Governmental Duties - Spending (soul)
- Defined Territory - Church/God (will)
- <u>Cut Throat</u> - Lamb: Blessing of Life = Submission (instant death)
- *Tabernacle of Forgiveness* - Free Redemption (soul)
- God's Blessing - Heaven with God (heart)
- Peace, Joy, and Happiness - Sainthood (mind)

This illustration shows that the "Life-experience" is based on <u>God's War of Good and Evil</u> which brings the **Harsh Reality** that **Each of God's Children** must **Choose** to be either a **<u>King of Glory</u>** (Jesus/save sinners) by **Fighting Evil** or become a **Priest of Holiness** (Christ/create saints) by **Saving Souls.** The point is to see that "Each of Us must Face" <u>Worldly Survival</u> (begging) to **Attain His** "Church Redemption (begging)," <u>If We are Going</u> to **Fulfill** the **Meaning of Life** (existence). Secondly, "Each of Us must Face" <u>Military Discipline/Power</u> (demanding) to **Attain His** "Civilian Authority (voting)," <u>If We are Going</u> to **Fulfill** the **Purpose of Life** (service). Finally, "Each of Us must Face" <u>Learning Business Skills</u> (earning) to "Attain His Government Duties (spending)," <u>If We are Going</u> to **Fulfill** the **Value of Life** (happiness). At each of these "Three Levels of Perfection," a <u>Person is to Establish</u> his **Own Physical Identity** (mind/flesh), **Spiritual Character** (heart/spirit), and **Mystical Personality** (soul/soul) before **God** (sacrifice**), Society** (prayer), and **Man** (gift). This means that in "Each Life," a <u>Soul is Striving</u> to **Establish a Fixed Frame of Reference** based on either

Learning Truth or Experiencing Truth to **Know the Difference** between <u>Wrong, Evil, and Man's Will</u> versus <u>Right, Good, and God's Will</u> to have a **Mind of Its Own** (thinking).

We can now recognize that through a "Person's Submission (spirit/God)" and "Sacrifice (flesh/Man)," **He can See** the **Lord's Two Truths of Life** (paradox): 1) <u>Divine Truth</u> (God becomes Man) - Faith: Spiritual Dimension = God/Man (reason for living); and 2) <u>Human Truth </u>(Man becomes God) - Law: Physical Dimension = Man/God (price for dying). Through both the "Divine and Human Truths," <u>We See the Conversion</u> of the **Mind, Heart, and Soul** to bring forth one's **Divine Holiness** (heart/spirit/church/robot) and **His Human Righteousness** (mind/flesh/world/animal). This means that the "Jews of the Old Testament (title deed to earth)" <u>Represent the Creation</u> of **Heaven on Earth** (Sadducees), while the "Christians of the New Testament (title deed to Heaven)" <u>Represent the Creation</u> of **Heaven with God** (Pharisees). Through these "Two Separate Missions of Life," we see the new <u>Mystical Union</u> between **God's Divinity** (Christ/intercessor/faith) and **Man's Humanity** (Jesus/interpreter/law). The idea here is that the "Jewish People" or the <u>People of Death</u> were **Created** to **Redeem the Damned** (empty hell/free redemption), while the "Christian People" or the <u>People of Life</u> were **Created** to **Save the Saints** (fill Heaven/earned salvation). To this end, the "Lord Jesus Christ has Come" so that <u>His Spirit could Surrender</u> (blood shed) to **God** to **Glorify Heaven's Saints** (give divinity) and <u>His Flesh could be Sacrificed</u> (body broken) to **Glorify Earth's Sinners** (take-sin). In this way, the "Glory of God (God becomes Man/Christmas)" can be <u>United</u> with the "Glory of Man (Man becomes God/Easter)" as **They Come Together** in **Truth, Law, Will, and Love** to bring forth <u>Man's</u> **Righteousness** (new body), **Holiness** (eternal life), **and Perfection** (kingdom) **before God.**

The following tabular information indicates God's "Two-Truth System of Life" as it is manifested within the <u>Perfection of Heaven</u> and the <u>Imperfection of Earth</u> to **Balance** the **Love of God** (obedience) with the **Love of Man** (pleasure):

The "Two Truths of God" are Manifested
in the Two Natures of Jesus Christ, Our Savior
(the spiritual dimension surrenders to,
while the physical dimension is sacrificed, for God)

2nd Truth - Physical Dimension	1st Truth - Spiritual Dimension
• Love of Man - Jesus as Man/God (chaos)	• Love of God - Christ as God/Man (order)
• Sacrifice of the Flesh – Take-sin	• Submission of Spirit - Give Divinity
• Born-again to Unselfishness	• Dying to a Soul's Selfishness
• Reason for Living – Challenge	• Price for Dying – Adventure
• M i n d - Intellect: See Limitations	• F l e s h - Knowledge: See Potential
• Circumcision - Blood Sacrifice	• Scourging - Sin (venial)
• H e a r t - Emotions: Feel Limits	• S p i r i t - Self-aware: Feel Hope
• Baptism - Water Blessing	• Crucifixion - Evil (mortal)
• S o u l - Instincts: Experience Limits	• S o u l - Conscious: Experience Life

• Calvary - Death Offering	• Cursed Tomb - Death (capital)
Righteousness - Learn Right from Wrong	Holiness - Learn Good from Evil
• Free Redemption - Offer Promise	• Earned Salvation - Fulfill Promise
• Earth - World: Saving the Lost	• Heaven - Church: Creating Saints
• Conversion of Babies: Ethics (death)	• Conversion of Adults: Morals (life)
• Exterior Blessing of Informality	• Interior Blessing of Formality
(Jewish Inheritance - Repentance)	(Christian Birthright - Forgiveness)

This illustration shows that there is both a "Reason for Living (challenge)" and a "Price for Dying (adventure)," which are made One in the **Mystical Dimension of Perfection** in the **Person** of **Jesus Christ**. It can be seen that through the "Forces of Chaos (2nd truth/illusion)" and the "Forces of Order (1st truth/reality)," the whole Human Race can come into **Balance** with the **Expectations of Heaven** (God) and the **Hopes of Earth** (Man). This means that the "Lord God Almighty" has been Working Feverishly on finding a way to **Save the Pagan World from Damnation** (Jesus/Man) as well as being able to **Create Saints Out of Sinners** (Christ/God). During the "Fall of Adam/Eve," Truth became Lies (deceit); the Law became Evil (deception); and God's Will became the Curse of Death (defiance), leaving **Mankind** in a **Pit of Death Agony/Hopelessness/Separation**. With the coming of "God's Son, Jesus Christ," this Pit of Torment (death agony/hopelessness/separation) would be **Transformed** into a **New Creation** (new nature) of **Peace, Joy, and Happiness**.

Obviously, the "Lord has been Working Diligently" on Creating both **Righteous Citizens** (Jews/blood) for the **Earth** (body broken) and **Holy Saints** (Christians/water)" for **Heaven** (blood shed). This "Great Effort" has been Performed by God to bring **Perfection to His** whole **Kingdom of Glory** through the **Redemptive Sacrifice** of **His Son, Jesus Christ**. This means that "God's Son, Christ (change nature)" created Christmas (surrender spirit/eternal life) to **Honor Heaven's Saints** (stars) with His **Shed Blood** (submission/lamb), while "Mary's Son, Jesus (wash away sin)" created Easter (sacrifice flesh/new body) to **Honor Earth's Sinners** (dust) with **His Body Broken** (sacrifice/goat). Now, try to imagine "Going the 1st Mile with Christ (1st truth/holiness)" and then "Going the 2nd Mile with Jesus (2nd Truth/righteousness)" to Unite the 1st (redemption) and 2nd (salvation) Truths into **One Perfect Lifestyle**.

1. **1st Mile** - Create Righteous Nature; God Thinks of Child.... See Limitations
2. **2nd Mile** - Create Holy Behavior: God Speaks to Child.... See Potential
3. **3rd Mile** - Create Perfect Lifestyle: God Touches Child ..... See Self-worth

This "Awesome Journey" from Death to New-life allows the **Lord God Almighty** to **Force All Souls** to **Decide, for themselves**, whether to **Offer God** a **Blood Sacrifice** to make **God's Acquaintance** (think of), offer a **Death Sacrifice** to become **God's Neighbor** (speak to), offer a **Damnation Sacrifice** to become **God's Friend** (touch), offer an **Oblivion Sacrifice** to enter **God's Family** (sup with), and/or offer a **Resurrection Sacrifice** to become **God's Beloved Treasure** (adopted son). The **Choice is Theirs**. At each of these "Levels of Sacrifice," the Human Race has a chance to **Show** the **Depth of Its Commitment** (sacrifice/prayer/gift) in trying its very best to **Meet, Know, Love, and Serve Its God** <u>No Matter What the Cost</u> in **Time, Money, and/or Effort.** In this explanation, we see that "If a Person Wants" even <u>One Thought from God,</u> he must be willing to **Pay the Lord** in a **<u>Devout Sacrifice of his Own Blood</u>** just to make **God's Acquaintance.** Secondly, "If He Wants" just <u>One Word from God,</u> he must be willing to **Pay the Lord** in his **<u>Sacrifice of Death</u>** just to become **God's Neighbor.** Thirdly, "If He Wants" just <u>One Touch from God,</u> he must be willing to **Pay the Lord** in his **<u>Sacrifice of Damnation</u>** just to become **God's Friend.** Fourthly, "If He Wants" just <u>One Supper from God,</u> he must be willing to **Pay the Lord** in his **<u>Sacrifice of Oblivion</u>** to become welcomed into **God's Family.** Finally, "If He Wants" just <u>One Overnight Stay from God,</u> he must be willing to **Pay the Lord** in his **Blessing of Resurrection** to be **<u>Legally Adopted</u>** (sonship) by the **Lord God Almighty Himself.**

Through each of these "Five Offerings," a <u>Person can Expect God</u> to **Think of him, Speak to him, Touch him, Sup with him,** and finally, **Adopt him** into the **Royal Family of God.** The implication is that "God is Asking Each Soul" to first make its own <u>Offering of Promise,</u> then **Live its Life to the Fullest,** and then **Compare** its **Physical Actions** (sinner's effort) or **Free Will** with its **Spiritual Accomplishments** (Christ's effort) or **Divine Will.**

===

*****Perfect Faith** means: Having <u>Divine Knowing without Proof</u> (100 belief) making **One's Mind** (intellect/earth) and **Heart** (emotions/Heaven) **<u>One</u>** in **<u>Infinite Truth</u>** (righteousness/holiness)**,** thereby **<u>Transforming a Christian's Soul</u>** (instinct/kingdom) into **Perfection** (Sonship/Priesthood/Kingship) **before God.**

===

Obviously, the "Lord God Almighty" is <u>Asking Each of Us</u> to **Compare** his **Physical Actions** (intellect) with his **Spiritual Accomplishments** (emotions) by **Examining** the **<u>Value of his Life</u>** on **Earth** (righteousness/ethics) as it **Relates** to the **<u>Value of his Life</u>** in **Heaven** (holiness/morals). Note that "Man's Earthly Experience (baby)" is <u>Defined</u> by his **Physical Conversion** as he **Removes his Ignorance** and **Gains Wisdom** by **<u>Learning God's Right</u>** and **man's wrong** to **See his Own Limitations** (knowing God). Secondly, "Man's Heavenly Experience (teenager)" is <u>Defined</u> by his **Spiritual Conversion** as he **Removes his Cowardice** and **Gains Courage** by **<u>Learning God's Good</u>** and **man's evil** to **See his Own Potential** (loving God). Finally, "Man's Kingdom Experience (adult)" is <u>Defined</u> by his **Mystical Conversion** as he **Removes his Greed** and **Gains Generosity** by **<u>Learning God's Will</u>** from **man's will** to **See his Own Self-worth.** Through these "Three Conversion Experiences," a Person can Comprehend that the **Life-experience** is **Comprised of Three Seven-Step Cycles** or **<u>Twenty-One Individual Changes,</u>** thereby making a **Person More and More Valuable to God, Angels, and Men.**

Now, let's examine "Man's Seven Physical Changes (flesh/mind)" based on: (1) <u>Being Saved,</u> (2) <u>Mastering the Home,</u> (3 <u>Learning Man's</u> Laws, (4) <u>Becoming a Citizen,</u> (5) <u>Believing Correctly,</u> (6) <u>Seeing Limitations,</u> and finally, (7) coming to <u>Know God.</u> In like manner, let's examine "Man's Seven Spiritual Changes (spirit/heart)" based on: (1) <u>Saving Oneself,</u> (2) <u>Mastering the Church,</u> (3) <u>Learning God's Laws,</u> (4) <u>Becoming a Saint,</u> (5)

Being Faithful, (6) Seeing Potential, and finally, (7) coming to Love God. Next, let's examine "Man's Seven Mystical Changes (soul/being)" based on: (1) Saving Others, (2) Mastering the Government, (3) Learning God's/Man's Laws,(4) Becoming a Son of God, (5) Knowing Truth, (6) Seeing Self-worth, and finally, (7) coming to Serve God. By "Passing" through this Cycle of Transformation (21 steps), a **Person** is able to both **Grow and Mature** into a **Righteous King, Holy Priest, and Perfect Son of God.** The question is: "Just How Must Effort" is a Child of God **Willing to Put Into** his **Life-experience** based on the **Lord's Call** to **Righteousness, Holiness, and Perfection** via **His Earthly Home** (baby), **Heavenly Church** (teenager), and **Kingdom Government** (adult)?

The following tabular information indicates that the "Human Race must Pass" through Three Conversion Experiences via the **Influence** of **Earth** or **Physical Transformation** (baby level), then **Heaven** or **Spiritual Transformation** (teenage level), and finally, **God's Kingdom** or **Mystical Transformation** (adult level):

Facing Three Conversion Experiences of Earth, Heaven, and Kingdom to become a True Son of God
(baby is converted physically, teenager is converted
spiritually, and an adult is converted mystically)

—————————Breaking Chains of Slavery – Set Free from Sin—————————

Flesh   A. **Physical Conversion** - Earth (chains)....Remove Ignorance and Gain Wisdom

(mind)
1. Baby Level of Growth - Being Saved
2. Learn Right from Wrong – Home
   (remove faults - sacrifice self)
3. Taught Ethical Behavior - Man's Laws
4. Become a Righteous Man – Citizenship   **Just Freedom**
5. Wash Away Sin - Water: Belief   (individual rights)
6. Born-again Christian - See Limitations
7. *New Body* – Transfiguration
   • Live with Self - Know God

(father's table - God's/Abraham's Union: toil changed to rest = home blessed/obedience)

—————————Opening Prison Doors - Escape from Evil —————————

Spirit   B. **Spiritual Conversion** - Heaven (doors)....Remove Cowardice and

(heart)
1. Teenage Level of Maturity - Saving Self   Gain Courage
2. Learn Good from Evil - Church
   (gain virtues - sacrifice enemies)
3. Taught Moral Behavior - God's Laws
4. Become a Holy Man – Sainthood   **Loving Liberty**
5. Change Nature - Blood: Faith   (social rights)
6. Mystical Saint - See Potential
7. *Eternal Life* – Glorification
   • Live with Society - Love God

(church's altar - Priest/Laity Union: pain changed to pleasure = church sanctified/prayer)

Soul   C.   **Mystical Conversion** - <u>Kingdom</u> (guards) … Remove Greed and Gain Generosity

(being)   1. Adult Level of Fulfillment - Saving Others

               2. Learn God's Will/man's will - Government

                   (become holy - bless goodness of God)

               3. Taught Perfect Behavior - God's/Man's Laws

               4. Become Perfect Man – Sonship   **Peaceful Independence**

               5. Becoming Divinity - Spirit: Works   (divine rights)

               6. Divine Son of God - See Self-worth

               7. *Royal Kingdom* – Exaltation

                  • Live with God - Serve God

(courtroom bench - Angels/Saints Union: death changed to life = government anointed/works)

This illustration shows that "Mastering" one's <u>Physical Conversion</u> (break chains) means **Entering God's Just Freedom** (new body) to attain his **Personal Independence from Sin** and **Receive God's Blessing of Individual Rights** (kingship). Secondly, "Mastering" his <u>Spiritual Conversion</u> (open doors) means **Entering God's Loving Liberty** (eternal life) to attain his **Social Liberty from Evil** and **Receive God's Blessing of Social Rights** (priesthood). Finally, "Mastering" his <u>Mystical Conversion</u> (overcome guards) means **Entering God's Peaceful Independence** (royal kingdom) to attain his **Divine Independence from Death** and **Receive God's Blessing of Divine Rights** (sonship). We see that one way to "Imagine" <u>Our Conversion Experience</u> on **Earth** is to visualize a **Prisoner in Chains** (sin) as he **Struggles** to **Break Free** using only his **Mind** (flesh), **Heart** (spirit), and **Soul** (being). Secondly, "Imagine" <u>Our Conversion Experience</u> in **Heaven** is to visualize a **Prisoner Unlocking the Prison Doors** (evil) as he **Seeks Freedom** using **God's Mind** (intellect), **God's Heart** (emotions), and **God's Soul** (instincts). Finally, "Imagine" <u>Our Conversion Experience</u> within **God's Kingdom** is to visualize a **Prisoner Overpowering the Guards** (death) as he **Seeks his Own Free Will** using the **God/Man Mind** (authority), **God/Man Heart** (responsibility), and **God/Man Soul** (duty).

Through the "Forces" of both <u>God and Man,</u> the **Whole Human Race** will be **Set Free** from <u>Sin, Evil, and Death</u> to **Defeat Man's Sin-nature,** the **World's Temptations,** and **Lucifer's Demonic Possession.** Only when "Man," the "World," and "Lucifer" will be <u>Defeated</u> **will God Get His** *Loving Home* (flesh/obedience), **Worshiping Church** (spirit/devotion), and **Government of Service** (soul/honesty). Yes! Only through "Freedom (break chains)," "Liberty (open doors)," and "Independence (overpower guards)," will the <u>Human Race</u> **Defeat** <u>Sin, Evil, and Death</u> to attain a **New Earthly Body, Eternal Life from Heaven,** and its own **Royal Kingdom from God.** We see in the "Creation of a Triune Society (earth/Heaven/Kingdom)" that <u>God the Father</u> came to **Establish His Kingdom** (Jews/Earth); then <u>Jesus Christ</u> (good son) came to **Establish His Kingdom** (Christians/Heaven); and finally, the <u>Prodigal Son</u> (bad son) will come to **Establish His Kingdom** (pagans/Kingdom). Out of these "Three Kingdoms of Glory," <u>God will Bless Man</u> with a special <u>Gift</u> to **Be Saved** (baptism), to

Save himself (confession), and then to **Save Others** (communion) based on God's **Divine Forgiveness** (love).

This concept is like being given the "Title Deed" to a **Free Gold Mine** (redemption), yet one must still **Dig Out the Gold** (salvation), and finally, he must **Share his Gold with Others** (rewards). The idea is to see that "God Saves One Man (Jesus Christ)," He teaches <u>Lost Souls</u> (Christians) how to **Save Themselves,** and then these **Saints** go out to **Save the Whole World** (pagans). In this sequence of "Saving the Lost" through the <u>Good News</u> (redemption), <u>Gospel Message</u> (salvation), and <u>Doctrinal Truths</u> (rewards), the **Three Kingdoms of God** are to be **Created.** The idea here is to see that the "Messiah Comes (1st advent)" as <u>God the Father</u> or as a **Priest on a Donkey** to **Transform the Earth** from **Sinfulness to Righteousness**, thereby **Giving the Jewish People** their own **Title Deed to Earth** (new body). Secondly, the "Messiah Comes (2nd advent)" as the <u>Son of God</u> (Jesus Christ) or as a **Thief in the Night** (man's spirit) to **Transform Heaven** from **Evilness into Holiness** (seal saints)**,** thereby **Giving the Christian People** their own **Title Deed to Heaven** (eternal life). Finally, the "Messiah Comes (3rd advent)" as the <u>Holy Spirit</u> (man's soul) or as a **Just Judge on a Cloud** (man's soul) to **Transform God's Kingdom** from **Death into New-life** (royal kingdom), thereby **Giving God's Saintly People** their own **Title Deed to God's Kingdom** (royal kingdom).

The following tabular information indicates that God is "Creating Three Kingdoms" to house the <u>Jews</u> (Earth), the <u>Christians</u> (Heaven), and <u>Saints</u> (Kingdom) through the manifestation of the Lord's **Church** (spiritual), **Government** (physical), and **Home** (mystical):

Establishment of God's Three Kingdoms
of the Jews, Christians, and the Saints Peoples
(Father's Jewish Kingdom,
Jesus' Christian Kingdom, and Prodigal Son's Pagan Kingdom)

Mystical (home)	1.	**God the Father** - <u>1st Kingdom:</u> Jewish Earth…Being Saved by Law
		• Good News - Free Redemption: Circumcised Blood/Water Baptism
		• Learning God's Will/man's will - Create Perfect Men: Perfection
		• Heaven on Earth - Repentance through Submission: Sonship = Sons
		• Free Gold Mine - God Pays Man's Sin-debt of Original Sin (capital)
		• Father Calls Only "Perfect People" - A = Students
		• Graded on Pass/Fail System - Direct Will: Superior Expectations
		• *Receive Royal Kingdom* - Perfect Man within the Kingdom
Spiritual (church)	2.	**Jesus Christ** - <u>2nd Kingdom:</u> Christian Heaven…Saving Self by Grace
		• Gospel Message - Earned Salvation: Soul Changing Confession
		• Learning Good from Evil - Create Perfect Society: Holiness
		• Heaven in God's Presence - Prayers through Sacrifice: Priesthood = Priests
		• Digging Out Gold - Paying One's Own Sin-debt of Personal Sins (mortal)
		• Son of God Calls "Semi-perfect People" - B/C/D Students

- Graded on a Curve System - Permissive Will: High Expectations
- *Receive Eternal Life* - Holy Man in Heaven

Physical 3. **Prodigal Son** - <u>3rd Kingdom:</u> Saintly Kingdom… Saving Others by Love
(government)
- Doctrinal Truths - Bonus Rewards: Inspirational Communion
- Learning Right from Wrong - Create Perfect Set of Friends: Righteousness
- Freedom in God's Kingdom - Works through Reconciliation: Kingship = Kings
- Sharing One's Gold - Paying Sin-debt of Other Sinners (venial)
- Son of Man Calls "Imperfect People" - F/drop-outs = Students
- Graded on Trying - Compromised Will: Rehabilitation Expected
- *Receive New Body* - Righteous Man on Earth

This illustration shows that the "Father's Kingdom Demands" <u>Absolute Perfection</u> so that He will one day establish **His Kingdom on Earth** (kingship), where **He will Live** with **His** most **Beloved Saints** in **Peace, Joy, and Happiness Forever.** Secondly, the "Son's Kingdom" expects <u>High Standards</u> so that He will one day establish His **Kingdom in Heaven** (priesthood), where **He will Live** with **His Holy Church** in **Peace, Joy, and Happiness Forever.** Finally, the "Prodigal Son" expects to <u>Rehabilitate the Lost</u> so that He will one day establish **His Kingdom of Glory** (sonship), where **He will Live** with His **Righteous/Holy/Perfect World** in **Peace, Joy, and Happiness Forever**. By visualizing the coming "Kingdom of God" in <u>Three Stages of Perfection,</u> it becomes clear that **Everyone in Society** will find his place in **God's Creation** either as a **Son** (home), **Priest** (church), or a **King** (government). We see that the "Sons of God" will be <u>Graded on a Pass/Fail System</u> as they **See Themselves** as **100% Perfect** in their **Own Self-evaluation.** Secondly, we see that the "Priests of God" will be <u>Graded on the Curve</u> (average) as God must **See Them** as **Getting a Passing Grade** based on **God's Judgment** (teenage level). Finally, we see that the "Kings of God" will be <u>Graded on Just Trying</u> (failures) as **Everyone will See Them** as **Failing Life** based on facing **Lucifer's Test of Ignorance** (baby level). In short, whether one is a "Son (God's Face)," "Priest (God's Temple)," and/or "King (God's City)," he must <u>See Himself</u> as a **Beloved Human being,** who has been **Chosen to Exist** (job) in the **Kingdom of God Somewhere.**

To comprehend "God's Kingdom," we must see the <u>Lord's Grand Design,</u> where **Earth is a Physical Realm** (flesh/kingship) which **Represents Death** (baby obedience) as **God becomes a Man** (Christmas) by **Teaching** the **Human Intellect** (mind) **Wrong** (human) and **Evil** (demonic). Secondly, "Heaven is a Spiritual Realm (spirit/priesthood)" which <u>Represents Life</u> (teenager/limitation) as **Man becomes God** (Easter) by **Teaching** the **Human Emotions** (heart) **Right** (human) and **Good** (angelic). Finally, the "Kingdom is a Mystical Realm (soul/sonship)" which <u>Represents Life/Death</u> (adult thinking) as **God and Man become One** (Halloween) by teaching Man's **Human Instincts** (soul) the difference between **God's Will** (divine) and **Man's Will** (human). Through these "Three Realms of Existence," a person can <u>Journey</u> from the **Nothingness of Ignorance** (baby) to the **All of Wisdom** (adult) via the **New Nature of Christ.**

Now, we must associate each of these "Three Realms of Education" with its Teaching Staff based on those who have the most experience with **Positive Forces** (right/good) and **Negative Forces** (wrong/evil). We see that obviously, the "Angels will Teach Good (emotions)" and the "Saints will Teach Right (intellect);" while the "Demons will Teach Evil (emotions)," and the "Damned will Teach Wrong (intellect)." But who will **Teach God's Will** and **Man's Will?** The answer is that "God's Will" is to be taught by God's Son, Christ (truth) via the **Eternal Father**; while "Man's Will" is to be taught by Mary's Son, Jesus (law) via the **Holy Spirit.** We can now see that "Earth" is God's Elementary School (baby farm) which will be **Taught** by the **Virgin Mary** with assistance from **Demons** (evil) and the **Damned** (wrong); while "Heaven" is God's High School (teenagers) to be **Taught** by **Saint Joseph** with assistance from **Angels** (good) and **Saints** (right). Next, the "Kingdom" will be God's College (adults) to be **Taught** by **Jesus Christ** with assistance from the **Holy Spirit** (man's will) and the **Eternal Father** (God's Will). This means that the Lord is creating His "Divine School of Higher Learning" out of Earth, Heaven, and the Kingdom based on how well one masters **God's Law** (height), **Man's Faith** (width), and **God's/Man's Knowing** (depth).

We are being told that "Earth" will define each child's Fixed Frame of Reference (truth) based on establishing his **Identity** (mind), **Character** (heart), and **Personality** (soul) by forcing him to **Face the Tests of Lucifer** (individual rights). Secondly, we are told that "Heaven" will define each person's Relative Focused Existence (law) based on establishing his **Righteousness** (mind), **Holiness** (heart), and **Perfection** (soul) by requiring each soul to **Face God's Judgment** (social rights). Finally, we are told that the "Kingdom" will define each person's Perception of Reality (will) based on establishing each individual's **Kingship** (mind), **Priesthood** (heart), and **Sonship** (soul) by **Facing** his own **Self-evaluation** (divine rights). This means that the whole "Process of Human Existence" is based on attaining one's New Body (obey law) from **Earth**, his Eternal Life (imitate Christ) from **Heaven,** and his Own Personal Kingdom (think for self) from **God**.

The following tabular information indicates that God's "Divine School of Higher Learning" is comprised of the Earth (life), Heaven (body), and the Kingdom (home) teaching **God's Children** the subjects of **Fixed Frame of Reference** (wrong/evil), **Relative Focused Existence** (right/good), and the **Perception of Reality** (God's/Man's Wills):

Earth, Heaven, and Kingdom Teach Man Fixed Reference,
Focused Existence, and Perceiving Reality
(obtaining a free body, gaining eternal life,
and getting own kingdom of glory before God)

Flesh   1. **Earth** - Fixed Frame of Reference (truth): Learning Wrong and
(mind)   Evil....Obey Law
                 • God becomes Man - Christmas: Life ....Individual Rights (self)
                 • Elementary School - Taught by *Virgin Mary*: Face Lucifer's Test
                   (passport)

- Assistant Teacher - **Damned** Teach Wrong: Intellect = Baby Grows
- Celestial Court - Judge Positive People: Repentant Sinners (criminal)
- Assistant Teacher - **Demons** Teach Evil: Emotions = Baby Matures
- Celestial Court - Judge Negative People: Lost Fools (insane)
- Graduation - Free New Body: Transfigured Human Body =
  Title Deed to Earth

(free redemption gives kingship - see life bottom to top/height: identify self)

Spirit 2. **Heaven** - <u>Relative Focused Existence</u> (law): Learning Right and
(heart)   Good...Imitate Christ
- Man becomes God - Easter: Death.... Social Rights (society)
- High School - Taught by **Saint Joseph**: Face God's Judgment (scored
  on curve)
- Assistant Teacher - **Saints** Teach Right: Intellect = Teenager Grows
- Temple Court - Judge Negative People: Remove Faults (innocent)
- Assistant Teacher - **Angels** Teach Good: Emotions = Teenager Matures
- Temple Court - Judge Positive People: Gain Virtues (sainthood)
- Graduation - Earned Eternal Life: Glorified Angelic Body = Title Deed
  to Heaven

(earned salvation gives priesthood - see life left to right/width: own character)

Instinct 3. **Kingdom** - <u>Perception of Reality</u> (will): Learn God's/Man's Wills ...
(soul)   Think for Self
- God and Man become One - Halloween: Resurrection—-Divine Rights
  (God)
- College - Taught by **Jesus Christ**: Face Self-evaluation (handicap system)
- Assistant Teacher - **Holy Spirit** Teaches Man's Will: Intellect =
  Adult Grows
- Royal Court - Judge Negative People: Sons of God (Christ-like)
- Assistant Teacher - **Eternal Father** Teaches God's Will: Emotions =
  Adult Matures
- Royal Court - Judge Positive People: Free Men (God-like)
- Graduation - Bonus Kingdom: Mystical Body of Christ = Title Deed to
  Kingdom

(bonus rewards give sonship - see life back to front/depth: create personality)

This illustration shows that "God is Running" a <u>Massive Processing Plant</u> **Using** (babies) **Spirit** (heart), **Flesh** (mind), **Souls** (being), and **Life-forces** (God) as **His Raw Materials** which are **Transformed** (crushed) into **Righteous Citizens** (earth), **Saintly People** (Heaven), **Sons of God** (Kingdom), and **Free Men** (God). We see that this "Eternal Process Begins" with <u>Mother Nature</u> (babies) **Creating** an **Infinite Number** of **Spiritual Life-forms** which are **Selected by God** (chosen) to be <u>**Made into Various Types**</u> of **Human Beings**. We are being told that "Raw Life-forms" are being <u>Processed</u> through the **Lord's Divine School of Higher Learning** to **Create Lost**

Fools, **Repentant Sinners, Innocent Children, Righteous Citizens, Holy Saints, Sons of God,** and **Free Men of Glory** <u>All in the Name</u> of *Divine Perfection* (God). This means a "Person can Possibly End Up" in <u>God's Royal Household</u> (Kingdom) **If he Dies to his Own Selfishness 100%,** or can become a **Nobleman** (Heaven) in **God's Leadership,** assuming he **Dies to his Own Selfishness 99% to 50%.** We see that "If a Person" Dies to Selfishness between **49% and 0%,** then he will become **Among** the **Work-a-Day Class, Destined to Live** an **Eternal Life of Mediocrity** or **Choose to Spend an Eternity Trying to** become **More** in the **Eyes of God** than in the **Selfish Eyes of himself.**

Now, we see that "Our Current Life-experience" is <u>Not some Silly Game</u> as it is <u>Dead Serious</u> when it comes to **Pleasing God,** by **Creating** an **Infinite Kingdom of Treasures** for the **Lord's** <u>Personal Enjoyment</u> as **Gifts of Life** to **All Who Love Him.** This means that "If a Person Graduates from Earth (elementary)," he will be <u>Given a Free Redemption</u> (defined in truth) in the **Form** of a **Kingship** (transfigured body) so that he **Sees his Own Life-experience, Bottom to Top** (height), thereby **Allowing him to Attain** his **Own Personal Identity.** Secondly, "If a Person Graduates from Heaven (high school)," he will be <u>Given an Earned Salvation</u> (obedience to the law) in the **Form** of a **Priesthood** (glorified body) to see **Life Left to Right** (width), thereby **Allowing him to Attain** his **Own Character.** Finally, "If a Person Graduates from God's Kingdom (college)," he will be <u>Given a Bonus Reward</u> (following the will) in the **Form** of a **Sonship** (mystical body) to see **Life Back to Front** (depth), thereby **Allowing him to Attain** his **Own Personality.**

In this way, a "Person" will be "Defined in Truth (identity)" as a <u>Member </u>of **Human/Angelic/Divine Society** and **Travel through All** of the <u>**Dimensions of Exis-tence**</u> by **Personal Recognition.** Secondly, a "Person" will become "Obedient to God's Law (character)" as a <u>Citizen</u> of <u>Earth, Heaven,</u> and the <u>Kingdom</u> to **Participate in All Aspects** of the **Life-experience** via his **Citizenship Eligibility** (passport). Finally, a "Person" will "Follow God's Will" as a <u>Royal Heir</u> to **Eternal Life, to a Perfect Body,** and His **Own Kingdom,** to **Own a Portion** of the <u>**Divine Nature**</u> by **God's Own De-cree.** We now see that by "Personal Recognition (face)," "Citizenship (passport)," and by "Ownership (title)," a **Person** can become a **beloved Member** of **Human, Angelic, and Divine Society,** thereby <u>Making him</u> a **King, Priest, and Son of God.**

Unfortunately, for a "New-born Soul" to <u>Reach this Awesome</u> **Divine State of Perfection** before **God,** it must **Begin** this **Eternal Journey** by becoming **Spiritually Perfect** (believe 100%) from <u>**Within its Own Nature**</u> (Christ-like) through its **Own Submission** (dying to self). We see that this "State of Perfection" has its <u>Centerpiece</u> within the **Four Cups** of the **Holy Mass** as seen through a **Marriage Union** between **God's Son, Jesus Christ** (groom) and **Man's Holy Church** (bride) via the <u>**Exchange**</u> of **God's Name** (divinity) for **Man's Virginity** (holiness). The idea here is to "See that Each" of the <u>Four Cups of the Mass</u> brings forth a **Union** of **Fathers, Couple, Friends, and Two Families** to bring <u>**Peace, Joy, and Happiness**</u> (universal harmony) to both **God and Man.** This "Need for Perfection" in <u>All Its Forms</u> of **Divine/Human Relations Demands** the <u>**Human Race**</u> to <u>**Wash Away Its Sins**</u> and also **Demands** that <u>**God Change His Nature**</u> from **Divine to Human.**

We see this "Process of Conversion" actually <u>Taking Place</u> within the **Holy Mass** through **the Offering of its Four Cups of Union, thereby bringing forth a New Set of Supernatural Laws** (canon) to <u>**Govern**</u> the **Divine/Human Wills of God and Man**. The idea here is to see that "Mankind" must <u>Wash Away Its Sins</u> (dowry/faith/holiness) to **Offer the Groom** a **Worthy Virgin** (honor God); while the "Lord God Almighty" must <u>Change His Nature</u> (bride price/law/divinity) to **Offer His Bride** a **Worthy Name** (honor man). Note that "During the Offering" of the <u>1st Cup</u> (exchange of bride price/dowry), **Father Abraham** is **Promising** to **Wash Away Sin** to become a **<u>Holy Saint</u>** before **God** (divinity); while **Father God** is **Promising to Change His Nature** to become a **<u>Righteous Human</u>** before **Man** (humanity). Secondly, in the "2nd Cup," the <u>Bride</u> (Church) is **Offering Her Virginity** as **Her Dowry** (wash/existence); while the <u>Groom</u> (Jesus) is **Offering His Respected Name** as **His Bride Price** (change/service). Thirdly, in the "3rd Cup," the <u>Bridesmaid of Honor</u> (laity) is **Offering Her Prayers** to **Save Sinners** (man's will); while the <u>Best Man</u> (priesthood) is **Offering His Works** to **Create Saints** (God's Will). Finally, in the "4th Cup," the <u>Bride's Family</u> (saints) is **Offering Planet Earth** to **Manifest Heaven on Earth** (man's illusion); while the <u>Groom's Family</u> (angels) is **Offering Heaven** to **Manifest Paradise in Heaven** (God's Reality). We see that in each of these "Four Cups of Unity," <u>God and Man</u> are becoming **Closer and Closer** to **Their Mutual Perfection** in **Mind, Heart, Soul, and Life-force** to **<u>Make Them One</u>** in **Friendship, Companionship,** and **Marriage** (oneness).

The following tabular information indicates that the "Four Cups" of the <u>Holy Mass</u> are **Defining the Union** of the **Fathers, Couple, Friends,** and **Families** during a **Marriage Ceremony** to bring forth an **<u>Ocean of Babies</u>** to become the **Future Children of God**:

Four Cups are Offering-up the Marriage Contract, Betrothal, Wedding Supper, and Wedding Feast
(1st cup is promise, 2nd cup is wash/change, 3rd cup removes sin/new-life, and 4th cup is new earth/new Heaven)

1st Cup	1. **Marriage Contract** - <u>Union of Two Fathers</u> ..... Offer Dowry/Bride Price
	• Father Abraham - Bread/Promise to Wash Away Sin: Become Saints (wrong)
Purify	• Gift - Number of Earthly Babies: Sand/Stars
Grave	• Father God - Wine/Promise to Change Man's Nature: Become Perfect (right)
	• Gift - Number of Heavenly Saints: Jews/Christians
	(learning right from wrong - righteous citizen on earth: given new body)

2nd Cup	2. **Betrothal** - <u>Union of Couple</u> .... Offer Virginity/Name
	• Bride/Church - Eat Raw Sin: Become Death (evil)
Purify	• Gift - Number of Sins Confessed: Repentance/Sacrifices
Host	• Groom/Jesus - Drink Repentance: Become New-life (good)
	• Gift - Number of Absolutions: Forgiveness/Washed Souls
	(learn good from evil - holy saint in Heaven: given eternal life)

3rd Cup	3. **Wedding Supper** - <u>Union of Friends</u> .... Offer Prayers/Works

3rd Cup   3. **Wedding Supper** - <u>Union of Friends</u> .... Offer Prayers/Works

- Bridesmaid/Laity - Eat Prayers: Save Sinners (man's will)

Purify

- Gift - Number of Living Prayers: Holy Graces/Earthly Wealth

Life

- Best Man/Priesthood - Drink Works: Create Saints (God's will)
- Gift - Number of Soldiers-of-the-Light: Holy Money/Heavenly Wealth

(learn God's will/man's will - perfect son within Kingdom: given royal kingdom)

4th Cup   4. **Wedding Feast** - <u>Union of Families</u>........... Offer Earth/Heaven

- Bride's Family/Saints - Eat Earth: Heaven on Earth (man's illusion)

Purify

- Gift - Number of Saintly Daughters: New Earth/kingdom

Eternal Life

- Groom's Family/Angels - Drink Heaven: Paradise in Heaven (God's reality)
- Gift - Number of Saintly Sons: New Heaven/New Jerusalem

(learn God's Reality/man's illusion - free man is master of all: given freedom)

This illustration shows that through the "Four Cups" of the <u>Holy Mass,</u> the **Marriage Vows** of **God and Man** are <u>**Given**</u> via the **Marriage Contract** (fathers), **Betrothal** (couple), **Wedding Supper** (friends), and **Wedding Feast** (family). This means that the "Two Fathers" must <u>Come Together</u> within the **Lord's Physical Dimension** (earth) to **Determine** the <u>Value</u> of **Man's Dowry** ($/number of babies) versus the <u>Value</u> of **God's Bride Price** ($/number of saints). Secondly, the "Couple (bride/groom)" must <u>Come Together </u>within the **Lord's Spiritual Dimension** (Heaven) to **Determine** the <u>Value</u> of **Man's Repentant Sinners** ($/conversions) versus the <u>Value</u> of **God's Forgiven Christians** ($/transformations). Thirdly, the "Friends (maid of honor/best man)" must <u>Come Together</u> within the **Lord's Mystical Dimension** (Kingdom) to **Determine** the <u>Value</u> of **Man's Living Prayers** ($/graces) versus the <u>Value</u> of **God's Soldiers-of-the-Light** ($/money). Finally, the "Families (saints/angels)" must <u>Come Together</u> within the **Lord's Divine Dimension** (God) to **Determine** the <u>Value</u> of **Man's Saintly Daughters** ($/slaves) versus the <u>Value</u> of **God's Saintly Sons** ($/free men).

We now see that through the "Treasure House (perfection)" of both <u>Man and God,</u> we can **Visualize Their Joint Venture** in **Building** a <u>**Universal Kingdom of Glory**</u> to **Serve** the **Needs/Wants of All God's Creatures.** Unfortunately, this "Mystical Joint Venture" requires that <u>Mankind becomes Perfect</u> and requires <u>God to become Human</u> to bring **Them Together** in a **Life of Peace, Joy, and Happiness.** The theme here is that "God Wants to become Man (Christmas)" and "Man Wants to become God (Easter)" and this can <u>Only be Done,</u> if they will **Unite Their Natures** via **Christ's Spiritual Perfection.** We now see that man's "Spiritual Perfection" will come from within to be <u>Manifested</u> in a **Person's Life** through a most strange **Power of Instinctive Compulsion** (automatic mode) leading a **Chosen Saint** to the **Holy Life** (knowing good/evil) of **Christ.** Recall that having a "Holy Life" occurs without <u>Experiencing any Conscious Realization</u> of any **Change in Behavior** either **Good or Bad.**

A "Christian" does not <u>Make himself Holy</u> by conquering **Faults** and practicing **Virtues** as is **Commonly Thought in Our Misled Churches Today. . . No**. We are miraculously given (gift) "Spiritual Form" which is placed within our <u>Humble and Contrite Hearts</u> (evil bears good fruit) of <u>Holy Love</u> bringing us to a **New State** of **True Spiritual Obedience** without **Our Conscious Knowledge** (instinctive compulsion) or without any **Noticeable Physical Change**. Anyone who seeks "God's Holy State" via his <u>Own Fleshly Pretense,</u> no matter how good he might be at **Acting Holy** or at pretending to **Practice** the **Saintly Virtues** of **Divine Truth** means that <u>He</u> is simply a **Self-righteous Fool,** who one day will **See himself** as he really is, a **<u>Conniving Fake</u>** (false face), who has **Achieved Nothing at All**. This means that what is "Going On in the Spirit" cannot be either <u>Seen or Felt</u> in the **Flesh**, implying that what a "Person is Doing in the Flesh" in the form of <u>Good Works</u> (meaningless) has absolutely **No Effect on his Spirit**.

Note that the "Human Flesh" must <u>Die to the Spirit of Christ</u> and then be <u>Born-again in the Person of Jesus</u> as a **Divine Spiritual Man** made **Perfect** in both **Destiny** (blood son/blessed) and **Free Will** (obedient son/lessons). It is written in "Numbers: Chapter 6," if an <u>Adult Jew</u> desires to enter the "Holiness of God" to communion with the Lord, a special provision has been made within the <u>Mosaic Law</u> (contemplative prayer) to **Allow a Person** to take a **<u>Nazarite Vow</u>** of **Absolute Obedience** to the **Divine Will of God**. A Jew could actually become "Holy" by spending <u>Seven Days</u> (week) in strict **Prayer and Fasting** within the **<u>Mosaic Tabernacle</u>** to experience the **Perfection of God for himself**. This means that **<u>God</u>** is creating an "Interior State of Formality (church)" out of **God's Divine Son** (perfection/time); while **<u>Man</u>** is creating an "Exterior State of Informality (home)" out of **Mary's Human Son** (imperfection/space). By "Blending" both the <u>Formal</u> (serious) and the <u>Informal</u> (relaxed) **Qualities of Man** into a **well-balanced Son of God**, the **<u>Lord Hopes to Create</u>** that most **Perfect Man for All Seasons** (righteous citizen/holy saint). The implication here is that "God has Cursed the Human Spirit" to <u>Pay Its Sin-debt</u> (temple tax); while "Man has Cursed himself with Ignorance," forcing the <u>Human Race</u> to <u>Work Hard</u> (offer lamb sacrifice/righteous man) enough to subdue **All the Forces of Evil** and **Set Itself Free**.

This concept for having "Christ Redeem Man's Spirit (heart/surrender)" and for having "Each Person Save himself (mind/fight evil)" <u>Explains why Neither</u> the **Redeemed Spirit** (Heaven) nor **<u>Man's Prosperous Flesh</u>** (earth) are **Connected in Any Way**. For this reason, "God Desires" both a "Divine Marriage (God/Mary)" and a "Human Marriage (Jesus/Church) to <u>Unite</u> the **Spirit World** (emotions) with the **Physical World** (intellect) in **Truth** (blood), **Law** (death), **Will** (damnation), **and Love** (oblivion). This "Two-Truth Concept (paradox)" of <u>Existence</u> (time/space) is causing so much **Confusion** and **Mystical Contradiction** in the **<u>Mind</u>** of **Every Person on Earth** be he either **great and small**. We see this "Confusion" in a "Devout Jew," who desires to <u>Enter God's Holiness</u> by promising to **Not Cut his Hair, Drink Wine,** or **Touch the Dead** during this sacred period; then on the eighth day, **Shave his Head** and **Burn his Hair** upon the **<u>Brazen Altar</u>** as a **Sacrifice unto the Lord**. This "Rite of Passage (Nazarite vow)" must be accomplished in both <u>Man's Spirit</u> (church/heart) and in <u>Man's Flesh</u> (world/mind) by **Dying to Selfishness** (nothing) and then by being **Born-again** (all) in God's **Truth** (fixed reference), **Law** (relative focus), **Will** (perception of reality), and **Love** (living reality).

The significance attached to this most unique "Nazarite Vow (holiness)" or <u>Contemplative Prayer</u> is that **Jesus was Called** the **Nazarene** in the **Spirit of Samson,** who made the **Nazarite Vow Famous** when he **Defeated the Philistines** by destroying the **Evil Temple of Baal.** Obviously, Jesus would also destroy the "Evil Jews" by destroying <u>Herod's Temple</u> and rebuilding it in **Three Days without Hands** by simply **Dying on Mount Calvary** and being **Resurrected** on the **Third Day.** In this lesson, we see that God has made a special arrangement with the "Jewish People (Nazarite Vow)" to allow them to become <u>Holy as God is Holy</u> for at least **One Week.** In contrast, when the "Messiah" would come, then <u>All Men</u> could become **Holy as God is Holy** at least in **Spirit** (heart) by simply being **Baptized, Confessing,** and going to **Communion** in the **Lord's Catholic Church.**

Recall that the whole reason for creating the "Mosaic Tabernacle" was to allow the <u>Human Race</u> to approach the <u>Lord without Fear</u> of being **killed by God's Fiery Glory,** for simply *Not being Holy.* We see that "Aaron's Two Sons (Nabad/Abihu)" were both <u>killed by</u> **God's Fiery Glory,** when they offered the **Lord Foreign Fire** and fell out of *Holiness* just for an *Instant.* We see that the "Two Sons of Aaron" found out that there were <u>No Mistakes Permitted</u> *If a Person* is in the *Presence of God.* This startling event shows us what happens when a person faces the "Divine Judgment of God" and <u>Pays the Ultimate Price</u> in a single *Moment of Truth.* This logic explains why "Jesus Christ" was "Executed on Mount Calvary" after He <u>Gave-up His Divinity to Humanity</u> (Mary's Son) during His **Agony in the Garden** and went to His **Death as a Worthless Sinner,** without *God's Divine Holiness* (Nazarite Vow) to *Protect Him* from the *Forces of Sin, Evil, and Death.* Obviously, the "Lord" was willing to Go to Calvary (sin/evil/death/damnation) to give Him the **Authority** to **Convert the World** (Jews), **Church** (gentiles), **Angels** (good), **Saints** (holy), **Earth** (son of man), **Hell** (damned), **Gehenna** (demons), all in the name of *Divine Fairness.*

Jesus Christ Creates Eight Tickets to God's Forgiveness
(God's son paid in fear, pain, evil, death, damnation, oblivion, and resurrection)

1. Convert World - Save Traitors: My God, My God, Why
   Have You Forsaken Me ....Jews
2. Convert Church – Save Neighbors: I Thirst.............................Gentiles
3. Convert Angels – Save Family: Son, behold your Mother/Mother,
   Behold your Son ....Good
4. Convert Saints – Save Friends: This Day You will be with
   Me in Paradise ....Holy
5. Convert Earth – Save Strangers: It is Finished ....Sons of Man
6. Convert Heaven – Save Self: I Release My Spirit ....Sons of God
7. Convert Hell – Save Enemies: Forgive Them for They Know
   Not What They Are Doing ....Damned

Through this "Awesome Sacrifice," <u>God</u> would bring forth His <u>Physical World</u> of **Jews/Gentiles** (earth), His <u>Spirit World</u> of **Angels and Saints** (Heaven), His <u>Mystical World</u> of **Blood/Adopted Sons**, and finally, His <u>Divine World</u> of **Damned/Demons**, all to teach God's **Infinite Truths** to **His New-born babies**. Through the "Creation" of God's <u>Divine School of Higher Learning</u>, **God, Angels, and Men** would become **One** in **Truth, Law, Will, and Love Forever**. This means that God is "Creating Eight Stages of Existence," each designed to <u>Produce</u> something of **Great Value to God** which are: 1) <u>Transfigured Bodies</u> - Feed Starving Christ's Host, 2) <u>Eternal Lives</u> - Clothe Naked in God's Glory, 3) <u>Personal Kingdoms</u> - Remove Slavery (servanthood), 4) <u>Universal Freedom</u> - Homeless Receive New Homes, 5) <u>Glorified Bodies</u> - Sinfulness Forgiven, 6) <u>Divine Life</u> - Evil Souls are Pardoned, 7) <u>Kingdom of Glory</u> - Dead Souls are Given New-life, and 8) <u>Independence</u> - Damned Souls are Resurrected. At each of these "Levels of Conversion," the entire <u>Kingdom</u> can be **Saved** from **Starvation** (world), **Nakedness** (church), **Slavery** (Angels), **Homelessness** (saints), **Sinfulness** (earth), **Evilness** (Heaven), **Death** (hell), and **Damnation** (demons) by the **Sacrifice of Jesus Christ**.

We can now imagine the "Symbolism" of <u>God Saving Eight People</u> at the **Time of Noah.** The Lord was saying that the **Ark** would be **Christ's Church** and that the **Eight People in the Ark** would be: (1)the **World**, (2) **Church**, 3) **Angels**,(4) **Saints**, (5) **Earth**, (6) **Heaven**, (7) **Hell**, and (8) **Gehenna** . Through these "Eight Dimensions of Existence," we see God's coming <u>Divine School of Higher Learning</u> which will **Teach Each of God's Children** his own **Fixed Frame of Reference** (identity), giving him a **Relative Focused Existence** (character), and a new **Perception of Reality** (personality) to allow him to *See, Hear, and Speak to his Creator God.*

The following tabular information indicates that "God has Focused" His <u>Redemptive Power</u> on **Saving** the **Jewish World, Gentile Church, Good Angels, Holy Saints, Earthly Sonship, Heavenly Sonship, Damned of Hell,** and the **Demons of Gehenna**:

Saving the World, Church, Angels, Saints, Earth,
Heaven, Hell, and Gehenna as Divine Teachers
(the physical world, spirit world, mystical world,
and divine world serve the needs of God)

Man's Truth	1. **Jewish World** - <u>Physical Nature:</u> Air Contract (solemn word)...... Knowledge
	• First Person Saved - Father Noah: God Bless You = Man's Friendship
	• Forgive Them for They Know Not What They Do - Save Strangers
	• Save Physical Mind - Starvation: Christ's Host = Transfigured Body
	• Learn Right - Righteous Citizen of Earth: Thought of by God
Man's Law	2. **Gentile Church** - <u>Physical to Spiritual:</u> Water Contract (bless)....Self-awareness

		• Second Person Saved - Noah's Wife: God Keep You = Guest of Honor
		• On This Day You shall be with Me in Paradise - Save Friends
		• Save Physical Heart - Nakedness: God's Glory = New Eternal Life
		• Learn Wrong - Righteous Citizen of Earth: Spoken to by God
Man's Will	3.	**Good Angels** - <u>Spiritual Nature:</u> Oil Contract (anoint)…Consciousness
		• Third Person Saved - Son Ham: God's Face Shines on You = God's Love
		• Mother behold Thy Son, Son behold Thy Mother - Save Family
		• Save Physical Soul - Slavery: Servanthood = New Kingdom
		• Learn Good - Holy Saint in Heaven: Touched by God
Man's Love	4.	**Holy Saint** - <u>Spiritual to Mystical:</u> Blood Contract (sanctify)…..Sentience
		• Fourth Person Saved - Son Ham's Wife: God's Grace upon You = God's Wealth
		• I Thirst - Save Closest Neighbors
		• Save Physical Life-force - Homelessness: New Homes = Freedom
		• Learn Evil - Holy Saint in Heaven: Sup with God
God/Man Survival	5.	**Earthly Sonship** - <u>Mystical Nature:</u> Death Contract (consecrate)…Calling
		• Fifth Person Saved - Son Shem: God Lifts-up His Countenance = God's Adoption
		• My God, My God, Why have You Forsaken Me - Save All Traitors
		• Save Spiritual Mind - Sinfulness: Forgiveness = Glorified Body
		• Learn God's Will - Son of God within Kingdom: Adopted by God
God's Truth	6.	**Heavenly Sonship** - <u>Mystical to Divine:</u> Damnation Contract (worship) … Enlightenment
		• Sixth Person Saved - Son Shem's Wife: God Gives You His Peace = Citizenship
		• It is Finished – Save All Enemies
		• Save Spiritual Heart - Evilness: Pardoned = Divine Life
		• Learn man's will - Son of Man within Kingdom: Blood Son of God

- -

God's Love	7.	**Damned of Hell** - <u>Divine Nature:</u> Oblivion Contract (praise)… Awakening
		• Seventh Person Saved - Son Japheth: God shall put His Name on You = Ownership
		• I Release My Spirit - Save All Lost Humans
		• Save Spiritual Soul - Death: New-life = New Kingdom of Glory
		• Learn God's Reality - Damned in Hell: Divine Son of God
Free Choice	8.	**Demons of Gehenna** - <u>Divine to God:</u> New-life Contract (thanks)….. Indwelling
		• Eighth Person Saved - Son Japheth's Wife: God shall Set You Free = Freedom
		• Moment of Silence - Save All Murderers
		• Save Spiritual Life-force - Damnation: Resurrection = Independence
		• Learn Man's Illusion - Demons in Gehenna: Set Free by God

This illustration shows that "Father Noah" was bringing <u>God's Blessing</u> (helping hand); his "Wife" was bringing <u>God to Keep You</u> (offer room); his "Son Ham" was bringing <u>God's Face to Shine upon You</u> (God's smile); "Ham's Wife" was bringing <u>God's Grace upon You</u> (God's forgiveness); through "Noah's Son Shem," <u>God Lifts-up His Countenance upon You</u> (royal seat); "Shem's Wife" insures that <u>God Gives You Peace</u> (personal kingdom); "Noah's Son Japheth" reveals that <u>God will put His Name on You</u> (new name); and finally, his "Wife" reveals that <u>God will Set You Free</u> (freedom). We see that each of "God's Children" can receive each of these <u>Eight Gifts of Conversion,</u> if he will simply **grow-up** and **Learn his Lessons of Life** by **Surrendering his Life** to **Nature, Man, Angels, and God**.

Recall that when "Jesus" was on <u>His Cross of Death,</u> He **Spoke Seven Last Words** plus a **Moment of Silence** to <u>Save the Lost of the World</u> at **Any Cost**. The Lord said: "Forgive Them for They Know Not What They Do" to <u>Save All Strangers.</u> "This Day You will be with Me in Paradise" to <u>Save All His Friends.</u> "Mother, behold Thy Son and Son, behold Thy Mother" to <u>Save All His Family.</u> "I Thirst" to <u>Save All His Close Neighbors.</u> "My God, My God, Why have you Forsaken Me?" to Save All Traitors. "It is Finished" to Save All God's Enemies. "Into Your Hands I Release My Spirit" to <u>Save Lost Humans.</u> Finally, "Christ's Moment of Silence" to <u>Save All Murderers</u> (Barabbas). Through these "Eight Redemptions of Life," we can find <u>Our Own Redemption</u> either as an **Enemy to God** (Demons of Gehenna), a **Traitor to God** (Damned of Hell), a **Wicked Murderer of God's Son** (Jewish World), a **Stranger to God** (Gentile Church), a **Neighbor to God** (Holy Saints), a **Friend of God** (Good Angels), or finally a **Family Member to God** (Earthly Sonship), and a **Son of God** (Heavenly Sonship). The implication is that the "Life-experience" is divided into <u>Two Truths:</u> one of **Physical Life** (Man/earth/evil spirit/curse), and one of **Spiritual Life** (God/Heaven/Holy Spirit/blessing), thereby giving God **Enemies, Traitors, Murderers,** and **<u>Strangers</u>** on **One Side** (negative) with **<u>Neighbors,</u> Friends, <u>Family,</u>** and **Sons** on the **Other Side** (positive).

The following tabular information indicates that there are "Four Negative Groups" <u>Against God's</u> **Divine Countenance** (enemies/traitors/murderers/ strangers); while there are "Four Positive Groups" <u>For God's</u> **Divine Countenance** (neighbors, friends, family and sons):

Enemies, Traitors, Murderers, Strangers, Neighbors, Friends, Family, and Sons of the Almighty
(God saves demons of Gehenna, damned of hell,
Jews, gentiles, saints, angels, and God's sons)

Friendship (knowledge)	1.	**Enemy of God** - <u>Demons of Gehenna:</u> Eternal Slave to God......Truth
		• Overcome Demonic Possession - Sacrifice of Lucifer (1st angel)
		• Attend School of Evil - Learn Not to be Ignorant
Honor (self-awareness)	2.	**Traitors to God** - <u>Damned of Hell</u>: Eternal Servant to God..... Law
		• Overcome Worldly Temptations - Sacrifice of Adam (1st man)
		• Attend School of Death - Learn Not to be a Coward
God's Love	3.	**Murderer of God's Son** - <u>Jewish World</u>: Eternal Citizen to God.... Will

(consciousness)
- Overcome Man's Sin-nature - Sacrifice of 1st Society (1st family)
- Attend Elementary School - Learn Right from Wrong

Wealth   4. **Stranger to God** - <u>Gentile Church:</u> Eternal Employee to God ...... Love
(sentience)
- Overcome Man's Wicked Faults - Sacrifice of Chosen People (1st nation)
- Attend High School - Learn Good from Evil

- -

Adoption   5. **Neighbor to God** - <u>Holy Saints:</u> Eternal Leader of God .... Venerate
(calling)
- Gain Man's Righteous Virtues - Sacrifice of Messiah (1st Son of God)
- Attend College - Learn God's Will from man's will

Citizenship   6. **Friend unto God** - <u>Good Angels:</u> Eternal Nobleman to God.... Adore
(enlightenment)
- Gain Man's Holy Virtues - Sacrifice of Holy Church (1st holy nation)
- Attend On-the-Job Training Classes - Learn God's Reality/man's illusion

Ownership   7. **Family of God** - <u>Earthly Sonship:</u> Eternal Royalty before God ..... Exalt
(awakening)
- Gain Man's Perfect Virtues - Sacrifice of Pagan World (1st world)
- Enter One's Professional Career - Teach the Meaning of Life

Independence   8. **Son of God** - <u>Heavenly Sonship:</u> Eternal Son on Right of God .... Worship
(indwelling)
- Serve God with Whole Being - Sacrifice of Whole Creation (1st life)
- Enter God's Royal Palace - Teach the Purpose of Life

This illustration shows that the "Redemption of Noah's Family" of <u>Eight Members</u> had a **Great Significance** as it **Symbolized** the **Lord's Coming Eight Categories** or **Dimensions of Life** that are to be **Included** within **God's Kingdom of Glory**. This meant that "All of God's" <u>Physical</u> (earth), <u>Spiritual</u> (Heaven), <u>Mystical</u> (Kingdom), and <u>Divine Creation</u> (Messiah) would **Play a Role** in the **Birth** and **Raising** of **His Human Babies** as **They Come** forth from **Nothing** (never-created life) to **All** (created life). We can now grasp the importance of "Noah's Ark as he Faced" the <u>Absolute Wrath of God</u> and **Passed the Lord's Divine Judgment**, when **Everyone Else** had **Failed** and was **Washed Away in God's Great Flood of Divine Hatred.** We see this same theme being applied to the "Jewish People," the "Christian Church," the "Righteous World," and even "God's Kingdom of Glory" as <u>They Each Faces</u> the **Tests of Lucifer** (demonic possession), the **Judgment of God** (worldly temptations), and one's **Own Self-evaluation** (sin-nature).

We see that out of the "Personal Actions of Noah," God has created both the <u>Jewish</u> (earth/law) and <u>Christian</u> (Heaven/faith) <u>Religions:</u> one comprised of **Seven Feasts** (being saved), and the other comprised of **Seven Sacraments** (saving self). The idea here is that out of the "Jewish Feasts" is to come <u>Seven Sacrificial Offerings</u> designed to **Convert the Physical Life-experience** into **Heaven on Earth** (kingship). Secondly, out of the "Christian Sacraments" is to come <u>Seven Divine Blessings</u> designed to **Convert the Spiritual Life-experience** into **Paradise in Heaven** (priesthood). The question is "Why Noah's Ark has" been selected to represent the <u>Conversion</u> of both **Man's Physical Nature** and **Man's Spiritual Nature** based on the following **Seven Events**: 1) <u>Animals Placed in Ark</u> - Believe God, 2) <u>Family Placed in Ark</u> - Trust God, 3) <u>God Closed Ark's Door</u> - Faith in God, 4) <u>Land on Mt. Ararat</u> - Know God, 5) <u>Dry Land Returns</u> - Love God, 6) <u>Release Birds</u> (raven/dove) - Serve God, and 7) <u>Olive Branch</u> - Adopted by God.

The answer is that "Noah's Ark" represents a <u>Lost Broken Sinner</u> entering his **Transformation like an Animal** going through the **Process of Conversion** (sainthood) and then **Coming Out of the Ark** in a **Newly Cleaned Creation** ready to live in a **Holy World of Perfection.** Secondly, we see that "Noah's Ark" also represents both the <u>Jewish Temple</u> (Ark of the Covenant) and the <u>Christian Church</u> (Virgin Mary as the Ark) where they perform the same function as **Noah's Ark** by both **Transforming** (flesh) and **Purifying** (spirit) **People** into **Righteous Citizens on Earth** (take-sin/repentance) and **Holy Saints in Heaven** (give divinity/forgiveness).

The following tabular information indicates the "Basic Functions" governing "Noah's Ark (animals)," the "Jewish Temple (feasts)," and the "Catholic Church (sacraments)" as they <u>Come from God</u> to **Change** (nature), **Convert** (people), and **Transform** (saints) His most **Perfect Creation into New-life:**

Noah's Ark, the Jewish Temple, and Christian Church Convert Death into New-life
(nature becomes people who become saints
through the transformation of flesh and spirit)

Noah's Ark (nature/life)	Jewish Temple (people/flesh)	Christian Church (saints/spirit)
1. Animals Enter Ark	**Feast of Passover**	**Sacrament of Baptism**
• Believe God	• Master Good Taste	• Forgive Capital Sin
2. Family Enters Ark	**Feast of Unleavened bread**	**Sacrament of Confession**
• Trust God	• Master Honesty	• Forgive Mortal Sin
3. **God Closes Ark Door**	**Feast of Firstfruits**	**Sacrament of Communion**
• Faith in God	• Master Charity	• Forgive Venial Sin
4. **Lands on Mt. Ararat**	**Feast of Pentecost**	**Sacrament of Confirmation**
• Know God	• Master Love	• Remove Wicked Faults
5. **Dry Land Returns**	**Feast of Trumpets**	**Sacrament of Marriage**
• Love God	• Master Good Values	• Gain Virtue of Righteousness
6. Releases Birds (raven/dove)	**Feast of Atonement**	**Sacrament of Holy Orders**
• Serve God	• Master Good Judgment	• Gain Virtue of Holiness
7. **Olive Branch**	**Feast of Tabernacles**	**Sacrament of Last Rites**
• Adopted by God	• Master Humility	• Gain Virtue of Perfection
8. Dove Never Returns	**Feast of Last Supper**	**Sacrament of Resurrection**
• Set Free	• Master Unselfishness	• Gain Virtue of Sainthood

This illustration shows that the "Nature of Earth" has been <u>Washed and Renewed by Noah</u> leading to the "Purification of Man" via the <u>Jewish People,</u> their **Temple** (priesthood), **Throne** (kingship), and **Messiah/Palace** (sonship). Secondly, "Noah" leads to the "Transformation of Man" via the <u>Christian People</u> through their **Worship** (give life), **Praise** (give wealth), and **Thanksgiving** (give labor).

Finally, "Father Noah" leads to the Conversion of Man via the **Righteous World** through its **Government** (truth), **Church** (law), and **Home** (will). Through the "Creation of Each of these Institutions," the Human Race is able to get a grasp of the very **Meaning of Life** (exist), **Purpose of Life** (serve), and the **Value of Life** (happiness) based on the **Level of Maturity** of one's **Mind** (intellect), **Heart** (emotions), **Soul** (instincts), and **Life-force** (nature). To comprehend "God's Grand Design," a Person must be Introduced to the **Lord's Five Dimensions:** 1) Physical Dimension - Noah's Ark: Temple, Throne, and Messiah (palace); 2) Spiritual Dimension - Jewish Temple: Worship, Praise, and Thanksgiving; 3) Mystical Dimension - Christian Church: Government, Church, and Home; 4) Divine Dimension - Righteous World: Meaning, Purpose, and Value; and 5) Godly Dimension - Kingdom of Glory: Self, Society, and God. In truth, there are "Two More Dimensions" but only attributed to God's Divinity or His Paradox which is (6) **Nothing** and (7) **All,** but these **Concepts of Existence** are far above the **Human Mind**. Through the "Five Dimensions" depicted here, a person can get a Composite View of the **Entire Life-experience** as it relates to **Nature, Oneself, Earth, Kingdom, and God Himself.**

The following tabular information indicates that the function of "Noah's Ark," the "Righteous World," and God's "Kingdom of Glory" is to **Change** (nature), **Convert** (earthly life) and **Transform** (eternal life) the **Lord's Chaotic Existence** (death) into **God's most Perfect Order** (life):

Noah's Ark, Righteous World, and Kingdom of Glory Convert Wicked Sinners into Holy Saints
(nature becomes citizens who become sons
through the transformation of flesh and spirit)

Noah's Ark	Righteous World	Kingdom of Glory
(nature/life)	(citizen/soul)	(sonship/life-force)
1. Animals Enter Ark	**Love of Parents**	**Thinking for Himself**
• Believe God	• Growing-up	• Believe in Christ
2. Family Enters Ark	**Properly Behaved**	**Vibrant Imagination**
• Trust God	• Submission	• Fight Evil
3. God Closes Ark Door	**Educated**	**Celestial Government**
• Faith in God	• Good Judgment	• Save Souls
4. Lands on Mt. Ararat	**Career**	**Sacred Church**
• Know God	• Hard-working	• Learn Lessons
5. Dry Land Returns	**Loving Family**	**Royal Home**
• Love God	• Self-control	• Righteous (right/wrong)
6. Releases Birds	**Prosperity**	**Perfect Self**
• Serve God	• Leadership	• Holy (good/evil)
7. Olive Branch	**Family Name**	**Beatific Vision**
• Adopted by God	• Ownership	• Perfect (God's/Man's Wills)

8. Dove Never Returns	Saintly Life	Friendship of God (covenant)
• Set Free	• Honors	• Divinity (reality/illusion)
New World	**New Soul**	**New Life-force**
• Natural	• Mystical	• Divine

This illustration shows that the "Human Race" is being called to Grow-up and <u>Love One's Parents</u> to become <u>Properly Behaved, Study to be Educated, Work hard, and Build a Career</u>, establish a <u>Loving Family,</u> become <u>Prosperous in the Community,</u> have a <u>Good Family Name,</u> and <u>Lead a Saintly Life.</u> This means that if a person "Grows-up Correctly" and strives to become a <u>Man for All Seasons,</u> he can then expect to **Master the Institutions** of <u>**Government**</u> (flesh), **Church** (spirit), and **Home** (soul) allowing an **Awakened Soul** to be **Called from Death to New-life.** Recall that when "Father Noah" overcame both the <u>Hatred of Man</u> and the <u>Elements of Nature,</u> he then established a **New-life** in a **New World** and then he was **Richly Rewarded by God** via his **Own Covenant** (rainbow). If we consider the fact that "Noah (physical)," "Abraham (spiritual)," and "Jesus (mystical)" have cleared the path from <u>Nothing</u> (life) to <u>All</u> (eternal life), we can see it is simply **Our Job to Try Our Best** to become **Great in the Eyes of God, Society, and Ourselves.** It is said that the "Life-experience" is comprised of facing <u>Lucifer's Test</u> (physical), <u>God's Judgment</u> (spiritual), and <u>Our Own Evaluation</u> (mystical) and you can imagine that the **Hardest of these Evaluations** will be **Our Own.**

Obviously, life is about "Time (life)" and "Resources (bodies)." Thus, we must <u>Learn the Lessons</u> of **Balancing and Synchronizing Everything** to get the greatest amount of **Efficiency** to produce the **Best Results Possible.** The question is: do we "Master" the <u>Physical, Spiritual, Mystical, Divine,</u> and/or <u>Godly Dimensions</u> or simply **Try to Balance Them All** into one **State of Perfection** and then **Present these Results to God** for **His Blessing**? The answer is to "Surrender" to <u>Christ's Church,</u> and then adopt a philosophy of **Unto Thine Own Self be True** by following one's **Guilty Conscience** to the **Letter,** and then simply **Fight Evil,** and **Learn the Lessons of Life** (instinctive compulsion). This is a more roundabout way of saying that "God Calls Mankind" to <u>Holiness</u> by learning the important <u>Lessons of Life</u> and by being **Smart where the Skin is Off** (thinking for oneself/bear fruit). In this way, "God is Making" <u>Every Struggling Soul Worthy</u> of **His Divine Light of Truth** through the **Power of Submission** (abandonment), **Power of Sacrifice** (conversion), and the **Power of Reconciliation** (freedom). Obviously, this means that everyone must "Find God the Hard-way" and <u>Do It Right</u> the next time as the **Lesson** (becoming truth) is more **Important** than the **Sweet Taste of Success** (thrill of victory). Certainly, this is the way that most of us have had to "Learn Our Lessons of Life," become <u>Truly Wise,</u> **Out** of the **Painful Experiences** of **Our** most **Humiliating Failures** (agony of defeat).

Yes! It is out of "One's Failures" that a <u>Person</u> becomes **Smart, Where the Skin is Off** (experience) showing that through both **Growth and Maturity,** a **Person Masters** his **Own Ignorant, Criminal, Insane, and Evil Behavior.** We see that one's "Ignorant Behavior" can be <u>Overcome</u> by **Surrendering to Christ** as a **Person** (baby) is **Taught Right from Wrong** through the **Forces of Correct Instruction** (knowledge). Secondly, his "Criminal Behavior" can be <u>Overcome</u> by **Using Effective Teaching Techniques** as He (teenager) is **Taught Good from Evil** through the **Forces of Dynamic Education** (self-awareness). Thirdly, his "Insane Behavior" can be <u>Overcome</u> by **Dedicated Policing** as a **Person** (adult) is **Taught God's Will from man's will** through the **Forces of Personal Rehabilitation** (consciousness). Finally, his "Evil Behavior" can be <u>Overcome</u> by becoming a **Law-abiding Citizen** as **He** (wise man) is **Taught God's Reality from man's Illusion** through the **Forces of Self-control** (sentience).

In each of these "Stages of Growth," a <u>Person can See</u> his **Limitations, Potential, Self-worth,** and finally, **See God Himself.** The idea here is that a "Baby" <u>Faces being Excommunicated from the Temple</u> for **Violating his Family's Rules** and must **Repent** to be **Forgiven for his Sins** and **Restored Back to his Family's Good Graces.** Secondly, a "Teenager" <u>Faces becoming an Outcast from his People</u> for **Violating Society's Laws** and must **Pay his Debt** to be **Honored** with the <u>**Gift of Life**</u> and a **Place Within His Community.** Thirdly, an "Adult" <u>Faces being Banished from Earth</u> (executed) for **Violating both Man's and God's Laws** and must **Pay the Ultimate Price** to **Reconcile himself Back as a Man of Virtue** (fruits) **in Good Standing.** Finally, a "Wise Man" <u>Faces being Forsaken by God</u> (damned) for **Violating God's Will** and must **Pay with his Soul** to **Resurrect** (treasure) from **Damnation by Defeating his Own Sinfulness.** At each of the "Stages of Conversion," a <u>Person</u> can **Overcome** <u>**Ignorance, Criminal, Insane,**</u> **and** <u>**Evil Behavior**</u> to become an **Eternal Servant unto the Lord.**

Man is Called to Parenting, Teaching, Policing, and being a Law-abiding Citizen before God
(parenting brings righteousness/teaching brings
holiness/policing brings perfection/law brings freedom)

Ignorance 1. **Parenting** - <u>Righteous Man:</u> Knows Right from Wrong .... Knowledge
(home)
- Kingship - Rules Physical Creation: In-charge of *New Bodies* (tasks)
- 1st Faces Excommunication from Temple - Caiaphas (stick): Guilty
- 2nd Receives Forgiven Sin (virtues) from Church - Christ (carrot): Innocent
- Book of Matthew - Jews become Righteous: Think of God (see limitations)

(righteousness creates righteous citizen on earth - worthy of new body)

Criminal 2. **Teaching** - <u>Holy Man:</u> Knows Good from Evil ...... Self-awareness
(government)
- Priesthood - Rules Spiritual Creation: In-charge of *Eternal Life* (duty)
- 1st Faces being Outcast from People - Herod (stick): Abstained
- 2nd Receives God's Gift (life) from Saints - Christ (carrot): Neutral Book of Luke - Gentiles become Holy: Speak to God (see potential)

(holiness creates holy saints in Heaven - worthy of eternal life)

Insane	3.	**Policing** - <u>Perfect Man:</u> Knows God's Will/man's will...... Consciousness
(church)		• Sonship - Rules Mystical Creation: In-charge of ***Royal Kingdoms*** (responsibility)
		• 1st Faces being Banished from Earth - Pilate (stick): Innocent
		• 2nd Receives God's Fruits (new-life) from Angels - Christ (carrot): Guilty
		• Book of Mark - Christians become Perfect: Touch God (see self-worth)

(perfection creates perfect son within Kingdom - worthy of royal kingdom)

Evil	4.	**Law-abiding** - <u>Free Man:</u> Know God's Reality/man's illusion .... Sentience
(God)		• Freedom - Rules Divine Creation: In-charge of ***Personal Freedom*** (authority)
		• 1st Faces being Forsaken by God - Lord God Almighty (stick): Convicted
		• 2nd Receives God's Treasures from God - Christ (carrot): Pardoned
		• Book of John - Saints become Free: Becoming God (see God)

(freedom creates free man within Self - worthy of freedom from death)

This illustration shows that through "God's Kingship (Earth)," <u>Righteousness Creates</u> **Righteous Citizens on Earth** to become **Worthy of Supplying God's Kingdom with All** the **New Bodies the Lord might Ever Need.** Secondly, through "God's Priesthood (Heaven)," <u>Holiness Creates</u> **Holy Saints in Heaven** to become **Worthy of Supplying God's Kingdom with All** the **Eternal Lives the Lord might Ever Need.** Thirdly, through "God's Sonship (Kingdom)," <u>Perfection Creates</u> **Perfect Sons within God's Kingdom** to become **Worthy of Supplying God's Kingdom with All** the **Royal Kingdoms the Lord might Ever Need.** Finally, through "God's Free Man (God)," <u>Divinity Creates</u> **Free Men within God's Kingdom** to become **Worthy of Supplying God's Kingdom with All** the **Natures of Freedom the Lord might Ever Need.**

Note that in the "Book of Matthew," the <u>Author is Describing</u> the **Righteous Man** or a **Jew** who desires to **Raise a Family, Build a Home,** and **Perform his Job** with **Excellence, All in the Name of Righteousness.** Secondly, in the "Book of Luke," the <u>Author is Describing</u> the **Holy Man** or a **Gentile,** who desires to **Worship, Praise, and Thank his God** in **Absolute Submission, All in the Name of Holiness.** Thirdly, in the "Book of Mark," the <u>Author is Describing</u> the **Perfect Man** or a **Christian,** who desires to **Help his Community** and **Save the Souls of Others, All in the Name of Perfection.** Finally, in the "Book of John," the <u>Author is Describing</u> the **Free Man** or a **Saint** who desires to come to **Know, Love, and Serve his God, All in the Name of Eternal Freedom.** Now, we see that "Matthew," "Mark," "Luke," and "John" have <u>All Mentioned</u> the **Righteousness, Holiness, Perfection, and Freedom of God** to **Show Mankind** the **Way to Eternal Life.** This means that "Life is a Beautiful Fantasy" where a <u>Child Can Dream</u> the **Impossible Dream** of a **Future World of Magical Wonders and Infinite Possibilities.**

Now, we might better "Understand the Fantasies" which We Find at Our Local Magic Kingdom (Disneyland) that **Gives Us a Perfect Analogy** for **Comprehending** the coming **Kingdom** of **Mystical Growth** and **Maturity** (learning) that brings **Us God's Divine Fulfillment** (knowing). We are fully aware that a "Child must have the Maturity" to go on the "Big Scary Rides" to Experience the Spiritual Pain of his **Own Fiery Love and Share the Fantasy** with the **Future Heroines and Heroes** of the **Fairy tale World** of **Make-believe**. In ancient times, a "Fairy" was thought to be a goddess of Joyous Fates bringing a **Person** the **Treasures of Eternal Happiness Out** of the **Blessings of Youthful Thinking** (playful), thereby **Making Life** truly **Fun** and a **Joy for All Ages**. This "Power of Youthful Imagination (creativity)" is Taken Away from the **Human Race** as **Each Generation** is **Forced to Shoulder** more and more **Responsibility** (toil), in **Service to its Growing Massive World System**. In this theme of being "Worked to Death (toil)," the Men of the World are **Overwhelmed**; then the **Women,** and finally, even the **Children** are **Pressed into Service** as **Slaves** to the **System of Material Wealth**. This "Work, Work, and then Work" some more mentality (bucket) has finally Crushed Out Any and All Hope of **Finding** a **Happy Life**, much **Less Allowing Any Room** for a **Person's Unrestricted Imagination**. This means that the "Life-experience" is a Hell of Continual Work (money) and an Endless Prayer (worship) **Leaving No Time** to **Dream One's Dream** of **Delightful Fantasies** (happiness).

By "Conquering the Demand" for Endless Work and Endless Prayer, a **Person is Set Free** from his **Meaningless Existence** and can then **Start his New-life** of **Challenge, Adventure, and Fun** with **Men, Angels, and God**. The question is just: "What Ends the Drudgery of Life" and "Begins the Joys of Life?" The answer is by Mastering **Grammar, Mathematics, Symbols, Wants, Likes, Loves, Needs, Possessions,** and finally, **Ownership**. In short, the "Mind is Called (logic)" to Learn **Syntax Structure** (words), the Formulation of **Numeric Expressions** (equations), and Define **Symbolic Meaning** (signs). Secondly, the "Heart is Called (feelings)" to Learn **Personal Wants, Individual Likes, and Devotional Loves** as **They Reflect** the **Meaning** (existence), **Purpose** (service), and **Values** (happiness) **of Man**. Finally, the "Soul is Called (instincts)" to Learn one's **Needs, Possessions, and Ownership** as **They Reflect** the **Righteousness** (earth), **Holiness** (Heaven), and **Perfection** (Kingdom) **of Man**. We now see that by "Mastering the Mind (logic), Heart (feelings), and one's Soul (instincts), a **Person** can **Prepare himself** to **Leave Earthly Life** (elementary school) and **Enter Heavenly Life** (high school).

This "Journey" from Death to New-life means that a **Person** has **Mastered Individuality, Social Order, and Divine Perfection** by **Striving to Learn** Mathematics, **Grammar, Symbols, Wants, Likes, Loves, Needs, Possession, and Ownership**. The idea here is to see that by "Becoming a Righteous Man," he can Attain the **Respect of Others,** thereby **Making him** a **Citizen on Earth** (king) **Worthy** of **Receiving a New Body**. Secondly, by "Becoming a Holy Man," he can Attain the **Honors of Society,** thereby **Making him** a **Holy Saint in Heaven Worthy** of **Receiving Eternal Life**. Finally, by "Becoming a Perfect Man," he can Attain an **Exalted Position in Life,** thereby **Making him** a **Perfect Son** within **God's Kingdom Worthy** of his **Own**

Royal Kingdom. Through this "Journey" from his <u>Intellectual Achievements,</u> via his <u>Emotional Maturity,</u> to his <u>Instinctive Adult Behavior,</u> a **Person can Enter** a **State** of **Knowing,** then **Understanding,** and finally, **Fully Comprehending** the **Meaning of Life**. This means that to "Know All Things" is to <u>Master Logic;</u> and to **Learn the Difference** between **God's Right** and **man's wrong** is to **See the Meaning of Existence**. Secondly, to "Understand All Things" is to <u>Master One's Feelings</u> by **Learning the Difference** between **God's Good** and **man's evil** to **See the Purpose of Service to Others**. Finally, to "Comprehend All Things" is to <u>Master One's Instincts</u> by **Learning the Difference** between **God's Reality** and **man's illusion** to **See the Value of Eternal Happiness**. Yes! through "Existence," "Service to Others," and "Eternal Happiness," <u>God, Angels, and Men</u> will **Find** the **Meaning, Purpose, and Value of Life**.

   The following tabular information indicates that the "Human Experience" on **Earth** involves **Mastering** one's **Mind of Logic, Heart of Feelings,** and **Soul of Instincts** to **Learn the Meaning, Purpose, and Value of Life**:

Mastering the Logic of Mind, Feelings of Heart, and Instincts of Soul to Become a Son of God
(learning God's mathematics/grammar/symbols, wants/likes/loves, needs/possession/ownership)

Logic   1. **Mind** - Knowing: Learning God's Right from Man's Wrong .... Knowledge
   - Righteous Man (respect) - Citizen of Earth (king): Attain New Body
   - Mathematics – Formulation
   - Grammar – Syntax   **Individuality**
   - Symbols - Meaning
            (meaning of existence - baby level: use one's intellect to see his own limits)

Feelings   2. **Heart** - <u>Understanding:</u> Learning God's Good from Man's Evil ...
            Self-awareness
   - Holy Man (honor) - Holy Saint in Heaven (priest): Attain Eternal Life
   - Wants - Desires
   - Likes – Selection   **Social Order**
   - Loves - Oneness
            (purpose of service to others - teenage level: use one's feelings to see his potential)

Instincts   3. **Soul** - <u>Comprehending:</u> Learning God's Will/man's will...Consciousness
   - Perfect Man (exalted) - Perfect Son within Kingdom (son): Attain Royal Kingdom
   - Needs - Survival
   - Possession - Control   **Divine Perfection**
   - Ownership - Title
            (value of happiness - adulthood level: use one's instincts to see his self-worth)

This illustration shows that for a "Baby to See his Limits (mind)," he must Learn **Mathematics, Grammar, and Symbols** to **Recognize the Difference** between the **Right Way** Leading to Prosperity and the Wrong Way **Leading to Poverty**. Secondly, for a "Teenager to See his Potential (heart)," he must Learn **Wants, Likes, and Loves** to **Recognize the Difference** between the **Good of God Leading to Heaven** and the **Evil of Man Leading to Hell**. Finally, for an "Adult to See his Own Self-worth," he must Learn **Needs, Possession, and Ownership** to **Recognize the Difference** between **God's Reality Leading to Knowing God** and **Man's Illusion Leading to Knowing Lucifer**. Via "Mastering" one's Mind, Heart, and Soul, a **Person** can both **Grow and Mature** on **Earth**, in **Heaven**, and within **God's Kingdom** to become a **Righteous Citizen, Holy Saint,** and **Perfect Son** before the **Throne of God**.

We are "All Called" to Learn to **Think** for **Ourselves, Develop** a **Healthy Imagination,** and **Comprehend** the **Grand Design of God** to **Befriend God, Angels, Men, and One and All**. This means that as "Individuals," We can Respect Ourselves; within the "Social Order," we can Respect Others; and via "God's Divine Perfection," the Lord will **Come to Respect Us All**. Obviously, in "Our Youth," We are Able to **See a Bright** and **Happy Future**, yet as **We Grow Older**, the **Life-experience Takes on** a **More Serious Note** until **We Realize** that **What We Are** is a **Reflection of Our Own Value**. The truth is that this most "Happy Theme of Youthful Imagination" will Last Forever as **Every Chosen Soul of God** will be **Challenged Each Day to Try Harder to Defeat his Pure Innocence** (adventure), thereby **Forcing himself** to **Grow One Tiny Step Closer** to the **Love and Respect of God**. This "Automated System of Spiritual Maturity" is ignited in the very Soul of Every Christian, who is willing to **Surrender** (die to self) his whole being to the **Divine Will** of the **Eternal Father**. Through this "Commitment," a Person must **Take his Sonship Training** like a man and **Face** the **Challenges of Life** (fight evil), without a **Single Complaint** to **Prove the Depth of his Faith**. We must "Never Believe" for a second that once this painful Struggle of Flesh (lost fool) against Spirit (wise man) ends on earth, that we will **Escape** the **Blessings of Pain**. We are being told that at the "End of Life," all will become a Bed of Roses; yet, the **Challenge to be Perfect** will **Never End** for those who truly **Love God**. No! "Life" is Created from a "Love for Self-achievement (value/money)" and where there is **No Painful Sacrifice**, there will be **No Holy Works of God;** there will be **No Human Gain** or **Divine Gratitude** without **Sacrifice,** leading to the **Lord's Perfect Gift of Divine Love** (existence/benevolent force).

We see in the fact that the "Lord Needed to Create a Person," such as the Blessed Virgin Mary, **Indirectly Confirms the Premise** for an **Eternal Life** of **Dynamic Spiritual Fire** rising from **God's Divine Flame** of **Perfect Love**. This fact reveals that the "Lord God Almighty's" new perfect Game of Love (eternal addiction) Hurts so Good that everyone Loves to Play It and can't get enough no matter how **Long and Hard They Try**. In real terms this "Pleasurable Pain (fun)" occurs in Loving God to the **Extent** that it actually **Begins to Hurt** to think about experiencing so much **Pure Pleasure,** when one is only an **Unworthy Foolish Broken Sinner**.

The future desire of "Humanity" will be to Serve a Supreme Being (benevolent force), **Whose Only True Joy** comes with **Serving His** most **Beloved Children** in an **Unending Mutual Admiration Society** of **Perfect Love**. This will truly be a "Kingdom of Perfect Love" with One Hope that is to be Filled with Divine Love, yet, the **Blessed Mother** will be the **Only One** who **Can't Get Enough Infinite Love,** even from the **Lord God Almighty Himself.** It can now be seen that the "Virgin Mary" is to be Paradise's **Horn of Plenty** as **She Steals** the **Evil One's Bottomless Pit** to make it the depths of Her **Human Love for Her God** and **His most Beloved Children.** With "Her Infinite Grace," the Virgin Mary will capture the **Evil One's Lake of Fire** to **Transform** it into **Her Children's Fiery Love** for their most **Worshiped** and **Praised Eternal Father.** Finally, the "Blessed Mother (emphatic)" will Invade the Evil One's Outer Darkness with Her infinite **Light of Righteousness** to bring forth the **Fruits** of **Her Son's Triumph over Death** and the **Redemption of All Men.** By "Conquering Sin (lake of fire)," "Evil (bottomless pit)," and "Death (outer darkness)," the Blessed Virgin will be able to **Set Humanity Free** from its **Paralyzing Fear** (ignorance), a **Lifetime of Pain** (cowardice), and its **Curse of Eternal Death** (greed).

This concept of the "Blessed Virgin" as an "All-Consuming Love Machine" must be continually Served and Feed **Her Son's Divine and Human Love** to keep **Her Absolutely Happy** at **All Times.** This "Love Machine Concept" sits at the heart of God's coming Civilization of Love or **1,000 Years of Peace** (forgiveness/seal saints) which has been **Created** to **Transform the Earth** from **Sin, Evil, and Death** into a **New Creation** of **Peace, Joy, and Happiness.** The "Virgin Mary's" insatiable Appetite for Affection is all **Embracing** in **Spirit and in Truth** bringing **Peace** (mind), **Joy** (heart), and **Happiness** (soul) to all the **Kingdom of God.** The "Blessed Mother" can best be compared to a Pair of Divine Dice in **God's Game of Life**, who never wearies of keeping the **Lord and His Children Amused**, because She knows that He just **Loves to Play** the **Divine Game of Creation** on and on **without end.**

- -

Physical Life - Earth: Righteous Citizen

We see in the "Game of Creation" that the Central Theme is **Centered** upon **Raising Children** of **Quality** and **Respectability** to become of **Great Value to Human Society** by **Striving** to **Honor Themselves, Society, and God.** This means "Each of God's Children" is Called to Master the **Seven Steps of Physical Life**: 1) Develop a Righteous Mind - Intellect: Defeat Gluttony (food), 2) Master Babyhood - Elementary School: Defeat Sloth (cheating), 3) Enter Laity - Vestibule: Defeat Envy (wanting things), 4) Become a Jewish Citizen - Israel: Defeat Lust (sexuality), 5) Eligible to Enter Outer Court - Offering: Defeat Avarice (money), 6) Crowned as King - Duty: Defeat Anger (power), and 7) Title Deed to Earth - Heaven on Earth (God becomes Man): Defeat Pride (ownership).

- -

Spiritual Life - Heaven: Holy Saint

Secondly, "Mastering" the **Seven Steps of Spiritual Life:** 1) Develop Holy Heart - Emotions: Gain Virtue of Good Taste, 2) Master Teenage Stage - High School: Gain Virtue of Honesty, 3) Enter Priesthood - Church: Gain Virtue of Charity, 4) Become

Roman Citizen - Christianity: Gain Virtue of Loving, 5) <u>Enter Holy Place</u> - Acceptance: Gain Virtue of Good Values, 6) <u>Ordination as Priest</u> - Responsible: Gain Virtue of Good Judgment, and 7) <u>Title Deed to Heaven</u> - Heaven with God (Man becomes God): Gain Virtue of Humility.

- -

<u>Mystical Life</u> - Kingdom: Son of God

Finally, "Mastering" the **Seven Steps of Mystical Life:** 1) <u>Develop Perfect Soul</u> - Instincts: Attain Good Health, 2) <u>Master Adulthood</u> - College: Become Highly Educated, 3) <u>Ordained High Priest</u> - Sanctuary: Develop Good Manners, 4) <u>Become Greek Citizen</u> - Pagan: Become Perfect Mate, 5) <u>Enter Holy of Holies</u> - Consideration: Establish Successful Career, 6) <u>Given Sonship</u> - Authority: Leader of Men, and 7) <u>Title Deed to the Kingdom</u> - God's Glory: Respected Family Name.

At each of these "Twenty-One Stages" of <u>Growth</u> and <u>Maturity,</u> a person can be **Physically Transformed, Spiritually Purified, and Mystically Converted** as he **Passes** through the Lord's **Divine School of Higher Learning** (awakened).

The following tabular information indicates the "Physical," "Spiritual," and "Mystical Journeys" that the <u>Human Race</u> will take as each of **God's Children Struggles** through <u>Life</u> to find out the **Meaning of Life** (existence), the **Purpose of Life** (service), and the **Value of Life** (happiness):

**Finding the Meaning, Purpose, and Value of Life
via Physical, Spiritual, and Mystical Truths**
(removing faults, then gaining virtues,
and finally, developing a new nature of perfection)

Meaning of Life	Purpose of Life	Value of Life
Physical Journey	Spiritual Journey	Mystical Journey
<u>(remove faults)</u>	<u>(gain virtues)</u>	<u>(create nature)</u>
Earthly Realm	**Heavenly Paradise**	**Kingdom of Glory**
1. **Mind** - Intellect	1. **Heart** – Emotions	1. **Soul** - Instincts
• Gluttony (food)	• Good Taste	• Good Health
2. **Baby** – Elementary	2. **Teenager** - High School	2. **Adult** - College
• Slothful (cheating)	• Honesty	• Highly Educated
3. **Laity** - Vestibule	3. **Priesthood** – Church	3. **High Priest** – Sanctuary
• Envious (things)	•. Charitable	• Good Manners
4. **Jewish** – Israelites	4. **Roman** – Christians	4. **Greek** - Pagans
• Lustful (sex)	• Loving	• Perfect Mate
5. **Outer Court** - Offering	5. **Holy Place** – Acceptance	5. **Holy of Holies** – Consideration
• Avarice (money)	• Good Values	• Successful Career
6. **King** – Duty	6. **Priest** – Responsibility	6. **Son** - Authority
• Anger (power)	• Good Judgment	• Leadership

7. **Earth** - Heaven on Earth	7. **Heaven** - Presence of God	7. **Kingdom** - God's Glory
• Pride (ownership)	• Humility	• Family Name
(home - good grades)	(church - many graces)	(government - high points)

- -

New Nature – Transfigured Body	**New Behavior** - New Glorified Spirit	**New Lifestyle** – New Holy Soul
• Man becomes God	• God becomes Man	• God and Man become One
• Righteousness	• Holiness	• Perfection

This illustration shows that the "Life-experience Involves" <u>Taking a Long Journey</u> from **Death to New-life** by **Mastering the Art of Human Behavior** in the **Home, Government,** and within the **Church** to be a **Productive Citizen on Earth** (home), in **Heaven** (government), and within the **Kingdom of God** (church). This means that a "Person must Simultaneously" <u>Develop his Mind, Heart,</u> and <u>Soul</u> into **Their Mature States of Perfection** by **Mastering Jesus' Babyhood, Christ's Teenage Years,** and **Jesus Christ's Adulthood** to **Earn God's Blessing** and to be **Forever Set Free.** Once a "Born-again Soul" has <u>Reached</u> **Full Maturity,** it will be **Capable of Distinguishing** the **Difference** between **Man's Illusion** (lie) and **God's Reality** (truth) and can now **Think for itself** (wisdom). We must all clearly understand "God's Reality" as it <u>Relates</u> to the **Tremendous Price** the **Lord** had to <u>Pay to Wash</u> and **Purify** (sin-debt) the **Body** (mind), **Spirit** (heart), and **Soul** (instincts) **of Man.** This "Divine Payment" might <u>One Day</u> **Allow Man to Find** that **Awesome Life** of **True Fulfillment** (love) that the **Lord has Always Desired** for **Each of His Children** to <u>Make Them</u> into **Righteous, Holy, and Perfect Citizens of God's Kingdom.**

This meant that "Our Blessed Mother" had to "Wash the Evil Flesh of Man (mind)" with <u>Her Son's Living Waters</u> (baptism) which **Poured** forth from **His Dying Words of Righteousness** to <u>Purify the Minds</u> of **All Sinful Men** (damned/sin-nature). We see that the "Blessed Virgin Mary" was also <u>Required</u> to **Wash Away the Evil Spirit** (heart) of **Her Lost Children** with **Her Son's Sacrificial Blood** (penance) **Poured** forth from **His Open Wounds of Purification** to <u>Purify the Hearts</u> of **All Evil Sinners** (damned/worldly temptations). Finally, the "Queen Mother, Mary" of the "Divine Will" had to <u>Wash the Evil Soul</u> (instincts) of <u>Man</u> with **Her Son's Igno-minious Death** (forgiveness) **Poured** forth from **His Death of Redemption** to **Purify the very Being** (nature) of **Damned Humanity** (hell fire/demonic possession). The most essential concept to be aware of is that "Heaven would be Worse" than the <u>Evil Demons in Hell,</u> **If Eternity** is to become **Boring** even for an **Instant** as it would **Take Only One Flaw** to **Destroy** its <u>Eternal Promise</u> of **Divine Perfection.** The "Job of the Blessed Virgin (co-redemptrix/advocate/mediatrix)" as the <u>Mother of God</u> is to be **All Things to All People** in **Keeping** the **Whole Kingdom Progressing** <u>Along To-ward</u> the **Prideful Loving Eyes of God**. Obviously, "God is Creating" a <u>Perfect King-dom</u> to **Forever Admire** the **Great Works of His Hands** (babies) **When His Children Grow-up** into **Righteous Citizens of Earth, Holy Saints in Heaven,** and into **Sons of God within God's Kingdom.** This means that the "Lord is a Creator" of <u>Infinite Differences</u>, **Creating** an **Infinite Series of Choices** (challenges) for **Every Life**, thereby **Making Them <u>Perfectly Unique</u>** (one of a kind) in a **Land of Infinite Harmony** (paradise).

The "Lord God Almighty" is obviously <u>Making Repetition of Man's Cup of Tea,</u> yet, with a **Touch** of the **Unexpected** to **Add** that **Special Spice, Giving** it a **Perfect Flavor**, a **Wine Bouquet** of **Infinite Love** so that <u>**Every Child**</u> can be **All he can Be before God.** To accomplish this great feat of "Holy Perfection," the <u>Lord Came to Earth</u> with **Three Distinct Missions**: 1) <u>Disseminate God's Truth</u> (word/new body) and to bring Redemption (free) through His Holy Church (graces)**; 2)** <u>Bring Salvation</u> (earned/eternal life) to man's body, spirit, and soul through His Sacred Government (points); and 3) <u>Build a Highway of Love and Honors</u> (rewards/kingdom) to the Eternal Father (will) so that all might come to Live in His Divine Home (grades). This most "Painful Task" has <u>Required</u> **Our Jewish Messiah, Jesus Christ** to **Solve and Untie** the **Gordian Knot of Death** (take-sin) by **Actually <u>Marrying</u>** the **Prostitute of Death** (sinners/church). The Lord will then "Transform Her" into a <u>Perfect Flaw of Life</u> (give divinity) bringing **Her Virginity** before **His Father's Divine Justice** to **<u>Set All the Captives</u> Free** from **Sin, Evil, and Death.**

This reveals that "Our Lord is Begging Us" to <u>Do Our Tiny Part</u> in **Helping Him Carry** some **Portion** of **Man's Mountain of Sin** (cross) to the **Divine Flame of Forgetfulness** so **that We might All Share** (earn) in <u>**Our Own Gifts**</u> of **Righteousness, Holiness,** and **Perfection**. This theme of having a "Second Chance" to <u>Make Amends</u> (repentance) for **Our Childish Actions Sits at the Center** of the **Lord's New <u>Perfect Justice System</u>** of **Infinite Forgiveness** (full restitution). The question before the "Children of God" and "All Humanity" is: are <u>They Willing</u> to put in the <u>Necessary Effort</u> **Required by God** to **Earn Their Way to Heaven** by **<u>Striving</u>** to become of **Eternal Service to God?**

CPSIA information can be obtained
at www.ICGtesting.com
Printed in the USA
BVHW040304040821
613530BV00029B/329